VOLUME

# 13

## K–Lyre
## pages 1-400

# Compton's
# Encyclopedia

## and Fact-Index

# F.E. Compton Company

### Division of Encyclopaedia Britannica, Inc.

THE UNIVERSITY OF CHICAGO
COMPTON'S ENCYCLOPEDIA IS PUBLISHED WITH THE EDITORIAL ADVICE
OF THE FACULTIES OF THE UNIVERSITY OF CHICAGO

*"Let knowledge grow from more to more and thus be human life enriched"*

# HERE AND THERE IN VOLUME 13

AT ODD TIMES when you are just looking for "something interesting to read," without any special plan in mind, this list will help you. With this as a guide, you may visit faraway countries, watch people at their work and play, meet famous persons of ancient and modern times, review history's most brilliant incidents, explore the marvels of nature and science, play games—in short, find whatever suits your fancy of the moment. This list is not intended to serve as a table of contents, an index, or a study guide. For these purposes consult the Fact-Index and the Reference-Outlines.

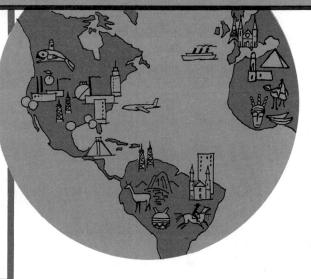

## Picture Highlights

A Tour of Korea . . . . . . . . . 76a
A Ruby Laser . . . . . . . . . 129a
The Red and Gold of Autumn Leaves . . 179
Central London . . . . . . . . . 338–9

## Reading for Pleasure

"In Days of Old, When Knights
  Were Bold" . . . . . . . . . . . 65
Landseer, Painter of Animals . . . . . 109
Some Famous Lighthouses . . . . . . 270
Androcles and the Lion . . . . . . . 296
David Livingstone, British Explorer of
  Africa . . . . . . . . . . . . . 316

## School and Home; Work and Play

Kindergarten—The First Step
  from Home . . . . . . . . . . . 51
Kites and How They Are Used . . . . . 62
Putting the Communication
  Skills Together . . . . . . . . . 120

## Learning for the Enrichment of Living . 169
Leisure—How to Use It Wisely . . . . 185
Talking by Mail—The Art of Letter
  Writing . . . . . . . . . . . . . 197
Literature That Speaks to Children . . . 309

## Historical Highlights

"The First City Founded After
  the Flood" . . . . . . . . . . . 61
The Battle of Lexington and Concord . . 203
Louis—Kings of France . . . . . . . 358

## Famous People

John Keats, Poet of Beauty . . . . . . 23
Helen Keller's Triumph over Handicaps . 24
John F. Kennedy—35th President
  of the United States . . . . . . . 24a
Martin Luther King, Jr.—Champion of
  Black Rights . . . . . . . . . . 54
Rudyard Kipling, English Storyteller
  and Poet . . . . . . . . . . . . 59
Lafayette—Hero of Three Revolutions . 101

# HERE AND THERE IN VOLUME 13

Lee—Hero of the Southern Confederacy . 180b
Lenin, the Professional Revolutionary . . 188
Abraham Lincoln—16th President
  of the United States . . . . . . . . 279
Lindbergh—America's "Lone Eagle
  of the Sky" . . . . . . . . . . . 288

## The Plant and Animal Kingdoms

The "Old Man" of Australia . . . . . . 1
Leaves—Food Factories of Plant Life . . 177
The Lion—Feared Hunter and Killer . . 296
The Scaly Dragons of Modern Times . . 317

## The Wide World of Facts

Knots, Hitches, and Splices . . . . . . 70
Labor and Labor Unions . . . . . . . 81
Lacemaking by Hand and by Machine . 93
Latitude and Longitude—The
  Earth's Grid System . . . . . . . . 156
Laundry—Washing and Ironing Today . 159a
Leather—A Product of Hides and Skins . 173
Life—What It Means to Be "Alive" . . 253
Lumber—The Major Forest Product . . 388

## Marvels of Science and Invention

Lasers and Masers . . . . . . . . . 129a
Lenses—The Magic in a Curve of Glass . 190
Light—For Seeing and Growing . . . . 260
Lightning—A Gigantic Electric Spark . . 274
Linotype—The Machine That Casts
  Lines of Type . . . . . . . . . 292
Locomotive—A Power Plant on Wheels . 326

## The Arts

Charles Lamb's Charming Essays . . . 103
The Sea of Language Around Us . . . . 114
Latin America's Creative Writers . . . . 148
Basic Language of the Western World . . 153
A Library Is A Way of Sharing . . . . 206
Literary Awards for Writers and
  Illustrators . . . . . . . . . . . 303
Literature—A Way of Seeing,
  A Way of Feeling, A Way of Knowing . 305
Longfellow—Best Loved of
  American Poets . . . . . . . . . 346

## At Home and Abroad

Kansas—The Wheat-Growing State . . 3
Kentucky—Gateway to the South . . . 26
Kenya—East African Equatorial Land . 44
Korea—A Divided Land . . . . . . 75
Labrador—The Northeast Corner of
  North America . . . . . . . . . . 92
The People's Republic of Laos . . . . 125a
Latin America—Its Problems and
  Promise . . . . . . . . . . . . 130
Lebanon—Mediterranean Gateway
  to Asia . . . . . . . . . . . . 180
Leningrad—Russia's "Window
  to the West" . . . . . . . . . 188b
London—Capital of the
  United Kingdom . . . . . . . . . 336
Los Angeles—City of Sunshine
  and Industry . . . . . . . . . . 350
Louisiana—Gateway to the
  Mississippi Valley . . . . . . . . 362
The Toy Country of Luxemburg . . . . 397

Where was the first Labor party launched? 91.

What animal can cast off its tail and then grow a new one? 319.

Why do some plants "form partnerships"? 250 pictures.

What large animal is only an inch long at birth? 2.

To what family does the lion belong? 296.

Who learned to "hear" through her fingertips? 24.

Why do leaves change color in the fall? 178, 180.

**What reptile runs on its hind feet like a man? 320.**

What color is a live lobster? 322.

What lawyer wrote a famous national song? 46.

Where did Peter the Great build a magnificent "window" toward Europe? 190.

What city was said to be built on human bones? 190.

What explorer gave France its claim to the entire Mississippi Valley? 128.

What state is noted for its thoroughbred horses? 29.

Whose teachings on nonviolent resistance impressed young Martin Luther King, Jr.? 54.

What strenuous game was learned from the American Indians? 98–99.

How much of the land area of the United States is not privately owned? 108.

What British institution is called the Old Lady of Threadneedle Street? 339.

What African town is named for a president of the United States? 204.

Who was the most famous of all the pirates? 48b.

When and why was handmade lace smuggled into England? 95.

Which of the Seven Wonders of the World was built to save lives? 270.

In what state are two of the world's largest telescopes? 356.

What will boil on a cake of ice? 301.

What toy helped Franklin find electricity in the lightning? 64.

How do Moslems believe the Koran originated? 74.

What kind of rock is made up of animals' shells? 278.

How long have forks been used in Europe? 69.

What sovereign received a pair of the first machine-knit silk stockings? 67.

What invention was the first step toward the reliable calculation of longitude? 158.

How did British sailors get the nickname of "limeys"? 278.

What is a time lock? 325.

Why are green leaves important to man? 177.

Who was America's "lone eagle of the sky"? 288.

Why does a kite fly? 63.

What were the "turtle ships"? 76g, 77a pictures.

What are the duties of the famous "beefeaters"? 341.

How do natural and man-made laws differ? 165.

Why is Liberia of special interest to Americans? 204.

What French nobleman took part in three revolutions? 101.

Who introduced the resolution in the Continental Congress to declare the colonies independent? 180b.

One out of five Koreans has the same surname. What is it? 75b.

How was the territory of the United States doubled at one stroke? 383.

What missionary lived to tell of his lion bite? 316.

What reformer made Scotland Protestant? 73.

Who said: "I am the state"? 359.

Who built the first West Point fortifications? 78c.

How was Martin Luther saved from death on his return from the Diet of Worms? 397.

How do we know that European lakes were inhabited 10,000 years ago? 103.

What is a "sheepshank"? 72.

What world language did not have to be invented? 153.

What British author told of India in stories and verse? 59.

Who was the first Republican president of the United States? 284d.

In what season of the year do most lemons ripen? 188.

Which is the only bird that gives us leather? 175.

Why are skyscrapers seldom damaged by lightning? 275.

How did the expression "crazy as a loon" originate? 350.

What insect lays its eggs in overlapping rows, like shingles? 23.

How does the ladybug defend itself? 100.

**What relative of the leopard is trained to aid in hunting? 196a.**

What birds are hatched out on a bed of fishbones? 56.

Why can the lynx hunt so well at night? 399.

Who was the first American to win the Nobel prize in literature? 202.

How did the lyrebird get its name? 400 picture.

Which is better: to practice for five hours continuously or for one hour on five different days? 171.

Explain why lemurs were called "ghosts." 188.

# KEY TO PRONUNCIATION

*Pronunciations have been indicated in the body of this work
only for words which present special difficulties.
For the pronunciation of other words, consult the FACT-INDEX.
Marked letters are sounded as in the following words:*

cāpe, ăt, fär, fȧst, whạt, fạll; mē, yĕt, fẽrn, thêre;

īce, bĭt; rōw, wȯn, fôr, nŏt, dọ; cūre, bŭt, rựde, fụll, bûrn; out;

ü = French *u*, German *ü*; ġem, ḡo; *th*in, *th*en;

ṅ = French nasal (Jeaṅ); *zh* = French *j* (*z* in azure); K = German guttural *ch*.

**K2.** The earth's second highest mountain is officially named K2. Also known as Mount Godwin Austen and as Dapsang, the 28,250-foot-high peak is in the Karakoram mountain system of northern Kashmir near the border of Pakistan and China.

K2 was long considered unclimbable because of its great height and almost unbroken slopes of rock and ice. The ascent is precipitous and full of overhangs, and there are few areas where climbers can camp.

The first of several attempts to reach K2's summit was made in 1902. Several persons were killed in these climbs. In 1954 an Italian expedition succeeded. It was led by geologist Ardito Desio and consisted of 11 climbers, 6 scientists, and more than 500 porters. Achille Compagnoni and Lino Lacedelli, the team chosen to attempt the final portion of the climb, are credited with having reached the summit.

THESE ARTICLES ARE IN THE FACT-INDEX

Kabotie, Fred
Kadar, Janos
Kaesong, North Korea
Kafir
Kafka, Franz
Kaganovich, Lazar
  Moiseevich
Kagawa, Toyohiko
Kagera River
Kagoshima, Japan
Kahanamoku, Duke
Kahn, Otto Hermann
Kahului, Hawaii
Kaibab National Forest
Kaifeng, People's
  Republic of China
Kailua, Hawaii
Kailyard school
Kairouan, Tunisia
Kaiser, Georg
Kaiser, Henry J(ohn)
Kaiserslautern, West
  Germany
Kajima Peace Award

Kala azar
Kalah, Assyria
Kalakaua, David
Kalamazoo, Mich.
Kalamazoo Case, The
Kalamazoo College
Kalantian, Code of
Kalat, Pakistan
Kaleidoscope
Kalgan, People's Republic
  of China
Kalidasa
Kalinin, Mikhail
  Ivanovich
Kalinin, Russia
Kaliningrad, Russia
Kalispell, Mont.
Kallikak
Kalm, Peter
Kalmar, Sweden
Kalmus, Herbert Thomas
Kalthoeber, Charles
Kamakura, Japan
Kama River

**KAMCHATKA** (*kăm-chăt′kạ*). From the eastern part of Soviet Siberia the long, bleak peninsula of Kamchatka extends south about 750 miles between the Sea of Okhotsk and the Bering Sea. From its tip a chain of islands, the Kurils, leads to Japan. Coastal plains are covered with tundra growth, and forests clothe the lower mountain slopes. In the southeast a higher range is covered with volcanoes, some active. Klyuchevskaya (15,192 feet) is Siberia's highest peak. The peninsula's area is about 105,000 square miles. Its population is estimated at 210,000.

THESE ARTICLES ARE IN THE FACT-INDEX

Kamehameha I
Kamel, George Joseph
Kamerlingh Onnes, Heike
Kamikaze
Kamimura, Hikonojo, Baron
Kamloops, B. C.
Kampen, Netherlands
Kanawha River
Kanazawa, Japan

Kanchenjunga
Kandahar, Afghanistan
Kandinski, Vasili
Kandy, Sri Lanka
Kane, Elisha Kent
Kane, Harnett Thomas
Kane, Paul
Kaneohe, Hawaii

**KANGAROO.** When Capt. James Cook was exploring the coast of Australia in 1770, his men were amazed by a strange animal. At times it stood upright, braced on its hind legs and huge tail. It moved by great leaps. Thus white men first met the great gray kangaroo, the "boomer" or "old man" of Australia.

More than a hundred species of the kangaroo family live in the open spaces of Australia, New Guinea, and

This baby kangaroo, or "joey," is leaning out of the pouch of its watchful mother to nibble on vegetation.
Australian Tourist Commission

nearby islands. They belong to the *marsupial* order (animals that carry their young in pouches). The kangaroo's body is specially built for jumping. In this way it differs from other marsupials. However, the kangaroo family should not be confused with the so-called kangaroo rats, the jerboas, and similar jumping rodents of America, Africa, and Asia.

The great gray kangaroo reaches a weight of 200 pounds and a length of ten feet from nose to tip of tail. The tail alone is about four feet long, and the strong muscles at the base make it nearly as thick as the animal's body. There are four toes on each of the two hind feet. The second toe from the outside is much stronger and longer than the others and ends in a huge claw. This toe and the shorter outside toe are used in the great leaps that the kangaroo makes. It can leap along the ground at 30 miles an hour.

Three fourths of the animal's size and weight are in its hindquarters. The front legs are short and slender, with two small five-toed paws. These are used like hands in taking hold of food. They are drawn up against the chest in jumping.

The female has a large pouch on the belly made by a fold in the soft furry skin. When the single, inch-long, naked baby kangaroo is born, it finds shelter in this pouch. There it attaches itself to one of the mother's nipples, which swells inside the baby's mouth so that for several weeks it cannot loosen its grip. It is unable at first to draw out milk for itself or to swallow it. The mother has muscles that pump her milk down the baby's throat.

The young kangaroo is called a "joey" in Australia. When the joey is about four months old, it is able to lean out of the sheltering pouch and nibble grass. Soon it climbs out and learns to hop around in search of food. It continues for several weeks longer to climb back into the pouch for sleep and safety. If sudden danger threatens while the young kangaroo is some distance away, the mother starts toward it at full speed, gathers it up in her forepaws as she passes, and tucks it into her pouch.

## Other Kinds of Kangaroos

The red kangaroo and the wallaroo are nearly as large as the great gray kangaroo. Next in size are various species popularly known as wallabies. These larger types are usually found in small groups, or "mobs." They move from place to place, feeding on grass, shrubs, and the leaves of small trees. Their keen noses, ears, and eyes warn them of danger from hunters or wild dogs. Kangaroos are hunted because of the damage they do to crops and for their tender flesh and their skins, which produce fine leather.

Timid as it is, the kangaroo fights hard when cornered. It stamps its hind feet and growls. With its front paws it pushes its attackers within reach of a blow from its back feet. It can rip a dog to death with a single stroke. When chased by a pack, a kangaroo sometimes jumps into a lake or stream.

The smaller kangaroos include the rock wallabies, the hare wallabies, and the rat kangaroos. They live in hidden places in cliffs or in thick brush. A few species live in trees. These tree kangaroos have much shorter hind legs and longer forelegs than the others. They do not hop but climb among the branches like small bears. Some of these smaller kangaroos eat berries and small insects as well as grass and leaves.

## Scientific Facts About Kangaroos

Fossil remains of about 30 different kangaroo species have been found in Australia. Among them were several giant types, one of which is estimated to have stood fully ten feet tall.

Kangaroos make up the family *Macropodidae* of the marsupial order (*Marsupialia*). The great gray kangaroo is *Macropus giganteus*. Other marsupials are the phalangers (*Phalangeridae*), including the cuscus, koala, and several Australian opossums; wombats (*Phascolomyidae*); bandicoots (*Peramelidae*); Tasmanian devil (*Dasyuridae*); Tasmanian wolf (*Thylacynidae*); banded anteater (*Myrmecobiidae*); marsupial mole (*Notoryctidae*); and true opossums (*Didelphidae*), including the opossum of North America.

Helplessness at birth is typical of all marsupials. The young do not reach the same degree of development inside the mother's body as do the young of higher mammals. They are born sooner and complete the early stages of their growth in the mother's pouch.

The marsupials lie between the most primitive egg-laying mammals, such as the duckbill, or platypus, and the spiny anteater of the order *Monotremata*, and the higher orders, which include all the remaining mammals. (*See* Australia; Duckbill; Opossum; Tasmania.)

**HOPPING AT HIGH SPEED**
Powerful hind-leg muscles enable some kangaroos to move at speeds of about 30 miles an hour over short distances.

THESE ARTICLES ARE IN THE FACT-INDEX
**K'ang Hsi**
**Kankakee, Ill.**
**Kannapolis, N. C.**

# KANSAS—

# The Wheat-Growing

# State

The fertile plains of central and western Kansas usually produce more wheat than any other section of the country. This wheat field near Sublette is ready for harvesting.

**KANSAS.** One of the greatest farming states in the nation is Kansas. Its fertile prairies yield from 200 million to nearly 300 million bushels of wheat yearly. In most years this is more than is grown in any other state. The state's output is usually about one fifth of the total United States crop. Kansas is also one of the top five states in broomcorn, rye, and sorghum for grain, forage, and silage.

Kansas is the most centrally located state, not including Alaska and Hawaii. It lies halfway between Canada and Mexico. Until Alaska and Hawaii became states, the geographic center of the United States was in Smith County, two miles northwest of Lebanon. Just 42 miles to the south, in Osborne County, is the geodetic center of North America. All geodetic surveys on the continent are keyed to this point. (*See also* Surveying.)

The state is named for the Kansa tribe of Sioux Indians who once lived along the Kansas (or Kaw) River. *Kansa* is a Sioux word meaning "wind people." Because of its many sunflowers Kansas is nicknamed the Sunflower State. It is also called the Jayhawker State, from a Civil War term for Kansas troops and for guerrilla forces operating in the state.

**Population** (1980): 2,363,208—rank, 32d state. Urban, 66.7%; rural, 33.3%. Persons per square mile, 28.9—rank, 37th state.

**Extent:** Area, 82,264 square miles, including 477 square miles of water surface (14th state in size).

**Elevation:** Highest, Mount Sunflower, 4,135 feet, in Wallace County; lowest, Verdigris River at Oklahoma border, 686 feet; average, 2,000 feet.

**Geographic Center:** 15 miles northeast of Great Bend.

**Temperature** (° F): Extremes—lowest, −40° (Lebanon, Feb. 13, 1905); highest, 121° (near Alton, July 24, 1936, and other locations and earlier dates). Averages at Topeka—January, 28.8°; July, 79.9°; annual, 54.9°. Averages at Wichita—January, 32.0°; July, 80.9°; annual, 57.1°.

**Precipitation** (inches): At Topeka—annual average, 32.36 (including 20.5 snowfall). At Wichita—annual average, 28.41 (including 14.7 snowfall).

**Land Use:** Crops, 57%; pasture, 35%; forest, 3%; other, 5%.

**For statistical information about Agriculture, Communication, Education, Employment, Finance, Fishing, Forests, Government, Health Care, Manufacturing, Mining, Population Trends, Trade, Transportation, Vital Statistics, and Welfare, see KANSAS FACT SUMMARY.**

3

## Survey of the Sunflower State

Kansas is in the north-central region of the United States. It is bordered by four states—Oklahoma on the south, Colorado on the west, Nebraska on the north, and Missouri on the east. Its only natural boundary is in the northeast, where the Missouri River flows between Kansas and the state of Missouri before turning eastward at Kansas City.

The state is shaped like a rectangle, almost twice as long as it is wide. Its greatest length, from east to west, is 411 miles. Its greatest width, from north to south, is 207 miles. The total area of Kansas is 82,264 square miles, including 477 square miles of inland water surface.

## The State's Four Natural Regions

Although Kansas is generally level, it consists of four distinct natural regions. In the east are the Osage Plains and the Glacial Plains. Both regions are part of the Central Lowland of the United States. Western Kansas, a part of the Great Plains, is divided into the High Plains and the High Plains Border.

In Wallace County, near the western border, is Mount Sunflower (4,135 feet), the highest point in the state. From here the surface slopes down to a low of 686 feet along the Verdigris River at the Kansas-Oklahoma boundary in the southeast.

**The High Plains** cover the western end of the state. This is a rolling tableland with little rainfall and few trees. From west to east the elevation slopes from 4,000 to 3,000 feet above sea level.

**The High Plains Border** occupies west-central Kansas. It is an intermediate zone between the higher region of the west and the lower plains to the east. In the south-central part of this region are the prairies of the Great Bend of the Arkansas River.

**The Glacial Plains** lie in the northeastern corner of the state. During the Ice Age, glaciers deposited a layer of fertile soil in this region. To the west are the low, grass-covered Flint Hills.

**The Osage Plains** extend over southeastern Kansas. This is gently rolling, rich farmland. In Cowley and Butler counties and to the north are the Flint Hills. These hills cross the state in a north-south direction.

Most of the rivers of Kansas flow from west to east. The northern half of the state is drained by the Kansas (Kaw) River, formed by the junction of the Republican and Smoky Hill rivers in Geary County. The chief river of southern Kansas is the Arkansas. Its tributaries include the Cimarron in the southwest and the Verdigris and Neosho in the east.

## Climate and Weather

Because it is about 600 miles from any large body of water, Kansas has a continental climate. Summers are hot and winters are cold.

Stanton County receives the least precipitation (rain and melted snow)—about 15 inches a year. From west to east the rainfall gradually increases until it reaches a maximum of 40 inches in the extreme southeast. The growing season varies from 160 days a year in the northwest to 200 days a year along the southeast border. Like the other plains states, Kansas is subject to occasional droughts and tornadoes.

## Natural Resources and Conservation

The Sunflower State's chief natural resource is its soil. The flat plains of western Kansas are ideal for large-scale wheat growing. The fertile farmland of eastern Kansas produces corn and other crops. There are also extensive grazing lands, chiefly bluestem grass in the east and buffalo grass in the west.

Kansas farm products help make food processing one of its most important manufacturing industries. Petroleum and natural gas are the state's principal mineral resources.

The chief conservation problem in Kansas has been the protection of the soil from erosion by wind and water. This has been partly accomplished by improved farming practices and by the planting of trees. (*See also* Conservation.) In the northern half of the state the rivers of the Missouri Basin are being developed primarily for flood-control and irrigation purposes. Since 1925 many of the state's natural resources have been administered by the Kansas Fish and Game Commission.

## People of the Sunflower State

What is now Kansas was the home of several tribes of Plains Indians. These included the Kansa, Osage, Pawnee, and Wichita. Several tribes of Indians came into the area from the East after 1830, when Congress authorized their removal west of the Mississippi River. After Kansas was opened to white settle-

Kansas Industrial Development Commission

Castle Rock, a 70-foot chalk spire near Utica, is visible for miles. Gove County has many of these unusual chalk formations.

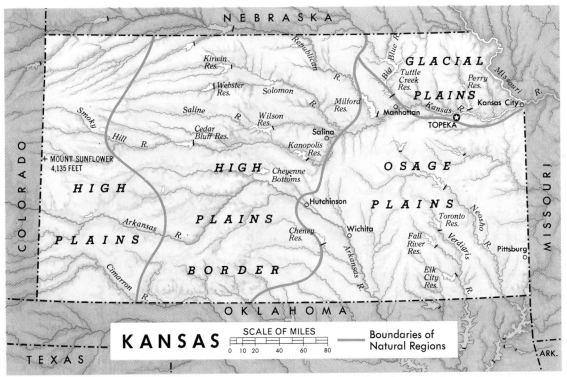

KANSAS
SCALE OF MILES
0 10 20 40 60 80
Boundaries of Natural Regions

This map shows the four natural regions and the surface features of Kansas. The use that can be made of the land is related to the physical features of each region.

ment in 1854, the Indians began to surrender their lands. By about 1880 most of the tribes had been resettled in Indian Territory (now Oklahoma). Today there are only about 8,500 Indians in Kansas.

The Kansas-Nebraska Act of 1854 brought a rush of settlers into the region. Proslavery men from Missouri and antislavery groups from as far away as New England fought for control of the territory. In 1855 there were only about 8,600 people in Kansas. Five years later the population had increased to more than 107,000.

The state's greatest growth in population came during the 25 years that followed the Civil War. Many of the new settlers were farmers from the Eastern states. They took up land opened by the Homestead Law of 1862. Only a few foreign immigrants came to Kansas. Today the number of foreign born is 2 percent of the population. Of the total foreign stock, Germans are the most numerous. Blacks make up 5 percent of the population.

### Products of the Land

About 90 percent of Kansas is cropland or pasture. There are about 90,000 farms in the state. More than 10,000 of these are larger than 1,000 acres. The size of the average farm is about 550 acres.

The most important crop by far is wheat. Most of it is a hard, winter variety grown on large farms that are highly mechanized. The record yield was some 308 million bushels produced in 1952. The chief wheat-growing counties are Sumner, Reno, Ford, Thomas, Barton, Harper, McPherson, and Finney.

Sorghum for grain is the second most valuable crop. It is produced largely in the southwest. Hay, especially alfalfa and sweet clover, is grown throughout the state. Other important crops are corn, soybeans, sugar beets, and barley. Of the state's livestock, cattle and calves produce the largest cash income. Cattle and sheep are grazed mainly in the central part and in the west. Dairying and the raising of hogs and poultry are important in the east.

Petroleum accounts for about three fifths of the value of the state's mineral production. The western part of Kansas is the most productive area. Next in value is natural gas. Other valuable minerals are helium, cement, stone, and salt.

### Manufacturing and Cities

Only about one out of every six workers in Kansas is engaged in manufacturing. The chief industry is the manufacture of aircraft, motor vehicles, and other transportation equipment. Second in importance is the processing of foodstuffs, such as flour and meal, meat, bakery goods, and dairy products.

The third most important industry is the making of chemicals and related products. These include explosives, soap, and vegetable and animal oils. Next in value is the refining of petroleum. The manufacture of nonelectrical machinery and clay and glass products is also important.

The largest city in the state is Wichita, on the Arkansas River. It is noted for its food processing,

## TWO SOURCES OF KANSAS' WEALTH

The cattle industry is the state's largest source of farm income. This herd of Herefords (left) is being fattened in a feedlot.

Petroleum is by far the state's most important mineral. Much of the oil is processed in this modern refinery (right) at Augusta.

oil refineries, and aircraft manufacture (see Wichita). Kansas City, second in size, is a livestock and meat-packing center where the Kansas and Missouri rivers meet. Nearby is rapidly growing Overland Park. Across the state line is the twin city, Kansas City, Mo. (see Kansas City, Kan.). About 60 miles upstream from the mouth of the Kansas River is Topeka, the state capital and third largest city (see Topeka).

In the northeast are Lawrence, on the Kansas River, and Leavenworth, on the Missouri. Salina, a flour-milling and meat-packing city, is on the Smoky Hill River. Hutchinson is located on the Arkansas River. Its industries are based on wheat, oil, and salt. Pittsburgh and Coffeyville are the largest cities of the southeast. Manhattan lies near the junction of the Big Blue and Kansas rivers.

### The Development of Transportation

The first "highway" for wheeled vehicles across the Kansas region was the Santa Fe Trail, which was opened by William Becknell in 1821. It ran from Independence, Mo., west and south through Council Grove and Pawnee Rock to Santa Fe, N. M. The second great route to the West that passed through Kansas was the Oregon Trail (see Oregon Trail).

Today the Sunflower State is served by a network of modern roads. Kansas maintains some 10,000 miles of primary highways and other state roads. The chief east-west routes are Interstate 70 (which incorporates parts of US 40) and US 36, 24, 50, 54, and 160; the major north-south highways are US 83, 283, 183, 281, 81, 77, 75, 59, and 69. In 1956 the state opened Interstate 35, a 236-mile turnpike from Kansas City through Topeka and Wichita to the Oklahoma border.

The first railroad in the state was a five-mile line from Elwood to Wathena, opened in 1860. By 1873 the Atchison and Topeka Railroad (now The Atchison, Topeka and Santa Fe Railway) had been completed across the state. Today more than a dozen railroads serve Kansas, with most of the trackage in the eastern half. Another important form of transportation is the barge line on the Missouri River.

### Recreation in Kansas

About 60 state parks and state lakes have been established to provide fishing, swimming, and other

### MANUFACTURING IN WICHITA

One of the great airplane-production centers of the world is Wichita. Busy assembly lines turn out both military and commercial aircraft.

recreation for the people of the Sunflower State. Some of the leading points of interest in Kansas are mementos of pioneer days. Boot Hill Cemetery at Dodge City, the Pawnee Capitol at Fort Riley, Fort Scott, and Fort Hays are among these. Fort Larned, once an important military post on the Santa Fe Trail, is administered by the National Park Service.

At Abilene are the Dwight D. Eisenhower Library, the Eisenhower Museum, and the president's boyhood home. Wichita is the site of the annual National Baseball Congress. The Kansas State Fair is held at Hutchinson and the Mid America Fair at Topeka.

### Growth of the School System

The first schools in Kansas were religious missions established among the Indians in the 1820's. In 1827 the federal government sent Daniel Morgan Boone, son of Daniel Boone, to teach farming to the Indians in Jefferson County. In 1855 the first territorial legislature provided for a system of free public schools. From this law came the organization of school districts administered by county superintendents.

Compulsory attendance for children of school age has been in effect since 1874. The first high school was built in Chapman in 1889. Today the public educational system is directed by the State Board of Education, composed of seven members.

The largest school of higher learning is the University of Kansas, at Lawrence, with the University of Kansas Medical Center, at Kansas City. Also state supported are Kansas State University of Agriculture and Applied Science, at Manhattan; Wichita State University, at Wichita; and three other state universities, at Emporia, Pittsburg, and Fort Hays. Other schools are Washburn University of Topeka; Benedictine College, at Atchison; Ottawa University, at Ottawa; and Bethany College, at Lindsborg.

### Government and Politics

The capital of Kansas was chosen by popular vote in 1861. Topeka was the winner over Lawrence. The state is governed under its original constitution, adopted in 1859 and effective 1861.

The chief executive officer is the governor, elected every four years. Lawmaking is in the hands of the Senate and the House of Representatives. The judiciary is headed by the Supreme Court. Kansas pioneered in the development of a legislative council, which studies public problems and prepares bills for the legislature. The legislative coordinating council consists of three senators and four representatives.

In politics Kansas has long been a predominantly Republican state. It has elected only seven Democratic governors in its history. In presidential elections Kansas has voted Republican each time except in 1892, 1896, 1912, 1916, 1932, 1936, and 1964. Alfred M. Landon, governor from 1933 to 1937, was the unsuccessful Republican candidate for president in 1936. Dwight D. Eisenhower, whose boyhood home was in Abilene, was elected the 34th president of the United States in 1952 and reelected in 1956.

Wolfe Commercial Photo Service

The Shawnee Methodist Mission was opened in 1839 to teach Indian children. Its site is just south of Kansas City.

## HISTORY OF KANSAS

On May 30, 1854, Kansas was organized as a territory out of what had been the old Missouri Territory, sometimes called "Indian country." Three of its boundaries were the same as they are today—the state of Missouri on the east, the 40th parallel on the north, and the 37th parallel on the south. Its western border extended to the Rocky Mountains. When Kansas became a state, on Jan. 29, 1861, its western boundary was set at the "twenty-fifth meridian of longitude west from Washington (D. C.)." The area west of this line was made a part of Colorado Territory. The following sections tell how Kansas developed into a modern state.

### Exploration to Statehood

In 1541 Coronado and his party of Spanish explorers became the first white men to enter what is now Kansas (see Coronado). Little was known of the region when the United States acquired all but the southwestern corner of the present state in 1803 (see Louisiana Purchase). The remainder was secured by the United States from Texas in 1850.

During the first half of the 1800's, the chief settlements in the Indian country were forts erected to keep peace on the frontier. Fort Leavenworth was built in 1827, Fort Scott in 1842, and Fort Riley in 1853. By 1850 the population numbered only about 1,500 whites and some 34,000 Indians.

In 1854 the territory was opened to white settlement by the Kansas-Nebraska Act (see Kansas-Nebraska Act). Congress left it up to the settlers to decide whether they wanted Kansas to become a free state or a slave state. The earliest arrivals were proslavery people from Missouri. They founded Leavenworth and Atchison. Later, free-state forces established settlements at Lawrence and Topeka.

For four years the two groups battled for control of "bleeding Kansas." In 1856 Lawrence was sacked by a proslavery party. In revenge John Brown and his followers massacred five men along Pottawatomie Creek near Lane. Gradually the antislavery settlers became dominant. In 1859 a convention at Wyandotte (later Kansas City) adopted a free-state constitution that was ratified by popular vote. In 1861 Kansas was admitted to the Union as the 34th state.

### Growth of the Modern State

In 1867 the first herd of Texas longhorn cattle was driven along the Chisholm Trail to the railroad at Abilene. This began the cattle boom that lasted until the 1880's. Meanwhile Mennonite pioneers from Russia introduced a hardy new type of wheat, called Turkey Red. First grown near Hillsboro in 1874, it provided the basis of today's bountiful crops of Kansas wheat.

During the 1890's farmers expressed their discontent with low farm prices by joining the Granger movement and the Populist party. This was also the era when Carry Nation became nationally famous for smashing Kansas saloons that disregarded antiliquor laws.

By 1900 most of the state's farmland had been claimed by settlers. Because of the drought-created Dust Bowl and low farm prices, Kansas lost almost 80,000 residents between 1930 and 1940. During the 1940's and 1950's this loss was more than made up by an increase of some 379,000 persons. Between 1970 and 1980 the population increased by 114,137 persons, a gain of 5.1 percent but 6.3 percent less than the national growth. During the 1960's the major industries of Kansas were expanding at a slow rate. They were unable to provide job opportunities for all of the Kansas farm workers who had been displaced by mechanization. (*See also* United States, sections "North Central Plains" and "Great Plains"; individual entries in the Fact-Index on Kansas persons, places, products, and events.)

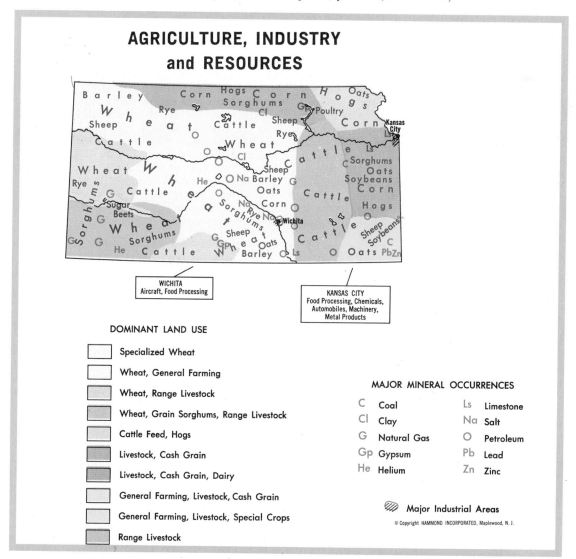

**AGRICULTURE, INDUSTRY and RESOURCES**

WICHITA
Aircraft, Food Processing

KANSAS CITY
Food Processing, Chemicals, Automobiles, Machinery, Metal Products

**DOMINANT LAND USE**

- Specialized Wheat
- Wheat, General Farming
- Wheat, Range Livestock
- Wheat, Grain Sorghums, Range Livestock
- Cattle Feed, Hogs
- Livestock, Cash Grain
- Livestock, Cash Grain, Dairy
- General Farming, Livestock, Cash Grain
- General Farming, Livestock, Special Crops
- Range Livestock

**MAJOR MINERAL OCCURRENCES**

| | | | |
|---|---|---|---|
| C | Coal | Ls | Limestone |
| Cl | Clay | Na | Salt |
| G | Natural Gas | O | Petroleum |
| Gp | Gypsum | Pb | Lead |
| He | Helium | Zn | Zinc |

Major Industrial Areas

© Copyright HAMMOND INCORPORATED, Maplewood, N. J.

# Notable Events in Kansas History

1541—**Coronado, searching for city of Quivira, reaches central Kansas.**

1723—Étienne de Bourgmont builds Fort Orléans.

1803—France sells Louisiana, including most of Kansas, to U. S.

1804—Kansas included in District of Louisiana under Indiana Territory; made part of Louisiana Territory in 1805. Lewis and Clark enter Kansas.

1806—Zebulon M. Pike explores Republican River area.

1812—Territory of Missouri created.

1819—*Western Engineer*, first steamboat in Kansas, carries Stephen H. Long's expedition.

1821—William Becknell opens route of Santa Fe Trail.

1824—Presbyterian mission founded on Neosho River.

1825—Kansa (Kaw) and Osage Indians cede land.

1827—**Fort Leavenworth established.** Daniel Morgan Boone founds Indian school in Jefferson County.

1830—Shawnee Methodist Mission for Indians established near Turner; moved to site near Shawnee in 1839.

1842—John C. Frémont leads first of several expeditions through Kansas. Fort Scott established.

1843—Wide-scale migration to Oregon country begins.

1849—California gold seekers follow Kansas trails.

1853—Fort Riley established.

1854—Kansas-Nebraska Act creates Kansas Territory; temporary capital, Fort Leavenworth; governor, A. H. Reeder. Leavenworth, Lawrence, Atchison, and Topeka founded.

1855—First territorial legislature meets at Pawnee, then at Shawnee Mission; legalizes slavery. Free State party forms separate government. Wakarusa War occurs over slavery.

1856—Proslavery men sack Lawrence. **John Brown leads free-state raiders in massacre along Pottawatomie Creek.**

1857—Proslavery Lecompton Constitution rejected.

1859—Antislavery Wyandotte Constitution adopted. Atchison and Topeka Railroad chartered.

1860—Pony Express crosses Kansas en route to West. First oil well in Kansas drilled near Paola.

1861—Kansas becomes 34th state, January 29; capital, Topeka; governor, Charles Robinson.

1863—Confederates led by William Quantrill sack Lawrence.

1864—University of Kansas organized at Lawrence. Confederate Gen. Sterling Price raids Kansas.

1867—First herd of Texas cattle driven to Kansas.

1874—**Mennonites introduce Turkey Red wheat to U. S.**

1878—Cheyenne raid is last Indian skirmish in state.

1880—Kansas adopts state prohibition amendment.

1899—Carry Nation begins her saloon-smashing raids.

1903—Present State Capitol completed.

1948—Kanopolis Dam on Smoky Hill River completed; Fall River Dam, in 1949; Cedar Bluff Dam on Smoky Hill River, in 1951.

1951—Floods cause great damage.

1952—Dwight D. Eisenhower, who spent his boyhood in Abilene, elected 34th president of U. S.

1954—Eisenhower Museum, adjacent to boyhood home, opens in Abilene; Dwight D. Eisenhower Library founded in Abilene in 1962. In historic Brown *vs.* Topeka Board of Education decision, U. S. Supreme Court bans segregation in public schools.

1956—Construction of Kansas Turnpike completed.

1965—Agricultural Hall of Fame and National Center opened near Kansas City. Fort Scott designated national historic monument.

1976—Mid-American All-Indian Center opens in Wichita.

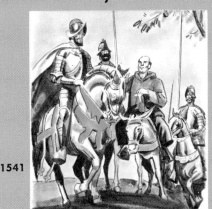

1541

1827

1856

1874

STATE FLOWER:
Wild Sunflower

STATE TREE:
Cottonwood

STATE BIRD:
Western Meadowlark

STATE SEAL: Plowman represents
agriculture; steamboat symbolizes
commerce; wagon train, Indians,
and buffalo depict early history.

# Kansas Profile

FLAG: *See* Flags of the United States.
MOTTO: Ad Astra per Aspera
(To the Stars Through
Difficulties).
SONG: 'Home on the Range'—words,
Brewster Higley; music, Dan Kelly.

Visitors to the Sunflower State are struck by the extent of its flat terrain. To many Kansans the vast plains are a blessing, for the wealth of the state lies in and under its soil. Record wheat crops are often harvested. Kansas is a leading producer of sorghum, hay, and corn. Plump cattle graze throughout the state. Kansas packinghouses prepare Kansas-bred livestock for national markets. In addition, rich petroleum and natural-gas deposits lie beneath the western part of the state.

The early settlers' conflicting views jeopardized the stability of young Kansas. Proslavery and abolitionist groups fought savagely during the brief territorial years of "bleeding Kansas." Then, after the Civil War, gunmen and outlaws terrorized the cow towns—Dodge City, Abilene, Wichita—that arose at railroad cattle-shipping terminals. With great determination, the people of Kansas survived these trials and brought peace to their land.

Before the settlers staked out Kansas, it was a windswept grassland across which great herds of buffalo roamed. These herds had vanished by the end of the 19th century, destroyed largely by hunters who furnished meat to transcontinental railroad workers. Much of the grass had also disappeared, plowed under by farmers who came to the state from New England and the South.

Modern Kansas has experienced floods and droughts, falling farm prices, and a dwindling of owner-operated farms. Steps have been taken to cope with these problems. Large reservoirs have been built for flood control and irrigation. These also serve as recreational sites. The state has made successful efforts to attract industry and thus provide jobs for displaced farmers. In such cities as Topeka, Kansas City, and Wichita flourishing manufacturing enterprises are preparing the way for the further urbanization of Kansas.

The University of Kansas, at Lawrence, was organized in 1864 and opened two years later. Its campanile, a 53-bell, 120-foot-high war memorial, has been a campus landmark since 1951. Kansas State University, at Manhattan, opened as an agricultural college in 1863.

The State Capitol, built between 1866 and 1903, is in Topeka, one of the largest cities in the Sunflower State. The state legislature has held its sessions at Topeka since 1861. During the restless territorial history of Kansas, lawmakers met at many different sites.

Wichita, the largest city in Kansas, is best known for its aircraft industry. The city is also an agricultural and petroleum center. This is a portion of downtown Wichita.

Kansas rail centers, known as cow towns, flourished until the great cattle drives ended in the 1880's. The jail of the famed Western lawman Wyatt Earp has been restored in Wichita, a former cow town.

11

Eisenhower Chapel

Eisenhower Home

Eisenhower Library

Kansans can enjoy water-skiing, camping, and other outdoor activities at state, county, and city parks and lakes. Here a water-skier skims over the surface of Topeka's Shawnee Lake.

Dwight D. Eisenhower, the 34th president of the United States, spent his boyhood in Kansas. His home in Abilene, now part of the Eisenhower Center, has become a national shrine. The center also includes a chapel, a museum, and a library which houses Eisenhower's military and presidential papers.

Dodge City, in southwestern Kansas, was one of the tough frontier towns that characterized the old West. Today it features replicas of the shops and saloons of the past.

Gypsum Hills, a cluster of curiously eroded rocks, stand in the south-central part of Kansas, near Medicine Lodge. This town became famous as the home of Carry Nation, the prohibitionist saloon wrecker.

Cavalry troops played an important part in the pacification of Kansas in frontier days. At Fort Riley, birthplace of the United States Seventh Cavalry, the Old Trooper monument honors the horse soldier.

During its brief life the Pony Express performed a valuable communications service. This Pony Express station at Hanover was one of the points where the mail-carrying riders changed their horses.

Winter wheat (below) is the most valuable Kansas crop. These huge grain elevators at Hutchinson (left) have a combined capacity of 27 million bushels. For agricultural statistics, see KANSAS FACT SUMMARY.

DWIGHT D. EISENHOWER

*some famous people**

BENJAMIN (PAP) SINGLETON

CARRY NATION

JOHN BROWN

WILLIAM ALLEN WHITE

AMELIA EARHART

KARL A. MENNINGER

EDGAR LEE MASTERS

EMMETT KELLY

WILLIAM C. MENNINGER

ALFRED M. LANDON

ARTHUR CAPPER

*Only a few of Kansas' famous people are shown here. The persons depicted are generally associated with the state, though not all of them were born there. For biographical information, *see* entries in the Fact-Index.

# KANSAS FACT SUMMARY

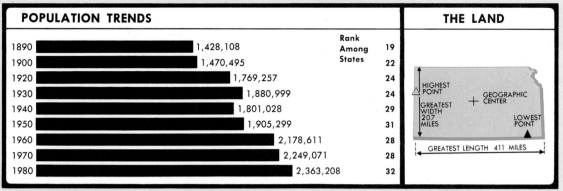

## POPULATION TRENDS

| Year | Population | Rank Among States |
|------|-----------|-------------------|
| 1890 | 1,428,108 | 19 |
| 1900 | 1,470,495 | 22 |
| 1920 | 1,769,257 | 24 |
| 1930 | 1,880,999 | 24 |
| 1940 | 1,801,028 | 29 |
| 1950 | 1,905,299 | 31 |
| 1960 | 2,178,611 | 28 |
| 1970 | 2,249,071 | 28 |
| 1980 | 2,363,208 | 32 |

## THE LAND

HIGHEST POINT
GEOGRAPHIC CENTER
GREATEST WIDTH 207 MILES
LOWEST POINT
GREATEST LENGTH 411 MILES

## GOVERNMENT

**Capital:** Topeka (since 1861).

**Statehood:** Became 34th state in the Union on Jan. 29, 1861.

**Constitution:** Adopted 1859. Amendment may be passed by two-thirds vote of State Legislature; ratified by majority voting on it in an election.

**Representation in U. S. Congress:** Senate—2. House of Representatives—5. Electoral votes—7.

**State Legislature:** Senators—40; term, 4 years. Representatives—125; term, 2 years.
Convenes 2d Tuesday in January annually. Session limit —90 legislative days (even years); no limit in odd years. Special session limit—none.

**Executive Officers**
Governor—term, 4 years. May succeed himself once.
Other officials—lieutenant governor, secretary of state, treasurer, and attorney general; all elected; terms, 4 years.

**Judiciary:** Supreme Court—7 justices; appointed by the governor from list submitted by nominating commission; run for reelection at large; term, 6 years. Appellate court—7 judges selected by same process as Supreme Court justices; term, 4 years. District courts—69 judges; term, 4 years.

**County:** 105 counties. Governed by a county board of 3 members; elected; term, 4 years. Other county officers elected; term, 2 years.

**Municipal:** Mayor-council plan most common; also commission and council-manager forms.

**Voting**
Residency requirements—none.
General election—1st Tuesday after 1st Monday in November.
Primary election—1st Tuesday in August in even years.
Preferential presidential primary—none.

## EDUCATION

**Private Elementary and Secondary Day Schools**
Enrollment—elementary, 25,700; secondary, 7,100.
Classroom teachers—1,900.

**Public Elementary and Secondary Schools***
Operating school districts—307.
Compulsory school age—7 to 16.
Enrollment—elementary, 237,940; secondary, 200,260.
Average daily attendance—409,279.
High school graduates—32,470.
Administrative officials
State Board of Education, 10 members; elected; term, 4 years.

County superintendents; elected; term, 2 years.
Superintendents of schools; appointed by city boards of education.
Instructional staff—total, 28,533; principals and supervisors, 1,375; elementary teachers, 13,597; secondary teachers, 11,920.
Teachers' average annual salaries—elementary, $11,081; secondary, $12,716.
Revenue receipts—$700,737,000.
Source of receipts (% of total)—federal, 7.8; state, 44.4; local, 47.8.
Nonrevenue receipts†—$45,000,000.
Current expenditures
For day schools—$636,620,000.
For other programs—$29,285,000.
State expenditure on education—$1,458 per pupil.
Head Start programs—participants, 2,710; funds allocated, $4,005,389.

**Universities and Colleges‡**
Number of institutions—total, 52; public, 29; private, 23.
Degree-credit enrollment—120,000.
Earned degrees conferred—bachelor's and first professional, 12,761; master's except first professional, 3,046; doctor's, 448.

**Special Institutions** (for the handicapped): Kansas School for the Blind, Kansas City; Kansas School for the Deaf, Olathe; Parsons State Hospital and Training Center.

**Libraries:** City, town, and village public libraries—360. State Library and Traveling Libraries Commission provide loan service to public libraries, schools, and individuals. Traveling Library Division provides consultant service to aid in organization and development of local library units. Noted special libraries—State Historical Library, Topeka; Eisenhower Presidential Library, Abilene.

**Outstanding Museums:** Museum of Art and Museum of Anthropology, University of Kansas, Lawrence; Wichita Art Museum; Wichita Historical Museum; Kansas State Historical Society Museum, Topeka; Dwight D. Eisenhower Center, Abilene.

## CORRECTIONAL AND PENAL INSTITUTIONS

**State**
Adult—Kansas State Penitentiary, Kansas Correctional Institution for Women, and Kansas Correctional Industries, all in Lansing; Kansas State Reception and Diagnostic Center and Kansas Correctional-Vocational Training Center, both in Topeka; Kansas State Industrial Reformatory, Hutchinson. Work release centers—Wichita, Topeka. Honor camp—Toronto.
Juvenile—youth centers in Atchison, Beloit, and Topeka.
**Federal**
United States Penitentiary, Leavenworth.

All Fact Summary data, including estimates, are based on current government reports.
*Kindergartens are included in the elementary schools; junior high schools, in the secondary schools.
†Money received from loans, sales of bonds, sales of property, and insurance adjustments.
‡Excludes data for service academies.

# KANSAS FACT SUMMARY

## PRODUCTION—YEARLY VALUE: $3,186,000,000

Manufacturing* 46%     Agriculture† 38%     Mining 16%

The chart at left shows the state's major product categories and each category's percentage of the total value.

The charts below list the leading items in each of three important product groups and indicate their dollar values.

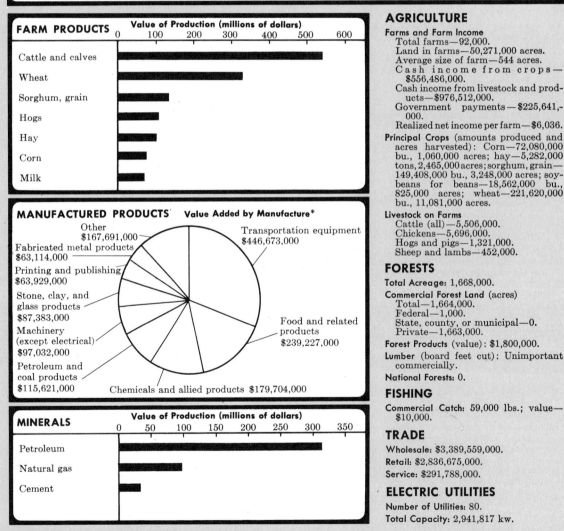

## FARM PRODUCTS
### Value of Production (millions of dollars)

0   100   200   300   400   500   600

- Cattle and calves
- Wheat
- Sorghum, grain
- Hogs
- Hay
- Corn
- Milk

## MANUFACTURED PRODUCTS
### Value Added by Manufacture*

Other $167,691,000
Fabricated metal products $63,114,000
Printing and publishing $63,929,000
Stone, clay, and glass products $87,383,000
Machinery (except electrical) $97,032,000
Petroleum and coal products $115,621,000
Chemicals and allied products $179,704,000
Transportation equipment $446,673,000
Food and related products $239,227,000

## MINERALS
### Value of Production (millions of dollars)

0   50   100   150   200   250   300   350

- Petroleum
- Natural gas
- Cement

## AGRICULTURE

**Farms and Farm Income**
Total farms—92,000.
Land in farms—50,271,000 acres.
Average size of farm—544 acres.
Cash income from crops—$556,486,000.
Cash income from livestock and products—$976,512,000.
Government payments—$225,641,000.
Realized net income per farm—$6,036.

**Principal Crops** (amounts produced and acres harvested): Corn—72,080,000 bu., 1,060,000 acres; hay—5,282,000 tons, 2,465,000 acres; sorghum, grain—149,408,000 bu., 3,248,000 acres; soybeans for beans—18,562,000 bu., 825,000 acres; wheat—221,620,000 bu., 11,081,000 acres.

**Livestock on Farms**
Cattle (all)—5,506,000.
Chickens—5,696,000.
Hogs and pigs—1,321,000.
Sheep and lambs—452,000.

## FORESTS

**Total Acreage:** 1,668,000.

**Commercial Forest Land** (acres)
Total—1,664,000.
Federal—1,000.
State, county, or municipal—0.
Private—1,663,000.

**Forest Products** (value): $1,800,000.

**Lumber** (board feet cut): Unimportant commercially.

**National Forests:** 0.

## FISHING

**Commercial Catch:** 59,000 lbs.; value—$10,000.

## TRADE

Wholesale: $3,389,559,000.
Retail: $2,836,675,000.
Service: $291,788,000.

## ELECTRIC UTILITIES

Number of Utilities: 80.
Total Capacity: 2,941,817 kw.

All Fact Summary data are based on current government reports.
*Value Added by Manufacture—value of manufactured products as they leave the factory, less the cost of materials, supplies, fuel, etc. For complete definition, see Fact-Index.
†Cash receipts.

# KANSAS FACT SUMMARY

## TRANSPORTATION

**Roads and Streets**
Total state mileage—134,700.
Municipal mileage—11,600.
Rural mileage—123,100.
National Interstate Highway System
Total designated mileage—821.
Mileage open to traffic—797.
Mileage under construction or projected—24.
**Automobiles, Trucks, and Buses** (registrations)*
Total motor vehicles—1,848,000.
Automobiles—1,257,000.
Trucks and buses—591,000.
**Motorcycles** (registrations): 91,000.
**Railroads**
Total mileage owned—7,524.
First railroad—Elwood to Wathena, 1860.
**Airports:** 334.
**Pipelines** (mileage)†: 17,152.

## COMMUNICATION

**Post Offices:** 694.
**Radio Stations** (commercial): AM—59; FM—39. First station —WEY, Wichita, licensed March 23, 1922.
**TV Stations:** Commercial—12; educational—2. First station— KTHV, Hutchinson, began operation June 25, 1953.
**Telephones:** Total—1,635,000; residence—1,234,000; business—401,000.
**Newspapers**
Daily—50; circulation—645,000.
Weekly—204.
Sunday—14; circulation—434,000.
First newspaper—*Shawnee Sun* (in Shawnee language), Wyandotte County, 1835; *Kansas Weekly Herald*, Leavenworth, 1854.
**Periodicals:** 85.

## FINANCE‡

**Revenue:** $1,459,443,000.
**Expenditures:** Total—$1,441,458,000; education—$613,004,-000; highways—$240,303,000; public welfare—$245,187,-000; hospitals—$97,895,000.
**Debt:** Total—$408,101,000; issued (long term only)—$124,520,000; retired (long term only)—$22,735,000.
**Taxation**
State tax collections—$853,936,000; general sales—$300,365,000; individual income—$193,730,000.
Intergovernmental—$408,861,000.
**Personal Income per Capita:** $6,495.
**Banks:** 615; total assets or liabilities—$11,127,000,000.
**Savings and Loan Associations:** 86; total assets—$4,881,000,000; per capita assets—$2,113.
**Life Insurance Policies:** 4,279,000; value—$25,778,000,000.

## VITAL STATISTICS§

**Birthrate:** 15.0.
**Death Rate:** 9.6.
**Marriage Rate:** 10.5.
**Divorce Rate:** 5.5.

## HEALTH CARE

**Hospitals:** 164; beds—18,183.
**Nursing Homes:** 468; beds—22,889.
**Physicians:** 3,221.
**Dentists:** 1,049.
**Licensed Practical Nurses:** 4,170.

All Fact Summary data are based on current government reports.
*Excludes vehicles owned by military services.
†Petroleum and products only.
‡Figures for one-year periods.
§Rates per 1,000 population.
◆Data are based on state reports to United Way of America.

## EMPLOYMENT

**Total Number of Persons Employed:** 863,900.

THOUSANDS OF WORKERS
0   40   80   120   160   200

- Trade
- Professional services
- Manufacturing
- Agriculture, forestry, and fisheries
- Transportation, communication, and utilities
- Construction
- Government
- Finance, insurance, and real estate
- Personal services
- Business and repair services
- Mining
- Recreation services
- Not accounted for

## WELFARE‡

**Old-Age and Survivors Insurance:** Beneficiaries—330,719; benefits—$786,296,000.
**Disability Insurance:** Beneficiaries—31,830; benefits—$70,779,000.
**Unemployment Insurance:** Beneficiaries (weekly average)—9,918; benefits—$3,323,709.
**Workmen's Compensation Benefits:** $39,436,000.
**Vocational Rehabilitation**
Disabled persons rehabilitated—3,012; in process of rehabilitation—4,023.
Total federal and state funds—$8,929,000.
**Public Assistance**
Dependent children—recipients, 73,096; average payment, $84.16.
General assistance—recipients, 5,483; average payment, $123.26.
**Supplementary Security Income**
Old age—recipients, 10,251; total $752,000.
Permanently and totally disabled—recipients, 11,872; total, $1,289,000.
Blind—recipients, 339; total, $40,000.
**Maternal and Child Health Services**
Federal grants—maternal and child health services, $1,833,000; crippled children, $844,000.
**United Way Campaigns◆:** amount raised—$10,139,050.

# KANSAS FACT SUMMARY

## LARGEST CITIES*

**Wichita** (279,835): industrial center; flour mills, grain elevators, meat-packing plants, stockyards, oil refineries, airplane factories, railroad shops; Wichita State University; Friends University; Riverside Park; Art Museum; restoration of Wyatt Earp's jail (*see* Wichita).

**Kansas City** (161,148): industrial city across Missouri River from Kansas City, Mo.; stockyards; grain elevators; oil refineries; meat-packing, flour milling, soap; auto assembly plant (*see* Kansas City, Kan.).

**Topeka** (115,266): state capital; Kansas State Historical Museum; manufacturing city in farm area; railroad shops; flour mills; meat-packing; insurance center; Menninger Foundation; Gage Park (*see* Topeka).

**Overland Park** (81,784): community near Kansas City; dairying.

**Lawrence** (52,738): flour mills; canning; University of Kansas; Haskell Indian Junior College.

**Salina** (41,843): trade center; flour mills; Kansas Wesleyan (formerly Kansas Wesleyan University); Marymount College; Indian Burial Pit nearby.

**Hutchinson** (40,284): salt mines; oil refineries; flour mills; meat-packing plants; railroad shops.

**Olathe** (37,258): residential suburb of Kansas City; Mid-America Nazarene College.

**Leavenworth** (33,656): industrial city in farm area; Fort Leavenworth, federal penitentiary; Saint Mary College.

**Manhattan** (32,644): farm center; dairy products; Kansas State University; Tuttle Creek Dam nearby.

## PLACES OF INTEREST

**Cedar Bluff State Park:** near Ellis; water sports.

**Chase County State Lake:** near Cottonwood Falls; fishing, swimming.

**Cheyenne Bottoms:** near Great Bend; wildlife refuge; hunting, fishing.

**Clark County State Lake:** near Kingsdown; deep canyon of Bluff Creek; fishing, picnicking.

**Coal Strip Mines:** near Pittsburg; some of world's largest power shovels; fishing lakes.

**Council Grove:** Indian treaty signed for survey of Santa Fe Trail (1828); Kaw Mission (1849).

**Dodge City:** former cowboy capital; Boot Hill, gunman cemetery; Beeson Museum, pioneer relics.

**Eisenhower Boyhood Home, Museum, and Library:** in Abilene; papers and memorabilia of former president.

**Fall River State Park:** near Fall River; hiking, picnicking, water sports.

**Finney County State Game Refuge:** near Garden City; buffalo herd; other animals and birds.

**Fort Hays:** in Hays; frontier military post (1865).

**Fort Leavenworth:** near Leavenworth; established in 1827; museum; federal penitentiary.

**Fort Riley:** Santa Fe Trail military post (1853); territorial capitol (1855).

**Fort Scott:** military post built in 1842.

*1980 census.

**Greensburg:** Big Well, one of world's largest hand-dug wells; Pallisite Meteorite, rare meteor.

**Hugoton:** world's largest natural-gas field.

**Indian Burial Pit:** near Salina; many remains.

**John Brown Memorial Park:** in Osawatomie; log-cabin home of abolitionist.

**Kanopolis State Park:** near Salina; hiking, water sports, camping.

**Kirwin Reservoir:** on North Fork of Solomon River.

**Lebanon:** near old geographic center of U. S.

**Leavenworth County State Lake:** near Tonganoxie; boating, fishing.

**Lindsborg:** annual Messiah Festival; Birger Sandzen Memorial Art Gallery.

**Marais des Cygnes Refuge:** near La Cygne; wildlife refuge; fishing, hunting.

**Meade County State Lake:** near Meade; fishing lake; buffalo, elk, deer, game birds; pheasant farm.

**Meade's Ranch:** near Osborne; geodetic center of North America.

**Monument Rocks:** near Russell Springs; chalk rocks.

**Natural Bridge:** near Sun City; rock arch.

**Neosho County State Lake:** near Parsons; artificial lake in deep ravine; water sports.

**Pawnee Rock:** near Great Bend; on Santa Fe Trail.

**Pony Express Station:** near Hanover; only original unaltered Pony Express station extant.

**Rock City:** near Minneapolis; rock spheres.

**Shawnee Methodist Mission:** near Kansas City; founded in 1830; educated Indians (1839–62).

**Sod House:** Colby fairgrounds; reconstructed house and furnishings.

**Tuttle Creek State Park:** near Manhattan; camping, fishing, hiking, picnicking.

**Waconda Springs:** near Beloit; health resort.

**Woodson County State Lake:** near Toronto; scenic woodland; boating, picnicking.

## BOOKS ABOUT KANSAS

**Bailey, B. F.** Picture Book of Kansas, rev. ed. (Whitman, 1969).

**Coatsworth, E. J.** The Sod House (Macmillan, 1967).

**Corder, Eric.** Prelude to Civil War: Kansas-Missouri (Macmillan, 1970).

**Drury, J. W. and others.** The Government of Kansas, rev. ed. (Univ. of Kan. Press, 1970).

**Howes, C. C.** This Place Called Kansas (Univ. of Okla. Press, 1961) o.p.

**Miller, N. H.** Kansas: a Students' Guide to Localized History (Teachers College, 1965).

**Rawley, J. A.** Race and Politics: "Bleeding Kansas" and the Coming of the Civil War (Lippincott, 1969).

**Wilder, L. I.** Little House on the Prairie (Harper, 1975).

**Writers' Program.** Kansas: a Guide to the Sunflower State (Somerset, 1939).

**Zornow, W. F.** Kansas: a History of the Jayhawk State (Univ. of Okla. Press, 1971).

# KANSAS

## COUNTIES

| | | |
|---|---|---|
| Allen | 15,043 | G 4 |
| Anderson | 8,501 | G 3 |
| Atchison | 19,165 | G 2 |
| Barber | 7,016 | D 4 |
| Barton | 30,663 | D 3 |
| Bourbon | 15,215 | H 4 |
| Brown | 11,685 | G 2 |
| Butler | 38,658 | F 4 |
| Chase | 3,408 | F 3 |
| Chautauqua | 4,642 | F 4 |
| Cherokee | 21,549 | H 4 |
| Cheyenne | 4,256 | A 2 |
| Clark | 2,896 | C 4 |
| Clay | 9,890 | E 2 |
| Cloud | 13,466 | E 2 |
| Coffey | 7,397 | G 3 |
| Comanche | 2,702 | C 4 |
| Cowley | 35,012 | F 4 |
| Crawford | 37,850 | H 4 |
| Decatur | 4,988 | B 2 |
| Dickinson | 19,993 | E 3 |
| Doniphan | 9,107 | G 2 |
| Douglas | 57,932 | G 3 |
| Edwards | 4,581 | C 4 |
| Elk | 3,858 | F 4 |
| Ellis | 24,730 | C 3 |
| Ellsworth | 6,146 | D 3 |
| Finney | 19,029 | B 3 |
| Ford | 22,587 | C 4 |
| Franklin | 20,007 | G 3 |
| Geary | 28,111 | F 3 |
| Gove | 3,940 | B 3 |
| Graham | 4,751 | C 2 |
| Grant | 5,961 | A 4 |
| Gray | 4,516 | B 4 |
| Greeley | 1,819 | A 3 |
| Greenwood | 9,141 | F 4 |
| Hamilton | 2,747 | A 3 |
| Harper | 7,871 | D 4 |
| Harvey | 27,236 | E 3 |
| Haskell | 3,672 | B 4 |
| Hodgeman | 2,662 | C 3 |
| Jackson | 10,342 | G 2 |
| Jefferson | 11,945 | G 2 |
| Jewell | 6,099 | D 2 |
| Johnson | 220,073 | H 3 |
| Kearny | 3,047 | A 3 |
| Kingman | 8,886 | D 4 |
| Kiowa | 4,088 | C 4 |
| Labette | 25,775 | G 4 |
| Lane | 2,707 | B 3 |
| Leavenworth | 53,340 | G 2 |
| Lincoln | 4,582 | D 2 |
| Linn | 7,770 | H 3 |
| Logan | 3,814 | A 3 |
| Lyon | 32,071 | F 3 |
| Marion | 13,935 | E 3 |
| Marshall | 13,139 | F 2 |
| McPherson | 24,778 | E 3 |
| Meade | 4,912 | B 4 |
| Miami | 19,254 | H 3 |
| Mitchell | 8,010 | D 2 |
| Montgomery | 39,949 | G 4 |
| Morris | 6,432 | F 3 |
| Morton | 3,576 | A 4 |
| Nemaha | 11,825 | F 2 |
| Neosho | 18,812 | G 4 |
| Ness | 4,791 | C 3 |
| Norton | 7,279 | C 2 |
| Osage | 13,352 | G 3 |
| Osborne | 6,416 | D 2 |
| Ottawa | 6,183 | E 2 |
| Pawnee | 8,484 | C 3 |
| Phillips | 7,888 | C 2 |
| Pottawatomie | 11,755 | F 2 |
| Pratt | 10,056 | D 4 |
| Rawlins | 4,393 | A 2 |
| Reno | 60,765 | D 4 |
| Republic | 8,498 | E 2 |
| Rice | 12,320 | D 3 |
| Riley | 56,788 | F 2 |
| Rooks | 7,628 | C 2 |
| Rush | 5,117 | C 3 |
| Russell | 9,428 | D 3 |
| Saline | 46,592 | E 3 |
| Scott | 5,606 | B 3 |
| Sedgwick | 350,694 | E 4 |
| Seward | 15,744 | B 4 |
| Shawnee | 155,322 | G 2 |
| Sheridan | 3,859 | B 2 |
| Sherman | 7,792 | A 2 |
| Smith | 6,757 | D 2 |
| Stafford | 5,943 | D 3 |
| Stanton | 2,287 | A 4 |
| Stevens | 4,198 | A 4 |
| Sumner | 23,553 | E 4 |
| Thomas | 7,501 | A 2 |
| Trego | 4,436 | C 3 |
| Wabaunsee | 6,397 | F 3 |
| Wallace | 2,215 | A 3 |
| Washington | 9,249 | E 2 |
| Wichita | 3,274 | A 3 |
| Wilson | 11,317 | G 4 |
| Woodson | 4,789 | G 4 |
| Wyandotte | 186,845 | H 2 |

## CITIES AND TOWNS

| | | |
|---|---|---|
| Abbyville | 143 | D 4 |
| Abilene | 6,661 | E 3 |
| Ada | 120 | E 2 |
| Adams | 29 | E 4 |
| Admire | 144 | F 3 |
| Agenda | 107 | E 2 |
| Agra | 294 | C 2 |
| Agricola | 43 | G 3 |
| Alamota | 30 | B 3 |
| Albert | 235 | C 3 |
| Alden | 238 | D 3 |
| Alexander | 129 | C 3 |
| Aliceville | 50 | G 3 |
| Allen | 175 | F 3 |
| Alma | 905 | F 2 |
| Almena | 489 | C 2 |
| Altamont | 845 | G 4 |
| Alta Vista | 402 | F 3 |
| Alton | 214 | D 2 |
| Altoona | 475 | G 4 |
| Americus | 441 | F 3 |
| Ames | 65 | E 2 |
| Amy | 30 | B 3 |
| Andale | 500 | E 4 |
| Andover | 1,880 | E 4 |
| Angola | 40 | G 4 |
| Anson | 30 | E 4 |
| Antelope | 25 | F 3 |
| Anthony | 2,653 | D 4 |
| Antonino | 55 | C 3 |
| Arcadia | 388 | H 4 |
| Argonia | 591 | E 4 |
| Arkansas City | 13,216 | E 4 |
| Arlington | 503 | D 4 |
| Arma | 1,348 | H 4 |
| Arnold | 60 | B 3 |
| Arrington | 45 | G 2 |
| Ash Grove | 28 | D 2 |
| Ash Valley | 20 | C 3 |
| Asherville | 52 | D 2 |
| Ashland | 1,244 | C 4 |
| Ashton | 30 | E 4 |
| Assaria | 303 | E 3 |
| Atchison | 12,565 | G 2 |
| Athol | 108 | D 2 |
| Atlanta | 216 | F 4 |
| Attica | 639 | D 4 |
| Atwood | 1,658 | B 2 |
| Auburn | 261 | G 3 |
| Augusta | 5,977 | F 4 |
| Aurora | 120 | E 2 |
| Axtell | 456 | F 2 |
| Baileyville | 110 | F 2 |
| Bala | 26 | F 2 |
| Baldwin City | 2,520 | G 3 |
| Barnard | 190 | D 2 |
| Barnes | 209 | F 2 |
| Bartlett | 138 | G 4 |
| Basehor | 724 | G 2 |
| Bassett | 62 | G 4 |
| Bavaria | 80 | E 3 |
| Baxter Springs | 4,489 | H 4 |
| Bazaar | 40 | F 3 |
| Bazine | 386 | C 3 |
| Beagle | 80 | G 3 |
| Beattie | 288 | F 2 |
| Beaumont | 135 | F 4 |
| Beaver | 90 | D 3 |
| Beeler | 75 | B 3 |
| Bellaire | 21 | D 2 |
| Belle Plaine | 1,553 | E 4 |
| Bellefont | 34 | C 4 |
| Belleville | 3,063 | E 2 |
| Belmont | 35 | D 4 |
| Beloit | 4,121 | D 2 |
| Belpre | 191 | C 4 |
| Belvidere | 25 | C 4 |
| Belvue | 161 | F 2 |
| Bendena | 80 | G 2 |
| Benedict | 91 | G 4 |
| Bennington | 561 | E 2 |
| Bentley | 260 | E 4 |
| Benton | 517 | E 4 |
| Bern | 191 | F 2 |
| Berryton | 60 | G 3 |
| Beverly | 193 | E 2 |
| Big Bow | 90 | A 4 |
| Bird City | 671 | A 2 |
| Bison | 285 | C 3 |
| Blaine | 38 | F 2 |
| Blair | 40 | H 2 |
| Bloom | 63 | C 4 |
| Blue Mound | 308 | H 3 |
| Blue Rapids | 1,148 | F 2 |
| Bluff City | 109 | E 4 |
| Bogue | 257 | C 2 |
| Boicourt | 22 | H 3 |
| Bonner Sprs. | 3,662 | H 2 |
| Brantford | 35 | E 2 |
| Brazilton | 91 | H 4 |
| Bremen | 60 | F 2 |
| Brewster | 320 | A 2 |
| Bridgeport | 64 | E 3 |
| Bronson | 397 | H 4 |
| Brookville | 238 | E 3 |
| Brownell | 98 | C 3 |
| Bucklin | 771 | C 4 |
| Bucyrus | 196 | H 3 |
| Buffalo | 321 | G 4 |
| Buhler | 1,019 | E 3 |
| Bunker Hill | 181 | D 3 |
| Burden | 503 | F 4 |
| Burdett | 285 | C 3 |
| Burdick | 120 | F 3 |
| Burlingame | 999 | G 3 |
| Burlington | 2,099 | G 3 |
| Burns | 268 | F 3 |
| Burr Oak | 426 | D 2 |
| Burrton | 808 | E 3 |
| Bush City | 28 | G 3 |
| Bushong | 39 | F 3 |
| Bushton | 397 | D 3 |
| Byers | 46 | D 4 |
| Cairo | 38 | D 4 |
| Caldwell | 1,540 | E 4 |
| Cambridge | 110 | F 4 |
| Caney | 2,192 | G 4 |
| Canton | 893 | E 3 |
| Carbondale | 1,041 | G 3 |
| Carlton | 40 | E 3 |
| Carlyle | 50 | G 4 |
| Carneiro | 28 | D 3 |
| Cassoday | 123 | F 3 |
| Catharine | 126 | C 3 |
| Cawker City | 726 | D 2 |
| Cedar | 46 | D 2 |
| Cedar Bluffs | 20 | B 2 |
| Cedar Point | 73 | F 3 |
| Cedar Vale | 665 | F 4 |
| Centerville | 45 | H 3 |
| Centralia | 511 | F 2 |
| Chanute | 10,341 | G 4 |
| Chapman | 1,132 | E 3 |
| Charleston | 25 | B 4 |
| Chase | 800 | D 3 |
| Chautauqua | 137 | F 4 |
| Cheney | 1,160 | E 4 |
| Cherokee | 790 | H 4 |
| Cherryvale | 2,609 | G 4 |
| Chetopa | 1,596 | G 4 |
| Chicopee | 300 | H 4 |
| Cimarron | 1,373 | B 4 |
| Circleville | 178 | G 2 |
| Claflin | 887 | D 3 |
| Claudell | 20 | C 2 |
| Clay Center | 4,963 | E 2 |
| Clayton | 127 | B 2 |
| Clearwater | 1,435 | E 4 |
| Clements | 35 | F 3 |
| Clifton | 718 | E 2 |
| Climax | 64 | F 4 |
| Clyde | 946 | E 2 |
| Coats | 152 | D 4 |
| Codell | 100 | C 2 |
| Coffeyville | 15,116 | G 4 |
| Colby | 4,658 | A 2 |
| Coldwater | 1,016 | C 4 |
| Collyer | 182 | B 2 |
| Colony | 382 | G 3 |
| Columbus | 3,356 | H 4 |
| Colwich | 879 | E 4 |
| Concordia | 7,221 | E 2 |
| Conway | 64 | E 3 |
| Conway Sprs. | 1,153 | E 4 |
| Coolidge | 102 | A 3 |
| Copeland | 267 | B 4 |
| Corbin | 50 | E 4 |
| Corning | 162 | F 2 |
| Corwin | 25 | D 4 |
| Cottonwood Falls | 987 | F 3 |
| Council Grove | 2,403 | F 3 |
| Countryside | 403 | *H 2 |
| Courtland | 403 | E 2 |
| Coyville | 93 | G 4 |
| Crestline | 102 | H 4 |
| Crystal Springs | 35 | D 4 |
| Cuba | 290 | E 2 |
| Cullison | 117 | D 4 |
| Culver | 148 | E 3 |
| Cummings | 826 | G 2 |
| Cunningham | 483 | D 4 |
| Damar | 245 | C 2 |
| Danville | 80 | E 4 |
| De Soto | 1,839 | H 3 |
| Dearing | 338 | G 4 |
| Deerfield | 474 | A 4 |
| Delavan | 55 | F 3 |
| Delia | 168 | G 2 |
| Delphos | 599 | E 2 |
| Denison | 248 | G 2 |
| Denmark | 40 | D 2 |
| Dennis | 120 | G 4 |
| Densmore | 34 | C 2 |
| Denton | 162 | G 2 |
| Derby | 7,947 | E 4 |
| Detroit | 90 | E 3 |
| Devon | 80 | H 4 |
| Dexter | 286 | F 4 |
| Dighton | 1,540 | B 3 |
| Dodge City | 14,127 | B 4 |
| Dorrance | 234 | D 3 |
| Douglass | 1,126 | F 4 |
| Dover | 122 | G 3 |
| Downs | 1,268 | D 2 |
| Dresden | 103 | B 2 |
| Duluth | 34 | F 2 |
| Dunlap | 102 | F 3 |
| Durham | 143 | E 3 |
| Dwight | 322 | F 3 |
| Earlton | 102 | G 4 |
| Eastborough | 1,141 | E 4 |
| Easton | 435 | G 2 |
| Edgerton | 513 | H 3 |
| Edmond | 90 | C 2 |
| Edna | 418 | G 4 |
| Edson | 77 | A 2 |
| Edwardsville | 619 | H 2 |
| Effingham | 605 | G 2 |
| Elbing | 128 | E 3 |
| El Dorado | 12,308 | F 4 |
| Elgin | 115 | F 4 |
| Elk City | 432 | G 4 |
| Elk Falls | 124 | F 4 |
| Elkhart | 2,089 | A 4 |
| Ellinwood | 2,416 | D 3 |
| Ellis | 2,137 | C 3 |
| Ellsworth | 2,080 | D 3 |
| Elmdale | 102 | F 3 |
| Elmo | 25 | E 3 |
| Elmont | 112 | G 2 |
| Elsmore | 116 | G 4 |
| Elwood | 1,283 | H 2 |
| Elyria | 100 | E 3 |
| Emmett | 156 | F 2 |
| Emporia | 23,327 | F 3 |
| Englevale | 29 | H 4 |
| Englewood | 158 | C 4 |
| Ensign | 237 | B 4 |
| Enterprise | 868 | E 3 |
| Erie | 1,414 | G 4 |
| Esbon | 206 | D 2 |
| Eskridge | 589 | F 3 |
| Eudora | 2,071 | G 3 |
| Eureka | 3,576 | F 4 |
| Everest | 304 | G 2 |
| Fairport | 41 | C 2 |
| Fairview | 283 | G 2 |
| Fairway | 5,133 | *H 2 |
| Fall River | 191 | G 4 |
| Falun | 105 | E 3 |
| Farlington | 95 | H 4 |
| Fellsburg | 25 | C 4 |
| Florence | 716 | E 3 |
| Fontana | 160 | H 3 |
| Ford | 246 | C 4 |
| Formoso | 180 | D 2 |
| Fort Dodge | 450 | C 4 |
| Fort Leavenworth | 8,060 | H 2 |
| Fort Scott | 8,967 | H 4 |
| Fostoria | 63 | F 2 |
| Fowler | 588 | B 4 |
| Frankfort | 960 | F 2 |
| Franklin | 620 | H 4 |
| Frederick | 39 | D 3 |
| Fredonia | 3,080 | G 4 |
| Freeport | 21 | E 4 |
| Friend | 35 | B 3 |
| Frontenac | 2,223 | H 4 |
| Fulton | 213 | H 4 |
| Galatia | 78 | D 3 |
| Galena | 3,712 | H 4 |
| Galesburg | 146 | G 4 |
| Galva | 522 | E 3 |
| Garden City | 14,790 | B 4 |
| Garden Plain | 678 | E 4 |
| Gardner | 1,839 | H 3 |
| Garfield | 261 | C 3 |
| Garland | 125 | H 4 |
| Garnett | 3,169 | G 3 |
| Gas | 438 | G 4 |
| Gaylord | 211 | D 2 |
| Gem | 80 | B 2 |
| Geneseo | 453 | D 3 |
| Geuda Springs | 223 | E 4 |
| Girard | 2,591 | H 4 |
| Glade | 180 | C 2 |
| Glasco | 767 | E 2 |
| Glen Elder | 422 | D 2 |
| Glendale | 22 | E 3 |
| Goddard | 955 | E 4 |
| Goessel | 386 | E 3 |
| Goff | 207 | G 2 |
| Goodland | 5,510 | A 2 |
| Gordon | 30 | F 4 |
| Gorham | 379 | D 3 |
| Gove | 172 | B 3 |
| Grainfield | 374 | B 2 |
| Grandview Plaza | 734 | F 2 |
| Grantville | 190 | G 2 |
| Great Bend | 16,133 | D 3 |
| Greeley | 368 | G 3 |
| Green | 163 | E 2 |
| Greenleaf | 448 | E 2 |
| Greensburg | 1,907 | C 4 |
| Grenola | 290 | F 4 |
| Gridley | 328 | G 3 |
| Grinnell | 449 | B 2 |
| Gypsum | 391 | E 3 |
| Haddam | 289 | E 2 |
| Hallowell | 135 | H 4 |
| Halstead | 1,716 | E 4 |
| Hamilton | 349 | F 4 |
| Hamlin | 95 | G 2 |
| Hanover | 793 | F 2 |
| Hanston | 282 | C 3 |
| Hardtner | 300 | D 4 |
| Harlan | 62 | D 2 |
| Harper | 1,665 | D 4 |
| Harris | 41 | G 3 |
| Hartford | 478 | F 3 |
| Harveyville | 279 | F 3 |
| Havana | 144 | G 4 |
| Haven | 1,146 | E 4 |
| Havensville | 163 | F 2 |
| Haviland | 705 | C 4 |
| Hays | 15,396 | C 3 |
| Haysville | 6,483 | E 4 |
| Hazelton | 176 | D 4 |
| Healy | 251 | B 3 |
| Hedville | 35 | E 3 |
| Heizer | 85 | D 3 |
| Hepler | 152 | H 4 |
| Herington | 3,165 | E 3 |
| Herkimer | 75 | F 2 |
| Herndon | 268 | B 2 |
| Hesston | 1,926 | E 3 |
| Hewins | 70 | F 4 |
| Hiattville | 60 | H 4 |
| Hiawatha | 3,365 | G 2 |
| Hickok | 70 | A 4 |
| Highland | 899 | G 2 |
| Hill City | 2,071 | C 2 |
| Hillsboro | 2,730 | E 3 |
| Hillsdale | 250 | H 3 |
| Hoisington | 3,710 | D 3 |
| Holcomb | 272 | B 3 |
| Hollenberg | 47 | F 2 |
| Holmdel Gardens | 1,960 | *E 3 |
| Holton | 3,063 | G 2 |
| Holyrood | 593 | D 3 |
| Home | 120 | F 2 |
| Homewood | 60 | G 3 |
| Hope | 438 | E 3 |
| Horace | 137 | A 3 |
| Horton | 2,177 | G 2 |
| Howard | 918 | F 4 |
| Hoxie | 1,419 | B 2 |
| Hoyt | 420 | G 2 |
| Hudson | 181 | D 3 |
| Hugoton | 2,739 | A 4 |
| Humboldt | 2,249 | G 4 |
| Hunnewell | 77 | E 4 |
| Hunter | 150 | D 2 |
| Huron | 106 | G 2 |
| Hutchinson | 36,885 | D 3 |
| Hymer | 30 | F 3 |
| Idana | 96 | E 2 |
| Independence | 10,347 | G 4 |
| Industry | 60 | E 2 |
| Ingalls | 235 | B 4 |
| Inman | 836 | E 3 |
| Iola | 6,493 | G 4 |
| Ionia | 100 | D 2 |
| Iowa Point | 35 | G 2 |
| Isabel | 147 | D 4 |
| Iuka | 210 | D 4 |
| Jamestown | 470 | E 2 |
| Jarbalo | 73 | G 2 |
| Jennings | 224 | B 2 |
| Jetmore | 936 | B 3 |
| Jewell | 569 | D 2 |
| Johnson | 1,038 | A 4 |
| Junction City | 19,018 | E 2 |
| Kackley | 24 | E 2 |
| Kalvesta | 33 | B 3 |
| Kanopolis | 626 | D 3 |
| Kanorado | 278 | A 2 |
| Kansas City | 168,213 | H 2 |
| Kansas City | †1,256,327 | H 2 |
| Keats | 75 | F 2 |
| Kechi | 229 | E 4 |
| Kelly | 50 | G 2 |
| Kendall | 160 | A 4 |
| Kensington | 653 | C 2 |
| Kimball | 60 | G 4 |
| Kincaid | 189 | G 3 |
| Kingman | 3,622 | D 4 |
| Kingsdown | 45 | C 4 |
| Kinsley | 2,212 | C 4 |

*No room on map for name. †Population of metropolitan area.

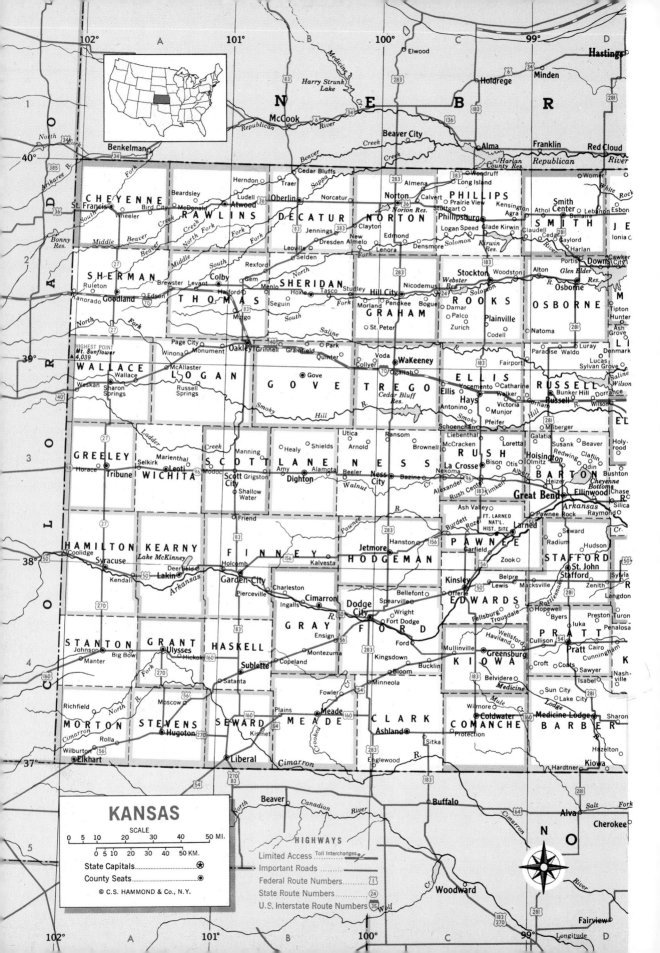

# KANSAS

SCALE

0 5 10 20 30 40 50 MI.

0 5 10 20 30 40 50 KM.

State Capitals ............ ⊛

County Seats ............ ◉

© C.S. HAMMOND & Co., N.Y.

## HIGHWAYS

Limited Access — Toll Interchanges ✱

Important Roads ..........

Federal Route Numbers ..........

State Route Numbers ..........

U.S. Interstate Route Numbers ..........

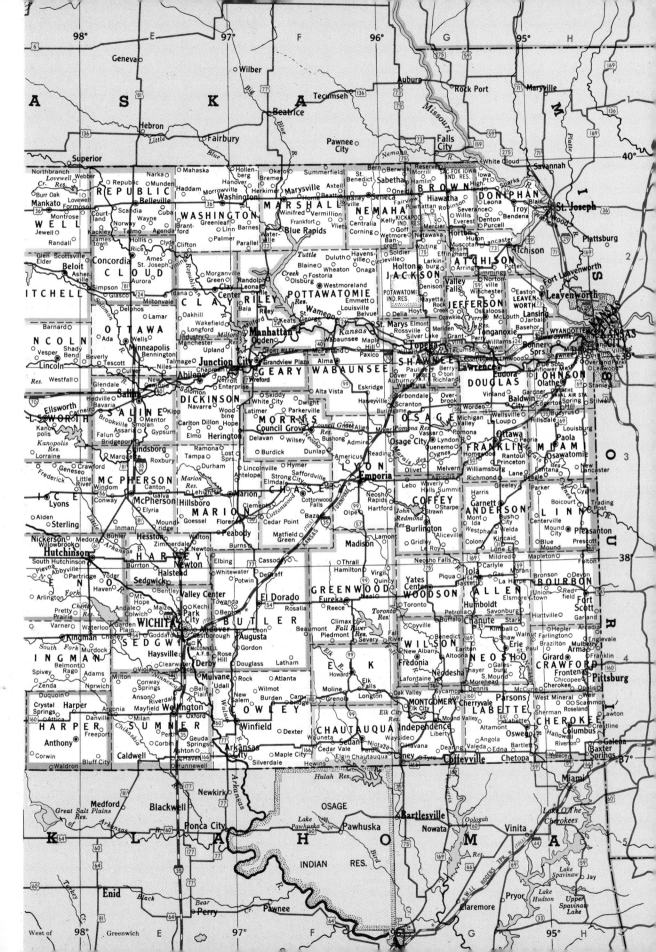

| | | |
|---|---|---|
| Kiowa | 1,414 | D 4 |
| Kipp | 77 | E 3 |
| Kirwin | 293 | C 2 |
| Kismet | 294 | B 4 |
| La Crosse | 1,583 | C 3 |
| La Cygne | 989 | H 3 |
| La Harpe | 509 | G 4 |
| Labette | 105 | G 4 |
| Lafontaine | 140 | G 4 |
| Lake City | 65 | D 4 |
| Lakin | 1,570 | A 4 |
| Lamont | 65 | F 3 |
| Lancaster | 279 | G 2 |
| Lane | 254 | G 3 |
| Langdon | 93 | D 4 |
| Lansing | 3,797 | H 2 |
| Larkinburg | 30 | G 2 |
| Larned | 4,567 | C 3 |
| Latham | 156 | F 4 |
| Latimer | 29 | F 3 |
| Lawrence | 45,698 | G 3 |
| Lawton | 60 | H 4 |
| Le Loup | 82 | G 3 |
| Le Roy | 551 | G 3 |
| Leavenworth | 25,147 | H 2 |
| Leawood | 10,349 | H 3 |
| Lebanon | 517 | D 2 |
| Lebo | 589 | G 3 |
| Lecompton | 434 | G 2 |
| Lehigh | 168 | E 3 |
| Lenexa | 5,242 | *H 3 |
| Lenora | 439 | C 2 |
| Leon | 510 | F 4 |
| Leona | 72 | G 2 |
| Leonardville | 412 | F 2 |
| Leoti | 1,916 | A 3 |
| Leoville | 70 | B 2 |
| Levant | 425 | A 2 |
| Lewis | 525 | C 4 |
| Liberal | 13,789 | B 4 |
| Liberty | 185 | G 4 |
| Liebenthal | 169 | C 3 |
| Lincoln | 1,582 | D 2 |
| Lincolnville | 218 | F 3 |
| Lindsborg | 2,764 | E 3 |
| Linn | 388 | E 2 |
| Linwood | 323 | G 2 |
| Little River | 493 | E 3 |
| Logan | 760 | C 2 |
| Lone Elm | 66 | G 3 |
| Longford | 99 | E 2 |
| Long Island | 195 | C 2 |
| Longton | 304 | F 4 |
| Loretta | 42 | C 3 |
| Lorraine | 153 | D 3 |
| Lost Springs | 103 | E 3 |
| Louisburg | 1,033 | H 3 |
| Louisville | 204 | F 2 |
| Lovewell | 30 | D 2 |
| Lucas | 524 | D 2 |
| Ludell | 100 | B 2 |
| Luray | 303 | D 2 |
| Lyndon | 958 | G 3 |
| Lyons | 4,355 | D 3 |
| Macksville | 484 | D 4 |
| Madison | 1,061 | F 3 |
| Mahaska | 122 | E 2 |
| Maize | 785 | E 4 |
| Manchester | 92 | E 2 |
| Manhattan | 27,575 | F 2 |
| Mankato | 1,287 | D 2 |
| Manter | 219 | A 4 |
| Maple City | 20 | F 4 |
| Maple Hill | 327 | F 2 |
| Mapleton | 112 | H 3 |
| Marienthal | 120 | A 3 |
| Marion | 2,052 | F 3 |
| Marquette | 578 | E 3 |
| Marysville | 3,588 | F 2 |
| Matfield Green | 77 | F 3 |
| Mayetta | 246 | G 2 |
| Mayfield | 110 | E 4 |
| McCracken | 333 | C 3 |
| McCune | 487 | G 4 |
| McDonald | 269 | A 2 |
| McFarland | 209 | F 2 |
| McLouth | 623 | G 2 |
| McPherson | 10,851 | E 3 |
| Meade | 1,899 | B 4 |
| Medicine Lodge | 2,545 | D 4 |
| Medora | 110 | E 3 |
| Melvern | 455 | G 3 |
| Menlo | 48 | B 2 |
| Mentor | 75 | E 3 |
| Mercier | 85 | G 2 |
| Meriden | 472 | G 2 |
| Merriam | 10,851 | H 3 |
| Michigan Valley | 70 | G 3 |
| Milan | 162 | E 4 |
| Milberger | 28 | D 3 |
| Mildred | 42 | G 3 |
| Milford | 296 | F 2 |
| Miller | 50 | F 3 |
| Milton | 75 | E 4 |
| Miltonvale | 718 | E 2 |
| Minneapolis | 1,971 | E 2 |
| Minneola | 630 | C 4 |
| Mission | 8,376 | H 2 |
| Mission Hills | 4,177 | *H 2 |
| Mission Woods | 242 | *H 2 |
| Modoc | 50 | A 3 |
| Moline | 555 | F 4 |
| Mont Ida | 45 | G 3 |
| Montezuma | 606 | B 4 |
| Montrose | 44 | D 2 |
| Monument | 101 | A 2 |
| Moran | 550 | G 4 |
| Morehead | 20 | G 4 |
| Morganville | 257 | E 2 |
| Morland | 300 | B 2 |
| Morrill | 308 | G 2 |
| Morrowville | 201 | E 2 |
| Moscow | 228 | A 4 |
| Mound City | 714 | H 3 |
| Moundridge | 1,271 | E 3 |
| Mound Valley | 467 | G 4 |
| Mount Hope | 665 | E 4 |
| Mulberry | 622 | H 4 |
| Mullinville | 376 | C 4 |
| Mulvane | 3,185 | E 4 |
| Munden | 123 | E 2 |
| Munjor | 200 | C 3 |
| Murdock | 65 | E 4 |
| Muscotah | 206 | G 2 |
| Narka | 130 | E 2 |
| Nashville | 107 | D 4 |
| Natoma | 603 | D 2 |
| Navarre | 88 | E 3 |
| Neal | 78 | F 4 |
| Nekoma | 36 | C 3 |
| Neodesha | 3,295 | G 4 |
| Neosho Falls | 184 | G 3 |
| Neosho Rapids | 234 | F 3 |
| Ness City | 1,756 | C 3 |
| Netawaka | 192 | G 2 |
| New Albany | 59 | G 4 |
| New Almelo | 85 | B 2 |
| New Cambria | 160 | E 3 |
| New Salem | 100 | F 4 |
| Newton | 15,439 | E 3 |
| Nickerson | 1,187 | D 3 |
| Nicodemus | 62 | C 2 |
| Niles | 90 | E 2 |
| Niotaze | 83 | F 4 |
| Norcatur | 284 | B 2 |
| North Newton | 963 | E 3 |
| Northbranch | 30 | D 2 |
| Norton | 3,627 | C 2 |
| Nortonville | 727 | G 2 |
| Norway | 55 | E 2 |
| Norwich | 414 | E 4 |
| Oak Valley | 50 | G 4 |
| Oakhill | 41 | E 2 |
| Oakley | 2,327 | B 2 |
| Oberlin | 2,291 | B 2 |
| Odin | 117 | D 3 |
| Offerle | 212 | C 4 |
| Ogallah | 110 | C 3 |
| Ogden | 1,491 | F 2 |
| Oketo | 133 | F 2 |
| Olathe | 17,917 | H 3 |
| Olivet | 64 | G 3 |
| Olmitz | 161 | D 3 |
| Olpe | 453 | F 3 |
| Olsburg | 151 | F 2 |
| Onaga | 761 | F 2 |
| Oneida | 112 | G 2 |
| Opolis | 160 | H 4 |
| Osage City | 2,600 | G 3 |
| Osawatomie | 4,294 | H 3 |
| Osborne | 1,980 | D 2 |
| Oskaloosa | 955 | G 2 |
| Oswego | 2,200 | G 4 |
| Otis | 387 | C 3 |
| Ottawa | 11,036 | G 3 |
| Overbrook | 748 | G 3 |
| Overland Park | 79,034 | H 3 |
| Oxford | 1,113 | E 4 |
| Ozawkie | 137 | G 2 |
| Page City | 60 | A 2 |
| Palco | 398 | C 2 |
| Palmer | 166 | E 2 |
| Paola | 4,622 | H 3 |
| Paradise | 145 | D 2 |
| Park | 178 | B 2 |
| Park City | 2,529 | E 4 |
| Parker | 255 | H 3 |
| Parkerville | 25 | F 3 |
| Parsons | 13,015 | G 4 |
| Partridge | 302 | D 4 |
| Pauline | 800 | G 3 |
| Pawnee Rock | 442 | D 3 |
| Paxico | 216 | F 2 |
| Peabody | 1,368 | E 3 |
| Peck | 150 | E 4 |
| Penalosa | 32 | D 4 |
| Penokee | 97 | C 2 |
| Peoria | 100 | G 3 |
| Perry | 664 | G 2 |
| Perth | 63 | E 4 |
| Peru | 289 | F 4 |
| Petrolia | 69 | G 4 |
| Pfeifer | 175 | C 3 |
| Phillipsburg | 3,241 | C 2 |
| Piedmont | 116 | F 4 |
| Pierceville | 175 | B 4 |
| Piqua | 107 | G 4 |
| Pittsburg | 20,171 | H 4 |
| Plains | 857 | B 4 |
| Plainville | 2,627 | C 2 |
| Pleasanton | 1,216 | H 3 |
| Plevna | 124 | D 4 |
| Pomona | 541 | G 3 |
| Portis | 178 | D 2 |
| Potter | 96 | G 2 |
| Potwin | 497 | F 4 |
| Powhattan | 111 | G 2 |
| Prairie View | 201 | C 2 |
| Prairie Vill. | 28,138 | H 2 |
| Pratt | 6,736 | D 4 |
| Prescott | 222 | H 3 |
| Preston | 239 | D 4 |
| Pretty Prairie | 561 | D 4 |
| Princeton | 159 | G 3 |
| Protection | 673 | C 4 |
| Quenemo | 429 | G 3 |
| Quincy | 35 | F 4 |
| Quinter | 930 | B 2 |
| Radium | 55 | D 3 |
| Rago | 53 | D 4 |
| Ramona | 121 | E 3 |
| Randall | 195 | D 2 |
| Randolph | 106 | F 2 |
| Ransom | 416 | C 3 |
| Rantoul | 163 | G 3 |
| Raymond | 133 | D 3 |
| Reading | 247 | F 3 |
| Redfield | 138 | H 4 |
| Redwing | 54 | D 3 |
| Reece | 60 | F 4 |
| Republic | 243 | E 2 |
| Reserve | 117 | G 2 |
| Rexford | 231 | B 2 |
| Richfield | 82 | A 4 |
| Richland | 100 | G 3 |
| Richmond | 464 | G 3 |
| Riley | 668 | F 2 |
| Riverdale | 79 | E 4 |
| Riverton | 500 | H 4 |
| Robinson | 278 | G 2 |
| Rock | 102 | F 4 |
| Rock Creek | 93 | G 2 |
| Roeland Park | 9,974 | H 2 |
| Rolla | 400 | A 4 |
| Rosalia | 130 | F 4 |
| Rose Hill | 387 | E 4 |
| Roseland | 113 | H 4 |
| Rossville | 934 | G 2 |
| Roxbury | 110 | E 3 |
| Rozel | 236 | C 3 |
| Ruleton | 50 | A 2 |
| Rush Center | 237 | C 3 |
| Russell | 5,371 | D 3 |
| Russell Sprs. | 83 | A 3 |
| Sabetha | 2,376 | G 2 |
| Saffordville | 23 | F 3 |
| Saint Benedict | 75 | F 2 |
| Saint Francis | 1,725 | A 2 |
| Saint George | 241 | F 2 |
| Saint John | 1,477 | D 3 |
| Saint Joseph | 80 | E 2 |
| Saint Marys | 1,434 | G 2 |
| Saint Paul | 804 | G 4 |
| Saint Peter | 60 | C 2 |
| Salina | 37,714 | E 3 |
| Satanta | 1,161 | B 4 |
| Savonburg | 109 | G 4 |
| Sawyer | 164 | D 4 |
| Scammon | 457 | H 4 |
| Scandia | 567 | E 2 |
| Schoenchen | 182 | C 3 |
| Scott City | 4,001 | B 3 |
| Scottsville | 46 | D 2 |
| Scranton | 575 | G 3 |
| Sedan | 1,555 | F 4 |
| Sedgwick | 1,083 | E 4 |
| Seguin | 40 | B 2 |
| Selden | 271 | B 2 |
| Selkirk | 25 | A 3 |
| Seneca | 2,182 | F 2 |
| Severance | 128 | G 2 |
| Severy | 384 | F 4 |
| Seward | 66 | D 3 |
| Shady Bend | 28 | D 2 |
| Shallow Water | 106 | B 3 |
| Sharon | 265 | D 4 |
| Sharon Springs | 1,012 | A 3 |
| Shaw | 40 | G 4 |
| Shawnee | 20,482 | H 2 |
| Sherman | 53 | H 4 |
| Shields | 110 | B 3 |
| Silver Lake | 811 | G 2 |
| Silverdale | 64 | F 4 |
| Simpson | 131 | E 2 |
| Skiddy | 25 | F 3 |
| Smith Center | 2,389 | D 2 |
| Smolan | 175 | E 3 |
| Soldier | 173 | G 2 |
| Solomon | 973 | E 3 |
| South Haven | 413 | E 4 |
| S. Hutchinson | 1,879 | D 3 |
| South Mound | 46 | G 4 |
| Sparks | 71 | G 2 |
| Spearville | 738 | C 4 |
| Speed | 58 | C 2 |
| Spivey | 78 | D 4 |
| Spring Hill | 1,186 | H 3 |
| Stafford | 1,414 | D 4 |
| Stanley | 450 | H 3 |
| Stark | 124 | G 4 |
| Sterling | 2,312 | D 3 |
| Stilwell | 350 | H 3 |
| Stockton | 1,818 | C 2 |
| Strawn | 100 | G 3 |
| Strong City | 545 | F 3 |
| Studley | 53 | B 2 |
| Stuttgart | 90 | C 2 |
| Sublette | 1,208 | B 4 |
| Summerfield | 254 | F 2 |
| Sun City | 119 | D 4 |
| Sunflower | 1,744 | H 3 |
| Susank | 59 | D 3 |
| Sycamore | 125 | G 4 |
| Sylvan Grove | 403 | D 2 |
| Sylvia | 390 | D 4 |
| Syracuse | 1,720 | A 3 |
| Talmage | 125 | E 2 |
| Talmo | 35 | E 2 |
| Tampa | 154 | E 3 |
| Tasco | 20 | B 2 |
| Tecumseh | 250 | G 2 |
| Tescott | 393 | E 2 |
| Thayer | 430 | G 4 |
| Timken | 123 | C 3 |
| Tipton | 315 | D 2 |
| Tonganoxie | 1,717 | G 2 |
| TOPEKA | 125,011 | G 2 |
| Topeka | †155,322 | G 2 |
| Toronto | 431 | G 4 |
| Towanda | 1,190 | E 4 |
| Trading Post | 35 | H 3 |
| Traer | 35 | B 2 |
| Treece | 225 | H 4 |
| Tribune | 1,013 | A 3 |
| Trousdale | 50 | C 4 |
| Troy | 1,047 | G 2 |
| Turon | 430 | D 4 |
| Tyro | 206 | G 4 |
| Udall | 668 | E 4 |
| Ulysses | 3,779 | A 4 |
| Uniontown | 286 | G 4 |
| Upland | 20 | E 2 |
| Utica | 297 | B 3 |
| Valeda | 100 | G 4 |
| Valley Ctr. | 2,551 | E 4 |
| Valley Falls | 1,169 | G 2 |
| Varner | 47 | D 4 |
| Vassar | 79 | G 3 |
| Vermillion | 191 | F 2 |
| Vesper | 48 | D 2 |
| Victoria | 1,246 | C 3 |
| Vining | 84 | E 2 |
| Vinland | 102 | G 3 |
| Viola | 193 | E 4 |
| Virgil | 179 | F 4 |
| Vliets | 55 | F 2 |
| Wabaunsee | 75 | F 2 |
| Wakarusa | 90 | G 3 |
| WaKeeney | 2,334 | C 3 |
| Wakefield | 583 | E 2 |
| Waldo | 123 | D 2 |
| Waldron | 24 | D 4 |
| Walker | 72 | C 3 |
| Wallace | 112 | A 3 |
| Walnut | 330 | G 4 |
| Walton | 211 | E 3 |
| Wamego | 2,507 | F 2 |
| Washington | 1,584 | E 2 |
| Waterloo | 60 | E 4 |
| Waterville | 632 | F 2 |
| Wathena | 1,150 | H 2 |
| Waverly | 510 | G 3 |
| Wayne | 26 | E 2 |
| Wayside | 85 | G 4 |
| Webber | 49 | D 2 |
| Weir | 740 | H 4 |
| Welda | 149 | G 3 |
| Wellington | 8,072 | E 4 |
| Wells | 75 | E 2 |
| Wellsville | 1,183 | G 3 |
| Weskan | 350 | A 3 |
| West Mineral | 232 | H 4 |
| Westmoreland | 485 | F 2 |
| Westfall | 65 | D 3 |
| Westphalia | 185 | G 3 |
| West Plains (Plains) | 857 | B 4 |
| Westwood | 2,329 | *H 2 |
| Westwood Hills | 414 | *H 2 |
| Wetmore | 392 | G 2 |
| Wheaton | 106 | F 2 |
| Wheeler | 35 | A 2 |
| White City | 458 | F 3 |
| White Cloud | 210 | G 2 |
| Whitewater | 520 | E 4 |
| Whiting | 256 | G 2 |
| Wichita | 276,554 | E 4 |
| Wichita | †389,352 | E 4 |
| Wilburton | 40 | A 4 |
| Willard | 124 | G 2 |
| Williamsburg | 286 | G 3 |
| Williamstown | 89 | G 2 |
| Willis | 82 | G 2 |
| Willowbrook | 100 | D 3 |
| Wilmore | 96 | C 4 |
| Wilmot | 24 | F 4 |
| Wilsey | 169 | F 3 |
| Wilson | 870 | D 3 |
| Winchester | 492 | G 2 |
| Windom | 183 | E 3 |
| Winfield | 11,405 | F 4 |
| Winifred | 30 | F 2 |
| Winona | 293 | A 2 |
| Woodbine | 170 | E 3 |
| Woodruff | 30 | C 2 |
| Woodston | 211 | C 2 |
| Worden | 57 | G 3 |
| Wright | 173 | C 4 |
| Yates Center | 1,967 | G 4 |
| Yoder | 155 | E 4 |
| Zenda | 142 | D 4 |
| Zenith | 100 | D 4 |
| Zimmerdale | 20 | E 3 |
| Zook | 45 | C 3 |
| Zurich | 189 | C 2 |

### OTHER FEATURES

| | | |
|---|---|---|
| Arkansas (riv.) | | D 3 |
| Beaver (creek) | | A 2 |
| Big Blue (riv.) | | F 1 |
| Cedar Bluff (res.) | | C 3 |
| Cheney (res.) | | E 4 |
| Cheyenne Bottoms (lake) | | D 3 |
| Chikaskia (riv.) | | E 4 |
| Cimarron (riv.) | | B 4 |
| Cottonwood (riv.) | | F 3 |
| Crooked (creek) | | B 4 |
| Elk (riv.) | | F 4 |
| Fall (riv.) | | G 4 |
| Forbes A.F.B. | | G 3 |
| Ft. Larned Nat'l Hist. Site | | C 3 |
| Ft. Riley | 14,779 | F 2 |
| Hulah (res.) | | F 5 |
| John Redmond (res.) | | G 3 |
| Kanopolis (res.) | | D 3 |
| Kansas (riv.) | | F 2 |
| Kickapoo Ind. Res. | 255 | G 2 |
| Ladder (creek) | | A 3 |
| Little Arkansas (riv.) | | E 3 |
| Little Blue (riv.) | | E 1 |
| Marais des Cygnes (riv.) | | H 3 |
| Marion (res.) | | E 3 |
| McConnell A.F.B. | | E 4 |
| McKinney (lake) | | A 3 |
| Medicine Lodge (riv.) | | D 4 |
| Milford (res.) | | E 2 |
| Missouri (riv.) | | G 1 |
| Nemaha (riv.) | | G 1 |
| Neosho (riv.) | | G 4 |
| Ninnescah (riv.) | | F 4 |
| Olathe Naval Air Sta. | | H 3 |
| Pawnee (riv.) | | B 3 |
| Potawatomi Ind. Res. | 663 | G 2 |
| Rattlesnake (creek) | | D 4 |
| Republican (riv.) | | E 2 |
| Sac-Fox-Iowa Ind. Res. | 125 | G 2 |
| Saline (riv.) | | D 3 |
| Sappa (creek) | | B 2 |
| Smoky Hill (riv.) | | C 3 |
| Solomon (riv.) | | E 2 |
| Sunflower (mt.) | | A 2 |
| Toronto (res.) | | F 4 |
| Tuttle Creek (res.) | | F 2 |
| Verdigris (riv.) | | G 5 |
| Walnut (creek) | | B 3 |
| Walnut (riv.) | | E 4 |
| Webster (res.) | | C 2 |
| White Rock (creek) | | D 2 |

*No room on map for name. †Population of metropolitan area.

THIS ARTICLE IS IN THE FACT-INDEX
**Kansas, University of**

**KANSAS CITY, Kan.** Only the state line divides Kansas City, the second largest city of Kansas, from its twin city on the Missouri side. The two cities are really one industrially and commercially. Both are served by the same bus system and telephone exchange. The Kansas metropolis is situated on both sides of the Kansas (Kaw) River, west of Kansas City, Mo. It rises in the west to bluffs and hills upon which many of the city's residences are built.

The bottomlands in the river valley are devoted to many great industries and factories. The slaughtering and meat-packing plants are the most important. Owing to their position among the corn and beef states of the Southwest, the two Kansas Citys rank high as a livestock market. They also make shortening, soap, and other important by-products of the meat-packing industry.

The advantages of natural gas and oil, combined with excellent railway facilities, have helped greatly in building up the industries of Kansas City, Kan. In addition to its stockyards it has flour and feed mills, grain elevators, and varied food-product plants. It has oil refineries, iron- and steelworks, foundries, electrical- and transportation-equipment plants, and lumber- and brickyards. There are 28 parks, with a total area of 375 acres. Educational institutions include the University of Kansas Medical Center and the state school for the blind. West of the city the Agricultural Hall of Fame and National Center is being built on a 275-acre site. Modern Kansas City was formed in 1886 by a merger of several towns. It is governed by a commission. (*See also* Kansas.) Population (1980 census), 161,148.

**TWIN CITIES ON THE KANSAS RIVER**
This view is westward from Kansas City, Mo., toward the industrial area of Kansas City, Kan., along the Kansas River. On both sides of the river are the great stockyards.

**KANSAS CITY, Mo.** Missouri's second largest city is the marketplace and manufacturing center for a vast area of the West and Southwest. It lies on the western boundary of the state, at the point where the Kansas (Kaw) River enters the waters of the Missouri.

Here the winding Missouri leaves the state border, checks its southward course, and turns sharply eastward. This location has been a natural trading center for more than 100 years. Fur trappers along both rivers brought their pelts to the bend where François Chouteau established a trading post in 1821. Westport Landing grew up nearby. At this transfer point, settlers coming upstream by boat outfitted their wagons for the long journey to the Far West over either the Santa Fe or the Oregon Trail. At first Independence, ten miles to the east, was the main outfitting center. But the great Missouri flood of 1844 destroyed the Independence wharves, and West-port Landing gained most of the Santa Fe trade. In 1853 Westport Landing was renamed City of Kansas, and in 1889 it became Kansas City.

Kansas City's industries have developed out of the rich agricultural lands which surround it. Lying between the Western range country, where cattle are raised in great numbers, and the corn belt, where they are fattened, it became a big livestock market and meat-packing center. Important by-products of the meat-packing industry include soap, gelatin, oleomargarine, and leather goods. It is the world's largest winter wheat market. With Kansas City, Kan., its twin city, it is second only to Buffalo in flour milling. Other large industries include bakery and other food products, garmentmaking, printing and publishing, automobile assembling, petroleum refining, and the manufacture of iron and steel, machinery and equipment, cereals, stock feed, and chemicals.

Kansas City is situated on bluffs which rise in terraces above the river bottoms. An extensive boulevard and expressway system links the various parts of the city and the suburbs. In the heart of the city is the Municipal Auditorium, where conventions, stage productions, and sports events are held. The auditorium's Music Hall is the home of the Kansas City Philharmonic Orchestra. Baseball's Kansas City Royals and football's Kansas City Chiefs play in separate stadiums in the Harry S. Truman sports complex. The city's Union Station is one of the largest railway terminals in the country. Facing it across a plaza stands the shaft of the Liberty Memorial.

The William Rockhill Nelson Gallery of Art and the Mary Atkins Museum of Fine Arts contain notable collections. Nearby is the Kansas City Art Institute and School of Design. Also in the city are the University of Missouri at Kansas City, Rockhurst College, Central Institute of Technology, Avila College, and the Penn Valley Community College. The Midwest Research Institute is noted for scientific research in many fields. Midcontinent Airport, opened in 1963, and the Municipal Airport serve the city.

An extensive rebuilding program was begun in the early 1960's. Many government buildings are concentrated in the Civic Center. Kansas City has the city manager form of government. (*See also* Missouri.) Population (1980 census), 448,159.

**KANSAS-NEBRASKA ACT.** The Kansas-Nebraska Act, passed by Congress in 1854, has been called the most momentous piece of legislation in the United States before the Civil War. It set in motion events which led directly to the conflict over slavery.

In January 1854, with the support of President Franklin Pierce, Senator Stephen A. Douglas of Illinois laid before the Senate a report of the Committee on Territories. This provided for the organization of the territories of Kansas and Nebraska. The bill allowed the people of these regions to decide for themselves whether they would allow slavery within their borders. The bill as finally enacted into a law expressly repealed the Missouri Compromise, which had prohibited slavery north of latitude 36° 30'. A whole generation had regarded the Missouri Compromise as a binding agreement between the North and the South. (*See also* Missouri Compromise.)

The news that such an act was being considered fell like a thunderbolt upon the people of the North. Mass meetings were held to denounce the measure. Ministers preached against the "Nebraska iniquity," and Douglas was accused of weakly yielding to the South in the hope of winning the presidency.

In spite of Northern anger, Congress passed the bill on May 30, 1854. The fight over slavery was then transferred to the two territories. Proslavery men of the South and antislavery men of the North rushed into Kansas. Each side determined to win the state. The first elections, in 1855, were carried by the settlers from the South, aided by the "border ruffians" of Missouri. They crossed the border the night before election and seized the polls, illegally casting their votes for a proslavery candidate for governor.

The settlers from the North refused to accept the results of this fraudulent election. They held an election of their own, at which the proslavery men refused to vote. As a result two rival governments

were set up in the territory, and a civil war started. The antislavery party under the leadership of John Brown returned violence for the violence of the proslavery men. The attention of the whole country was fixed on "bleeding Kansas."

The settlers from the South were supported by President Pierce. Eventually he sent United States troops into the territory to quell the disturbance and to disperse the free-state legislature. A new election was then called. Again the illegal methods of the proslavery party won the day. Congress refused to recognize the constitution adopted by such methods as legal, and Kansas was forced to remain a territory for a while longer.

As time went on, the free-state settlers became more numerous, and finally the South gave up the attempt to make Kansas a slave state. A new constitution was then drawn up, and on Jan. 29, 1861, on the eve of the Civil War, Kansas was admitted to the Union as a free state. (*See also* Kansas.)

THESE ARTICLES ARE IN THE FACT-INDEX

Kansas River
Kansas State
College of
Pittsburg
Kansas State Teachers
College

Kansas State University
of Agriculture and
Applied Science
Kansas Wesleyan
Kansu, People's Republic
of China

**KANT, Immanuel** (1724–1804). The philosopher of the 1700's who ranks with Aristotle and Plato of ancient times is Immanuel Kant. This mild little man set forth a chain of explosive ideas that have kept men thinking ever since his time. He created a link between the idealists—those who thought that all reality was in the mind—and the materialists—those who

The Bettmann Archive

thought that the only reality lay in the things of the material world. Kant's ideas on the relationship of mind and matter provide the key to understanding the writings of many 20th-century philosophers.

Kant was born April 22, 1724, in Königsberg, East Prussia, Germany. His father was a saddle and harness maker. Young Kant was the fourth of ten children. The boy attended school at the Collegium Fredericianum. He studied religion and the Latin classics. When he was 16 years old he entered the University of Königsberg. He enrolled as a student of theology, but he soon became more interested in physics and mathematics.

After leaving college he worked for nine years as a tutor in the homes of rich families. In 1755 he took his doctor's degree at the university and became a lecturer to university students. He lived on the small fees his students paid him. He turned down offers from other schools, and finally the University of Königsberg offered him the position of professor of logic and metaphysics.

Kant never married. He never traveled farther than 50 miles from Königsberg, where he died in 1804. He lived a regular life, dividing his time between his lectures, his writing, and his daily walks. He was small, thin, and weak, but his ideas were powerful.

### Kant's Great Ideas

Kant's most famous work was the 'Critique of Pure Reason' (published 1781, revised 1787). In it he tried to set up the difference between things of the outside world and actions of the mind. He said that things which exist in the world are real, but the human mind is needed to give them order and form and to see the relationships between them. Only the mind can surround them with space and time. The principles of mathematics are part of the space-time thoughts supplied by the mind to real things.

For example, we see only one or two walls of a house at any one time. The mind gathers up these sense impressions of individual walls and mentally builds a complete house. Thus the whole house is being created in the mind while our eyes see only a part of it.

Kant said that thoughts must be based on real things. Pure reason without reference to the outside world is impossible. We know only what we first gather up with our senses. Yet living in the real world does not mean that ideals should be abandoned. In his 'Critique of Practical Reason' (published 1788) he argued for a stern morality. His basic idea was in the form of a Categorical Imperative. This meant that men should act so well that their conduct could give rise to a universal law.

THESE ARTICLES ARE IN THE FACT-INDEX

Kantor, MacKinlay
Kantorovich, Leonid
Kantrowitz, Adrian
Kantrowitz, Arthur
  (Robert)

Kaohsiung, Republic of
  China
Kao K'o-kung
Kapitza, Peter
  Leonidovich
Kaplan, Joseph

**KAPOK** (kā′pŏk). From the branches of the ceiba tree dangle pods filled with silky fibers called kapok. These fibers are fine, air-filled tubes, valuable for making mattresses, upholstery, lifesaving equipment, and insulation. In life preservers kapok supports 30 times its own weight and is seven times more buoyant than cork. Fiberglas, foam rubber, and other substitutes are replacing kapok in some uses. Highly flammable, kapok can be rendered reasonably fireproof by a simple chemical treatment.

The ceiba tree grows in all tropical and semitropical climates. It thrives best at altitudes of less than a thousand feet and on porous volcanic soil.

Almost all the kapok used in the United States is imported from Thailand and Indonesia. Other important producers are Vietnam, Ecuador, the Philippines, and Sri Lanka. Most kapok is obtained from wild trees. Less than 10 percent is grown on plantations. A mature tree yields about 7,000 pods, or 60 pounds of cleaned floss, and about 135 pounds of seeds. The seeds furnish oil for making soap. The down of milkweed can be used as a substitute for kapok (see Milkweed).

THESE ARTICLES ARE IN THE FACT-INDEX

Kapp, Wolfgang von
Kappa Delta Pi
Kapteyn, Jacobus

**KARACHI, Pakistan.** When Pakistan became a nation in 1947, Karachi in West Pakistan was chosen its first capital. A sea- and airport on the Arabian Sea, near the mouth of the Indus River, it had a population of some 300,000. The city quickly tripled in size  and continued to grow, as throngs of Moslems from Hindu India poured in (see Pakistan).

The Pakistan central government started projects to ease the severe housing and employment problems. Huge refugee colonies were developed on the city's outskirts. An industrial estate was laid out to set aside land for new factories, built both by the government and by private capital. The port was expanded and modernized to handle the increasing commerce. In 1959 the capital was shifted to Rawalpindi and in 1967 to Islamabad.

Karachi is the largest city in Pakistan and is the nation's principal commercial and industrial center. There are many popular attractions, including fishing in the city's harbor and bathing at nearby beaches. Other places of interest are a zoological garden, the national museum, and an aquarium. Population (1975 estimate, metropolitan area), 4,465,000.

THESE ARTICLES ARE IN THE FACT-INDEX

Karaganda, Russia
Karageorge
Karajan, Herbert von
Karajich, Vuk Stefanovich
Karakoram Range
Karakorum, Mongolian
  People's Republic
Karamzin, Nikolai
  Mikhailovich
Kara Sea
Karate
Karbala, Iraq
Karelian Isthmus
Karikal, India
Karlfeldt, Erik Axel
Karl-Marx-Stadt, East
  Germany
Karloff, Boris

Karlovy Vary,
  Czechoslovakia
Karlowitz, Yugoslavia
Karlskrona, Sweden
Karlsruhe, West Germany
Karnataka, India
Karok
Károlyi, Mihály, Count
Kárpathos
Karrer, Paul
Kars, Turkey
Karsavina, Tamara
Karsh, Yousuf
Karun River
Kasai River
Kasavubu, Joseph
Kashgar, People's
  Republic of China

Suraj N. Sharma

Many Indians make their homes in houseboats such as these craft on the Jhelum River of Kashmir and Pakistan. The Jhelum flows through the fabled Vale of Kashmir.

papier-mâché articles, wood carvings, and silverware. Hindus form an influential minority in Kashmir. Most of them live in the Jammu area. In the high Ladakh region of the east are Buddhists of Mongoloid stock.

Kashmir's natural resources include extensive forests and coal deposits. These resources, however, have been little developed.

## History of Kashmir

Owing to its seclusion, Kashmir experienced few political changes until modern times. In 1586 Akbar brought Kashmir into the great Mogul Empire (*see* India). The Afghans conquered it in 1756 and held it until 1819, when it fell to the Sikhs of the Punjab. In 1846 the British took Kashmir under their protection and established a princely Hindu family of Jammu, the Singhs, on the throne. Kashmir and Jammu were thus united.

The Indian Empire was dissolved in 1947. Kashmir was granted independence. At once Pakistan claimed it, and 10,000 Moslems invaded Kashmir from Pakistan. Fearing the loss of his throne, Kashmir's Hindu maharajah called on India for aid. India moved in troops, and an undeclared war broke out. The United Nations called for a plebiscite. In 1949 India and Pakistan ordered a cease-fire; but India would not agree to a plebiscite. A truce line split Kashmir into Indian and Pakistani sectors.

Indian-controlled Kashmir abolished the monarchy in 1952, and in 1957 a new constitution formalized the accession to India. In 1965 war between Indian and Pakistani forces flared briefly in Kashmir. A local Moslem movement aimed at achieving a plebiscite added to the unrest in the mid-1960's. Total area, 86,024 square miles; population in Indian-controlled section (1971 preliminary census), 4,615,176.

**KASHMIR** (in full, **JAMMU AND KASHMIR**). The state of Kashmir occupies the northernmost part of the peninsula of India. Much of it is wild and uninhabited. Great mountain ranges sweep across it from east to west. The highest range is the Karakoram, in the northeast. Within it rises K2, or Godwin Austen (28,250 feet), the second highest peak in the world (*see* K2). Kashmir is bordered on the south by India, on the west by Pakistan and Afghanistan, and on the north and east by Communist China's Sinkiang-Uigur Autonomous Region and Tibet.

From towering ranges in the north the land slopes southward in a series of steps. The first step is to the valley of the Indus River, which separates the northern ranges from the Himalayas. The second step is to the valley of the Jhelum. The third is to the basin of the Chenab River, in the semimountainous Jammu section of Kashmir. Near the center of Kashmir the Jhelum River winds through the beautiful Vale of Kashmir. The Vale is an oval basin, 84 miles long and 20 to 25 miles wide, once the bed of a vast lake. Loveliest of all its gardens is Shalimar, a royal pleasure ground on lotus-covered Dal Lake.

The chief cities (1971 preliminary census) are Srinagar (403,612), summer capital, on the Jhelum, and Jammu (155,249), winter capital, on a tributary of the Chenab.

Moslems make up the bulk of the population. A majority of them are poor farmers who raise rice and corn on irrigated fields. Kashmiri Moslems, who are noted craftsmen, also make silk fabrics, woolen textiles (such as the famous cashmere shawls and carpets),

---

THESE ARTICLES ARE IN THE FACT-INDEX

Kaskaskia
Kaskaskia, Ill.
Kaskaskia River
Kassel, West Germany
Kassites
Kastler, Alfred
Kästner, Erich
Kat
Kataev, Valentin
Katahdin, Mount

Katanga, Republic of Zaire
Katayama, Tetsu
Kater, Henry
Katherine
Kathmandu, Nepal
Katmai, Mount
Kato, Takaakira, Viscount
Katowice, Poland
Katrine, Loch
Katsura, Taro, Prince

**KATYDID.** Throughout the late summer nights the katydid sings unceasingly in the tops of the tallest trees: *"Katy did; Katy didn't; she did; she didn't."* Only the male katydids are the music makers. The song they sing is the mating call. They make the sound by rubbing a scraper at the base of one of the front wings across a file on the base of the other.

Katydids are green and blend with the leaves where they live. Like their cousins the grasshoppers they are good jumpers. The two antennae, or feelers, upon the head are long and fragile. The body is rather broad and boat-shaped. A full-grown katydid is one and one half to about two inches long. The insects feed upon leaves and tender twigs.

Early in autumn katydids lay some 200 or more flattened, slate-colored eggs. The eggs are laid in overlapping rows, like shingles. The following spring each egg splits along the top, and the young "katys" squirm out. They are pale in color but soon turn leaf green, like the adults. The mature insects die with the frost.

Katydids belong to the order *Orthoptera*, which includes grasshoppers, crickets, and cockroaches. The scientific name of the oval-winged katydid is *Pterophylla camellifolia;* of angular-winged katydid, *Microcentrum retinervis*. Both live east of the Rockies.

THESE ARTICLES ARE IN THE FACT-INDEX

| | |
|---|---|
| Katyn, Russia | Kazakh |
| Katz, Sir Bernard | Kazakh Soviet Socialist |
| Katzenbach, Nicholas | Republic |
| deBelleville | Kazan, Elia |
| Kauffmann, Angelica | Kazan, Russia |
| Kaufman, George S(imon) | Kazantzakis, Nikos |
| Kaulbach, Wilhelm von | Kazbek, Mount |
| Kaunas, Lithuanian S.S.R. | Kazvin, Iran |
| Kaunitz, Prince Wenzel | Kean, Charles John |
| Anton von | Kean, Edmund |
| Kava | Kean, Ellen |
| Kawabata, Yasunari | Keane, John Joseph |
| Kawasaki, Japan | Kearney, Denis |
| Kay, John | Kearney, Neb. |
| Kay, Ulysses (Simpson) | Kearney State College |
| Kayans | Kearny, Philip |
| Kaye, Danny | Kearny, Stephen Watts |
| Kaye, Nora | Kearny, N. J. |
| Kaye-Smith, Sheila | Keating, Kenneth B. |
| Kayseri, Turkey | Keats, Ezra Jack |

**KEATS, John** (1795–1821). "Here lies one whose name was writ in water." This is the epitaph which the poet John Keats prepared for himself. He thought of it in the dark days when he felt death drawing near and despaired of winning fame. His whole poetical career had lasted only seven years. During this brief period he had written some of the greatest poems

in the English language. They were filled with lines of haunting beauty that will live as long as the language is spoken.

John Keats was born in London, England. His father was a livery-stable keeper. He did not spend his early years close to nature, as did most of our poets, but in the city of London. Yet in some marvelous manner there was born in him an intense love of beauty. "A thing of beauty is a joy forever" is the first line of his 'Endymion'. In the 'Ode on a Grecian Urn', in which he seems to have caught much of the ancient Greeks' worship of beauty, he declares:

> Beauty is truth, truth beauty,—that is all
> Ye know on earth, and all ye need to know.

Unlike his contemporaries Shelley and Wordsworth, Keats had no desire to reform the world or to teach a lesson. He was content if by his magic power he could make his readers see and hear and feel with their own senses the marvelous forms, colors, and sounds that his imagination brought forth.

Keats was apprenticed to a surgeon in early youth and studied surgery faithfully for seven years, but his heart was elsewhere. "I find I cannot exist without Poetry," he said, "—without Eternal Poetry." In 1816 he became acquainted with Leigh Hunt, and through Hunt with Shelley. The next year, at 22, he gave up his profession and devoted the rest of his short life entirely to the writing of poetry.

In 1818 his first long poem, 'Endymion', appeared. It was harshly attacked by the reviewers. They overlooked its beauties and failed to see that its faults were due to immaturity. Other troubles crowded upon the young poet. He was in money difficulties, and he was tormented by a hopeless love affair. His health had begun to fail. He rapidly developed tuberculosis. In the autumn of 1820 he went to Italy with his friend Joseph Severn. Early in 1821 he died in Rome.

Keats's chief poems are: 'Endymion'; 'Lines on the Mermaid Tavern'; 'Isabella, or The Pot of Basil'; 'I Stood Tiptoe upon a Little Hill'; 'The Eve of St. Agnes'; 'La Belle Dame sans Merci'; 'Ode to a Nightingale'; 'Ode to Autumn'; 'Lamia'; 'Hyperion'; and a number of sonnets. Among them are 'On First Looking into Chapman's Homer' and 'When I Have Fears That I May Cease to Be'.

THESE ARTICLES ARE IN THE FACT-INDEX

| | |
|---|---|
| Keble, John | Keene State College |
| Kebnekaise | Keewatin, District of |
| Kecskemet, Hungary | Kefauver, Estes |
| Kedah, Malaysia | Keighley, England |
| Kedron, Valley of | Keitel, Wilhelm |
| Keefe, Tim(othy J.) | Keith, Sir Arthur |
| Keeler, William H. (Wee | Keith, Harold |
| Willie) | Keith, James Francis |
| Keeley, Leslie E. | Edward |
| Keelung, Republic of | Kekulé, Friedrich August |
| China | Kelantan, Malaysia |
| Keen, William Williams | Kelland, Clarence |
| Keene, Charles Samuel | Budington |
| Keene, Laura | Keller, Gottfried |
| Keene, N. H. | |

**KELLER, Helen Adams** (1880–1968). "Once I knew only darkness and stillness.... My life was without past or future. . . . But a little word from the fingers of another fell into my hand that clutched at emptiness, and my heart leaped to the rapture of living." This is how Helen Keller described the beginning of her "new life," when despite blindness and deafness she learned to communicate with others.

Helen Keller was born June 27, 1880, at Tuscumbia, Ala. Nineteen months later she had a severe illness which left her blind and deaf. Her parents had hope for her. They had read Charles Dickens' report of the aid given to another blind and deaf girl, Laura Bridgman. When Helen was six years old, her parents took her to see Alexander Graham Bell, famed teacher of the deaf and inventor of the telephone (see Bell, Alexander G.). As a result of his advice, Anne Mansfield Sullivan (who became Mrs. John Albert Macy in 1905) began to teach Helen on March 3, 1887. Until her death in 1936 she remained Helen's teacher and constant companion. Miss Sullivan had been almost blind in early life, but her sight had been partially restored.

Helen soon learned the finger-tip, or manual, alphabet as well as braille. By placing her sensitive fingers on the lips and throat of her teachers, she learned to "hear" them speak. Three years after mastering the manual alphabet, she learned to speak herself.

At the age of 20 she was able to enter Radcliffe College. She received her Bachelor of Arts degree in 1904 with honors. She used textbooks in braille, and Miss Sullivan attended classes with her, spelling the lectures into her hand.

Miss Keller helped to found the Massachusetts Commission for the Blind and served on the commission. She raised more money for the American Foundation for the Blind than any other person. She lectured widely and received honors and awards from foreign governments and international bodies.

At her home near Easton, Conn., she wrote and worked for the blind and deaf (see Blind, Education of the). She died at her home on June 1, 1968.

Miss Keller's writing reveals her interest in the beauty of things taken for granted by those who can see and hear. Her books include 'The Story of My Life' (1903); 'Optimism' (1903); 'The World I Live In' (1908); 'Out of the Dark' (1913); 'Midstream: My Later Life' (1929); 'Journal' (1938); 'Let Us Have Faith' (1940). (For pictures, see Alabama Profile.)

**KELVIN, William Thomson, first Baron** (1824–1907). Although he was a brilliant theorist, William Thomson believed that science should have a practical value as well. He became one of Great Britain's foremost scientists and inventors.

The Bettmann Archive

Thomson published more than 650 scientific papers and patented some 70 inventions. He was the first to suggest accurate temperature readings from gas thermometers, using −273° C as absolute zero. This scale is called the Kelvin thermodynamic scale. (See also Heat.)

Thomson supervised the laying of the first transatlantic cable in 1866. To improve cable communication, he also invented and put into use the mirror galvanometer for signaling and the siphon recorder for receiving. For his work he was knighted by Queen Victoria. (See also Cables; Galvanometer.)

William Thomson was born on June 26, 1824, in Belfast, Ireland. His parents were James and Margaret Thomson. When William was six years old, his mother died. His father then undertook his education.

When he was 11, William entered the University of Glasgow in Scotland, where his father was a professor of mathematics. William was a brilliant student. By the time he was 21 years old he had studied in Glasgow, Cambridge, and Paris and had published 12 scientific papers. In 1846 he became a professor of natural philosophy in Glasgow. There he established the first physics laboratory in Great Britain. His investigations into the properties of matter made him famous.

In 1852 he married Margaret Crum. She died in 1870, and in 1874 Thomson married Frances Ann Blandy. He had no children. In 1892 Thomson was named first Baron Kelvin of Largs. Before his death on Dec. 17, 1907, he had become an honorary member of many foreign academies and held honorary degrees from many well-known universities. He was buried in Westminster Abbey in London, England.

### THESE ARTICLES ARE IN THE FACT-INDEX

Kellermann, Bernhard
Kellermann, François Christophe de
Kelley, Florence
Kelley, Joseph James
Kelley, Oliver H(udson)
Kellgren, Johan Henrik
Kellogg, Frank Billings
Kellogg, Vernon Lyman
Kellogg, W(ill) K(eith)
Kellogg, Idaho
Kells, Ireland

Kelly, Colin P(urdie), Jr.
Kelly, Eric Philbrook
Kelly, George
Kelly, John
Kelly, Michael Joseph (King)
Kelly, Walt(er)
Kelly, William
Kelowna, B. C.
Kelsey, Henry
Keltie, Sir John Scott

### THESE ARTICLES ARE IN THE FACT-INDEX

Kemal, Yashar
Kemal Atatürk
Kemble
Kemble, Fanny
Kemerovo, Russia
Kemmel, Mont
Kemmerer, Edwin Walter
Kemp Coast
Kempis, Thomas à
Ken, Thomas
Kenaf
Kenai Peninsula
Kendall, Amos

Kendall, Edward C(alvin)
Kendall, Henry Clarence
Kendrew, John C(owdery)
Kendrick, John
Kendrick, John Benjamin
Kenilworth, England
Kenilworth ivy
Kenna, John Edward
Kennan, George Frost
Kennebec River
Kennedy, David M(atthew)
Kennedy, Edward Moore

# JOHN F. KENNEDY—
## 35th President of
## the United States

KENNEDY, John Fitzgerald (1917–63; president 1961–63). In November 1960, at the age of 43, John F. Kennedy became the youngest man ever elected president of the United States. Theodore Roosevelt had become president at 42 when President William McKinley was assassinated, but he was not elected at that age. On Nov. 22, 1963, Kennedy was shot to death in Dallas, Tex., the fourth United States president to die by an assassin's bullet.

Kennedy was the nation's first Roman Catholic president. He was inaugurated in January 1961, succeeding Republican President Dwight D. Eisenhower. He defeated the Republican candidate, Vice-President Richard M. Nixon, by little more than 100,000 votes. It was one of the closest elections in the nation's history. Although more than 68 million votes were cast, Kennedy and his vice-presidential running mate, Lyndon B. Johnson, got less than half of them. Kennedy thus became the 14th minority president.

Because of the close vote, election results were challenged in many states. The official electoral vote was Kennedy 303, Nixon 219, and Senator Harry F. Byrd of Virginia 15. (*See also* President.)

### Kennedy's Family

President Kennedy's great-grandparents immigrated to the United States from Ireland in 1858. They settled in Boston, Mass. His grandfathers, Patrick J. Kennedy and John F. ("Honey Fitz") Fitzgerald, were born there. Both men became influential in state politics. "Honey Fitz" served several terms as Boston's mayor and as a member of the United States House of Representatives. Patrick Kennedy was a powerful ward boss and served in both houses of the Massachusetts legislature.

Patrick's son, Joseph, was a brilliant mathematician. At the age of 25 he became the youngest bank president in the United States. His fortune continued to grow, and he was one of the few financiers to sense the stock market crash of 1929. He made hundreds of millions of dollars.

Joseph married Rose Fitzgerald, daughter of Honey Fitz, Oct. 7, 1914. Their first child, Joseph, Jr., was born in 1915. John was born May 29, 1917. Seven other children followed: Rosemary, Kathleen,

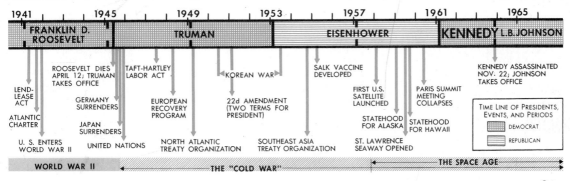

**YOUNG FOOTBALL PLAYER, COLLEGE ATHLETE, AND WAR HERO**
An active athlete, John Kennedy played football (left) at Dexter School, in Brookline, Mass., and was a star swimmer (cen-ter) at Harvard University in 1938. He served courageously as a naval officer (right) during World War II.

Eunice, Patricia, Robert, Jean, and Edward (called Teddy). All but Teddy were born in Brookline, Mass. Teddy was born in Hyannis Port, Mass.

### Training Pays Off

Joseph Kennedy, Sr., set up a million-dollar trust fund for each of his children. This freed them from future financial worry and allowed them to devote their lives to public good, if they desired. As the children grew, their parents stressed the importance of competitive spirit. One of their father's favorite mottoes was: "Second place is a loser." The drive to win was deeply embedded in the children, and they never did anything halfheartedly.

Their parents were careful to neglect neither the intellectual nor the physical development of the children. As they grew older, the children would eat their evening meals in two groups, divided by age. Mr. and Mrs. Kennedy ate at both meals. This allowed them to discuss subjects which were of interest to each group. All the children attended dancing school while very young, and all, with the exception of Rosemary, loved sports activities. Rosemary did not take part in rough-and-tumble play. The other children, however, thrived on it. Even when they

were adults, one of their favorite pastimes was a rousing and often bruising game of touch football.

On pleasant days, Mrs. Kennedy took her children for long walks. She made a point of taking them into church for a visit each day. "I wanted them to form a habit of making God and religion a daily part of their lives," she said later in life.

With this background, it was quite natural for John Kennedy and his brothers and sisters to excel in school and in sports. John attended public schools in Brookline. Later he entered private schools in Riverdale, N. Y., and Wallingford, Conn. In 1935 and 1936 he studied at the London School of Economics. Then he followed his older brother, Joe, into Harvard University. An excellent athlete, John was a star swimmer and a good golfer. His athletic activities, however, were cut down after he suffered a back injury in a Harvard football game. The injury was to plague him later in life.

John and his older brother were very close. While a young boy, Joe said that someday he would be president of the United States. The family took him at his word. Of all the children Joe seemed the one most likely to enter the political field.

Joseph, Sr., was named ambassador to Great Britain in 1937. John and his older brother then worked as international reporters for their father. John spent his summers in England and much of the rest of his time at Harvard. The brothers often traveled to distant parts of the world to observe events of international importance for their father. The clouds of World War II were hovering over Europe at that time.

### Return to the United States and College

The senior Kennedy was a controversial ambassador. His candid remarks about the progress of the

**KENNEDY'S ADMINISTRATION**
1961–1963

Peace Corps established (1961)
Alliance for Progress announced (1961)
23d Amendment adopted (1961)
First United States astronaut orbits earth (1962)
Trade Expansion Act passed (1962)
Nuclear test ban treaty (1963)
Kennedy assassinated (Nov. 22, 1963)

war in Europe earned him the disfavor of the English and of some of his countrymen in the United States. His family returned home in 1939, and he followed the next year.

John finished his studies at Harvard and was graduated with honors in 1940. Later that same year he did graduate work in economics at Stanford University. He also expanded a college thesis into a full-length book entitled 'Why England Slept'. It dealt with England's unpreparedness for World War II and was based on John's own experiences while working for his father. The book became a best seller.

### Serves with Navy in the Pacific

A few months before the Japanese attacked Pearl Harbor in December 1941, John attempted to enlist in the United States Army. His old back injury kept him from being accepted. After several months of exercise, he was granted a commission in the Navy. Eventually he became the commander of a torpedo boat and saw extensive action in the South Pacific.

In August 1943, during a night action in the Solomon Islands, John's torpedo boat was rammed and cut in half by a Japanese destroyer. The force of the collision threw him to the deck, reinjuring his back. Despite this, he gathered the ten members of his crew together. One of the crew members was so badly injured that he was unable to swim. He was put into a life jacket.

Kennedy gripped one of the jacket's straps between his teeth and towed the man as the crew swam to a nearby island. It took them five hours to reach it. For his heroism, Kennedy was awarded the Navy and Marine Corps medal, the Purple Heart, and a citation. The back injury, however, put him out of action for the remainder of the war.

Nearly one year after John's narrow escape, Joe, Jr., a Navy pilot, was killed when his plane exploded in the air over the English coast. To his brother's memory John wrote 'As We Remember Joe', a collection of tributes. In 1948 John's sister Kathleen died in an airplane crash in the south of France. She

**THE KENNEDY SUMMER HOMES**
In his father's spacious home (bottom center) at Hyannis Port, Mass., Kennedy spent the early years of the 1930's. Later he occupied the home at top center with his own family.

was the widow of the marquess of Hartington of England. He too had been killed in action during World War II, while leading an infantry charge in Normandy, France.

### Begins Political Career

The death of his brother deeply affected John Kennedy. Before the war Joe had decided to carry on with his ambition to enter politics. This caused a certain degree of disappointment for John, because he too had considered that field. He felt, however, that one Kennedy in politics was enough and determined to become a newspaperman. After his discharge from the Navy he worked for a short time as a correspondent for the *Chicago Herald American* and the International News Service. In 1946 he decided to take up where his older brother had left off

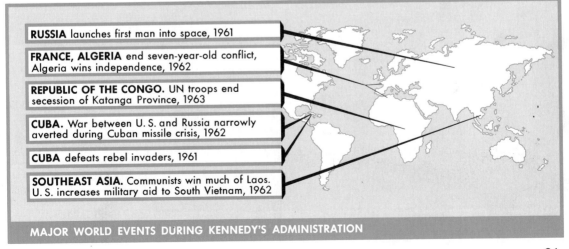

**RUSSIA** launches first man into space, 1961

**FRANCE, ALGERIA** end seven-year-old conflict, Algeria wins independence, 1962

**REPUBLIC OF THE CONGO.** UN troops end secession of Katanga Province, 1963

**CUBA.** War between U. S. and Russia narrowly averted during Cuban missile crisis, 1962

**CUBA** defeats rebel invaders, 1961

**SOUTHEAST ASIA.** Communists win much of Laos. U. S. increases military aid to South Vietnam, 1962

**MAJOR WORLD EVENTS DURING KENNEDY'S ADMINISTRATION**

and enter politics. To the family this was the most natural thing for him to do.

For his first target, Kennedy chose to try for a seat in the United States House of Representatives. He would represent the 11th Massachusetts Congressional District. His family rallied to his side as he began his campaign for the nomination. Because the 11th district was predominantly Democratic, the candidate for the office would. have no trouble being elected once he had gained the nomination. Kennedy and his family worked tirelessly. Their efforts, Kennedy's own impressive war record, and his family's political background greatly aided his campaign. He easily defeated eight other candidates running for the same nomination.

In office, Kennedy quickly established himself as a moderately independent thinker. Occasionally he voted against proposed measures which had met with the approval of his own Democratic party. He was re-elected in 1948 and 1950. An accomplished orator, the young congressman became a popular speaker.

His back injury, however, continued to bother him. He often appeared on the House floor and at speaking engagements supported by crutches. In 1946 he was named by the United States Chamber of Commerce as one of the nation's outstanding men of the year.

### Elected to the Senate

In 1952 Kennedy decided to run for the United States Senate. His opponent was Republican senator Henry Cabot Lodge, Jr. Again the Kennedy family worked side by side to get John elected. Kennedy defeated Lodge by more than 70,000 votes. The victory was particularly impressive because across the rest of the nation Republican candidates were swept into office along with the landslide of votes for the new Republican president, Dwight D. Eisenhower.

**KENNEDY SAILING WITH HIS FUTURE WIFE**
During their courtship, John Kennedy and his fiancée, Jacqueline Lee Bouvier, enjoyed sailing this small boat.

In the Senate Kennedy had woolen textile tariffs raised and urged President Eisenhower to obtain an agreement with Japan to cut textile imports. The president agreed to do so. Kennedy helped pass several other measures important to Massachusetts' textile industry. He also sponsored bills which improved his state's conservation programs.

One of the many committees Kennedy served on was the Select Committee of the Senate to Investigate Improper Activities in Labor-Management Relations. His younger brother Robert was chief legal counsel for this group. The two Kennedys were frequently in the public eye in 1959 as the committee investigated racketeering among top labor union officials. As a result of these hearings, John sponsored a labor bill which did a great deal to eliminate criminal practices in unions.

### Weds Long Island Beauty

Kennedy met his future wife, Jacqueline Lee Bouvier, at a Washington, D.C., party shortly after his election to the Senate. Described as a cameo beauty, "Jackie" was the daughter of a Long Island family. At the time they met, she was a photographer and a pen-

**THREE KENNEDY BROTHERS**
The president chats with his younger brothers, Robert (left) and Teddy (center). The oldest Kennedy son, Joseph, was killed in action in World War II.

and-ink artist for a Washington, D. C., newspaper. They were married on Sept. 12, 1953. Their daughter, Caroline, was born in 1957. Their son, John Fitzgerald, was born on Nov. 25, 1960, 17 days after Kennedy was elected president of the United States. As wife of the president, Jackie became one of the most gracious and most beautiful White House hostesses.

Jackie was born on July 28, 1929, at Southampton, Long Island. She attended several private American schools and the Sorbonne, in Paris, France. She was graduated from George Washington University, in Washington, D. C. (*See also* White House, sections "Hostesses of the White House" and "Children in the White House.")

### Back Surgery

Kennedy's old back injury still gave him a great deal of pain. Beginning in October 1954 he underwent a series of spinal operations.

While he was recuperating in 1955 he decided to write a book he had been contemplating for several years. It was a series of portraits of eight of the most courageous senators in the nation's history. Entitled 'Profiles in Courage', it became a best seller and won Kennedy the 1957 Pulitzer prize for biography.

### Misses Vice-Presidential Nomination

During his campaign for the 1960 Democratic nomination, Kennedy often began his speeches with this remark: "Thanks for not voting for me in 1956." That was the year he barely missed being nominated vice-president on the Democratic ticket. Senator Estes Kefauver of Tennessee, who won the nomination, and Adlai E. Stevenson, the presidential nominee, were defeated in the election. Had Kennedy won the nomination and been defeated in the election, his chances for the presidency might have been lost.

### The Presidential Nomination

Following the 1956 national election, Kennedy began an elaborate campaign for the 1960 Democratic presidential nomination. His popularity increased. In 1958 he was re-elected to the Senate by a margin of some 874,000 votes, more than any other Massachusetts senator had ever received. His brother Robert managed John's senatorial campaign. In 1958 Teddy, the youngest of the Kennedy family, worked with Robert in managing John's campaign for the Democratic nomination.

In the early months of 1960 Kennedy entered and won seven primary elections across the nation. At the 1960 Democratic convention in Los Angeles he received his party's nomination on the first ballot.

During the campaign Kennedy and Vice-President Richard M. Nixon met in four nationally televised "debates." It was generally conceded that these television appearances helped Kennedy more than Nixon.

### Problems Facing the New President

As Kennedy took office, cold-war tensions between Communist and Western nations increased. Communist forces pushed into Laos and threatened South Vietnam. The new president pledged strong efforts to halt the spread of Communism. As one step toward this end, he created a Peace Corps of young American men and women to work in underdeveloped countries.

After Russia successfully launched the first man into outer space in April 1961, Kennedy asked for a greatly increased budget for space research. This new phase of the cold war was called the "space race." The first United States manned space flight was in May. (*See also* Space Travel.)

**THE DEMOCRATIC CANDIDATES**
Kennedy and Johnson confer before making their acceptance speeches at the 1960 Democratic National Convention.

**MRS. KENNEDY AND THE CHILDREN**
Jacqueline Kennedy, wife of the president, poses with their children, John, Jr., and Caroline.

In the spring of 1961 Cuba was invaded by opponents of its Communist premier, Fidel Castro. The rebels were defeated quickly. The invasion had been aided by the United States Central Intelligence Agency (CIA). Kennedy was criticized by some for having approved the CIA's support of the invasion. Others blamed him for the operation's failure.

Kennedy met with Premier Nikita Khrushchev of Russia in Vienna in June to discuss world problems. The conference apparently did not alter Communist goals. Khrushchev immediately made new attempts to drive the Western powers from Berlin.

### Domestic and Latin American Affairs

At home Kennedy won Congressional approval of a number of his proposals, including greater social security benefits, a higher minimum wage, and aid to economically depressed areas in the country. The 23d Amendment to the Constitution was ratified early in Kennedy's Administration. It gave Washington, D. C., citizens the right to vote in presidential elections. (*See also* United States Constitution.)

In March 1961 Kennedy proposed an Alliance for Progress in the Americas. In August a conference of the Organization of American States formally ratified the charter for the Alliance for Progress (*see* South America, subhead "Alliance for Progress").

### Events of 1962

In March 1962 Kennedy used his influence to get a steel-industry wage settlement generally regarded as noninflationary. Early in April, however, several companies announced increases in their steel prices. Kennedy was angered. He exerted unusual pressure by shifting government orders to rival steel manufacturers and by threatening tax and antitrust suits. Within four days the price increases were canceled.

Kennedy's most important legislative success of 1962 was the passage of the Trade Expansion Act. It gave the president broad powers, including authority to cut or eliminate tariffs. The act was designed to help the United States compete or trade with the European Economic Community (Common Market) on equal terms. Kennedy's medical care project was defeated in Congress. Under this plan certain hospital expenses for most elderly persons would have been paid through the social security system.

In October 1962 Kennedy faced the most serious international crisis of his Administration. Aerial photographs proved that Russian missile bases were being built in Cuba. Declaring this buildup a threat to the Americas, Kennedy issued an ultimatum to Russia. He warned that any attack by Cuba would be regarded as an attack by the Soviet Union and the United States would retaliate against Russia. He also imposed a quarantine on ships bringing offensive weapons to Cuba. Negotiations were carried on between the president and Premier Khrushchev. By the end of November the missiles had been shipped back to the Soviet Union, the United States had lifted the quarantine, and the month-long crisis had abated. (*See also* Cuba.)

### The Civil Rights Crisis of 1963

In 1963, clashes between the police and demonstrating Negroes in Birmingham, Ala., and elsewhere induced the president to stress civil rights legislation. Kennedy's new civil rights message was sent to Congress in June. It included bills to ban discrimination in places of business; to speed up desegregation of public schools; and to end discrimination in the hiring of workers on federal construction projects.

An agreement to set up a teletype link between Kennedy and Khrushchev was signed in June 1963. This limited but promising achievement was intended as a precaution against war by accident or miscalculation.

The president also paid increasing attention to strengthening the North Atlantic Treaty Organization (NATO). Visiting Europe early in the summer of 1963, he conferred with government leaders in West Germany, Italy, and Great Britain. In West Germany, the president pledged that United States military forces would remain on the European continent. Kennedy also visited Ireland, from which his great-

**KENNEDY AND ADENAUER**
Chancellor Konrad Adenauer welcomed President Kennedy to Bonn, the West German capital, in June 1963. They discussed a unified nuclear missile force.

grandparents had emigrated to the United States.

A limited nuclear test ban treaty was signed by representatives of the United States, Russia, and Britain in the summer of 1963. The agreement permitted underground nuclear tests, and signatory nations could withdraw after 90 days' notice. Kennedy called the treaty a "victory for mankind."

Mrs. Kennedy gave birth to her second son, Patrick Bouvier, on Aug. 7, 1963. Born prematurely, the infant died after only 39 hours of life.

### The Last Campaign

In November, looking forward to the 1964 presidential election, Kennedy made a political visit to Florida and Texas, the two most populous Southern states. His wife, Vice-President Johnson, and Mrs. Johnson accompanied him on the Texas trip.

He had been warned that Texas might be hostile. In Dallas, only a month earlier, Adlai Stevenson, United States ambassador to the United Nations, had been spat upon and struck with a picket's placard. In San Antonio, Houston, and Fort Worth, however, the crowds were friendly, and obviously delighted with the charming young Jacqueline Kennedy.

### Kennedy Is Assassinated

A large and enthusiastic crowd greeted the presidential party when it arrived at the Dallas airport on the morning of November 22. Along the route of the motorcade into downtown Dallas the people stood 10 to 12 deep, applauding warmly. Next to the president in the big open limousine sat his wife. In front of them, on "jump seats," were John B. Connally, the governor of Texas, and his wife, Nellie. The third car in the procession carried Vice-President and Mrs. Johnson. As the cars approached a triple underpass, Mrs. Connally turned around and said, "You can't say Dallas doesn't love you, Mr. President."

At that moment three shots rang out. The president, shot through the head and throat, slumped over into his wife's lap. The second bullet hit Governor Connally, piercing his back, chest, wrist, and thigh. A reporter, glancing up, saw a rifle slowly disappear into a sixth-floor corner window of the Texas School Book Depository, a textbook warehouse overlooking the highway. It was 12:30 P.M. in Dallas.

President Kennedy died in Parkland Memorial Hospital without regaining consciousness. The time of death was set at 1:00 P.M. Governor Connally recovered from his multiple wounds.

Six minutes after the shooting, a description of a man seen leaving the textbook warehouse went out

**THE PRESIDENT IS ASSASSINATED**

As Mrs. Kennedy frantically seeks help, secret serviceman Clinton J. Hill leaps onto the car and flings himself over her and the dying president. Kennedy is slumped in the back seat. Governor Connally and his wife have fallen to the floor of the car.

over the police radio. At 1:18 P.M. patrolman J. D. Tippit stopped and questioned a man who answered the description. The man shot him dead. At 1:35 P.M. Dallas police captured Lee Harvey Oswald in a motion-picture theater, where he had hidden after allegedly killing patrolman Tippit.

**A GRIEVING FAMILY**

John F. Kennedy, Jr., salutes the American flag, as his father had taught him. Behind him is Robert F. Kennedy. Behind Caroline, standing next to her mother, is Edward M. Kennedy.

**LEE HARVEY OSWALD**

Although a mass of circumstantial evidence, including ballistics tests, pointed to Oswald as the slayer of President Kennedy, the 24-year-old professed Marxist and Castro sympathizer never came to trial. On Sunday, November 24, as he was being led across the basement of the City Hall for transfer to another prison, Jack Ruby (born Rubenstein), a Dallas nightclub owner, broke through a cordon of police and shot Oswald. The murder was committed in full view of television cameras as millions watched.

### The Return to Washington

The casket bearing Kennedy's body was removed to the presidential jet plane, Air Force One, where Lyndon B. Johnson took the oath of office as president of the United States (for picture, *see* Johnson, Lyndon B.). Only 98 minutes had elapsed since Kennedy's death.

All that long afternoon and into the early morning of the next day, Mrs. Kennedy refused to leave her husband's body. Close by her side at all times after her return to Washington, D.C., was her husband's brother and closest adviser, Attorney General Robert F. Kennedy. Mrs. Kennedy directed the details of the funeral, consulting with historians as to the burial procedures for other presidents who had died in office.

### Burial at Arlington

The body lay in repose for a day in the East Room of the White House. On November 24, in a solemn procession to the slow beat of muffled drums, the casket was removed to the rotunda of the Capitol and placed on the catafalque which had borne President Abraham Lincoln's casket.

The following day the funeral procession moved from the Capitol to the White House and then to St. Matthew's Cathedral. Here Richard Cardinal Cushing, Roman Catholic archbishop of Boston, celebrated Low Mass. From the White House to the cathedral, Mrs. Kennedy walked in the procession between her husband's brothers, Robert and Edward. In a scene unduplicated in history, 220 foreign leaders followed them.

Burial was at Arlington National Cemetery, on a hillside overlooking the Potomac and the city of Washington. At the conclusion of the service Mrs. Kennedy lighted an "eternal flame" at the grave.

Two Kennedy infants were later reburied on either side of their father. They were Patrick Bouvier and an unnamed daughter who was stillborn in 1956.

On June 8, 1968, the Kennedy family and a host of other mourners again gathered at the Kennedy gravesite—this time for the burial of Robert F. Kennedy. The president's brother, who had become a United States senator, was shot on June 5 in Los Angeles, Calif., while campaigning for the Democratic presidential nomination. He died on June 6 of brain damage. Sirhan Bishara Sirhan, a Jordanian immigrant who was seized at the scene of the shooting, was indicted for the murder.

For the second time President Johnson declared a day of mourning for a Kennedy. Many Americans who honored Robert Kennedy's memory on June 9, 1968, were reminded of an earlier day of mourning.

In his proclamation declaring November 25, 1963, a "National Day of Mourning" for John Kennedy, President Johnson paid this tribute to the slain president, quoting in conclusion from Kennedy's inaugural address of January 1960: "As he did not shrink from his responsibilities, but welcomed them, so he would not have us shrink from carrying on his work beyond this hour of na-

**THE FUNERAL PROCESSION LEAVES THE CAPITOL**

The flag-draped casket holding the body of John F. Kennedy is borne on a caisson drawn by six gray horses. It is followed by the traditional riderless black horse, the empty boots turned backward in the stirrups, the sword sheathed in its scabbard.

# Important Events in the Administration of John F. Kennedy

## ADVANCES ON WORLD FRONTIERS

Alan B. Shepard, Jr., made America's first manned space flight, May 5, 1961.

The Peace Corps was established in 1961. The corps provides trained men and women to work and teach in underdeveloped countries.

The Alliance for Progress in the Americas was inaugurated in 1961.

At Kennedy's demand, Oct. 22, 1962, Russian missiles in Cuba were removed.

The nuclear test ban treaty was ratified by the Senate, Sept. 24, 1963.

## ACHIEVEMENT AND TRAGEDY AT HOME

The civil rights movement gained momentum during 1961-63.

The assassination of John F. Kennedy in Dallas, Tex., Nov. 22, 1963, shocked the world. The funeral was attended by 220 foreign leaders from almost every nation.

tional tragedy. He said it himself: 'The energy, the faith, the devotion which we bring to this endeavor will light our country and all who serve it—and the glow from that fire can truly light the world'."

### The Warren Commission

On Nov. 29, 1963, President Johnson created the President's Commission on the Assassination of President John F. Kennedy to investigate and report on the facts relating to the tragedy. Chief Justice Earl Warren was appointed chairman. Other members of the commission were Senator Richard B. Russell (D., Ga.), Senator John Sherman Cooper (R., Ky.), Representative Hale Boggs (D., La.), Representative Gerald R. Ford (R., Mich.), Allen W. Dulles, and John J. McCloy. J. Lee Rankin was the general counsel. The report was published on Sept. 24, 1964.

The commission's function was to uncover all the facts concerning the assassination and to determine if it was in any way directed or encouraged by unknown persons at home or abroad. It functioned neither as a court nor as a prosecutor.

If Oswald had lived he could have had a trial by American standards of justice. Since he was unable to defend himself, and in fairness to him and his family, the commission requested Walter E. Craig, president of the American Bar Association, to participate in the investigation and to advise the commission whether the proceedings conformed to the basic principles of American justice.

The commission found that the shots which killed President Kennedy and wounded Governor Connally were fired by Lee Harvey Oswald. There was no evidence that either Oswald or Jack Ruby was part of any conspiracy, domestic or foreign, to assassinate President Kennedy. No direct or indirect relationship between Oswald and Jack Ruby was discovered. On the basis of the evidence before it, the commission concluded that Oswald acted alone.

The commission criticized both the Secret Service and the Federal Bureau of Investigation (FBI). Some of the advance preparations and security measures in Dallas made by the Secret Service were found to have been deficient. In addition, although the FBI had obtained considerable information about Oswald, it had no official responsibility to refer this information to the Secret Service. "A more carefully coordinated treatment of the Oswald case by the FBI might well have resulted in bringing Oswald's activities to the attention of the Secret Service," the report stated.

The commission made suggestions for improved protective measures of the Secret Service and better liaison with the FBI, the Department of State, and other federal agencies. Other recommendations were:

That a committee of Cabinet members, or the National Security Council, should review and oversee the protective activities of the Secret Service and other agencies that help safeguard the president.

That Congress adopt legislation which would make the assassination of the president and vice-president a federal crime.

That the representatives of the bar, law-enforcement associations, and the news media establish ethical standards concerning the collection and presentation of information to the public so that there will be no interference with pending criminal investigations, court proceedings, or the right of individuals to a fair trial.

**PRESIDENT JOHNSON RECEIVES THE "WARREN REPORT"**
Chief Justice Earl Warren, chairman, hands the report of the President's Commission on the Assassination of President John F. Kennedy to President Lyndon B. Johnson. Others, left to right, are John J. McCloy, J. Lee Rankin, Senator Richard B. Russell, Representative Gerald R. Ford, Allen W. Dulles, Senator John Sherman Cooper, and Representative Hale Boggs.

### Books About John F. Kennedy

Bishop, J. A.   A Day in the Life of President Kennedy (Random, 1964).

Donovan, R. J.   PT 109: John F. Kennedy in World War II (McGraw, 1961).

Graves, C. P.   John F. Kennedy (Garrard, 1965).

Lichtenstein, Nelson and Schoenebaum, E. W., eds.   Political Profiles: the Kennedy Years (Facts on File, 1976).

Manchester, W. R.   Death of a President (Harper, 1967).

Manchester, W. R.   Portrait of a President, rev. ed. (Little, 1967).

Salinger, Pierre.   With Kennedy (Doubleday, 1966).

Schlesinger, A. M., Jr.   A Thousand Days (Houghton, 1965).

Schoor, Gene.   Young John Kennedy (Harcourt, 1963).

Sorensen, T. C.   Kennedy (Harper, 1965).

Steinberg, Alfred.   The Kennedy Brothers (Putnam, 1969).

United Press International and American Heritage (Periodical), eds.   Four Days (Simon & Schuster, 1964).

White, T. H.   The Making of the President: 1960 (Atheneum, 1961).

THESE ARTICLES ARE IN THE FACT-INDEX

| | |
|---|---|
| Kennedy, John Pendleton | Kenney, George Churchill |
| Kennedy, Joseph P(atrick) | Kenny, Elizabeth |
| Kennedy, Robert F(rancis) | Kenora, Ont. |
| Kennedy, Mount | Kenosha, Wis. |
| Kennelly, Arthur Edwin | Kensington, P. E. I. |
| Kenner, La. | Kensington and Chelsea |
| Kennesaw Mountain | Kent, Edward Augustus, |
| Kenneth I, MacAlpine | duke of |
| Kennewick, Wash. | Kent, James |

**KENT, Rockwell** (1882–1971). Few modern artists can claim a more adventurous life than Rockwell Kent. In search of subjects for his pictures he lived in such faraway places as Newfoundland, Alaska, and Tierra del Fuego. Once he was shipwrecked off Greenland. A talented author, he wrote and illustrated books of his travels.

Rockwell Kent grew up in Tarrytown, N. Y., his birthplace, and in New York City. His father died when Rockwell was a young boy. Although he liked to draw, Rockwell did not seriously think about becoming an artist. He attended Horace Mann School in New York City and was an average pupil.

Kent studied architecture at Columbia University but left in his junior year. He had already begun to study painting. Not until 1914, however, was he able to make a living by art. Meanwhile he had worked as a carpenter, gravedigger, lobster fisherman, draftsman, engraver, and illustrator—painting all the time.

In 1916 the artist moved to Newfoundland. This was the first of many journeys that he took to wild and lonely places outside the United States. Among his books about his trips are 'Wilderness' (1920), about his stay in Alaska; 'Voyaging Southward from

**PAINTING BY ROCKWELL KENT**
This oil painting of Mount Equinox in Vermont is typical of Kent's stark, powerful landscapes. His lines are economical.

the Strait of Magellan' (1924); and 'Salamina' (1935), a story of his Eskimo housekeeper. Kent illustrated special editions of 'Moby-Dick', 'Candide', 'Leaves of Grass', and Shakespeare. In 1955, when he was 73, he wrote a long autobiography, 'It's Me O Lord'. Kent died in Plattsburgh, N. Y., on March 13, 1971.

THIS ARTICLE IS IN THE FACT-INDEX
Kent, England (kingdom)

**KENT, England.** The "garden of England" is Kent. This beautiful, fertile county, or shire, is in southeast England on the Strait of Dover. Winding rivers, including the Thames, thread through its rich plains and wooded hills, or downs.

Kent is chiefly agricultural. Much of its land is planted to hops. Vineyards and orchards border green fields. Kent supplies market vegetables to London. The region is noted for the Southdown and Kent breeds of sheep.

The coastal towns are busy with fisheries. Kentish shrimp and oysters are especially prized. The north has coal and iron. Industries include pottery, paper, textiles, brewing, munitions, and shipbuilding.

The capital is Maidstone. The principal cities include the cathedral town of Canterbury and the city of the "white cliffs," Dover (see Canterbury; Dover).

Kent is famous for picturesque antiquities. The oldest standing building in England is a Roman lighthouse at Dover. Later, in the 5th century, the Kentish coast was the first invasion spot of the Anglo-Saxons. Ruins of medieval abbeys loom in the countryside. In World War II Nazi bombs, shells, and rockets battered Kent for five years. Area, 1,525 square miles; population (1969 estimate), 1,388,820.

THESE ARTICLES ARE IN THE FACT-INDEX

| | |
|---|---|
| Kent, Ohio | Kenton, Stan(ley Newcomb) |
| Kenton, Simon | Kent State University |

Trim white fences and spacious barns mark the thoroughbred horse farms of the Bluegrass section of Kentucky. Fine horses have been raised on this fertile plain since the late 1700's.

# KENTUCKY—
# Gateway to the South

**KENTUCKY.** The oldest state west of the Appalachian Highlands is Kentucky. Originally a part of the western lands of Virginia, Kentucky was first settled in 1774. During the next 15 years its population grew to more than 73,000. In 1792, with the permission of Virginia, Kentucky was admitted to the Union as the 15th state.

Kentucky has a well-balanced economy. Its chief source of income is manufacturing, which amounts to more than $2\frac{1}{2}$ billion dollars a year. Next in importance is farming, headed by tobacco and cattle. Mining ranks third in value, with coal the chief mineral.

The state is noted for its many political leaders. Henry Clay, author of the Compromise of 1850, served in Congress for more than 30 years (*see* Clay, Henry). The two opposing leaders of the Civil War, Abraham Lincoln and Jefferson Davis, were both born in Kentucky (*see* Lincoln, Abraham; Davis, Jefferson). The state has also had three vice-presidents of the United States—Richard M. Johnson, John C. Breckinridge, and Alben W. Barkley.

The state's name probably comes from the Indian word *Kentake*, meaning "meadowland" or "prai-

**Population** (1980): 3,661,433—rank, 23d state. Urban, 50.8%; rural, 49.2%. Persons per square mile, 92.3—rank, 23d state.

**Extent:** Area, 40,395 square miles, including 745 square miles of water surface (37th state in size).

**Elevation:** Highest, Black Mountain, 4,145 feet, near Lynch; lowest, Mississippi River near Hickman, 257 feet; average, 750 feet.

**Geographic Center:** 3 miles northwest of Lebanon.

**Temperature** (° F): Extremes—lowest, −34° (Cynthiana, Jan. 28, 1963); highest, 114° (Greensburg, July 28, 1930). Averages at Lexington—January, 34.5°; July, 77.4°; annual, 55.6°. Averages at Louisville—January, 35.0°; July, 77.6°; annual, 55.7°.

**Precipitation** (inches): At Lexington—annual average, 44.73 (including 15.0 snowfall). At Louisville—annual average, 41.32 (including 17.1 snowfall).

**Land Use:** Crops, 37%; pasture, 8%; forest, 46%; other, 9%.

For statistical information about Agriculture, Communication, Education, Employment, Finance, Fishing, Forests, Government, Health Care, Manufacturing, Mining, Population Trends, Trade, Transportation, Vital Statistics, and Welfare, see KENTUCKY FACT SUMMARY.

26

rie." During pioneer days, Kentucky was called the "dark and bloody ground," for the many battles between the settlers and the Indians. The nickname Bluegrass State is from the unusual grass that grows in various parts of Kentucky and is most abundant in the Lexington area.

## Survey of the Bluegrass State

Kentucky lies in the south-central section of the United States. On the north the Ohio River separates the state from Ohio, Indiana, and Illinois. To the northeast is West Virginia, separated from Kentucky by the Big Sandy River and its Tug Fork. Virginia is to the southeast. To the south is Tennessee. On the west the Mississippi River is the boundary between Kentucky and Missouri.

The state's greatest length, from east to west, is 425 miles. Its greatest width is 182 miles, from north to south. The area of Kentucky is 40,395 square miles, with 745 square miles of inland water surface.

## The State's Three Natural Regions

From highlands in the southeast the surface of Kentucky slopes generally north and west. The highest point in the state is Black Mountain (4,145 feet), at the Virginia border. Here the average elevation is about 2,800 feet. Central Kentucky has an average elevation of about 1,000 feet; western Kentucky, about 400 feet. The lowest point in the state is 257 feet, along the Mississippi River near Hickman. There are three distinct natural regions.

**The Appalachian Plateau** covers the eastern fourth of Kentucky. The southeastern edge of this region is formed by the Cumberland and Pine Mountain ranges, known also as the Cumberland Mountains. From these highlands a series of sharp ridges and narrow valleys extend north (Kanawha section) and west (Cumberland Plateau section). Another name

that is sometimes used to designate the Appalachian Plateau is the Eastern Coal Field.

**The Interior Low Plateaus** extend from the eastern mountains to the Tennessee River in the west. This region is by far the largest in the state. It contains four separate areas. In the northern bulge of Kentucky is the *Bluegrass* area, named for its bluish-tinted grass. The area is also known as the Lexington Plain. Around the edge of the Bluegrass is a semicircle of rounded hills called the *Knobs*. To the south and west is the *Pennyroyal* (Pennyrile) Plateau, named for a variety of the mint plant found here. Another low plateau, the *Western Coal Field*, lies on both sides of the Green River, from Edmonson County north to the Ohio River.

**The Coastal Plain** occupies the eight westernmost counties. It is part of the great lowland that sweeps north from the Gulf of Mexico. This region is also called the Jackson Purchase, or Purchase. It is so named because Andrew Jackson helped buy the land between the Mississippi and Tennessee rivers from the Chickasaw Indians in 1818.

Most of Kentucky's rivers flow north and west into the Ohio. These include, from east to west, the Licking, Kentucky (with its branch, the Dix), Salt, and Green. The Cumberland River rises in the southeast, makes a loop in Tennessee, then reenters Kentucky to join the Ohio. The Tennessee flows through the western end of the state. Along the northern and western boundaries are the Ohio and Mississippi rivers (*see* Ohio River; Mississippi River).

## Climate and Weather

Kentucky has a continental climate, with warm summers and cool winters. The coldest part of the state is the far north, which has an average annual temperature of about 55° F. This is about five degrees lower than that of the extreme southwest, the

Early in May the spectacular Kentucky Derby is run at Churchill Downs in Louisville. The racing event attracts people from many states and countries. First held in 1875, it is for three-year-olds over a distance of 1¼ miles.

The *Louisville Courier-Journal*

This map shows the three natural regions and the surface features of Kentucky. The use that can be made of the land is related to the physical features of each region.

warmest section. The growing season varies from 180 days a year in the eastern highlands to 210 days in the west.

The average precipitation (rain and melted snow) varies from 40 inches a year in the extreme north to 52 inches in the extreme south-central part of the state. The heaviest rainfall falls along the southern border between Allen and Bell counties. Boone, Kenton, and Campbell counties in the far north receive the least amount.

### Natural Resources and Conservation

Kentucky's chief agricultural resources are fertile soil, a favorable climate, and plenty of rainfall. About two fifths of the land is forested, with the heaviest stands of timber in the east. About 500 million board feet of hardwood and softwood lumber are cut each year.

Deposits of coal, petroleum, and natural gas provide fuels for manufacturing. The state's rivers are an important means of transportation. Kentucky has fine water for making distilled and malt liquors. Horse farms and horse racing are tourist attractions.

A major conservation problem has been the erosion of topsoil. This condition is being corrected by crop rotation and other improved farming methods.

Several large dams have been built, primarily to improve navigation and to supply power. The reservoirs formed by these dams also offer boating, fishing, and swimming, and facilities for camping are available along their shores. Kentucky Dam, on the Tennessee River, is part of the Tennessee Valley Authority (*see* Tennessee Valley Authority). Barkley Dam, on the Cumberland River, was built and is maintained by the United States Army Corps of Engineers. Wolf Creek Dam, on the Cumberland, and Dale Hollow Dam in Tennessee, on the Obey, a branch of the

Cumberland, have aided the economy of the Cumberland Basin. Other important dams are the Rough River, Nolin, Green River, Buckhorn, and Dewey.

Much of the state's conservation work is done by the Department of Fish and Wildlife Resources. The Department of Natural Resources includes agencies for forestry, flood control and water usage, soil and water resources, and parks.

### People of the Bluegrass State

Kentucky was the site of savage battles among Indian tribes long before white men entered the re-

**LOUISVILLE'S CITY HALL**
The City Hall (left) of Kentucky's largest city was completed in 1873. It faces the Jefferson County Courthouse.

gion. During the 1600's the Iroquois Confederacy, operating from what is now New York State, drove most of the Indians out of the area. The only tribe the white men found living in the region was the Shawnee.

The first pioneers to settle in Kentucky came from Virginia and North Carolina. Until about 1830 the state was settled largely by people of English and Scottish descent who worked their way over the Appalachian Mountains. Then, as new routes to the West came into use (by way of the Deep South and the Great Lakes), the mountain region became somewhat isolated. It was not until the 1900's that improved methods of transportation and communication forged a close link between eastern Kentucky and the rest of the state. One of the greatest aids to the mountain people was the Frontier Nursing Service, a public health agency founded by Mary Breckinridge in 1925.

Kentucky has attracted few immigrants from abroad. Today over one half of one percent of its people are foreign born. Of the total foreign stock the Germans and the English are the largest groups. Seven percent of the people are black.

## Manufacturing and Cities

During World War II the value of manufacturing in Kentucky increased almost four times, reaching a total of some 740 million dollars. Today the value of work done in the state's mills, factories, and processing plants is more than $2\frac{1}{2}$ billion dollars a year. Most of the large manufacturing centers are on the Ohio River.

The most important industry in Kentucky is the processing of food and related items, such as distilled and malt liquors, grain, and dairy products. Next in value is the manufacture of electrical machinery. Also important are the manufacture of chemicals and allied products; the tobacco industry; the production of construction equipment, conveyors, and other nonelectrical machinery; and the manufacture of transportation equipment.

The largest city and chief industrial center is Louisville, on the Ohio River (see Louisville). Lexington, the second largest city, is a tobacco and livestock market in the heart of the Bluegrass region. Owensboro, third in size, is an industrial city on the Ohio which produces oil, coal, and tobacco.

Covington, Paducah, Ashland, and Henderson are industrial cities on the Ohio River. Covington stands at the mouth of the Licking River. Across this river is Newport, a residential city with metal-manufacturing plants. Bowling Green and Hopkinsville are farm centers in the east-central part of the state. Middlesboro, in the southeastern section, is noted for its mountain resorts and nearby coal mines. Frankfort,

Kentucky Department of Public Information

Now held safely in place by a huge 101-foot chain, towering Chained Rock once seemed a constant menace to Pineville.

on the Kentucky River, is Kentucky's state capital (see Frankfort).

## Products of the Land

About six percent of all the workers in Kentucky are engaged in agriculture. The state has about 102,000 commercial farms. The average size of these farms is about 141 acres. Tobacco, the principal cash crop, accounts for two fifths of the total farm income. The chief growing region is between the Green and Cumberland rivers. Only North Carolina produces more tobacco than Kentucky.

Corn, the second most valuable field crop, is grown throughout the state. Other important crops are hay, soybeans, wheat, barley, potatoes, sorghum, and oats. Kentucky also raises many cattle (for beef and milk), hogs, chickens, and sheep.

The Bluegrass State takes great pride in its thoroughbred horses. Breeders have produced strains of saddle horses which combine speed with endurance. The chief breeding area, which also develops horses for harness racing and for show, is around Lexington.

Coal is by far the most valuable mineral. The major coal-mining counties are Hopkins and Muhlenberg in western Kentucky and Pike and Harlan in the eastern part of the state. Only West Virginia and Pennsylvania mine more coal than Kentucky. Other important minerals are petroleum, stone, natural gas, sand and gravel, natural-gas liquids, and clays.

## Development of Transportation

The first "highway" into Kentucky was the Wilderness Road blazed by Daniel Boone in 1775. It led through Cumberland Gap northwest to Boonesborough, Harrodsburg, and later to Louisville. The second important "road" into the state was the Ohio River, which carried flatboats down to landings at what are now Maysville, Louisville, and Owensboro.

**KENTUCKY'S TWO BASIC PRODUCTS**
The state's chief cash crop is tobacco. Here buyers (left) bid for lots of loose-leaf tobacco sold by an auctioneer. Much of

Kentucky's coal is obtained by strip mining. The electric shovel (right) can handle 30 cubic yards at one bite.

Railroad transportation began in 1832 with the opening of the Lexington and Ohio line between Lexington and Frankfort. This route is now part of the Louisville and Nashville Railroad. Today the state is served by nearly 30 railroads and several airlines.

Kentucky has an extensive multilane highway system. Interstate 64, a major east-west route, extends east from Louisville into West Virginia. Western Kentucky Parkway begins at Princeton and extends northeast to Elizabethtown. Interstate 75 crosses the state from north to south, skirting Lexington. Interstate 65, which extends south through Louisville, incorporates a 40-mile turnpike from Louisville to Elizabethtown.

### Recreation in Kentucky

The state's scenic mountains, valleys, and historical landmarks are visited by many tourists. Three of the chief attractions are maintained by the federal government—Mammoth Cave National Park, Abraham Lincoln Birthplace National Historic Site, and Cumberland Gap National Historical Park (*see* National Parks, United States).

Man-made lakes such as Kentucky, Cumberland, and Herrington are noted for fishing and other sports. Louisville is the site of the Kentucky State Fair and the Kentucky Derby. There are a variety of state parks.

### Growth of the Educational System

The first school in what is now Kentucky was opened in the fort at Harrodsburg in 1775. By 1800 many private academies had been established. One of these schools was Transylvania Seminary, which was founded at Danville in 1780. Moved to Lexington in 1788, it was one of the first schools of higher learning west of the Appalachians.

The state legislature passed the first public school law in 1838. There was little progress, however, until 1847, when Robert Breckinridge became superintendent of education. By 1853 a public school system had been established in every county. The Civil War temporarily halted further development. Since that time Kentucky has continued to improve its schools.

**FORT BOONESBOROUGH STATE PARK**
This natural sandy beach beside the Kentucky River is near the site where Daniel Boone built his famous homestead fort.

The University of Kentucky, at Lexington, is the largest school of the state's educational system. Also state-supported are the University of Louisville, at Louisville; Western Kentucky University, at Bowling Green; Eastern Kentucky University, at Richmond; Murray State University, at Murray; Morehead State University, at Morehead; and Kentucky State University, at Frankfort. Other schools are Bellarmine College and Catherine Spalding College, both at Louisville; Cumberland College, at Williamsburg; Georgetown College, at Georgetown; and Berea College, at Berea.

Ewing Galloway

Billions of dollars in gold are stored in the Gold Bullion Depository built by the United States at Fort Knox in 1936.

## Government and Politics

When Kentucky was admitted to the Union on June 1, 1792, the capital was Lexington. Later in 1792 Frankfort was selected as the permanent seat of government. Although generally referred to as a "state," Kentucky calls itself a "commonwealth." It is governed under a constitution adopted in 1891.

The chief executive officer is the governor, elected every four years. Lawmaking is in the hands of the General Assembly, made up of the Senate and the House of Representatives. The judiciary is headed by the Supreme Court.

Kentucky usually votes Democratic in both local and state elections. In presidential campaigns it has supported the Democratic candidate in every election since the Civil War except those of 1896, 1924, 1928, 1956, 1960, 1968, and 1972. Kentucky was the second state, after Georgia, to lower the voting age from 21 to 18.

## HISTORY OF KENTUCKY

The Big Sandy River, its Tug Fork, and the Cumberland Mountains have formed the eastern boundary of Kentucky since 1776. The state's western boundary, the Mississippi River, was fixed by the peace treaty of 1783. Its northern border, along the Ohio River, was established by the Northwest Ordinance of 1787. Although Kentucky was admitted to the Union in 1792, its boundary with Tennessee was not settled until 1820. This line was based upon two earlier surveys —from Cumberland Gap to the Tennessee River and from the Tennessee to the Mississippi River. The sections below tell the history of Kentucky to the present.

## Exploration and Settlement

For almost 150 years the American Colonies were blocked from expanding westward by the mountain ranges of the Appalachians. Then, in 1750, Dr. Thomas Walker led a party of Virginians into what is now Kentucky through a pass in the Cumberland Mountains. He named the pass Cumberland Gap.

Later John Finley, Daniel Boone, and others came through the Gap looking for fertile land (*see* Boone). Many of these adventurers stayed in Kentucky so long that they were called "long hunters." Meanwhile the region was organized by Virginia as Fincastle (later Kentucky) County.

In 1774 James Harrod and a group of Virginians made the first permanent settlement in the region at Harrodstown (now Harrodsburg). The next year Daniel Boone led a party from North Carolina along the famous Wilderness Road from Cumberland Gap. He founded Boonesborough (now Boonesboro) on the Kentucky River in what is now Madison County. There was some rivalry between the two settlements of Boonesborough and Harrodstown, but they united their efforts in fighting off Indian attacks.

Ewing Galloway

Abraham Lincoln Birthplace National Historic Site, near Hodgenville, houses the log cabin where he was reputedly born.

Much of the danger from Indians was removed by the victories of George Rogers Clark in the Revolutionary War (*see* Clark). The last Indian battle in the state was at Blue Licks (near Mount Olivet) in 1782. The Indians retreated across the Ohio River.

### Statehood to the Civil War

In 1784 a group of Kentuckians meeting at Danville asked to be separated from Virginia. This was the first of ten such conventions that prepared the way for statehood. Finally, on June 1, 1792, Kentucky was admitted to the Union.

The new state joined with Virginia in 1798 in passing the resolutions denouncing the Alien and Sedition Laws (*see* Alien and Sedition Laws; States' Rights). The resolutions were guided through the state legislature by John Breckinridge of Lexington.

The name Breckinridge became one of the most famous in Kentucky. Three of John's sons—Joseph, John, and Robert—were noted as either lawyers or Presbyterian clergymen. Robert served as Abraham Lincoln's Kentucky adviser during the Civil War. Two grandsons, however, fought for the Confederacy—John C. Breckinridge, son of Joseph and vice-president of the United States under James Buchanan; and William C. Breckinridge, son of Robert.

During the Civil War Kentucky was as divided as the Breckinridge family. A slave state, it tried to remain neutral. Some of its men joined the Confederacy, others fought for the North. Late in 1861 a separate state government at Bowling Green was recognized by the Confederate government. The following year Gen. Braxton Bragg led a Southern army into Kentucky. He was turned back at the battle of Perryville by a Union force under Gen. Don Carlos Buell. (*See also* Civil War, American.)

### Growth into a Modern State

Following the reconstruction period, Kentucky showed a steady growth in agriculture and manufacturing (*see* Reconstruction Period). Coal mining on a large scale was started during the 1870's. There were a number of clashes between miners and operators until the United Mine Workers of America won recognition as the miners' bargaining agent in 1939.

The first Kentucky Derby was held at Louisville's Churchill Downs in 1875. Another major attraction, Mammoth Cave, became a national park in 1936. In the same year the nation's gold reserve was moved to Fort Knox for safekeeping. In 1962 the Kentucky legislature passed a law regulating the strip mining of coal. Unchecked, this mining technique ravages the soil. The law was made more comprehensive in 1965. (*See also* United States, section "The South"; individual entries in the Fact-Index on Kentucky persons, places, products, and events.)

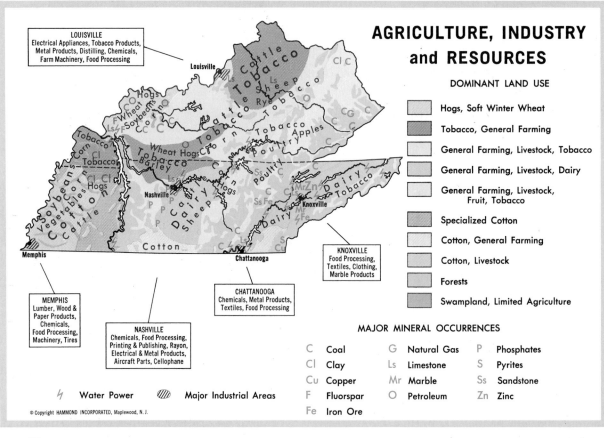

© Copyright HAMMOND INCORPORATED, Maplewood, N.J.

# Notable Events in Kentucky History

1671—Thomas Batts and Robert Fallam of Virginia reach Ohio Valley.

1739—Capt. Charles de Longueuil discovers Big Bone Lick, near Walton.

1750—Dr. Thomas Walker discovers Cumberland Gap.

1751—Christopher Gist explores area along Ohio River.

1763—France cedes area including Kentucky to Britain.

1769—Daniel Boone and John Finley explore Kentucky.

1774—James Harrod starts building Harrodstown (Harrodsburg); Indians force settlers to withdraw; settlers return in 1775.

1775—Boiling Springs and St. Asaph settled. Indians give Richard Henderson land between Ohio and Cumberland rivers for Transylvania Land Company. **Boone blazes Wilderness Road; Boonesboro founded.**

1776—Harrodsburg settlers, jealous of Boonesboro, send George Rogers Clark and John Jones to ask Virginia's aid; Virginia declares Transylvania Land Company illegal; creates Kentucky County.

1778—Indian siege of Boonesboro repulsed. Clark organizes expedition against British beyond the Ohio.

1782—**"Last battle of American Revolution" fought at Blue Licks, near Mount Olivet.**

1784—First of ten conventions held to prepare way for separation of Kentucky from Virginia.

1792—Kentucky becomes 15th state, June 1; governor, Isaac Shelby; capital, Lexington, then Frankfort.

1794—Gen. "Mad Anthony" Wayne's victory at Fallen Timbers in Ohio ends Indian attacks in Kentucky.

1796—Wilderness Road opened to wagons.

1798—Legislature passes Kentucky Resolutions opposing U. S. Alien and Sedition Laws.

1811—Henry Clay elected to Congress from Kentucky. *New Orleans,* first steamboat on Ohio River, stops at Louisville; *Enterprise* reaches Louisville from New Orleans, La., in 1815.

1812—Kentuckians bear brunt of war with England north of the Ohio and in New Orleans.

1830—Louisville and Portland Canal, around Falls of Ohio River, opened.

1849—Zachary Taylor, Kentucky hero of Mexican War, becomes 12th president of U. S.

1861—Kentucky declares its neutrality in Civil War.

1862—Last major battle in state fought near Perryville.

1865—University of Kentucky founded at Lexington.

1875—**First Kentucky Derby run at Churchill Downs.**

1891—Present state constitution adopted.

1909—Present State Capitol completed.

1936—U. S. gold depository built at Fort Knox. Mammoth Cave National Park established.

1937—Worst Ohio River flood occurs.

1944—**Kentucky Dam on Tennessee River completed by Tennessee Valley Authority.**

1946—Frederick M. Vinson, born 1890 in Louisa, is appointed chief justice of the U. S.

1950—Atomic energy plant built near Paducah.

1951—Wolf Creek Dam on Cumberland River dedicated.

1959—Cumberland Gap National Historical Park dedicated.

1962—Kentucky is first state given control of certain nuclear energy materials by federal government.

1964—Western Kentucky Parkway opened; Kentucky Central Parkway, in 1965.

1966—Kentucky is first Southern state to pass a comprehensive civil rights law. Barkley Dam on Cumberland River dedicated.

1977—Nightclub fire in Southgate kills 164 persons.

1775

1782

1875

1944

STATE FLOWER:
Goldenrod

STATE TREE:
Kentucky Coffee Tree

STATE BIRD:
Cardinal

# Kentucky Profile

**FLAG:** *See* Flags of the United States.
**MOTTO:** United We Stand, Divided
We Fall.
**SONG** 'My Old Kentucky Home'—
words and music by Stephen
Collins Foster.

STATE SEAL: Two friends shaking
hands, surrounded by state motto.

When Daniel Boone explored the Kentucky region in 1769, herds of bison roamed the grassy areas and its forests offered a seemingly unlimited supply of bear, deer, and wild turkey. Describing his determination to settle in this lush, wild country, the great woodsman called Kentucky "a second paradise."

Today the bison are gone, and the bear, deer, and wild turkey populations survive only through careful restocking. Kentucky is well on its way to becoming an industrial state. Yet Daniel Boone's paradise lives on in the tough, individualistic spirit and strong feeling for tradition that continue to characterize its citizens. The mountains near the West Virginia border are still home to descendants of such famous feuding families as the Hatfields and the McCoys. Although the shotgun is rarely used to settle disputes, family loyalties and antagonisms among families remain extremely strong.

Kentucky is still a decidedly rural state, but it is developing a rich manufacturing industry that yields more income and becomes increasingly varied with each passing year—as the burgeoning Louisville aluminum industry and the new chemical plants on the Ohio River testify. Yet farming is also vital to the economy of the Bluegrass State. Tobacco is the leading crop. Increasingly, however, farms are becoming larger and their number fewer. The high cost of labor is driving many small tobacco farmers out of business, and agriculture is diversifying as many farms change over to crops more easily managed by machines than tobacco.

The automation of the large coal mines and the consequent unemployment of the miners, especially in the eastern part of the state, is probably the state's major problem. Efforts are being made to attract tourists and industry to Kentucky, so that the economic level of this area can be raised.

Louisville, Kentucky's largest city, is noted for tobacco products, fine whiskey, and the Kentucky Derby. Founded in 1778 by George Rogers Clark, the city was later named in honor of Louis XVI of France.

The University of Kentucky, at Lexington, was chartered as the Kentucky Agricultural and Mechanical College in 1865 and opened at its present location in 1881. Shown is the university's Medical Center.

The State Capitol at Frankfort was completed in 1909. It stands on a wooded slope overlooking the Kentucky River. The dome is a reproduction of the dome over Napoleon's tomb.

Cumberland Gap, a famous pass through a range of the Appalachian Highlands, is in Cumberland Gap National Historical Park, one of two such parks in Kentucky. The first settlers from Virginia entered Kentucky through this pass.

The 68-foot-high waterfall is the most impressive sight in Cumberland Falls State Park. A beautiful moonbow often forms over it. The park occupies nearly 2,000 acres on the Cumberland River.

# Kentucky picture profile

Boating is popular on Kentucky Lake, one of the longest man-made lakes in the world. This Tennessee Valley Authority project is about 180 miles long and encompasses some 2,400 miles of shoreline.

This is the central attraction at Natural Bridge State Park, a 1,372-acre area in the Red River valley near Slade. There are more than 30 state parks in Kentucky.

Much-visited Mammoth Cave National Park is noted for its more than 150 miles of charted underground passageways. The cave's high, vaulted rooms are filled with unusual onyx and limestone formations.

Every October the Daniel Boone Festival is held in Barbourville. The town is on the Wilderness Road, the trail that the famous frontiersman blazed in 1775.

Ashland, in the city of Lexington, was the home of Henry Clay, for whom it was built in 1806. In 1857, five years after Clay's death, the mansion was rebuilt. Clay raised cattle and horses on his estate.

The museum in Audubon State Park is a tribute to John J. Audubon, the renowned artist and ornithologist. It houses many of his works as well as relics of the period in which he lived. The park is also a bird sanctuary.

In Pioneer Memorial State Park at Harrodsburg stands a reconstruction of Fort Harrod. It was erected on the site of the first permanent white settlement in Kentucky, established by James Harrod in 1774.

Tobacco is Kentucky's chief field crop. The buds are usually cut off to give the leaves more nourishment. The green leaves turn brown in curing. For agricultural statistics, see KENTUCKY FACT SUMMARY.

37

JOHN C. BRECKINRIDGE

IRVIN S. COBB

FREDERICK M. VINSON

DANIEL BOONE
© Art Grossmann

MARY BRECKINRIDGE

HENRY CLAY

JOHN MARSHALL HARLAN

WHITNEY M. YOUNG, JR.

DAVID WARK GRIFFITH
*Chicago Historical Society*

LOUIS D. BRANDEIS

ROBERT PENN WARREN

HENRY WATTERSON

ALBERT S. JOHNSTON

*Only a few of Kentucky's famous people are shown here. The persons depicted are generally associated with the state, though not all of them were born there. For biographical information, see entries in the Fact-Index.*

# KENTUCKY FACT SUMMARY

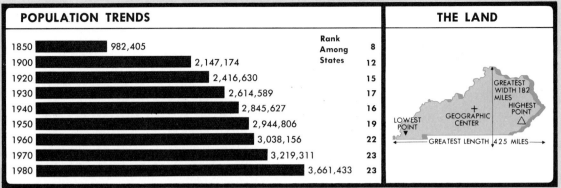

## POPULATION TRENDS

| Year | Population | Rank Among States |
|------|-----------|-------------------|
| 1850 | 982,405 | 8 |
| 1900 | 2,147,174 | 12 |
| 1920 | 2,416,630 | 15 |
| 1930 | 2,614,589 | 17 |
| 1940 | 2,845,627 | 16 |
| 1950 | 2,944,806 | 19 |
| 1960 | 3,038,156 | 22 |
| 1970 | 3,219,311 | 23 |
| 1980 | 3,661,433 | 23 |

## THE LAND

GREATEST WIDTH 182 MILES
HIGHEST POINT
LOWEST POINT
GEOGRAPHIC CENTER
GREATEST LENGTH 425 MILES

## GOVERNMENT

**Capital:** Frankfort (since 1792).

**Statehood:** Became 15th state in the Union on June 1, 1792.

**Constitution:** Adopted 1891. Amendment may be passed by three-fifths vote of both houses; ratified by majority voting on it in an election.

**Representation in U. S. Congress:** Senate—2. House of Representatives—7. Electoral votes—9.

**General Assembly:** Senators—38; term, 4 years. Representatives—100; term, 2 years.
Convenes on Tuesday after 1st Monday in January in even years. Session limit—60 legislative days. Special session limit—no special session provided for.

**Executive Officers**
Governor—term, 4 years. May not succeed himself.
Other officials—lieutenant governor, secretary of state, attorney general, and treasurer; all elected; terms, 4 years.

**Judiciary:** Supreme Court—7 justices; elected; term, 8 years. Circuit courts—83 judges; elected; term, 6 years. County courts—1 in each county; judges elected; term, 4 years.

**County:** 120 counties. Governed by fiscal courts consisting of a judge and magistrates or a judge and 3 commissioners; all elected; terms, 4 years.

**Municipal:** Mayor-council plan most common; also commission and council-manager plans.

**Voting**
Residency requirements—30 days.
General election—1st Tuesday after 1st Monday in November.
Primary election—1st Tuesday after 4th Monday in May.
Preferential presidential primary—1st Tuesday after 4th Monday in May.

## EDUCATION

**Private Elementary and Secondary Day Schools**
Enrollment—elementary, 54,800; secondary, 16,600.
Classroom teachers—3,440.

**Public Elementary and Secondary Schools***
Operating school districts—181.
Compulsory school age—7 to 16.
Enrollment—elementary, 430,280; secondary, 263,720.
Average daily attendance—635,650.
High school graduates—41,500.
Instructional staff—total, 36,195; principals and supervisors, 1,925; elementary teachers, 19,960; secondary teachers, 12,340.
Administrative officials
Superintendent of public instruction; elected; term, 4 years.
County superintendents; appointed.
Superintendents of schools; appointed by school board members, who are elected.

Teachers' average annual salaries—elementary, $10,700; secondary, $11,450.
Revenue receipts—$881,640,000.
Source of receipts (% of total)—federal, 12.2; state, 58.4; local, 29.3.
Nonrevenue receipts†—$70,000,000.
Current expenditures
For day schools—$696,300,000.
For other programs—$3,200,000.
State expenditure on education—$1,019 per pupil.
Head Start programs—participants, 12,948; funds allocated, $12,883,860.‡

**Universities and Colleges‡**
Number of institutions—total, 38; public, 9; private, 29.
Degree-credit enrollment—118,000.
Earned degrees conferred—bachelor's and first professional, 13,135; master's except first professional, 4,517; doctor's, 251.

**Special Institutions:** Kentucky School for the Blind, Louisville; Kentucky School for the Deaf, Danville; Lexington Deaf Oral School; The Louisville Deaf Oral School, Inc.; Outwood Hospital and School, Dawson Springs.

**Libraries:** City and county libraries—127; regional libraries—19; bookmobiles—104. Department of Libraries aids in developing public libraries. Department of Education aids in developing school libraries. Noted special libraries—Filson Club, *Courier-Journal* and *Louisville Times* libraries, all in Louisville; Kentucky Historical Society, Frankfort.

**Outstanding Museums:** Behringer-Crawford Memorial Museum of Natural History, Covington; Kentucky Historical Society, Frankfort; Audubon Museum, Henderson; J. B. Speed Art Museum and Museum of Science and History, both in Louisville; Old Fort Harrod Mansion Museum, Harrodsburg.

## CORRECTIONAL AND PENAL INSTITUTIONS

**State**
Adult—Kentucky State Reformatory, La Grange; Bell County Forestry Camp, Chenoa; Harlan County Forestry Camp, Harlan; Boone County Correctional Center, Burlington; Blackburn Correctional Complex, Lexington; Frenchburg Correctional Facility; Frankfort Career Development Center; Roederer Farm Center, La Grange; Western Kentucky Farm Center, Eddyville; Kentucky Correctional Institution for Women, Peewee Valley; Kentucky State Penitentiary, Eddyville.
Juvenile—Lake Cumberland Boys' Camp, Monticello; Woodsbend Boys' Camp, West Liberty; Jewel Manor Treatment Center, Louisville; Central Kentucky Treatment Center, Lynden; Frenchburg Boys' Center; Green River Boys' Camp, Cromwell; Lynwood Treatment Center, Anchorage; Morehead Treatment Center; Northern Kentucky Treatment Center, Crittenden.

**Federal**
Federal Correctional Institutions, Ashland and Lexington.

All Fact Summary data, including estimates, are based on current government reports.
*Kindergartens are included in the elementary schools; junior high schools, in the secondary schools.
†Money received from loans, sales of bonds, sales of property, and insurance adjustments.
‡Excludes data for service academies.

# KENTUCKY FACT SUMMARY

## PRODUCTION—YEARLY VALUE: $3,726,700,000

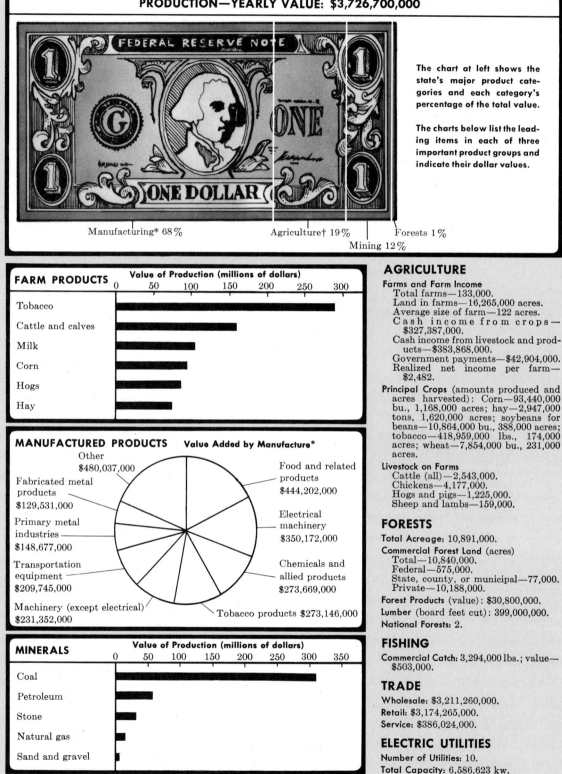

The chart at left shows the state's major product categories and each category's percentage of the total value.

The charts below list the leading items in each of three important product groups and indicate their dollar values.

Manufacturing* 68%  Agriculture† 19%  Forests 1%  Mining 12%

## FARM PRODUCTS
Value of Production (millions of dollars)
0   50   100   150   200   250   300

- Tobacco
- Cattle and calves
- Milk
- Corn
- Hogs
- Hay

## MANUFACTURED PRODUCTS
Value Added by Manufacture*

Other $480,037,000

Fabricated metal products $129,531,000

Primary metal industries $148,677,000

Transportation equipment $209,745,000

Machinery (except electrical) $231,352,000

Food and related products $444,202,000

Electrical machinery $350,172,000

Chemicals and allied products $273,669,000

Tobacco products $273,146,000

## MINERALS
Value of Production (millions of dollars)
0   50   100   150   200   250   300   350

- Coal
- Petroleum
- Stone
- Natural gas
- Sand and gravel

## AGRICULTURE

**Farms and Farm Income**
Total farms—133,000.
Land in farms—16,265,000 acres.
Average size of farm—122 acres.
Cash income from crops—$327,387,000.
Cash income from livestock and products—$383,868,000.
Government payments—$42,904,000.
Realized net income per farm—$2,482.

**Principal Crops** (amounts produced and acres harvested): Corn—93,440,000 bu., 1,168,000 acres; hay—2,947,000 tons, 1,620,000 acres; soybeans for beans—10,864,000 bu., 388,000 acres; tobacco—418,959,000 lbs., 174,000 acres; wheat—7,854,000 bu., 231,000 acres.

**Livestock on Farms**
Cattle (all)—2,543,000.
Chickens—4,177,000.
Hogs and pigs—1,225,000.
Sheep and lambs—159,000.

## FORESTS
Total Acreage: 10,891,000.
**Commercial Forest Land** (acres)
Total—10,840,000.
Federal—575,000.
State, county, or municipal—77,000.
Private—10,188,000.
Forest Products (value): $30,800,000.
Lumber (board feet cut): 399,000,000.
National Forests: 2.

## FISHING
Commercial Catch: 3,294,000 lbs.; value—$503,000.

## TRADE
Wholesale: $3,211,260,000.
Retail: $3,174,265,000.
Service: $386,024,000.

## ELECTRIC UTILITIES
Number of Utilities: 10.
Total Capacity: 6,586,623 kw.

All Fact Summary data are based on current government reports.
*Value Added by Manufacture—value of manufactured products as they leave the factory, less the cost of materials, supplies, fuel, etc. For complete definition, see Fact-Index.
†Cash receipts.

# KENTUCKY FACT SUMMARY

## TRANSPORTATION

**Roads and Streets**
Total state mileage—70,100.
Municipal mileage—6,100.
Rural mileage—64,100.
National Interstate Highway System
Total designated mileage—737.
Mileage open to traffic—679.
Mileage under construction or projected—58.

**Automobiles, Trucks, and Buses** (registrations)*
Total motor vehicles—2,350,000.
Automobiles—1,740,000.
Trucks and buses—610,000.

**Motorcycles** (registrations): 63,000.

**Railroads**
Total mileage owned—3,517.
First railroad—Lexington to Frankfort, 1832.

**Airports:** 90.

**Pipelines** (mileage)†: 2,444.

## COMMUNICATION

**Post Offices:** 1,267.

**Radio Stations** (commercial): AM—117; FM—83. First station—WHAS, Louisville, licensed July 18, 1922.

**TV Stations:** Commercial—11; educational—14. First station—WAVE-TV, Louisville, began operation Nov. 24, 1948.

**Telephones:** Total—1,912,000; residence—1,447,000; business—465,000.

**Newspapers**
Daily—27; circulation—769,000.
Weekly—119.
Sunday—12; circulation—595,000.
First newspaper—*Kentucky Gazette*, Lexington, 1787.

**Periodicals:** 66.

## FINANCE‡

**Revenue:** $2,447,532,000.

**Expenditures:** Total—$2,355,861,000; education—$961,-590,000; highways—$420,943,000; public welfare—$404,-545,000; hospitals—$71,396,000.

**Debt:** Total—$1,996,558,000; issued (long term only)—$97,500,000; retired (long term only)—$44,349,000.

**Taxation**
State tax collections—$1,403,735,000; general sales—$409,193,000; individual income—$292,546,000. Intergovernmental—$742,466,000.

**Personal Income per Capita:** $5,423.

**Banks:** 342; total assets or liabilities—$12,290,000,000.

**Savings and Loan Associations:** 108; total assets—$3,991,-000,000; per capita assets—$1,164.

**Life Insurance Policies:** 6,371,000; value—$29,911,000,000.

## VITAL STATISTICS§

**Birthrate:** 16.1.

**Death Rate:** 9.8.

**Marriage Rate:** 9.4.

**Divorce Rate:** 4.3.

## HEALTH CARE

**Hospitals:** 125; beds—19,432.

**Nursing Homes:** 312; beds—18,177.

**Physicians:** 4,320.

**Dentists:** 1,393.

**Licensed Practical Nurses:** 6,624.

## EMPLOYMENT

**Total Number of Persons Employed:** 1,096,561.

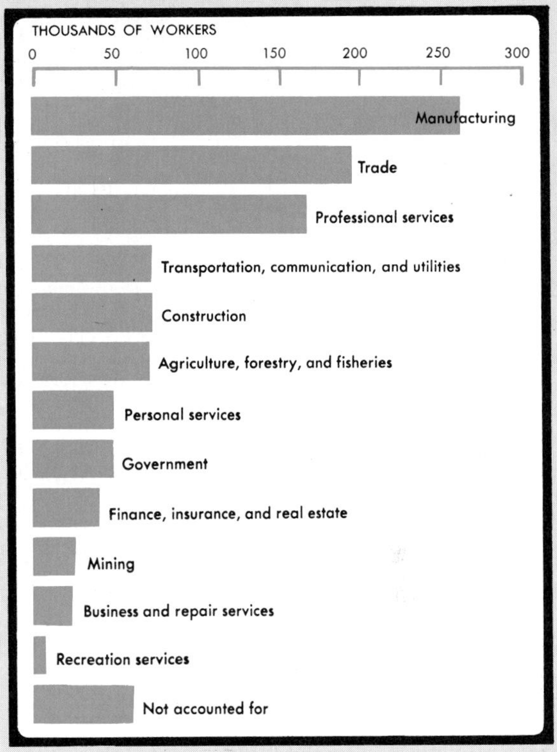

THOUSANDS OF WORKERS
0  50  100  150  200  250  300

Manufacturing
Trade
Professional services
Transportation, communication, and utilities
Construction
Agriculture, forestry, and fisheries
Personal services
Government
Finance, insurance, and real estate
Mining
Business and repair services
Recreation services
Not accounted for

## WELFARE‡

**Old-Age and Survivors Insurance:** Beneficiaries—467,759; benefits—$941,724,000.

**Disability Insurance:** Beneficiaries—103,130; benefits—$196,765,000.

**Unemployment Insurance:** Beneficiaries (weekly average)—17,040; benefits—$4,934,970.

**Workmen's Compensation Benefits:** $75,591,000.

**Vocational Rehabilitation**
Disabled persons rehabilitated—9,002; in process of rehabilitation—12,960.
Total federal and state funds—$19,135,000.

**Public Assistance**
Dependent children—recipients, 176,428; average payment, $57.66.

**Supplementary Security Income**
Old age—recipients, 48,550; total, $4,185,000.
Permanently and totally disabled—recipients, 43,804; total, $5,726,000.
Blind—recipients, 2,025; total, $306,000.

**Maternal and Child Health Services**
Federal grants—maternal and child health services, $4,778,000; crippled children, $1,855,900.

**United Way Campaigns♦:** 15; amount raised—$9,121,821.

All Fact Summary data are based on current government reports.
*Excludes vehicles owned by military services.
†Petroleum and products only.
‡Figures for one-year periods.
§Rates per 1,000 population.
♦Data based on state reports to United Way of America.

# KENTUCKY FACT SUMMARY

## LARGEST CITIES AND OTHER PLACES*

**Louisville** (298,840): industrial center at Falls of the Ohio; port; railroad shops, distilleries, cigarette plants; chemicals; University of Louisville; Churchill Downs track; J. B. Speed Art Museum (*see* Louisville).

**Lexington–Fayette** (204,165): in Bluegrass region; horse farms; Keeneland track; tobacco and livestock market; University of Kentucky; Transylvania College; Ashland, Henry Clay's home; Hopemont, Gen. John Hunt Morgan's home; Kentucky Horse Park, with Man O' War statue.

**Owensboro** (54,450): oil and tobacco center; varied industries; radio tubes; Kentucky Wesleyan College.

**Covington** (49,563): industrial city on Ohio River; Devou Park; St. Mary's Cathedral; Dan Beard Home.

**Bowling Green** (40,450): farm center; livestock and tobacco market; Western Kentucky University.

**Fort Knox†** (31,055): federal gold depository; Patton Museum of Cavalry and Armor; historical armored vehicle show.

**Paducah** (29,315): port on Ohio River; tobacco market; rail shops; near atomic plant.

**Pleasure Ridge Park†** (27,332): suburb south of Louisville.

**Hopkinsville** (27,318): manufacture of precision springs, lighting fixtures, wire; tobacco auctions; Fort Campbell military installation.

**Ashland** (27,064): industrial center; steel, oil, and chemical products.

**Frankfort** (25,973): state capital on Kentucky River; distilleries, quarries; Old State Capitol; Liberty Hall; Frankfort Cemetery; state university (*see* Frankfort).

## PLACES OF INTEREST

**Abbey of Our Lady of Gethsemane:** near New Haven; Trappist monastery, founded in 1848.

**Abraham Lincoln Birthplace National Historic Site:** near Hodgenville; memorial building encloses Lincoln's reputed birthplace cabin.

**Ancient Buried City (King Mounds):** in Wickliffe; 5 of 40 prehistoric Indian mounds explored; museum.

**Audubon State Park:** near Henderson; museum.

**Bardstown:** Georgian colonial homes; paintings in St. Joseph's Cathedral; John Fitch Monument; Knob Creek farm, a Lincoln home (1811–16), nearby.

**Berea:** Berea College, mountain school; Boone Tavern, college hotel; Churchill Weavers.

**Blue Licks Battlefield State Park:** near Carlisle; site of "last battle of American Revolution" (1782).

**Breaks Interstate Park:** in mountains bordering Kentucky and Virginia; area of rugged scenic beauty.

**Columbus-Belmont Battlefield State Park:** on Mississippi River bluff near Columbus; fortified in Civil War.

**Constitution Square State Shrine:** in Danville; site of framing of Kentucky's first constitution, in 1792.

**Cumberland Gap National Historical Park:** in Kentucky, Virginia, and Tennessee; near Middlesboro; pass used by Daniel Boone and pioneers.

**Dr. Thomas Walker Memorial State Shrine:** near Barbourville; first white man's cabin in Kentucky (1750).

**Fort Knox:** U. S. gold depository houses major part of gold

*1980 census.
†Unincorporated.

reserve of U. S.; Patton Museum of Cavalry and Armor.

**Harlan:** coal capital of Kentucky; in heart of magnificent mountain scenery.

**Herrington Lake:** near Danville; Dix River Dam; fishing.

**Horse Farms:** in Bluegrass area near Lexington.

**Isaac Shelby Memorial State Shrine:** near Danville; grave of first governor of Kentucky.

**Jefferson Davis Monument State Shrine:** near Hopkinsville; honors Confederate president; 351-foot shaft.

**Kentucky Lake:** huge TVA lake; fishing.

**Kentucky Woodlands National Wildlife Refuge:** near Cadiz; state's largest game preserve.

**Levi Jackson Wilderness Road State Park:** near London; Indian massacre site (1786); pioneer buildings.

**Lincoln Homestead State Shrine:** near Springfield; museum.

**Mammoth Cave National Park:** near Cave City; more than 150 miles of passages; stalactites and stalagmites in vast chambers.

**Murray:** monument to Nathan Stubblefield, a radio inventor.

**My Old Kentucky Home State Shrine:** near Bardstown; Foster said to have written song here.

**Old Mulkey Meeting House State Shrine:** near Tompkinsville; oldest log meetinghouse in Kentucky (1798).

**Paris:** Duncan Tavern, built in 1788; Claiborne Stud, famous thoroughbred horse farm, nearby.

**Perryville Battlefield Monument State Shrine:** near Perryville; site of bloody Civil War battle (1862).

**Pine Mountain Settlement School:** near Harlan; school for mountain boys and girls.

**Pioneer Memorial State Park:** in Harrodsburg; replica of Fort Harrod, state's first white settlement (1774).

**Shakertown:** near Harrodsburg; communal town called Pleasant Hill founded by Shakers in 1805.

**William Whitley House State Shrine:** near Stanford; first brick house west of Alleghenies.

## BOOKS AND FILMS ABOUT KENTUCKY

**Bailey, B. F.** Picture Book of Kentucky, rev. ed. (Whitman, 1967).

**Carpenter, Allan.** Enchantment of Kentucky (Childrens, 1967) o.p.

**Channing, S. A.** Kentucky: a Bicentennial History (Norton, 1977).

**Clark, T. D.** The Kentucky (Henry Clay, 1969).

**Clark, T. D.** Kentucky: Land of Contrast (Harper, 1968).

**Filson, John.** The Discovery, Settlement and Present State of Kentucky (Univ. Microfilms, 1966).

**Giles, J. H.** The Kentuckians (Houghton, 1953).

**Kentucky Pioneers,** film (Encyclopaedia Britannica Films).

**McMeekin, I. M.** Journey Cake (Messner, 1942) o.p.

**Steele, W. D.** The Old Wilderness Road (Harcourt, 1968).

**Stuart, Jesse.** The Thread That Runs So True (Scribner, 1958).

**Wilkie, K. E. and Moseley, E. R.** Kentucky Heritage (Steck, 1966) o.p.

**Writers' Program.** Kentucky: a Guide to the Bluegrass State (Somerset, 1939).

# KENTUCKY

## COUNTIES

| Name | Pop. | Ref. |
|---|---|---|
| Adair | 13,037 | G 6 |
| Allen | 12,598 | E 7 |
| Anderson | 9,358 | H 5 |
| Ballard | 8,276 | C 3 |
| Barren | 28,677 | F 7 |
| Bath | 9,235 | K 4 |
| Bell | 31,121 | K 7 |
| Boone | 32,812 | H 3 |
| Bourbon | 18,476 | J 4 |
| Boyd | 52,376 | M 4 |
| Boyle | 21,090 | H 5 |
| Bracken | 7,227 | J 3 |
| Breathitt | 14,221 | L 5 |
| Breckinridge | 14,789 | E 5 |
| Bullitt | 26,090 | F 5 |
| Butler | 9,723 | D 6 |
| Caldwell | 13,179 | E 3 |
| Calloway | 27,692 | D 4 |
| Campbell | 88,561 | J 3 |
| Carlisle | 5,354 | C 3 |
| Carroll | 8,523 | G 3 |
| Carter | 19,850 | L 4 |
| Casey | 12,930 | H 6 |
| Christian | 56,224 | C 7 |
| Clark | 24,090 | J 5 |
| Clay | 18,481 | K 6 |
| Clinton | 8,174 | G 7 |
| Crittenden | 8,493 | E 2 |
| Cumberland | 6,850 | G 7 |
| Daviess | 79,486 | C 5 |
| Edmonson | 8,751 | E 6 |
| Elliott | 5,933 | L 4 |
| Estill | 12,752 | K 5 |
| Fayette | 174,323 | J 4 |
| Fleming | 11,366 | K 4 |
| Floyd | 35,889 | M 5 |
| Franklin | 34,481 | H 4 |
| Fulton | 10,183 | C 4 |
| Gallatin | 4,134 | H 3 |
| Garrard | 9,457 | H 5 |
| Grant | 9,999 | H 3 |
| Graves | 30,939 | D 3 |
| Grayson | 16,445 | E 5 |
| Green | 10,350 | F 6 |
| Greenup | 33,192 | M 3 |
| Hancock | 7,080 | D 5 |
| Hardin | 78,421 | F 5 |
| Harlan | 37,370 | L 7 |
| Harrison | 14,158 | J 4 |
| Hart | 13,980 | F 6 |
| Henderson | 36,031 | B 5 |
| Henry | 10,910 | G 4 |
| Hickman | 6,264 | C 3 |
| Hopkins | 38,167 | B 6 |
| Jackson | 10,005 | J 6 |
| Jefferson | 695,055 | F 4 |
| Jessamine | 17,430 | H 5 |
| Johnson | 17,539 | M 5 |
| Kenton | 129,440 | H 3 |
| Knott | 14,698 | M 6 |
| Knox | 23,689 | K 7 |
| Larue | 10,672 | F 5 |
| Laurel | 27,386 | J 6 |
| Lawrence | 10,726 | M 4 |
| Lee | 6,587 | K 5 |
| Leslie | 11,623 | L 6 |
| Letcher | 23,165 | M 6 |
| Lewis | 12,355 | L 3 |
| Lincoln | 16,663 | H 6 |
| Livingston | 7,596 | D 2 |
| Logan | 21,793 | D 7 |
| Lyon | 5,562 | E 3 |
| Madison | 42,730 | J 5 |
| Magoffin | 10,443 | L 5 |
| Marion | 16,714 | G 5 |
| Marshall | 20,381 | D 3 |
| Martin | 9,377 | M 5 |
| Mason | 17,273 | K 3 |
| McCracken | 58,281 | D 3 |
| McCreary | 12,548 | J 7 |
| McLean | 9,062 | C 5 |
| Meade | 18,796 | E 5 |
| Menifee | 4,050 | K 5 |
| Mercer | 15,960 | H 5 |
| Metcalfe | 8,177 | F 7 |
| Monroe | 11,642 | F 7 |
| Montgomery | 15,364 | K 4 |
| Morgan | 10,019 | L 5 |
| Muhlenberg | 27,537 | C 6 |
| Nelson | 23,477 | F 5 |
| Nicholas | 6,508 | J 4 |
| Ohio | 18,790 | D 6 |

## CITIES AND TOWNS

| Name | Pop. | Ref. |
|---|---|---|
| Aberdeen | 200 | D 6 |
| Adairville | 973 | D 7 |
| Adams | 195 | M 4 |
| Adolphus | 100 | E 7 |
| Aflex | 475 | N 5 |
| Albany | 1,891 | G 7 |
| Alcorn | 56 | K 5 |
| Alexandria | 3,844 | J 3 |
| Allegre | 200 | C 7 |
| Allen | 724 | M 5 |
| Allen Sprs. | 50 | E 7 |
| Allensville | 266 | C 7 |
| Allock | 61 | L 6 |
| Almo | 100 | D 3 |
| Alpha | 145 | G 7 |
| Alpine | 100 | H 7 |
| Alton | 220 | H 4 |
| Altro | 250 | L 6 |
| Alva | 175 | L 7 |
| Alvaton | 100 | E 7 |
| Amburgey | 430 | M 6 |
| Ammie | 200 | K 6 |
| Anchorage | 1,477 | F 4 |
| Anco | 375 | L 6 |
| Anna | 380 | E 6 |
| Anneta | 200 | E 6 |
| Annville | 500 | K 6 |
| Arabia | 100 | H 6 |
| Arjay | 975 | K 7 |
| Arlington | 549 | C 3 |
| Artemus | 425 | K 7 |
| Arvel | 50 | K 5 |
| Ashbyburg | 28 | C 5 |
| Ashland | 29,245 | M 4 |
| Ashland–Huntington | †253,743 | M 4 |
| Athertonville | 175 | F 5 |
| Auburn | 1,160 | D 7 |
| Audubon Park | 1,862 | F 4 |
| Augusta | 1,434 | J 3 |
| Austin | 150 | F 7 |
| Auxier | 900 | M 5 |
| Bagdad | 160 | G 4 |
| Bakerton | 85 | G 7 |
| Balkan | 200 | K 7 |
| Bandana | 290 | C 2 |
| Banner | 550 | M 5 |
| Barbourmeade | 884 | *F 4 |
| Barbourville | 3,549 | K 7 |
| Bardstown | 5,816 | G 5 |
| Bardwell | 1,049 | C 3 |
| Barlow | 746 | C 3 |
| Barnrock | 150 | M 5 |
| Barterville | 45 | J 4 |
| Baskett | 375 | B 5 |
| Battletown | 200 | E 4 |
| Bayou | 50 | D 2 |
| Bays | 96 | P 5 |
| Beals | 100 | C 5 |
| Beattyville | 923 | K 5 |
| Beauty | 800 | N 5 |
| Beaver Dam | 2,622 | D 6 |
| Bedford | 780 | G 3 |
| Bee Spring | 500 | E 6 |
| Beech Creek | 100 | C 6 |
| Beech Grove | 233 | C 5 |
| Beechwood | 1,788 | F 4 |
| Belfry | 800 | N 5 |
| Bell Farm | 53 | H 7 |
| Bellefonte | 966 | *M 4 |
| Bellemeade | 576 | *F 4 |
| Bellevue | 8,847 | L 1 |
| Bellewood | 410 | *F 4 |
| Belmont | 250 | F 5 |
| Belton | 280 | D 6 |
| Benham | 1,000 | M 7 |
| Benton | 3,652 | D 3 |
| Berea | 6,956 | J 5 |
| Bernstadt | 400 | J 6 |
| Berry | 266 | J 3 |
| Berrys Lick | 25 | D 6 |
| Bethel | 80 | K 4 |
| Bethelridge | 188 | H 6 |
| Bethlehem | 189 | G 4 |
| Betsy Layne | 975 | M 5 |
| Beverly | 350 | L 7 |
| Big Clifty | 432 | E 5 |
| Big Creek | 473 | K 6 |
| Big Spring | 120 | E 5 |
| Birdsville | 100 | D 2 |
| Blackford | 150 | B 6 |
| Blaine | 300 | M 4 |
| Blairs Mills | 181 | L 4 |
| Blanche | 225 | K 7 |
| Blandville | 116 | C 3 |
| Bloomfield | 1,072 | G 5 |
| Blue Diamond | 150 | L 6 |
| Blue Ridge Manor | 596 | *F 4 |
| Boaz | 52 | D 3 |
| Boldman | 500 | M 5 |
| Bond | 150 | J 6 |
| Bondville | 85 | H 5 |
| Bonnieville | 328 | F 6 |
| Bonnyman | 800 | L 6 |
| Boone | 300 | J 5 |
| Booneville | 126 | K 6 |
| Boreing | 52 | J 6 |
| Boston | 400 | F 5 |
| Bowen | 65 | K 5 |
| Bowling Green | 36,253 | D 7 |
| Bradford | 115 | J 3 |
| Bradfordsville | 338 | G 6 |
| Brandenburg | 1,637 | E 4 |
| Breeding | 139 | G 7 |
| Bremen | 299 | C 6 |
| Brewers | 300 | D 3 |
| Briarwood | 327 | *F 4 |
| Brightshade | 50 | K 7 |
| Broad Fields | 534 | *F 4 |
| Brodhead | 769 | J 6 |
| Bromley | 1,069 | K 1 |
| Bronston | 350 | H 7 |
| Brooklyn | 50 | D 6 |
| Brooks | 850 | F 4 |
| Brookside | 400 | L 7 |
| Brooksville | 609 | J 3 |
| Browder | 450 | D 6 |
| Brownsboro Farm | 823 | *F 4 |
| Brownsboro Village | 494 | *F 4 |
| Brownsville | 542 | E 6 |
| Bruin | 500 | L 4 |
| Brushart | 100 | L 3 |
| Bryantsville | 140 | H 5 |
| Buchanan | 100 | M 4 |
| Buckner | 300 | G 4 |
| Buechel | 5,359 | F 4 |
| Buffalo | 142 | F 6 |
| Bulan | 800 | L 6 |
| Burgin | 1,002 | H 5 |
| Burkesville | 1,717 | G 7 |
| Burkley | 100 | C 3 |
| Burlington | 500 | J 2 |
| Burna | 300 | D 2 |
| Burning Sprs. | 100 | K 6 |
| Burnside | 586 | H 6 |
| Burton | 145 | M 6 |
| Burtonville | 100 | L 4 |
| Bush | 75 | K 6 |
| Buskirk | 100 | L 5 |
| Butler | 558 | J 3 |
| Cadiz | 1,987 | B 7 |
| Cains Store | 350 | H 6 |
| Calhoun | 901 | C 5 |
| California | 90 | J 3 |
| Calvary | 400 | G 6 |
| Calvert City | 2,104 | D 3 |
| Calvin | 375 | K 7 |
| Cambridge | 251 | *F 4 |
| Camp Dix | 50 | L 3 |
| Campbellsburg | 479 | G 3 |
| Campbellsville | 7,598 | G 6 |
| Campton | 419 | K 5 |
| Canada | 300 | N 5 |
| Cane Valley | 250 | G 6 |
| Caney | 150 | L 5 |
| Caneyville | 530 | E 6 |
| Canmer | 166 | F 6 |
| Cannel City | 100 | L 5 |
| Canton | 200 | B 7 |
| Carlisle | 1,579 | J 4 |
| Carpenter | 200 | K 7 |
| Carrollton | 3,884 | G 3 |
| Carrsville | 110 | D 2 |
| Carter | 94 | L 4 |
| Casey Creek | 130 | G 6 |
| Caseyville | 50 | B 5 |
| Catlettsburg | 3,420 | M 4 |
| Cave City | 1,818 | F 6 |
| Cawood | 800 | L 7 |
| Cayce | 200 | C 4 |
| Cecilia | 500 | F 5 |
| Cedarville | 140 | *N 6 |
| Center | 90 | F 6 |
| Centertown | 323 | C 6 |
| Centerville | 209 | *N 6 |
| Central City | 5,450 | C 6 |
| Cerulean | 253 | B 7 |
| Chance | 70 | G 7 |
| Chaplin | 360 | G 5 |
| Chappell | 95 | L 7 |
| Charley | 25 | M 5 |
| Charters | 50 | L 3 |
| Chavies | 500 | L 6 |
| Chenoa | 165 | K 7 |
| Cherrywood Village | 481 | *F 4 |
| Cherokee | 115 | M 4 |
| Chevrolet | 300 | L 7 |
| Chilesburg | 35 | J 4 |
| Clarkson | 660 | E 6 |
| Clay | 1,426 | B 6 |
| Clay City | 983 | K 5 |
| Claymour | 50 | C 7 |
| Claypool | 30 | E 7 |
| Clearfield | 550 | K 4 |
| Clermont | 150 | F 5 |
| Clifford | 160 | N 4 |
| Clifty | 175 | C 7 |
| Climax | 35 | J 6 |
| Clinton | 1,618 | C 3 |
| Clintonville | 100 | J 4 |
| Closplint | 324 | L 7 |
| Clover Bottom | 600 | J 5 |
| Cloverport | 1,388 | D 5 |
| Co-operative | 190 | H 7 |
| Coakley | 50 | C 3 |
| Coal Run | 234 | *N 6 |
| Cobb | 50 | B 6 |
| Cold Spring | 1,406 | L 2 |
| Colesburg | 100 | F 5 |
| College Hill | 225 | J 5 |
| Collista | 300 | M 5 |
| Colson | 50 | M 6 |
| Columbia | 3,234 | G 6 |
| Columbus | 371 | C 3 |
| Combs | 900 | L 6 |
| Concord | 108 | L 3 |
| Concordia | 300 | D 4 |
| Confluence | 200 | L 6 |
| Constance | 265 | J 1 |
| Conway | 150 | J 6 |
| Cooper | 500 | H 7 |
| Coopersville | 400 | H 7 |
| Corbin | 7,317 | J 7 |
| Corinth | 236 | H 3 |
| Cornishville | 200 | H 5 |
| Corydon | 880 | B 5 |
| Cottle | 250 | L 5 |
| Cottonburg | 50 | J 5 |
| Covington | 52,535 | K 1 |
| Cowan | 89 | K 4 |
| Cowcreek | 105 | K 6 |
| Coxton | 300 | L 7 |
| Crab Orchard | 861 | H 6 |
| Crane Nest | 157 | K 7 |
| Crayne | 200 | E 2 |
| Creekville | 200 | L 6 |
| Creelsboro | 75 | G 7 |
| Crescent Park | 598 | *K 2 |
| Crescent Springs | 1,662 | K 1 |
| Creston | 60 | G 6 |
| Crestview | 659 | L 1 |
| Crestview Hills | 1,114 | K 2 |
| Crestwood | 290 | G 4 |
| Crider | 80 | B 6 |
| Crittenden | 359 | H 3 |
| Crofton | 631 | C 6 |
| Cromwell | 250 | D 6 |
| Cropper | 150 | G 4 |
| Crossgate | 220 | *F 4 |
| Crummies | 75 | L 7 |
| Crutchfield | 500 | C 4 |
| Cub Run | 200 | E 6 |
| Cubage | 275 | K 7 |
| Cumberland | 3,624 | M 6 |
| Cundiff | 338 | G 7 |
| Cunningham | 700 | C 3 |
| Curdsville | 136 | C 5 |
| Custer | 125 | E 5 |
| Cutshin | 200 | L 6 |
| Cynthiana | 6,356 | J 4 |
| Daisy | 500 | L 6 |
| Dalton | 150 | B 6 |
| Danville | 11,542 | H 5 |
| David | 200 | M 5 |
| Dawson Springs | 3,009 | B 6 |
| Daysville | 30 | C 7 |
| Dayton | 8,751 | L 1 |
| De Mossville | 100 | J 3 |
| Decoy | 83 | L 5 |
| Defoe | 100 | G 4 |
| Dekoven | 125 | B 5 |
| Delphia | 140 | L 6 |
| Denton | 375 | M 4 |
| Depoy | 269 | C 6 |
| Devondale | 1,071 | *F 4 |
| Dewitt | 400 | K 7 |
| Dexter | 238 | D 3 |
| Dixon | 572 | B 5 |
| Donansburg | 40 | F 6 |
| Donerail | 25 | J 4 |
| Dorton | 750 | M 6 |
| Dover | 277 | K 3 |
| Drakesboro | 907 | D 6 |
| Dreyfus | 100 | J 5 |
| Druid Hills | 416 | *F 4 |
| Dry Ridge | 1,100 | H 3 |
| Dublin | 300 | C 3 |
| Dundee | 150 | D 5 |
| Dunmor | 156 | C 6 |
| Dunnville | 200 | H 6 |
| Dwale | 300 | M 5 |
| Dycusburg | 89 | E 3 |
| Dyer | 91 | E 5 |
| Earlington | 2,321 | B 6 |
| E. Bernstadt | 550 | J 6 |
| East Point | 225 | M 5 |
| Echols | 648 | D 6 |
| Eddyville | 1,981 | E 3 |
| Edgewood | 4,139 | K 2 |
| Edmonton | 958 | F 7 |
| Eighty Eight | 200 | F 7 |
| Ekron | 190 | E 5 |
| Elamton | 64 | L 5 |
| Elias | 50 | K 6 |
| Elihu | 300 | H 6 |
| Elizabethtown | 11,748 | E 5 |
| Elizaville | 145 | K 4 |
| Elk Creek | 150 | G 4 |
| Elkatawa | 135 | K 5 |
| Elkfork | 60 | L 5 |
| Elkhorn City | 1,081 | N 6 |
| Elkton | 1,612 | C 7 |
| Elliottville | 100 | L 4 |
| Elmrock | 36 | L 6 |
| Elsmere | 5,161 | K 2 |
| Eminence | 2,225 | G 4 |
| Emlyn | 300 | J 7 |
| Emma | 100 | M 5 |
| English | 105 | G 3 |
| Ennis | 150 | D 6 |
| Eolia | 768 | M 6 |
| Erlanger | 12,676 | K 2 |
| Essie | 140 | L 6 |
| Etoile | 42 | F 7 |
| Etty | 210 | M 6 |
| Eubank | 230 | H 6 |
| Evarts | 1,182 | L 7 |
| Ewing | 525 | K 4 |
| Ezel | 400 | L 5 |

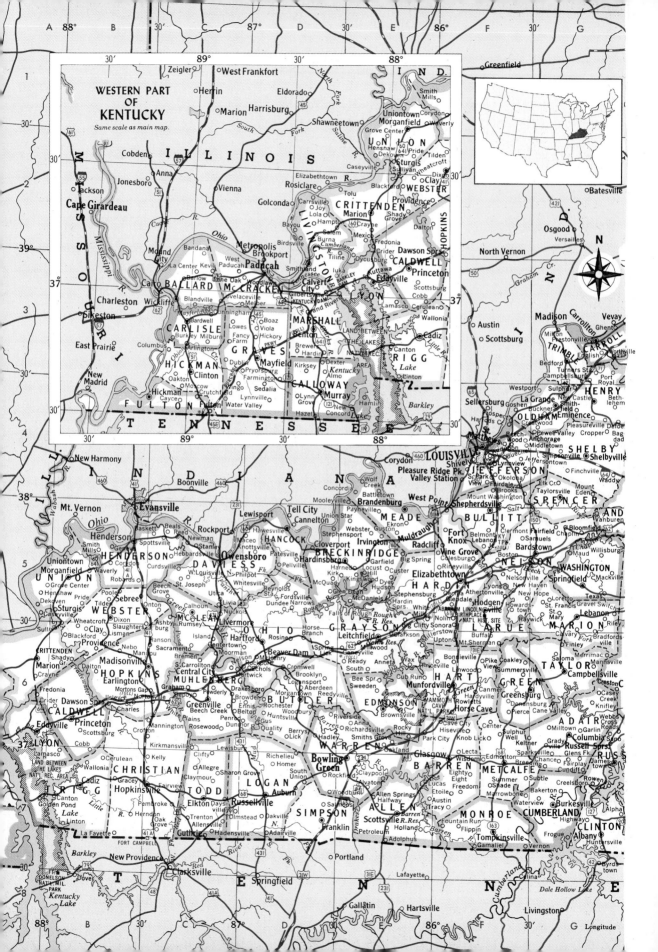

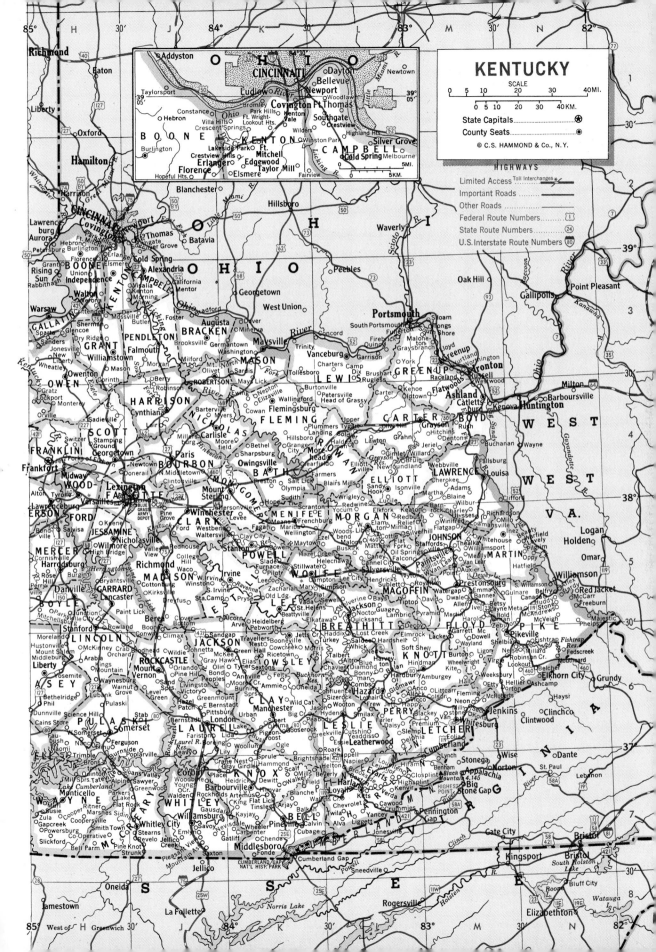

# KENTUCKY

SCALE

State Capitals.............⊛
County Seats..............◉

© C.S. HAMMOND & Co., N.Y.

HIGHWAYS

Limited Access   Toll Interchanges *
Important Roads
Other Roads
Federal Route Numbers
State Route Numbers
U.S. Interstate Route Numbers

| Name | Pop. | Map |
|---|---|---|
| Fagan | 30 | K 5 |
| Fairdale | 12,079 | F 4 |
| Fairfield | 163 | G 5 |
| Fairmeade | 317 | *F 4 |
| Fairplay | 95 | G 7 |
| Fairview | 300 | C 7 |
| Fairview | 235 | K 2 |
| Falcon | 450 | L 5 |
| Falls of Rough | 700 | E 5 |
| Falmouth | 2,593 | J 3 |
| Fancy Farm | 850 | C 3 |
| Fariston | 125 | J 6 |
| Farler | 350 | L 6 |
| Farmers | 240 | L 4 |
| Farmington | 200 | D 4 |
| Faubush | 496 | H 6 |
| Fedscreek | 950 | N 6 |
| Felty | 150 | K 6 |
| Ferguson | 507 | H 6 |
| Field | 50 | K 7 |
| Finchville | 125 | G 4 |
| Finley | 40 | G 6 |
| Firebrick | 325 | L 3 |
| Fishtrap | 338 | N 6 |
| Flat | 150 | K 5 |
| Flat Fork | 500 | L 5 |
| Flat Lick | 1,750 | K 7 |
| Flat Rock | 25 | H 7 |
| Flatgap | 450 | M 5 |
| Flatwoods | 7,380 | M 4 |
| Fleming | 473 | M 6 |
| Flemingsburg | 2,483 | K 4 |
| Flippin | 100 | F 7 |
| Florence | 11,661 | J 2 |
| Fonde | 150 | K 7 |
| Ford | 300 | J 5 |
| Fordsville | 489 | D 5 |
| Forest Hills | 469 | *F 4 |
| Forks of Elkhorn | 300 | H 4 |
| Fort Knox | 37,608 | F 5 |
| Fort Mitchell | 6,982 | K 2 |
| Fort Thomas | 16,338 | L 1 |
| Fort Wright—Lookout Hts. | 4,819 | K 1 |
| Foster | 91 | J 3 |
| Fountain Run | 128 | F 7 |
| FRANKFORT | 21,902 | H 4 |
| Franklin | 6,553 | D 7 |
| Fredonia | 450 | B 6 |
| Freeburn | 300 | N 5 |
| Freedom | 60 | F 7 |
| Frenchburg | 467 | K 5 |
| Frew | 80 | L 6 |
| Frogue | 180 | G 7 |
| Fullerton | 950 | L 3 |
| Fulton | 3,250 | C 4 |
| Furnace | 40 | K 5 |
| Gamaliel | 431 | F 7 |
| Gapcreek | 120 | H 7 |
| Garfield | 100 | E 5 |
| Garlin | 100 | G 6 |
| Garrett | 985 | M 6 |
| Garrison | 800 | L 3 |
| Gatliff | 125 | K 7 |
| Gausdale | 150 | J 7 |
| Geneva | 80 | B 5 |
| Georgetown | 8,629 | H 4 |
| Germantown | 332 | K 3 |
| Ghent | 385 | G 3 |
| Gilbertsville | 241 | D 3 |
| Gimlet | 100 | L 4 |
| Girdler | 500 | K 7 |
| Glasgow | 11,301 | E 7 |
| Glen Dean | 114 | E 5 |
| Glencoe | 500 | H 3 |
| Glendale | 250 | F 5 |
| Glens Fork | 183 | G 6 |
| Glenview Manor | 140 | *F 4 |
| Glomawr | 400 | L 6 |
| Goshen | 200 | F 4 |
| Gracey | 450 | B 7 |
| Gradyville | 100 | G 6 |
| Graham | 500 | C 6 |
| Grahn | 450 | L 4 |
| Grand Rivers | 438 | E 3 |
| Grange City | 75 | K 4 |
| Grant | 150 | H 3 |
| Gratz | 105 | H 4 |
| Gravel Switch | 50 | G 5 |
| Gray | 800 | K 7 |
| Gray Hawk | 500 | J 6 |
| Graymoor | 1,419 | *F 4 |
| Graysbranch | 50 | M 3 |
| Grayson | 2,184 | M 4 |
| Green Hall | 85 | K 6 |
| Greenmount | 100 | J 6 |
| Greensburg | 1,990 | F 6 |
| Greenup | 1,284 | M 3 |
| Greenville | 3,875 | C 6 |
| Greenwood | 175 | J 7 |
| Grove Center | 85 | E 1 |
| Guage | 450 | L 5 |
| Gulnare | 219 | N 5 |
| Gus | 100 | D 6 |
| Guston | 125 | E 5 |
| Guthrie | 1,200 | C 7 |
| Haddix | 406 | L 6 |
| Hadensville | 50 | C 7 |
| Hadley | 300 | D 6 |
| Haldeman | 300 | L 4 |
| Halfway | 200 | E 7 |
| Hall | 500 | M 6 |
| Hamlin | 150 | E 4 |
| Hammond | 500 | K 7 |
| Hampton | 150 | D 2 |
| Hanson | 378 | C 6 |
| Happy | 350 | L 6 |
| Hardburly | 300 | L 6 |
| Hardin | 522 | D 3 |
| Hardin Sprs. | 300 | E 5 |
| Hardinsburg | 1,547 | D 5 |
| Hardshell | 430 | L 6 |
| Hardy | 950 | N 5 |
| Hardyville | 250 | F 6 |
| Harlan | 3,318 | L 7 |
| Harned | 325 | E 5 |
| Harold | 400 | M 5 |
| Harrods Ck. | 380 | F 4 |
| Harrodsburg | 6,741 | H 5 |
| Hartford | 1,868 | D 6 |
| Harveyton | 150 | L 6 |
| Hatfield | 700 | N 5 |
| Hawesville | 1,262 | D 5 |
| Hazard | 5,459 | L 6 |
| Hazel | 424 | D 4 |
| Hazel Green | 250 | K 5 |
| Hazel Patch | 50 | J 6 |
| Head of Grassy | 127 | L 4 |
| Hebbardsville | 125 | C 5 |
| Hebron | 550 | J 1 |
| Heidelberg | 200 | K 5 |
| Heidrick | 400 | K 7 |
| Helechawa | 120 | L 5 |
| Hellier | 100 | N 6 |
| Helton | 350 | L 7 |
| Henderson | 22,976 | B 5 |
| Hendricks | 340 | L 5 |
| Henshaw | 225 | B 5 |
| Herndon | 78 | C 7 |
| Hickman | 3,048 | C 4 |
| Hickory | 173 | D 3 |
| High Bridge | 300 | H 5 |
| Highland Heights | 4,400 | L 1 |
| Highsplint | 75 | L 7 |
| Highway | 125 | G 7 |
| Hillsboro | 150 | K 4 |
| Hima | 600 | K 6 |
| Himyar | 225 | K 7 |
| Hindman | 808 | M 6 |
| Hiram | 400 | L 7 |
| Hiseville | 152 | F 6 |
| Hitchins | 500 | M 4 |
| Hodgenville | 2,562 | F 5 |
| Holland | 150 | E 7 |
| Hollyvilla | 907 | *F 4 |
| Homer | 22 | D 7 |
| Hope | 300 | K 4 |
| Hopeful Hts. | 473 | J 2 |
| Hopkinsville | 21,250 | B 7 |
| Horse Branch | 150 | D 6 |
| Horse Cave | 2,068 | F 6 |
| Houston Acres | 684 | *F 4 |
| Howardstown | 150 | F 5 |
| Huddy | 175 | N 5 |
| Hudson | 35 | E 5 |
| Huntersville | 150 | G 7 |
| Huntsville | 100 | D 6 |
| Hurstbourne Acres | 289 | *G 4 |
| Hustonville | 413 | H 6 |
| Hyden | 482 | L 6 |
| Ilsley | 500 | B 6 |
| Independence | 1,784 | H 3 |
| Indian Hills | 600 | *F 4 |
| Indian Hills Cherokee Section | 282 | *F 4 |
| Inez | 469 | N 5 |
| Irvine | 2,918 | K 5 |
| Irvington | 1,300 | E 5 |
| Island | 410 | C 6 |
| Isonville | 95 | L 4 |
| Iuka | 50 | D 3 |
| Ivel | 400 | M 5 |
| Ivyton | 125 | L 5 |
| Jackson | 1,887 | L 5 |
| Jamestown | 1,027 | G 7 |
| Jason | 120 | K 6 |
| Jeff | 615 | L 6 |
| Jeffersontown | 9,701 | G 4 |
| Jeffersonville | 800 | K 5 |
| Jellico Creek | 300 | J 7 |
| Jenkins | 2,552 | M 6 |
| Jeriel | 150 | M 4 |
| Jett | 300 | H 4 |
| Jetts Creek | 150 | K 6 |
| Johnetta | 65 | J 6 |
| Jonesville | 150 | H 3 |
| Joy | 50 | D 2 |
| Junction City | 1,046 | H 5 |
| Kayjay | 225 | K 7 |
| Keaton | 250 | L 5 |
| Keavy | 500 | J 6 |
| Keene | 300 | H 5 |
| Keeneland | 587 | *F 4 |
| Kehoe | 100 | L 4 |
| Kelly | 100 | C 7 |
| Keltner | 22 | F 6 |
| Kenton | 300 | J 3 |
| Kenton Vale | 178 | K 1 |
| Kenvir | 800 | L 7 |
| Kevil | 274 | C 3 |
| King | 150 | K 7 |
| Kings Mtn. | 300 | H 6 |
| Kingsley | 504 | *F 4 |
| Kingswood | 295 | E 5 |
| Kirk | 200 | D 5 |
| Kirkmansville | 100 | C 6 |
| Kirksey | 150 | D 3 |
| Kirksville | 125 | J 5 |
| Kite | 280 | M 6 |
| Kitts | 950 | L 7 |
| Knifley | 225 | G 6 |
| Knob Lick | 168 | F 6 |
| Knottsville | 250 | D 5 |
| Kona | 250 | M 6 |
| Krypton | 100 | L 6 |
| Kuttawa | 453 | E 3 |
| La Center | 1,044 | C 3 |
| La Fayette | 158 | B 7 |
| La Grange | 1,713 | G 4 |
| Lackey | 294 | M 6 |
| Lair | 102 | J 4 |
| Lake | 150 | K 6 |
| Lake Louisvilla | 430 | *F 4 |
| Lakeside Park | 2,511 | K 2 |
| Lakeview | 478 | *K 1 |
| Lamasco | 200 | E 3 |
| Lambric | 120 | L 5 |
| Lancaster | 3,230 | H 5 |
| Latonia Lakes | 428 | *J 3 |
| Lawrenceburg | 3,579 | H 4 |
| Lawton | 100 | L 4 |
| Leatherwood | 750 | L 6 |
| Lebanon | 5,528 | G 5 |
| Lebanon Junction | 1,571 | F 5 |
| Lecta | 100 | F 6 |
| Lee City | 50 | L 5 |
| Leeco | 475 | K 5 |
| Leitchfield | 2,983 | E 6 |
| Lejunior | 597 | L 7 |
| Levee | 350 | K 5 |
| Level Green | 75 | J 6 |
| Lewisburg | 651 | C 6 |
| Lewisport | 1,595 | D 5 |
| Lexington | 108,137 | J 4 |
| Lexington † | 174,323 | J 4 |
| Liberty | 1,765 | H 6 |
| Lida | 250 | K 6 |
| Liggett | 200 | L 7 |
| Ligon | 500 | M 6 |
| Lily | 800 | J 6 |
| Lincolnshire | 222 | *F 4 |
| Linton | 45 | E 3 |
| Linwood | 50, | F 6 |
| Lisman | 93 | B 6 |
| Littcarr | 550 | M 6 |
| Livermore | 1,594 | C 5 |
| Livia | 50 | C 5 |
| Livingston | 338 | J 6 |
| Lloyd | 350 | M 3 |
| Lockport | 105 | H 4 |
| Locust Hill | 100 | E 5 |
| Logansport | 75 | D 6 |
| Lola | 600 | D 2 |
| London | 4,337 | J 6 |
| Lone Oak | 3,759 | D 3 |
| Lookout | 600 | N 6 |
| Loretto | 985 | G 5 |
| Lost Creek | 500 | L 6 |
| Lothair | 800 | L 6 |
| Louellen | 150 | L 7 |
| Louisa | 1,781 | M 4 |
| Louisville | 361,958 | F 4 |
| Louisville † | 826,553 | F 4 |
| Lovelaceville | 400 | C 3 |
| Lovely | 500 | N 5 |
| Lowes | 200 | C 3 |
| Lowmansville | 500 | M 5 |
| Loyall | 1,212 | L 7 |
| Lucas | 125 | F 7 |
| Lucile | 125 | L 4 |
| Ludlow | 5,815 | K 1 |
| Lynch | 800 | M 7 |
| Lyndon | 460 | *F 4 |
| Lynn Grove | 120 | D 4 |
| Lynnview | 1,494 | F 4 |
| Lynnville | 100 | D 4 |
| Lyons | 50 | F 5 |
| Maceo | 400 | D 5 |
| Mackville | 229 | G 5 |
| Madisonville | 15,332 | B 6 |
| Majestic | 600 | N 5 |
| Malone | 250 | L 5 |
| Maloneton | 200 | M 3 |
| Manchester | 1,664 | K 6 |
| Manitou | 112 | B 6 |
| Mannington | 200 | C 6 |
| Mannsville | 197 | G 6 |
| Mariba | 50 | K 5 |
| Marion | 3,008 | E 2 |
| Marrowbone | 325 | F 7 |
| Marshes Siding | 950 | H 7 |
| Martha | 200 | M 4 |
| Martin | 786 | M 5 |
| Martwick | 110 | D 6 |
| Mary | 150 | K 5 |
| Maryhill Estates | 211 | *F 4 |
| Mason | 125 | H 3 |
| Matthew | 75 | L 5 |
| Maud | 63 | G 5 |
| Mayfield | 10,724 | D 3 |
| Mays Lick | 430 | K 3 |
| Maysville | 7,411 | K 3 |
| Maytown | 125 | K 5 |
| McAndrews | 975 | N 5 |
| McCarr | 200 | N 5 |
| McDaniels | 125 | E 5 |
| McDowell | 400 | M 6 |
| McHenry | 420 | D 6 |
| McKee | 255 | K 6 |
| McKinney | 475 | H 6 |
| McQuady | 100 | D 5 |
| McRoberts | 1,037 | M 6 |
| McVeigh | 700 | N 5 |
| Meadow Vale | 1,231 | *F 4 |
| Meadowview Estates | 139 | *F 4 |
| Meally | 300 | M 5 |
| Means | 50 | K 5 |
| Melber | 250 | D 3 |
| Melbourne | 500 | L 2 |
| Mentor | 300 | J 3 |
| Merrimac | 150 | G 6 |
| Meta | 600 | N 5 |
| Mexico | 175 | E 2 |
| Middleburg | 300 | H 6 |
| Middlesboro | 11,878 | K 7 |
| Middletown | 2,500 | G 4 |
| Midway | 1,278 | H 4 |
| Milburn | 150 | C 3 |
| Milford | 100 | J 3 |
| Mill Springs | 100 | H 7 |
| Millard | 600 | N 6 |
| Millersburg | 788 | J 4 |
| Millerstown | 95 | E 6 |
| Mills | 400 | K 7 |
| Millstone | 400 | M 6 |
| Milltown | 200 | G 6 |
| Millwood | 213 | E 6 |
| Milo | 200 | M 5 |
| Milton | 756 | G 3 |
| Mima | 43 | L 5 |
| Minerva | 100 | K 3 |
| Minor Lane Heights | 2,217 | *F 4 |
| Mitchellsburg | 285 | H 5 |
| Mockingbird Valley | 255 | *F 4 |
| Monterey | 205 | H 4 |
| Monticello | 3,618 | H 7 |
| Mooleyville | 106 | D 4 |
| Moorefield | 200 | K 4 |
| Moores Creek | 140 | K 6 |
| Moorland | 705 | *F 4 |
| Moorman | 215 | C 6 |
| Morehead | 7,191 | L 4 |
| Moreland | 350 | H 6 |
| Morgan | 40 | J 3 |
| Morganfield | 3,563 | E 1 |
| Morgantown | 1,394 | D 6 |
| Morning View | 150 | J 3 |
| Morris Fork | 211 | K 6 |
| Mortons Gap | 1,169 | B 6 |
| Moscow | 60 | C 4 |
| Mount Eden | 225 | G 4 |
| Mount Olivet | 442 | J 3 |
| Mount Salem | 50 | H 6 |
| Mt. Sherman | 145 | F 6 |
| Mt. Sterling | 5,083 | J 4 |
| Mt. Vernon | 1,639 | J 6 |
| Mount Washington | 2,020 | F 4 |
| Mountain Ash | 150 | J 7 |
| Mouthcard | 350 | N 6 |
| Muldraugh | 1,773 | E 5 |
| Munfordville | 1,233 | E 6 |
| Murl | 100 | H 7 |
| Murray | 13,537 | D 4 |
| Myers | 72 | K 4 |
| Nancy | 600 | H 6 |
| Naomi | 120 | H 6 |
| Napier | 150 | L 7 |
| Nebo | 274 | B 6 |
| Ned | 103 | L 6 |
| Nelse | 55 | M 6 |
| Nelson | 150 | C 6 |
| Nelsonville | 100 | F 5 |
| Neon | 705 | M 6 |
| Nepton | 90 | K 4 |
| Nevisdale | 125 | J 7 |
| New Castle | 755 | G 4 |
| New Concord | 85 | E 4 |
| New Haven | 977 | F 5 |
| New Hope | 200 | G 5 |
| New Liberty | 150 | H 3 |
| Newfoundland | 300 | L 4 |
| Newman | 75 | C 5 |
| Newport | 25,998 | L 1 |
| Newtown | 75 | J 4 |
| Nicholasville | 5,829 | J 5 |
| Noctor | 500 | L 5 |
| Nolin | 50 | F 5 |
| Norbourne Estates | 467 | *F 4 |
| North Middletown | 433 | J 4 |
| Northfield | 192 | *F 4 |
| Nortonville | 699 | C 6 |
| Nuckols | 40 | C 5 |
| Oak Grove | 200 | C 7 |
| Oakland | 144 | E 6 |
| Oakton | 115 | C 4 |
| Oakville | 50 | D 7 |
| Offutt | 125 | M 5 |
| Ogle | 110 | K 6 |
| Oil Springs | 900 | L 5 |
| Okolona | 17,643 | F 4 |
| Old Landing | 158 | K 5 |
| Oldtown | 250 | M 4 |
| Olin | 80 | J 6 |
| Olive Hill | 1,197 | L 4 |
| Olmstead | 90 | D 7 |
| Olympia | 250 | K 4 |
| Oneida | 700 | K 6 |
| Onton | 121 | C 5 |
| Oppy | 250 | N 5 |

*No room on map for name.   †Population of metropolitan area.

| Place | Pop. | Map |
|---|---|---|
| Orlando | 65 | J 6 |
| Orville | 41 | H 4 |
| Owensboro | 50,329 | C 5 |
| Owensboro † | 79,486 | C 5 |
| Owenton | 1,280 | H 3 |
| Owingsville | 1,381 | K 4 |
| Paducah | 31,627 | D 3 |
| Paint Lick | 200 | J 5 |
| Paintsville | 3,868 | M 5 |
| Paris | 7,823 | J 4 |
| Park City | 567 | E 6 |
| Park Hills | 3,999 | K 1 |
| Parkers Lake | 115 | H 7 |
| Parksville | 560 | H 5 |
| Parkway Village | 829 | *F 4 |
| Patesville | 50 | D 5 |
| Payneville | 248 | E 5 |
| Peabody | 200 | K 6 |
| Pebworth | 175 | K 5 |
| Pellville | 110 | D 5 |
| Pembroke | 634 | C 7 |
| Penrod | 375 | C 6 |
| Peoples | 35 | J 6 |
| Perryville | 730 | H 5 |
| Petersburg | 430 | H 2 |
| Petersville | 75 | L 4 |
| Petroleum | 60 | E 7 |
| Pewee Valley | 950 | G 4 |
| Phelps | 770 | N 6 |
| Phil | 25 | H 6 |
| Philpot | 531 | D 5 |
| Pierce | 60 | F 6 |
| Pigeonroost | 300 | K 6 |
| Pike View | 30 | F 6 |
| Pikeville | 4,899 | N 6 |
| Pilgrim | 250 | N 5 |
| Pilot | 40 | K 5 |
| Pine Grove | 96 | J 5 |
| Pine Hill | 186 | J 6 |
| Pine Knot | 950 | H 7 |
| Pineville | 2,817 | K 7 |
| Pittsburg | 938 | J 6 |
| Place | 275 | J 7 |
| Plantation | 895 | *F 4 |
| Pleasant Valley | 251 | *N 6 |
| Pleasant View | 300 | J 7 |
| Pleasure Ridge Park | 28,566 | E 4 |
| Pleasureville | 747 | G 4 |
| Plum Sprs. | 185 | *E 7 |
| Plummers Landing | 100 | L 4 |
| Plymouth Village | 230 | *F 4 |
| Poole | 300 | B 5 |
| Poplarville | 49 | J 6 |
| Port Royal | 140 | G 3 |
| Powderly | 631 | C 6 |
| Powersburg | 225 | H 7 |
| Premium | 489 | M 6 |
| Preston | 200 | K 4 |
| Prestonsburg | 3,422 | M 5 |
| Prestonville | 252 | G 3 |
| Priceville | 80 | F 6 |
| Pride | 65 | E 2 |
| Princeton | 6,292 | B 6 |
| Prospect | 500 | F 4 |
| Providence | 4,270 | B 6 |
| Pryorsburg | 200 | D 3 |
| Pryse | 100 | K 5 |
| Pulaski | 200 | H 6 |
| Pyramid | 200 | M 5 |
| Quality | 50 | D 6 |
| Quicksand | 250 | L 5 |
| Quincy | 300 | L 3 |
| Quinton | 125 | H 7 |
| Rabbithash | 50 | H 3 |
| Raceland | 1,857 | M 3 |
| Radcliff | 7,881 | E 5 |
| Ravenna | 784 | K 5 |
| Raywick | 195 | G 5 |
| Ready | 65 | E 6 |
| Redbush | 300 | L 5 |
| Redhouse | 40 | J 5 |
| Redwine | 60 | L 4 |
| Reed | 400 | C 5 |
| Reedyville | 172 | D 6 |
| Relief | 200 | L 5 |
| Revelo | 500 | J 7 |
| Reynolds Sta. | 125 | D 5 |
| Ricetown | 100 | K 6 |
| Richardson | 45 | M 5 |
| Richardsville | 300 | E 6 |
| Richelieu | 108 | D 7 |
| Richlawn | 578 | *F 4 |
| Richmond | 16,861 | J 5 |
| Ridgeview Heights | 189 | *J 2 |
| Riley | 100 | G 5 |
| Rineyville | 125 | F 5 |
| Ritner | 72 | H 7 |
| Riverside | 100 | K 6 |
| Roark | 75 | L 6 |
| Robards | 701 | B 5 |
| Robinson | 60 | J 4 |
| Robinson Ck. | 300 | N 6 |
| Robinswood | 353 | *F 4 |
| Rochester | 252 | D 6 |
| Rockfield | 300 | E 7 |
| Rockholds | 289 | J 7 |
| Rockport | 377 | D 6 |
| Rocky Hill | 139 | E 6 |
| Rolling Fields | 737 | *F 4 |
| Rolling Hills | 1,313 | *F 4 |
| Rose Hill | 325 | K 5 |
| Rosewood | 69 | C 6 |
| Rosine | 349 | D 6 |
| Rowena | 90 | G 7 |
| Rowland | 200 | H 5 |
| Rowletts | 250 | F 6 |
| Royalton | 300 | M 5 |
| Royville | 54 | *G 6 |
| Rugless | 40 | L 3 |
| Rumsey | 200 | C 5 |
| Rush | 175 | M 4 |
| Russell | 1,982 | M 3 |
| Russell Sprs. | 1,641 | G 6 |
| Russellville | 6,456 | D 7 |
| Sacramento | 437 | C 6 |
| Sadieville | 272 | H 4 |
| Saint Charles | 373 | B 6 |
| Saint Francis | 250 | G 5 |
| Saint Helens | 300 | K 5 |
| Saint Joseph | 110 | C 5 |
| Saint Mary | 400 | G 5 |
| Saint Matthews | 13,152 | F 4 |
| Saint Regis Pk. | 1,527 | *F 4 |
| Saldee | 52 | L 5 |
| Salem | 650 | D 2 |
| Salmons | 100 | D 7 |
| Saloma | 100 | G 6 |
| Salt Lick | 441 | K 4 |
| Salvisa | 500 | H 5 |
| Salyersville | 1,196 | L 5 |
| Samuels | 245 | G 5 |
| Sand Springs | 150 | J 6 |
| Sanders | 268 | H 3 |
| Sandgap | 400 | J 6 |
| Sandy Hook | 192 | L 4 |
| Sano | 50 | G 6 |
| Sardis | 183 | K 3 |
| Savoy | 200 | J 7 |
| Sawyer | 26 | J 7 |
| Saxton | 100 | J 7 |
| Scalf | 500 | K 7 |
| Science Hill | 470 | H 6 |
| Scottsburg | 70 | E 3 |
| Scottsville | 3,584 | E 7 |
| Scranton | 35 | K 5 |
| Sebree | 1,092 | B 5 |
| Seco | 88 | M 6 |
| Sedalia | 185 | D 4 |
| Seneca Gardens | 822 | *F 4 |
| Sewell | 500 | L 5 |
| Sextons Ck. | 975 | K 6 |
| Shady Grove | 50 | B 6 |
| Sharon Grove | 245 | C 7 |
| Sharpsburg | 307 | K 4 |
| Shelbiana | 800 | M 6 |
| Shelbyville | 4,182 | G 4 |
| Shepherdsville | 2,769 | F 4 |
| Sherman | 200 | H 3 |
| Shively | 19,150 | F 4 |
| Sibert | 500 | K 6 |
| Siloam | 300 | M 3 |
| Silver Grove | 1,365 | L 2 |
| Silverhill | 250 | L 5 |
| Simpson | 300 | L 5 |
| Simpsonville | 628 | G 4 |
| Sizerock | 280 | L 6 |
| Slade | 100 | K 5 |
| Slaughters | 276 | B 6 |
| Slemp | 500 | L 6 |
| Slickford | 190 | H 7 |
| Sloans Valley | 158 | *J 7 |
| Smilax | 856 | L 6 |
| Smith Mills | 395 | B 5 |
| Smith Town | 500 | H 7 |
| Smithfield | 185 | G 4 |
| Smithland | 514 | D 3 |
| Smiths Grove | 756 | E 6 |
| Soft Shell | 250 | L 6 |
| Soldier | 600 | L 4 |
| Somerset | 10,436 | H 6 |
| Sonora | 390 | F 5 |
| South | 175 | E 6 |
| South Carrollton | 218 | C 6 |
| South Irvine | 100 | J 5 |
| South Park View | 287 | F 4 |
| South Portsmouth | 950 | L 3 |
| South Shore | 676 | M 3 |
| South Union | 57 | D 7 |
| South Williamson | 850 | N 5 |
| Southgate | 3,212 | L 1 |
| Sparksville | 175 | G 6 |
| Sparta | 213 | H 3 |
| Spottsville | 914 | C 5 |
| Spring Lick | 110 | D 6 |
| Springfield | 2,961 | G 5 |
| Springlee | 583 | *F 4 |
| Sprule | 72 | K 7 |
| Stab | 250 | J 6 |
| Staffordsville | 700 | M 5 |
| Stamping Ground | 411 | H 4 |
| Stanford | 2,474 | H 5 |
| Stanley | 350 | C 5 |
| Stanton | 2,037 | K 5 |
| Station Camp | 150 | J 5 |
| Stearns | 900 | J 7 |
| Stephensburg | 400 | E 5 |
| Stephensport | 500 | D 5 |
| Stillwater | 25 | K 5 |
| Stone | 850 | N 5 |
| Strathmoor Gardens | 337 | *F 4 |
| Strathmoor Manor | 464 | *F 4 |
| Strathmoor Village | 540 | *F 4 |
| Strunk | 240 | J 7 |
| Sturgis | 2,210 | B 5 |
| Sublett | 200 | L 5 |
| Subtle | 50 | G 7 |
| Sudith | 250 | K 4 |
| Sullivan | 255 | A 6 |
| Sulphur | 300 | G 4 |
| Sulphur Well | 81 | F 6 |
| Summer Shade | 250 | F 7 |
| Summersville | 360 | F 6 |
| Susie | 82 | H 7 |
| Sweeden | 200 | E 6 |
| Switzer | 150 | H 4 |
| Talbert | 150 | L 6 |
| Tateville | 680 | H 7 |
| Taylor Mill | 3,194 | K 2 |
| Taylorsport | 150 | J 1 |
| Taylorsville | 897 | G 4 |
| Texas | 92 | G 5 |
| Thealka | 550 | M 5 |
| Tilden | 125 | B 5 |
| Tiline | 250 | D 3 |
| Tinsley | 300 | K 7 |
| Tiptop | 130 | L 5 |
| Tollesboro | 500 | K 3 |
| Tolu | 200 | E 2 |
| Tompkinsville | 2,207 | F 7 |
| Tongs | 85 | M 3 |
| Tracy | 50 | F 7 |
| Travellers Rest | 195 | K 6 |
| Trenton | 496 | C 7 |
| Trimble | 145 | H 6 |
| Trinity | 75 | K 3 |
| Turkey | 250 | L 6 |
| Turners Sta. | 100 | G 3 |
| Twila | 32 | L 7 |
| Tyner | 590 | K 6 |
| Tyrone | 135 | H 4 |
| Ulysses | 300 | M 5 |
| Union | 500 | H 3 |
| Union Star | 105 | D 5 |
| Uniontown | 1,255 | B 5 |
| Upper Tygart | 150 | L 4 |
| Upton | 552 | F 6 |
| Urban | 50 | K 6 |
| Utica | 300 | C 5 |
| Vada | 85 | K 5 |
| Valley Sta. | 24,471 | F 4 |
| Valley View | 25 | J 5 |
| Van | 200 | M 6 |
| Van Lear | 1,033 | M 5 |
| Vanburen | 75 | G 5 |
| Vanceburg | 1,773 | L 3 |
| Verda | 950 | L 7 |
| Vernon | 40 | F 7 |
| Verona | 500 | H 3 |
| Versailles | 5,679 | H 4 |
| Vicco | 377 | L 6 |
| Victory | 168 | J 6 |
| Villa Hills | 1,647 | K 1 |
| Vine Grove | 2,987 | F 5 |
| Viola | 75 | D 3 |
| Virgie | 600 | M 6 |
| Visalia | 250 | J 3 |
| Waco | 200 | J 5 |
| Waddy | 250 | G 4 |
| Walden | 150 | J 7 |
| Walker | 250 | K 7 |
| Wallingford | 52 | K 4 |
| Wallins Creek | 369 | K 7 |
| Wallonia | 100 | B 7 |
| Walnut Grove | 150 | H 4 |
| Waltersville | 175 | J 5 |
| Walton | 1,801 | H 3 |
| Warfield | 236 | N 5 |
| Warsaw | 1,232 | H 3 |
| Washington | 439 | K 3 |
| Water Valley | 285 | C 4 |
| Watergap | 300 | M 5 |
| Waterview | 41 | G 7 |
| Waverly | 335 | B 5 |
| Wax | 200 | E 6 |
| Wayland | 384 | M 6 |
| Waynesburg | 250 | H 6 |
| Webbs Cross Roads | 150 | G 6 |
| Webbville | 400 | M 4 |
| Webster | 180 | E 5 |
| Weeksbury | 950 | M 6 |
| Wellington | 727 | *F 4 |
| Wellington | 100 | K 5 |
| W. Buechel | 1,581 | *F 4 |
| West Irvine | 305 | J 5 |
| West Liberty | 1,387 | L 5 |
| W. Louisville | 100 | C 5 |
| West Paducah | 100 | C 3 |
| West Point | 1,741 | E 4 |
| West Somerset | 850 | H 6 |
| West Van Lear | 975 | M 5 |
| Westbend | 400 | J 5 |
| Westport | 185 | F 4 |
| Westwood | 777 | *F 4 |
| Westwood | 2,900 | M 4 |
| Wheatcroft | 229 | B 5 |
| Wheatley | 95 | H 3 |
| Wheeler | 100 | K 7 |
| Wheelwright | 793 | M 6 |
| Whick | 200 | L 6 |
| Whipps Millgate | 529 | *F 4 |
| White Mills | 150 | E 5 |
| White Plains | 729 | C 6 |
| Whitehouse | 300 | M 5 |
| Whitesburg | 1,137 | M 6 |
| Whitesville | 752 | D 5 |
| Whitley City | 1,060 | J 7 |
| Wickliffe | 1,211 | C 3 |
| Wilbur | 40 | M 5 |
| Wild Cat | 100 | K 6 |
| Wilders | 823 | N 1 |
| Wildie | 100 | J 6 |
| Wildwood | 412 | *F 4 |
| Willard | 100 | M 4 |
| Williamsburg | 3,687 | J 7 |
| Williamsport | 424 | M 5 |
| Williamstown | 2,063 | H 3 |
| Willisburg | 225 | G 5 |
| Wilmore | 3,466 | H 5 |
| Winchester | 13,402 | J 4 |
| Windy Hills | 1,692 | *F 4 |
| Wingo | 593 | C 4 |
| Winifred | 35 | M 5 |
| Winston | 170 | J 5 |
| Winston Park | 1,108 | L 2 |
| Wisdom | 25 | F 7 |
| Wolf Creek | 175 | E 4 |
| Wolverine | 500 | L 5 |
| Woodbine | 700 | J 7 |
| Woodburn | 351 | E 7 |
| Woodbury | 139 | D 6 |
| Woodland Hills | 1,233 | *F 4 |
| Woodlawn | 1,639 | D 3 |
| Woodlawn | 525 | L 1 |
| Woodlawn Park | 1,237 | *F 4 |
| Woodsbend | 100 | L 5 |
| Woollum | 215 | K 6 |
| Wooton | 750 | L 6 |
| Worthington | 1,364 | M 3 |
| Worthville | 258 | G 3 |
| Wrigley | 290 | L 4 |
| Wurtland | 350 | M 3 |
| Yancey | 200 | L 7 |
| Yeaddiss | 430 | L 6 |
| Yocum | 70 | L 5 |
| York | 100 | L 3 |
| Yorktown | 174 | *N 6 |
| Yosemite | 250 | H 6 |
| Youngs Creek | 50 | J 7 |
| Zachariah | 110 | K 5 |
| Zebulon | 80 | M 5 |
| Zula | 15 | H 7 |

### OTHER FEATURES

| Feature | Map |
|---|---|
| Abraham Lincoln Birthplace Nat'l Hist. Site | F 5 |
| Barkley (lake) | E 3 |
| Barren (riv.) | D 6 |
| Barren River (res.) | E 7 |
| Beech Fork (riv.) | G 5 |
| Big Sandy (riv.) | M 4 |
| Black (mt.) | M 7 |
| Buckhorn (res.) | K 6 |
| Chaplin (riv.) | G 5 |
| Clarks, East Fork (riv.) | D 3 |
| Cumberland (lake) | H 7 |
| Cumberland (mt.) | L 7 |
| Cumberland (riv.) | F 8 |
| Cumberland Gap Nat'l Hist. Park | K 7 |
| Dale Hollow (lake) | M 5 |
| Dewey (lake) | M 5 |
| Dix (riv.) | H 5 |
| Fishtrap (res.) | N 6 |
| Fort Campbell | 13,616 | B 7 |
| Grayson (res.) | L 4 |
| Herrington (lake) | H 5 |
| Kentucky (lake) | E 3 |
| Kentucky (riv.) | G 3 |
| Land Between The Lakes Nat'l Rec. Area | E 3 |
| Laurel River (res.) | J 6 |
| Licking (riv.) | J 3 |
| Little (riv.) | B 7 |
| Mammoth Cave Nat'l Park | F 6 |
| Mud (riv.) | D 7 |
| Nolin (res.) | E 6 |
| Nolin (riv.) | E 6 |
| Ohio (riv.) | C 2 |
| Paint Lick (riv.) | J 5 |
| Panther (creek) | C 5 |
| Pond (riv.) | G 6 |
| Red (riv.) | C 7 |
| Red (riv.) | K 5 |
| Rockcastle (riv.) | J 6 |
| Rolling Fork (riv.) | F 5 |
| Rough (riv.) | D 5 |
| Rough River (res.) | E 5 |
| Salt (riv.) | F 5 |
| Tennessee (riv.) | D 3 |
| Tradewater (riv.) | B 6 |
| Tug Fork (riv.) | N 5 |

THESE ARTICLES ARE IN THE FACT-INDEX

Kentucky, University of    Kentucky State College
Kentucky coffee tree    Kentucky Wesleyan College
Kentucky River    Kentwood, Mich.

**KENYA.** The country of Kenya is named for the mountain that dominates the land. Kenya is on the Indian Ocean and is crossed almost in the center by the equator (for map, *see* Africa).

Until it gained its independence in 1963, Kenya was a British colony and protectorate. The protectorate—a narrow strip of land and islands along the southern coast—was leased from the sultan of Zanzibar. Kenya is bordered by Tanzania on the south, Uganda on the west, Sudan and Ethiopia on the north, and Somalia on the northeast. Its area is 224,960 square miles, somewhat smaller than Texas. It has 10,942,705 people (1969 census). A small percentage of the population is composed of Asians and Europeans.

### Land and Climate

Kenya lies on the East African plateau. In the west the plateau is split from north to south by a rift valley. Africa's highest mountains rise from the sides of the rift: Mount Kenya (17,058 feet); Mount Elgon (14,178); and, just across the border in Tanzania's Tanganyika, Mount Kilimanjaro (19,340). (*See also* Africa, subhead "The Great Rift Valley.")

Most of Kenya north of the equator has little rain. It is an arid waste of dry grasses, scrub, thorn, and acacia trees. It is a hunter's paradise—a land of lions, zebras, elephants, giraffes, antelopes, and other game animals (*see* Grasslands; for pictures in color, *see* Africa).

The highlands of southwest Kenya are sometimes called the "white man's country." The days are warm and sunny and the nights are cool. The highlands get about the same amount of rain as the Midwestern

Nairobi, the capital of Kenya, boasts many handsome buildings. The largest city in the nation, it is used by hunters as an outfitting point for safaris.

Pix

Pix

Mount Kenya's snow and glaciers are almost on the equator. Africa's second highest mountain looms behind a tropical lobelia.

United States. The soil is volcanic, usually deep and rich. The western slopes of the highlands are mostly grassland (savanna). The land descends gradually to the level of Lake Victoria. East of the highlands it drops to the Indian Ocean coast. The climate in the lowlands ranges from tropical to subtropical. The malaria mosquito and the tsetse fly make it unhealthy for white settlers.

### The Peoples of Kenya

There are more than a hundred tribes in Kenya. The principal tribes are the Masai and the Kikuyu.

The Masai are a nomadic people of mixed Hamitic and Negro parentage (*see* Africa). They are handsome, proud, and aggressive. Their living depends upon their cattle. Masai villages are built around a cattle enclosure called a kraal. For protection from lions the huts are covered with thorn-tree branches. Grazing herds are guarded by young Masai warriors. The Masai live mostly on the milk and blood of the cattle. Their scanty clothing is made of cattle hides.

The Kikuyu are Bantu Negroes. Most of them are farmers. For years they cultivated the rich soil of the highlands. Then the white men came. Gradually they took over the Kikuyu lands. The Kikuyu were crowded into areas where the soil was poor. Their tribal system began to break down. They envied the large, fertile farms of the whites. The resentment of the Kikuyu grew and finally exploded in the terror and violent murders of the Mau Mau secret society. The Mau Mau were determined to drive the whites from Kenya.

Pix

Much has been done in recent years to educate Kenya's adults. These women of the Kikuyu tribe are learning to read and write in an outdoor classroom.

As in South Africa, a large number of British emigrants have settled in Kenya. Nearly all of them live in the highlands. Parts of the highlands look like the English countryside. There are pink brick manor houses set in green parks. There are farms where sheep and cattle graze. In contrast, antelope, giraffes, and other wild animals roam in the savannas and forests of the highlands.

Arabs, Pakistani, and Asian Indians are a minority group. Many are descendants of early traders and settlers. Until Kenya became independent, they dominated small-scale trade. After independence the government began a drive to replace Asians in trade and in government with Africans. Many Asians who retained British citizenship emigrated.

Nairobi, the capital, population (1969 census), 509,286, is one of the most cosmopolitan cities in Africa. It blends features of both East and West. A tall, modern apartment house may tower over the dome and minaret of a Moslem mosque.

Britain began giving more self-government to Kenya, moving it along the road to independence. Emergency restrictions imposed in 1952, at the beginning of the Mau Mau resistance, were lifted in 1960 after order had been restored and preliminary to a conference in London to discuss steps leading toward self-government.

The wide range of climate provides a variety of crops. In the temperate to semitropical highlands the major crops are wheat, maize (corn), tea, coffee, and pyrethrum. The dairy and wool industries are important. The tropical lowlands produce sisal, cotton, coconuts, and pineapples. Rice and tobacco are grown in the Lake Victoria region.

Forests are divided into two zones: highland and tropical coast. Valuable highland trees are the pencil cedar, African camphor, African olive, and podo

(widely used for lumber). The coast produces the aromatic *muhugu* (exported to India as a substitute for sandalwood), mangroves, and others.

Mineral resources are not fully explored. The most important are salt, soda ash, gold, asbestos, manganese, graphite, gypsum, and diatomite.

## Trade, Transportation, and Communication

The principal exports are coffee, tea, sisal, cattle hides, and pyrethrum. The chief imports are cotton goods, blankets, gasoline, kerosine, iron and steel, machinery, electrical equipment, and motor vehicles.

There are more than 25,000 miles of roads, varying from all-weather hard surfaces to faint tracks in remote areas. The main railway runs from Mombasa to Nairobi and goes on to Kampala in Uganda. Nairobi is an important air center served by East African Airways and other airlines. There is steamer service on Lake Victoria. Nairobi has a broadcasting station.

### History

Arabs and then Portuguese first settled Kenya's coast. In the 19th century Britain gained commercial control through the British East Africa Company. A protectorate was established in 1890 and a crown colony in 1920. After 1897 Kenya received a flow of immigrants from the British Isles and South Africa.

Kenya won self-government in mid-1963; independence came in December. In 1964 a republican form of government was adopted. Jomo Kenyatta, Kenya's first prime minister, became its first president. Kenya is a member of the Commonwealth of Nations and of the United Nations.

THESE ARTICLES ARE IN THE FACT-INDEX

| | |
|---|---|
| Kenya, Mount | Keogh, James |
| Kenyahs | Keokuk |
| Kenyatta, Jomo | Keokuk, Iowa |
| Kenyon College | Kephallenia |

**KEPLER, Johannes** (1571-1630). The German duchy of Würtemberg was Kepler's birthplace. He was a sickly child but had a brilliant mind. At the University of Tübingen he was greatly influenced by the theories of the astronomer Copernicus (*see* Copernicus). He later taught astronomy and mathematics at the university in Graz, Austria. While there he corresponded with two other great astronomers of the time—Galileo and Tycho Brahe. In 1600 he became

Tycho's assistant in Prague. When Tycho died Kepler succeeded him as astrologer and astronomer to Rudolph II of Bohemia. His task of casting horoscopes at births and other important events in the royal family was of first importance; astronomy was secondary. Kepler, however, gave all the time he could to the outstanding astronomical problem of the day.

By Kepler's time, many astronomers believed that the sun was the center of the solar system and that the earth turned on its axis. These astronomers, however, still believed that the planets moved in circular orbits. Because of this, they failed completely when it came to explaining the motions of the planets as seen from the earth. Mercury and Venus stand higher in the evening or morning sky, then lower, but always near the sun. Mars, Jupiter, and Saturn, on the other hand, move eastward night after night against the background of stars but occasionally shift backward (retrogress to the west).

Kepler decided to try explaining these motions by finding another shape for the planetary orbits. Because Mars offered the most typical problem and he had Tycho's lifelong, accurate observations of this planet, Kepler began with it. He first tried every possible combination of circular motions in attempts to account for Mars's observed positions. These all failed, though once a discrepancy of only eight minutes of arc remained unaccounted for. "Out of these eight minutes," he said, "we will construct a new theory that will explain the motions of all the planets!"

After six years of incredibly laborious work, hampered by poor eyesight and the clumsy mathematical methods of the day, he found the answer. Mars follows an elliptical (oval) orbit at a speed which varies according to the planet's distance from the sun. In 1609 he published a book on the results of his work, boldly titling it 'The New Astronomy'.

Next he turned his attention to the other planets and found that their motions corresponded to those of Mars. He also discovered that their periods of revolution (time required to go around the sun) bore a precise relation to their distances from the sun.

Kepler's great work on planetary motion is summed up in three principles which have been known since his day as "Kepler's laws": (1) The path of every planet in its motion about the sun forms an ellipse, with the sun at one focus. (2) The speed of a planet in its orbit varies so that a line joining it with the sun sweeps over equal areas in equal times. (3) The squares of the planets' periods of revolution are proportional to the cubes of the planets' mean distances from the sun.

These laws removed all doubt that the earth and planets go around the sun. Later Newton used Kepler's laws to establish his law of universal gravitation (see Newton).

Kepler could now proceed with his task of revising the Rudolphine tables, an almanac of stellar positions which, although unsatisfactory, was the best available at the time. Kepler's new laws enabled him to predict positions of the planets by date and hour that have proved to be substantially accurate even to our day.

Kepler was one of the first to hear from Galileo about the invention of the telescope, and he went on to do valuable pioneer work in optics. It was he who invented the present-day form of astronomical telescope (see Telescope). His book on optics, 'Dioptrice', published in 1611, was the first of its kind and founded the scientific study of light and lenses.

---

THESE ARTICLES ARE IN THE FACT-INDEX

Keppel, Frederick Paul
Kerala, India
Kerch', Russia
Kerensky, Alexander Feodorovich
Keres
Kerguelen Island
Kerguélen-Trémarec, Yves Joseph de
Kermadec Islands
Kerman, Iran
Kermanshah, Iran
Kermit, Tex.
Kerosine
Kerr, Jean (Collins)
Kerr, Robert Samuel
Kerr, Walter F(rancis)

Kerry, Ireland
Kerst, Donald William
Kerulen River
Kerwin, Joseph P.
Kerwin, Patrick
Kesselring, Albert
Kestrel
Ketchel, Stanley
Ketchikan, Alaska
Kettering, Charles F(ranklin)
Kett's Rebellion
Keuka College
Kewanee, Ill.
Kewaunee, Wis.
Key, Ellen

---

**KEY, Francis Scott** (1779-1843). The man who composed the stirring words of the 'Star-Spangled Banner' was a lawyer who wrote verses only as a hobby. He might be forgotten now if he had not seen the American flag flying over besieged Fort McHenry in the War of 1812. How this sight inspired him to write the verses is told in the article National Songs.

Francis Scott Key was born on his family's estate, Terra Rubra, in western Maryland. His birth date is usually given as Aug. 1, 1779. Until he was ten he was taught at home. After attending preparatory school at Annapolis he entered St. John's College. Key went on to prepare himself for a legal career in the office of Judge Jeremiah Chase. A fellow student there was Roger Brooke Taney, who later became the chief justice of the Supreme Court.

In 1802 Key married Mary Tayloe Lloyd. They had six sons and five daughters. Soon after their wedding the Keys moved to Georgetown, then just outside Washington, D. C. In Georgetown Key's law practice prospered and he met many government leaders. Taney, who had married Key's sister Ann, and John Randolph of Roanoke were constant visitors. A devout man, Key once thought seriously of becoming a clergyman. He was a lay reader and a delegate to Episcopal church conventions.

Key served briefly in the War of 1812 but was a civilian again when he wrote the 'Star-Spangled Banner'. He was active in the American Colonization Society, which helped free Negroes to settle in Liberia. In 1833 President Jackson appointed him attorney for the District of Columbia. Still active at 63, he was visiting his daughter in Baltimore when he caught cold and died of pleurisy Jan. 11, 1843.

Ewing Galloway

Fort Jefferson National Monument was a Civil War prison. It is on Garden Key, 60 miles from Key West, in the Gulf of Mexico.

---

THESE ARTICLES ARE IN THE FACT-INDEX

**Keyes, Frances Parkinson**
**Keynes, John Maynard, first Baron**
**Keyserling, Hermann, Count**

---

**KEY WEST, Fla.** The southernmost city in the United States, outside of Hawaii, is Key West. It spreads over a small island, four miles long and less than two miles wide, some 60 miles southwest of the tip of the mainland. The island, or key, is the westernmost in a chain called the Florida Keys. Its location (latitude 24° 33′ north) provides sunny year-round warmth; its shores are bathed by the Gulf Stream and the southeast trade winds bring warm breezes.

Key West's history has been colorful. Spanish adventurers of the 16th century were early inhabitants. Pirate ships hid in the passes and waterways between the keys. The offshore reefs still hold the sunken wrecks of ships scuttled in sea battles of long ago.

A settlement on the island was incorporated as a city in 1828. Cuban cigar makers built a prosperous industry after 1869, and sponge fishing flourished. During the 1890's Key West, with 18,000 people, was Florida's largest city.

In 1912 a railroad was built along the keys, and Key West became an important port for trade with the Caribbean islands. The railway was abandoned after a hurricane in 1935 destroyed many of the bridges and viaducts between the islands. The federal government used much of the roadbed and bridgework to build a road across the keys.

Since 1938 the Overseas Highway has linked Key West to Miami, 156 miles away. Many tourists use the "seagoing highway" to the island city. Hotels, motels, and other tourist facilities have been built.

Today the tourist trade, the naval air station, and fishing provide the greatest employment. Shrimp are caught in the Gulf of Mexico. Giant sea crayfish are sold as "Florida lobsters." A cannery turns sea turtles into green turtle soup.

An aqueduct, about 130 miles long, was built by the federal government to supply badly needed fresh water to Key West and the other islands. During World Wars I and II naval and air bases were established at Key West to guard the entrance to the Gulf of Mexico. Population (1980 census), 24,382.

The small islands off Florida are called "keys," from the Spanish word *cayo*. It means "rock" or "islet." The name Florida Keys is restricted to the chain of about 60 keys from Miami Beach to Key West.

The northern end of the chain is a remnant of an

U.S. Navy

Key West is the westernmost island of the Florida Keys. The keys lie between the Atlantic Ocean and the Gulf of Mexico.

old coral reef. Living corals are still building reefs here (*see* Coral). The southern keys are of limestone. Mangrove thickets line the shores and cover some of the low islands. The growth that rises on the higher ground is composed of tropical hardwoods and palms. Some small keys are submerged at high tide.

The largest of the keys is Key Largo—about 30 miles long and less than 2 miles wide. John Pennekamp Coral Reef State Park is located in the Atlantic waters off this key. Its chief attractions are underwater scenery and living coral formations.

Settlements have sprung up on some of the larger keys. There is little agriculture because of the thin soil. Fishing resorts entertain sportsmen who come for deep-sea fishing.

The Marquesas keys lie 26 miles west of Key West. The Dry Tortugas keys spread about 60 miles to the west. A Civil War fort on Garden Key is preserved as Fort Jefferson National Monument. On Loggerhead Key in the Tortugas is a marine laboratory.

---

THESE ARTICLES ARE IN THE FACT-INDEX

| | |
|---|---|
| Khabarovsk, Russia | Khamsin |
| Khachaturian, Aram | Khan |
| Khairpur, Pakistan | Khaniá, Crete |
| Khalkidike | Khan Tengri |

---

Bernadine Bailey

The architectural form shown in this view of Khar'kov has been much used in Russia to house the huge bureaucracy. Flying ramps connect sections of the building across streets.

**KHAR'KOV** (*kär′ kôf*), **Russia.** In the Russian Ukraine all roads lead to Khar'kov. From its early days as a fort in the 17th century down through World War II, Khar'kov has been repeatedly ravaged by war. Each time a new city was erected. Today Khar'kov is one of Russia's great manufacturing centers. It is also one of the largest cities in the Ukraine (*see* Ukrainian Soviet Socialist Republic).

Khar'kov became important because of its central position in the upper Donets Basin. This is one of Russia's richest districts. The city stands midway between the Dnieper and Don rivers—each about 125 miles away. Moscow is 400 miles to the north.

### From Farming Center to Machinery Maker

Khar'kov is a collecting point for grain from the Ukraine fields, fruit from the Crimea, and oil from the Caucasus. Late in the 19th century the great Donets coal fields and the iron deposits of Krivoy Rog, to the southwest, were developed. Thus supplied, Khar'kov developed iron and steel industries and related manufacturing. Six railroads and, later, several airlines were established to serve the area's ever-expanding industries. Machinery of many kinds is manufactured —tractors, coal-mining and oil-drilling equipment, diesel motors, ball bearings, machine tools, combines, and locomotives. The Dnieper Dam was built in 1932 at Zaporozh'ye, about 150 miles southwest. The flood of hydroelectric power created another large industry —the manufacture of electrical equipment.

The city grew from an agricultural trading center into the "Pittsburgh of Russia." Scientific laboratories, technical schools, and libraries were built.

The University of Khar'kov (founded in 1805) was enlarged. These and a fine collection of Ukrainian art made Khar'kov a cultural center.

Khar'kov began in 1654 as a Cossack outpost to defend Moscow in its wars against the Poles and Tatars. At times it replaced Kiev as capital of the Ukraine. The Russian civil wars of 1917–20 overran Khar'kov. In World War II it was seized by the Germans. Some 100,000 citizens died during the occupation. The battle to free it in 1943 destroyed half its buildings. The government rebuilt the city and added new factories. Population (1970 preliminary census), 1,223,000.

---

THESE ARTICLES ARE IN THE FACT-INDEX

Khartoum, Republic of the Sudan
Khaya
Kherson, Russia
Khios

Khmers
Khorana, Har Gobind
Khorasan, Iran
Khotan, People's Republic of China

---

Sovfoto

**KHRUSHCHEV, Nikita Sergeevich** (1894– 1971). Joseph Stalin, dictator of Russia for 29 years, died March 5, 1953. The next day the government radio announced that to "prevent panic" a collective leadership had been formed to rule Russia. Nikita Khrushchev was not mentioned in the bulletin. Yet within a few years he triumphed over his rivals to become sole dictator of the Soviet Union. (*See also* Russian History; Stalin.)

At Stalin's funeral services Khrushchev shared the platform with the Soviet Union's top leaders. He was, however, merely the chairman who introduced the members of the ruling committee. The most important offices went to Georgi M. Malenkov. The other members of the collective leadership were Lavrenti P. Beria, the head of the secret police, and Vyacheslav M. Molotov, who was Stalin's brilliant foreign minister (*see* Molotov).

### Khrushchev's Early Years

Nikita Khrushchev was born April 17, 1894, in a peasant's hut in the poverty-stricken village of Kalinovka, in southern Russia. Like his father, he became a coal miner. He joined the Communist party in 1918, during the civil war, and became an untiring organizer. Little is known about his first wife, whom he married in 1920. They had two children, Leonid and Yulia. (Leonid was killed in World War II.) Khrushchev was reported to have married his second wife, Nina Petrovna, in 1938; but she insisted the marriage took place in 1924. They had one son, Sergei, and two daughters, Yelena and Rada.

48

Khrushchev entered an industrial school in Moscow in 1929. In the mid-1930's he played a major part in carrying out Stalin's purges. In 1938 Stalin sent him back to the Ukraine to purge the party of anti-Stalinists. After the government had taken almost all the peasants' land, Khrushchev tried to deprive them of the small private plots they still held.

For the last 14 years of Stalin's rule, Khrushchev was party secretary of the Moscow region and a member of the Politburo (later Presidium), the highest organ of the Communist party. When Stalin died, many of Khrushchev's supporters were in important posts.

### Rise to Power

About a week after Stalin's death, Khrushchev wrested control of the party machinery from Malenkov. Then he moved against Beria, head of the secret police. With the help of Marshal Georgi K. Zhukov he had Beria arrested in June 1953. In December Beria and many of his aides were executed. Meanwhile Khrushchev had been named first secretary, the acknowledged head of the Communist party.

In 1955 Khrushchev forced Malenkov to resign as premier, on the ground of "inexperience." The title of premier went to Marshal Nikolai Bulganin. Marshal Zhukov then replaced Bulganin as minister of defense.

### The Plot Against Khrushchev

As first secretary, Khrushchev was not only the most powerful man in Russia but leader of the world Communist movement. In February 1956 he delivered his famous two-day "secret" speech (later released) before the 20th Communist Party Congress. In this speech Khrushchev denounced Stalin's rule, accusing the dead dictator of infamous crimes. The revelations shocked Communists throughout the world who had blindly followed Stalin's dictates.

Russia's satellite countries were encouraged by the speech to take a more independent line. The Poles rioted, and the Hungarians openly revolted. Stalinists in the Russian government blamed Khrushchev. Khrushchev put down the revolt in Hungary with Stalinist terroristic methods and eased his stand on Stalinism. (See also Hungary; Poland.)

In June 1957 Khrushchev's enemies gained the upper hand in the 11-member Presidium and voted secretly to oust Khrushchev as party secretary. Khrushchev refused to accept the decision and took the fight to the large Central Committee of the party. There, after two days of debate, his leadership was confirmed. Four members of the Presidium—including Molotov and Malenkov—were dropped and forced to confess their "mistakes." In October even Zhukov, who had helped Khrushchev defeat the conspiracy, was dropped from the Presidium. There remained, however, powerful Stalinist dissenters in both the government and the army. In March 1958 the "collective leadership" was ended when Khrushchev took over Bulganin's title as premier.

Wide World

Khrushchev lashed out against President Eisenhower before a huge press conference in Paris in May 1960. With him were Andrei Gromyko (left) and Marshal Rodion Malinovsky.

### Personality and Policies

Correspondents from Western nations described Khrushchev as a man of enormous energy and drive, talkative, sociable, earthy, tough, and shrewd. With great self-confidence he took colossal gambles in both foreign and domestic policy. As a dictator he did not have to fear opposition from a parliament or criticism from the press. He could not, however, completely ignore the discontent of the Russian people. His announced goals were to overtake the United States in productivity and to spread Communism throughout the world. (See also Russia.)

At home Khrushchev continued to build up armaments and heavy industry, at the same time promising the people a huge expansion in consumer goods. In foreign affairs he was bold and unpredictable, making quick turnabouts that put the free nations at a disadvantage. While talking peace, he made no concessions—except when forced to withdraw missiles from Cuba in 1962 and his agreeing to the nuclear test ban treaty of 1963. In the early 1960's Khrushchev's de-Stalinization policy caused a rift with Red China that split the Communist world into two camps. In 1964 Khrushchev was removed from office. In his remaining years, he lived quietly. He died in a Moscow hospital Sept. 11, 1971, following a heart attack. (See also Russian History. For relations with the United States, see Eisenhower; Kennedy; Cuba.)

THESE ARTICLES ARE IN THE FACT-INDEX

Khwarizmi, al-
Khyber Pass
Kiangsi, People's
  Republic of China
Kiangsu, People's
  Republic of China

Kiaochow, People's
  Republic of China
Kickapoo Indians
Kickinghorse Pass
Kidd, Benjamin
Kidd, Michael

**KIDD, Captain William** (1645?–1701). Numberless legends cluster around the name of Captain Kidd. They have made him the most famous of pirates. Oddly enough, the charge of piracy was never definitely proved against him. Some authorities now doubt if he was ever a pirate at all.

William Kidd was a Scottish minister's son. He followed the sea from his youth. In King William's War between the English and the French he became known as the bold captain of a privateer in the West Indies. By the end of the 17th century he had become a successful shipmaster sailing from New York City. British commerce then suffered greatly from marauding pirates.

At the request of the governor of New York, Kidd was given two commissions from the English king addressed to "our trusty and well-beloved Captain Kidd." One was given for suppressing piracy. The other commissioned him to cruise as a privateer against the French. With his 30 guns and his crew of 155, the captain jauntily set sail in his ship *Adventure* for Madagascar, Malabar, and the Red Sea region— the chief haunts of the pirates.

### Why Kidd Became a Pirate

Now Kidd's troubles began. No pirates were found. A cholera plague destroyed some of his crew. The ship grew leaky, and supplies began to give out. Then, apparently, the crew mutinied. The men seized his vessel and turned to piracy. They captured several small Moorish vessels, fought with a Portuguese man-of-war, and finally took the *Quedagh Merchant*, a rich Armenian prize.

At this point, according to Kidd's later testimony, he regained his command. He abandoned the old *Adventure* and transferred the captured booty to a sloop. He then set sail for America, intending to turn over the loot to the colonial authorities. He was arrested in Boston, where he landed, and sent to London for trial. There he was convicted of murder for killing a mutinous sailor. During his trial for piracy the evidence was inconclusive. He kept protesting that he was "the innocentest person of them all," but he was pronounced guilty. He was hanged at Execution Dock with several of his companions. His body hung in chains for a long time, as a warning to all would-be robbers of the sea.

His fame was spread abroad by the popular ballad "My name is Captain Kidd, as I sailed, as I sailed." Many a romance, such as Robert Louis Stevenson's 'Treasure Island', has been inspired by stories of his adventures. From time to time people still search fruitlessly along the Hudson River or on the shores of Long Island Sound for the hoard of gold, silver, and precious stones said to have been buried by him.

THESE ARTICLES ARE IN THE FACT-INDEX

**Kidderminster, England
'Kidnapped'
Kidney diseases**

**MUTINY ON THE 'ADVENTURE'**
This is the incident that brought Captain Kidd to the gallows. It was the crew, he said, that forced him to piracy.

**KIDNEYS.** The paired kidneys lie one on each side of the backbone. They are located about as high as a person's elbows if he holds his arms at his sides. All the blood in the body flows through the kidneys every few minutes. Their function is to remove from the blood the waste products of living cells and any excess water and acid. The fluid that they remove is called urine.

Blood enters each kidney through a *renal* (kidney) *artery*, which comes directly from the main artery of the body, the aorta. It leaves through a *renal vein*. A third tube, the *ureter*, carries urine down to the bladder, a storage sac. From the bladder the urine is expelled from the body through the *urethra*.

Inside each kidney the renal artery fans out into finer and finer branches, in the *renal pyramids*. In the *cortex*, the thick outer rind of the kidney, the arteries break up into tufts of capillaries called *glomeruli*. Each glomerulus pushes into a *capsule*, the cup-shaped end of a *tubule* (microscopic tube). One glomerulus, with its entire winding tubule, makes up a *nephron*. In each nephron blood is filtered and urine is formed. It is estimated that there are from 1 million to $4\frac{1}{2}$ million of these filtration units in each kidney. Each tubule descends from the cortex deep into the *medulla* (inner tissue). There it makes

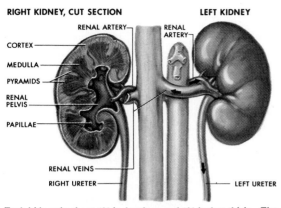

**RIGHT KIDNEY, CUT SECTION**     **LEFT KIDNEY**

RENAL ARTERY — RENAL ARTERY

CORTEX

MEDULLA

PYRAMIDS

RENAL PELVIS

PAPILLAE

RENAL VEINS

RIGHT URETER — LEFT URETER

Each kidney is about 4½ inches long and 1¼ inches thick. The right kidney is a little lower and smaller than the left.

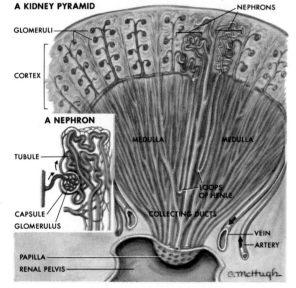

**A KIDNEY PYRAMID**     NEPHRONS

GLOMERULI

CORTEX

**A NEPHRON**

TUBULE

MEDULLA     MEDULLA

LOOPS OF HENLE

CAPSULE

GLOMERULUS

COLLECTING DUCTS

VEIN — ARTERY

PAPILLA

RENAL PELVIS

*e. mcHugh*

The dots in the cortex of the pyramid are balls of capillaries. Each ball (glomerulus), with its tubule, makes up a filtration unit (nephron), which is shown enlarged at the left.

a hairpin turn (loop of Henle) that carries it back to the cortex. After more twists, the tubule enters a collecting duct. Drop by drop, urine passes from the ducts in the pyramid through a *papilla* (nipplelike projection) of the *renal pelvis*. The pelvis is the collection chamber of the ureter.

Ordinarily the kidneys discharge three or four pints of urine every day. Anything that interferes with their activity causes an accumulation of harmful waste matter in the blood.

THESE ARTICLES ARE IN THE FACT-INDEX

| | |
|---|---|
| Kido, Takayoshi | Kielce, Poland |
| Kieft, William | Kielland, Alexander |
| (Wilhelmus) | Kienzl, Wilhelm |
| Kiel, West Germany | Kiepura, Jan |
| Kiel, Peace of | Kierkegaard, Sören |
| Kiel Canal | Kiesinger, Kurt Georg |

**KIEV** (*kē'yĕf*), **Russia.** Ancient Kiev, known as the "mother of Russian cities," is now the capital of the Ukrainian Soviet Socialist Republic. It is beautifully situated on the hilly right bank of the great Dnieper River. It has so many parks and gardens that it is called the "green city." The climate is mild and winters are not severe.

The city lies in a rich agricultural district. Sugar refineries, distilleries, and flour mills process the sugar beets and wheat of the area. Shipyards make boats for the Dnieper River traffic. Much of Kiev's heavy industry was moved to Siberia after World War II, but it still produces machines and machine tools, electrical equipment, and textiles. Many of the factories are located at Darnitsa, a leftbank suburb. The city is also a railway center.

Kiev is a city of lovely churches. The Byzantine St. Sophia Cathedral is noted for its soaring blue bell tower and its 11th-century frescoes and mosaics. The 11th century also saw the rise of the famous monastery Petcherskaya Lavra, "the city of caves." Until the Russian revolution of 1917, the Lavra's catacombs were visited yearly by thousands of pilgrims. Much of the monastery was destroyed by the Germans during World War II. The Lavra is now a museum city. The Cathedral of St. Vladimir (completed 1896) is still used as a place of worship.

The University of Kiev is one of the most important educational institutions in Russia. Kiev also has an academy of sciences, agricultural colleges, engineering and trade schools, and numerous other technical and scientific institutes.

Kiev was founded in the 5th century as a trading settlement. It became the center of the Russian Orthodox faith in the 10th century, when Grand Duke Vladimir, ruler of Kiev, had all the people baptized in the Dnieper (*see* Russian History). From 1320 to 1668 Kiev was under the rule first of Lithuania and then of Poland. It grew into two parts—the old city, on the hills, and the low-lying business section, the Podol, which included a large Jewish quarter.

In 1920 the capital of the Ukraine was moved to Khar'kov. During World War II the Germans held Kiev from 1941 to 1943. When the Russians reentered the city, they found the population had dwindled from 846,000 to about 305,000. About 85 percent of the center of the city was demolished. In 1946 a major rebuilding program was begun. Population (1970 preliminary census), 1,632,000. (*See also* Ukrainian Soviet Socialist Republic; Dnieper River.)

THESE ARTICLES ARE IN THE FACT-INDEX

| | |
|---|---|
| Kigoma-Ujiji, Tanzania | Kildare, Ireland (town) |
| Kikuyu | Kilgore, Tex. |
| Kildare, Ireland | Kilimanjaro |
| (province) | Kilkenny, Ireland |

Associated British and Irish Railways

This is Lough Leane, the Lower Lake. In the foreground is a slender peninsula called Ross Island. It cuts the lake nearly in half. Part of the beauty of the lakes of Killarney lies in the deep, rich greenness of the surrounding grass and trees.

**KILLARNEY, Ireland.** One of the world's most beautiful places is the region around the little town of Killarney, in County Kerry, southwest Ireland. Here three island-dotted lakes lie one below the other in a green valley encircled by low-lying mountains.

Lough Leane, the Lower Lake at the north, is the largest, about five miles long by two miles wide. On its northeast side stands the little town of Killarney. Many small islands break the blue surface of Lough Leane. Most beautiful is Innisfallen, with its groves of holly and the ruin of St. Finian's Abbey, built in the 6th century. On the east shore of Lough Leane stand the ivy-covered ruins of Ross Castle and of Muckross Abbey, built in the 15th century.

From the southern end of Muckross, or Middle, Lake rises Torc Mountain. A winding stream called the Long Range links Middle Lake with the small Upper Lake, where trees of Kerry arbutus (*Arbutus unedo*) blossom. To the west lie the highest mountains in Ireland, Macgillycuddy's Reeks. Not far from the lakes, between Purple Mountains and the Reeks, is the Gap of Dunloe. Legends say that the great hero Finn MacCool slashed it into the mountains with one mighty blow of his sword.

The fame of their beauty draws throngs of visitors to the lakes each year. Much of the area around them is a national park. Killarney town provides hotels and guest houses for the travelers. Boatmen and drivers of jaunting carts entertain them with poetic tales and legends about the region. Fishing for trout and salmon is good. Population of Killarney (1966 census), 6,877.

**KILMER, (Alfred) Joyce** (1886–1918). American schoolchildren know the poem 'Trees', by Joyce Kilmer. It first appeared in *Poetry: A Magazine of Verse* in 1913. Like so much of his poetry, 'Trees' celebrated an ordinary thing with lyric simplicity.

Kilmer was born in New Brunswick, N.J. As a boy, his interest turned to writing. He attended Rutgers College, then transferred to Columbia University. In 1908 he married Aline Murray.

Wide World

Kilmer taught Latin a year and later served as literary editor of the *Churchman*, a publication of the Episcopal church, to which he belonged. He wrote book reviews and newspaper articles. He was converted to Roman Catholicism, which influenced his writing.

In World War I the writer enlisted as a private. He became a sergeant in France. During the second battle of the Marne he was killed, on July 30, 1918. He is buried in the American cemetery at Fère-en-Tardenois. He was awarded a posthumous Croix de Guerre. Kilmer's best-known books are 'Trees and Other Poems' (1914), 'Main Street and Other Poems' (1917), and the war poem 'Rouge Bouquet'.

THESE ARTICLES ARE IN THE FACT-INDEX

Killeen, Tex.
Killian, James R(hyne), Jr.
Killiecrankie
Kill van Kull
Killy, Jean Claude
Kilmainham Treaty
Kilmarnock, Scotland

THESE ARTICLES ARE IN THE FACT-INDEX

Kilpatrick, Hugh Judson
Kilpatrick, William Heard
Kilwa Kivinje, Tanzania
'Kim'
Kimbrough, Emily
Kim Il Sung
Kim Koo
Kimmel, Husband E(dward)
Kim Sowol
Kim Yusin
Kinck, Hans

# KINDERGARTEN—The First Step from Home

**KINDERGARTENS AND NURSERY SCHOOLS.** In the years before children reach school age, it becomes more and more difficult to keep them happily occupied at home. They are able to run, to climb well out of reach, to pedal a tricycle a considerable distance. They are tremendously curious not only about electrical and mechanical appliances in the home, but the steam shovel three blocks down the street. They want to know about the man who brings the mail, the bus driver, the old lady who walks with a cane, and about other children—the little girl with the doll carriage and the twins next door.

They begin to ask questions which are enough to "stump the experts." But they are satisfied with simple answers. When they ask what a book says and begin to notice words and letters, they are not demanding to be taught the alphabet. They often attempt more than they can finish. They lay out an airplane hangar on the living-room floor, but fatigue overtakes them and they leave it for "grownups" to trip over. Sometimes they surprise themselves and their parents. They may carry a list to the grocery store and bring home every item. They may dry the dishes and pick up their toys. But these efforts are spurts. Parents cannot expect such mature behavior consistently.

Carol Ann Bales

Her small charges watch intently as a kindergarten teacher, with the aid of a librarian, shows them how to check out a library book. One class member learns from the inside.

## How Kindergartens Work with Children

What kind of living goes on in a good kindergarten? First of all, a child can be himself. His ideas are respected, while he learns gradually to respect the ideas of others. His teacher knows that no two children start with the same abilities or grow in quite the same way. Six youngsters who have lived near each other and played together a good deal will carry on with some of the play ideas they have been using in their own backyards. Other children have had an older brother or sister who has fought at least some of their battles for them. Now they need some protection from children their own age. Some children will

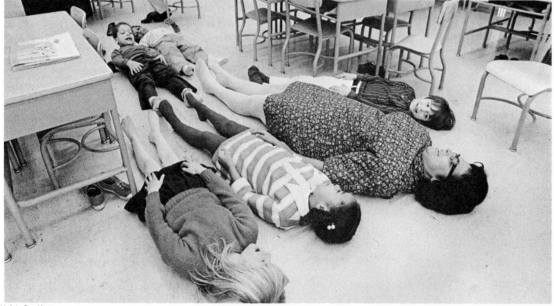

Hal A. Franklin I.

Preschoolers at the Ancona Montessori School in Chicago, Ill., stretch out along with their teacher to take a brief rest between exercises. To help develop the young bodies, exercise is a regular part of the progressive school's schedule.

51

seize new experiences. They will try everything in the room and chatter about it all when they get home. Others will look, listen, and really enjoy themselves, but say very little. Knowing all this, the teacher plans at the start activities for small groups, which let the children become acquainted with one another.

What kind of learning takes place in kindergarten? Social learning—getting along with other people—is important. The setting, however, must provide for other kinds of learning as well. The paint, clay, building blocks, and housekeeping toys found in kindergartens are not solely for enjoyment.

A child stands with brush in hand, chooses his favorite color, and sweeps it over a big piece of white paper. Then he dots it with blobs of black. He may comment to his teacher, "That's the way the sun is. All red. And the buildings black." She does not check his accuracy. She knows that as he paints what he sees and feels, he develops his ability to observe. As he grows older he will become more self-critical and will want to make the sun and buildings look right.

Three boys are working on a large block construction. One says, "It does so have a second story. And there is an elevator." The teacher asks a question, finds they have enough blocks to make a second story, discusses with them how they could raise things from the first to second floor, sends one child for the suggested pulleys, helps the others select wood for the elevator. She does not discuss with the children the physical forces of gravity and friction, but obviously the children are learning to deal with them.

There are no arithmetic lessons, but the children learn a great deal about numbers. Sally collects a pile of pie plates in the sandbox. Jane protests, "She has them all. A whole bunch." The teacher helps them

### LEARNING FROM PICTURES
The Montessori Method used in this classroom permits children, under supervision, to concentrate on what they wish most to learn from the learning tools at hand.

Hal A. Franklin II

count how many there are and plan how they can be shared. "There are six: two for Sally, two for Jane, and two for Rita." Arnold tells his willing helper that four more blocks will be needed to complete their building. When cookies are served, halves and quarters are carefully measured.

Over in one corner, Mary and Susan are washing doll clothes. "I like to do this," says Mary, "but my mother doesn't. The laundryman takes our clothes every Tuesday and brings them back on Friday." Susan considers this as she carefully dumps her pile of washed and rewashed clothes back into the soapy water for another rub. "We have a washing machine," she murmurs. How people live, different ways of doing things—these are part of important learning in kindergarten.

In dramatic play the child lives over many of the things that have happened to him and acts out events as he sees them. A girl scolds her dolls; a boy drives a big truck. Each one telephones the neighbors. These dramatic creations usually spring from the child's own life experiences. They mean more than the stories and poems that are read to him. Fairies, elves, and dragons may enter into dramatic play. Most five-year-olds, however, are absorbed with the problems of understanding what goes on immediately around them. Too-fanciful material confuses them. Teachers accept whatever fantasy the children introduce, but they do not offer it unless the children are clearly ready for it.

## Music Plays an Important Role

Music is always associated with the kindergarten and seems to permeate the program. Children have both listening and creating experiences. An alert teacher picks up the music the children make as they play. She notes the rat-tat-tat of Jerry's hammer as he fastens a railing of nails to his boat, and the chant which Mary sings as she sets the table for lunch. Sometimes the whole group joins in making up a song. This is in addition to all the favorites they have learned together.

Music is not just to be sung. It is something they have in their muscles too. They love to run, to skip, and to turn somersaults. The teacher's drum is accompaniment enough, but it is fun to have a piano sometimes. Recorded music brings added richness.

## Preparing Children for Reading

In many ways children in kindergarten learn to appreciate what it means to be able to read. They learn to identify their own names and sometimes those of their friends on their various belongings. They know that a sign saying "Do not disturb" left on a half-finished block building is something to be respected. Sometimes they ask questions which can only be answered by consulting books. They watch their teacher and listen carefully to what she reads. They observe that she frequently writes notes so that important items will not be forgotten.

Children's vocabularies expand in kindergarten. The children talk to each other, to the teacher, and to visitors. They delight in knowing the correct term for everything they see, and in an environment in which they can question freely, their vocabularies increase rapidly.

While they are having all these experiences, some children become interested in reading. They ask questions about words they see in books and magazines or on signs and packages. They may indicate that they know some of the letters. Their teacher recognizes these signals of developing reading ability, but she does not sit the children down with a primer. Nor is she concerned about children who show less interest. Those black symbols on the white page are extremely complicated for the young child. It takes a long, long period of seeing other people read and write, of noting how those strange black figures stand for things one knows, before any child is ready to concentrate on learning to read.

## Measures to Promote Health

Kindergartens emphasize the health of children. Good programs provide for thorough physical examinations and continuous health supervision. An effort is made to balance vigorous physical activity, quiet activity, and rest, according to the needs of each child.

Outdoor exercise is a vital part of a good health program for young children. Boards to balance on, bars to swing from, places to climb, heavy things to push and pull—all help strengthen their growing muscles.

## Rise of Kindergartens and Nursery Schools

The story of the kindergarten begins with the work of Friedrich Froebel, who founded a school for young children at Blankenburg, Germany, in 1837 (see Froebel). At this kindergarten, as he named the school, children learned through play activities. Kindergarten is German for "child garden."

Kindergartens were introduced into the United States between 1850 and 1860 by German immigrants. The first distinctly American kindergarten was opened in Boston, Mass., by Elizabeth Peabody in 1860. In 1873, through the efforts of Susan Blow, St. Louis, Mo., became the first city to make kindergartens a part of the public-school system.

In 1913 California enacted a law which provided that the board of education of a city, town, county, or district must establish a kindergarten when petitioned to do so by the parents of 25 or more children of kindergarten age. Similar legislation was later adopted by other states.

Many communities have kindergartens or nursery schools which enroll children at the age of three or four. Group training of children below kindergarten age gained impetus in England shortly before World War I. Under the guidance of Margaret and Rachel McMillan, nursery schools were established in the slum districts of London to help improve the physical

Luba Dinkin

Learning to share is not easy. The expression of the child in the top picture shows how much she would like to keep all the blocks for herself. The children in the bottom picture have learned to share.

condition of children living in those poorer areas.

In the United States, the nursery school began in research centers established at various universities and colleges in the early 1920's. An increasing awareness of the needs of young children spread from these centers to professional workers and to parents. Nursery school programs were subsidized by the federal government during the depression years in the 1930's to provide employment for teachers and other workers and during World War II to free mothers for work in industry. In 1965 the government instituted the Head Start program to help children with limited backgrounds prepare for school or kindergarten.

Current materials on kindergartens and nursery schools may be obtained from the Association for Childhood Education International. Its headquarters are located at 3615 Wisconsin Avenue N. W., Washington, D. C. 20016.

THESE ARTICLES ARE IN THE FACT-INDEX

Kinesics

King, Basil (William Benjamin)

King, Clarence

King, Coretta (Scott)

King, Ernest Joseph

# MARTIN LUTHER KING, JR.—Champion of Black Rights

KING, Martin Luther, Jr. (1929–1968). Inspired by the belief that love and peaceful protest could end social injustice, Martin Luther King, Jr., became one of the outstanding black leaders in the United States during his short but active life. He aroused whites and blacks alike to protest racial discrimination, poverty, and war. A champion of nonviolent resistance to oppression, he was awarded the Nobel peace prize in 1964.

Martin Luther King, Jr., was born in Atlanta, Ga., on Jan. 15, 1929. His father, Martin, Sr., was the pastor of the Ebenezer Baptist Church, a black congregation. His mother, Alberta Williams King, was a schoolteacher. Martin had an older sister, Christine, and a younger brother, Alfred Daniel.

Martin encountered racism at an early age. When he was six, his friendship with two white playmates was cut short by their parents. When he was 11 a white woman struck him and called him a "nigger." Martin and his family, like all black people in their community, met with discrimination in stores and on buses and trains.

Martin was a bright student. At 15 he was admitted to Morehouse College without first completing high school. He decided to become a minister, and at 18 he was ordained in his father's church.

After graduating from Morehouse in 1948, Martin entered Crozer Theological Seminary in Chester, Pa. He was the valedictorian of his class in 1951 and won a graduate fellowship. At Boston University he received a Ph.D. degree in theology in 1955.

In Boston King met Coretta Scott. They were married in 1953 and had two sons, Martin Luther III and Dexter Scott, and two daughters, Yolanda Denise and Bernice Albertine.

## Civil Rights Campaigns

King was concerned with social problems as well as spiritual matters. He was impressed by the teachings of Henry David Thoreau and Mohandas K. Gandhi on nonviolent resistance. King wrote, "I came to feel that this was the only morally and practically sound method open to oppressed people in their struggle for freedom."

King became pastor of the Dexter Avenue Baptist Church in Montgomery, Ala., in 1954. In December 1955 he was chosen to head the Montgomery Improvement Association, formed by the black community to lead a boycott of the segregated city buses.

During the tense months of the boycott King's home was bombed. He urged his angered followers to heed the Biblical command to love one's enemies. He persuaded them to remain nonviolent despite threats to their lives and property. Late in 1956 the United States Supreme Court forced desegregation of the buses. King regarded the boycott as a milestone in the struggle for civil rights. It proved, he said, that "there is a new Negro in the South, with a new sense of dignity and destiny."

Early in 1958 King became president of a group that later became known as the Southern Christian Leadership Conference (SCLC). This conference was formed to carry on civil rights activities in the South. He spent the next few years writing, lecturing, and participating in civil rights demonstrations. He inspired blacks throughout the South to hold peaceful sit-ins and "freedom rides" protesting segregated shopping, eating, and transportation facilities. The SCLC financed many of these efforts.

In 1957 King became the youngest recipient of the Spingarn Medal, awarded annually to an outstanding black person by the National Association for the Advancement of Colored People. A visit to India in 1959 gave him a long-awaited opportunity to study Gandhi's techniques of nonviolent protest. In 1960 King became copastor of his father's church in Atlanta. The following year he led a "nonviolent army" to protest discrimination in Albany, Ga. King was jailed in 1963 during a campaign that won the desegregation of many public facilities in Birmingham, Ala. In a moving appeal, known as the "Letter from Birmingham Jail," he replied to several white clergymen who felt that his efforts were ill timed. King argued that Asian and African nations were fast achieving political independence while "we still creep at a horse-and-buggy pace toward gaining a cup of coffee at a lunch counter."

In December 1964 King became the youngest man to receive the Nobel peace prize. He regarded it not only as a personal honor but also as an international tribute to the nonviolent civil rights movement in the United States.

In 1965 King led a drive to register black voters in Selma, Ala. The drive met with violent resistance. In protest of this treatment thousands of black and white demonstrators conducted a five-day march from Selma to the State Capitol at Montgomery.

On Dec. 21, 1956, King rode the first desegregated bus in Montgomery, Ala. His leadership of a black boycott to desegregate the city's buses had attracted national attention.

UPI Compix

King was disappointed that the progress of civil rights in the South had not been matched by improvements in the lives of Northern blacks. He was greatly disturbed in 1965 by riots in the poverty-stricken black Watts section of Los Angeles, Calif. He resolved to focus the nation's attention on the living conditions of blacks in Northern cities.

In 1966 King established a headquarters in a Chicago, Ill., slum apartment. From this base he organized protests against the city's discrimination in housing and employment. He reached an agreement with the city administration, but its provisions were attacked by many blacks as vague and limited.

### Attacks on War and Poverty

King combined civil rights protests with a strong stand against the Vietnam conflict. He believed that the money and effort spent on war could be used to combat poverty and discrimination. King also felt that he would be a hypocrite if he protested racial violence without condemning the violence of war as well.

Militant black leaders began to attack King's appeals for nonviolence. They accused him of being influenced too much by whites. Government officials criticized his stand on Vietnam. Some black leaders felt that King's statements against war diverted public attention from civil rights. Despite these criticisms, King continued to attack discrimination, violence, and war.

He inspired and planned the Poor People's March on Washington, D. C., in 1968 to dramatize the rela-

King, like Dr. Benjamin Spock (left), actively opposed American participation in the Vietnam conflict. His concern was for "the survival of a world in which to be integrated."

John Goodwin—Pictorial Parade

On Aug. 28, 1963, King was the principal speaker at a giant civil rights march on Washington. His eloquent "I Have a Dream" address was the high point of the demonstration.

tionship of poverty to urban violence. But he did not live to take part in it. Early in 1968 he traveled to Memphis, Tenn., to support a strike of poorly paid sanitation workers. There, on April 4, he was assassinated by a sniper. King's death shocked the nation and precipitated rioting by blacks in many cities. He was buried in Atlanta under a monument inscribed with the final words of his famous "I Have a Dream" address. Taken from an old slave song, the inscription read: "Free at Last,/ Free at Last,/ Thank God Almighty,/ I'm Free at Last."

King's brief career greatly advanced the cause of civil rights in the United States. His efforts spurred the passage of the Civil Rights Act of 1964 and the Voting Rights Act of 1965. His energetic personality and persuasive oratory helped unite many blacks in a search for peaceful solutions to racial oppression. In his last years King's views were challenged by blacks who had lost faith in nonviolence. But his belief in the power of nonviolent protest remained strong. His writings include 'Stride Toward Freedom' (1958), the story of the Montgomery bus boycott; 'Strength to Love' (1963); 'Why We Can't Wait' (1964); and 'Where Do We Go from Here: Chaos or Community?' (1967). (*See also* Black Americans.)

### Books and Films About Martin Luther King, Jr.

King, Coretta. My Life with Martin Luther King, Jr. (Avon, 1969).
Martin Luther King, Jr., film (Encyclopaedia Britannica Films).
Preston, Edward. Martin Luther King (Doubleday, 1968).
Wilson, B. P. Martin Luther King, Jr. (Putnam, 1971).

THESE ARTICLES ARE IN THE FACT-INDEX

| | |
|---|---|
| King, Rufus | King, Wayne |
| King, Thomas Starr | King, William |

## KING, William Lyon Mackenzie (1874–1950).

Between 1921 and his retirement in 1948, Mackenzie King was prime minister of Canada for a total of more than 21 years. No other statesman in the history of the British parliamentary system had headed a government for so many years.

William Lyon Mackenzie King was born on Dec. 17, 1874, at Berlin (now Kitchener), Ont. His mother was the daughter of William Lyon Mackenzie, leader of the Rebellion of 1837 (see Mackenzie).

King was educated at the universities of Toronto and Chicago and at Harvard. In Chicago he lived at Hull-House, where he first studied the social and labor problems which were his greatest interest for many years. As a traveling fellow at Harvard, he studied labor conditions in Europe.

During a summer vacation King wrote newspaper articles exposing sweatshop conditions in the federal post office of Canada and then conducted a government investigation that helped end the abuses. In 1900 he was asked to organize a bureau of labor in Canada and to become its deputy minister.

Sir Wilfrid Laurier, the Liberal prime minister, was impressed by King's ability (see Laurier). At his urging, King ran for and won a seat in the House of Commons in 1908. In 1909 Laurier named him Canada's first Cabinet minister of labor. In 1911 the Liberals were defeated, and during World War I King was a labor adviser for the Rockefeller Foundation and for business firms in the United States.

Upon Laurier's death in 1919, Mackenzie King was chosen to lead the Liberal party. On Dec. 29, 1921, he became prime minister. During the years in office that followed, King helped lead Canada from the status of a British dominion to full sovereignty. As early as 1922 he asserted Canada's independence by refusing to supply troops to back up Britain in a dispute with Turkey. At the 1926 Imperial Conference in London, England, King successfully argued for "separate and equal status" for British dominions. This principle was formalized in the 1931 Statute of Westminster.

In 1926 King lost his post briefly, following a scandal involving customs officials. He skillfully forced a new election that overturned the rule of the Conservative Arthur Meighen (see Canadian History; Meighen). In 1930, after a depression struck Canada, King's party was again defeated.

He returned to office in 1935 and soon faced the task of leading his nation through World War II. As his own foreign minister, King negotiated defense and economic pacts with the United States. At home he used his great gift for compromise to maintain unity between French- and English-speaking Canadians. King took an active part in the formation of the United Nations in 1945 and in the Allies' postwar conferences on atomic power and defense.

Mackenzie King never married. He was deeply devoted to his mother and maintained a shrine to her memory after her death. King died on July 22, 1950, at Kingsmere, his country home near Ottawa.

---

THESE ARTICLES ARE IN THE FACT-INDEX
**King, William Rufus**
**King**

---

**KINGBIRD.** The kingbirds are flycatchers. They can often be seen perching on telephone wires along roads. They are somewhat smaller than robins. The eastern kingbird is black above and white below. A scarlet crown patch is usually concealed by overlapping feathers. Across the bottom of the black tail is a white band. This bird is found east of the Rockies from southern Canada to tropical America.

The western, or Arkansas, kingbird has a gray head and back, yellow underparts, and a black tail with white feathers on the sides. (For pictures in color, see Birds.) The scientific name of the eastern kingbird is *Tyrannus tyrannus;* western kingbird, *T. verticalis.* (See also Flycatcher.)

---

THESE ARTICLES ARE IN THE FACT-INDEX
**King College**
**Kingfish**

---

**KINGFISHER.** The kingfisher family includes some 80 species, distributed over the greater part of the globe. They are known for their swift dives. From its perch the kingfisher swoops like an arrow to seize a fish underwater or an insect on land.

The commonest species in North America is the belted kingfisher (for picture in color, see Birds). It nests east of the Rocky Mountains from northern Canada to the Gulf coast and winters in the central and southern parts of the United States. The bird is 11 to 14 inches long and has a shaggy, black crest. Its feathers are bluish gray on the upper parts and white on the underparts. The male has a gray belt across the breast. The female has a chestnut belt. The belted kingfishers nest in holes which they dig in banks beside lakes and streams. The eggs—five to eight in number—are laid on a bed of fish bones. The kingfisher call is a loud rattle.

The kingfisher family is most numerous in the East Indies, where there are many vividly colored species. The common kingfisher of Europe is also brightly colored, with iridescent, blue-green upper parts and a rich chestnut breast.

The ancient name of the kingfisher was *halcyon.* The scientific name of the kingfisher family is *Alcedinidae;* of the belted kingfisher, *Megaceryle alcyon;* green kingfisher, *Chloroceryle americana.*

**KING GEORGE'S WAR.** This war took place in the American colonies in the 18th century during the reign of King George II of England. It was a part of a general conflict in Europe.

In the European war Prussia, France, and Spain were lined up against Austria and England in the War of the Austrian Succession (1740–48). This was a struggle for balance of power, commerce, and colonial possessions (*see* Maria Theresa). The colonial war was fought from Canada to the Caribbean Sea, with the English against both the French and the Spanish. English expeditions against Cartagena, great Spanish stronghold on the South American coast, and St. Augustine, Fla., came to nothing.

The chief event of the war was the capture in 1745 of the French fortress of Louisbourg on Cape Breton Island by an English fleet and an army of New England colonials. This fort was built to protect the southern entrance to the Gulf of St. Lawrence. From it the French had hoped to recapture Acadia, which they had lost in Queen Anne's War. In the Peace of Aix-la-Chapelle (1748) Louisbourg was restored to the French. This, however, was a mere truce before the final struggle in which the French lost New France to the English (*see* French and Indian War).

---

THESE ARTICLES ARE IN THE FACT-INDEX

'King Henry IV'            'King Henry VIII'
'King Henry V'             'King John'

---

**'KING LEAR'.** This tragedy by Shakespeare is ranked by many judges as the finest piece of dramatic literature ever written. It contains some of the most beautiful poetry in the English language.

Lear, a headstrong old ruler of ancient Britain, divides his kingdom into three parts. Each of his three daughters is to receive her share according to the love she professes for him.

The evil Goneril and Regan insult reason with their extravagant claims. The youngest daughter, simple, honest Cordelia, becomes disgusted with them and states her own dutiful love too modestly to please the proud old king. He casts her off penniless. She would have been poor indeed had not the pitying king of France made her his queen. Having thus foolishly thrown away his kingdom, Lear learns—

> How sharper than a serpent's tooth it is
> To have a thankless child!

Betrayed by the two false daughters, he rushes out into the stormy night and goes mad with grief. There is an obscure subplot involving Lear's only faithful follower, the duke of Gloucester. Gloucester has done injustice to his son Edgar in favor of another villainous son Edmund. Lear, Gloucester, and the disinherited Edgar, who pretends to be mad, form a pathetic group. Cordelia and Lear are reunited as the armies of France battle the English. But Cordelia is captured and hanged in prison on the orders of her sisters. The French are victorious. Goneril, Regan, and Edmund are killed. Lear dies of grief.

**KINGLETS AND GNATCATCHERS.** Midgets of the bird world are the kinglets and gnatcatchers. Only the hummingbirds are smaller. Though they are not shy, it is difficult to observe these tiny birds. They are always on the move.

Kinglets are only $3\frac{1}{2}$ to $4\frac{1}{2}$ inches long. They have olive-green backs and yellowish under parts. The golden-crowned kinglet (*Regulus satrapa*) has a golden-yellow crown patch, bordered with black, which is always visible. The ruby-crowned kinglet (*Regulus calendula*) has a ruby-red patch which it displays or conceals at will. It is also distinguished by pale wing bars and a white eye ring. It has a beautiful song. Both kinglets nest in spruce forests of the northern United States and Canada. They winter from the central states southward.

The blue-gray gnatcatcher (*Polioptila caerulea*) is somewhat larger than the kinglets ($4\frac{1}{2}$ to 5 inches). It is blue gray above and white below, with a long tail, black in the center and white on the sides (for picture in color, *see* Birds). It nests in woodlands throughout the continental United States (except Alaska) and winters from the Southern states through Mexico. The western plumbeous gnatcatcher (*Polioptila melanura*) has a black cap and less white in the tail. Kinglets and gnatcatchers belong to the family *Silviidae*, to which the Old World warblers also belong.

---

THESE ARTICLES ARE IN THE FACT-INDEX

Kingman, Dong (Moy Shu)
'King of the Golden River, The'

---

**KING PHILIP'S WAR.** One of the most tragic of all the wars between the colonists and the Indians was King Philip's War. In 1662 Metacomet, or Philip, younger son of the Pilgrims' friend Massasoit, succeeded his father as chief of the Wampanoags. He tried for some years to keep peace and to meet the demands of the white settlers. They were increasing in numbers and advancing more and more on the Indians' lands. The English suspected Philip of secretly plotting against them and forced the Wampanoags to surrender their arms (1671). Whether or not their suspicions were justified is a disputed point. At any rate, an Indian who was acting as informer to the colonists was murdered in 1675. Three Wampanoags were executed for the crime.

This act precipitated a bloody war which involved the Nipmucs and Narragansets, as well as the Wampanoags. Up and down the Connecticut Valley in Massachusetts and in the colonies of Plymouth and Rhode Island the war raged. The Indians raided and burned settlements and killed men, women, and children. The colonists resorted to similar measures. Gradually the colonists cleared the country of Indians. Philip was hunted down in a swamp in Rhode Island and killed Aug. 12, 1676. At his death the war in southern New England was over. In New Hampshire and Maine the Saco Indians continued to raid defenseless settlements for a year and a half longer.

THESE ARTICLES ARE IN THE FACT-INDEX

'King Richard II'    King's College,
Kings    University of
King's College    Kingsford, William

**KINGSLEY, Charles** (1819–1875). In his own lifetime this tall, thin clergyman was known chiefly as a social reformer. Today Kingsley is beloved by children everywhere for his delightful fairy story 'Water-Babies'.

Charles Kingsley was born June 12, 1819, in Devonshire, England. His father was a clergyman. Charles attended King's College in London. Later he entered Cambridge University. In 1842 he went as curate to the parish of Eversley, in Hampshire, and soon was appointed rector. He held the position for the rest of his life, except for brief intervals when he accepted other appointments. In 1859 he was chaplain to Queen Victoria. From 1860 to 1869 he was professor of modern history at Cambridge. He died Jan. 23, 1875, and was buried in his own churchyard at Eversley.

Kingsley risked his position in the church by his speeches and writings in behalf of the laboring classes. It was he who originated the term "sweatshop system" to describe abusive working conditions in the manufacturing industries. He associated himself with the Christian Socialists, a group which proposed radical solutions for England's industrial problems. 'Alton Locke' (1849) is a novel dealing with social problems.

He is chiefly remembered for his historical novels. 'Westward Ho!' (1855) tells the story of a Devonshire knight in the stirring days of Queen Elizabeth I. 'Hypatia' (1853) deals with the former glories of Alexandria, in Egypt. 'Hereward the Wake' (1866) is a tale of Saxon England.

For his children Kingsley wrote delightful stories, such as 'The Heroes', a retelling of the old Greek myths. 'Water-Babies' (1863) is a fairy story and nature story combined. Its hero, a little chimney sweep, is changed by the fairies into a water baby. He learns about the habits of the water creatures.

THESE ARTICLES ARE IN THE FACT-INDEX

Kingsley, Henry    Kings Point, N. Y.
Kingsley, Mary Henrietta    Kingsport, Tenn.
Kingsley, Sidney    Kingston, Charles Cameron
Kings Mountain    Kingston, Jamaica
Kings Park, N. Y.    Kingston, N. Y.

**KINGSTON, Ontario.** The city of Kingston stands near the east end of Lake Ontario, on a channel from the lake to the St. Lawrence River. Its harbor is the southern outlet of the Rideau Canal from Ottawa. The city is an educational center and

a summer resort. It has a considerable trade, chiefly in the transshipment of grain.

Kingston is the seat of the Royal Military College and of Queen's University. Its industries include the manufacture of locomotives, textiles, machinery, boats, aluminum, nylon, cigars, and chemicals. Nearby are large feldspar and mica mines.

Kingston got its start in 1673 when Count Louis de Frontenac, governor of New France, built a fort on the site. The fort bore his name for more than a hundred years. It was a leading French center of government and trade until it fell into the hands of the British in 1758 during the French and Indian War. United Empire Loyalists who emigrated to Fort Frontenac during the American Revolution changed the name to Kingston in honor of King George III. From 1841 to 1844 Kingston was the capital of Canada. Population (1971 census), 59,047.

THESE ARTICLES ARE IN THE FACT-INDEX

Kingston, Pa.    Kingtehchen, People's
Kingsville, Tex.    Republic of China
    King William Island

**KING WILLIAM'S WAR.** From 1689 until the battle of Waterloo in 1815 the French and the British fought a series of wars in a struggle for power on the European continent. Several of these wars were fought in America as well, for there too the French and English were rivals. The American wars resulted in the conquest of New France by the British.

The first of these European wars began after William of Orange, the chief enemy of Louis XIV of France, was given the English throne. It was fought chiefly to check the attempt of Louis XIV to push his boundaries east to the Rhine (*see* William III).

The American phase of the struggle is called King William's War. Both the French and English were helped by their Indian allies. The French resorted to Indian methods of warfare, making raids along the frontiers of New York and New Hampshire and against the settlements of Maine. The English planned expeditions against Montreal and Quebec. A fleet commanded by Sir William Phips captured Port Royal (now Annapolis Royal, Nova Scotia), but Phips's sea expedition against Quebec was defeated by Frontenac, the French governor (*see* Frontenac). Iberville, in command of French ships, took Newfoundland and Hudson's Bay.

The Peace of Ryswick, signed in 1697, restored all territorial gains in the colonies. But peace was of short duration, for five years later Queen Anne's War (1702–13) broke out as part of the War of the Spanish Succession in Europe.

THESE ARTICLES ARE IN THE FACT-INDEX

Kinkajou    Kino, Eusebio
Kinley, David    Kinsey, Alfred Charles
Kinnaird, Mary Jane

## KINSHASA, Republic of Zaire.

The capital of Zaire (formerly the Democratic Republic of the Congo) is Kinshasa, one of the largest cities in Africa south of the Sahara. The city, formerly Léopoldville, is in the western part of the republic. It sprawls along the south bank of the Congo (Zaire) River for about eight miles, downstream of the expansion of the river known as Stanley Pool. Across the river is Brazzaville, capital of the People's Republic of the Congo.

Kinshasa is connected with the Atlantic port city of Matadi by a railroad that parallels an unnavigable stretch of the Congo. Oil pipelines and a motor road also facilitate commerce between the two cities. The city is a vital inland port, collecting and processing goods for export from Matadi and distributing imported goods upstream to the interior.

The city of Kinshasa grew out of two nearby villages, Kinshasa and Kintambo. It was named Léopoldville in honor of Belgium's King Leopold II. In the 1920's Léopoldville became the capital of the Belgian Congo. It was renamed Kinshasa in 1966.

Kinshasa is a modern city with many tall buildings and broad boulevards lined with palm trees and flowers. The climate is hot and humid. The western part of the city houses administrative buildings and an industrial sector. The commercial section of the city is in the east, near the port facilities. Many ministerial buildings and official residences are in the riverside suburb of Kalina.

Kinshasa is a center for education. The Lovanium University of Kinshasa was founded in 1954. The National School of Administration (1960) and the National School of Postal and Telecommunications (1967) are also in the city. In addition to an institute of arts, where painting, sculpture, and ceramics are taught, in or near the city are a zoological garden and museums of ethnography and geology. A school of architecture was founded in 1962. Ndjili Airport provides local and international service.

An important industrial center, Kinshasa produces textiles, food products, chemicals, and construction materials. There are also large cotton factories. Because of the extensive use of the Congo for transportation, Kinshasa has developed an important shipbuilding and ship-repairing industry.

Although most of Kinshasa's inhabitants are poor, life in the city is considered better than that in the rest of the country. As a result, the population has been growing by about 10 percent a year, as more people move in from the countryside. Population, greater city (1966 estimate), 1,200,000. (*See also* Zaire, Republic of.)

---

THESE ARTICLES ARE IN THE FACT-INDEX

**Kinston, N. C.**
**Kinzie, John**

---

# RUDYARD KIPLING, English Storyteller and Poet

Gramstorff

**KIPLING, Rudyard** (1865–1936). Millions of children have spent happy hours with Kipling's 'Jungle Books' and 'Just So Stories'. They are about the land and people of the India of long ago—a country of heat, rain, and green jungles—and about animals that talk. Kipling was a master storyteller, whether he wrote in prose or in verse. His ballads, which are written in a strong marching rhythm, have the same popular style as his prose.

Rudyard Kipling knew India well. He was born there, in Bombay, on Dec. 30, 1865. His parents, John Lockwood Kipling and Alice Macdonald, had been married in England early in the same year. John Kipling had gone to Bombay to teach architectural sculpture in the Bombay School of Art.

India at this time was part of the British Empire. Beyond the cities and highways of British India, where the English lived, lay strange primitive country. Rudyard and his younger sister, Alice, had an Indian nurse who told them wonderful tales about the jungle animals. These stories remained in the boy's memory to appear later in his books about Mowgli, Shere Khan, and the gray wolves.

This happy period ended when Rudyard was five. It was the custom for English people living in other lands to send their children back to England to be educated. In 1871 Rudyard and his sister were taken to England and left in the home of a retired naval officer at Southsea. In 'Baa, Baa, Black Sheep' Kipling later described the six miserable years they spent in this "house of desolation." The woman who cared for the children seems to have been the worst possible guardian for the sensitive boy. Nearly everything that a small boy wanted to do was a "sin" to this woman. As a punishment, even reading was forbidden. Rudyard almost ruined his eyes by reading in secret every book he could lay his hands on.

In 1877 his mother came home from India and remade his world. He and his sister were taken to Devonshire to spend the summer with their mother and their cousins. The next year his father came home on leave and took Rudyard to Paris to see the great Paris Exhibition. This trip, Rudyard Kipling said, was the beginning of his lifelong love for France.

**"TIGER! TIGER!"**

"Once started, there was no chance of stopping." Mowgli, on the back of the great herd bull Rama, leads the buffalo charge against Shere Khan, the tiger. Illustration by Kurt Wiese from 'All the Mowgli Stories'. (Doubleday.)

At the end of this holiday the boy was sent to the United Service College at Westward Ho in Devonshire to be educated for the army. His years there are recorded in 'Stalky & Co.', one of the best stories about schoolboys ever written. Led by Stalky, the three boys plotted and carried out endless mischief. Rudyard, the only boy in the school who wore glasses, was Beetle, a studious youth with a talent for writing verses. The poems he wrote while at this school were later published privately by his father.

The headmaster wisely encouraged the boy's passion for reading. Rudyard read French literature, the English Bible, English poets, and storytellers such as Defoe. In this school also he developed a passionate faith in England and the English people. He voiced this faith over and over again in his writings.

John Kipling was now principal of the Mayo School of Art at Lahore, in northwest India. When Rudyard was just short of 17, he joined his family there. He became a reporter on the one daily newspaper in the Punjab, the *Civil and Military Gazette*. To get material for his newspaper articles he traveled around India and came to know the country as few others did.

Now Kipling began to write the poems and short stories about the British soldier in India that were to establish his reputation as a writer. 'Plain Tales from the Hills', 'Soldiers Three', and 'Barrack-Room Ballads' are known now wherever English is spoken. The slim volume of 'Departmental Ditties' he edited, printed, published, and sold himself. From these books emerged the British soldier, "Tommy Atkins."

In 1887 Kipling was transferred to a larger and more important newspaper at Allahabad, the *Pioneer*. Here he had more time for creative writing, and he made the most of it.

### To England and Fame

In 1890 Kipling sailed for England, going by way of Japan, China, and North America. He stopped in New York City long enough to offer his stories to a publisher; but they were rejected and he went on to England. Again he faced hard times. His effort to make a living as a writer is reflected in 'The Light That Failed'. He did find a publisher and some recognition; but it was several years before the man in the street discovered him.

### Kipling Marries an American

Two years later, his reputation firmly established, he married an American girl, Caroline Balestier, and started off with her on a trip around the world. Her brother, Wolcott Balestier, was a writer too and a great friend of Kipling's. Together they wrote 'The Naulahka'.

After their honeymoon Kipling and his wife settled down in Vermont, in a little house on the outskirts of Brattleboro. In this house their first child was born, and there Kipling wrote the tales that were to make up his 'Jungle Books'. Kipling's father visited them and made the famous drawings that were published first, with the stories, in *St. Nicholas*. Soon after the birth of their daughter, the Kiplings built a larger house not far away, which they called Naulahka. The family physician, Dr. Conland, had once served with the Gloucester fishing fleet, and he persuaded Kipling to go to Gloucester for the annual memorial service for the men who had been lost or drowned during the year. The two men listened, fascinated, to the stories of life on the Grand Banks, and Kipling went home to write 'Captains Courageous'.

After four years in America, the Kiplings decided that their real home was in England. They rented a house in a Sussex village near his uncle, Edward Burne-Jones, and his cousin Stanley Baldwin. There in 1897 their only son, John, was born.

### The Writing of 'Kim'

The story that is known as 'Kim' had been in Kipling's mind for years. Now, stimulated by his father's keen interest, he began to write it. The book was first published in 1901. A year later John Lockwood Kipling made low-relief plaques which were photographed for an illustrated edition.

Long visits to South Africa, where they formed a friendship with Cecil Rhodes, and another trip through

North America varied the Sussex life. Early in 1902 Kipling and his wife bought a house near the Sussex Downs. All about it was land that had been cultivated since before the Norman Conquest. It was called, and is called today, Bateman's. Dredging in a pond, Kipling found a Stone Age axhead and two Elizabethan "sealed quarts." "Just beyond the west fringe of our land," he wrote, "in a little valley running from Nowhere to Nothing-at-all, stood the long overgrown slag heap of a most ancient forge, supposed to have been worked by the Phoenicians and Romans."

One day his cousin, Ambrose Poynter, said to him: "Write a yarn about Roman times here." So 'Puck of Pook's Hill' and 'Rewards and Fairies' were begun. Volumes of history cannot give the vital impression that these stories give of England's past. Puck—the only fairy left in England, old and wise and kind—brings to life one by one the men and women who tell their own tales. Together they form a chain of "scents and sights and sounds" that reach to the very heart of England. Reading them, one can see the glint of a crude edge as the Flint-Worker lifts his knife to defy the wolves, hear the Roman centurions chatting in their camp behind the Roman Wall, and smell the potatoes roasting in Old Hobden's fire. The reader comes to understand why King John signed the Magna Carta and why the Norman Conquest affected the Anglo-Saxon race so deeply.

## Rewards and Sorrows

In 1907 he was awarded the Nobel prize for literature, and he and his wife went to Stockholm to receive it from Sweden's king. The first World War brought him personal tragedy. His only son was killed fighting in France with the Irish Guards.

With the social and political changes that followed the war Rudyard Kipling had little sympathy. More and more he withdrew from the active scene, spending the greater part of the year in his Sussex farmhouse. When he was nearly 70 years old, he sat down to write his autobiography, 'Something of Myself'. It was published after his death. This is a curiously revealing book. In it may be seen the background and the events that made Rudyard Kipling, the writer. In it also are revealed, perhaps more than he himself intended, the prejudices and the convictions that made Rudyard Kipling, the man.

Kipling died Jan. 18, 1936, in the same month that brought the death of England's king, George V. He was buried in Westminster Abbey with England's honored sons.

Kipling's principal works are 'Departmental Ditties' (1886); 'Plain Tales from the Hills', 'Soldiers Three', 'The Story of the Gadsbys', 'Wee Willie Winkie' (1888); 'The Light That Failed' (1891); 'Barrack-Room Ballads' (1892); 'The Jungle Books' (1894, 1895); 'Captains Courageous' (1897); 'Stalky and Co.' (1899); 'Kim' (1901); 'Just So Stories' (1902); 'Puck of Pook's Hill' (1906); 'Rewards and Fairies' (1910); 'The Irish Guards in the Great War' (1923); and 'Something of Myself' (1937).

## Books About Rudyard Kipling

Amis, Kingsley. Kipling and His World (Scribner, 1975).
Charles, Cecil. Rudyard Kipling, His Life and Works (Folcroft, 1972).
Fido, Martin. Rudyard Kipling (Viking Press, 1974).
Manley, Seon. Rudyard Kipling (Vanguard, n.d.).
Wilson, Angus. The Strange Ride of Rudyard Kipling: His Life and Works (Viking Press, 1977).

THESE ARTICLES ARE IN THE FACT-INDEX

Kiplinger, W(illard) M(onroe)
Kipnis, Alexander
Kirby, Rollin
Kirby, William
Kirchhoff, Gustav Robert
Kirghiz
Kirghiz Soviet Socialist Republic
Kirin, People's Republic of China (province)
Kirin, People's Republic of China (city)
Kirk, Grayson (Louis)
Kirklareli, Turkey
Kirksville, Mo.
Kirkuk, Iraq
Kirkwall, Orkney Islands
Kirkwood, Samuel Jordan
Kirkwood, Mo.
Kirsten, Dorothy
Kiruna, Sweden
Kisaeng
Kisangani, Zaire

**KISH.** The once majestic city of Kish is today only a mound of ruins. It lies between the Tigris and Euphrates rivers, about 100 miles south of Baghdad, Iraq. Inscriptions in the ruins state that it was "the first city founded after the Flood." As the traditional first capital of the Sumerians, Kish was an early center of civilization (see Babylonia and Assyria).

In ancient times, the plain was fertile, watered by the Euphrates. The Sumerians settled along a bend of the river. They built a fortified city, more than five miles long and almost two miles wide. Until as late as the time of Sargon (about 2750 B.C.), Kish dominated the Near East. Then it declined, for the Euphrates changed its course. Finally it was abandoned and drifting desert sand covered its ruins.

Archaeologists from the Field Museum of Natural History and Oxford University excavated the ruins in 1923–33. Digging to virgin soil, 60 feet below the top of the mound, the expedition found remains of several cultures, from Neolithic times to the Christian Era. A band of alluvial soil, about 40 feet below the surface, indicated that Kish had been flooded about 3200 B.C. Many take this to be evidence of the great Biblical flood. Astounding also was the discovery, below the flood stratum, of a four-wheeled chariot, the earliest known wheeled vehicle. Other discoveries showing the highly developed Sumerian civilization were thick-walled ziggurats (temple towers), canals, painted pottery, and a library with some of the earliest writing known to have existed in the world.

THESE ARTICLES ARE IN THE FACT-INDEX

Kishi, Nobusuke
Kishinev, Russia
Kismayu, Somalia
Kiss, August
Kissinger, Henry A(lfred)
Kistiakowsky, George B(ogdan)
Kistna River
Kisumu, Kenya
Kitakyushu, Japan
Kitazato, Shibasaburo
Kit-Cat Club
"Kitchen Cabinet"

The Bettmann Archive

**KITCHENER, Horatio Herbert** (Earl of Khartoum) (1850–1916). "Your country needs you." With this poster appeal in World War I, Earl Kitchener, British field marshal and secretary of state for war, assembled and organized one of the mightiest armies in his country's history.

Horatio Herbert Kitchener was born of English parents in County Kerry, Ireland, on June 24, 1850. He was educated at the Royal Military Academy at Woolwich, England, and in 1871 was commissioned in the Royal Engineers.

After serving in various civil service and military posts, he became commander in chief of the Anglo-Egyptian army in 1892. With this army he began a campaign to conquer the Sudan in 1896. At the battle of Omdurman in 1898, he crushed the Arab Mahdists and captured Khartoum, avenging the death there of Gen. Charles George Gordon (see Gordon; Sudan). For this feat he was made a baron and was awarded a large grant of money.

Kitchener was governing the Sudan when the Boer War began. In 1899 he was sent to South Africa as chief of staff. In 1900 he was named commander in chief. Slowly and ruthlessly he overcame the Boer resistance, ending the war in 1902 (see Boer War). Honors were heaped upon him, and he became a viscount. From 1902 to 1909 Kitchener served in India as commander in chief. In 1911 he was named consul general of Egypt. For his work there, including his economic reforms, he was made an earl.

When World War I broke out in 1914, Kitchener entered the British Cabinet as field marshal and secretary of state for war. By the end of 1915 he had expanded Britain's expeditionary force from 160,000 to more than 2,250,000 men. Until mid-1915 he was also charged with mobilizing Britain's industries for the war effort—a task for which he was unsuited. Worshiped by the people, he could not get along with his colleagues. He died en route to Russia in 1916, when his ship struck a German mine off the Orkneys.

---

THESE ARTICLES ARE IN THE FACT-INDEX
**Kitchener, Ont.**
**Kitchen middens**

---

**KITE.** A bird of prey, the kite belongs to the same family (*Accipitridae*) as the hawk. Kites are strong and graceful fliers. The four species found in the United States vary in length from 14 to 24 inches. The swallow-tailed kite, with a white head and underparts and black upperparts, is the largest of these species. Smallest of the species is the Mississippi kite, which has dark gray upperparts, light gray underparts, and a black tail. (*See also* Hawk.)

**KITES.** Flying kites is a popular pastime all over the world. A kite is a device that soars through the air at the end of a line. It may be large or small, light or heavy, simple or ornate. Kites are flown in competitive sports, for military or scientific purposes,

## HOW TO MAKE A BOX KITE

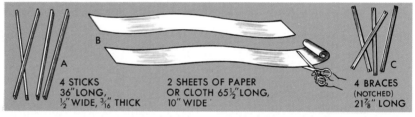

4 STICKS 36" LONG, ½" WIDE, 3/16" THICK

2 SHEETS OF PAPER OR CLOTH 65½" LONG, 10" WIDE

4 BRACES (NOTCHED) 21⅞" LONG

A box kite is simple to construct. Basic materials include four light, smooth corner sticks of spruce or pine (A); two cover sheets of stout paper or cloth (B); four notched wood cross braces to hold corner sticks when covers are stretched in place (C).

Glue together the ends of each cover sheet, overlapping 1½ inches (D). When ends are dry, stretch sheets over opposite ends of two corner sticks. Glue corner sticks on one narrow edge so that they will adhere to sheets (E). When sticks are nearly dry, mark the exact center of cover sheets between the two corner sticks. Glue remaining two corner sticks into position at these points and allow glue to dry thoroughly. When two adjacent corner sticks are lifted (F), assembly will swing down, forming a square (G).

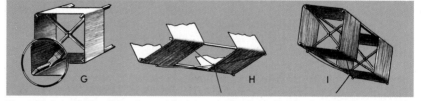

Next, bind notched edges of cross braces with string to prevent splitting. Fit notched braces diagonally over corner sticks and push into position. Tie braces where they cross (G). Now fasten a bridle (crossed strings) at adjacent corners and near opposite ends of the corner sticks on one side of kite (H). Attach the kite line at the point where the bridle strings cross (I), and the kite is ready to fly.

and as a means of relaxation.

## Types of Kites

There are many kinds of kites. Most of them are simple, lightweight wooden frames covered with paper or cloth and attached to a long line held in the hand. The best-known types in the United States are *plane surface* and *box* kites.

The simplest form of plane surface kite is the two-sticker illustrated on this page. A variation of the plane surface kite was invented in 1902 by Silas J. Conyne, an American. The Conyne kite has a rectangular vertical framework. A cross stick is attached near the top of this framework to form a six-sided kite.

The box kite was invented in the 1890's by Lawrence Hargrave, an Australian. Box kites are harder to make than plane surface kites, but many boys prefer them. In addition to the rectangular type shown in the diagram on the preceding page, box kites of other shapes can be built using the same general instructions.

The Eddy, or bow, kite was developed in the 1890's by William A. Eddy, an American, from a similar kite made in Malaya. The cross stick of the kite is bent in the form of a bow, and the kite string is attached so that the concave undersurface faces the wind when the kite is flown. The Eddy kite is similar in appearance to the two-stick plane surface kite. However, it does not need a tail.

## How Kites Fly

The principle that makes a kite fly also keeps an airplane aloft (*see* Airplane Flight Theory). An airplane creates its own wind by its speed through the air. On a calm day, running with a kite in an open space produces the same effect. The kite rises because currents of air, moving parallel to the ground, strike the face of the kite and force it backward. The best wind for kiteflying is a steady breeze. Stronger winds may drive the kite to the ground before it has a chance to rise to a safe height. The string holds the

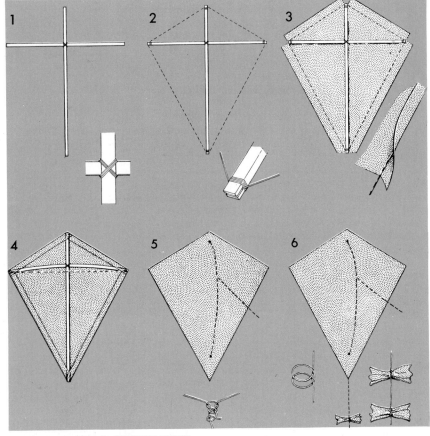

## HOW TO MAKE A SIMPLE KITE

1. Use two sticks, one about 30 inches long, the other a little shorter. Cross the sticks and tie them together with string. 2. Notch the ends of the sticks and bind near the notches to prevent splitting. Stretch a string through the notches to form a frame. 3. Cut strong tissue paper or light treated cloth to fit, leaving wide flaps. Fold the flaps over the frame and glue or staple down. 4. With another piece of string, draw the shorter stick in to form a bow. 5. Fasten a bridle to the long stick. Tie the kite string to the bridle with the knot shown. 6. For a tail, which helps keep the kite upright, tie strips of cloth to a string.

kite steady, with the face of the kite tipped forward, and the wind pushes up on the tipped face to lift the kite, much as a wedge pushed under an object lifts it. If the kite were not held by the kite string, it would be whirled away and would fall to the ground. The kite rises also because of the reduction in pressure on the upper surface that takes place because of the greater distance that is traveled by the airstream moving over it.

A kite should not be flown on rainy days, since a wet kite string is a conductor of electricity. Wire should never be used for a kite string, and the kite should never be flown where there are electric power lines. Many boys have been electrocuted when their kite strings touched live electric wires.

## Kiteflying as a Sport

In eastern Asia, kiteflying is an ancient custom. It may have begun as a religious rite. Some Asian kites are "musical." When the wind whistles through the reeds or bamboo tubes of the kites, the sound is thought to frighten away evil spirits.

In Korea men, women, and children fly kites during the first days of the New Year. In the Republic of China (Formosa), the ninth day of the ninth month—Kites' Day, or the Festival for Climbing Heights—is a holiday honoring kites. Chinese and Japanese kites are brightly colored and elaborately decorated. They may have the shapes of birds, insects, dragons, or various geometric forms.

Kiteflying is especially popular in Thailand, where the air is filled with a great variety of kites during the spring months. Here *kite fighting* is a major league sport. The All-Thailand championships are held in Bangkok every spring. In the Thai variety of kite fighting, each of the two contending teams seeks to bring the other team's kite to earth. The diamond-shaped *pakpao* is flown by one team, the star-shaped *chula* by the other. The superior speed and maneuverability of the smaller pakpaos often enable them to defeat the larger chulas.

Kite fighting is also popular in India. There the object is to cut the string of the opponent's kite, and the kite string is coated with ground glass. In South American kite fights, the kite frames may be armed with razor blades.

Kite competitions for boys and girls are held in many parts of the United States. Prizes may be given for the best kite of each type as well as to the winning participants in different age groups. Awards may also be presented for the kite with the strongest pull, the highest flight, or the most interesting design. Originality and quality of workmanship may also be used as prizewinning categories.

A comparatively recent pastime in the United States is *ski-kiting*. In this sport, water skiers cling to large, nonsinkable kites and are pulled behind speeding motorboats to heights ranging from 50 to 75 feet. The skier is able to maneuver the kite by shifting his body weight.

### Other Uses of Kites

Throughout history, kites have had many practical uses. In ancient times kites were employed to carry lines across streams or gorges as the first step in building bridges. In 1752 Benjamin Franklin drew electricity from a storm cloud with a kite and a key. Aerial photography by kite was achieved during the 1880's and was employed extensively in the Spanish-American War. In the early 1900's the United States Weather Bureau measured wind velocity, temperature, and humidity with instrument-carrying kites. During one of these operations—on May 5, 1910, at Mount Weather, Va.—the bureau achieved a record height for kites (23,835 feet) by using a train of ten kites.

During World War II the United States used kites that could be made to move like enemy airplanes as targets for antiaircraft gunnery practice. Life rafts on United States ships carried kites that served as radio transmission aerials, greatly simplifying searches for lost seamen and fliers. At this time man-carrying kites were launched from German submarines for observation purposes.

THESE ARTICLES ARE IN THE FACT-INDEX

Kitimat, B. C.
Kitksan
Kitson, Henry Hudson
Kittatinny Mountain
Kittinger, Joseph
  William, Jr.
Kittiwake
Kitt Peak National
  Observatory
Kittredge, George Lyman
Kittson, Norman Wolfred
Kitty Hawk, N. C.
Kivu, Lake

Kiwanis clubs
Kiwi
Kizilirmak
Kjelgaard, James Arthur
Klabund
Klagenfurt, Austria
Klamath Falls, Ore.
Klamath River
Klaproth, Martin Heinrich
Klassen, Elmer Theodore
Klaus, Karl Karlovich
Kléber, Jean Baptiste
Klebs, Edwin

**KLEE** (*klā*), **Paul** (1879–1940). One of the most inventive painters to emerge from the 20th-century rebellion against representational art was Paul Klee. Fantasy and striking use of color characterize his work.

Paul Klee was born on Dec. 18, 1879, near Bern, Switzerland. His parents, Hans and Ida Marie Frick Klee, were musicians. After attending school in Bern, he went to Munich,

The Bettmann Archive

Germany, where he studied art from 1898 to 1901. In 1906 he married Lily Stumpf.

Klee taught at the Weimar Bauhaus from 1921 to 1924 and at the Dessau Bauhaus from 1926 to 1930. When the Nazis came to power in 1933, they condemned his work. Klee then returned to Switzerland. He died at Muralto, near Locarno, on June 29, 1940.

Klee was one of the Blue Rider artists, who led Germany's experiments in nonobjective art before World War I. His early works were chiefly drawings and etchings. After a trip in 1914 to Tunisia, where he was deeply impressed by the colors he saw, he turned to painting. Later Klee contributed to the art theory of the Bauhaus school, which influenced industrial design, architecture, and painting. He developed pictorial themes in the way a composer develops musical themes. His output ranges from highly realistic portraiture to the abstractionism of such paintings as 'Villa R' and 'Fugue in Red'. Later works —'Fear' and 'Death and Fire', for example—reflect his concern with the approach of his death and of war. (For pictures, *see* Drawing; Painting.)

THESE ARTICLES ARE IN THE FACT-INDEX

Kleiber, Erich
Klein, Herbert G(eorge)
Kleist, Heinrich von
Klem, William J. (Bill)
Klemperer, Otto
Kleptomania

Klerk, Michel de
Kleve, West Germany
Klinger, Friedrich
  Maximilian von
Klinger, Max

**KLONDIKE.** The Klondike region, in the Yukon Territory of Canada, became famous for the great gold rush of 1897. It was named for the Klondike River, a tributary of the Yukon. In August 1896 gold was discovered in gravel along Bonanza Creek. News reached the United States in January 1897. More than 30,000 men and a small number of women made the difficult trip in the first winter. They had to carry their luggage on their backs, and many did not bring enough provisions. Some froze to death. (For picture, *see* McKinley, William.)

Peak gold production was reached in 1900. In Dawson, a trading center at the junction of the Klondike and the Yukon, are two national historic sites—a restored 1899 theater, the Palace Grand, and the SS *Keno*, an old riverboat housing a museum of the Gold Rush period. (*See also* Yukon Territory.)

THESE ARTICLES ARE IN THE FACT-INDEX

Klopstock, Friedrich Gottlieb
Kluck, Alexander von
Knapweed
Kneisel, Franz
Knelier, Sir Godfrey
Knickerbocker, Diedrich

Knight, Charles Robert
Knight, Eric Mowbray
Knight, Frank H(yneman)
Knight, John Shively
Knight, Dame Laura
Knight, William J.

# "In Days of Old, When Knights Were Bold"

**KNIGHTHOOD.** A knight in armor would present a very strange appearance on a modern battlefield. His prancing steed and coat of mail, the heavy iron helmet which covered his head, the shield which he carried on his left arm, his lance and shining sword—all these belong to bygone days and have little place among the swift airplanes, the rapid-shooting automatic weapons, and the scorching flame throwers of modern warfare.

Knighthood flourished before the time of guns and gunpowder when battles still were won by hand-to-hand conflicts of heavy-armored knights. Fighting was almost an everyday occurrence, and the common people generally could not protect themselves against an invading foe. In times of danger they fled to the castles or strongholds owned by the nobles. To obtain protection the poorer folk became the serfs or villeins of their powerful neighbors, and those in turn were the vassals of those still more powerful. The institution of knighthood was part of this feudal system.

## Training of a Knight

The education of a knight began at the age of seven, when he was taken from his home and sent to the castle of some famous nobleman, perhaps his father's lord. Here he served the lord and lady as a page until he was 14 years old. It was his duty, and he esteemed it a privilege, to accompany them at all times. He waited on them at table and went with them to the chase. He received religious instruction from the chaplain and training in arms from the squires. He was taught by his mistress and her ladies to honor and protect all women. He also learned to sing and to play the lute, to hunt and to hawk. But above all else he learned to ride a horse.

At the age of 14, he became a squire. He now learned to handle sword and lance and to bear the weight of the heavy armor. In addition to his other duties, he had now to carve at table and to accompany his knight to war. He assisted him in putting on the heavy armor. He saw to it that the knightly sword as well as other arms were polished until they shone. He stood by to give aid in conflict should his lord be overmatched; to lend his horse should the master lose his own. It was the squire who raised his knight when he fell and who bore his body away if he were wounded or killed in battle.

In the Prologue to the 'Canterbury Tales' there is this beautiful description of a squire: "His clothes were embroidered red and white, as it were a meadow of fresh flowers. All the day he was singing or playing upon a lute, he was as fresh as the Month of May. His coat was short, with long wide sleeves.

Well could he sit a horse and ride, make songs, joust and dance, draw and write. He loved so ardently that at nighttime he slept no more than a nightingale. He was courteous, modest, and helpful, and carved before his master at table."

## The Knighting Ceremony

At the age of 21, if he had acquitted himself well as page and squire, the young man was made a knight. This was an occasion of elaborate ceremony and solemn vows. After a purification bath, the candidate for knighthood knelt or stood all night in prayer before the altar on which lay the precious armor he would don on the morrow. In the morning there was a religious ritual, with perhaps a sermon on the knight's duty to protect the weak, to right wrongs, and to honor women. Then in the courtyard in the presence of the assembled knights

**EQUIPPING THE YOUNG KNIGHT FOR ADVENTURE**

In a few days this young squire will be "knighted" with elaborate ceremonies. Here he is seen trying on the honored armor of a knight while his family watches him proudly. The armorer is fitting the metal "garments" with the aid of hammer and pincers.

and fair ladies, a knight's armor was buckled on, piece by piece, a sword was girded about his waist, and spurs were attached to the candidate's feet. He then knelt to receive the accolade. This was a blow upon the neck or shoulder, given by the officiating lord or knight with his fist or with the flat of a sword. As he gave it he said, "In the name of God and St. Michael and St. George, I dub thee knight; be brave and loyal." The ceremony was followed by exhibitions of the young knight's skill in arms.

Sometimes on the occasion of a knighting, the lord at whose castle the ceremony took place gave a tournament. This was often a very gorgeous and extravagant entertainment. Knights for miles around were invited to come and take part, while many persons of distinction came to see the events. Sometimes the visitors came in such numbers that the lodgings of the castle were filled and tents were put up to accommodate the later arrivals. Each knight's shield with its coat of arms served as a sort of doorplate to the passersby, who when they saw a familiar device displayed would say, "Sir Percival is within this tent."

In the morning, after attending mass, the knights would go to the tourney field, or lists. Here the combats or jousts between the knights were fought. Sometimes two knights fought alone, sometimes whole companies met in combat. When all were

assembled, the heralds announced the names of the contestants, and the new knight looked upon the most brilliant scene that the times had to offer. Along the sides of the field were handsome pavilions filled with beautiful ladies, lighthearted young pages, and jewel-bedecked nobles. The knights were resplendent in shining armor, with swords and golden spurs giving back the sunlight. Banners fluttered, and here and there gleamed gorgeous cloth of gold.

The combats which took place in this gay setting were not gentle ones. The points of the weapons, to be sure, were usually encased in blocks of wood to make the encounter less dangerous, but the sport was so rough and the knights jousted in such earnest that many were wounded and some were killed. About each knight's helmet was tied the favor his lady had given him, and he fought to do her honor quite as much as to do himself credit. The joust was attended by much excitement, with the blowing of trumpets, the clash of steel, the shouts of heralds, and the applause of the spectators. It continued until one or the other of the knights was overcome. The defeated knight then yielded his horse and armor to his adversary and was assisted from the field by the squires.

Sometimes a tournament lasted for several days, feasting, dancing, and hawking filling the hours not given to fighting. Hawking was a sport indulged in by the ladies and the squires as well as by the knights.

Almost every lady had her own hawk or falcon which when unhooded was trained to rise into the air and attack game birds. (*See also* Hawk.)

Often during the festivities of a tournament a large pie was baked and live birds concealed inside. Then in the great hall the pie was opened, the birds flew about, and the falcons were loosed at them. This was considered great sport and has been immortalized in the nursery rhyme—

Sing a song of sixpence, pocket full of rye,
Four and twenty blackbirds baked in a pie;
When the pie was opened, the birds began to sing;
Wasn't that a dainty dish to set before a king?

### Into the Great World of Adventure

After the festivities attending the conferring of knighthood, the young knight was free to go where he pleased. Usually he rode forth in quest of adventure, armor on his back, his spurs on his heels, and with sword, shield, and lance ready to hand. As a knight-errant he sought a fair maiden in need of a champion or a strange knight with whom to joust. Sometimes he stationed himself at a bridge or crossroad to challenge to combat any knight who happened by. He was usually sure of hospitality at any castle to which he came. After a time he might return to his father's castle or join the following of some great lord or become one of the multitude of crusaders who journeyed to rescue the Holy Sepulcher. Whenever or however he went he took with him the three watchwords of a knight: Religion, Honor, Courtesy. The ideal knight is thus described by the poet Chaucer: "And though he was valorous, he was prudent and as meek as a maid of his bearing. In all his life he never yet spake discourteously but was truly a perfect gentle knight." Sometimes, of course, knights were false to those high ideals.

With the rise of the longbow and the crossbow carrying wounds or death from a distance, and the invention of gunpowder and cannon rendering useless the feudal castle, the knight in armor passed out of existence. Knighthood then came to be merely a title of honor conferred for valuable service to the king or state, with the title "Sir" as its only distinction. In recent times in England, it has been conferred on eminent scholars, lawyers, physicians, artists, and civil officers, as well as on soldiers. The United Kingdom has a number of honorary orders of knighthood. Among these are the Garter, the Thistle, St. Patrick, the Bath, St. Michael and St. George, and the British Empire. (*See also* Armor; Castle; Feudalism.)

**KNIGHTS OF COLUMBUS.** This great Roman Catholic fraternal organization was founded in New Haven, Conn., in 1882 by a Catholic priest, Michael J. McGivney. Its purpose is to provide insurance for its members, to assist those who are sick and disabled, and to promote education.

The association now has a branch in every state, in every Canadian province, and in Cuba, Puerto Rico,

the Philippines, and the Canal Zone. The total membership is about half a million. It is governed by a supreme council, elected by the various state councils. During World War I it contributed notably to welfare work among the soldiers at home and overseas. It has since aided employment and contributed to relief funds.

---

THESE ARTICLES ARE IN THE FACT-INDEX
**Knights of St. Gregory**
**Knights Templar**
**Kniphofia**

---

**KNITTING MACHINES.** Knitting is a way of looping yarn so that the loops interconnect to form a fabric. Like many other old handicrafts, it is now an important machine industry.

Hand knitting is done with a single yarn looped back and forth, or around and around, on two or more needles. The knitter catches the yarn with a needle to form new loops as she transfers rows of loops from one needle to another. Machine knitting is done with many needles, and these look more like hooks than like needles. There may be one yarn or many yarns. Yet the principle is the same as in hand knitting; that is, the yarn is *looped* into a fabric.

Because of its looped construction, knitted material is elastic and pliable. It is especially suitable for garments in which both fit and comfort are important. Stockings, sweaters, underwear, and gloves are examples. Knitted material has other advantages. It has many little air pockets. These make it warm, since air pockets are a form of insulation. They also make it absorbent and light in weight. Knitted cloth does not wrinkle easily and sometimes does not have to be ironed after washing.

Little is known about the early history of knitting. Prehistoric people may have looped fibers into fishnets by a crude sort of hand knitting. Whatever method they used was gradually improved through the ages. By the 15th century hand-knit garments were common in Western Europe.

William Lee, a young curate of Nottinghamshire, England, made the first knitting machine in 1589. It knit stockings flat, and they had to be sewed up the back. There was a needle for every loop across the width of the stocking, eight needles to the inch. These were so arranged that they formed and gave off loops alternately.

Lee presented a pair of wool stockings to Queen Elizabeth I and asked for a patent on his machine. She asked him to try to make silk stockings, perhaps because she was afraid the new machine would take work from thousands of her subjects who made their living by hand knitting wool stockings.

In 1598 Lee produced a pair of silk stockings for Elizabeth on a machine with 20 needles to the inch. Although pleased, the queen refused to grant him a patent. He then inaugurated manufacturing operations in France at the invitation of King Henry IV.

By courtesy of American Textile Manufacturers Institute, Inc.

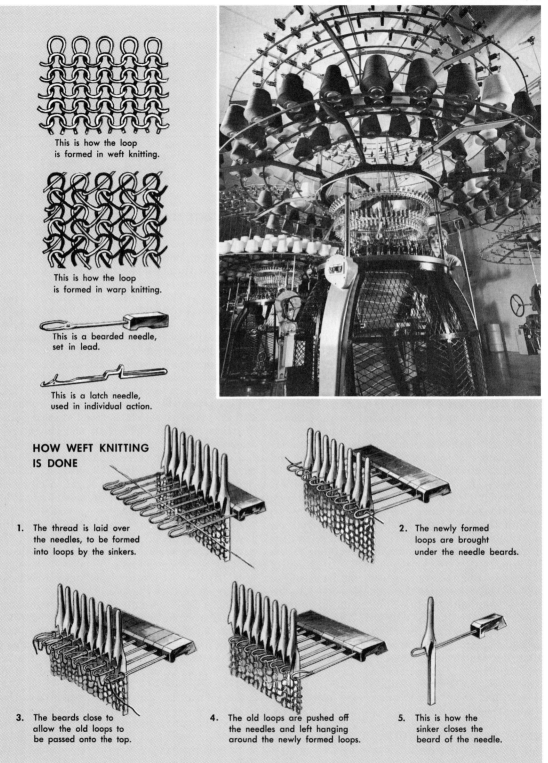

This is how the loop
is formed in weft knitting.

This is how the loop
is formed in warp knitting.

This is a bearded needle,
set in lead.

This is a latch needle,
used in individual action.

## HOW WEFT KNITTING IS DONE

1. The thread is laid over
the needles, to be formed
into loops by the sinkers.

2. The newly formed
loops are brought
under the needle beards.

3. The beards close to
allow the old loops to
be passed onto the top.

4. The old loops are pushed off
the needles and left hanging
around the newly formed loops.

5. This is how the
sinker closes the
beard of the needle.

# A KNITTING MACHINE AND HOW IT WORKS

The photograph (upper right) shows a circular machine knitting tubular fabric. The drawings at the left show plain weft knitting (top), warp knitting, and two kinds of needles. The drawings below show weft knitting. After the thread, or yarn, has been laid over the needles (1) the sinkers dip down to form loops in the thread. With the same movement these loops are pushed under the needle beards as shown (2) and the beards are closed. As the sinkers rise again (3) the old loops are ready to slide over the new ones (4) and complete the row. No. 5 shows detail of operation.

Not long after Queen Elizabeth's death, Lee's knitting machine was reintroduced into England.

Knitting machines did not come into widespread use, however, until the mid-18th century. At that time flatbed machines modeled after Lee's were developed. Early in the 19th century circular knitting machines appeared. For a time these tended to displace the flatbed type.

## Modern Knitting Machines

Today manufacturers make tubular fabrics and seamless stockings and socks on circular machines. Flat fabrics and flat-shaped pieces, such as those that are made up into sweaters, gloves, and full-fashioned hosiery, are produced on flatbed machines.

All knitting machines, whether circular or flatbed, have a needle for every loop. The needles are moved up and down by cams or similar devices. Their hook-like heads close as they pull newly forming loops through other loops that are being slipped off to form the body of the fabric or the garment.

## Weft Knitting and Warp Knitting

The two basic types of machine knitting are *weft knitting*—also known as *filler knitting*—and *warp knitting*. In weft knitting, one yarn travels around and around if the machine is circular, back and forth if the machine is flat. Since weft knitting produces a more elastic fabric than does warp knitting, it is used to make stockings, sweaters, and other garments. If a thread in a weft-knit garment breaks, a "run," or "ladder," results.

Warp knitting, the more recent of the two methods, is generally faster than weft knitting and can produce a greater variety of patterns. It has been slow to develop, however, because it is costlier.

As many yarns are used in warp knitting as there are loops in the width of the fabric. These yarns travel up in loops, zigzagging so that loops directly above one another are formed by different yarns. Thus the loops are all interconnected.

Warp knits are firmer than weft knits and therefore less likely to sag—an advantage for some purposes. They are also practically runproof. Filament yarns, particularly viscose rayon, nylon, and rayon acetate, are especially well suited to warp knitting. Warp knitting is often used to make fabrics rather than finished articles. (*See also* Fabrics.)

**KNIVES, FORKS, AND SPOONS.** The first tools a child learns to handle are his eating utensils—knives, forks, and spoons. Although these tools are made in many forms and serve many purposes, it is for eating that they are most useful to modern man.

The knife was the first eating utensil. During the Stone Age, knives were made of flint, slate, or bone, and the same knife with which animals were killed and skinned was used in eating them. Bronze Age knives have been found in Europe. The ancient Greeks and Romans ate with copper and iron knives as well as with bronze knives.

The spoon, invented after the knife, was the first utensil to be developed primarily for eating. Seashells may have served as the first spoons, but the first man-made spoons were of clay. Ornately carved wooden, ivory, and stone spoons have been found in the tombs of ancient Egypt. Bronze and silver spoons were made in ancient Greece and Rome.

Only in modern times has the fork been used widely as an eating utensil. The first European forks had two prongs, were made of iron, bone, or hardwood, and were used only in cooking. They were probably introduced from the Orient in the 11th century, but their use as flatware spread slowly. In the 17th century they were still regarded as a curiosity.

## Stainless Steel and Other "Silverware"

Regardless of their composition, knives, forks, and spoons are generally called *silverware*. Strictly speaking, however, this term applies only to articles made of or plated with silver. *Flatware* and *tableware* are other common designations for eating utensils.

*Stainless steel*, an alloy developed early in the 20th century, is the material most widely used for tableware. Stainless steel tableware has a chromium content of 14 to 18 percent and a nickel content of 4 to 8 percent—the higher the chromium and nickel content, the better the tableware. As the name implies, stainless steel is very resistant to rust and discoloration. (*See also* Alloys.)

*Silver plate* is silverware with a layer of pure silver over a core of base metal. The plating is applied by electrolysis (*see* Electroplating).

*Sterling* silverware is $92\frac{1}{2}$ percent silver combined with $7\frac{1}{2}$ percent copper or other metal—a ratio authorized by Queen Elizabeth I of England. The alloy is much harder and more durable than pure silver. (*See also* Silver.)

## Manufacture

The manufacture of knives, forks, and spoons has become highly mechanized. Refined metal in the form of ingots is heated, rolled, and stamped into rough blanks. The blanks are rolled again, lengthwise as well as crosswise, until the desired thickness is achieved. Dies stamp out the bowls of spoons and the prongs of forks. Abrasive belts smooth and taper edges. The handles and blades of some knives are made separately, then joined.

In the Middle Ages, Sheffield, England; Solingen, Germany; and Thiers, France, began to specialize in the production of knives, forks, and spoons. Today these same cities are still leading producers of flatware. Other important manufacturing centers are located in Sweden, Italy, and the United States. Massachusetts, Connecticut, and Rhode Island are the chief producing states.

---

THIS ARTICLE IS IN THE FACT-INDEX
**Knopf, Alfred A(braham)**

---

# KNOTS, HITCHES, AND SPLICES

**KNOTS, HITCHES, AND SPLICES.** The ability to tie knots is a skill that can prove valuable to everyone. Children learn at an early age that they must tie a good knot in their shoelaces to keep shoes firmly on their feet. They also discover that if such a knot is made properly, it can be untied with only a little effort.

A *knot*, correctly made, remains secure but may be easily untied. A *hitch* is a knot that is less secure and is usually looped around a stationary object. A *splice* is a permanent knot formed by interweaving the strands of a single rope or of two ropes.

The professions and trades in which knots are used are many and varied. The surgeon must be able to tie knots deep within an incision. The rancher, fisherman, and seaman must all know many good knots and how to apply them to best advantage.

Many types of knots have been employed for decorative purposes. Some have served as badges in heraldry. The carrick bend—a knot now used for tying two ropes together—was the heraldic badge of Hereward Wake, a Saxon leader of the 11th century.

Knot-making was a highly developed skill long before the Christian era. Stone Age men made fishnets by knotting together strands of fiber. The sailors of ancient Egypt were proficient knot makers. Pottery and sculpture reveal that the ancient Greeks were familiar with the square knot.

## KNOTS

Some knots are especially valuable because of the speed with which they can be made. The best, however, are those that hold firmly without slipping, yet do not bind so tightly that they are difficult to untie. The long portion of a rope, about which the loose end is woven, is called the *standing part*. A loop of rope is termed a *bight*.

**Overhand Knot.** The simplest of all knots is the *overhand*, or *thumb*, *knot*. Although usually a part of other, more complex, knots, it may also be employed by itself, to provide a handhold on a rope, to prevent a rope from raveling, and to keep a rope end from running through a pulley or a sewing thread from pulling through cloth. The overhand knot is made by holding the standing part in one hand, forming a closed loop with the free end, and drawing the end around and through the loop.

**OVERHAND KNOT**

**SQUARE KNOT**

**SHEET BEND**

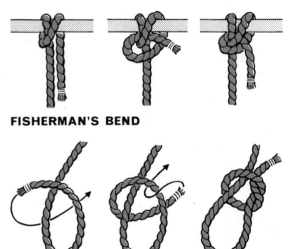

**FISHERMAN'S BEND**

**SLIPKNOT**

**Square Knot.** The knot that is most commonly used for fastening ropes or strings together is the *square knot*, also known as the *sailor's*, or *reef*, *knot*. Shoelaces, for example, are customarily tied by means of the square knot. The square knot is always used by sailors in *reefing* a sail, that is, shortening a sail by tying back a portion. Made with ropes of the same thickness, the square knot is extremely reliable and easy to untie. It is less reliable if it is made with ropes of different thicknesses. Even if the ropes are stiff and wet, they can be loosened without difficulty by pushing the free ends back against the knot, then completely untied by pulling out the loops—as one does when untying shoelaces.

To tie a square knot the loose ends of two ropes are passed around each other once and then again in such a way that the standing part and the end of each rope come out on the same side of the loop.

If the standing parts and the ends of the ropes are brought out on opposite sides of the loop, the result is a *granny*, or *lubber's*, *knot*. The granny knot is unreliable, for it slips easily and gives way under strain.

**Sheet Bend.** The term *bend* is generally applied to knots that connect two ropes or that connect one rope with a solid object. The *sheet bend*, or *weaver's knot*, is one of the most useful of these. Weavers tie ends of thread together with this knot because it passes smoothly through the needle. The sheet bend is begun like the square knot, but one of the ends is then turned back under itself.

**Fisherman's Bend.** The *fisherman's*, or *anchor, bend* is commonly used by sailors to fasten a rope to a buoy or an anchor ring. The rope is looped twice around the securing object, the second loop passing over the first. The end is looped again, this time passing through the first two loops. The knot is frequently made secure by binding the end with string against the standing part.

**Slipknot.** One of the easiest knots to tie is the *slipknot*, or *running knot*. It is made by first forming a bight, then making an overhand knot around the standing part. The slipknot is not strong and will give under strain. It frequently serves a temporary purpose.

**Bowline.** One of the most useful of all knots, the *bowline* is sometimes called the "king of knots." It is quickly and easily tied and will never slip. The bowline is tied by forming a loop in the standing part and passing the end through this loop, around the standing part above it, then back through the loop. The *bowline on a bight* is formed with a length of rope that has been doubled back upon itself. It is begun in the same way as the bowline; but after being passed through the loop, the bight is spread open and the parts of the knot already formed are pulled through it. The bowline on a bight is used to support a person working along the side of a ship or along other steep worksites.

## HITCHES

Usually a hitch is formed around a solid object, such as a spar, post, or ring. Some types of hitches work loose by themselves if the standing part is not subjected to a constant strain.

**Clove Hitch.** Perhaps the most widely used of the hitches is the *clove*, or *ratline, hitch*. It is especially

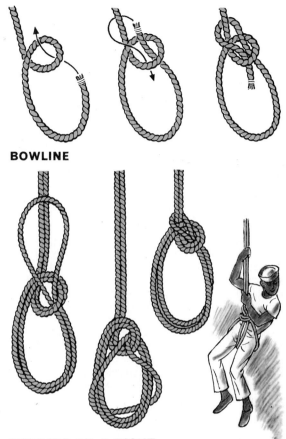

**BOWLINE**

**BOWLINE ON A BIGHT**

practical for making a rope fast to a pole or similar object. The end is passed over the object twice, the second loop crossing back over the standing part; it is then pulled through the inside of the loop so that it lies along the standing part.

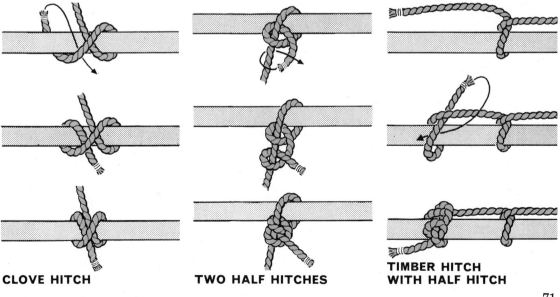

**CLOVE HITCH**    **TWO HALF HITCHES**    **TIMBER HITCH WITH HALF HITCH**

**Half Hitch.** A basic segment of many knots is the *half hitch*. This is a simple loop around a pole or other stationary object, with the end and the standing part in tension against each other. Two half hitches—providing considerably more security than a single half hitch—are commonly used for such purposes as tying up a boat to a dock post.

**Timber Hitch.** The *timber hitch* is often used in towing logs or other cylindrical objects. These can be towed lengthwise by adding one or more half hitches to the timber hitch. The timber hitch is formed by making a half hitch and then winding the end around the loop.

**Sheepshank.** The *sheepshank* is the most practical knot for shortening a rope without cutting it. The rope is first folded back and forth along its length. A clove hitch is then made at each end to secure the folds.

**Figure Eight Halter Hitch.** Among the most valuable of the hitches are the *halter hitches*, which are customarily employed to fasten the halters of horses and cows to posts and hitching rings. The *figure eight halter hitch* has a special advantage—it can be untied quickly. To tie a figure eight halter hitch, the end is passed through a hitching ring or a similar secure object, then turned against itself to form a closed loop; the remaining part of the end is passed around the standing part and doubled to form a bight; the bight is then drawn through the first loop, and the hitch is tightened by pulling on the standing part. It is easily untied by pulling on the end of the rope. However, an animal that has been restrained by means of this hitch cannot free itself, no matter how hard it struggles.

**SHEEPSHANK**

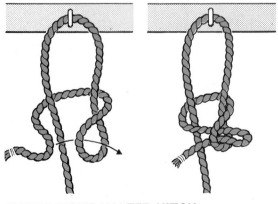

**FIGURE EIGHT HALTER HITCH**

**SHORT SPLICE**

## SPLICES

A splice is used to connect the ends of two ropes or to form a loop at the end of a rope. Splices are considerably stronger than knots, but they do not have the advantage of being easily undone. Wire rope is always repaired by splicing, since it is too stiff for the satisfactory formation of knots.

**Short Splice.** The simplest type of splice is the *short splice*, in which the strands of two ropes are *unlaid*, or untwisted, to a convenient length and then interwoven to form one rope. When the strands have been untwisted, the ropes are placed end to end with the strands spread out. The ropes may be temporarily tied into this position with a string. Each strand of one rope is then laced under one strand and over a second strand of the other. This process is repeated until the unlaid portions of both ropes have been completely interwoven. The resulting splice is somewhat bulkier than the rest of the rope, since it contains twice as many strands.

**Eye Splice.** The *eye splice* is made in the same way as the short splice. In the eye splice, however, the end of a single rope is woven back into itself, to form a loop, or eye.

In splicing Manila rope, the openings between strands are made with a pointed wooden *fid*. For wire rope, a metal or metal-tipped *marlinespike* is used. The art of working with fiber and wire rope is known as *marlinespike seamanship*. (*See also* Rope and Twine; Fishing.)

**EYE SPLICE**

THESE ARTICLES ARE IN THE FACT-INDEX

| | |
|---|---|
| Knotweed | Knox, Frank |
| Knowland, William F(ife) | Knox, Henry |
| Knowles, Lucius James | |

**KNOX, John** (1505?–1572). The leader of the Protestant Reformation in Scotland was John Knox. For years he lived in exile or was hunted as an outlaw at home. Courageous and dogmatic, he finally established Presbyterianism as Scotland's national church.

Little is known of John Knox's early life. Probably he was born at Giffordgate in Haddington. He may have entered Glasgow University but was never graduated. He received minor orders in the Roman Catholic church; then he turned to tutoring.

## A Call to Preach

Knox was a tutor when he became involved in church reform in 1546. At the time, Scotland was a Catholic nation, but many were angry at church abuses. Knox became a follower of George Wishart, a Lutheran reformer. When Cardinal Beaton had Wishart burned as a heretic, a mob killed the cardinal and occupied his castle. Knox joined the castle garrison and began teaching the gospel. Soon the leaders of the revolutionaries asked him to act as their preacher.

In July 1547 the Catholics regained the castle with French help, and the defenders were made French galley slaves. In February 1549 Knox was released. For a time he preached in England and Germany. Later he was pastor of an English congregation in Geneva, Switzerland. There he became a student of the Protestant leader John Calvin (*see* Calvin).

By 1559 Scotland was ready for the new doctrine. Knox returned home and his preaching soon roused the people to wreck churches and monasteries. In 1560 the Scottish Parliament established Presbyterianism as the national faith. Thereafter Knox devoted himself to strengthening the new church. One of his chief targets was Mary Stuart Catholic ruler of Scotland. In 1567 she was deposed. Knox then knew his church was safe. (*See also* Mary, Queen of Scots.)

John Knox married when he was about 48 and had two sons. Following the death of his first wife he remarried at 59 and had three daughters. Knox died in Edinburgh on Nov. 24, 1572.

THESE ARTICLES ARE IN THE FACT-INDEX

Knox, John Jay
Knox, Philander Chase
Knox College

**KNOXVILLE, Tenn.** The industrial city of Knoxville prospers because of the nearness of raw materials and because it is the center for a vast recreational area. Burley and other tobaccos are grown in the fertile Tennessee Valley. Marble is quarried and coal mined nearby. About 20 miles west is Oak Ridge, an atomic research and production center. Great Smoky Mountains National Park begins 35 miles southeast. Close by are beautiful lakes, formed by the dams of the Tennessee Valley Authority.

Knoxville is located in east-central Tennessee, just four miles below the point where the Holston and French Broad rivers join to form the Tennessee River. The city is a wholesale- and retail-trade center for a large area and the headquarters for the Tennessee Valley Authority (*see* Tennessee Valley Authority). Great tobacco auctions are held in Knoxville from December to March. The city's industries produce textiles and clothing; machinery and other metal goods; processed foods; stone, glass, and clay products; chemicals; plastics; and wooden articles. Knoxville is host to many conventions. The Tennessee Valley Agricultural and Industrial Fair is held annually in September. The University of Tennessee and Knoxville College are here. The Blount Mansion, built in 1792, is now a museum. The Lawson McGhee Library houses the McClung historical collection.

Knoxville's first settler, James White, built a log fort on the site in 1786. The town was named for Gen. Henry Knox, President Washington's secretary of war. From 1792 to 1796 it was the capital of the Territory South of the River Ohio and then of the state until 1812. Knoxville's first rail line, from Chattanooga, reached the town in 1855. Knoxville gained population steadily after the Civil War and rapidly in the 1900's.

### HUB OF INDUSTRY AND RECREATION
Downtown Knoxville, on the far side of the Tennessee River, serves a 42-county primary trade area in Tennessee.

By courtesy of the Greater Knoxville Chamber of Commerce

Water, gas, and electricity supplies are municipally owned. In 1948 the city adopted the mayor-council form of government. (*See also* Tennessee.) Population (1980 census), 175,030.

THESE ARTICLES ARE IN THE FACT-INDEX

Knoxville College
Knubel, Frederick Hermann
Knudsen, William S(ignius)
Koa

Kobe, Japan
Koberger, Anton
Koch, Karl
Koch, Lauge

**KOCH, Robert** (1843–1910). A German country doctor helped raise the study of microbes to the modern science of bacteriology. By painstaking laboratory research, Robert Koch at last demonstrated how specific microbes cause specific diseases.

Robert Koch was born on Dec. 11, 1843, in Clausthal, a mining town in the Harz Mountains. He was a thin, wiry boy. He studied geology; made collections of minerals, plants, and small animals; and dreamed of being a great explorer. In 1862 he entered the university at Göttingen and began the study of medicine. He hoped to explore as an expedition doctor. After graduation, Koch interned at a hospital for the insane in Hamburg. In Hamburg he met and married Emmy Fraatz. Emmy wanted a safe, settled life. So he buried his dreams and became a country doctor.

Koch began studying bits of matter through a magnifying glass. He wanted a microscope. By much scrimping, Emmy managed to buy one for his 28th birthday. Koch began his study of anthrax. He identified and raised cultures of anthrax microbes. With these cultures he gave the disease to well animals. His work took four years. When he brought the results before the scientists of the University of Breslau, his proofs—the first of their kind—were undeniable.

In 1880 Koch became a member of the National Health Department. In 1882 he isolated the tubercle bacillus. The next year he became head of a commission to study cholera in Egypt and India. He announced the discovery of the cholera microbe in 1883.

Germany acclaimed him. The spare, bearded little man was given $25,000 and made director of a great institute to pursue his researches. In 1890 he announced tuberculin. This substance, at first wrongly thought to be a cure for tuberculosis, is now widely used to detect the presence of the disease. He followed this discovery with other investigations of tuberculosis. Koch went on to study tropical diseases in East and West Africa. In 1905 he was awarded the Nobel prize in medicine. Koch died of a heart attack on May 28, 1910.

THESE ARTICLES ARE IN THE FACT-INDEX

Kochanowski, Jan
Kocher, Emil Theodor
Kochi, Japan
Kochia
Kodály, Zoltán
Kodiak Island
Kodok, Sudan
Koerner, Theodor
Koestler, Arthur
Koffka, Kurt
Koga, Mineichi
Köhler, Wolfgang
Koiso, Kuniaki
Kokomo, Ind.
Kokoschka, Oskar
Kola nut
Kola Peninsula
Kolbe, Adolf Wilhelm Hermann

Kolbe, Georg
Kolin, Czechoslovakia
Kollwitz, Käthe
Kol Nidre
Koltsov, Alexis Vasilevich
Komárno, Czechoslovakia
Komodo Island
Kondylis, George
Konev, Ivan Stepanovich
Konigsburg, Elaine L.
Konoye, Fumimaro, Prince
Konstanz, West Germany
Konti, Isidore
Konya, Turkey
Koo, V(i) K(yuin) Wellington
Kootenay River

**KORAN.** On the Koran, the sacred book of the Moslems, is based the religion of more than 400 million people. The name means "the reading," or the book to be read. The Koran is used in public worship, is the chief textbook in Mohammedan schools, and is the standard of all practice for devout Moslems.

The Koran is regarded by the Moslems ("the faithful") as the word of God revealed to the prophet Mohammed, through the angel Gabriel. Its various parts were written down from the prophet's lips, gathered together, copied, and arranged roughly in the order of length regardless of content. Thus the book has "neither beginning, middle, nor end."

The Koran, which is written in Arabic, is about as long as the New Testament and is divided into 114 *suras*, or chapters. Each of these begins, "In the name of God, the merciful and compassionate." The book consists of history, legends, prophecies, moral precepts, and laws. The histories are chiefly about Old Testament characters, and many of the doctrines and laws are the same as those of Judaism or of Christianity. Moses, Jesus, and Mohammed are named as the greatest of the prophets sent by God to lead mankind in the path of truth.

The fundamental doctrine is the oneness of God, expressed in the simple statement, "There is no God but God (Allah)"; and submission to His will (Islam) is the highest virtue. Much emphasis is laid also on the Last Judgment, when everyone shall receive reward or punishment for his deeds. The faithful Moslem is commanded to pray five times a day, turning his face toward Mecca, to fast at stated times, to give alms, and to make at least one pilgrimage in his lifetime to Mecca, the sacred city. The civil and criminal laws of Islam are based on the teachings of the Koran. (*See also* Islam; Mohammed and Mohammedanism.)

THIS ARTICLE IS IN THE FACT-INDEX
**Kordofan, Republic of the Sudan**

A link with Korea's past, the ancient South Gate of Seoul
stands in the new city that has risen from the ruins of war.

# KOREA

**KOREA.** On a mountainous peninsula jutting southward from the eastern Asian mainland is Korea, the historic land bridge and buffer between China and Japan. Today Korea is a land divided into a Communist north and a non-Communist south. It is torn by rival political and economic systems and by bitterness stemming from the Korean War. However, the people of both North Korea and South Korea are still united by a common cultural heritage and continue to regard themselves as a single nation.

The two halves of Korea have been rebuilt from the devastation of the Korean War. But they still suffer from huge military expenditures, dependence on foreign aid, and economies unbalanced by the partition of Korea after World War II. In addition new difficulties are being created by the growing conflicts between their traditional and modern ways of life.

Most of Korea lies on the Korean peninsula, between the Sea of Japan on the east and the Yellow Sea on the west. South Korea occupies the southern

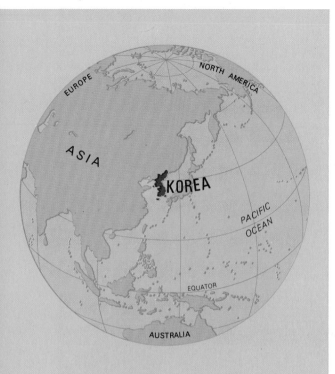

part of the peninsula, while North Korea spreads north and northeast beyond the peninsula's base. Between them is the demilitarized zone, set up by the truce ending the Korean War in 1953. It runs from about 40 miles north of the 38th parallel on the east to about 20 miles south on the west. Korea extends more than 600 miles from northeast to southwest. The Korean peninsula is about 150 miles wide.

South Korea's only land border, on the north, is with North Korea. North Korea is bounded by South Korea on the south, by China on the northwest. It touches the Soviet Union in the extreme northeast. The main islands of Japan lie 120 miles southeast of the South Korean coast across the Korea Strait.

Korea is about the size of Utah. Its total area is 85,000 square miles—47,000 in the north, 38,000 in the south. Korea's total population is more than 54 million—37 million in the south, 17 million in the north. South Korea is one of the world's most densely populated countries. Its capital, Seoul, is the largest city in Korea. Pyongyang is the largest city and the capital of North Korea.

**Preview**

The article Korea is divided into the following sections:

Introduction . . . . . . . . . . . . . . . . .K-75–75a
People. . . . . . . . . . . . . . . . . . . . . .K-75b–d
Government . . . . . . . . . . . . . . . . . .K-75e–f
Economy . . . . . . . . . . . . . . . . . . .K-75g–76a
Culture . . . . . . . . . . . . . . . . . . . . .K-76b–c
Natural Features . . . . . . . . . . . . . .K-76d–e
History. . . . . . . . . . . . . . . . . . . . . .K-76f–77a
Fact Summary . . . . . . . . . . . . . . . .K-77b
Reference-Outline; Bibliography. . .K-77c
Political Map . . . . . . . . . . . . . . . . .K-77d–e

Included in the article are the following special features: "A Tour of Korea," K-76a; "Korea—North vs. South," K-76h; "Notable Events in Korea's History," K-77a.

At the end of the sections "People," "Government," "Economy," "Culture," "Natural Features," and "History" are two study aids—"Words to Remember" and "Questions to Think About."

**Facts About Korea**

**Official Name:** South Korea—Republic of Korea (*Taehan Minguk*); North Korea—Democratic People's Republic of Korea (*Choson Minjujuui Inmin Konghwaguk*).

**Capital and Largest City:** South Korea—Seoul; North Korea—Pyongyang.

**Population (1978 estimate):** South Korea—37,018,932; North Korea—17,078,000.

**Area (in square miles):** Korea—84,969 (South Korea—38,169; North Korea—46,800, including demilitarized zone—487).

**Population Density (1978):** Korea—637 persons per square mile (South Korea—955; North Korea—356).

**Form of Government:** South Korea—Republic; North Korea—People's Republic.

**Flag:** *See* Flags of the World.

**Extent:** Northeast to southwest—635 miles.

**Highest Elevation:** Mount Paektu, 9,003 feet.

**Climate:** Warm, moist summers; cool to cold winters.

**National Anthem:** South Korea—*Aegug-ga*.

**Monetary Unit:** Won—South Korea ($.0021, or 484 per dollar); North Korea ($1.14, or 0.88 per dollar).

**Major Language:** Korean.

**Major Religions:** Buddhism, Christianity.

**Chief Products:** Rice, barley, corn, millet, soybeans, fish, graphite, magnesite, tungsten, iron ore, coal, textiles, food products, iron and steel.

The following contributors and consultants assisted in the preparation of this article: Byong-uk Chung, Professor of Korean Literature, Seoul National University; Earle Ernst, Senior Professor and Chairman, Department of Drama and Theatre, University of Hawaii; John D. Eyre, Professor of Geography, University of North Carolina; Pyong-choon Hahm, Professor of Law, Yonsei University; William E. Henthorn, Professor, Department of Oriental Studies, Princeton University; Jun-yop Kim, Professor of History, Korea University; Kyung-sung Kim, Professor of Geography, Seoul National University; Kwang-rin Lee, Professor of History, Sogang University; John Roderick, Foreign Correspondent; Jack Sewell, Curator of Oriental Art, The Art Institute of Chicago; Suk-kee Yoh, Professor of English Literature, Korea University.

# KOREA —People

## THE PEOPLE OF KOREA

The Koreans are a culturally and racially homogeneous people. They have a common language and, like the Chinese and the Japanese, are of Mongoloid stock.

Korea's population from the 17th to the late 19th centuries has been estimated at between 7 and 10 million. The first modern census, taken in 1925, recorded 19,020,000 inhabitants. By the 1975 census, South Korea alone had a population of 34,678,972, and the 1978 population estimate totaled 37,018,932. The 1978 population estimate for North Korea was 17,078,000.

Both South Korea and North Korea have high annual birthrates—about 30 per 1,000 population. Their death rates are less than 10 per 1,000. The rate of population growth in Korea is about 2 percent per year. Medical advances have raised the average life expectancy of Koreans to about 63 years. But the population of Korea is young. About half its people are under 20.

Korea's population is heavily concentrated on the coastal plains, particularly along the west coast of South Korea. South Korea is one of the most densely populated nations in the world, averaging more than 900 persons per square mile. North Korea's population density averages more than 400 persons per square mile.

Until recently the Koreans were a mainly rural people. In 1925, less than 5 percent of the population lived in cities. By 1975, however, about half of all South Koreans and probably almost as high a proportion of North Koreans were city dwellers. Seoul, Korea's largest city and South Korea's capital, has about 7,800,000 inhabitants; Pusan, also in South Korea, is second, with about 2,450,000; and Pyongyang, the largest city and the capital of North Korea, is third, with about 1,500,000.

## EVERYDAY LIFE

Under the impact of the West, the everyday life of the Korean people has been gradually changing. The Japanese occupation, the post-World War II partition, and the Korean War—all helped to spur this change and to deepen the differences between the old rural traditions and a newly developing urban way of life.

### The Family

Historically, Korean families were formed into clans that shared the same family name. As a result, only a few hundred major surnames are used today. Kim, the most common, is the surname of about one fifth of all Korean families. In Korea, family names are customarily placed first and women do not change their names when they marry.

The Korean family has been traditionally domi-

nated by the husband. The wife has had only a secondary influence in family affairs, though her status improved after she bore one or more sons.

A first son is especially welcomed because his arrival ensures the continuity of the family line. On his first birthday, a baby usually has a big party at which he is formally introduced to his family and their friends. As a child grows up, he is taught to behave properly and to respect and obey his elders.

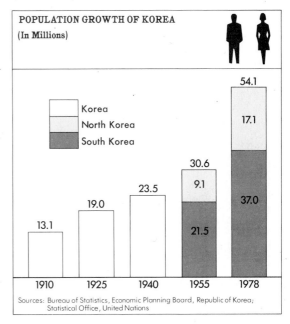

**POPULATION GROWTH OF KOREA**
(In Millions)

Korea
North Korea
South Korea

13.1 (1910)
19.0 (1925)
23.5 (1940)
30.6 — 9.1 / 21.5 (1955)
54.1 — 17.1 / 37.0 (1978)

Sources: Bureau of Statistics, Economic Planning Board, Republic of Korea; Statistical Office, United Nations

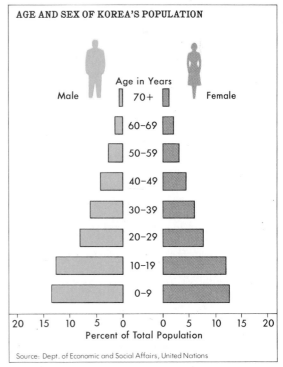

**AGE AND SEX OF KOREA'S POPULATION**

Male     Age in Years     Female

70+
60–69
50–59
40–49
30–39
20–29
10–19
0–9

20  15  10  5  0  0  5  10  15  20
Percent of Total Population

Source: Dept. of Economic and Social Affairs, United Nations

## WHERE THE KOREAN PEOPLE LIVE

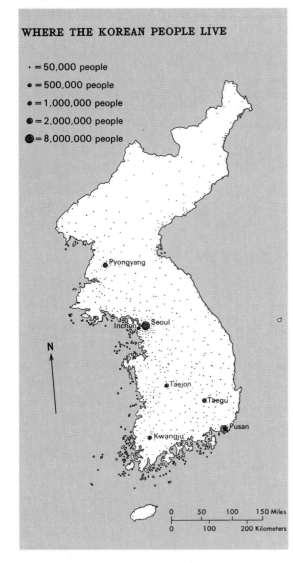

- · = 50,000 people
- • = 500,000 people
- ◉ = 1,000,000 people
- ◕ = 2,000,000 people
- ● = 8,000,000 people

Pyongyang

Inchon • Seoul

N

Taejon

Taegu

Kwangju • Pusan

| 0 | 50 | 100 | 150 Miles |
| 0 | | 100 | 200 Kilometers |

### Everyday Expressions in Korean

Yes. *Nye.*
No. *Anio.*
Good-bye. *Annyong i kasio.*
How are you? *Annyonghasipnika?*
What is your name? *Irum ul muorago hasimnika?*
My name is Jones. *Jones io.*
I am very glad to see you. *Tcham pankap so.*
What time is it? *Myossi-yo?*
What is this? *Igosi muosio?*
What is that? *Chogosun muosio?*
What are these? *Ikosi muosio?*
I know. *Ao.*
I don't know. *Moruo.*
Thank you. *Komapsupnida.*
Please. *Sipsiyo.*
Excuse me. *Yongso hasipsiyo.*

In the past, marriages were arranged by parents or by go-betweens called *chungmae.* Today, however, young people—particularly those living in cities—more often choose their own mates. Men usually marry at about the age of 21; women, at about 18. City dwellers tend to marry at a somewhat later age.

One of the most important milestones in a Korean man's life is his *hangab* (60th birthday). This date symbolizes the completion of a full life cycle and is marked by a big anniversary party.

### Housing, Food, and Clothing

Traditional rural houses in Korea were one-story structures, with mud-plastered wood walls and a thatched roof of rice straw. There were usually three rooms—a kitchen with a dirt floor, a bedroom, and a living room—arranged in an L or U shape. Flues under the floor carried hot smoke from a wood or coal stove in the kitchen to a chimney at the opposite end of the house. This provided a system of radiant heating called *ondol.* The living room usually had a board floor. Koreans removed their shoes before entering it from the kitchen or the outdoors. They sat on mats and slept on quilts spread out on the floor. Traditional city houses were similar, although slate or tile was used for roofs.

Houses today are commonly built of concrete, but radiant heating is still often used. City houses generally have modern conveniences such as electricity. The construction of large housing projects—including Western-style apartment buildings—has helped ease the housing shortage caused by the destruction of the Korean War and by the rapid growth of the urban population.

Rice, the staple food of the Korean diet, is eaten at most meals. Millet, wheat, barley, corn, and sorghum are also eaten, especially in the north. The vegetables Koreans eat include potatoes, Chinese cabbage, turnips, and onions. Garlic and red peppers are used as seasoners. *Kimchi* (pickled vegetables) is a favorite dish. Fish and other seafoods are the usual sources of proteins. Eggs have also become popular. Milk is now drunk by youths, especially in the cities, a practice unheard of a generation ago. *Ttog,* or rice cake, is a popular confection.

Traditional clothing, made of cotton or synthetic materials, is worn only by some people in the rural areas and by others on special occasions. Loose-fitting, long-sleeved jackets and oversized trousers that are tied at the waist and bound or left loose at the ankles are traditional garments for men. Nearly all men in the cities and most of the farmers have adopted Western-style shirts, trousers, and suits. Western-style shoes have largely replaced the traditional sandals, which were made of various materials.

The traditional dress of Korean women includes the *chima,* a long, high-waisted, pleated skirt worn over a slip or loose trousers called *paji.* The *chogori,* a short, flared blouse, is worn open in front over a tight-fitting undergarment. In the cities today, nearly all Korean women wear Western-style clothing.

## Education, Recreation, and Welfare

In South Korea, elementary education is compulsory for children 6 to 11 years of age. Secondary education is provided in middle schools for 12- to 14-year-olds and in academic and vocational high schools for 15- to 18-year-olds.

Higher education is offered in two- and four-year colleges and universities. Seoul National University is South Korea's largest institution of higher education. Among its better-known private universities are Yonsei University, Ewha Women's University, and Korea University, all in Seoul.

In North Korea, 4- and 5-year-olds attend preschools, while 5- and 6-year-olds attend kindergartens. Education in primary schools is compulsory for 7- to 10-year-olds, and 11- to 15-year-olds are required to attend middle schools that provide general and technical courses. Graduates may go on to a vocational school, a higher technical school, or a college-preparatory high school. There are 11-year postkindergarten programs for specialization in music, ballet, drama, the arts, or foreign languages. Kim Il Sung University, in Pyongyang, is the principal institution of higher education.

For recreation and relaxation, Koreans enjoy weddings, family gatherings, picnics, and sight-seeing. The Lunar New Year, in late January or early February, and the Harvest Moon Festival, in late September, are widely celebrated traditional holidays. Folk dancing and zither playing are very popular. Movies are well attended. Hiking, swimming, and Western sports—soccer, baseball, basketball, track, and boxing, for example—have large followings.

Among the social services provided by the South Korean government are day nurseries and old-age, maternity, and children's homes. The number of public health services, hospitals, and clinics staffed by trained medical personnel has been increasing. In some rural areas, however, midwives and herb doctors still provide the only available medical assistance. North Korea is a welfare state. Government and industrial workers are entitled to free medical care, and factories have kindergartens and nurseries for the children of working mothers.

## Religion

Most Koreans do not belong to an organized religion. The Confucian ethical system, however, has greatly influenced Korean culture. Buddhism, introduced from China in the 4th century, has a following of about 13 million persons in South Korea. Confucianists number about 4.7 million. There are about 6 million Christians, mostly Protestants. Chondogyo, a native Korean religion known originally as *Tonghak* (Eastern Learning), had about 815,000 adherents in the late 1970's. It was founded in the mid-19th century in opposition to foreign cultural influences. Shamanism, the superstitious worship of spirits, is widespread in rural areas. Religion is discouraged by the North Korean government.

Marilyn Silverstone—Magnum

In lowland South Korea, farmers usually live in compact villages near a stream, surrounded by their fields. They plant, cultivate, and harvest their crops cooperatively.

Modern South Korean schools stress science and technology to train students for industrial careers. Many South Koreans feel that an academic education offers greater prestige.

K. M. Lee

---

**Words to Remember**

*chungmae*—a go-between in Korean marriages.
*hangab*—a Korean man's 60th birthday.
*ondol*—the radiant heating system in Korean homes.
*kimchi*—pickled vegetables.
*chima* and *chogori*—a Korean woman's traditional skirt and blouse.
Chondogyo—a Korean religion founded in the mid-19th century to combat foreign cultural influences.

---

**Questions to Think About**

1. Give possible reasons why the population of Korea has been predominantly rural.
2. How might the regimes of North Korea and South Korea differ in their impact on the traditional Korean way of life?
3. What social problems are South Korea and North Korea likely to face in the future?

# KOREA—Government

## NATIONAL ANTHEM OF THE REPUBLIC OF KOREA

### 'Aegug-ga'

Dong-hae- mul-gwa  Baeg-du- san- i   ma-reu-go dal - to-rog
Un - til the East  Sea goes dry and   Paek-tu Moun- tain falls,

Ha - neu-nim-i   bo-u - ha-sa   u - ri- na-ra-man- se.
May our glor-ious na-tion last,   and God pre-serve its walls.

Mu - gung-hwa sam- cheon-li hwa-ryeo-gang - san.
Rose of Sha-ron, fair-est blos-som, flow-er of our land!

hwa ryeo gang san.
flower of our land!

Dae- han - sa-ram Dae-hane-u - ro  gi- ri-bo-jeon-ha - se.
God pre-serve this folk as one,   the peo-ple of Dae-han.

Source: Ministry of Culture and Information

The government administrative agencies of the Republic of Korea are housed in the Capitol in Seoul.

## South Korea

The Republic of Korea, or South Korea, was established in 1948 as a democratic republic. Its constitution provides for three separate and independent branches of government—the executive, the legislative, and the judicial.

The executive branch is headed by the president of the republic. He is empowered to make treaties with other nations, to appoint many government officials, and to act as supreme commander of the armed forces. Under constitutional revisions adopted in 1972, the president can have an unlimited number of six-year terms and has virtually unlimited emergency powers. He is chosen by the National Conference for Unification, a body of up to 5,000 delegates elected by popular vote for a six-year term.

The State Council, which functions as a presidential cabinet, consists of the president, the prime minister, the deputy prime minister, and the heads of administrative ministries. The prime minister is appointed by the president and directs the State Council. The heads of the ministries are appointed by the president upon the recommendation of the prime minister.

The one-house National Assembly has only limited legislative authority. One third of its 231 members are appointed by the president of the republic with the approval of the National Conference for Unification; two thirds are elected by popular vote. Elected members of the National Assembly serve six-year terms; appointed members, three-year terms.

The Supreme Court heads the judicial branch. It has a maximum of 16 justices, including the chief justice. The chief justice is appointed by the president, with the consent of the National Assembly, for a term of six years. The other Supreme Court justices, who are appointed by the president on the chief justice's recommendation, serve ten years. The Supreme Court interprets the constitution and hears appeals from lower courts. Its decisions are final.

The lower courts of the Republic of Korea consist of the district courts, family courts, and appellate courts. The district courts have primary jurisdiction over civil and criminal cases. The family courts also try cases for the first time, but they deal only with such matters as domestic relations and juvenile delinquency. The appellate courts hear appeals from the district and family courts. Military courts try members of the armed forces and may also try civilians accused of such military crimes as espionage.

The two major political parties in South Korea are the Democratic Republican party and the New Democratic party. Since 1963, the year of its organization, the Democratic Republican party has controlled the government. It was headed by President Park Chung Hee until his assassination in 1979. The opposition New Democratic party was formed in 1967 as a coalition of two other parties, the New Korea party and the Masses party.

The electoral system in South Korea is based on direct, equal, and secret suffrage. All citizens over the age of 20 have the right to vote. Political participation has been high, with about 80 percent of the registered voters casting ballots in presidential elections. In addition to the ballot, South Koreans often use other forms of political expression, such as protest demonstrations. The press has also been an important voice of political opinion.

## North Korea

North Korea, or the Democratic People's Republic of Korea, has a Communist government. According to the North Korean constitution, the country's highest legislative body is the Supreme People's Assembly. It is made up of representatives who are supposed to be elected every four years. A permanent presidium is empowered to act on behalf of the assembly when it is not in session.

The Administration Council, or cabinet, which is legally accountable to the assembly, acts as the government's executive branch. It includes the premier and several vice-premiers. Since 1972, the secretary-general of the Workers' (Communist) party has been the president of North Korea and its head of state. There are three vice-presidents.

North Korea's judicial structure functions on three levels, with the Central Court at the top, the provincial courts at the intermediate level, and people's courts in the cities, counties, and districts at the base. Closely linked to the courts is the Procuracy, or law-enforcement agency. The Procuracy is headed by a procurator-general with broad powers. He participates in sessions of the Central Court and has the authority to issue directives on judicial procedure to the lower courts.

The Workers' party has almost complete control over the government of North Korea. As a result, the government functions differently than the nation's constitution prescribes. Elections to the Supreme People's Assembly are held irregularly, and the cabinet has assumed absolute power.

**GOVERNMENT ORGANIZATION OF THE REPUBLIC OF KOREA (EXECUTIVE BRANCH)**

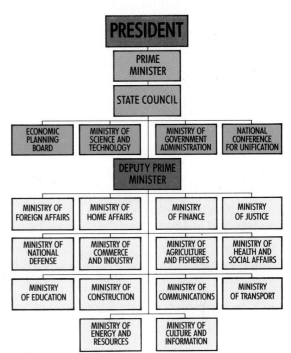

Source: Foreign Area Studies of the American University

There are no opposition parties of any influence in North Korea. All of the country's major political decisions are made within the Korean Workers' party.

In recent years the Korean Workers' party has begun to educate a new corps of industrial managers and technicians and to incorporate them into the party structure. As a result of these efforts more North Koreans have been participating in the affairs of the Korean Workers' party, and North Korea's one-party government has to that extent become somewhat more representative. However, most of the North Korean people still have little voice in the policies and operation of their government.

---

**Words to Remember**

Republic of Korea—the official name of South Korea.
Democratic Republican party—the ruling political party in South Korea.
Democratic People's Republic of Korea—the official name of North Korea.
Korean Workers' party—the ruling political party in North Korea.

---

**Questions to Think About**

1. Compare the role of political parties in the governments of North and South Korea.
2. Which of the two Korean governments is best suited to maintain social order? Explain.

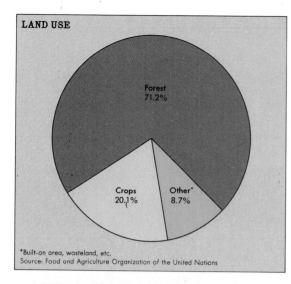

LAND USE

Forest
71.2%

Crops
20.1%

Other*
8.7%

*Built-on area, wasteland, etc.
Source: Food and Agriculture Organization of the United Nations

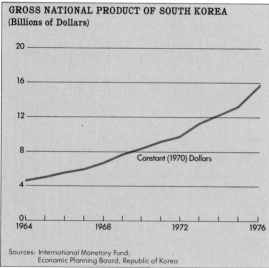

GROSS NATIONAL PRODUCT OF SOUTH KOREA
(Billions of Dollars)

20

16

12

8

4

0
1964        1968        1972        1976

Constant (1970) Dollars

Sources: International Monetary Fund;
Economic Planning Board, Republic of Korea

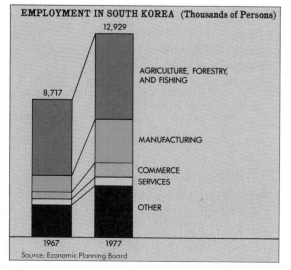

EMPLOYMENT IN SOUTH KOREA (Thousands of Persons)

12,929

8,717

AGRICULTURE, FORESTRY,
AND FISHING

MANUFACTURING

COMMERCE
SERVICES

OTHER

1967        1977
Source: Economic Planning Board

# KOREA—Economy

Korea's traditional economy was agricultural. Not until the late 1800's did industry begin to develop. Under Japanese rule, Korea became a source of Japan's raw materials and a market for its products. Modern transportation, communications, and electric power facilities were built, but on the whole Japanese rule stunted Korea's economic development. The partition of Korea after World War II dislocated its economy. Most of the factories and electric power plants, the bulk of the mineral deposits, and the largest forests were in North Korea. The best ports, most of the railway mileage, most of the good farmland, and over two thirds of the people were in South Korea.

South Korea and North Korea have taken different paths of economic development since the partition. The South Korean government provides central guidelines for economic development and some financing for industry. But it encourages private enterprise and capital investment by foreign companies. South Korea's economy has been financed in part by aid and loans from the United States. The Communist regime of North Korea controls all the means of production and has a highly centralized economy. It stresses the development of heavy industry. North Korea has received economic aid from the Soviet Union, China, and other Communist nations.

## The Economy of South Korea

Agriculture is the economic mainstay of South Korea. About two fifths of the people work in agriculture, forestry, and fishing. The average farm household has less than $2\frac{1}{2}$ acres of land, usually on several scattered plots. Some farming is now done with modern machines. The generally low yields have been rising with the increased use of fertilizer. The mild winters permit double-cropping on most lowland fields. In irrigated areas, rice is generally grown in the summer; other grains, in the winter.

Rice is by far the major crop—in tonnage, acreage, and value. Other leading crops include sweet potatoes, barley, soybeans, wheat, corn, millet, cotton, mulberry leaves, fruits, and vegetables. Pigs and chickens are the principal livestock.

The government has sought to raise agricultural output by increasing fertilizer production and reclaiming farmland from west coast tidal flats. A program to increase the number of farm owners has made progress.

The fishing industry is an important source of food for South Korea. The catch is sufficient to meet domestic demand and to allow some exports. Pusan is the largest fishing port.

South Korea's forests were badly overcut during and after World War II. There has been some reforestation, but the fast-rising demand for lumber must be met through imports. Because of the government's forest preservation policies, coal has mostly replaced wood as the fuel used in homes.

Most of South Korea's electric power is generated by coal- and oil-fired thermal plants in the coastal cities. Some comes from hydroelectric plants in the northeastern mountains. South Korea's petroleum refineries use imported crude oil. The nation's first major refinery was built at Ulsan in 1964. The chief mineral product of South Korea is anthracite coal. The nation is a leading producer of tungsten and graphite. Other commercially important minerals are iron ore, limestone, fluorite, gold, silver, and kaolin.

Before partition, South Korea had little manufacturing industry. Its few plants produced textiles, machinery, and foodstuffs. Since partition, emphasis has been placed on the development of heavy industry. The new stress on heavy industry has greatly boosted the output of cement, fertilizer, petrochemicals, ships, and automobiles. However, the textile industry is still one of the largest. It now uses not only cotton but also nylon, rayon, and other synthetic fibers. In addition to textiles, South Korea's light industries produce foodstuffs, plastics, plywood, plate glass, porcelain, cutlery, tires, wigs, cosmetics, sewing machines, toys, and leather goods. Artisans in small shops still engage in traditional handicrafts. South Korea's industry is heavily concentrated in the Seoul-Inchon area and at Pusan and Ulsan. An integrated steel mill has been built at Pohang.

A modern transportation network is being built in South Korea. Main railroad lines have been electrified; new lines have been built to the northeast; and old rolling stock has been replaced. Modern expressways, beginning with one between Seoul and Inchon (1968) and one between Seoul and Pusan (1970), have been built. Trucks carry more than one half of the country's domestic freight traffic. South Korea's principal seaports are at Pusan, Ulsan, and Inchon. Modern air service links the major cities with each other and with the rest of the world. The nation has modern telephone, telegraph, and postal services as well as many newspapers and radio and television stations.

South Korea's foreign trade grew substantially in the 1970's. Manufactured goods, especially clothing and textiles, make up two thirds of the value of its exports. Other leading exports are wood veneers, foods, and raw materials. The chief imports are machinery, transportation equipment, petroleum, textiles, foods, chemicals, and wood. The United States and Japan are South Korea's main trading partners.

The South Korean government owns and operates the major transportation services, communications facilities, and electric power plants. Private companies dominate most other sectors of the economy.

## The Economy of North Korea

Agriculture is one of the weakest segments of North Korea's economy. Since the winters are long and cold, most of the farmland supports only a summer crop. Yields are low. Rice is well over a half of the total

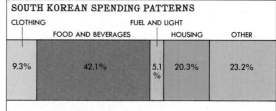

### SOUTH KOREAN SPENDING PATTERNS

| CLOTHING | FOOD AND BEVERAGES | FUEL AND LIGHT | HOUSING | OTHER |
|---|---|---|---|---|
| 9.3% | 42.1% | 5.1% | 20.3% | 23.2% |

Source: Economic Planning Board

### Principal Products of Korea

| CROPS | NORTH KOREA Acres (In Thousands) | NORTH KOREA Tons (In Thousands) | SOUTH KOREA Acres (In Thousands) | SOUTH KOREA Tons (In Thousands) |
|---|---|---|---|---|
| Rice | 1,927 | 5,082 | 3,039 | 9,193 |
| Barley | 457 | 375 | 1,275 | 897 |
| Corn | 1,013 | 2,006 | 124 | 99 |
| Potatoes* | 383 | 1,940 | 356 | 1,647 |
| Soybeans | 988 | 342 | 692 | 375 |
| Wheat | 346 | 342 | 99 | 99 |
| Millet | 1,161 | 461 | 67 | 29 |

| MINERALS | Tons (In Thousands) | Tons (In Thousands) |
|---|---|---|
| Coal | 44,092 | 19,009 |
| Iron ore | 10,361 | 871 |
| Tungsten | 2,370 | 5 |
| Graphite | 83 | 72 |
| Limestone | † | 25,059 |
| Magnesite | 1,874 | † |

| ELECTRIC POWER | Kilowatt-Hours (In Millions) |
|---|---|
| | 16,500     23,117 |

| MANUFACTURES (South Korea) | Value Added (Millions of Dollars) |
|---|---|
| Food, beverages, tobacco | 630 |
| Textiles, wearing apparel, leather | 756 |
| Chemicals, petroleum, coal, rubber, plastic products | 693 |
| Basic metal industries | 262 |
| Fabricated metal products, machinery and equipment | 561 |
| Paper and paper products, printing and publishing | 153 |
| Other | 415 |
| Total | 3,470 |

*Includes Sweet Potatoes.
†Data not available.
Sources: Food and Agriculture Organization of the United Nations; Economic Planning Board, Republic of Korea; The Mining Journal

The sea is an important source of food for South Koreans. Here a day's catch is being cleaned.

John Launois—Black Star

In North Korea, emphasis has been placed on the expansion of steelmaking and other heavy industries. Less stress has been given to increasing the production of consumer goods.

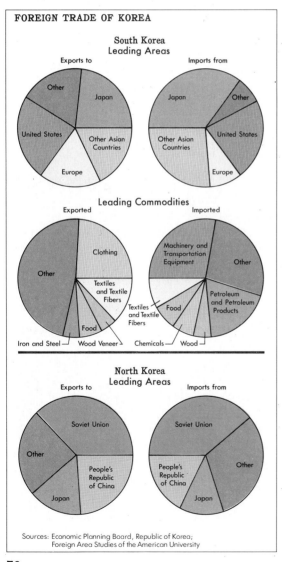

FOREIGN TRADE OF KOREA

South Korea
Leading Areas

Exports to    Imports from

Other    Japan          Japan    Other

United States    Other Asian    Other Asian    United States
Countries    Countries

Europe    Europe

Leading Commodities

Exported    Imported

Clothing    Machinery and
Transportation
Equipment    Other

Other    Textiles
and Textile
Fibers    Petroleum
and Petroleum
Textiles    Food    Products
and Textile
Fibers
Food

Iron and Steel    Wood Veneer    Chemicals    Wood

North Korea
Leading Areas

Exports to    Imports from

Soviet Union    Soviet Union

Other    People's    People's    Other
Republic    Republic
of China    of China

Japan    Japan

Sources: Economic Planning Board, Republic of Korea;
Foreign Area Studies of the American University

grain harvest. Other leading crops are corn, potatoes, millet, barley, soybeans, and wheat. More than 90 percent of the cultivated land is in state-controlled collective farms; the remainder in state-operated farms. Farm machinery is in only limited use. Crop production falls short of the nation's needs and is supplemented by imports, mainly wheat.

Fish are an important part of North Korea's food supply. Cod, herring, sardines, salmon, swordfish, and crabs are leading marine products. The major fishing ports are Kimchaek (Songjin), Chongjin, and Nampo.

Although North Korea's forests were depleted under Japanese rule, enough stands remain to support logging operations. Spruce, fir, larch, pine, and oak are the main commercial species. Sinuiju, Hoeryong, and Pyongyang are the major centers of the lumber, woodworking, and pulp industries.

North Korea is rich in mineral deposits. It is a leading producer of tungsten, graphite, and magnesite. Other principal mineral products are coal, iron ore, limestone, nickel, zinc, copper, lead, titanium, fluorite, mica, and gold. Power is provided by hydroelectric plants on the Yalu River and its tributaries and by thermal plants.

Manufacturing dominates North Korea's economy. Although the nation's industries were largely destroyed during the Korean War, they have since been rebuilt and expanded. Important products include iron and steel, nonferrous metals, machinery, machine tools, chemicals, cement, tractors, automobiles, railway rolling stock, and small ships. Consumer goods include textiles, foodstuffs, medicines, and plastics. Pyongyang is the leading manufacturing center.

Railways serve the main industrial areas of North Korea, but until the early 1970's the Pyongyang-Wonsan line was the only transpeninsular link. Other lines connect with Chinese and Soviet railways. There are domestic air links and flights from Peking and Moscow. The principal ports are Unggi, Najin, Wonsan, and Nampo. North Korea's foreign trade is mainly with the Soviet Union and China. Japan is its principal non-Communist trading partner. Major imports are machinery, oil, coking coal, rubber, and wheat. Iron ore and processed metals are the major exports.

---

**Words to Remember**

double-cropping—raising two crops a year on the same plot of soil.

collective farm—a form of state-controlled co-operative farm in North Korea.

---

**Questions to Think About**

1. What might be advantages and disadvantages of living under the economic system of North Korea? Of South Korea?
2. Would consolidating the small farms in South Korea help its economy? Why or why not?

# A Tour of Korea

1. **KYONGBOK PALACE** and its grounds in Seoul are now a public park. This old Buddhist pagoda stands in the park.

2. **POPJU TEMPLE** is at the foot of Mount Songni. Its huge Buddha—nearly 95 feet high—is the tallest statue in Korea.

3. **BULGUKSA TEMPLE**, at Kyongju, was built about A.D. 540. It houses many historic treasures of the Silla Dynasty.

4. **CHOMSONGDAE**, an early astronomical observatory, is in Kyongju. It was erected in the mid-7th century A.D.

5. **CHONJEYON WATERFALL** is one of the many scenic attractions on rugged Cheju Island.

76a

# KOREA—Culture

## The Korean Language

Korean is not closely related to any other modern language. Despite the longtime cultural influence of China upon Korea and the use of Chinese as the official written language of Korea until the late 19th century, Korean and Chinese belong to entirely different linguistic families. However, some experts believe that Korean may belong to the Ural-Altaic family—along with Japanese, Mongolian, and Turkish.

Spoken Korean is soft and lilting. There are no heavy nasal tones and no strong accents to emphasize words in sentences. Although half a dozen dialects are spoken in Korea, the differences among them are not very great. People from various sections of the nation can understand one another easily.

Formal manuscripts did not appear in Korea until the 4th century A.D., when educated Koreans wrote in

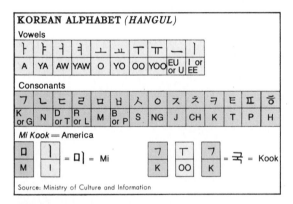

**KOREAN ALPHABET (HANGUL)**

Vowels

| ㅏ | ㅑ | ㅓ | ㅕ | ㅗ | ㅛ | ㅜ | ㅠ | ㅡ | ㅣ |
|----|----|----|-----|---|----|----|-----|------|------|
| A | YA | AW | YAW | O | YO | OO | YOO | EU or U | I or EE |

Consonants

| ㄱ | ㄴ | ㄷ | ㄹ | ㅁ | ㅂ | ㅅ | ㅇ | ㅈ | ㅊ | ㅋ | ㅌ | ㅍ | ㅎ |
|-----|---|------|------|---|------|---|----|---|----|---|---|---|---|
| K or G | N | D or T | R or L | M | B or P | S | NG | J | CH | K | T | P | H |

*Mi Kook* = America

ㅁ M + ㅣ I = ㅁㅣ = Mi    ㄱ K + ㅜ OO + ㄱ K = 쿡 = Kook

Source: Ministry of Culture and Information

Ceramics is regarded as Korea's most notable fine art. This Yi Dynasty porcelain jar has designs in underglaze iron.

**76b**

Chinese. Later, systems were developed by which Korean words could be written in Chinese ideograms. The mastery of Chinese ideography was very difficult, however, and only scholars could read and write.

*Hangul*, an alphabet suited to the Korean language, was developed at the direction of King Sejong and introduced in 1446. It was used by the common people, but educated Koreans continued to write in Chinese. Hangul did not come into general use until the end of the 19th century, when it became the official alphabet for all laws and decrees.

After the Japanese assumed complete control of Korea in 1910, they discouraged and then abolished the use and teaching of Korean. With the liberation of Korea at the end of World War II, hangul was revived. Today Korean texts and parts of Korean newspapers are printed in hangul. Chinese ideography is still taught, but most writers use hangul.

## Korean Literature

The first Korean literature is thought to have been primitive poetry which, accompanied by music and dance, was used in prehistoric religious rites. The evolution of Korean poetry as an independent art form is believed to have begun in the 1st century A.D. The brief *Sijo* probably developed late in the Koryo period and is still popular today. It was used as a vehicle for romantic and naturalistic themes.

Under the Yi Dynasty, the novel gradually replaced poetry as the most popular literary form. The early Korean novelists sought primarily to edify their readers. The works of later novelists mocked the *yangban* (aristocracy).

The late 17th and early 18th centuries are known as "the golden age of the classic novel" in Korea. The most popular novel of this era, 'Chunhyangjon' (The Story of Spring Fragrance), is about the love of an aristocrat's son for a lower-class girl. Many of the classic Korean novels had romantic themes.

Growing Western influence in the last half of the 19th century inspired the "new novel." The "new novels" promoted such ideas as political democracy and social equality. The best known of these novels was 'The Tears of Blood' by Yi Injik.

New writers in many branches of literature emerged. Such authors as Yi Kwangsu, Ch'oe Namson, Kim Tongin, and Kim Sowol assimilated Western literary trends and contributed to the development of modern Korean literary forms.

During World War II, the progress of Korean literature was blocked by a Japanese ban on native culture. After the Korean War, however, new writers emerged who drew their inspiration from contemporary trends in world literature. There was a surge of activity in poetry, the novel, and literary criticism.

## The Fine Arts

Korea's artists have been strongly influenced by the cultures of neighboring nations. Nevertheless, they have always produced sculptures, paintings, and pottery that are peculiarly their own.

Little early Korean sculpture has survived, though a few fine stone figures and relief carvings remain. The golden age of Korean sculpture reached its height in the late 7th century during the reign of the Silla Dynasty. Most of the sculpture of this period is of bronze, small in scale, and dedicated to Buddhist deities.

Except for some tomb frescoes dating from the 4th through the 7th centuries, few examples of early Korean painting have survived. Painters of the last Yi Dynasty (1392–1910), however, left a rich legacy. Their paintings were executed on silk or paper scrolls and album leaves. They depicted towering landscapes, important personages, and scenes of daily life.

The ceramics of Korea almost certainly represent the country's most significant artistic contribution. Functional as well as decorative, Korean ceramics have an unmistakable character. The utilitarian vessels of the Silla period are of sturdy dark-gray earthenware with modest, usually incised, decoration. The rich-green celadons of the Koryo period are adorned with brilliant brushed or inlaid designs that are admirably adapted to their forms. The heavier wares of the Yi Dynasty bear designs, usually on a white porcelaneous base, which seem swiftly executed, almost offhand, yet masterly.

Early Korean architecture is exemplified by the tombs of Koguryo and the remains of great walled fortresses. From the late 7th century into the Koryo Dynasty many Buddhist temple complexes—actually small villages—were built. Although their general features were Chinese, they were adapted to local materials and landscape by their Korean builders.

Under the Yi Dynasty the increasing popularity of Confucianism was mirrored in the construction of Confucian shrines. There was also an upsurge of nonreligious architecture, including imposing palaces, town gates, and watchtowers.

## The Performing Arts

Korea's performing arts were greatly influenced by those of China, whose dance, music, and instruments the Koreans adopted. Korea, in turn, played a major role in transmitting music and dance to Japan.

Among the earliest extended performances in Korea were the danced mask plays that originated around the 9th century. Their purpose was magical—to make crops grow, to ward off evil spirits and disease, to placate the spirits of the dead. Toward the end of the 14th century, various elements of these plays were combined in the "typical" mask play, the *Sandae*. Accompanied by drums, flutes, and the Korean harp, or *kayageum*, the Sandae satirized the nobility and corrupt priests.

Korea's puppet plays may have originated at about the same time as the mask plays. The puppet plays were performed on a two-story stage. The puppets—one to three feet tall—were in the upper story; their manipulators were hidden below.

A kind of musical drama was created by combining a narrative with folk tunes. The first permanent Korean theater for performances of this type was built in Seoul in 1902. This genre survives partially in the popular *Pan-Sori* (folk opera).

Unlike other Asian countries, Korea failed to develop a classical theater from its popular theatrical forms. Folk dances and mask plays, once established, remained unchanged over the centuries.

During the 20th century the Korean performing arts were greatly influenced by the West, at first by way of Japan, where a type of play called *shimpa* developed about 1890. The shimpa plays were patterned on realistic Western drama. In later decades adaptations of shimpa plays became very popular in Korea. The Earth-Moon Society, formed by men who had studied theater in Tokyo, began presenting plays by Anton Chekhov, Henrik Ibsen, and George Bernard Shaw in 1923. Familiarity with the work of contemporary Western playwrights led, increasingly, to the writing of Korean plays that dealt with existing social conditions.

Since 1945 much has been done to encourage the performing arts of Korea. A government-sponsored National Theater opened in April 1950. The Seoul Cultural Center for the performing arts and a new National Theater, also located in Seoul, were opened during the 1970's.

---

**Words to Remember**

*hangul*—the Korean alphabet.
*Sijo*—a brief poetic form developed in the Koryo period.
*kayageum*—a 12-stringed Korean harp.
*Pan-Sori*—a form of Korean folk opera.
*shimpa*—a play based on Western realistic drama.

---

**Questions to Think About**

1. How did the lack of a written Korean language affect Korea's development?
2. How did Korea develop a distinctive culture despite the influence of its neighbors?

The Kang Gang Su Wol Lae is one of Korea's many traditional folk dances. The circling women chant rhythmically to the beat of the accompanying music.

# KOREA — Natural Features

## Land

The Korean peninsula is dominated by mountains. From the northern interior, where several peaks reach over 8,000 feet, a mountainous backbone—the Taeback Mountains—extends southward along the east coast. The range has many spurs to the west and south. The longest spur—the Sobaek Mountains—extends to the southwestern corner of the peninsula.

There are no active volcanoes in Korea today, nor are there any earthquakes. But volcanic activity in past geologic times helped shape the rugged Korean landscape. Korea's highest point is Mount Paektu (9,003 feet), an extinct volcano on the North Korean-Chinese border. The highest point in South Korea is Mount Halla (6,398 feet), on Cheju (Quelpart Island).

Many short, swift, and shallow rivers flow from the mountains to the coast. Most of them drain to the south and west, into the Yellow Sea and the Korea Strait. Korea's two longest rivers—the Yalu and the Tumen—are along the boundary with China and the Soviet Union. The Yalu flows west for 491 miles into the Yellow Sea. The Tumen flows east for 324 miles into the Sea of Japan. Other important rivers are the Taedong, which flows through the North Korean capital of Pyongyang; the Han, which flows through the South Korean capital of Seoul; and the Naktong,

in southeastern Korea. The lower courses of the larger rivers are navigable by small boats. Some rivers have been dammed to generate hydroelectric power. Korea has no large lakes.

Most of Korea's plains are small and nestled among mountains or between mountains and the sea. Except for the plain around Wonsan, the plains along the east coast are especially narrow. Most of the plains in the southeast are clustered around the Naktong River and its tributaries. The most extensive lowlands are along the west coast, but even these are broken into pockets by hills and mountains. The southeastern and western lowlands comprise most of Korea's productive cropland and its major urban centers and support the bulk of the Korean population. Many of the significant historical developments in Korea have taken place on these plains.

The Korean peninsula has a long, varied coastline. The east coast is relatively straight and rocky, with a tidal range of only one or two feet. The west coast is low and deeply indented and has long stretches of mud flats. It has a tidal range of more than 17 feet. Major ports are Pusan and Masan on the south coast; Inchon and Chinnampo, on the west coast; and Ulsan, Unggi, and Wonsan on the east coast.

The south and west coasts are fringed with more than 3,300 islands, of which about 200 are inhabited. The largest islands of Korea are Cheju, Koje, Kanghwa, Chin, and Namhae, off the south and west coasts, and Ullung, in the Sea of Japan.

## Climate

Most of Korea has a humid, continental climate marked by sharp seasonal changes. In winter, cold, dry air from the Asian interior—warmed somewhat as it crosses the Yellow Sea—moves across Korea. In summer, air flows across Korea from the opposite direction. Regional variation in climate is greatest during the winter and slight during the summer. In general, however, the south is warmer than the north and the coasts are warmer than the mountainous interior. The Korean peninsula juts far enough south to reach the warm waters of the Kuroshio, or Japan Current. Korea's southern coast has a humid, subtropical climate. The length of the frost-free period ranges from about 130 days in the northern interior to 220 days in the extreme south.

Cool weather begins in October and November, when winds start to come from the north and northwest. A long winter follows. Winter in the northern interior is bitterly cold. From November to April, the average monthly temperature there is below 32° F. and sub-zero readings are common. Temperatures in the south for the same period are considerably higher. The cold weather is relieved by numerous warm spells. January is Korea's coldest month.

Spring arrives in April and is noted for its pleasant, sunny weather. Summer comes in June. By July, it is hot and humid everywhere in Korea except the higher mountains and the northeast coast. Daytime temperatures commonly reach the high 80's and low

### TOPOGRAPHY OF KOREA

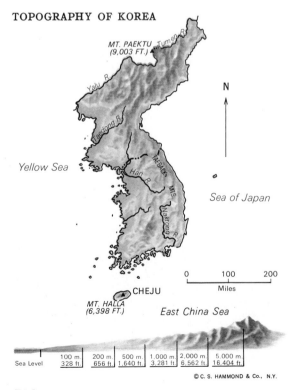

MT. PAEKTU (9,003 FT.)

Tumen R.

Yalu R.

Taedong R.

N

Yellow Sea

Han R.

TAEBACK Mts.

Sea of Japan

Naktong R.

0    100    200
Miles

CHEJU

MT. HALLA (6,398 FT.)

East China Sea

| Sea Level | 100 m. 328 ft. | 200 m. 656 ft. | 500 m. 1,640 ft. | 1,000 m. 3,281 ft. | 2,000 m. 6,562 ft. | 5,000 m. 16,404 ft. |

© C. S. HAMMOND & Co., N.Y.

90's. In September, humidity decreases and clear, cloudless days become more frequent. The first cold spells come at night in October, but the October days remain sunny, dry, and warm. October and May are Korea's pleasantest months.

Precipitation is moderate in Korea, ranging from less than 25 inches to more than 55 inches annually. Most falls as rain, which is heaviest in the period from April to September. The remainder of the year is relatively dry. Summer downpours often cause flooding. In late summer and early autumn, torrential rains accompany the typhoons that strike the peninsula from the south and east. Winter snows accumulate to a depth of several feet in the northern mountains, but snow that falls in the south soon melts.

The heaviest precipitation, more than 55 inches annually, is along the south and east coasts and on Cheju. Parts of the mountainous north receive less than 25 inches annually.

## Plant and Animal Life

Korea's plants and animals are transitional between those of Manchuria and Siberia and those of the Japanese islands. The original vegetation of the Korean peninsula was notable for its many varieties of trees, shrubs, and flowering plants. But the rich forests that once covered most of Korea have been largely removed from the plains and adjacent mountain slopes. Some species were merely thinned out, but broad areas were cut too often to allow new trees to mature, and artificial plantings favored a few fast-growing species. Both North Korea and South Korea have undertaken reforestation. Fir, spruce, larch, and pine forests prevail in the northern mountains. Central and southern Korea have mixed forests of oak, pine, elm, beech, and poplar. The natural vegetation of the south coast is broadleaf evergreen forest and bamboo.

Early in the 20th century, Korea still had a rich variety of wild animals, including sables, marten, foxes, beaver, otter, deer, antelope, goats, tigers, and leopards. Most of these wild animal species have either disappeared completely or are found only in small numbers in remote northern mountain areas. They were killed for their fur or their forest habitat was destroyed. Pheasants and rabbits are now the most common wildlife. There are also many smaller mammals and birds, as well as reptiles and fish.

### Words to Remember

Mount Paektu—Korea's highest peak.
Yalu—Korea's longest river.
Kuroshio—the warm Pacific current that washes the southern shores of Korea.

### Questions to Think About

1. How has Korea's topography and peninsular location affected its history and economy?
2. How does Korea's climate compare with that of the New England section of the United States?

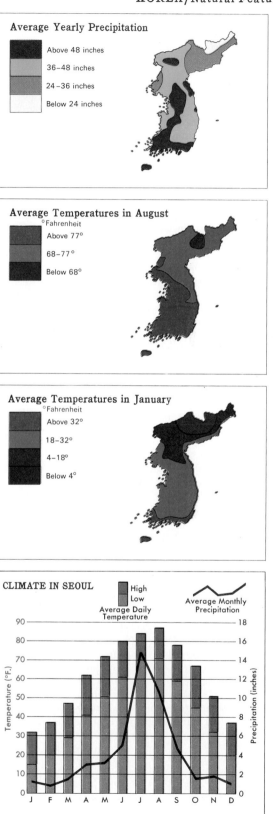

Average Yearly Precipitation
- Above 48 inches
- 36–48 inches
- 24–36 inches
- Below 24 inches

Average Temperatures in August
°Fahrenheit
- Above 77°
- 68–77°
- Below 68°

Average Temperatures in January
°Fahrenheit
- Above 32°
- 18–32°
- 4–18°
- Below 4°

CLIMATE IN SEOUL
High / Low
Average Daily Temperature
Average Monthly Precipitation

# KOREA —History

## Early History and the Three Kingdoms

Archaeological evidence indicates that men lived in southwestern Korea well before 10,000 B.C. Later, Korea was inhabited by at least two distinct groups of people who migrated from the north. One group consisted of fishermen and shellfish gatherers, who settled along the rivers and the seacoast about the third millennium B.C. They produced an earthenware which is known as "comb ceramic" from the linear decoration on its surface. The second group entered the Korean peninsula around the 7th century B.C. It was made up of hunters and gatherers who produced *mumun* (undecorated pottery). They developed a primitive agriculture and may have built the great stone-slab tombs, or dolmens, found throughout Korea. Wet-field rice agriculture and the use of metal appear to have been introduced from China by 300 B.C.

By the 2d century B.C. the state of Choson had developed in northwestern Korea, with its capital at the present city of Pyongyang. In 108 B.C., Choson and the northern part of the peninsula fell to the armies of the Chinese Han Dynasty. Four Chinese commanderies were established; the great walled city of Lo-lang was built; and the advanced civilization of China began to penetrate the Korean peninsula. Native resistance soon compelled the Chinese to abandon three of the commanderies.

Confederations of the many Korean tribes led to the rise in the 1st century B.C. of the Three Kingdoms—Koguryo, in the Yalu River basin in the north; Paekche, in the Han River basin in the west; and Silla, in the southeast. In the following centuries Buddhism was introduced into the Korean peninsula from China. It was adopted by Koguryo in 372, by Paekche in 384, and by Silla in 528. Buddhism was accompanied by T'ang Dynasty art and the study of Chinese characters, which remained the basic written language of Korea until the 20th century.

The Korean states battled for primacy. After centuries of warfare, the combined forces of Silla and T'ang China defeated Paekche in 660 and Koguryo in 668. The greater part of Korea was now unified under Silla, and a period of peace and strong Chinese influence followed. A great cultural and technical flowering centered at the capital of Silla (the present Kyongju). Astronomy, medicine, metal casting, sculpture, and textile manufacture reached especially high levels. Hundreds of Buddhist temples were built. A brisk maritime trade was conducted with China.

## The Koryo and Yi Dynasties

In the 9th century, the ruling clans of Silla lost control over warlords in the outlying provinces. After a century of fighting, the peninsula was reunified under the state of Koryo (935–1392), from which

the modern Western name of Korea is derived. During the Koryo period, hundreds of Buddhist monasteries were built in the mountains around the Koryo capital of Kaesong. Maritime trade with Sung Dynasty China fostered a new flowering of culture. The Korean authorities modeled their methods of government on the example of China, including a system of civil service examinations.

In the 11th century, Korea was invaded by the Ch'itan people of Manchuria. During the 12th century, it was ruled by military overlords. The Mongols launched the first of a series of invasions against Korea in 1231. To gain divine assistance in removing the invaders, the Koreans carved over 81,000 wood blocks for the printing of the entire Buddhist canon, the Tripitaka. The enterprise took 16 years. In 1270 Korea made peace with the Mongols and became a partner in Mongol campaigns of conquest, including two disastrous attempts to invade Japan in 1274 and 1281. By 1368 the Koreans had ousted the Mongols, who had suffered defeats in China that drove them back to their homeland. In 1392 a Korean general, Yi Songgye, seized the throne as the ruler of the new Yi Dynasty.

Under the Yi Dynasty, landowners formed a ruling elite called the *yangban*. They were firmly anti-Buddhist, and the withdrawal of their patronage from the Buddhist establishment led to the decline of Buddhism in Korea. The social attitudes of the yangban were expressed in Confucian terms. In their view relationships of superiority and inferiority existed between ruler and subject, father and son, husband and wife, elder and younger brother, and among friends. The Yi class system was rigidly hierarchical and hereditary, from the royal caste down to the peasants and slaves. There was little social mobility.

Comparative peace and increasing international trade fostered a period of intellectual achievement. Under the direction of King Sejong, the fourth ruler of the Yi Dynasty, an alphabet called *hangul*, or "script of the Korean people," was completed in 1446. Although hundreds of years passed before it was widely used, the alphabet made it possible for any Korean to read his language. Literacy and knowledge were no longer the monopoly of the yangban.

From 1592 to 1598 Korea was devastated by two invasions under the Japanese military ruler Hideyoshi Toyotomi. Aided by the armies of Ming Dynasty China and the brilliant tactics of a native naval genius, Yi Sunsin, the Koreans drove the Japanese out. Yi Sunsin invented the ironclad Korean "turtle ship" early in 1592. From 1627 to 1637 Korea was invaded by the Manchus, who founded the Ch'ing Empire in China. Korea remained tributary to this empire until the late 19th century. The strict political, social, and economic controls imposed by the Yi authorities were thoroughly disrupted by the wars. The destruction of land, tax, and slave registers enabled many Koreans to escape the bonds of caste and class.

In the first half of the 17th century a number of Dutchmen visited Korea. Several of them fought with the Koreans against the Manchu invaders. They were among the first Westerners in Korea, though knowledge of Europe had been brought back earlier by Korean embassies to Peking.

In the first half of the 19th century, Jesuit priests entered Korea from China and Western ships began to appear off the Korean coast. A few of the ships requested trading privileges for their nations, which the Koreans refused to grant. Korean shore batteries at times exchanged fire with ships entering Korean bays or rivers. In 1876, negotiations resulting from a Korean attack on a Japanese naval vessel led to the signing of the Treaty of Kanghwa, which opened three Korean ports to Japan. Acting on advice from the Chinese, the Korean authorities attempted to dilute Japanese influence by also signing treaties with Western nations. The first of these was a treaty of friendship with the United States, signed in 1882.

## Japanese Occupation

The period from 1876 to 1910 was marked by power struggles between the pro-Chinese conservative ruling Min family and rival factions which wanted to modernize Korea along Japanese or Russian lines. Meanwhile, the antiforeign *Tonghak* movement, which advocated "Eastern Learning" as opposed to *Sohak*, or "Western Learning," was developing in the countryside. In 1894, antiforeign sentiment, coupled with peasant demands for political and social reforms, culminated in the Tonghak Rebellion. Both Japan and China sent armies to help quell the rebellion. Their rival interests led to the Sino-Japanese War of 1894–95. The victory of Japan ended China's influence over Korea. Japanese-backed administrations unsuccessfully attempted to institute reforms in 1894.

John Holstein

Admiral Yi Sunsin's statue towers over Seoul's Sejong Avenue. The admiral's "turtle ships," believed to have been the world's first ironclads, routed Japanese invaders in the 1590's.

Rivalry between imperial Japan and czarist Russia over dominance in the Korean peninsula led to the Russo-Japanese War of 1904–5. The victorious Japanese declared Korea to be a protectorate of Japan. In 1910 they formally annexed Korea as a Japanese colony, bringing the end of the Yi Dynasty.

The Japanese helped modernize the Korean economy, but during their occupation many Korean government workers, farmers, and businessmen lost their positions to Japanese immigrants. The Japanese

Japan and China clashed over Korea in the Sino-Japanese War of 1894–95. The defeat of China was followed by a long period of Japanese domination in Korea.

The Bettmann Archive

*Continued on page 77*

# Korea—North vs. South

by John Roderick

Relations between South Korea and North Korea have been strained by a clash of ideologies, memories of their bitter military conflict, and differences over how to reunify the divided country.

In 1945 the people of Korea hailed Japan's defeat in World War II. It marked the end of 35 years of Japanese colonial rule. But the joy of the Koreans was short-lived. They were denied independence and unity by the two great antagonists of the cold war—the Soviet Union and the United States.

Through an agreement made in 1945, Soviet troops occupied the portion of Korea north of the 38th parallel and United States forces occupied the portion south of the 38th parallel. From this agreement stemmed much of the tragedy of postwar Korea.

Initially, the Soviets cooperated in a move to establish a provisional, united Korean government. In 1947, however, the Soviet Union resisted a United Nations General Assembly resolution that elections be held throughout Korea. The following year, because of Soviet obstruction, no elections were held north of the partition line. Meanwhile, Soviet advisers had been creating a strong military machine.

Korea has always been a strategic factor in the Asian policies of Russia's rulers. This continued to be the case after World War II, when Soviet Premier Joseph Stalin viewed Korea as vital to the existence of the Far Eastern sphere of influence the Russians had gained by invading Manchuria after entering the war against Japan in August 1945. By 1949, the newly established Communist Chinese People's Republic of Mao Tse-tung was also coveting Korea, a historic route of China-bound invasion armies.

With the encouragement of the Soviet Union and Communist China, North Korea's premier, Kim Il Sung, undertook to destroy the Republic of Korea. On June 25, 1950, North Korean troops invaded

**Improved North Korean-South Korean relations were encouraged by talks on reuniting families that had been separated by the division of Korea. Official meetings were held in 1972–73.**

Korean Overseas Information Service

South Korea. The move was influenced by a United States decision to exclude Korea from the area in the western Pacific that it was prepared to defend.

Reacting quickly to the invasion, United States President Harry S. Truman reversed his country's position and brought the United States and other members of the United Nations into the conflict. The initial successes of the North Koreans, the intervention of Communist China, and widespread destruction in the south hardened South Korea's opposition to Communism. When the war ended, Korea remained a divided country. (*See also* Korean War.)

Having failed to unify Korea militarily, Kim Il Sung launched a campaign of infiltration and subversion. With North Korea's population less than half that of South Korea and with no assurance that aid from the quarreling Soviets and Chinese would be forthcoming, Kim realized that North Korea could not enforce its will on South Korea through a new war.

Since the early 1960's Kim Il Sung has asserted that the question of unification must be settled by the Koreans themselves. He proposed the withdrawal of all United Nations forces from the south, the reduction of the armed forces of each of the country's two sections to a maximum of 100,000 men, and the beginning of economic and cultural relations between North Korea and South Korea. These moves would be followed by a confederation permitting the continuation of independent activities by the two Korean governments. Kim's overtures were rejected both by the Republic of Korea and the United Nations General Assembly, which maintained the position that unification could be achieved only through general elections supervised by the United Nations. South Korean officials also said that, if United Nations forces left, another North Korean attack might succeed.

His political overtures rebuffed, in 1966 Kim spelled out a detailed blueprint for the overthrow of President Park Chung Hee's South Korean government. He called for the creation of a South Korean Marxist-Leninist workers' and peasants' party. He increased infiltration into the south by propaganda-terrorist teams. On Jan. 21, 1968, a group of North Korean guerrillas on a mission to assassinate President Park were stopped less than a mile from the presidential mansion in Seoul. On January 23, the United States intelligence ship *Pueblo* was seized by North Korea off Wonsan. These acts inflamed public opinion in South Korea and the United States.

As the decade of the 1970's opened, shooting incidents were common in the demilitarized zone between North Korea and South Korea, and the two nations continued to strengthen their military forces. In 1971, however, the rival regimes opened discussions to reunite millions of Korean families that had been separated by the division of their country after World War II. A South-North Coordinating Committee was established in 1972, but in mid-1973 the north began boycotting its sessions. As the decade ended, the south sought further reunification talks; joint political meetings were short-lived, however.

Shinto religion was taught in Korean schools, while the Korean language was forbidden and the study of Korean history was discouraged.

Korean missions abroad made unsuccessful appeals to the great powers for help in restoring their kingdom. In 1919 the Koreans staged a passive resistance campaign known as the *Samil* (March First) Independence Movement. Thousands of unarmed people were killed, wounded, and imprisoned in the brutal repression instituted by the Japanese authorities. The same year a Korean provisional government-in-exile was formed in Shanghai, China, with Syngman Rhee as president.

### Recent Times

Korea was liberated in 1945, after Japan's defeat in World War II. Under a wartime agreement concerned solely with the surrender of the Japanese forces, Soviet troops occupied the area north of the 38th parallel and United States troops the area south of the 38th parallel. For the next three years there were fruitless negotiations on how to reunify Korea. The United Nations proposed nationwide elections. Although the north refused, elections were held in the south. As a result, the Republic of Korea was established in the south in August 1948, and Syngman Rhee was elected president by its new National Assembly. In September the Democratic People's Republic of Korea was established in the north, with Kim Il Sung, a Communist, as its premier. Kim had gained prominence in the 1930's as a leader of anti-Japanese Korean guerrillas based in Manchuria.

By 1950 all United States and Soviet troops had been withdrawn from Korea. But in June the Soviet-equipped North Korean army invaded South Korea, beginning the Korean War. The United Nations

K. M. Lee

South Korea was left in ruins by the Korean War. Modern Seoul symbolizes the rapid reconstruction and modernization of South Korea after the conflict.

voted to aid South Korea, but most of the troops sent to fight the North Koreans were furnished by the United States. At the end of 1950 Communist China entered the war in support of North Korea. In 1953 a truce was signed, with the truce line at approximately the prewar border. (*See also* Korean War.)

The Korean War severely crippled industrial and agricultural production in both North and South Korea. In North Korea an economic recovery program was begun in 1953, with substantial aid from the Soviet Union and Communist China. Most private farms were replaced by state-controlled cooperatives. The development of heavy industry was stressed.

In the south, the Korean War left Rhee's government weak and unstable. Increasingly, Rhee turned to force in an effort to maintain his rule. Students protested against his manipulation of elections. In 1960 Rhee was ousted, and he fled to Hawaii.

A military junta seized control of South Korea in 1961. Gen. Park Chung Hee, a junta leader, was elected president in 1963. His Democratic Republican party won a majority in the National Assembly. The country's rapid economic growth led to Park's re-election in 1967 and again in 1971. Despite improved relations between North and South Korea, Park then declared a state of emergency, invoking the threat of invasion from the north. In 1972 he declared martial law, banned all political activity, and dissolved the National Assembly. A revised constitution, giving Park almost unlimited powers, was adopted; he was reelected for six-year terms in 1972 and 1978.

North Korea also revised its constitution in 1972. Premier Kim was named to the new post of president.

On Oct. 26, 1979, Park was slain in a shootout. The caretaker president, Choi Kyu Hah, restored the civil rights of dissidents, but a return to democratic rule depended upon revision of the constitution.

Reunification meetings, begun in 1972, were stalemated in 1973. In 1979 summit talks were resumed, and preliminary conferences were held in 1980.

---

### Words to Remember

*mumun*—undecorated ancient Korean pottery.
*yangban*—the Yi Dynasty's landowning elite.
*hangul*—the Korean alphabet.
*Tonghak* (Eastern Learning)—an antiforeign Korean movement of the late 19th century.
*Samil* (March First)—a 1919 resistance movement against Japan's occupation of Korea.

---

### Questions to Think About

1. How has Korea's history been affected by its location between China and Japan?
2. Give possible reasons why some 19th-century Koreans preferred *Sohak*, or "Western Learning," while others advocated *Tonghak*, or "Eastern Learning."
3. Could the political division of Korea after World War II have been prevented? Explain.

# Notable Events in Korea's History

**1592–98**—Korea's Adm. Yi Sunsin uses ironclad vessels—the so-called "turtle ships"—to battle Japanese invaders. Ming Dynasty China helps Korea repel Japanese land forces.

Hakwon-Sa Co., Ltd.

**1950–53**—Korean War, an attempt by North Korea to forcefully reunify Korea, ends in stalemate; truce signed between North Korea and United Nations, 1953.

Wide World

1600 1900 1950 2000

UPI Compix

**1919**—Mass arrests and executions put down Samil Independence Movement against Japan's occupation of Korea. Syngman Rhee heads Korean government-in-exile based in China.

Wide World

**1963**—Park Chung Hee is elected president of South Korea; served until assassination, 1979; Park's administrations distinguished by political stabilization and economic advances.

## THE KOREAN PEOPLE BUILD THEIR NATION

**2d century B.C.**—Choson state established.
**108 B.C.**—Northern Korea conquered by Han China.
**1st century B.C.**—Rise of the Three Kingdoms.
**4th century A.D.**—Buddhism introduced into Korea.
**660–68**—Paekche and Koguryo kingdoms conquered by T'ang China and Silla kingdom.
**935**—Koryo kingdom gains control of Korea.
**1392**—Yi Dynasty established.
**1592–98**—Japanese invade Korea.
**1627–37**—Manchus invade Korea; Korea becomes vassal of Ch'ing China.
**1876**—Korea signs Treaty of Kanghwa with Japan; signs treaties with Western powers, 1882–86.
**1894–95**—Antiforeign Tonghak Rebellion quelled. Sino-Japanese War ends China's influence over Korea.
**1905**—Japan establishes protectorate over Korea after victory in Russo-Japanese War, 1904–5.

**1910**—Japan annexes Korea; Samil Independence Movement against Japanese occupation crushed, 1919.
**1945**—United States and Soviet troops occupy Korea after Japan's defeat in World War II.
**1948**—Separate North Korean and South Korean governments set up.
**1950**—North Korea's invasion of South Korea triggers Korean War; truce signed, 1953.
**1960**—April Revolution in South Korea forces Syngman Rhee's resignation; military coup ousts successor, 1961.
**1963**—Constitutional rule restored in south. Park elected president; reelected, 1967, 1971, 1972, 1978.
**1972**—North Korea and South Korea revise constitutions. South-North Coordinating Committee established; reunification sessions disbanded, 1973; attempts to reopen joint talks resumed, 1979, 1980.
**1979**—Park assassinated.

# KOREA – Fact Summary

## HOW KOREA COMPARES . . .
### . . . IN AREA AND POPULATION

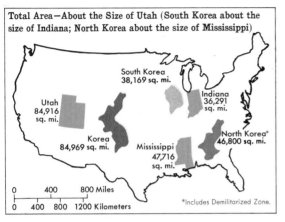

Total Area—About the Size of Utah (South Korea about the size of Indiana; North Korea about the size of Mississippi)

South Korea
38,169 sq. mi.

Indiana
36,291 sq. mi.

Utah
84,916 sq. mi.

Korea
84,969 sq. mi.

Mississippi
47,716 sq. mi.

North Korea*
46,800 sq. mi.

0    400    800 Miles
0    400    800    1200 Kilometers

*Includes Demilitarized Zone.

---

Population—About as Large as the States of Massachusetts, Michigan, Ohio, Illinois, Texas, and Minnesota (1978 Population Estimates in Millions)

| Mass. 5.8 | Michigan 9.2 | Ohio 10.7 | Illinois 11.2 | 36.9 |

| South Korea | 37.0 |

| Texas 13.0 | Minn. 4.0 | 17.0 |

| North Korea | 17.1 |

Sources: Bureau of the Census, U.S. Dept. of Commerce;
Statistical Office, United Nations

---

—South Korea Near the Top in Population Density*

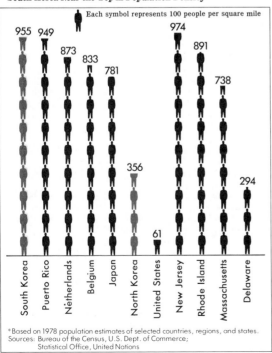

Each symbol represents 100 people per square mile

955  949  873  833  781  974  891  738
South Korea  Puerto Rico  Netherlands  Belgium  Japan  356 North Korea  61 United States  New Jersey  Rhode Island  Massachusetts  294 Delaware

*Based on 1978 population estimates of selected countries, regions, and states.
Sources: Bureau of the Census, U.S. Dept. of Commerce;
Statistical Office, United Nations

## . . . IN ECONOMIC ACTIVITY

Slow Increase in Gross National Product (GNP)*

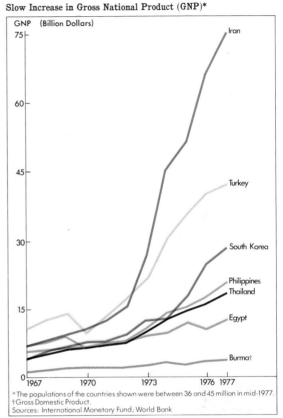

GNP   (Billion Dollars)

75 — Iran

60

45 — Turkey

30 — South Korea

Philippines
Thailand

15 — Egypt

Burma†

0
1967      1970      1973      1976 1977

* The populations of the countries shown were between 36 and 45 million in mid-1977.
†Gross Domestic Product.
Sources: International Monetary Fund; World Bank

---

Korea Ranks High in the Output of Several Products

| Product | SOUTH KOREA World Rank | SOUTH KOREA Share of World Output | NORTH KOREA World Rank | NORTH KOREA Share of World Output |
|---|---|---|---|---|
| Graphite | 5 | 10.7% | 2 | 17.5% |
| Magnesite | * | * | 2 | 17.0% |
| Tungsten | 6 | 6.2% | 8 | 5.0% |
| Cabbages | 4 | 4.8% | 15 | 1.3% |
| Soybeans | 10 | 0.4% | 11 | 0.4% |
| Rice | 10 | 2.3% | 12 | 1.3% |
| Sweet potatoes | 3 | 1.3% | 18 | 0.3% |
| Salted and dried herring, anchovies, and sardines | 8 | 1.6% | * | * |

*Data not available.

Sources: Food and Agriculture Organization of the United Nations;
The Mining Journal

77b

# KOREA

## Reference-Outline

### THE PEOPLE AND THEIR CULTURE

I. The people K-75b: population K-75a, 75b, charts K-75b, 77b, map K-75c; race K-75b, 76f; language K-75c, 76b, 76f, L-116 (alphabet, table K-76b)
II. How the people live K-75b–d: social services K-75d
  A. The family K-75b–c: family names K-75b; children K-75b
  B. Food K-75c: rice R-199
  C. Clothing K-75c, pictures K-75d, 76c
  D. Shelter K-75c, picture K-75d
  E. Recreation K-75d, K-64, picture K-76c
  F. Education: South Korea K-75d, S-111; North Korea K-75d
  G. Religion K-75d
III. Korean arts K-76b–c: Chinese influence K-76b, 76c
  A. Architecture K-75c, 76c, pictures K-75, 76a
  B. Literature K-76b, L-310f, S-468, 479
  C. Painting and sculpture K-76c, picture K-76a
  D. Crafts K-76c, P-473, pictures K-76b, M-231
  E. Music, dancing, drama, puppets K-75e, 76c
IV. Government: South Korea K-75e–f, 77, chart K-75f (flag F-210–11, picture F-209); North Korea K-75f, 77 (flag F-210, picture F-209)

### THE LAND AND THE ECONOMY OF KOREA

I. Location and size K-75–75a: location in world, map W-243; in Asia, maps A-636, C-313, P-4; political divisions, map K-77d
II. Structure of the land K-76d, maps K-76d, C-291
  A. Mountains and plains K-76d, picture K-76a
  B. Coastline and islands K-76d, maps K-77d, C-313
III. Climate K-76d–e, A-618, map K-76e: winds W-183
IV. Plant and animal life K-76e
V. Principal cities K-75b, 76d: South Korea—Seoul S-111; North Korea—Pyongyang (Fact-Index)
VI. Resources and industries, tables K-75h, 77b: land use, chart K-75g

A. Agriculture: South Korea K-75g, table K-75h; North Korea K-75h-6, table K-75h
B. Fisheries: South Korea K-75g; North Korea K-76
C. Forests and forest products: South Korea K-75g; North Korea K-76
D. Fuels and power sources: South Korea K-75g–h; North Korea K-76
E. Manufacturing: South Korea K-75h, S-111, table K-75h; North Korea K-76, picture K-76
F. Mining and minerals A-627, 628, G-178, T-288: South Korea K-75h; North Korea K-76
VII. Trade: South Korea K-75h; North Korea K-76
VIII. Transportation and communication: South Korea K-75h, picture S-111; North Korea K-76

### HISTORY OF KOREA

I. Early history K-76f: silk culture introduced S-202; Chinese Han Dynasty conquers land K-76f, C-295g–h
II. Three Kingdoms—Koguryo, Paekche, and Silla K-76f: Buddhism introduced K-76f; Korea unified under Silla, Chinese culture imitated K-76f, A-630
III. Koryo Dynasty (935–1392): K-76f: land invaded by Ch'itan (11th century) and by Mongols (13th century) C-295h; Korean invasion of Japan J-405
IV. Yi Dynasty (1392–1910) K-76f–g
  A. Alphabet (hangul) completed (1446) K-76b, 76f
  B. Ironclad ships used against Japanese K-76f
  C. Manchu invasions; Korea becomes a vassal state of China K-76f
  D. First Europeans visit Korea (17th century) K-76f
  E. Korean ports opened to Japan by treaty (1876); United States treaty signed (1882) K-76g
  F. Tonghak Rebellion; Sino-Japanese War (1894–95) K-76g, J-407: independence recognized C-296
V. Korea in the 20th century K-76g–7
  A. Russo-Japanese War (1904–5); Japan gains control of Korea R-362, K-75g, 76g, J-407, P-17
  B. Japanese annexation and occupation (1910–45) K-76g, 77, J-407: Samil Independence Movement suppressed K-77, picture K-77a; government-in-exile formed by Syngman Rhee (1919) K-77
  C. Aftermath of World War II K-75, 75g, 76h, 77, K-77g: Soviet and American occupation K-77; a land divided—North and South Korea K-77
  D. Korean War (1950–53) K-77f–78b, K-76h, 77, U-24, R-357, C-302, M-2, map K-77h, table K-78b: the truce K-78–78a, K-75a, U-193–4
  E. Uneasy peace; economic reconstruction; internal conflicts K-75, 75b, 76h, 77, K-78a: South Korea K-77; North Korea K-77

## Bibliography

Gosfield, Frank and Hurwood, B. J. Korea: Land of the 38th Parallel (Parents, 1969).
Gurney, Gene and Claire. North and South Korea (Watts, 1973).
Hatada, Takashi. A History of Korea (ABC-Clio, 1969).
Henderson, Gregory. Korea: the Politics of the Vortex (Harvard Univ. Press, 1968).
Johnston, R. J. Getting to Know the Two Koreas (Coward, 1965).
Lawson, Don. The United States in the Korean War: Defending Freedom's Frontier (Abelard, 1964).
Solberg, S. E. The Land and People of Korea, rev. ed. (Lippincott, 1973).
Vreeland, Nena and others. Area Handbook for North Korea, 2d ed. (U. S. Govt. Printing Office, 1976).
Vreeland, Nena and others. Area Handbook for South Korea, 2d ed. (U. S. Govt. Printing Office, 1975).

# KOREA

POLYCONIC PROJECTION

### SCALE OF MILES
0  20  40  60  80

### KILOMETERS
0  20  40  60  80

Capitals of Countries ....... ☆
Provincial Capitals ........... ⊙
International Boundaries ---·---
Provincial Boundaries ......-·-·
Railroads ...........................

## PROVINCES

| NORTH KOREA | REF. | SOUTH KOREA | REF. |
|---|---|---|---|
| 1. Chagang | B2 | 12. Cheju | B6 |
| 2. Kaesong (city) | B3 | 13. Kangwon | C4 |
| 3. Kangwon | B3 | 14. Kyonggi | B4 |
| 4. N. Hamgyong | C2 | 15. N. Cholla | B5 |
| 5. N. Hwanghae | B3 | 16. N. Chungchong | B4 |
| 6. N. Pyongan | A2 | 17. N. Kyongsang | C4 |
| 7. Pyongyang (city) | A3 | 18. Pusan (city) | C5 |
| 8. S. Hamgyong | B3 | 19. Seoul (city) | B4 |
| 9. S. Hwanghae | B3 | 20. S. Cholla | B5 |
| 10. S. Pyongan | B3 | 21. S. Chungchong | B4 |
| 11. Yanggang | C2 | 22. S. Kyongsang | C5 |

© C. S. HAMMOND & Co., Maplewood, N.J.

Longitude East B of Greenwich

# KOREA*


Aechang B 3
Anak, 25,185 A 3
Anbyon B 3
Andong, 95,449 C 4
Anju, 21,861 A 3
Ansan-ni, 12,326 B 5
Ansong, 27,723 B 4
Anui, 16,112 B 5
Anyang, 134,862 B 4
Aoji-ri, 39,616 D 1
Bonghwa, 20,344 C 4
Chaeryong, 22,227 A 3
Chagang (province), 885,000 B 2
Chaho, 20,328 C 2
Changbaek-sanmaek (mts.) B 2
Changhowon-ni, 18,395 B 4
Changhung, 22,227 B 5
Changhung-ni B 2
Changjin (reservoir) B 2
Changjin (river) B 2
Changjon C 3
Changnyon A 3
Changnyong, 22,763 C 5
Changpai B 2
Changsan-got (point) A 3
Changsong, 17,661 A 2
Changsong, 26,266 B 5
Changsungpo-ri, 17,051 C 5
Changyon, 18,072 A 3
Changyong-gap (point) C 4
Chasong B 2
Chechon, 74,239 B 4
Cheju, 135,189 B 6
Cheju (island), 412,021 B 6
Cheju (province), 412,021 B 6
Cheju (strait) A 6
Chido, 24,475 B 5
Chinan, 19,305 B 5
Chinchon, 20,347 B 4
Chin-do (island) A 5
Chinhae, 103,657 C 5
Chinju, 154,676 B 5
Chinyong-ni, 20,468 C 5
Chiri-san (mountain) B 5
Chochiwon, 29,198 B 4
Cho-do (island) A 3
Cholsan, 12,501 A 3
Chonan, 96,789 B 4
Chonchon (Mupyong-ni) B 2
Chongchon (river) A 3
Chongdan B 3
Chongdo, 25,577 C 5
Chongha, 13,025 C 4
Chongjin, 308,000 C 2
Chongju, 18,633 A 3
Chongju, 192,734 B 4
Chongpyong B 3
Chongsan, 12,318 B 4
Chongson, 21,002 C 4
Chongsong, 6,834 C 1
Chongup, 54,864 B 5
Chonju, 311,432 B 5
Chorwon, 8,180 B 3
Chosan, 18,239 A 2
Chulpo, 12,410 B 5
Chumunjin, 34,185 C 4
Chunchon, 140,521 B 4
Chungju, 105,143 C 4
Chungmu, 66,817 C 5
Chungsan, 12,932 A 3
Chunyang, 15,618 C 4
Chuuronjang, 37,134 C 2
Dagelet (Ullungdo) (island) D 4
East Korea (bay) B 3
Hadong, 20,400 B 5
Haeju, 131,000 A 3
Haeju-man (bay) A 4
Haemi, 16,096 B 4
Haenam, 26,766 B 5
Hamchang, 20,426 C 4
Hamhung-Hungnam, 680,000 B 2
Hamjong-ni, 11,824 A 3
Hampyong, 21,383 B 5
Hamyang, 26,780 B 5
Han (river) B 4
Hanchon, 11,412 A 3
Hapsu C 2
Hochon (river) C 2
Hoengsong, 19,541 C 4
Hoeryong, 24,330 C 1
Hoeyang B 3
Hongchon, 29,499 B 4
Hong-do (island) A 5
Hongsong, 26,995 B 4
Hongwon, 25,663 B 2
Huchang B 2
Huichon, 14,619 B 2
Hungnam-Hamhung, 680,000 B 3
Hupkok B 3
Hwachon (reservoir) C 3
Hwachon-ni B 3
Hwangju, 16,993 A 3
Hwasun, 22,862 B 5
Hyesanjin C 2
Ichon, 22,825 B 4
Imjin (river) B 3
Inchon, 799,982 B 4
Ipyong-dong B 2
Iri, 117,111 B 5
Iwon C 2
Japan (sea) D 4
Kaesong, 379,000 B 3
Kampo-ri, 15,030 C 5
Kang-dong, 12,848 B 3
Kanggye, 30,013 B 2
Kanggyong, 23,659 B 4
Kanghwa, 21,577 B 4
Kanghwa (bay) A 3
Kanghwa-do (island) B 4
Kangnung, 85,040 C 4
Kangso, 12,264 A 3
Kangwon (province), 1,421,000 B 3
Kangwon (province), 1,862,107 C 4
Kansong, 10,051 C 3
Kapsan C 2
Kapyong, 19,716 B 4
Kasan-dong B 2
Kigye, 20,230 C 4
Kijang, 19,762 C 5
Kilchu, 30,026 C 2
Kimchaek (Songjin), 67,778 C 2
Kochang (North Cholla), 23,721 B 5
Kochang (South Kyongsang), 41,624 B 5
Kogum-do (island), 16,777 B 5
Kogunsan-kundo B 5
Kohung, 17,654 B 5
Koje (island) C 5
Koksan, 7,213 B 3
Koksong, 16,121 B 5
Komdok-san (mountain) C 2
Kongju, 39,756 B 4
Korea (strait) C 5
Kosan, 11,371 B 5
Kosanjin A 2
Kosong, North Korea, 14,842 C 3
Kosong, South Korea, 27,096 C 5
Kosong-ni C 2
Koto-ri B 2
Kowon B 3
Kujang-dong B 3
Kum (river) B 4
Kumchon, 67,066 C 4
Kumhae, 55,635 C 5
Kumhwa, 5,619 B 3
Kumje, 35,974 B 5
Kumo-do (island) B 5
Kumsan, 28,968 B 4
Kumsong B 3
Kunsan, 154,485 B 5
Kunu-ri B 3
Kunwi, 14,960 C 4
Kurye, 19,930 B 5
Kuryongpo-ri, 31,781 C 5
Kusong, 11,191 A 2
Kwangchon-ni, 24,623 B 4
Kwangju, 607,058 B 5
Kwangyang, 26,381 B 5
Kwanmo-bong (mountain) C 2
Kyebang-san (mountain) C 4
Kyomipo, 53,035 A 3
Kyonggi (province), 4,039,885 B 4
Kyonghung D 1
Kyongju, 108,447 C 5
Kyongsan, 30,648 C 5
Kyongsong, 25,925 C 2
Manpojin B 2
Masan, 371,937 C 5
Mayang-do (island) C 3
Miryang, 42,951 C 5
Mokpo, 192,927 B 5
Muju, 18,130 B 5
Mukhojin-ni, 55,154 C 4
Munchon, 12,005 B 3
Mungyong, 22,958 B 4
Mupyong-ni B 2
Musan, 20,717 C 1
Musu-dan (point) C 2
Myohyang-san (mountain) B 2
Myongchon C 2
Najin, 34,338 D 1
Naju, 30,727 B 5
Naktong, 14,134 C 4
Naktong (river) C 5
Nam (river) C 5
Namchonjom A 3
Nampo (Chinnampo), 153,000 A 3
Namsi A 3
Namwon, 50,859 B 5
Nan (river) B 3
Nanam, 20,936 C 2
Nonsan, 30,844 B 4
North Cholla (province), 2,456,455 B 5
North Chungchong (province), 1,552,155 B 4
North Hamgyong (province), 1,800,000 C 2
North Hwanghae (province), 1,294,000 B 3
North Korea, 17,078,000 B 2
North Kyongsang (province), 4,858,809 C 4
North Pyongan, 2,051,000 A 2
Obok-tong C 2
Odaejin, 9,083 C 2
Okchon, 26,139 B 4
Ongjin, 32,965 A 4
Onsong, 10,116 D 1
Onyang, 41,519 B 4
Osan, 31,207 B 4
Paektu-san (mountain) C 1
Paengnyond-do (island) A 4
Pakchon, 17,184 A 3
Pango-ri C 5
Panmunjom B 4
Panpyong-dong A 2
Pigum-do (island), 15,404 A 5
Pihyon A 3
Piro-bong (mountain) B 3
Pohang, 134,404 C 5
Pohari (Poha-dong) C 2
Polgyo-ri, 38,857 B 5
Pongdu-ri C 2
Popsongpo, 16,344 B 5
Port Hamilton (So-do) (island) B 5
Posong, 20,256 B 5
Poun, 20,961 B 4
Puan, 27,284 B 5
Puchon, 109,236 B 4
Pujon (reservoir) B 2
Pukchin A 2
Pukchong, 30,709 B 2
Pukhan (river) B 3
Puksubaek-san (mountain) B 2
Punggi, 24,012 C 4
Pungsan, 17,453 C 2
Pusan, 2,454,051 C 5
Pusan (city-province), 2,454,051 C 5
Puyo, 31,176 B 4
Pyoktong, 11,567 A 2
Pyongchang, 18,054 C 4
Pyonggang, 20,524 B 3
Pyonghae-ri, 23,816 C 4
Pyongsong A 3
Pyongtaek, 51,470 B 4
Pyongyang (capital), North Korea, 1,157,000 A 3
Pyongyang (city-province), 2,147,000 A 3
Quelpart (Cheju) (island), 412,021 B 6
Saji-dong C 2
Sakchu, 13,568 A 2
Samchok, 42,526 C 4
Samchonpo, 59,721 C 5
Samga, 13,327 C 5
Samnangjin, 19,374 C 5
Sangju, 52,889 C 4
Sang-ni B 2
Sariwon, 42,957 A 3
Seoul (capital) South Korea, 6,889,470 B 4
Seoul (city-province), 6,889,470 B 4
Sinanju A 3
Sinchang, 21,770 C 2
Sinchang-ni B 3
Sinchon, 22,611 A 3
Singosan B 3
Sinmak B 3
Sinmi-do (island) A 3
Sinnyong, 11,960 C 4
Sinpo, 26,086 C 2
Sinuiju, 210,000 A 2
Sinwon-ni A 3
Soan-kundo (island), 10,200 B 5
So-do (island) B 5
Sodu (river) C 2
Sogwi-ri, 53,420 B 6
Sohuksan-do (island) A 5
Sokcho, 71,475 C 3
Somjin (river) B 5
Sonchon, 22,725 A 2
Songchon, 9,148 B 3
Songhwan, 27,596 B 4
Songjong-ni, 41,909 B 5
Songju, 18,822 C 5
Sonsan, 17,900 C 4
Sosan, 38,081 B 4
Sosura D 1
South Cholla (province), 3,984,849 B 5
South Chungchong (province), 2,948,649 B 4
South Hamgyong (province), 2,241,000 B 3
South Hwanghae (province), 1,735,000 A 3
South Korea, 34,708,542 B 4
South Kyongsang (prov.), 3,280,091 C 5
South Pyongan (province), 2,589,000 B 3
Suan B 3
Sunan A 3
Sunchon, 20,682 A 3
Sunchon, 108,034 B 5
Supung (reservoir) A 2
Susang-ni C 2
Suwon, 224,177 B 4
Taean, 23,112 B 4
Taean-dong A 2
Taebaek-san (mountain) C 4
Taebaek-San Maek (mountains) C 4
Taechon, 42,282 B 4
Taedong (river) B 3
Taegang-got (point) B 3
Taegu, 1,311,078 C 5
Taehuksan-do (island) A 5
Taein, 17,275 B 5
Taejon, 506,703 B 4
Taejong, 24,964 B 6
Takeshima (Tok-Do) (isls.) D 4
Tamyang, 15,494 B 5
Tanchon, 32,761 C 2
Tangjin, 22,645 B 4
Tokchok-kundo (islands) A 4
Tokchon, 15,711 B 3
Tok-Do (Takeshima) (isls.) D 4
Tolsan-do (island) B 5
Tongchon, 12,443 C 3
Tongno (river) B 2
Tumen (river) C 1
Tungsan-got (point) A 4
Tuun-bong (mountain) B 2
Uijongbu, 108,365 B 4
Uiju, 27,378 C 4
Uisong, 26,480 C 4
Ulchin, 27,607 C 4
Ullung-do (island), 29,517 D 4
Ulsan, 252,639 C 5
Unggi, 20,882 D 1
Waegwan, 31,076 C 5
Wando, 22,171 B 5
West Korea (bay) A 3
Wi-do (island), 4,619 B 5
Wiwon B 2
Wonju, 120,335 C 4
Wonsan, 295,000 B 3
Yalu (river) A 2
Yangdok B 3
Yanggang (prov.), 536,000 C 2
Yangmun-ni B 3
Yangpyong, 17,385 B 4
Yangyang, 10,819 C 3
Yean, 12,243 C 4
Yechon, 27,577 C 4
Yellow (sea) A 3
Yesan, 35,775 B 4
Yesong (river) B 3
Yoju, 20,928 B 4
Yonan, 29,743 B 4
Yongam, 16,427 B 5
Yongampo, 17,873 A 3
Yongchon, 50,765 C 5
Yongdok, 18,671 C 4
Yongdong, 26,572 B 4
Yonggwang, 21,967 B 5
Yonghae, 15,305 C 4
Yonghung, 18,445 B 3
Yonghung-man (bay) B 3
Yongil-man (bay) C 4
Yongju, 70,793 C 4
Yongsapo A 3
Yongwol, 31,619 C 4
Yonpo B 3
Yonsanpo, 25,991 B 5
Yosu, 130,641 B 5
Yudam-ni B 2


* All population figures are taken from the latest census or official estimate available.

Delivering fire support to United Nations ground forces in Korea, the battleship USS *Wisconsin* looses a salvo of one-ton, 16-inch projectiles at a Communist position.

**KOREAN WAR.** Early in the morning of June 25, 1950, the armed forces of Communist North Korea smashed across the 38th parallel of latitude in an invasion of the Republic of Korea (South Korea) that achieved complete surprise. Although attacks came all along the border, the major North Korean thrust was in the west of the Korean peninsula, toward Seoul, the capital of South Korea.

South Korea's army, smaller and not as well trained and equipped as that of North Korea, was unable to stem the onslaught. By June 28, Seoul had fallen, and across the peninsula, everywhere south of the Han River, the shattered remnants of South Korea's army were in full retreat.

## The World Reacts

Within hours after the invasion of South Korea began, the United Nations Security Council called for an immediate cease-fire and the withdrawal of North Korean forces from South Korea. North Korea ignored the resolution. Two days later the Security Council urged United Nations members to assist South Korea in repelling its invaders. Both resolutions passed because Russia was boycotting Security Council meetings. Had the Soviet delegate been present, he surely would have vetoed the measures.

In response, 16 nations sent troops to the aid of South Korea. The United States sent an army; Great Britain, a division; and other nations, lesser units. The heaviest burden of the war, however, was borne by South Korea itself. Its army reached a peak strength of some 400,000 men, maintained that strength only by a steady flow of hastily trained replacements, and sustained an estimated 850,000 combat casualties. The United States Army in Korea ultimately numbered some 300,000 men, supported by about 50,000 Marine, Air Force, and Navy combatants.

The United States reacted even more quickly than did the United Nations. Upon hearing of the North Korean attack, President Harry S. Truman directed General of the Army Douglas MacArthur, commander of the United States occupation forces in Japan, to insure the safe evacuation of United States civilians and to supply weapons and ammunition to South Korea.

On June 26, United States air and naval forces were directed to support South Korean ground units. The commitment of United States ground forces was authorized after General MacArthur inspected the battlefront. The ground forces available to General MacArthur in Japan were four understrength Army divisions composed largely of inexperienced, undertrained men and lacking in heavy weapons.

Early in July the United Nations asked the United States to appoint a commander for all United Nations forces in Korea. President Truman named General MacArthur. Soon thereafter, South Korea placed its forces under the United Nations command.

After the fall of Seoul, North Korea's forces paused briefly to regroup, then resumed their southward drive. South Korea's army resisted bravely

David Douglas Duncan, *Life* © Time Inc.

Members of the first Marine brigade to reach Korea advance during the defense of the Pusan perimeter. The Marines, though few in number, were instrumental in thwarting the initial Communist offensive that nearly overran South Korea.

but was pushed back steadily. Three United States divisions sent to its aid were committed in small units. They too were driven into retreat. By late July the remnants of South Korea's army and the United States units had been pressed into a small, roughly rectangular area surrounding the port of Pusan at the southeastern tip of Korea. Here, defending a perimeter roughly 150 miles long, the United Nations forces finally were able to hold as reinforcements poured in.

## The Origins of a War

The roots of the Korean War are deeply embedded in history. While few regions are less suited to warfare than is the mountainous, river-slashed Korean peninsula, few have known more conflict. For centuries, Korea's three powerful neighbors—China, Japan, and the Soviet Union—vied for its control. By 1910, Japan had established a supremacy that it was to maintain until its defeat in World War II.

Seven days before the Japanese surrender that ended World War II, the Soviet Union declared war on Japan. Soviet troops entered Korea. By agreement, the Soviet Union accepted the surrender of all Japanese forces in Korea north of the 38th parallel of latitude, while the United States accepted the surrender of Japanese units south of the 38th parallel.

The Soviet Union quickly sealed off the 38th-parallel border. It soon set up an interim civil government for the 9 million Koreans of the north, which contained most of Korea's industry. The government was run by Soviet-trained Communist officials.

The United States maintained a military government in the south. The 21 million Koreans of the largely agricultural region were not satisfied with it.

A United States–Soviet commission that was established to make plans for the reunification of Korea under a free government made no progress. In 1947 the United States took the problem before the United Nations, which voted that free elections—under its supervision—should be held throughout Korea in 1948 to choose a single government. The Soviet Union refused to permit the United Nations election commission to enter the north. Elections were thus held only in the south, where a National Assembly and a president—Syngman Rhee—were chosen. The new democracy was named the Republic of Korea.

In the north, the Soviet Union proclaimed a Communist dictatorship called the Democratic People's Republic of Korea (North Korea). Pyongyang was named its capital. Late in 1948, Soviet forces began to withdraw from North Korea, leaving behind an entrenched Communist regime and a well-trained, well-equipped North Korean army. United States occupation forces left South Korea in 1949. They left behind a government still "feeling its way" and an army ill-trained compared with that of the north. This army also lacked air power, tanks, and artillery.

South Korea, however, successfully resisted North Korean attempts at subversion, Communist-supported guerrilla activities, and border raids by North Korean forces. Frustrated, North Korea early in 1950 decided upon war to achieve its goal of Korean unification under Communist rule.

In June 1950 North Korea's army totaled some 135,000 men. North Korea's infantry was supported by some 150 Soviet-made medium tanks, ample artillery, and a small air force. South Korea's ground

## THE HUMAN COST OF THE KOREAN WAR

| UNITED NATIONS | Dead | Wounded and Missing | Total |
|---|---|---|---|
| Republic of Korea | 591,285 | 1,293,592 | 1,884,877 |
| United States | 33,629 | 103,308 | 136,937 |
| Turkey | 725 | 2,234 | 2,959 |
| United Kingdom | 493 | 1,680 | 2,173 |
| Canada | 320 | 1,211 | 1,531 |
| France | 219 | 815 | 1,034 |
| Australia | 180 | 748 | 928 |
| Thailand | 114 | 799 | 913 |
| Greece | 187 | 615 | 802 |
| Netherlands | 120 | 648 | 768 |
| Colombia | 140 | 517 | 657 |
| Ethiopia | 120 | 536 | 656 |
| Belgium | 101 | 354 | 455 |
| Philippines | 81 | 233 | 314 |
| New Zealand | 37 | 80 | 117 |
| South Africa | 22 | 12 | 34 |
| Totals | 627,773 | 1,407,382 | 2,035,155 |
| **COMMUNIST** | | | |
| North Korea | | | 926,000 |
| People's Republic of China | | | 900,000 |
| Total | | | 1,826,000 |

**SCALING THE SEAWALL AT INCHON**
Marines of the first assault wave scramble over the seawall at the port of Inchon in September 1950. The daring amphibious attack led to the recapture of Seoul and the complete destruction of North Korea's army as an effective fighting force.

forces included a 45,000-man national police force and an army of 98,000 men. South Korea was armed largely with light infantry weapons supplied by the United States. It had no tanks or combat aircraft, and its artillery was inferior to that of North Korea. Its officers and men had generally less training and experience than did those of North Korea.

## Masterstroke Reverses Course of War

While North Korea continued to hurl furious but ineffective attacks at the Pusan perimeter, General MacArthur readied the counterstroke that was to reverse the course of the war—an amphibious assault in his enemy's rear at the port city of Inchon, southwest of Seoul. On September 15, a Marine division swarmed ashore after preparatory bombardment by aircraft and naval guns. An Army division followed. Simultaneously, the Eighth Army—by now a well-equipped and cohesive force—broke out of the Pusan perimeter. Although bloody fighting was required, Seoul was recaptured within a few days. Thereafter the North Korean army—its supply line severed and its principal withdrawal route blocked by the capture of Seoul—rapidly collapsed. By October 1, utterly destroyed as a fighting force, its remnants had retreated above the 38th parallel.

North Korea had also met disaster in the air. Late in June, United States jet fighters had streaked westward from Japan after a North Korean fighter fired on an American transport. Within two weeks the North Korean air force had ceased to exist, and the United Nations had established an air superiority that it generally was to maintain throughout the war. Even when, later in the war, the Communist forces were supplied with Russian-built jet fighters equal or superior to the United States aircraft flown by the United Nations, their Chinese—and sometimes Russian—pilots proved no match for those of the United Nations. In the course of the war, 14 Communist aircraft were shot down for every United Nations plane lost in aerial combat. At sea, under the guns of United States and British warships, North Korea's minuscule navy—a few patrol boats—suffered a fate similar to that of its air force.

## North to Disaster

In the United Nations, Communist delegates indicated that North Korea would now be willing to accept restoration of the 38th parallel as the border between the two Koreas. The United States and South Korea, however, decided to forcibly reunite North and South Korea under the government of South Korea. They disbelieved the threat of Communist China that it would intervene if United Nations forces entered North Korea.

United Nations forces began in early October 1950 to press northward. They met only light resistance and by late November had captured virtually all of North Korea. At two points, units reached the Yalu River, the border between North Korea and Red China.

Shortly after the United Nations advance into North Korea began, however, Communist China had secretly begun to infiltrate troops into North Korea. United Nations air patrols detected no sign of them.

United Nations forces had advanced northward in two columns, the Eighth Army in the west and the X

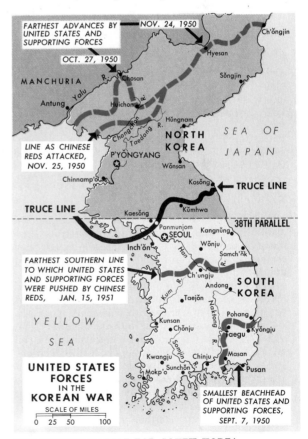

**THE SEESAW BATTLE FOR SOUTH KOREA**
This map shows how the conflict surged back and forth. The truce line added 850 square miles to North Korea below the 38th parallel, 2,350 square miles to South Korea above it.

Corps in the east, separated by up to 50 miles by the central mountain chain of North Korea. Units of both columns were also dispersed and open to attack.

Contacts with Communist Chinese units—some in strength—began in late October and continued into early November. Chinese aircraft—Russian-built MiG-15 jet fighters—first appeared early in November. However, the United Nations command underestimated the strength of the Chinese forces and misread China's intentions. The command planned a final offensive that would bring all of North Korea under United Nations control, confident that United Nations air power could prevent the Chinese from crossing the Yalu River in sufficient strength to stop the offensive. By this time, however, Chinese Communist troops in North Korea numbered 300,000.

**AGGRESSORS ON THE MARCH**
Soldiers of the North Korean army advance toward the front. Severed telephone lines offer mute evidence that United Nations air forces had previously patrolled the road.

Late in November, across the snow that heralded a harsh North Korean winter, the Chinese struck. Attacking largely at night, the Chinese—though they suffered tremendous casualties—rapidly dislodged the Eighth Army and X Corps.

In the east, X Corps units were withdrawn by sea from the ports of Hungnam and Wonsan. Surrounded far inland, the 1st Marine Division reached Hungnam in one of the great fighting retreats of history. In the west, by land and sea, the Eighth Army also fell back. By the end of December the United Nations forces had been pushed back to a line just south of the 38th parallel. In the face of a renewed Chinese offensive, they withdrew from Seoul and the Han River line early in January 1951.

In the more open terrain of South Korea, the United Nations forces were able to form a fairly continuous line of resistance. They continued to withdraw slowly, exacting a terrible toll of the advancing Chinese, until in mid-January the front stabilized along an undulating line running from the 37th parallel in the west to a point midway between the 37th and 38th parallels in the east.

## Reunification Abandoned

The entry of Red China into the war had a heavy impact upon the United States. Draft calls were increased, and more reservists were called to active duty. President Truman declared a state of national emergency, and economic controls were imposed.

Fearing that the wider war with China that would be necessary to reunify Korea would cost too many American lives and raise the risk of nuclear war with Russia, the United States abandoned the idea of forcibly reuniting the two Koreas. Instead, it decided to accept a rough restoration of the situation that had existed before the war. Although the United Nations declared Communist China an aggressor, it agreed with the new United States policy. United Nations forces would repel China from South Korea but would not seek to retake the north.

By late January 1951 the Eighth Army—reformed and strengthened and incorporating the X Corps—was ready to advance against the now-weakened Chinese and North Korean armies. Thrusts of infantry and armor were supported by the vastly superior United Nations artillery and air power. Where the Communist forces chose to stand, they were slaughtered. In one action alone, 6,000 Chinese men were killed, 25,000 wounded. Seoul was reoccupied by the United Nations in mid-March. By March 31 the battle line stood roughly along the 38th parallel.

Enraged at China's intervention, General MacArthur had dissented vigorously from the new United Nations policy. He wished to press an expanded war against Communist China, including forbidden attacks upon "sanctuaries" above the Yalu River. He made his views public. Believing the general's actions to be both insubordinate and dangerous, President Truman relieved him of his commands in April (see MacArthur; Truman). General MacArthur was replaced by Lieut. Gen. Matthew B. Ridgway, who had commanded the Eighth Army in the field since the death of Lieut. Gen. Walton H. Walker in a jeep accident in December 1950. Command of the Eighth Army was passed to Lieut. Gen. James A. Van Fleet.

## Truce Talks Begin

Above the 38th parallel, the Chinese and North Korean forces once again regrouped. In April and in May, their commanders hurled them against the United Nations lines. In response, General Van Fleet's forces slowly withdrew, scourging their attackers with superior firepower. When their adversaries were exhausted by massive casualties and supply shortages, the United Nations forces counterattacked. By mid-June, save for a small sector north of Seoul in the west, the United Nations line stood well above the 38th parallel.

Late in June, the Soviet Union indicated that the Communists might be prepared to seek a truce. On

Helicopters were used to transport troops into combat for the first time in the Korean War. The versatile aircraft were also used extensively in the evacuation of the wounded.

June 30, General Ridgway offered to open truce negotiations. North Korea and China accepted.

Truce talks opened on July 10 at Kaesong, some 35 miles northwest of Seoul. It quickly became apparent that the opposing sides had different goals at the truce table. The United Nations sought only an honorable end to the war. North Korea and Red China, however, undertook to win in conference what they had been unable to attain on the battlefield. The Communists made every effort to embarrass and humiliate United Nations delegates, to force concessions through intransigence and delay, and to use the conference as a propaganda forum.

Although it was agreed that hostilities were to continue during the truce talks, no more major offensives were conducted during the war. A lull in the fighting developed as the talks opened; both sides used it to strengthen their forces. The Communist buildup was hampered—though not halted—by United Nations naval and air forces.

Late in August, the Communists broke off the truce talks. General Van Fleet promptly launched a limited offensive to straighten and improve the United Nations lines. By mid-October, defeated again, the Communists offered to reopen the truce talks.

The meeting site was moved to Panmunjom, some five miles east of Kaesong. Here the armistice talks were to drag on, with intermittent recesses, for another year and a half, stalling repeatedly over such issues as the establishment of a truce line and the repatriation of prisoners. Along the front, meanwhile, the fighting settled into a modernized version of the grinding trench warfare of World War I.

## A Long and Uneasy Truce

In order to maintain the military pressure that seemed essential to serious negotiations, the United Nations insisted that the truce line be the line of contact between the opposing armies at the time the truce was signed. Finally, a line was agreed upon. Finally, too, the Communists agreed that prisoners who did not wish to return to their homelands did not have to. At first, they had insisted that the United Nations return, by force if necessary, all the Communist prisoners it held. Nearly half of all the prisoners held by the United Nations—and three quarters of the Chinese—did not wish to return to Communist rule. The truce agreement was finally signed July 27, 1953, and that day, at 10:00 P.M., Korean time, the guns fell silent along the blood-soaked main line of resistance.

The conclusion of the cease-fire had probably been hastened by events outside of Korea. First, General of the Army Dwight D. Eisenhower, who succeeded Truman as president of the United States in January 1953, had hinted broadly that military pressure might be sharply increased if the fighting did not end soon. Second, the death in March 1953 of Soviet dictator Joseph Stalin caused a general turning inward of the Communist world.

After the cease-fire, the opposing forces each withdrew two kilometers from the truce line. The armistice agreement had provided for a conference to seek a permanent peace, but—in the face of Communist intransigence—it was delayed for many years. Today, United States troops remain in South Korea, and heavily armed North Korean and South Korean forces still face each other across a narrow demilitarized zone. Truce violations are common.

Despite the beginning of talks aimed at reuniting families divided by the war and looking toward eventual reunification of North Korea and South Korea, permanent peace seemed remote in the early 1970's. It was believed, however, that the long, bloody war had had a positive result. It was the first time in history that an invasion by a military aggressor had been halted through the combined action of members of a world organization.

A lonely sentinel watches a sector of the demilitarized zone between the two Koreas. To his left, the South Korean defense line stretches westward across the rugged peninsula.

# CHRONOLOGY OF THE KOREAN WAR*

## 1950

**June**

25. North Korean (Red) armored forces invade South Korea, or Republic of Korea (ROK), Sunday morning at dawn (Saturday afternoon, June 24, Eastern Standard Time), starting the conflict.
25. At 5:45 P.M. EST (Sunday), the United Nations (UN) issues cease-fire order. Reds ignore it.
26. President Harry S. Truman orders the United States air and naval forces in Far East to give armed aid to South Korean forces.
27. The UN empowers its members to send armed forces to aid South Korean forces.
28. Seoul abandoned.
30. Truman orders U. S. ground troops into action.

**July**

1. First U.S. troops arrive from Japan.
5. U. S. troops in first battle.
7. The UN asks U. S. to create a unified command.
8. Truman names Gen. Douglas MacArthur commander of UN forces in Korea.
10. First Red atrocities reported.
12. U. S. troops and ROK forces retreat toward Taejon.
13. Lieut. Gen. W. H. Walker takes command of U. S. forces.
20. Reds take Taejon.
31. First reinforcements land direct from U. S.

**August**

5. U. S. and ROK troops pushed back to Naktong River line in a small defense perimeter based on Pusan; Reds within 40 miles of Pusan.
7. U. S. troops counterattack.

**September**

1. Reds within 30 miles of Pusan.
15. Amphibious landing at Inchon.
16. UN forces launch counterattack.
24-28. UN forces regain Seoul.

**October**

1. ROK pushes across 38th parallel; Reds ignore MacArthur's demand to surrender.
7-11. U. S., British, Australian forces join ROK beyond 38th parallel.
15. Truman, MacArthur confer.
19. UN forces take Pyongyang, North Korean capital.
26. ROK reaches Yalu River at Chosan; UN forces capture first Chinese Communist troops.

**November**

1. Peiping (Peking) radio announces Red China "will let volunteers fight in defense of Yalu area"; UN pilots engage first Russian-built MiG-15 jet fighters. U. S. forces hard hit by Red Chinese at Unsan.
24. UN forces launch "end of war" offensive.
26. Red counterattack smashes UN drive; UN forces begin long retreat.
27. U. S. forces cut off in Chosen Reservoir area.

**December**

5. Pyongyang abandoned to Reds.
23. Lieut. Gen. W. H. Walker killed. Lieut. Gen. Matthew B. Ridgway takes command of UN forces.
24. End evacuation, by ship, of 105,000 U. S. troops from Hungnam.

## 1951

**January**

1. Reds launch general offensive.
4. UN forces again abandon Seoul.
17. Reds reject UN cease-fire request.
25. UN forces launch offensive for "war of maneuver."

**February**

1. UN denounces Red China as "aggressor."
12. ROK drives across 38th parallel.

**March**

7. MacArthur asserts conflict will stalemate if UN forces are not permitted to attack Red bases in Manchuria.
14. UN forces retake Seoul.
24. MacArthur invites retreating Communist leaders to confer with him in the field to end the war "without further bloodshed." Refused. UN forces resume northward drive.

**April**

11. General MacArthur relieved of all his commands by Truman. General Ridgway made Supreme Commander of Allied Powers. Lieut. Gen. James A. Van Fleet takes command in Korea.
22. Reds launch counteroffensive with some 600,000 troops.
29. Red offensive halts on outskirts of Seoul in west and 40 miles below 38th parallel in central Korea.

**May**

3. UN forces launch limited counterattack.
16. Reds advance in offensive drive.
19-21. UN forces stem drive and counterattack.

**June**

23. Russia's delegate to the UN suggests possibility of a cease-fire.
30. General Ridgway proposes meeting to discuss armistice.

**July**

10. First meeting of UN and Red representatives, at Kaesong.

**August**

23. Reds suspend armistice talks.

**September**

13. UN launches attack on "Heartbreak Ridge."

**October**

25. Armistice talks resume, after move to Panmunjom.

**December**

18. UN and Red commands exchange prisoner of war lists. Reds list 11,559 names; UN has 132,474 Red POWs.

## 1952

**January**

24. Armistice talks stalemated.
27. Talks resumed.

**February**

6. Chinese Reds drop their title of "volunteer troops" and list themselves as equal partners with North Korea in "opposing the UN in Korea."
18. Red prisoners riot in UN camp on Koje Island off Pusan.
22. Reds broadcast charges that UN wages "germ warfare" in Korea.
24. U. S. Navy starts second year of shelling Wonsan.

**March**

4. Syngman Rhee protests armistice talks; insists on unified Korea and withdrawal of Chinese Reds.

**April**

12-15. Battle lines seesaw in intensified fighting.

**May**

7. Red prisoners on Koje Island seize Brig. Gen. F. T. Dodd, compound commander; hold for 3 days.
12. Gen. Mark W. Clark succeeds General Ridgway.

**June**

21-22. U. S.-Philippine troops hold hills against savage Red attacks.
23. UN bombers blast hydroelectric plants on the Yalu.

**July**

3. Russia vetoes U. S. request in UN to have International Red Cross investigate North Korean charges that UN forces engage in germ warfare.
10. Armistice talks enter second year.
11-12. UN land and carrier-based planes bomb Pyongyang.

**August**

1. U. S. troops win "Old Baldy."
6-7. ROK takes "Capitol Hill."
12. U. S. Marines take "Siberia Hill" and "Bunker Hill."

**September**

17. U. S. Navy uses guided missiles on North Korean plants.
28-30. Reds seize three hill positions.

**October**

6. Reds attack 35 UN positions.
8. Truce teams take indefinite recess in armistice talks.

**November**

1-30. Hill positions change hands repeatedly in hard fighting.

**December**

2-5. Dwight D. Eisenhower, U. S. president-elect, tours combat zone.

## 1953

**January**

25. UN launches heavy attack.

**February**

11. Lieut. Gen. Maxwell D. Taylor takes over command from General Van Fleet, retiring from Army.
22. General Clark proposes exchange of sick and wounded prisoners.

**March**

17. UN throws back heavy attack on "Little Gibraltar."
26. Reds capture "Old Baldy."

**April**

11. Reach agreement on wounded prisoner exchange: 605 UN troops for 6,030 Reds.
20. Exchange starts.

**May**

1-31. Ground and air fighting sharpen.

**June**

9. South Korean assembly votes against truce terms.
12-15. Reds step up attack.
18. President Syngman Rhee defies UN and releases 27,000 anti-Red North Korean prisoners.
20. Truce talks stall.

**July**

8. Reds agree to renew truce talks.
27. Armistice signed at Panmunjom at 10:01 A.M., after 3 years and 32 days of conflict; hostilities ended 12 hours later.

*All dates of action in Korea are Korean time, which is 14 hours ahead of Eastern Standard Time.

THESE ARTICLES ARE IN THE FACT-INDEX

Korea Strait
Kornberg, Arthur
Körner, Karl Theodor
Korngold, Erich Wolfgang

Kornilov, Lavr
  Georgievich
Korolenko, Vladimir
Korzybski, Alfred Habdank

## KOSCIUSKO (käs-ē-ŭs'-kō), Thaddeus (1746–1817).

The gallant Polish general Thaddeus Kosciusko fought for freedom on two continents. In 1776 he came to America from Warsaw to serve in the Revolutionary War. He became an engineer and a colonel of artillery in the Continental army and built the first fortifications at West Point. After the war he was rewarded with the rank of brigadier general, a grant from the public lands, and an annual pension.

Poland meanwhile was suffering from external aggression and internal anarchy. Kosciusko returned to fight valiantly but unsuccessfully at Dubienka and elsewhere in 1792 against the Russian invasion.

In 1794 Kosciusko became dictator and commander in chief and successfully defended Warsaw against siege by the Russian and Prussian armies. On Oct. 10, 1794, his army of 7,000 Poles was defeated by 16,000 Russians at Maciejowice, where he was wounded.

Kosciusko was released from a Russian prison in 1796. He revisited America, living for a time in Philadelphia, Pa. Unlike many Polish patriots, he refused to serve under Napoleon Bonaparte. He died in Switzerland on Oct. 15, 1817. A statue honoring him stands in Washington, D. C. (See also Poland.)

THESE ARTICLES ARE IN THE FACT-INDEX

Kosher
Kosice, Czechoslovakia

Koslov, Peter Kuzmich
Kossel, Albrecht

## KOSSUTH (kä' suth), Louis (Hungarian Lajos) (1802–1894).

Hungarians cherish the memory of Louis Kossuth as the fiery revolutionary who led a revolt against their hated Austrian rulers in 1848. Kossuth belonged to one of the poorer noble families of Hungary. He was a brilliant lawyer, orator, and journalist. For years he had sought greater freedom for Hungary, which Austria then regarded as little more than an eastern province of its empire. His liberal publications, many written as letters to avoid censorship, angered the Austrian Hapsburg monarchy. In 1837 the royal government arrested Kossuth. He was charged with treason and imprisoned.

People protested so widely that he was released in 1840. He became the leader of the Liberals and a member of the Hungarian diet. His savage political attacks on the feudal rights of nobles led to the abolition of serfdom in Hungary (see Hungary).

In March 1848, inspired by the revolution in France, Kossuth demanded parliamentary government for Hungary. When it seemed that Austria would try to end the freedom movement by force, he rallied the Hungarians to rise "in self-defense." He became the virtual dictator of Hungary, declaring it independent of Austria on April 19, 1849. Kossuth's rashness and egotism, however, alienated other Hungarian leaders. His forces were defeated, and he fled to Turkey.

He visited the United States, where he spoke eloquently for Hungarian independence. In 1852 he went to England, where he stayed for most of the next 17 years. He died on March 20, 1894, in Turin, Italy.

THIS ARTICLE IS IN THE FACT-INDEX
Kostelanetz, André

## KOSYGIN (kō-sē'ḡ'n), Aleksei Nikolaevich (1904–1980).

When Aleksei Kosygin was 13, his native Russia was swept by Communist revolution. Some 47 years later this son of poor parents became Russia's premier.

Aleksei Nikolaevich Kosygin was born on Feb. 20, 1904, in St. Petersburg (now Leningrad), then the capital of Russia. His father, Nikolai, was a lathe operator. When Aleksei was 15 years old, he joined the Red army to fight in his country's civil war. He served until 1921, when he became a student at the Leningrad Cooperative Technical School. Later he worked in cooperatives in Siberia. From 1929 to 1935 he attended the Leningrad Kirov Textile Institute, and at the same time began to rise in the Communist party, which he had joined in 1927. In 1939 he was elected to the party's Central Committee and became a member of the national government as commissar of the textile industry.

In 1940 Kosygin was elected a deputy premier of the Soviet Union. From 1943 to 1946 he also headed the government of Russia's largest republic. Under the regime of Joseph Stalin, he advanced to the head of the finance and light-industry ministries and was appointed to the Politburo, the Communist party's highest decision-making body.

After Nikita Khrushchev succeeded Stalin in 1953, Kosygin became chairman of the State Planning Commission. He was made a first deputy premier in 1960 and by 1964 ranked second to Khrushchev.

On Oct. 14, 1964, when Khrushchev was deposed, Kosygin was elected premier; he promoted a policy of peaceful coexistence with the West. Kosygin and his wife, Klavdia, who died in 1967, had two children. In failing health, Kosygin resigned on Oct. 23, 1980. He died in Moscow on Dec. 18, 1980.

THESE ARTICLES ARE IN THE FACT-INDEX

Koto
Kotor, Yugoslavia
Kotzebue, August
  Friedrich von
Koufax, Sanford (Sandy)
Koussevitzky, Serge
Kovalevsky, Sonya
Kozhikode, India
Kozlov, Frol Romanovich
Kraepelin, Emil
Krafft, Adam
Kramer, Jack
Krasnodar, Russia
Krasnoyarsk, Russia
Krebs, Sir Hans Adolf
Kredel, Fritz
Krefeld, West Germany
Krehbiel, Henry Edward
Kreisler, Fritz
Krenek, Ernst
Kresge, Sebastian Spering
Kress, Samuel Henry
Kreuger, Ivar
Kreutzer, Konradin
Kreutzer, Rodolphe
Krieghoff, Cornelius
Krishna Menon, V(engalil)
  K(rishnan)

Kristiansand, Norway
Kroeber, Alfred Louis
Kroger, Bernard Henry
Krogh, (Schack) August
  (Steenberg)
Krohg, Christian
Krol, John Joseph,
  Cardinal
Kroll, Leon
Krone
Kronshtadt, Russia
Kropotkin, Peter, Prince
Kru
Krueger, Karl
Krug, J(ulius) A(lbert)
Kruger, Paul
Kruglov, Sergei
  Nikiforovich
Krumgold, Joseph
Krupa, Gene
Krupp, Alfred
Krupp, Friedrich
Krupp, Friedrich
  Alfred
Krupp von Bohlen und
  Halbach, Bertha
Krutch, Joseph Wood
Krylov, Ivan Andreevich

## KUALA LUMPUR

(*kwäl'ạ lụm'pụr*), **Malaysia.** One of the fastest-growing cities in Southeast Asia is Kuala Lumpur, the national capital of Malay-

sia. Kuala Lumpur is also the capital of Selangor, one of the country's Malay states.

Kuala Lumpur is in the south-central part of the Malay Peninsula, near the west coast. It lies at the junction of the Gombak and the Klang rivers. The Klang provides a waterway westward to the Strait of Malacca, 27 miles away. Across the strait is the Indonesian island of Sumatra. The city is built on hilly land near equatorial rain forests.

In the population of Kuala Lumpur, Chinese outnumber Malays. There are also many people of Indian and European origin. The varied backgrounds of Kuala Lumpur's inhabitants are reflected in the city's architectural medley of Chinese shops, Muslim minarets, and modern skyscrapers. Among the newer landmarks are the largest war memorial in Asia, the gigantic National Mosque, and the 20-story Parliament Building, which is part of a complex of government buildings. The city's educational facilities include a national university.

Kuala Lumpur is a commercial, banking, and transportation center in an area rich in tin and rubber. It has access to deepwater shipping facilities at Port Swettenham, at the mouth of the Klang. Light industry abounds in Kuala Lumpur proper as well as in Petaling Jaya, a satellite industrial area.

Immigrant Chinese tin miners founded Kuala Lumpur in the mid-1800's. Since 1895 it has been the capital, successively, of the Federated Malay States, the Federation of Malaya, and Malaysia. Most of its expansion has taken place since 1950. Population (1980 estimate), 1,081,000.

THESE ARTICLES ARE IN THE FACT-INDEX

Kuban' River
Kubelik, Jan
Kubelik, (Jeronym) Rafael
Kubik, Gail
Kubitschek, Juscelino
Kublai Khan
Kudu
Kudzu

Kufra Oasis
Kuhio, Prince
Kuhlmann, Richard von
Kuhn, Bowie
Kuhn, Richard
Kuhn, Walt
Kuiper, Gerard Peter
Ku K'ai-chih

## KU KLUX KLAN.

An antiblack terrorist organization, the Ku Klux Klan began as a Pulaski, Tenn., social club established late in 1865 by six former Confederate officers. The Klan then spread rapidly throughout the South.

Early in 1867, Klans from several states formed an alliance. Nathan Bedford Forrest, a Confederate general, was named the leader, or Grand Wizard. The Ku Klux Klan soon became so powerful that it was called "the Invisible Empire." It was the most notorious of many violent, all-white Southern orders pledged to overthrow the postwar Reconstruction state governments and to maintain white supremacy.

At first, the Klan's tactics were confined to night-riding in ghostly robes to frighten former slaves. Soon, however, it used bribery, arson, whipping, and murder to prevent blacks and their white sympathizers from voting or running for public office.

Alarmed by the Klan's violent activities, several Southern states enacted "Ku Klux laws" banning masked, night-riding societies. Although the Klan was formally disbanded in 1869, many Klansmen continued their activities. When they were prosecuted for violating the right of blacks to vote, sympathetic juries usually refused to convict them. In 1871 Congress authorized the use of federal troops to combat lawlessness in the South. Federal intervention, however, was inadequate to save the Reconstruction governments, and all-white control was restored in the South. Its goals achieved, the Ku Klux Klan virtually disappeared after the 1870's.

The Klan was revived in Georgia in 1915 by William J. Simmons, a professional organizer of fraternal orders, but it did not expand rapidly until after World War I. The new Klan was pledged to create an all-white, Protestant, "pure American" culture.

It appealed to racists and to people fearful of competing with immigrants for jobs in the postwar depression. By the mid-1920's the Klan had at least 3 million members and was active in nearly every state. It added hostility toward Roman Catholics, Jews, and "foreigners" to its fierce hatred of blacks. Partly because of internal power struggles and press exposure of its violence, the Klan declined during the late 1920's. It did not become widely active again until the mid-1950's, when it opposed school desegregation and other civil rights measures. By the late 1970's several competing Klan organizations had a total membership of about 10,000 in more than 20 states, and incidents of Klan violence were increasing.

---

THESE ARTICLES ARE IN THE FACT-INDEX

| | |
|---|---|
| Kukui | Kunlun Mountains |
| Kumamoto, Japan | Kunming, People's |
| Kuma River | Republic of China |
| Kun, Béla | Kunz, George Frederick |
| Kunersdorf, Poland | Kunzite |
| Kung, Hsiang-hsi | Kuomintang |
| Kunitz, Stanley | Kuprin, Aleksandr |
| (Jasspon) | Ivanovich |
| Kuniyoshi, Yasuo | Kurbash |

---

**KURDS.** For some 4,000 years the fiercely brave and proud Kurds have held to their love of liberty. These people of Indo-European stock fought the Sumerians, Assyrians, Persians, Mongols, crusaders, and Turks. Saladin was a great Kurdish leader (see Saladin). Gradually they withdrew into the fortresslike mountains and sheer valleys of the Iranian Plateau, where most of them live today. Their rugged region, called Kurdistan, spreads over an area where Turkey meets Iran, Syria, and Iraq. Many Kurds also live in the Caucasus region of Russia. The total number of Kurds is estimated at 11 million.

The Kurds are Moslems. Their many dialects are part of the Indo-Iranian language family. They are superb horsemen and daring raiders. A tragic chapter in Kurdish history was their slaughter of Armenians, instigated by Turkey (see Armenian Soviet Socialist Republic).

Many Kurds are nomads, taking their livestock to mountain pastures in summer and returning to valley villages in winter. Most Kurds today are settled farmers, however.

The Kurds have repeatedly tried to become independent. Between 1919 and the mid-1950's Turkey, Iran, and Iraq put down 11 major Communist-led Kurdish uprisings. After Kurds in northern Iraq revolted in 1961, a 1970 agreement finally granted them several concessions, including autonomous local government. A Kurdish group led by Mustafa Barzani opposed the final implementation of the agreement in 1974, and fighting broke out again. Although the rebellion collapsed within a year, occasional hostilities continued (see Iraq). Following the 1979 revolution in Iran, there was severe fighting between government forces and Kurds demanding autonomy (see Iran).

THESE ARTICLES ARE IN THE FACT-INDEX

| | |
|---|---|
| Kure, Japan | Kushiro, Japan |
| Kurelek, William | Kut, Iraq |
| Kuria Muria Islands | Kutaisi, Russia |
| Kuril Islands | Kutani ware |
| Kuroki, Tamesada, Count | Kutaradja, Sumatra |
| Kuropatkin, Alexei | Kutb-ud-Din |
| Nikolaievich | Kutch, India |
| Kurtz, Efrem | Kutchuk-Kainardji, Treaty |
| Kurumba | of (1774) |
| Kurusu, Saburo | Kutenai Indians |
| Kusch, P(olykarp) | Kutztown State College |

**KUWAIT** (*kŭ-wāt'*). A tiny desert monarchy in the Middle East, Kuwait might be called a "Cinderella state." Since the discovery of rich oil resources in 1937, it has been transformed from a poverty-ridden British protectorate into a wealthy independent Arab nation.

Kuwait is situated on the Arabian peninsula, on the northwestern coast of the Persian Gulf. It is bordered on the north and northwest by Iraq and on the south and southwest by Saudi Arabia. Its area is about 7,400 square miles, of which some 1,200 square miles were acquired in 1969, when the Neutral Zone between Kuwait and Saudi Arabia was divided between the two nations. Kuwait's territory also includes a number of islands in the Persian Gulf.

The climate of Kuwait is generally hot and dry. Average maximum daily temperatures range from 111° F. in July and August (the hottest months) to 64° in January (the coolest month). Average minimum daily temperatures vary from 84° in July to 46° in January. Kuwait's average yearly rainfall of less than six inches occurs almost entirely between the months of November and May.

The native population of Kuwait is derived from a number of Arab tribes. However, only half of the people in Kuwait are natives. The rest were attracted from other countries by the nation's oil boom. Most of the people live in or around Kuwait, the capital city, or in the oil-producing center of Ahmadi, 20 miles to the south. Nearly all Kuwaitis are Moslems. The official language of Kuwait is Arabic.

Symbolic of the source of Kuwait's wealth, an oil truck passes air-conditioned buildings on the streets of the city of Kuwait.
Arab Information Center

Kuwait's government is a constitutional monarchy. The head of state is the amir, who is chosen from the members of the ruling family. The amir selects a cabinet of 14 ministers who are responsible to the National Assembly. The 50 members of the National Assembly are chosen in popular elections.

Kuwait is a highly developed welfare state. It provides liberal subsidies for housing. Medical care and education—including university education abroad—are furnished free to Kuwaitis.

Since World War II oil has been the mainstay of Kuwait's economy. Kuwait controls nearly 20 percent of the world's known oil reserves. The Burgan oil field in southeastern Kuwait is believed to be the world's richest single oil pool. The field accounts for about 80 percent of the nation's output of crude oil. About 97 percent of Kuwait's oil is exported. Oil refining is the most important manufacturing industry.

Only about one percent of the land is cultivated. Nearly all of Kuwait's foodstuffs, manufactured goods, and raw materials are imported. The three major ports are Shuwaikh, Shuaiba, and Mina al Ahmadi.

Archaeological excavations have shown that Kuwait was already a center of trade for the Middle East as far back as 3000 B.C. At that time, however, the civilization of the area centered upon the island of Failaka.

Kuwait did not become a nation until the 18th century. It was then that the clan of al-Sabah migrated to the little coastal trading town that became the city of Kuwait. Kuwait's independence was threatened by the Ottoman Empire, so in 1899 Kuwait concluded a protective treaty with Great Britain. In 1914 Great Britain recognized Kuwait as an independent state under its protection. Kuwait achieved complete independence in 1961. It joined the United Nations in 1963. Population (1970 preliminary census), 738,663.

THESE ARTICLES ARE IN THE FACT-INDEX

Kuybyshev, Russia
Kuznets, Simon
Kuznetsk Basin
Kwajalein
Kwammu
Kwangju, South Korea
Kwango River
Kwangsi Chuang Autonomous Region
Kwangtung, People's Republic of China

Kwantung
Kweichow, People's Republic of China
Kweiyang, People's Republic of China
Kyakhta, Russia
Kyanite
Kyd, Thomas
Kyne, Peter B(ernard)
Kyodo News Service
Kyongju, South Korea

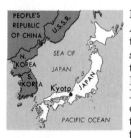

**KYOTO** (kē-ōt′ō), **Japan.** A city important in the history of Japan, Kyoto lies on a fertile plain in south-central Honshu, between Lake Biwa and the Inland Sea. Ranking fifth among Japan's cities in population, it is the capital of Kyoto Prefecture in Kinki District. It was the capital of Japan for over a thousand years and was the birthplace of the nation's culture. The many Shinto shrines and Buddhist temples and the palaces with their elaborate gardens have made it one of Japan's most visited cities.

Kyoto is also an important industrial center. Traditional industries include silk weaving, dyeing, embroidery, and the making of porcelain, lacquerware, and cloisonné (decorative enamelware) products. Modern industries include the making of heavy machinery, copper products, and chemicals. It is noted for the production of foodstuffs and as a center of the *sake* (rice wine) industry.

Residents of Kyoto enjoy a mild, moist climate. Mean temperatures range from an average of about 80° F. in July (the hottest month) to an average of about 38° in January (the coldest month). Average annual precipitation is about 70 inches.

In Kyoto's early days it was known as Heian-kyo, or "capital of peace and tranquillity." The city grew up around the court of Emperor Kwammu in the late 8th century. It later became known as Kyoto, or "capital city."

Kyoto was originally laid out according to Chinese concepts, with long streets intersected by broad avenues. The city was surrounded by a low earthen wall pierced by 18 gates.

Kyoto was the scene of several conflicts during Japan's medieval era. After 1336 it was continually ravaged by feuding warlords. It was not rebuilt to any extent until the second half of the 16th century, when Hideyoshi restored its temples and laid out the streets once more.

Kyoto was the only major Japanese city that escaped bombing raids during World War II. The Allies spared the city because it held so many of Japan's cultural treasures. Among Kyoto's historic landmarks are the Kyoto Imperial Palace, Higashi Honganji Temple, Sanjusangendo (a 13th-century hall), Yasaka Shrine, Daitokuji Temple, Koryuji Temple, and Toji Temple. Its important modern edifices include the 430-foot-high Kyoto Tower in front of Kyoto Station and Kyoto International Conference Hall, which is representative of present-day Japanese architecture. Exhibits of Japan's traditional and industrial arts are housed in Kyoto National Museum, Nishijin Textile Museum, and Gion Corner.

Kyoto is the principal center of education for western Japan. In 1875 Joseph Niijima and Yamamoto Kakuma, in cooperation with the American Board of Foreign Missions, established the Christian Doshisha University in Kyoto. Kyoto University, which incorporates a school of agriculture, was founded in 1897. Other institutions of higher education in Kyoto include Kyoto Prefectural University and the Kyoto Municipal College of Fine Arts. (*See also* Japan.) Population (1970 census), 1,419,165.

THESE ARTICLES ARE IN THE FACT-INDEX

Kyrie eleison
Kyushu

# LABOR
# and LABOR UNIONS

Airplanes line up for takeoff on a runway (below) because of major delays resulting from a work slowdown by air traffic controllers (above) who want improved working conditions.

**LABOR.** Most of the men and women who make a living in the United States work for wages and salaries. They "hire out" their services and thus provide the general term *labor* in an economy called *laboristic*.

A laboristic economy is a relatively recent development in the United States. As late as 1870, more than half of all workers were engaged in agriculture. Now only about one worker in 25 is so engaged. A rapid expansion of industry and trade has led to more and more persons becoming dependent upon wages and salaries earned in nonfarm work. (*See also* United States, section "How the People Meet Their Needs.")

The United States became a great industrial nation largely after 1900 (*see* Industry, American). Since that time sweeping changes have taken place in the ways people live and work together. Many ideas and institutions are still undergoing change. *Labor unions*, formed by wage earners for mutual aid and protection, are an example. The functions and responsibilities of these unions have not been fully defined or accepted. This has given rise to a long series of controversies with many of the old problems still in existence. Solutions to these problems are urgently needed.

### The Labor Force and Bargaining Power

Wages and salaries account for about two thirds of the national income. Some employees who receive salaries are not included in the group called "labor."

Persons who are hired for a year or more at a time and who exercise wide judgment or determined policy in their jobs are usually considered to be in the managerial or the professional classes. Business executives and college professors are examples.

The labor group consists of those who are paid salaries on a weekly or monthly basis or wages on an hourly basis. In general these people carry out the plans laid by others, working at routine tasks or following the instructions of supervisors. Thus labor is made up of the routine workers who, in the United States, form a highly essential part of the greatest economic and industrial machine ever created. Bricklayers, bookkeepers, coal miners, coat makers, farm laborers, longshoremen, locomotive engineers, laundry workers, machinists, television assemblers, and waiters—these are only a very few of the people who are "labor." (*See also* Vocations.)

**STRIKING TEACHERS ON PICKET LINE**
Members of a teachers' union picket before their city's board of education building after walking off the job to demand better schools and salaries.

The service performed by any one worker is not vital to the employer, and he can be eliminated. When the services of all the workers in a craft, trade, or industry are combined, however, they cannot be eliminated. In such a combination the relative bargaining power of labor, *collective bargaining*, is greater. Terms of employment can be fixed for all workers at one time rather than for each worker individually. This is important in business recessions or depressions when wages and working standards may be deflated in a disorderly manner under individual bargaining. Some observers maintain that collective bargaining is "monopolistic." During times of business prosperity, the "control" of all labor in a trade or industry may result in inflationary increases in wages and working standards. This issue has been fought heatedly in the United States.

### Basis of the Labor Problem

Despite opposition, workers in every wage-earning class have formed unions to bargain collectively and to advance their interests by united action. Employers often resisted the formation of these unions. In the United States especially, employers emphasized their interest in preserving the right of the individual worker to stand on his own feet. Many of the most bitterly contested strikes in the nation were fought over employee demands for union recognition and collective bargaining.

Governments also sought to repress unions when they were first being organized. Because unions often won increases in wages which resulted in higher prices, they were widely regarded as being against the "public interest." As unions grew in power and prestige, governments have gradually come to recognize and even to encourage them. Today the workers' right to collective bargaining in the United States has been recognized as a matter of law, first under the Wagner act (National Labor Relations Act) of 1935 and then under the Taft-Hartley act (Labor-Management Relations Act) of 1947. Strikes are no longer conducted over union recognition but directly about wages and working conditions.

### Unemployment and the Depression

Even where wage earners have gained collective bargaining rights they are usually subject to being laid off with little or no prior notice. When the opportunity to earn wages disappears, often overnight, the average worker has no other way of providing for the necessities of life. This economic insecurity is not so keenly felt in times of prosperity when jobs are plentiful. During periods of declining business, however, when jobs are scarce, layoffs and the threat of layoffs can become the most critical factors in the lives of wage earners.

The widespread unemployment during the serious depression from 1929 to 1933—and the poverty and lowered morale which it generated—left a permanent mark upon an entire generation of wage earners. The careful specification and regulation of "seniority rights" in most factories are direct evidences of this mark. Seniority rights favor workers who have the longest terms of service. At times of production cutbacks, these rights often determine who gets laid off and who is kept on the job.

The government has had to recognize the critical importance of the unemployment problem in a laboristic economy. Since 1936 there has been a system of unemployment insurance, operated by the federal and the various state governments. This provides certain out-of-work benefits to wage earners who lose their jobs. The government has also tried to maintain full employment within the private enterprise system. This

**MONTH OF LABOR—THE SEPTEMBER HARVEST**
A page of 'Trés riches Heures du Duc de Berry' (1413–16), in the Musée Condé, Chantilly, France, depicts September labor.

idea is found in the Employment Act of 1946. Some unions favor "guaranteed annual wages" (GAW) for employees. This rarely means an actual guarantee of an annual wage to all employees. Rather, it aims to have employers regularize production so there will be more steady employment. In 1955 the United Automobile Workers got GAW contracts from Ford and General Motors providing benefits to supplement government unemployment compensation.

### The Need for Teamwork

The problems of collective bargaining and economic insecurity are only two aspects of labor relations. Equally important is the problem of how to get good teamwork in a laboristic economy. Everyone has experienced the difficulties of getting even a few people in a club or in a social organization to pool their efforts toward a common goal. Such difficulties are magnified many times in the factory or business enterprise. Here the individual efforts of many workers —up to the hundreds of thousands—have to be correlated and directed. The planning of output and the co-ordination of efforts to achieve production goals are the exacting tasks of management.

In management's use of "man power," much more is involved than merely hiring people. The productivity of labor depends in large measure upon the will of the individual to work and upon the teamwork which exists. People tend to resist arbitrary orders issued in a dictatorial manner; the orders have to "make sense" to them. Workers may work listlessly if they fail to appreciate the importance of their relatively small tasks to the over-all program.

Workmen are not cogs. They are human beings who must be led and not directed arbitrarily. The manner in which labor is used not only affects output but has much to do with the kind of person and

citizen the worker will be. In recognition of these considerations many companies have established personnel departments to deal with wage earners not simply as "labor" but as people.

Still another problem has a direct bearing on each worker's take-home pay. How is the money value of labor to be determined and how are wages to be allocated among the various specialized services needed to produce goods? For example, in the operation of a railroad train, how much should be paid to the locomotive engineer and how much to the locomotive fireman? Or, what should be paid to those who assemble radios and what to those who drive the trucks which deliver the radios to distributors? This is a problem requiring the closest kind of teamwork between labor and management. To solve such problems, collective bargaining gradually developed. This permits workers' representatives to participate as equals with the employer in determining the terms of employment.

### The Question of Free or Slave Labor

Labor problems have arisen over the years in every society whenever individuals have joined to work together toward a common objective. In a modern democracy, the common objective is an improved standard of living for all.

More of the necessities of life—and more of the luxuries—can be provided through joint undertakings than could be obtained if each person tried to take care of all his own needs by his own individual efforts. American industry has shown that a bigger pie (gross national product) can be made when tasks are broken down for performance by specialists. (*See* Industry, American.) Controversies arise, however, about how to cut up the bigger pie for distribution among the many who contributed to its making. Another deep concern is the protection of the dignity and the rights of each individual who is on the production team. In a democracy, the freedom of the individual is vital. Men cannot be compelled to work under any certain terms or for any particular employer. Workers have the right to bargain about the terms and conditions of their employment. They can withhold their services if they believe the offer for such services is not enough.

The rights of the men and women who labor have varied greatly through the years. In ancient Greece and Rome, much of the labor was performed by slaves who were supplied with the necessities of life by their masters. In the Middle Ages, serfs were "bound to the soil" and were required to do certain work for the lord of the manor (*see* Slavery and Serfdom). Apprentices and journeymen under the guild system were paid largely in the form of food, clothing, and shelter provided by the master (*see* Guilds). Even today, under totalitarian regimes, workmen do not have the right to choose their employment or to bargain over their share of the value added to the product by their labor. Their services and their returns are determined by a "master plan" designed to use the individual for the state.

Americans would doubtless choose to follow a system of free labor in preference to a system of forced labor even if more goods and services would be secured by a dictatorial use of labor. It is a part of democratic faith that workmen who voluntarily accept employment are not only more free but also more productive than slaves or serfs. In other words, free labor outproduces slave labor. High production achieved in the United States proves this.

### Individual or Collective Bargaining?

There has been a considerable difference of opinion about how the freedom of the individual can be reconciled with the necessities of collective bargaining. Proponents of individual bargaining believe that wages should be paid according to the worth of each particular man's services. They say that some workers are underpaid and some are overpaid when all the workers in a group receive the same wage or the same wage increase through collective bargaining. On the other hand, it is often impossible to measure differences in ability or performance among workers on routine and machine-tending operations. Attempts of foremen and supervisors to make such measurements frequently give rise to charges of favoritism and discrimination.

In individual bargaining the worker may find that he has to accept far less than he believes his services are worth. Because he is under pressure to provide week by week for the needs of his family, the individual worker usually needs his job more urgently than the employer needs his services. When jobs are scarce, individual workers with the greatest family needs are under a strong compulsion "to get a job at any wage." Workers then "undercut" each other and break established standards. Some observers believe that such "flexibility" of wages is an essential factor in reducing costs and in getting business to move upward again.

Others believe that undercutting of wage standards to obtain scarce jobs demoralizes the workers. They argue that this makes worse the already poor business situation by creating a chaotic downward spiral. At any event, since 1935 the national policy of the United States has been for the government to support collective bargaining when that method of fixing wages is desired by a majority of the employees. There is considerable concern, however, that the unions may get too strong and that the union leaders may dictate the terms of employment to both employers and employees. An important expression of this concern was the Taft-Hartley act, which regulated the conduct of unions in many particulars.

When collective bargaining prevails, no individual employee can bargain with the employer about his wages. Union representatives and the management negotiate wages for all workers—for the majority who belong to the union and also for any workers who do not. Under collective bargaining then, the individual workman participates in establishing the terms of his employment only through the union and

**REGISTERING FOR A JOB ASSIGNMENT**
When employment is seasonal or irregular, workers find jobs through a placement agency, or "hiring hall." This San Francisco longshoreman "plugs in" a board for a job as dockman.

not directly. Collective bargaining is a form of representative government in industry.

### The Issue of Union Security

What if an individual workman does not want to join the union? Trade unionists believe it is a rejection of the very idea of collective bargaining for a worker to deal separately with an employer. They say "union security," or collective bargaining security, is involved, and they insist that once a majority of workers choose collective bargaining, all should be made to join the union. This issue is highly important. What responsibility has each wage earner to all wage earners? How far should majority rule subordinate individual rights? How can minority rights be guarded without threat to majority rights?

Three chief plans to insure union security have been advanced. In the now illegal *closed shops* employers could hire only union members. The union largely determined who was hired. In *union shops* employers may hire anyone, but new employees are expected to join the union within a specified period. The company thus largely determines who will be union members. In *agency shops* employees need not join a union, but they must pay the union a "service fee" to cover the cost of representing a nonmember in collective bargaining. (In an *open shop* employers may hire anyone, and new employees need not join a union.)

Union security remains one of the most controversial issues in labor relations, because a worker may in effect be made to pay union fees as a condition of employment. Closed shops were outlawed by the Taft-Hartley law. On June 3, 1963, the Supreme Court ruled agency shops legal, under the Taft-Hartley act, in states where they are not prohibited. Under the same law, where states concur, union shops are

**A SHOW OF HANDS**
In organized labor, many decisions are made by vote of the union membership.　Hundreds of workers vote (above) in England, where the labor movement started.

even be unable to get another job if he were *blacklisted* by the employer as a troublemaker.

To seek higher wages and improved conditions, workers in a trade or in a factory combined to form one organization, called a trade union or a labor union, with one spokesman to represent them. If the employer refused the united demand of the workers, all the workers could stop work—that is, they could *strike* until their demands were granted. There were usually a few workers who did not want to join the union. The other workers looked upon them as enemies to their own class; the employers looked upon them as "loyal employees."

During a strike, the plant would be *picketed*—strikers would march up and down before the factory and seek to induce reluctant or timid employees not to work. Those who "went through the picket line" to work were called *scabs*. Employers would sometimes hire professional *strikebreakers* to man the struck jobs, and then violence would often develop on the picket lines. The employer could easily discharge one man; he could not discharge all the employees if he wanted to stay in business. Strikers insisted that they retained the right to their jobs; they reasoned that they had temporarily withdrawn their services while negotiations were going on. By united action, employees could press their demands more effectively with less chance of losing their jobs. The need for income, however, often resulted in the employees giving in to the employer and ending their strike.

permissible, but an employee may be discharged if he fails to pay the regular union dues. The idea seems to be that since every employee receives the benefits of collective bargaining every employee should contribute to its financial support.

### Early Labor Movements Abroad

Labor movements began the same way in each country. The factory system of production led to workers being hired to work for a wage (*see* Factories and Factory Laws). Dissatisfied with their wages and conditions of employment, the wage earners developed a "class consciousness." They then combined their efforts to secure improved status and working conditions. They sought these goals by presenting a united front in bargaining with the employer and in pressing for favorable legislation.

The labor movement began in England in the 1700's when the Industrial Revolution brought sweeping changes in the way men earned a living (*see* Industrial Revolution). Power machinery had been invented. Large numbers of people were employed to operate this machinery in factories. Others were hired to produce the materials needed by the factories. Still other employees were needed to transport great quantities of products to consumers. The wage earners did not share very much in the greater output because of their intense competition for jobs. Often paid barely enough to sustain life, everyone in the family had to work in order to eat. Workers, including women and children, often labored from 12 to 14 hours a day (*see* Child Labor Laws).

Individual workers could do little to improve their lot. Anyone who protested too vigorously—or who failed to show the "proper respect" to the employer— placed his job in danger. A discharged employee might

### Legislative and Political Action

When the Industrial Revolution spread to other countries, the labor movement did also. All attempts of the workers to form unions were fought by the employers and severely repressed as conspiracies by the governments. Despite such opposition, the workers persisted until their right to organize unions was recognized. Such recognition came gradually. The British government first passed legislation approving the right of workers to form unions in 1825 and under the Trade Union Acts of 1871 and 1876 gave unions full legal recognition, including the right to strike. At the same time, Great Britain began adopting legislation to reduce industrial hazards and to promote social insurance. In advance of most countries, Great Britain made legislative provision for workers' old age, unemployment, and sickness.

From their very start, the labor movements in England and on the Continent were largely associated with political movements. The workers in Europe exerted great efforts to elect their own representa-

**HONORING AN AMERICAN LABOR LEADER**
The first great champion of American labor was Samuel Gompers, honored in this memorial in Washington, D.C. It was erected by the American Federation of Labor; the designer, Robert Aitken.

tives to the government in order to press for legislation covering minimum wages, old-age pensions, and the like. They believed that an improvement in the lot of the workers could be more readily gained from the government than from the employer. Germany pioneered in the field of accident, sickness, and old-age insurance under Bismarck's rule in the 1880's. The Scandinavian countries later assumed leadership in extending social insurance.

Despite the legislative support for their needs, European workers did not believe they could substantially improve their lot in a capitalistic system in which the "tools of production" were owned by the employers. In this, they were strongly influenced by the views of Karl Marx (*see* Marx). These workers believed their well-being ultimately depended upon their ownership of the tools of production through the government. Seeking to supplant capitalism with socialism, the European labor movements supported far-reaching political as well as economic reforms. (*See also* Labor Parties.)

In marked contrast to the "class conscious" attitude of European labor, wage earners in the United States organized primarily to improve their bargaining position with their employers. They were long suspicious of government "intervention" in industrial relations. American workmen accepted as desirable the private ownership of the tools of production. At the same time, they insisted that they must have strong unions to get "equality of bargaining power." Once such a bargaining status was attained, the wage earners believed they could take care of their own interests in collective bargaining. This point of view has been called a "limited objective."

### Beginnings of American Labor Movement

In the United States management and labor have demonstrated an ability to settle their differences and to co-operate for the common objective of economic progress. American labor history has been stormy, however. Even the "limited objective" attitude has been vigorously opposed by many employers and often by the government.

The factory system was relatively late in starting in the United States. As late as about 1890, workers did not have to labor in a factory if conditions became too oppressive. They could "go West" and take up farming on free land. As a result, the bargaining position of American workers was never as poor as that of European workers.

American wage earners rejected individual bargaining very early. They strove, usually against strong obstacles, to form unions. The cordwainers (shoemakers) of Philadelphia started a union in 1792 and conducted a strike in 1799. Early unions in the United States were *craft unions*—formed by skilled craftsmen of particular trades in a certain city.

The first efforts of craftsmen to form such unions resulted in the so-called Conspiracy Cases decided from 1806 to 1815. In these cases, the cordwainers who struck against their employers were found guilty of conspiracy. This doctrine was rejected in 1842, however, in the famous Massachusetts decision of Commonwealth *vs.* Hunt. It was ruled that unions, even if formed to strike in order to maintain a closed shop, were not illegal. It was held, however, that the methods employed by unions could be illegal.

### Problems of Early Unions

For many years unions remained weak. On the upswing of the business cycle, when wages lagged behind increases in the cost of living, workers joined unions. This helped to secure wage increases from the employer who could not afford a complete stoppage of work. When the business cycle turned downward, unions lacked the power to halt wage decreases. Workers then dropped out of unions because they thought the unions could not do anything for them.

The first relatively permanent national labor organization in the United States was the Knights of Labor. Organized in 1869 by Uriah Smith Stephens, the K. of L. admitted all workers without regard to skill or craft and included farmers and small shopkeepers. For some time the K. of L. was a secret order with special handclasps and rituals. Secrecy was abandoned about 1880; thereafter the membership grew to about 700,000 in less than a decade.

The program of the K. of L. was varied and included an emphasis upon producers' and consumers' co-operatives. Although the leaders of the organization favored arbitration, many strikes were conducted. Employers' opposition and dissension within the labor organization, however, seriously weakened the Knights and they formally disbanded in 1917.

### The History of A.F.L.

While the Knights of Labor was still a power, the groundwork for the American Federation of Labor was laid. In 1881, six craft unions met in Pittsburgh and founded the Federation of Organized Trades and Labor Unions. Five years later, at Columbus, Ohio, this group was absorbed by the newly created American Federation of Labor, which was soon recognized as the leading spokesman for organized labor in the United States. The leaders of the A.F.L. have been Samuel Gompers, William Green, and George Meany, who became president in 1952 (*see* Gompers).

A principal function of the A.F.L. has been to charter national unions, thus giving such unions an exclusive jurisdiction over certain jobs—that is, the right to organize those who work on the specified jobs. Some of these chartered unions are "international," which means they have local unions in Canada or Mexico. The jurisdiction of a national union may be designated on a craft basis, covering various industries, called *horizontal jurisdiction*; or, it may be designated on an industrial basis, covering various crafts, called *vertical jurisdiction*.

The A.F.L. developed the principle of horizontal organization. Workers in each of several crafts in a factory or in an industry joined with the same craftsmen employed elsewhere to form a union. Thus, electricians are in the same A.F.L. union regardless of the plant or industry by which they are employed. The craft unions have frequent "boundary disputes" over the jurisdictions allocated to them, and the A.F.L. is responsible for settling them. Strikes over union jurisdictional disputes have come to be recognized as unfair because the employer may be hurt, although he is not usually a party to the dispute.

### Policies of the A.F.L.

Unions chartered by the A.F.L. are autonomous. Their operations and policies are not subject to regulation by the A.F.L. If the actions or policies of a national union are considered improper, however, the A.F.L. may withdraw the charter and assign jurisdiction to another union. In such cases the Executive Council of the A.F.L., the co-ordinating body, makes recommendations to the Convention, which is the final authority of the A.F.L. Such an action was taken in 1953, when the International Longshoremen's Union was expelled because of an alleged tie-in between the heads of that union and certain racketeers. A new union was then chartered to exercise jurisdiction in behalf of longshoremen.

Except for such disciplinary action, each affiliated national union of the A.F.L. is free to make its own rules and to develop its own policies. Local unions are chartered by the national unions. It is the local union—close to the workers—which is largely responsible for actually bargaining with the employer and representing the employees in day-by-day affairs. The local union may always seek the assistance of the national office.

Various local unions, affiliated with A.F.L. national unions but operating in the same area, form Central Labor Unions in their cities. They also form State Federations under direct charter from the A.F.L. and not from their national unions. The city and state federations represent the workers in various kinds of local problems. In the same manner

the A.F.L. speaks for its membership with respect to various national problems.

The A.F.L. and its affiliated unions have exerted their main efforts toward establishing and developing collective bargaining. These unions have traditionally not agitated for large-scale economic reforms and, with few exceptions, have not supported particular political parties. The political attitude of the A.F.L. was stated by its first president, Samuel Gompers, who advised: "Reward your friends and punish your enemies." Gompers distrusted government intervention.

### Craft Versus Industrial Unions

Although the A.F.L. consists principally of horizontal craft unions, some of its affiliates have long been industrial unions. The International Ladies' Garment Workers' Union is an example of a national union with jurisdiction over all workers, regardless of craft, who work in and about women's clothing factories. In most cases, however, the craft setup predominates and for very good reasons. It is not easy to replace craftsmen when they strike. They therefore have had a greater economic bargaining power than the semiskilled and unskilled employees who could more readily be replaced.

During and after World War I, however, the number of unskilled and semiskilled workers increased greatly in the rapid expansion of such mass-production industries as steel and automobile. In seeking to unionize these factory employees, the craft unions engaged in heated disputes. The factory jobs in question did not fall easily into the craft classifications. Moreover, many of the workers in these industries strongly opposed being represented by several unions. They believed one union should represent all the workers employed by the company. Some of the craft unions, it was alleged, cared little about taking semiskilled workers into their organizations.

### The Revolt of the C.I.O.

In 1935 arguments over organizing workers in the mass-production industries split the A.F.L. John L. Lewis and seven other union leaders then formed the Committee for Industrial Organization. They claimed that the A.F.L. organization program was inadequate and began organizing on a vertical basis workers employed by such industries as automobile, steel, rubber, and textiles. The participants in the rebel Committee were expelled from the A.F.L. in 1936. Two years later they held a constitutional convention and formed the Congress of Industrial Organizations under the leadership of John L. Lewis (*see* Lewis, John L.). Philip Murray of the Steelworkers was elected to the presidency of the C.I.O. when Lewis resigned in 1940. Following the death of Murray, Walter Reuther of the Automobile Workers was elected president in 1952.

The C.I.O. is a national union organization which charters affiliates and gives them jurisdictional rights to organize workers in specified industries.

Like the A.F.L. affiliates, the C.I.O. national unions charter local unions which are united into city and state federations or councils. Both A.F.L. and C.I.O. unions claimed the right to organize particular groups of workers.

### The Two Groups Merge

Many efforts have been made to create a "united labor movement." They were directed chiefly at bringing together the A.F.L. and the C.I.O. After much negotiation, these two giant unions were merged in 1955 and took their combined name—A.F.L.-C.I.O. The head of the old A.F.L., George Meany, became president of the merged unions. They then created an Industrial Union Department to expand industrial unions. The powerful IUD was headed by Walter Reuther, president of the old C.I.O.

Despite the merger, union labor was not wholly united. About 55 unions do not belong to the A.F.L.-C.I.O. One of the largest is the United Mine Workers. Affiliated at first with the A.F.L. and then with the C.I.O., it became independent in 1947.

Some national unions have always been independent. One of the most powerful of these independent labor groups is the railway brotherhoods of engineers, conductors, and railroad trainmen (the firemen and enginemen joined the A.F.L.-C.I.O. in 1956). There are also many "independent unions" or "company unions" composed of employees of a particular company. These are not affiliated with a national union.

### The Wagner Act Aids Labor

The rise of the C.I.O. was rapid. It quickly organized workers in many previously unorganized plants and industries. It established collective bargaining relationships where only individual bargaining had existed. Affiliates of the C.I.O. secured labor agreements with such great companies as the Goodyear Tire and Rubber Company, the United States Steel Corporation, and the General Motors Corporation.

The most bitterly contested C.I.O. strike was launched in 1937 against the Republic Steel Company. Like many other C.I.O. strikes it was primarily an *organizational* one. This type of strike was undertaken not simply to secure higher wages but rather to win management's recognition of the union and management's assent to collective bargaining.

Then labor obtained a new way to win union recognition. It was provided by the Wagner act, passed in 1935. The Wagner act was deliberately one-sided in favor of labor. Its principal purposes were (1) to outlaw certain actions of employers which interfered with the formation of unions and (2) to guarantee collective bargaining to employees whenever a majority of the employees wanted it. These rights were to be protected by a newly created National Labor Relations Board (NLRB). Workers did not have to win a strike to get collective bargaining; they could get collective bargaining by winning an industry election. After 1937 the representation election supplanted the organizational strike.

Protected and assisted by the Wagner act and encouraged by the industrial expansion during World War II, unions increased their membership rapidly from 1937 until about 1947. Then a leveling-off period began. Today the total union movement consists of about 20 million members, including almost 4 million women workers. About 16 million workers belong to the A.F.L.-C.I.O. The remainder are members of various independent unions.

There are some 130 unions affiliated with the A.F.L.-C.I.O. About half of these unions have a membership of more than 100,000 each. The International Brotherhood of Teamsters, Chauffeurs, Warehousemen & Helpers of America, with over 1,700,000 members, was expelled from A.F.L.-C.I.O. in 1958. This was the result of a Senate committee investigation which revealed corruption on the part of the union's leaders. Also expelled were the bakery union and the laundry union.

### Postwar Problems

During World War II, with but few exceptions, labor co-operated with the War Labor Board to resolve disputes without interrupting production. By 1946 many unions had become so powerful that certain of their practices were subjected to critical attack. There developed a demand for some restricting of the right to strike. For example, industry-wide strikes in coal or steel brought great inconvenience to the public.

Such union power was called "monopolistic." Strikes broke out in many industries in 1946 and 1947. Wages, which had been controlled during World War II, moved upward by great leaps in the so-called wage-pattern increases. It was claimed the unions helped inflation by their wage policies. It was also charged that individual employees were being bullied by union leaders. Out of these circumstances came the Taft-Hartley act.

### Passage of the Taft-Hartley Act

The Taft-Hartley act was passed by Congress in 1947 over the veto of President Truman. Many parts of the Wagner act were retained but a large number of new rules and regulations were introduced. The closed shop was outlawed and only a limited kind of union shop was allowed. Boycotts were made illegal. Some unions, such as those of the Teamsters and the Building Trades, had long used the *boycott* weapon. One local union of the Teamsters, for example, would not make delivery of apples to a store if such apples were purchased from a company which was in dispute with another local of the Teamsters. Such pressure on the third party was deemed to be improper. So-called *wildcat strikes* also became the subject of legislation. Such strikes occur when employees stop work in violation of the terms of a labor contract. Under the Taft-Hartley act the union was made subject to suits for damages for such occurrences. Special procedures were provided by the act for dealing with public emergency disputes; specifically, an injunction could be secured by direction of the president

**A VACATION RESORT FOR UNION MEMBERS**
One of the pioneers in providing benefits for workers has been the International Ladies' Garment Workers' Union. In addition to operating medical centers, schools, and gymnasiums, the I.L.G.W.U. owns this thousand-acre resort at Forest Park, Pa.

of the United States, forbidding the union to strike for a certain period. In addition, the NLRB was increased to five members, with administrative functions given to a general counsel.

The Taft-Hartley act has come to have symbolic importance. Most labor union officials condemn the act as grossly unfair to workers. Long arguing for outright repeal, most union officials now seek amendments which would make the act less "antilabor." Some public opinion polls, however, seem to show that individual union members are in favor of many parts of the act. A number of management organizations, such as the National Association of Manufacturers and the United States Chamber of Commerce, have championed the act. They have suggested "strengthening" it in the form of additional regulation of unions and of union power.

The Taft-Hartley act has been a controversial political issue. In 1954 the secretary of labor, James P. Mitchell, said that the continuous argument for changes in the Taft-Hartley law had become "a battle of the professionals." In other words, the arguments were so technical as to have little meaning either for the people who work for a living or for the management group.

### Dealing with Labor Problems

Labor unions and industrial relations attract the most attention when bargaining fails and a strike is called. Far more often than not, however, union and management reach an agreement around the conference table. Despite the undue attention given to strikes, there is strong evidence that union and man-

agement are developing an understanding of each other's functions and a respect for each other. There is a growing conviction that collective bargaining will work as a democratic institution and will contribute to economic progress.

Perhaps the greatest progress has been made in dealing with day-by-day problems. Management must make thousands of decisions which affect the workers. One man receives a disciplinary layoff for insubordination; another man is passed over for a promotion; a piece rate is fixed for a new operation. When workers feel that their rights are infringed upon by such decisions, they file *grievances*. Nowadays provision is made in most labor agreements for a careful step-by-step appraisal of these grievances by various union and company representatives.

### Arbitration of Grievances

If no agreement is reached, it is customary to submit grievances to an outside arbitrator. He will decide the issue with both parties having agreed in advance to accept his ruling. About 90 per cent of all labor agreements in the United States make provision for *arbitration* as the final step of the grievance procedure (*see* Arbitration). Through such procedures a system of industrial jurisprudence is gradually being developed in many companies and in many industries.

Voluntary arbitration is now used extensively in the United States to settle grievance disputes arising *under the terms* of a labor contract. For example, was Employee A or Employee B entitled to promotion under the seniority clause of a labor agreement?

89

Arbitration is usually unacceptable to both unions and employers in disputes *over the terms* of the contract. Should wages go up $0.15 an hour? Both parties think the stakes too high to trust such decisions to outsiders. If necessary, they prefer a strike. This encourages both parties to modify their extreme positions in order to reach agreement.

To help the parties agree before a strike begins, the federal government and some state governments provide *conciliation and mediation services.* Such services have been available to the railroads since 1926. Railroad grievance disputes can be submitted to an adjustment board. The National Mediation Board deals with disputes over terms. If a dispute threatens to interrupt railroad operations, the president can select an emergency board. A strike is prohibited while this board investigates and for 30 days after it makes its recommendations. In 1963 Congress passed the first compulsory arbitration bill when negotiations failed in a major railroad dispute. This was seen as a failure for collective bargaining.

Under the Taft-Hartley act disputes in other industries are administered by the Federal Mediation and Conciliation Service. The president may appoint a special board to investigate a major dispute. A court injunction can postpone a strike for 80 days. At any time during this "cooling-off period" the NLRB may hold a vote among employees on the company's latest offer. (*See also* United States Government, section "Department of Labor.")

### Union Accomplishments

Some unions have done much more for their members than to act as collective bargaining representatives. Active membership in such organizations as the Amalgamated Clothing Workers or the International Ladies' Garment Workers' Union can be a way of life.

Both of these unions have medical centers, schools, and gymnasiums. With the employers, broad pension and vacation programs have been worked out. The "Amalgamated" has a bank which provides capital to bolster weak companies and to make jobs more secure. The I.L.G.W.U. has a leadership development course to train employee representatives. Almost every union in the country has taken some steps to help the general well-being of its members.

Organized labor has also helped to bring about many humanitarian reforms through legislation. Laws have been passed to regulate the conditions of employment of women and children and to specify maximum hours of employment and minimum wages for all workers. Legislation was also passed to protect against industrial accident, unemployment, and old-age dependency. Prior to the 1930's it was believed that jurisdiction over labor legislation was denied to the federal government by the Constitution. Such jurisdiction thus remained subject to control of the state legislatures. This was changed by the Supreme Court ruling on the constitutionality of the Wagner act in 1937. The court held that Congress had a right to regulate industrial relations on the ground that such relations affected the flow of interstate commerce.

Before 1937, the drive of organized labor for legislative reforms had to be conducted state by state. Massachusetts was a leader in labor legislation. In blazing new trails, however, its industry was often placed at a competitive disadvantage with the industry of other states which lagged. Over many years, the A.F.L. and other unions have worked in each state to secure the passage of Workmen's Compensation Acts providing for payments in the case of industrial accidents. Even today such protection is not uniform; wide variations exist in the benefits available in the various states (*see* Employers' Liability).

**HEADQUARTERS OF THE DEPARTMENT OF LABOR**
One of the major executive departments of the federal government is the Department of Labor, which has occupied this imposing building since 1935. It is located at Constitution Avenue (foreground) and 14th Street in Washington, D.C.

One of the first federal aids to workers was the Social Security Act, passed in 1935. This provided a combination of federal and state assistance to the aged and the unemployed. (*See also* Social Security.) The Fair Labor Standards Act, first passed in 1938, required concerns engaged in interstate commerce to pay overtime for work in excess of 40 hours a week. It also set a minimum wage.

In 1950 an agreement in the steel industry set a pattern for old-age pensions. That same year the Automobile Workers and General Motors Corporation signed an agreement periodically adjusting wages to changes in the cost-of-living index. This was the so-called *escalator clause*. (*See also* Living Costs.)

In 1959 the Landrum-Griffin labor law was approved by Congress. It imposed a variety of new restrictions on trade unions. These included several limitations on picketing and secondary boycotts. The new law also ordered labor leaders to respect rank-and-file rights under pain of jail sentences.

### Foreign and International Labor Groups

One of the largest labor groups abroad is Great Britain's Trades Union Congress, with a membership of about 8 million. The German Trade Union Federation (of West Germany) has more than 6 million members. In France, the General Confederation of Labor claims about 5 million members. Italy's Communist-dominated General Confederation of Labor has about 5 million members. Canada has more than one million labor unionists, about half of them belonging to the Trades and Labour Congress. Russian trade unions include almost all wage earners.

The first international labor organization was the International Secretariat of National Trade Union Centers, formed in 1901. In 1949 the C.I.O., A.F.L., U.M.W., and the unions of other free countries formed the International Confederation of Free Trade Unions (ICFTU). This organization was recognized by the United Nations in 1950.

The International Labor Organization (ILO) was created along with the League of Nations in 1919. In 1946 it became affiliated with the United Nations. The ILO represents governments, employers, and workers. It seeks to eliminate child labor, secure safe working conditions, and aid the spread of free unions.

### Labor Day and May Day

In the United States and Canada, the first Monday in September is celebrated as Labor Day in honor of all wage earners. This celebration grew out of an annual September parade in New York City by the Knights of Labor during the 1880's.

Oregon, in 1887, was the first state to recognize Labor Day as a legal holiday. Seven years later Congress made the day a public holiday. In many nations organized labor and radical political parties hold demonstrations and parades on May 1.

**LABOR PARTIES.** After workingmen had organized unions to deal with employers they also founded political parties in some countries. Their purpose was to influence government and secure favorable legislation. (*See also* Labor.)

In England various socialist societies, notably the Fabians and the Social Democratic Federation, became active in the late 1800's. These societies, working with the Independent Labor party founded by James Keir Hardie in 1893, sought to send members to Parliament. In 1899 the Trades Union Congress began backing the movement. As a result the Labor party was created, and it won nearly 30 parliamentary seats in the 1906 election. After World War I the Labor party became the chief opposition group to the Conservatives (*see* English History). In Australia and New Zealand also, labor parties have held a prominent place in government since World War I.

On the continent of Europe, labor parties grew out of trade unions but generally they took the name of some political doctrine such as Socialism. During the 1930's Germany, Italy, and Spain suppressed these parties, but most of them sprang up again after World War II. The workers in Asian countries and in Central and South America also began asserting themselves. In some nations the party members disagreed on the political and economic changes they wanted. Usually the majority of the members favored Socialism, but a strong minority supported Communism (*see* Communism; Socialism).

The first Labor party in the world was launched in the United States. This was the Working Men's party, formed by trade unionists in Philadelphia in 1828. This party soon died. A Socialist Labor party was founded in 1874. In 1901 some members split off to form the Socialist party. This group in turn was weakened by the rise of the Communist party.

Labor unions gave little support to the national labor parties. They preferred to campaign for the prolabor candidates of the regular political parties. After World War I, however, there arose several state parties which helped effect local reforms. This was true of the Farmer-Labor party in Minnesota and the American Labor party in New York.

The rapid growth of union membership since the mid-1930's has given the large unions great political power. Working within the framework of the Democratic and Republican parties they played the political role of rewarding friends and punishing enemies.

The American Federation of Labor and the Congress of Industrial Organizations merged in 1955. They formed a Committee on Political Education (C.O.P.E.). Its aim is to inform members on political issues and candidates and to get out the labor vote. The C.O.P.E. is a merger of the A.F.L.'s Labor's League for Political Education and the C.I.O.'s Political Action Committee.

---

THESE ARTICLES ARE IN THE FACT-INDEX

**Labor party (Great Britain)**
**Labouchère, Henry du Pré**
**Labouchère, Pierre Antoine**

---

**LABRADOR.** The northeastern corner of the North American continent is the peninsula of Labrador. This peninsula extends from Hudson Bay to the Atlantic Ocean and from the Gulf of St. Lawrence to Hudson Strait. In 1949 Labrador joined with the island of Newfoundland to become the tenth province of Canada (*see* Newfoundland).

The name Labrador refers to the eastern triangle of the peninsula only. This section is also sometimes called the Coast of Labrador. It covers 112,826 square miles. The Quebec section of the peninsula is known as Ungava or New Quebec. The boundary between Labrador and Quebec runs along the "height of land" separating the watersheds. It was established in 1927 by the English Privy Council. (For map, *see* Canada.)

### Rugged Land

The peninsula is a part of the rocky Canadian Shield, or Laurentian Plateau (*see* Laurentian Plateau). Over the southern part stretches a great spruce forest. The forest thins out toward the north, and the upper third of the peninsula is tundra.

At least a fourth of the peninsula is covered with marshes, lakes, and streams. The Atlantic coastline, about 1,200 miles long, is fringed with islands and deep arms of the sea. These sea arms are called fjords. The south coast is low. Toward the north, however, bold rocky cliffs rise 2,500 to 5,500 feet out of the sea.

The cold Labrador Current flows down from the Arctic Ocean and makes the climate along the coast very severe. Inland it is somewhat milder, but winter temperatures reach −50° F. Summers are short and cool. A few hardy vegetables are raised in village gardens, but agriculture can never be highly successful in Labrador. Usually snow covers the ground from September to June.

The coast of Labrador is treeless and rocky. Trading vessels bring supplies to coastal villages during the summer months.

Except for fishing villages on the coast, the peninsula was unbroken wilderness until 1941. Then Goose Airport was built at the head of Hamilton Inlet. This airport is on the great circle air route between North America and Western Europe. It is an important military and commercial base.

One of the world's largest deposits of iron ore lies along the Ungava-Labrador border 350 miles north of the Gulf of St. Lawrence. At Lake Allard, 22 miles north of the gulf, is the world's largest deposit of ilmenite (titanium ore). The 357-mile-long Quebec North Shore and Labrador Railway hauls about 12 million tons of iron ore a year from the rich Labrador mines.

Waterpower in the peninsula is enormous. Over the edge of the plateau the rivers descend in foaming rapids and mighty waterfalls. The Churchill River, 600 miles long, empties into Lake Melville, an arm of the Atlantic Ocean. About 230 miles from its mouth it drops 1,038 feet in 16 miles. At Churchill Falls it plunges 245 feet into Bowdoin Canyon (*see* Waterfalls). The Churchill Falls Power Station was officially opened in 1972, with full operation at a capacity of 7 million horsepower scheduled for 1975. An additional estimated 3 million horsepower is available downstream.

### How the People Live

Labrador has only 28,166 permanent residents (1971 census). The white people, of English and Scottish ancestry, are called *Livyeres* ("live heres"). Almost all of them live in tiny villages perched on the bleak rocks of the south coast. Goose Airport (Goose Bay), on Lake Melville, is the largest town. In the north are Eskimos. A few wandering Indians of the Montagnais and Naskapi tribes live in the interior forests. In summer several thousand fishermen come to fish for cod.

The people of Labrador lived in great poverty until an English doctor, Wilfred Grenfell, arrived to help them. The International Grenfell Association, founded to carry on his work, maintains schools, churches, hospitals, and nursing stations along Labrador's south coast (*see* Grenfell). The Moravian Church of Labrador has four stations among the people. Moravian missions have been maintained since the 1750's.

The United States has a radar base in northern Labrador. This is part of the American-Canadian radar network designed to supply early warning of enemy attack.

Labrador was visited by the Norse as early as 986 and by Leif Ericson in the year 1000. John Cabot rediscovered the peninsula in 1498.

THESE ARTICLES ARE IN THE FACT-INDEX

| | |
|---|---|
| Labrador Current | Labuan Island |
| Labrador duck | Laburnum |
| Labrador tea | Labyrinth |
| La Bruyère, Jean de | Laccadive Islands |

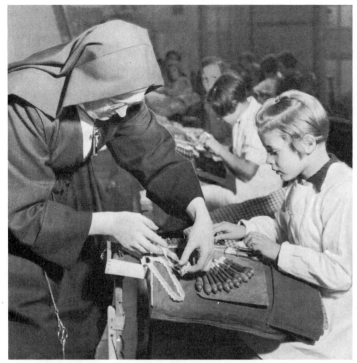

In the Belgian town of Bruges lacemaking by hand is still an important occupation. The community's girls are taught the art from an early age.

# LACEMAKING
# by Hand and by Machine

LACE. The most delicate of textile fabrics is lace. Wealthy women once wore dresses made entirely of lace. Now, however, it is used mostly as decoration.

Until the end of the 18th century lacemaking was an art, produced by hand. Today the fabric generally is made of cotton thread by machine. The modern lacemaking machine weighs about 17 tons and covers about 10 by 50 feet of floor space.

On one of these huge machines shining little flattened bobbins swing through threads which spin from reels. The bobbins dart swiftly over one thread and under the next. Sometimes they stop and vibrate rapidly a fraction of a second before they go on. This vibration twists the threads. Patterns are made by these twisted threads. Machine-made lace in many cases is so delicate that only an expert can tell it is not handmade. In one day a machine can produce a piece of lace which would have required six months' work by a skillful hand worker.

### The Development of Lace Machines

The first machine-made lace was produced on a stocking machine. This turned out a lacy material which was really a knitted fabric. By about 1780 net machines were at work in France and England. Net produced by these devices was used as a background on which lace designs were worked by hand. In 1802 Robert Brown invented an excellent machine that produced nets of all sizes.

John Heathcoat in 1809 patented a bobbin net device, so-called because the threads were wound on bobbins. This was the forerunner of the lace machine that we know today. Joseph M. Jacquard meanwhile had perfected a pattern-weaving device in 1800. In 1813 John Leavers used the principles of the Heathcoat machine and of the Jacquard machine to invent a device which would produce a fancy pattern at the same time that the background of net was being made. Although laws forbade the export of lace machines, the Leavers models were taken apart and smuggled into France.

By 1837 French lacemakers had achieved the final goal. Using a punched-card system incorporated into the machine they reproduced the fine designs that had been possible only by handwork.

### Machine-Made Lace

Washing, bleaching, dyeing, and finishing are now done by machine. Loose threads are clipped by machine, and scallops are also machine-cut.

The United States lace industry began early in the 20th century. It had a slow start. England forbade the export of lace machines to protect its industry. Many, however, were brought to the United States in parts. They were assembled by workers who had also been imported from England.

In 1909 England lifted the ban on lace-machine exports, and the United States Congress permitted them to be imported duty free for a period of 17 months. Many of the machines were brought into the country during this time. The American lace industry was then well under way.

For a time the industry grew steadily despite the fact that a three-year apprenticeship was required to learn the trade. In recent years, however, the demand for lace has declined sharply. The industry has suffered as a consequence. The main centers of machine-made laces today are Nottingham, England; Calais and Caudry, France; and several areas of the United States.

### How Lace Is Made by Hand

Handmade lace is still produced all over the world. The manufacture of it in quantities is confined to China, France, Belgium, Ireland, Italy, England, and the Philippines. The infinite care and the great amount of time required to produce handmade lace will always make it expensive. There are many

**MAKING LACE BY MACHINE**
On this huge lace-curtain loom many pieces of fabric can be made at one time. Cotton is most often used in machine-made lace. Silk, rayon, nylon, and wool threads are also used.

different grades of these laces. They vary in value according to the fineness and the design of the fabric and the time needed to make each piece.

There are two types of handmade lace—(1) needle point, or point, and (2) bobbin, or pillow. Needle point is made with a needle and a single thread. The pattern is drawn on parchment and then stitched to a piece of heavy linen in order to hold it straight. Threads are laid on the many lines of the pattern and are lightly fastened through to the linen. The entire figure is then worked. When it is completed the stitches holding it to the linen are cut, and the lace comes free.

In making bobbin lace the design is drawn on stiff parchment which is carefully stretched over a *pillow*. This is a round or oval board which is stuffed to form a cushion. The lacemaker places the pillow on her knees. The pattern is picked out along the outline of the drawing, and small pins are stuck in at close intervals. Around these pins threads wound on bobbins of varying size are twisted and crossed to form the various meshes and openings. The pattern, called a *gimp*, is formed by interweaving a much thicker thread. Needle point is the heavier of the two types of lace. Pillow lace is very supple and is prized for the way it can be draped.

### History of Handmade Lace

The ancient Persians, Greeks, Chinese, and Egyptians made a kind of lace, but little is known about its appearance. The arts of drawn thread work and netting practiced by the ancient Egyptians were completely lost for centuries. They were rediscovered in the 15th century in Italy.

The earliest specimens of Italian lace were produced in convents. Nuns had the time, patience, and skill to produce these works of art. As a decoration lace has long been important to religion. Priceless altar cloths and vestments made of the delicate fabric are still stored in cathedrals. At the height of the Venetian lace industry, in the 16th century, the doge (chief magistrate) required that material be submitted to him before it was put on sale so that he could choose the best for religious use.

Lacemaking became a pastime for gentlewomen and a means of livelihood for the workers. The art spread to France, Flanders, Belgium, England, and Ireland. Countries and regions competed to create new patterns which were jealously guarded. Ambassadors acted as spies. They were required to report on developments in the lace industry of the countries to which they were sent.

### Lace in France

In 1533 Catherine de' Medici came to France from Italy to marry the future King Henry II. She introduced the art of lacemaking at the French court. In an inventory of her household goods were 381 squares of unmounted lace in one chest and 538 in another. She kept her waiting women constantly at work making lace to decorate her bedchamber.

The French royal court became the center of new designs. Venice remained the source for the heavier needle lace. French workers made lighter types of new grace and delicacy. These were worn as cravats and ruffles by men and were used for fans, handkerchief borders, and gowns for women.

Until the last quarter of the 17th century French lace was similar to the Italian. Jean Baptiste Colbert, the finance minister under extravagant Louis XIV, used lacemaking to increase France's prosperity and was responsible for creating a distinct French type of lace. He imported workers from Venice. These artisans and others whom they taught spread the art throughout the country. Schools and workshops were set up in many French towns.

## Lace in England

During the reign of Elizabeth I close relations between the courts of France and England encouraged the use of lace in England. Elizabeth's high ruff of lace is familiar to everyone who has seen her portraits. (For picture, see Elizabeth I.)

Both the art and the fine materials for lacemaking were limited in England. In 1662 such huge sums of money were going out of the country for the material that Parliament prohibited its importation. This posed a problem for merchants who had to fill large orders for the court of Charles II. They began smuggling the choicest Brussels lace into England and selling it as "English point." Today Brussels lace is still called *point d'Angleterre*.

## Belgian Lace

Belgium, with Flanders, was a leading lace center in the 16th century. Even at the height of production, in the 18th century, Belgian lace was very expensive. An artisan working 12 hours a day could turn out only one third of an inch a week. As many as 1,200 bobbins were sometimes used on one pillow. Today schools in Belgium teach children the art of making the fabric from an early age.

## American Lace

When French officers came to the American Colonies to help fight the Revolution, they brought with them the fashion of wearing lace. Nearly all that was used in the colonies was imported. The manufacture of handmade lace was never an industry in the United States. Soon after lace became popular with Americans, it could be made by machine.

## Modern Handmade Lace

Belgium produces some of the finest modern handmade lace. The flax which grows there is an important factor in this Belgian industry. In the town of Bruges almost every woman makes lace. Special ordinances require that only the handmade article can be so labeled. *Point d'Angleterre* is still made in Belgium, as are handmade fabrics of Italian, French, and English origin.

France produces *point d'Alençon*, which is still the high luxury lace. It is very expensive. It is used for the finest lingerie. The art of making it is taught at a school in Alençon. In convents at Argentan is taught the making of a light lace which is less expensive. It is used for household decoration rather than for clothing. Lace is also produced at Bayeux, Le Puy, and Lyons.

## FAMOUS HANDMADE LACES

Alençon is a fine French needle-point lace. It is made in small segments, joined with invisible seams. Each part is done by a different workman. It dates from the 1600's.

Brussels lace (left) is the finest of all. It is made on the pillow with fine thread. In

bridelace (right) the ground is made entirely of bars without a net foundation.

## FAMOUS HANDMADE LACES

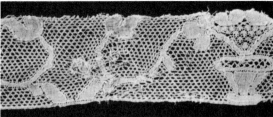

Valenciennes (left) is a durable pillow lace originally produced in France, now handmade in Belgium and machine-

made elsewhere. Antwerp (right) is a pillow lace. It is recognized by the vase of flowers which always appears in it.

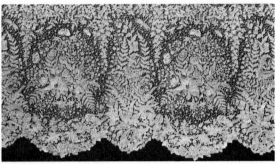

Cluny (left) is a coarse, strong lace with a leaf motif. It is principally used for interior decoration. Honiton (right) is

an English pillow variety still made in the county of Devonshire. A lacemaking school is conducted there.

In Italy the island of Burano, near Venice, is the center of lacemaking. When girls there are eight years old they go every afternoon to the Royal School of Lace to learn their art. Each girl specializes in some aspect of manufacture. The finished products of Burano are the work of many co-operating hands. Burano lace is used for larger articles such as tablecloths, curtains, and bridal gowns.

### Types of Handmade Lace

There are many types of lace. With a few exceptions each bears the name of the town from which it originally came, and each one is different from all others. These are some of the most famous.

**Alençon** is a fine needle-point lace of linen thread. Its manufacture was established by Colbert, who brought Venetian lacemakers to his château near Alençon. They could not teach the French to make true Venetian stitches, so they invented a new kind of lace.

It is made with a fine needle on a parchment pattern. Small sections are joined together with invisible seams. About a dozen steps are required to complete this lace. It is now made in France and Italy. Patterns in the handmade variety are heavier than in the machine-made type.

**Argentan** is a needle-point lace which originated in Argentan, France. It is similar to Alençon, and like Alençon it was originally called *point de France*.

Designs are still made in Argentan. They are larger and bolder than Alençon and less expensive. It is reproduced by machine.

**Arras** is a strong, firm, very white lace made in France. It has little variety in its patterns. Workers

have acquired great skill and speed in the production of Arras lace.

**Binche** is of the Brussels bobbin type. Floral or bowknot designs and sprigs made with bobbins are appliquéd to net. The earlier, finer type of this lace was popular in Paris in the middle of the 18th century. It is similar to Valenciennes in texture and pattern.

**Brussels** is the finest and filmiest of all lace. It is made on the pillow of an amazingly fine thread. Before the cost became prohibitive, this thread was hand-spun underground. Because of its fineness contact with the air made it break. Brussels has less "relief" than Alençon; that is, the motifs are not raised from the background.

**Carrickmacross** is the oldest Irish type. Lacemaking is still done near Carrickmacross, where the industry was established about 1820. A pattern is cut from fine cambric and applied to net with point stitches. The rose and the shamrock are the most popular patterns.

**Chantilly** is a bobbin lace made of silk. Its patterns usually consist of vases, baskets of flowers, and elaborate combinations of flowers, sprays, and leaves. Modern Chantilly is often even more beautiful than old laces. No handmade fabric is now produced in Chantilly, France. Machinery has taken over the making of this material.

**Chinese** lace was introduced to China by the Syrians. The technique is the same as that of the Venetian type, but the thread and the designs are inferior. When good thread and well-drawn patterns are used, the Chinese Venise lace is excellent.

**Cluny** is a coarse, strong fabric still made by hand

**LACEMAKERS OF BURANO**
Girls are taught the ancient craft practiced by every woman on the island. Burano is famous as "the island of laces."

in France, Belgium, and China. Its name was taken from the Cluny Museum in Paris. It is also made by machine. Heavy linen thread is used, and the design is so open that the product is light and pleasing.

**Duchesse** is also called *point de Flandre*. It is widely regarded as the most beautiful of the pillow laces. It is pure white and has a graceful, rhythmic pattern. The designs consist of leaves, flowers, and scrolls. Bridal veils of the Flemish Duchesse lace are often heirlooms.

**Honiton** is a form of *point d'Angleterre*. It was the favorite of Queen Victoria, whose coronation gown was made of Honiton. It is a pillow lace, first produced about 1568 in Honiton, England. The pattern parts are worked on a pillow and then fastened to a net ground which is made separately.

**Lille** has a simple design. It was originally made at Lille, France. The plain net ground often has a heavy sprinkling of dots. The formal patterns are outlined with thick, flat thread.

**Limerick** was originally made in Ireland about a hundred years ago. There are two types—tambour and run. Run is finer and lighter.

**Macramé** is a heavy fabric of the Venice type which was used in Spain and Italy during the 15th, 16th, and 17th centuries to decorate church vestments. It is one of the oldest laces and is still made in convents of the Riviera where nuns teach its manufacture to children.

**Maltese** is a heavy, attractive pillow lace. The pattern is of geometrical forms, often a Maltese cross, joined by a purled background. It was originally made on the island of Malta. Now it is produced in England, France, and Ireland.

**Mechlin** is a valuable lace that looks like Lille. It is very fine, but added strength is given by extra stitches at every mesh of the grounding. It is made in one piece on the pillow. All laces of Flanders up to 1665 were called Mechlin except Brussels.

**Spanish** includes many varieties of lace, the most famous called *point d'Espagne*. It is usually gold or silver, sometimes embroidered with colored silk.

**Torchon** is a coarse pillow lace made of a soft, loosely twisted thread. The patterns are simple, and this lace is used to trim muslin and heavy linen garments. It is manufactured in many places in Europe, especially in Saxony, where it is made by men.

**Tulle** is a silk net that is very fine. During the 17th and 18th centuries a type of pillow lace used for women's sleeves was made at Tulle and Aurillac, in France, and also in Germany.

**Valenciennes** is one of the best-known varieties. It is a durable pillow lace in which the pattern and ground are worked together. Great skill is required to do this. First made in Valenciennes, France, in the 18th century, many fine types of this lace are now made by machine.

THESE ARTICLES ARE IN THE FACT-INDEX

| | |
|---|---|
| Lace-bark tree | Laclede, Pierre |
| La Ceiba, Honduras | Lacombe, Albert |
| Lachaise, Gaston | La Condamine, Charles |
| Lachine, Que. | Marie de |
| Lachish, Palestine | Laconia, Greece |
| Lachlan River | Laconia, N. H. |
| Lackawanna, N. Y. | La Coruña, Spain |

**LACQUER AND SHELLAC.** The glossy film often applied for protection to metal and wood is lacquer. Nearly all the lacquer used today is manufactured by a chemical process.

Military forces use a great deal of lacquer. It guards tanks, airplanes, and other military vehicles against weathering. Lacquer serves many other purposes as well. It is used in coating phonograph records, in fingernail polish, and in covering for refrigerators, kitchen ranges, and automobiles.

### How Lacquer Is Made

Lacquer manufacture is a complex process. Various ingredients are used. They are combined in different proportions according to the purpose for which the lacquer will be used.

A typical lacquer contains about six types of ingredients. These may include film-forming materials, pigments, solvents, thinners, plasticizers, and stabilizers. Each of these has a definite use.

Film-forming materials give the lacquer its waterproofness, hardness, durability, and luster. Pigments color the lacquer. They are not used in clear lacquer. Solvents keep the film-forming substances in liquid form before use. Thinners prevent the lacquer from drying before and during application. Plasticizers reduce brittleness. Stabilizers stop decomposition.

### Oriental Lacquer

Originally lacquer was made from the sap of the varnish tree (*Rhus vernicifera*). The varnish tree grows abundantly in China. It was in that country that the art of lacquering was discovered more than 3,000 years ago.

The Chinese lacquering process was a long and laborious one. It required putting as many as 18 or 20 coats of lacquer over paper-covered or cloth-covered wood to get the hard film desired. Each coat of lacquer was rubbed with fine charcoal before the next one was brushed on.

The Japanese lacquering process was similar, but in time they learned to surpass the Chinese in this work. By the 17th century the Oriental art of lacquering was known as *japanning*.

### Lacquer in Europe and America

In Europe and America, where varnish trees do not thrive, the early lacquers were simple spirit varnishes of which shellac was the most common example. These spirit varnishes were either clear or colored. They were sometimes used on wood but more often on metals such as brass. This lacquer coating prevented tarnishing and gave a soft, pleasing luster to the wood or metal.

Other spirit-soluble gums such as sandarac and elemi were often added to the mixture of shellac and alcohol. This preparation produced a lacquer which, after many applications, gave a more durable and adhesive coating to metalwork.

### Uses of Shellac

Shellac is a natural resin. It is not made chemically as is lacquer. It is produced by tree lice, which are cultivated chiefly in northern India. Like lacquer, it gives a smooth, glossy coating.

At one time shellac was widely employed for the same general purposes that lacquer is used today. Shellac, however, is inferior to the more newly developed lacquer and, consequently, has been replaced by it in most cases.

Shellac is still important to some extent in the manufacture of oilcloth, glue, linoleum, sealing wax, and some types of phonograph records. It is also used in electrical work as a binder and insulator.

### Insects Make Lac Resin

The tree lice which make shellac "sweat" resin (*see* Scale Insects). Their long scientific name, *Tachardia lacca*, is shortened to *lac*. The word comes from the Hindustani word *lakh*, which means "one hundred thousand." Scholars are not certain why the name was chosen. It may be because thousands of insects are needed to make even a little shellac or because the lacs swarm in vast numbers.

The lac grows from about one fortieth of an inch to one twenty-seventh. Lacs attach themselves to tender shoots of the fig tree and to some kinds of acacia. They suck sap through tiny sharp beaks,

then emit resin from their pores as humans excrete perspiration. The resin hardens into a protective shell.

### Harvesting Resin

In late summer and early fall Indian workers cut the twigs or scrape off the shells. The mass of resin hardens further into *stick-lac*. The Indians crush this with stone hammers or in a stone mill, separating it into fragments called *seed lac*.

After several washings, seed lac is dried and graded. Some is sold as a raw product, but most is made into shellac, button lac, and garnet lac. The most important is shellac. In shellac the resin is stretched into thin sheets, or shells. Button lac is composed of round, flat discs. Garnet lac gets its name from its deep red color.

### Making Shellac

To make shellac, two workers pack seed lac in a long thin cloth bag. They twist this bag over a charcoal fire. Hot resin falls to a stone slab, where workers stretch it to very thin sheets about four feet square.

Garnet lac is unstretched sheet shellac. Button lac is shaped into little lumps about three inches in diameter, usually stamped with the maker's initials. Nearly all shellac and other lac are produced by hand. Workers increase the natural crop by spreading the lac colonies. They do this by tying twigs coated with lac eggs to other trees.

---

THIS ARTICLE IS IN THE FACT-INDEX
**La Crosse, Wis.**

---

**LACROSSE.** The oldest organized sport played in North America is lacrosse. French and English colo-

**DIAGRAMING A PLAY**
During a practice session the coach uses a diagram to explain a play to the members of the Cornell University lacrosse team.

nists found the Indians playing a fast, rough contest called "baggataway." White men in Canada adopted the game about 1840. They revised the rules and called it *lacrosse* because the curved end of the playing stick resembled a bishop's staff, or *crosier*. In 1867 an act of Parliament made lacrosse the national game of Canada.

From Canada the game soon spread to the United States, particularly along the Atlantic seaboard. To-day it is a popular summer sport of Eastern schools and athletic clubs.

Lacrosse is played with a rubber sponge ball $7\frac{3}{4}$ to 8 inches around and 5 to $5\frac{3}{4}$ ounces in weight. Each player carries a *crosse*, a 6-foot hickory stick shaped like a long-handled tennis racket. At the end of the crosse a 12-inch crook is bent at right angles to the main shaft. Within this crook a net of cord and rawhide lacings provides a pocket to catch and carry the ball.

### Scoring a Goal

At each end of the playing field is a goal, 6 feet wide and 6 feet high. The goal posts support a pyramid-shaped cord netting which slopes back to the ground 7 feet from the mouth of the goal. Each team tries to advance the ball to a position where it can be thrown into the opponent's goal net. One point is scored for each goal.

There are 10 men on a team—the *goalkeeper* defends his team's goal. The *point* is the first defense man in front of the goal crease. The *cover point* plays ahead of the point. The *first defense* and the *second defense* protect their goal. The *center* represents his team on the *facing line* at the beginning of each quarter. The *first attack* and *second attack* carry the play into the opponent's territory. The *out home* and *in home* provide much of the scoring punch.

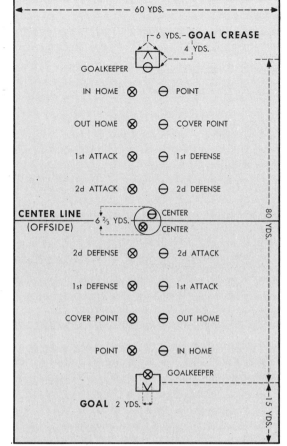

**TEAMS LINE UP**

This diagram shows the layout of a lacrosse field. It also gives the general positions taken by the players at the start of a game. Each quarter starts with a "face-off."

**PLAY BEGINS**

Play is started by "facing" the ball in a ten-foot circle. The referee places the ball between the reverse surfaces of two crosses. Only the two players (centers) who are facing the ball are allowed into the circle until the ball has cleared it.

Each player wears a padded helmet and a wire face mask to protect himself against an accidental blow from a crosse. Other equipment includes thick gloves, hip pads and shoulder pads worn under the uniform, and canvas shoes with cleats to take a firm grip on the ground.

### How the Game Is Played

Each quarter of play starts with a *face-off* in the center of the field. The referee places the ball between the two rival centers. At a signal from the official each center tries to get the ball by scooping it up with his crosse.

The team with the ball then works it toward the opponent's goal. It may be passed from one man to another or carried on the crosse. Opponents may knock the ball out of a player's crosse or *check* a rival by running in front of him.

A goalkeeper may bat the ball away with his hand, but other players are not permitted to touch the ball or another player with the hand. A player who violates the rule may be suspended from the game for one to three minutes, or his opponents may be given the ball to put in play (*free throw*).

During play each team must have at least four men in their own half of the field and no less than three men across the center line in their opponent's territory. A lacrosse game is divided into quarters of 15 minutes each.

THESE ARTICLES ARE IN THE FACT-INDEX

| | |
|---|---|
| Lactose | Ladd-Franklin, Christine |
| Ladanum | Ladies tresses |
| Ladd, Edwin Fremont | Ladislaus, Saint |
| Ladd, George Trumbull | |

**LADOGA** (*lăd'ō-ga*), **LAKE.** Some 70 rivers pour their icy waters into Lake Ladoga, Europe's largest fresh-water lake. The lake lies in northern Russia near the Finnish border. It has an area of 7,000 square miles. This is about the area of Lake Ontario.

Ladoga is ice-free only about six months of the year. Severe storms and rocks and shoals make navigation dangerous. Several canals have been built along the southern shore. Through these canals pass many vessels and rafts. They carry timber, iron, granite, and other products from the northern shores of Leningrad by way of the Neva River.

Through the broad Neva the lake's surplus waters flow into the Gulf of Finland. A system of waterways, including the Svir' River and Lake Onega, connects Ladoga with the White Sea many miles to the north.

**LADYBUG.** The policemen of the insect world are the ladybugs, or ladybirds. They are really beetles. These small bright-colored creatures live in orchards, fields, and gardens. They are always busy clearing plants and trees of insect pests. Friendly as they are to man, ladybugs are like hungry tigers among other insects. (*See also* Scale Insects.)

**THE HELPFUL LADYBUG**
As soon as the larvae hatch they begin devouring insect pests on the leaves of plants where the eggs were laid.

There are 150 species of ladybugs. The most common member of this large family in the United States is red with two black spots. Other types are a more brilliant red with black, yellow, or white spots. Some are shining black with red spots. Still others are yellow with black or red spots.

Ladybugs defend themselves by ejecting drops of an ill-smelling liquid from their knee joints. This makes them extremely distasteful to birds and to most other insect eaters. The eggs are laid under the leaves of plants that have been infested with insect pests. When the larvae hatch they rid the plant of the pests. The scientific name of the common red ladybug is *Adalia bipunctata*.

THESE ARTICLES ARE IN THE FACT-INDEX

Ladycliff College
Lady of the Lake
Ladysmith, South Africa

**LADY'S-SLIPPER.** In May and June the lady's-slipper, or moccasin flower, blossoms. This fragrant genus of orchids grows from southern Canada south to North Carolina and westward to the Rockies.

There are two yellow lady's-slippers. One is larger than the other. Both have twisted petals of yellowish-brown streaked with red or purple. The pink lady's-slipper has dark-brown or green petals and a rose pouch veined with a darker color. (For picture in color, *see* Flowers, Wild.) The showy lady's-slipper has white petals and a rose- and white-striped pouch.

The scientific name of the yellow lady's-slipper is *Cypripedium parviflotum* (the large yellow lady's-slipper is the variety *pubescens*); pink lady's-slipper, *C. acaule*; showy lady's-slipper, *C. reginae*.

THESE ARTICLES ARE IN THE FACT-INDEX

| | |
|---|---|
| Lae, New Guinea | La Farge, Oliver (Hazard |
| Laënnec, René Théophile | Perry) |
| Hyacinthe | Lafayette, George |
| La Farge, John | Washington Motier de |

## LAFAYETTE, Marquis de (1757–1834).

Among the heroes of the American Revolution only the name of Washington ranks above that of Lafayette. He was a gallant Frenchman who generously placed his life and his fortune at the disposal of the American colonists.

By birth he belonged to one of the old noble families of France. His father had been killed in the battle of Minden, in 1759. The young man, whose family name was Du Motier, inherited from his father a castle and the title of Marquis, and from his mother a princely fortune. When he was 16 years old he married a young girl who belonged to one of the greatest families in France.

Three years later, when Lafayette was 19 and a captain in the French army, came the news that the American colonies had declared their independence of England, France's ancient foe. "At the first news of this quarrel," Lafayette afterward wrote, "my heart was enrolled in it." So he disobeyed the commands of his king and his angry father-in-law, purchased a ship, and after many difficulties sailed for America in 1777. He offered to serve without pay, and Congress gave him the rank of major general. Washington soon became a firm friend—almost a father—to the young Frenchman.

Lafayette proved a good officer and a wise adviser. He was slightly wounded in his first battle, that of the Brandywine, in September 1777. Next year he was commended for a masterly retreat from Barren Hill and played an honorable part in the battle of Monmouth and in the Rhode Island expedition.

More important, however, was his influence in inducing the French government to sign a treaty of alliance with the colonies, in 1778. Without this treaty America could not have won the war. To aid this alliance he was back in France in 1779; but he returned to America in time to assist in the Virginia campaign and in the final movements which led to Cornwallis' surrender at Yorktown in 1781.

Lafayette's love for liberty led him to join those French noblemen who favored the Revolution of 1789 in his own country. He was elected to the Estates-General and in that body presented a draft for a Declaration of Rights modeled on the American Declaration of Independence. On the day after the storming of the Bastille (July 14, 1789) he was made commander in chief of the new National Guard, organized to safeguard the Revolution. It was he who proposed for the Revolutionary armies the famous tricolor.

Lafayette rescued Queen Marie Antoinette from the mob that stormed the Palace of Versailles on Oct. 5, 1789, and issued orders to stop King Louis XVI when he sought to escape from France. But gradually he became dismayed at the growing excesses of the Revolution. As the head of an army raised to defend France against Austria, he planned to overthrow the Jacobins and to support a limited monarchy. He was therefore proclaimed a traitor. To escape arrest and the guillotine he fled to Belgium, where he was imprisoned by the Austrians. For five years (1792–97), he remained there in captivity; then Napoleon obtained his release.

Lafayette disapproved of the rule of Napoleon, however, and took no part in public affairs until after his overthrow. Under the restored Bourbon monarchy, Lafayette generally was politically inactive until the people were again oppressed. Then he led the opposition, and in 1830 he took part in his third revolution. He commanded the Army of National Guards that drove Charles X from France and placed on the throne Louis Philippe, the "citizen king."

Twice after the close of the American Revolution Lafayette visited the United States—in 1784 and 1824. On the latter visit, Congress voted him $200,000 and a township of land. This was a welcome gift, for his own property had been taken during the French Revolution.

Lafayette's death, in Paris, saddened both the French and the American people. He was not a great general or a great statesman. He was, however, a lifelong lover of liberty and played a vital part in three important revolutions.

THESE ARTICLES ARE IN THE FACT-INDEX

LaFayette, Marie
  Madeleine, comtesse de
Lafayette, Ind.
Lafayette, La.

Lafayette College
Lafayette Square
La Fère, France

## LAFITTE (lȧ-fēt'), Jean (1780?–1826?).

The pirate Jean Lafitte was also a patriot. Little is known about his early life. No one knows who his parents were. A dozen French cities claim to be his birthplace. His exact birth date is also unknown.

Jean Lafitte appeared in New Orleans about 1806. He opened a blacksmith shop as a cover for his smuggling business. He sold goods captured by pirates from ships sailing the Caribbean Sea.

For two years Lafitte prospered. He was handsome, educated, and pleasant. When the United States outlawed the importing of slaves, in 1808, smugglers had a new source of profit. Lafitte became the leader of smugglers who had a base on Grand Terre Island, 60 miles south of New Orleans. From here he controlled imports into New Orleans. He insisted that his captains operate as privateers, legally commissioned to capture ships and cargoes of enemy nations. At that time this meant British and French ships.

Because other business suffered from Lafitte's monopoly, he and his men were indicted as pirates. In 1814 his base on Grand Terre was destroyed by a United States Navy force. Lafitte escaped.

At this time an English captain offered Lafitte $30,000 and a commission to help the British attack New Orleans. Instead, Lafitte told Governor Claiborne of the planned attack and offered his help. During the battle Lafitte fought well. Later President James Madison pardoned him and his men for piracy.

Lafitte's successful days were over. Many of his men deserted him as he sailed for three years looking for a new base. In 1817 he settled on the island that is now Galveston, Tex. In 1821 Lieut. Lawrence Kearney of the United States Navy ordered Galveston evacuated. After that, Lafitte operated from Mujeres Island off Yucatán, but his forces were small. He died about 1826 at Teljas, on the Yucatán mainland.

People have called Lafitte patriot and privateer, smuggler and pirate. He was all these things. Above all, he was an interesting individual and the last great figure in history's line of dashing pirates.

THESE ARTICLES ARE IN THE FACT-INDEX

La Follette, Philip F(ox)
La Follette, Robert Marion
La Follette, Robert Marion, Jr.
La Fontaine, Henri

**LA FONTAINE, Jean de** (1621–1695). One of the world's favorite storytellers was Jean de la Fontaine. He wrote the beloved 'Fables'. French children have for years learned these verse stories. They have been translated into many languages. Adults never tire of the wisdom in these tales. (*See also* Fables.)

Jean de la Fontaine was born at Château-Thierry, in the French province of Champagne. His father was a government official in charge of forests. Young Jean attended school at Reims. In 1641 he went to the Oratory of St. Magloire in Paris, intending to become a priest. He never took his studies seriously, however, and soon returned home.

In 1647 La Fontaine succeeded to his father's job. He was married in that same year. Before long, however, he gave up his job, separated from his wife, and went to live in Paris.

La Fontaine was a genius at making and keeping friends. Rich patrons took a liking to his wit, and they were happy to support him. A kinsman introduced the young man to Nicolas Fouquet, finance minister to Louis XIV. The minister gave La Fontaine a pension in return for four poems a year.

From 1672 to 1693 La Fontaine lived at the home of Madame de la Sablière, a wise and studious woman. In 1683 he was elected to the French Academy. About 1685 he met M. d'Hervart, his last patron. With him he spent the last two years of his life.

The first six books of 'Fables' appeared in 1668. They were followed by two more in 1678 and 1694. Today only scholars read his other books, but the 'Fables' are read everywhere.

The 'Fables' are both realistic and fantastic. In one story, a fool thinks it is wrong for big pumpkins to grow on small vines and little acorns on great oaks. He changes his mind when a falling acorn awakens him from a nap under an oak tree.

THESE ARTICLES ARE IN THE FACT-INDEX

Lafontaine, Sir Louis Hippolyte
Laforgue, Jules
Lagado
Lagash, Babylonia
Lagerkvist, Pär Fabian

**LAGERLÖF** (*lä′gĕr-lûv*), **Selma Ottiliana Lovisa** (1858–1940). The first woman to win the Nobel prize for literature was Selma Lagerlöf, a Swedish novelist. This was in 1909. She was also the first woman to become a member of the Swedish Academy (1914). In her books she skillfully pictured Swedish life. She had a remarkable knack for turning the commonplace into enjoyable fantasy. She used for her subject matter folklore, magic, her family, and the countryside in which she grew up.

Selma Lagerlöf was born Nov. 20, 1858, in the Swedish province of Värmland. Her parents, Lieut. and Mrs. Erik Gustaf Lagerlöf, were landowners. Selma was frequently sick as a child and spent her time reading. At the age of 15 she had exhausted the library at her home and had begun to write poetry.

When she was 22, Selma Lagerlöf went to Stockholm to study for a teaching career. She spent a year at Sjoberg's Lyceum for girls. In 1882 she entered the Royal Women's Superior Training College where she finished her education. Three years later she became a teacher at Landskrona, in Skåne, in southern Sweden. She was there from 1885 to 1895.

While she was teaching, Selma Lagerlöf began to write in earnest. Her first published book, 'Gösta Berling's Saga', brought her fame. She submitted the first five chapters in a magazine contest and won. When the complete novel was published, it was praised for its imaginative treatment of legends.

After her second book, 'Invisible Links', was published, in 1894, she gave up teaching to devote all her time to writing. In 1904 she received the gold medal of the Swedish Academy. The high point of her career was the Nobel prize award five years later. Her two volumes of 'The Wonderful Adventures of Nils' (1906–7) have always been loved by children. Her other works include 'Miracles of the Anti-Christ' (1897); 'The Outcast' (1918); 'Memories of My Childhood' (1934); 'Diary of Selma Lagerlöf' (1936).

Selma Lagerlöf cherished and worked for peace. In the early days of the Third Reich, Nazi critics praised her. Later, she helped German refugees, and the Nazis no longer approved her work.

In 1924 she made her only visit to the United States, as a delegate to the Women's Congress in Washington, D. C. She came hoping that the United States would lead the world to peace. She died at the age of 81 at her family home in Värmland.

THESE ARTICLES ARE IN THE FACT-INDEX

Lagomorpha
Lagos, Nigeria
Lagrange, Joseph Louis
La Grange, Ga.
La Grange, Ill.
La Grange College
La Grange Park, Ill.
La Guaira, Venezuela
La Guardia, Fiorello
 Henry
Laguna, N. M.
Laguna Beach, Calif.
La Habra, Calif.
Lahaina, Hawaii
La Hogue, battle of
Lahore, Pakistan
L'Aiglon
Laird, Melvin R(obert)

Laissez faire
Lajoie, Napoleon (Larry)
La Jolla, Calif.
La Jonquière, Jacques
 Pierre Taffanel,
 marquis de
La Junta, Colo.
Lake, Simon
Lake Charles, La.
Lake Erie College
Lake Forest, Ill.
Lake Forest College
Lake Geneva, Wis.
Lakeland, Fla.
Lakeland College
Lake of the Woods
Lake Placid, N. Y.

**LAKES.** Technically a lake is an inland body of water surrounded by land. It is larger than a pool or pond. The name, however, is sometimes given to the widened parts of rivers and to bodies of water which are in direct connection with the sea.

Other inland bodies of water, such as the Caspian and Dead seas, are true lakes although not so called. Like Great Salt Lake, these seas are salty. They have no outlet to the ocean. They lose their water by evaporation. This leaves an excessive amount of mineral matter behind. The Caspian Sea is the largest inland body of water in the world. Lake Superior is the greatest freshwater lake.

Lakes are found in any sizable depression of the land surface where there is a sufficient supply of moisture. Hundreds of thousands of lakes owe their origin to the great glaciers of ancient times. These filled many river valleys with their deposits. They also created new hollows by gouging out rock or by distributing their debris unequally. Because of glacial action North America has larger and more numerous lakes than any other continent.

Many lakes are formed by obstructions in river channels. These can be caused by lava flows, landslides, the operations of the beaver, or by tributaries that bring down sediment. The abandoned *meanders*, or windings, of a river often become the sites of lakes. They are called *oxbow lakes* or *bayous*.

Occasionally the warping of the earth's crust creates depressions. Lake Geneva, in Switzerland, was formed by the subsidence of part of the Alps. Sometimes *sink lakes* are formed by the sinking of land due to the washing away of underlying soluble rocks. Lakes are often found also in the craters of inactive volcanoes. The deepest freshwater lake in North America is Crater Lake in Oregon, where the volcano formation is perfectly evident.

Many European lakes, especially in Switzerland and northern Italy, show signs of having been inhabited by prehistoric lake dwellers who lived between 4500 and 2500 B. C. Their houses were built on wooden piles driven into the lake bottom along the shore. Study of the bones, implements, and other remains found in the mud and sands underlying such sites provides much information about the life of these peoples. (*See also* Earth, and separate articles under the names of different lakes.)

THESE ARTICLES ARE IN THE FACT-INDEX

Lakeview, Mich.
Lakewood, N. J.
Lakewood, Ohio
Lake Worth, Fla.
Lalande, Saint Jean de
Lalande, Joseph Jérôme
 Le François
Lalemant, Saint Gabriel
Lalique, René
'Lalla Rookh'
'L'Allegro'
Lalo, Édouard

La Malbaie, Que.
Lamar, Lucius Quintus
 Cincinnatus
Lamar, Mirabeau
 Buonaparte
Lamarck, Jean Baptiste
 Pierre Antoine de
 Monet, chevalier de
La Marque, Tex.
Lamar University
Lamartine, Alphonse de

**LAMB, Charles** (1775–1834). An Englishman of letters, Charles Lamb was an essayist, critic, and poet. He was also a brave and tender man whose life was full of tragedy and whose writings were full of light. Although the world held only brief moments of happiness for Lamb, he brought joy to others. As long as the English language is spoken or read, he will be remembered as one of the most lovable figures in English literature. People of all ages love him. He was not only the most delightful of essayists but one of the cheeriest and bravest spirits that ever lived.

Record Press

Charles Lamb was born in the heart of London in the Inner Temple, a great rambling old building filled with lawyers' offices and lodgings. His father was a poor lawyer's clerk. At the age of seven Charles was sent to Christ's Hospital School. Here he met another poor boy who became his lifelong friend—the poet Samuel Taylor Coleridge. These days are delightfully described in Lamb's essay 'Christ's Hospital Five-and-Thirty Years Ago'. At the age of 17 Lamb became a clerk in the accountant's office in the East

India House. There he remained until he retired on a pension 33 years later.

When he was 21 his sister Mary fell a victim to the insanity that was hereditary in their family. She killed her mother and was confined in an asylum. She recovered temporarily and was released upon her brother's promise that he would care for her the rest of her life.

Thenceforth Charles Lamb sacrificed everything for his sister. When her illness returned, he would take her by the hand and brother and sister would walk mournfully to the asylum. In the intervals which he called "between the acts," there was much that was cheerful and beautiful in their lives. They became famous for their evenings "at home." The brightest wits of London gathered for talk and laughter and good cheer. Mary Lamb shared in many of her brother's literary labors. They wrote together the 'Tales from Shakespear' which have given pleasure to so many children.

### The 'Essays of Elia'

Charles Lamb's fame today rests chiefly on the essays written under the name of "Elia." (He intended this pseudonym to be pronounced ĕ'lĭ-à.) In these essays he has taken the most trivial subjects and put into them his own whimsical, pathetic, quaintly humorous personality. Whether he writes 'A Chapter on Ears', 'Imperfect Sympathies', 'The Praise of Chimney-Sweepers', 'Old China', or a 'Complaint on the Decay of Beggars', he says something worth while. Probably no essay in the English language has aroused more laughter than his 'Dissertation on Roast Pig', and none is more full of pathos than his beautiful 'Dream Children'.

In addition to the 'Essays of Elia', Lamb's most important prose works include the critical notes in his 'Specimens of English Dramatic Poets who lived About the Time of Shakspeare', 'The Adventures of Ulysses', and his romance 'Rosamund Gray'. His best-known poem is 'The Old Familiar Faces'.

---

THESE ARTICLES ARE IN THE FACT-INDEX

| | |
|---|---|
| Lamb, Willis E(ugene), Jr. | Lamé |
| | Lamentations |
| Lamballe, Marie Thérèse de | Lamesa, Tex. |
| | Lamia |
| Lambaréné, Gabon | Laminated Fabrics |
| Lambert, Johann Heinrich | La Mirada, Calif. |
| Lambert, Richard Stanton | Lamoille River |
| Lambkill | Lamon, Ward Hill |
| Lamb's-ears | Lamont, Robert Patterson |
| Lamb's quarters | La Motte-Fouqué, |
| Lambuth College | Friedrich, baron de |

---

**LAMPREY.** Fishermen everywhere dread the eellike lamprey. It destroys millions of valuable food fish every year. The lamprey has no jaws. The mouth is a cuplike sucker disk lined with sharp projections, and the tongue also has sharp files. With these the lamprey rasps a hole in its victim's body and sucks the blood and body juices.

Lampreys are distributed throughout the world. They thrive in fresh water as well as in the sea. Before World War II sea lampreys invaded the Great Lakes through the St. Lawrence River canals. Lake trout were their favorite prey. They virtually destroyed the trout fisheries of Lakes Michigan and Huron and threatened to deplete Lake Superior.

Like the salmon, lampreys migrate upstream to spawn. Soon thereafter they die. The eggs hatch as larvae. The larvae drift downstream until they reach mud flats. There they bury themselves with only the head protruding. They feed on minute organisms that float past their mouths. The larval life lasts four years. Then the larva develops into a mature lamprey, emerges from the mud, and drifts down to the lake or sea, where it lives for about a year. It grows two to three feet long. In late spring the lamprey re-enters the streams to spawn and die.

### New Control Method Discovered

For many years the United States and Canadian governments sought means to control or eliminate these eellike creatures. None of the measures tried was entirely satisfactory. In August 1958, however, scientists announced that they had discovered a selective lamprey poison. It kills the eel but is harmless to other fish and wildlife. The poison is used against the larvae of the lamprey.

Besides the naturalized sea lampreys, there are several relatively harmless native varieties. The lamprey is a primitive fish with a skeleton of gristle. The scientific name of the sea lamprey is *Petromyzon marinus.* (*See also* Fish; Animal Migration.)

**A KILLER AND ITS PREY**
The deadly sea lamprey (left) is a parasitic eel that almost destroyed fishing on the Great Lakes. The fisherman (right) holds a lake trout that was attacked by a lamprey.

**LAMPS OF PREHISTORIC MAN AND ANCIENT CIVILIZATIONS**

The prehistoric stone lamp (top left) is carved out to hold fuel. The shell lamp (top right) was made in Palestine about 1600 B.C. The alabaster lamp (lower left) and the pottery lamp (lower right) are fine examples of ancient lampmaking.

**LAMPS.** Early man used fire to cook his food and to light the darkness (*see* Fire; Man; Science). The torch was probably the first portable source of illumination. Later, the first lamps were developed. These were hollowed and shaped stones which held animal grease and burned natural-fiber wicks. Some stone lamps found in caves have been estimated to be 30,000 years old.

In the East and in the Mediterranean area the first lamps were probably made of sea shells. Shells from oysters, clams, scallops, and whelks were the most commonly used. Later, stone lamps were carved in the form of shells. The earliest traces of the shell lamp come from Mesopotamia.

### Lamps of Ancient Times

Lamps manufactured of man-made materials first appeared in the ancient civilizations of Palestine, the Indus River valley, Sumeria, and Egypt between 3500 and 2500 B.C. They appeared in China about 2000 B.C. Most of these were of earthenware. Alabaster and metallic lamps were rare.

As civilization advanced lamps were slowly improved. A groove for the wick was added. The bottom of the lamp was tilted toward the wick end to concentrate the oil. A resting place away from the flame was added for the hand.

Animal fats and vegetable and fish oils were burned in these lamps. In Sumeria the seepage from petroleum deposits was used as fuel. The wicks were made of twists of natural fibers.

### Greek and Roman Lamps

The history of the Greek lamp began about the 6th century B.C. Its origin was probably the simple open-bowl, or saucer, lamp. Lamps from Crete, dating before 1000 B.C., were also of the simple bowl type, although they had nozzles for the wicks.

**GREEK LAMP**      **"BETTY" LAMP**      **KEROSENE LAMP**

This Greek lamp had its own stand and was made of bronze. A wick projected from the spout. The Dutch iron "Betty" lamp was like those brought to America by the Pilgrims. The kerosene lamp appeared in the latter part of the 18th century.

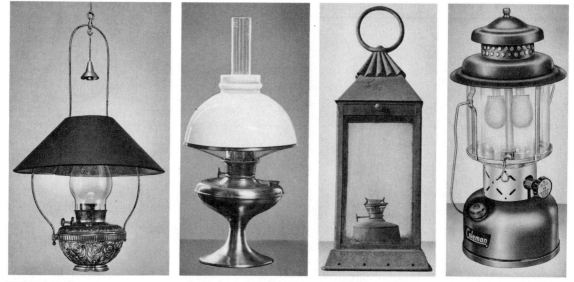

**HARP LAMP**      **ROCHESTER LAMP**      **COLONIAL LANTERN**    **COLEMAN LANTERN**

The harp lamp was symbolic of the early Western frontier in America. Rochester lamps, named for the type of burner they used, were produced in the late 19th century. They were still being made during the 1920's. A colonial lantern of 1780 had a screw to move the wick. The gasoline pressure Coleman lantern, with its incandescent mantles, is in use today.

The Greek lamp was quickly improved. The rim was turned in to prevent spilling, and the nozzle was bridged. Greek lamps were made on the potter's wheel.

Roman lamps appeared about the 3d century B.C. They were similar to Greek lamps at first but soon developed a distinctive appearance. The two main differences were that Roman lamps had concave tops instead of flat or convex tops and they were made in two pieces instead of one. They were also completely enclosed. It was during Roman times, particularly after the 1st century A.D., that the use of metal for making lamps became common.

### Improvements in Lamps

Very little progress was made in the lighting efficiency of lamps until the 18th century. The Cardan lamp, invented in the 16th century, had an improved fuel supply system. It was the only improvement for the next 200 years. The lamps that were brought to America by the Pilgrims were simple pan-shaped types.

The greatest advance in design was made by Aimé Argand, a Swiss chemist. In 1784 he produced a lamp in which a flat wick was placed around a hollow tube. A glass chimney encircled the tube. With more air and a better draft the flame burned more brightly and produced no smoke. The Argand lamp gave far more light than had ever come from a single wick.

Many improvements in the Argand lamp followed. The Carcel lamp, developed in 1798, used a little clockwork pump to feed oil to the wick. A powerful spring in the oil reservoir performed the same function in the Moderator lamp, invented in 1836.

### Advances After 1860

The development that made these improved lamps available for general use, however, was the large-scale production of kerosene, which began about 1860. This comparatively clean, safe, cheap fuel replaced such liquids as camphene, a dangerously explosive combination of turpentine and alcohol. Other fuels were too inefficient or expensive for popular use.

Although the last half of the 19th century saw the rise of gas and electric lighting, improvements in lamp efficiency continued. In 1865 a duplex burner was introduced. It consisted of two parallel flat wicks about an eighth of an inch apart. Later, incandescent mantles for lamps increased brightness greatly (*see* Gas, Manufactured). The last major advancement in the evolution of the oil lamp was the burner patented in 1888 by Henry E. Shaffer. It was used in the Rochester lamp. Meanwhile electric light gradually began to replace the oil lamp (*see* Electric Light; Lighting).

### The Lantern

The lantern is a portable shield for a source of light such as a candle or a lamp. The first true lantern appeared in Roman times. Roman lanterns of the 1st century A.D. had horn windows and carried small oil lamps. Candles were used in lanterns of the Middle Ages and the period following.

Flat glass panes for lanterns gained popularity during the 18th century. Previously the panes were made of mica or similar material or they were simply panels of tin or iron with holes punctured to let the light through.

Lanterns lighted with mineral fuels are still occasionally used by railroad men, road repairmen, and campers. They are kept in many places for emergency lighting. Some portable electric lights, such as those carried by railroad men and miners, retain the familiar shape of lanterns (*see* Davy).

THESE ARTICLES ARE IN THE FACT-INDEX

Lampsacus, Asia Minor       Lancashire, England
Lanai                       Lancaster, Calif.
Lanao, Lake

**LANCASTER, England.** The city of Lancaster is in northwestern England. It is the county seat of Lancashire (sometimes also called Lancaster). The city lies along the Lune River, about 230 miles northwest of London.

The city of Lancaster began as a Roman fortification. During the Norman conquest it became the possession of Roger of Poitou. In 1266 its ownership passed from Henry III to his son Edmund. In 1362 John of Gaunt obtained a charter giving him exclusive rights to hold meetings in Lancaster. Parliament accepted the claim of Henry, duke of Lancaster, to the English throne in 1399. As Henry IV he became the first of the Lancastrian dynasty, which ruled England from 1399 to 1461. Henry IV's son and grandson, Henry V and Henry VI, were the only other members of the Lancaster family to rule England. Henry VI's son, the last of the line, was killed in the Wars of the Roses (see Roses, Wars of the).

Lancaster is an important river port and manufacturing center. Its leading products are cotton, rayon, and silk textiles. Linoleum, furniture, beer, book cloth, matting, and knitwear are also produced. Population (1969 estimate), 48,170.

THESE ARTICLES ARE IN THE FACT-INDEX

Lancaster, N. Y.
Lancaster, Ohio

**LANCASTER, Pa.** The city of Lancaster is located in one of the most highly cultivated and productive regions in the United States. It lies along the Conestoga River, about 65 miles west of Philadelphia. It is the seat of Lancaster County.

The Lancaster area was originally settled by German, Moravian, English, Scottish, Welsh, and Irish immigrants. In 1729 Lancaster County, named after Lancaster, England, was established. The city of Lancaster, founded as Hickory Town, was laid out in 1730. The borough of Lancaster was the state capital from 1799 to 1812. In 1818 it was chartered as a city.

The rich, rolling countryside surrounding Lancaster yields a variety of agricultural products. The chief crops are tobacco, wheat, and corn. The city is one of the largest livestock markets located in the East. Lancaster's manufactures include linoleum, cork, watches, television tubes, and toys. Ball bearings, machinery, candy, and cotton, silk, and woolen textiles are other products. The city is the wholesale and retail center of the entire Lancaster region.

President James Buchanan's home, Wheatland, has been preserved in Lancaster as a memorial. Franklin and Marshall College, Lancaster Theological Seminary of the United Church of Christ, and Thaddeus Stevens Trade School are also in the city. (See also Pennsylvania.) Population (1970 census), 57,690.

THESE ARTICLES ARE IN THE FACT-INDEX

Lancelot            Lanciani,
Lancewood              Rodolfo
Lanchow, People's   Lancret, Nicolas
   Republic of China

**LAND, Edwin Herbert** (born 1909). The inventor of many optical devices, including the Polaroid Land camera, was Dr. Edwin H. Land. He was a basic as well as an applied research scientist, and his theories on color perception challenged long-accepted views.

Edwin Herbert Land was born in Bridgeport, Conn., on May 7, 1909. He attended Norwich

Polaroid Corp.

Academy and Harvard University. In 1929 he married Helen Maislen. They had two daughters.

While still at Harvard, Land experimented with polarized light (see Light). This led to his invention of a light polarizer that proved to be a superior new camera filter. Land was a government adviser on guided missile technology in World War II. He also developed many optical instruments that helped the war effort. In 1947 he introduced the Polaroid camera. It delivers a black-and-white picture seconds after a subject has been photographed.

In the 1950's, Land began experimenting with three-dimensional color photography. Dissatisfied with current knowledge about how the eye sees color, he performed experiments which produced a new concept of color perception. In 1963, he introduced Polacolor film, which makes a colorphoto in less than a minute, and in 1972, completely automatic pocket-sized cameras and films. (See also Photography, History of.)

### The Land Theory of Color Vision

Until 1959 scientists generally believed that the eye's ability to perceive color could be compared with the action of color-sensitive photographic film. Such film contains many different chemicals. Each chemical is sensitive to only one particular color. Similarly, the eye's retina was said to contain three types of color-receptor cells (see Eye). One type received only the wave lengths of red light, another only those of blue, a third only those of green.

In 1959 Land made two identical black-and-white transparent photographs of the same colored scene. One photograph was made through a red filter. This exposed the film to the longer wave lengths of red light. The other was made through a green filter, exposing the film to shorter wave length light. Each photograph was next inserted in its own projector and flashed on a screen. Two black-and-white images appeared. When the two images were superimposed, however, the resulting single image contained all the colors in the original scene.

Land concluded that the retina does not select each specific wave length of various colors. Rather, he decided, color perception by the retina depends upon a broad interplay of long and short wave lengths over the entire scene.

THESE ARTICLES ARE IN THE FACT-INDEX

Land, Emory S(cott)
Landau, Lev Davidovich

Lander, Richard Lemon
  and John
Lander, Wyo.
Lander College

**LAND GRANT.** When the United States government makes a gift of land to a state, a municipality, an institution, a private organization, or an individual, the transaction is called a *land grant* (*see* Lands, Public). The federal government first used the land-grant idea to liquidate the public debt incurred by the Revolutionary War.

In 1780 Congress passed a resolution asking the states to cede their vacant, unappropriated lands to the federal government. The government was then to sell or otherwise dispose of them for the common good. New York complied first (1781). Virginia was next (1784), followed in order by Massachusetts, Connecticut, South Carolina, and Georgia.

There are two general types of land grants. The first is given for improvement of facilities such as railroads or canals. The second is granted to the various states for the building or expanding of colleges and universities and for internal improvement.

### Land-Grant Colleges

In 1862 Congress passed the Morrill Act. Sponsored by Representative Justin S. Morrill of Vermont, the bill granted every state 30,000 acres of land for each senator and representative it had in Congress. This land was to be sold by the states. The proceeds of such sales were to be invested, and the income used to finance the building and maintenance of agricultural and mechanical arts colleges. The act gave more than 11 million acres to the states. In 1890 the second Morrill Act was passed. It called for additional cash gifts to land-grant colleges (*see* Education).

The states did not all use their land-grant funds according to the stipulations. Many of them could not sell the lands. What land they could sell brought such low prices that profits were small.

Some states did manage to finance new colleges of agriculture and mechanical arts with land-grant funds. Other states turned the money over to state universities. These were to establish colleges of agriculture and mechanical arts. A few states made outright gifts of their grants to private colleges.

The land-grant idea, however, proved to be generally successful. The universities of Illinois, California, Texas, and Washington, for example, were developed with land-grant funds.

THESE ARTICLES ARE IN THE FACT-INDEX

Landis, James McCauley
Landis, Kenesaw Mountain
Land of Nod

Landon, Alf(red) Mossman
Landor, Walter Savage

**LANDOWSKA, Wanda** (1879–1959). One of the world's most famous musicians was Wanda Landowska. She was particularly noted for her interpretations of early music, which she played on the harpsichord.

Brown Brothers

Wanda Landowska was born in Warsaw on July 5, 1879. Her father, Marjan, was a lawyer and amateur musician. Her mother, Eve, was a linguist.

At the age of 4 Wanda began to study the piano. While a little girl she became fascinated by old music, especially the compositions of Bach. She studied at the Warsaw Conservatory, where her teacher was Aleksander Michalowski, the famous interpreter of the music of Chopin. She was graduated from the conservatory when she was only 14 years old.

In 1900 Wanda Landowska went to Paris. Here she married the folklorist Henri Lew. In 1906 she began a series of extended concert tours through Europe and Africa. These tours established her fame as an accomplished pianist. Meanwhile she had become an enthusiastic student of 17th-century French, Flemish, and English music. She was convinced that this music could be played only on the harpsichord, a forerunner of the piano (*see* Piano). A French piano-manufacturing firm built a harpsichord especially for her.

Madame Landowska made her North American debut, as a soloist with the Philadelphia Symphony Orchestra, in 1923. She returned to Paris in 1925. She founded a school dedicated to the study of early music. This school, the École de Musique Ancienne, was located near Paris. In 1940, to escape the Nazis, Wanda Landowska came to the United States. Here she continued her concert work. She died in Lakeville, Conn., Aug. 16, 1959.

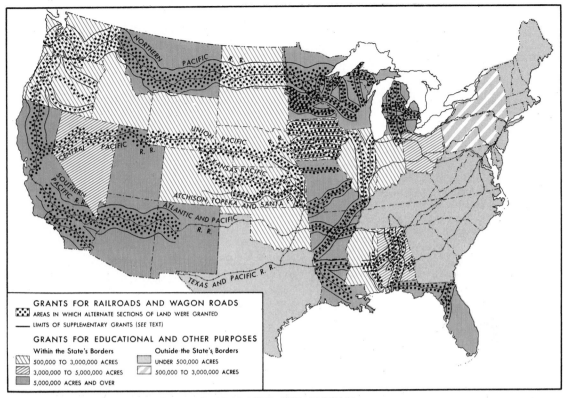

GRANTS FOR RAILROADS AND WAGON ROADS
▨ AREAS IN WHICH ALTERNATE SECTIONS OF LAND WERE GRANTED
— LIMITS OF SUPPLEMENTARY GRANTS (SEE TEXT)

GRANTS FOR EDUCATIONAL AND OTHER PURPOSES
Within the State's Borders
▨ 500,000 TO 3,000,000 ACRES
▨ 3,000,000 TO 5,000,000 ACRES
▨ 5,000,000 ACRES AND OVER
Outside the State's Borders
▨ UNDER 500,000 ACRES
▨ 500,000 TO 3,000,000 ACRES

**GRANTS OF PUBLIC LAND (EXCEPT IN ALASKA AND HAWAII)**

Every state has received federal grants of land for educational and other purposes. The 29 states shown in color (solid and hatched) received land from the public domain within their own borders. The others shown contained little federal land, but they were given the right to sell land in other parts of the public domain. Special grants were given for railroads and wagon roads.

# How Public Lands Helped the United States Grow

**LANDS, PUBLIC.** At one time or another the federal government has been the "private owner" of about three fourths of the land area within the United States. Today it still controls some 770 million acres.

Congress maintains the right to dispose of such lands as it sees fit. The lands may be used for building or expanding Indian reservations; naval or military installations; reclamation projects; wildlife refuges; monuments, cemeteries, and other national shrines; and federal buildings. Public lands may also be given as land grants (see Land Grant).

## The First Public Lands

The first public lands were those ceded to the federal government by the states of New York, Virginia, Massachusetts, Connecticut, South Carolina, and Georgia. The Louisiana Territory was purchased from France in 1803. Florida was obtained from Spain in 1819. Texas was annexed in 1845. Parts of the Oregon country south of the 49th parallel were incorporated in 1846. In 1848 California and the New Mexico region were acquired. Alaska was purchased from Russia in 1867. In all, 1½ billion acres of land were acquired by the United States government.

Most additions to the national area consisted of land held originally by the Indians. Among the Indians no individual ever owned land. The government therefore became owner of the new lands wherever it made treaties by which the Indians surrendered their "hunting rights."

## Public Lands Promote Settlement

Thus the United States, almost alone among modern nations, had a large portion of a rich continent at its disposal for national purposes. As soon as the federal government was formed, it began using public lands to promote settlement (see Northwest Territory). Acreage was sold to "land companies" and to individuals. Land grants were given to many veterans of the Revolutionary War. Men who had performed distinguished service received choice tracts.

Early in the 19th century the government began giving land to companies in return for agreements that they would build roads, canals, or railroads. Railroad grants alone amounted to about 207,000 square miles. These grants consisted of alternate sections of land within a tract extending a certain number of miles on each side of the right of way. The total width of the tract varied from 10 to 80 miles.

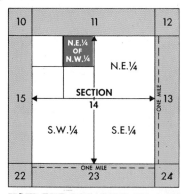 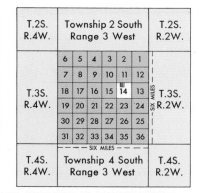

## HOW THE LOCATION OF A PIECE OF LAND IS DETERMINED

The dark-colored square is our 40 acres of land. This diagram shows how it is located in section 14. (Parts of surrounding sections are numbered 10 through 24, as shown. Every whole section is one mile square.) Section 14 is shown divided into quarters. The northwest quarter is also divided into quarters. Our land is the northeast quarter of the northwest quarter. Any section may be divided further into still smaller parts.

This diagram shows how section 14 is located in a township. Every township is six miles square and divided into 36 numbered sections. The third diagram shows how our township is located in the state. Description of location starts at the spot where the state's base line crosses the principal meridian. Divisions east or west of the principal meridian are ranges. Divisions north or south of the base line form townships.

This third diagram also shows a guide meridian and a guide parallel. They are surveyed every 24 miles. Putting all the description together, we see that our land is in "northeast quarter of northwest quarter of section 14 of township 3 south in range 3 west." This will be abbreviated on our land deed to "N.E. ¼, N.W. ¼, Sec. 14, T. 3 S, R. 3 W." This method of measurement for location is the "rectangular system" of surveying.

Settlers were allowed to claim unoccupied lands by a short residence and payment of $1.25 an acre. In 1862 Congress passed the first Homestead Act. This permitted any citizen over 21 years old or any head of a family to acquire 160 acres of public land by giving legal notice of his intention (called "making entry"). He had to live on the land for five years and make certain improvements.

Later laws provided for homesteads up to 640 acres in semiarid regions or where soil was poor. War veterans could count their wartime service as part of the five-year residence period.

Huge grants were made to states to support public education. Until 1850 each new state usually got 1/36 of its area for public school support. The amount then rose to 1/18 and 1/9. The Morrill Acts of 1862 and 1890 provided grants to states to establish agricultural colleges. (See also Education.)

### Public Lands in the 20th Century

By 1900 nearly all good farm land had passed to state or private ownership. Under President Theodore Roosevelt, the government adopted a policy of conservation. It withdrew most of the mineral-bearing lands and forest lands from settlement (see Conservation).

In 1934 President Franklin D. Roosevelt withdrew *all* public lands. This was to give the government time to study the best future use of them. As a result, the Taylor Grazing Act was enacted later in 1934 to permit controlled grazing on public lands. Today the government selects certain public lands and transfers them to state and private ownership.

In 1962 the public domain in the continental United States was 770.8 million acres, or about one third of the nation's total land acreage. These lands are administered chiefly for such uses as national forests and flood control. The secretary of the interior has the authority to lease grazing, mineral, and recrea-

tional rights and open some reclaimed areas for crops.

Most of the public lands are administered by the Department of Agriculture or by the Bureau of Land Management of the Department of the Interior.

### The Township Survey System

Under our system of surveying, the lands are laid out into "townships" six miles square. Each township is subdivided into 36 "sections," each containing one square mile, or 640 acres. The sections are subdivided into quarter sections of 160 acres. Certain parallels of latitude are taken as *base lines*, and certain meridians of longitude as *principal meridians*. Townships are described by *number*, north or south of the base line, and in *ranges*, numbered east or west of the principal meridian. This system of land description is used in legal documents to describe land in all states formed out of the public domain.

### Public Lands in Canada

In Canada, the federal government administers the Yukon and the Northwest Territories, totaling 1,458,-784 square miles, or 41 percent of the land surface of Canada. Other federal lands include the Arctic Archipelago; the islands in Hudson Strait, Hudson Bay, and James Bay; the national parks and historic sites; Indian reserves; forest experiment stations; experimental farms; and ordnance and admiralty lands. In general, the holdings include all lands connected with the administration of the federal government.

Other public lands in all provinces are controlled by the provincial legislature. Requirements for obtaining such lands vary among the provinces. A common requirement for obtaining agricultural land is residence for three years and payment of a small purchase price. Land bearing valuable timber usually is leased rather than sold. (For federal and provincial lands in Canada, see Canada Fact Summary.)

**LANDSEER, Sir Edwin Henry** (1802–1873). No English artist of his time enjoyed a wider popularity than Sir Edwin Landseer. Engravers turned out thousands of copies of his paintings and the public eagerly bought them. His chief subjects were animals, especially dogs. He gave all his animals human qualities—sometimes humorous but more often sentimental.

Edwin Landseer was born in London in 1802. His father, John Landseer, was a fine engraver. Edwin had little love for books, and his father did not believe in formal education. He took the boy with him into the fields and taught him to sketch sheep, goats, and donkeys. He also encouraged him to visit the zoo so that he could study and sketch wild beasts as well. The boy developed technical ability at an early age. He worked quickly and could draw equally well with either hand. When he was 14 he entered the schools of the Royal Academy. He is described at this time as a curly-headed boy who divided his time between his classes and the zoo. Dogs soon became Landseer's favorite subjects, but he loved all animals.

Landseer was elected a full member of the Royal Academy in 1831. He became popular in society and soon found favor at the palace. He made many portraits of Queen Victoria, her children, her gamekeepers, and her pets. He even gave her lessons in engraving. Victoria knighted him in 1850. He died in 1873 and was buried in St. Paul's Cathedral.

Of Landseer's dog pictures, the most popular were 'Dignity and Impudence', 'The Old Shepherd's Chief Mourner', and 'A Distinguished Member of the Human Society'. His stag pictures were almost as popular as his dogs—particularly 'The Stag at Bay' and 'The Monarch of the Glen'. As a sculptor, he is remembered for the colossal lions that stand at the base of the Nelson Monument in Trafalgar Square, London.

THESE ARTICLES ARE IN THE FACT-INDEX

**Landshut, West Germany**
**Landsteiner, Karl**
**Landsting**

# Right and Wrong Ways of Using Land

**LAND USE.** Anyone who has even a back yard has to think about land use. Where should the garage go; the clotheslines; the lawn; the rose bed; the vegetable garden? These are problems in land use that anyone can understand.

The American pioneers who helped to establish towns or took up farms in the wilderness had to settle larger problems in land use. They probably asked themselves three simple questions before deciding what to do: (1) How can we do it? (2) Will it pay? (3) Shall we enjoy the result? Scientists speak of these aspects of land use as: (1) the technical or scientific; (2) the economic or business; and (3) the social or human.

In earlier days it was thought that if every user of land were free to answer these questions for himself— to do what he could, what paid him, and what he enjoyed—the problem of land use would work itself out for the good of all. But after a century and a half many people in America began to realize that something was wrong.

### Some Good and Bad Uses of Land

Many millions of acres are not now returning a living to those who own or occupy them. A map of the lands on which taxes have not been paid for a long

Most of the brush in this area of a Texas ranch was destroyed by fire. Careful conservation methods, such as resting the land, were used to restore the growth of grasses and shrubs.

time will show this; so will a map of relief payments to farmers. These maps would not differ much from the map on the following page showing regions where people are trying to farm land that is better suited to other uses. On this map one can see that the wrong use of land is most marked in three regions. These are

(1) the Southeastern states, (2) the Great Plains, and (3) northern Michigan and Wisconsin.

The Southeastern region has many good farming districts, such as the beautiful Shenandoah Valley of Virginia. Much of the land, however, is too rough and thinly covered with soil to make good farms. This land was once covered with fine forests, and it should be put back to growing trees. The country needs lumber, and the forests would check floods (see Flood Control).

In the Great Plains, where the average rainfall is less than 20 inches a year, most of the land is best suited to cattle grazing. In many places the ground has been plowed for dry farming. Skillful dry farming can be made to pay; but it is a dangerous gamble. If the wrong kind of soil is plowed in the wrong way, it will start to blow and there will be dust storms, drifts, and general destruction. Dry years will produce crop failures. A farmer must have money enough to carry himself over when this happens. Many dry farmers do not. Much of the land they have plowed should be put back into grass.

The bad spots in Wisconsin and Michigan are cut-over pine forests; this land cannot be farmed profitably.

The map also has some bright spots, where the land is properly used. The land of eastern Pennsylvania is rich and was settled in colonial days by skillful farmers who have kept it so. Westward from central Ohio through eastern Kansas and Nebraska stretches a natural tall-grass prairie, which has the deepest, richest soil in the country. This region has in the main been wisely used by good farmers and has become the breadbasket of the nation. So it forms one of the largest areas on the map. Many irrigated lands in the Far West also are very productive.

Why should there be good and bad spots on a map showing American farms? The answer lies in what happened when the country was settled.

### Mistakes Made by Early Settlers

The surveyors who came West before 1800 often indicated in their notes just what use could be made of the land which they examined. But in the rush of settlement not much attention was paid to their reports, and much land was put to uses for which it was not best suited. The situation was made worse by the rapid development of transportation, which gave poor land access to markets and tempted men to farm it. Many new inventions enabled men to work land intensively, beyond its natural power to produce. For reasons such as these, much land has been exploited rather than used wisely and in moderation. The forests have been largely destroyed and so has much of the natural grassland. Streams have been silted full of mud, floods have become steadily worse, and the underground water level has dropped greatly since

## REGIONS IN CONTINENTAL UNITED STATES (EXCEPT ALASKA) WHERE MANY FARMS DO NOT PAY

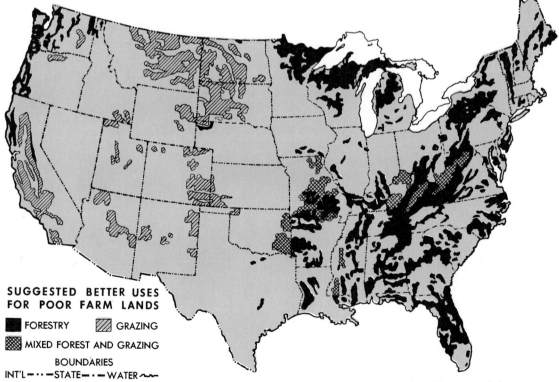

SUGGESTED BETTER USES
FOR POOR FARM LANDS

■ FORESTRY  ▨ GRAZING

▩ MIXED FOREST AND GRAZING

BOUNDARIES

INT'L — ·· — STATE — · — WATER ∼∼

The black and shaded areas are regions where many farmers cannot earn satisfactory livings because the land is not suitable for farming. In general, the owners would do better if they used the land as indicated by the key. The map and the recommendations are adapted from a study made by the Land Planning Committee of the National Resources Board.

## LAND USE IN THE UNITED STATES
Each complete symbol equals 100,000,000 acres

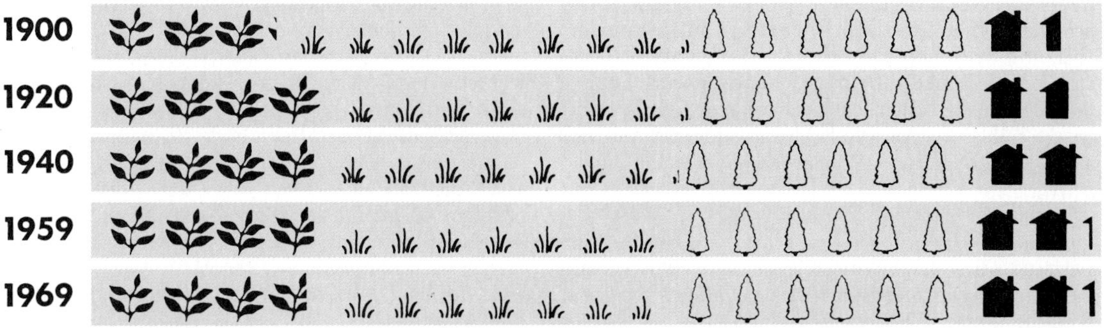

| | | | | |
|---|---|---|---|---|
| 1900 | | | | |
| 1920 | | | | |
| 1940 | | | | |
| 1959 | | | | |
| 1969 | | | | |
| | CROPLAND | GRASSLAND | FOREST LAND | OTHER* |

*Includes cities, roads, parks, game refuges, farmsteads, and wasteland.

Source: U.S. Dept. of Agriculture

In all the mainland except Alaska (not included in the chart) cropland and farm pastures have increased at the expense of forests and grazing land. Alaska's great forests are almost untouched. Other land uses include buildings and roads.

settlement. The country's soil has suffered a loss of about 30 percent by being washed away. All this has seriously reduced the nation's wealth in land.

The continental United States (excluding Alaska) has a land area of almost 3 million square miles, or about 1,900 million acres. The people have put land to different uses, as shown on the chart above. Land uses may be classified in various ways because a single acre may be used for crops, pasture, grazing, or forest, or for combinations of these. The chart follows a classification adopted by the United States Department of Agriculture.

### Land Uses Present and Future

About half of the United States land area is farmland. In addition, about 300 million acres of Federal land is used for livestock grazing. This means that about 58 percent of the land area is used for agricultural purposes (excluding forestry). Another fourth is in forests and an eighth is wasteland.

Urban land accounts for only $2\frac{1}{2}$ percent of the total land area. This includes land in airports, railroads, and highways, as well as all places with a population of more than 1,000.

By the year 2000, with the possibility of an additional 100 million people, urban areas will need only about 4 percent of the land area. To feed this increased population, only slightly more cropland will be needed. Some undeveloped land can be made productive by irrigation, drainage, or clearing. Some pasture can also be rotated with crops. A large amount of misused cropland, however, should be converted to pasture or woodland.

Only a small additional amount of cropland will be required because the yield per acre will be increased by better conservation farming and by technological progress, such as improved farm machinery, seed, livestock, and disease and insect control (see Conservation). A greater food supply could also result from a reduction in the export of farm products or an increase in the import of such products.

The country will also need more wood for its larger population. To meet this demand, some poor farmland can be reforested. Timber supply, however, is as much a matter of land management as of land use. If the existing forests were properly managed, they could probably supply all needs (see Forests; Alaska).

Special uses will also require some additional land. As more people move into cities or leave the cities for suburban homes, they will need more room for living and recreation.

### How Culture Affects Land Use

Planners must consider what people will be wanting to do with land 20 or even 50 years from now. For in the end the pattern of human activity, or culture pattern, largely determines how land will be used.

If a tribe lives by hunting or gathering wild food, ten square miles may be needed to support it, and the plants and animals must be kept in nearly their natural state. This was true of the Sioux Indians. If a group, however, should live by intensive cultivation of irrigated land, one square mile might support hundreds of people, as in Egypt and China. Or a few farmers working a large area might provide food for hundreds of people in cities. So too, a small land rich in minerals might support hundreds of people, if they get their food elsewhere.

### Choosing and Using Farmland Wisely

The capacity of land to produce depends upon what is in it. This is clear enough if we are talking about minerals. It is also true, however, for crops. We cannot profitably grow food in the wrong type of soil.

The kind of soil depends somewhat upon the kind of rock from which it was formed. Thus the Atlantic coastal plain is excellent for market gardening because it is sandy, having only recently been sea bottom. It requires much fertilizer, however. Kentucky and Kansas, whose land is sweet because it is underlain by limestone, are remarkable for their pastures. Capacity to produce depends also upon climate, for

111

climate determines the amount of water, the vegetation, the soil structure, and even to some extent the mineral contents of the soil (*see* Soil). These factors are often difficult to weigh separately; but nature does this for us with her types of natural vegetation. Pine-forest land is likely to be acid and poor in humus; trees which shed their leaves every year usually make better soil. Tall grass indicates good water and rich soil; sparse bunch grass suggests good grazing land.

## Location and Land Use

Location with reference to markets is another important factor in planning use of land. The accompanying diagram shows how location affects the use of land for farms. The expensive land near big cities is used largely for intensive farming of the more perishable and valuable truck crops. Farther away trucking gives way to dairy farming, this in turn to grain farming, and finally, on the least costly land farthest from the city, we have hay and pasture—the most extensive, least intensive, use of land.

Land values in general vary according to this pattern; and nearness to cities is often more important in determining how the land is used than is the kind of land. For example, if manufacturing or mining draws many people to a certain region and a demand for food arises, farmers can afford to work naturally poor land nearby, using fertilizers and perhaps irrigation. On the other hand, naturally good land may hardly be worth farming, because of its location. The Whiskey Rebellion during Washington's Administration was caused by the fact that farmers in the Pennsylvania hills could not afford to haul their grain to market. Only by changing it to whiskey could they make money; they therefore resisted the new whiskey tax.

## Agencies Interested in Planning

Since 1900 the belief has grown that the man who owns land should not have the right to destroy its value for the future. Instead he should look upon himself as a trustee, charged to pass the land on in as good condition as it came to him. Back of the owner's rights lie the rights of all the people. Freedom should mean freedom to use and enjoy, not to wreck.

Since the United States is a democracy, land-use problems cannot be settled by force. What means do we have to make possible a national program?

1. *National Planning.* Several government agencies and departments are assisting by collecting information and promoting local efforts. The Agricultural Adjustment measures were designed to encourage proper land use. The Department of the Interior has withdrawn all public lands from private entry (*see* Lands, Public). The Taylor Grazing Act permits this department to regulate grazing on public land. A model state conservation law drafted by the Department of Agriculture provides a democratic method whereby local districts may adopt land-use regulations, with expert help.

2. *State Planning.* Each state, through a planning board, can cooperate with federal efforts. Wisconsin and Michigan have taken great steps forward in the problem of land use. Many counties in Wisconsin have adopted county zoning plans, which indicate the proper use of land in each county.

3. *Regional Planning.* The states can be divided into a number of more or less natural geographical groups. These groups correspond roughly to groupings used by the national government in handling soil conservation, forestry, and related work. States within these regions can form agreements to cooperate.

4. *Education.* This is the most hopeful means of bringing about wise land use. The United States Commissioner of Education has sponsored public discussion forums and has developed material on land use and conservation for schools. A flood of books and magazine articles is rousing popular interest.

Today the United States leads the world in land-use planning and in soil conservation work. Since 1937, more than 80 per cent of the nation's farms have been enrolled in voluntary conservation programs. With the technical aid of the Soil Conservation Service, farmers treat gullied and worn lands to stop erosion and to determine the best use for each acre.

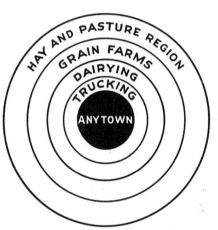

**USE OF FARM LAND NEAR CITIES**
The use of farm land tends to change with its distance from a large city, as the chart shows. (After a diagram by Dr. A. E. Waller.)

## Foreign Land-Use Planning

Representatives of many nations have studied conservation methods on United States farms. American experts have aided projects in other lands—notably in Latin American countries.

Before World War II, Mussolini set in motion a huge drainage project to fit the Pontine marshes near Rome for intensive farming. The Russian government laid extensive plans for the use of each part of its vast land. Some signs suggest that Russia may have repeated some of the mistakes Americans have made, particularly in practicing dry farming too widely. The British Empire had also set up projects in many areas. Huge dams and storage basins in India reclaimed thousands of desert acres. In parts of Africa, reclamation efforts came too late. Some tribes had so increased in numbers under British protection that they had overworked their land until soil erosion caused widespread damage.

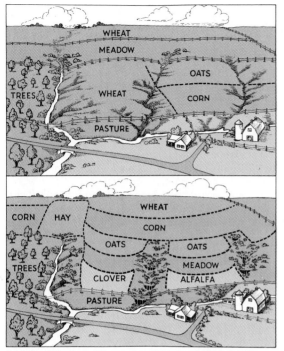

**GOOD AND BAD WAYS TO USE SLOPING LAND**
Top, a farm was being eroded because the land had been culti-vated regardless of slope. Bottom, rearrangement of fields and cultivation along contours, or level lines, are saving the soil.

In a changing world, present practices may need re-vision. For example, decentralization of industry may require more land near rural factories for part-time employment in farming.

Inventions may affect land use. If *hydroponics*, or *tray agriculture*, could grow crops on a commercial scale, less farmland would be needed (*see* Plants). Nylon and other man-made fibers may diminish the demand for land for cotton and sheep raising. Syn-thetic foods may also release farming land.

The United States is steadily consuming its mineral fuels. In time, fuel scarcity may cause a popu-lation shift south. Or men may learn to use another force, such as nuclear energy, for heating and power.

THESE ARTICLES ARE IN THE FACT-INDEX

| | |
|---|---|
| Lane, Edward William | Lang, Cosmo Gordon |
| Lane, Joseph | Langdell, Christopher |
| Lane, Sir William | Columbus |
| Arbuthnot | Langdon, John |
| Lane College | Lange, Christian Louis |
| Lanfranc | Langensalza, East Germany |
| Lang, Andrew | Langer, William |

**LANGLEY, Samuel Pierpont** (1834–1906). On May 6, 1896, a strange machine flew a half mile over the Potomac River near Washington, D.C. The odd craft was about 16 feet long and weighed some 26 pounds. It flew about a minute and a half. This was the first time a power-driven, heavier-than-air ma-chine stayed in the air more than just a few seconds.

**A FAMOUS INVENTOR AND HIS FLYING MACHINE**
Langley's man-carrying *Aerodrome* is shown plunging into the Potomac River as its attempt to fly fails. It was patterned after his steam-powered model but had a gasoline engine.

The builder of this airplane model was Samuel P. Langley, secretary of the Smithsonian Institution. After many laboratory experiments he had finally shown that mechanical flight was possible. Later, for the War Department, he built a 56-foot machine. Two attempts to launch it in 1903 failed. The Wright brothers, however, proved the worth of Langley's ideas in their successful airplane (*see* Airplane History; Wright Brothers).

### Early Interest in Science

Langley's interest in aeronautics began as a boy in Roxbury, Mass., where he was born. He watched gulls wheel and soar, using their wings only to meet new currents of wind. His father's telescope gave him his first knowledge of astronomy. He attended Boston Latin School but did not go to college.

After seven years with a Chicago engineering firm, Langley held positions with the astronomical observa-tories of Harvard University and the United States Naval Academy. In 1870 he became director of the Allegheny Observatory at Western University in Pitts-burgh, Pa. He helped raise money for the observatory by selling the first standard time service to the Penn-sylvania Railroad. Time signals were flashed to all stations on the road for engineers to set their watches. In 1878 he invented the bolometer, a sensitive electric thermometer for measuring the distribution of heat in the energy rays of the sun.

Langley was appointed secretary of the Smithsonian Institution in 1887. He made the exhibits interesting for people of ordinary education and ordered the in-stitution's books to be written in simple language. He established the famous Children's Room. Langley put into it the things children liked—stuffed birds with their nests and eggs, odd sea animals, bright shells, and coral formations. He collected animals for a zoo, and from this grew the National Zoological Park.

THESE ARTICLES ARE IN THE FACT-INDEX

| | |
|---|---|
| Langmuir, Irving | Langston University |
| Langres, France | Langton, Stephen |
| Langston, John Mercer | Langtry, Lily (Emily) |

# The Sea of Language Around Us

**LANGUAGE.** There is a sea of language around us. From that sea comes a constant flow of messages in Brooklynese and Basque, teenybop and Tibetan. And all those messages are wrapped in sounds and silences and signals.

### Language Isn't: Animal Language

In a sense, animals talk to one another. But it is different from human talk. Every human language uses sounds. Not all animal languages do, though. The language of the bees, for instance, uses body movements.

Every person has to learn his language. A human baby raised by apes would learn only the language of apes and other animals. To learn a human language, he would have to hear it from humans. But much animal talk is not learned. It's inborn. A cat will purr and meow even if it never hears another cat.

With any human language, a person can talk about the future and the past. He can discuss ideas—kindness, truth, honesty, justice. He can make almost any number of sentences—including sentences he never heard before. No animal language is so rich in uses and possibilities.

### Language Isn't: Written Language

Speech is what most writing starts out from. Writing is a secondhand way of trying to say what the sounds and the signals of language say. (*See also* Punctuation; Spelling.)

Written language is separate from spoken language. Children learn to speak without any special training. But reading and writing—written language—have to be specially taught.

Written language has a life of its own. Every written language was invented long after spoken language began. In fact, not all languages have a written form (*see* Writing).

Written language also has its own style. For one thing, written language doesn't change as fast as spoken language. For another thing, people do not commonly write the way they speak. Often writing is more formal. (*See also* Sentence.)

## THE SOUNDS OF LANGUAGE

Sounds are what language comes wrapped in. But not all sounds made by people are language. A person can't say a sneeze, for instance. Or a burp. Burps and sneezes are sounds he can't usually help. The sounds of language are those a person wants to make—and that carry a message.

### Bits of Sound

There are strings of sound called sentences, strings of sound called words, strings of sound called syllables. Syllables are strings of vowel and consonant sounds. And even vowels and consonants are strings of smaller sounds. But the smallest bits of sound people recognize are vowels and consonants.

Strictly speaking, no two language sounds are ever the same. But a person learns to ignore some differences between sounds, depending on his language. To a speaker of English, the sounds of *p* in *pot* and *spot* are alike. Actually, the first *p* is followed by a small puff of air. The second *p* isn't. But whether or not the *p* is puffed, the meanings of *pot* and *spot* do not change. So in English, no one pays attention to the difference. In other languages though—Northern Chinese, for instance—a puffed *p* may change meaning. So speakers of Northern Chinese learn to hear the difference.

English has one *p* sound. Northern Chinese has two—a puffed *p* and an unpuffed one. Such classes of sounds are called *phonemes*. A phoneme is the smallest bit of sound that may change meaning. Most often phonemes are vowels or consonants.

Below is a voiceprint, or *sound spectrogram*. It is a picture of the way one speaker is saying "the sea of language around us."

Other spectrograms of the same words—even by the same speaker—will be a little different.

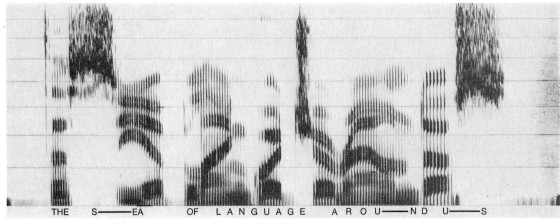

THE S——EA OF LANGUAGE AROU——ND U——S

Bell Telephone Laboratories, Inc.

114

Phonemes combine in patterns. And these patterns vary from language to language. In Spanish, for instance, the *sp* combination never begins a word. But many words in English begin with *sp*. So an English word like *Spanish* is difficult for a Spanish speaker to pronounce. Often he will say *Espanish*.

In English the sound *ng* comes only at the end of a syllable—*ring, ringer, ringworm*. But in some languages of Africa, *ng* may begin as well as end a syllable. The last name of Kenyan novelist James Ngugi is an example.

### Strings of Sound

Most phonemes have no meaning. But they form strings of sound that do. The smallest string of sound with meaning is called a *morpheme*. A morpheme can be what we call a word, or it can be a piece of a word. Take *eater*, in English. *Eat* is a morpheme —it can't be broken down into anything smaller with meaning. The other morpheme is *-er*, meaning "someone who ——s." In *eaters*, there is still a third morpheme, *-s*, meaning "plural" or "more than one."

### The Trouble with Words

If *eater* is a word, *eat* is a piece of that word. But in *anteater*, *eater* is only a piece of a word. Of course, *eater* can be used as a word in English. So can *eat* and *ant*. So on that basis they might be called words. This would set them apart from morphemes like *-er* and *-s*, which are commonly used only as pieces of words.

All languages have what might be called words. But the nature of a word varies from language to language. For instance take Chukchi, a language spoken in Siberia. In Chukchi, *the-big-reindeer-a-person-has-killed* is one unit, one word. It can't be broken up into smaller units the way it would be in English. There are many such words in Chukchi, Eskimo, and other languages. In Northern Chinese, on the other hand, many syllables—and even parts of syllables— are what might be called words in English.

Boundaries between words may shift or disappear in actual speech. In English, for instance, *found it* often comes out *foun dit; don't know* becomes *dunno;* and so on. This is one of the things that makes it hard for people learning a second language to understand speakers of that language.

### Spoken Signals

The sounds of language include spoken signals. The voice rises and falls. It stresses some sounds. And it pauses between some sounds.

Such spoken signals may change meaning. In English, stress makes a difference between *con′ tract* and *con tract′*. A pause makes a difference between *careless* and *care less*. And pitch—the rise and fall

This article was contributed by Harold B. Allen, formerly professor of English and Linguistics, University of Minnesota.

of the voice—makes a difference between "Really?" and "Really."

In languages such as English, pitch is added in a sentence. And it belongs to a place in the sentence, not to a word. Compare "Really?"; "Truly?"; "Honest?" The rising pitch goes with a certain place in that type of sentence. It doesn't matter what the word is. In fact the same words will take different pitches in other sentences.

But in some languages, called *tone languages*, certain pitches belong to certain words. In Northern Chinese, for instance, *chyan* spoken in a level tone means "thousand." In a rising tone it means "money"; in a dipping tone, "shallow"; in a falling tone, "owe." In such languages, the same pitches and the same words always go together.

## THE MECHANICS OF LANGUAGE

Language is in strings of sound. And it's in spoken signals. And these sounds and signals fit together in different ways.

### Word Clumps and Word Order

Words and pieces of words clump together to form larger words. Prefixes and suffixes are added to a root. Or words are combined to form a compound

In English, intonation—the movement of the voice—sometimes makes a difference in the meanings of words.

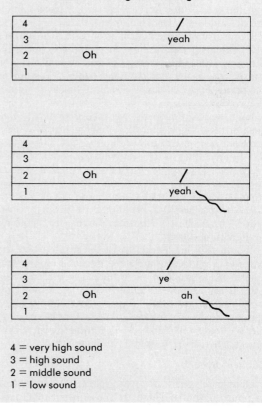

**How Intonation Changes Meaning**

4 = very high sound
3 = high sound
2 = middle sound
1 = low sound

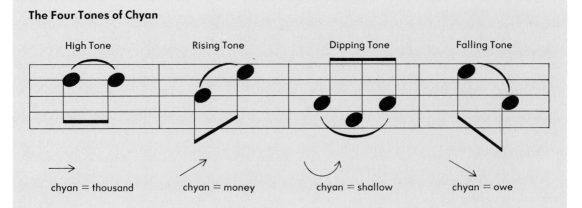

**The Four Tones of Chyan**

High Tone     Rising Tone     Dipping Tone     Falling Tone

chyan = thousand     chyan = money     chyan = shallow     chyan = owe

In Northern Chinese, the movement of the voice makes a difference in the meanings of most words. Northern Chinese has four tones. And the meaning of a word commonly depends on which tone it is spoken in.

word. How words combine with other words and pieces depends on the language. In English, for instance, nouns often add *-s* or *-es* to form the plural (book, books; box, boxes). (*See also* Noun.) Some languages, such as Japanese, usually add no endings for plural. Japanese *hon* means "book" or "books"; *hako* means "box" or "boxes." But Japanese verbs, like many English verbs, add an ending for past tense (*-mashita*). *Arukimasu* (walk) becomes *arukimashita* (walked). (*See also* Verb.)

Languages most often add prefixes and/or suffixes to a root. But sometimes changes are made inside a root instead. Thus, Arabic *bint* (girl) becomes *banāt* (girls), and English *mouse* becomes *mice*.

Words clump together in groups called phrases (*see* Sentence). Again, how they clump depends on the language. An Arabic speaker would say *the caliph rotten* instead of *the rotten caliph*. Instead of the phrase *in the kitchen*, a Swahili speaker would use the word *kitchen-in*.

Each language has its own special phrases. One type is what might be called a *usage clump*. These are words clumped together so often that they sound odd in any other order. *Stars and stripes* and *bread and butter* are examples in English. Another type of special phrase is the *idiom*. An *idiom* doesn't mean what its individual words mean. In Italian, *"In the mouth of the wolf"* is an idiom. It means "Good luck." And *kick the bucket* in English has nothing to do with buckets.

Words also clump together in clauses, but how the parts of a clause are arranged depends on the language. An example of one common type of arrangement is the English sentence *Bobby Joe* (subject) *ate* (verb) *my fortune cookie* (direct object). A Japanese speaker would use another common type of arrangement—*Bobby Joe* (subject) *my fortune cookie* (direct object) *ate* (verb). (*See also* Sentence.)

### Parts of Speech

Chunks of speech are often grouped by types, such as nouns or verbs. These are sometimes called *parts of speech* (*see* Grammar). Parts of speech are not the same in every language. Nor is the way they act the same. Turkish, for instance, has postpositions instead of prepositions. Instead of *in your hat*, a Turkish speaker would say *hat-your-in*.

Parts of speech have jobs to do. Nouns in English, for instance, may act as subjects. And verbs may act as predicates (*see* Grammar).

### The Shapes of Spoken Signals

The spoken signals of language form patterns in phrases and clauses. No two languages have exactly the same patterns. But in many languages a statement commonly has a special shape. Often it drops at the end and fades into silence. (I guess I'll get the papers and go home.) A question that can be answered *yes* or *no* often has a different shape. At the end it usually goes up and breaks off. (Did you see that?) (*See also* Sentence.)

## THE MEANING OF LANGUAGE

Language is, above all, meaning. Meanings are attached to pieces of words, words, word groups. Meanings are attached to the spoken signals of language. Meanings are attached to the shifts and changes of grammar.

### Meaning and No Meaning

The sounds of words have no meaning to begin with. It's people who attach meaning to them.

Every day someone thinks up a new word. Or he uses an old word in a new way. He might suddenly say, "Hey, that's *zonko*, you know? Boy, that's really *zonko!*" If no one pays much attention to him, that's the end of *zonko*. But maybe his friends and other people begin to use the word, too—"Wow! *Zonko!*" Then another word has been born.

### Meaning More or Less

Some words have more of what might be called outside meaning than others. *Orange*, for instance, means "a reddish-yellow color, a fruit," etc. But it also means tigers and sunsets and excitement—meanings outside the dictionary definitions. Words like *the*, *and*, *to* have little outside meaning. They are sometimes called *function words* (*see* Grammar).

Much-repeated words may mean less after a while. *Clichés* are an example. A cliché is an expression that loses its punch through overuse. Used sparingly, "That's really great!" may get a listener's special attention. If it's used too often, however, it doesn't mean much.

Common expressions of courtesy often lose meaning. Chances are that a casual acquaintance who asks "How are you?" doesn't really want to know.

### Same and Different Meaning

Few words have exactly the same meaning. Not only are the Burmese and Arabic words for "house" different, they mean different things to a Burmese villager and a desert Arab. *Return* and *take back* are much alike in English. But like all synonyms they do not always mean the same. There's a world of difference between "We *took* Ralphie *back* to the monkey house" and "We *returned* Ralphie to the monkey house." But in practice, speakers accept certain words as more or less the same. This helps them communicate more easily.

The same word often has different meanings, depending on how it's used with other words. In English, *go* can mean "leave" (Please don't *go*.); "work" (My watch won't *go*.); "reach" (It doesn't *go* far enough.); etc. Homonyms, or homophones, like *bear* and *bare* are more or less the same word to a listener. It's how they're used with other words that gives them different meanings.

Not only do the same words have different meanings; the same groups of words often do. "She drove into the bank this morning" is an example. Was it a drive-in bank? Or did she zig when she should have zagged? Or what? The surrounding sentences will give clues to the meaning.

A phrase or clause doesn't always mean the same as its words. Idioms are an example. Another example is the way the words are spoken. "Oh, sure I will!" in a sarcastic tone means something very different from what the words say.

### Ways of Meaning

A word commonly has different ways of meaning. What a word refers to is only one way it means. Thus, the word *prunes* refers to a food. But much of the meaning of words has to do with the speaker's attitude. So the meaning of *prunes* depends also on how the speaker feels about them. The word has a pleasant meaning if he likes them, an unpleasant meaning if he doesn't.

The meaning a word refers to is its *denotation*. What a word suggests because of the speaker's or listener's attitude is its *connotation*.

Languages have different ways of separating meaning. Eskimo has separate words for falling snow, snow on the ground, etc. English has only one—*snow*. Shona, a language of Rhodesia, has three words for all the colors. One word means "red, purple, orange." Another means "white, yellow, green."

### Social Meaning

People don't usually talk to themselves. They talk to other people. And their talk has social meaning.

Only part of the social meaning of a conversation is carried by the words. Take saying hello or talking about the weather. Often such talk has little dictionary meaning. It is a way of being friendly or polite.

Choice of language often has social meaning. An informal "Yeah" in the neighborhood carries a relaxed meaning. Often it is replaced by a formal "Yes" in a classroom or at a job interview. Spanish-speaking Americans often switch from Spanish at home to English in the classroom. Use of special work words may mean a speaker is an architect or plumber or foundry worker. In many countries, the words a speaker uses label him a member of the upper or lower classes.

Dirty words have social meaning. So do expressions using God's name in vain. The same goes for conversation about such things as going to the toilet. Usually these are no-no's, and they have that meaning attached to them.

### Grammatical Meaning

Some meanings attach to words. These are dictionary meanings. And some meanings, called *grammatical meanings*, attach to the signals of grammar.

The form a word takes may have grammatical meaning. In English, *-s* or *-es* added to a noun means "plural" or "more than one." A *-mashita* ending on a Japanese verb means "past tense."

Word order may have grammatical meaning. Take the English sentence "Mary bit John." In English, the common order for statements is subject-verb-direct object. So *Mary* means "subject," and John means "direct object." It's Mary who does the biting, John who gets bitten.

Function words have grammatical meaning. In English, *the* or *a* means that a noun is coming up. *Quién* (who) at the beginning of a Spanish sentence means that the sentence is a question.

Spoken signals can have dictionary meaning. Pitch in the words of tone languages is an example. But spoken signals can also have grammatical meaning. In English, for example, stress on *sus-* in *suspect* signals that the word is a noun. Stress on *-spect*, on the other hand, means "verb." At the end of a clause, a drop in pitch with a fading into silence commonly means "statement."

### The Trouble with Translation

The words of one language seldom mean the same as the words of another. Take the Russian "*Ja govorila*." It can be translated into English as "I said." But the meanings are not exactly the same. The verb *govorila* tells a Russian that "I" is a female.

It also tells a Russian she spoke more than once or that she hadn't finished speaking. Neither of these meanings is carried by the English words.

Even the same word may not have the same meanings. English borrowed *sputnik* from Russian. It means "artificial satellite." But in Russian, the word also means "fellow-traveler" and "guide." So *sputnik* the English word does not mean the same as *sputnik* the Russian word.

A translation is, at best, something like. It tries to transfer meanings from one language to another. But different words and different mechanics of language must be used. Take the Japanese "*Musukosan wa hebi wo tabemashita.*" Word by word it reads,

**Japanese sentences are not built like English sentences. So in translating, parts of a sentence must be shifted around.**

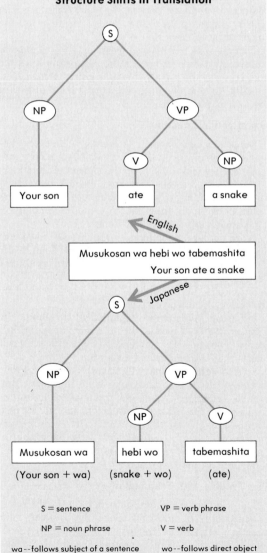

**Structure Shifts in Translation**

Musukosan wa hebi wo tabemashita
Your son ate a snake

(Your son + wa)    (snake + wo)    (ate)

S = sentence      VP = verb phrase

NP = noun phrase      V = verb

wa--follows subject of a sentence      wo--follows direct object

"Your son+*wa*+snake+*wo*+ate." But that's not a translation. *Wa* and *wo* have no dictionary meaning, only grammatical meaning—*wa* comes after a subject, *wo* after a direct object. So *wa* and *wo* are dropped in translation. Thus, "Your son snake ate." But in English the direct object (snake) follows the verb (ate). So the words must be switched around to read "Your son ate snake." That's not comfortable English, though. Japanese has no word for *a*, so it must be added. The result is "Your son ate a snake." Still that doesn't carry over all the meanings. *Musukosan*, for instance, has a meaning of respect that is missing in *your son*. Just the same, it's a good translation. A Japanese speaker trying to translate "Your son ate a snake" into Japanese faces the same problems in reverse.

A translation doesn't usually take the same form as the original. Sometimes a noun can be translated by a noun, a phrase by a phrase. But it doesn't work that way very often. German "*Guten Tag*" means "Good day," but it's better translated as "Hello"—people don't usually say "Good day" in English. French *s'il vous plaît* (if it pleases you) is better translated in English as *please*.

The idea of one correct translation is false. For instance, Italian "*La casa è a Sua disposizione*" can be translated as "The house is at your disposal," "Make yourself at home," etc. It is partly a matter of choice. It is also partly a matter of style—whether the words were used in a formal or informal way.

When computers are used in translation, it is called *machine translation*. A computer can work much faster than a human—in looking up a word, say. But the machines have many problems. They have trouble identifying the same sounds made by different people. Sometimes different sounds are spelled with the same letters. (Compare the sounds of the *s* in *cats* and in *dogs*.) Computers have trouble with those. And computers have much trouble with meaning—words with different· possible meanings, sentences with different possible meanings.

A computer is only as good as the information put into it. And that's the heart of the machine translation problem. No one has all the answers to how any language works.

### BEYOND LANGUAGE

When people talk, they don't stop short at language. They use their voices in ways that go along with language. People also talk with their bodies. And they use substitutes for language.

### Paralanguage

The voice carries more than the sounds of language. It carries sounds that go along with language.

A voice may tell whether the speaker is sick or healthy, sleepy or wide awake, drunk or sober. A voice can cry or laugh, moan, groan, or giggle—apart from the words. A voice can drawl. It can hiss or hesitate. It can even fall silent in a special way—the silence of shame, the silence of anger, the

Body talk is closely related to language. People speak with their bodies, their hands, their eyes, their faces.

silence of bitter disappointment. None of these sounds is language. They are *paralanguage*, sounds that go along with language.

### Body Talk

Body movements, too, go along with language. Sometimes they take the place of actual speech.

Some body signals probably can't be helped. Someone who says "Wha-a-at?" may show disbelief by actions as well as words. His eyes may widen, his mouth open a little wider perhaps. Eyebrows may draw together as angry words are spoken. A slight hunch of the shoulders may go along with a confession of fear.

Body signals that can't be helped sometimes contradict the messages of spoken language. A look may say *yes*, even if the words say *no*. The way a person stands may say "I don't like you," even if the words say "We're friends."

Some body signals are deliberate. Deliberate signals, called *gestures*, have to be learned. People in different places use different gestures and attach different meanings to them.

In many places, an up-and-down nod of the head means *yes*. But in the Middle East, an upward jerk of the head may mean *no*. People of western Europe often shake the head from side to side to say *no*. But in some Arab countries, that same gesture means *yes*. Most Chinese motion "Come here" with palm down instead of palm up. French people often substitute a shrug for "I don't know."

Even among the same group of people, a gesture can have many possible meanings. In the United States, for instance, a wink can mean "Hi, there." Or it might mean "This is our secret," or "You'll get a laugh out of this," and so on.

### Language Substitutes

People have many ways of getting through to one another (*see* Communication). And some of these are substitutes for language.

Most written languages are substitutes for spoken language. Morse code and semaphore code, too, are language substitutes. (*See also* Signaling.) Their signals stand for letters of the alphabet, which in turn stand for spoken language. The same is true of braille, the reading alphabet for the blind. Another substitute for language is the hand alphabet for deaf-mutes.

Another system of hand signals is Indian sign language. But it isn't a substitute for language, at least not in a direct way. Indian sign language is used by people speaking different languages. So the signs cannot stand for words. Instead the signs themselves have meaning. For instance, two spread fingers moving past the mouth mean "lie," or "forked tongue." Each person translates the meaning of the hand signals into the words of his own language.

Other language substitutes include whistle talk and drum talk. Whistle talk is used for communicating over long distances by people of the Canary Islands. Drums are used to send messages in many

**115d**

Sometimes body talk takes the place of speech. Without words, the woman at right is saying something like, "I can't take it any more!"

parts of Africa. The signals of these systems stand for the words of spoken language.

## LANGUAGE CHANGE

A language is always changing. And it keeps changing as long as it is spoken.

### Borrowing from Without

One way a language changes is by borrowing words from other languages. It's easier to borrow a word for a new thing than to make one up. English, for instance, borrowed *hula* from Hawaiian, *karate* from Japanese, *pizza* from Italian. Words are often borrowed from a language that has prestige. In the far East, Chinese culture was much admired from early times. As a result, many Chinese words were adopted by languages of Asia. In Europe, Greek culture had great prestige. Today there are many Greek words in European languages.

Borrowed words are often changed somewhat. For one thing, they're not pronounced the same. *Sauerkraut*, for instance, begins with a *z* sound in the original German. For another thing, borrowed words often don't mean exactly the same. The word *dancing*, borrowed from English, means "night club" in French, for instance.

Not just words are borrowed. Sometimes a way of saying something is borrowed, though the actual words are not. For instance, German *Wolkenkratzer* (cloud-scratcher) is borrowed from English *skyscraper*. Sounds also are borrowed. A few languages

of South Africa, for instance, have borrowed a kind of click sound from neighbor languages. Sometimes even a way of putting words together is borrowed. Take "The children want that they eat" instead "The children want to eat." Languages of the Balkans have borrowed such an arrangement from each other.

### Borrowing from Within

Borrowing from other languages is a way a language changes from the outside. But some changes come from the inside.

Sometimes a language borrows from itself. New words are made from the old stuff of the language. Or old words take on new meanings. *Hamburger* dropped the *ham* to become *cheeseburger*, *chiliburger*, etc. The French *traire* used to mean "to pull" or "to draw." Now it means "to milk."

Sometimes old words take on new sounds, new forms, and even new ways of acting. English *brethren* became *brothers*. *Bug* stopped being just a noun (Eek! A *bug!*) to become a sometime verb (Don't *bug* me.).

Sometimes there is a sort of minus borrowing— words slowly fade out of use. Hardly anyone wears *breeches* anymore. People rarely say *verily* or *"Lo!"* And *lamplighters* and *organ grinders*, *iceboxes* and *3-D movies* are mostly things of the past.

### Changing the Rules

Another way of changing from within has to do with the way a language works. A language changes its rules, so to speak.

115e

In Old French a phrase like *my back* used to have *the* in front of it—*the my back*. French doesn't work that way any more. In English, *not* used to follow any verb. Now it can follow only a few. Thus, people still say "You had better not" or "I did not." But they would no longer say "I like it not" or "The mailman comes not."

Language sounds, too, work by what might be called rules. In Latin, a word of fewer than three syllables was stressed on the first syllable. Thus, *nav′ is* (ship), *pu′ er* (boy). But in French, one of the languages that grew out of Latin, stress no longer works that way. Thus, *che val′* (horse), *a mi′* (friend).

## KINDS OF LANGUAGE

People speak many kinds of language. There is the language of different places, and there is the language of different groups.

### Language and Dialect

A speaker of Arabic and a speaker of Malay have different speech habits and don't understand one another's speech. A speaker from the Tennessee hills and a speaker from Chicago have different speech habits too. But they can pretty much understand each other. Arabic and Malay are called languages.

The origin of a word—its etymology—often reveals borrowings from other languages. English is especially rich in borrowed words. For instance, many roots, prefixes, and suffixes in English were long ago borrowed from Greek.

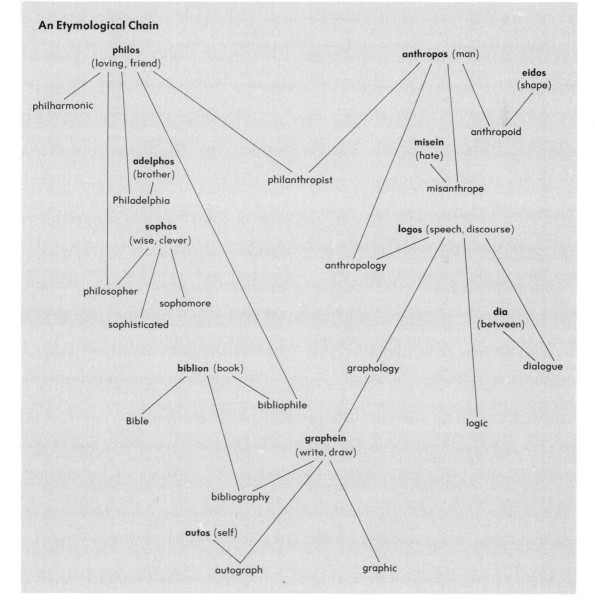

An Etymological Chain

Chicagoese and Tennessee mountainese are called *dialects*. A dialect is a variety of a language.

The line between languages and dialects is not always clear. Dialects are sometimes called languages, and languages are sometimes called dialects. Northern Italians and Sicilians commonly do not understand each other's speech. Yet both speak so-called dialects of Italian. Danish and Norwegian are called different languages. Yet Danes and Norwegians pretty well understand one another.

A country's boundaries can be marked on a map. But language boundaries can't—at least, not in the same way. A line between two languages would mean everyone on one side of the line spoke one language. It would also mean everyone on the other side of the line spoke another language. But language just doesn't work that way.

For one thing, some people use two or more languages. French and English are spoken by many Canadians. Many people of Paraguay are fluent in both Spanish and Guarani, an American Indian language. Quite a number of Israelis understand Hebrew, Yiddish, and a European language, such as Russian.

For another thing, languages have dialects. And often the dialects of one language merge into the dialects of a neighbor language. Take French and Italian. Anyone going from Paris to Naples can hear small language differences between each town and the next. At no point can a sharp line be drawn. Yet the French of Paris and the Italian of Naples are different languages.

### The Difference in Dialect

Differences in speech habits are what make dialects. Speakers pronounce words differently. They use different words for the same thing. And they sometimes put words together in different ways.

A London cockney will say *'arry* for *Harry*, *'orrible* for *horrible*. *Hot dog, frankfurter, wiener*, and *red hot* are all words for the same thing in the United States. "Goin' git me some" and "I'm going to get some" are two ways of saying much the same thing. Each way of pronouncing words, of using words, is right for a particular dialect. No dialect is better or worse than another—only different.

### All Kinds of Dialect

Strictly speaking, no two people have exactly the same dialect. Every speaker pronounces at least some words a little differently from everyone else. Probably no two persons know exactly the same set of words. Everyone puts his words together in his own ways. And to complicate matters, a person's dialect is always changing.

Just the same, there are patterns of dialect. People in certain neighborhoods, certain cities, certain regions speak a lot alike—even if there are some differences. Many New Yorkers have a way of speaking that sets them apart. The speech of most people from the South is distinctive. American English is distinct from Australian English, which is distinct from English English. Such dialects, spoken by people of different places, might be called *geographical dialects*.

Another type of dialect is the *social dialect*. Social dialects are spoken by people of different groups. In many countries, people in high society speak differently from working-class people. People who work together—astronauts, doctors, gangsters—often share special work words, a sort of shop talk. Men's talk is a little different from women's talk. The language of older people is not the same as that of the young.

In many places one dialect has more social standing than the others. Often it becomes the language of government and is taught in the schools. Such a dialect is called a *standard dialect*. Take the dialect of Paris. Originally it was one of many dialects spoken in what is now France. As Paris became more important, so did the Parisian dialect. Now it is the standard French dialect.

All people have more than one dialect. A person's dialects depend on where he lives, what groups he moves with, his education, and so on. For instance, a Tokyo engineer from Kyoto might use his own Kyoto dialect at home, the standard dialect of Tokyo at work. His speech would differ in some ways from that of his wife. And it would differ from that of his teen-age son. With other engineers he would use a kind of engineering shop talk. Such switching from one dialect to another is common.

People also have more than one way of using their dialects. There is a relaxed way—for talking with friends, for instance. And there is a formal way—for talking with a job interviewer, say.

### Standard Languages

Language has no boundaries. Speakers of the same language may live in many countries. And every country has many languages. But often, one of the languages of a country is chosen as the standard language. And this is the language taught in the schools and used for official business.

In France, for instance, the standard language is French. But not all Frenchmen speak French. There are German speakers in Alsace-Lorraine, Breton speakers in Brittany, Basque speakers in the Pyrenees mountains. And in southern France the Provençal dialects are so different from standard French that they can be considered a separate language. The standard language is used for easier communication. It is also used to unite the people of a country.

Often a standard language does make communication easier. French is taught in all the schools of France. So most Frenchmen can get through to each other. A Basque speaker can use French to talk to a Breton speaker, for instance. A standard language can also help give speakers of different languages a feeling of oneness. An example is Modern Hebrew, the standard language of Israel.

The trouble is, a standard language doesn't always work the way it's supposed to. There are no first-class or second-class languages. But because a standard language is the official language, it often has a higher social standing. And nonstandard languages are often considered less important, even looked down on.

In such instances, a nonstandard speaker learns the standard language only if he has to. And even then he resents it. His resentment may take the form of not learning it well—just enough to get by with. Or he may simply refuse to learn it at all.

Some countries have more than one standard language. Belgium uses French and Flemish. Canada uses French and English. Yugoslavia uses Serbo-Croatian, Slovenian, and Macedonian. India has no less than 14 standard languages. But often even such countries have language problems.

Problems arise because one language is—or seems to be—more favored than another. In Belgium, Flemish speakers have protested the favored position of French. In India, many have protested the favored position of Hindi. Problems also arise because most people in most places use only one language. So unless all a country's languages are taught in the schools, which usually isn't practical, most people can't understand speakers of another language.

In some countries, an outside language is sometimes chosen as a standard language. Take Ghana. Its people speak perhaps 50 or more languages. So English was adopted as an official language. And it was used for teaching in the schools.

## Second Languages

Most people speak only their first language—the language learned in the home. But many also learn a second language. There are several kinds of second languages. One kind is the language of the other speaker. When a Basque speaker uses French to talk to a French speaker, for instance, he is using the other speaker's language.

But sometimes speakers of different languages don't use the language of the other speaker. They use a third language. Such a language is sometimes called a *lingua franca*. A speaker of Telugu from southern India and a speaker of Hindi from northern India may talk to each other in English. Then English is being used as a *lingua franca*. A Ukrainian speaker and a Yakut speaker from Siberia may use Russian as their common language. In that case, Russian is their *lingua franca*.

Another kind of second language is a *pidgin language*. Pidgins are often used for brief contacts between people—between two traders, say. A pidgin is a sort of hybrid of both the speakers' languages. But the vocabulary is greatly reduced. And the way words fit together is greatly simplified. The first known Pidgin English was used by English speakers and American Indians. One justice of the peace wrote to an Indian policeman, "You, you big constable, quick you catch um Jeremiah Offscow, strong you hold um, safe you bring um afore me." Russonorsk was a pidgin of Russian and Norwegian. It was used

by Russian and Norwegian fishermen for about a hundred years before World War I. A pidgin of Dutch and Malay, known as Bazaar Malay, was used in the Dutch East Indies. *Bahasa Indonesia*, the official language of Indonesia, is based on Bazaar Malay.

Sometimes a pidgin becomes the first language of a group of speakers. Then it is a *creole language*. In the Caribbean, African slaves from the same tribe were often separated. This was to reduce the danger of revolt. So the slaves on a plantation had no common language. They could only talk to each other in a pidgin of their owner's language—such as Pidgin French or Pidgin Spanish. In time the slaves married and had children. The children learned the pidgin as their only language. At that point, their language was a creole language.

Gullah is a creole language. It is spoken on and near the Sea Islands off Georgia. Louisiana Creole is a French-based language. Another French-based creole is Haitian Creole, the language of Haiti. Speakers of Louisiana Creole and Haitian Creole commonly understand each other. Jamaican Creole is an English-based language of Jamaica. So-called Hawaiian Pidgin English is actually a creole language. It is the speech of a large number of people brought up in the Hawaiian Islands.

## Interlanguages

The Old Testament tells of a time when there was one world language. And how Nimrod ruined it all by building a tower to reach Heaven. And how the Lord made the workmen speak different languages. So the Tower of Babel was never finished.

The idea of a world language, or *interlanguage*, is very old. Hundreds have been invented. But few have received much attention. The first one to become well known was Volapük. It was introduced by a Bavarian clergyman, Johann Martin Schleyer, in 1879. Schleyer based his language mostly on German and English, with many words also from languages like Latin—French, Italian, Spanish, and so on. The name *Volapük* meant "world speech."

Volapük was popular in Europe for a while, but it didn't last. For one thing, some of its sounds were difficult for non-German speakers. The ü sound in Volapük is an example. For another thing, the way its words fit together was complicated. Volapük went out of use shortly after the invention of another—and simpler—interlanguage, Esperanto.

Esperanto is probably the best known interlanguage. It was introduced in 1887 by a Polish doctor, L. L. Zamenhof. The name *Esperanto* is based on a word for "hope." Zamenhof felt that language was at the root of problems between people. He believed a world language would bring peace and understanding.

Esperanto is based mostly on languages like French, Italian, and Spanish, with a number of words also from German and Greek. Both the sounds and the mechanics of the language are fairly simple—for most Europeans. Esperanto is used in many countries. Schools teach it, and books are published in Esperanto.

## Major Living Languages of the Indo-European Family

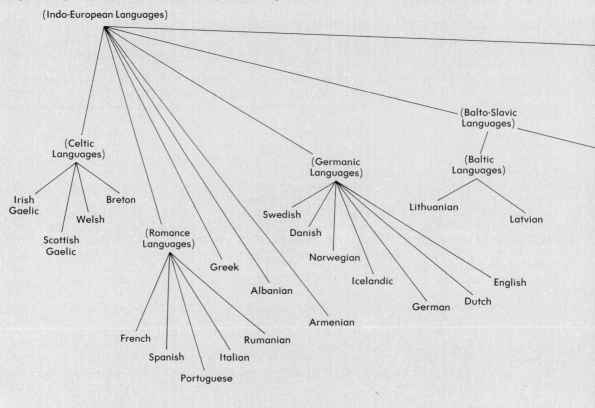

(Indo-European Languages)

(Balto-Slavic Languages)

(Celtic Languages)

(Germanic Languages)

(Baltic Languages)

Irish Gaelic

Breton

Welsh

Scottish Gaelic

(Romance Languages)

Swedish

Lithuanian

Latvian

Danish

Greek

Norwegian

Albanian

Icelandic

English

Armenian

German

Dutch

French

Rumanian

Spanish

Italian

Portuguese

The trouble with world languages is that they're not. Mostly they are made for speakers of English, German, French, Spanish, Portuguese, Italian, and a number of related languages. A speaker of Northern Chinese, for instance, would have as much trouble with Esperanto as with French or German. The same is true of a speaker of Eskimo or a speaker of Tamil, a language of southern India. Esperanto ignores the sounds and mechanics and meanings of most of the world's languages.

Another problem with world languages has to do with language change. Suppose Esperanto, say, were adopted as a world language. It would soon be spoken in many different dialects. For one thing, people have different speech habits. For another thing, language is always changing. Dialects of people far apart would become more and more different. This would be especially true of people in remote places, people having little or no contact with speakers of other dialects. It would probably also be especially true of people who felt that Esperanto was not "their" language, that it represented the languages of other people. Given time enough, resistance or resentment enough, and separation enough, speakers of different dialects would no longer be able to understand one another. And a new interlanguage would have to be invented all over again.

### Related Languages

Languages have dialects. And some of those dialects grow so far apart that they become languages. And the new languages separate into dialects. And some of those become languages. Such related languages are called a *language family*.

**Indo-European.** The family to which English belongs is the Indo-European family. It consists of many groups of languages.

The Germanic, or Teutonic, group includes the Scandinavian languages—Danish, Norwegian, Swedish, and Icelandic. German is commonly divided into High German and Low German. High German includes the dialects of southern Germany, the dialects of Austria, and the German dialects of Switzerland. Dutch, Flemish (spoken in Belgium), and the dialects of northern Germany make up Low German. Afrikaans, an offshoot of Dutch, is spoken in South Africa. English, which is also a Germanic language, is closely related to Dutch. But even closer to English is Frisian, spoken mostly in the northern Netherlands. Yiddish, a language of the Jewish people, is for the most part a High German of the Middle Ages.

The Romance group descended from Latin. After the Roman Empire fell apart, the Latin dialects of the different regions grew farther and farther apart.

115i

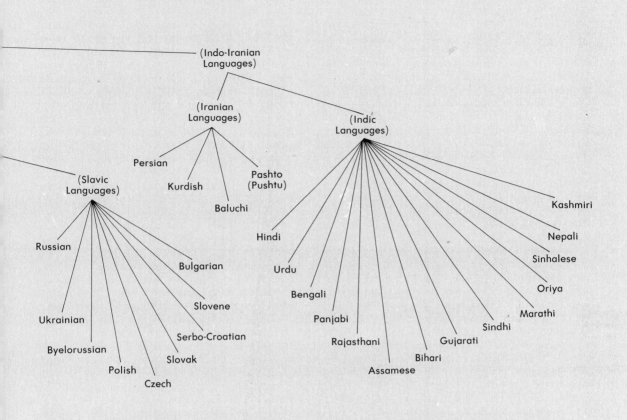

Best known of the Romance languages are French, Spanish, Portuguese, Italian, and Rumanian. Provençal, a name for the dialects of southern France, is sometimes considered a separate language. Catalan is spoken mostly in eastern Spain. Romansh is spoken in Switzerland. And Sardinian is spoken on the island of Sardinia.

The Balto-Slavic group consists of the Baltic languages and the Slavic languages. Lithuanian and Latvian (or Lettish) are Baltic languages. The Slavic languages include Russian, Ukrainian, and Byelorussian (or White Russian), all spoken in the Soviet Union. Czech and Slovak, spoken in Czechoslovakia, are very closely related. Indeed they might be called varieties of the same language. Serbo-Croatian is one language written in two alphabets—Croatian in Roman letters, Serbian in the Cyrillic alphabet. (*See also* Writing.) It is spoken chiefly in Yugoslavia, as is the Slovenian language. Other well-known Slavic languages include Polish and Bulgarian.

The Celtic group of languages, once spoken over a large territory, today are used only in the British Isles and northwestern France. And the number of speakers is small. Irish Gaelic and Scottish Gaelic are Celtic languages. Welsh, spoken in Wales, and Breton, a language of Brittany in northwestern France, form another branch of Celtic.

The Indo-Iranian group consists of Indic languages and Iranian languages. Persian is an Iranian language. So are Pashto (or Pushtu), spoken in Afghanistan and Pakistan; and Kurdish, spoken in Kurdistan. Baluchi, spoken mostly in Pakistan and Iran, also is an Iranian language. Sanskrit is an Indic language. It is the oldest living Indo-European language, now used chiefly as the sacred language of Hinduism. Hindi, the leading language of northern India, and Urdu, the national language of Pakistan, are also Indic languages. Both Hindi and Urdu are varieties of the same language. But Urdu has more Persian and Arabic words and is written with a different alphabet. Other Indic languages include Bengali, Panjabi, Gujerati, Marathi, Rajasthani, Bihari, Kashmiri, Oriya, Sindhi, Assamese, and Nepali. Sinhalese, spoken in Ceylon, is also an Indic language. And so is the language of the Gypsies, Romany.

Greek belongs in a separate group. The same is true of Armenian. And the same is true of Albanian. An Indo-European language called Tocharian was once spoken in what is now Sinkiang, China. The language of the Hittites, a people mentioned in the Bible, was also Indo-European.

**Uralic.** The Uralic family has two main groups: Finno-Ugric and Samoyed. Of the Finno-Ugric group, the best known Ugric language is Hungarian (or

Magyar). Finnish, Estonian, and Lapp are the best known Finnic languages. Lapp, the language of the Lapps, is spoken mostly in Norway, Sweden, and Finland. Two other Finnic languages, Mordvin and Cheremis, are spoken in the Soviet Union. The Samoyed group of languages are spoken in Siberia.

**Altaic.** The Altaic family is commonly divided into three main groups: Turkic, Mongolian, and Manchu-Tungus (or Manchurian). Turkish is the best-known Turkic language. Other Turkic languages include Azerbaijani, Uzbek, Kazakh, Tatar, Kirghiz, and Turkoman (or Turkmenian), all spoken mostly in the Soviet Union. Azerbaijani is also spoken in Iran. Another Turkic language, spoken mostly in Sinkiang, China, is Uighur. Yakut, spoken in Siberia, is also a Turkic language. The Mongolian group of languages are spoken in Mongolia and China. The Manchu-Tungus group of languages are spoken in Manchuria and Siberia.

**Sino-Tibetan.** The Sino-Tibetan family has many groups of languages. Of these, the best known is the group called Chinese. Chinese has about half a dozen main dialects, so-called. But they are, for practical purposes, separate languages. They are very different—in sounds and vocabulary mostly. And the speakers of one dialect cannot understand the speakers of another. Northern Chinese (or Mandarin) is considered the standard language of China. Other Chinese languages include Wu, Min (or Fukienese), Hakka, and Cantonese (or Yue). Most Chinese on Formosa speak Min. Cantonese is used by most of the Chinese speakers in the United States.

Tibetan and Burmese also belong to the Sino-Tibetan family. Sometimes they are considered one group, sometimes two. Another group includes Thai and Lao. Thai is spoken in Thailand mostly, Lao mostly in Laos. The Miao-Yao languages are sometimes considered Sino-Tibetan. They are spoken by tribespeople in southwest China, northern Burma, and Indochina.

**Austronesian.** The Austronesian, or Malayo-Polynesian, family is spoken from Madagascar, off the coast of Africa, to Hawaii. One of its best-known languages is Malay. The standard languages of Malaysia and Indonesia are varieties of Malay. Tagalog, Visayan, and Ilocano, all spoken in the Philippines, also belong to this family. So does Malagasy, a language spoken on the island of Madagascar.

Maori, spoken in New Zealand, is an Austronesian language. And related languages are spoken in many of the South Sea Islands. These include Fiji in the Fiji Islands, Samoan in the Samoan Islands, Tahitian in the Society Islands, Hawaiian in the Hawaiian Islands, and Chamorro on Guam.

**Congo-Kordofanian.** The Congo-Kordofanian family has two main groups: the Niger-Congo and the Kordofanian. The Kordofanian languages are spoken in the Sudan. The Niger-Congo languages are spoken over a great part of central and southern Africa.

Well-known languages of the Niger-Congo group include Ibo, Yoruba, and Efik, spoken in Nigeria. Fulani (or Fula) is spoken mostly in Nigeria and Guinea; Mandingo mostly in Mali, Ivory Coast, and Guinea. Twi has many speakers in Ghana. Mossi, Wolof, Ewe, and Tiv also are Niger-Congo languages.

The Bantu languages are only one branch of one division of the Niger-Congo group. But they are very numerous. A few better-known Bantu languages are Swahili, Ruanda and Rundi, Sotho and Tswana, Ganda, Shona, Kongo, Kikuyu, Xhosa, Zulu, and Swazi.

**Afroasiatic.** The Afroasiatic family is divided into four main groups. The best known is Semitic. Arabic, with its many dialects, is the most widely used Semitic language. It is spoken in many countries of the Near East and North Africa. Modern Hebrew, the standard language of Israel, is also a Semitic language. So is Amharic, the standard language of Ethiopia.

The other groups of Afroasiatic are Berber, Cushitic, and Chad. The Berber languages are spoken in North Africa. The Cushitic languages are spoken over a wide area in East Africa. Somali is the best known Cushitic language. Hausa, the best known Chad language, is widely spoken in West Africa.

**Other Families.** The Dravidian family of languages are spoken mostly in southern India. They include Telugu, Tamil, Kanarese (or Kannada), and Malayalam. Tamil is also spoken in Ceylon. Brahui, a Dravidian language, is spoken in Pakistan and Iran.

The Munda family consists of a few languages in central India. The Mon-Khmer family is spoken in Southeast Asia. Its best-known language is Cambodian, or Khmer, spoken in Cambodia. Most Mon speakers live in Burma and Thailand.

Among the better-known languages of the Nilo-Saharan family are Kanuri, Dinka, Luo, and Masai. Kanuri is spoken in Nigeria and Niger, Dinka and Luo in Kenya, Masai in Tanzania. The Khoisan family of languages are spoken mostly in South Africa. The best known of these languages are Bushman and Hottentot. Khoisan speakers use special click sounds. Some of these sounds have spread to nearby Bantu languages like Zulu, Sotho, and Xhosa.

Japanese seems to be the only member of a family. The same is true of Korean. And the same is true of Vietnamese. Basque is spoken mostly in the Pyrenees mountains region of France and Spain. It has no ties with any other language. Another language without ties is Burushaski. It is spoken in and around Hunza, in the Karakoram mountains of Kashmir. Andamanese, spoken by a handful of people in the Andaman Islands, has no known relatives. Neither has Ainu, once the language of a non-Japanese people of northern Japan. The Ainu people survive, but only a few words of their language are still used.

About 25 or so languages spoken in the Caucasus Mountains have no known relatives. Some of them seem to be related, but the language picture there as a whole is not clear. Sometimes they are divided into two groups, a northern group and a southern. Among the better known of these languages are Circassian and Georgian. How the languages of Australia are related also is not known. The same is true of most languages of New Guinea.

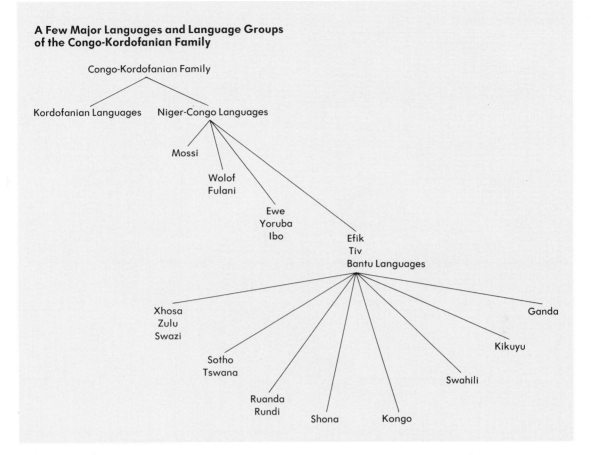

A Few Major Languages and Language Groups of the Congo-Kordofanian Family

A few languages of Siberia do not belong to families elsewhere. These are sometimes called Paleosiberian languages. Some of these are related. But it is not certain that all are. Probably the most numerous group, the Chukchi group, includes Chukchi and Koryak. The American Indian languages in North and South America are sometimes called Amerindian languages. Like the Paleosiberian languages, they are not clearly understood. Some Amerindian languages are related—Eskimo and Aleut, for instance. And most seem to fit into families such as Iroquoian, Siouan, etc. But many do not.

## LANGUAGE THROUGH LANGUAGE: GUIDELINES FOR A MODEL SECOND-LANGUAGE PROGRAM

No language is hard for a child. He picks up any language easily and naturally—by listening and talking. But that ability soon fades. And then he must learn a new language through the one he already has. And that's where the second-language teacher comes in. The following are some guidelines for a model second-language program.

1. Sounds are first. Students concentrate on listening and speaking, especially to begin with.

2. Students get lots of practice in listening—to the teacher, to records and tapes, and so on. Then they imitate. They try to hear groups of words, not just one word at a time.

3. Students get lots of practice in speaking, too. Everyone gets to do some talking every period, especially slow learners. And the students do most of the talking—the teacher already knows the language.

4. Learning a new language is hard. Students are told—slow learners especially—not to worry about making mistakes, that everybody makes them.

5. The teacher explains about the new language when necessary. But mostly students practice using the language. Practice helps them understand how the language works.

6. Students get drill. They need it to break old language habits and form new ones. But the teacher doesn't overdo drill and tries to make it interesting.

7. Students don't translate from the new language to English. That builds the wrong skill—making sentences in English. And they go easy on translating from English. Instead they concentrate on thinking in and using the new language.

8. Students are surrounded with second language. As much as possible, the teacher teaches in it.

9. Students practice in lifelike situations—asking directions, ordering a meal, shopping, and so on. That

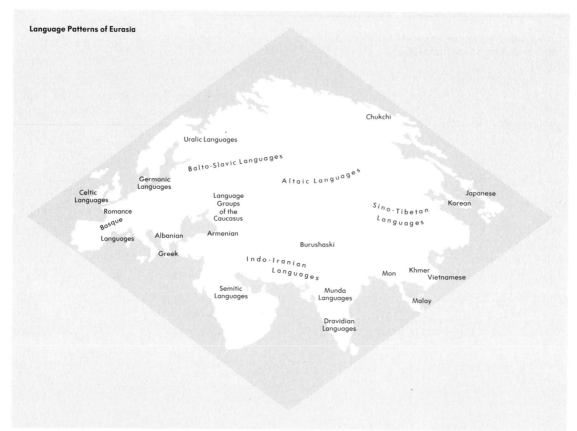

**Language Patterns of Eurasia**

Chukchi

Uralic Languages

Balto-Slavic Languages

Altaic Languages

Germanic Languages

Celtic Languages

Language Groups of the Caucasus

Japanese
Korean

Romance

Sino-Tibetan Languages

Basque Languages

Albanian

Armenian

Greek

Burushaski

Indo-Iranian Languages

Mon
Khmer
Vietnamese

Semitic Languages

Munda Languages

Malay

Dravidian Languages

The above diagram is not a language map. It is meant only to give a rough idea of language patterns in Europe and Asia.

Languages shown are not the only languages spoken in a particular area. And they are not confined to that area.

way, they get to feel the new language is as alive as their own. And they get to understand about varieties of language.

10. Students learn the body talk that goes along with language. They watch live speakers. Or they see films and videotapes. Then they practice using language and body talk together.

11. Class time is used for live language interchange—between teacher and student, between student and student. Outside time is set aside for language lab work, for practice work of various kinds.

12. Many kinds of materials are used—no one kind works best with all students. Practice materials are available for use outside of class.

13. Students use the hardware of second-language learning—a language lab, tape recorders, records, and other aids. These are sometimes used at random. But they are also part of every student's program.

14. The teacher uses many approaches to language learning. He knows the best method is the one that works with a particular student at a particular time.

15. The teacher adjusts the program to each student's abilities, especially with slow learners.

16. Classes are small—small enough for everyone to have a chance to talk every day, small enough for the teacher to get around to everyone.

17. The teacher aims for interest and excitement in materials and in the daily work.

## LINGUISTICS: THE THEORY OF THE LITTLE BLACK BOX

Linguistics is the study of language in a scientific way. But the linguist, or language scientist, has a problem. How can he study something he can't get at?

In the mind of every speaker is what might be called a mysterious little black box. And it powers the machinery of language. But the linguist can't open that box without destroying the mechanism inside. So he can't directly examine how language works. What he can do is observe the effects of that mechanism on the organs—such as the larynx and the tongue—that produce the sounds of language. And he can study those sounds—how they're made, how they fit together, what the difference sound patterns mean, and so on. That's what linguistics is mostly about.

Linguists also study how language influences people and affects society. That's called *sociolinguistics*. Another branch of linguistics is *psycholinguistics*. It deals with how language is learned and how it can be taught. *Computational linguistics* deals with computers and language. Machine translation is part of it.

# REFERENCE-OUTLINE FOR STUDY OF LANGUAGE

## LANGUAGE USAGE AND MEANINGS

I. **What language is**
  A. **Language is learned** L-114, C-481, W-308a, B-299b, C-268-9, C-495-7
  B. **Language is sounds** L-114-15, C-268-9, W-308
  C. **Language is spoken signals** L-115, L-120-1, P-268b, W-308-308a
  D. **Language is patterns of sound** L-115: tone languages L-115, diagram L-115a
  E. **Language is meaning** L-115a-b, diagram L-115: attitude, denotation, connotation L-115b; social meaning L-115b; grammatical meaning L-115b, G-168
  F. **Spoken language is not written language** L-114

II. **The sounds of language** L-114-15, picture L-114
  A. **Elements of language sounds** L-115-115a, P-268b-d: words L-115
  B. **Spoken signals:** tone languages L-115, diagram L-115a; pause and pitch L-115, diagram L-115

III. **The mechanics of language—words and word order** L-115-115a
  A. **Grammar** G-166-8: nouns N-372; pronouns P-507-8; verbs V-281-2; adjectives A-33; adverbs A-37; conjunctions C-518; prepositions P-491; phrases, idioms, and clauses L-115a, 115b, G-167, S-110-11, V-282
  B. **Effective language usage:** rhetoric R-176-7; figures of speech F-109, W-310b-c
  C. **Translation and the problems of translation** L-115b-c, diagram L-115c: machine (computer) translation L-115c, C-502e
  D. **Paralanguage** L-115c-d
  E. **Body talk** L-115d, pictures L-115d-e

IV. **Spoken language changes constantly** L-115e-f, 114, W-308b-9
  A. **Borrowing words from other languages** L-115e
  B. **New words from old within a language** L-115e
  C. **Rules of language usage change** L-115e-f

V. **Language substitutes** L-115d-e, C-481-3: written language W-306, A-284; codes and ciphers C-342a-3; International code, picture T-50; International Signal Code, pictures S-194a-b; semaphore code, pictures S-195; drums L-115d-e, C-514, D-200e; numeration systems N-379, 379c, R-248

## THE STUDY OF LANGUAGE

I. **Linguistics—the scientific study of language** L-118
II. **Etymology—study of the origin of words** E-251-2, L-153, diagram L-115f
  A. **Personal names** N-3 (nicknames N-285)
  B. **Slang** S-212, C-139
III. **Invention and development of writing** C-489-90, C-368, W-306-7, W-308, L-114, A-484-6, A-44. See also Reference-Outlines for Ancient History and Communication
  A. **Prehistoric beginnings** C-489, W-306, W-308-308a
  B. **The alphabet** A-284-7. See also each letter in Fact-Index for its history and development
IV. **Semantics—word meanings** L-115a: effect of translation L-115b-c; machine translation L-115c; propaganda C-488; usage of language changes L-115e-f
V. **The language arts** L-120-4
  A. **Listening and speaking** L-121-2, C-496, A-702, pictures L-121-2 (phonics P-268a-d): conversation C-550; debate D-43; public speaking P-526

B. **Reading** R-100-103h, L-122, P-268a-d, C-496-7, K-52-3: children's literature L-309-12, N-126i-j, R-104-11e; libraries L-206; storytelling S-460-82; folklore F-291-306. See also Reference-Outline for Literature
C. **Writing** L-122-3, W-308, 309, C-489-90, C-497, W-310: expressing thought in writing L-123-4, W-308a, W-310-12 (letter writing L-197, report writing R-151a-b)
D. **Grammar** G-166-8
  1. Sentence S-110-11: punctuation P-534; figures of speech F-109, W-310b-c
  2. Parts of speech: adjective A-33; adverb A-37; conjunction C-518; noun N-372; preposition P-491; pronoun P-507-8; verb V-281-2
  3. Spelling L-123, S-375-7: abbreviations A-4, table A-4a-b

VI. **Guidelines for the study of a second language** L-117-18: use of audio-visual devices A-702, T-17, pictures A-697, C-502e, F-360

## LANGUAGES OF THE WORLD

I. **Kinds of language** L-115f
  A. **Language** L-115f-g: language families L-115i-17, diagram L-118
  B. **Dialects—differences in speech habits** L-115f-g, 115i: geographical, social, and standard dialects L-115g
  C. **Standard (official) language of a nation or people** L-115g-h, diagram L-118
  D. **Second languages** L-115h, A-623: lingua franca L-115h; pidgin L-115h; creole L-115h
  E. **Interlanguage (world language)** L-115h-i: Volapük L-115h; Esperanto E-289, L-115h-i

II. **Indo-European languages** E-313-14, L-115i-j
  A. **Germanic (Teutonic)** T-108, L-115i, diagrams L-115i, 118: English E-251-2, E-224; German G-96, table A-286; Scandinavian (Danish, Norwegian, Swedish, Icelandic) S-52g, N-361, N-366, S-524; Afrikaans S-264; Yiddish L-115i, H-121
  B. **Romance (Latin)** R-239, L-115i-j, diagrams L-115i, 118
    1. Latin L-153-4, table A-284
    2. Modern Romance languages: French F-436; Italian I-321, I-330; Portuguese P-456; Rumanian R-318; Spanish S-365, S-353-4
  C. **Balto-Slavic (Baltic and Slavic)** S-214, 215, L-115j, diagrams L-115i-j, 118: Bulgarian B-370; Lithuanian L-313; Polish P-412; Russian R-359, R-325, table A-286
  D. **Celtic** C-185, L-115j, diagrams L-115i, 118: Irish Gaelic I-292, picture I-285; Breton F-385; Scottish Gaelic S-67; Welsh W-3
  E. **Indo-Iranian** L-115j, diagrams L-115j, 118
    1. Iranian languages L-115j: Persian P-211, I-278; Kurdish K-79; Pashto (Pushto) A-68
    2. Indic languages L-115j: Sanskrit and the dialects derived from it I-69, Fact-Index (Hindi I-69, Urdu P-78); Romany G-268; Sinhalese B-56, M-69
  F. **Greek** G-216, G-232-3, 235-6, A-285, A-44, A-485-6, diagram L-115i, table A-286
  G. **Hittite (extinct language)** H-180, A-485

III. **Uralic languages (Finno-Ugric, Samoyed)** L-115j-16, diagram L-118: Estonian E-292; Finnish F-119; Hungarian (Magyar) H-274; Lapp L-125d

IV. Altaic languages (Turkic, Mongolian, Manchu-Tungus) L-116, diagram L-118: Turkish T-301, L-115a; Tatar T-29

V. Sino-Tibetan languages L-116, diagram L-118: Burmese B-382; Chinese C-295c–d, diagram L-115a, pictures C-289, 295d; Lao L-125a; Thai T-143

VI. Austronesian (Malayo-Polynesian) L-116, diagram L-118: Hawaiian H-55; Malagasy M-23; Tagalog and Pilipino P-253b, 255a, 255b, 257c

VII. Congo-Kordofanian languages (Niger-Congo, Kordofanian) L-115b, 116, diagram L-117, map A-89: Bantu A-78, C-514. See also Africa Fact Summary

VIII. Afroasiatic (Semitic, Berber, Cushitic, Chad) L-116, diagram L-118: Arabic A-469, E-109–10, K-79, A-285, table A-286; Hebrew H-120–1, table A-286; Amharic E-294; Coptic E-110, Fact-Index

IX. Other language families L-116–17, diagram L-118
   A. Dravidian I-69, L-116, diagram L-118
   B. Munda I-69, L-116, diagram L-118
   C. Japanese J-390, 365, 376, L-115a, 115c, W-307, A-285, diagrams L-115c, 118, pictures J-390
   D. Korean K-76b, 75e, diagram L-118, table K-76b
   E. Basque S-354, L-116, diagram L-118
   F. In the Caucasus Mountains L-116, diagram L-118
   G. American Indian (Amerindian) language families L-117, I-133–8, W-306a, picture F-182, table I-136–7: Aztec A-839; Eskimo E-288; Mayan M-180, A-486, W-306b, picture W-306a

## BIBLIOGRAPHY FOR LANGUAGE

### Books for Children

Adler, Irving and Joyce. Language and Man (John Day, 1970).

Alexander, Arthur. The Magic of Words (Prentice, 1962).

Davidson, Jessica. What I Tell You Three Times Is True (McCall, 1970).

Dugan, William. How Our Alphabet Grew (Golden Press, 1972).

Epstein, Samuel and Beryl. The First Book of Words (Watts, 1954).

Frimmer, Steven. The Stone That Spoke and Other Clues to the Decipherment of Lost Languages (Putnam, 1969).

Hofsinde, Robert. Indian Sign Language (Morrow, 1956).

Ludovici, L. J. Origins of Language (Putnam, 1965).

Ogg, Oscar. The 26 Letters, rev. ed. (Crowell, 1971).

Scott, J. H. and Lenore. Hieroglyphs for Fun (Van Nostrand-Reinhold, 1974).

Selsam, M. E. The Language of Animals (Morrow, 1962).

Showers, Paul. How You Talk (Crowell, 1975).

Thomson, D. S. and others. Language (Time-Life, 1975).

Wolff, Diane. Chinese Writing (Holt, 1975).

### Books for Young Adults and Teachers

Bernstein, T. M. The Careful Writer: a Modern Guide to English Usage (Atheneum, 1977).

Chase, Stuart. Danger—Men Talking! A Background Book for Young People on Semantics and Communication (Parents, 1969).

Fowler, H. W. A Dictionary of Modern English Usage, 2d ed. rev. (Oxford, 1965).

Gallant, R. A. Man Must Speak (Random, 1969).

Garrison, Webb. What's in a Word? (Abingdon, 1975).

Hayakawa, S. I. Language in Thought and Action, 3d ed. (Harcourt, 1972).

Helfman, E. S. Signs and Symbols Around the World (Lothrop, 1967).

Hendry, J. F. Your Future in Translating and Interpreting (Rosen, 1969).

Laird, Helene and Charlton. The Tree of Language (Collins, 1977).

Lenneberg, E. H., ed. New Directions in the Study of Language (MIT Press, 1964).

Norman, James. Ancestral Voices: Decoding Ancient Languages (Scholastic, 1975).

Partridge, Eric. A Dictionary of Slang and Unconventional English, 7th ed. (Macmillan, 1970).

Pei, Mario. All About Language (Lippincott, 1954).

Pei, Mario. The Story of the English Language, rev. ed. (Lippincott, 1967).

Rogers, Frances. Painted Rock to Printed Page (Lippincott, 1960).

(See also bibliographies for Ciphers and Codes; Communication; Phonics; Reference Books, subhead "Selected List of Modern Dictionaries"; Spelling.)

### Learning Foreign Languages

Colyer, Penrose. I Can Read Spanish (Watts, 1976).

Cooper, Lee. Fun with German (Little, 1965).

Feelings, Muriel. Jumbo Means Hello: Swahili Alphabet Book (Dial, 1974).

Hautzig, Esther. At Home: a Visit in Four Languages (Macmillan, 1968).

Hautzig, Esther. In School: Learning in Four Languages (Macmillan, 1969).

Joslin, Sesyle and Barry, Katharina. There Is a Bull on My Balcony (Harcourt, 1966).

Maeda, Jun. Let's Study Japanese (C. E. Tuttle, 1965).

Magocsi, P. R. Let's Speak Rusyn (Transworld, 1976).

Pays francophones, film (Encyclopaedia Britannica Films).

Pei, Mario. Talking Your Way Around the World, 3d ed. (Harper, 1971).

Viajando por México y España, film (Encyclopaedia Britannica Films).

Wiese, Kurt. You Can Write Chinese (Viking Press, 1945).

# Putting the Communication Skills Together

**LANGUAGE ARTS.** Writing is a communication skill. So is reading. So are speaking and listening. The language arts program in elementary school puts them all together. In high school, another name for the same kind of program is English studies. (See also Communication; Communication Skills.)

Children learn best when they use what they learn. So the emphasis in language arts programs is on using language skills—and using them in a meaningful way. Thus, children spend more time writing than they spend in the study of writing.

Children also learn best when they can associate ideas. So language arts programs interweave language arts as much as possible. An example is the language experience approach to reading. A child tells the teacher about an experience he had. The teacher prints the story on a large chart. And from that chart, the child learns to read back his own words. Later on, he himself writes his stories and shares them with his classmates. Thus he learns the importance of speaking clearly, organizing thoughts, spelling, handwriting, and punctuation.

In learning a language, a child begins with listening and speaking. Later on, typically in the first years of school, he learns to read the written code

> This article was contributed by Carl B. Smith, Director, Measurement and Evaluation Center in Reading Education, Indiana University.

of language. Finally he learns to write his thoughts and make them understandable to others. The order in which language arts develop shows how important the home background is. It shapes the child's listening and speaking habits. It helps him develop the spoken language skills he will need for reading and writing. It forms his vocabulary and the way he puts words together.

## Listening

Listening is the first language art a child develops. Children—and adults—spend more time listening than they do speaking, reading, or writing.

Being able to speak and read well depends partly on listening. Children have to hear sounds clearly in order to speak them clearly. And a child needs the memory of those sounds to help him sound out words in reading. (*See also* Reading; Phonics.)

But the art of listening takes practice. Children sometimes practice listening to street sounds on a record. Then they pick out a sound, describe it, and tell what probably made it. Sometimes teachers ask children how word groups like *grump, groan,* and *grind* are alike. These kinds of exercises help children identify sounds in words.

Just hearing and understanding words is not enough, though. Children also need practice in critical listening. This helps them remember and weigh the value of a speaker's ideas. Critical listening is sometimes hard. A reader can adjust his reading speed to the difficulty of the ideas in a book. But someone listening to radio or TV has no control over the speed of the speaker.

## Speaking

Most communication is through speaking and listening, especially in the early grades. And both reading and writing are based partly on the skills of spoken language.

One goal of the language arts program is to have children express and compare ideas. So children are encouraged to speak freely on matters of interest to them. Teachers promote discussions and debates. And they have children tell about their experiences. Thus children learn to organize their thoughts. They learn to speak clearly and in ways that are easy to understand.

Teachers also set up real or make-believe speaking situations. Children make introductions, talk on a play telephone, give directions to someone who is lost, etc. These activities help polish speaking skills.

Literature is often read aloud in language arts programs. Younger children act out stories they already know. Or they dramatize experiences they have had. Such activities strengthen reading as well as speaking skills. And they help build an appreciation of literature.

Children tend to speak in the home or neighborhood dialect. They can express their ideas more easily that way. And it's important that the teacher ac-

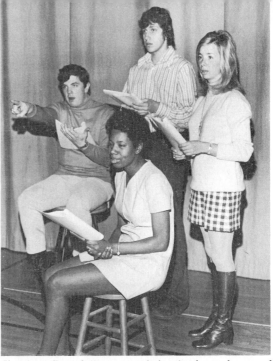

Choral reading of literature unlocks the frozen beauty of printed language. It involves several language arts.
National College of Education

cept that home dialect. The teacher must not say— or imply—that the child's way of speaking is wrong. It really isn't wrong. *He tired,* for instance, is just another way of saying *he is tired.* Neither way is more correct than the other. (*See also* Grammar.)

Another thing, a child's home dialect is an important part of him. To reject the way he talks is to reject him—not to mention his family, friends, and neighbors. And a rejected child is not a child who's going to learn very much.

Still, teachers must help children learn standard English, in which most books are written. Some teachers turn children's home dialect sentences into standard English. Then they have the children repeat the standard sentences. Some teachers just

Listening to the sounds of words and word patterns will help these kindergartners recognize them in print later on.

National College of Education

121

turn home dialect sentences into standard English without having the child repeat. These teachers feel that the child will begin to imitate standard English sooner or later. Some teachers give children pattern drill in standard English. Children repeat spoken sentence patterns, using tape recorders and other such equipment.

## Reading—The Heart of the Language Arts Program

Reading is the heart of most language arts programs. Most efforts to tie the language arts together build listening, speaking, and writing exercises around a reading selection. In most schools, reading is still a separate course. But the trend is to teach it as part of language development in general.

The reading program usually begins with reading readiness activities. Children are encouraged to talk or draw. Or they listen to stories and follow picture stories. Such activities prepare children to decode words and to follow events in a story. (*See also* Reading.)

Reading is often taught with a series of textbooks called *readers*. Many beginning textbooks help build a vocabulary of words that can be recognized on sight. They also help build skills to recognize new words with. These word analysis skills include phonics and context clues (*see* Phonics; Reading). The goal is for the child to understand the printed page. Skills are developed to the point where he can pretty much read on his own. When a child has a reading problem the teacher can't handle, a reading specialist is called in. The specialist uses various tests to diagnose the problem and suggests a possible solution.

Learning to read is important. But learning to appreciate literature is just as important in the language arts program. So language arts teachers are concerned with what children read as well as how they read. Fortunately, an enormous selection of good literature is available at all reading levels. (*See also* Reading/Books for Children; Reading/Books for Young Adults.)

Teachers today try to make reading personal, to tailor it as much as possible to each child. Children have different tastes, different interests. And they learn differently. So the teacher must not only use different approaches to teaching reading but must also use different kinds of reading material.

Reading in special subjects requires a special vocabulary. It also requires special skills. So children are taught how to read in social studies, and science, and math. (*See also* Reading.) They are also taught how to use reference books of various kinds (*see* Reference Books; "How to Use Compton's" at beginning of Vol. 1).

## Handwriting

A child should write legibly. Otherwise no one can read what he puts on paper. Children usually begin by learning to print the letters of the alphabet. Later they are shown how to form letters in cursive script. Today, handwriting practice is related to spelling and reading. Writing exercises help show the connection between letters and the corresponding sounds in words.

Print is called the manuscript alphabet. Most authorities believe that manuscript writing is easier than cursive writing for young children. Many young children do not yet have full control over the small muscles. So it is difficult for them to form the cursive letters. Practice in manuscript writing also helps children recognize the printed letters they read in books.

Children usually print in the first and second grades. As they gain control of the manuscript

A second grader (below) reads out loud. This helps him translate unfamiliar written symbols into the familiar sounds and patterns of speech. At right, a girl is absorbed in reading a good book—one of the things language arts instruction is all about.

Children learn spelling patterns by seeing them, listening to them, and writing them down.

Imperial International Learning

forms, they are shifted gradually to cursive. Little time is spent in teaching or practicing handwriting after the third grade. And then it is mostly a matter of correcting individual handwriting problems. (*See also* Writing, Communication by.)

## Spelling

Spelling is important in writing. Poor spelling may confuse a reader. Or it may turn him away. Or it may cast doubts on the value and accuracy of what the writer has to say.

Learning to spell is not memorizing words in a list. Teachers today work with spelling patterns like *cat, fat, sat* or *date, hate, late*. The patterns are then related to reading. Children are helped to see that a speller writes a word in a code, and that a reader decodes that word. In either case, the same pattern is used. The pattern approach helps children sound out, read, and spell new words. (*See also* Spelling.)

Spelling improves when children know the meaning of the words they spell. It also improves when the spelling words are taken from the child's own writing. Other than that, it's not so much a question of which spelling words to teach. It's a question of which spelling patterns to teach. Learning to spell individual words is useful. And it's sometimes necessary because not all words fit a spelling pattern. But most words do fit a pattern. So learning the patterns makes it possible to spell an almost unlimited number of words. Schools also teach children how to use a dictionary, the speller's best friend.

Parents can help a child improve his spelling by giving him practice. He can write the grocery list his mother dictates. Or he can make up a list of school supplies he needs before school begins. Or he can be asked to write a thank-you note. He can also learn spelling by using guide words in dictionaries and encyclopedias.

## Composition

Listening and reading are ways of receiving ideas. Written and oral composition are ways of sending them. Oral composition is spoken instead of written. Some form of it is done at all grade levels. But it is more common in the early grades, where the skills of written composition have not yet been fully developed.

Children use language best when they have something to say. Both home and school should provide opportunities for speaking. A teacher should not forbid talking, but encourage it. This does not mean the teacher need allow idle chatter. But he can make it easy for children who want to discuss interests, books, projects, etc. He can provide a comfortable atmosphere for speaking and oral composition of all kinds.

A writer does his best writing about something he knows, something he has experienced. That's why many teachers encourage children to draw on their own backgrounds for writing. Teachers also try to provide children with more experiences. Children go on nature walks and field trips to various places of interest. They are shown films, filmstrips, videotapes, etc. Tapes and records are played for them to listen to. And all the while, they are prompted to use their senses—to see, hear, smell, touch, and taste. Afterwards, the children talk about their experiences. And they write about their experiences.

A first-grade teacher writes on an experience chart as a pupil dictates to her.

National College of Education

123

A class newspaper provides practice in all the language arts for these eighth graders.

National College of Education

Sooner or later almost everyone has to write letters—letters of invitation, thank-you notes, etc. Language arts classes arrange writing experiences around simple—and natural—situations such as these. Writing is also arranged around book reports, science reports, and the class or school newspaper. These strengthen handwriting, spelling, and reading skills as well as those of composition.

Children need to know how to write in different forms. They need to do information-type writing such as reports. And they need to do creative writing. (*See also* Writing, Communication by; Writing, Creative.) A child must learn to choose the form that lends itself best to what he is trying to say.

One of the biggest problems facing teachers today is how to correct and grade compositions. Two extremes can be found. There is the teacher who is afraid to correct anything for fear he will hamper the child's creativity. And there is the teacher who marks all errors of spelling, punctuation, etc., without giving any constructive guidance.

A more effective approach lies somewhere between the two extremes. Creativity and unhampered expression are vital. But communication is still the primary reason for most writing. And some of the tools of written communication need to be shaped and sharpened. By the time he leaves elementary school, the child should know how sentences are formed. He should know standard punctuation. He should know how to construct a paragraph. He should know the standard English equivalents for common nonstandard usages. Much of what the pupil needs to know can be taught through actual writing. But this must be followed by a discussion of other, possibly better, ways of saying the same thing.

One technique now used for grading is a rating scale that indicates how effective the composition is. Number 1 on the scale means no communication at the sentence level. Number 5 means communication with impact and originality, and with excellent use of the mechanics of composition.

**LANIER** (*la-nēr′*), **Sidney** (1842–1881). Despite years of sickness and financial hardship, Lanier became a fine poet and a musician of rare ability.

Sidney Lanier was born Feb. 3, 1842, in Macon, Ga. As a boy he loved to play the flute and to read and write poetry. He graduated from Oglethorpe University in 1860. When the Civil War began he joined the Confederate army. In 1864 he was captured and held in a disease-ridden Union prison. He probably contracted tuberculosis there—the disease from which he died.

Culver Pictures

He married in 1867 and moved to Baltimore, Md., in 1873. There the Peabody Symphony Orchestra engaged him as a flutist. He knew that he had only a few years to live. He decided to devote himself to music and poetry. He was a master of English rhythms and the melody of English sounds. This is shown in his rollicking 'Song of the Chattahoochee' and the somber 'Marshes of Glynn'.

Lanier's best-known works are 'Tiger-Lilies: A Novel' (1867); 'Poems' (1876, 1884, 1891); 'Florida: Its Scenery, Climate, and History' (1876); 'The Boy's Froissart' (1878); 'The Science of English Verse' (1880); and 'Music and Poetry' (1898).

THESE ARTICLES ARE IN THE FACT-INDEX

Lankester, Sir Edwin Ray
Lansdale, Pa.
Lansdowne, Henry Charles Keith Petty-Fitzmaurice, 5th marquis of
Lansdowne, Henry Petty-Fitzmaurice, 3d marquis of
Lansdowne, Md.
Lansdowne, Pa.
Lansing, Robert
Lansing, Ill.

## UNIVERSITY AND GOVERNMENT CENTER

The Beaumont carillon bell tower (left) is a landmark on the Michigan State University campus. It is a meeting place for students and faculty. This air view (right) shows the business center of the city, with the tower of the Capitol Building at the upper left center. The Grand River and countless trees help make Lansing a beautiful city.

**LANSING, Mich.** The capital of Michigan is Lansing. It was settled in the 1830's on densely wooded land. The first industry was lumbering. In 1847 the state capital was moved to Lansing from Detroit. It then consisted only of a sawmill and a log cabin.

A plank road to Detroit was open in 1852, and the first rail line reached the town in the 1870's.

Forests were cleared from the countryside, and farms were started. The townspeople began making horse-drawn vehicles. In the 1900's, under the leadership of Ransom E. Olds, the manufacture of automobiles and trucks was begun. Lansing soon became an industrial center, with metalworking the leading industry. Today its Oldsmobile and Fisher Body plants are nationally known. Other factories make automotive parts, farm tools, machinery, and refrigerating units. Lansing is also a trade center for the fertile farming area of south-central Michigan.

The city lies in a shallow, cuplike valley formed by the Grand and Red Cedar rivers. The business area and the ten-acre capitol park are set in the city's center, atop a slight elevation bordered on three sides by the Grand. The Capitol was completed in 1879. It contains the War Relic Museum and the state library. Nearby are the Lewis Cass and Stevens T. Mason state office buildings.

On the fringe of the downtown business district is the Civic Center, dedicated in 1955. In Lansing are the Michigan Historical Commission Museum, a replica of Mount Vernon, George Washington's home; Kresge Art Center; Lansing Community College; a state school for the blind; and a state vocational school for boys. The city has about 35 parks, including Arboretum Park, with its flower gardens and nature trails, and Potter Park, which contains a zoo.

East Lansing, which is separately incorporated, adjoins the capital city. It is the home of Michigan State University of Agriculture and Applied Science, opened in 1857, the first agricultural school in the United States.

Lansing was chartered as a city in 1859. It owns its water and electric supply systems and a sewage-disposal plant. It has the mayor-council form of government. (*See also* Michigan.) Population (1980 census), 130,414.

---

THIS ARTICLE IS IN THE FACT-INDEX

**Lanston, Tolbert**

---

**LANTANA.** A garden flower useful as a perennial border and in window boxes and hanging baskets is the lantana. It is a member of the verbena family (*Verbenaceae*). The blossoms grow in dense, nearly flat-topped heads. The colors of the lantana are usually yellow or pink when the flower first opens, changing to orange or scarlet.

The plant is native to tropical America, north to Texas and southern Georgia. In the wild it may grow into a shrub ten feet high. The cultivated lantanas of temperate climates are usually dwarf forms. The lantana has been introduced into India, Ceylon, and the state of Hawaii. In Hawaii it has become a noxious weed, and insects are imported to prey on it.

---

THESE ARTICLES ARE IN THE FACT-INDEX

| | |
|---|---|
| Lantern fish | Laodicea |
| Lanuvium, Italy | Laomedon |
| Laoag, Philippines | Laon, France |
| 'Laocoon' | |

---

125

Black Star

The historic palace of the Laotian royal family sits beside the Mekong River. In the garden grows the lush tropical vegetation of a hot, rainy region.

**LAOS.** The People's Democratic Republic of Laos is the only country of Southeast Asia without an outlet to the sea. The former kingdom occupies a rugged central strip of the Indochinese peninsula, surrounded by Vietnam on the east, Cambodia on the south, Thailand on the west, Burma on the northwest, and the People's Republic of China on the north. (For map, *see* Indochina.)

This country of 91,429 square miles is commonly divided into two parts—Upper and Lower Laos. Upper Laos is a roughly circular region of highlands, rising to 6,500 feet in height. The chief ridges run from north to south, separating the narrow valleys of swift-flowing streams. In places the valleys broaden into small alluvial basins.

Lower Laos is a slender panhandle for the wider upper section. Its eastern border lies along the crest of the Annamite Chain, where elevations reach more than 8,000 feet. Passes cut through the range. The lowest is only 1,600 feet above sea level. Most of Lower Laos consists of several plateaus. Those underlaid by limestone are eroded into fantastic formations of the type known as *karst*. The Bolovens Plateau in the far southeast is underlaid by volcanic basalt. Its fertile, reddish soils are well suited for such plantation crops as rubber.

### The Mekong River and Its Valleys

The Mekong is the master stream of Laos. Although it flows along the edge of the country, most Laotian rivers drain into it. In Upper Laos its deep valley forms the boundary with Burma. At about 18° N. latitude the Mekong curves eastward then southward in a gigantic bend which forms most of the boundary with Thailand. Flood plains of varying width are found along the streams. These lowlands are the most fertile areas of Laos. Most of the highland and plateau soils are thin and poor. The highlands support forests. Savanna vegetation and coarse grasses are found on the plateaus and lowlands.

The monsoon climate in Laos varies with altitude and latitude. In the lowlands it is hot the year around and there is an all-year growing season. In the uplands the nights grow cool and frost is known at the highest elevations. Differences in seasonal temperatures are greater in Upper Laos than in Lower Laos. The chief seasonal contrast is between the wet season, from May to October, and the dry season, from November to April. Rainfall varies from 40 to 80 inches annually in the lowlands and is higher in the uplands. More than 80 percent falls in the wet season.

### The Peoples of Laos

In this setting live 3,383,000 people (1976 estimate). More than half are the Lao or Lao-Thai, who speak virtually the same language as the Thai and live mainly in the lowlands. The hill peoples may be classed in three groups: Thai tribes, who believe in spirits rather than in Buddhism; the Miao and Man, who have migrated from southwest China in the past 100 years; and tribes who speak Indonesian languages and are known collectively as Kha (savages). There are also a few thousand Vietnamese and some Chinese town dwellers.

The typical Lao village is strung along a road or a stream. Houses are raised on timber stilts. They have steep thatched roofs and verandas. Animals find shelter beneath the houses. Tropical fruit trees and vegetable gardens grow nearby. Rice fields surround the village.

The Lao, like the Thai, are Theravada (or Hinayana) Buddhists. Village life has long centered about the temple, with its guesthouse, monastery, and monastery school. Each Lao youth traditionally spends some time as a Buddhist monk, with shaven head, saffron robe, and begging bowl. Buddhism prevails, but there is widespread belief in spirits, called *phu*.

Physically the Lao resemble the Thai of Thailand. They are slight in stature and graceful. They have light-brown skin and black hair. Typical Lao clothing consists of a saronglike garment, worn by both men and women, and a blouse or jacket. Shoes are seldom worn.

The diet is barely adequate. It consists chiefly of rice combined with a pungent fish sauce. Little meat is eaten, largely because of Buddhist beliefs.

Only a few Laotians live in cities or large towns. There is little manufacturing to offer employment, and most trade is carried on by Chinese. Vientiane, the national capital, has a population of 176,637 (1973 census). Luang Prabang, formerly the dynastic capital, has a population of 43,924. Thakhek, Savannakhet, and Pakse are regional centers.

Most Laotians depend upon agriculture for a livelihood, though less than 6 percent of the country is under permanent cultivation. Rice accounts for about 90 percent of the permanently tilled acreage. Also raised are corn, potatoes, tobacco, citrus fruits, coffee, tea, and plants yielding spices and drugs, especially opium poppies.

Each village aims to meet its own needs. Weaving, basketmaking, forest gathering, and fishing help supply its wants. Some lumbering is carried on. Tin is produced in Lower Laos.

### Transportation and Trade

The Mekong River system is the chief transportation route, though it is only partly navigable. Between Vientiane and Savannakhet it can handle vessels up to 200 tons. Navigation on other sections is hampered or blocked by shallows, rapids, and falls.

In 1956 the Thai railroad system was extended to the Mekong, near Vientiane. This provided Upper Laos with access to the sea through Bangkok. Good roads are scarce.

### Political History

Laos came into history in the 9th century as Thai-speaking peoples moved southward from China. The powerful kingdom of Lan Xang was founded in the 14th century. It split into the kingdoms of Vientiane and Luang Prabang in the 18th century. In 1828 Vientiane was destroyed by Thailand.

The French established a protectorate over the kingdom of Luang Prabang in 1893 and governed the rest of Laos as a colony. The Japanese occupied Indochina in World War II. The French recognized the king of Luang Prabang as king of all Laos before they returned in 1946. In 1953 Laos became independent. Both Communist and Western nations recognized its neutrality. Its two northernmost provinces, however, were controlled by Communists. Military and technical aid came from North Vietnam and China.

In keeping with its policy of halting Communist expansion in Southeast Asia, the United States gave massive aid to the anti-Communist government. The Royal Laotian Army, however, was unable to stem the advances of the pro-Communist Pathet Lao forces, and by early 1961 the Communists controlled much of the country. In May a cease-fire was signed. A coalition government of neutralist, Communist, and pro-Western factions was formed in June 1962. In July, 14 nations signed a pact guaranteeing the neutrality of Laos. All foreign troops were ordered removed. United States forces withdrew, but the International Control Commission found no evidence that North Vietnamese troops had left.

Three Lions        Black Star

Two women in Laotian dress (left) shop in a market. The baby rides in a sling on his mother's back. The man, a member of the Lu tribe, carries produce in a basket hung from a yoke.

Prince Souvanna Phouma, neutralist premier of the coalition government, failed to get cooperation among the contending factions. Political assassinations and military and political coups harassed the government. The Pathet Lao and its North Vietnamese allies fought to extend and strengthen their control over Laotian territory. Their grip on the strategic corridor paralleling the Vietnamese border enabled them to protect the Ho Chi Minh Trail, the network of jungle trails over which North Vietnam sent men and arms to South Vietnam.

Souvanna sanctioned the bombing of the trail by United States planes. The Royal Laotian Air Force bombed the trail and Pathet Lao positions. The premier's position became stronger when a rightist coup failed in 1965.

In 1968 the Pathet Lao dislodged royalist troops from their last position on South Vietnam's frontier. By 1968 about one tenth of the Laotian people were refugees from areas held by the Pathet Lao. In 1969 and 1970 government and Pathet Lao military activity increased. In 1971 a South Vietnamese invasion into southern Laos failed to cut North Vietnamese supply routes along the Ho Chi Minh Trail. In 1973 the Laotian government and the Pathet Lao signed a peace pact setting up a coalition government, which was established in April 1974.

In late 1975, after Communist victories in Vietnam and Cambodia, the Pathet Lao took full control. With the proclamation of the People's Democratic Republic of Laos, both the coalition regime and the monarchy were abolished. Premier Souvanna resigned. (*See also* Vietnam Conflict.)

---

THIS ARTICLE IS IN THE FACT-INDEX
**Lao-tse**

## LA PAZ, Bolivia.

The highest government seat in the world is La Paz, Bolivia. It lies 12,400 feet above sea level in a deep gorge cut in the Andean Plateau by the La Paz River. Snowclad peaks of the Cordillera Real (Royal Range) on the east give it a magnificent setting. Mount Illimani (21,185 feet) sweeps directly above the city like a stage back-drop.

La Paz is Bolivia's unofficial capital. Although Sucre is the official capital, only the Supreme Court meets there. A crossroads between the interior and the sea, La Paz is the country's largest city and the center of industry, commerce, and culture.

### An Up and Down City

The traveler approaches La Paz by El Alto Airport on the plateau. The tableland stops abruptly, and a long narrow canyon opens out. Its walls slope almost straight down to a green-floored valley, 4,000 feet below, where the city lies.

The main street is Avenida 16 de Julio, popularly known as the Prado (for picture, see Bolivia). Along the Prado are the modern hotels, shops, restaurants, and theaters. Here the people stroll in the evenings and on holidays, while the military band plays in a plaza at one end and the municipal band plays in a plaza at the other end. Indians, the women wearing shawls and odd derby hats, and an occasional llama train add color to the scene.

The Prado is part of a series of avenues, actually the same street but with different names, linked by plazas. Near Plaza Roma is the University of San Andres, housed in a 16-story skyscraper. On Plaza

**THE LOFTY CITY OF LA PAZ**
La Paz lies 12,400 feet above sea level in a deep river-carved gorge. Snowy Mount Illimani (21,185 feet) rises above the city.

Tamayo is the national library. Across the La Paz River from the Prado is Plaza Murillo. On this broad square are the huge cathedral, the Presidential Palace, and the national Capitol. A few blocks away is the big Indian market.

The manufacture of textiles is the chief industry. There are flour mills, breweries, and a match factory. In small home workshops the people make jewelry and wood carvings.

The Spanish conquerors founded La Paz in 1548. The name (*Paz* is Spanish for "peace") reflects the desire at the time to encourage trade along the route between the old Inca capital at Cuzco and the Potosí silver mines. Population (1961 estimate), 350,142.

THESE ARTICLES ARE IN THE FACT-INDEX
La Paz, Mexico
La Peltrie, Marie Madeleine de
La Pérouse, Jean François de Galaup, count de

**LAPLACE** (*là-plàs'*), **Marquis de** (1749–1827). One of the most brilliant astronomers in history was Pierre Simon Laplace. This Frenchman predicted many things with mathematics that men were to see later with powerful telescopes.

Pierre Simon Laplace was born March 28, 1749, in Beaumont-en-Auge, a village in Normandy. His father was poor, and Pierre could have expected only a little education. Wealthy neighbors took an interest in him and sent him to the university at Caen. There he made a fine record in mathematics. At 18 he went to Paris with a letter of introduction to Jean Le Rond d'Alembert, a leading mathematician. D'Alembert refused to see him, so Laplace sent him an outline of mathematical principles. This deeply impressed d'Alembert, and he helped the young man to a position as professor of mathematics at the École Militaire.

One of Laplace's first investigations was to disprove the notion that the moon would some day crash into the earth. From this work grew one of his great principles—that variations in the movements of planets are regular and predictable.

With Joseph Lagrange, another mathematician, Laplace reviewed the studies made since Isaac Newton's time on gravitational forces in the universe. Then he wrote 'Mécanique céleste' ('Celestial Mechanics'), issued in five volumes from 1799 to 1825. A condensed version contained his *nebular hypothesis*, a theory of the origin of the solar system (*see* Earth). Laplace won many awards for his studies, but he remained humble. Before his death he said, "What we know is little. What we know not is immense."

LAPLAND
Indefinite
Boundary

Lapland is not a nation but an area across northern Scandinavia, Finland, and western Russia occupied by the Lapp people.

**LAPLAND.** The region called Lapland lies across Arctic Norway, Sweden, Finland, and western Russia. The Lapps have no country of their own but are considered to be citizens of the country in which they maintain permanent villages.

The origin of the Lapps is uncertain. They are believed to be a Mongoloid people who migrated northwestward from Siberia near Lake Baikal (Baykal) long ago. They speak a Finno-Ugric language related to that of the Finns and Hungarians. In their own tongue they are the Same (sä′mē), or Samelats.

They are Europe's smallest people, averaging only 4½ to 5 feet tall. They are stocky in build, strong and agile, and fair-skinned and blue-eyed.

### A Nomadic Life of Herding Reindeer

The traditional way of life is nomadic. The Lapps live by herding reindeer. They go wherever the animals can find lichens (reindeer moss) to eat. Reindeer provide the people with milk, cheese, and meat for food and skins for tents, blankets, moccasins, leggings, and harnesses. From the sinews they make thread, cord, and braided lassos. Bones and antlers are carved into tools and household utensils. To foreigners they sell sinew, for use as surgical thread, and reindeer hair, for stuffing life belts.

When they are following the grazing herds, the Lapps live in a tent of skins stretched over poles. There is a smoke hole about four feet in diameter in the center of the top. Dried reindeer meat and fish hang from overhead poles. The smoke from cooking fires helps cure and preserve these meats. Reindeer-drawn sleds, called *pulkas*, provide transportation over frozen rivers and plains. Many prosperous Lapps own outboard motorboats for summer travel.

Their dress is very colorful. They wear bright blue pull-over tunics, decorated with red and yellow trim, and wide leather belts. The women don fringed shawls and gay red and blue bonnets. The men wear blue breeches and large four-cornered blue caps with red pompons. They use no stockings inside the reindeer-hide moccasins but pack fresh hay around their bare feet. Pounded to a silky soft consistency and changed every day, the hay provides perfect insulation and absorbs perspiration.

Most of the Lapps today are only partially nomadic. The men, in addition to owning reindeer herds, are engaged in fishing or farming. They work in the iron

**REINDEER TAXIS MEET THE AIRLINER**

These Lapps (left) are in front of the airport at Rovaniemi, Finland. Notice the sleds, called pulkas. Shaped like a boat, they have a single runner. The men wear loose, belted tunics, leather moccasins with pointed, upturned toes, and four-cornered caps. The women (right) wear the same kind of moccasins and tunics and colorful shawls, hoods, and mittens.

mines and in the lumber and pulp mills. In the winter they live in permanent villages in cabins of hand-hewn logs. A wooden church, usually Lutheran, and a school are found in every village. Town meetings are held in which such problems as grazing and fishing rights are settled with the authorities of the country in which they live.

The Lapps number about 38,000. Some 25,000 of them live in Norway. There are about 10,000 in Sweden and 2,500 in Finland. Only a few of these people remain in the Soviet Union.

THESE ARTICLES ARE IN THE FACT-INDEX

La Plata, Argentina     Laramie, Jacques
La Porte, Ind.     Laramie, Wyo.
La Puente, Calif.     Larboard
Lapwing

**LARCH.** The larch is unusual among conifers because its needlelike leaves are shed each year. About ten species of larch are widely distributed throughout the Northern Hemisphere. Of these, four grow in North America.

Photographs, U.S. Forest Service

The western larch has very fine needles, arranged in dense whorls on a short stem attached to the branch. They are light green. The cones are broad and short. The tree (left) has an open, spirelike type of growth. The trunk is very straight.

The eastern larch is called the American tamarack, or hackmatack. It grows in the Great Lakes and New England states, in Alaska, and throughout Canada east of the Rocky Mountains as far north as the Arctic Ocean. In its northern range it thrives on well-drained uplands. In the Great Lakes and New England areas it is found more commonly in swamps. It is a slender, graceful tree, 40 to 80 feet tall and 1 to 2 feet in diameter. The threadlike needles are triangular and arranged in whorled bunches. The tree matures in 100 to 200 years.

The western larch is a much larger tree, growing to a height of 100 to 180 feet, with a diameter of 3 to 4 feet. It reaches maturity in 300 to 400 years. Trees over 700 years old have been reported. The strong, tough resinous wood is used for railroad ties, fence posts, telephone and telegraph poles, and boats. The western and small alpine larches grow on mountain slopes in a limited area in the northwestern states (except Alaska) and British Columbia.

The Alaska larch is a small tree restricted to coastal Alaska. The common European larch is planted in the eastern states for ornamental purposes and for reforestation projects.

The larches belong to the genus *Larix* of the pine family (*Pinaceae*). Their scientific names are tamarack, *Larix laricina;* western larch, *L. occidentalis;* alpine larch, *L. lyalli;* Alaska larch, *L. alaskensis;* and European larch, *L. decidua.*

THESE ARTICLES ARE IN THE FACT-INDEX

Larcom, Lucy     Largetooth aspen
Lardner, Ring(gold     Larghetto
  Wilmer)     Largo, Fla.
Laredo, Tex.     Largs, Scotland
Lares     Lárisa, Greece

**LARK.** The lark is primarily a bird of the Old World. Only one species, the horned lark, is native to North America. The meadowlark and the pipit, sometimes called titlark, are not true larks (*see* Meadowlark; Titlark).

All larks wear modest coats of brown streaked with dark brown or black. The breast is buff, yellow, or white, with dark streaks. The outer tail feathers are white. The horned lark has two black tufts on the top of the head and black patches on head, cheeks, and throat. Throat and eyestreaks may be yellow. (For picture in color, *see* Birds.)

Larks nest on the ground in open fields and prairies. They rarely perch on trees. As they move over fields in search of grain and insects they walk instead of hop. The male usually sings on the wing.

The larks form the family *Alaudidae*. The skylark (*Alauda arvensis*) is widely distributed across Europe and Asia. The bird has been introduced into the United States but has never established itself there. On Vancouver Island, British Columbia, however, it has become a resident.

The horned lark (*Eremophila alpestris*) is also widely distributed. It ranges from Alaska and the

**HORNED LARK AT THE NEST**
This horned lark stands near its hungry young in a nest on the ground. The black ear tufts, or "horns," show plainly.

Arctic coast of Canada to northern Europe and Asia and south to Egypt and Africa in the Eastern Hemisphere and to South America in the Western Hemisphere. The horned lark migrates in winter from the more northern parts of its range. There are 21 subspecies in North America.

THIS ARTICLE IS IN THE FACT-INDEX
**Lark sparrow**

**LARKSPUR.** The tall blue and purple spires that border garden walls and paths are known to gardeners as *Delphinium*. The Greeks so named the flower because they thought the long black sepal resembled a dolphin. This sepal also resembles the rear toenail of a lark's foot, hence the name "larkspur."

**"GLITTERS," A VARIETY OF LARKSPUR**
The tall blue spires of the larkspurs make beautiful backgrounds and accents in the perennial border of the garden.

The blossoms grow compactly around a stalk from 18 inches to 6 feet high, which rises above low-growing decorative leaves. Blue is the predominating color, but there are also shades of purple, white, yellow, pink, and rose. The larkspurs are annual and perennial flowers, native to cool, temperate regions north of the equator. There are about 150 species, of which some 60 are represented in North America. They form the genus *Delphinium* of the crowfoot family, *Ranunculaceae*.

The annual larkspurs grow wild from coast to coast. They fall into two general groups—the rocket, or spikelike, forms and the candelabrum, with a number of short spired heads of different heights. These are poisonous to cattle.

Native to the Mississippi Valley and eastward is the perennial *D. exaltatum*. Most of the cultivated garden flowers are perennials derived principally from the species *D. grandiflorum*, a native of Siberia; *D. hybridum*, from Asia; *D. formosum*, possibly from Asia Minor; and *D. exaltatum*.

Delphiniums should grow in full sunshine, in deep, well-drained but moisture-retentive soil. They are most vigorous in cool weather. Some bloom only in the spring; others become dormant in hot weather and bloom again in the fall. They are usually propagated from seed, which may be planted early in the spring if the springs are long and cool. Otherwise planting should be done in late spring or early fall.

THESE ARTICLES ARE IN THE FACT-INDEX

| | |
|---|---|
| La Rochefoucauld, François, duc de | Larsa, Mesopotamia |
| La Rochelle, France | Larsen Ice Shelf |
| | Larson, (Lewis) Arthur |

**LARVA.** The word larva is applied to the young of certain animals that must undergo profound changes before they become adults. A young frog hatches from the egg as a water-living tadpole and gradually becomes transformed into the air-breathing adult. A tadpole is therefore a larva.

Many insects go through a larval stage. This is one way of meeting the difficulty all insects have in growing. The outer covering (*exoskeleton*) of an adult insect is made of a tough substance (*chitin*) that cannot stretch or grow bigger. Many insects, such as grasshoppers, acquire this skin when young and must shed, or molt, it several times while they are growing. Other insects remain soft-skinned during the growing period, usually with altogether different shapes and habits from those they will have later on. Young insects in this stage are called larvae. Before they are ready for adult life, they pass through another stage, called the pupal stage, in which they get their hard outer skin (*see* Pupa). Insects that go through the four stages of egg, larva, pupa, and adult are said to have complete metamorphosis (*see* Insects).

Many insect larvae have special names. The larvae of beetles are grubs; of flies, maggots; of butterflies and moths, caterpillars.

**LA SALLE, Sieur de** (1643–1687). The father of the great Louisiana Territory was the French explorer René Robert Cavelier, sieur de La Salle. He was the first to voyage down the Mississippi River to the Gulf of Mexico. As a result of this exploration France laid claim to the entire Mississippi Valley under the name of Louisiana.

René Cavelier was born Nov. 22, 1643, at Rouen, France. The son of a rich merchant, he was educated by the Jesuits. When he was only 23 years old he sailed for Montreal, Canada, to seek his fortune. He got a grant of land at Lachine, near Montreal, from the Seminary of St. Sulpice, where his older brother was a priest. He was more interested, however, in Montreal's greatest activity, the fur trade, than he was in farming. Every spring Indians in hundreds of canoes, led by French agents called *coureurs de bois* (wood runners), came to trade bales of furs for trinkets, cloth, firearms, and brandy. For ten days or two weeks Montreal hummed with business and riotous celebrations. Then the Indians vanished into the West until the following year.

### La Salle's First Explorations

Soon La Salle learned the Iroquoian language and several other Indian dialects. From the Indians he heard that south of the Great Lakes a broad river ran southwest to "the Vermilion Sea." La Salle thought that this sea might be the Gulf of California. If so, "the great river" would be a splendid route to China, and by discovering the route La Salle could become rich.

La Salle sold his land to finance an expedition in 1669–70. He ascended the St. Lawrence River to Lake Ontario. His men paddled along the southern shore until they came to the west end of the lake. The records of his exploration from here on were lost. Historians today cannot say where he went next. He may have made his way to a branch of the Ohio River and descended the Ohio as far as the rapids at Louisville, Ky. Upon his return he found Count Louis de Frontenac in power (*see* Frontenac).

### A Grand Plan for an Inland Empire

In 1673 Louis Joliet and Father Jacques Marquette had explored the Mississippi far enough to prove that the river emptied into the Gulf of Mexico. Frontenac and La Salle at once proposed to build a chain of forts and trading posts along the Great Lakes and the Mississippi to hold the region and its fur trade for France. This protection was needed because the Iroquois Indians were trying to force the fur trade through New York into the hands of their allies, the Dutch and English traders at Albany.

Frontenac had made a start on this plan by building Fort Frontenac (1673), where the St. Lawrence flows out of Lake Ontario (*see* Kingston). La Salle was to be made governor of the West and given a monopoly of trade in the region. In return, he was to build and maintain the needed forts. La Salle made two trips to France, in 1674 and 1677, before he received the monopoly and was given his title of *sieur* ("sir," in English).

In the winter of 1678–79 an advance party built a fort at the Niagara River and started to build a 40-ton ship, the *Griffon*. On Aug. 7, 1679, La Salle with his lieutenant, Henri de Tonti, started for Green Bay on the first voyage ever made by a ship on the Great Lakes.

Tonti was an able, bold adventurer who served La Salle faithfully in the New World. The Indians called him the "man with the iron hand." He had a metal claw at the end of one arm to replace a hand blown off in battle.

La Salle and Tonti reached Green Bay in September and sent the ship back laden with furs. In December 1679 they established Fort Miami on the southeastern shore of Lake Michigan. Then La Salle followed the route to Lake Peoria, shown on the map on the facing page. Here, early in 1680, he built Fort Crèvecoeur ("heartbreak"). From this fort he sent Father Louis Hennepin with two companions to explore the upper Mississippi (*see* Hennepin).

Leaving Tonti in charge of the new fort, La Salle made a fast trip back to Fort Frontenac, where he found out that the *Griffon* never had been heard from. On his return westward, he learned the Iroquois had ravaged the country. Fort Crèvecoeur was in ashes. Tonti and his men had vanished. La Salle traced him northward to Mackinac. The veteran had fought his way out through the Green Bay region.

**LA SALLE TAKES POSSESSION OF LOUISIANA**
On April 9, 1682, La Salle gave the name Louisiana to the entire Mississippi Valley and claimed the territory for France.

## Exploring the Mississippi in 1682

La Salle now spent a year organizing the Illinois Indians to resist the Iroquois. Early in 1682 the explorer followed the Illinois River and the Mississippi to the Gulf of Mexico. On April 9 he named the entire Mississippi Valley Louisiana and claimed it for France. Retracing his steps La Salle built Fort St. Louis at Starved Rock, Ill., as a rallying point for the Illinois Indians.

In 1683 he returned to civilization, to find that Frontenac had been recalled and his own rights canceled by the new governor. He went to France and persuaded Louis XIV to renew his rights and to help him procure four ships and about 400 men for a post at the mouth of the Mississippi.

## The Final Disaster of 1684-87

This expedition by sea ruined La Salle. The naval commander, Beaujeu, who had charge of the ships, opposed him constantly. In the West Indies La Salle fell sick. Many men deserted. When the explorer set sail again with only about 180 men he lost his way. He had not known how to fix the longitude of the Mississippi's mouth at the time he had discovered it, in 1682. Now he could not choose the right opening from among the river's many bays and bayous. Finally he landed at Matagorda Bay, Tex., where Beaujeu left him with one small ship on March 12, 1685.

La Salle started to build a second Fort St. Louis (Texas) and scouted for the Mississippi. His ship was wrecked, and he lost all but 36 of his men. In January 1687 he took half the men on an overland trip to reach Tonti in Illinois. On March 19 in eastern Texas three of his men shot him.

### LA SALLE EXPLORES AMERICA

- ■ Fort already established
- ▬ Exploration of 1679-80
- ▭ Forts established
- •••• Exploration of 1682
- ▣ Forts established
- ⋮⋮⋮⋮ Exploration of 1684-87
- ▢ Fort established
- ▪▪▪▪ Hennepin exploration of 1680

**THE EXPLORATIONS OF LA SALLE**
La Salle explored the lower Great Lakes and the Mississippi River valley. He tried to establish a chain of forts to control the rich fur trade for France.

THESE ARTICLES ARE IN THE FACT-INDEX
La Salle, Ill.
La Salle, Que.

**LAS CASAS, Bartolomé de** (1474-1566). As soon as the Spaniards settled in the West Indies, their need of laborers for mines and plantations led them to enslave the natives. Bitterly hard labor and brutal treatment killed the Indians by the thousands. The first man to interfere in their behalf was Bartolomé de Las Casas.

Las Casas was a lawyer in Spain when his father, who had accompanied Christopher Columbus on his second voyage, sent him to Hispaniola to manage a newly acquired estate. In 1510 he became a priest, the first to be ordained in the New World. He began his life's work by freeing the Indians under his control. He journeyed to Spain and obtained from Charles V an order that Indians must be paid for their work unless they were cannibals. He himself was appointed "protector of the Indians." In his zeal for the red men, he advocated the substitution of Negro slaves— a measure he bitterly regretted later on.

In 1523 he entered the Dominican Order and gained the help of this powerful organization. In 1530 he won a decree freeing the Indians of Peru. Yet the government made little effort to enforce the new laws. Opposed by numerous enemies, Las Casas retired to Spain in 1547. Before his death he had the satisfaction of seeing the emancipation of the Indians begun.

THESE ARTICLES ARE IN THE FACT-INDEX
Las Cruces, N. M.
La Serena, Chile

# LASERS AND MASERS

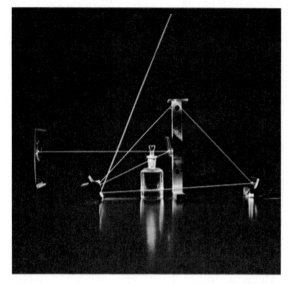

Orville Andrews

The thin beam of intense green light was produced by an argon laser. Smoke blown in the path of the light made it visible.

**LASERS AND MASERS.** The first men to land on the moon left a quartz reflector—the lunar laser reflector. Later, a beam of light was sent from earth all the way to the moon, where it bounced off the reflector and returned to earth. The instrument that produced this intense beam of light was a *laser* (from light amplification by stimulated emission of radiation).

Light emerges from a laser in a narrow beam that can be focused down to less than 0.001 inch in diameter. Such concentrated beams are so powerful that they are used to drill tiny holes in diamonds, taking minutes where old methods took days. Ultrathin wires are also made by pulling metal through these holes. Laser light can then be used to weld these tiny wires.

Laser beams are used in delicate eye surgery. A beam of light can be aimed through the pupil onto a detached retina, forming a tiny scar that "welds" the retina back in place. No incision is made in the eye.

Lasers mark a straight line with extreme accuracy. A laser beam guided the construction of the linear accelerator at Stanford University, in Stanford, Calif., and is still used to signal when parts of the two-mile-long accelerator move out of line.

Laser light has several features that are significantly different from white light. To begin with, light from most sources spreads out as it travels, so that much less light hits a given area as the distance from the light source increases (*see* Light). Laser light travels as a parallel beam and spreads very little.

Furthermore, laser light is *monochromatic* and *coherent*. White light is a jumble of colored light waves (*see* Light; Color). Each color has a different wavelength. If all the wavelengths but one are filtered out, the remaining light is monochromatic. If these waves are all parallel to one another, they are also *coherent:*

the waves travel in a definite phase relationship with one another. In the case of laser light, the wave crests coincide and the troughs coincide. The waves all reinforce one another. One special application of coherent light is the recording of three-dimensional images called holograms (*see* Color).

The laser uses a process called *stimulated emission* to amplify light waves. (One method of amplification of an electromagnetic beam is to produce additional waves that travel in step with that beam.) A substance normally gives off light by *spontaneous emission*. One of the electrons of an atom absorbs energy. While it possesses this energy, the atom is in an *excited state*. If the electron gives off this excess energy (in the form of electromagnetic radiation such as light) with no outside impetus, spontaneous emission has occurred.

If a wave emitted by one excited atom strikes another excited atom, it stimulates the second atom to emit energy in the form of a second wave that travels parallel to and in step with the first wave. This *stimulated emission* results in amplification of the first wave. If the two waves strike other excited atoms, a large coherent beam builds up. But if they strike unexcited atoms, they are absorbed, and the amplification is lost. In normal matter on earth,

The diagrams below show the structure and workings of a ruby laser. Light from the flash tube excites the chromium atoms in ruby. When an atom emits a light wave, it may hit a second excited atom, stimulating emission of a second wave. The beam grows stronger and bursts out of the cylinder.

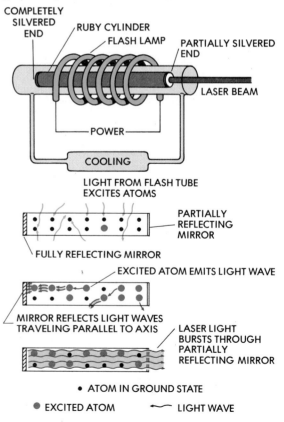

COMPLETELY SILVERED END
RUBY CYLINDER
FLASH LAMP
PARTIALLY SILVERED END
LASER BEAM
POWER
COOLING

LIGHT FROM FLASH TUBE EXCITES ATOMS
PARTIALLY REFLECTING MIRROR
FULLY REFLECTING MIRROR

EXCITED ATOM EMITS LIGHT WAVE
MIRROR REFLECTS LIGHT WAVES TRAVELING PARALLEL TO AXIS
LASER LIGHT BURSTS THROUGH PARTIALLY REFLECTING MIRROR

• ATOM IN GROUND STATE
● EXCITED ATOM
⌒ LIGHT WAVE

129a

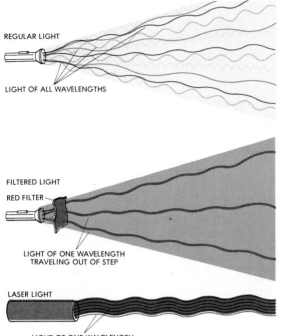

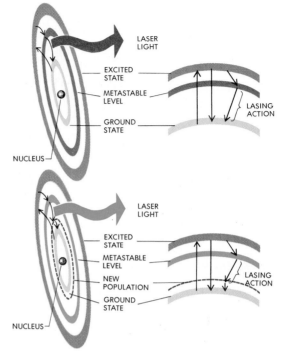

White light contains many wavelengths of light. A filter transmits light of one wavelength (monochromatic light) but weakens the original beam. Lasers produce light that is monochromatic and coherent (traveling in step).

When atoms in a ruby laser (top) emit light, they return to the ground state, where they can absorb light. In the helium-neon laser (bottom) atoms form a new population at a lower excited level that does not absorb the laser light.

the great majority of atoms are not excited. As more than the usual number of atoms become excited, the probability increases that stimulated emission rather than absorption will take place.

The first laser, invented in 1960 by T. H. Maiman, contained a synthetic ruby shaped like a cylinder, with a completely reflecting silver layer on one end and a thin, partially reflecting silver layer on the other. Ruby is composed of aluminum oxide with chromium impurities. The chromium atoms absorb blue light and become excited; they then drop first to a metastable level and finally to the ground (unexcited) state, giving off red light.

Light from a flash lamp enters the ruby and excites most of the chromium atoms, many of which fall quickly to the metastable state. Some atoms then emit red light and return to the ground state. The light waves strike other excited chromium atoms, stimulating them to emit more red light. The beam bounces back and forth between the silvered ends until it gains enough energy to burst through the partially silvered end as laser light. When most of the chromium atoms are back in the ground state, they absorb light, and the lasing action stops. In continuous-wave lasers, such as the helium-neon laser, electrons emit light by jumping to a lower excited state, forming a new atomic population that does not absorb laser light, rather than to the ground state.

The principle of stimulated emission was first successfully applied in 1954 when Charles Townes constructed the *maser* (microwave amplification by stimulated emission of radiation). Townes bombarded excited ammonia molecules with microwaves. The ammonia molecules were in a box that vibrated at the same wave frequency as the microwaves, so the waves bounced back and forth, causing the ammonia molecules to emit more microwaves, until an amplified microwave pulse was emitted. The stable and accurate ammonia maser amplifies microwave signals from radio stars and in satellite communications.

## Books and Films About Lasers and Masers

Carroll, J. M. The Story of the Laser, rev. ed. (Dutton, 1970).

Harrison, G. R. Lasers (Watts, 1971).

Introduction to Lasers, film (Encyclopaedia Britannica Films).

Klein, H. A. Masers and Lasers (Lippincott, 1963).

Mims, F. M., III. Lasers (McKay, 1977).

THESE ARTICLES ARE IN THE FACT-INDEX

Lashley, Karl Spencer
Lasker, Eduard
Lasker, Emanuel
Laski, Harold Joseph
Laskin, Bora
Lasky, Jesse L(ouis)
Las Palmas, Canary Islands
La Spezia, Italy
Lassalle, Ferdinand
Lasso, Orlando di
'Last Days of Pompeii, The'
Lastex

'Last of the Mohicans, The'
Las Vegas, Nev.
Las Vegas, N. M.
Latakia, Syria
Lateran, The
Lateran Councils
Latham, Jean Lee
Lathrop, Dorothy Pulis
Lathrop, George Parsons
Lathrop, Julia Clifford
Latimer, Hugh
Latina, Italy

# LATIN AMERICA— Its Problems and Promise

These mestizo lads are sitting on the steps of a Peruvian cathedral. What does the future hold for them? Latin America's democratic leaders are urging gradual reform to bring justice, education, and opportunity. The Communists urge revolution.

LATIN AMERICA. Twenty independent nations lying to the south of the Rio Grande and the Straits of Florida make up Latin America. Ten comprise Middle America. These are Mexico, Guatemala, El Salvador, Honduras, Nicaragua, Costa Rica, and Panama and the West Indian countries of Cuba, Haiti, and the Dominican Republic. The remaining ten countries are located in South America. They are Venezuela, Colombia, Ecuador, Peru, Bolivia, Chile, Paraguay, Argentina, Uruguay, and Brazil. Latin America includes almost half the area of the Western Hemisphere and accounts for about half the total population.

## Similarities and Differences

Many similarities as well as striking differences are found among these countries. Racial composition ranges from mostly white in several nations to chiefly Indian in others. In most countries the majority of the inhabitants are racially mixed.

In the United States of Brazil, which makes up nearly half of the continent of South America, Portuguese is spoken. In little Haiti the language is French. In all other countries Spanish is the official language, though in many sections Indian dialects are more commonly heard. Remarkable differences among countries, and parts of countries, are also found in their physical features and natural resources, in the character and level of their economic growth, and in their cultural development.

As the name implies, however, the republics of Latin America, situated together in the same portion of the globe, possess a considerable number of similarities. They share a common cultural heritage from Mediterranean Europe, and they have had similar colonial experiences.

Each of the countries of Latin America is predominantly Roman Catholic in religion. To varying degrees, they are faced with the same social, economic, and political problems.

## What Is Latin America?

The term Latin America has increased in usage in recent years as a convenient way to designate collectively those countries located south of the United States. The basis for the term, like the basis for the term Anglo-America, lies in the origin of the inhabitants. Latin Americans reflect the Latin cultural traditions of southern Europe. The peoples of the United States and Canada, on the other hand, reflect largely the Anglo-Saxon traditions of northern Europe. It must be remembered, however, that Latin America and Anglo-America are both broad terms. There are differences between Bolivia and Uruguay that are just as distinct as some differences between Mexico and Canada.

Not all people find the term Latin America acceptable. Other names that are sometimes used include Spanish America, Hispanic America, Ibero-America, and Indo-America.

130

## World Significance

The world significance of Latin America is greater today than at any other time in history. Latin America's importance lies not only in its continued production and export of needed commodities but also in the trend of its social development and the influence it exerts in the field of international affairs.

To the free nations of the West it is of vital concern that Latin American countries speak for democracy and peace in the United Nations and other international bodies. It is even more essential that the peoples of these countries take the way of democracy in their drive to raise the level of living and to foster economic development.

The forces of totalitarianism also recognize the importance of Latin America, and they are seeking to dominate its peoples. Military dictators, who are ruling in the interest of a powerful landholding minority, have held back democracy and progress in many Latin American nations. World Communism recently has attained a foothold through the revolution in Cuba (see Cuba).

Latin America is vital to the security of the Western Hemisphere. Globally the major world centers of economic and military strength in Europe are located in a northerly direction from Canada and the United States. Latin America holds the flank and rear. Many of its nations help guard approaches to the strategic Panama Canal.

## Possibilities in Foreign Trade and Immigration

Latin America has long been recognized for its output of minerals and agricultural products. Some people think it has great possibilities for settlement of immigrants. It does have a small population in relation to total land area. Much of the good land, however, is overcrowded even now. Critical problems, dealing with land tenure and transportation, will have to be solved in order to provide enough desirable land for the natural increase in population alone.

**SUGAR—TROPICAL AMERICA'S FIRST BIG EXPORT CROP**
Here sugarcane is being harvested much as it was when slaves brought in the richest lowland crop of the Spanish and Portuguese colonies.

**PLANTING COFFEE AND HARVESTING BANANAS**
These men (left) are planting a young coffee tree. Coffee is the chief upland crop of Latin America. This man (right) is harvesting bananas. The fruit is grown in the hot lowlands of Central America and tropical South America.

With advances in education, individual income, and the general level of living, Latin America can become a large and growing market for both domestic and foreign manufactured goods. In an interdependent world the improvement of conditions in one part makes it easier and less costly to maintain high living standards in another.

# Physical Diversity of Latin America

THE MANNER in which Latin America has developed is related in many ways to the nature, arrangement, and diversity of its physical features. Mountain systems form the framework and influence the shapes of the landmasses. Agriculture, transportation, and general progress have been retarded by the mountains, but the minerals found in them have been a leading source of wealth to the highland regions.

The land link between the United States and South America is for the most part high, rugged country. From the broad plateau of Mexico, the highland backbone of ridges, intermontane basins, and volcanic peaks tapers through Central America to the width of a single range in Panama. In southern Mexico,

Guatemala, Honduras, and northern Nicaragua, the bedrock structures have an east-west trend. The submerged extensions of these structures rise from the Caribbean Sea to form the Greater Antilles, which are linked to South America by the volcanic island chain of the Lesser Antilles. Except for the limestone platform of the peninsula of Yucatán and parts of Cuba, flatland in Middle America is mainly limited to narrow coastal margins, river valleys, and intermontane basins.

### South America's Mountain Systems

The geologic framework of South America consists of: (1) the relatively young and high Andes on the west and (2) the older and lower Guiana and Brazilian highlands on the east. The Andes, extending for some 4,500 miles from the Caribbean Sea to Cape Horn, make up the world's longest continuous mountain system. Composed of high ranges and intermontane basins, the Andes form a great barrier between the west coast and eastern South America. (See also Andes.)

The Guiana Highlands are remote in their location and very sparsely populated. South from the Orinoco River, rounded hills give way to flat-topped plateaus and mesas that rise to more than 6,500 feet. Deep gorges, swift rivers, and spectacular waterfalls offer magnificent scenery.

In contrast, the extensive Brazilian Highlands support many towns and cities. Through the course of history the highlands have provided commodities of economic importance. They consist of a low rolling plateau surmounted in the southeast by an occasional mountain range less than 10,000 feet in elevation. The surface of the plateau slopes away from an abrupt wall-like edge near the Atlantic. The streams flow inland from this escarpment. No navigable stream gives access from the interior to the ocean.

### Tropical and Middle-Latitude Plains

Between the mountain systems lies a central lowland. This lowland is formed by the great river basins of the Orinoco, Amazon, and Paraná-Paraguay. The lowland is composed of material eroded from the highlands on either side. The plains of the Orinoco and, especially, the Amazon suffer from the handicaps of tropical temperature and rainfall conditions. They support little commercial activity and few people. The cooler and much more productive plains bordering the Paraná and the Plata in Argentina have great commercial importance.

South America possesses little coastal plain. Few good harbors exist, the major exception being Guanabara Bay, on which Rio de Janeiro is located. At most stops along the west coast of the continent, ships anchor well offshore. Passengers and cargo are then transferred to and from the ports in small boats.

### Variations in Climate

Diversity is found in climate as well as in land surface. Although most of Latin America lies in the tropics, differences in elevation, ocean currents, and prevailing winds have combined with differences in latitude to produce a highly varied pattern. Climatic contrasts, in turn, produce a variety of natural vegetation and soil conditions.

The great elevation of many Andean peaks in the tropics gives them an Arctic climate and a year-round snowcap. The narrow southern part of Latin America does not have the temperature extremes of

**PUMPING OIL AND HAULING IRON ORE IN VENEZUELA**

Latin America has abundant minerals. At the left is one of the oil fields that make Venezuela the world's greatest petroleum exporter. The iron-ore train at the right is moving toward an Orinoco River port. From there the ore will be shipped to mills in the United States. Other Latin American countries with rich iron reserves are Brazil, Chile, Peru, and Mexico.

**TIN MINERS IN BOLIVIA AND A COPPER WORKER IN CHILE**

The Indians at the left mine tin at an elevation of 15,000 feet in Bolivia. At the right a worker in Chile hauls a load of copper ore from an underground mine. These metals make up a large share of the exports of the two countries. When the world market price of tin or copper declines, the whole economy of the producing country suffers.

similar latitudes in the interior of North America. This is because southern South America is much closer to the moderating influence of the oceans. Winters are not severe in Latin America, and only in northern Mexico and northern Argentina do steady midsummer daytime temperatures exceed 100° F.

Rainfall extremes are characteristic. The Atacama Desert in northern Chile, for example, is one of the world's driest areas. Years often pass with no rain. Because of this lack of moisture, the world's largest deposit of sodium nitrate, a highly soluble fertilizer mineral, is found here. On the other hand, areas such as the Isthmus of Panama, the Caribbean coast of Guatemala, and the upper Amazon Basin are drenched with more than 100 inches each year. (For further information on climates, *see* South America; Central America; West Indies; and country articles.)

### Resources of Different Regions

The various parts of Latin America have quite different natural resources. The mountains of Mexico, Peru, and Chile hold the greatest and the most varied reserves of ores. Venezuela and Mexico lead in petroleum resources. Brazil has vast deposits of iron ore.

Coal resources, however, are scattered and scanty.

Latin America's industrial development suffers from the shortage of coal for power and for the making of iron and steel. Brazil ranks first in potential hydroelectric sites. Most countries, however, have waterfalls that are not harnessed for power. Many of these are deep in mountains or rain forests—far from industries or cities that need power.

The Amazon Basin contains the largest area of tropical forest in the world, but little of its valuable timber has been harvested. The tropical hardwoods of the Central American coastlands are easier to reach and to cut.

Good farmland is also unevenly distributed. The Argentine Pampa is one of the world's great stretches of level, fertile, middle-latitude farmland. Its rich prairie soils are ideal for growing grains and many other crops. These prairies and those of Uruguay and the southeastern part of Brazil are excellent pastures. This region has the additional advantage of a location near the sea. Its output moves into the world market through nearby harbors.

The west coast countries are limited in level land and have large desert areas. Too much rain is the problem in many of the tropical lowlands. The downpours leach the fertility from the soil.

## Racial Variety of Latin America

THE VARIETY of races and cultures adds to the complexity of Latin America. The primary racial stocks are Indian, white European, and Negro. These three elements have mixed and produced a variety of combinations. Intermarriages of white Europeans and Indians have resulted in the common racial type known as the mestizo.

### The Indians

The Indians that the Spanish and Portuguese conquerors found in the New World were of two general types. Numerous uncivilized migratory tribes lived in the Caribbean area and in the lowlands of South America. In contrast, sedentary farming tribes lived

133

## TWO CAPITAL CITIES AND THEIR PEOPLE

School is out in Panama City, Panama, and the children fill the street (left). Narrow streets and balconied buildings are found in the older Latin American cities. At the right is a business section of San José, Costa Rica. Two monks talk at the corner. Foreign cars and trucks and the signs on buildings suggest the extent of the country's imports of manufactured goods.

primarily in the highlands. These farming Indians inhabited four distinct areas. They made up about three quarters of all the native peoples in the Western Hemisphere.

Two of the advanced culture groups were in Middle America—the Aztecs and related peoples of the central plateau of Mexico and the Mayas of Guatemala and Yucatán. Two groups were in the highlands of South America—the Chibchas of Colombia and the Inca peoples who controlled the territory from Ecuador to the central part of Chile. (*See also* Aztecs; Incas; Indians, American; Mayas; South America, section "Peoples, Industries, and Occupations.")

### The Europeans

The Spanish and the Portuguese came to the New World seeking wealth and prestige. The Spanish conquered a vast empire. Particularly attractive to them were the four areas of concentrated Indian settlement.

The Spaniards conquered these civilizations in a relatively short time. Although the conquerors were greatly outnumbered, they had several advantages. The Indian cultures had passed their points of greatest development. They were all suffering from internal political difficulties. The Europeans had firearms, armor, and horses; and many Indians thought that the white men were gods.

The sedentary peoples possessed gold. After looting the Indians of this treasure, the Spanish put them to work in the mines and as laborers on large landholdings. Disease and overwork greatly reduced the Indian populations in all Latin America. In the high-

lands, however, sufficient numbers remained to greatly outnumber the Spaniards. Today these areas are still heavily populated by Indians and mestizos.

The Portuguese were faced with different conditions in eastern South America. The Indians were primitive and many quickly died of disease. Unlike the Spanish, the Portuguese found no gold or other ready sources of wealth. Prosperity in Brazil did not come until after 1550, when the great wave of sugar planting took place along the northeastern coast. Because Indian labor was lacking, Negro slaves were brought over from Africa to work on the sugar estates. This coastal belt still has a large Negro and mulatto population. (*See also* Brazil.)

### Immigration in the 19th and 20th Centuries

After the Latin American colonies gained their independence, an important period of modern immigration began. Italians outnumbered those of any other single nationality coming in, with 4 million landing between 1825 and 1900. By the latter date they made up about one third the population of Argentina, Uruguay, and southern Brazil.

From 1885 to 1956 nearly 7 million immigrants were added to the population of Latin America. They came primarily from Italy, Spain, and Portugal, but some migrated from Germany and the Slavic countries. Today the Germans probably form the largest non-Latin group. In addition, the present population includes small but influential groups of English, Scottish, and Irish people. Japanese are most numerous in Brazil and Peru; and Chinese are found chiefly in Mexico, Peru, Panama, and Cuba.

### The Negro in Latin America

The Negroes make up a large third racial stock in the population of Latin America. The greatest number of Negroes and mulattoes are found in areas where, in the past, commercial plantation agriculture produced a heavy demand for field labor.

Negroes are an important part of the national life of Cuba, Brazil, and several other countries. Haiti has been a Negro republic since its founding in 1804. In countries such as Argentina, Chile, Peru, and Mexico, which brought in fewer slaves, Negroes have been so thoroughly absorbed in the population that persons with African ancestry are hardly recognizable.

### Population Distribution

Two facts are outstanding with regard to the population of Latin America. The total number of people, more than 250 million, is small in relation to the land area of 7,800,000 square miles. The rate of growth (2.9 percent a year) is higher than in any other major region of the world. Latin America makes up about one seventh of the total land area of the earth, but it has only about one fifteenth of the world's population. West Germany and East Germany together have almost as many people as Brazil—yet Brazil is more than 20 times as large.

The high rate of increase is part of a worldwide population explosion. Between 1920 and 1960 the population of Latin America more than doubled, whereas that of the world expanded about two thirds. It is estimated that by 1990 Latin America will have 400 million people, or considerably more than the United States and Canada combined. This spectacular growth is due to a continuing high birthrate with a rapidly falling death rate brought about by improved health conditions.

### A Youthful, Growing Population

The population of Latin America is young, and the proportion of children to adults is increasing. The ratio of school-age children to each adult is twice what it is in Europe. Improvement in the general level of living is difficult when so much effort is required just to supply food to the increasing population.

Most Latin Americans live in villages or cities. Between these the land is usually sparsely settled, in some places almost empty.

In Mexico and Central America the people are concentrated largely in the highland basins and valleys. The Central American lowlands, except in Panama, are thinly settled.

Most South Americans live in a wide belt around the edge of the continent. Clusters of people in western South America are most numerous in the high valleys and basins of the Andes. The larger communities maintain connections with the ports, but many villages are in almost complete isolation. In Chile the heavy population is in the Central Valley.

Since World War II urban growth has been rapid. The metropolitan areas of Buenos Aires, São Paulo, Rio de Janeiro, and Mexico City hold several millions, and Bogotá, Lima, Caracas, Santiago, Montevideo, Recife, and Havana are around the million mark.

**MARKET DAY AT SOLOLÁ, GUATEMALA**
The market has attracted the Indians from the countryside. They have walked many miles carrying their wares. The women wear the handwoven dresses traditional in their villages, whereas the men wear "store clothes."

**A DWELLING IN THE SAN BLAS ISLANDS**
These Indians have kept their old ways by forbidding outsiders to settle on the islands. The women wear skirts and *molas* (blouses) in bright patterns, gold nose rings, and many beads. The shells and coral fans will be bartered.

135

# Culture, Recreation, and Education

THE CULTURE of the Indians in the New World was as varied as the land itself. The nomadic tribes depended upon hunting, fishing, and collecting. They gave little evidence of artistic development.

In central Mexico, Guatemala and Yucatán, and the Andean lands, however, a high state of civilization with well-developed art forms had evolved. The ornate textile art of the Andean peoples has rarely been surpassed (see Textiles). The many examples of their pottery reveal a mastery of techniques in ceramic sculpture.

The Indians of the central plateau region of Mexico were able to express great beauty and feeling in both clay and stone. Although the true arch was unknown in the New World, the offset principle was used in a false arch in constructing massive and ornately decorated temples. The temples of the Mayas in what is now Yucatán and Guatemala rivaled the pyramids of Egypt. (See also Mayas, subhead "Architecture and Other Arts.")

Exquisite ornaments of gold and silver were produced throughout the three areas. Much of the Indian art, including objects fashioned from the precious metals, was of a religious nature. The Spaniards, despising that which to them was pagan, destroyed or looted objects expressing the Indians' religious symbolism. The artistic spirit, however, could not be destroyed.

## Early Architecture and Sculpture

During the colonial period, Spain and Portugal reached the greatest heights of their civilization.

**A MAYAN TEMPLE AT TIKAL IN GUATEMALA**
Tikal probably flourished from A.D. 300 to 900, and beneath it are earlier ruins. Archaeologists have stripped away the rain forest to reveal the city's temples, palaces, and monuments.

Wealth from the possessions enabled the people at home and in the colonies to build elaborate churches and houses. Indian craftsmen in Latin America were under the direction of Europeans. Nevertheless they superimposed their own ideas on the Renaissance forms of Europe and created a "mestizo" art form. The extreme curves and trim of the baroque style of architecture, which characterized the 17th and 18th centuries, can be seen today in many of the older towns of Latin America. Buildings here were elaborately decorated with paintings, tapestries, and figures done in clay, stone, and wood.

The wars for independence disrupted cultural activities and exhausted the economies of the new nations. Continued turmoil and upheaval during the 19th century impeded the further development of art. Latin American artists for the most part remained culturally dependent upon European schools of art.

## Modern Painting and Architecture

During the first half of the 20th century art expression reawakened in Latin America. Mexico's dramatic, colorful murals and frescoes, dealing chiefly with social and historical themes, are world famous. The walls of numerous public buildings have paintings by Diego Rivera, José Clemente Orozco, and David Alfaro Siqueiros. The Brazilian artist Candido Portinari is noted for his portrayal of Brazilian life as well as for frescoes in buildings in Rio de Janeiro and Washington, D. C.

Mexican artists influenced those of other Latin American countries in paintings depicting everyday life, especially Indian life. By the 1940's the younger painters had turned to the international modernist movements for their inspiration. In Latin American exhibits of the 1960's a large share of the canvases showed abstract, or nonobjective, compositions.

In architecture, functional designs were adopted as a host of new buildings were constructed in the prosperous decades following World War II. Their severe lines contrasted oddly with the baroque and other lavish designs of the older buildings. Brasília, the new capital city in the interior of Brazil, is one of the architectural triumphs of the 20th century (for pictures, see Brasília.) It is the product of Brazilian architects who are famous abroad as well as at home. Oscar Niemeyer, who also aided in designing United Nations buildings in New York City, designed all of Brasília's public buildings.

## Music of the Latin Peoples

Musical activities are universally enjoyed in Latin America. Popular and folk music are highly regionalized. With few exceptions, both forms are gay and lively. At the fiesta, a spectacle of brightly colored costumes, rhythmic, sensuous music of Spanish flavor is played. Music is one of Latin America's biggest items of "export." Millions over the world dance to the captivating rhythms of mambos, rumbas, tangos, boleros, and sambas. The masses of Latin America, despite widespread poverty, possess a capacity for participating joyously in the many holiday festivals and carnivals. This is well illustrated by the samba schools of Rio de Janeiro. These schools are neighborhood Negro groups organized for the purpose of dancing and parading at Carnival time. Throughout the year the groups spend most of their leisure practicing and making the costumes for Carnival.

Aside from the gay music, there are ballads of love and sorrow. The lover is often portrayed with a guitar serenading *la señorita*. The guitar is as much a part of the *gaucho* (cowboy) as his horse. His music and songs reflect the loneliness of the empty plains of Argentina.

In the Andean highlands the Indians are little affected by outside influence. Instruments played today—clay or bamboo flutes, panpipes, cymbals, drums, and various rattles—are much the same as those played by the Indians prior to the Spanish conquest. The land is stark; life is harsh; the music and songs are melancholy. The group dances reflect the sorrowful songs dealing with love or death.

## Opera, Theater, and Other Entertainment

Much of the classical music enjoyed has been and still is European. With the rising tide of nationalism in the 19th century, native composers turned to their own environment for stimuli to develop music of a national character. The younger musicians today tend to be international in their outlook.

Latin American culture still looks to aristocratic and humanistic ideals. A fondness for the drama, opera, symphonies, dancing, and political debate persists. The major cities have great opera houses and national, state, or municipal theaters where the world's finest artists perform. Going to the movies is very popular. Because most films shown are made in Hollywood, they spread both accurate and inaccurate impressions of life in the United States.

## Amusements and Sports

The village folk of Latin America find most of their recreation in the traditional fiestas. City people enjoy a variety of sports and amusements.

Only in recent times have vigorous sports such as tennis, rugby, soccer, baseball, and rowing come into wide favor. Horsemanship has always been popular, and Argentine polo teams compete internationally. The favorite sport of Spain, bullfighting, is the chief spectator sport in numerous Latin American countries. Jai alai is another sport introduced from Spain.

## Education in the Latin American Republics

Educational facilities are inadequate in most of Latin America. This situation is related to the traditional feudalism established by the Spanish and Portuguese. Education was in the hands of the Roman Catholic church in colonial times. Little attention was given to education for the masses.

By the end of the 17th century many of the major

**STIRRUP SPOUT JUGS OF EARLY PERU**
The Mochican Indians, who lived in a fertile valley of northern Peru before A.D. 1000, were fine potters. They portrayed gods, people, and animals in ceramics later buried with the dead.

**PRE-COLUMBIAN TAPESTRIES FROM PERU**
The Indians of Peru wove fine textiles of cotton and wool 1,000 years before Columbus discovered America. These tapestries, found in tombs, were preserved by the dry climate.

Spanish colonial cities had universities. Their enrollments were small and almost entirely restricted to sons of wealthy landowners. Brazil had no universities until later. Fortunate young men were often sent to college in Portugal.

## Early Colonial Universities

The University of Santo Domingo, in what is now the Dominican Republic, was the first institution of higher learning in the Americas. It was founded in 1538. Both the University of San Marcos in Lima, Peru, and the National Autonomous University of Mexico in Mexico City were established in 1551. By the time Harvard University was founded, in 1636, as the first college in the English colonies, Latin America had several more universities. The National University of Colombia, at Bogotá, grew from a college founded in 1573; the Central University of Ecuador, at Quito, traces its origins to 1594; the University of Córdoba, in Argentina, was founded in 1613.

The few elementary and secondary schools were mainly college preparatory. Scholasticism, the system of thought based on the teachings of Aristotle and the doctrines of the church, dominated teaching. Applied science was neglected. Mission schools operated by Roman Catholic orders, such as the Society of Jesus (the Jesuits), offered some instruction in religion and the manual arts to a few Indians in their immediate area. The great majority of Negro and Indian slaves received no schooling. (*See also* South America, subhead "Schools and Universities.")

After the Jesuits were expelled from the colonies by Portugal in 1759 and by Spain in 1767 the schools lost many of their ablest teachers. By the time most of the colonies had won their independence, early in the 19th century, intellectual activity was at a virtual standstill.

### Free Schools and Private Schools

With independence there was a rise in demand for education, and some progress was made against the opposition of the landed aristocracy. The outstanding champion of free public schools was Domingo Sarmiento of Argentina.

By the end of the 1800's most Latin American governments were on record as providing free and compulsory education. In reality, however, illiteracy remained widespread. It is still extensive, especially outside the largest cities. Most areas are without enough schoolrooms, teachers, or books. In many cases the legally required three-to-six-year elementary program is not available. Teachers are generally poorly paid, and many are inadequately trained.

Some of the schools in the large cities are as good as any in the world. Where secondary schools exist, they are usually of better quality than elementary schools. Private schools carry a significant portion of the educational load. Those operated by the Roman Catholic church are overwhelmingly in the majority. Communities of foreigners, especially those from the United States, Great Britain, France, Germany, and Italy, have well-equipped schools for their children. Because these schools have, in some cases, been used as centers of political propaganda, they are now largely under governmental supervision.

### Facilities and Students of the Universities

About 85 percent of the total school enrollment is at the elementary level. Less than 2 percent is at the college level. Few of the children who start elementary school ever graduate from high school or college. As a result there are not enough college graduates to provide intellectual and technical leadership in local communities.

The universities differ considerably from those in North America. Faculties are mainly composed of men who practice a profession and teach only part time. Students have a strong voice in running the universities. They often go on strike if they feel examinations are too difficult. They also influence national politics and sometimes demonstrate or strike in attempts to change government policies.

### ART OF THE SPANISH AND PORTUGUESE COLONIES

Torre Tagle Palace in Lima (left) was begun in 1715. Its owner was the marqués of Torre Tagle, treasurer of Peru. Notice the richly carved balconies and the iron-studded door. For this church (right) the Brazilian sculptor Antônio Francisco Lisboa (1730-1814) carved 'Jonas' (foreground) and 77 other statues. Crippled, he worked with tools strapped to his wrists.

## Campaigns for Technical Training and Literacy

Most university students study law or medicine, the two most popular vocations for an educated man. Many graduates enter politics, and public officeholders frequently have a doctor's degree. Attempts are being made to increase enrollments in engineering, agriculture, industrial management, and other technical fields to help ease the most pressing needs.

Renewed efforts are now being made to wipe out illiteracy. Adult education programs are being launched. In some cases government teams travel from village to village offering vocational training and basic instruction in reading and writing. In Mexico's "Each one, teach one" campaign, every literate person was required to teach an illiterate fellow citizen how to read and write.

**THE GARDEN OF ART IN MEXICO CITY**
Public interest in art is shown by the popularity of the Sunday art exhibit in Sullivan Park, Mexico City. Artists of Mexico and other Latin American countries display their canvases here to interested audiences each week.

# Some Heroes and Patriots of Latin America

COLONIAL LATIN AMERICA was molded by the swashbuckling conquistadores who had quickly subdued most of the Indian populations. Seeking gold and personal power, these men possessed a fanatical zeal for spreading the influence of their church and their king. Their exploits demanded the utmost in human endurance and heroism. They are noted for their cruelty and treachery. Such men as Hernando Cortez (1485–1547), Vasco Nuñez de Balboa (1475–1517), and Francisco Pizarro (1471?–1541), wearing

**CRUELTY OF THE CONQUEROR**
In their zeal, the conquistadores were guilty of appalling excesses of cruelty. A 16th-century engraving depicts their use of vicious dogs to destroy the native Indians.

steel armor and riding strange monsters, struck terror in the hearts of the Indians. Firearms and vicious dogs gave them victory against superior numbers. By the end of the 16th century the conquistadores had laid claim for Spain to nearly half of the New World. (*See also* Cortez; Balboa; Pizarro.)

Other Spaniards were as idealistic as the conquistadores were ruthless. Bartolomé de Las Casas (1474–1566) was the first priest to be ordained in the New World. He resolved to devote his life to helping the Indians. He became known as a protector of the Indian and a prince of peace. (*See also* Las Casas.)

Juana Inés de la Cruz (1651–95) embodied the virtues of Latin womanhood and the persistence of Spanish culture and religion in the wild frontier life of America. At 17 she was a lady-in-waiting at the viceroy's court in Mexico City. Like England's Queen Elizabeth I she was so familiar with the classics and philosophy that her reputation for scholarship spread over America and Europe. Tiring of the admiration which her beauty and brilliance brought her, she sought quiet in a convent. The exquisite quality of her love poems earned her a position of immortality in the realm of Spanish literature. She was one of the first champions of woman's rights. At the age of 44 she died, exhausted from nursing the victims of a smallpox epidemic in Mexico City.

### The Great Liberators

The three outstanding leaders in the movement to break away from Spain were educated in Europe. These men—Simón Bolívar (1783–1830), José de San Martín (1778–1850), and Bernardo O'Higgins (1778–1842)—were as brave as any conquistador.

Bolívar's earliest revolts in South America failed; but after a period of exile in the West Indies, one success followed another. Venezuela and Colombia were free of Spain by 1821. San Martín began his fight to liberate the south at the battle of Lorezeno, in Argentina, in 1813. The next year Bernardo O'Higgins was defeated by the Spaniards in Chile. He fled to Argentina and joined San Martín.

With the skill of a Hannibal, San Martín led his army across the snowy Andes into Chile and engaged the Spanish forces. In 1817 O'Higgins led a charge which won the decisive battle for the independence of Chile. San Martín then turned his attention to Peru while Bolívar was liberating Ecuador. The two men met in July 1822, after which San Martín retired from the scene. Bolívar cleared the last remnants of Spanish rule from the area. (*See also* Bolívar; San Martín; O'Higgins.)

The revolutionary movement in Mexico began as a social and racial revolt. The leader, Miguel Hidalgo (1753–1811), was a Mexican-born village priest and onetime dean of the College of San Nicolás at Valladolid (now Morelia). Like Father Las Casas, he tried to help the Indian masses. Although his army of insurrection was defeated and he was executed in 1811, he is today called the Father of Mexican Independence. (*See also* Mexico, subhead "Spanish Conquest—Then Independence.")

José Martí (1853–95) was a leader in the Cuban independence movement. He took up arms in the civil war of 1895 and was one of the first to be killed. Pierre Toussaint L'Ouverture (1746?–1803), Negro slave and grandson of an African king, led the Haitian rebellion of the 1790's. He was captured in 1802, and he died in a French prison in 1803, the year before Haiti became free.

# Economic Conditions and Critical Problems

THE ECONOMIC aim of Spain and Portugal in founding colonies was to obtain precious metals, foodstuffs, and raw materials. The colonies also provided an expanding market for the manufactured goods of the homeland. Rigid trade restrictions limited a colony to commerce with the founding country only. The pattern of exporting raw materials and foodstuffs and importing manufactured goods has continued to the present time. Today the independent nations are, of course, free to trade with any country.

Large areas, as in the past, are almost entirely dependent upon the production and export of a single commodity, such as sugar, coffee, bananas, beef, wool, copper, tin, or petroleum. Mexico, Bolivia, Venezuela, and Chile lean heavily upon minerals. Argentina, Brazil, Colombia, Ecuador, Uruguay, Paraguay, the republics of Central America, and the three island countries depend upon farm, pastoral, and forest products. Peru exports important amounts of farm products and minerals. The countries that depend upon selling a single commodity are at the mercy of the fluctuating world market. When the price of the commodity collapses, the nation suffers.

Profits, meager or large, must balance off imports consisting of iron and steel, metal products, machinery, fuels and lubricants, transportation equipment, electrical goods, pharmaceuticals and chemicals, and a variety of other products. The price levels of manufactured products are likely to be more stable than those of raw materials.

## The Drive to Industrialize

The Latin American nations, as well as other countries that depend upon raw materials, are eager to advance in manufacturing. They want the "value added by manufacture" to bolster the price of their output, and they need the jobs afforded by industries.

Manufacturing has increased in parts of Latin America in recent years but only in the face of many obstacles. Capital is scarce, for few wealthy Latin Americans have been inclined to invest in factories. Most prefer land investments. Taxes on land have been traditionally low and easy to evade. Some of the rich also send their money overseas to a country whose economy is more stable than that of their own.

Foreign investment has been heavy in Latin America. Foreign concerns control many of the bigger mining, petroleum, and manufacturing establishments. United States and British financiers have built railways and public utilities.

**MEXICANS WORK FOR BETTER SCHOOLS**
Although the Mexican government spent 20 percent of its budget on education in 1960, some old school buildings were neglected. A campaign with the slogan "Restore the school nearest your heart" set pupils and parents to work.

The United States is the leader in private investment today. It invested some 9 billion dollars by 1960—about 80 percent of all foreign investment in Latin America. Substantial interests are held by British, French, Dutch, and German citizens and corporations. Petroleum investment accounts for more than one third of United States private financing. One third of all United States investment in Latin America is in Venezuela.

### Conflicts from Foreign Investment

Foreign investment has brought difficulties as well as benefits. In the past there have been cases in which foreign investments were used as an excuse for foreign military interference. In a number of instances foreign firms have received special concessions from corrupt local officials. Some Latin Americans are consequently antagonistic toward foreign investing and look upon it as exploitation of resources and labor. They take the view that the profits earned are all sent abroad, though statistics show that the national governments collect more from foreign companies in taxes than is remitted to stockholders abroad. Some three fourths of the gross income of United States-owned companies is spent in Latin America for wages to nearly one million workers, for materials, and for taxes.

On the other hand, many foreigners hesitate to place capital in Latin America because some of the governments have seized foreign-owned mines, wells, transportation lines, utilities, and plantations. Although they may promise payment for the property in the currency or bonds of the country, such expropriation usually brings serious losses to the investors.

### Government Investment

In recent decades, many governments have set up development agencies and have used federal money to build key industries and other economic and social projects. Often the governments have borrowed abroad to finance these enterprises. Since the 1930's the United States Export-Import Bank has furnished over $2\frac{1}{2}$ billion dollars to Latin America—more than one third of its total loans. The United Nations World Bank loaned over one billion dollars between 1947 and 1960. The Inter-American Development Bank was set up under the Organization of American States (OAS) in 1959 to supply additional loan funds to Latin America.

The shortage of skilled workers is another serious handicap to industrialization. Rural people have flooded into the cities seeking factory work, but

**PATIO OF SOUTH AMERICA'S OLDEST UNIVERSITY**
The University of San Marcos was founded in Peru in 1551, well before England began colonizing North America. It was directed by the Jesuits until the order was expelled in 1767. It is now a national institution.

**TRAINING TEACHERS IN BOLIVIA**
Bolivia is trying to meet its need for teachers by building rural normal schools like this one at Warisata. Teachers are trained to instruct in agriculture, rural industries, and domestic science as well as in academic subjects.

without skills and education they have only swelled the number of unemployed and spread the slums. The lack of good coal and the shortage of power are other obstacles to industrialization.

### Leading Industrial Areas

The chief industrial areas are the São Paulo-Rio de Janeiro area of Brazil; the Paraná-Plata area of Argentina and Uruguay; the Valparaiso-Santiago-Concepción region of Chile; the Bogotá-Medillín area of Colombia; and the Caracas area of Venezuela.

141

**CARNIVAL TIME IN COLÓN, PANAMA**

These young Panamanians wear traditional costumes to dance the *tamborito* in the carnival festivities. The woman's dress, the *pollera*, consists of a full skirt and an off-the-shoulder blouse colorfully embroidered and frosted in lace.

building on a large scale must precede the general use of trucks. Rail networks are inadequate in most sections of Latin America.

The vast distances, rugged, mountainous surfaces, and swampy or forested tropical areas of Latin America make road and railway building difficult and expensive. Some sections are so distant and unproductive that their output does not warrant the construction of transportation lines.

Communication has not been adequately developed. Telephone and telegraph lines, radio and television broadcasting facilities, and even regular mail service do not exist in many areas.

### Need for Land Reform

The landownership problem, like many other problems in Latin America, can be traced to the colonial period. The best lands of the New World were given by the crown to an aristocratic minority, except in Costa Rica. The huge estates were worked by people bound to the soil in a semifeudal system. Land meant wealth and power to the owner. He was influential in political affairs. The farm workers were landless then, and most remain so today. Their meager earnings depress the average income of Latin Americans.

Land reform is a major rallying point for political reformers throughout most of Latin America. Actual redistribution, however, is difficult to achieve. Landowners oppose reform, though their estates may contain hundreds of acres of unused land. In some countries there is not enough known good land to be distributed. Studies are needed to determine actual settlement possibilities.

### Mexico's Land Distribution History

Although some progress has been made in Venezuela, Bolivia, Chile, Colombia, Ecuador, and Guatemala, only Mexico has carried on a plan long enough to bring fundamental changes. Following the revolution of 1910, the constitution of 1917 gave the government the right to expropriate private property. Today the large estates, or *haciendas*, no longer exist.

Two systems of landholding have developed. The *ejido* is a peasant community. Each family works a parcel of land as its property but may not sell it. The title to the land remains in the ejido when a family moves away. Land is also distributed to private owners. The size of the plot may vary from

Mexico has made overall progress. Industry is, however, mainly concentrated in the central basins around Mexico City and in the Monterrey region, where pig iron and steel have been produced since 1903.

The leading types of industry in Latin America are food processing and light manufacturing. The countries are trying to develop heavy industry. Many have established steel mills.

### Problems of Latin America

Latin America's critical problems are so interwoven that efforts on many fronts will be necessary to bring about genuine progress. The problem of education is fundamental to the others. The estimated 70 to 80 million people unable to read or write are a drag on the economy. A sound educational program probably holds the key to advancement. Responsible political and business leaders must be developed.

Another major problem is inadequate transportation. Latin America is off the main trade routes linking the industrialized areas of the world. More significant than external isolation is the internal isolation that many of the countries suffer. Large areas are completely without roads. Rugged mountains block the development of transcontinental routes.

### Transportation and Communication

Aviation has been greatly advanced in recent decades. It is exceedingly important to the movement of passengers and mail. It has helped tie isolated places to the main routes. Airfreight, however, is too expensive for shipping bulky materials. Road

25 acres of irrigated land to more than 500 acres of grazing land too dry for crops. (*See also* Mexico.)

## Land Programs in Bolivia, Venezuela, and Chile

Expropriation came out of revolution in Bolivia in 1952. Progress in land distribution was slow due to economic problems and weak administration.

The Venezuela Agrarian Reform Law of 1960 had as its objective the relocation of 400,000 families of farm tenants, sharecroppers, squatters, and agricultural workers in ten years. In the first year 24,000 families received an average of 50 acres each. Other aspects of the plan moved slowly. These included provisions for agricultural credit, research and extension services, and market organization. Also provided for were the formation of cooperatives and the building of roads, irrigation systems, and rural housing, schools, and hospitals. Redistribution is aided by Venezuela's possession of extensive public land.

A sample survey in Venezuela in 1956 revealed that 1.7 percent of farm families owned 75 percent of the land in use, whereas 81 percent worked farms of less than 25 acres. These parcels totaled only 4 percent of the land.

Evolution rather than revolution describes the breaking up of haciendas in Chile. Some have been subdivided and sold to members of the rising middle class. Others have been bought by the government and made into small farms.

Puerto Rico's Operation Bootstrap has inspired the land reform programs of its neighbors. As a possession of the United States, Puerto Rico had marketing and other economic advantages, but the republics have adapted its methods. The resource base and use of the land were carefully surveyed before distribution. The farm population received instruction in modern tillage and in the use of improved varieties of plants and animals. Marketing cooperatives helped sell the produce. Manufacturing was developed to employ the surplus rural population. (*See also* Puerto Rico.)

## Communist Inroads in Latin America

Communists have made serious inroads in many countries. After Cuba became a Communist-controlled nation under Fidel Castro, Havana became the center of subversive activities in Latin America (*see* Cuba). In November 1963 Venezuela charged before the OAS that Cuba had smuggled arms onto Venezuela's territory with the intent of overthrowing the country's government. An OAS investigating committee confirmed the charges.

On March 31, 1964, President João Goulart of Brazil was ousted by the army, which charged him with having Communist ties. Brazil's new government severed relations with Cuba. Communists took part in the Dominican Republic revolt in 1965 and obstructed OAS peace efforts. In 1967 Ernesto "Che" Guevara, a leading Cuban revolutionary, was killed while organizing a guerrilla uprising in rural Bolivia. The Organization for Latin American Solidarity (OLAS), formed in Cuba in 1967 to promote revolt and guerrilla action, sought the support of Latin America's Communist parties. In 1970 Salvador Allende of Chile became the first freely elected Marxist president in the Western Hemisphere; he was ousted in 1973.

Philip D. Gendreau

In Latin America many scenic spots and historic monuments are set aside in parks for the enjoyment of the people. Here bathers in a pool at the National Park of Atecozol, in El Salvador, can watch steam rise from Izalco volcano.

Philip D. Gendreau

Colombians view the parade opening a bullfight in Bogotá. The favorite sport of Old Spain is very popular in some countries of Latin America. The elaborate costumes of the matadors are called "suits of lights."

143

**AUTOMOBILE FACTORY IN SÃO PAULO**
This industrial plant was financed by foreign capital and set up by foreign technicians. More than half its stock, however, is Brazilian-owned, and nearly all employees are Brazilians.

**WEIGHING SHRIMPS IN A PACKING PLANT**
The countries bordering the Caribbean have increased their shrimp fisheries in recent years. The Food and Agriculture Organization helped with a study of the sea's shrimp resources.

# The Struggle for Hemispheric Solidarity

PROGRESS TOWARD unity among the countries of the Western Hemisphere has been slow. Distance and geographic obstacles formed almost insuperable barriers when the nations were young. Cities that are now only hours apart by jet plane were separated by long weeks of difficult travel in colonial times. The chief sea routes crossed the Atlantic, and the American nations continued their close relations with their mother countries instead of establishing new ties in the Western Hemisphere.

### Conditions That Molded North Americans

Contrasts in background and development led to differences in politics, economics, and viewpoint that further separated the peoples of the New World. British and Dutch colonists and later settlers from northern Europe came to a cold climate in Anglo-America. They had to work or freeze and starve. They found no skilled Indian farmers to help them.

The Puritans who came to New England, the Roman Catholics who settled Maryland, the Quaker founders of Pennsylvania—all were trying to get away from religious persecution. They sought political liberty as well as religious freedom. They brought their families and built new homes and new social institutions.

These colonists of many nationalities and creeds were influenced by the political and economic upheavals that changed northern Europe in the 17th and 18th centuries. Their material progress was later promoted by the Industrial Revolution in Europe (see Industrial Revolution). The people of the 13 colonies fought the American Revolution not only for freedom from England but also for the right to rule themselves. They established a republican form of government which guaranteed that right.

### Latin Americans Cling to Iberian Ways

The conquistadores of the south came to America to get gold for themselves and their king and to win converts for their church. They had no thought of setting up new forms of government or religion. The colonists who followed the conquistadores remained faithful subjects of the Spanish and Portuguese monarchs. Living under autocratic rule, they gained no experience in self-government.

In several areas they found Indians farming the land. The Iberians took over the land and made serfs of the people. Huge tracts were granted by their kings to military and political leaders. Thus began the great landed estates that have continued to handicap Latin America. With the best land owned by a few families and worked by peon laborers, the Latin American countries did not attract the many European farmers and other middle-class folk who helped develop Anglo-America.

The settlers of Central and South America were under the sole influence of either Spain or Portugal. Trade was confined to the mother countries, where the Industrial Revolution had not yet penetrated. Thus there were few influences tending to encourage political change and such striking economic progress as arose in Anglo-America. When the colonies won their liberty, they freed themselves from Spain and Portugal but not from the tradition of autocratic rule. Republics were founded, but they were often

144

**LISTENING TO THE "VOICE OF THE ANDES"**
Cut off from the world by illiteracy and poor communications, these Ecuadorian Indians hear their first radio programs on a transistor set assembled by HCJB, a mission station in Quito.

ruled by military dictators. Economic life in many countries was dominated by the few wealthy landowners. The mass of the people were not educated for self-government and individual enterprise.

### Efforts to Link the Spanish Nations

After the colonists of Spain gained their liberty, they made attempts to create federations. Simón Bolívar dreamed of a union of the American states. At Panama City in 1826 a Treaty of Perpetual Union, League and Confederation was drawn up. Only Colombia ratified it. Bolívar's dreams were shattered. Upon his death in 1830, his own Gran Colombian Federation broke up into the present countries of Colombia, Venezuela, and Ecuador. In 1823 the five Central American states north of Panama formed a federation, but it collapsed in 1838.

Some of the circumstances operating against unity were indefinite boundaries, great distances between cities, intrigue by political refugees across international boundaries, and expansionist activities of political leaders. The forces causing strife and division were stronger than the urge for unity. Brazil, which was successful in maintaining its boundary claims and had little to fear from abroad, showed no inclination to cooperate during the 19th century.

### Wars Between the Nations

Frontier skirmishes occurred often, but they generally were localized events. Only three major wars were fought between Latin American countries during the 19th century. The first was the Argentine-Brazilian War (1842–52), concerning the sovereignty of Uruguay. Argentina finally lifted an eight-year siege of Montevideo and hostilities ceased, leaving Uruguay free.

The Paraguayan War (1865–70) pitted the well-disciplined army of Paraguay against the combined forces of Argentina, Brazil, and Uruguay. Paraguay lost the war and most of its male population.

The last of the three wars is known as the War of the Pacific or the Nitrate War (1879–83). After several decades of boundary disputes in the Atacama Desert, Chile declared war on both Peru and Bolivia. Chile was victorious and annexed all the Bolivian territory bordering on the Pacific plus the Peruvian province of Tarapacá.

Meanwhile the rising power of the United States was expressed through the Monroe Doctrine (1823) and its subsequent liberal interpretations (*see* Monroe Doctrine). This statement of policy warned the nations of Europe not to intervene in the affairs of the Western Hemisphere. Toward the middle of the 19th century certain Latin Americans began to fear the United States more and Europe less. As a result of the Mexican War (1846–48) the United States annexed half of Mexico's territory. Special congresses were held by Latin American nations relative to the question of security against aggressive acts of all foreign powers.

### Pan-American Conferences

The first of the international conferences of American states (popularly called Pan-American or inter-American conferences) met in Washington, D.C., in 1889. It set up a Commercial Bureau of the American Republics. At the fourth conference, in 1910, this bureau became the Pan American Union.

Other inter-American conferences held in various capital cities of Latin America have brought about significant agreements, resolutions, and treaties. Between conferences work has been carried on by special commissions and councils. Much effort has been

**BUILDING THE ROAD FROM BRASÍLIA TO BELÉM**
Thousands of men and hundreds of road machines worked three years to carve this highway through the rain forest. It is opening Brazil's thinly populated interior to settlement.

Peace Corps

As this Peace Corpsman teaches Spanish to village children in Colombia, he is also working for closer friendship and understanding between the peoples of the United States and Colombia.

devoted to the fields of economic cooperation, education, and health.

At the seventh conference, at Montevideo in 1933, the nations agreed not to intervene in one another's internal affairs. The "good neighbor" policy of President Franklin D. Roosevelt was inaugurated there. At Lima in 1938, under the totalitarian threats of Germany, Italy, and Japan, the delegates adopted the Declaration of Lima, proclaiming the unity of the hemisphere. All 21 nations were committed to defend the two continents against aggression. Immediately after war broke out in Europe the foreign ministers met in Panama and established a zone, av-

When Fidel Castro addressed a Havana crowd on May Day 1961, radio carried his speech to Cuba's Spanish-speaking neighbors. His promises of land and bread had great appeal.

eraging 300 miles in width, around the Americas into which ships of the belligerents were not to enter. At Havana in 1940 the foreign ministers arranged for the provisional administration of European colonies in America should political changes in Europe make such action necessary.

Following the attack on Pearl Harbor most Latin American nations either declared war on the Axis or severed diplomatic relations. The foreign ministers met in Mexico City in 1945 and passed the Act of Chapultepec, strengthening inter-American unity and cooperation. Because of its prolonged neutrality and the Nazi sympathies of its military government, Argentina was not included. The same year the Western Hemisphere nations took part in creating the United Nations. The conference at Rio de Janeiro in 1947 made formal the Act of Havana and made permanent the Act of Chapultepec.

At a conference in Bogotá in 1948, the Organization of American States (OAS) was chartered. The OAS functions as a regional agency within the United Nations. In 1962, OAS foreign ministers voted to expel Cuba because its Communist rule was "incompatible with the inter-American system." In July 1964 the OAS condemned Cuba for "acts of aggression" in connection with its terrorist campaign during Venezuela's 1963 election. Except for Mexico, all OAS members severed diplomatic relations with Cuba. By 1974, eight Latin American nations, including Venezuela, had defied the OAS policy against Cuba, but a motion to end the sanctions officially fell two votes short of a two-third majority. The following year, however, the OAS voted to lift the sanctions, allowing each member country to formulate its own trade, political, and economic policies toward Cuba. (*See also* Organization of American States.)

As an alternative to the United States-dominated OAS, a new organization was proposed by Mexico and Venezuela. The Latin American Economic System (SELA) was established in 1975 with 23 Latin American and Caribbean member countries (not including the United States).

## Other Joint Action

Decade by decade, cooperation among the republics increased. Through the Inter-American Highway Act of 1941, the United States aided in the construction of the separate sections of the Pan American Highway. The Inter-American Development Bank was chartered in 1959. Through intergovernmental arrangements, students and professors were exchanged between the countries of Latin America and the United States. Technical, economic, and cultural aid was furnished to the developing countries by the United States, by various international agencies, and by philanthropic organizations.

The growth of Western Hemisphere travel and trade in the postwar years had brought the peoples of the various countries into closer contact and had given them greater understanding of their neighbors' problems. The poor and illiterate of the Latin nations

Wide World

had been aroused by the world "revolution of rising expectations" and were demanding change and justice. Europe's success with the Common Market had set an example of the value of cooperation.

## Common Markets

In 1961 two organizations were formed to further mutual economic development, primarily by eliminating tariff barriers to intraregional trade. One, the Central American Common Market (CACM), consists of Costa Rica, El Salvador, Guatemala, Honduras, and Nicaragua. A major organ of CACM has been the Central American Bank for Economic Integration (CABEI). Each member nation subscribed 4 million dollars and the United States 10 million dollars.

The second, the Latin American Free Trade Association (LAFTA), consists of Argentina, Bolivia, Brazil, Chile, Colombia, Ecuador, Mexico, Paraguay, Peru, Uruguay, and Venezuela. An Andean Group within LAFTA was formed in 1969 for cooperation in industrial planning. Its members are Bolivia, Chile, Colombia, Ecuador, Peru, and, since 1973, Venezuela.

The Caribbean Community, including the Caribbean Common Market, was established in 1973. In 1978 the Amazon Pact was established by eight countries with frontiers in the Amazon River Valley in order to promote cooperative development of the area.

## The Alliance and the Peace Corps

At the Inter-American Economic and Social Council meeting at Punta del Este, Uruguay, in August 1961, President John F. Kennedy's proposal for an Alliance for Progress in the Americas was ratified. A flow of 20 billion dollars in private and public capital into Latin America was anticipated. The program progressed slowly. Many countries lagged in passing tax and land reform laws and in making development plans required for loans or grants. By 1964, however, encouraging advances in education, housing, and health had been made. The United States contributed over one billion dollars a year during the ten-year period after the alliance was formed.

The United States Peace Corps undertook many projects in Latin America during the 1960's and 1970's (*see* Peace Corps). Their aim was people-to-people understanding as well as technical assistance. Corpsmen lived in villages and worked on projects with the people. (For further information about Latin American people, history, culture, industries, and trade, *see* Central America; Latin American Literature; South America; West Indies; and articles on the various countries.)

### BIBLIOGRAPHY FOR LATIN AMERICA

#### Books and Films for Children

**The Amazon**, film (Encyclopaedia Britannica Films).
**Baum, Patricia.** Dictators of Latin America (Putnam, 1972).
**Bishop, C. H.** Martin de Porres, Hero (Houghton, 1954).
**Caldwell, J. C.** Let's Visit Central America, rev. ed. (John Day, 1973).
**Central America**, film (Encyclopaedia Britannica Films).
**Clayton, Robert.** Mexico, Central America, and the West Indies (John Day, 1971).
**Joy, C. R.** Getting to Know the River Amazon (Coward, 1963).
**Quinn, Vernon.** Picture Map Geography of Mexico, Central America and the West Indies, rev. ed. (Lippincott, 1965).
**Skiles, Jacqueline.** Columbus Started Something (Friendship, 1970).
**Syme, Ronald.** Bolívar (Morrow, 1968).

Pix

The construction business boomed in Latin America after World War II as new sections, like this one in Panama City, sprang up around many of the older cities. Architects have adapted modern designs and materials to tropical conditions.

Pan American Union

This hotel in Port-au-Prince, Haiti, is one of many built in Latin America in recent years to develop tourism. Sunny winter weather and bathing, fishing, and other sports have attracted a host of visitors from the Anglo-American countries.

**AGRARIAN REFORM UNDER WAY IN VENEZUELA**
As he receives title to cropland and the key to a new home, a farmer shakes the hand of President Rómulo Betancourt (left).

### Books for Young Adults and Teachers

Adams, R. N. and others. Social Change in Latin America Today (Random, 1960).

Alexander, R. J. Prophets of the Revolution (Macmillan, 1962).

Bailey, H. M. and Nasatir, A. P. Latin America: the Development of Its Civilization, 3d ed. (Prentice, 1973).

Butland, G. J. Latin America: a Regional Geography, 3d ed. (Halsted, 1973).

Fisher, J. R. Latin America: From Conquest to Independence (John Day, 1972).

Goetz, Delia. Neighbors to the South, rev. ed. (Harcourt, 1956).

Gordon, W. C. Political Economy of Latin America (Columbia Univ. Press, 1965).

Herring, H. C. and H. B. A History of Latin America, from the Beginnings to the Present, 3d ed. rev. (Knopf, 1968).

James, Preston. Latin America, 4th ed. (Odyssey, 1969).

Lamb, R. S. Latin America (Ocelot, 1963).

Madariaga, Salvador de. Latin America Between the Eagle and the Bear (Greenwood, 1976).

Nevins, A. J. Away to the Lands of the Andes (Dodd, 1962).

Parker, F. D. The Central American Republics (Oxford, 1964).

Perkins, Dexter. The United States and Latin America (La. State Univ. Press, 1961).

Prago, Albert. The Revolutions in Spanish America (Macmillan, 1970).

Robertson, W. S. Rise of the Spanish-American Republics As Told in the Lives of Their Liberators (Free Press, 1965).

South American Handbook (Rand, annual).

Tannenbaum, Frank. Ten Keys to Latin America (Random, 1966).

Von Hagen, V. W. Incas: People of the Sun (Collins, 1961).

Walton, R. J. The United States and Latin America (Seabury, 1972).

Williams, Byron. Continent in Turmoil (Parents, 1971).

Worcester, D. E. and Schaeffer, W. G. The Growth and Culture of Latin America, 2 vols., 2d ed. (Oxford, 1970–71).

Wythe, George. Industry in Latin America (Greenwood, 1949).

Yoder, H. W. This Is Latin America (Friendship, 1961).

Young, Bob and Jan. Liberators of Latin America (Lothrop, 1970).

(*See also* bibliographies for **Latin American Literature; Mexico; South America.**)

# Latin America's Creative Writers

**LATIN AMERICAN LITERATURE.** Literature and the other arts were cultivated in Latin America long before they were cultivated in the Anglo-American countries. This was partly because there were flourishing settlements in Middle and South America nearly a century before Jamestown and Quebec were founded. In addition, the colonists of the south had the leisure for scholarly pursuits earlier than the settlers of the north. The Indians in many sections of Latin America had the skills needed to till the soil, mine the ores, and work on the construction of churches and homes for the colonists. The Indians of Canada and of the 13 colonies lacked these skills. (*See also* Latin America.)

Universities and printing presses were also established far earlier in Latin America than they were in Anglo-America. The first book published in the New World was printed in Mexico City about 1539.

Only one language influence was felt in a given Latin American country—Portuguese in Brazil, French in Haiti, and Spanish in all others. In the 13 colonies and in Canada, on the other hand, there was competition among the languages and cultures of the settlers, who came from England, France, Spain, Germany, Holland, and other lands. English became dominant everywhere in Anglo-America except in French Canada.

Similarities existed in spite of these differences.

The first writings in both Latin America and English-speaking America were the works of writers from the Old World who had migrated to the New. The early 'Letters' of Hernando Cortez can be compared to 'The True Relation . . .' written by Capt. John Smith.

It was necessary in both Latin America and Anglo-America that settlers struggle against the tendencies to develop new languages by adopting and exaggerating differences in vocabulary and grammatical usage. Noah Webster, a lexicographer of the United States, had his counterpart in Andrés Bello of Venezuela. Both tried to keep the languages in the New World as similar as possible to those of the Old.

## PERIODS OF LATIN AMERICAN LITERATURE

Although there is no fully satisfactory chronological division of the literature of Latin America, a useful one is as follows:

**Colonial,** beginning with the date of the 'Diary' of Christopher Columbus, written during his first voyage in 1492, and extending to the "Cry of Dolores" of Father Miguel Hidalgo of Mexico, 1810.

**The Struggle for Independence,** extending to the battle of Ayacucho, 1824.

**The 19th Century Before Modernism,** extending to the publication of 'Azure', by the Nicaraguan poet Rubén Darío, 1888.

**Modernism,** extending to the resignation of Porfirio Díaz from the presidency of Mexico, 1911.

**Contemporary,** extending to the present.

## The Colonial Period

Pre-Columbian Indian literature was entirely oral except for Mayan hieroglyphic "books" (*see* Writing). The following works of explorers and others illustrate a gradual change from a literature by foreigners, using forms, languages, and loyalties brought from the Old World, to productions as characteristic of the New World as anything written by Benjamin Franklin:

'Diary', Christopher Columbus (1451–1506).

'History of the Indies', Bartolomé de Las Casas (1474–1566).

'Letters', Hernando Cortez (1485–1547).

'Shipwrecked', Alvar Núñez Cabeza de Vaca (1490–1557).

'The True History of the Conquest of New Spain', Bernal Díaz del Castillo (1492–1581?).

'The Chronicle of Perú', Pedro de Cieza de León (1518–60).

'The Araucaniad', Alonso de Ercilla y Zúñiga (1533–94).

'Florida of the Inca', "El Inca" Garcilaso de la Vega (1540?–1616). This author, the son of an Inca princess, tells a story sympathetic to his people.

'Arauco Subjugated', Pedro de Oña (1570–1645?).

'The Truth Suspected', Juan Ruiz de Alarcón y Mendoza (1580?–1639). Born in Mexico, the author went to Spain when quite young. He did all his writing there, but Mexico justly claims him.

## The Struggle for Independence

Most of the Spanish American countries began their struggle for political independence soon after the Napoleonic invasion of Spain. Puerto Rico and Cuba, however, remained a part of the Spanish empire until 1898. Haiti, with its uneasy freedom gained in 1804, and Brazil, with its status as an empire gained in 1822 and its change into a republic in 1889, had slightly differing histories.

The struggle for independence lasted about 14 years and provided subject matter and inspiration for nationalistic literatures. Some young Latin American writers who had been living abroad hurried back to their native countries to continue their careers. Among them was Manuel Eduardo de Gorostiza, a Mexican who had won recognition as a dramatist in Spain.

The temptation to exaggerate language differences was greater after independence but fortunately was not allowed to progress too far. Representative writers of this period who showed the influence of the political events are: Andrés Bello, of Venezuela, poet and grammarian; José Joaquín Fernández de Lizardi, Mexican novelist; José María Heredia, of Cuba, poet; and José Joaquín de Olmedo, of Ecuador, poet.

## The 19th Century Before Modernism

During this period European influences, particularly French, became more pronounced. Romanticism was represented by such writers as the Cuban poet Gabriel de la Concepción Valdés (pen name Plácido); Jorge Isaacs, Colombian novelist; Ignacio Manuel Altamirano, Mexican historioromantic novelist; and the Argentine folklore poet José Hernández. *Costumbrismo*, a type of literature similar to the essays of Addison and Steele, is best represented by Ricardo Palma, the Peruvian short-story writer.

## Modernism

Modernism was characterized by freedom of the individual to strike out on his own, rejecting European models. It was also characterized by a Pan-Americanism that rejected the leadership and influence of the United States and by a desire to invent new forms in poetry and fiction. The Nicaraguan poet Rubén Darío is accepted as the spokesman for modernism. Others, however—such as Julián del Casal, Cuban poet; José Asunción Silva, poet of Colombia; and Manuel Gutiérrez Nájera, Mexico's leading poet— were either contemporary to or slightly before him.

## Contemporary Period

The contemporary period was ushered in by the Mexican Revolution, which had repercussions in many other Latin American countries. The period showed a definite shift to the essay and prose fiction. Poetry and drama have continued to be cultivated, though the latter has found difficulty in competing commer-

**A POETESS OF COLONIAL MEXICO**
Juana Inés de la Cruz, 17th-century Mexican nun, won renown for her beauty, her poetic talent, and her self-sacrifice in the care of the poor and the afflicted.

Newberry Library  **OLMEDO**   Pan American Union  **BELLO**   Library of Congress  **HEREDIA**   Pan American Union  **PALMA**

cially with motion pictures. The novel has grown in popularity as the number of persons able to buy and read books has increased. The following five types of novels have been the most popular:

**Indianista novel**, the first being 'Birds Without a Nest', by a Peruvian, Clorinda Matto de Turner. This type is now represented by hundreds of titles.

**Gaucho (cowboy) novel**, especially popular in Argentina, Chile, Mexico, Uruguay, and Venezuela. The best of this class is 'Don Segundo Sombra', translated with the title 'Shadows on the Pampas', by the Argentine Ricardo Güiraldes.

**Novel of the Mexican Revolution**, which also became popular outside Mexico. The best and one of the earliest of this type is 'The Under Dogs', written by Mariano Azuela.

**Urban novel**, gaining in popularity as cities become increasingly important. One of the best of this type is 'Nacha Regules', written by the Argentine novelist Manuel Gálvez.

**Novel of escape**, rather widely cultivated as writers wish to get away from national and regional themes. One of the best novels of escape is 'The Spell of Seville' by the Uruguayan Carlos Reyles.

Three Latin American writers have so far received the Nobel prize for literature. In 1945 it was awarded to Gabriela Mistral of Chile for her poetry. (Her real name was Lucila Godoy Alcayaga.) Miguel Angel Asturias of Guatemala received the Nobel prize in 1967 for his novels, legends, and poetry. And in 1971 the prize was awarded to Pablo Neruda (Neftalí Ricardo Reyes) of Chile for his poetry.

# Summary of Latin American Literature by Countries

## ARGENTINA

The great names in the literature of Argentina are mainly those of the 19th and 20th centuries. After the ousting of the dictator Juan Manuel de Rosas in 1852 the republic was strongly united with centralized authority. Under a new constitution it encouraged a rapid advance in education, political stability, and art. Domingo Faustino Sarmiento, educator, politician, and writer, was one of the great creators of modern Argentina.

Argentina's chief contribution to Latin American literature was the *Gaucho* theme, used in both poetry and prose fiction. Some of Argentina's finest writers are:

**Andrade, Olegario Víctor** (1841–82)—'Song to the Future of the Latin Race in America'.

**Borges, Jorge Luis** (born 1900)—'Ficciones'.

**Echeverría, Esteban** (1805–51)—'Rhymes'.

**Gálvez, Manuel** (1882–1962)—'Nacha Regules'.

**Güiraldes, Ricardo** (1886–1927)—'Shadows on the Pampas'.

**Hernández, José** (1834–86)—'Martín Fierro'.

**Larreta, Enrique** (1875–1961)—'The Glory of Don Ramiro'.

**Lugones, Leopoldo** (1874–1938)—'Golden Mountains'.

**Lynch, Benito** (1885–1951)—'The Englishman of the Bones'.

**Mármol, José** (1818–71)—'Amalia'.

**Obligado, Rafael** (1851–1920)—'Argentine Legends'.

**Ocantos, Carlos María** (1860–1949)—'León Zaldívar'.

**Payró, Roberto J.** (1867–1928)—'Upon These Ruins'.

**Rojas, Ricardo** (1882–1957)—'Ollantay'.

**Sarmiento, Domingo Faustino** (1811–88)—'Facundo'.

**Storni, Alfonsina** (1892–1938)—'The Rosebush's Restlessness'.

## BOLIVIA

Bolivia, in spite of its chronic economic difficulties, its large number of unassimilated Indians, many of whom do not speak Spanish, and its relative isolation from major cultural centers of the world, has produced some important literature.

The greatest of Bolivia's poets, Ricardo Jaimes Freyre, spent much of his life in Argentina. Some contemporary writers, especially Alcides Arguedas, are interested in presenting the problems of the lower economic classes. Some notable Bolivian writers are:

**Arguedas, Alcides** (1879–1946)—'The Bronze Race'.

**Calvo, Daniel** (1832–80)—'Rhymes'.

**Cerruto, Oscar** (born 1907)—'Rain of Fire'.

**Chirveches, Armando** (1883–1926)—'The Rojas Candidacy'.

**Galindo, Nestor** (1830–65)—'Tears'.

**Jaimes Freyre, Ricardo** (1870–1933)—'The Conquistadores'.

**Lenz, Benjamín** (1836–78)—'Poems'.

149a

Pan American Union
**HOSTOS Y BONILLA**

Library of Congress
**ANDRADE**

Hispanic Society of America
**MEDINA**

Pan American Union
**MARTÍ**

## BRAZIL

Brazil holds a unique place among the countries of the New World—it is the only one in which Portuguese is the official language. The literature of Brazil, like that of Mexico, Peru, and Chile, started in colonial times. Although the primary inspiration for writing came from a well-developed motherland literature, the influence of French letters also was felt at the outset.

José de Anchieta, one of the earliest Brazilian writers, set the tone and spirit still to be found in the nation. His description of the beauties of the country and his recognition of the white man's responsibility for the Indian's welfare make him truly Brazilian though he was born in Europe.

Antonio José da Silva worked to keep the drama alive in the 18th century, while Thomaz Antonio Gonzaga in his 'Chilean Letters' shows the influence of Rousseau. Literature soon became more realistic, and even pessimistic, with Brazil's greatest writer, Joaquim Maria Machado de Assis. Stories dealing with the socioeconomic problems continue to be of primary importance among Brazilians writing today. Brazil's best writers include:

Amado, Jorge (born 1912)—'Limitless Lands'.
Anchieta, José de (1534–97)—'Poems'.
Azevedo, Aluizio (1857–1913)—'The Mulato'.
Castro Alves, Antonio de (1847–71)—'Poems'.
Da Cunha, Euclydes (1866–1909)—'Rebellion in the Backlands'.
Da Silva, Antonio José (1705–39)—'Life of the Great Don Quixote'.
Escragnolle Tounay, Alfredo de (1843–99)—'Innocence'.
Gonçalves Dias, Antonio (1823–64) — 'American Poems'.
Gonzaga, Thomaz Antonio (1744–1807?)—'Chilean Letters'.
Graça Aranha, José Pereira da (1868–1931)—'Canaan'.
Lima, Jorge de (1893–1953)—'Poems'.
Machado de Assis, Joaquim Maria (1839–1908)—'Posthumous Memoirs of Braz Cubas'.
Martiniano de Alencar, José (1829–77) — 'The Guaraní'.
Monteiro Lobato, José Bento (1883–1948)—'Light Tales'.
Oliveira, Antonio Mariano Alberto de (1859–1937)—'Sonnets and Poems'.
Verissimo, Erico (born 1905)—'Night'.

## CHILE

Chile's literature is most significant. It began in the colonial period with 'The Araucaniad' by Alonso de Ercilla y Zúñiga. Two Chilean poets have received the Nobel prize for literature—Gabriela Mistral, in 1945, and Pablo Neruda, in 1971. Alberto Blest Gana, called the Balzac of Chile, wrote for nearly 70 years. A few of the outstanding writers are:

Alegría, Fernando (born 1918)—'Four White Feet'.
Barrios, Eduardo (1884–1963)—'The Men Within the Man'.
Blest Gana, Alberto (1831–1920)—'Martín Rivas'.
Ercilla y Zúñiga, Alonso de (1533–94)—'The Araucaniad'.
Lillo, Baldomero (1867–1923)—'The Devil's Pit and Other Stories'.
Medina, José Toribio (1852–1930)—Bibliographical, historical works.
Mistral, Gabriela (Lucila Godoy Alcayaga) (1889–1957)—'Desolation'.
Neruda, Pablo (Neftalí Ricardo Reyes) (1904–73)—'Twenty Love Poems and a Song of Despair'.
Prado, Pedro (1886–1952)—'Alsino'.
Subercaseaux, Benjamín (born 1902)—'Jemmy Button'.
Vicuña Mackenna, Benjamín (1831–86)—Histories, biographies.

## COLOMBIA

Colombians—especially in the three main cities of Bogotá, Cali, and Medellín—have always prided themselves on a tradition of culture. Colonial traditions and customs are strong in 'María', by Jorge Isaacs. 'The Vortex', by José Eustacio Rivera, pictures life in the dense tropical jungles. In José Asunción Silva is found a source of the modernism of the great Nicaraguan Rubén Darío. Best-known writers of Colombia include:

Alvarez Lleras, Antonio (1892–1956)—'The Claw'.
Arboleda, Julio (1817–61)—'Poems'.
Caro, José Eusebio (1817–53)—'Poems'.
Carrasquilla, Tomás (1858–1940)—'The Marquise of Yolombó'.
Gutiérrez González, Gregorio (1826–72)—'Poems'.
Isaacs, Jorge (1837–95)—'María'.
Palacios, Eustaquio (1830–98)—'The Royal Ensign'.
Rivera, José Eustacio (1889–1928)—'The Vortex'.
Sanín Cano, Baldomero (1861–1957)—'Literary and Philological Disquisitions'.

**149b**

Silva, José Asunción (1865–96)—'Poems'.
Tablanca, Luis (Enrique Pardo y Farelo) (born 1883)—
'The Country Girl'.
Valencia, Guillermo (1873–1943)—'Poems'.

## COSTA RICA

Costa Rica is one of the most progressive Central American countries. Several Costa Rican intellectuals have been leaders in the advancement of education—particularly Roberto Brenes Mesén and Joaquín García Monje. Some notable Costa Rican writers are:

Brenes Mesén, Roberto (1874–1947)—'The Gods Return'.
Echeverría, Aquileo (1866–1909)—'Rustic Rhymes'.
Fallas, Carlos Luis (born 1910)—'Mother United'.
Fernández Guardia, Ricardo (1867–1950)—'Tican Stories'.
García Monje, Joaquín (1881–1958)—'Daughters of the Soil'; editor, *Repertorio Americano*.
Lyra, Carmen (María Isabel Carvajal) (1888–1949)—'Stories of My Aunt Panchita'.
Pacheco Cooper, Emilio (1865–1906)—'Poetry'.
Sotela, Rogelio (1894–1943)—'Writers and Poets of Costa Rica'.

## CUBA

The fact that independence came much later in Cuba than it did in the other Spanish American republics affected the development of its literature. The leading poets of the extended colonial period were José María Heredia and Gertrudis Gómez de Avellaneda y Arteaga. The finest writer of the struggle for independence was the journalist, poet, and patriot José Martí. Cuba's great modernist was Julián del Casal. Carlos Loveira y Chirino, a labor organizer, was the country's best novelist. Some Cuban writers are:

Baralt, Luis Alejandro (1892–1969)—'The Moon in the Swamp'.
Casal, Julián del (1863–93)—'Poems'.
Gómez de Avellaneda y Arteaga, Gertrudis (1814–73)—'Poems'; (also stories, novels, and plays).
Heredia, José María (1803–39)—'Niágara'.
Hernández Catá, Alfonso (1885–1940)—'Stories of Passion'.
Loveira y Chirino, Carlos (1882–1928)—'Generals and Doctors'.
Martí, José (1853–95)—'Poems, Essays . . .'.
Plácido (Gabriel de la Concepción Valdés) (1809–44)—'A Prayer to God'.
Villaverde, Cirilo (1812–94)—'Cecilia Valdés'.

## DOMINICAN REPUBLIC

The Dominican Republic has gone through a relatively long period of political difficulties in the 20th century. As the first Latin American republic to be permanently settled, however, it has developed a worthwhile literature. The best-known writers of the Dominican Republic include:

Galván, Manuel de Jesús (1834–1911)—'Enriquillo'.
Henríquez Ureña, Max (1885–1968)—'Historical Panorama of Dominican Literature'.
Henríquez Ureña, Pedro (1884–1946)—'Dominican Literature'.
Monte, Felix María del (1819–99)—'Poems'.
Pérez, José Joaquín (1845–1900)—'Native Fantasies'.
Ureña de Henríquez, Salomé (1850–97)—'Poems'.

## ECUADOR

Ecuador has contributed significantly to Latin American literature. The first poet to eulogize the independence of Latin America in epic style was José Joaquín de Olmedo. The high percentage of Indians in the population has helped make racial themes popular. Some of the writers are:

Carrera Andrade, Jorge (born 1903)—'Place of Origin'.
Gil Gilbert, Enrique (born 1912)—'Our Daily Bread'.
Icaza, Jorge (born 1906)—'Huasipungo'.
Mera, Juan León (1832–94)—'Cumandá or a Drama Among Savages'.
Montalvo, Juan (1832–89)—'Chapters Cervantes Forgot to Write'.
Olmedo, José Joaquín de (1780–1847)—'The Victory of Junin, Song to Bolívar'.
Zaldumbide, Gonzalo (1885–1965)—'Bitter Fruits'.

## GUATEMALA

Guatemala has begun to lead the Central American republics in publishing. The educational system has been reorganized. Many people believe that a real literary renaissance is on the way. A few of the writers worthy of mention are:

Arévalo Martínez, Rafael (born 1884)—'Depths'.
Asturias, Miguel Ángel (1899–1974)—'The President'.
Batres y Montúfar, José de (1809–44)—'Traditions of Guatemala'.
Diéguez, Juan (1813–66)—'April Afternoons'.
Irisarri, Antonio José de (1786–1868)—'Satirical and Burlesque Poems'.
Jil, Salom (José Milla y Vidaurre) (1827–82)—'Don Bonifacio'.

ZORILLA DE SAN MARTÍN

OLIVEIRA

SANÍN CANO

DARÍO

## HAITI

Haitian literature deals, on the whole, with the nation's history and its problems concerning its socioeconomic development. Many of the writers have spent some time in France and have come under the influence of contemporary French writers. Among the country's notable authors are:

Coicou, Massillon (1867–1908)—'Emperor Dessalines'.
Marcelin, Fréderic (1848–1917)—'Mama's Vengeance'.
Marcelin, Pierre (born 1908)—'Canapé-Vert' (with Philippe Thoby-Marcelin).
Roumain, Jacques (1907–44)—'Masters of the Dew'.
Sylvain, Georges (1866–1925)—'Cric! Crac!'.
Thoby-Marcelin, Philippe (1904–75)—'Canapé-Vert' (with Pierre Marcelin).

## HONDURAS

The literature of Honduras had early beginnings, but the country's output was not large. Since the second half of the 19th century a real awakening has been noted. Some of the best-known writers are:

Carcoma, Jacob (1914–59)—'Pines of Honduras'.
Castro, Jesús (born 1906)—'Fragrance of Spring'.
Díaz Lozano, Argentina (born 1909)—'Pearls from My Rosary'.
Durón, Jorge Fidel (born 1902)—'American Stories'.
Molina, Juan Ramón (1875–1908)—'Song to the Río Grande'.
Reyes, José Trinidad (1797–1855)—'Pastorals'.
Turcios, Froilán (1875–1943)—'Almond Blossoms'.

## MEXICO

Mexico, with the largest population of the Spanish-speaking countries of the New World, has one of the richest literatures of Latin America. From the earliest times, even during the days of the conquistadores, important writing was done. Cortez' 'Letters' and Bernal Díaz del Castillo's 'True History of the Conquest of New Spain' are two interesting works produced by the conquistadores.

The Spanish Golden Age was enriched by the Mexican-born dramatist Juan Ruiz de Alarcón y Mendoza. The 17th-century nun Juana Inés de la Cruz produced great love poems. The best picaresque novel of the New World, 'The Itching Parrot', was written by a Mexican, José Joaquín Fernández de Lizardi.

During the 19th century several Mexican poets contributed significantly to modernism. It is probable, however, that in the novel of the Mexican Revolution Mexico developed a new type of fiction. Notable Mexican writers include:

Altamirano, Ignacio Manuel (1834–93)—'Christmas in the Mountains'.
Azuela, Mariano (1873–1952)—'The Under Dogs'.
Delgado, Rafael (1853–1914)—'La Calandria'.
Díaz Mirón, Salvador (1853–1928)—'Poems'.
Fernández de Lizardi, José Joaquín (1776–1827)—'The Itching Parrot'.
Gamboa, Federico (1864–1939)—'The Highest Law'.
Gorostiza, Manuel Eduardo de (1789–1851)—'The Clown's Daughter'.
Gutiérrez Nájera, Manuel (1859–95)—'Poems'.
Guzmán, Martín Luis (born 1887)—'The Eagle and the Serpent'.
Juana Inés de la Cruz (1651–95)—'Poems'.
López y Fuentes, Gregorio (1897–1966)—'El Indio'.
Nervo, Amado (1870–1919)—'The Moment That You'll Love Me'.
Reyes, Alfonso (1889–1959)—'Sea Gulls'.
Romero, José Rubén (1890–1952)—'The Useless Life of Pito Pérez'.
Ruiz de Alarcón y Mendoza, Juan (1580?–1639)—'The Truth Suspected'.
Sierra, Justo (1814–61)—'The Jew's Daughter'.
Torres Bodet, Jaime (born 1902)—'Poems'.
Usigli, Rodolfo (born 1905)—'The Apostle'.
Vasconcelos, José (1882–1959)—'Ulises Criollo'.

## NICARAGUA

Rubén Darío was the leader, if not the founder, of modernism. Because of his international acceptance and reputation, he has overshadowed the other writers of this turbulent and interesting country.

The several invasions of Nicaragua have been the subject of hundreds of poems, essays, and works of fiction. The fear of Yankee imperialism was expressed by Rubén Darío in his famous poem 'To Roosevelt'. A few of the outstanding writers of Nicaragua are:

Aguilar Cortés, Jerónimo (born 1890)—'The Necklace of False Pearls'.
Calero Orozco, Adolfo (born 1899)—'Rustic Tales'.
Cuadra, Pablo Antonio (born 1912)—'Nicaraguan Poems, 1930–1933'.
Darío, Rubén (1867–1916)—'Azure'.
Robleto, Hernán (born 1895)—'Blood in the Tropics'.

## PANAMA

Panama has been an independent country only since 1903. As the youngest of the Spanish American republics,

RODÓ

LARRETA

CHOCANO

VASCONCELOS

GARCÍA MONJE

P. HENRÍQUEZ UREÑA

MISTRAL

A. REYES

it is often given scant recognition by literary historians. Even before its independence, however, Panama's writers were showing characteristics distinct from those of authors in Colombia. A marked trend toward cosmopolitanism was noteworthy. A few outstanding writers are:

Fábrega, José Isaac (born 1900)—'The Crucible'.
Geenzier, Enrique (1888–1943)—'Dusk and Shadows'.
Méndez Pereira, Octavio (1887–1954)—'The Treasure of the Dabaibe'.
Miró, Ricardo (1883–1940)—'Silent Paths'.
Obaldía, María Olimpia de (born 1891)—'Orchids'.
Sinán, Rogelio (Bernardo Domínguez Alba) (born 1904)—'Holy Week in the Mist'.

## PARAGUAY

Paraguay has passed through very difficult times. It has been engaged in an almost continuous series of wars since it became independent. Now it is finally emerging from its "dark ages" into a period of enlightenment.

Paraguay is virtually bilingual. The Guarani Indian language has reached the status of a literary language. Writers of note include:

Alsina, Arturo (born 1897)—'The Brand'.
Barrett, Rafael (1877–1910)—'Short Stories'.
Casaccia, Gabriel (born 1907)—'La Babosa'.
Pla, Josefina (born 1909)—'Here Nothing Has Happened'.
Ramos Giménez, Leopoldo (born 1896)—'Eros'.
Roa Bastos, Augusto Antonio (born 1918)—'Nightingale of Dawn'.

## PERU

Several evidences of pre-Columbian literature are found in Latin America. Perhaps the most interesting is an Inca drama, 'Ollantay', first set down by a Peruvian priest in the 18th century. Early literature in Spanish is represented by the historical writings of "El Inca" Garcilaso de la Vega and the poet Juan del Valle y Caviedes.

A famous Peruvian prose writer of the modern period was Ricardo Palma. His nine-volume 'Peruvian Traditions' is a mixture of history and fiction. The stories are amusing and delightfully written tales and anecdotes from Peruvian history. José Santos Chocano was second to Rubén Darío among the great modernists. A few of the many Peruvian writers are:

Alegría, Ciro (1909-67)—'Broad and Alien Is the World'.
Chocano, José Santos (1875–1934)—'Song to the Future'.

Diez Canseco, José (1905–49)—'Mulatto Types'.
García Calderón, Ventura (1886–1959)—'Worth a Peru'.
Garcilaso de la Vega, "El Inca" (1540?–1616)—'Florida of the Inca'.
González Prada, Manuel (1848–1918)—'Peruvian Ballads'.
Matto de Turner, Clorinda (1852–1909)—'Birds Without a Nest'.
Palma, Ricardo (1833–1919)—'Peruvian Traditions'.
Valle y Caviedes, Juan del (1652–92)—'Poems'.

## PUERTO RICO

Although Puerto Rico is not a Latin American republic, its literature is in the same vein. Its first important writer was the philosopher-educator Eugenio María de Hostos y Bonilla. The Association of Puerto Rican Writers has been influential in inspiring creative writing. Some leading authors are:

Balseiro, José (born 1900)—'The Watch Tower'.
Hostos y Bonilla, Eugenio María de (1839–1903)—'The Wanderings of Bayoán'.
Laguerre, Enrique (born 1906)—'The 30th of February'.
Palés Matos, Luis (1898–1959)—'Poems'.

## SALVADOR, EL

The small, densely populated republic of El Salvador claims with Guatemala a pre-Columbian literary work. This is the 'Popol-Vuh', the history or mythology of the Quiche Indians. It is said to have been written in the 17th century in Latin characters, reproducing in part a pre-Columbian original in Mayan hieroglyphics. A few of El Salvador's writers are:

Avila, Julio Enrique (born 1892)—'The World of My Garden'.
Cañas, Juan José (1826–1918)—'Departure of the Ship *Gold Hunter*'.
Lars, Claudia (Carmen Brannon de Samayoa) (born 1899)—'Stars in the Pool'.
Quijano Hernández, Manuel (born 1871)—'Stories of My Country'.
Salazar Arrué, Salvador (born 1899)—'That and More'.
Ulloa, Juan (born 1898)—'Humble Lives'.

## URUGUAY

The small country of Uruguay is one of the most literate and progressive of the Latin American nations. It has a rich literature. Its best-known poet is Juan Zorilla de San Martín. The novelist Carlos Reyles was both an escapist and a psychological analyst.

Many Uruguayan writers are claimed both by their home country and by Argentina. Florencio Sánchez and Horacio Quiroga were born in Uruguay and moved to Argentina. Quiroga wrote of the Argentine Chaco and Misiones. Sánchez became a newspaperman and a playwright in Buenos Aires. A few of Uruguay's notable writers are:

**Acevedo Díaz, Eduardo** (1851–1924)—'Soledad'.
**Agustini, Delmira** (1886–1914)—'Poems'.
**Herrera y Reissig, Julio** (1875–1910)—'Lyrical Anthology'.
**Ibarbourou, Juana de** (Honorary name: Juana de América) (born 1895)—'The Hour'.
**Quiroga, Horacio** (1879–1937)—'Stories of Love, Madness and Death'.
**Reyles, Carlos** (1868–1938)—'The Spell of Seville'.
**Rodó, José Enrique** (1872–1917)—'Ariel'.
**Sánchez, Florencio** (1875–1910)—'My Son the Doctor'.
**Viana, Javier de** (1868–1926)—'Yuyos'.
**Zorilla de San Martín, Juan** (1855–1931)—'Tabaré: Novel in Verse'.

## VENEZUELA

Venezuela was influential in the Latin American movement for intellectual and political emancipation from Spain. One of its leaders, Andrés Bello, was notable in the fields of journalism, poetry, law, history, philology, and literary criticism. Today fiction is more accepted than poetry and drama. A distinguished contemporary novelist, Rómulo Gallegos, was a former president of the republic. Rufino Blanco-Fombona was a poet, critic, and novelist. Among the best-known writers are:

**Bello, Andrés** (1781–1865)—'Eulogy to the Agriculture of the Torrid Zone'.
**Blanco-Fombona, Rufino** (1874–1944)—'Man of Gold'.
**Gallegos, Rómulo** (1884–1969)—'Doña Bárbara'.
**Padrón, Julián** (1910–54)—'Spring Nights'.
**Parra, Teresa de la** (1895–1936)—'Mama Blanca's Souvenirs'.
**Picón-Febres, Gonzalo** (1860–1918)—'Sergeant Phillip'.
**Rosales, Julio** (born 1885)—'Under the Golden Skies'.
**Uslar Pietri, Arturo** (born 1906)—'Red Lances'.

### Books About Latin American Literature

**Anderson Imbert, Enrique.** Spanish-American Literature: a History, 2 vols., 2d rev. ed. (Wayne State Univ. Press, 1969).

**Fitts, Dudley, ed.** Anthology of Contemporary Latin-American Poetry (Greenwood, 1976).

**Foster, D. W. and V. R., eds.** Modern Latin American Literature, 2 vols. (Ungar, 1975).

**Franco, Jean.** An Introduction to Spanish-American Literature (Cambridge Univ. Press, 1969).

**Holmes, H. A.** Spanish America in Song and Story (Gordon Press, n.d.).

**Oliver, W. I., ed. and tr.** Voices of Change in the Spanish American Theater: an Anthology (Univ. of Texas Press, 1971).

**Torres-Ríoseco, Arturo.** The Epic of Latin American Literature (Univ. of Calif. Press, 1942).

# LATIN—Basic Language of the Western World

**LATIN LANGUAGE AND LITERATURE.** When people talk of inventing a world language, the idea sounds visionary. But such a language really existed for many centuries—from just before the dawn of the Christian Era almost to our own times. This world language was Latin. It began its career by following the victorious Roman legion over Europe, Asia, and Africa. It finally became the speech of Western civilization. It was spoken in one form or another from the British Isles to the Persian Gulf.

The Latin of everyday life kept steadily changing in pronunciation, grammar, and vocabulary. Various dialects grew up in different localities. In the course of a few centuries these dialects developed into the group of related tongues called the Romance languages (*see* Romance Languages).

Literary Latin remained the language of religious, scholarly, and political life. It underwent little change. In the Middle Ages scholars, priests, and statesmen could travel the length of Europe without learning the languages of the various countries. In every community there were sure to be men of learning who talked Latin. State documents, as well as scientific, philosophical, and other scholarly works, were written only in Latin.

Even today Latin might be considered a world language. One third of the English that we write is Latin. We can hardly speak a sentence without using

These countries speak the Romance languages, derived directly from Latin. Languages such as English owe Latin a large debt.

words such as "wall," "street," "city," "army," "justice," "religion," and thousands of others that we have inherited from the Romans (*see* English Language). In the Romance languages of Europe—Italian, French, Spanish, Portuguese, and Rumanian—the proportion of Latin words is even higher than it is in English.

In the Indo-European family of languages, Latin might be called a sister of Sanskrit and Greek (*see* Language). When Greek was already a major world language, Latin was still a tongue spoken only by a few tribes in Latium, a district that included Rome. It was not until the 3d century B.C. that it was spoken throughout Italy. It superseded for the

153

CICERO

most part the other Italic dialects. It was not until the first century, however, that it had been developed into a superb literary language, a marvelous instrument for prose and poetry. The Latin of this so-called Golden Age had a stateliness and an artistic finish of style that have never been surpassed in any tongue. The masters knew the limitations of their instrument. Latin did not lend itself to expressing fine shades of meaning. Therefore the great Roman writers strove rather for clearness and precision. The language did not have the variety of sound that Greek possessed through its more numerous vowels and diphthongs and its musical accent. The monotony of Latin was further increased by the great number of long syllables. But this very monotony in the right hands gave weight and dignity and a beautiful rhythmic cadence.

## The Beginnings of Literature

Before the influx of Greek culture about 270 B.C., the Romans had already developed a type of literary form, called Saturnian verse. The meter of this verse was based upon accent. Its form was capable of adaptation to a variety of poetical purposes. The Greek measures that Latin afterward followed were based not on accent but on long and short syllables.

The first Roman book, however, seems to have been a translation of the Greek 'Odyssey'. This was made in the latter half of the 3d century B.C. by a Greek slave, Livius Andronicus, who also translated some Greek plays. The next poet, Gnaeus Naevius (died about 200 B.C.), continued to translate or imitate Greek drama, often using subjects from Roman history and introducing allusions to contemporary politics. He also used the pattern given by Andronicus' 'Odyssey' to write an epic of the First Punic War. Thus from its beginnings, Roman literature was based upon Greek models.

On this foundation Quintus Ennius (239–169 B.C.), the most important Roman writer before the age of Cicero, reared the stately edifice of his 'Annales'. This tremendous epic history of the Roman state is unfortunately known today from only a few fragments. In his poem Ennius remolded the still rude and clumsy Latin to fit the stately flow of the Greek hexameter verse form (see Greek Language and Literature). Thus he influenced the whole later history of the language. A tireless and prolific worker, Ennius also produced an astonishing number of translations from the Greek tragedy and comedy, as well as many original dramas and other works which won for him the title "father of Roman poetry."

The first Latin writer whose works have survived in any considerable body is Titus Maccius Plautus (254?–184 B.C.), the greatest comic dramatist of Rome. Twenty of his farcical plays have been preserved more or less intact through the centuries, making him one of the world's chief dramatic influences. His plots—which he borrowed from the Greek comic poets—have in turn furnished a rich mine for later playwrights, including Shakespeare and Molière. Many of the stock characters of the comic stage of today are mere adaptations of the types which he took from Greek comedy. (See also Drama.)

Though Plautus got the substance of his plots and characters from Greek sources, his manner and spirit were essentially Roman. His great successor Terence, who was born about the year Plautus died, avoided as a blemish any impulse toward originality or the expression of national quality. Terence copied his Greek originals with slavish fidelity. There is nothing Roman about his work but the language. His merit is that he thus brought into Roman literature the Greek standards of elegance, artistic perfection, and moderation. His defect is that he "struck Latin literature at the root with the fatal disease of mediocrity." His six plays, which all survive, have served as models of classical perfection to every generation of playwrights since. Some of his exquisitely polished lines—such as *Homo sum: humani nihil a me alienum puto* ("I am a man; and I think nothing pertaining to mankind foreign to me")—have passed into the currency of common speech.

In addition to these poets, there was Cato the Censor (234–149 B.C.), the first writer of prose history in Rome to use his native tongue. His published speeches were greatly admired by Cicero. Another poet was Lucilius (about 180–103 B.C.), whose satires were the first written in the modern sense of witty social criticism. These were the most important contributors to the early period of Latin literature.

## The Golden Age

The Golden Age, that great period when Latin literature reached its fullest splendor, covers about a century (80 B.C.–A.D. 14). It started with the beginning of Cicero's rise as an orator and ended with the death of the Emperor Augustus, under whose patronage arts and letters flourished as never before in Italy. Cicero brought Latin prose as an instrument for oratorical, philosophical, literary, and epistolary expression to such a pitch of perfection that the adjective "Ciceronian" is a synonym for "classically perfect," "polished" (see Cicero). A leading modern critic of Latin literature, J. W. Mackail of Oxford University, once wrote: "Cicero's unique and imperishable glory is that he created a language which remained for 16 centuries the language of the civilized world, and used that language to create a style which 19 centuries have not replaced, and in some respects have hardly altered." Different but in no way inferior to the stately sonorous periods of Cicero was the simple straightforward style of

Caesar. Caesar's 'Gallic Wars', recording his campaign in Gaul, remains a model of prose narration (*see* Caesar).

The other chief writers of the Ciceronian period are Sallust, Lucretius, and Catullus. Sallust (86–34 B.C.) is placed in the front rank of Roman historians because of his accounts of the Catilinarian conspiracy and the Jugurthine War. The philosophical epic *De rerum natura* ("Concerning the Nature of Things") of Lucretius (96?–55 B.C.) is perhaps the most original and certainly, next to the 'Aeneid', the greatest poem in Latin. The love poems of Catullus (84–54 B.C.) present the joy and pain of the passing moment with the same vividness that is found in the sonnets of Shakespeare. These authors wrote during the period of the Roman Republic.

As the significant authors of the Ciceronian era had perfected Latin prose, so the poets of the Augustan age perfected Latin verse. First of these was Virgil, or Vergil, (70–19 B.C.), the "Homer of Rome." His great national epic, the 'Aeneid', written in a deftly handled Latin hexameter, is one of the supreme masterpieces of the world, second only to the 'Iliad' and the 'Odyssey' (*see* Virgil).

In the field of lyric and satiric verse, the genial and accomplished Horace (Quintus Horatius Flaccus, 65–8 B.C.) triumphed as surpassingly as did Virgil with the epic. He embodied his philosophy of "idealized common sense" in phrases of such unforgettable charm that many of them have become as familiar as proverbs. In his mildly ironical 'Satires' and 'Epistles' he left what is still the most complete and vivid picture of life in the Augustan age.

## The Elegiac Poets

There was nothing of Horatian self-restraint and even-souled calm in the brief erratic life of Sextus Propertius (50?–15 B.C.). He flashed on the Roman world when he was 20 with a volume of passionate colorful poems celebrating his love for the capricious "Cynthia." A gentler and more refined young poet was Tibullus (54?–19 B.C.), in whom grace and melodiousness took the place of Propertius' fire. These two poets both used the metrical form called the "elegiac." Their brilliant contemporary Ovid (43 B.C.–A.D. 17?) polished this form to the same perfection to which Virgil had brought the hexameter and Horace various lyrical forms. Ovid was a facile and copious writer. He became the uncrowned laureate of the later Augustan age, whose glittering coldness and cynical worldliness he perfectly embodied in his licentious 'Art of Love'. His greatest work is the romantic 'Metamorphoses'. In this fascinating narrative poem he interwove a vast number of stories from ancient mythology.

The Augustan age was the Golden Age of Latin poetry, but to this time belongs also the most famous Roman historian. Livy (59 B.C.–A.D. 17) is noted for his splendid rhetoric. He preferred literary effectiveness to historical accuracy. Thus his narrative of Rome from its founding is more like a prose epic, a series of splendid pictures, than history.

## The Silver Age

After Ovid and Livy the decline of Roman literature set in rapidly. All writing suffered from the custom of public readings. The author was tempted to write brilliant passages to win his listeners' praise, even though he injured his work as a whole.

Historical Pictures Service, Chicago

**VIRGIL**

The satirist Juvenal (A.D. 60?–140) and the epigrammatist Martial (A.D. 40?–104) belong to this Silver Age period. Juvenal's savage castigations of Roman life have been translated and imitated by many English poets. These men are chiefly interesting now for the picture they give of life in the days of the empire.

The tragedies of Seneca were models for early English dramatists. Today they are read as curiosities, but Seneca's philosophical studies can still be enjoyed (*see* Seneca).

Tacitus (A.D. 55?–120?) in his terse and vivid style provides a number of illuminating historical pictures. The 'Germania' is the only view of central Europe under the early Roman Empire. His 'Agricola' is a fine biography. What remains of his 'Annals' and 'Histories' is a chief source for the events of the first century of the Roman Empire. Suetonius (A.D. 75?–160), was a writer of much less distinction than Tacitus. He was one of Hadrian's private secretaries and could therefore write his very gossipy 'Lives of the Twelve Caesars' from documentary sources.

Perhaps the most interesting writings in the Silver Age are the letters of Pliny the Younger (A.D. 61?–113). The most famous one tells of the death of his uncle Pliny the Elder in the eruption of Vesuvius that buried Pompeii. As a whole these letters give a racy picture of the time that is also described by Juvenal and Tacitus. Pliny the Elder (A.D. 23–79) was the author of a 'Natural History', a priceless storehouse of information about the science of ancient times. Two other works of the Silver Age strike a more modern note—the literary criticism of Quintilian and the 'Satyricon', the prose novel of Petronius Arbiter.

With the gradual breakdown of the Roman Empire after the death of Marcus Aurelius (A.D. 180), Latin literature almost disappeared. Although Latin survived as a learned language, Latin literature may be said to have ended in the 2d century A.D.

THESE ARTICLES ARE IN THE FACT-INDEX

Latin League

Latins

Latinus

# LATITUDE
# AND LONGITUDE—

## The Earth's Grid System

**LATITUDE AND LONGITUDE.** A system of lines is used to find the location of any place on the surface of the earth. Commonly called a *grid system*, it is made up of two sets of lines that cross each other. One set—*lines of latitude*—runs in an east-west direction. The other set—*lines of longitude*—runs in a north-south direction. Although these are only imaginary lines encircling the earth, they can be drawn on globes and maps as if they actually existed.

### Drawing the Earth Grid

To draw the lines of the grid system on a globe or map, it is necessary to have starting points, or points of reference. There are two such points of reference on the earth. These are the *North Pole* and the *South Pole*. The poles are the points at which the earth's *axis* meets the earth's surface.

Halfway between the poles is an east-west line called the *equator*. It encircles the earth and divides it into two equal parts, or hemispheres. The North Pole is in the hemisphere north of the equator—the *northern hemisphere*. The South Pole is in the hemisphere south of the equator—the *southern hemisphere*.

One set of lines in the earth's grid system is drawn around the globe parallel to the equator. These are east-west lines, or lines of latitude. In the basic grid there are 89 such equally spaced lines to the north of the equator, 89 to the south. Where the 90th east-west lines would be are two points—the North and South poles. Each east-west line is a circle. The farther it is from the equator the shorter its length. The 60th east-west line, for example, is only half as long as the equator.

East-west lines are numbered from 0 at the equator—the east-west base line—to 89 near the poles. The east-west lines between the equator and the North Pole are north of the equator; those between the equator and the South Pole, south of the equator. The city of New Orleans, La., is located on the 30th east-west line north of the equator. But many other places in the world are also situated on this line. That is why a second set of lines is needed to locate the exact position of New Orleans—or of any other place.

The second set of lines in the earth's grid system is drawn from pole to pole. These are north-south lines, or lines of longitude. One north-south line has been chosen by international agreement as the zero, or base, line. It passes through Greenwich, England, a borough of London. In the basic grid there are 180 such equally spaced lines to the east of the Greenwich base line, 180 to the west. Unlike east-west lines, all north-south lines have the same length.

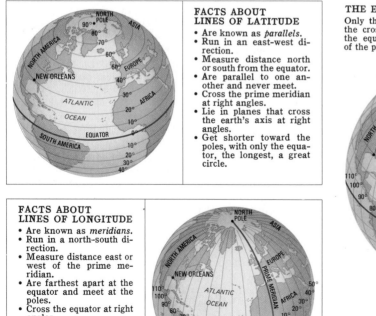

**FACTS ABOUT LINES OF LATITUDE**
- Are known as *parallels*.
- Run in an east-west direction.
- Measure distance north or south from the equator.
- Are parallel to one another and never meet.
- Cross the prime meridian at right angles.
- Lie in planes that cross the earth's axis at right angles.
- Get shorter toward the poles, with only the equator, the longest, a great circle.

**FACTS ABOUT LINES OF LONGITUDE**
- Are known as *meridians*.
- Run in a north-south direction.
- Measure distance east or west of the prime meridian.
- Are farthest apart at the equator and meet at the poles.
- Cross the equator at right angles.
- Lie in planes that pass through the earth's axis.
- Are equal in length.
- Are halves of great circles.

**THE EARTH'S GRID SYSTEM**
Only the city of New Orleans, La., is located at the crossing of the 30th east-west line north of the equator and the 90th north-south line west of the prime meridian.

- Lines of latitude cross lines of longitude at right angles.
- Although only a few lines of latitude and longitude are shown on globes and maps, their number is infinite.

North-south lines are numbered from 0 at the north-south base line both east and west to the 180th north-south line. The zero line and the 180th line together form a complete circle that, like the equator, cuts the earth into two hemispheres. The half west of the zero line can be called the *western hemisphere;* the half east of the zero line, the *eastern hemisphere.*

The north-south lines and the east-west lines together form the global grid system used to find the exact location of any place on earth. New Orleans, on the 30th east-west line north of the equator, is also on the 90th north-south line west of the north-south base line. Many places in the world—among them, Memphis, Tenn.; East St. Louis, Ill.; and the Galápagos Islands of Ecuador—are on or near the same north-south line as New Orleans. Many other places —for example, Port Arthur, Tex.; St. Augustine, Fla.; and Cairo, Egypt—are on or near the same east-west line as New Orleans. But only New Orleans is situated on both lines—exactly where they cross each other. Likewise, each place in the world—and only that place—is situated at the intersection of a given east-west line and a given north-south line.

### Parallels and Meridians

All east-west lines are equidistant from the equator and from each other. This means that they are all parallel to the equator and to each other. Every point on a given east-west line, therefore, is the same distance from the equator, the same distance from the North Pole, and the same distance from the South Pole. For this reason east-west lines, or lines of latitude, are commonly referred to as parallels of latitude, or simply *parallels.*

The north-south lines, or lines of longitude, also have another name. They are commonly referred to as meridians of longitude, or simply *meridians.* The zero meridian, or base line for numbering the north-south lines, is called the *prime meridian.* Each meridian goes only halfway around the earth—from pole to pole. Each has a twin on the other side of the earth. Like the prime meridian and the 180th meridian, all such pairs of meridians form circles that cut the earth into hemispheres. These circles are known as *great circles.* Only one parallel, the equator, is a great circle.

### Measurements of Angular Distance

A cutaway drawing of the earth demonstrates how latitude is determined. It makes clear that latitude is a measure of the angle between the plane of the equator and lines projected from the center of the earth. For example, the angle between a line drawn from New Orleans on the 30th line of latitude to the center of the earth and a line drawn on the plane of the equator is 30 *degrees* (30°). In each hemisphere the 30th line of latitude connects all points whose pro-

This article was contributed by Clyde Kohn, Professor of Geography, The University of Iowa.

jections to the center of the earth form a 30° angle with the plane of the equator.

The latitude of the equator is zero degrees (0°). Lines of latitude north and south of the equator are numbered to 90° because the angular distance from the equator to each pole is one fourth of a circle, or one fourth of 360°. There is no latitude higher than 90°. The North Pole is situated at 90° north latitude, or simply 90° N. The South Pole is at 90° south latitude, or 90° S.

The cutaway drawing of the earth also shows how longitude is determined. Longitude is seen to be a measure of the angle between the planes of two meridian circles, one of which is the prime meridian. For example, the plane of the 90th line of longitude, on which New Orleans is located, forms a 90° angle with the plane of the prime meridian. All places on the 90th line of longitude west of the prime meridian, therefore, are at 90° west longitude.

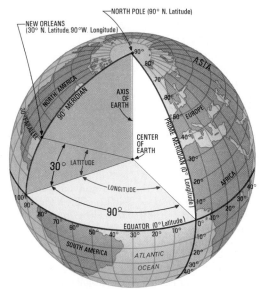

**ANGLES OF LATITUDE AND LONGITUDE**
This cutaway drawing shows that the latitude and longitude of any place are based on the sizes of two angles that originate at the center of the earth. For New Orleans these angles are 30 degrees (north latitude) and 90 degrees (west longitude).

The prime meridian is designated zero degrees (0°) longitude. Lines of longitude are numbered east of the prime meridian from 0° to 180° east longitude and west from 0° to 180° west longitude. There is no longitude higher than 180°, and the 180th meridian east and the 180th meridian west are identical.

Degrees of latitude and longitude can be divided into sixtieths, or *minutes* ('). Any location on earth can be described as lying at a certain number of degrees and minutes of latitude either north or south of the equator and at a certain number of degrees and minutes of longitude either east or west of the prime meridian. For example, the United States Capitol in Washington, D. C., is at 38 degrees 53 minutes north latitude (38°53' N.) and 77 degrees 0 minutes west

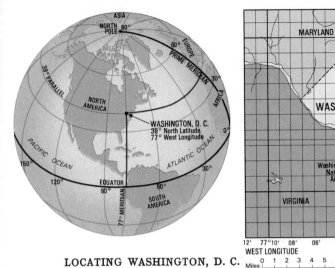

**LOCATING WASHINGTON, D. C.**

As shown on the small-scale globe perspective, Washington, D. C., is located at the crossing of the 39th east-west line north of the equator (39 degrees north latitude) and the 77th north-south line west of the prime meridian (77 degrees west longitude).

The large-scale map locates the city more precisely and pinpoints specific places of interest within it. The dome of the United States Capitol, for example, is at 38 degrees, 53 minutes, 23 seconds north latitude and 77 degrees, 0 minutes, 34 seconds west longitude (38°53′23″N., 77°0′34″W.). To the nearest minute, what are the latitude and longitude of the White House? the National Airport?

longitude (77°0′ W.). Minutes of latitude and longitude can be divided into sixtieths, or *seconds* (″), when more precise information on the location of a place is needed, for example, by navigators, surveyors, or map makers.

A degree of latitude can easily be changed into miles. Since the circumference of the earth is roughly 25,000 miles, the length of each degree of latitude is about 69 miles (1/360 of 25,000 miles). Degrees of latitude vary a little in length—the variation between the shortest and the longest is less than a mile—because the earth is not a perfect sphere but is flattened slightly toward the poles and bulges slightly around the equator (*see* Earth). The length of a degree of longitude, however, varies from about 69 miles at the equator to zero at the poles, where the meridians come together.

### Finding Latitude and Longitude

The navigator of a ship or an airplane can determine the latitude of his position by using an instrument called a *sextant*. With it he measures the *altitude* (angle above the horizon) of the sun as the sun *transits*, or crosses, his meridian (longitude).

**HOW DEGREES OF LATITUDE AND LONGITUDE VARY IN LENGTH**

| Lat. | Length of 1° of Lat. | Length of 1° of Long. | Lat. | Length of 1° of Lat. | Length of 1° of Long. |
|---|---|---|---|---|---|
| 0° | 68.70 mi. | 69.17 mi. | 50° | 69.12 mi. | 44.55 mi. |
| 5° | 68.71 | 68.91 | 55° | 69.18 | 39.77 |
| 10° | 68.73 | 68.13 | 60° | 69.23 | 34.67 |
| 15° | 68.75 | 66.83 | 65° | 69.28 | 29.32 |
| 20° | 68.79 | 65.03 | 70° | 69.32 | 23.73 |
| 25° | 68.83 | 62.73 | 75° | 69.36 | 17.96 |
| 30° | 68.88 | 59.96 | 80° | 69.39 | 12.05 |
| 35° | 68.94 | 56.73 | 85° | 69.40 | 6.05 |
| 40° | 68.99 | 53.06 | 90° | 69.41 | 0.00 |
| 45° | 69.05 | 49.00 | | | |

He then calculates his latitude by combining the observed altitude with information from an *almanac*—a book of data about the movement of the sun and stars. In the evening, latitude may similarly be found by observing stars (*see* Navigation).

Longitude is more difficult to determine than latitude because the sextant and the almanac together do not yield enough information. To calculate his longitude, a navigator must also know the exact time at which he is making his observations. The time is needed because the sun and stars, as they appear to move across the sky, look the same at all places in a given latitude at some time during each day.

The invention of clocks during the Renaissance was the first step toward the reliable calculation of longitude. The clocks of that era, however, were too inaccurate for use in navigation. In 1714 the British Board of Longitude offered a large cash prize to anyone who could build a clock that would meet certain standards of accuracy throughout long ocean voyages. By 1735 John Harrison, a British clockmaker, had submitted the first of several clocks, the last of which won the prize for him. They were called chronometers (*see* Watches and Clocks). In 1766 Pierre Le Roy, a Frenchman, built a chronometer more accurate than Harrison's. From that time on, sailors have been able to determine longitude accurately by comparing local time with Greenwich mean time (GMT). (*See also* Time.)

Shipboard chronometers are set to show GMT. Because of the speed and direction of the earth's rotation, local time at a given place will be one hour behind GMT for every 15 degrees west of the prime meridian and one hour ahead of GMT for every 15 degrees east of the prime meridian. For example, if a ship's chronometer reads 0300 (3:00 A.M.) and the ship's local time is 0800 (8:00 A.M.), the ship is 75 degrees east of Greenwich, or at 75° E. Special radio time signals allow navigators to check the accuracy of their chronometers.

## How the Prime Meridian Was Selected

Before a prime meridian was agreed upon, map makers usually began numbering the lines of longitude at whichever meridian passed through the site of their national observatory. In the United States, for example, this was the Naval Observatory at Washington, D. C.; in France, the Paris Observatory; and in Great Britain, the Royal Greenwich Observatory, at Greenwich. Since Britain was a world leader in exploration and map making, navigators of other nations often used British maps. As a result, in 1884 the meridian of Greenwich was adopted throughout most of the world as the prime meridian. In the 1950's the Royal Greenwich Observatory was moved about 60 miles southeast of Greenwich. The Greenwich meridian, however, remained the prime meridian.

There was still another reason for the selection of the Greenwich meridian as 0° longitude. Travelers must change time by an entire day when they cross the 180th meridian (*see* Time). If this meridian crossed a large country, timekeeping and the establishment of calendar dates would be difficult. But with the Greenwich meridian set at zero, the 180th meridian is near the middle of the Pacific Ocean. It crosses only a small land area in northeastern Asia and divides some island groups in the Pacific. To avoid differing dates in those areas, the nations of the world established a special line across which dates change. It swerves from the 180th meridian whenever convenient. This line is called the *international date line* (*see* International Date Line).

## Special Lines of Latitude and Longitude

Several lines of latitude have special significance. One of these is the equator. Two other special lines of latitude are the 30th parallels. The area between

them, straddling the equator, is commonly referred to as the *low latitudes*. The low latitudes are generally warm lands. The two 60th parallels are also special lines of latitude. The areas north and south of the 60th parallels, which center on the North and South poles, are commonly referred to as the *high latitudes*. The high latitudes are generally cold lands. The areas between the 30th and 60th parallels in both hemispheres are commonly referred to as the *middle latitudes*. Generally, middle-latitude lands have four seasons—fall, winter, spring, and summer (*see* Seasons).

The latitude of a place, accordingly, is a clue to its climate. The yearly average of insolation, or heat energy received from the sun, depends in large measure on the angle or slant of the sun's rays. This angle varies with distance from the equator (latitude). Regions in high latitudes, both north and south, get less insolation and are therefore usually colder than regions in low latitudes. (*See also* Climate.)

Four other special lines of latitude are the *Tropic of Cancer* ($23\frac{1}{2}$° N.), the *Tropic of Capricorn* ($23\frac{1}{2}$° S.), the *Arctic Circle* ($66\frac{1}{2}$° N.), and the *Antarctic Circle* ($66\frac{1}{2}$° S.). These lines relate to the tilt of the earth's axis as the earth revolves around the sun. The Tropics of Cancer and Capricorn mark the limits of the zone astride the equator in which the sun appears directly overhead at some time during the year. The Arctic and Antarctic circles mark the limits of the areas around each pole in which the sun at some time during the year does not rise or set for a period of 24 hours or more.

The only special line of longitude is the prime meridian. Time zone boundaries and the international date line are based on certain lines of longitude but do not follow them exactly. (*See also* Directions; Maps and Globes.)

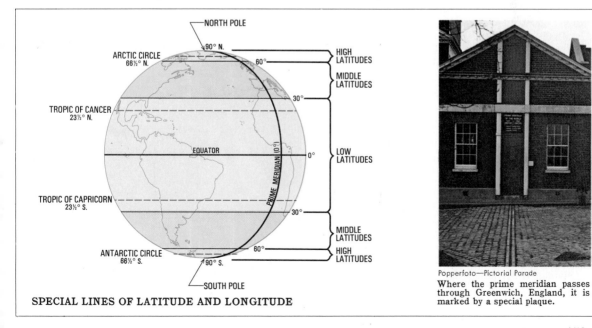

**SPECIAL LINES OF LATITUDE AND LONGITUDE**

Popperfoto—Pictorial Parade

Where the prime meridian passes through Greenwich, England, it is marked by a special plaque.

THESE ARTICLES ARE IN THE FACT-INDEX

La Tour, Charles Amador de
La Tour, Georges de
Latreille, Pierre André
Latrobe, Benjamin Henry

Latrobe, Pa.
Lattimore, Eleanor Frances
Lattimore, Owen
La Tuque, Que.

## LATVIAN SOVIET SOCIALIST REPUBLIC.

One of the three Baltic States that enjoyed brief freedom after the Russian Revolution of 1917 was Latvia, or Letvia, land of the Letts. Today it is a republic of the Soviet Union.

Latvia comprises most of the former czarist provinces of Courland and Livonia and lies between the Estonian and Lithuanian Soviet republics. It has good harbors at Riga, the capital, Liepaja, and Ventspils. Its area is 24,710 square miles; population (1970 preliminary census), 2,365,000.

Much of Latvia is low and marshy, though Livonia has wooded hills and pretty lakes. One man, Baron Osten Sacken, once owned a large part of Courland. After 1917 many of the big estates were divided. The Letts make up 76 per cent of the population. With the Lithuanians they form a branch of the Indo-European family akin to the Slavs. More than half the people are Lutherans.

Latvia is chiefly an agricultural country, but industries are claiming more workers. Rye, barley, oats, potatoes, and flax are the main crops. Timber, flax, and butter are the chief exports. There are about 2,000 miles of railroads and some 600 miles of paved roads.

In the 13th century what is now Latvia was part of the territory conquered and Christianized by Teutonic knights. In the 16th century the region came under Poland's rule. In 1629 Sweden annexed Livonia. A century later it fell to Russia. Courland was annexed by Russia in the third partition of Poland (1795). The two provinces formed part of the czar's realm until the Russian Revolution of 1917. Latvian nationalists proclaimed a new republic in 1918.

Latvia existed as an independent nation only until World War II began. Russia exacted military concessions from Latvia in 1939. In July 1940 the Latvian parliament voted to become a soviet republic. The Germans made Latvia a province of the Reich in 1941. In 1944 the Red army drove the Germans back, and Russia reclaimed Latvia. (*See also* Russia; Union of Soviet Socialist Republics.)

THESE ARTICLES ARE IN THE FACT-INDEX

Lauan
Laubach, Frank Charles
Laud, William
Lauder, Sir Harry Maclennan
Laudonnière, René Goulaine de

Laue, Max (Theodor Felix) von
Laughlin, James
Laughlin, James Laurence
Laughton, Charles
Launceston, England
Launceston, Tasmania

# LAUNDRY—Washing and Ironing Today

**LAUNDRY.** Washing and ironing clothing and fabrics is called laundering. In the home Monday has traditionally been laundry day. New products have made home laundering easy and efficient.

Commercial laundries now do much of the work that was once done in the home. Their services are available to individuals, families, and institutions throughout the United States.

## COMMERCIAL LAUNDRY

About one fourth of the families in the United States use commercial laundries. Many institutions have their laundry done by commercial establishments. Others, such as big hospitals, have their own facilities. These may be as large as professional laundries.

### First Steps in Laundering

**Weighing and sorting.** At the laundry, the bundle of clothes is weighed or the pieces in it are counted. The items are then sorted by color and fabric. In the average bundle there may be five different classifications, each of which is washed separately.

**Washing temperatures.** The five principal classifications of articles are white, light-colored, dark-colored, man-made fiber, and wool. In the first category are linens, towels, and white garments. These are washed

at a high temperature (about 160° F.). Light-colored garments, such as cotton dresses, slacks, shorts, pajamas, prints, and rugs are washed at a temperature no higher than 120°.

Clothes drying on a line in the wind and the sun is still a common sight in some areas, though perhaps a fourth of the families in the United States use commercial laundries.

Stephen L. Feldman

## WASHING AND EXTRACTING

These workers (left) are transferring washed loads of laundry to extractor containers. Two containers at a time are whirled around in an extractor (right, foreground) until the clothing is sufficiently dried for ironing.

Items such as socks, sport shirts, and housedresses and those of darker colors are washed at a temperature of 90°. Hotter water is likely to make the colors run. Rayons, nylons, and other fabrics composed of man-made fibers, as well as silk, are also washed in water at a temperature no higher than 90°.

Wool is one of the most difficult fabrics to wash because it will shrink if the water is too hot. Woolens are washed at a temperature of 80°.

### The Washing Process

In most laundries each family's laundry is put into porous net bags. Each bag has a numbered identification tag. The bags of clothes are then put into large cylinders that revolve within the washers. The suds in the cylinders go freely through the net bags, so washing is thorough.

Each load of washing is accurately weighed. Overloading of the equipment would result in unsatisfactory washing. A measured amount of fresh soft water is then pumped into the washer.

The water must be at the proper temperature. Thermostatic controls assure an even temperature for each classification.

Several kinds of soaps are used. The amount and the type depend upon the articles to be washed and the temperature of the water. For an average family wash there are from 3 to 5 complete changes of soap and from 11 to 13 complete changes of water. From 4 to 6 changes of water are used for rinsing alone. During the washings and rinsings the clothes are gently tumbled through the water as the cylinder turns. Every few minutes the washer automatically reverses its motion for thorough cleansing action.

Bleach is added to the suds for stain removal and as a germicide. The amount depends upon the weight and type of fabric washed. Then bluing is added. A special rinsing agent is added to the final rinse.

After the washing and rinsing, the bundles are placed in *spinners*, or extractors, to throw off excess water. These work by centrifugal force. They leave the wash with just enough moisture for ironing.

Knitted garments and similar articles are fluffed in *tumblers* until they are dried. By gentle rolling action each load is tumbled in clean, fresh, warmed air.

### How the Laundry Is Ironed

The numbered net bags are next reassembled, and the various items are ready to be ironed. Sheets, pillowcases, table linens, and handkerchiefs are called flat pieces, or flatwork. These are mangled; that is, pressed smooth on padded rollers that move them over a steam-heated surface. Linens are pressed flat and folded afterward so that no creases are ironed in.

Shirt sleeves are pressed on special forms. Collars and cuffs are ironed on forms curved to fit the contours of the neck and wrists. Another form is used for the body of the shirt. There are also small presses for the cuffs, collars, and upper parts of work clothes other than shirts. Larger equipment is used for trouser legs and skirts. All presses have thick, resilient padding for different thicknesses of materials, seams, and buttons. If the garments have puffed sleeves, they are placed on heated round irons that conform to the contour of the sleeves.

### Specialty Work

Articles that require individual care are handled in separate departments. Laundering such items is called specialty work. Curtains and lace tablecloths are carefully shaped on frames, and there is special equipment for ruffles.

**DRYING IN A COMMERCIAL LAUNDRY**
Here a load of clothing is being taken from a tumbler-dryer and put back into its original net bag.

Laundering blankets is another specialty. Careful attention is necessary to wash a wool blanket thoroughly without shrinking or matting it. After the blankets are dried, they are combed, or carded. on equipment designed for this purpose. Carding raises the nap so air can get between the fibers, making the blankets softer and warmer.

## HOME LAUNDRY

In about 75 per cent of the households in the United States, all the washing is done in the home. Automatic washers, dryers, and combination washer dryers have simplified laundering for the housewife There have also been many improvements in wringer-washers, ironers. and steam-dry irons.

**Pretreatment.** Some of the tasks that should precede washing are emptying dirt from cuffs, removing loose objects from pockets, mending rips and tears, fastening loose buttons, removing non-washable trim, and treating nonwashable stains (*see* Dry Cleaning). Ground-in dirt on cuffs and collars can be pretreated by rubbing with soap or detergent and water before washing.

**Sorting.** Sheer and delicate articles should be separated from those that are heavy and sturdy. White and colorfast materials may be washed together but never with nonfast colors. Heavily soiled articles and lightly soiled pieces should be separated. Lint producers should be kept out of dark loads.

**Detergents and soap.** All-purpose detergent is used in hard water and all-purpose soap in soft water. In a tumbler washer or combination washer-dryer, a detergent that yields a minimum of suds produces a cleaner wash.

**Bleach.** Overbleaching is harmful. Bleaches should be chosen according to the type of fabric being washed. Chlorine bleaches will harm silk and wool and *some* resin-treated fabrics. Sodium perborate bleaches may be used safely on all colorfast fabrics. Liquid chlorine bleach must be diluted before it comes in contact with fabrics.

**Other aids.** Flake- or bead-type bluing is used in the wash water. Liquid-type bluing goes into the rinse water. Nylon brighteners may occasionally be added to the wash water.

Water softeners or conditioners added to the rinse prevent soap-film grayness on clothes. They are ideally used when water is under 12 grains hardness (the equivalent of 12 grains of calcium carbonate per gallon of water). Otherwise a mechanical water softener is more efficient.

Fabric softeners may sometimes be added to the *final rinse* to give extra fluffiness to the clothes. It is important *not* to put them in the wash water or to use them if a water conditioner went into the rinse.

Dyes should be used after the wash-and-rinse cycles are completed. Starches add stiffness or crispness to fabrics. Starching is done after the washing is completed. When clothes are to be dried in an automatic dryer twice the usual amount of starch is needed.

## Washing, Drying, and Ironing

**Setting the washer controls.** Some washers have predetermined settings marked according to the type of fabric that makes up the load. Others have a combination of the following controls: timer, for length of washing; wash-water temperature (warm, cold, or hot); rinse-water temperature (warm or cold); washing speed; spin speed; and load setting, for amount of water. The more controls there are on a particular washer, the easier it is to adapt the machine to a particular problem.

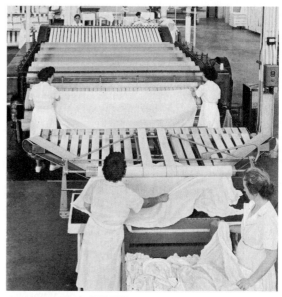

**IRONING FLAT PIECES**
Sheets, table linens, and other flatwork are pressed smooth on this machine after excess water is extracted from them.

**Washing.** The remaining washing steps are automatic. The washer removes soil from garments by agitation. It rinses them and then spins out the water, leaving the clothes damp dry. Agitation is accomplished in top-loading washers by eccentric, oscillating, reciprocating, or undulating washing action. In front-loading types it is accomplished by tumbling.

**Drying.** Generally all garments that can be washed automatically can be dried automatically. Clothes are put in the dryer, the heat and time needed are selected, and the clothes are taken out when the time is up. Prompt removal from the dryer minimizes wrinkling. Overdrying should be avoided.

**Ironing.** Many fabrics shed wrinkles easily and require little or no ironing if smoothed and put away as soon as the dryer stops. Most fabrics still require ironing after drying, however. Much "wash-and-wear" type clothing looks even better when ironed. It also stays fresh-looking longer.

## HISTORY OF LAUNDERING

Centuries before the modern power laundry came into existence, ancient civilizations had their own unique methods of washing and ironing clothes. The first known record of laundering goes back almost 4,000 years. It was found in a tomb at Beni Hasan, in Egypt. On the wall of the tomb is a representation of two slaves washing a cloth. One pours water over the material while the other rubs it. The water runs into a trough below. In some parts of the world women still wash clothes by similar crude methods.

### Laundering in Ancient Rome

The early Romans were proud of the garments they wore draped in graceful folds as they strolled in the Forum. (*See* Dress.) Because the cloth was mainly wool, it needed skillful manipulation to retain its size and shape. Garments were ordinarily sent to a public laundry where the laundryman, or "fuller", washed whitened, redyed, and pressed the garments.

After they washed the clothes, the fullers placed them in a "fuller's press." This consisted of two uprights, two planks, and a large screw top. Turned by cranks, it flattened the cloth between the planks. This press was probably the first step toward the development of calenders and manglers. These appeared in England many centuries later and were the forerunners of the present-day commercial laundry's flatwork ironer.

### Laundering in the United States

In the United States the first patent on "washing cloaths" was issued to Nathaniel Briggs in 1797. In the next half century more than 200 patents were granted on washing machines alone. (Until about 1850, models instead of drawings were filed with the patent office.) No drawings or descriptions of these washing-machine models are available.

The first laundry is thought to have been started in 1837 by Independence Stark in Troy, N. Y. Stark had a collar factory and opened a plant for laundering his product. He called it the Troy Laundry. Many laundries today are named Troy after the first one.

The first complete power laundry in the United States was probably born of the needs of the "forty-niners" during the gold rush days of California. Oakland was then a struggling settlement with a population made up almost entirely of men. There were no women to wash their clothes. A few Chinese operated individual laundries along creek banks. Some men sent their laundry all the way to Hawaii. They had to wait up to six months for delivery. In 1851 a man named D. Davis established the Contra Costa Laundry in Oakland. At first all the work was done by hand. Later a 12-shirt washing machine was built. It was operated by a ten-horsepower donkey engine.

The man who is credited with making power laundries commercially practical is Hamilton E. Smith of Philadelphia, Pa. In 1863 he patented the reciprocating mechanism to reverse the movement of the revolving drum in the washing machine. That same year he established a power laundry in the St. Charles Hotel and the Monongahela House in Pittsburgh, Pa.

Companies were soon formed for the manufacture of laundry machinery. As they worked to perfect their

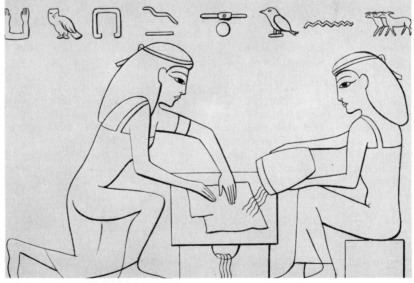

**ANCIENT LAUNDERING SCENE**
This scene was depicted on a wall of an Egyptian tomb dating back almost 4,000 years. It is the earliest historical record of laundering methods.

161

Walter Turrentine, Jr.—Coin Launderer & Cleaner

**SELF-SERVICE LAUNDRY**
A child helps her mother with the family wash at a self-service laundry, where customers may use as many washing machines as necessary at one time.

products, the laundry business grew rapidly. In 1898 the editor of the *National Laundry Journal* estimated that United States laundry owners collected 52 million dollars a year. In 1909 the United States census figures showed that earnings had increased to $104,-680,000. In spite of this phenomenal growth it remained chiefly a shirt-and-collar business until about 1915. Then, along with the development and successful marketing of electrically operated washing machines, came "wet-wash laundries." Today the industry grosses a billion dollars yearly.

### Change in the Laundry Business

Laundries had priced what little family wash they had formerly done on a per-piece basis. With the introduction of the "wet wash" they began to charge on a per-pound basis for all classes of work. Up until this time the routemen delivered the laundry to their customers on a bicycle or in horse-drawn wagons. Soon afterward, however, the industry's pickup and delivery service became motorized.

Laundry machinery continued to develop and improve. The revolving cylinder was the first major development in washers. It failed to do the job at first because centrifugal force caused the wet clothes to cling to the sides of the cylinder. There was not enough action to remove the dirt. This problem was solved by the rotary washer with reversing action. It turned over the clothes inside the cylinders and splashed them in sudsy water.

Similar progress was made in apparel presses. Instead of imitating a traditional hand iron, with its sliding action, pressure was applied through a steam-heated chest, or "buck," which closed over the garment.

The industry is now equipped with such modern devices as controls for washers which automatically add water and supplies. The worker simply presses a button to begin the entire washing cycle. Thus one man can control an entire roomful of washers. Other marvels include an electric eye for counting pieces and an ultraviolet light for reading otherwise invisible identification marks. Manufacturers have also developed presses for finishing every type of garment, including socks, blankets, and curtains.

### Recent Trends

The end of World War II saw the beginning of self-service laundry stores. These are equipped with a number of home-type washers and dryers. At first, customers came in and did the laundry themselves. In a short time, however, the self-service laundries became attendant-operated. Housewives demanded this service so they could merely drop off their laundry and perhaps go shopping while the attendant handled their wash.

This trend lasted until about 1955, when many "launderettes" were converted into completely coin-operated establishments, open 24 hours a day. There are usually no attendants in these laundries.

Many laundries have opened branch stores for pickup and delivery services. Some of these establishments have a minimum of operating equipment. They are called "activated" units.

A major development is a trailer-type receiving and pickup station. This is simply a converted automobile trailer, specifically designed to serve as a laundry pickup station. It gives the owner the opportunity of trying it out in a particular location. If business is poor there, he can easily move it to another spot.

Since 1955 large family laundries that have gone out of business because of poor management or consolidation have generally remained closed. On the other hand, there is an increasing growth in the number of small branch establishments, activated units, and coin-operated stores.

THESE ARTICLES ARE IN THE FACT-INDEX

Launfal, Sir
La Unión,
  El Salvador

Laura Ingalls Wilder
  Award
Laurana, Francesco da
Laurel, Miss.

**LAUREL.** One of the most spectacular of wild shrubs is the laurel. Its masses of pink, crimson, or white blossoms may blanket whole mountainsides and tinge great marshy areas with rich color. The laurels are hardy evergreen shrubs. The flowers grow in clusters. Each blossom has five sepals and a saucer-shaped corolla with five lobes. There is one pistil. The ten stamens curve outward and over from the center of the blossom, their tips (anthers) hidden in pouches below the rim of the corolla. At the touch of an insect, the anthers spring out of their pouches and dust the visitor with pollen. Thus the insect fertilizes the plants as it travels from flower to flower. There are several kinds of laurels in North America, all members of the heath family (*Ericaceae*).

Mountain laurel (*Kalmia latifolia*) is the state flower of Connecticut and Pennsylvania. It grows in the mountains of eastern North America from New Brunswick to the Gulf coast. The shrubs may reach 20 feet in height. Thick clusters of pinkish-white flowers grow at the ends of the branches. The large leathery leaves are pointed at both ends, smooth-edged, and bright glossy green on both sides.

Sheep laurel, or lambkill (*Kalmia angustifolia*), is much smaller than the mountain laurel. It grows in swamps and wet pastures from Labrador to Georgia and westward to the Pacific coast. Crimson flowers cluster around the stem, which is terminated by the new leaves. Its leaves are poisonous to young animals.

### Bay, or Sweet, Laurel

The bay, or sweet, laurel (*Laurus nobilis*) is a small tree found in the Mediterranean region of Europe, in Great Britain, and in southern Asia. It has yellowish-green flowers. It belongs to the laurel family (*Lauraceae*), not, like mountain laurel and sheep laurel, to the heath family. The laurel family includes sassafras, camphor, and spicebush, or wild allspice—trees and shrubs which are noted for their aromatic qualities. From the berries and other parts of the sweet laurel is distilled an aromatic oil used in the manufacture of toilet waters. Dried bay leaves are used for flavoring in cookery and pickling.

The ancient Greeks used the entwined twigs of bay, or sweet, laurel to crown victors of the Pythian games. The tree was sacred to Apollo. The nymph Daphne, when pursued by Apollo, was, in answer to her prayers, changed into a laurel. The custom of placing a laurel crown on the brow of poets dates from the Middle Ages (*see* Poet Laureate).

THESE ARTICLES ARE IN THE FACT-INDEX

| | |
|---|---|
| Laurençin, Marie | Laurens, John |
| Laurens, Henri | Laurent, Robert |
| Laurens, Henry | |

**LAURENTIAN PLATEAU, or CANADIAN SHIELD.** About half of Canada's area consists of some of the oldest rock in the world. This Precambrian igneous rock exists in a vast mass called the Laurentian Plateau, or Canadian Shield. It was dry land ages ago when the oceans still rolled over the sites of the Appalachian and the Rocky mountains. Throughout geologic time it has been a firm anchor for the continent. It was uplifted to form a plateau, and then it was carved by stream erosion. Finally it was planed almost level by glaciers.

This combination of uplift and erosion gave eastern Canada its present-day appearance as a rocky tableland deeply carved by rivers. The Saguenay, a tributary of the St. Lawrence, with great cliffs rising in some places to 1,500 and 1,700 feet, has some of the most sublime river scenery in the world. The whole plateau is so covered with winding waterways and lakes that, by making occasional portages, one can travel in almost any direction by canoe.

Shaped like a great "V," with Hudson Bay in the center, the Laurentian Plateau comprises some 1,850,-000 square miles—about half of Canada. On the east it underlies most of Quebec and Labrador. On the south it extends through Ontario as far as Lake Superior and the Adirondack Mountains. Portions of its southern edge are exposed in northern Michigan and Wisconsin. Its western edge borders the interior plains and lowlands. It may be traced by the line of lakes running northwest from Lake Winnipeg to Great Slave and Great Bear lakes. The plateau is tilted from a clifflike edge in Quebec and Labrador to sea level around Hudson Bay. The average elevation is 600 to 1,200 feet above sea level. The highest point is Cirque Mountain (5,160 feet) in the Torngats.

The plateau is rich in minerals of all kinds except coal and petroleum. Thick forests cover much of the region, but the soil is mostly too poor for farming. Great herds of caribou and musk oxen; fur-bearing animals; and ducks, geese, and other birds make the plateau their home. (*See also* Canada, subhead "The Canadian Shield," and the discussion of the Canadian Shield under the Natural Regions subhead in the following articles: Alberta; Manitoba; Newfoundland; Ontario; Quebec; Saskatchewan.)

**LAURIER** (*lȯr′ē-ā*), **Sir Wilfrid** (1841–1919). The first French Canadian to become prime minister of Canada was Wilfrid Laurier. Although French was his native tongue, he became a master of English oratory. His eloquence and picturesque personality made him popular throughout Canada, and he led the young dominion in a 15-year period of great development.

Wilfrid Laurier was born at St-Lin, Quebec, and studied law at McGill University. After three years in the Quebec legislature, he was elected to the Canadian House of Commons in 1874. There he rose rapidly to leadership. Although he was a French Canadian and a Roman Catholic, he was chosen leader of the Liberal party in 1887. Nine years later he became prime minister. He was knighted in 1897.

"Build up Canada" was the watchword of Laurier's government. Laurier was loyal to Great Britain, sent Canadian volunteers to help in the Boer War, established a tariff favorable to British goods, and worked to strengthen the ties between the two countries. But he saw the British Empire as a worldwide alliance of free and equal nations, and he opposed every attempt to limit Canada's freedom.

Laurier's liberal immigration policy brought hundreds of thousands of settlers to the western provinces. He reduced postal rates, promoted the building of railroads needed for national expansion, and appointed a commission to regulate railroad rates. After 15 years in office his government was defeated, presumably on the issue of reciprocal trade with the United States. Laurier believed, however, that his political defeat was caused primarily by opponents in Ontario who considered him too partial to Roman Catholic interests in Quebec.

Prior to World War I, Laurier ardently supported the formation of a Canadian navy. His own Liberal party defeated this measure, however, and Canada entered the war without a fleet of its own. During the early years of World War I, Laurier supported the war policy of Sir Robert Borden's Conservative government. In 1917, nevertheless, he refused to join a coalition government that was formed to uphold conscription. Laurier felt that he could not back a measure so unpopular in the province of Quebec. He died in Ottawa on Feb. 17, 1919. (*See also* Canadian History, subhead "The Age of Laurier.")

THESE ARTICLES ARE IN THE FACT-INDEX

Lauritsen, Charles Christian
Laurium, Greece
Lausanne, Switzerland
Lausanne, Treaty of
Laut, Agnes Christina
Lauzon, Que.

**LAVA.** The more or less completely melted rock discharged from volcanoes is called lava. Molten lava is a thick fluid permeated with gases and steam. Its fluidity depends upon its temperature, the amount of vapors it contains, and its chemical composition. When first ejected, lava may flow as fast as 50 miles an hour, but it generally slows down to less than a mile an hour.

If lava contains not more than 58 percent of silica it is called basic. *Basic* lava comes from deeper levels of the earth and melts at about 2,250° F. *Acid* lava contains 66 percent or more of silica. It comes from the upper shell of the earth and remains pasty even at 3,000° F. Lavas of Stromboli (in the Lipari Islands), Hawaii, and Skaptar Jökull (in Iceland), are basic. Basic lava flows faster than acid lava and goes farther before it cools, making a low cone with gentle slopes. Mount Shasta, Mount Hood, and Mount Rainier on the West coast of the United States and Vulcano of the Lipari Islands were formed by the accumulation of acid lava and have high, steep cones.

If acid lava cools too quickly for its minerals to crystallize, it forms glasslike *obsidian*. A partial crystallization produces *rhyolite*. Acid lava having large crystals embedded in a matrix of small crystals is called *porphyry*. Basic lava cooled to a prismatic structure that forms columns and stairs is called *basalt*. The top of lava is often frothy from bubbles of gas. *Pumice* is rock froth light enough to float on water. Powdered pumice is used in grinding glassware, in making soaps for mechanics, and for polishing various materials. Great quantities are exported from the Lipari Islands. (*See also* Volcanoes.)

THESE ARTICLES ARE IN THE FACT-INDEX

Laval, Pierre
Lavalleja, Juan Antonio
Laval-Montmorency, François, Xavier de
Laval University
Lavater, Johann Kaspar
Lavatera
'Lavengro'
Laver, Rod(ney George)
Laveran, Charles Louis Alphonse
La Vérendrye, Pierre Gaultier de Varennes, sieur de
La Verne College
Lavery, Sir John
Lavinia
Lavinium, Italy
Lavisse, Ernest

**LAVOISIER** (*lȧv-wäz′ē-ā*), **Antoine Laurent** (1743–1794). One of the most honored men in the history of science is the Frenchman Lavoisier. For more than a century before his day, chemists had been hampered by a false theory about fire and the burning of matter. By revealing the truth about fire and burning Lavoisier helped chemistry make its remarkable advance from that time on.

Antoine Laurent Lavoisier was born in Paris, the son of a rich lawyer and landowner. His father bought a title of nobility and wanted an aristocratic career for the boy. Young Antoine preferred science, however, so his father sent him to many famous scholars. Antoine studied mathematics at Mazarin College under Abbé Lecaille. He also studied chemistry and botany, the latter under the renowned botanist Bernard de Jussieu.

When Lavoisier was only 23 years old, he won a prize from the Academy of Science for an essay on the lighting of cities. In 1768 he was elected to the academy, an unusual honor for so young a man. The same year he was appointed to the *ferme générale*—a body of men who held the right to "farm" (collect) taxes. In 1776 he began his career as director of the government arsenal.

The American Colonies issued their Declaration of Independence in the same year, and soon afterward colonial troops were using his improved gunpowder. By 1783 Lavoisier had solved the most significant chemical problem of the day by proving the connection between oxygen and fire.

At the time, Joseph Priestley, Henry Cavendish, and Joseph Black had identified the gases oxygen, hydrogen, and carbon dioxide in air. But they misinterpreted their discoveries in terms of a false theory that burning involved an invisible "essence" called *phlogiston*. Black, for example, thought that carbon dioxide was air combined with phlogiston. Cavendish explained oxygen as "dephlogisticated air." By brilliant experiments and delicate measurements Lavoisier proved that burning, the rusting of metals, and the breathing of animals all consisted of the union of oxygen with other chemicals. Since this union (oxidation) is one of the most important chemical processes, his discovery started the development of modern chemistry.

Lavoisier had become commissioner of weights and measures, and in 1791 he was appointed a commissary of the treasury. In 1794, however, the French revolutionists accused him and other members of the *ferme générale* of plotting to cheat the government. Because of this he was executed by the Revolutionary Tribunal.

---

THESE ARTICLES ARE IN THE FACT-INDEX
**Law, Andrew Bonar**
**Law, John**

---

**LAW.** We use the word law with at least three fundamentally different meanings. In its widest sense, law expresses the relation between cause and effect. Students of the sciences found, after long observation, that natural objects and forces can be depended upon to act in certain ways; these ways are natural laws. In this sense the chemist speaks of the law of the conservation of matter; the physicist, of the laws of motion; the biologist, of the laws of heredity.

In a narrower sense the word law refers to the social life of man. Thus we speak of laws of etiquette, laws of honor, and the moral law. When people first began to live in groups they had no rules or laws, but they soon realized that each man had to pay attention to the needs and welfare of his neighbors in order to make life not only pleasant but possible for the greatest number of people. These rules or customs were at first unwritten. When law in this second sense failed, the state made laws in a third sense. The state set up a positive set of rules, or codes, and enforced them.

### Development of Positive Law

The best known of the earliest codes to come down to us is that of Hammurabi, king of Babylon, who lived about 1800 B.C. (*see* Babylonia and Assyria). Another Babylonian king, Lipit-Ishtar, had set up a similar code of laws perhaps 150 years earlier. (Parts of these laws were discovered on four pieces of clay tablet in the University of Pennsylvania Museum. The tablets had been unearthed before 1900 but were overlooked until 1947.) In the 7th century B.C. Draco compiled the first Athenian code. However, it proved to be too harsh and gave way to the laws of Solon (*see* Solon).

The Romans built up a remarkable body of laws based on custom. But they let their judges and lawmakers modify laws or add to them as need arose. Finally the Emperor Justinian codified them as the Roman Civil Law. Roman law has determined the general character of the laws of every nation in Western Europe, with the exception of England. (*See also* Justinian I.)

Before the Normans invaded England, each manor, borough, or shire had its rules based on established custom—laws of tradition. After the Norman Conquest, judges appointed by the king moved from place to place to administer these local laws, and gradually popular custom gave way to judicial custom. In time, the decisions of the judges, constantly modified by later decisions, were accepted as the body of English "common law." Except in Louisiana, where the Code Napoléon prevails, civil law in the United States is based on English common law.

Statute law, or legislation, is yet another kind of law. It grew up because new conditions arose to which judge-made, or common, law did not apply. Statute law is made by legislative bodies, such as parliaments, congresses, and legislatures. Two chief types of statute law came to be recognized: civil law, which sets forth the rights of persons, with methods for maintaining or regaining them; and criminal law, which deals with harmful actions and with punishments for offenders. A constitution is the basic law of a state; it provides the framework of government for that state.

### Canon and Martial Law

Canon law arose in the Middle Ages to deal with church matters. The New Code of the Canon Law is a collection of all the disciplinary laws of the Roman Catholic church. Military law is used for governing the members of a military organization. Martial law is imposed upon a civilian population after civil laws have been suspended in time of emergency. Martial law applies military law to civilians, to any extent that seems advisable. Both military and martial law are enforced by the military powers. Under military and martial law trial decisions are reached by courts-martial.

Parliamentary law is not "law." It is a body of rules to regulate the procedure of a deliberative group, such as a legislature. Jurisprudence is the science that deals with the nature of law and the content and classification of laws.

The legal profession is crowded, but many find training in law good preparation for business. The various states admit candidates to the practice of law if they pass a bar examination. The amount of education required before taking the examination differs from state to state. The American Bar Association standard is two years of college followed by three years in law school. (*See also* Courts of Justice; International Law; Jury; Parliamentary Law. For a list of the terms most commonly used in law, *see* the table on the following pages.)

# TERMS COMMONLY USED IN LAW

**Acquittal.** The action taken by a jury when, upon trial, they find that the accused is not guilty and enter a verdict accordingly.

**Administrator.** A person appointed by probate court to manage and to distribute the estate of a person who has died without a will; distinguished from an executor.

**Affidavit.** A written statement which is sworn to before an officer who has authority to administer an oath.

**Alias** (ā'lĭ-ás). A description of the defendant that results from adding to his real name other names by which he is known.

**Alibi** (ăl'ĭ-bī). Proof offered by one accused of a crime that he was in a different place from that at which the crime was committed at the time it was committed.

**Alien.** A resident of a country who was born outside that country and who has not become a naturalized citizen.

**Arraignment.** The calling of a prisoner before a judge (sitting in his courtroom) to answer the accusations contained in an indictment.

**Arson.** Under common law, the malicious burning of the house owned by another person; under statutes, the house need not be one owned by another person.

**Assault.** Force unlawfully directed or applied to another under circumstances of personal violence.

**Assignment.** Transfer of a property right or title to some particular person under an agreement, usually in writing.

**Attachment.** Preliminary legal seizure of property to force compliance with a decision which may be obtained in a pending suit.

**Bailment.** Delivery of possession of, but not title to, tangible personal property by one person to another under an agreement that it will be held in trust for a special purpose and that it will be returned when the purpose has been accomplished.

**Bankruptcy.** The condition of being unable to pay one's debts as they become due.

**Bench warrant.** An order issued by a judge for the attachment or arrest of a person.

**Bequest.** A gift by will of personal property. A bequest is the same as a legacy.

**Blue laws.** A name applied to certain laws, originally in force in the New England states, which were extremely rigorous.

**Brief.** A written or printed argument furnished to the court by an attorney which sets forth the pertinent facts of the case being tried and the laws applicable to it.

**Carte blanche** (kärt blänsh'). Unlimited authority—granted by one person to another—to impose conditions which will be binding upon the person granting such authority.

**Chattel.** Personal property, movable or immovable, which is less than a freehold; for example, a book, a coat, a pencil, growing corn, a lease.

**Codicil.** A written instrument that adds to or qualifies a last will and testament.

**Common law.** The body of law which includes both the unwritten law of England and the statutes passed before the settlement of the United States.

**Confiscation.** Appropriation of private property for public use without compensation.

**Contempt of court.** Any willful disobedience to, or disregard of, a court order or any misconduct in the presence of a court; punishable by fine or imprisonment or both.

**Contract.** An agreement between two or more competent persons to do or not to do some lawful act for a consideration.

**Copyright.** The exclusive privilege of printing, publishing, and vending copies of writings or drawings.

**Corespondent** (kō-rē-spŏn'dĕnt). A term sometimes applied to a third person, who is accused of committing unlawful acts with the defendant, by the party seeking a divorce from the defendant.

**Corporation.** A fictitious legal person which has rights and duties independent of the rights and duties of real persons and which is legally authorized to act in its own name through duly appointed agents.

**Decree.** The judgment or sentence of a court of equity which corresponds to the judgment of a court of law.

**Deed.** A written document for the transfer of land or other real property from one person to another. A quitclaim deed conveys only such rights as the grantor has. A warranty deed conveys specifically described rights which together comprise good title.

**De facto.** A term used to denote a thing done in fact but without strict legal authority as contrasted with *de jure*, which denotes a thing done according to law.

**De jure.** *See* De facto in this table.

**Dower.** The provision which the law makes for the support of a widow during her lifetime out of income produced by the real estate owned by her husband during the marriage. This provision for the support of a widow is usually favored over the claims of her deceased husband's creditors.

**Easement.** A right enjoyed by the owner of one parcel of land, by reason of this ownership, to use the land of another for a special purpose.

**Endorsement** (also **indorsement**). The act of transferring title to a written negotiable instrument by having the temporary owner write his name on the back of the document.

**Equity.** A system of law designed to furnish remedies for wrongs which were not legally recognized under the common law of England or for which no adequate remedy was provided by the common law.

**Escrow.** A written agreement between two parties providing that a third party hold money or property until the conditions of the agreement are met.

**Estate.** A term commonly used to denote the sum total of all types of property owned by a person at a particular time, usually upon his death.

**Evidence.** In law, all facts, testimony, and documents presented for the purpose of proving or disproving a question under inquiry.

**Executor.** In law, the person designated by a testator in his will to carry out the terms of that instrument.

**Ex officio** (ĕks ŏ-físh'ĭ-ō). Term used to designate powers exercised by public officials by virtue or because of the office they hold.

**Ex parte** (ĕks pär'tē). Term used to designate action taken by one party in the absence of the opposite party, usually after giving notice.

**Ex post facto.** Term used to designate action taken to change the effect given to a set of circumstances. This action relates back to a prior time and places this new effect upon the same set of circumstances existing at that time.

**Extradition.** The surrender by one state to another of a person charged with a crime. This surrender is made in response to the demand of the latter state that the accused be returned to face the charge.

**Felony.** A serious crime, such as murder, larceny, or robbery, punishable by death or by imprisonment in a state or federal penitentiary.

**Fine.** Payment of money demanded of a person convicted of a crime or a misdemeanor; the fine is imposed by a court as punishment.

**Fixture.** An article which was once a chattel but which has now become a part of the real estate because the article is permanently attached to the soil or to something attached to the soil.

**Foreclosure.** The legal process by which the mortgagor's equitable or statutory right to redeem mortgaged property is terminated.

**Forgery.** The act of criminally making or altering a written instrument for the purpose of fraud or deceit; for example, signing another person's name to a check.

**Freehold.** An interest in land which permits the owner to enjoy possession of real estate during his life without interference from others.

**Garnishment.** The process by which a judgment creditor seizes money, which is owed to his judgment debtor, from a third party known as a garnishee.

**Grand jury.** At common law, a group of persons consisting of not less than twelve nor more than twenty-four who listen to evidence and determine whether or not they should charge the accused with the commission of a crime by returning an indictment. The number of members on a grand jury varies in different states.

**Guarantee.** In law, a contract under which one person agrees to pay a debt or perform a duty if the other person who is bound to pay the debt or perform the duty fails to do so.

**Habeas corpus.** An order signed by a judge directing a sheriff or other official, who has a person in his custody, to bring that person before the court to determine whether or not he should be released from custody.

**Hearsay.** That kind of evidence which is not entirely within the personal knowledge of the witness but is partly within the personal knowledge of another person.

**Heir.** At common law, this term was restricted to lawfully born children who could inherit land from an ancestor; under statutes, it includes all those who have the right to inherit from a deceased person.

**Honorarium.** Money or other valuable property given in gratitude for services rendered; for example, payments to ministers for presiding at weddings and funerals.

**Indemnity.** An agreement whereby one party agrees to secure another against an anticipated loss or damage.

**Indictment.** A formal written charge against a person which is presented by a grand jury to the court in which the jury has been sworn.

**Indorsement.** *See* Endorsement in this table.

**Injunction.** A court order which restrains one of the parties to a suit in equity from doing or permitting others who are under his control to do an act which is unjust to the other party.

**Ipso facto.** By the fact itself or by the very nature of the case.

**Joint tenancy.** A method by which one person mutually holds legal title to property with other persons in such a way that when one of the joint owners dies his share automatically passes to the surviving joint owners by operation of law.

**Judgment.** The declaration, by a court, of the rights and duties of the parties to a lawsuit which has been submitted to it for decision.

**Larceny.** Illegal taking and carrying away of personal property belonging to another with the purpose of depriving the owner of its possession.

**Lease.** An instrument conveying the possession of real property for a fixed period of time in consideration of the payment of rent.

**Legacy.** A gift of money or of personal property, title to which is passed under the terms of a will.

**Libel.** In law, a false defamation expressed in writing, printing, or picture which injures the character or reputation of the person defamed or which exposes him to public ridicule; distinguished from slander.

**Lien.** In law, the right to retain the lawful possession of the property of another until the owner fulfills a legal duty to the person holding the property, such as the payment of lawful charges for work done on the property.

**Manslaughter.** The unlawful killing of a human being without malice or premeditation; distinguished from murder, which requires malicious intent.

**Misdemeanor.** A crime—less serious than a felony—which is punishable by fine or imprisonment in a city or county jail rather than in a penitentiary.

**Mortgage.** The transfer of title to real estate which is made to secure the performance of some act such as payment of money by the person making the transfer. Upon the performance of the act, the grantee agrees to convey the property back to the person who has conveyed it to him.

**Murder.** *See* Manslaughter in this table.

**Notary public.** An official authorized by the state to attest or certify legal documents.

**Option.** A contract whereby one person purchased the right for a certain time, at his election, to purchase property at a stated price.

**Patent.** A grant made by the government to one or more individuals entitling them to exercise some privilege not granted to others during the period they are so authorized to exercise that privilege.

**Per capita.** Term used to designate a system of inheritance under which an individual descendant takes a share which is equal in size to the shares of each of the other descendants, regardless of whether that descendant is the child, grandchild, or great-grandchild of the decedent.

**Perjury.** The offense of willfully making a false statement when one is under oath to tell the truth.

**Per se** (*pĕr sē*). By or of itself; for example, slander *per se*, where the words spoken are obviously defamatory and the injured party is not required to prove damage to his character.

**Per stirpes** (*pĕr stĕr'pēz*). Term used to designate a system of inheritance under which children take among them the share which their parent would have taken had he survived the decedent. Thus the children are said to claim their shares by representing their parent.

**Petit jury.** The ordinary trial jury of twelve persons whose duty it is to find facts as opposed to the grand jury whose duty it is to return an indictment.

**Power of attorney.** An instrument by which one person authorizes another to act for him in a manner which is as legally binding upon the person giving such authority as if he personally were to do the acts.

**Precedent.** The body of judicial decisions in which were formulated the points of law arising in any case.

**Prima-facie** (*prī'mạ-fā'shĭ-ē*) **evidence.** Evidence that is sufficient to raise a presumption of fact or to establish the fact in question unless rebutted.

**Probate.** In law, the process of proving before a probate court that a will has been properly executed according to the statutory requirements.

**Pro rata** (*prō rā'tạ*). Term used to designate the system of distributing the assets of an estate in equal proportion among all the members of the same class of beneficiaries.

**Referendum.** A system of legislation whereby proposed laws are submitted to popular vote.

**Replev'in.** A proceeding employed by a party to regain possession of personal property which was illegally taken from him.

**Riparian rights.** Legal rights of owners of land bordering on a river or other body of water; also, law which pertains to use of the water for that land.

**Sedition.** Conduct which is directed against a government and which tends toward insurrection but does not amount to treason. Treasonous conduct consists of levying war against the United States or of adhering to its enemies, giving them aid and comfort.

**Slander.** In law, a false defamation (expressed in spoken words, signs, or gestures) which injures the character or reputation of the person defamed; distinguished from libel.

**Statute.** A law established by an act of the legislature.

**Subpoena** (*sŭb-pē'nạ*). An order directed to an individual commanding him to appear in court on a certain day to testify in a pending lawsuit.

**Summons.** The proceeding to commence an action in a court of law which consists of a notice to the defendant requiring him to serve an answer to the complaint.

**Testator.** One who has made a last will and testament.

**Title.** The sum total of legally recognized rights to the possession and ownership of property.

**Tort.** In law, a wrong or injury which does not grow out of a breach of contract and for which one is entitled to damages; for example, fraud, slander, or libel.

**Treason.** *See* Sedition in this table.

**Trespass.** In law, an unlawful intentional intrusion upon another's property or person.

**Trust.** An agreement under which one person transfers title to specific property to another who agrees to hold or manage it for the benefit of a third person.

**Usury.** An illegal profit received on a loan of money.

**Venue** (*vĕn'ū*). The county in which the facts are alleged to have occurred and in which the trial will be held.

**Verdict.** The unanimous decision made by a jury and reported to the court on matters lawfully submitted to them in the course of the trial of a case.

**Warranty.** A statement or agreement by a seller of property which is a part of the contract of sale. The truth of the statement is necessary to the validity of the contract.

**Will.** In general, any instrument, executed with the required formalities conferring no present rights but intended to take effect on the death of the maker, which contains his intention respecting the disposition of his property.

THESE ARTICLES ARE IN THE FACT-INDEX

Lawes, Sir John Bennet
Lawless, Theodore Kenneth
Lawn
Lawn bowling
Lawndale, Calif.
Lawrance, Charles Lanier
Lawrence, Saint
Lawrence, Abbott
Lawrence, Amos Adams

Lawrence, Charles
Lawrence, D(avid) H(erbert)
Lawrence, Ernest O(rlando)
Lawrence, Gertrude
Lawrence, Sir Henry Montgomery
Lawrence, Jacob

## LAWRENCE, James

(1781–1813). "Don't give up the ship!" cried Captain Lawrence, commander of the United States frigate *Chesapeake*, as he was carried below, mortally wounded. These words were used later by Oliver H. Perry on his flag at the battle of Lake Erie.

James Lawrence was born Oct. 1, 1781, in Burlington, N. J. He entered the Navy as a midshipman at the age of 17 and rose to the rank of lieutenant in 1802. During the war with the Tripoli pirates (1804–5) he was second in command to Stephen Decatur. At different times he commanded the *Argus*, *Vixen*, *Wasp*, and *Hornet*.

On June 1, 1813, commanding a poorly trained crew on the *Chesapeake*, he sailed out of Boston Harbor to meet the British frigate *Shannon*. The two ships were about equal in size and guns, but the crew of the *Shannon* was experienced and well-trained.

Soon the *Chesapeake* was disabled and Lawrence fell fatally wounded. He died a few days later in Halifax, where his captured vessel was taken. His body was later returned to the United States and buried in the yard of Trinity Church, New York City.

THESE ARTICLES ARE IN THE FACT-INDEX

Lawrence, John Laird Mair Lawrence, Baron

Lawrence, Josephine
Lawrence, Sir Thomas

## LAWRENCE, Thomas Edward

(1888–1935). One of the most remarkable careers of World War I was that of "Lawrence of Arabia." He became famous for his exploits as leader of the Arab revolt against the Turks (1916–18); and his dislike of publicity made him an almost legendary figure.

Lawrence was born Aug. 15, 1888, in Portmadoc, Wales. After secondary school he enrolled in Oxford. He rarely attended classes, but he read continually. Lawrence was interested in the Middle Ages, and after college this interest took him to the Near East to study the castles of the crusaders. He tramped all over Palestine, Syria, and Mesopotamia.

When World War I began in 1914 Lawrence was rejected for active service because of his short stature. He found a place in the War Office and was transferred to the intelligence service in Egypt. Soon he was sent to Arabia with the rank of colonel.

To weld the scattered Arab forces into a fighting unit, Lawrence became almost an Arab himself. He wore an Arab's flowing robes and a chieftain's headdress and rode on camels. Under his leadership attacks against supply trains and other surprise maneuvers routed the Turks from strong positions. In a series of battles his forces destroyed the Fourth Turkish Army and captured Damascus.

When the war was over Lawrence looked after Arab interests at the peace conference and took part in the Middle Eastern Settlement of 1921. Then he retired to write 'Seven Pillars of Wisdom', his account of the revolt. An abridged edition, 'Revolt in the Desert', appeared later. Meanwhile he had enlisted in the armed services as a private. To escape attention he had changed his name, first to Ross, then to Shaw. He refused any reward or decorations for his war service. He died May 19, 1935, following a motorcycle accident.

THESE ARTICLES ARE IN THE FACT-INDEX

Lawrence, William
Lawrence, Kan.

## LAWRENCE, Mass.

This city was long known as the chief center for the manufacture of worsted cloth in the United States and as a leading producer of cotton goods. In the 1920's Lawrence began to lose some textile business to the South. Its decline continued until the 1950's, when an aggressive campaign brought in new industries. The most important of these are the making of electrical and electronic machinery and ordnance manufacture. Leather, rubber, and plastic products; chemicals; paper; and clothing are also produced.

Lawrence lies on the Merrimack River, 30 miles from the ocean and about 25 miles northwest of Boston. It was founded in 1847 when a dam was being built on the Merrimack. When the dam was completed, in 1848, it furnished waterpower for textile mills and other factories. Lawrence was chartered as a city in 1853. It was named for Abbott Lawrence, a director of the company that built the dam.

Lawrence is the center of Greater Lawrence, which also includes Andover, North Andover, and Methuen. Merrimack College is in North Andover, and Phillips Andover Academy is in Andover. Lawrence is governed by a mayor and four aldermen. (*See also* Massachusetts.) Population (1970 census), 66,915.

THESE ARTICLES ARE IN THE FACT-INDEX

Lawrence University
Lawrie, Lee
Lawson, Don
Lawson, Henry
Lawson, John Howard
Lawson, Robert
Lawson, Victor Fremont
Lawton, Henry Ware
Lawton, Okla.
Laxness, Halldor
 (Kiljan)
Layamon

Layard, Sir (Austen)
 Henry
Layne, Robert (Bobby)
Laysan Island
Layton, Utah
Lazarus
Lazarus, Emma
Lazear, Jesse William
Lea, Henry Charles
Lea, Homer
Lea, Tom
Leacock, Stephen Butler
Lead, S. D.

**LEAD.** Few if any metals surpass lead for a variety of uses. In the United States about one third of all the lead used goes into electric storage batteries (*see* Battery). The next largest consumption is in antiknock fluid (tetraethyllead) for gasoline. Large quantities go into coverings for electric-wire cables and into paints and pigments. Lead bullets have made gunpowder effective in firearms, and lead is the main ingredient in type metal, used in printing.

Lead is both the heaviest and the softest of common, or base, metals. It is employed in making electric-cable coverings because it bends easily and resists corrosion. Alloys for solder, safety plugs, and fuses are only a few which contain lead (*see* Alloys). Collapsible tubes are made from lead. It adds brilliant luster to glassware (*see* Glass).

Lead serves well in the making of water pipes because it is almost insoluble in water. It also resists attack by strong chemicals. Hence it is used to line working chambers in laboratories for many chemical processes, such as making sulfuric acid (*see* Sulfuric Acid). Lead screens are important for protection against X rays, gamma rays, and products of radioactivity because lead absorbs these radiations.

World production of lead varies between 2 and $2\frac{1}{2}$ million tons or more a year. The United States produces

about 15 percent of the total. Other major producers are the Soviet Union, Australia, Mexico, West Germany, and Belgium. Idaho and Missouri supply over 60 percent of the United States output.

The United States uses more than half the world's production. To help meet this demand worn-out lead products are reworked whenever practical. Some lead also must be imported.

In the United States the most abundant lead ore is *galena* (lead sulfide, $PbS$). Other important ores are *cerussite* (lead carbonate, $PbCO_3$) and *anglesite* (lead sulfate, $PbSO_4$). Most ores contain zinc as well as lead. Some also have a valuable content of silver, gold, or other metal.

The ore is first pulverized, and the heavy metal-bearing material is separated from the rock. The ore is then treated by the *flotation process*. It is mixed with water and certain oils and chemicals. The lead-bearing particles are wetted by the oil and float to the surface attached to air bubbles. The *gangue*, or waste, is wetted by the water and sinks.

The concentrated lead-bearing particles are roasted to drive off sulfur, and the remainder is smelted in a blast furnace or open-hearth furnace with coke and a flux of silica or lime. The lead settles to the bottom of the melt, and other metals (except gold and silver) are skimmed off in the slag. Lead may be purified further by electrolysis.

Lead belongs to the carbon family of elements (*see* Periodic Table). Like carbon it can form compounds with both acids and bases.

Red oxide of lead, or *minium* ($Pb_3O_4$), is used to protect iron and steel from rust. Basic lead carbonate ($PbCO_3 \cdot 2Pb(OH)_2$) is the white pigment used in paint. Litharge (lead monoxide, $PbO$) is used in optical glass. Lead arsenate ($Pb_3(AsO_4)_2$) is a poison used as an insecticide. All lead compounds are poisonous and "cumulative." Regular small doses remain in the body and build up diseased conditions that range from colic to nerve paralysis and death.

Certain isotopes of lead result from the radioactive decay of uranium (*see* Radioactivity). The lead end product of uranium decay has an atomic weight of 205.97446. Ordinary lead has an atomic weight of 207.19. Its four stable isotopes are Pb-204, Pb-206, Pb-207, and Pb-208 (*see* Chemistry).

Lead was used in ancient times. As far back as 2000 B.C. lead was used to purify gold and silver. The Romans used lead for water pipes. From *plumbum*, the Latin word for lead, come our word "plumber" and the chemical symbol Pb for lead. Some lead pipe dug up in Rome appears from an inscription to have been made about A.D. 70.

These men have spliced a coaxial television cable on the Mississippi River. Such cables have lead coverings.

Wide World

THESE ARTICLES ARE IN THE FACT-INDEX

Leadbelly (Huddie Ledbetter)
Leadville, Colo.
Leadwort family
Leaf, Munro
Leaf-cutting ant

Leaf fish
Leafhoppers
Leaf insect
Leaf rollers
League

**LEAGUE OF NATIONS.** The League of Nations was created in 1920. Its covenant was written into the peace treaties that closed World War I. After World War II, 26 years later, it passed quietly out of existence. At its last meeting, April 18, 1946, it gave the United Nations its technical services and buildings.

This international group was the first real attempt to set up an organization to maintain peace. It was to be a world-wide institution, with all the great powers participating. However, the United States, which had fathered the covenant, refused to join. Other nations withdrew when League decisions went against them. Japan left in 1933, Germany in 1935, Italy in 1937, and Russia in 1939. When a second world war threatened, the League was powerless.

The League of Nations was first suggested in the Fourteen Points presented Jan. 8, 1918, by Woodrow Wilson, president of the United States, as a basis for armistice negotiations. After the peace negotiations opened, the work was continued by a commission headed by Wilson. A working plan, called The Covenant of the League of Nations, became Section I of the Treaty of Versailles. The League came officially into existence with the ratification of this treaty on Jan. 10, 1920. The first Assembly met in Geneva, Nov. 15, 1920, with 41 nations represented. More than 20 nations joined later but there were numerous withdrawals. In 1946 the League had a membership of 44 nations. (*See also* Wilson.)

The organization, powers, and purposes of the League were stated in 26 articles of the Covenant. Its specific aims were to promote arbitration for settling international disputes; to bring about reduction of armaments; to study and remove the causes of war; and to promote world interests in all fields of human work. The organization consisted of the Secretariat, headed by a secretary-general; the Council, normally 14 members, five permanent and nine nonpermanent; and the Assembly. The Council early set up the Permanent Court of International Justice, or World Court, at The Hague, Netherlands.

All the member nations agreed to submit to the League's procedure any international dispute that was likely to lead to armed conflict. If the Council made a unanimous report (the votes of the disputing states not counting), the League members were bound not to declare war on the disputant complying with the Council's report. The members agreed to use "sanctions" (economic blockades) against any member nation that went to war instead of submitting its dispute to the League. The Council had no international army to carry out its decisions, but it could recommend the use of force against an offending nation.

After World War I, the League helped stabilize finances and bring relief to the war victims. It aided in suppressing slavery and the illicit narcotics trade, helped improve working conditions, established institutions for the study of disease, and found havens for political and religious refugees. It set up many committees, such as the Mandates Commission, which examined the reports of the mandatory powers governing territories taken from Germany and Turkey. It successfully arbitrated a number of international disputes until its later years, when it suffered a series of defeats. In defiance of the League, Japan invaded Manchuria and China; Germany absorbed Austria and Czechoslovakia; and Italy took Ethiopia and Albania. (*See also* Europe, History of; World War I.)

---

THESE ARTICLES ARE IN THE FACT-INDEX

Leah
Leahy, William Daniel

Leakey, Louis Seymour
  Bazett
Leamington, England

---

**LEAR, Edward** (1812–1888). The English humorist Edward Lear made famous the limerick form of verse and illustrated his work with amusing pictures. The gentle, friendly man was always fond of children, and most of his writing was done for their pleasure.

Edward Lear was born May 12, 1812, in London, England. He was the youngest of a huge family of 21 children. Their father, once a wealthy stockbroker, was imprisoned for debt; and Edward had to start earning his own living at 15.

Lear had always enjoyed drawing pictures of birds, animals, and plants, and he soon began to specialize in natural history and medical drawings. He was hired to make drawings of the brilliantly colored parrots in the Regent's Park Zoo in London, and in a year he had produced 42 lithographic plates. Precise in line and faithful in color, these won the acclaim of many scientists.

Seeing them, the 13th earl of Derby invited Lear to come to Knowsley Hall, his estate near Liverpool, and make drawings of his private menagerie. Lear became the favorite of the earl's nieces, nephews, and grandchildren. He entertained the children with comic drawings and with limericks.

These verses were published in 1846 as 'A Book of Nonsense', dedicated to the Knowsley Hall children. It was followed years later by 'Nonsense Songs, Stories, Botany, and Alphabets' (1871), 'More Nonsense Pictures, Rhymes, Botany, Etc.' (1872), and 'Laughable Lyrics' (1877). For several years, Lear traveled in Europe and Asia, making sketches for landscape paintings and writing illustrated travel journals. He gave painting lessons to Queen Victoria, and she and the Prince of Wales maintained a constant interest in his work.

Lear never married. He depended upon his friends, among them Alfred Tennyson and the painter Holman Hunt, for companionship. He died in 1888, in San Remo, Italy, where he had spent his last years.

# LEARNING
# for the
# Enrichment
# of Living

A mother takes pleasure in watching her child develop coordination by using building blocks to make shapes and structures that her fancy and experience suggest.

**LEARNING.** At birth a child is the most dependent of creatures. He could not live without help from others. As he grows older he becomes increasingly independent. Aimless kicking and crying are replaced by asking for what he wants and by getting things for himself. He buttons his clothes without help. He speaks new words every day. The tricycle that gave him so much trouble at first he can now ride with little effort. Soon he is counting, repeating the alphabet, and printing his name.

Thousands upon thousands of basic skills are acquired during childhood. All these things must be learned. Learning is both acquiring new reactions and changing old ones. Skills and certain other acquisitions are called habits (*see* Habit). Learning itself is sometimes referred to as "habit formation." In addition to skills there are study habits, habits of thought, the smoking habit, and so on. The learning process is much the same whether the habits are good or bad and whether they are primarily muscular (like riding a bicycle) or verbal (like counting).

## Growth of Learning Ability

The brain of a newborn baby is only one fourth of its adult size. It is also immature in other ways. Millions of nerve fibers must grow and interconnect before it is fully developed. This immaturity explains in part the baby's poor learning ability. He has not yet learned that he can learn.

Within a few weeks after birth, however, learning is well under way. Having learned that crying brings attention the baby soon learns to stop crying when he is picked up. Soon he becomes quiet when he just hears his mother's voice. He has learned to connect sounds and persons. Although he is not aware of it, he has begun to learn that it is possible to change his environment through his own actions. He is learning how to learn.

When the child discovers his hands and feet, his clothes, and the objects around him he soon develops motor skills. His verbal skills begin when he understands what is said to him. A much greater development occurs when he can use the words himself. When he can speak he can ask questions. As skills develop, the child increases his power to learn new things. When he has learned to read, a new tool for learning is available. Having learned arithmetic, he is ready for algebra, then for higher mathematical skills. These open up the fields of science. The more we learn, the better we are equipped for further learning.

## Stimulation and Response

Learning requires stimulation. Learned reactions are responses to stimulation. The child touches a hot stove and jerks away his hand. Heat is the stimulus, jerking is the response. With one or two such experiences the child learns not to touch a hot stove. The sense organs and muscular mechanisms, therefore, are of great importance to the learner. Normally the most important sense is vision. Hearing is second in importance and touch is third. People born with neither vision nor hearing are very greatly handicapped. Only through intensive use of their sense of touch can they be taught to take care of themselves

169

**DETOUR PROBLEM TESTS LEARNING FROM EXPERIENCE AND OBSERVATION**

A barrier open at each end separates food or a toy from the subject. The baby (left) persists in trying to get the doll through the glass instead of reaching around the side. The monkey grasps the solution quickly. The dog observes and imitates the monkey. But the dull-witted chicken will never have sense enough to walk around the end of the fence to reach the coveted corn.

and to communicate with others. Helen Keller is an illustration of what careful training through touch can accomplish in a person who is both blind and deaf.

We learn to put on warm clothes when our temperature sense tells us it is cold. We recognize many objects through taste and smell. Muscle sense (kinesthesia) likewise plays a part. Muscular defects may hinder or prevent the learning of motor skills. As in the case of sensory defects, it is sometimes possible to overcome such handicaps by making unusual uses of the muscles that remain unimpaired.

Once motor skills are acquired, the kinesthetic sense becomes extremely important. After we have learned through vision where the electric-light button is, this sense enables us to go directly to it in the dark. It also accounts for the fact that we can carry on complex motor skills more or less automatically. Driving an automobile or operating a typewriter by the touch system are examples.

Specialized kinesthetic sense organs called receptors are located in the muscles, tendons, and joints. Muscle movements stimulate them, sending nerve impulses into the spinal cord and brain, then back again to the muscles. These impulses provide the succession of stimuli, or cues, necessary to carry on a learned sequence of movements. (*See also* Muscles.)

### Learning and the Brain

Although sense organs and muscles are necessary to learning, the most important structure of all is the brain (*see* Brain; Nerves). This not only interconnects sense organs and muscles, but its billions of nerve cells somehow retain a record of what has happened to us. How they do this is not known. There are many theories. One scientist likens the nerves of the brain to the wires of a wire recorder. The wire is changed magnetically. This modification then makes possible a "playback" (chiefly through the brain) of what has gone into the mechanism.

Learning ability increases as the brain grows in size and complexity. Animals without brains cannot learn much and the little they do learn is not re-

tained very long. The rat has only a small brain, but it learns to find the correct path through a maze, it learns to associate food with certain signs and not with others, and it even learns to solve simple problems which require recall of past experience and elementary reasoning. It also retains what it learns, sometimes for months.

The dog, with a much larger brain, can learn skills and solve problems too complex for the rat. Confronted by a barrier placed between itself and food, the rat will attack the barrier. A bright dog grasps the uselessness of such an approach and makes a detour around the obstruction. This is an example of learning through insight rather than a simple trial-and-error attack.

Learning by insight is more evident in the apes, such as the chimpanzee. These animals have brains far in advance of the dog's. Their learning ability is "almost human" because they also have superior sense organs and their fingers possess almost human powers of manipulation. All three superior factors— brain, sensory ability, and powers of manipulation— enable chimpanzees to acquire complex skills and solve involved problems.

Learning ability decreases as a result of brain injury, usually in proportion to the extent of brain damage. The handicap is greater for complex learning than it is for simpler learning. Injury to the front part of the brain interferes with ability to grasp the meaning of situations and to act appropriately. Insight and reasoning are impaired.

### How Learning Is Studied

Many psychological studies of learning are carried on in laboratories with animals, children, or college students as subjects. When motor skills are being investigated, the most widely used apparatus is some form of maze. An animal runs through the maze or along the top of an elevated maze pathway. Human subjects usually trace a smaller maze with a stylus while blindfolded. The animal learns the correct pathway because it is hungry and food is found at

**LEARNING BY INSIGHT**
The chimpanzee is placed in a cage with a bunch of bananas hanging overhead. He tries to reach the fruit and realizes he cannot. The solution of stacking the boxes and climbing on them shows learning by insight instead of by trial and error.

period. Along the vertical axis progress in learning (errors or successes) is indicated. In a typewriting test, for example, the line may show the number of errors or words correctly typed in five-minute tests.

## Plateaus of Learning

When very complex skills are being learned, there is often a period of little or no progress. This is known as a "plateau." Poor motivation may be one explanation for plateaus. In one industrial situation, the average worker reached a level of skill which would enable him to "get by," and he showed no further improvement. When a bonus based upon piecework was offered, however, the average output soon increased.

When motivation is at its highest possible level and methods of maximum efficiency are used, performance often reaches a point where no further improvement is possible. This is the *physiological limit*. It is reached when errors cannot be reduced and when correct movements are made as fast as brain and muscles will allow. Very few people ever reach their physiological limit in any skill.

## Efficient Learning

Three factors are especially important in learning. Keeping them in mind will greatly improve the effectiveness of learning (*see* Study).

The first factor is the *principle of rest*. Experiments in the laboratory, in the classroom, and in industrial situations have shown that much more efficiency is attained with frequent rests than with practicing continually for long periods. In general, a one-hour period without a rest is long enough. In the case of intensive study, a half-hour period may be better. If the student spends 15 to 30 minutes getting settled and trying to concentrate on what he is doing, a half-hour study period is largely wasted. In any case, when one finds that he is reacting automatically, going through the motions without grasping what he is doing, it is time for a rest. Continued work without rest will bring diminishing returns. Rest periods need not be long. Often a few minutes may be effective. What happens during the interval is especially important. The best retention occurs during sleep (*see* Memory). One cannot have a nap between each work period, but he can relax as much as possible. The principle of work and rest applies equally well to learning motor and verbal skills and to study.

The *principle of recitation* should be applied when we try to memorize something. Without recitation

the end of the path. As it learns to avoid blind alleys, it gets its reward more quickly and with less effort. Experiments have shown that it does not learn unless it has a need and its efforts satisfy this need. Thus nonhungry rats fail to learn a maze when food is the only reward. Make them hungry and they soon learn. Likewise, hungry rats who find no food at the end of the pathway fail to learn. Place food there and the maze is soon mastered.

Learning in human beings also requires rewards. Sometimes this is the knowledge that one is making progress toward mastery of a task. Perhaps his reward is a "well done" from an observer. Children who were given money when they reached the end of a maze pathway learned more quickly and with fewer errors than those given no reward.

Mazes are widely used because a pathway may be arranged which is new to all learners. A fair comparison of the learning performances of different subjects could not be made if some had already had practice. When verbal learning is being studied, subjects are often required to memorize lists of such nonsense syllables as TOJ, XUH, and GIK.

Progress can be followed by plotting a learning curve. Along the base one marks off trials or practice periods. Each trial may be a five-minute practice

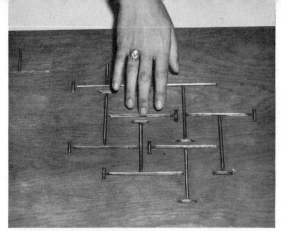

**A FINGER RELIEF MAZE**
Mazes are used in psychology laboratories to test comparative learning ability. In this test the subject is blindfolded and traces a raised wire pattern with the fingertips.

one merely reads the material again and again until he is able to repeat it. With recitation he reads, then tries to recall. After the first reading or so, he looks at the material only when he is unable to recall some of it. He follows this procedure, with rest periods, until the entire material is recalled.

The third factor is the *principle of whole versus part learning*. In memorizing a long poem, for example, the results of research suggest that one should begin with the entire poem, then concentrate on the verses which give most difficulty. In studying a textbook assignment, also, it is preferable to begin by skimming through the entire assignment, then concentrating on parts which seem to require detailed study. Finally, one should go over the entire poem or assignment again. This might be called the "whole-part-whole" method of procedure.

Learning ability shows its greatest growth during the first 15 to 20 years of life. In the late teens one has a brain that is about as mature as it will ever be. After we reach adulthood there is a period of about 20 years during which learning ability remains at a high level. Beyond this period it becomes increasingly difficult to learn new things. The slow-

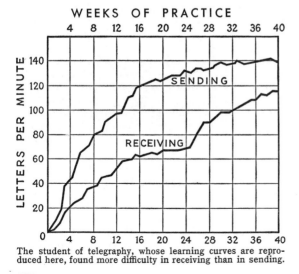

**WEEKS OF PRACTICE**

SENDING

RECEIVING

LETTERS PER MINUTE

The student of telegraphy, whose learning curves are reproduced here, found more difficulty in receiving than in sending.

ing down is evident when we attempt to learn entirely new things, as in the case of a person who has never learned mathematics and who now attempts to master mathematical skills. The chief reason is that the brain is no longer as easily modified or as retentive as it once was.

### Transfer of Learning

Learning one skill often helps in learning others. Similarity between tasks is an obvious reason for transfer of learning. To the degree that activities have similar aspects, use similar methods, and follow similar principles one can expect that learning one will aid in learning the others.

Some school subjects transfer a great deal to other subjects. Students who first study mathematics are helped in their study of the physical sciences, which make much use of mathematical symbols, methods, and principles. Latin aids in the study of Spanish because many Spanish words are derived from Latin.

Occasionally transfer is a hindrance. This is sometimes referred to as habit interference. When one has achieved skill in typing by the visual "hunt-and-peck" method, he has unusual difficulty in learning the touch method.

### "Discipline" of the Mind

It was once believed that certain difficult subjects, especially Latin and mathematics, "discipline the mind." This concept of transfer is referred to as the "doctrine of formal discipline." Large-scale experiments on high-school students have shown that students who take Latin and mathematics are usually brighter than average to begin with. Thus their superiority cannot be attributed to the subjects studied.

In a carefully controlled study of a large group of high-school students, all students were given a test. On the basis of their scores they were divided into groups of the same average intelligence. They studied certain subjects in common. In addition some groups took Latin, some mathematics, and so on. At the end of the year they were all given another test which would indicate whether any particular study improved their intelligence more than another. The conclusion was against the doctrine of formal discipline. No one study had a general mental effect which differed from that of other studies.

We do not learn merely to improve our minds in any general sense. We learn specific facts and skills. We should acquire habits which aid further learning; information which enriches our everyday lives and helps us to understand the world we live in; skills which enable us to earn our living; and above all, interests to carry us through the later years of life. We begin the learning process in early infancy. It need never stop during the rest of our lifetime.

---

THIS ARTICLE IS IN THE FACT-INDEX
**Leary, Herbert Fairfax**

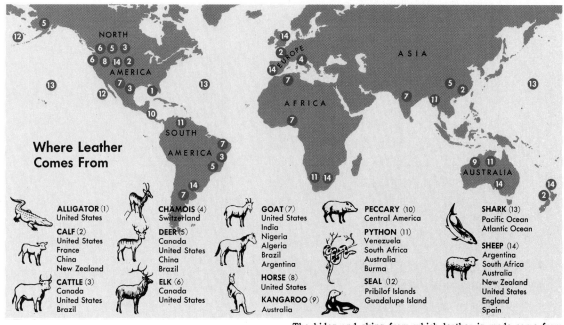

## Where Leather Comes From

**ALLIGATOR** (1)
United States

**CALF** (2)
United States
France
China
New Zealand

**CATTLE** (3)
Canada
United States
Brazil

**CHAMOIS** (4)
Switzerland

**DEER** (5)
Canada
United States
China
Brazil

**ELK** (6)
Canada
United States

**GOAT** (7)
United States
India
Nigeria
Algeria
Brazil
Argentina

**HORSE** (8)
United States

**KANGAROO** (9)
Australia

**PECCARY** (10)
Central America

**PYTHON** (11)
Venezuela
South Africa
Australia
Burma

**SEAL** (12)
Pribilof Islands
Guadalupe Island

**SHARK** (13)
Pacific Ocean
Atlantic Ocean

**SHEEP** (14)
Argentina
South Africa
Australia
New Zealand
United States
England
Spain

The hides and skins from which leather is made come from many countries, as this map illustrates. Leather follows food and wool as man's most important gift from the animal world.

# LEATHER—A Product of Hides and Skins

**LEATHER.** Nearly everyone uses leather in some way each day. Most people, all over the world, wear shoes that are made of it. Many industries depend upon the product for belting in their machines. Cowboys ride on leather saddles. Lumberjacks' boots are made of it. Baseballs, footballs, and basketballs are covered with leather. Aviators wear leather jackets. Many people use gloves and carry handbags or billfolds of leather.

### Modern Leather Manufacture

The hides and skins of domestic animals are the main sources of leather. The skins of larger animals, such as cattle and horses, are called *hides*. Those of smaller animals, such as sheep, goats, and peccaries, are called *skins*.

In the manufacture of leather, the skin, as nearly whole and undamaged as possible, is first removed from the animal. With modern tools this is done quickly. At the *tannery* skins are examined. The hoofs, tails, ears, and other unusable parts are trimmed off and sent to gelatin producers or to glue-makers. The skins then are put into large tanks of water called *soaks* and left to soften for two days.

The *fleshing* machine next removes all the fat and tissue. The skins are then partly dehaired in a lime-water bath. Any remaining hair is removed by a machine. After the hides are dehaired they are treated with pancreatic enzymes for two days in order to further soften the skin and to remove the lime. The hides are then ready for *tanning*.

### Two Methods of Tanning

In *vegetable tanning* the extract, or tannin, from the bark and wood of trees is used. This is a long process. It produces a firm leather which is water resistant. Most shoe soles, industrial beltings, luggage, and upholstery are made by this method.

The tanning is done by soaking the skins in several baths, starting with very weak solutions and becoming progressively stronger. This takes about one month. The skins are then dried by artificial heat, oiled, and finally ironed by large rollers.

*Chrome tanning* was invented in 1884 and is now the most popular method of dressing light leathers. Most shoe uppers, gloves, and garment leathers are made from chrome-tanned light hides or skins. The chrome treatment takes only about a third as long as the vegetable process.

The skins are pickled in a bath of salt and sulfuric acid. The hides are then soaked with a solution of sodium dichromate. Next they are treated with sodium thiosulfate in the reduction drum. The chromium salts are set on the fibers by adding borax to the skins in the settling drums. After washing, the leather is ready for finishing.

### Leather Finishing

Finishing operations are the same for chrome-tanned and vegetable-tanned leather. The processes vary with the use for which the leather is intended.

Leather as it dries after tanning is stiff and rough.

**COLD STORAGE**
Hides and skins are kept in cold storage until the tanning process begins. This prevents rotting and stiffening.

**TRIMMING**
Hoofs, tails, ears, and other unusable parts of the skin are trimmed off and sent to gelatin or glue manufacturers.

**SOAKING**
Trimmed hides are soaked in clean, cool water at about 60° F. for at least two days. This softens the hides.

Oil is rubbed into it to make it soft and pliable. This process is called *currying*. Dull leather, such as that used in cheaper grades of shoes, may simply be oiled and worked so it will be pliable. Harness and sole leathers are put in great presses to make them hard and durable.

If a luster is desired, a dressing is applied to the grain side of the leather. Then it is run through pressure rollers, which polish the surface. If a dull polish is desired, a revolving brush is passed over the surface. Grained and decorated surfaces may be attained by embossing the pattern on the skin with heat and pressure.

The coloring of leather is an art that requires great care in order to bring about a uniform result. Different skins going through the same color bath will have different shades. Various portions of the same skin too may take the color unevenly so that the leather may appear spotted.

### The Leather "Zoo"

**Cowhide** comes from cattle and is tough and long wearing. It is used in shoe soles and some shoe uppers, as well as in machine beltings and harnesses. Thinned, or split, hides are made into luggage, gloves, clothing, and many other articles. Cowhide is the most useful of all leathers.

**Calfskin** has a fine grain. It is good for shoes because it withstands scuffing and hard wear. It is also used for handbags, gloves, bookbindings, luggage, and garments.

**Goatskin** and **kidskin** are mostly imported. They are used in women's fine shoes. Goatskin is also used in garments. Kid is one of the sturdiest leathers and also one of the softest and most pliable. It is an excellent material for suède leather.

**Sheepskin** and **lambskin** are good for shoe uppers and linings, gloves, garments, handbags, chamois, parchments, textile-mill rollers, hat sweatbands, and

**FLESHING AND HAIR REMOVAL**
In fleshing, all fat and tissue are removed (left), leaving a uniform surface on the hide. This is a mechanical operation.

A solution of lime and water or sodium sulfide is used to remove hair on the hides (right). They are then washed.

piano parts. Lambskins with the wool left on them are used for coats and boots.

**Pigskin** comes mainly from the peccary. This is a kind of wild hog found in North and South America. When the bristles are removed from the skin, pores are left which give it an unusual texture. Pigskin is used for gloves, saddles, wallets, sport shoes, bookbindings, upholstery, and razorstrops.

**Buckskin** is made from deer. Almost all buckskin consumed in the United States is imported from Latin America and Canada. It is used for garments, gloves, and the uppers of high-quality shoes.

**Alligator** comes from Latin America, Florida, and Louisiana. The beautifully textured skins are made into high-priced shoes, handbags, luggage, belts, and billfolds. These accessories are also made from the skins of water snakes, lizards, pythons, and cobras.

Some other animals also yield leather. Kangaroo, which comes exclusively from Australia, makes strong, flexible leather for shoe uppers.

The ostrich is the only bird that provides leather. Its pinkish skin is used for fine handbags and wallets. Many unusual leathers come from seals, sharks, whales, and water buffaloes.

### Leather Substitutes

Because of the increasing demand for leather and its consequent rise in price, various substitutes have been devised. Some of these man-made products closely resemble leather in feel and appearance. Others differ from leather in appearance and texture but can be put to the same uses.

Artificial leather is made of many layers of strong fabrics which are coated or ground together with plastic compounds.

Scrap leather, wood pulp, or some other insoluble ingredient may be included in the mixture. The cloth used is dyed the desired shade of the imitation leather being made. Large embossing roll presses or bed presses imprint designs which make the fabric resemble real leather.

### Early History of Leather

The story of leather is long and colorful. Many years before man kept a written record of his history, he must have wrapped himself in dried animal pelts. When he found that the skins turned stiff and rotted, he discovered ways of preserving them. In this way he learned to make leather.

How primitive man treated the hides to keep them soft and durable is unknown. At first, he probably dried them in air and sunlight. Later he

**DYEING AND COLORING**
Skins and hides are placed in these huge drums. Hot water and dye are added, and the door is closed. The drum then is set in motion.

**BUFFING AND EMBOSSING**

A buffing machine (left) has a sandpaper roll which removes the grain from skins. This produces a smooth leather. To emboss a skin, it is placed under tons of pressure (right). A heated plate of the desired pattern is pressed on the leather.

may have soaked them in water and dried them over a fire. Still later he discovered that certain twigs, barks, and leaves soaked in the water with the hides helped preserve the skins. From these early discoveries developed the leather industry as it is known today. The art of leathermaking is very old. The records show that it was highly developed thousands of years ago.

Among the pictures which Egyptians carved on stone 5,000 years ago are some showing leather dressers at work. The New York Metropolitan Museum of Art owns a pair of Egyptian leather sandals that is more than 3,300 years old. There is, at Cairo, an Egyptian queen's funeral tent of gazelle hides which was made in 1100 B.C.

The Israelites learned how to make leather from the Egyptians. A passage in the Old Testament reads, "Unto Adam and also unto his wife did the Lord God make clothes of skins and clothe them." By the time that St. Luke wrote the Book of Acts, tanning had become a common trade.

### Greek and Roman Tanning Methods

The Greeks and Romans left evidence that their methods of tanning were highly developed. Both Herodotus and Homer mention the use of leather.

In Rome leather served as money, and leather shoes of different types indicated the rank of the wearer. Our word "pecuniary" comes from the Latin *pecus*, meaning "cattle."

Pliny the Elder, writing in the first century A.D., gives the Roman recipe for tanning. "Hides were tanned with bark, and gallnuts, sumac and lotus were used," he wrote. Gallnuts are caused by insects laying eggs on the leaves or buds of oak trees. These eggs produce a growth which yields a high percentage of tannic acid. Gallnuts are still used in one type of tanning process.

### Tanning in Early America

When the first settlers arrived in America they found that the Indians' tanning method was much like the ancient "shamoying." This method was used by the Arabs and mentioned by Homer. The Indians taught the pioneers how to use the process in making buckskin.

The colonists brought oak-bark tanning methods from England. The first leathermaker arrived in Plymouth in 1623. His name was Experience Miller. In 1629 two shoemakers arrived. By 1650 there were 51 tanners in Massachusetts.

The early leathermakers simply dug holes in the ground and walled them with planking. In these holes hides were covered with oak bark and left for at least six months. This method was no more advanced than that used by the ancient Hebrews.

In 1805 Sir Humphry Davy discovered that materials from other trees—hemlock, mimosa, chestnut, and ash—could be used in tanning. These trees were plentiful in the United States and helped make it the center of the leather trade.

Samuel Parker, in 1809, invented a machine that could split hides to any thickness. Until then it took one workman an entire day to divide four hides. Now he could split one hundred in the same length of time. From these beginnings grew the scientific process of modern leather manufacture.

---

THESE ARTICLES ARE IN THE FACT-INDEX

**Leather beetle**                                    Leavenworth, Henry
**'Leatherstocking Tales'**                    Leavenworth, Kan.

---

hollow tubes, called *veins*. They are the blood vessels of the leaf. Water and dissolved minerals are carried from the soil through the roots and stems of the plant into the leafstalk and finally through the veins into the leaf. The liquid food materials formed in the leaf are carried back into the plant through the veins. (*See also* Plants; Plants, Physiology of.)

There are two principal kinds of veining—parallel and net. The grasses and lilies have the veins running side by side (parallel) from the leafstalk to the tip of the blade. In net veining, some leaves have the veins branching from a large central midrib. From its featherlike appearance, this type is called *pinnate venation*. In other leaves large veins of equal size fan out from a common point. This is *palmate venation* (shaped like the fingers and palm of the hand).

If the leaf is a single blade it is called *simple*. If it has two or more distinct parts, called *leaflets*, the leaf is *compound*. Leaves are said to be *opposite* if two are attached at the same point on opposite sides of the stem. If three or more are attached at the same point they are *whorled*. Single leaves attached to the stem first on one side and then on the other are said to be *alternate*.

The leafstalk twists and bends to hold the blade in the best position relative to light. Leafstalks on the same plant vary in length so that the leaves do not overlap and cut off light from one another. A leafy vine growing on a brick wall turns all its leaves outward to face the sun, forming a *mosaic* pattern. Most leaves expose their largest surface area to the sun. In very hot, dry regions they would lose too much moisture in this position; so some plants turn their leaves edgewise to the midday sun, and

# LEAVES—The Food Factories of Plant Life

**LEAVES.** The green color of forest, field, and garden is caused by leaves. They are the dress of trees and other plants. They are far more important than mere dress, however. The foods by which the plant lives and grows are made in the leaves. All the food eaten by human beings and other animals can be traced back to plants and the green leaf. Even our bacon and eggs start with plants, for pigs and chickens live on plant food. Without green leaves there would be no animal life on earth.

Most leaves are broad and very thin, but they have many different shapes. The needles of the pine trees are leaves. The long ribbon streamers of the seaweeds, the fronds of ferns, the tiny hairs of mosses, the hollow traps in which the pitcher plant catches insects, and the climbing tendrils of the garden pea are also leaves. The leaves of water plants show many interesting differences from those of land plants (*see* Water Plants).

### The Structure of a Leaf

The broad, thin part of the leaf is called the *blade*. It is attached to a stemlike *leafstalk*, or *petiole*. The leafstalk grows from the stem of the plant. The blade holds its shape because it has a framework of

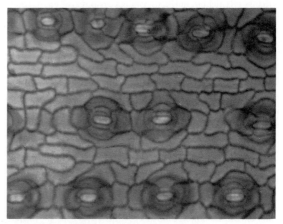

**THE BREATHING PORES OF A LEAF**
This is a magnified leaf surface. It shows breathing pores, called stomata (the light spots), surrounded by guard cells. Gases and water vapor enter and leave the leaf through stomata.

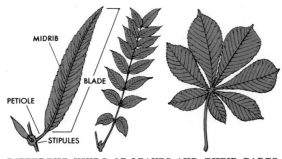

**DIFFERENT KINDS OF LEAVES AND THEIR PARTS**
The willow is a simple leaf. Compound leaves have several leaflets. The walnut is pinnately compound, or feather-shaped. The horse chestnut is palmately compound, or hand-shaped.

the flat surface only to the morning and evening rays (*see* Compass Plants).

### How the Leaf Makes Food

Between the veins of the leaf is a spongy mass of cells filled with green material which gives the leaf its color. The green cells are called *chloroplasts*. The coloring matter is *chlorophyll*. Food is made by action of the chlorophyll in the plant.

On the lower surface of the leaf, and sometimes on the upper surface, are many pores known as *stomata* (singular, *stoma*). Each stoma is a tiny opening between two bean-shaped guard cells. In most plants these pores are open all day and closed all night. There are great numbers of pores in a single leaf. An oak leaf may have 1,400 in one square millimeter of area. A square millimeter is no larger than the tip end of a lead pencil.

As sunlight shines on the leaf, carbon dioxide, in the form of gas from the air, enters the stomata. Inside the tissues of the leaf the carbon dioxide mixes with the water carried into the leaves from the roots. Then the green coloring matter, with the energy from sunlight, produces a wonderful chemical change. The carbon dioxide and the water are broken down into their separate parts (molecules), and the molecules are put together again in a new order to form sugars and starches (carbohydrates). These are the food materials of the plant. The chemical process, basic to all life, is called *photosynthesis*. The word comes from Greek words meaning "light" and "putting together." (*See also* Plants, Physiology of.)

The sugars and starches in liquid form pass back through the veins and leafstalk into the plant to nourish it. The hard woody material (cellulose) of the stem and branches is a carbohydrate (*see* Cellulose). Proteins are formed when the carbohydrates manufactured by the plant combine with dissolved minerals carried into the plant from the soil.

In the process of making food the plant uses only about 4 per cent of the water that it soaks up through its roots. The other 96 per cent evaporates into the air through the stomata. The process is called *transpiration*. Thus leaves keep the air which surrounds them fresh and moist. (*See* Trees; Water.)

In food making the plant also sends oxygen into the

air through the stomata. Here again plants make life possible for animals and man. All animals use oxygen and must have a constant supply.

### Why Leaves Change Color and Fall

In the autumn, leaves turn from green to brilliant shades of scarlet, gold, orange, and purple. Then they finally fall to the ground. It is not a season of dying. The tree or shrub is preparing for winter.

In late summer, as the growing period slows down, a corky layer of cells forms at the base of the leafstalk where it joins the stem. It is called the *separation layer*. It does not pass through the woody fibers which connect the leafstalk with the stem. These fibers hold the leaf in place until frost or wind tear it free. After the leaf has fallen the scar where it was attached to the stem is sealed and protected by the layer of cork.

As the separation layer forms, the manufacture of food materials slows down. The cells and veins in the leaf become clogged. No more chlorophyll is produced, and the green color disappears. Other colors were present in the leaf, but they were hidden by the stronger green. Now they appear in all their beauty.

All leaves contain yellow pigments called *carotene* and *xanthophyll*. The yellow pigments are formed in the protoplasm of the leaf cells. The reds and purples are due to pigments called *anthocyanins*. They are formed in cell sap which is rich in sugar. Sugar maples, oaks, and sumacs have the most brilliant scarlet and purple colors. To develop such high color they must be exposed to the sunlight. Sugar maples which are heavily shaded by larger trees do not become red but show only yellow coloring.

Jack Frost is usually given credit for autumn color. Actually frost has very little to do with it. A combination of favorable weather conditions is required. Red pigments are formed in the sunlight in leaves which have stored sugar. Cloudy, rainy weather or a very hot, dry summer prevents the pigments from developing. If warm days are followed by warm nights the sugars drain out of the leaves and into the woody portions of the plant. Ideal conditions are bright, sunny days followed by cool nights.

Frost is chiefly responsible for freeing the leaves from the twigs. On a cold, frosty night ice crystals

**THREE LEAF PRINTS**
A collection of leaves may be made without the labor of pressing and mounting them. Leaf prints are made from fresh leaves. They are attractive and fun to make.

*Direct-color photograph*  *By John Kabel*

## THE RED AND GOLD OF AUTUMN LEAVES

Like the flaming bush that appeared to Moses, a red maple rises here from among the evergreens and seems to blaze against the blue sky. A group of quaking aspens forms a golden background for this autumn scene, which was photographed along a roadside in northern Ohio.

form in the separation layer and break the woody fibers which hold the leaf in place. Then when the ice melts in the morning sun the leaves flutter in a gold and scarlet shower to the ground. In some oaks the separation layer does not develop fully and the leaves remain on the tree all winter.

The wise gardener does not burn fallen leaves but adds them to the compost pile. Rotted leaves (leaf mold) are a valuable soil conditioner. (*See* Compost; Gardens and Gardening.)

### How to Make a Leaf Collection

Late spring, when leaves are fresh and green, is the time to start a leaf collection. Fresh leaves may be mounted on paper in the same way as flowers (*see* Flowers, Wild, subhead "Making a Herbarium").

Leaf *prints* are less work to prepare than a pressed and mounted collection. A collection of *spatter prints* is interesting and easy to make. A bottle of ink, an old toothbrush, a piece of wire screening, and sheets of white paper are needed. Place a fresh leaf on the paper and pin it down flat. Then dip the toothbrush into the ink bottle, letting the excess ink drain off. Hold the wire screen over the paper and rub the bristles over it, working from side to side and from top to bottom. Draw the bristles *toward* you so the ink will spatter *away* from you. When the ink is dry remove the leaf. The imprint will remain.

For leaf *blueprints* use blueprint paper, a piece of window glass, and a basin filled with clear water. Working in dim light, lay the leaf on the treated side of the blueprint paper and cover with the window glass. Expose it to sunlight until the paper turns dark blue. Remove the glass and the leaf and quickly wash the paper in the basin of water until the color "sets." Dry the paper on a smooth, flat surface so it will not curl. The impression of the leaf will be white or pale blue on a darker blue background.

A *printer's ink print* shows the veins as well as the outline of the leaf. Needed materials are a tube of printer's ink, a sheet of window glass, two rubber rollers, and several sheets of paper. Spread a thin film of ink over the glass with one of the rollers. Place a leaf, underside down, on the inked glass. Cover it with a sheet of paper. Run the second (clean) roller over the paper several times. Now the leaf is thoroughly inked on its underside. Discard the inky paper and place the leaf, inked side down, on clean paper. Cover with a sheet of clean paper, and again work the clean roller over the paper. Finally remove the top paper and the leaf. Let the finished print dry.

A *plaster cast* may be made by putting a leaf in a greased saucer and covering it with plaster of Paris. After the plaster has set, the leaf may be removed. Its imprint in the plaster may then be painted and trimmed to the outline of the leaf.

Philip D. Gendreau

Today Baalbek is only a tiny village in central Lebanon. Once it was a magnificent city of ancient Rome. These columns are all that remain of a temple dedicated to Jupiter.

# LEBANON—Mediterranean Gateway to Asia

**LEBANON.** The small republic of Lebanon is in Southwest Asia. It is a long and narrow strip of land at the eastern end of the Mediterranean Sea. The length of the coast is about 135 miles. The average width of the land is 30 miles. Lebanon is bordered

on the north and east by Syria, and on the south by Israel. Its area is 4,015 square miles, almost twice the size of the state of Delaware. Lebanon is the second smallest country in the Arab League.

### Land and Climate

Lebanon is a rugged land. It has two almost parallel mountain ranges. The Lebanon Mountains extend the length of the country close to the narrow Mediterranean coastal plain. In the east the Anti-Lebanon Mountains divide Lebanon from Syria.

Between the two ranges is a high fertile valley called the Bekáa. The Bekáa is watered by Lebanon's chief river, the Litani (in ancient times called the Leontes). The Litani flows south through the valley.

Beirut's modern office and apartment buildings (left) rise above the blue Mediterranean. At the right is the main entrance to the

American University of Beirut. Since it was founded it has been one of the most important schools in the Middle East.

Then it turns abruptly westward, flows through a deep gorge in the Lebanon Mountains, and empties into the Mediterranean Sea.

Lebanon's coast has a Mediterranean (subtropical) climate, with warm, dry summers and mild, rainy winters. Summers in the Bekáa are hot and dry; winters are cool. In the winter the mountains, particularly the western slopes, are lashed by high winds and heavy rains and snows.

Plant life varies with the altitude and climate. Tropical and semitropical plants grow in the coastal plain. The rich soil supports large groves of orange and olive trees. Bananas, figs, grapes, and other fruits are also grown. Apples and potatoes are cultivated in the foothills. The Bekáa is another rich farming region, producing tobacco, vegetables, cotton, grains, and mulberries.

In the mountains much of the soil is barren. Erosion has destroyed almost all the natural vegetation, leaving only scattered bush and scrub. Of the famous cedars of Lebanon, only a few remain in protected groves.

### The People of Lebanon

Lebanon is fairly densely populated, but the people are unevenly distributed. The population (1979 estimate) is 3,254,000.

Most Lebanese are of Arab descent, but many racial and cultural groups are represented. Arabic is the chief language; French and English are also widely spoken. The people are almost equally divided between Christians and Moslems.

Religious groups control Lebanese politics. The Maronite Catholics are the largest Christian sect. Other Christian sects include the Greek Orthodox, the Greek Catholic, the Armenian Orthodox, and the Armenian Catholic. The chief Moslem sects are the Sunnites and Shiites. The Druses are an independent sect. Protestants and Jews are minority groups. The president must be a Maronite Christian; the prime minister, a Moslem Sunnite; the speaker of the legislature, a Moslem Shiite.

Members of the republic's one-house parliament, the national assembly, are elected for four-year terms. They represent religious rather than political groups. The president is chosen by parliament for a six-year term. He appoints the prime minister. He can also dissolve parliament and call for new elections.

### Cities, Industry, and Trade

The capital and largest city is Beirut, a Mediterranean port. Its population (1975 est.) is 1,172,000, including suburbs. A center of learning, Beirut has St. Joseph University (founded as a seminary in 1846), the American University of Beirut (founded in 1866), and the Lebanese University (1951). Other coastal towns are Tripoli, Tyre, and Saida (ancient Sidon). Tripoli and Saida are terminals for oil pipelines from Iraq and Saudi Arabia. (*See also* Beirut.)

Industries include oil refining, food processing, and textile manufacturing. Foods, textiles, and manufactured goods are important exports.

Lebanon's prosperity has traditionally been based on trade and on Beirut's position as the banking center of the Middle East. Civil war during the 1970's severely disrupted the economy.

### History

The region that includes modern Lebanon had many rulers in ancient times. It fell under Arab control in the 7th century. About the same time a Christian sect called Maronites was establishing itself in Lebanon. The Druses, who also settled in the Lebanon-Syria region, fought bitterly with the Maronites.

Turkey conquered the region in the 16th century; and, until World War I, Lebanon was part of the Ottoman Empire. After the war Lebanon was put under French mandate. When France fell in World War II, the Free French government agreed to end the mandate. Elections were held in 1943. Lebanon became a charter member of the United Nations (UN) in 1945.

In 1958, discontented religious groups in Lebanon (particularly the Moslems) revolted against the government of President Camille Chamoun (a Maronite). After Chamoun appealed to the West for support, the UN sent observers. In July the parliament chose a president, Gen. Fuad Chehab (also a Maronite), who was acceptable to the major factions.

In 1967, when war erupted between Israel and the Arab states, Lebanon supported the Arabs and declared a state of emergency. Lebanon was the only nation bordering Israel that did not lose territory to Israel in the war. Increasing numbers of Palestinians displaced from their homes sought refuge in Lebanon, however. Armed clashes between Palestinian guerrillas and Lebanese groups were common, producing frequent crises within the government.

In 1969 the Palestinians agreed to restrictions on their activities, but the government continued to allow the guerrillas to use southern Lebanon as a base for attacks on Israel. These attacks produced Israeli reprisals that caused loss of Lebanese lives and damage to the country. The violent situation, coupled with Moslem demands for increased power in the government, led to civil war between Moslems and Christians in April 1975. An estimated 60,000 Lebanese were killed, and much of Beirut was destroyed. The intervention of Syrian troops helped to restore order, and an effective cease-fire was established in October 1976. Although Lebanon began to rebuild itself, Palestinian guerrilla attacks on Israel continued, as did Israeli reprisals, civil religious strife, and breakdown of Lebanese government control. This instability continued into the early 1980's, culminating in an Israeli invasion of Lebanon in June 1982. A ten-week war ensued, causing enormous destruction as well as the evacuation of Palestinian guerrilla forces.

### THESE ARTICLES ARE IN THE FACT-INDEX

| | |
|---|---|
| Lebanon, N. H. | Le Conte, Joseph |
| Lebanon, Pa. | Leconte de Lisle, |
| Lebanon, Tenn. | Charles Marie |
| Lebanon Valley College | Lecoq de Boisbaudran, |
| Le Bel, Joseph Achille | Paul Émile |
| Lebensraum | Le Corbusier |
| Leblanc, Maurice | Le Creusot, France |
| Leblanc, Nicolas | Lecuona, Ernesto |
| Le Blon, Jacques | Leda |
| Christophe | Lederberg, Joshua |
| Le Bris, Jean Marie | Ledyard, John |
| Lebrun, Albert François | Ledyard, Conn. |
| Lebrun, Charles | Lee, Ann |
| Le Caron, Joseph | Lee, Arthur |
| Le Chatelier, Henry Louis | Lee, Charles |
| Lech River | Lee, Dennis |
| Lecky, William Edward | Lee, Doris (Emrick) |
| Hartpole | Lee, Fitzhugh |
| Leclaire, Edmé Jean | Lee, Harper |
| Leclerc, Jacques Philippe | Lee, Henry |
| Lecocq, Alexandre Charles | Lee, Jason |
| Lecompton, Kan. | Lee, Joseph |

**LEE, Richard Henry** (1732–1794). On June 7, 1776, Richard Henry Lee offered the resolution in Congress "that these colonies are, and of right ought to be, free and independent states." Lee's fame rests on this history-making resolution, but he served his country in many other ways.

Richard Henry Lee was born Jan. 20, 1732, in Virginia. At 25 he took a seat in the Virginia House of Burgesses. He was among the first to suggest that the colonists organize committees to achieve unified action against the British. Lee was a signer of the Declaration of Independence and president of the Continental Congress in 1784–86.

Lee was opposed to the idea of a Constitution. He and Patrick Henry were its most violent critics. They feared that it would deprive the states of their rights and might become an instrument of tyranny. In 1789 he accepted appointment as senator from Virginia. In the Senate Lee became one of the strongest advocates of the first ten amendments, the Bill of Rights. Ill health forced him to retire in 1792. He died June 19, 1794.

# LEE—Hero of the Southern Confederacy

**LEE, Robert E.** (1807–1870). The Confederacy's greatest soldier, Robert E. Lee, once wrote to one of his sons: "Duty is the sublimest word in our language. Do your duty in all things . . ." Duty to others and discipline of self—these were two of the strongest traits in Lee's character.

The Lees were an old and honored family. Several of Lee's forebears had played distinguished roles in Virginia's history. His father was the Revolutionary War hero Light-Horse Harry Lee, the friend of Washington's. The family were living at Stratford, their ancestral home in Westmoreland County, when Robert was born on Jan. 19, 1807. He was the fourth of five children. Shortly after his birth, the family moved to Alexandria, near the nation's capital, where the tradition of George Washington lived on. Washington was young Lee's hero.

Partly because of the military tradition in his family and partly because an army career was attractive to Southern boys, young Lee decided to become a soldier. He entered West Point and was graduated in 1829, standing second in his class. He specialized in military engineering, and for several years he supervised various construction projects for the army. On June 30, 1831, he married Mary Custis, great-granddaughter of Washington's wife and heiress of the estate of Arlington, across the Potomac from Washington. The Lees had seven children.

Lee's application to his work won him promotion to the rank of captain. His first experience in actual

battle came in the Mexican War. He was one of a group of young engineer officers on the staff of Gen. Winfield Scott, the general in chief of the army. Scott headed an army which landed on the east coast of Mexico and moved inland to capture Mexico City, the capital. The commanding general used the engineers to scout out the enemy positions, and he relied heavily on them for tactical advice. Lee was the ablest of the engineer officers and served with distinction in all the operations of Scott's victorious campaign. He came out of the war in 1848 with the brevet rank of colonel. More important, Scott had marked him as an officer with a brilliant future.

After the Mexican War, Lee's next big assignment was as superintendent of West Point. From the academy, he went to Texas in 1855 as lieutenant colonel of the Second Cavalry Regiment. Here he served several years, policing the border areas against Indians. In 1859 he was home on leave when the abolitionist John Brown tried to start a slave uprising at Harpers Ferry in Virginia. Lee led a party of Marines from Washington which captured Brown and his band. He returned to Texas for a short tour of duty but was recalled to Washington early in 1861. The secession movement had started. Some Southern states had left the Union, others were about to go. Lee's own Virginia was considering secession.

## Lee's Fateful Decision

Old General Scott, loyal to the Union, was too infirm to be active if war came. He wanted Lee near him and offered the colonel an important command in the national army. Lee had a momentous decision to make. Should he accept Scott's offer and stay with the nation or go with his state, which was obviously going to secede? What was his duty? Lee loved the Union, and he was saddened and dismayed by the prospect of its being broken up by Southern action. At the same time, he could see little attraction, as he put it, in a Union that had to be held together by force. In the end, his course was determined by his devotion to his state. As much as he venerated the Union, he was first of all a Virginian and loved the Old Dominion. He could not bear to think of a national army invading Virginia to coerce it back into the Union or of himself as possibly leading that army. After days of deliberation, he decided his right course was to resign his commission, return home, and offer his services to Virginia. His action has been called the decision he was born to make.

Virginia had seceded from the Union but had not yet formally joined the Confederacy when Lee reached Richmond. The state appointed him commander of the Virginia military forces then being gathered. At this time, Lee was 54 years of age and a splendid figure of a man. He was about five feet eleven inches in height and weighed 175 pounds. He seemed larger than he actually was because of his massive head and wide shoulders. His face was ruddy, his eyes were brown, and his dark wavy hair was beginning to show marks of gray. In manner, he was grave, some-

times reserved, and always kind. His dignity, like that of Washington, repelled familiarity.

After Virginia joined the Confederacy, the capital of the new Southern nation was established in Richmond. The Confederate government took over the direction of all military forces in Virginia, including Lee's state troops. Although Lee was made a full general, he was a general without an army. Finally the president of the Confederacy, Jefferson Davis, sent him to repel the Federal forces that were invading western Virginia, the region that would be the future West Virginia. Lee failed to halt the Federal advance. He was then ordered to South Carolina and Georgia to build coastal fortifications.

## General in Chief of Confederate Armies

Lee was recalled to Richmond early in 1862 and appointed by Davis to be general in chief of all Confederate armies under authority of the president. His title was important, but his position was not. Davis kept the direction of the war largely in his own hands and entrusted only minor matters to Lee.

Soon after Lee took office, a large Federal army approached Richmond and penetrated to the gates of the city. In the fighting before the capital, the commander of the Confederate army was seriously wounded. Davis appointed Lee commander of the organization known as the Army of Northern Virginia. Lee's great military career was about to begin.

## Command in the Field

If there can be such a person as a natural field general, Lee was one. He was aggressive and combative. In his strategy, he was original, sometimes brilliant. Realizing that the weaker side must take chances, he was daring. His character and personality aroused the devotion of his men, who called him "Marse Robert." He was big enough to take the blame for failure, as when after Gettysburg he said: "It is all my fault." He knew how to handle his generals and make them work as a team.

Lee demonstrated many of his military characteristics soon after he assumed command in June 1862. The Union army, under the command of General McClellan, was a few miles from Richmond and astride the Chickahominy River before the city. Lee decided to mass his army and attack the smaller part of the enemy army on the north side of the river. He hoped to destroy this fraction and then smash the Federals on the south side. He took the planned risk that McClellan would not discover there was only a small defending Confederate force directly in front of Richmond. Lee was partly successful in the battle of the Seven Days that followed. He drove the Union army back about 25 miles but was not able to destroy it.

The Union government then withdrew McClellan's army to northern Virginia to regroup it with the smaller force of General Pope. Lee hurried northward to hit Pope before McClellan could arrive. In August he fought Pope, who had received some of McClellan's troops, at the second battle of Manassas. Again making a daring plan, he divided his army and sent part of it around to Pope's rear. Following with the rest of his troops, he defeated the confused Pope and drove him back into Washington. Lee next decided to invade Maryland, a state which had not seceded. His object was to get the armies out of Virginia during the harvest season and possibly win a victory in a Union state. McClellan, in command of the Union forces again, moved to meet him. The two met in September at the battle of Antietam, where McClellan attacked Lee but failed to break his lines. Lee, realizing that he was in a dangerous position and far from his supplies, retreated and took up a defensive

**THE LEE MANSION ON THE POTOMAC RIVER**
At Arlington, Va., stands the Lee Mansion, where the Lees lived from 1831 to 1861. Lee's wife had inherited this beautiful stucco-covered brick house from her father. Restored as a museum and national memorial, it was opened to the public in 1925.

position behind the Rappahannock River in northern Virginia. Here General Burnside, who succeeded McClellan, attacked Lee in December at the battle of Fredericksburg and met a bloody repulse. As the year 1862 closed, Lee had given the Confederacy its greatest victories and had become the idol of the Southern people.

In the spring of 1863, General Hooker, the new Federal commander, crossed the Rappahannock above Fredericksburg to attack Lee's left flank. When Lee confronted him, Hooker drew back. In Lee's most daring move of the war, he sent Stonewall Jackson to turn the Federal right while he attacked from the front. His objective was to cut the Federal army in two and destroy it. In this engagement, the battle of Chancellorsville, Lee hit the Federals hard; but they managed to withdraw across the river.

After Chancellorsville, Lee started an offensive movement he hoped would win the war—an invasion of Pennsylvania. In the southern part of that state, he met the defending Federal army at Gettysburg in a three-day battle, July 1–3, the greatest ever fought in North America. On the second and third days Lee threw strong attacks against the Union lines and was repulsed with heavy losses. He has been criticized for attacking a larger army in a strong position. (He had about 75,000 men to the 88,000 Federals.) However, it must be remembered that he had great faith in his men and that even the best Civil War generals did not understand that the firepower of the new rifles was making frontal attacks dangerous to attempt. (*See also* Gettysburg, Battle of.)

### The Last Campaign

After Gettysburg, Lee fell back into northern Virginia. For the rest of the war, with an army ever getting smaller, he had to employ a defensive strategy. In the spring of 1864, General Grant assumed direction of the Federal army in Virginia. His ob-

jective was to bring Lee to battle in northern Virginia and to destroy the Confederate army. Lee showed great skill in this campaign. He evaded attempts to trap him into decisive battle and inflicted heavy losses on Grant at the battles of the Wilderness, Spotsylvania, and Cold Harbor. Finally Grant swung south of Richmond to Petersburg, hoping to reach the railroads which carried supplies to Lee's army and make Lee fight there. Lee got to Petersburg first. Grant then decided the only way he could get at Lee was by the slow method of running siege trench lines around to the railroads in Lee's rear. Grant started his siege in the summer of 1864. Not until the spring of 1865 did he seize the railroads. Lee then abandoned Petersburg and Richmond. He retreated to the west, but Grant was right on his heels. With only 25,000 men left, Lee realized that his cause was hopeless. To continue fighting meant the needless loss of lives. Early in April he met Grant at Appomattox and surrendered the Army of Northern Virginia.

In the years after the war, Lee was the hero of the South. With dignity and without bitterness, he accepted defeat and preached to his people the necessity of peace and national unity. Offered many jobs, he accepted the presidency of Washington College at Lexington, Va. Later it was renamed Washington and Lee. It was his duty, he thought, to guide the youth of the South in the postwar years. He died on Oct. 12, 1870. His body rests in a mausoleum in the chapel of the college.

THESE ARTICLES ARE IN THE FACT-INDEX

Lee, Sir Sidney
Leeboard
Leech, John

**LEECH.** The leeches are bloodsuckers which belong to the worm family. Like many worms, they have soft, flat bodies divided into segments. At each end is a rounded sucker, a large one at the tail end and a smaller one where the mouth is. Most leeches live in the water, where they attach themselves to fishes, turtles, and frogs, and even to persons and cattle. They fasten themselves with their hind sucker. Then with the mouth sucker they suck up the blood through three little holes which they make in the skin with their sharp teeth. Leeches swim well, curving their bodies like eels and moving with the tail end foremost (for pictures, *see* Worm). A few leeches live on land. These are found chiefly in the damp forests of Asia and are terrible pests.

The stomach of a leech extends almost the entire length of the body. Numerous little sacs along its sides greatly increase its capacity. The leech can swell out its body with the blood it has sucked almost as if it were made of rubber. One meal may last for several months. Leeches were formerly much used by physicians for bleeding feverish patients.

Along its body the leech has rows of sense organs, which look like pimples. These organs detect the temperature of the water and the presence of food or enemies. Near the head they are modified as eyes.

There are two common species. The *horse leech* is jet black. It may grow to a length of six or eight inches. The smaller *medicinal leech* is cross-barred with brown and black. This kind is most often found attached to the underside of stones in clear running streams. Turtles often have leeches attached to the fleshy underparts of their bodies. The scientific name of the medicinal leech is *Hirudo medicinalis;* of the horse leech, *Aulastoma gulo*.

THIS ARTICLE IS IN THE FACT-INDEX

**Lee College**

**LEEDS, England.** For centuries England has been noted for the quality of its woolen cloth. Its manufacture centers in Leeds, Yorkshire, one of the largest cities in England.

Leeds owes its importance to two factors: its transport facilities and its situation on the edge of the great Yorkshire coal fields. The Aire River connects it with the east coast. The Leeds and Liverpool Canal provides cheap transportation to the west coast. Iron manufactures are nearly as important as woolens. Leeds also ranks high in the manufacture of boots and shoes, felt, ready-made clothing, artificial silk, glass, and pottery. The city is also noted for the University of Leeds and for the music festival held there every three years.

A suggestion of its history, which goes back for 13 centuries, is found in the ruins of Kirkstall Abbey, a Cistercian monastery of the 12th century. Population (1969 estimate), 503,720.

THESE ARTICLES ARE IN THE FACT-INDEX

| | |
|---|---|
| Leeming, Joseph | Lehar, Franz |
| Leesburg, Fla. | Lehigh River |
| Lee's Summit, Mo. | Lehigh University |
| Leeuwarden, Netherlands | Lehman, Herbert H(enry) |
| Leeuwenhoek, Anthony van | Lehmann, Lilli |
| Leeward Islands | Lehmann, Liza |
| Lefebvre, Jules Joseph | Lehmann, Lotte |
| Lefèvre d'Étaples, | Lehmbruck, Wilhelm |
| Jacques | Lei |
| Le Gallienne, Eva | Leibniz, Gottfried |
| Le Gallienne, Richard | Wilhelm, Baron von |
| Legal tender | Leicester, Robert Dudley, |
| Legaspi, Philippines | earl of |
| Legate | Leicester, England |
| Legend | (county) |
| Legendre, Adrien Marie | Leicester, England (city) |
| Léger, Alexis Saint-Léger | Leiden, Netherlands |
| Léger, Fernand | Leidesdorff, William |
| Léger, Paul Émile, | Leidy, Joseph |
| Cardinal | Leigh, Vivien |
| Leghorn, Italy | Leigh, England |
| Legion | Leigh-Mallory, Sir |
| Legitimists | Trafford Leigh |
| Legler, Henry Eduard | Leighton, Frederick, |
| Legnano, Italy | Baron Leighton of |
| Legnica, Poland | Stretton |
| Legree, Simon | Leighton, Margaret |
| Legros, Alphonse | Leinsdorf, Erich |
| Legumes | Leinster, Ireland |

**LEIPZIG** (līp′sĭg), **East Germany.** The city of Leipzig grew up around a castle in Saxony named Libzi, in the 11th century. It lies at the junction of the Elster and Pleisse rivers in the middle of the broad plain at the crossing of two ancient trade routes. Its location made it a natural trade center, and Leipzig established a great medieval fair. Annual fairs are still held by the Communist government.

The city became the capital of Saxony and the economic and cultural center of the German Midlands. It also became the heart of the great German book trade. As a music center it won world fame. It was the birthplace of Wagner and the home of Schumann and Bach. Bach was organist at St. Thomas church.

The University of Leipzig, founded in 1409, became a great center of German education. In 1519, in the "Leipzig Disputation," Martin Luther and John Eck held a public debate on Christian doctrine.

Leipzig's history is stormy. It suffered six sieges in the Thirty Years' War. Napoleon met defeat here in 1813. In World War II, the Allies bombed it as a munitions center and rail hub. American troops took it in 1945, but it was included in the Soviet zone. Population (1970 estimate), 584,365.

THESE ARTICLES ARE IN THE FACT-INDEX

**Leipzig, University of
Leisler, Jacob**

# LEISURE—How to Use It Wisely

**LEISURE.** The problem of leisure is new. Until very recent times people worked each day to the limit of their strength. Of course there were always a privileged few who had leisure; but most men had to work 12, 14, or even 16 hours a day, six days a week. As late as 1840 the average factory worker labored 72 hours a week. "Sunup to sundown" was the farmer's working day, or as another phrase puts it, "from can to can't."

Today the average worker in a store, an office, or a factory spends about 39.8 hours a week at his job. Dividing his whole week of 168 hours into 39.8 for work and 56 for sleep, he has 72.2 hours a week left as leisure time (including hours spent for eating and personal care). His wife and children have at least as much leisure time.

This new leisure has been created by big improvements in methods of production. Today, working less than a 40-hour week, men enjoy a higher standard of living than when they worked 72 hours a week. If we today, using modern machines and methods, accepted the living standard of 1870 we would have to work much less than 40 hours a week to achieve it. (*See also* Industry, American.)

The wise use of leisure time is an important problem for everyone, young or old. It is a particularly difficult problem for the sick, the aged, and those who have retired from earning a living. These people have so much leisure that it is hard for them to find interesting and worthwhile ways to use it.

However short the work week becomes, work is still the most important part of life. We do not work to get leisure and the pleasures leisure brings us; rather, we use leisure wisely so that work itself can become rewarding and enjoyable. The feeling of success at doing one's daily work—whether it is a job, maintaining a home, or going to school—depends largely on coming to it each day with renewed energy and active interest.

Leisure and recreation go together, though they are not necessarily the same thing. "Recreation" has an obvious meaning. It is the kind of leisure activity that brings "re-creation" or refreshment of strength and spirit. When one speaks of making good use of leisure, he means choosing recreational activities which contribute to health, growth, and spirit.

A recreational activity may be a strenuous sport or a quiet hobby. It may only be a passing diversion or it may be simply an escape from care. It may be an earnest attempt to master a new skill or to help those who are in need of help. Recreational tastes differ. What is fun for one may be exhausting to another. Whatever the choice of recreation may be, its function is to keep a person fit for his daily work.

## Guiding the Child's Leisure Activities

Children need guidance in their recreation as much as they do in schoolwork or in developing good personal habits. Children welcome properly given guidance because it means new fun and new experiences. A child's leisure activity—reading, a handicraft problem, or a game—should offer both challenge and success. Children, like adults, quickly grow tired of activities that are too easy or too hard. If the activity is long or involved, it should be divided into units which can be successfully accomplished along the way. Then if the child does not complete the whole activity, he will at least derive satisfaction from goals he has reached or mastered. (*See also* Games; Play.)

In leisure activities, children should seldom be set in direct competition with one another. The aim of leisure is self-improvement, not winning. A child may "win" by accident or luck, or he may win because his competitor is not a fair match for him. In either case, "victory" is hollow and can only give a false sense of superiority, not a rebirth of spirit.

The child who consistently "loses," loses more than the game. He may lose interest in the activity, the desire for social contacts, and his self-respect. The desire for approval which comes from success may lead him to find unfair ways to win. Either consistent winning or losing may harm the personality of the child. (*See also* Child Development.)

Instead of competing with one another, children should be encouraged to develop their skills in a program of self-competition. The Boy Scout, Girl Scout, and 4-H Club programs are built on this idea. The children win ranks, badges, and other forms of recognition based on levels of accomplishment. (*See also* Boy Scouts; Camp Fire Girls; Girl Scouts; 4-H Clubs; Juvenile Organizations.)

Children naturally seek the company of others their own age. This is wholly normal and should be encouraged. However, because a child has his own friends, he should not be denied his parents' companionship during their leisure hours. Sharing leisure experiences with the whole family is important to a child's growth. Parents should plan activities which in-

## LEISURE TIME PUT TO GOOD USE
Many persons find that working on hobbies or reading about their special interests are among the most rewarding ways to use leisure time.

clude their children, even at the cost of giving up some (but not all) of their adult social functions.

These activities might include picnics, swimming parties, and outings where active fun is shared, or they might include learning experiences in which parents and children share. Children like to do things with an understanding family. It gives them emotional security and an all-important "sense of belonging." Parents benefit too. The wholesome results of such activities are rich rewards.

### Leisure-Time Activities for Adults

During one's leisure time, a little aimless loafing does no harm; but most people find excessive idleness more tiring than work or strenuous play. The greatest benefits from leisure come from planned programs of activity. The activities should be difficult enough to provide a real physical or intellectual challenge, yet not so hard that accomplishment is virtually impossible. A too-easy program leads to boredom; a too-difficult one exhausts strength and spirit instead of re-creating them.

The range of possible activities is wide. Many people choose to be active participants, others to be merely spectators. Some enjoy reading, sedentary games, or one of the collection hobbies, such as stamps or coins. Others choose one or more of the arts—music, dancing, drawing and painting, or photography. Still others find recreation in doing useful, or constructive, tasks such as carpentry or sewing.

Whatever the choice, one rule applies: enjoyment grows with doing. To find real pleasure in an activity, one must have some skill, and skill comes only with honest practice. Acquiring a skill brings indirect satisfaction as well. For example, the people who most enjoy a professional baseball game are those who have played some form of baseball themselves. Once people have begun to paint as a hobby, they see new values in great paintings. Amateur musicians get keener delight out of concerts than those who have had no musical training at all. The man who does home carpentry has a good understanding of the work involved when he hires a skilled carpenter to do a major job.

People sometimes reach professional skill at a leisure-time activity, then turn this skill to profit. The pleasure of the activity then becomes complicated with the work elements. Time schedules, economic pressure, and risk—all present in nearly everything that is done for gain—robs the activity of its recreational values. Fun becomes work, and new leisure activities must be found. (*See* Work and Fatigue.)

Competition for prestige or recognition also tends to rob activities of their recreational worth. A man's pleasure in his fine garden is heightened if he has produced it to beautify the whole area. His pleasure is less if he has worked only to outdo the man next door. A game must have its winners and losers, of course, but truly amateur players get their greatest satisfaction from sharing enjoyable experiences, no matter who wins.

Sharing experiences with family and friends is a vital part of any leisure program. Commercial amusements, where people sit and watch, have their place, but the best recreation is active participation. It is better to make your fun than to buy it.

### Group Co-operation

Fun, pleasure, enjoyment—these may be derived from self-centered activities, or they may come as a result of service to others. The person with a sense of social responsibility allots some of his leisure time to serving his community and his nation. He works in his church, lodge, parent-teacher association, or any worthwhile organization. He helps raise money for charity; he is active in service clubs such as Kiwanis or Rotary; he gives as much as he can of his time, money, and strength to many causes. He takes a serious interest in good government, keeping himself informed so that he can vote wisely. The quiet satisfactions that come from these interests are frequently more rewarding than the short-lived pleasures of essentially selfish activity.

Many community agencies are concerned with the wise use of leisure time. Education today is as much devoted to teaching young people to use leisure intelligently as it is to preparing them to earn a living. In many communities the school or the public library serves as a leisure activity center for both adults and children. A large share of the community's budget is spent on parks and playgrounds and to provide the band concerts, sports tournaments, and arts and crafts classes sponsored by these recreational centers.

Private organizations, such as churches, lodges, and veterans' groups, have their own constructive programs. They sponsor Scout troops, musical groups, and classes and clubs for the various arts and crafts. Such activities help the organization and its members. Families are brought together, new friendships formed, and experiences shared. All these strengthen the primary purpose of the organization. People in rural areas also have organizations of their own which provide recreational programs (*see* Farm Life).

### Some Suggested Leisure-Time Activities

Reading should be a part of everyone's leisure program. A planned schedule of related reading will prove more rewarding than a random selection of books. If you like historical fiction, for example, try reading factual histories of the same period. Increase your reading speed, and you will find that both enjoyment and comprehension will be increased. (*See also* Reading.)

Collection hobbies need not be expensive. United States commemorative stamps can be bought at face value from a post office (*see* Stamp and Stamp Collecting). Interesting coins may be found among those received in change (*see* Coin Collecting). Seashells, leaves or flowers, and butterflies or other insects make beautiful and informative collections (*see* Nature Study; Insect Collecting).

People who do sedentary work often find relaxation in handicraft. A workbench and a wide range of tools are not always needed. For example, with only a jackknife as a tool, attractive low-relief carvings can be made from the ends of fruit crates. Inexpensive kits for making automobile and ship models are available (*see* Ship Models). Even in small living quarters, space can be found to do such work as tooling leather or painting. (*See also* Arts, The.)

Parents and children can do many things together. They can grow flowers or vegetables, raise pets, or develop one of the many nature collections. They can share many kinds of reading matter. Even such pastimes as "Twenty Questions" and various word-building games are both fun and intellectually stimulating when the whole family joins in.

Among commercial amusements, such as movies and professional sports contests, there is a wide choice. These should not occupy the whole of one's leisure time, nor should the passive forms of home entertainment, such as radio and television. Read the reviews carefully and choose the shows or programs that are of genuine interest to you. As with any form of recreation, wise planning is needed if you want to derive real pleasure from these activities. (*See also* Hobbies; Vacation Activities.)

### The Spending of Time and Money

How do people actually spend their leisure time? Surveys show that the ten activities most frequently engaged in are newspaper and magazine reading, listening to radio and watching television, attending movies, visiting or entertaining visitors, reading fiction, automobile riding for pleasure, swimming, writing letters, reading nonfiction, and conversing. The home still occupies an important place as a recreational center, and it increases in importance as people grow older.

Every year the American people spend about one ninth of their total income on leisure-time activities. In other words, they spend nearly six weeks' income out of 52 on play, amusements, and other leisure-time pursuits. About 8 percent of the total area of a suburban district such as Westchester County, N. Y., is given over to recreational purposes. National parks and monuments cover an area larger than the state of Indiana and are visited by millions of people yearly. State parks and monuments also draw huge crowds of visitors. A quarter of the nation's huge expenditure on automobiles—their purchase, operation, and maintenance—is directly chargeable to their use in recreation.

These facts and figures show that leisure activity involves substantial personal and governmental expenditures. People sometimes need to be cautioned against spending money foolishly; more often they should be warned against foolish and wasteful expenditures of time. If leisure-time activities are to yield full returns, they must represent wise investments of both time and money. Only then can recreation become true "re-creation."

### Books About Leisure

Carlson, R. E. and others. Recreation in American Life, 2d ed. (Wadsworth, 1972).

De Grazia, Sebastian. Of Time, Work and Leisure (Kraus Reprint, 1973).

Ellis, M. J. Why People Play (Prentice, 1973).

Madow, Pauline, ed. Recreation in America (Wilson, 1965).

Neumeyer, M. H. and E. S. Leisure and Recreation, 3d ed. (Ronald, 1958).

THESE ARTICLES ARE IN THE FACT-INDEX

| | |
|---|---|
| Leith, Scotland | Lemaître, Jules |
| Leitrim, Ireland | Le Mans, France |
| Leix, Ireland | Lemare, Edwin Henry |
| Le Jeune, Paul | LeMay, Curtis E(merson) |
| Leland, Charles Godfrey | Lemay, Léon-Pamphile |
| Leland, Henry Martyn | Lemay, Mo. |
| Leloir, Luis F(ederico) | Lemke, William |
| Lely, Sir Peter | Lemnitzer, Lyman L(ouis) |
| | Lēmnos |

**LEMON.** As the mercury rises, the demand for lemons increases by leaps and bounds. In the long hot days of summer nothing seems more refreshing than a glass of sparkling ice-cold lemonade.

A citrus fruit, the lemon is a close relative of the orange. It was probably introduced into Europe from Asia about the same time as the sweet orange, in the 8th or 9th century. The lemon is much less hardy than the orange, however, and the area of its cultivation is therefore more restricted.

### Where Lemons Are Grown

Lemon culture has long been a commercial industry in Spain, Portugal, Italy, Sicily, and Corsica.

Ewing Galloway

The fruit of the lemon tree is cut as soon as it is just large enough to slip through a ring that measures 2¼ inches in diameter.

# LEMON

Until the cold wave of 1894–95, the lemon industry in Florida was of considerable importance. Since that time the great development of lemon culture in the United States has been in the irrigated lands of southern and central California. Today California grows practically all the commercial American crop and about half the world crop of lemons.

Lemons are cultivated in much the same manner and regions as oranges. The straggling branches of the lemon tree, however, are unlike the compact dense foliage of the orange tree. Also, the purplish flowers do not have the same agreeable fragrance of the white orange blossoms. (*See also* Orange.)

The lemon tree flowers continuously and has fruit in all stages of development most of the year. A tree bears as many as 3,000 lemons annually. If the lemons ripen on the tree, they lose their keeping quality. Thus they are picked green before there is any sign of the golden–yellow coloring. Each picker has a little ring $2\frac{1}{4}$ inches in diameter. The fruit is cut when it can just slip through the ring.

In dark storehouses, well ventilated but free of drafts, the lemons are carefully spread out and slowly ripened. In curing, the fruit shrinks a little; the skin becomes thinner and tougher and develops a silky finish. When the process is completed, the lemons are washed, dried, and sometimes wrapped in tissue paper. In this condition they will keep for months. This is important to the growers because most of the fruit ripens in the winter and the great market demand is in the summer.

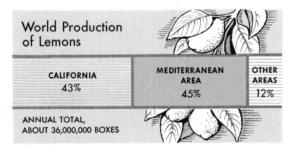

**World Production of Lemons**

| CALIFORNIA 43% | MEDITERRANEAN AREA 45% | OTHER AREAS 12% |
|---|---|---|

ANNUAL TOTAL, ABOUT 36,000,000 BOXES

The lemon is used in more ways than any other citrus fruit. The pulp yields juice which contains citric acid and citrate of lime. It is an excellent source of vitamin C. The juice is used in flavoring foods and drinks. About a third of the California production is processed as juice or concentrates. Lemon juice may also be used as a bleach in the printing of cotton fabrics. Lemon oil, or extract, is obtained from the rind. This extract is used in flavoring and in the making of perfume and some medicines. The rind can be cooked with sugar to make candied lemon peel. The lemon's scientific name is *Citrus limonia*.

THESE ARTICLES ARE IN THE FACT-INDEX

Lemon Grove, Calif.
Lemonnier, Pierre Charles
Lemon verbena
Le Moyne, Charles
LeMoyne-Owen College
Le Moyne College

188

**THE LEMURLIKE POTTO HAS FOUR FINGERS**
The furry little potto, native to west Africa, clings to branches by opposing its thumb to the other three fingers.

**LEMURS.** The lemurs resemble monkeys and are the size of cats and squirrels. They have big eyes, foxlike faces, and doglike nostrils. The name lemur comes from the Latin word *lemures*, meaning "ghosts." It was given to these animals because of the silent, ghostlike way they move about, mainly at night.

The lemurs are classified as primates, the group which also includes monkeys, apes, and man. Most of them have tails, but they cannot hang from trees by them as some monkeys can.

With their many relatives, lemurs form the family called *lemuroids*. Of the 90 or so species of lemuroids, 50 or more live in Madagascar. All of them are found only in the southern regions of the Old World— Africa, India, Ceylon, and the Philippines. The true lemurs, however, are found only on the island of Madagascar and the nearby Comoro Islands.

Included among the lemuroids are the ring-tailed lemur, whose tail is marked with alternate rings of black and white; the large *indri*, or babakoto ("little old man"), of Madagascar; the dark iron-gray lemur which lives in the bamboo jungles; and the aye-aye of Madagascar, so named from its cry. Lemuroids eat leaves, fruits, insects, small reptiles, birds, and birds' eggs. (*See also* Monkey.)

THESE ARTICLES ARE IN THE FACT-INDEX

Le Nain, Antoine, Louis, and Mathieu
Lenard, Philipp
Lenau, Nikolaus
Lenbach, Franz von
Lenepveu, Jules Eugène
L'Enfant, Pierre Charles
L'Engle, Madeleine
Lenglen, Suzanne

**LENIN, Nikolai** (1870–1924). The revolution that brought the Communist party to power in Russia in 1917 has been called the most important political event of the 20th century. Its leader was Nikolai Lenin, a Marxian socialist. Lenin spent years studying the technique of revolution and building up a band of revolutionaries. At the right moment he carried out his plan with great skill and no scruples.

Nikolai Lenin's real name was Vladimir Ilich Ulyanov. He was born April 22, 1870, in Russia at

**LENIN AND HIS WIFE, NADEZHDA KRUPSKAYA**
After suffering two strokes, Lenin retired to Gorky (Gor'kiy), near Moscow. This picture was taken a year before his death.

Simbirsk (now Ul'yanovsk), a town on the Volga River. His father, a teacher, rose to be a provincial director of schools. Vladimir was 16 when his father died. The next year his older brother, Alexander, was executed for taking part in a plot to assassinate Czar Alexander III. Lenin's hatred of the ruling and propertied classes began at this time.

### Lenin Becomes a Professional Revolutionary

A few months after his brother's execution Lenin was expelled from school for taking part in a political demonstration. For several years he lived with relatives, studying law, languages, and the writings of Karl Marx (*see* Marx). In 1891 he passed his law examinations. He soon gave up his law practice to spend full time in the revolutionary underground movement in St. Petersburg, then the Russian capital. The city is now called Leningrad in his honor.

In 1895 Lenin was arrested, jailed for more than a year, and later exiled to Siberia. There he married Nadezhda Krupskaya (exiled in 1898), whom he had known in the St. Petersburg underground. She later wrote: "As a whole the years of exile were not bad. These were years of serious study." It was in Siberia that he first used the pen name N. Lenin.

When his term ended, in 1900, Lenin went abroad. The next year his wife joined him. Most of the time until 1917 the couple lived as exiles, traveling from country to country, often with forged passports. With other Russian Marxists they published a newspaper, *Iskra* ('The Spark'), that was smuggled into Russia. Lenin soon built up a following in Russia and among the younger Russian exiles in Europe.

### Founds Bolshevik (Communist) Party

In 1903 some 60 Russian revolutionaries opened a congress in Brussels. The Belgian police ordered them to leave, and the congress was continued in London. Lenin's fanaticism made him unpopular with the more moderate old guard socialists. In a rage against them, he split the Russian Social Democratic party in two, calling his group the Bolsheviks (*Majority*).

The party also split in Russia. The Bolsheviks (actually the smaller group) followed Lenin's instructions implicitly. Funds could be raised, he told them, by breaking into banks. He also told them how to obtain and use bombs, how to set fires, and how to stop trucks with tacks. The party organized cells in trade unions, among transportation workers, and in the army and navy. (*See also* Communism.)

### Lenin Returns to Russia

The Lenins were in Switzerland during World War I. Most socialists supported their governments. Lenin called on the workers of all countries to revolt and end the war. This interested the German government, which wanted peace with Russia.

Russia's losses in the war were appalling. Revolution broke out in March 1917. The czar was dethroned by the new provisional government, but the war went on. The German government, hoping to change the course of the revolution, arranged to send the Lenins and 30 other revolutionaries back to Russia. The group arrived at Finland Station, in the Russian capital, on April 16. The next day Leon Trotsky arrived from New York City. Lenin and Trotsky made a formidable team. (*See also* Trotsky; World War I.)

In July the Bolsheviks took part in an unsuccessful uprising. The provisional government accused Lenin of being a German agent, and he fled to Finland. On October 22 he returned secretly. After instructing the Bolsheviks, he again went into hiding.

### The October Revolution

On November 6 Lenin reappeared to direct the revolution. Before daybreak on November 7 (October 25 in the old Russian calendar) the Bolsheviks seized the railway station, state bank, power stations, and telephone exchange. In the evening they arrested cabinet members meeting in the Winter Palace. On November 9 Lenin formed the world's first Communist government.

Lenin only began the revolution. It was left to his successor, Joseph Stalin, to establish firmly the Communist dictatorship (*see* Stalin).

Lenin suffered two strokes in 1922. A third, in 1923, resulted in loss of speech. The fatal stroke came on Jan. 21, 1924.

The Russians regard Lenin as their greatest national hero. His writings—particularly his directives for the Communist party—rank with the works of Karl Marx. His tomb, on Red Square in Moscow, is a shrine. (*See also* Russian History; Communism.)

THIS ARTICLE IS IN THE FACT-INDEX
**Leninakan, Russia**

In the center is the former Senate, seat of the czars' highest law courts. St. Isaac's Cathedral (right) is now an antireligious museum. At the left is a wing of the Admiralty.

# LENINGRAD—Russia's "Window to the West"

LENINGRAD, Russia. Russia's second largest city and chief seaport is Leningrad. Before the Communist revolution of 1917 it was one of Europe's brilliant capitals, a center of art and culture. It is still Russia's most beautiful city, although it has lost much of its former splendor. Its many palaces, churches, and monuments, now decaying, form a strange contrast to Russian life today. (*See also* Russia.)

The city has had three names. Czar Peter the Great, who founded it in 1703, called it St. Petersburg after his patron saint. In 1914, when the Russians were at war with Germany, they gave the name its Russian form—Petrograd—to get rid of the German *burg*. In 1924 the Communist government renamed it Leningrad after Nikolai Lenin, leader of the Bolshevik revolution, who died in that year (*see* Lenin).

## Location and Climate

Leningrad is located about 400 miles northwest of the city of Moscow. It lies in the delta of the Neva River, at the head of the Gulf of Finland, which is an inlet of the Baltic Sea. The site is divided into many islands by the Neva's delta arms; and the land is so low that it is sub-ject to floods. Granite levees guard the river banks, and canals crisscross the streets.

The city lies almost as far north as Anchorage, Alaska. The Baltic tempers the climate, however, and January temperatures are somewhat higher than in Moscow. Summer nights are so short that they are often called "white nights."

**NEVSKY PROSPEKT, LENINGRAD'S MOST FAMOUS STREET**
This was one of Europe's most fashionable avenues in czarist times. After the revolution it was called 25th of October Street. Now it is again Nevsky Prospekt.

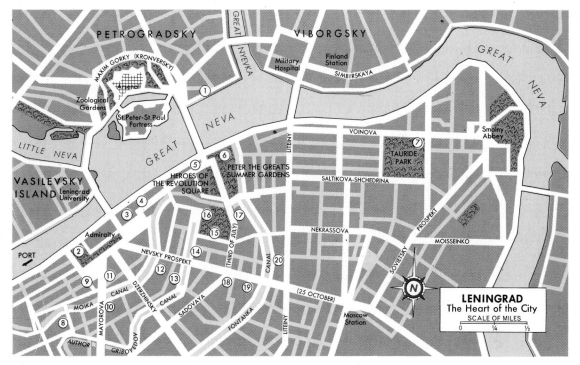

LENINGRAD
The Heart of the City
SCALE OF MILES
0    ¼    ½

**GUIDE TO PLACES OF INTEREST**

1. Peter the Great's Little House
2. Equestrian Statue of Peter the Great
3. Winter Palace
4. Hermitage
5. Marble Palace
6. Peter the Great's Summer Palace
7. Tauride Palace
8. Yussupov Palace
9. St. Isaac's Cathedral
10. Marinsky Palace
11. Hotel Astoria
12. Stroganov Palace
13. Kazan Cathedral
14. St. Catherine's Church
15. Russian National Museum (Michael's Palace)
16. Resurrection Church
17. Engineers' Palace
18. National Public Library
19. Pioneers' Palace (Anichkov Palace)
20. Fontanka Palace

## The Center of the City

The main part of the city occupies a peninsula formed by a bend in the Great Neva. Its center is the half-mile-long Admiralty on the river bank, which was begun by Peter the Great. Leningrad's principal streets radiate from the Workers' Gardens, which half surround the Admiralty. Near the Admiralty is the famous Étienne Falconet statue of Peter the Great, 'The Bronze Horseman'.

Czarist palaces are now museums and ministries, and imperial gardens serve as parade grounds or parks of culture and rest. Most famous of the many palaces are the 1,000-room Winter Palace, residence of the czars, and the adjoining Hermitage, which has 1,400 rooms in six different buildings. Peter the Great's Summer Palace is a Dutch-style structure set in the Summer Gardens.

## Museums and Cathedrals

Catherine the Great built the Hermitage and started its huge art collection. The Communist government added to it treasures they appropriated from private collectors. There are pictures here by Rembrandt, Peter Paul Rubens, Pablo Picasso, Henri Matisse, Paul Cézanne, Edgar Degas, and Vincent van Gogh. The Paul Gauguin collection is the largest in the world. In a basement, closely guarded, is a dazzling array of Scythian and ancient Greek gold objects.

Part of the Hermitage collection is now housed in the Winter Palace. In the palace also is a Museum of the Revolution. Here too the czars' apartments are preserved. The Russian National Museum (formerly Michael's Palace) illustrates Russian life and art.

Few churches are open for worship. St. Isaac's, the largest cathedral, has been converted into a museum. The Cathedral of Our Lady of Kazan has become an antireligious museum. Smolny Abbey is now used for government offices. Many noted writers and artists are buried in Alexander Nevsky Abbey, a group of 12 churches circled by walls and moats.

On an island in the Great Neva stands the fortress of St. Peter and St. Paul, built by Peter the Great. Within it is a cathedral of the same name, which contains the tombs of Peter and other Russian rulers. The fortress was a prison for political offenders.

## Leading Educational Institutions

Leningrad University (founded 1819) made tremendous contributions to Russian science and culture. Near it are the Academy of Sciences, where Ivan Pavlov did his work in conditioned reflexes; the Academy of Arts; and the Mining Academy.

Leningrad Public Library is one of the largest in the world. Tauride Palace, where the Russian duma (parliament) met, is now a school for Communist party members. The Marie Pavlovna Palace has become the House of Scientists.

### Industrial Districts and Seaside Resorts

Around the center of the city spread the factories and working-class districts. On Vasilevsky Island they crowd close around the students' quarters. To the south the old working-class district extends to the port warehouses and docks. The most important industrial district is Viborgsky, north of the Great Neva.

As in other Russian cities, housing in Leningrad has not kept pace with population growth. By law, each person is entitled to about a hundred feet of space; but it is common for several families to live in one apartment. Each family has one or two rooms, and all share the kitchen and bath.

Leningrad's subway stations are underground palaces, rivaling those of Moscow. People travel also by bus and trolley. There are few private cars. A favorite holiday excursion is taking a boat to Petrodvorets (formerly Peterhof) on the Gulf of Finland.

### Transportation and Industries

Airlines and a rail network radiate from the city, but there are few good highways. Canals connect the Neva with the upper Volga River and the White Sea. A deep-water canal allows passenger ships and freighters to reach the mouth of the Neva.

Leningrad was a machine-building center before the revolution, and it is still the only producer of certain specialized machine tools and electrical equipment. Its industries include also shipbuilding, chemicals, textiles, chinaware, pulp, and paper.

### History of the City

Peter the Great had traveled in Europe and was determined to bring Western culture to the backward Russians. "I want a window to look out upon Europe," he said. Thus in 1703 he founded and began to build the city that is now called Leningrad. (*See also* Peter the Great.) Piles had to be driven into the marshy ground to support the buildings. So many workmen died of disease and hardship that the city

**A HALL OF ITALIAN ART IN THE HERMITAGE**
The statue in the center is by Michelangelo. It is called 'Crouching Boy'. The frescoes are of the Raphael school.

was said to be built on human bones. In 1713 the capital was officially moved to the new city from Moscow. From the beginning the city's architecture was European. Learning and culture were also derived from the West; and in the 19th century the factory system was introduced.

The poverty of the workers made the city a hotbed of revolutionary activity. The 1905 revolution and the two 1917 revolutions began here. In 1918 the capital was moved back to Moscow. During World War II the Germans laid siege to Leningrad from August 1941 to January 1944. Many people died of starvation and disease. Population (1970 preliminary census), 3,513,000. (*See also* Russian History.)

THESE ARTICLES ARE IN THE FACT-INDEX

Lenin Peak
Lennep, Jacob van
Lenoir, (Jean Joseph) Étienne
Lenoir, William Benjamin
Lenoir, N. C.

Lenoir-Rhyne College
Lenormand, Henri René
Lenôtre, André
Lenroot, Katharine Fredrica
Lens, France

# LENSES—The Magic in a Curve of Glass

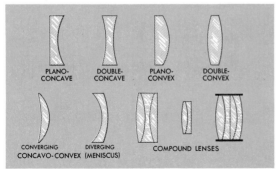

PLANO-CONCAVE   DOUBLE-CONCAVE   PLANO-CONVEX   DOUBLE-CONVEX

CONVERGING CONCAVO-CONVEX   DIVERGING (MENISCUS)   COMPOUND LENSES

**PRINCIPAL SHAPES OF LENSES**
Lens types are named from the shapes of the two faces. The properties of a lens vary according to the amount of curvature.

**LENS.** For thousands of years men could study only things they were able to see with unaided eyes. Today with help from lenses much more can be seen. Thus much more can be studied.

Millions of people use lenses as spectacles to correct defective vision. In telescopes lenses help astronomers study the stars and planets. Microscopes enable scientists to see things far too small to be seen by the eyes alone. In cameras lenses bring light to a small area. Picture projectors use lenses to spread light out over a large area.

Lenses do each of these things because of their shapes. The effect of the shape can be seen by comparing a windowpane with eyeglasses. Both are made of glass. When one looks through a windowpane,

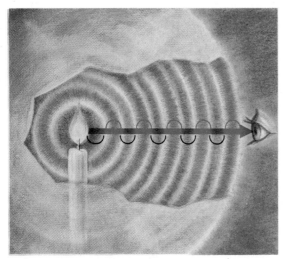

**WAVES AND RAYS OF LIGHT**
Light radiates from a source in ever-widening circles. Movement in one direction can be indicated as a ray or by waves.

he sees everything through it just as it is. Looking through eyeglasses makes everything seem larger and nearer. The glass in the windowpane is flat, but the glass in the eyeglasses is curved. It is the curve that makes a piece of glass a lens.

Curved glass is called a *lens* because in earlier days one common kind was shaped like a lentil. The Latin word *lens* means "lentil." The Roman emperor Nero is said to have used a lentil-shaped lens made from an emerald.

### Light Waves and Rays

A lens works by affecting the movement of light through it. This movement is often called wavelike; but it is not like water waves. Light comes from a source, such as the sun or an electric light bulb, as pulses of energy. These pulses swell out from the source in all possible directions. They are like concentric spheres expanding at great speed.

The pulses carry a rise and fall of energy, as waves do. Each pulse brings a burst of energy, like that in the crests of waves. Between pulses there is a fall

off in energy, as in the troughs of waves. The picture (left) shows how pulses can be compared to waves.

A complete explanation of lens action must use these wavelike characteristics of light pulses. Simple explanations can be given, however, by supposing that light travels along straight lines called *rays*. The rays fan out across the waves like spokes in a wheel. At any point a ray shows the direction of the waves as they move across that point. This simple description of light movement can be used for most explanations of how lenses work.

### Speed of Light in Air and in Glass

The speed of light across a vacuum is about 186,000 miles a second. It is almost as fast in air. It is only 124,000 miles a second through common glass. Lenses act by affecting the speed of light as it passes through them.

When a light wave passes through a windowpane, all parts of the wave are slowed down equally while passing through. They speed up equally upon leaving the windowpane. Thus the curvature and direction of the wave are not changed.

There is a change, however, if different parts of the wave pass through different thicknesses of glass. This happens whenever light passes through a shaped piece of glass such as a prism or a lens. The parts of each wave that pass through the thin part of the glass can resume speed in air sooner than the parts that pass through thicker glass. When the light which was slowed down leaves the glass, it travels in a new direction.

### Rays and the Handy Normal

The diagrams below show this action in a prism and in a simple lens both with waves and with rays. The last two drawings show how a *normal* line can be used with rays to help in tracing a change of direction.

A normal is a direction perpendicular to a surface at any point. If a ray passes from a lighter medium (air) into a denser medium (glass), it will be bent *toward* the normal at the point of entry. If it passes from a denser medium to a lighter one, it is bent *away* from the normal. Another way to state what hap-

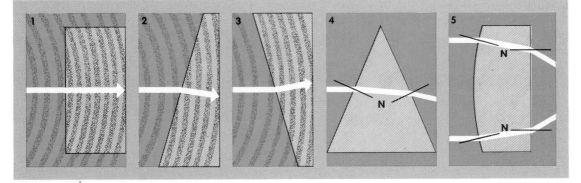

**HOW SHAPED GLASS BENDS LIGHT**
1. When light waves strike flat glass, they slow down but go straight through. 2, 3. A prism slows part of each wave un-

equally. This makes the light change direction (indicated by a ray). 4, 5. A normal (N) traces the bending (refraction).

pens is to say that light rays are bent toward the thicker part of the glass.

The amount of bending depends upon the ratio between the speeds of light in glass and in air. The ratio increases as the speed difference increases. The resulting change of direction is called *refraction*. The exact measure of the ratio which produces refraction is called the *index of refraction*. This is explained later in the article.

### Action of a Burning Glass

Even in ancient times men knew how to use a double-convex lens and sunlight for setting fire to materials such as cloth or paper. The lens is held at the right distance from the material to bring the light to a point on the material. The concentrated light and accompanying heat set it afire.

The concentration is produced by slowing down the sun's rays in the glass. Around the center of the lens each wave passes through more glass and is slowed down accordingly. Nearer the edges the waves pass through less glass and resume speed in air sooner.

This makes each wave *concave*, or curved toward all points ahead of it, when it leaves the lens. This effect is shown in a diagram at the bottom of the page. The concave shape assures that the energy in each wave will proceed toward some one point. This gives the focusing effect that produces burning.

### Focus and Optical Center

The point where the waves come together is called the *principal focus* of the lens. Its distance from the lens is called the *focal length* of the lens. Both the principal focus and the focal length are fixed partly by the kind of glass in the lens and partly by how the lens surfaces are curved.

Focal length is measured from a point called the *optical center* of the lens. In a double-convex or double-concave lens, this is on the *principal axis* that runs through the center of each face. It is also mid-

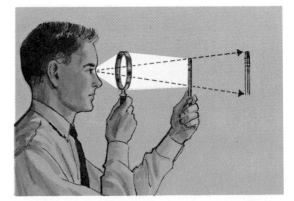

The simplest result with a double-convex lens is magnification. Both the lens and the object must be near the eye. The object will look larger and farther away than it actually is.

A magnifying glass makes a very distant object seem nearer and smaller than it is. The image, however, is not sharp. A better way to view distant objects is shown on the next page.

way between the faces. If the two faces of the lens have different curvatures, the optical center is on the principal axis but at the surface nearer the principal focus. In the lens of the plano-type, with one face flat, the optical center is where the principal axis cuts the curved face.

### A Lens as a Projector

When a burning glass is used to concentrate sunlight, the light waves that strike it have come a tremendous distance. The tiny portion of each curved wave front that strikes the lens is practically flat. The lens can produce enough change in direction to focus all these waves upon one point.

A burning glass can be used also to produce practically flat waves as a beam from a headlight or other projector. A strong but small source of light is placed at the focus. (This is one focal length from the optical center of the lens.) When light waves leave the lens, they are practically flat, and they move forward as a beam. (In actual headlights a mirror behind the light source helps the lenses in forming a sharp beam.)

### Seeing with Lenses and Making Images

Lenses can help in seeing or in making pictures, as in a camera. They are also used in projectors. Each

### MAKING A POINT OR A BEAM

A double-convex lens focuses light from a distant source upon a point. If sunlight is focused, it will set paper afire. A lens used to do this is called a burning glass.

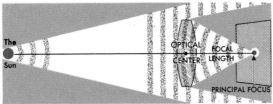

A source of light placed one focal length from a double-convex lens reverses the burning-glass effect. The lens sends on flat waves as a beam. This effect is used in projectors.

## MAGNIFYING GLASS

A magnifying glass can produce an image of a distant object on a screen. The image is smaller than the object and upside down. It is also dim. A second lens (below) gives a better image.

A small convex lens can be used to view an image formed by a larger magnifying glass. The image seen in this way will be larger than the object and upside down.

use can be demonstrated with a magnifying glass (a double-convex lens) as shown in the diagrams at the top of this and the facing page.

The diagrams at the top of the facing page indicate how the glass helps seeing. The top diagram on this page shows an image made on screen. The last diagram indicates how two lenses arranged like a simple telescope aid vision.

The lens is held at varying distances from the objects for these different purposes. The basic action however, is the one used for image making. Seeing with a lens depends upon this because the lens of the eye, in turn forms the image on its retina (see Eye).

### How a Lens Forms an Image

A convex lens does not act like a burning glass if the light source is so near that waves from it still have curvature when they reach the lens. Then the lens cannot focus all the light upon any one point. Instead, waves from each point on the object will strike the lens at different angles. These will cause an *image* of the object to form.

The image will be on a plane called the *focal plane*. The plane will be beyond the principal focus because the waves are still convex when they strike the lens. The lens cannot make such waves as sharply concave as it can the flat waves of sunlight. Being less con-

cave when they leave the lens, the waves must travel beyond the principal focus before they are brought to focus on the focal plane.

The lower diagrams on the bottom of the page show this action for only two points of an object. One is at the top of the object, the other at the bottom. Every point between these two will be placed correctly, however, to form an image of the complete object.

The diagrams also show one ray passing straight from the object to the image, through the optical center of the lens. Changes produced by one face of the lens upon this ray are canceled exactly by the other face. This happens only to rays that pass through the optical center.

The image must be caught on a screen or some other background to make it visible. It is called a *real* image because it can be made visible in this way. The real image is *inverted* (upside down).

### Images in a Camera

When a lens and screen alone are used, the image is focused closer to the lens as the object moves farther from the lens. Because light waves from distant objects have less curvature to be overcome, the lens needs less distance for making the image.

In a camera the image must be formed where the film is held. A good camera meets this need by having a device for moving the lens. Setting the lens at the right distance to form an image on the film is what a photographer calls *focusing*. Cameras are kept to convenient size by using lenses that have power enough to give short focal length.

### Reduced and Enlarged Images

In using a camera the object to be photographed is usually more than two focal lengths from the focal plane. The film, however, is less than two focal lengths from the lens. At these distances the image on the film will be smaller than the object. It has

### HOW A LENS MAKES IMAGES

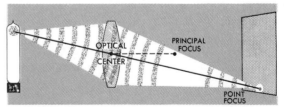

The diagram shows how a double-convex lens affects light from a point. If the waves are curved when they strike the lens, it will concentrate them at a point beyond the principal focus.

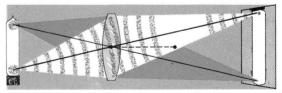

Here the action in the upper diagram is shown for a second point on the object. The focused images of the two points will be farther apart than they are on the object.

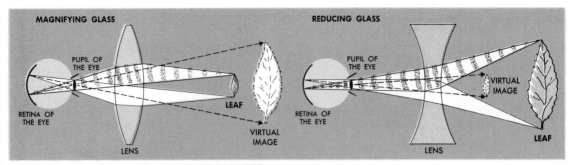

## SEEING MAGNIFIED AND REDUCED IMAGES

For objects less than a focal length away, a magnifying glass cannot form an image. It can, however, help the eye to do so.

When the eye views an object through a double-concave lens, it sees the object nearer and smaller than it actually is.

been *reduced*. When the object is exactly two focal lengths from one side of the lens, the image is formed at the same distance from the other side. It will also be the *same size* as the object. In enlarging cameras the distances are more like those in motion-picture projectors and stereopticons.

In these devices the picture (object) to be projected is between one and two focal lengths from the lens. The projected image is on a screen more than two focal lengths from the lens. It will also be *larger* than the object (the projected picture).

The closer objects are to being within one focal length of a convex lens, the more the lens acts like a beam projector. When an object is just near enough to bring this about, the image is fuzzy. If the object is any closer, the lens cannot form an image.

When light is focused upon a point on a screen, it produces a spot of light if the screen is opaque. If the screen is transparent, the waves go through and start spreading out again from the point. A ground-glass screen in a camera achieves both effects. The ground surface is opaque enough to show an image; but enough light shows through to make the image visible on the side away from the source of light.

### How the Eyes See Through Lenses

Whenever anything is seen, the crystalline lens of the eye focuses the light from each point of the object viewed upon some point on the retina of the eye.

The combination of eye, brain, and body then reacts

to the object seen on a line from the retinal point through the optical center of the crystalline lens. These lines of sight explain how a magnifying glass works.

The glass changes the direction of rays from different points on the object being viewed. After the rays are focused upon the retina of the eye, the changes make the eye and the brain see points on the object farther apart than they are. The brain also contributes a correction of its own.

The image formed on the retina of the eye is like that formed on the film in a camera. The image is reversed. It is upside down and with right and left interchanged. It does not match what the sense of touch says is "up" or "top" when standing alongside the object. The brain brings these sense reports into agreement by reversing the retinal image.

### Virtual Images

Convex lenses form images by changing all waves that strike them to concave ones that can focus upon a point. A concave lens, however, makes waves that pass through it more convex. If rays are used to trace wave directions, the rays diverge (spread apart). Therefore concave lenses never can form real images on a screen.

When the lens is held properly, however, between an object and an observer, the crystalline lens can bring the convex waves to a focus on the retina of the eye. The eye then gets an image, as shown by a diagram at the top of the page. The di-

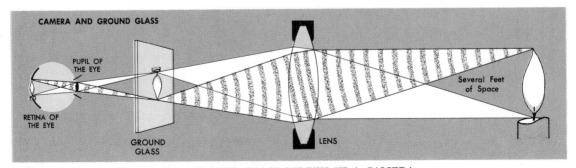

## SEEING THE IMAGE ON THE GROUND-GLASS SCREEN IN A CAMERA

Many cameras use a ground glass for a screen to permit viewing by the photographer. Each point on the screen radiates light to his eye and forms an upright image on the retina. The brain reverses this to a second inverted image.

rection of the rays placed across the wave shows that the brain will judge the object to be smaller than it actually is. Hence a concave lens used in this manner is called a reducing glass.

The image is called *virtual* because it cannot be caught on a screen or film. It can be seen only by the eye and the brain. A convex lens can also produce a virtual image when an object is less than one focal length from it.

The lens does this by reducing convexity of the waves from points in the object just enough to let the crystalline lens make them concave. This lens then focuses the waves on the retina. An observer looking through the lens then sees an erect, virtual image on the same side of the lens as the object. The image is larger than the object, and the convex lens so used is called a magnifying glass.

### Aperture, Brightness, and Focusing

The larger the area of a lens, the more light it gathers and focuses upon a point in the image. The width of the area available for light gathering is called the *aperture* of the lens. The larger the aperture, the brighter the image will be.

Many cameras have a diaphragm that can be changed to make the aperture larger or smaller. On bright days a small aperture admits all the light needed to make a good picture. On dull days more light can be gathered by opening the aperture wider.

Good cameras also have an aid for focusing called "f stops." These are fractions placed around the lens that are marked, for example, f/3.2, f/8, and so on. The symbol states a measure called the *relative aperture*. This is the focal length divided by the aperture being used. In the fraction the f is just a marker, and the denominator states the result of the division. For example, a focal length of three inches, working with an aperture of $1\frac{1}{2}$ inches, is being used at relative aperture f/2. The *f-rating* of a lens is the value of the fraction at maximum aperture. Low f-ratings mark lenses that can gather light enough to take fast exposures. (*See also* Photography, Cameras and their Operation in.)

### Remedying Aberrations of Lenses

Simple lenses have defects of action called *aberrations*. *Spherical* aberration arises near the edge of the lens. There light meets the lens at sharper angles. Refraction is thus greater, and the light is focused nearer the lens than light passing through central parts. This can be remedied by altering the usual spherical curvature of the lens or by combining convex and concave lenses into an *aplanatic doublet*.

Another defect is *chromatic* aberration. In the articles Color and Light, it is explained how light of a certain wave length looks red. A shorter wave length makes a viewer see yellow, and so down to blue and violet. White, or colorless, light contains all wave lengths. When white light strikes a simple lens made of glass, the glass does not refract each wave length (or color) equally. The lens brings the shorter violet

## Spherical Aberration

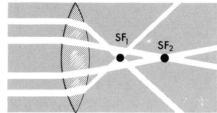

Light rays that are refracted near the edge of a lens are focused closer to the lens (SF₁) than the inner ones (SF₂). This gives some fuzziness to an image.

## Chromatic Aberration

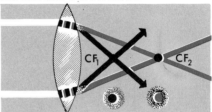

A simple lens breaks up white light slightly. Blue focuses nearer the lens (CF₁) than red (CF₂). At each focus there is a spot of the focused color and halos of the others.

waves to a focus in less distance than it does red. Other colors are focused between these extremes. As a result the colors are blurred.

For many years color dispersion hampered the development of optical instruments. Then in 1733 Chester Moor Hall found that flint glass disperses light into a longer spectrum than crown glass. He cut a convex lens of crown glass and combined it with a concave lens of flint glass. The concave lens canceled out the color fringe around the images. This was the first *achromatic* lens. John Dollond, an English optician, is often credited with the discovery because he made the new lens generally available.

### Manufacturing Lenses

Making a lens is a delicate and highly specialized task. The glass used in the lens must be of the highest quality, and the workmanship must be perfect. The huge telescope lenses are specially made. Eyeglass lenses are usually made in large lots. Optical glass comes from the furnace in rough broken chunks. These are tested for imperfections. Out of perfect pieces workmen form lens blanks. They heat the glass until it is soft and then mold it into disks about the size of a lens.

Lenses are ground from these blanks in several operations. "Roughing" is first. An iron dish coated inside with carborundum is revolved against the blank. This gives the general shape to the lens. Then the lens maker grinds it to shape. At each stage he uses a tool that is closer to the final form. From the last cut he uses an emery-coated tool of exact form.

Finer emery is used to smooth the lens. Next it is given a final polish with a fine ferrous oxide, called *rouge*. The lens is now cut, or *edged*, to the proper diameter on a lathe. After final inspection for flaws, the lens is ready for use.

### How Lens Action Is Figured

For the exact study of lenses, the science of optics uses many definitions and rules. One definition makes it possible to measure and figure refraction. Light travels more slowly in water than in air; the speed is even less in glass. The ratio of the speed in air to that in any other medium is the *refractive index* (or *index of refraction*) of the substance. Since light travels only three fourths as fast in water as in air, the index is 4/3 or 1.333. For window glass it is about 3/2 or 1.5.

The index can be found for any substance by comparing the angle of incidence with the angle of refraction. The ratio between the *sines* of the two angles is the index. (For the meaning of "sine," *see* Trigonometry.) For example, suppose a light beam passes into a medium at an angle of 30° from the normal and is refracted to 22°. The sine of 30° is .5 and for 22° it is .375. Dividing .5 by .375 gives 1.333, the index of refraction. Likewise, the angle of a refracted beam can be calculated from the incident angle and the index of refraction.

The shape of a lens can be defined by locating the center of curvature for each face. The curves and the refractive index determine where the principal focus will be and fix the focal length. The central point of a lens is called the *optical center*. Rays which pass through the optical center are refracted. But they emerge parallel to the incident ray.

---

THIS ARTICLE IS IN THE FACT-INDEX

**Lenski, Lois**

---

**LENTIL.** This food plant is a relative of the bean and pea. It is a legume grown chiefly in southern Europe, Egypt, and western Asia. Its pods contain seeds which are generally used to make soup. The small, lens-shaped seeds are reddish brown, gray, or black and have a distinct flavor. They are rich in carbohydrates and protein. The vines make excellent fodder for cattle and sheep. Thin, dry soil produces the best crop of lentils.

**LEO, Popes.** The first of the 13 popes of this name was called Leo the Great (pope, 440–461). He was a great scholar and did much to preserve the unity of the church. When Attila the Hun invaded Italy, Leo persuaded him to spare the city of Rome. His feast day is April 11. (*See also* Huns.)

**Leo III** (pope, 795–816) is chiefly remembered because it was he who placed the imperial crown on the head of Charlemagne on Christmas Day A.D. 800 (*see* Charlemagne). His feast day is June 12.

**Leo IV** (pope, 847–855) did much to repair the damage done to Rome by the Saracens. He also extended the walls of the city to include the Vatican quarter, on the right bank of the Tiber River.

**Leo IX** (pope, 1049–54) was a German. He was famed for spreading the reforms of the monks of Cluny. He became pope through the influence of Emperor Henry III and brought with him to Rome a young monk, Hildebrand. Hildebrand later became the great Gregory VII. Leo IX's feast day is April 19.

**Leo X** (pope, 1513–21) was a member of the Medici family of Florence, the son of Lorenzo the Magnificent. He was made a cardinal at the early age of 13. The wise and affectionate counsel which his father gave in a letter when the boy first set out for his duties in Rome still exists. He was elected pope at the age of 38. His reign saw the beginning of Luther's revolt against the church, increasing danger to eastern Europe from the Turks, and a continuance of the political struggles and wars involving the Papacy begun by his predecessor, Julius II. But Leo X is chiefly remembered for his part in the Italian Renaissance. He was the liberal patron of Raphael and other artists and of numerous scholars, poets, and other literary men. He was mainly responsible for making Rome the successor to Florence as the literary and artistic capital of Europe.

**Leo XIII** (pope, 1878–1903), the latest to bear this name, had one of the longest reigns in the history of the Papacy. He came to power at a time when the Papacy had recently been deprived of its authority as ruler of Rome and the surrounding country. Like his predecessor, Pius IX, he refused all offers of compromise with the new kingdom of Italy and remained a "prisoner" in the Vatican. He was a man of wide knowledge and strong character. In many ways he was a liberal statesman, but he never gave up in his efforts to restore to the Papacy its secular as well as religious authority.

---

THESE ARTICLES ARE IN THE FACT-INDEX

Leo III, the Isaurian     León, Mexico
Leo VI, the Wise     León, Nicaragua
Leofric     Leonard, William Ellery
Leominster, Mass.

---

**LEONCAVALLO, Ruggiero** (1858–1919). The fame of the Italian composer Leoncavallo rests upon his opera 'I Pagliacci'. First produced in 1892 in Milan, Italy, it has remained popular with operagoers to this day.

Ruggiero Leoncavallo was born in Naples, Italy, on March 8, 1858. He studied music at the conservatory there. At 18 he was graduated and began work on an opera. He gave the completed score—and all his money—to a producer who promised to arrange for the performance of the opera. Instead the man disappeared, leaving the young composer penniless. Then began a long period in which Leoncavallo made his living by giving lessons in singing and the pianoforte and by playing accompaniments at cafés concerts. His travels as an accompanist took him all over Europe and even to Egypt. Finally he returned to Italy, having completed the first part of a trilogy of operas concerning the Italian Renaissance.

New difficulties with producers postponed the performance of this work. In the meantime Leoncavallo wrote 'I Pagliacci'. When it was produced, it made the composer's name famous throughout Italy. The opera, whose story is based on an actual murder, is an example of the realistic school of Italian opera (see Opera). It tells of a clown whose jealousy leads him to murder his wife and her lover.

'I Medici', the first opera of his planned trilogy, was then performed. It was a failure. Some of his later operas were more favorably received. Of these 'Zaza' is probably the best.

Leoncavallo wrote the stories and dialogues not only for his own operas but occasionally for those of other composers as well. As a librettist, he showed great dramatic ability and skill in using theatrical effects. Leoncavallo died on Aug. 9, 1919.

---

THIS ARTICLE IS IN THE FACT-INDEX
**Leonov, Aleksei Arkhipovich**

---

**LEOPARD.** This spotted animal of the cat family lives in Africa, Asia, and the East Indies. Its length averages between six and seven feet from the nose to the end of the tail. It may weigh as much as 160 pounds. Leopards vary greatly, however, in size and color. The leopard, like its cousin the jaguar, is usually a buff or tawny color with dark spots. The undersurface of the body is somewhat lighter in color. There are also species which are solid black in color. The larger forms of southern Asia are commonly called panthers. The leopard lives in the forests and is a tree climber. It is agile and is a remarkable jumper. It attacks antelope, young cattle, pigs, and occasionally man.

New York Zoological Society
**For years the leopard's fur has been prized for use in coats. Excessive hunting has made the leopard an endangered species.**

The cheetah, or hunting leopard, of India is a slim species which is tamed and trained to aid in hunting. The ocelot is another leopardlike cat, with striped and spotted fur, found in tropical America and the extreme southwestern United States. A full-grown ocelot weighs 25 to 35 pounds. The scientific name of the common leopard, or panther, is *Panthera pardus;* cheetah, *Acinonyx jubatus;* ocelot, *Felis paradalis.*

---

THIS ARTICLE IS IN THE FACT-INDEX
**Leopardi, Giacomo, Count**

---

**LEOPOLD, Holy Roman Emperors.** Two emperors of the Holy Roman Empire were named Leopold.

**LEOPOLD I** (born 1640, ruled 1658–1705) was the second son of the Holy Roman emperor Ferdinand III. When the older son died, Leopold became a candidate for the throne. At the age of 16 Leopold was crowned king of Hungary; at 17, king of Bohemia. At 18 he was elected Holy Roman emperor.

During much of Leopold's long reign the empire was at war. His most persistent foe was Louis XIV of France, who repeatedly enlarged his domain at the expense of other European rulers. Louis further weakened Leopold's power by making alliances with German princes in the western empire.

The emperor also faced armed conflict with Protestant Hungarians, whom he had persecuted, and with the Turks. In the 1680's both united against him. Vienna, Leopold's capital, was saved from the Turkish army only through the intervention of King John III (Sobieski) of Poland. At the time of his death Leopold was again fighting Louis XIV in the War of the Spanish Succession.

**LEOPOLD II** (born 1747, ruled 1790–92) was the son of the emperor Francis I and Maria Theresa (see Maria Theresa). For 25 years he was a popular, progressive ruler in Tuscany. When he became emperor, the empire was endangered by many conflicts. With great diplomatic skill, he negotiated an agreement that ended threats from Prussia, made peace with Turkey, and appeased rebellious elements within the empire. Leopold's sister was Marie Antoinette, the ill-fated queen of France. His son became Francis II, the last Holy Roman emperor.

**LEOPOLD, Kings of Belgium.** Three kings of Belgium have borne the name Leopold.

**LEOPOLD I** (born 1790, ruled 1831–65) was the first king of an independent Belgium. The son of a German prince, Leopold married the heiress to the British throne, Princess Charlotte, but she died a year later. He was 40 when a Belgian national congress elected him the nation's king.

Leopold had a successful reign. Through wise administration, he helped the nation survive its early stresses and contributed to its economic growth. Although revolutions broke out in many European countries in 1848, his throne remained secure. Leopold also strengthened Belgium's position through skillful diplomacy. In 1832 he married Princess Louise, daughter of the French king Louis Philippe. Their oldest son became Leopold II.

**LEOPOLD II** (born 1835, ruled 1865–1909) was interested in acquiring colonial possessions in Africa. In 1876 he founded the International African Association to encourage exploration of the continent. In 1877 the explorer Henry M. Stanley returned from a long expedition to tell of the vast Congo region. Leopold eagerly commissioned Stanley to survey the area and sign treaties with the tribes. The king then claimed the territory and made himself sovereign of it. The abuses of the natives that developed under his administration were eventually brought to public attention. As a result the area was turned over to the government and made a Belgian colony in 1908.

Leopold's exploitation of the Congo made him unpopular. His only son died at an early age, and Leopold was succeeded by his nephew, Albert I.

**LEOPOLD III** (born 1901, ruled 1934–40; July 22 —Aug. 11, 1950) was the son of Albert I. He married Princess Astrid of Sweden, who died in an automobile accident in 1935.

In 1940, when the Germans invaded Belgium, Leopold ordered his army to surrender and refused to flee with officials to form a government-in-exile in England. His actions were widely resented in Belgium, and he aroused further criticism by his marriage in 1941 to a commoner, who was said to be pro-Nazi. Leopold was held prisoner by the Germans until the end of the war, when he went to Switzerland. In 1950 a plebiscite showed a small majority of the Belgians were in favor of his return. Protests arose as soon as he resumed office, however, and he delegated his powers to his son Baudouin on Aug. 11, 1950. On July 16, 1951, he abdicated.

THESE ARTICLES ARE IN THE FACT-INDEX

| | |
|---|---|
| Leopold V | Lermontov, Mikhail |
| Lepachys | Yurievich |
| Lepidus, Marcus Aemilius | Lerner, Alan Jay |
| Leprechaun | Lerwick, Scotland |
| Leprosy | Le Sage, Alain René |
| Leptis Magna, Libya | Lesage, Jean |
| Lepton | Lesbos |
| Le Puy, France | Lescaze, William |
| Lérida, Spain | Leschetizky, Theodor |
| Lerma River | Leslie, Sir John |

**LESOTHO.** The nation of Lesotho, formerly Basutoland, is completely surrounded by South Africa (for map, *see* South Africa). The mountainous country, with an area of 11,716 square miles, is about the size of Belgium. Most of Lesotho consists of scenic highlands, which rise in the Drakensberg range, in the east, to more than 11,000 feet. About two thirds of the people live on the western

AFRICA

LESOTHO

**A HOME IN THE RUGGED LAND OF LESOTHO**
This hut is typical of the homes in Lesotho. Rugged highlands cover most of the country.

lowlands. These, at an altitude of 5,000 feet, are low only by comparison with the other areas.

The climate of the lowlands is mild. Rainfall is variable but averages about 28 inches a year.

### How the People Live

Almost all the people are Basuto, a Bantu tribe. The few Europeans are traders and missionaries. Most of the people are Christians. Their language is Sesuto, a Bantu tongue.

Most Basuto farm or raise sheep, cattle, and other livestock. Wool and mohair, the chief exports, are sold to South Africa. Soil erosion is a major problem in Lesotho. Because of the shortage of tillable land, more than half of the Basuto men work in South Africa as laborers.

Lesotho's literacy rate is about 85 percent. Girls generally receive a better education than boys since the boys must serve as shepherds for the livestock. Students from several other African nations attend the university in Lesotho.

Lesotho has no industries. Some diamonds have been found, but there are no other known minerals. The only town of any size is Maseru, the capital (population, 1965 estimate, 10,000). A railroad runs from Maseru to South Africa. In many areas pack animals are the chief means of transport.

### History and Government

The Basuto nation dates from the early 1800's, when a chief named Moshesh gathered together the remnants of tribes scattered by the aggressive Zulu and Matabele. Intermittent warfare with Boers moving northward then developed. Moshesh obtained protection from the British government in 1868, and then his land became the British colony of Basutoland in 1884.

In 1960 a legislative assembly was introduced. In 1964 a parliamentary government headed by the tribal paramount chief was set up to prepare the people for independence, which was granted in 1966. Lesotho is also a member of the Commonwealth of Nations. (*See also* Africa; British Empire and the Commonwealth of Nations.) Population (1965 estimate), 745,000.

THESE ARTICLES ARE IN THE FACT-INDEX

Lespinasse, Julie Jeanne
  Eléonore de
Lesseps, Ferdinand,
  vicomte de
Lessing, Gotthold
  Ephraim

Lesueur, Charles
  Alexandre
Le Sueur, Pierre Charles
Lethbridge, Alta.
Leto
Letters of marque
Letters patent

# Talking by Mail—The Art of Letter Writing

**LETTER WRITING.** "I feel as though I were talking to you," wrote Cicero to a friend nearly two thousand years ago. That is the way a person should feel when he is writing friendly letters. Such letters are a kind of conversation carried on by mail and should follow the rules of conversation (*see* Conversation). A letter takes a person's place when he is separated from his friends, and it should reflect his own personality. When writing a letter, a person should write as he would talk and should be natural in what he says.

### Letter Writing in Ancient Times

Letter writing as an art began, so far as is known, with Cicero. His letters have the conversational quality and the personal touch that are found in the best letters of all ages.

More than a thousand years before Cicero's time, the rulers of western Asia were keeping up a lively correspondence with the pharaoh of Egypt. A collection of some 300 of their letters, written on clay tablets, was dug up at El Amarna, Egypt, in 1887.

The accounts of Homer and Herodotus show that the ancient Greeks sent letters. It was left for the Romans, however, to develop letter writing into an art. Their able men had to spend years in governing distant provinces. They could learn what was happening at Rome only from the letters of their friends.

### Letters as Literature, and Their Writers

Some letters have expressed so much of the charm and personality of their writers that they are regarded as part of the literature of the world. Two of the most famous letter writers in the English language are William Cowper, the poet, and Charles Lamb, the author of 'Essays of Elia' and 'Tales from Shakespear'. Neither of them led an exciting life, but they had an affectionate interest in their correspondents and found delight in writing about everyday scenes and events. Jane Carlyle, wife of the famous Thomas Carlyle, won a place in literature by her lively letters. Another woman remembered for her letters is Madame de Sévigné, a Frenchwoman of the 17th century (*see* Sévigné). Robert Louis Stevenson, William Dean Howells, and William

Ch. Ch. Oxford
Mar. 15. 1891.

My dear Enid,
    Please tell your Mother I was ever so much surprised, and ever so much pleased, with her letter. And I hope ever so much that she'll bring you here to tea, some afternoon when you happen not to be in a passion: for it won't do to have screaming children in College: it would vex the Dean ever so much. I send you ever so much of my love. Get a hammer, and knock it ever so hard, till it comes in two, and then give Winnie half.
    Yours ever so affectionately,
      C. L. Dodgson.

Miss Enid Stevens.

Charles L. Dodgson (Lewis Carroll) illustrated his letters. This charming note is from a collection 'Letters of Lewis Carroll to His Child-Friends'. Apparently he and Enid have two jokes—one about her excessive use of "ever so much" and the other about her disposition.

James wrote delightful letters. In this century there are the remarkable letters of Woodrow Wilson, the sparkling correspondence between George Bernard Shaw and Ellen Terry, and Thomas Wolfe's letters to his mother. Reading such letters is not only entertaining but also inspires people to write more readable letters.

### Ethics and Etiquette of Letters

Letters that have been published are meant for all to read, but there are other letters that are private property. Well-bred persons never open a

197

letter addressed to another—even to a member of the family, except with permission—or read an opened letter which they find. They do not permit others to read a letter sent them, unless they are sure that the writer would not object. And, to show that they trust others to be equally well bred, they do not seal a letter which is to be delivered by a friend.

Good manners are as important in letter writing as in any other social activity. You want to present a good appearance in your correspondence, as in your dress and your conversation.

Be careful to choose the right kind of stationery. Unruled paper, white or pale gray, blue, or buff, is in good taste for social letters. Fashions in the shape and design of letter paper change slightly from time to time, but paper of fantastic design should never be used. The paper you use for social letters may bear your monogram or your address. Many people today use paper that is imprinted with both name and address.

Good form requires that letters be written in ink, not pencil, and that margins be left at both sides and at the top and bottom of pages. Abbreviations (such as A.M. and Tues.) and figures, except in dates, should be avoided because they suggest discourteous haste. Omitting the date is careless. If your address is not on the letter paper, you should be sure to write it in the upper right-hand corner of the first sheet or at the end of the letter at the left below your signature.

### Salutation, Signature, Beginning of Letter

In writing to a mere acquaintance or to someone you have not met, you would probably begin your letter with, "My dear Mrs. Sterling." To a friend or a relative you would say less formally, "Dear John" or perhaps more intimately "Dearest Mary." The correct close for a letter which opens formally with "My dear Mrs. Sterling" is "Sincerely yours."

Mr. and Mrs. Carl Swann Holt

request the honor of your presence

at the marriage of their daughter

Geraldine

to

Mr. Enoch Hoe Garden

Saturday, the tenth of June

at twelve o'clock

St. Mark's Church

Chicago

*Invitation to Wedding Ceremony (⅔ actual size)*

Mr. and Mrs. Carl Swann Holt

request the pleasure of your company

at the wedding breakfast

at half after twelve o'clock

Sixteen Belmont Avenue

*Invitation to Wedding Breakfast*

A more intimate letter may end with "Affectionately yours," "Lovingly yours," or with some other variation which appeals to you. Young people do not use "Faithfully yours" or "Cordially yours." In writing to good friends or to relatives it is more important to be natural and sincere than to follow any set form of closing in your letter.

Except in letters to members of your family and to intimate friends, the proper signature is your first and last name, with a middle name or initial if you prefer. It is not necessary for an unmarried woman to put (Miss) before her name, and those of the best taste do not do it. A married woman signs her name this way:

Edith Wordsworth Prim
(Mrs. Barstow Prim)

or she omits her maiden surname if she chooses.

The start of a letter is important, just as first impressions are important in our contacts with people. Beginning with an apology such as, "I meant to write you before, but I haven't had time," is uninteresting. It would be much more pleasant to say, "I am glad today is a holiday, so that I have time to write you."

There is nothing amiss in beginning with "I" when that seems natural, but a letter studded with I's appears too full of self. Turning a sentence around will often make the I's less conspicuous. Instead of "I received your letter. I was glad to hear from you," you might say, "You were good to write me that jolly letter when I was ill."

Too few I's are as bad as too many. A chopped-off sentence, such as "Was glad to get your letter," is ungrammatical and impolite.

### Letters of Thanks and Informal Invitations

Among the special kinds of letters which must be written from time to time, letters of thanks come first. Writing these promptly shows one's appreciation. Moreover, a reply is certain to result in more enthusiastic letters.

To be gracious they should be specific. For example, instead of writing "Thank you for the present you sent me," mention the gift received and tell what you like about it. "Thank you for the book about stamps. It will help me to get my collection in order."

The "bread-and-butter letter" is the one sent to one's hostess after a visit. When you have spent a few days at the home of a friend, you write shortly after your return home not only to this friend but also to the mother of the household. Here is an example:

246 Wilmette Street<br>Malden, Michigan<br>July 10, 19—

Dear Mrs. Millmont:

Mother met me when I got off the train and wanted me to tell her at once about the good times I had at your house. It was fun just talking about them. I especially enjoyed the trip to Bald Mountain and the visit to the tile factory and swimming in the river every day. Thank you for all you did for me. Please remember me to Mr. Millmont.

Sincerely (or affectionately) yours,<br>Marion March

Before young people visit in one another's homes, it is customary for the mothers to exchange letters. But sometimes, when the families know each other well, a daughter may send an invitation in her mother's name.

Dear Lucia,

Mother wants me to ask you to spend the week of August fifth with us at the seashore. There is a good train which gets to Milford at four o'clock, and we could meet you there Monday afternoon. We'll swim, play tennis, and picnic on the beach. I do hope you can come.

Your loving<br>Emily

## Formal Invitations and Replies

Occasionally you will receive a formal invitation to a party or wedding, written or engraved in the third person. Your reply should be in the third person also. It would begin: "Miss Greta Swanson (or Mr. Herbert Harley) accepts with pleasure" and then follow the wording and the line division of the invitation (*see* example in next column). Repeating the date, place, and hour shows that you have correctly noted these details. Use white note paper about four by five inches in size. Never sign or date a formal reply.

"R.S.V.P." in the lower left-hand corner of an invitation stands for *Répondez s'il vous plaît,* French for "Reply, if you please." Sometimes "Please reply" is used. Even without such requests you should be considerate about answering written invitations.

When you receive a wedding invitation asking you to the church ceremony only, you need not reply. But if the wedding is to be at home, or if you are invited to the wedding breakfast or reception after the ceremony, you must send an answer. Let us suppose you receive a wedding invitation and a card to the wedding breakfast, like those on the opposite page. You would

answer the breakfast invitation only, like this:

Miss Elaine Tennyson<br>accepts with pleasure<br>Mr. and Mrs. Carl Swann Holt's<br>kind invitation to the wedding breakfast<br>Saturday, the tenth of June<br>at half after twelve o'clock<br>at Sixteen Belmont Avenue

The reply to an invitation to a home wedding would begin in the same way, but the latter part could be shortened to

kind invitation<br>for Saturday, the tenth of June<br>at half after twelve o'clock

A note of regret would be written like this:

Mr. Calvin Leighton<br>regrets that illness<br>prevents his accepting<br>Mr. and Mrs. Carl Swann Holt's<br>kind invitation<br>for Saturday, the tenth of June

It is not necessary to give the reason for declining an invitation, but it is more polite to do so. It might be "absence from town will prevent his accepting" or "a previous engagement prevents his accepting."

Hostesses who are very particular like to word their formal invitations entirely in the third person. Thus, instead of "request the honor of your presence," such an invitation will read:

request the honor of<br>Mr. Calvin Leighton's<br>presence

In an engraved invitation of this type a line is left blank and the name of the person invited is filled in by hand.

Invitations to informal dances or dinners or to teas are frequently written on visiting cards.

## How to Write Business Letters

A business letter must above everything else be clear and to the point, but it cannot be effective unless it sounds as natural as talk. Stilted expressions take all the life out of a letter. The roundabout "I beg to acknowledge your favor" and the formal close prevalent in Charles Lamb's time, "I am, Sir, with great respect, your humble servant" are equally out of fashion.

Unnecessary words and insincere phrases are also avoided by good letter writers. For example, "Enclosed is" or "I am enclosing" is preferable to "Enclosed herewith." "Your letter" or "your order" is simpler than "your esteemed favor." And "We are pleased to advise you" is both pompous and useless. Some of the rules for the format of social letters, such as leaving good margins and placing the letter so that it looks well on the page, apply to business letters as well, and should be carefully followed.

One of two endings will serve for nearly all business letters—"Sincerely yours" to one person, whether an acquaintance or a stranger, and "Very truly yours" to a firm. "Respectfully yours" is suitable in a letter to a person of high position in the church or government, and perhaps in a letter from a young employee to the company head, but not on other occasions.

In business letters it is important to include both the *heading* (the date and the address of the writer) and the *superscription* (the name and address of the person or the company to whom the letter is written).

Following the superscription, a letter to a firm may begin either with "Gentlemen" or with "Dear Sirs." Some think the latter more courteous.

## Letters of Application

A good letter of application is straightforward, definite, and confident but not boastful. It should sound as if the writer were thinking of the employer's needs and not simply following a form.

> 2440 Logan Avenue
> Atlanta, Ga.
> June 18, 19—

Messrs. Gray and Herbert
Lawyers Building
Atlanta, Ga.

Dear Sirs:

Please consider me as an applicant for the position of office assistant which you advertised in today's *Times*.

I have just received my diploma from the West Side High School and am eager to get in an office like yours, since I am especially interested in law.

During the last two summers I worked as a messenger in the Charters National Bank and the Farmers State Bank and learned something about office practice and routine. I can use a typewriter and an adding machine and handle a switchboard.

For information about my character and ability, I can refer you to

Mr. Marshall Drury, Charters National Bank
Mr. E. P. Small, Farmers State Bank
Dr. Wiley Ash, St. Paul's Episcopal Church

I shall be glad to come to your office for an interview at any time you suggest. My telephone number is 262-7648.

> Very truly yours,
> Mark Spencer

In this letter the applicant gives in a few simple paragraphs his education, his interests, his experience, —adding a detail or two that might be useful to an employer—and his references.

## Inquiry and Order Letters

In a letter of inquiry the important thing is to give the information necessary for an answer but no more.

> CENTRAL HIGH SCHOOL
> GRANADA, ARKANSAS
> November 25, 19—

Bombazine Costume Company
259 Forrest Place
Little Rock, Ark.

Gentlemen:

The senior class of Granada High School will present "The Rivals" on December 20. Can you supply us with suitable eighteenth-century costumes? What is the rental charge for costumes of this type?

> Very truly yours,
> Stephen Story

An order letter must be explicit.

> 45 Pembroke Road
> Cleveland, Ohio
> April 15, 19—

R. G. Watson Supply Company
1331 Chester Street
Philadelphia, Pa.

Dear Sirs:

Please send me the following items taken from your Spring Catalog Number 21:

```
4 baseballs, #617, @$3.00.............$12.00
3 baseball gloves, #242, @$20.00....... 60.00
                                        ───────
                                        $72.00
```

I enclose a money order for $72.00.

> Very truly yours,
> Robert Swenson

The *block form* for the heading and the superscription (shown in the above letters) is preferred today to the *indented form*:

> R. G. Watson Supply Company
> 1331 Chester Street
> Philadelphia, Pa.

Punctuation is omitted at the end of lines, except when an abbreviation calls for a period. In business correspondence (but not in social letters) names of states may be abbreviated. It looks better never to abbreviate "street," "avenue," and similar words. The address on the envelope should look like these:

Mrs. Robert South    National Cracker Company
1245 Barren Street    400 West 42nd Street
San Francisco, Calif.    New York, N.Y.

When you write either to a person or to a company requesting a reply that is merely a favor to you, always enclose a stamped, addressed envelope. This is not needed when you inquire about an article that is for sale or apply for a position which has been advertised.

It is important to know how to write a good business letter, for almost all of us have such letters to write.

### BIBLIOGRAPHY FOR LETTER WRITING
#### Art of Letter Writing

Blumenthal, L. A. The Art of Letter Writing (Grosset, 1976).

Jacobson, Helen and Mischel, Florence. The First Book of Letter Writing (Watts, 1957).

Joslin, Sesyle. Dear Dragon . . . and Other Useful Letter Forms for Young Ladies and Gentlemen Engaged in Everyday Correspondence (Harcourt, 1962).

Measures, Howard. Styles of Address, 3d ed. (St. Martin's, 1970).

Monro, K. M. and Taintor, S. A. The Handbook of Social Correspondence (Macmillan, 1936).

Monro, K. M. and Taintor, S. A. The Secretary's Handbook, rev. 9th ed. (Macmillan, 1969).

Shurter, R. L. Written Communication in Business, 3d ed. (McGraw, 1971).

Watson, L. E. The Bantam Book of Correct Letter Writing (Bantam, 1962).

#### Famous Letters

Bowen, Marjorie, ed. Some Famous Love Letters (Richard West, 1973).

Schuster, M. L., ed. A Treasury of the World's Great Letters (Simon & Schuster, 1940).

## THE FOUR MAIN TYPES OF LETTUCE

Crisphead lettuce (top left) has a firm head with crisp leaves. Butterhead lettuce (top right) typically has a soft head and tender leaves. This is a Big Boston. Cos, or romaine (bottom left), a leaf lettuce, grows upright. Black-seeded Simpson (bottom right) is also a leaf type.

THESE ARTICLES ARE IN THE FACT-INDEX

| | |
|---|---|
| Leucippus | Levine, Jack |
| Leucite | Levine, Philip |
| Leutze, Emanuel | Levinson, Salmon Oliver |
| Lev | Lévis, Que. |
| Levant, Oscar | Leviticus |
| Levant | Levittown, N. Y. |
| Levelland, Tex. | Levittown, Pa. |
| Levene, Phoebus Aaron | Lewes, George Henry |
| Leverhulme, William | Lewes, Del. |
|   Hesketh Lever, first | Lewin, Kurt |
|   Viscount | Lewis, Andrew |
| Leverrier, Urbain Jean | Lewis, C(live) S(taples) |
|   Joseph | Lewis, D(ominic) B(evan) |
| Levi |   Wyndham |
| Leviathan | Lewis, Elizabeth Foreman |
| 'Leviathan' | Lewis, Francis |
| Levin, Harry (Tuchman) | Lewis, Gilbert Newton |
| Levin, Meyer | Lewis, Isaac Newton |

**LETTUCE.** The world's most popular salad green is lettuce. It originated in western Asia and was popular with the ancient Persians, Greeks, and Romans. The milky juice in the plant stem was believed to induce sleep.

Lettuce is cultivated for its root leaves. It is a hardy annual and grows best in cool weather. It grows quickly and must be cut for table use before it produces its long, slender seed stalk. The small ray flower is yellow.

There are five types of lettuce—crisphead, butterhead, Cos, leaf, and stem. Stem, or asparagus, lettuce is little used in the United States. It is grown in China for its tall, thick, edible stems.

The most important lettuce commercially is crisphead. The chief varieties are New York (popularly called iceberg), Imperial, and Great Lakes. Butterheads include Big Boston and the small, tender bibb. Most popular of the Cos, or romaine, type is Paris white. Leaf lettuce is the easiest type to grow in the home garden. It includes Grand Rapids and the white-seeded and black-seeded Simpsons.

Lettuce is grown commercially in 22 states. By far the largest producer is California, followed by Arizona. These two states supply eastern markets the year around. California furnishes almost all the seed.

Lettuce belongs to the family *Compositae*. Its scientific name is *Lactuca sativa*.

**LEWIS, John Llewellyn** (1880–1969). For 40 years (1920–60), John L. Lewis was president of the United Mine Workers of America. He also worked for unionization of the steel, automobile, and other mass-production industries and organized the Congress of Industrial Organizations. Demanding and unyielding, he aroused passions with his thunderous oratory and kept industry in turmoil.

John Llewellyn Lewis was born in Lucas, Iowa, Feb. 12, 1880. His father, Thomas, a coal miner from Wales, was active in the Knights of Labor. John quit school at 12 to drive mules underground. At 17 he became a coal miner. With the help of a schoolteacher, Myrta Edith Bell, he educated himself. He also directed a debating club and engaged in amateur theatricals. In 1907 he married Myrta Bell. One of their three children died at an early age. His son, John, became a physician, and Kathryn worked with her father.

At 26 Lewis was a delegate to a United Mine Workers convention. In 1920 he was elected president. The membership was then about 700,000, the largest in the American Federation of Labor. The miners' basic daily pay was from $2.50 to $3.00. When competition from gas and oil lowered the demand for coal, Lewis pressed for more mechanization. This saved the coal industry but reduced the number of miners. When Lewis retired in 1960 there were only 200,000. However, their wages were high, and they were excellently insured. Lewis died in Washington, D. C., on June 11, 1969. (*See also* Coal; Labor.)

### JOHN L. LEWIS SPEAKS FOR THE MINERS

Lewis did not believe in speaking softly. Here, in an appearance before a Congressional hearing, the union leader challenges the government.

THESE ARTICLES ARE IN THE FACT-INDEX
**Lewis, Matthew Gregory**
**Lewis, Meade Lux**

**LEWIS, Meriwether** (1774–1809). The name of Meriwether Lewis is closely linked with that of another American explorer, William Clark. Together they led the expedition named for them (*see* Clark, William; Lewis and Clark Expedition).

Meriwether Lewis was born Aug. 18, 1774, on a plantation near Charlottesville, Va. Thomas Jefferson, a neighbor, was a friend of the family. Meriwether studied with private tutors, hunted, and learned nature lore. In 1791 he served in the Whiskey Rebellion. The next year he fought against Indians in the Northwest Territory. Between campaigns he learned Indian speech and customs.

Soon after Jefferson became president, Lewis moved into the White House as his private secretary. They often discussed the exploration of a land route to the Pacific Ocean. Lewis was eager to lead the expedition. Congress, at Jefferson's request, appropriated the sum Lewis estimated was needed ($2,500). Jefferson asked Lewis to choose a companion officer, and Lewis selected William Clark of Louisville. The success of the expedition was due to the combined abilities of the two leaders.

In 1806 Jefferson appointed Lewis governor of the Louisiana Territory, with headquarters at St. Louis. Lewis was an excellent administrator, but his service was brief. In 1809 he started on a trip to Washington, D. C. On the night of October 11 he was found shot to death at an inn in Tennessee. He was probably murdered, though there was no proof of it.

**LEWIS, Sinclair** (1885–1951). The novels that Sinclair Lewis wrote in the 1920's assure him a lasting place in American literature. Nothing he wrote before or after matches his work in 'Main Street' (1920), 'Babbitt' (1922), 'Arrowsmith' (1925), 'Elmer Gantry' (1927), and 'Dodsworth' (1929). In 1930 he won the Nobel prize in literature for 'Babbitt', a novel about a petty and dull small-town businessman. Lewis was the first American to receive the award.

In the 1920's Lewis was using material familiar to him. Gopher Prairie, the setting for 'Main Street', is actually his birthplace, Sauk Centre, Minn. Minneapolis, 100 miles away, is renamed Zenith in other books. His father, Edwin J. Lewis, was a country doctor, as were Will Kennicott in 'Main Street' and, for a time, Martin Arrowsmith.

As a boy Lewis read everything obtainable. He attended Yale University and was graduated in 1907. Years of editorial work and free-lancing preceded his first success. He wrote steadily, averaging a book every two years for over 30 years. He also wrote short stories. Lewis was married twice, the second time to Dorothy Thompson, a newspaper columnist. He died in Rome, Italy, on Jan. 10, 1951.

THESE ARTICLES ARE IN THE FACT-INDEX
**Lewis, William Berkeley**      **Lewis and Clark**
**Lewis, Wyndham**                   **Centennial Exposition**
                                                **Lewis and Clark College**

**LEWIS AND CLARK EXPEDITION** (1804–1806). Little was known about western America when the Lewis and Clark Expedition set out in 1804. Twelve years earlier Capt. Robert Gray, an American navigator, had sailed up the mouth of the great river he named the Columbia. Traders and trappers reported that the source of the Missouri River was in the mountains in the Far West. No one, however, had yet blazed an overland trail.

Thomas Jefferson was interested in knowing more about the country west of the Mississippi. In 1803, two years after he became president, he asked Congress to appropriate $2,500 for an expedition.

To head the expedition, Jefferson chose his young secretary, Capt. Meriwether Lewis. Lewis invited his friend William Clark to share the leadership. Both were familiar with the frontier and with Indians through their service in the Army. (*See also* Lewis, Meriwether; Clark, William.)

Before Lewis and Clark set out, word came that Napoleon had sold an immense tract of land to the United States (*see* Louisiana Purchase). The expedition would therefore be exploring American territory.

Plans for the expedition were carefully laid. The party was to ascend the Missouri to its source, cross the Continental Divide, and descend the Columbia River to its mouth. In preparation for the historic journey, Lewis studied map making and learned how to fix latitude and longitude.

In the winter of 1803–4 the expedition was assembled in Illinois, near St. Louis, Mo. The party consisted of the 2 leaders, Lewis and Clark; 14 soldiers; 9 frontiersmen from Kentucky; 2 French boatmen; and Clark's Negro servant, York.

On May 14, 1804, the explorers started up the Missouri in a 55-foot covered keelboat and two small craft. On July 30 they held their first powwow with Indians at a place the explorers named Council Bluff. (Council Bluffs, Iowa, across the river from the site, perpetuates the name with the slight change.) On October 26 they reached the camps of the Mandan Indians.

On a site close to present-day Stanton, N. D., the explorers built Fort Mandan and spent the winter. It was here that they hired Toussaint Charbonneau, a French interpreter, and his Indian wife, Sacagawea, the sister of a Shoshone chief. While at Fort Mandan, Sacagawea gave birth to a baby boy. This did not stop her from joining the group. She carried the child on her back for the rest of the trip. As an Indian interpreter she was to prove invaluable.

In the spring of 1805 the keelboat was sent back to St. Louis with dispatches for President Jefferson and with natural history specimens. Meanwhile, canoes had been built. On April 7 the party pushed on up the Missouri. On April 26 they passed the mouth of the Yellowstone, and on June 13 they reached the Great Falls of the Missouri. Making a 16-mile-long portage around the falls with their laden canoes caused a month's delay. On July 13 the canoes were launched again above the falls. On the 25th the expedition reached Three Forks, where three rivers join to form the Missouri. They named the rivers the Madison, the Jefferson, and the Gallatin.

For some time the explorers had been within sight of the Rocky Mountains. Crossing them was to be the hardest part of the journey. They decided to follow the largest of the three forks, the Jefferson.

They were now in the country of the Shoshone, Sacagawea's people. Sacagawea eagerly watched for her tribe, but it was Lewis who found them. The chief turned out to be Sacagawea's brother. He provided the party with guides and horses to cross the lofty Bitterroot Range. Owing to the lack of game, the entire party often went hungry.

After crossing the divide late in September, they reached a point on the Clearwater River. From here they were able to proceed by water.

On Nov. 7, 1805, Clark wrote in his journal, "Great

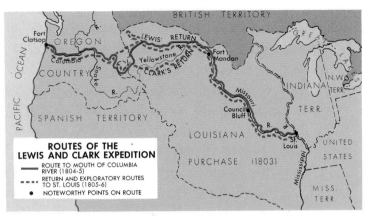

ROUTES OF THE
LEWIS AND CLARK EXPEDITION
—— ROUTE TO MOUTH OF COLUMBIA
RIVER (1804-5)
---- RETURN AND EXPLORATORY ROUTES
TO ST. LOUIS (1805-6)
● NOTEWORTHY POINTS ON ROUTE

joy in camp," for after a journey of over 18 months, the Pacific Ocean was within view. On the Pacific shore, near the mouth of the Columbia, they built a stockade, Fort Clatsop. There they spent the winter.

On March 23, 1806, the entire party started back. On June 24, with 66 horses, they began to cross the mountains. In the Bitterroot Valley the two leaders separated to learn more about the country.

Clark headed for the Yellowstone River and followed it to the Missouri. Lewis, with nine men, struck off toward the northeast to explore a branch of the Missouri which he named the Marias. On this trip he had a skirmish with Indians, the only one of the entire journey. Later, while out hunting, he was accidentally shot by one of his own men. He recovered after the party was reunited and had stopped at Fort Mandan. There they left Sacagawea and her family.

The party reached St. Louis Sept. 23, 1806. Their arrival caused great rejoicing, for they had been believed dead. They had been gone 2 years, 4 months, and 9 days, and had traveled about 6,000 miles.

Lewis and Clark brought back much new material for map makers and specimens of previously unknown wildlife. American settlers and traders soon began to travel over the route they had blazed. The expedition also provided one of the best grounds for the United States claim to the Oregon country.

**SACAGAWEA, A FAITHFUL COMPANION**
Clark had a deep regard for the Shoshone squaw who shared all the hardships of the journey. From a painting by N. C. Wyeth.

THESE ARTICLES ARE IN THE FACT-INDEX

Lewis College
Lewisohn, Ludwig
Lewisohn Stadium
Lewisporte, Newf.
Lewiston, Idaho
Lewiston, Me.

Lewistown, Mont.
Lewistown, Pa.
Lexington, Ky.
Lexington, N. C.
Lexington, Va.

**LEXINGTON AND CONCORD, BATTLE OF.**
The American Revolution began on April 19, 1775, with the battle of Lexington and Concord. Some time before, Gen. Thomas Gage, the military governor of Massachusetts, had received orders from England to arrest Samuel Adams and John Hancock, accused of stirring up rebellion in the colony. On the night of April 18 Gage sent a detachment of 800 troops to Lexington, where the "traitors" were staying. They were

203

to arrest the two men, then push on to Concord to destroy military supplies stored there by the colonists. News of the expedition leaked out, and two minutemen (as the colonial militia were called), William Dawes and Paul Revere, rode through the country warning people that the British regulars were coming. (*See also* Adams, Samuel; Hancock, John; Revere.)

When the troops reached Lexington they found about 50 minutemen drawn up on the common, an open square in the center of the town. John Pitcairn, the British commander, ordered the rebels to disperse. Both sides milled about in confusion, and shooting broke out. Eight Americans were killed and ten were wounded. The others scattered, and the British went on toward Concord. Hancock and Adams, warned of their coming, had already fled.

The soldiers arrived at Concord at seven o'clock that morning. During the night the colonists had hidden most of their stores and ammunition. What they had not been able to hide, the British set about destroying. Doing this, they met the minutemen at the Old North Bridge over the Concord River and fired upon them. The Americans fired back, and the war had begun. In this skirmish the British numbered about 200; the Americans, 400. The Americans poured over the bridge. The British retired and then began their retreat to Boston about noon.

Meanwhile, the farmers, from behind rocks, fences, and buildings, picked off the brightly clad soldiers along the road. At Lexington the fleeing redcoats met another detachment of 1,500 soldiers sent out by General Gage. Thus strengthened the British returned to Boston, having lost 274 killed and wounded and 25 missing. The American loss was 88 killed and wounded.

At Lexington, 12 miles northwest of Boston, visitors may still see Munroe Tavern, which the British used as their headquarters; Buckman Tavern, the rendezvous of the minutemen; and the Hancock-Clarke house, where Adams and Hancock lodged the night before the battle. The Minute Man National Historical Park, established in 1959, preserves these structures and such memorials as Daniel Chester French's statue of 'The Minute Man' in Concord.

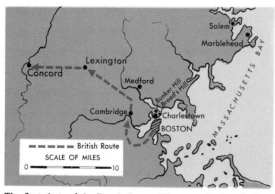

The first shots of the Revolutionary War were fired at Lexington. The first real battle was at Concord, where the minutemen forced the British to retreat.

THESE ARTICLES ARE IN THE FACT-INDEX

Ley, Robert
Ley, Willy
Leyte
Lhévinne, Josef
Liao
Liaoning, People's
  Republic of China
Liaotung Peninsula

Liaoyang, People's
  Republic of China
Liard River
Liatris
Libby, W(illard) F(rank)
Libby Prison
Liberal, Kan.
Liberal Republican party
Liberec, Czechoslovakia

**LIBERIA.** This small republic on the west coast of Africa, just north of the equator, is of special interest to Americans. It was founded as a refuge for liberated slaves from the United States. Its constitution and flag were modeled after those of the United States. Monrovia, its capital and chief port, was named for President James Monroe. Liberia was founded in 1822 by the American Colonization Society as a home for free blacks. On July 26, 1847, Liberia's independence was proclaimed.

Less than 2 percent of the people are descendants of American blacks. Living along the 350-mile coast, they made up a "ruling class" that controlled the economy and politics. The more deprived blacks of the interior still speak their tribal tongues, though English is the official language.

Five sixths of the land is covered by rain forests that grow dense and tall. The republic's exports include rubber, iron ore, gold, diamonds, palm kernels, coffee, cacao, and piassava fiber.

In 1926 an American rubber company leased a vast area where nearly 100,000 acres in rubber trees now produce most of the country's rubber. In 1951 an American mining company began exporting iron ore to the United States from deposits in the Bomi Hills. It built Liberia's first railway—43 miles of narrow-gauge road—and a parallel highway to Monrovia. Defense agreements between Liberia and the United States in World War II led to the construction of Monrovia's modern harbor and airport.

The republic had a progressive leader in William V. S. Tubman, who was reelected for his seventh successive term as president in 1971. After his death, in July 1971, Vice-President William R. Tolbert, Jr., succeeded him. In protest against a proposed increase in the price of rice, bloody riots broke out in Monrovia in April 1979. One year later Tolbert was assassinated in the country's first military coup. Area of Liberia, about 43,000 square miles. Population (1978 estimate), 1,716,900.

THIS ARTICLE IS IN THE FACT-INDEX
**Liberty, Mo.**

Port Authority of New York and New Jersey

The Statue of Liberty, which is nearly 152 feet tall, stands on a 150-foot pedestal on Liberty Island in New York Harbor.

**LIBERTY, STATUE OF.** The giant statue 'Liberty Enlightening the World' has become a symbol of freedom to oppressed people everywhere. It stands on Liberty Island in New York Harbor. The statue was a gift from the people of France to the people of the United States, commemorating the alliance of the two nations during the Revolutionary War.

Édouard de Laboulaye, a French historian, proposed in 1865 that his country present a suitable memorial to the United States on the 100th anniversary of the signing of the Declaration of Independence. The Franco-Prussian War intervened, but in 1874 a young Alsatian sculptor, Frédéric Auguste Bartholdi, was sent to New York City to confer with American authorities. As he sailed into the harbor, Bartholdi envisioned a colossal goddess of liberty at the gateway to the New World.

The Franco-American Union was formed to collect the funds. The total cost of about one million francs was contributed in France by popular subscription. Americans subscribed $250,000 for the pedestal. The statue was dedicated Oct. 28, 1886.

In her uplifted right hand the goddess holds a torch lighted by mercury-vapor lamps. In her left hand is the tablet of law bearing in roman numerals the date July 4, 1776. A broken shackle lies at her feet. The star-shaped wall around the base of the statue is the wall of old Fort Wood, which was built in 1808–11. The statue was made a national monument in 1924. The American Museum of Immigration in the base of the statue was opened in 1972.

On the pedestal appears the following sonnet by Emma Lazarus, entitled 'The New Colossus':

> Not like the brazen giant of Greek fame,
> With conquering limbs astride from land to land,
> Here at our sea-washed, sunset gates shall stand
> A mighty woman with a torch, whose flame
> Is the imprisoned lightning, and her name
> Mother of Exiles. From her beacon-hand
> Glows world-wide welcome; her mild eyes command
> The air-bridged harbor that twin cities frame.
> "Keep ancient lands, your storied pomp!" cries she
> With silent lips. "Give me your tired, your poor,
> Your huddled masses yearning to breathe free,
> The wretched refuse of your teeming shore.
> Send these, the homeless, tempest-tost to me,
> I lift my lamp beside the golden door!"

The figure is composed of more than 300 copper shells, $\frac{3}{32}$ of an inch thick. It is supported by an iron framework designed by Gustave Eiffel, builder of the Eiffel Tower in Paris. Bartholdi first built a 9-foot model. This was enlarged to a figure 36 feet tall, which was divided into sections. Each section was further enlarged to full size and patterns were made, over which the copper was hammered by hand. In the assembled statue each section of the shell was bolted to the central framework. The figure weighs 225 tons (100 copper and 125 iron).

---

THESE ARTICLES ARE IN THE FACT-INDEX
**Liberty cap**
**Liberty party**

---

'Library: 2001' is an abstract sculpture made for F. E. Compton Company by
Stan Smetkowski. The sculpture shows libraries as memory cells to the world.

# a library is a way of sharing

**The true university of the people is the library. And people is what it's all about. Opening the doors each morning is not enough— a library must also reach out to the unreached, the bypassed. Only in this way can the library enlarge the minds and the hearts and the spirits of all whom it serves.**

**LIBRARIES.** Walls cannot embrace a library. It is more than a place, more than books and films and records, more than the people who make it work. Basically a library is a gathering of ideas, of information—put in order and shared. And the sharing is the whole point of a library.

Reading Martin Luther King, Jr.'s "I have a dream" speech touches the mind and heart. But hearing it on tape or record sets the blood rushing and the ears tingling. Seeing the speech delivered on film or videotape adds a further visual dimension. The many ways of understanding come through books, records, tapes, films. That's why librarians today stock a great variety of materials.

## THE LIBRARY: AN INTRODUCTION

Different groups of people use libraries—teachers and learners, youngsters and oldsters, police and plumbers and politicians. Each group, each person has different library needs. Because no one library can handle all needs, there are different kinds of libraries, and there is sharing among libraries.

### A Difference in Libraries

No two libraries are exactly alike. But some have more in common than others.

Because the money to run a *public library* comes from taxes, it is a free library for the public—every-

one who lives in a certain neighborhood, city, county, or province. Such a library serves all ages and groups as an information center, as a reading-and-viewing-and-listening-for-pleasure library. There were early types of public libraries in ancient Greece and Rome. However, they did not lend materials freely as do the world's public libraries today.

Throughout the school day, students and teachers in elementary and secondary school need *school libraries* to work in. The modern school library in many countries is a learning center designed for both group and independent study. Besides books, the library may contain magazines, newspapers, maps, posters, charts, models, teaching machines, films and filmstrips and slides to look at, records and tapes to listen to, and the equipment to use these. There may be special study and listening areas, conference rooms, and even a recording or TV studio. Such a library is called a *materials center* or *media center*. A large secondary school library may have separate *resource centers* for science, social studies, and other subjects.

An *academic library* is found in a college or university. Like a school library, an academic library is a workshop for the students and teachers, but it often has anywhere from 50,000 to millions of books and other materials covering many special subjects. That's why scholars from outside the college or university often use such a library for research. A university

207

may include 50 or more libraries in its many schools —a Far Eastern studies library, a fine arts library, an engineering library, and so on. There may be separate libraries for undergraduates and for rare books and manuscripts. Because of the vast amount of materials they handle, some academic libraries use computers to keep track of the collections.

The medical library of a hospital is a *special library*. So are the libraries of a law office, a weather bureau, a labor union, or a museum. A special library is part of a hospital, business, or other organization, and it offers practical information to the workers or members. Such a library is not generally open

to the public. Usually it concentrates on a particular subject or subjects—medicine, law, climate and weather, labor, art. A special library may have few books, relying heavily instead on such materials as magazines, reports, and computer printouts. These enable the library to keep up in fast-moving fields such as aerospace.

Public, school, academic, and special libraries are the four main kinds the world over, but there are libraries that don't fit neatly into one of these groups. *Research libraries* are an example. Because scholars use them for study, they're much like academic libraries. Research libraries are not always attached to

Harrison Forman

Throughout the world, people who wish to enrich their lives with knowledge seek the services of a library to fill their needs.

Young Buddhist monks, for example, read American magazines in a school library in Thailand.

This article was contributed and critically reviewed by the following: Eleanor E. Ahlers, Professor, School of Librarianship, University of Washington, Seattle; John F. Anderson, Director, Public Library, Tucson, Ariz., Lester Asheim, Professor, Graduate Library School, University of Chicago; Augusta Baker, Coordinator of Children's Services, New York Public Library; Rebecca T. Bingham, Director, Library Media Services, Louisville Public Schools, Louisville, Ky.; Lillian M. Bradshaw, Director, Dallas Public Library, Dallas, Tex.; Henry C. Campbell, Chief Librarian, Toronto Public Libraries, Toronto, Ont.; David H. Clift, former Executive Director, American Library Association; Emma Cohn, Assistant Coordinator, Young Adult Services, New York Public Library; Robert L. Collison,

Head, Reference Department, University Research Library, University of California at Los Angeles; Compton's Encyclopedia Canadian Advisory Board; Richard M. Dougherty, University Librarian, University of California at Berkeley; Sara I. Fenwick, Professor, Graduate Library School, University of Chicago; Emerson Greenaway, former Director, Enoch Pratt Free Library, Baltimore, Md.; Dean Wright Halliwell, University Librarian, University of Victoria, Victoria, B.C.; John G. Lorenz, Deputy Librarian, Library of Congress; Jean E. Lowrie, Director, School Department of Librarianship, Western Michigan University, Kalamazoo; Alice B. McGuire, former Associate Professor, Graduate School of Library Science, University of Texas at Austin.

**Libraries reach beyond their walls to interest their communities in books and learning. This librarian from the Free Public** **Library in New Haven, Conn., tells stories to a front stoop audience of neighborhood children.**

a college or university, however. Also, a research library often concentrates on a special subject or subjects, much like a special library. The Folger Shakespeare Library in Washington, D.C., for instance, deals with William Shakespeare and his times.

Then there are *government libraries* of many kinds. Some, like those of a weather bureau or other government department, are special libraries, offering information and materials that government people need in their work. Others, like state or provincial libraries, are many things. They're public because they serve all the people of a particular region. But they also include research facilities and special libraries such as law libraries for officials.

National libraries are government libraries, too. These are the superlibraries of the world, with upwards of 80 million books and other materials in the largest. Because a national library serves the government of a country, it's a special library. It's also a research library for scholars. In addition, many national libraries are public in that they are for the people of an entire country.

Other libraries that don't fit neatly into one group include those for prisoners in jail, for visitors in such places as YMCA's, for members of the congregation in churches, shipboard libraries for sailors, and army post libraries for soldiers. These are sometimes considered special libraries. But like public libraries, they include much reading material for pleasure as well as for information.

Whatever type it is, every library serves a kind of community—a city, a school, a college or university, a hospital or engineering firm or labor union. Every library, also, shapes itself towards the people of its community—an aerospace library with its complicated computer printouts, an elementary school library with its bright decorations and children's furniture.

### A Sharing Among Libraries

No library, no matter how large, has every book or the answer to every question. So libraries share with each other as well as with the people who use them.

or *catalogs* are published by libraries. These list the materials a library has, thereby making them easier to find and share.

Libraries also form groups, called *systems* or *networks*, for sharing. A public library system in a city, for example, generally consists of a main library and its branches. The city system might be part of a larger system such as a county system. The county system, in turn, might be part of a state system. And that system might be part of a national system. Libraries within a system share books and other materials. In addition, they share services such as storage of little-used books, preparation of materials for library use, and on-the-job training of librarians.

Brooklyn Public Library, New York City

*A library is a way of sharing ... with city people ...*

If someone wants a book or magazine the library doesn't have, the library can borrow it from another library. This is called *interlibrary loan*. Should the book or magazine be needed where it is, a photographic copy, or *photocopy*, can be made of the pages wanted, and the photocopy can be sent instead. Some modern libraries use the Teletype to speed up requests for materials. Also, where equipment is available, photos of materials requested are sent back by electronic signals over telephone wire or via satellite. This is called *facsimile transmission*.

It's not just materials that are shared; it's information too. Larger libraries, for instance, often answer questions smaller libraries can't. Also, *union lists*

Libraries in different regions sometimes form networks. Tied in to each other by Teletype or TV or computer, they can exchange information faster and more easily. All the sharing among libraries are steps toward a giant memory cell, with all the world's libraries plugged in.

### The Why of a Library

People are what a library is all about. A library serves all who use it and reaches out to all who don't or can't. That's what the materials in a library, and the people who work there, are for.

It is common for a public library to have story hours for children, including preschoolers. There are also

UNESCO

*country people . . .*

Houston Public Library

*people who don't know . . .*

Library of Congress, Washington, D.C.

*people who don't see . . .*

Free Press, London, Ont.

*people who don't get out . . .*

picture books for them to page through, filmstrips and films to watch, and records to listen to. Children can see an exhibit of dolls or mobiles, watch a puppet show, or take part in an art contest. Some public libraries even have educational toys to play with and to take home. Tables, chairs, and shelves in a children's department are built to smaller and more convenient scale. Children's librarians introduce children's books to parents and help children choose books that are right for them. Sometimes storytellers are sent out into a community, and children in some places can call on the telephone to have a story read to them.

For those attending school, there is the school as well as the public library. Books and—where these

are available—records, even cassettes and cassette players, can be taken home. Study booths and tables allow youngsters to work alone or in groups. Screening rooms in some libraries are for viewing of films, filmstrips, and videotapes. For sound tapes and records there are usually special listening areas. Both school and public librarians teach students how to use a library.

From secondary school on, young people are served by many kinds of libraries. Public libraries may have young adult sections with books and other materials of interest to young people. Young adult librarians plan film programs, pottery or karate or origami workshops, and discussions on topics that concern the young in that particular community. In a few school and academic libraries, a student can dial to get a foreign language lesson or hear a lecture that has been stored in an *information retrieval bank*. Research libraries, when not part of a university, usually do not loan their materials. But all types of materials can be checked out of many other libraries. What can't be checked out can often be borrowed through inter-library loan or photocopied—many libraries have photocopy machines, or *copiers*, for people to use. There may also be machines called *microfilm, Micro-card,* and *microfiche readers*. With these, a person can read books, magazines, and newspapers that have been photographed and much reduced in size.

union halls, and housing projects. In special libraries, librarians not only find information for company workers but often summarize it for them.

For people of all ages, there are librarians specially trained to answer questions or help people get mate-rials. There are also reference books such as encyclo-pedias to use in finding information without help. Finding out is easier for people interested in special subjects because library collections are arranged by subject. Library interiors are designed to be inviting and comfortable for reading, listening, viewing, and studying. Special devices such as wheelchair ramps are installed for the physically handicapped. Many public libraries are community centers, with local

Brooklyn Public Library, New York City

*grown people ...*

Adults, too, are served by many kinds of libraries. Film programs and discussion groups, concerts and plays held in library auditoriums, and art exhibitions often are planned. In many places women's groups, business management groups, labor groups, and others can request materials and conference rooms for meet-ings. Librarians provide materials and guidance on recreation, income tax, travel, health, and retirement. Adults who don't speak the language of the country well or who have little schooling can attend special programs at public libraries. Public librarians also reach out with books and services to such places as schools, nursing homes for the elderly, jails, factories,

artists showing their work, or community leaders giving talks. A public library in the city reaches into the neighborhoods with branch libraries and book-mobiles. For people in the country, there are books by mail, bookmobiles, book sleds, book boats, book trains, and even book planes. "Talking books" and the record players to use them are sent to the blind. So are magazines and books in braille, as well as books with large type for people with poor eyesight. Libraries reach out to help deaf, sick, poor, and forgotten peo-ple. A library in ancient Egypt was called "The Heal-ing Place of the Soul." That goes a long way towards explaining the why of a library.

*teen people . . .*

*kid people . . .*

*working people . . .*                    *. . . and more*

## The How of a Library

A library is not just to learn about; it's to use. And using it begins with knowing how that particular library is arranged.

To make books easier to find, those of the same type are commonly kept together. Stories are kept in one section, science books in another, and so on. There are often separate sections for magazines and newspapers, and for films, records, tapes, and such.

**The Secret of Library Codes.** Books are marked, or coded, in different ways. On the spine of a storybook or novel there may be such marks as a PB for picture book, an E for easy, a J for juvenile, or an F for fiction. No matter how they are marked though, such storybooks and novels are put in alphabetical order by author's last name. So Paula Fox's books come before those of Astrid Lindgren. Books by the same author are in alphabetical order by title. Lindgren's 'Seacrow Island' comes after her 'Pippi Longstocking'.

The story of someone's life may be marked with a B for biography. Such biographies are put in alphabetical order by last name of the person the book is about. Thus, Howard Fast's 'Haym Salomon' comes before Earl Conrad's 'Harriet Tubman'. Biographies about many people—collective biographies—are grouped

213

separately. Such books are in alphabetical order by the last name of the person who wrote the book.

Of the many codes for marking books, two systems are used more often than the others in many parts of the world. One is called the Dewey decimal classification. It was designed by a librarian named Melvil Dewey, and school and public libraries use it most.

In the Dewey system, there are ten main subjects. Each subject has a three-figure number. The number 400, for instance, stands for language; 500 for science. In each Dewey number, the first figure is the key to the main subject. All books that begin with 5 are about science, and all books that begin with 4 are about language.

| Dewey Decimal Classification Main Subjects (Simplified) |
| --- |
| 000–099 many subjects (general works) |
| 100–199 man's ideas (philosophy) |
| 200–299 religion |
| 300–399 people in groups (social sciences) |
| 400–499 language |
| 500–599 science |
| 600–699 uses of science (technology) |
| 700–799 the arts |
| 800–899 literature |
| 900–999 history, geography, biography |

Author, subject, and title cards in the card catalog offer quick access to a library's information resources.

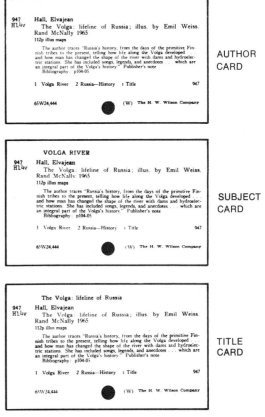

AUTHOR CARD

SUBJECT CARD

TITLE CARD

Each main subject is divided into ten parts. Literature (800) is divided into American literature (810), English literature (820), German literature (830), French literature (840), and so on. Each part of a subject can be divided into ten smaller parts. They, in turn, can be divided into ten still smaller parts. And that's what the decimal in the Dewey decimal classification is all about. Take 973. It includes all books on United States history. But that takes in books on the exploration of North America (973.1), the American Revolution (973.3), the Civil War (973.7), and so on. The smaller the part of a main subject, the more numbers after the decimal. Number 629.134354 stands for books about rocket engineering.

It isn't necessary to memorize the Dewey system. What is important, though, is to understand how it works. The same is true of the other much-used code, the Library of Congress (LC) classification. It was designed by librarians working in the Library of Congress, the national library of the United States. Academic and government libraries use it most.

In the LC system, there are twenty one main subjects instead of ten. The keys to subjects are capital letters, not numbers. For most main subjects, there is one key letter. But for the many books on North and South American history, two key letters are needed, so all books on that subject are coded with a beginning E or F.

The LC and Dewey systems also divide subjects differently. Dewey includes book lists and books about libraries in 000 (general works). LC separates them. Philosophy (100) and religion (200) are separated in Dewey, but in LC they are grouped together.

In the LC system, one capital letter stands for a main subject. Two capital letters together stand for part of that subject. World History (D), for instance, is divided into Great Britain (DA), Russia (DK), Asia (DS), Africa (DT), and so on. Each two-letter division can be further divided into 9,999 parts. For these, numbers are used. For smaller and smaller parts beyond that, a decimal point is used, followed by letters and numbers again. All books on the growing of carnations begin with LC number SB 413.C3.

A Dewey or LC number may be only part of a book's code number. In many libraries, there is another part, a bottom line. Dewey number 580, for instance, is for books on flowers. But there are many books on that subject, so they are set apart from one another by adding a second code. John Kieran's 'Introduction to Wild Flowers' ($\frac{580}{K54}$), Clarence J. Hylander's 'Flowers of Field and Forest' ($\frac{580}{H99}$), and Illa Podendorf's 'True Book of Weeds and Wild Flowers' ($\frac{580}{P75}$) are examples.

The bottom line is a code for the first few letters of the author's last name—K54 (or Kie) for Kieran, H99 (or Hyl) for Hylander, and P75 (or Pod) for

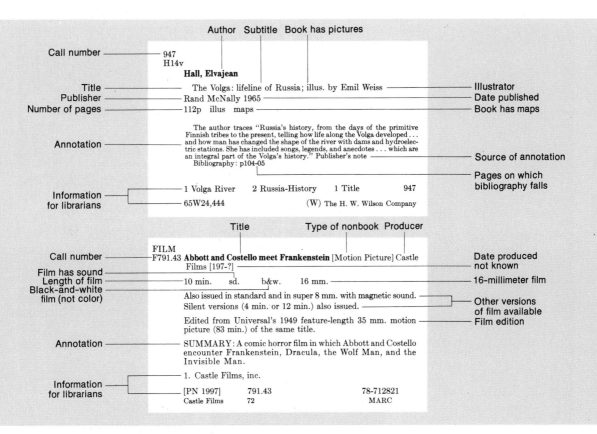

**Library of Congress Classification**
**Main Subjects (Simplified)**

| | | | |
|---|---|---|---|
| A | general works | M | music |
| B | philosophy, religion | N | the arts |
| C | subjects closely related to history | P | language, literature |
| D | world history (except American) | Q | science |
| E–F | North and South American history | R | medicine |
| G | geography, anthropology | S | agriculture |
| H | social sciences | T | technology |
| J | politics | U | armies |
| K | law | V | navies |
| L | education | Z | book lists, libraries |

Podendorf. A small letter after the numbers is used for books by the same author on the same subject. Author C. Clarke's 'Man and Space' ($^{629.25}_{C55m}$) and his 'Interplanetary Flight' ($^{629.25}_{C55i}$) are examples. The small letter stands for the first word in the title.

The top and bottom lines together are the book's *call number*. That's what people use to find the book on the shelves or ask for it at the call desk.

**Catalog: House of Cards.** A library is for browsing. But when information is wanted, finding the right books by browsing may take too long. That's when a catalog comes in handy.

Some catalogs are in book form. But most school and public libraries have card catalogs—stacks of slide-out drawers with printed cards inside, all in alpha-

betical order. The cards list and describe every book the library has. Other kinds of material are also listed, sometimes in the same catalog, sometimes in separate catalogs. On the outside of each drawer is a label: A–AK or AL–AM, for example. These are guides to the part of the alphabet covered by the cards inside. There are inside guides, too, cards which stand a little above the rest. In the A–AK drawer, for instance, inside guide cards might read: ADAMS, ADVENTURE, AFRICA, AGRICULTURE, AIRPLANES.

Different types of cards are found in a catalog. An *author card* has the name of a book's author on the top line. On a *title card*, the top line is the title of the book. The subject of the book is the top line of a *subject card*. Books are usually listed on more than

Libraries use labels to help patrons find books quickly. The label on the edge of a bookstack indicates the range of call numbers on its shelves. Labels above the shelves indicate the main subject or part of a main subject found below.

216

one type of card so that they will be easier to find. On all these types of cards, the call number will be in the upper left-hand corner.

Author, title, and subject cards also give other information. The author's birth and death dates are often given. If the book has drawings or photos, the card will say *illus.* or *illus. with photographs*. *Rev.* or *Rev. ed.* means that the book is a revised edition of the original. The card shows the date of publication. It tells the publisher's name and sometimes the place of publication. Number of pages is given. If the book is one of a series—Great Illustrated Classics, for example—the name of the series will appear in parentheses. Sometimes there is a short paragraph, called an *annotation*, that describes what the book is

"See also" cards, found at the end of all cards on a subject, direct a person to additional related subjects. The "see also" card for *Fish* might read:

> Fish
> see also
> Aquariums
> Fisheries
> Marine Animals

Cards for magazines and newspapers are listed by title only—*Sports Illustrated* and the *New York Times*. Cards for materials such as films, records, and tapes are sometimes kept in a separate catalog. Such cards may have the word *Film, Filmstrip,* or *Tape* above the call number. They may also be blue, red, or some other color to tell them apart from book cards.

The Dewey decimal call numbers on these books show that they are about philosophy and religion. Libraries can add extra symbols to call numbers. The library holding these books used the letters "y" and "s" to indicate reading level.

about. *Bibliography: p171–2* may appear on the card, meaning a list of books and other materials on the same subject can be found on those pages. Near the bottom of the card is information meant for librarians —other subjects the book will be listed under, and Dewey and LC numbers.

A catalog also has *cross reference* cards. These are of two types. "See" cards direct a person to a different subject or name. Someone looking for books by Mark Twain, might find cards that read:

> Twain, Mark
> see
> Clemens, Samuel L.

**The How of Finding a Book.** Here are some ABC's of bookfinding with the help of a catalog.

1. Unless you can memorize everything at a glance, bring pen or pencil and paper with you.
2. Save time with the outside and inside guides.
3. Keep these things in mind:
   a. Abbreviations are filed as if spelled out, as *Saint* for *St.* and *Mister* for *Mr.*
   b. The same is true of numbers. For '100 Famous Stories', read 'One Hundred Famous Stories'.
   c. Names beginning with *Mc* are filed as if spelled *Mac.* The Mac names may begin the M section, before *Maas* and *Mabinogion.*

217

d. Authors are listed last name first. But people with three names may be listed under the second one—some Spanish names, Von names, and De names. Some names may be filed under what looks like the first name—Kim Yong Ik under Kim, for example. Just because you can't find a non-English name right away doesn't necessarily mean it isn't there.

e. Titles are listed alphabetically by first word of title. But *a*, *an*, and *the* are not counted as first words, so look for 'The Coming of the Space Age' under C.

f. Just because you can't find a subject right away doesn't mean it isn't in the catalog.

5. Write down call numbers, titles, and authors.

6. Now go to the bookcases, or *stacks*, and use the *case labels*. In many libraries, labels on the side of each stack give the Dewey or LC numbers it holds: *202–238, 239–276*.

7. Use the *shelf labels* if the library has them. Shelf labels give code number and subject of books in that section—*Language 400, Poetry 808.1*.

8. Just because you can't find a book doesn't mean you should quit. Sometimes it's in the wrong place. Sometimes there's another copy around, maybe in another library. Sometimes another book will do just as well for you. Ask a librarian for help—that's what librarians are for.

Frank Verticchio

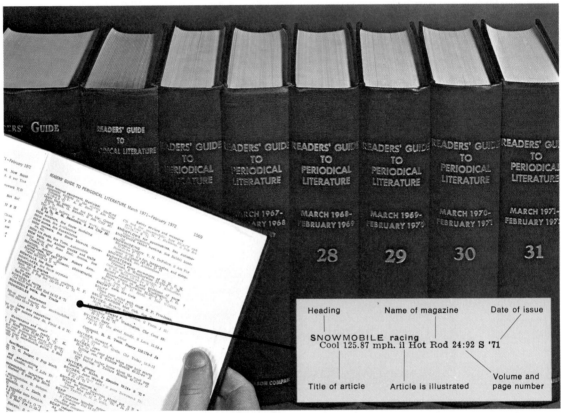

Try a similar subject—*petroleum* instead of *oil*. Or try a larger subject—*Civil War* instead of *Battle of Gettysburg*. Also try inverting the subject to bring out the key word —*Gettysburg, Battle of*.

g. Alphabetical order may be word by word, with *house fly* coming before *housebreaking*. Or the order may be letter by letter. Then *house fly* is considered as one word, and it comes after *housebreaking*. Find out which order you're using.

4. Cards are to read—make sure you're getting the books you want. Also follow up the "see" and "see also" cards.

**The How of Choosing a Book.** Finding books is not enough. Some may be too difficult, some too brief. The idea is to choose the most suitable ones.

1. Check out the author's special knowledge of the subject. Look at the *title page*—the one with

KAPLAN, Allan
    Poem: I don't know whether I am light or
    heavy. Poetry 115:227 Ja '70
KAPLAN, Johanna
    Babysitting; story. Commentary 50:60-6 D '70
    Dragon lady; story. il Harper 241:78-83 Jl '70
    Sudden luck; story. Redbook 136:84-5 D '70

In addition to subject entries, the 'Readers' Guide' lists authors, followed by an alphabetical inventory of their works.

title, author, and publisher. It may tell something about the author and other books he or she has written. If the book is a paperback or has a paper jacket, the cover may provide such information. If neither of these yields any clues, try the preface or introduction.

2. Check to see how recent the information is. On the back of the title page is the *copyright page*. A copyright date—© 1971—tells you that the information is new as of roughly that year. The title page may give a different year—1974, say—but that only means the book was reprinted in 1974 after all the 1971 copies were sold.

3. Find out more about what the book is trying to

and the index may be a glossary or bibliography. The *glossary* explains foreign or uncommon words. A *bibliography* may suggest materials for further reading. It may list the materials the author used in writing his book. Bibliographies are sometimes found at the end of chapters.

**Reference Power.** Some books are not to read through but to refer to for pieces of information. These are *reference books*. Because so many people use them, reference books usually have to stay in the library, though some may be taken home for a short time.

There are different types of reference books, differently arranged. Each answers different kinds of questions.

Frank Verticchio

A **dictionary** answers questions about words. It gives meanings and spellings of a word, tells how it may be pronounced, breaks it up into syllables, shows where it came from, even lists synonyms and antonyms. At the tops of pages, *guide words* show first and last words on a page. They help in finding words faster. In the back may be special sections—facts about famous people, facts about places. In the front, how to use the dictionary is usually explained.

cover, what kind of readers it's for. The preface or introduction will tell you. So will the *table of contents*, which gives an outline of the book. Skimming through parts of the *text*, or main body of the book, will tell you whether it's hard or easy to read. If you want to know whether a certain subject is discussed, check the *index* in the back. It lists all subjects alphabetically and tells what pages they're on.

4. Check for special features that may be useful. A list of illustrations often comes right after the table of contents. It includes the maps, charts, diagrams, or pictures in the book and tells where they can be found. Between the text

A **general encyclopedia,** usually a set of books, covers just about every subject. It has information about people, places, and things. Like a dictionary, an encyclopedia is alphabetically arranged. Every year parts of it are brought up to date, and a yearbook that goes along with it is put out. To help find information, an encyclopedia has *outside guides* (letters on each book, showing what part of the alphabet it covers), *inside guides* (guide words on top of each page), headings and subheadings to break up larger subjects, and an index. Some encyclopedias cover only one subject, such as religion or art. These are called *subject encyclopedias*.

An **atlas** is a book of maps. It also contains charts, tables, and other geographical facts. There are *political maps* to locate countries and cities, rivers and mountains; *physical maps* to show the highs and lows of the land; *economic maps* to show farming and business and industry; *historical maps* to show im-

Newspaper clippings, maps, photos, and sheet music are among the many items that are stored in a library's vertical files.

portant places and events in history. To read a map, a person needs to know the map symbols. These are explained in the front part of an atlas. The index in back helps locate places on a map.

A **gazetteer** is a geographical dictionary. Names of places, rivers, mountains, and so on are listed in alphabetical order. From a gazetteer a person can find out such facts as where a place is, how many people live in it, the height of a mountain, the length of a river. 'Webster's Geographical Dictionary' is a gazetteer.

Yearbooks, almanacs, and handbooks are sometimes hard to tell apart. A **yearbook** mostly reviews the important happenings or facts of a particular year. Ex-

amples include encyclopedia yearbooks. An **almanac,** too, comes out every year. But it concentrates more on giving up-to-date facts about hundreds of subjects —sports, births and deaths, foreign countries, famous people, radio and TV, dams and rivers. One of the best known is 'The World Almanac and Book of Facts'. It is one of the very few reference books in English with the index in front. A **handbook** is a guide to a particular subject—'Crowell's Handbook of Classical Mythology', 'Guinness Book of World Records', and 'Chilton's Auto Repair Manual'.

A **biographical dictionary** is a book of important people's names, with facts about their lives. Order is alphabetical by last name. Some biographical dictionaries list only living people ('Who's Who'), others only dead people ('Who Was Who'). Some list people from many countries, others from only one. Before using a biographical dictionary, it's important to know whether a person is still alive and what country that person comes from. Who is and isn't included is explained in the front part of the book.

A **book of quotations** is used to find out who said something worth quoting and exactly what the words were. It's a collection of phrases and sentences, usually from the works of many authors. But some such collections are from one author (Walt Whitman) or work (the Bible). Quotations may be arranged alphabetically by subject or by author—either alphabetically or by date, from ancient to modern times. Each such book has a large index that includes not only the subjects of quotations but also the key words.

An **index** can be a book by itself. It tells where to find information and items in other books or materials. 'Index to Plays in Collections', for instance, tells in which book or books a particular play can be found. To read an index, a person has to understand the many abbreviations explained in front of the book. A person may also have to ask the librarian for help in getting materials mentioned in the index. Generally not all of them are in the library.

A **bibliography,** too, can be a book by itself. Some bibliographies not only list books and other materials but tell something about them. Often a bibliography is on a particular subject.

A **directory** gives information about people, organizations, or institutions. Names and addresses are listed. A telephone book is a directory.

Of all the types of reference books, dictionaries and encyclopedias are probably the most used. They are also the first works to consult, as a rule. It's difficult to look up a subject that isn't spelled right or to find out about things that aren't clearly understood. Those are the problems a dictionary can help solve. An encyclopedia, too, can make things clearer. In trying to find out about a subject, the person who checks the encyclopedia first—even before the catalog—can get a fast focus on the big picture.

Even an encyclopedia is just the beginning. In each subject there are hundreds of special reference works such as handbooks, indexes, and bibliographies. Someone who wants to dig has to find out what the reference works in a particular subject have to offer. It's also important to check more than one reference work to compare different ways of looking at the same facts. (*See also* Reference Books.)

**Nonbooks: Magazines and Newspapers.** Because it takes time to put out a book, even a brand-new one is yesterday's facts. For many kinds of information—the height of a mountain, the spelling of a word—newness isn't too important. Such things aren't likely to change or change much for a long time. But for what's happening now, special kinds of materials are needed. These include magazines and newspapers.

A magazine comes out periodically—weekly, twice a month, monthly. So magazines are sometimes called

card for a magazine, won't help find articles on a certain subject. To locate such newspaper articles, 'The New York Times Index' is very useful. It's a key to other newspapers, too, because most of them have pretty much the same news on the same day. Like the 'Readers' Guide', 'The New York Times Index' comes in many volumes, each covering one year. To save space, many libraries keep back volumes of the *New York Times* and other newspapers on microfilm.

**'Readers' Guide': a Guide.** Anyone who can use the card catalog can learn to use 'Readers' Guide'. It is one of the easiest indexes to work with.

Authors and subjects of articles are listed in heavy type—**SPIRO, Howard M.; SPONGES; SPORTS;**

Large amounts of printed material can be photographically reduced for storage on microfilm. Microfilm is commonly seen as long strips of film wound on reels, with each frame of the film containing the image of at least one page of the material.

*periodicals*. Every six months or so, a library puts the back issues of some magazines together and has them bound in book covers. This is called a *volume*.

A card in the catalog tells the name of a magazine, which volumes are in the library, and so on. But if someone wants articles on a certain subject, the card won't help. For that kind of information, there are special indexes. Of these, probably the best known is the 'Readers' Guide to Periodical Literature', which indexes articles of about 150 magazines. Like those magazines, 'Readers' Guide' itself is a periodical. So it comes in volumes, each volume covering one or two years, with the dates printed on the spine.

The catalog card for a newspaper, like the catalog

**SPRAGUE, Marshall.** Under each author heading are listed articles by that author; under each subject heading, articles on that subject. Titles are in alphabetical order by first word. Some subjects are broken up into smaller and smaller subjects. **Manned flights** is a division of the subject **SPACE flight to the moon.** And *Apollo 17 flight* is a subdivision of **Manned flights.**

Sometimes a person is both a subject of articles and an author of other articles. Then articles by that person are listed first. And a subheading **about** is followed by articles about that person.

To use 'Readers' Guide', there are many abbreviations to figure out. The names of most magazines are abbreviated—*Pop Mech* for *Popular Mechanics*,

*Bsns W* for *Business Week,* and so forth. These are explained in front of each 'Guide'. So are the other abbreviations used. To understand a 'Readers' Guide' entry, a person has to learn its parts and the order of those parts. For instance, an entry on Mark Spitz, the Olympic swimmer, reads:

SPITZ, Mark
  All out to be number 1; with report by
   B. Bruns. il pors Life 63:47–8+ S15 '67

That translates into title of article ("All Out to Be Number One"), author (B. Bruns), illustrated article (il), with portrait photos (pors), name of magazine (*Life*), volume number (63), page numbers (47–48), continued on later pages (+), and date of issue

volumes or for John Dillinger in 1970's volumes. **Three** is to use the front of the *Guide* to clear up reading problems. **Four** is to copy entries that seem to do the job. That means title of article, author (if any), name of magazine, volume and page numbers, and date of issue. **Five,** of course, is to get hold of the actual magazines.

**More Nonbooks: Vertical File.** Every library has a place for clippings. Such things as newspaper articles on local people and places are worth cutting out and keeping. The same is true of special articles and pictures from magazines. Clippings are usually put in folders, alphabetically arranged by subject. The folders are kept in a deep-drawer cabinet called a

Microcard Editions, a division of Indian Head, Inc.

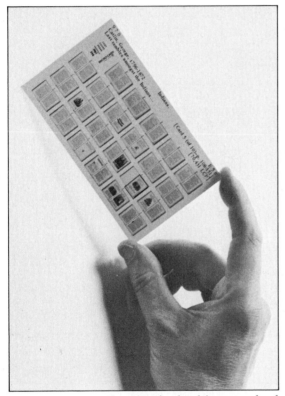

A Microcard is a positive print of reduced images produced from a microfilm negative. Because this reduction process uses opaque stock rather than transparent film, an array of images can be stored on both sides of the Microcard.

(September 15, 1967). It's important to keep in mind that the number before the colon is the volume number. Numbers after the colon are page numbers.

Some poems and stories are also indexed in 'Readers' Guide'. Poems are listed only under author, stories under author and title. Poems and stories in magazines can also be found with the help of such aids as 'Granger's Index to Poetry' and 'Short Story Index'.

There's a routine to 'Readers' Guide' that can save a lot of stumbling around. **One** is to find out what magazines are in the library. It's best to know beforehand which articles may take a while to get. **Two** is to get the right volumes of the *Guide*. There's not much point in looking for Elvis Presley in 1930's

*vertical file.* There are no catalog cards for individual clippings, but many catalogs have cross reference cards to the subjects in the file.

The vertical file has *pamphlets,* too. These are paperbound booklets, each often dealing with one subject. Like newspapers and magazines, many pamphlets give fast, up-to-date facts—on jobs, for instance—too new to be in books. Information that's hard to get elsewhere often comes in pamphlet form. Some libraries have special shelves or boxes for pamphlets, where they are arranged by subject. There are indexes for pamphlets as well as for magazines. *The Vertical File Index* is widely known. Also helpful is the *Monthly Catalog of United States Government Publications.*

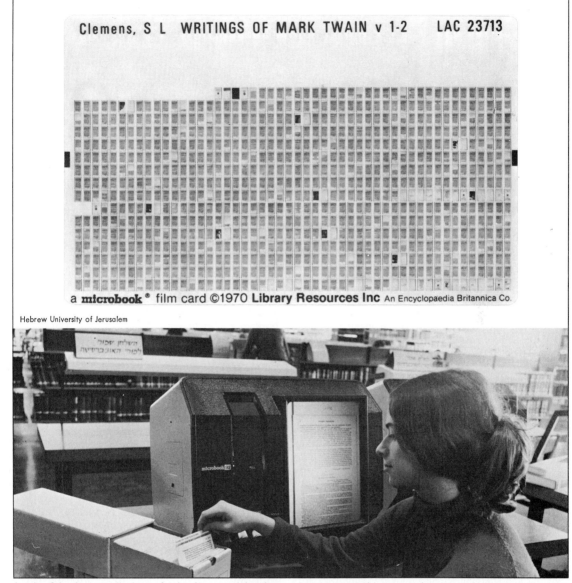

Clemens, S L  WRITINGS OF MARK TWAIN v 1-2   LAC 23713

a **microbook** ® film card ©1970 **Library Resources Inc** An Encyclopaedia Britannica Co.

Hebrew University of Jerusalem

A microfiche is a small sheet of microfilm containing from a few to many hundreds of negative or positive photographic images arranged in rows and columns. An entire book or even several books can be reproduced on a single microfiche.

A vertical file may also include maps, charts, graphs, posters, postcards, photos, and even sheet music. Some such items may be kept in a separate place—in a picture file or map file, for example.

**Nonbooks: Talking and Otherwise.** The what of a library is books, including paperbacks; magazines and newspapers; clippings and pamphlets and other vertical file material; and more, much more. Anything that's to learn with—and to dream with—is the stuff of libraries. There are records and sound tapes of music, poetry, language lessons; videotapes of neighborhood people and places, of amateur plays. For would-be artists and art lovers, color slides of buildings and paintings and sculpture are available. Films and filmstrips show the growth of a plant, the pollution of a stream, the agony of a violin lesson. Not even the best map shows relationships between places as well as a globe, so libraries have globes and other models. Specimens are sometimes arranged to show how a piece of tree becomes a pencil, or how crude oil is changed into gasoline.

Then there are mini-nonbooks: microfilm, Microcard, microfiche. These hold greatly reduced pictures of newspaper, magazine, and book pages that must be read with machines. The way records, films, and other nonbook materials are arranged varies from one library to another. Such materials may be listed in the main catalog or in separate catalogs near where they are kept.

223

A versatile and well-stocked library can offer its patrons many nonbook items, including motion picture films, filmstrips, photographs, color slides, phonograph records, and tape recordings.
Public Library of Cincinnati and Hamilton County, Ohio

## LIBRARY PEOPLE

Without people a library would be a mere place, a warehouse. Above all it is people using a library who make it come alive, but people are also needed to make a library work. Even the computerized memory cells of the future could not function without library people—the professionals called *librarians* and the many who help them.

### The Who of Library Service: Nonlibrarians

Most libraries are not run by librarians alone. If it were not for other library workers, in many places a person could not get a library card, find a clipping in the vertical file, use a microfilm reader, or take out a book.

On any given day, one person may return half a dozen books, a magazine or two, and several records to the library. Multiply that by several hundred or several thousand, and the result is a mountain of materials that must be sorted and put back in the right place. This is usually the work of a library *page*. Sorting and shelving are also done by temporary student employees, or *student assistants*. Pages have to be accurate—a book or magazine or record misplaced is as good as lost for days, weeks, or months.

*Library clerks* work out in front or behind the scenes. A clerk who deals with the public may help a youngster register for a library card, check materials in and out, collect overdue fines, help renew or reserve materials, or show someone how to operate a copying machine. A copying machine or charge-out machine can be mastered in a matter of minutes. What can't be mastered as easily is a pleasant attitude toward all people, springing from a desire to help them. Such an attitude is a must for all library people dealing with the public.

A clerk who prefers to work behind the scenes may file and keep records, check in new materials and get

them ready for use, type overdue notices in libraries where this isn't done by computer, operate a teletype, feed a computer the information needed to order a book or record or film. Both out-front and behind-the-scenes clerks need a high school diploma usually, or the ability to pass a civil service exam. All clerks work under the supervision of a librarian or library aide, and student assistants often do clerical work.

*Library aides* assist with many of the librarian's jobs. A library aide dealing with the public may help people find materials, answer easier reference questions, explain the library's services. Behind-the-scenes aides may operate audiovisual equipment, arrange displays, keep up the vertical file, look up prices and other information the librarian needs to order materials, supervise pages and clerks. For supervising others, aides must be tactful, firm, and able to follow the librarian's instructions as well as translate those instructions to others. A job as library aide requires at least a high school diploma, and many who do such work are *library technicians*, with two years of college. Aides who are college graduates are sometimes called *library associates*. Often they and library technicians do the more skilled types of library work.

Other library workers include audiovisual technicians to inspect and repair the audiovisual hardware of a library, book repairers to mend and rebind books and other materials, artists and photographers to prepare displays and public relations materials, and maintenance workers to keep library buildings in good condition. People with advanced training in related fields such as computer science and accounting also work in libraries.

### The Who of Library Service: Librarians

A librarian in a modern school may be called a *media specialist*. In a computerized business library, the librarian may be called an *information scientist*, or *documentalist*. There are children's librarians and young adult librarians in public libraries, institutional librarians in hospital and prison libraries, university librarians in university libraries. All librarians, whatever their work, have this in common: they are members of a profession in the service of mankind—like teachers, like doctors. Librarians also share knowledge and skills learned in college, in library school after college, and on the job.

**The Three Faces of Librarianship.** A librarian does three main kinds of work: selecting materials for the library, organizing them so that they'll be easy to find and use, and helping people get materials or information they need. To select materials, a librarian finds out what the library's users and potential users need. Rarely, if ever, can a library afford to buy all materials needed. So the librarian must be an expert not only on what materials are available but on which are more dependable, more useful to the library than others. To make room for new materials, the librarian regularly reviews the library collection, removing materials no longer useful. A good collection offers many points of view on any given subject. An important part of the librarian's job is to resist pressure from special groups who want to get rid of—or add—material because of the point of view.

If it weren't arranged, if it didn't have a catalog, a library would be a trackless jungle of information. That's where the organizer of materials comes in. This librarian examines every new book, record, film, or other item to determine what it's about. After the librarian decides what the subject is and how the item is related to other materials in the library, the item is *cataloged*, or described. Most libraries use card catalogs, but some modern libraries use a book catalog made and printed by computer.

Helping people get materials or information they need is circulation and reference work. The librarian in charge of circulation supervises the use of all materials. In many libraries, this librarian works behind the scenes. Clerks usually issue library cards, lend and receive materials, keep records of materials borrowed, even help people find materials they want. The way in which each such job is done is determined by the librarian in charge. Much circulation work is automated in libraries today—there are computerized systems to keep a record of materials lent and returned, for instance.

Nobody knows all the answers. The librarian in reference pursues a deeper wisdom—to understand all the questions. To learn what exactly the questioner is trying to find out, a reference librarian must be an expert interviewer. The whole point of reference work is personal assistance, either finding the answer or guiding a person to it. The same question may call for different types of help—for people of different ages and backgrounds, for example. Much reference work is done by phone.

**The Librarian as Specialist.** The three main kinds of library work are part of every librarian's education.

But, as in other professions, many librarians become specialists. An *acquisitions librarian* specializes in locating and ordering materials, a *cataloger* in organizing materials, a *reference librarian* in helping people get information. In many school and public libraries there are *media specialists* and *readers' advisers*. A media specialist is an expert on the use of all materials, both print and nonprint. A readers' adviser helps choose materials or prepares a special reading list for a particular person. Readers' advisers in hospital and prison libraries practice *bibliotherapy*, helping treat the sick, the disturbed, the downhearted with books and other materials.

Public librarians may specialize by age group of user. A children's librarian must know about such things as child behavior, what children study in school, nonprint materials and their uses, the teaching of reading, children's literature, and how to tell a story. Guiding children in their reading is an important part of the work. So are selecting materials, holding story hours, working with parents and Parent-Teacher Associations, visiting nearby classrooms, teaching the use of the library, and planning such special projects as Book Week.

A young adult librarian works with roughly the teenage group. Such a librarian must know what young adults are like, what they study in school, what they read and listen to and look at in their free time. It is especially important for a librarian working with this age group to be outgoing, unflappable, imaginative, and socially aware. The young adult librarian selects materials, keeping up with ever-changing teenage interests; acts as a readers' adviser; visits schools to talk about books and other materials; and explains how to use a library. An important part of work with young adults is planning programs for them.

The DIALOG information retrieval system of Lockheed Missiles and Space Company has thousands of references from material in the firm's technical library stored on computer tapes.

Lockheed Missiles and Space Co.

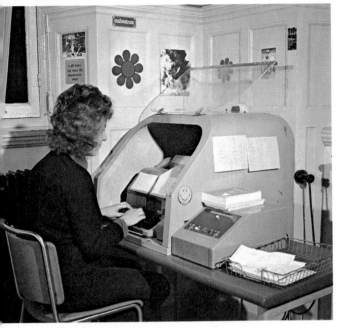

Librarians use Telex machines to receive and answer requests from other libraries for loans of library materials.

A public librarian may also specialize in the hard-to-reach, neglected, and unserved. These include school dropouts, the elderly, the uneducated, ghetto dwellers, the rural poor, and minorities. Many in such groups have reading problems and are reluctant or unable to come to a library. If there is one ingredient a librarian in such work needs above all, it is heart. To bring hope to the hopeless and a feeling of belonging to the outcast, professionalism is not enough. Also needed are initiative and imagination to draw such people to the library as well as to take the library to the people. A contagious enthusiasm for books is a must. So is a strong background in nonprint materials because they draw many people in such groups. The librarian should also know about the teaching of reading and the use of easy-to-read materials for adults.

Many academic and research librarians are subject or language specialists. Such librarians usually have special training in music, or African materials, or Spanish and Portuguese literature, or the sciences, or whatever. Subject specialists are found also in government libraries—*archivists* specializing in historical papers, librarians specializing in law.

There are many subject specialists in special libraries. The special librarian makes searches for information—helping an engineer gather materials for a report, preparing a reading list on water pollution for a steel company executive. Because engineers, doctors, and other specialists don't have time to read everything published in their field, the special librarian may review and summarize new articles and reports. Such summaries, or *abstracts*, keep busy people up to date and help them decide what to read

for more information. Another part of special library work is having important articles and reports translated. Information searches are made more and more with the help of computers. Some translation, too, is done by machine, but there are serious problems involved (*see* Language, section "The Trouble with Translation"). Because special librarians often make much use of other libraries, they must know not only their own but other library collections in their subjects. Special librarians often have advanced training in the field of concentration of their library. They should also have a background in library technology, automation being common in special libraries.

Many librarians do not specialize. They are *generalists*, working with a variety of groups and subjects. Included among generalists are most school librarians. School librarians work closely with teachers in helping students get the reading habit, learn study skills, and understand how to use a library. Besides an understanding of children or young adults, school librarians need a background in print and nonprint materials. In many places also, a school librarian must be qualified as a teacher. This is especially important as the school library becomes more and more a learning lab, an extension of the classroom.

**The Librarian as Information Scientist.** A librarian is a mover of ideas, of information from one mind to another. So it is not enough to know library science. A librarian must understand the bigger picture called *information science*, of which library science is only a part. To teach the use of a library, a librarian must understand how people think when they attack look-it-up problems. That's part of information science. To index a vertical file a librarian must understand how language works. That, too, is part of information science. A librarian often has to know something about computers to work with them. In addition he or she may need some math to use computer language. Both mathematics and computer technology are part of information science. To run a library, the librarian must learn techniques for analyzing and improving a system. Information science includes systems management, too.

Many librarians who work in automated libraries are called *information scientists*. But the term is not used by all such librarians. Basically every librarian must be an information scientist.

**The Librarian as People.** A librarian is not a little old lady with a built-in "Shhh. . . ." The libraries of the world have room enough—and work enough—for many types of people. There are reference jobs for the I-want-to-work-with-people type; jobs with the underprivileged for the I-want-to-improve-the-world type; jobs as catalogers and bibliographers for the I-want-to-do-research type. There are jobs for close-to-home and away-from-home types, for small-library and large-library types, for specialists and generalists, book addicts and nonbook addicts, teacher types, leader types. While librarians do not run to one type, though, they do have some things in common.

- **A librarian serves the people of a community**—a college, a school, a plastics company—either directly or indirectly.
- **A librarian is a matchmaker,** bringing people and knowledge together.
- **A librarian is sometimes the uninvited.** Not everyone who needs help asks for it, and being a "come-to" librarian isn't always enough.
- **A librarian is a bookeater.** Ideas come in many kinds of packages, most of them books, and a librarian has to know what's between the covers.
- **A librarian is curious.** He or she has not only an itch to know but an open mind that doesn't fear new ideas.
- **A librarian has a sense of order.** Everybody in a library has to know where things are and how to find them, quickly.

And that isn't all . . .

**Tips for Tomorrow's Librarian.** A library is not a place to get away from people, nor a sanctuary from the disagreements of the outside world. Even librarians behind the scenes must work with others. As for controversy, the librarian is where the action is, dealing with a continual flow of new ideas in the books and nonbooks that come to the library.

Anyone who wants to be a librarian must decide what type of work most interests him or her. As with any profession, it is necessary to plan ahead. A good general education is essential to someone who is going to guide and teach others. So are a good reading background and a knowledge of nonprint materials and automation. For specialist library work, training in that specialty is often required. An advanced degree is needed to teach in a library school or to run a large library. All librarians must have at least a college degree and library school beyond that.

Pamphlet material on library jobs and on scholarships is available in most libraries. Library school catalogs, found in large public and college libraries, tell what various schools have to offer. The schools listed on the following page meet certain requirements of the American Library Association. Many excellent schools in Canada, the United States, and elsewhere are not included in the list.

**Library Power: The Togetherness of Associations.** Librarians the world over work together in many associations to improve library service. Of these, the oldest and largest is the American Library Association, or ALA, founded in 1876 with the help of Melvil Dewey. Among the divisions of the ALA are associations for public librarians, school librarians, academic and research librarians. Most special librarians have their own associations—for medical librarians, law librarians, and so on.

The work of associations and other organizations friendly to libraries crosses national boundaries. The ALA has helped found library schools in several countries. It also works to improve library service in many parts of the world. So do agencies of various nations and of the United Nations (UNESCO, UNICEF). Private groups such as the Asia Foundation and Ford Foundation are also library builders, especially in Asia, Africa, and Latin America.

Just as libraries share with one another, so do the associations. The ALA and the Canadian Library Association (CLA), for instance, have worked closely together since the founding of the CLA in 1946. The International Federation of Library Associations, representing more than 50 countries, works at international library cooperation. So do international associations in particular fields—school library, medical library, and music library associations for instance.

### The Library in the Eye of Time

Libraries were born as collections of records—on animal bones and tortoise shells, clay tablets, papyrus and silk scrolls, or animal skins. Such collections go back some 4,500 to 6,000 years in Asia and Africa. Elsewhere, libraries developed much later.

Library science students learn to use the card catalog at the library of Makerere University in Kampala, Uganda. Trained librarians are instrumental in the efforts to decrease illiteracy in developing nations.

UNESCO

# SOME ALA-APPROVED SCHOOLS IN CANADA AND THE UNITED STATES

## Canada

School of Library Science, University of Alberta
Edmonton, Alta.

School of Librarianship, University of British Columbia
Vancouver, B.C.

School of Library Service, Dalhousie University
Halifax, N.S.

School of Library and Information Science, University of Western Ontario
London, Ont.

Faculty of Library Science, University of Toronto
Toronto, Ont.

Graduate School of Library Science, McGill University
Montreal, Que.

École de bibliothéconomie, Université de Montréal
(School of Librarianship, University of Montreal)
Montreal, Que.

## United States

School of Librarianship, University of California
Berkeley, Calif.

Graduate School of Library Service, University of California
Los Angeles, Calif.

School of Library Science, University of Southern California
Los Angeles, Calif.

Department of Librarianship, California State University
San Jose, Calif.

Graduate School of Librarianship, University of Denver
Denver, Colo.

Division of Library Science, Southern Connecticut State College
New Haven, Conn.

School of Library Science, Florida State University
Tallahassee, Fla.

School of Library Service, Atlanta University
Atlanta, Ga.

Graduate School of Library Studies, University of Hawaii
Honolulu, Hawaii

Department of Library Science, Northern Illinois University
DeKalb, Ill.

Graduate Library School, University of Chicago
Chicago, Ill.

Graduate School of Library Science, Rosary College
River Forest, Ill.

Graduate School of Library Science, University of Illinois
Urbana, Ill.

Graduate Library School, Indiana University
Bloomington, Ind.

School of Library Science, University of Iowa
Iowa City, Iowa

Department of Librarianship, Kansas State Teachers College
Emporia, Kan.

College of Library Science, University of Kentucky
Lexington, Ky.

School of Library Science, Louisiana State University
Baton Rouge, La.

School of Library and Information Services, University of Maryland
College Park, Md.

School of Library Science, Simmons College
Boston, Mass.

School of Library Science, University of Michigan
Ann Arbor, Mich.

Department of Library Science, Wayne State University
Detroit, Mich.

School of Librarianship, Western Michigan University
Kalamazoo, Mich.

Library School, University of Minnesota
Minneapolis, Minn.

School of Library and Informational Science, University of Missouri
Columbia, Mo.

Graduate School of Library Service, Rutgers University
New Brunswick, N.J.

School of Library and Information Science, State University of New York
Albany, N.Y.

Graduate School of Library and Information Science, Pratt Institute
Brooklyn, N.Y.

School of Information and Library Studies, State University of New York
Buffalo, N.Y.

Department of Library Science, Queens College, City University of New York
Flushing, N.Y.

School of Library and Information Science, State University of New York
Geneseo, N.Y.

Palmer Graduate Library School, Long Island University
Greenvale, N.Y.

School of Library Service, Columbia University
New York, N.Y.

School of Library Science, Syracuse University
Syracuse, N.Y.

School of Library Science, University of North Carolina
Chapel Hill, N.C.

School of Library Science, Case Western Reserve University
Cleveland, Ohio

School of Library Science, Kent State University
Kent, Ohio

School of Library Science, University of Oklahoma
Norman, Okla.

School of Librarianship, University of Oregon
Eugene, Ore.

Graduate School of Library and Information Science, University of Pittsburgh
Pittsburgh, Pa.

Graduate School of Library Science, Drexel University
Philadelphia, Pa.

Graduate Library School, University of Rhode Island
Kingston, R.I.

School of Library Science, George Peabody College for Teachers
Nashville, Tenn.

Graduate School of Library Science, University of Texas
Austin, Tex.

School of Library and Information Sciences, North Texas State University
Denton, Tex.

School of Library Science, Texas Woman's University
Denton, Tex.

Graduate Department of Library and Information Sciences, Brigham Young University
Provo, Utah

School of Librarianship, University of Washington
Seattle, Wash.

Graduate Department of Library Science, Catholic University of America
Washington, D.C.

Library School, University of Wisconsin
Madison, Wis.

## A World of Libraries: Yesterday

All libraries have their roots in ancient times. To understand the library of today, it is necessary to know something about the history of libraries.

**Bone Libraries and Others: Ancient Times.** The earliest known libraries were connected with palaces and temples. In China, records of the Shang dynasty (1767?–1123? B.C.) were written on animal bones and tortoise shells. An early library called "The Healing Place of the Soul," in the palace of Egypt's King Ramses II (1304?–1237 B.C.) at Thebes, consisted of thousands of papyrus scrolls. Among the most important libraries in the ancient Near East was the palace library of Ashurbanipal (668?–627? B.C.) at Nineveh in Assyria. This early type of national library, collected "for the sake of distant days," consisted of over 30,000 clay tablets. Early librarians were usually priests, teachers, or scholars. The first known Chinese librarian was the philosopher Lao Tse, who was appointed keeper of the royal historical records for the Chou rulers about 550 B.C.

Early types of public and academic libraries were founded in ancient Greece. Public libraries were opened in Athens perhaps as early as the sixth century B.C., but they weren't lending libraries. People who could read generally studied or copied scrolls in the library. A well-known Athenian library was that of the Lyceum, a kind of college founded by the philosopher Aristotle in 335 B.C. The most famous library built by the Greeks was attached to a kind of university called the Museum in Alexandria, Egypt. Scholars were encouraged to use and even borrow scrolls from the Museum Library, which had a vast collection.

A library located at Pergamum (near present-day Smyrna, Turkey) began using parchment instead of papyrus for its scrolls around 200 B.C. Parchment is made from thin layers of animal skin. Another animal-skin library was an important part of a Hebrew religious community founded at Qumran, Palestine, probably early in the first century B.C. This library contained the "Dead Sea Scrolls." In China, paper was invented about A.D. 100 and soon began to replace other book materials such as silk and bamboo.

Roman libraries were much like those of Greece. The most famous public library in the city of Rome was the Ulpian Library, founded in A.D. 114. It had separate sections for its Latin and Greek papyrus scrolls. The Romans were great builders of public libraries, establishing them throughout the empire. The Imperial Library, founded at Constantinople in the Eastern Roman Empire in about A.D. 330, attracted scholars from all over the world to its great collection. In early Roman libraries, scrolls were kept in pigeonholes or on shelves in the walls. Gradually papyrus scrolls were replaced by parchment sheets, folded and sewn in book form. These were kept in book chests.

None of the great libraries of ancient times survived. Some were destroyed in fires, some by volcanoes, others in wars and invasions. Many libraries simply died of neglect.

**Libraries for Saints and Scholars.** In ancient India, great libraries were built in the Buddhist monastery centers. Among the most famous was that of the Buddhist University of Nalanda, founded about A.D. 414 in what is today Bihar. Temple and pagoda libraries were common also in Buddhist monasteries in Asia.

Papyrus rolls lined the shelves of ancient Greek and Roman libraries. The Romans called the roll a *volumen*, from which the English word *volume* is derived. The great Museum Library at Alexandria, Egypt, held many thousands of these early books.

This earthenware statuette represents an oxcart used in China more than a thousand years ago to transport books. Imperial libraries, which originated as royal archives, were maintained by the emperors, many of whom were patrons of literature.

Christian monasteries were founded in Egypt, Palestine, and nearby areas during the second and third centuries A.D. But it was not until after the fall of the Roman Empire in A.D. 476 that monastery libraries became vitally important in the West. A famous monastery library was founded in about 550 by Flavius Cassiodorus, a Roman politician, on his family estate in Calabria, Italy. In Cassiodorus' Vivarium monastery was a *scriptorium*, where books were carefully copied by hand. Copying of books was also part of the routine in the Italian monastery at Monte Cassino, which was founded in 529 by St. Benedict. The scriptorium idea took hold in monastery libraries from Greece to Iceland, helping preserve the knowledge of the past in Europe throughout the Dark Ages. Other notable monastery libraries included those at St. Gallen in Switzerland, Corbie in France, and Fulda in Germany. The typical monastery library contained a small number of books kept in one or two book chests in or near the scriptorium. Most books were of parchment. There was some interlibrary loan, books being lent for copying as well as reading.

The cathedrals of Europe were also religious schools. Because their libraries were meant for educational reading, they commonly contained more books of a nonreligious nature than did the monastic libraries. Also, books were generally more plentiful in cathedral libraries. Reading desks with shelves replaced book chests in later cathedral libraries, with reference-type books often chained to the desks. To make information easier to find, libraries had devices such as bookwheels, which rotated so that the reader could refer to as many as a dozen books without changing position. Better known cathedral libraries were at Canterbury and York in England, Notre Dame and Rouen in France, Bamberg and Hildesheim in Germany, Toledo and Barcelona in Spain.

The early Moslems and Byzantines built many university and public-type libraries. Shortly after he became Caliph of Baghdad in 813, al-Mamun founded the "House of Wisdom," a great university. Its library was open to scholars from all over the Moslem world. A famous library was that of the University of Constantinople, opened by the Byzantines in about 850. One of the best academic libraries in Africa today is that of al-Azhar University, founded in Cairo, Egypt, in about 970. University and public-type libraries were scattered throughout the Moslem world—from North Africa to Central Asia, as well as in Moslem Sicily and Spain.

Books in Moslem libraries covered all subjects. Sometimes books on different subjects were located in different rooms, with a subject specialist in charge of each room. Students and scholars were generally encouraged to use and borrow books. In many public libraries, there were not only rooms for reading but for meetings and debates. Most of the early Moslem libraries were eventually destroyed through natural disasters, war, and neglect.

China, too, had early academic libraries. From Sung dynasty times (960–1279) on, libraries of the Imperial Academy and provincial colleges were open to all students. However, in Europe the earliest universities had no libraries at first.

**Great Libraries Take Shape.** From the 1200's on, some of today's great academic libraries began to take shape in Europe. France's University of Paris had a library by about 1250, when Robert de Sorbon gave them a collection of books. In England libraries were established at Pembroke College, Cambridge University in 1347 and at Merton College, Oxford University in 1377. The University of Prague (now Charles University) started a library in 1348, which eventually became the core of the national library of Czechoslovakia. In 1365 the University of Vienna began its library. The oldest library in Poland, that of the University of Cracow, dates from before 1400, as does the University of Coimbra library in Portugal. Other early universities that had some

sort of library by the 1400's included those at Bologna and Florence in Italy, Salamanca in Spain, Heidelberg and Cologne in Germany, Basel in Switzerland, and Copenhagen in Denmark.

Some of the world's outstanding research libraries started in the 1400's. The private family library begun by Cosimo de'Medici (1389–1464) and expanded by his grandson Lorenzo later became the Laurentian Library in Florence, Italy. A former librarian to Cosimo de'Medici, Pope Nicholas V began to build up the Vatican Library in Vatican City about 1450. It is a world-famous research library today. In Istanbul, Turkey, the Topkapi Museum library contains Islamic manuscripts collected by sultans, generals, and officials of the Turkish empire since 1452.

Many of today's national libraries began in the 1400's and 1500's. The Marcian national library in Venice, one of Italy's many national libraries, originated with the gift of a book collection to that city in 1468 by Johannes Cardinal Bessarion. The history of France's National Library in Paris dates back largely to the late 1400's, when it was the royal library of Louis XI, a continuation of an even earlier royal library founded by Charles V. Another royal library of the late 1400's, that of England's Henry VII, developed into the British Museum in London, one of the world's largest libraries. The origins of the Austrian national library in Vienna lie well before 1526, when it was the royal library of the Hapsburgs. Sweden's

Arabs founded great libraries throughout the Islamic world—such as those at Baghdad (now in Iraq), at Cairo, Egypt, and at Córdoba, Spain. This drawing from a 13th-century miniature depicts an Arab library in about A.D. 1000.

The Bettmann Archive

During the Middle Ages, monasteries and cathedrals were the guardians of classical learning, and many had large libraries.

Monastic scribes copied ancient manuscripts in a room called a "scriptorium" (above).

The Laurentian Library (below) in Florence, Italy, was founded by the Medici family during the Renaissance. The most fre-

quently used books and the valuable illuminated manuscripts were often chained to the shelves for safekeeping.

232

national library, the Royal Swedish Library in Stockholm, began as a collection of books brought together by the first Protestant king, Gustavus Vasa (1523–60).

After 1500 there were more and larger university libraries in Europe. Printing had come to Europe by about 1450, making large numbers of cheaper books available. In addition, as monasteries were closed in many places, the books and manuscripts often ended up in university libraries. One of Spain's great libraries, at the University of Madrid, began in the 1500's. So did those at the universities of Wittenberg and Leipzig in Germany, Graz in Austria, Wroclaw in Poland, Vilna in Lithuania, and Ljubljana in what is today Yugoslavia. In the 1500's also, academic libraries began to appear in Latin America. A library was established at the University of Santo Domingo in the Dominican Republic in 1538. Among the famous libraries of Latin America are those at the University of San Marcos in Lima, Peru, and the National Autonomous University of Mexico in Mexico City, both founded in the late 1500's. The University of Mexico library later became the National Library.

The year 1558 marks the beginning of one of Germany's great libraries—the Bavarian State Library in Munich. One of the great history libraries of Spain, the Escorial Library near Madrid, dates back to 1575. The University of Leiden in the Netherlands, with a small library, was founded in 1575. The Bodleian Library at Oxford University originated in about 1598 when Sir Thomas Bodley began to rebuild an Oxford library that had been largely destroyed. In Dublin, Ireland, the library of Trinity College began as a gift of books by the English army that defeated the Irish in the Battle of Kinsale (1601).

One of the many great libraries of Italy, the Ambrosian Library in Milan, was founded in 1609. Libraries were established at Córdoba National University in Argentina (about 1614) and at the University of Uppsala in Sweden (1620). Hungary's largest academic library, that of Eötvös Loránd University in Budapest, dates back to 1635. The first academic libraries in North America were those of the Jesuit College of Quebec (1635) and Harvard University in Massachusetts (1638). The Harvard library started with books and money donated by John Harvard, a Massachusetts clergyman. In gratitude the university was named after him, and the name of the city was changed from Newtowne to Cambridge because he had graduated from Cambridge University in England. Finland's national library, at Helsinki University, had its beginnings in Åbo (now Turku) in 1640. After a fire destroyed much of it, the library was moved to Helsinki and rebuilt there along with the new university. In Paris, France, a cardinals' college library was founded by Jules Cardinal Mazarin in 1643—the Mazarin Library. One of its librarians, Gabriel Naudé, worked out a system of running a library that is still used today.

Three important national libraries were formed in the late 1600's. Frederick III, who ruled Denmark from 1648 to 1670, acquired the collection that was to

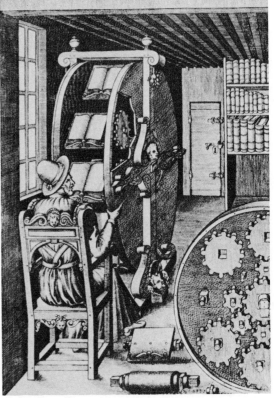

Newberry Library, Chicago

The book-wheel, a device somewhat resembling a waterwheel, was used to make several books readily available at one time. A reader turning the book-wheel could consult several volumes arranged on its shelves without ever having to leave his seat. Book-wheels began to be used in European cathedral and monastic libraries during the late Middle Ages.

Newberry Library, Chicago

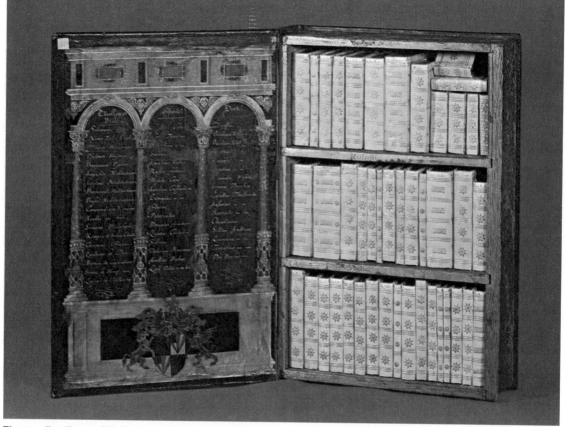

The traveling library of Sir Thomas Egerton, lord chancellor of England under King James I, was composed of miniature books on history, theology, and poetry. The Egerton family collection was one of the great private libraries of Europe.

become the Danish Royal Library in Copenhagen. The German State Library of East Berlin dates from 1661, where it began as the private library of Frederick William, ruler of Brandenburg. Later it was known as the Prussian State Library. When Germany was divided after World War II, part of the collection remained in East Berlin and part was moved to West Berlin and the University of Marburg. In Edinburgh the Advocates' Library was formed in 1682 as the private library of Scottish lawyers. It became the National Library in 1925.

**The Idea of a Public Library: Early Types.** The idea of a public library goes at least as far back as ancient Greece and Rome. There citizens able to read could study or copy the books in the library. Such libraries were also common throughout the Muslim world from about the 1200's. In Europe early types of public libraries began to appear from the 1400's on, as more and more people learned to read.

**Community or town libraries** were opened in such places as London, England (1423); Lyons, France (about 1530); Edinburgh, Scotland (1580); Antwerp, Belgium (about 1609); Boston, Massachusetts (about 1656); and Frankfurt-am-Main, Germany (1668). Generally such libraries did not *circulate*, or lend, books, and they were open for a few hours only.

Collections were often poorly arranged, and books were so scholarly or dull that few people used them. Frequently the person in charge was a "bookkeeper," neither experienced nor interested in library work.

**Parochial or parish libraries** for public use began to appear in the late 1600's. Many of them were founded by an Englishman, Reverend Thomas Bray of the Society for the Propagation of the Gospel in Foreign Parts. Collections of books—mostly of a religious nature—were put into parish churches. A Bray library was opened as early as 1698 in New York City. Churches in various places soon followed the example of the Bray libraries.

**Rental and subscription libraries** charged fees for the use of books. *Rental libraries*—in bookshops or peddlers' packs, on boats or carts or wagons—were known in many parts of the world. For small fees, people could read books they couldn't afford to buy— everything from religious books to joke books.

*Subscription libraries* were formed by groups of readers, usually well-to-do. These people paid dues that were used to buy books, rent a reading room, and perhaps hire a keeper of the books. In return for dues paid, members could use the reading room and borrow books from the collection. Perhaps the earliest subscription library was the Library Company of Phila-

The Bodleian Library at Oxford University in England (above) was dedicated in 1602 by Sir Thomas Bodley to replace a library destroyed by royal purges during the Reformation.

In the painting below, the poet Robert Burns stands at the door of James Sibbald's Circulating Library in Edinburgh, Scotland. The novelist Sir Walter Scott as a youth is at the right.

In about 1900, some public libraries in the United States began to provide rooms or corners with collections of juvenile litera- ture. In the 1920 photograph above, children in a Queens, N.Y., library are learning library rules.

As public libraries improved around the turn of the 20th century, many urban libraries extended their services to outlying areas. This early book wagon was used by the Evanston Public Library of Evanston, Ill.

delphia, Pa., founded by Benjamin Franklin in 1731. Canada's first such library, established in Quebec in 1780 by Governor Frederick Haldemand, stocked books in both French and English. The National Library of Singapore began as a subscription library. Subscription libraries went by many names—atheneums, lyceums, and others. The *social libraries* of the 1700's were a type of subscription library.

**Mercantile libraries and mechanics' institutes,** for office and shop workers, also charged small fees. They began as self-improvement libraries. One of the first mechanics' institutes was the Birmingham Artisans' Library in England (1795). Early mechanics' institutes were opened in the United States at Bristol, Conn. (1818), and in Canada at St. John's, Newfoundland (1827). A mechanics' institute in Toronto, Ont., later became the Toronto Public Library, and the Auckland Public Library in New Zealand owes its origin to an early mechanics' institute founded there. An early mercantile library was the Mercantile library in Philadelphia (1821).

Early **school district libraries,** in spite of the name, were a type of public library. The collections, usually kept in schools, were meant largely for adults. Libraries of this type were established in such places as France, Canada, and the United States from about the 1830's on. Later, school district libraries were planned more for students.

**YMCA libraries** began to appear in Canada and the United States in 1851, when the Young Men's Christian Association was founded. Open to the public even on Sunday's, YMCA reading rooms contained newspapers, magazines, and books. But the religious nature of such libraries tended to limit the number of users.

In the late 1800's **railroad libraries** appeared. They included popular books for the use of railroad employees as well as passengers. Beginning in 1881, employees of the Baltimore and Ohio Railroad could borrow books from its library in Baltimore, Md. The Atchison, Topeka and Sante Fe Railway had a passenger library on every long-distance train.

**Great Libraries Multiply.** Most of today's national libraries trace their beginnings to the 1700's and 1800's. But great libraries of other types developed during that time also.

Yale University in New Haven, Conn., was started by 11 ministers, each of whom brought a few books for a library. At the urging of Father Pedro Robinet of the Society of Jesus, King Philip V opened the Royal Library in Madrid in 1712. It is Spain's National Library today. One of the Soviet Union's great science libraries, that of the Academy of Science in Leningrad, was founded in 1714. At the University of Göttingen in Germany (1737), librarian Christian Heine began to build a great collection.

What is now the Princeton University library began at the College of New Jersey about 1750, as did the library of the University of Pennsylvania (then an academy) in Philadelphia. The Soviet Union's oldest university library, at the Moscow State University, was founded in 1755. At about the same time King's College (now Columbia University) opened its library in New York City. Dartmouth College in New Hampshire was chartered as a college in 1769, but its library began several years earlier as a collection of books gathered together by the school founder, Eleazar Weelock.

The children's story hour and cinema show has always been a popular activity at the Baroda Central Library in Baroda, India. The establishment of this library in the early 1900's spearheaded a public library movement throughout India.

Newberry Library, Chicago

A librarian at the Kenya Children's Library in Nairobi, Kenya, helps young patrons check out their favorite books.

the Two Sicilies, in 1782. In 1786 Italy's National Braidense Library in Milan opened. A library was begun at Central University in Quito, Ecuador, in 1787. Portugal's National Library in Lisbon was founded in 1796; that of the Netherlands—the Royal Library in The Hague—in 1798.

One of the world's largest libraries, the Library of Congress in the United States, started in 1800 when the government moved to the new city of Washington, D.C. Hungary's National Széchenyi Library in Budapest goes back to 1802, when Count Ferenc Széchenyi gave about 10,000 books to the nation for public use. National libraries were founded in Buenos Aires, Argentina (1810); Rio de Janeiro, Brazil (1810); and Santiago, Chile (1813). The University of Oslo library, established in 1811, now serves as Norway's national library. In 1815 the Library of Parliament in Ottawa, Ont., began to serve the legislatures of Upper and Lower Canada. Peru's National Library in Lima dates from 1821. In 1828 newly independent Greece opened a national library at Aegina, the capital. Both capital and library were later transferred to Athens. When McGill University in Montreal, Que., opened in 1829, a library had been established.

The National Library of Medicine in Bethesda, Md.—one of the great medical libraries of the world— began in 1836 as the library of the Surgeon General's Office. Belgium's national library in Brussels, the Albert I Royal Library, was created in 1837. One of the world's great technology libraries, the Technological Institute in Delft, Netherlands, started in 1842.

The collection of the library of Seoul National University in Korea dates back to 1776, when it was the Chang-Duk Palace Library. In 1778 the Museum Library in Djakarta began its collection of Indonesian culture. Sicily's National Library in Palermo was opened as the Royal Library by Ferdinand I, King of

The National Library of Singapore uses a bookmobile to provide service to children in rural areas. About half the library's holdings are in English—but the collection also includes works in the Chinese, Malay, and Tamil languages.

The National Museum Library in Colombo, Ceylon, was organized in 1845 as the library of the Royal Asiatic Society (Ceylon branch). Later it was combined with the Government Oriental Library to form a national library. In 1856 the General Assembly Library in Wellington, N.Z., was founded.

From the late 1800's important libraries began to appear more often in Asia and Africa. Libraries were founded at the universities of Bombay, Calcutta, and Madras, all in India, in 1857. In Africa the University of Liberia started a library in Monrovia in 1862. The Egyptian National Library in Cairo began as the Khedival Library in 1870. In 1872 the Emperor of Japan opened the Imperial Library in Tokyo. It was to become the National Diet Library, somewhat like the Library of Congress or Canada's Library of Parliament. A library was begun in 1880 at the University of Algiers, Algeria. The National Library in Saigon, South Vietnam, was founded in 1882, as was the library of the University of the Punjab in Lahore, Pakistan.

In 1887 the Newberry Library in Chicago, Ill., opened its doors to scholars. It is one of the great private research libraries. That same year marks the beginning of the State Library in Pretoria, South Africa, and the library of the University of Tokyo in Japan. The following year the National Library for the Blind opened in London, England. In Illinois the University of Chicago began with a considerable library in 1892. Jewish National and University Library in Jerusalem owes its origin to that city's B'nai B'rith Lodge library, started in 1892. Kyoto University in Japan founded a library in 1899.

**The Time of the Public Library.** The time of the modern public library, of the free lending library open to all, varied from place to place. There were few such libraries until the late 1800's. But before that, the idea of opening free libraries to the public—even if they didn't lend books—was spreading.

Antonio Magliabechi was a librarian and book lover who worked, ate, and slept among his books. In 1714 he died in Florence, leaving his collection to the people of the city. The Magliabechiana Library, opened in 1747, later became the National Central Library. In 1748 the Zaluski Library opened in Warsaw. It was given to the public by two bishops, Joseph and his brother Andrew Zaluski. It is today the National Library of Poland. From the mid-1700's, reference libraries were open to the public in many places in Japan. In China in 1783, Emperor Ch'ien-lung ordered six copies made of every important work in the imperial Four Treasures Library. Three of these duplicate libraries were opened for public study in other cities.

In St. Petersburg (now Leningrad), the Imperial Russian library opened in 1811. Later renamed for Russian writer Mikhail Evgrafovich Saltykov (Shchedrin), the Saltykov-Shchedrin Library is one of the U.S.S.R.'s largest. In what is today Czechoslovakia, a public reference library opened in Zlonice, Bohemia, in 1817. The South African Public Li-

Harrison Forman

**Future attorneys examine reams of court decisions at a law library in India.**

brary opened—but not to black people—in 1818. It is today one of South Africa's national libraries, the State Library in Pretoria being the other.

In Grossenhain, Germany, a library began lending books to the general public in 1828. It was one of the first. A public library was established in Bucharest, Rumania, in 1831. In 1833 one of the first public libraries in the United States opened at Peterborough, N.H. India's National Library in Calcutta began life as the Calcutta Public Library in 1836. The Red River Library was formed in Manitoba in 1847.

**At the university library in Samarkand, U.S.S.R., Uzbek students cram for examinations.**

Harrison Forman

Rich oriental carpets provide a magical setting for fairy tales at the Children's House of Books in Tashkent, U.S.S.R. Special children's libraries are a feature of the modern Soviet public library system.

In 1852 the Manchester Free Library began to lend books in England. Its first librarian, Edward Edwards, was a founding father of public libraries in his country. Dickson Public Library in Göteborg, Sweden, opened its doors in 1861.

At his death, Russian Count N. P. Rumyantsev left his collection of books in St. Petersburg for public use. Transferred to Moscow, it opened as the Moscow Public and Rumyantsev Museum Library in 1862.

Today it is the Lenin library, one of the largest in the Soviet Union. The people of Mexico City got their first public library in 1869. Many public libraries were established in Argentina after 1870, when President Domingo F. Sarmiento pushed through a law to found them throughout the country. In 1872 the Imperial Library was set up for the public in Tokyo, Japan. Some of the reading clubs started in Bulgaria about 1860 grew into public libraries after indepen-

The Oblast Library in Mogilev, U.S.S.R., provides music enthusiasts with a listening room and a fine literature-of-music collection. Many people attend evenings of music organized at the library.

dence from the Turks in 1878. Puerto Rico's Municipal Library in San Juan opened in 1880. The following year an American millionaire, Andrew Carnegie, offered a public library to Allegheny City (now part of Pittsburgh), Pa., where many of his steelworkers lived. It was the first of more than 2,500 public libraries he was to build in the United States and Canada.

In 1883 the Public Library in Tunis was founded. It is the Tunisian National Library today. Vienna, Austria, had its first free public library in 1887. That same year a free city library was established in Frederiksberg, Denmark. Alexandria Municipal Library opened in Egypt in 1892. In 1898 the Deichmann Library in Oslo, Norway, turned public. It had first been organized as a privately financed free library in 1780. In what is today the Netherlands, a public library opened in Dordrecht in 1899.

In many places free lending libraries open to all were not available until the twentieth century. Not until 1905 did China have such a library, the first one being in Hunan province. Malaysia's first public library, a Carnegie library, opened at Kota Bharu, Malaya, in 1938. Thailand had no public library until 1950. Black people in such places as the Congo (now Zaire) and the United States could not use all public libraries until the 1950's and 1960's. Despite blank spots and blemishes, the public library really came of age in the 1900's. Modern libraries were formed in more places, and library services were extended to all people wherever they were located.

**National and University Libraries: the 1900's.** Many national libraries formed in the 1900's were in Asia and Africa. The Philippines acquired a national library in Manila in 1901. Four years later King Chulalongkorn of Thailand formed the Vajiranana National Library out of three older collections in Bangkok. The National Library of Peking, by far the largest in Asia, opened in 1909. Another national library of China, the National Central Library, was later founded in Nanking. Part of it was taken by the Nationalist Chinese to Taipei, where it became Taiwan's national library. In 1923 national libraries were established in Phnom Penh, Cambodia, and Seoul, Korea. Korea's National Central Library was later augmented by the National Assembly Library, also located in Seoul. Liaquat Memorial Library in Karachi (1951) later became Pakistan's national library. The National Library of Burma (1952) was built upon the holdings of Rangoon's Bernard Free Library. National libraries were also begun by Iraq (Baghdad, 1963) and Malaysia (Kuala Lumpur, 1971).

In Africa national libraries opened in Rabat, Morocco (1920), and Addis Ababa, Ethiopia (1944). The French Institute of Black Africa libraries, begun by the French in 1946, later became national libraries in Yaoundé, Cameroon, and Lomé, Togo. Nigeria, the Malagasy Republic, and Ivory Coast set up national libraries in the 1960's in Lagos, Tananarive, and Abidjan respectively.

In Australia the National Library grew out of the Commonwealth Parliament Library, founded in Can-

Harrison Forman

A researcher gleans information from the newspaper collection at the library of the University of Warsaw in Poland.

Organization of American States

This youth at a library in São Paulo, Brazil, is fascinated by a coin-operated record player.

Internationale Jugendbibliothek, Munich

Youngsters enjoy browsing among displays of new books at the International Youth Library in Munich, West Germany.

241

A magnificent interior graces the Library of Parliament in Ottawa, Canada. The library, founded in 1815, is open to scholars as well as lawmakers. Most of its books were destroyed in a fire in 1855, but the collection was replaced.

berra in 1902. The world's greatest collection of Welsh materials started as the National Library of Wales in Aberystwyth in the 1900's. A country of many great libraries, Canada did not formally open a national library until 1953 in Ottawa, Ont. New Zealand's National Library, established in 1966 in Wellington, includes its General Assembly Library and the Alexander Turnbull Library, a great research library dating back to 1918.

In many places the greatest growth in university libraries occurred in the 1900's. Not only did already established libraries grow larger, but many new libraries were built, especially after World War II. Thailand's most outstanding academic library is that of Chulalongkorn University in Bangkok (1917). The approximately 40 libraries of National Taiwan University in Taipei date back to 1928, when the university was founded as Taihoku Imperial University by the Japanese. In Korea the great library of Seoul National University opened in 1946. Nanyang University in Singapore was founded in 1953, the University of Singapore in 1959. Each began with a library.

Notable northern African university libraries opened in the 1900's include those of Alexandria University in Egypt (1942) and the University of Khartoum in Sudan (1945). Among the largest and best libraries in central Africa are those of the University of Ghana in Legon (1948), the University of

Ibadan in Nigeria (1948), the University of Dakar in Senegal (1952), and National University in Kinshasa, Zaire, founded in 1954 as Lovanium University. A library at Ethiopia's Haile Selassie I University dates from 1950. The University of East Africa (1961) in 1970 became three independent universities, each with its own library—National University in Nairobi, Kenya; the University of Dar es Salaam in Tanzania; and Makerere University in Kampala, Uganda.

Even in countries rich in academic libraries, the 1900's were a period of great growth—especially the post-World War II period. Canada's University of Alberta and University of British Columbia libraries were formed in the early 1900's. So were the libraries of the University of Hawaii and the University of Alaska. When Czechoslovakia became independent in 1919, Comenius University in Bratislava and Purkyne University in Brno were founded, both with libraries. In the Soviet Union, Lenin established university libraries as early as 1920, including those at Tashkent State University and Urals State University in Sverdlovsk. Many eastern European university libraries such as those of the University of Lodz in Poland and the University of Sarajevo in Yugoslavia date from the 1940's. By World War I, many older university libraries were so large that they began to break up into separate libraries. There was a reverse trend after World War II toward combining the separate collections. From the 1950's on, numerous new university libraries were formed in many parts of the world.

**The Time of the Special Library.** There have been special libraries since earliest times. Shang dynasty historical records, or *archives*, made up a special library. So did medical collections of ancient Egyptian medical schools; business documents of Babylonian and Assyrian trading houses; sacred writings of early temples, pagodas, churches, and mosques. But it was not until the 1800's and especially the 1900's that the great growth in special library services took place. The Special Library Association in the United States was founded in 1909; the Association of Special Libraries and Information Bureaus (ASLIB) in England, in 1924.

Some modern special libraries date back to before 1900. The Lincoln's Inn library in London, England, for instance, was founded in 1497. It is one of the world's most famous law libraries. The Gazi Husrev Beg Library in Sarajevo, Yugoslavia, was begun under Turkish rule in 1537. It concentrates on the history and culture of the Balkans and Near East. In Antwerp, Belgium, the Plantin-Moretus Museum library specializes in, among other things, the early history of printing. It was established in 1640. Czechoslovakia's State Technical Library in Prague grew out of an engineering school library started in 1707. France's Arsenel Library in Paris, a great French literature library, was formed in the 1700's. So were the Royal Horticultural Library in Copenhagen, Denmark; the Library of the Academy of History in Madrid, Spain; the Library of the Society for the Literature of the Netherlands in Leiden; and the Library of the Royal Academy of Sciences in Stockholm, Sweden.

Toronto, Canada, Public Library

**Avid listeners enjoy a storytelling festival at the Toronto Public Library, the largest of Canada's public libraries.**

An important technical library, the Polish Society of Friends of Science Library in Warsaw, was opened in 1802. The Boston Athenaeum Library, a history collection, began as a subscription library in 1807. In the early 1800's, special libraries started to appear in public institutions—prisons, reformatories, mental hospitals. Early prison libraries were established in the State Penitentiary at Philadelphia, Pa., in 1829; at Sing Sing Prison in Ossining, N.Y., about 1840. The New York State Lunatic Asylum in Utica had a library in 1875. In London special library service took a leap forward with the founding of the National Library for the Blind in 1888.

**Players contemplate their opening moves during a chess tournament at a branch of the Chicago Public Library, Chicago, Ill.**
Art Shay—Chicago Public Library

Public Library of Cincinnati and Hamilton County, Ohio

Teachers often look to libraries in search of audiovisual materials for use in their classrooms. Two young teachers, above, listen to recordings in front of a background mural depicting the families of musical instruments. Another teacher, below, selects slides with the aid of a modern viewer.

Public Library of Cincinnati and Hamilton County, Ohio

Important special libraries formed in the first part of the 19th century include the Royal Conservatory of Music library in Brussels, Belgium (1832); the Royal Portuguese Reading Room in Rio de Janeiro, Brazil, which specializes in the history and literature of Brazil and Portugal (1837); and Advocates Library in Montreal, Que., a law library. The National Agricultural Library in Washington, D.C., one of the largest of its kind in the world, started as the library of the Department of Agriculture in 1862. In 1888 two outstanding Latin American libraries were founded—the Library of the National Academy of History in Caracas, Venezuela, concentrating on the history of Latin America, and the Pedagogic Museum and Library in Montevideo, Uruguay, for the use of teachers. The John Rylands Library, a great private research library in history and literature, opened in Manchester, England, in 1899. That same year, King Chulalongkorn founded the Siriraj Medical Library in Bangkok. It is one of Thailand's finest.

Important private research libraries opened in the first half of the 20th century include the Mitchell Library in Sydney, Australia (1910); the Alexander Turnbull Library in Wellington, N.Z., now part of the National Library of New Zealand (1918); the Henry E. Huntington Library in San Marino, Calif., with collections chiefly in English and American literature and history (1919); the Gennadius Library in Athens, Greece, devoted to materials on Greece and the Greeks (1926); and the Folger Shakespeare Library in Washington, D.C., which concentrates on Shakespeare and his times (1932). From the 1920's, the Soviet Union developed strong special libraries of many types. Trade union libraries, for instance, which served both as technical libraries on trade union history and popular reading collections for workers, were built under the direction of the Gorki Reference Library of the All-Union Central Council of Trade Unions in Moscow.

Beginning in the 1920s, library services for children were expanded in many places. Boys and Girls House in Toronto, Ont. (1922), was the first library building in North America specifically for young people. An outstanding example of services to youth in Latin America was the Children's Library in São Paulo, Brazil, founded in 1935. The International Youth Library in Munich, West Germany, opened in 1949, offers services to the young and encourages the publication of juvenile literature all over the world.

An important industrial library formed in the 1920's was that of the Rubber Research Institute in Kuala Lumpur, Malaysia. It is one of the world's most comprehensive sources of information on the growing of rubber. The National Science Library in Ottawa, Ont., founded in 1927, is the heart of Canada's national scientific and technical information network.

A great number of special libraries have been formed especially since the 1940's. Business libraries, such as those of banking and insurance companies, came into widespread use. Industries of all kinds found company libraries essential, as did magazines, professional societies, educational associations, and labor organizations. Hospital, prison, and other institutional libraries came into their own. The demands of industrial and scientific research led to the establishment of research and documentation centers, often with highly automated ways of storing, retrieving, and duplicating information. India set up its Indian National Scientific Documentation Center in 1952. It supplies photocopies of scientific material from India and abroad, has a translation service, and makes up bibliographies. Special library services are offered by the Brazilian Institute of Bibliography and Documentation, set up in Rio de Janeiro in 1954. Foremost among special libraries in the Arab world is the

National Information and Documentation Center in Cairo, Egypt, opened in 1955. Similar special library service was begun by the Pakistan National Scientific and Technical Documentation Center in 1955, the Japan Information Center of Science and Technology in 1957, the Korean Scientific and Technical Information Center in 1962, and the Iranian Documentation Center in 1968.

## The Libraries of Canada and the United States

Canada and the United States provide among the best library services in the world. School and public libraries are within the reach of most people. For those living in remote areas, there are bookmobiles,

These high school students are using a library of lessons recorded on computer tapes. Each student can study at his own speed, playing and replaying his selections. Students can also record their own comments, questions, and answers.

Ampex Corp.

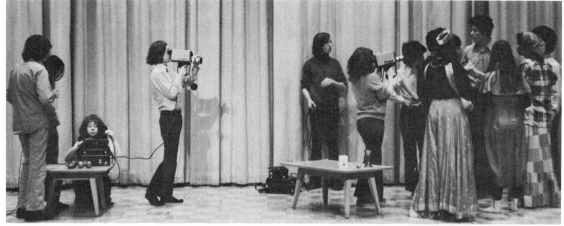

©Film Library Quarterly

Teenage drama students learn the technical aspects of their craft as they videotape their dress rehearsal at a New York Public Library sound stage. This facility is an example of the varied services offered by today's library system.

books by mail, and other types of extension services. State and provincial libraries also provide services for all the people living in a particular region. They plan statewide or province-wide library programs, serve as interlibrary loan headquarters, supply public and school libraries with expensive and little-used materials, and set up regional centers to more easily reach all with materials and services.

State and provincial libraries also act as special libraries, serving the government as well as the public. Not only is such a library a general information center for officials; it also includes special libraries— a law library for judges and lawmakers, a medical library for health officials, a technology library for highway and mining officials.

Every department of the two governments has its own library. Some of these also provide national and international services. The Library of Parliament in Ottawa, Ont., serves the needs of scholars as well as Canadian lawmakers. The National Science Library and the National Archives are also in Ottawa. Canada's National Library in Ottawa publishes a National Union Catalog, which lists materials in more than 300 Canadian libraries. In the United States, the National Union Catalog is published by the Library of Congress and lists materials in more than 700 United States and Canadian libraries. The Library of Congress also serves other government departments and agencies, libraries, scholars, and the general public. Other national libraries of the United States include the National Agricultural Library, the National Library of Medicine, and the National Archives.

There are important academic libraries in every province or state of Canada and the United States, many of them with outstanding library schools. The largest university libraries in Canada are those of the University of Toronto, the University of British Columbia, the University of Alberta, and Montreal's McGill University. Harvard University at Cambridge, Mass., has the world's largest academic library, with about 90 separate collections. Both Canada and the United States are rich also in special libraries such as industrial, technical, business, medical, and private research libraries.

## The Brave New World of Libraries

Every year a deluge of more and more information pours from the world's presses or appears on records, films, and tapes. How does the librarian keep track of the flood of materials, store them, and retrieve the information they contain? With a little help from some mechanical friends.

The photocopy has revolutionized the library. It

Modern advances in electronics have revolutionized information storage. Here, computer consoles display taped material.
Lockheed Missiles and Space Co.

is a fast, cheap, and easy way of getting parts of books, magazines, and other materials for everyone who wants them. Libraries can also enlarge their collections with photocopies of out-of-print books.

The library has also been revolutionized by the microform—the microfilm, the Microcard, the microfiche. These make it possible to store information in less space. One microfiche card, for example, can hold up to 1,000 pages of a book.

The magnetic tape, too, has revolutionized the library. Magnetic tapes called *data bases* provide a variety of information. To get information on magnetic tapes, it is necessary to use a computer. That, too, has contributed to the technological revolution in libraries. Computers are used by librarians to store and to find information, to order books or to keep records, and to produce book or card catalogs. The library has also been revolutionized by facsimile transmission machines, with which libraries can quickly send and receive a picture of a page.

In the past, libraries were largely for the learned and cultured. Even in highly literate countries, libraries existed to serve perhaps one third of the population. Many of today's librarians feel that the goal of the right book for the right library user is no longer enough. Today's libraries also reach out to nonusers, who generally include the uneducated, the poor, the minorities. Books are used, yes, but also films and records and tapes, easy-to-read materials, minority literature, job and health information. Storefront libraries and mobile libraries of various types carry the library to the people, serving their urgent needs. Often librarians go out of their way to help nonusers with practical problems, not only gathering information but putting it into easily understood form. Ignorance, poverty, and apathy are being attacked in many parts of the world, and libraries are in the forefront of that attack.

Reaching out to new users sometimes involves gathering nontraditional materials, materials they can relate to and understand—minority literature, for example. A library exists to serve its community. Unless it reflects the thinking of the entire community, it is serving only a portion of that community. One of the librarian's most important jobs is to preserve freedom of access to all kinds of ideas.

## BIBLIOGRAPHY FOR LIBRARIES

### A Multimedia Bibliography

Symbols used to indicate maturity level are as follows: P—primary; I—intermediate; J—junior high; S—senior high; L/T—librarian and/or teacher; T—teacher.

### How to Use Libraries

#### Books

Boyd, Jessie and others. Books, Libraries and You, 3d ed. (Scribner, 1965). J-S

Cleary, Florence D. Blueprints for Better Reading; School Programs for Promoting Skill and Interest in Reading, 2d ed. (Wilson, 1972). I-J

Mott, Carolyn and Baisden, L. B. Children's Book on How to Use Books and Libraries, 3d ed. (Scribner, 1968). P-I

Whitney, David C. The First Book of Facts and How to Find Them (Watts, 1966). I

Wisconsin Dept. of Public Instruction. Learning to Use Media (The Dept. 1970). P-I-J-S

#### Nonbook Materials

Advanced Library Reference Skills. Transparencies in spiral binding. (Encyclopædia Britannica Films). S-T

Introduction to the Library. (Schloat). Set of 4 sound filmstrips. Color. I-J

Lessons for Self Instruction in Basic Skills—Reference Skills. (California Test Bureau, 1965). I-J-S

Library Filmstrip Center. Some 18 sound filmstrips covering all phases of library use. (Wichita, Kansas). Color. Various age groups.

Library Reference Skills. Transparencies in spiral binding. (Encyclopædia Britannica Films). I-J

Library Skills. (Ideal, 1968). Eighteen charts and/or transparencies. I-J

National Test of Library Skills, by Frances Hatfield and others. (American Testing Co.). L/T

Using the Elementary School Library. (Society for Visual Education). Set of 6 filmstrips. Sound, color. P-I

Using Your Library. (Owen Publishing Co., 1965). Set of 32 posters. P-I

### Various Aspects of Libraries

#### Books

Broderick, Dorothy. An Introduction to Children's Work in Public Libraries (Wilson, 1965). L/T

Clarke, Joan D. Your Future as a Librarian (Rosen Press, 1963). J-S

Dunlap, Leslie W. Reading in Library History (Bowker Press, 1972). S-L/T

Greene, Carla. I Want to be a Librarian (Childrens, 1962). P

Hobson, Anthony. Great Libraries (Putnam, 1970). S-L/T

Klagsbrun, Francine. Read about the Librarian (Watts, 1970). P-I

Leopold, Carolyn C. School Libraries Worth Their Keep; a Philosophy Plus Tricks (Scarecrow, 1972). L/T

Logsdon, Richard and Irene. Library Careers (Walck, 1963). I

Meyer, Edith Patterson. Meet the Future; People and Ideas in the Libraries of Today and Tomorrow (Little, 1964). J-S

Oakes, Vanya. Challenging Careers in the Library World (Messner, 1970). J-S

Shay, Arthur. What Happens at the Library (Reilly & Lee, 1971). P-I

#### Audiovisual Materials

At the Center. (American Library Association) 16 mm film. Sound, color. 28 minutes. (School librarianship). L/T

Careers in Library Service. (National Film Board of Canada) Filmstrip with captions. Color. J-S

I Want to be a Librarian. (Educational Enrichment Materials) Sound filmstrip. Color. P

The Librarian. (McGraw-Hill Text Films) Filmstrip with captions. Color. P

Libraries Are for Sharing. (Neubacher Productions) 16 mm film. Sound, color. 11 minutes. P-I-L/T

The Library and the Librarian. (Eye Gate House) Filmstrip with captions. Color. P-I

A Library Is a Place Where. (Encyclopædia Britannica Films) 16 mm film. Sound. Color or B & W. P

The Library—A Place for Discovery. (Encyclopædia Britannica Films) 16 mm film. Sound, color. 16 minutes. I-T

Library of Congress. (Encyclopædia Britannica Films) 16 mm film. Sound. Color or B & W. 23 minutes. J-S

Your State Library. (Our Yank State) Filmstrip. Color. J-S

---

THESE ARTICLES ARE IN THE FACT-INDEX

**Libration**

**Libreville, Gabon**

---

**LIBYA** (*lĭb'ē-ȧ*). The oil-rich Libyan Arab Republic, in northern Africa, has more than 1,000 miles of Mediterranean coastline. From the coast the land extends southward into the Sahara. Libya has an area of 679,360 square miles—almost 93,000 square miles more than Alaska. Libya is bordered on the west by Tunisia and Algeria, on the south by Niger and Chad, and on the east by Egypt and Sudan. (*See also* Sahara; for map, *see* Africa.)

### The Land and the People

Most of Libya is a great limestone tableland, part of the African plateau. The plateau is a land of shifting sand or barren steppes. Occasional outcroppings of rock thrust up from the flat surface. The Arabs call them *jebels*. In the east and the west the coast rises sharply out of the Mediterranean. These regions are far enough north to have a climate like that of Southern California. In the middle, where the Gulf of Sidra bites southward into the land, the barren country is scorched by hot desert winds.

The population is 1,564,369 (1964 census), 1,682,-000 (1966 estimate). Tripoli, with a population of 213,506 (1964 census), is the administrative seat and the largest city. Next in size is Benghazi—population, 137,295. Most Libyans are Arabs or Berbers. There are also some Europeans, principally Italians. (*See also* Africa.)

Libya's chief industry is oil production. Oil was discovered in the Libyan Desert in 1959. By the late 1960's the income from petroleum was enabling Libya to undertake a development program of new roads, power stations, hospitals, and housing.

Other industries include sponge and tuna fishing, salt and sulfur mining, and the manufacture of tobacco products. Farming is limited to the coastal fringe and to a few desert oases. On the narrow coastal plain of Tripolitania, the western region, cereals, cotton, tobacco, and tropical fruits can be grown by dry farming or irrigation. Cyrenaica, in the east, has no coastal plain, but it can grow dates, olives, and barley for making beer or feeding cattle, sheep, and goats. Water for towns can be obtained by sinking wells to the water table which underlies most of Libya, even in the Sahara.

South of the coastal fringe the country slopes through ever-thinning pasturelands. Here, on the edges of the desert, little grows but the alfa plant (esparto grass), a tall grass which is exported to be made into paper. Then the sand and rocks of the Sahara stretch down toward the equator.

There are scattered oases in the Libyan Desert east of the Gulf of Sidra. These oases are found where the land is low and close to the water table. Water is obtained from shallow wells. A western group of oases, called the Fezzan, grows dates, olives, figs, almonds, and some grain.

### Early History

Libya was the ancient Greek name for all northern Africa. The region still called Cyrenaica was occupied by Greek colonists in the 7th century B.C. Modern geographers believe that Cyrenaica at that time had considerably more rainfall than it does today. The city of Cyrene, the capital, became one of the great centers of Greek culture. Here the sage Aristippus founded the Cyrenaic school of philosophy, which taught that "pleasure, tempered by intelligence" was the chief goal of life. At the height of its power Cyrene was a city of 100,000 inhabitants. Its splendid marble temples, baths, and cemeteries have

Publix                                          UPI Compix

These columns (left) of the ancient Roman city of Leptis Magna were uncovered by archaeologists in 1928. The modern highway (right), built when Italy controlled Libya, follows the coast from Tunisia to Egypt for more than 1,000 miles.

been recovered from the sands by modern archaeologists. Cyrenaica fell under Egyptian rule in the 4th century B.C. and was later conquered by Rome.

Roman Libya grew wheat enough for a large population and exported a large amount to Rome and other parts of Italy. The ruins of several ancient Roman cities have been uncovered along the coast. Chief of these is Leptis Magna, which was one of the most beautiful Roman colonial cities under the Emperor Septimius Severus. Leptis Magna and the neighboring cities of Sabrata and Oea gave the country the name of Tripoli ("three cities"). In the 5th century A.D. Libya was conquered by Vandal hordes from Spain (*see* Vandals). Two centuries later the country was overrun by Arabs.

Ewing Galloway
Date palms wave over the fertile oases of the Fezzan. Camel trains bring supplies from the outside world to the people who live in the oases.

During this time the climate was becoming drier, and it reached its present state during the late Middle Ages. In 1510 Ferdinand of Spain captured the city of Tripoli. From 1530 to 1551 it was occupied by the Knights of St. John (*see* Crusading Orders). Then the Turks seized the region and made it a pirate stronghold. In 1801 the United States fought a war with the Tripoli pirates who were preying on American ships sailing in the Mediterranean and seizing American sailors as slaves (*see* Decatur).

## Italy Gains Control

Italy took possession of Libya after fighting a war with the Turkish Empire in 1911–12. The coastal area was later divided into provinces and absorbed into the Italian kingdom. The desert region to the south (the Fezzan) was organized as a military district.

Italy supplied its new territory with thousands of settlers. Vast sums of money were spent for irrigation, buildings, roads, harbors, farm implements, and work animals. The ports of Tripoli and Benghazi were greatly improved. A naval base was established at Tobruk, which has one of the finest natural harbors on the North African coast. Bardia was made a modern town, with a good port. A paved highway was built along the entire length of the coast. Other roads were extended south to the chief oases. Airports dotted the land.

## World War II; Independence

Libya was one of the major battlegrounds in the African phase of World War II. There was heavy bombing as the British, entrenched in Egypt, fought the Italians and Germans back and forth across Libyan ground. Finally the Germans fled west to Tunisia, and the shattered Italian troops were captured. (*See also* World War II.)

After Italy's defeat, Libya was administered by Great Britain. In 1949 the United Nations began to prepare it for self-rule.

The independent kingdom of Libya was created in 1951. Cyrenaica's ruler was made king of Libya as Idris I. Originally a federal state of Tripolitania, Cyrenaica, and the Fezzan, Libya became a unitary state in 1963. In 1953 Libya joined the Arab League; in 1955, the United Nations. In 1971 it joined Egypt and Syria in the Confederation of Arab Republics.

In 1969 the monarchy was overthrown by a group of army officers. Libya is now governed by a premier, his cabinet, and a council of military officers.

Philip D. Gendreau
Modern Tripoli adjoins the native city which the Phoenicians founded as Oea over 3,000 years ago.

**LICHENS** (*lī'kĕns*). On tree trunks, rocks, old boards, etc., and also on the ground we often see those queer splotches of various-colored plant life which we call "lichens." They are of great scientific interest from the fact that they are not single plants, but unable to make food for itself owing to its lack of green coloring matter, uses the food made by the alga; while on the other hand the alga is protected from drying out by living on the sponge-like network of the fungus threads. There are others who

## PLANTS THAT FORM "PARTNERSHIPS"

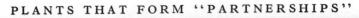

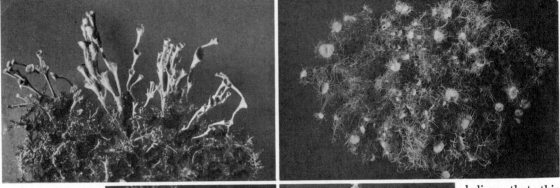

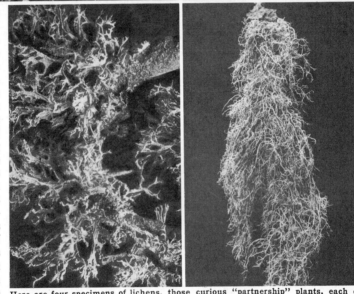

each lichen is formed of a fungus and an alga living together so intimately as to appear like a single plant. The lichens furnish one of the best illustrations of symbiosis ("living together"), as the scientists call this intimate relation of two different kinds of organisms. The fungus makes the bulk of the body with its interwoven threads, and in the meshes of the threads live the algae. The special fungi which take part in this arrangement are almost never found growing separately, but the algae are found growing free.

Here are four specimens of lichens, those curious "partnership" plants, each of which consists of a fungus and an alga. It is a peculiarity of the fungi, that, having no green coloring matter (chlorophyll), they are unable to manufacture their own food. So certain ones of them combine with the algae, which have the food-making power. In return the fungi shelter the algae and gather moisture for the partnership.

believe that this is a case in which the alga is not benefited by the presence of the fungus, but is held in slavery by it (*helotism*).

In any event the combination produces a structure which is able to exist where neither one could live alone. As a consequence, lichens are able to grow in the most unfavorable places. About the last plants one finds in the far north or up on a high mountain are the lichens; and they are about

Lichens have a peculiar and effective method of propagation. Upon the surface of the body there are commonly seen minute granules which give the body a dusty appearance. These granules (called *soredia*) each consist of a few cells of the alga surrounded by threads of the fungus. When these soredia are blown off they start new lichen bodies.

By many it is thought that the fungus and the alga are mutually helpful in this intimate relationship (*mutualism*). The claim is that the fungus, being

the first plants to be found upon rocks brought above the surface of the ocean. In such exposed situations the fungus could not live, because it depends upon other organisms; and the alga could not live, because it would be dried out speedily; but the two can live together. In this way lichens play a very important part in the first stages of soil formation on bare rocks.

Certain kinds of lichens, such as the ones called "Iceland moss" and "reindeer moss" are used as food by reindeer and even by man. Other kinds produce dyes, drugs, etc. (*See* Algae; Fungi.)

THESE ARTICLES ARE IN THE FACT-INDEX
Licinian laws
Licinius
Lick, James

**LICORICE.** The drops, sticks, and slender "whips" which are flavored with licorice owe their taste to a plant juice. The juice comes from the long pliant roots which extend straight down into the ground for more than a yard. The plant is cultivated chiefly in Mediterranean countries, including Spain, Italy, Greece, Turkey, and Syria, and in Iraq. The United States imports most of its supply. Some is grown in Louisiana and California. It takes three or four years before the crop of a new licorice plantation may be harvested.

Stick licorice is made by boiling the crushed roots and straining and concentrating the solution. For making cough drops, sirups, and candy, the solution is mixed with sugar. It is used also to cover the disagreeable taste of some medicines. Licorice paste, prepared from the first extract of the roots, is an ingredient in the manufacture of tobacco. A second extract is used in certain types of fire extinguishers. The roots remaining after extraction are used in the manufacture of boxboard and insulating wallboard.

There are a dozen or more varieties of licorice plants. *Glycyrrhiza glabra* is the most important. They are perennial herbs, 3 or 4 feet high, with fernlike leaves and with flowers that are usually pale violet.

THESE ARTICLES ARE IN THE FACT-INDEX
Lictor
Liddell, Henry George
Lie, Jonas
Lie, Trygve
Liebermann, Max

**LIEBIG** (*lē′bĭк*), **Justus, Baron von** (1803–73). Before Justus Liebig's time chemistry was mainly a mass of theory, of interest only to scientists. Liebig helped to make chemistry useful in man's daily life. His work with carbon compounds laid the foundations for modern organic chemistry.

Justus Liebig was born in Darmstadt, Germany, on May 12, 1803. He was the son of a dealer in paints. Justus began to learn chemistry as a boy when he first watched, then helped, his father improve the products of the family business. While serving as an apothecary's apprentice at 15, Justus read all the chemistry books he could find. Later he went to the University of Bonn, then transferred to the University of Erlangen. There he received a doctor's degree in 1822.

At 21 Liebig was invited to read his research report on fulminic acid to the French Academy of Sciences. The paper won praise and attention, and he gained the friendship of the scientists Alexander von Humboldt and Joseph Gay-Lussac. Liebig accepted a position at the University of Giessen in Germany. Here he set up the first experimental laboratory for college students. He was made a baron in 1845.

Liebig discovered chloral and chloroform, important contributions to medicine, and aldehyde, a chemical widely employed in industry. He improved methods for producing potassium cyanide, used in electroplating and in making ferrocyanides. Liebig's studies of meat juices resulted in meat extracts and special baby foods. With Friedrich Wöhler he made important investigations in the benzol compounds and uric acid.

Liebig showed that the mineral and organic worlds are composed of the same elements. He showed that plants use elements from the soil for growth and pass them on to animals that eat the plants. His studies of soil led to the use of chemical fertilizers to replace minerals withdrawn by crops and to supply minerals lacking in some soils.

Liebig taught at Giessen until 1852, when he became a professor at the University of Munich. He died in Munich on April 18, 1873.

THESE ARTICLES ARE IN THE FACT-INDEX
Liebknecht, Karl
Liebknecht, Wilhelm
Liebman, Joshua Loth

**LIECHTENSTEIN** (*lĭк′tĕn-shtīn*). One of the smallest independent states of Europe is Liechtenstein (61 square miles). It is situated between Switzerland and Austria. The Rhine forms the boundary with Switzerland. From its narrow valley the land rises eastward to rugged uplands.

The highest peak is Naafkopf (8,440 feet), on the southern border.

About one third of the land is devoted to raising crops. Farm products include beef and milk cattle, corn, cereals, grapes, and orchard fruits. Since World War II the country's industry has developed rapidly. Small-scale plants make calculating machines, precision instruments, needles, textiles, sausage casings, and canned foods.

Tax rates are low and business regulations are very liberal. As a result, thousands of foreign companies have established headquarters here. The moderate fees paid by these companies provide much of the country's revenue. The tourist trade and the sale of postage stamps are other sources of income.

Most of the people are German-speaking Roman Catholics. They are descendants of old German tribes and are ruled by a prince. Liechtenstein was made a principality in 1719 by the Holy Roman emperor Charles VI. In 1866 it became independent. It is a member of the Swiss customs union and uses Swiss currency. The capital is Vaduz. Population of Liechtenstein (1970 census), 21,078.

## LIE DETECTOR.

**LIE DETECTOR.** Sometimes it is hard to know when a person tells a lie. His eyes may be steady, his manner calm and sure. But except for very young children and some backward persons, most people feel guilty when they lie. Then they cannot control inward reactions, such as change in blood pressure.

A sensitive machine, however, can detect and record these hidden reactions. This instrument is popularly called a lie detector. It usually consists of an arm cuff to measure blood pressure and pulse, a pneumograph (chest tube) to record the rate of breathing, and a galvanograph to measure electrically the flow of sweat in the palm of the hand. One type of lie detector also provides special fittings in the subject's chair to note arm- and leg-muscle movements. The indicators (except the galvanograph) record fluctuations of pressure. Each indicator moves a pen that marks paper on a revolving cylinder. The pen lines thus make a graph of normally unnoticed reactions of the body. This is why the lie-detector apparatus is often called a *polygraph* (from the Greek word *polygraphos*, meaning "writing much").

Lie detectors are widely used in crime detection, including insurance investigations. They are also used in business—chiefly to test the honesty of applicants for responsible positions, especially those that involve the handling of money. After attaching the polygraph indicators to a subject, the trained examiner reads aloud the questions to be used in the test. This is to avoid startling the subject. Then the examiner begins the machine and again asks the questions. To each question, the subject answers only "yes" or "no" The examiner mingles irrelevant queries with questions pertinent to the issue. For example, he may first ask, "Do you live in the United States?" Then, "Did you steal the money?" The rise and fall of the graph lines indicate which answers are true and which are false.

The body's reactions to questions are traced on the lie detector's graph paper. The subject wears a blood-pressure arm cuff, a pneumograph tube, and galvanograph electrodes.

Compton's Encyclopedia

Lie-detector tests may not definitely prove guilt, but they often lead to signed confessions. They are also useful in clearing innocent persons of suspicion. In some states a lie-detector examiner may testify as a witness in a court trial, if there is no objection from the opposing counsel or the judge.

## LIÈGE

**LIÈGE** (*lē-āzh'*), **Belgium.** Situated on the Meuse River near the rich coalfields of the Meuse Valley, the city of Liège is one of the chief manufacturing centers in Belgium. Steel is the city's foremost finished product. For centuries Liège has been noted for its armaments industry. Even during the Middle Ages it was one of the arsenals of Europe, supplying lances and armor from its forges. Today machine tools, machinery, and bicycles are also produced in Liège, and aluminum, zinc, and rubber are processed. Brewing, paper milling, and flour milling are other industries.

The completion of the Albert Canal in 1939 gave Liège a shipping route to the sea. The city is also an important rail center, and a heliport was installed in 1955. It is the principal city in the Belgian province of Liège (*see* Belgium).

The history of Liège (in German, *Lüttich*) goes back to St. Monulph, who traveled through the Meuse Valley in the 6th century. Impressed with the beauty of the country, he stopped where the Ourthe and Meuse rivers meet and said, "God has chosen this place for the salvation of many people. Here must be raised a great town." The chapel he built was the start of the present city. From its beginnings until 1795, the city was ruled by bishops. For many centuries the "Prince-Bishops of Liège" sat in the diets of the Holy Roman Empire. The city was famous as a center of religion and learning long before its mineral wealth was discovered. Several times in the 1460's, when Belgium was under Burgundian rule, Charles the Bold ordered the destruction of the city as punishment for rebellions (*see* Charles the Bold).

Because of its strategic location on the Meuse Valley route through Belgium into France, Liège was the scene of fighting in both world wars. In the first major battle of World War I, the city fell after a heroic defense. It was seized again by the Germans in 1940 during World War II and suffered extensive damage from both German and Allied bombs.

Many old and stately buildings still stand amid the modern factories of Liège. The university, founded in 1817, is noted for its schools of science, including those of astrophysics and nuclear physics. Population (1961 census), 153,240.

---

THESE ARTICLES ARE IN THE FACT-INDEX

**Liepaja, Latvian S.S.R.**
**Lieutenant governor**

---

# LIFE—What It Means to Be "Alive"

**LIFE.** Living things include plants and animals. They live on the land, in the lakes, rivers, and seas and billions of tiny microbes live in both water and soil. These many plants, animals, and microbes are very different from one another. Yet all of them have one thing in common: they are *alive*. What do we mean by being "alive"? Anyone can think of such tests of living as *eating* and *moving*. But will *all* the tests apply to *every* living thing?

The picture on this page raises some of these questions. It shows, for example, that the test of motion is not easy to apply. Many nonliving things move, and many living things never seem to move. So if motion is a test of being alive, it must be motion *of a certain kind*. We must be able to find this *kind* of motion in moss and other plants that never seem to move. We must be able to say that this kind of motion cannot be found in nonliving things. The same is true of other tests for life. They must be true for all living things and not true for nonliving things.

## Tests of Life in Animals

A good way to find answers to questions about life is to study some common animals, such as dogs. They move even when asleep. They also respond to their surroundings. They dodge when we try to catch them but come when we offer them food.

Dogs use food in many ways. Young ones use it to grow. When they are older they use it to repair worn-out parts of their bodies. Dogs get energy from food. They use energy when they run, play, eat, and even while they sleep. Finally, dogs mate and reproduce, which means that they have young ones. Will these same tests apply to plants as well?

## Test of Life in Plants

Plants do not try to move when we touch them (except for the "sensitive" plants). But they do change position as they grow. A tree moves its branches and leaves to get sunlight. If a plant starts to grow in a dark spot, it will turn its stem to reach the light. Plants also turn their roots to reach water and minerals in the soil.

Plants therefore move in ways *that are useful to them*, just as animals do. This is the kind of motion that marks living things. Nonliving things move only if an outside force compels them to.

Although plants do not eat, they secure food and use it. Those we know best take water, nitrogen, and minerals from the soil and a gas called carbon dioxide

## WHAT MAKES PLANTS AND ANIMALS "ALIVE"?

**Because they MOVE?**
It is easy to say that the *man* is alive because he moves. But the *river* and the *clouds* also move. The *tree* is alive, but moves only in the wind. So movement is not a simple test for life.

**Because they EAT?**
*Fish* eat by swallowing food. If eating is a test of being alive, do the *grass* and *moss* "eat"? How do *microbes* in the pool eat? Eating by mouth then is not the only way to take nourishment.

**Because they GROW?**
Ability to grow may seem to be a good test of being alive. Some lifeless substances, however, expand and take on wonderful shapes. Freezing water forms *ice* or *snow*.

The picture shows various living and nonliving things. We say that the *trees, grass, man, fish, moss,* and *microbes* are alive. On the other hand, we say that the *ice, rivers, clouds,* and *snow* are not alive. The three questions above show that many "easy" tests of being alive are not so easy after all. The real tests of being alive are explained in the article.

from the air. They use these materials to make the foods they need for growth and energy. They also make some foods which can be stored for later use.

Plants reproduce in a number of ways. Many kinds have seeds which grow into new plants. Others grow from roots, pieces of stem, or bulbs. Some kinds even reproduce by means of leaves which grow into new plants when they fall on moist, rich ground.

### How Microbes Live

The tests for life described for the larger animals and plants also hold true for smaller and stranger forms of life. Microbes are living things which are too small to be seen clearly with our eyes alone. Enlarged pictures taken through microscopes tell us what they do. Many microbes swim, while others creep or twist to and fro. All respond to conditions around them by going toward things that are good for them and protecting themselves from things that are not.

Microbes get food in various ways. Many capture other tiny creatures. Some make food as large plants do. Other microbes, called germs of decay and disease, get food from dead or living plants and animals. We know that microbes use food when they move about. We can see that they grow and reproduce.

### Seven Functions of Living

Thus animals, plants, and microbes perform the *functions of living.* These are the tests of being alive. Here are seven of them:

**1. Movement.** All living things move *without outside help.* This makes them different from a stone that is thrown, a stream that runs downhill, or an engine which has to be started. No outside force has to start movements of a plant, a dog, or a microbe.

**2. Irritability.** This means that living things respond to conditions around them. Green plants, for example, grow toward sunshine. Certain microbes shrink into tiny balls when something touches them. Human beings show this kind of irritability by blinking when light shines into their eyes.

**3. Feeding.** All living things secure food. Some bite, some suck, and some soak up food through membranes ("skins") that cover their bodies. Green plants make food from water, gas, nitrogen, and minerals.

**4. Nutrition.** This is our name for processes by which food is used. Some food is turned into living material, bones, teeth, or wood. Some is used to provide energy, which living things need to keep going. We may compare this to the process in which an engine burns oil or coal and gets energy to move a train. But no engine can use coal or oil to make itself larger or mend parts, as living things do with food.

**5. Growth.** We say that snowballs grow when we roll them or that salt crystals grow in salty water as it evaporates. Actually, these lifeless objects only become larger. Living things grow by making new parts and changing old ones. This happens when a seed grows into a plant or a chick grows into a hen. Human beings add new parts, such as teeth, and change the proportions of other parts as they grow.

A special kind of growth heals injuries and replaces worn parts. Shrubs and trees mend injuries by covering them with bark and adding new layers of wood. Crabs grow new legs when old ones are lost. Human beings can heal cut skin and mend broken bones.

**6. Reproduction.** When living things reproduce, they make new living things. This is true even of simple microbes, which reproduce by dividing into two sections. Each section is able to move, feed, grow, and perform the other functions of living.

**7. Excretion.** This means getting rid of waste materials. Much waste comes from food. The rest is produced by movement, growth, and other functions of living. If this waste remained in living things, it would soon cause illness and death.

Common lifeless things, such as stones and machines, cannot carry on these seven functions of living. Some lifeless models have been made to perform *some* of these functions. But models are unable to carry on *all* of them.

### Living Material, Called Protoplasm

Since all living things perform these functions of life, the urge to do so must come from something within them. Do living things contain some special substance not found in lifeless things? If so, how does this substance form microbes, animals, and plants?

We find part of the answer in a creature known as an *amoeba.* It lives in ponds. To our eyes it looks like a milky speck, but a microscope shows it to be a lump of jelly. This jelly, called *protoplasm*, is the substance which makes up all living things.

When we watch an amoeba closely through a microscope, we see that its protoplasm moves and changes. It streams through the tiny body, especially when the creature changes shape. At one time the living jelly is clear. Then it becomes gray and grainy or

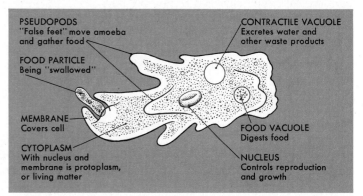

PSEUDOPODS
"False feet" move amoeba
and gather food

FOOD PARTICLE
Being "swallowed"

MEMBRANE
Covers cell

CYTOPLASM
With nucleus and
membrane is protoplasm,
or living matter

CONTRACTILE VACUOLE
Excretes water and
other waste products

FOOD VACUOLE
Digests food

NUCLEUS
Controls reproduction
and growth

**A ONE-CELLED ANIMAL THAT HUNTS FOR FOOD**
The amoeba consists of a single cell. It crawls by stretching out false feet, or *pseudopods*, and flowing into them. When a pseudopod touches a food particle the creature flows around it. The *food vacuole* then appears and digests it.

seems to fill itself with bubbles or droplets. A clear stiff network may appear too. Its threads are rather like tiny crystals of mineral matter. It serves as a support, or framework, for bubbles, droplets, and thin watery parts of the jelly.

This complex mixture moves and changes according to conditions inside the amoeba as well as around it. The mixture also takes in food, uses it, grows, and finally reproduces. The protoplasm which forms an amoeba also makes the little creature live.

## Cells Form Living Things

Although protoplasm is living material, the amoeba is not just a simple lump of protoplasm. It is protoplasm in the form of one definite body called a *cell* (*see* Cell). Several parts fit together, or are organized, in the amoeba's cell. Its surface is a clear, tough membrane which covers and protects a thinner, darker-looking *cytoplasm* inside. The membrane is flexible and permits the amoeba to change shape. By doing so the amoeba can move to get food.

The amoeba shows *irritability* by these movements. It feeds and also excretes waste material by forming little droplets called *vacuoles* in its protoplasm. As it absorbs food, it grows.

All these activities seem to be controlled by a structure called the *nucleus*. The nucleus also performs the function of reproduction. In due time it divides and each half takes its share of the cytoplasm. The two halves of the amoeba become two new amoebas.

## Life in a Single-Celled Plant

Another example of life in the form of a single cell may be seen in the tiny green plant known as *Protococcus*. Layers of these plants form green scum on damp trees, rocks, and brick walls.

Each Protococcus cell contains protoplasm, a nucleus, and a thin membrane. The nucleus controls the life of the cell and in time divides for reproduction. Inside the cell is a large structure filled with grains of a green substance termed *chlorophyll*. These grains make food for the plant from water and carbon dioxide. Since the plant can make food in this way,

it does not have to move about like an amoeba. Therefore it can have a stiff, protecting wall, made of a transparent substance called *cellulose*.

These two substances, chlorophyll and cellulose, make plant life quite different from animal life. With them a plant can stay in one place and make its food inside its colorless wall. Since animals do not have chlorophyll, they must get food from other living things or from dead material. To do this they have to move, which means that at least some of their cells must be covered with soft, flexible membrane. In one-celled creatures such as the amoeba, the whole tiny body moves freely.

## Simple and Complex Cells

There are many kinds of one-celled plants and animals related to the amoeba. Some one-celled creatures look like slippers, vases, or balls, and have more than one nucleus. Many swim by waving lashes. Others use hairlike structures. One kind has two nuclei, a mouth, and a ring of moving "hairs" that bring in food. It also has a stalk that can stretch or coil up and pull the creature away from danger.

All these parts are organized, which means that they fit and work together. For this reason, we call living things *organisms*. Not all organisms have as many parts as the ones described. Many microbes have no separate nuclei. Their food-making chlorophyll is scattered through the cell. Other microbes, called *bacteria*, have neither nuclei nor green grains. They get their food from other organisms or from dead material.

Bacteria once were said to be the simplest organisms. Then *viruses* and *bacteriophages* were discovered. Bacteriophages are tiny things that kill bacteria. Viruses include the germs that cause colds, yellow fever, and other diseases of animals and plants. Even the largest viruses are too small to be cells. They seem unable to grow or reproduce unless they are in animals or plants. Some scientists think viruses and bacteriophages are almost alive. Others think they are living things that have degenerated, losing most of their parts. The remaining substance gets along by taking material from other organisms.

## Many-Celled Organisms

The common plants and animals we know are much larger than viruses and microbes. They also are too big to be formed by a single cell. They therefore are made of many cells that live and work together.

Some of the simplest many-celled organisms are plants that live in ponds and streams. Each plant consists of a chain of cells that drifts to and fro in the water. Most cells in the chain are alike, but the one at the bottom, called a "holdfast," is different. It is long and tough. Its base holds to rocks or pieces of wood to keep the plant from floating away.

| SINGLE CELL | CELLULOSE WALL — Protects cell and makes it rigid | COLONIES OF CELLS |
|---|---|---|

CHLOROPLAST — Contains green chlorophyll for food making

CYTOPLASM — With nucleus and membrane is protoplasm, or living matter

NUCLEUS — Controls reproduction and growth

MEMBRANE — Covers cell

**A ONE-CELLED PLANT THAT MAKES FOOD**
This is Protococcus, a one-celled plant. Inside it is *chloroplast*, which contains *chlorophyll*. The chlorophyll uses energy from sunlight to make food from carbon dioxide and water. Colonies of cells form green scum on mud or moist rocks.

Sea lettuce also has a holdfast. The rest of the plant contains boxlike cells arranged in two layers. These layers are covered and protected by two sheets of clear cellulose that is very tough.

Trees, weeds, and other familiar land plants contain many more cells than sea lettuce and are much more complex. Their cells form organs such as roots, stems, leaves, and flowers. Millions of individual cells are needed to form these complex plants.

No animals consist of chains of cells or of cells arranged in two flat layers like the sea lettuce. But the body of a pond-dwelling creature called *Hydra* has two layers of cells arranged in a tube. The bottom of the tube is closed, but its top contains a mouth. Slender branches of the tube form tentacles that catch food and put it into the mouth.

Great numbers of cells of many kinds form the bodies of such creatures as insects, fish, and horses. Similar

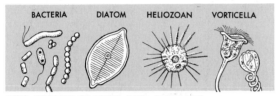

**ONE-CELLED PLANTS AND ANIMALS**
*Bacteria* are common single microscopic cells. The *diatom* plant has a glassy shell. The animal *heliozoan* has pseudopods. The animal *vorticella* has a stalk that coils away from danger.

**CHAINS AND LAYERS OF CELLS**
The plant called *Ulothrix* has its cells joined in a chain. Its bottom cell, called a "holdfast," anchors it. The *sea lettuce* plant and the tubelike animal *Hydra* have cells in two layers.

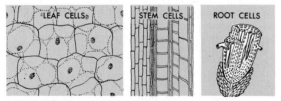

**SPECIALIZED CELLS IN HIGHER PLANTS**
Higher plants have specialized kinds of cells. Some *leaf cells* have chlorophyll for making food. *Stem cells* stiffen the plant. *Root cells* take in water and minerals.

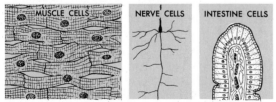

**SPECIALIZED CELLS IN HIGHER ANIMALS**
Higher animals also have specialized cells. They cannot make food from lifeless materials as plant cells do. *Muscle, nerve,* and *intestine cells* help to secure and use ready-made foods.

cells that work together make up *tissues*. Tissues that work together form *organs*. A dog's heart, for example, is an organ composed of muscle tissue, nerve tissue, connective tissue, and covering tissue. Another kind of tissue, the blood, nourishes them. All tissues work together when the dog's heart contracts.

## Parts and Cells Are Controlled

Varied parts and cells work together because they are controlled. In plants, control is carried out by chemical particles called *hormones*. They go directly from cell to cell or are carried about in sap. When something touches a sensitive plant, for instance, the touched cells produce a hormone that goes to countless other cells and makes them lose water and collapse. As cell after cell does this, leaves begin to droop. They will not spread out again until the effect of the hormones is lost.

In many-celled animals, hormones regulate growth, keep muscles in condition, and perform many similar tasks. Other types of control are carried out by nerve cells. They carry impulses to and from various parts of the body. These impulses tell when things are seen, felt, or heard. They also make muscle cells contract or relax, so that animals run, lie down, catch food, and do countless other things. Nerve cells may even deliver the impulses that cause other cells to produce hormones.

## Living Things Are Specialized

In the amoeba and Protococcus all parts of the protoplasm—other than structures such as the nucleus—are much alike and can do almost anything. This is not true of one-celled creatures that have lashes, hairs, and other definite parts. The lashes or hairs are used in swimming or in setting up currents that bring food. The food is swallowed through a mouth and digested in droplets that stay in the bubbly body. Special fibers that work like nerves control the hairs and lashes. Several one-celled organisms even possess "eyespots" that are affected by light.

These structures are *specialized*. Each one does its own part in the work of living. Many-celled organisms have tissues and organs that are still more specialized. Roots, leaves, flowers, eyes, and brains are examples of organs that do specialized work.

Specialization is carried from parts to entire living things. Cactus plants, for example, can live well only in dry regions, but cattails must grow in wet places. Herring swim near the surface of the sea, but the deep-sea angler fish lives on the bottom. Certain caterpillars eat only one kind of leaf.

This specialization of whole organisms is called *adaptation*. Every living thing is adapted to its surroundings—to the sea, fresh water, land, or even to living in other organisms. During the ages since life began, organisms have become adapted to all sorts of conditions. Today there are millions of different combinations between organisms and surroundings. With the possible exception of bacteriophages and viruses, however, all the different organisms consist of pro-

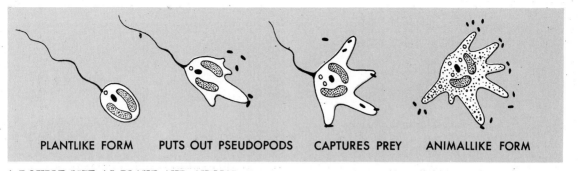

PLANTLIKE FORM    PUTS OUT PSEUDOPODS    CAPTURES PREY    ANIMALLIKE FORM

**A DOUBLE LIFE AS PLANT AND ANIMAL**

In its ordinary form the single-celled Chrysamoeba swims with a long lash. It makes food with the two large chloroplasts within its body just as a plant cell does. At times, however, the Chrysamoeba puts out pseudopods, or false feet. It may even absorb its long lash. It then moves about and captures food. It digests its food just as the animal amoeba does.

toplasm that is organized into cells. Cells are the "building blocks" of the living world.

### The Elements in Protoplasm

Since protoplasm differs from lifeless materials, people once thought it contained "principles" not to be found in the earth. It is now known that both the earth and protoplasm consist of simple substances called *chemical elements* (*see* Chemistry). These elements may exist alone, as the element carbon does in coal. Generally, however, elements combine into compounds, which may be very complex. Chemists who have studied the compounds in living things have found:

*First*, that protoplasm contains only elements that are common in the earth.

*Second*, that only 13 elements are found in *all* kinds of protoplasm. The most important of these "universal" elements are carbon, hydrogen, oxygen, nitrogen, phosphorus, sulfur, magnesium, and iron.

*Third*, that different varieties of protoplasm contain other elements, such as copper, zinc, and chlorine. These are also plentiful in the earth, which is where plants get them for use in protoplasm. Animals get them by eating plants or other animals.

### Atoms in Living Molecules

When elements form compounds, tiny particles called atoms combine and build up molecules. The molecules in protoplasm are complex. A molecule of the substance that makes a horse's blood red contains 2,359 atoms of six different elements. The red material in our blood contains about the same number of atoms.

The complexity is made possible by carbon, which may be called the "framework" element. It links atoms of different kinds in various proportions and arrangements. Carbon atoms also join with each other in long chains, rings, and other arrays.

Oxygen and hydrogen are most important in using energy, while nitrogen enables living things to vary and become specialized. Large amounts of nitrogen are found in protein, or "body-building" compounds. Nitrogen also is used in wood and in the substance called chitin which forms the shells of crustaceans, insects, jointed worms, and related creatures.

### How Plants Obtain Food

All living things get food in one of two ways. They make it or they get it ready-made. The one-celled plant Protococcus uses both methods. It combines water, carbon, and mineral matter dissolved in the water by the process called *photosynthesis*. The process requires energy, but the green chlorophyll grains can obtain this from sunlight. After several steps the food-making process results in a kind of sugar called *glucose*.

Protococcus may use glucose molecules almost as fast as it makes them. It also may turn them into starch or droplets of oil, which it stores for use when it cannot get sunlight. Finally, Protococcus may combine atoms from glucose with some ready-made food combinations in the dissolved minerals. In this way it builds up protoplasm and cellulose.

Many-celled plants also get ready-made foods and make glucose. In doing so, however, they use many different cells, tissues, and organs, such as leaves, roots, and sap-carrying channels in the stem.

### How Animals Change Food

Although many animals are green, no true animal contains grains of chlorophyll. Therefore no true animal can make food from carbon dioxide and water. This means that animals must get ready-made food from plants or other animals.

Animals, however, can change foods after they are eaten. When a horse eats more grain than it can use, it turns the extra grain into fat and stores the fat in tissues. Animals can turn sugary food into animal starch (*glycogen*) and store it in the liver, ready for use when needed.

### Securing Energy from Food

When plants make glucose from water and carbon dioxide, they subtract some atoms of oxygen from the combined materials. More oxygen is lost when glucose is turned into common sugar, starch, fat, or other food substances. As oxygen is lost, more and more energy is stored in the made-over molecules.

When energy is needed for living, the process must be reversed. Food is first digested (dissolved in liquid). Then oxygen is combined with food molecules.

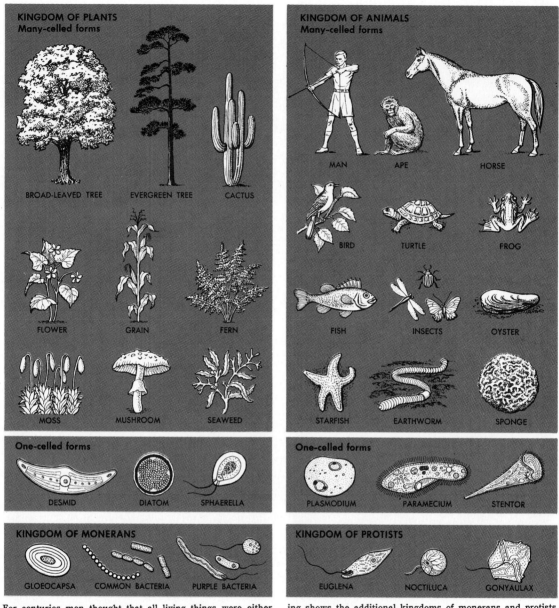

**KINGDOM OF PLANTS**
Many-celled forms

BROAD-LEAVED TREE  EVERGREEN TREE  CACTUS

FLOWER  GRAIN  FERN

MOSS  MUSHROOM  SEAWEED

One-celled forms

DESMID  DIATOM  SPHAERELLA

**KINGDOM OF MONERANS**

GLOEOCAPSA  COMMON BACTERIA  PURPLE BACTERIA

**KINGDOM OF ANIMALS**
Many-celled forms

MAN  APE  HORSE

BIRD  TURTLE  FROG

FISH  INSECTS  OYSTER

STARFISH  EARTHWORM  SPONGE

One-celled forms

PLASMODIUM  PARAMECIUM  STENTOR

**KINGDOM OF PROTISTS**

EUGLENA  NOCTILUCA  GONYAULAX

For centuries men thought that all living things were either plants or animals. Today scientists believe that two or more other kingdoms may exist, as the article explains. The draw-ing shows the additional kingdoms of monerans and protists. It should be noted that both the plant and animal kingdoms are further divided into many-celled and one-celled forms.

They are changed into simpler substances and give up energy. This process is called *oxidation*. If oxida-tion is complete, the food becomes water and carbon dioxide again and gives up all its stored energy. Part of this energy is lost but most of it remains in protoplasm to be used in the work of living.

Some one-celled plants and many parasites or dis-ease germs live where oxygen cannot be had. These organisms secure energy by dividing foods into sim-pler compounds. Yeast plants in bread dough, for ex-ample, turn starch into sugar while they can get oxy-gen. Later they secure energy by dividing sugar into

alcohol and carbon dioxide. These become wastes for the yeast plants. When yeast is used for making bread, this carbon dioxide is what makes the dough rise. The alcohol evaporates as the bread is baked.

### Carrying Food and Oxygen

One-celled plants such as Protococcus get food-making substances and energy through the cell wall. In many-celled plants each cell also absorbs and gives out substances through its wall. To provide what every cell needs and to carry off wastes the plant uses a liquid called *sap*, which travels through the

258

## LIVING THINGS CANNOT BE CLASSIFIED BY APPEARANCE
Although the sea anemone looks like a large flower with long, graceful petals, it belongs to a group of animals called "flower animals," which includes the sea fan and corals. They live in shallow sea waters and in tide pools.
Ron Church

cells. The larger many-celled animals provide for the needs of their cells with circulating liquids called *blood* and *lymph*. Blood carries the oxygen needed to release energy from food and it carries away the carbon dioxide and water produced as wastes.

### Kingdoms of Living Things

More than a million kinds of organisms are known. For centuries scientists divided them into two kingdoms—plants and animals. According to this classification, most members of the plant kingdom have chlorophyll and cellulose. Those that have no chlorophyll are supposed to be descended from organisms that lost it long ago. The animal kingdom consists of creatures that never possessed chlorophyll or cellulose.

These two kingdoms seemed to include all living things until scientists studied one-celled organisms. Some seemed to fit neither kingdom and others seemed to fit both. Bacteria, for example, are too simple to be animals. Yet they contain no cellulose and may never have had chlorophyll. Some organisms swim, crawl, and capture food like animals but contain chlorophyll. Others are also covered with plates of cellulose.

Such "in-betweens" have been called plants by botanists and animals by zoologists. More and more, however, scientists are deciding that these puzzling organisms require a new system of classification. One system divides living things into four kingdoms:

**Kingdom 1—Monerans.** These one-celled organisms have no distinct nuclei. They belong to two subkingdoms—bacteria and blue-green algae.

One important group of bacteria is purple and swims by means of lashes. Greenish particles in these purple bacteria can make food from carbon dioxide and water but are not true chlorophyll. Blue-green algae have no swimming lashes and often live together in chains or clumps covered by jelly. They contain true chlorophyll and can make food. They also can soak up ready-made food as many bacteria do.

**Kingdom 2—Protists.** Some scientists say that the only protists are the things that have been called both plants and animals. They are one-celled and have definite nuclei. They swim by means of lashes that whip to and fro. They act like animals and may catch other organisms and eat them. In spite of this, they have chlorophyll and can make glucose, as plants and the purple bacteria do.

Other scientists say that the protists include one-celled creatures such as amoebas, which generally are called protozoans, or "first animals." Still others include sponges, seaweeds, and even fungi, such as mushrooms. It seems best to confine the kingdom to one-celled creatures or to "in-betweens."

**Kingdom 3—Plants.** Plants probably began as one-celled organisms with nuclei, chlorophyll, and two lashes that were used for swimming. Some plants still drift about. Although some of these attached ("sessile") plants are one-celled, most of them have great numbers of cells. Plants such as fungi (which include mushrooms and molds) have lost their chlorophyll and live on other animals and plants or on dead material.

**Kingdom 4—Animals.** Animals are organisms whose cells contain nuclei but no chlorophyll. Except for certain one-celled forms, they also have no cellulose. Most animals move and change shape more freely than plants.

This classification does not include viruses and bacteriophages. If they prove to be living things, one or two kingdoms will have to be provided for them.

THESE ARTICLES ARE IN THE FACT-INDEX

Lifesaving

Liffey River

Ligature

Liggett, Hunter

# LIGHT

Life on earth depends on light from the sun. Green plants provide food for the world by changing light energy into food energy. The plants are eaten by animals that may, in turn, be eaten by other animals or by humans.

**LIGHT.** One of the most familiar and important forms of energy is light. Light is what makes it possible to see things. Nothing is visible when light is totally absent. But light is even more important for other reasons. Many scientists believe that millions of years ago light from the sun triggered the chemical reactions that led to the development of life on earth. Without light the living things now on earth would be unable to survive. Light from the sun provides energy for the inhabitants of the earth. Plants change the energy of sunlight into food energy. When light rays strike a green plant, some of their energy is changed to chemical energy, which the plant uses up as it makes food out of air and minerals. This process is called *photosynthesis*. Very nearly all living organisms on earth depend directly or indirectly on photosynthesis for their food energy. (*See also* Plants, Physiology of.)

Some of the energy of sunlight is absorbed by the earth's atmosphere or by the earth itself. Much of this energy is then changed to heat energy, which helps warm the earth, keeping it in the temperature range that living things have adapted to.

## LIGHT AND ELECTROMAGNETIC RADIATION

Different kinds of light are visible to different species. Humans see light in what is called the visible range. It includes all the colors beginning with red and continuing through orange, yellow, green,

This article was reviewed by Dr. John H. Pomeroy, Assistant Director, Lunar Sample Program, National Aeronautics and Space Administration, and by Dr. A. A. Strassenburg, Director, Office of Education and Manpower, American Institute of Physics.

blue, and violet (*see* Color). Some people can see farther into the violet region or the red region than other people. Some animals have a different "visible range." Pit vipers, for example, have sense organs (pits) that "see" rays that humans feel as heat. These rays are called *infrared radiation*. Bees, on the other hand, not only see some of the colors that humans see but are also sensitive to *ultraviolet radiation*, which is beyond the range visible to humans. So, though human eyes cannot detect them, infrared rays and ultraviolet rays are related to visible light. Instruments have been built that can detect and photograph objects by means of infrared rays or ultraviolet rays. *X rays*, which can be used to photograph objects, are also known to be related to light.

Scientists have learned that all these forms of energy—visible light, infrared rays, ultraviolet rays, X rays—and many other kinds of energy, such as radio waves, microwaves, and gamma rays, have the same structure. They all consist of electrical and magnetic fields that move together and are all called *electromagnetic radiation*. (*See also* Radiation; Infrared Radiation; Ultraviolet Radiation; X Rays.)

## SOURCES OF LIGHT

Unlike many animals, humans depend primarily on sight to learn about the world around them. During the day primitive man could see by the light that came from the sun; but night brought darkness and danger. One of the most important steps man has taken to control his environment occurred when he learned to conquer the dark by controlling fire—a source of light.

Torches, candles, and oil lamps are all sources of light. They depend on a chemical reaction—burning—to release the energy we see as light. Plants and animals that glow in the dark—glowworms, fireflies, and some mushrooms—change the chemical energy stored in their tissues to light energy. Such creatures are called *bioluminescent*. Electric-light bulbs and neon lights change electrical energy, which may be produced by chemical, mechanical, or atomic energy, into light energy.

Light sources are necessary for vision. An object can be seen only if light travels from the object to an eye that can sense it. When the object is itself a light source, it is called *luminous*. Electric lights are luminous. The sun is a luminous object because it is a source of light. An object that is not itself a source of light must be *illuminated* by a luminous object before it can be seen. The moon is illuminated by the sun. It is visible only where the sun's rays hit it and bounce off toward earth—or to an observer in a spacecraft.

In a completely dark room, nothing is visible. When a flashlight is turned on, its bulb and objects in its beam become visible. If a bright overhead bulb is switched on, its light can bounce off the walls, ceiling, floor, and furniture, making them and other objects in its path visible.

Heating some things causes them to give off visible light rays as well as invisible heat rays. This is the case for electric-light filaments, red-hot burners on electric stoves, and glowing coals. The light of such objects is *incandescent*. Other light sources emit light energy but no heat energy. They are known as *luminescent*, or *cold light*, sources. Neon and fluorescent lights are luminescent.

## MEASURING LIGHT

The clarity with which an object can be seen depends in part on the amount of light that falls on it, on how well it is illuminated. The amount of light that a light source gives off (called its *intensity*) is one factor in determining how well a surface will be illuminated by it. Other factors are the slant of the illuminated surface in relation to the light source and the distance between the surface and the source. As a light beam travels outward from most light sources—the exceptions include lasers and searchlights—the beam spreads to cover a larger area. Distance greatly weakens illumination from such sources. The same amount of light will cover a larger area if the surface it reaches is moved farther away. This results in weaker illumination, following the inverse-square law. If the distance from the source is doubled, the amount of light falling on a given area is reduced to one fourth—the inverse of two squared. If the distance is tripled, the area receives only one ninth of the original illumination—the inverse of three squared.

One way of varying the amount of illumination on a surface is to vary the intensity of the light source. Intensity is measured in *candles* (or *candelas* in the international system). A candle used to be the amount of light given off by a carefully constructed wax candle. It is now more precisely defined as one sixtieth of the light intensity of one square centimeter of a perfectly black object at the freezing point of platinum (2,046° K, or 3,223.4° F). *Photometers* are devices that are used to measure the intensity of light sources.

People are often more interested in measuring the illumination of a surface—a desk top or the floor and walls of a room—than in measuring the light that leaves the light fixture. When distance is measured in feet, the illumination of a surface is measured in *footcandles*. At a distance of one foot the illumination provided by a light source of 100 candles is 100 footcandles. Under the inverse-square law, the same source gives one fourth as much illumination, or 25 footcandles, at a distance of two feet.

Another measurement that scientists find useful is the total amount of light energy that a source gives off over a certain period of time. This amount of light

The inverse-square law describes the light received from most sources. If the distance between an object and the light source is doubled, a given area receives only one fourth as much light; if the distance is tripled, only one ninth.

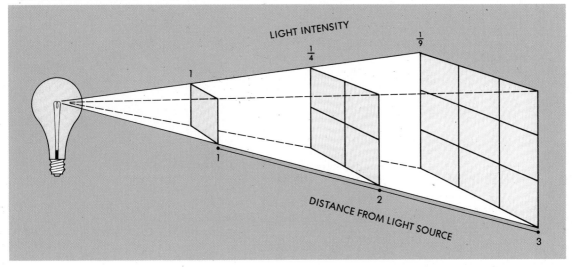

energy is called the *luminous flux* of a source and is measured in *lumens*. An ideal one-candle source gives off 4 $\pi$ lumens. One footcandle is equal to one lumen per square foot.

## LIGHT AND MATTER

The way substances look depends greatly on what happens when light hits them. It is possible to see through *transparent* substances more or less clearly because light can pass through them without being scattered or stopped. Light that bounces off the objects behind a transparent substance can pass right through it almost as if it were not in the way. Clear window glass, clean water, clear plastic, and air are all transparent, at least for short distances.

Only the surfaces of *opaque* substances are visible. Light cannot pass through them, and it is not possible to see through them. Opaque substances either absorb or reflect light. The light energy they absorb usually turns into heat and raises their temperature. Mercury, steel, and wood are examples of opaque substances.

*Translucent* substances permit some light to pass through them, but the light is scattered, and the images of objects behind them are not retained. Usually, if translucent substances are made thinner they become transparent; if they are made thicker they become opaque. Frosted light bulbs, waxed paper, and some kinds of curtain materials are translucent.

### Reflection

*Reflection* occurs when a light ray hits a surface and bounces off. The angle at which the ray hits the surface is equal to the angle at which it bounces off. If the surface is made very flat and smooth by polishing, all the light rays bounce off in the same direction.

This type of reflection is called regular, specular, or mirror reflection.

A mirror surface forms an image of things that reflect light onto it. This occurs because the light rays maintain the same pattern, except reversed from left to right, that they possessed before being reflected. Mirrors are usually made of smooth glass with a thin layer of a shiny metal such as silver bonded to the rear side (*see* Mirrors).

When an opaque surface is rough, even on the microscopic level, the light rays that hit it are scattered, causing the surface itself to become visible. This is diffuse, or irregular, reflection. If a piece of raw steel with a rough opaque surface is polished smooth and flat, it reflects light rays regularly and takes on the qualities of a mirror.

### Refraction and Dispersion

Light travels in a straight line as it passes through a transparent substance. But when it moves from one transparent material to another of different density— for example, from air to water or from glass to air— it bends at the interface (where the two surfaces meet). This bending is called *refraction*. The amount, or degree, of refraction is related to the difference between the speeds of light in the two materials of different densities—the greater the difference in densities, the more the speed changes, and the greater the bend. A slanting object partly out of water displays refraction. The object appears to bend at the interface of the air and water.

Lenses refract light. Those with concave (hollowed-out) surfaces spread light rays apart. Those with convex (bulging) surfaces bring light rays closer together (*see* Lens).

In the reflection of light, the angle of incidence is equal to the angle of reflection, measured from the normal (the line perpendicular to the point of impact). When the surface is smooth, so that all the normals are parallel, the rays maintain their spatial pattern. When the surface is rough, so that the normals are not parallel, the rays are scattered.

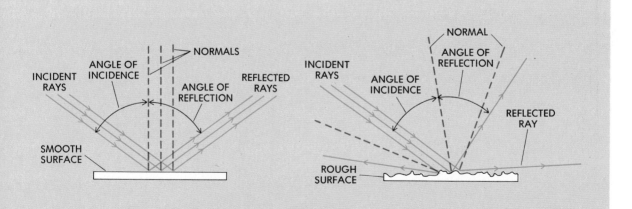

For centuries before the 1600's, scientists had known that when a ray of white light shines on a prism, a broad band containing several colors emerges. Some thought that the colors were caused by variations in lightness and darkness. But in 1672 Isaac Newton published the results of his experiments with light. He showed that a second prism placed in the path of a beam of one color could not add more color to the beam. It did, however, spread the beam farther apart. Newton concluded that the first prism broke white light down into its separate parts by spreading them apart, and he was able to establish that white light is not a pure color but a combination of all the colors in the spectrum. (*See also* Color.)

A prism spreads white light into the spectrum because each color has a slightly different speed within the prism, so each color bends (refracts) a slightly different amount as it enters and again as it leaves the prism. Violet light slows up the most, so it is bent the most; red light slows up the least, so it is bent the least. This spreading apart of white light into a spectrum is called *dispersion*.

Physicists often define dispersion as the fact that different colors move at different speeds within a substance, not necessarily causing a spectrum. For example, when white light enters a glass block that has parallel faces, the colors all have different speeds and bend different amounts as they travel through the glass. This, according to a physicist, is also dispersion. But the colors all bend back to form white light as they leave the second parallel face, so separate colors are not observed.

Opaque materials absorb all the colors of white light except their own, which they reflect. A piece of pure red material absorbs orange, yellow, green, blue, and violet but reflects red. Transparent colored materials absorb all colors except their own, which they both transmit and reflect. A piece of pure blue cellophane absorbs red, orange, yellow, green, and violet but transmits blue (it looks blue on the side opposite the light source) and reflects blue (it looks blue on the same side as the light source).

## MEASURING THE SPEED OF LIGHT

Light can travel through a vacuum. Stars are easily visible on clear nights, though their light must travel for years through empty space before it reaches earth. A laboratory experiment demonstrates that light can travel through a vacuum. When air is pumped out of a glass vacuum chamber that contains a ringing bell, the bell remains visible while the sound fades away. The vacuum cannot transmit sound waves, but the light rays continue to pass through it.

It is much easier to describe the interaction of light with matter than to explain what light is. One reason for this is that light cannot be seen until it interacts with matter—a beam of light is invisible unless it strikes an eye or unless there are particles that reflect parts of the beam to an eye. Also, light travels very fast—so fast that for centuries men disputed whether it required any time for light to move from one point to another. Many scientists thought that the movement of light was instantaneous.

Galileo suggested one of the first experiments to measure the speed of light, and Italian scientists carried out his idea. Two men were stationed on two hilltops. Each had a shaded lantern. The first man was to uncover his lantern. As soon as the second man saw the light, he was to uncover his lantern. The scientists tried to measure the time that elapsed

Light rays bouncing off the ruler on the left, in mineral oil, are bent (refracted) more than light rays from the ruler on the right, which is in water.

This alligator appears to be cut in half at the water line. Light reflected from the alligator underwater is refracted compared with the light reflected from above the water.

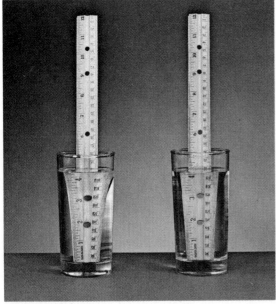

E F. Hoppe—Alfa Studio

Buddy Gaines—Artstreet

between the moment the first lantern was uncovered and the moment a return beam was detected. The speed of light was much too fast to be measured in this way, and the scientists therefore concluded that light might well travel instantaneously.

Olaus Roemer, a Danish astronomer, was dealing with an entirely different problem when he came across the first workable method for measuring the speed of light. He was timing the eclipses of Jupiter's moons and noticed that the time between eclipses varied by several minutes, depending on the position of the earth in its orbit. As the earth approached Jupiter, the time between eclipses grew shorter. As the earth receded from Jupiter, the time between eclipses grew longer. In 1676 Roemer proposed that these discrepancies be used to calculate the time required for light to travel the diameter of the earth's orbit. Since the exact size of the earth's orbit was not yet known, and since Jupiter's irregular surface caused errors in timing the eclipses, he did not arrive at an accurate value for the speed of light. But he had demonstrated that light took time to travel and that its speed was too quick to measure on earth with the instruments then available.

In 1849 Armand Fizeau, a French physicist, devised a way to measure the speed of light on earth instead of relying on uncertain astronomical measurements. His experimental apparatus included a beam of light that was sent through a notch in a rotating disk, was reflected from a mirror, and returned to the disk. The disk had 720 notches cut into it. When the returning light passed through a notch, an observer could detect it; if it hit between notches, the light was eclipsed. The distance light would travel (from the open notch to the mirror and back to the point where a tooth

could eclipse the light) was measured. Fizeau timed the eclipses and observed the rotational speed of the disk at the time of the eclipses. With this information he calculated that the speed of light in air was 194,000 miles per second. Later investigators refined this method. Jean Foucault, for example, replaced the disk with rotating mirrors and arrived at a value of 186,000 miles per second.

One of the most surprising and confusing facts about light was discovered by Albert Michelson and his co-worker, Edward Morley. They measured the speed of light very accurately as it traveled both in the same direction as the earth's movement and in the direction opposite to the earth's movement. They expected to get slightly different values, believing that the speed of the earth would be added to or subtracted from the speed of light. The situation, as they saw it, was similar to that of a person looking out the window of a car traveling at 60 miles per hour. If another car going 80 miles per hour overtakes it, the second car then seems to be moving at a speed of 20 miles per hour, or its own speed *minus* the speed of the car it has passed. If a car going 80 miles per hour approaches a car going 60 miles per hour, it seems to be traveling at 140 miles per hour, or its own speed *plus* the speed of the car that it is approaching. Light, the two men discovered, does not behave that way. Its speed appears to be the same, no matter what the speed or direction of movement of the observer making the measurement. Albert Einstein developed his theory of relativity to help explain this phenomenon (*see* Relativity).

The accepted value for the speed of light in a vacuum is $2.997924562 \times 10^8$ meters per second (about 186,282 miles per second), a fundamental

The distance between Jupiter and the earth differs at different times of the year. Olaus Roemer noted that the time between eclipses of Jupiter's moons decreased as the earth approached Jupiter and increased as the earth receded from Jupiter. He suggested that the discrepancies were caused by the time that light took to cross the diameter of the earth's orbit.

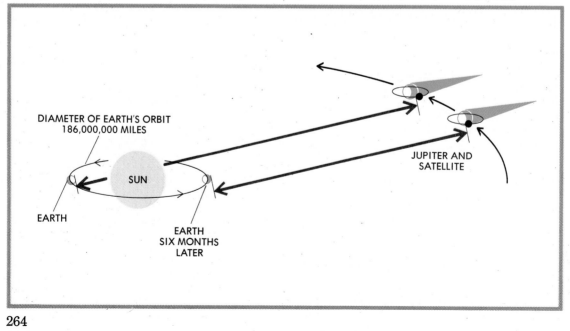

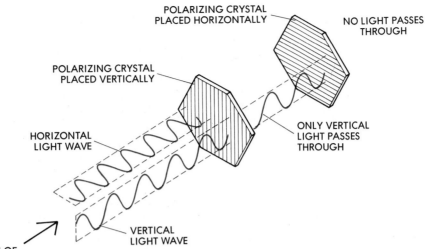

The polarization of light can be explained by the theory that light acts like transverse waves. Light vibrating parallel to some part of the polarizing crystal can pass through it. But light vibrating at a different angle is stopped by the crystal.

constant of the universe. According to the theory of relativity, time and distance may change as the speed of an object approaches the speed of light (its length shrinks and any changes it regularly undergoes take longer to occur, *relative* to a stationary observer), but the measured value for the speed of light always remains the same.

## LIGHT—WAVE OR PARTICLE?

The question remains, what is light? By the 17th century enough was known about the behavior of light for two conflicting theories of its structure to emerge. One theory held that a light ray was made up of a stream of tiny particles. The opposing theory regarded light as a wave. Both of these views have been incorporated into the modern theory of light.

Newton thought that light was composed of tiny particles given off by light sources. He believed that the different colors into which white light could be broken up were formed by particles of different sizes. He thought refraction resulted from the stronger attraction of the denser of two substances for the particles of light. Since the attraction was greater, the speed of light in denser mediums should also be greater, according to his theory. A basic piece of evidence supporting the particle view of light is that light travels in straight lines. This can be seen when a small, steady light source shines on a relatively large object. The shadow of the object has sharp borders. Newton felt that if light were a wave, it would curve slightly around obstacles, giving fuzzy-edged shadows. He pointed out that water waves curve as they pass an obstacle (for example, dock pilings) and that sound waves curve over hills and around the corners of buildings. Newton realized, however, that simple variations in the size of particles did not explain all light phenomena. When he tried to understand the shimmering coloration of soap bubbles, he had to introduce the idea that the particles vibrated.

Newton's contemporary Christian Huygens, a Dutch physicist, proposed that light was a wave. He postulated that a substance called the *ether* (not to be confused with the class of chemicals called ethers) filled the universe. Waves were generated in this pervasive substance when light traveled through it. Huygens assumed that light waves were like sound waves—the movement of alternately compressed and rarefied ether. Such waves are called longitudinal waves because the vibration of the wave is parallel to the direction in which it is traveling.

### Polarized Light

One aspect of the behavior of light posed a problem for both the particle and wave theories. Neither could really explain the polarization of light by certain transparent crystals. Both Newton and Huygens knew that when light was directed through certain crystals, it would emerge much dimmer. If a second crystal of this class were placed at a certain angle in the path of the dimmed light, the light could pass through it. Then, as either of the two crystals was slowly turned, the light emerging from the second crystal grew dimmer until it was completely blocked. Evidently, something in the structure of the first crystal allowed only part of the light to pass. When the second crystal was lined up properly with the first, it allowed the same amount of light to pass; when it was at the wrong angle to the first crystal, it screened out the light from the first crystal.

Newton speculated that polarization occurred because light particles had various shapes on their sides, some of which were rejected by the crystal structure. This was not a very satisfactory explanation. However, Huygens had to make even more complicated assumptions to explain how crystals could polarize longitudinal waves. Neither the wave theory nor the particle theory was sufficiently developed to account for all the observed light phenomena, but the weight

265

Fritz Goro, *Life*© Time Inc.

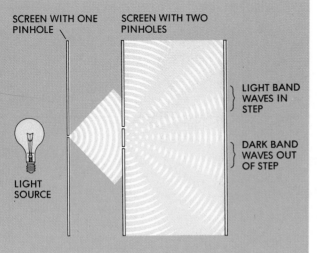

SCREEN WITH ONE PINHOLE

SCREEN WITH TWO PINHOLES

LIGHT BAND
WAVES IN
STEP

DARK BAND
WAVES OUT
OF STEP

LIGHT SOURCE

In Young's interference experiment, light that passes through the pinholes in the second screen sets up an interference pattern on the back wall. Such patterns are caused by waves.

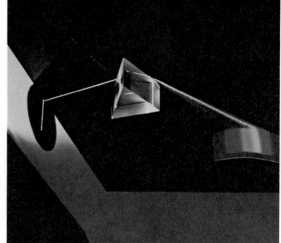

White light is a mixture of all the colors of the rainbow. A prism breaks up white light into its component colors by bending each color a different amount.

of Newton's reputation caused the particle theory to be accepted by most scientists.

## Light Bends Around Corners

In the early 19th century Thomas Young, a British physician, took the next step in developing the wave theory. He demonstrated that light waves were so short that the amount they curved as they passed an object was too small to be visible. He showed that, though shadows from point sources of light appear to have sharp edges, there are thin light-and-dark bands along their borders that are caused by the bending of some light rays into the shadow. This scattering of light, called *diffraction*, can be observed under certain conditions. A thin tubular source, such as a fluores-

Matter cannot travel faster than the speed of light in a vacuum. In a transparent substance, however, particles can travel faster than light travels in that substance. When that happens, they give off visible light, called Cherenkov radiation. The photograph shows the core of an atomic reactor submerged in water. The blue glow is Cherenkov radiation. It is caused by charged particles whose movement through the water is faster than that of light in water.

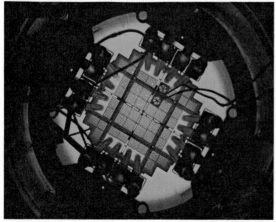

Argonne National Laboratory

cent light, is good. A very thin slit in an opaque material, or even two fingers squeezed loosely together so that light may pass between them, may cause diffraction. The slit is held a foot or two in front of one eye, parallel to the light source; the other eye is closed. Light shines through the slit, and a pattern of colored bands, or a colored glow, can be seen outlining the slit. The outline is colored because diffraction disperses white light into its separate colors in much the same way that a prism does. Young observed diffraction and concluded that it occurred because light was a wave.

Three important measurements describe a wave—speed, frequency, and wavelength. Frequency is a measure of the number of waves that pass a given point in a specified amount of time. Wavelength is the distance from one crest (the highest point) to the next crest, or from one trough (the lowest point) to the next. If all the waves have the same speed, a great many short waves will pass a point in the same time that only a few long waves pass it. Speed equals the wavelength times the frequency.

Young set up an experiment to measure the wavelength of light; using the principle of *interference*. When two sets of waves meet, they interfere with each other in a predictable way. Water waves, such as those made by the wakes of two boats, illustrate this. When two wakes meet, the water becomes choppy. Parts of the waves are very high and parts are very low; the individual waves can reinforce each other or cancel each other. Where two crests meet, the wave becomes higher. Where two troughs meet, the wave becomes deeper. And if a crest and a trough meet, they cancel each other and the water is level.

In his interference experiment Young used a single light source, a pinhole that admitted a single beam of sunlight. This beam fell on a screen that had two pinholes close together. As light passed through each

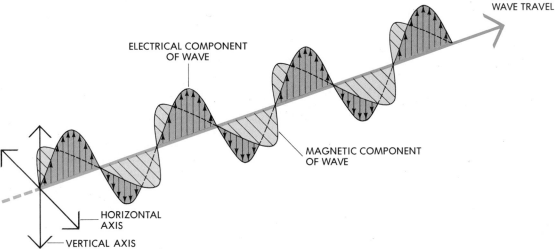

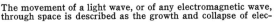

DIRECTION OF WAVE TRAVEL

ELECTRICAL COMPONENT OF WAVE

MAGNETIC COMPONENT OF WAVE

HORIZONTAL AXIS

VERTICAL AXIS

The movement of a light wave, or of any electromagnetic wave, through space is described as the growth and collapse of electrical and magnetic fields. The fields are at right angles to each other and to the direction of travel.

pinhole, it curved and spread out (diffracted). Because the pinholes were close enough together, the two light beams met and interfered with each other. Their interference pattern was seen on a screen behind the pinholes. With this pattern and knowing the distance between the screens, Young was able to calculate that the wavelength of visible light was about one millionth of a meter.

Subsequent measurements show that the wavelengths of visible light range from $7.60 \times 10^{-5}$ cm. to $3.85 \times 10^{-5}$ cm. ($2.99 \times 10^{-5}$ in. to $1.51 \times 10^{-5}$ in.). Each color is associated with a range of wavelengths. Red has the longest lengths. The wavelengths decrease from orange through yellow, green, and blue. Violet has the shortest wavelengths visible to the human eye.

### Transverse Waves Explain Polarization

Young and Augustin Jean Fresnel, a French physicist, cooperated in developing the idea that light waves are transverse, that they resemble the waves made when a rope stretched from a post is jerked up and down rather than longitudinal sound waves. The rope itself moves only up and down, at right angles to the forward travel of the wave. Young and Fresnel suggested the wave motion of light might also be at right angles to the direction in which the wave was traveling. The motion could be in any direction between sideways and up-and-down just so long as it was at right angles to the direction of travel. Wave motion of this kind could explain polarization. If a polarizing crystal admitted only those waves that were vibrating in a certain direction, then a second crystal would block those waves if it were turned at an angle to the first. The second one would be oriented to accept only waves vibrating in a different direction, and the first cyrstal would have already blocked all those waves. Fresnel made calculations that accounted for all the light behavior he knew of by assuming that light was made up of transverse waves.

Measurements of the speed of light in substances other than air presented additional difficulties for Newton's particle theory of light. The theory had assumed that light travels faster in dense substances than in rarefied substances. Fizeau and Foucault measured the speed of light in various transparent substances and discovered that it was slower in denser materials than in air.

### "Invisible Light"

Around 1800—while Young was developing his wave theory—three scientists discovered that the color spectrum was bordered by invisible rays. Sir William Herschel, a British astronomer, was measuring the temperature of the colors dispersed by a prism. As he moved the thermometer down the spectrum from violet to red, he observed a rise in temperature. As he moved the thermometer beyond the red beam, the temperature grew even higher. Herschel had discovered a hot, invisible radiation that appeared to be a continuation of the spectrum. This radiation is called infrared radiation because it occurs just below red in the spectrum. (See also Infrared Radiation.)

Ultraviolet rays were discovered by Johann Wilhelm Ritter and by William Hyde Wollaston, who were independently studying the effects of light on silver chloride. Silver chloride placed in violet light grew dark. When the chemical was placed in the area beyond the violet of the spectrum, it darkened even more rapidly. They concluded that a chemically powerful kind of invisible radiation lay beyond the violet end of the spectrum. (See also Ultraviolet Radiation.)

In 1864 James Clerk Maxwell, a Scottish physicist, published a theory of electricity and magnetism. He had developed equations that predicted the existence of electromagnetic waves caused by electrical disturbances. He calculated the speed of such waves and

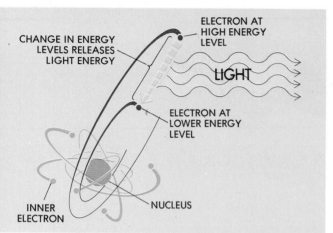

Modern theory explains the emission of light by matter in terms of electronic energy levels, diagramed above. An electron of relatively high energy may jump to a condition of lower energy, giving off the energy difference as electromagnetic radiation.

found it to be the same as the speed of light. Maxwell concluded that light was an electromagnetic wave. As a single light wave travels through space, its movement consists of the growth and collapse of electrical and magnetic fields. The electrical fields are at right angles to the magnetic fields, and both are at right angles to the direction in which the wave is moving.

Maxwell's theory implied that other electromagnetic radiations with wavelengths longer than infrared or shorter than ultraviolet might be found. In 1887 Heinrich Hertz produced radio waves, which have longer wavelengths than infrared rays, thus confirming Maxwell's theory. (*See also* Radiation.)

## LIGHT: WAVE AND PARTICLE

In 1900 the German physicist Max Planck advanced a theory to account for the behavior of *blackbodies*. A blackbody is an ideal substance with a perfectly black surface that absorbs all the radiation that falls on it and emits radiation in specific ways dependent on temperature. While such an ideal material does not actually exist, some materials resemble it closely enough to provide experimental tests of blackbody theory. The observed behavior is that blackbodies do not emit all wavelengths in equal amounts.

Instead, certain wavelengths are emitted more often than others. As the temperature increases, the wavelengths that are emitted preferentially decrease in length. In other words, the wavelength of maximum emission varies inversely with temperature. Planck explained this behavior by suggesting that matter can handle energy only in specific amounts, called *quanta*, and that amounts of energy between these quanta cannot be absorbed or emitted. The amounts must be exactly right.

In 1905 Einstein expanded this idea in his explanation of the *photoelectric effect*. If light falls on certain metals, electrons in those metals are freed and can form an electric current. Einstein was trying to account for the observation that the energy of the electrons is independent of the amount of radiation falling on the metal. The maximum energy of the electrons was observed to depend on the wavelength of the radiation. Einstein suggested that not only does matter handle energy in precise amounts (quanta), but the photoelectric effect could also be accounted for by assuming that electromagnetic energy, including light, always occurs in these bundles. This reintroduced the particle theory. The results of many subsequent experiments supported the idea that light energy travels in quanta. An individual light "particle" possesses one quantum of energy and is called a *photon*.

The way matter becomes a light source can be explained in terms of quantum theory. When certain elements are heated, they give off light of a specific color. This light can be separated into a spectrum that is made up of many distinct bright lines (*see* Spectrum and Spectroscope). Each element has its unique spectrum, which can be accurately measured. Since a spectrum positively identifies each element, the chemical composition of astronomical bodies is determined by an analysis of their spectra.

Scientists wondered why the atoms of each element, when provided with a wide range of energies by the heating process, give off only the specific energies in their spectra. The modern theory of atomic structure makes this phenomenon understandable. An atom is made up of a heavy, positively charged nucleus which is surrounded by light, negatively charged electrons.

The electromagnetic spectrum ranges from very energetic gamma rays, which have high frequencies and short wavelengths, to radio waves, which have low frequencies and long wavelengths. The visible light region is a very small part of the entire spectrum.

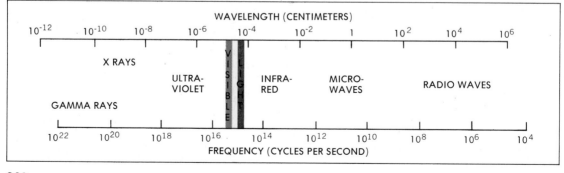

Modern theory states that the electrons of an atom can assume certain fixed energy relationships, called *energy levels*, to one another and to the nucleus. These energy levels are the same for all the atoms of a single element. An electron must occupy one of the energy levels; it cannot possess any energy between levels.

When an atom is heated, enough energy may be given to one of the electrons to raise it to a higher energy level. But it usually jumps back to a lower level, giving off an electromagnetic wave—the energy difference of the two levels. When this energy is in the visible light range, it shows up as one of the lines in the element's visible spectrum. Each element has a different spectrum because each element has a different number of electrons and different energy levels available to these electrons.

Atomic theory had not yet explained why both a wave theory and a particle theory were needed to describe light. Physicists used both, depending on which was more useful in a given situation. The paradox was finally resolved in 1924 by Louis de Broglie. He postulated that matter, which had always been treated as a collection of particles, had a wave aspect as well. This wave nature has been demonstrated in experiments with electrically charged moving particles, such as electrons. (*See also* Matter; Energy.)

### BIBLIOGRAPHY FOR LIGHT

#### Books and Films for Children

Asimov, Isaac. Light (Follett, 1970).
Beeler, N. F. and Branley, F. M. Experiments in Optical Illusion (Crowell, 1951).
Light and Color, film (Encyclopaedia Britannica Films).

#### Books and Films for Young Adults and Teachers

Beeler, N. F. and Branley, F. M. Experiments with Light (Crowell, 1957).
Cook, J. G. We Live by the Sun (Dial, 1957).
Mueller, C. G. and others. Light and Vision (Time-Life, 1966).
Rainwater, Clarence. Light and Color (Golden Press, 1971).
The Speed of Light, film (Encyclopaedia Britannica Films).
(*See also* bibliographies for **Color** and **Lasers and Masers**.)

The candle and the fireworks convert chemical energy to light. The incandescent light bulb, the fluorescent lights, and the neon lights convert electrical energy to light. The steel slabs have been heated until they give off light.

## LIGHTHOUSES AND LIGHT TOWERS.

In the days when Columbus and other bold mariners set sail on uncharted seas, they were in constant peril from shoals and submerged rocks. Now the ocean lanes are dotted with hundreds of lighthouses, light towers, and lightships to guide the seaman.

The history of the lighthouse is alive with the tales of heroic keepers. In the face of great perils they have performed their duties of guiding ships safely to port. One classic example is that of Grace Darling (1815–42), daughter of an English lighthouse keeper. She and her father rescued nine exhausted survivors of the *Forfarshire* after hours of struggle in a hurricane.

Most modern lighthouses are equipped with automatic lights and are serviced at periodic intervals by a tender. The modern keepers must be technically trained to operate diesel engines, air compressors, and radio beacon transmitters. (*See also* Radio.)

Until recent years, lighthouses were made of huge piles of very thick masonry that could withstand the buffeting of wave and wind. Today the typical lighthouse is a tapering cylindrical steel tower rising from 100 to 400 feet above the base. It is bolted into the solid rock of a reef or a masonry foundation. A winding staircase leads up to the gigantic lantern at the top. The blinding shaft of the lantern's light can be seen from the deck of a ship 20 miles away.

The lantern consists of from two to eight lenses held in a light metallic frame. Reflectors, lenses, and prisms magnify the intensity and focus the light into a beam. The beam turns as the lantern rotates at a controlled speed. The time between flashes enables an observer to tell one lighthouse from another. In early days the light was produced by coal fires, candles, or whale-oil lamps. Today electricity is the main source of light and power. Fuel cells and thermoelectric devices are being studied as possible methods of producing power for navigational aids.

Lighthouses were in use centuries before the Christian Era began. The source of light was a brazier of burning coals which hung from a pole. As far back as the 7th century B.C., there was a lighthouse at Cape Sigeum on the Asiatic side of the Dardanelles. The most famous lighthouse of antiquity was the tower built on the island of Pharos in the bay of Alexandria.

**AN OLDER TYPE OF LIGHTHOUSE LAMP**
Intense light (white spot at center) was produced by a gas-burning mantle. The light was magnified, focused, and emitted as powerful horizontal beams. A timing device (lower right) regulated the lamp's rotation.

It was completed in the 3d century B.C. and was considered one of the Seven Wonders of the World. For a long time the name "pharos" was given to all lighthouses. At Boulogne, on the French coast, the Romans built a great tower 200 feet high and 192 feet in circumference. It was a reliable guide for mariners for more than 14 centuries.

Famous lighthouses in operation today include the Eddystone, 13 miles off Plymouth, England; the Bell Rock, off the coast of Scotland; and Minot's Ledge, a very difficult engineering feat which rises from a sunken wave-swept reef in the open Atlantic 20 miles southeast of Boston, Mass.

Off dangerous coasts and at the entrance to harbors where lighthouses cannot be built, steel lightships

**A LIGHTHOUSE THAT GUIDED SHIPS FOR 1,400 YEARS**
The picture below is taken from an old print of a famous structure that was built by the Romans at Boulogne, on the north coast of France. This building served as a lighthouse for 14 centuries.

Although the sources of power that are used today were not known, the light from great bonfires provided a signal of safety for navigators.

# THE DESIGN AND CONSTRUCTION OF A MODERN LIGHTHOUSE

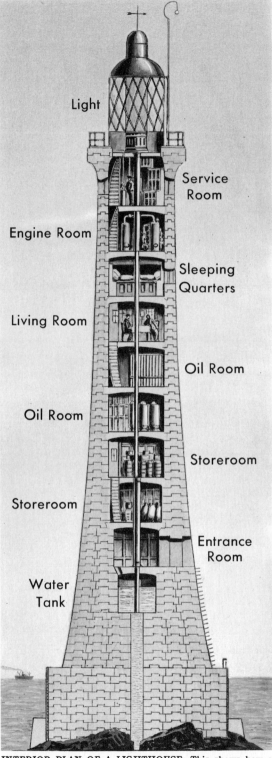

Light

Service Room

Engine Room

Sleeping Quarters

Living Room

Oil Room

Oil Room

Storeroom

Storeroom

Entrance Room

Water Tank

INTERIOR PLAN OF A LIGHTHOUSE. This shows how a modern lighthouse of the stone masonry type is built. Notice how heavy the walls are at the bottom where they have to withstand the heaviest shocks.

LAYING THE FOUNDATION. This part of the work often must be done from a temporary stage set up beside the lighthouse site. When the sea is rough, the work is very dangerous.

DELIVERING MATERIALS. Building materials for the lighthouse sometimes have to be delivered along cables, strung like giant spiders' webs from nearby cliffs. Here we see a great block of stone on its perilous journey.

A THRILLING TRIP TO WORK. Workmen as well as materials must make that dizzy trip along the cables when such lighthouses as the Beachey Head light on the southern coast of England are being erected.

George Fred Keck & William Keck, Architects; Hedrich-Blessing Photo

The walls of this contemporary house include large expanses of glass that, in the daytime, let sunlight brighten its interior.

Drapes help govern the intensity of the light. Indirect artificial-light fixtures are concealed above the windows.

Taken at night, this exterior view of the same house shows how its modern ceiling fixtures provide light that comes from the

direction of the windows and above, simulating the effect of daylight. Reading lights offer supplementary illumination.

<small>U.S. Coast Guard</small>

In 1961 this light tower at Buzzards Bay, Mass., became the first of its type to replace a lightship. A beacon producing 9 million candlepower is used during periods of low visibility.

are moored. Their masts carry powerful lights, and they have foghorns to sound warning in fog and storms. Many have radio beacons and radar.

### Government Aids to Navigation

During the early 1970's the United States began replacing its many lightships and some of its lightship stations. Most have been replaced by large automated buoys that operate at a fraction of the cost of maintaining lightships. In addition, a number of offshore light towers were in operation.

Buoys mark channels and minor obstructions. Channels are marked on the right, as ships come in, by red, cone-shaped buoys called "nuns"; black "cans," or flat-topped buoys, mark the left edge (for illustration of buoys, see Navigation). About 26,000 buoys are used in United States waters. Many have steady or flashing lights, which may be red, white, or green. Some sound warnings with bells or whistles. Electric storage batteries provide power for illumination.

One of the major services of the Coast Guard is the establishment and operation of aids to navigation. It maintains more than 46,000 such aids, including about 170 fully manned lighthouses. The Coast Guard is part of the Department of Transportation (see Coast Guard, United States). In Canada, the Marine Services of the Department of Transport administers lighthouses; in Britain, the Corporation of Trinity House.

**LIGHTING.** In the well-lighted homes of North America, it is hard to imagine the darkness in houses of a few generations ago. In the 19th century people read or worked at night by the light of oil lamps or gaslights. Before that time they used candles.

Houses have had good windows for several centuries, but in ancient and medieval times they were small and poor (see Shelter). The first glass windows were probably used in early Rome. They were made of small pieces of glass set in bronze frames. After the Dark Ages, glazed windows with tiny panes joined by strips of lead were used. However, the poorer homes received daylight only through windows covered with parchment or oiled paper.

As manufacturers made better and cheaper glass, windows became larger and more numerous. Even after glass became generally available, however, the number of windows in a house was kept at a minimum in some countries because a tax was levied on them. Such a tax was imposed in England in 1696 and was not repealed for 155 years. The early American colonists used oiled-paper windows, for glassworkers were scarce. Not until the 19th century did cheap glass become common.

Materials besides glass have been used for windows. Horn and isinglass have served like oiled paper to admit light. In Oriental lands costly alabaster is cut to paper thinness for windows. In warm climates windows are often not sealed.

Introduction of the incandescent electric lamp revolutionized artificial lighting. It provided new efficient lighting and, in time, added new beauty to dwellings, offices, and public buildings.

The light of the early carbon-filament bulbs was harsh and yellowish. Yet when mounted in shaded lamps it was a welcome improvement over oil and gas. Later, frosting and the tungsten filament gave electric light greater whiteness and softness. In time, fluorescent lights were developed.

Among the greatest improvements in home illumination has been indirect lighting. Light from either incandescent or fluorescent lamps is projected on a light-colored wall or ceiling. From there it is reflected and diffused over a large part of the room. Such lighting is far easier on the eyes than direct illumination. Skillfully handled, it can be used to produce pleasing patterns of light and shade.

The introduction of electric lighting gave rise to the profession of *illuminating engineering*. Illuminating engineers determine the amount of illumination required in buildings, decide on the placement of lights to provide the best working conditions and greatest economy, and design lighting devices. Some illuminating engineers specialize in airport, harbor, marine, theater, or decorative lighting. (See also Electric Light; Engineering; Lamps.)

---

THIS ARTICLE IS IN THE FACT-INDEX
**Lightner Museum of Hobbies**

---

This magnificent and frightening display of lightning performs a valuable service for nature. It may also cause great damage to life and property. In this photograph, strokes from cloud to ground and from cloud to cloud can be seen.

# LIGHTNING—A Gigantic Electric Spark

**LIGHTNING.** A violent thunderstorm, with its bright flashes of lightning and loud claps of thunder, is an awesome thing. Everyone has seen, and probably been frightened by, these sudden jagged streams of electricity. It is estimated that, at any given moment, about 3,500 thunderstorms are occurring around the world. These storms produce more than 100 bright strokes of lightning every second. The strokes act as electrical conductors joining the earth to its atmosphere. Thunderstorms and lightning are nature's ways of balancing the electrical forces that exist between the earth and the upper atmosphere.

In ancient times men believed that lightning bolts were thrown from the heavens by angry gods. No scientific explanation of the cause of lightning appeared until the 1700's. In 1745 the invention of the Leyden jar (the first electrical condenser) proved that electricity could be collected and stored for indefinite periods. Benjamin Franklin applied this information in a series of experiments he performed in 1752. He proved that lightning was an electrical discharge whose actions were in agreement with the principles of electricity known at that time. During the 20th century, research scientists, electric-utility companies, and weather bureaus have joined forces to study the causes and occurrences of lightning. Many useful facts have been learned. However, lightning activity is a very complicated subject, and much more work must be done before it is fully understood.

## The Build-up and Discharge of Lightning

Great electrical changes occur in the atmosphere when a large cloud forms above the earth. Inside the cloud, rapid heating and cooling of air masses produce violent activity. Rain falls, air currents rise, and water droplets freeze. Some drops of water in the cloud become charged with positive electricity. These are carried to the upper part of the cloud by air currents and form a positive-charge center. Ice crystals which are formed have a negative charge. Due to their weight, they move down and produce a negative-charge center at the base of the cloud. To balance this negative charge, positive charges on the earth are concentrated in the region just below the cloud. The cloud's negative charge induces a positive charge at the ground (see Electricity).

As cloud formation continues, the two opposite charges increase in strength. Since unlike charges attract, there is a powerful tendency for the charges to join and neutralize each other. Each charge exerts a strong electrical potential, or pressure, in an effort to bridge the air gap from cloud to ground. Air, a poor electrical conductor, resists the passage of the

---

**PROPERTIES OF A LIGHTNING STROKE**

Length—From 500 feet to more than two miles.

Pilot Streamer Speed—0.05 per cent of speed of light.

Return Streamer Speed—10 per cent of speed of light.

Duration—The entire visible discharge may last from 1/500 second to as much as 1.6 seconds. Total period of discharge depends upon the number of return strokes produced.

Width—From 1/3 inch to a foot at the stroke's peak.

Temperature—Up to 54,000° F. (30,000° C.).

Number of Return Streamers—An average of 6 or 7.

Current and Power—Up to 200 coulombs of electricity released. This is equivalent to many billions of kilowatts of power. (For definitions, see Electricity.)

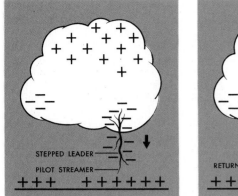
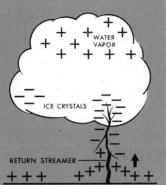
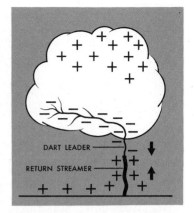

## NATURE PRODUCES A POWERFUL STROKE OF LIGHTNING

A lightning stroke begins when a pilot streamer moves down from a negative-charge center in a cloud (left). The stepped leader, a more powerful current, follows the pilot streamer. A return streamer, a current of very high density (center), leaps from the earth and travels upward along the path of ionized air created by the stepped leader. Discharge of a second negative-charge center in the cloud occurs when the dart leader (right) moves to the ground and is met by another return streamer.

charges. At some critical point, however, the resistance of the air is overcome. A small discharge, called a *pilot streamer*, moves toward the earth carrying negative charge. A stronger current, called a *stepped leader*, follows and ionizes the air in its path (*see* Ions). The stepped leader moves in a series of jagged spurts, each about 150 feet long. When the pilot streamer touches the earth, a high-current *return streamer* leaps from the ground toward the cloud. It travels along the path of ionized air created by the stepped leader. This is the part of the stroke that produces the brilliant flash we see.

As charge in one cloud center is dissipated, negative charge from an adjacent charge center moves in to replace it. A *dart leader* from the second charge center moves to the ground along the original current channel. This produces another return streamer which also travels up to the cloud. Discharging continues until all negative charges in the cloud have been drained off, restoring electrical balance between earth and atmosphere. Lightning strokes also travel between two clouds, and, in the case of *heat lightning*, between charge centers in the same cloud.

*Thunder* follows a lightning flash. During the electrical discharge, the flow of electricity along the discharge path ionizes the gases of the air and produces great heat. The gases expand violently, causing compression waves which travel outward at the speed of sound. Thunder is the sound produced by these compression waves.

### The Effects of Lightning

The destructive powers of lightning are much more spectacular than its beneficial effects. In an average year about 500 people are killed by lightning and 1,500 more are injured. This is more than twice the number killed by tornadoes and more than six times the number of deaths caused by floods. Lightning strokes cause more than 20 million dollars' worth of property damage every year in the United States.

On the credit side, lightning produces important chemical changes in the atmosphere. As a stroke moves through the air, it generates tremendous heat which unites nitrogen and oxygen to form nitrates and other compounds. The nitrate falls to earth with the rain. In this way, the atmosphere is able to continually replenish the supply of fertilizer which the soil needs to produce our food.

### Protection Against Lightning Damage

The attraction of tall structures for lightning has been known for centuries. This is easily explained by modern electrical theory. Lightning is an electrical current that tries to bridge the air gap between the ground and a cloud. It follows the path of least resistance—the route that crosses the shortest air gap. Thus the positive ground charge will concentrate at the highest point on the ground, and the stroke will usually be between that point and the cloud. For this reason, a lightning rod or shield is higher than all other objects near it. A shield may be a single pole set in the ground or a group of masts supported in a framework that completely surrounds a building. The shield provides a good target for a lightning stroke and thus protects other nearby structures.

For personal protection, remember that lightning normally strikes the tallest object in its range. A person standing in the middle of a field is the tallest object and therefore the main target. A tall tree attracts lightning and is a poor conductor of electricity. It offers so much resistance to the passage of current that a part of the current may flash out at the sides and strike any neighboring object. Steel buildings, trains, automobiles, and aircraft provide good paths to ground for electricity and are well insulated.

THESE ARTICLES ARE IN THE FACT-INDEX

Lignin
Lignum vitae
Ligny, Belgium
Liguria

Ligurian Republic
Ligurians
Li Hung-chang

**A LILAC-FRAMED GATEWAY**
This profusion of blossoms is typical of the lilac. The shrubs form beautiful and spectacular hedges up to 25 feet in height.

**LILAC.** A beautiful and fragrant shrub, the lilac is one of the most popular of garden plants. Its pyramidal clusters of blossoms are white, lavender, blue, violet, pink, or purple. There are both single and double varieties—all with glossy green leaves.

Lilacs are native to eastern Europe and Asia. The colonists brought them to America. They are often planted in groups to form masses of shrubbery or hedges. Some famous lilac gardens which display several hundred varieties are the Lemoine gardens at Nancy, France; the Arnold Arboretum at Jamaica Plains, Mass. (for picture, *see* Botanical Gardens and Arboretums); the gardens in Highland Park, Rochester, N. Y.; and Lilacia Park in Lombard, Ill.

Lilacs grow best in full sunlight, nonacid soil, and where there is good drainage. They need a winter freeze to provide a dormant, or rest, period. Single shrubs, given plenty of room, grow full and tall, reaching a height of 10 to 25 feet. For maximum bloom, however, they should be kept to a moderate height. Pruning back young growth to keep the interior open also helps flowering.

Lilacs belong to the olive family, *Oleaceae*. The name of the genus, *Syringa* ("little pipe"), was given it because lilac stems were once hollowed out and used as pipe stems. Syringa is also the common name for an unrelated shrub, the mock orange (*see* Syringa). The scientific name of the common lilac with purple flowers is *Syringa vulgaris;* of the Persian lilac, a smaller shrub with white flowers, *Syringa persica.*

THESE ARTICLES ARE IN THE FACT-INDEX

Liliencron, Detlev,     Lilienthal, Otto
  baron von             Lilith
Lilienthal, David E(li)    Liliuokalani

**LILLE** (*lēl*), **France.** In the Middle Ages, Lille grew up around a feudal castle on the Deule River, seven miles from the present Belgian frontier. It was the capital of French Flanders. Today it is the largest city in Northern France and the capital of the Nord (North) Department. It is also an important railroad and manufacturing center.

Lille has long been noted for the making of fine linen and flax thread for lacemaking and sewing. "Lisle" thread gets its name from the city. Cotton and woolen goods are also produced in Lille.

The old town has kept much of its 17th and 18th century appearance. There are still fine 17th-century gates in the ancient walls of the city. The Palais des Beaux Arts has one of the richest picture galleries in France. The Lille library is famous for its rare editions and historical documents. Among the city's educational institutions is Lille University, where the great Louis Pasteur once taught.

Lille was ruined and rebuilt in the wars between the Flemish and the French in the 13th century. Later it fell under Austrian rule, then Spanish, and was not restored to France until 1667. In 1792 it withstood a nine-day Austrian bombardment. In both World Wars it was occupied by Germany. Population (1962 census), 191,863.

THESE ARTICLES ARE IN THE FACT-INDEX
Lillie, Beatrice (Lady Peel)
Lillie, Gordon William

**LILY.** The white lily stands for purity. Artists for centuries have pictured the angel Gabriel coming to the Virgin Mary with a spray of lilies in his hand, to announce that she is to be the mother of the

**TURK'S-CAP LILY**
This orange-red flower is a common wild lily. Notice the recurved petals and the whorled leaves (bottom right of picture).

Christ child. The lily is also the sign of the Resurrection. The lovely white Madonna lily of southern Europe was used for years as the Easter lily. It often failed to bloom in time for Easter, so Bermuda lilies were substituted.

Some familiar colored lilies are the dark-red tiger lily, of Japan; the Siberian coral lily; the gold-banded, or Japan, lily, with yellow-banded purple-spotted white flowers; and the Japanese showy lily, with red-dotted pink flowers. Wild lilies of North America are the Turk's-cap, Canada, and wood lilies.

The bulb of a true lily is made up of loose scales that easily peel off. The bulbs never become completely dormant and must be kept moist in peat moss until they are planted. Professional breeders of lilies pull the bulbs apart and plant the scales. Each scale grows into a small bulb which in two or three years produces flowers. New varieties are created by shaking the pollen of one kind onto the stigma of another and planting the resulting seed.

True lilies belong to the genus *Lilium* of the family *Liliaceae*. Several hundred species and thousands of varieties are known. They have six-part flowers (three petals and three sepals colored alike) and usually six stamens.

The family includes many food plants—asparagus, onion, leek, garlic, and chives. Some of the flowers are the lily of the valley, mariposa, sego lily, tulip, hyacinth, and yucca, all members of different genera. The popular day lilies belong to the genus *Hemerocallis*. The plantain lily, or funkia, comprises the genus *Hosta*. Calla lilies belong to the unrelated *Arum* family (*Araceae*), of which Jack-in-the-pulpit is a member. (For pictures in color, *see* Flowers, Garden; Flowers, Wild.)

---

THIS ARTICLE IS IN THE FACT-INDEX
**Lilybaeum, Sicily**

---

**LILY OF THE VALLEY**
The dainty lily of the valley is a spring favorite.

**LILY OF THE VALLEY.** This fragrant flower, with its dainty white bells, is a popular spring blossom. The six-toothed, nodding bells grow on one side of a slender stem, clasped by two broad, oblong-shaped green leaves. The leaves spring from a horizontal underground rootstock.

The lily of the valley is native to Europe, Asia, and America. It prefers moist shady places. Planted in gardens, it easily escapes and runs wild. The plants grow for years without care by a gardener and spread to form large patches. The flower is a member of the lily family (*Liliaceae*). The scientific name is *Convallaria majalis*. There is a pink-flowered form, *Convallaria rosea*.

THIS ARTICLE IS IN THE FACT-INDEX
**Lima, Ohio**

**LIMA, Peru.** Francisco Pizarro, the Spanish conqueror of Peru, founded the city of Lima in January 1535. He named it the City of Kings, in honor of the Three Wise Men of the Orient. The name was changed to that of the Rimac River on which the city stands.

Eventually Rimac became mispronounced Lima. For centuries Lima was the capital of Spain's vast realm in South America.

The heart of the old city is the broad Plaza de Armas, laid out by Pizarro himself. On one side rises the Cathedral (1657). There Pizarro's shriveled body lies exposed to view in a glass coffin. The modern government palace also flanks the Plaza. It replaces the palace of Pizarro, but the gardens and fountains of the conqueror have been preserved.

In the narrow crowded streets nearby are many ancient churches and colonial mansions. Among the finest buildings are San Augustín Church (1551), famous for its magnificent façade; and the Torre Tagle Palace (about 1750), now the foreign office, probably the most beautiful example in the Western World of a Spanish-Moorish palace.

Lima is the seat of the oldest university in South America, the national University of San Marcos. It received its charter from Emperor Charles V in 1551. In the National Museum of Archaeology are rich remains of Inca and pre-Inca Indian civilizations.

Lima is the largest city of Peru and the center of its political, social, cultural, commercial, and economic life. Handsome suburbs have been built and wide avenues constructed. Its factories produce cotton and woolen textiles and many products for local use. The port of Callao, six miles distant on the Pacific Ocean, handles most of Peru's foreign trade. Limatambo airport is a principal stop on the air route between the Americas.

Lima lies at an altitude of 500 feet, near the center of the arid Peruvian coastal plain. The Rimac River supplies water for irrigation. Though the city is only 12 degrees south of the equator, the chill Humboldt Current of the Pacific Ocean cools the air. The annual mean temperature is 66.7° F. Rain seldom falls but fogs are common in winter. Numerous earthquakes have shaken the region. Population (1961 census), 1,436,231, including suburbs.

---

THESE ARTICLES ARE IN THE FACT-INDEX
Liman von Sanders, Otto
Limber pine
Limbo
Limbourg, Pol, Hermann, and Hannequin de

---

**LIME.** Quicklime, or lime, as it is more commonly called, is a white alkaline substance having considerable power to corrode, or "eat," animal tissues. Quicklime is usually obtained by roasting limestone in a kiln or furnace at about 1,800° F. This changes the calcium carbonate of limestone to calcium oxide (CaO), or quicklime (see Limestone). Since quicklime is alkaline and chemically active, it is useful in many processes. These include removing hair from hides and correcting acidity in soils and various liquids, for example, sugarcane juice. Another common use is in making mortar and plaster.

To make mortar, lime is *slaked* by adding water. This changes the oxide to a hydroxide (CaOH). Coarse sand, cinders, or pulverized stone is mixed in, and the mixture is used to bind or cover bricks or stones. As the mixture dries, it absorbs carbon dioxide from the air to form calcium carbonate, and also combines with the silica of the sand to form calcium silicate. These substances bind the bricks or stones together. Quicklime exposed to air is ruined for mortar making by absorption of carbon dioxide (air-slaking). Lime plaster is made by mixing hair with water-slaked lime.

Pure calcium oxide is formed by melting limestone in an electric furnace. Under intense heat this gives a strong white light. Limelights (also called calcium lights or Drummond lights) were formerly used for stage lighting.

A solution of calcium hydroxide in water is called *limewater*. This is used in medicine to correct acidity, to prevent milk from curdling in large lumps, and with certain oils as a liniment for burns. Limewater reveals the presence of carbon dioxide by becoming cloudy. It is an antidote for poisoning by mineral or oxalic acids.

---

THESE ARTICLES ARE IN THE FACT-INDEX

**Limerick, Ireland (county)**
**Limerick, Ireland (borough)**
**Limericks**

---

**LIMESTONE.** Without help from chemistry and a microscope we might find it hard to believe that the rock called limestone came from sea shells and corals. But chemistry tells us that shells and corals owe their stiffness to calcium carbonate (CaCO₃), often called "carbonate of lime." Limestone also is mainly calcium carbonate; and the microscope enables us to see the remains of animals which formed it.

Hence we know that limestone is sedimentary rock, formed from shells and other "limey" material in the oceans that in past ages covered the limestone regions. Outstanding regions of this sort in the United States are the present site of the Rocky Mountains, the valleys of the Mississippi, Ohio, and St. Lawrence rivers, and much of Texas (see Geology).

Limestone has many important uses. It is the chief source of lime. It is used in making portland cement (see Cement) and in smelting iron and lead (see Iron and Steel, Making of); and it is an important building material. It wears better than sandstone, is more easily shaped than granite, and weathers from nearly white to a beautiful gray. Oolitic limestone, quarried in Lawrence, Monroe, and Owen counties in Indiana, is particularly fine building stone. Its texture resembles fish eggs, hence its name, from the Greek *oion*, meaning "egg." Bedford, Ind., is an important limestone quarrying center. (See also Quarrying.)

Crushed limestone is used on macadam roads. Farmers use ground limestone to neutralize soil acids that attack calcium and other salts needed by plants. Such protection is given naturally when soils have a limestone foundation.

Travertine limestone and calcareous tufa consist of calcium carbonate deposited from hard water. Stalactites and stalagmites in caves are formed in the same way. Limestone rock is often riddled with caves because water and carbon dioxide dissolve the limestone. Chalk is a soft white limestone containing the shells of foraminifera (see Chalk). Marble is a metamorphic, or transformed, limestone crystallized by pressure and perhaps heat (see Marble).

---

THIS ARTICLE IS IN THE FACT-INDEX
**Limestone College**

---

**LIME TREE.** No flavor is more refreshing in a cold drink on a hot day than a dash of lime juice. This comes from a fruit like a small, green lemon. Limes are smaller and rounder than lemons and have a thinner rind and more sharply acidic juice.

The lime tree is a native of southeastern Asia, particularly India. Most of the limes sold in the United States come from plantations in the West Indies, Mexico, and Florida. The trees, which do not grow more than eight feet high, start bearing the third year and attain full growth when six or seven years old. Since the fruit spoils rapidly, it is shipped green. A cross, or hybrid, between the lime and the kumquat, called a limequat, is hardier than the lime and yields more juice and pulp.

Lime juice, often concentrated by evaporation, is marketed both for flavoring and as a source of citric acid. British sailors are called "lime-juicers" or "limeys" because of the British law requiring a regular allowance of lime or lemon juice at sea to prevent scurvy (see Vitamins).

The name lime tree is also applied to various species of linden (see Linden). The scientific name of the true lime tree is *Citrus aurantifolia*.

---

THESE ARTICLES ARE IN THE FACT-INDEX

| | |
|---|---|
| **Limitations, Statutes of** | **Limpkin** |
| **Limmat** | **Limpopo River** |
| **Limoges, France** | **Linacre, Thomas** |
| **Limón, José (Arcadio)** | **Linanthus** |
| **Limón, Costa Rica** | |

# ABRAHAM LINCOLN—
## 16th President of
## the United States

LINCOLN, Abraham (1809–1865; president, 1861–1865). Every boy and girl who knew Abraham Lincoln loved him as a friend. All the children around his home in Springfield, Ill., and around the White House in Washington felt that "Mr. Lincoln" understood them and truly liked them. Men and women who knew him admired him and called him "honest Abe." People throughout the world said he was one of the greatest men of all time.

He was an unusual man in many ways. One minute he would wrestle with his sons or tell a joke and slap his bony knees in laughter. The next minute he might be deep in thought and not notice anything around him. He was gentle and patient, but no one was more determined. He was tall—nearly six feet four inches—very thin, and stooped. He spent less than a year in school, but he never stopped studying. All his life he was a "learner." Born in a log cabin on the frontier, he made his own way in life and became the president who kept the United States united.

### His Family Came from England

The first of the Lincoln family to come to America was Samuel Lincoln. He had been a weaver's apprentice at Hingham, England. He settled in Hingham, Mass., in 1637. From there the family spread southward to Virginia, where Abraham's father, Thomas Lincoln, was born in 1778.

When Thomas was four years old the family moved to Kentucky. There his father, who was a farmer, was killed by Indians. Thomas grew up in Kentucky. He never went to school, but he learned to be a carpenter. He was a strong, heavy-built man, who sometimes spoke sharply and at other times entertained his friends with jokes and stories.

Some historians have called him shiftless. True, he moved many times in his life, but he worked hard enough at carpentry to buy farms. He did not, however, make much of a living, because most of the land he cleared was too poor for good crops.

### Marries Nancy Hanks, Mother of Abraham

In 1806 Thomas married Nancy Hanks. She had been born in Virginia, but little else is known of the Hanks family. Nancy was only a baby when her mother Lucy brought her to Kentucky. When Nancy married Thomas Lincoln she was 22 years old, tall, and slender. Some historians say she could neither read nor write, which was not unusual for pioneer women. Others say that she read the Bible daily.

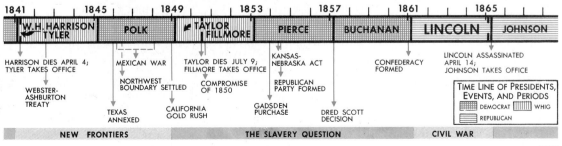

279

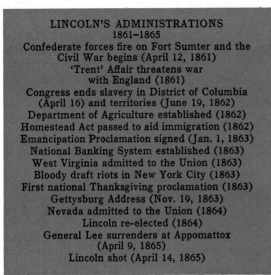

Thomas and Nancy settled in Elizabethtown in Hardin County, Ky. Their first child, Sarah, was born there. In 1808 Thomas bought a half-cleared farm at Sinking Spring on the Nolin River near Hodgenville. He hopefully moved his family to this first farm—a rolling stretch of thin, poor land on a lonely river.

### Abraham Born in a Log Cabin

About sunrise on Feb. 12, 1809, the son of Thomas and Nancy Lincoln was born. They named him Abraham after his grandfather Lincoln. Abraham's birthplace was a one-room log cabin, 16 feet long and 18 feet wide. The logs were chinked with clay and light came dimly through the single window. The floor was earth, packed down hard, and the bed was made of poles and cornhusks. A roaring fire on the hearth and rough bearskin blankets kept Nancy and her son Abraham warm on that cold winter morning.

In the spring of 1811 Thomas Lincoln moved his family to a farm he had bought on Knob Creek, about ten miles northeast. In later years Abraham Lincoln said that the Knob Creek farm was the first home he remembered and he loved it. Like all farm boys in those busy days young Abe learned to plant, hoe, husk corn, build hearth fires, carry water, and chop wood.

When he was six years old, Sarah and he tramped "up the road a piece," some two miles each way, to a log schoolhouse. Here he learned to read, write, and "do sums" (arithmetic). He liked writing best of all. Later he said that he practiced writing "anywhere and everywhere that lines could be drawn." He wrote with charcoal on the back of a wooden shovel and even in dust and snow.

Between chores young Abe climbed the rocky cliffs at Knob Creek, roamed among the dark cool pines and cedar trees in the valley, or waded in the pebbly creek. Sometimes he stood in the hot, dusty clay to watch the covered wagons carrying settlers along the nearby Cumberland Trail. His buckskin breeches were pulled high on his spindly legs and his thin arms stuck out from his rough linen shirt.

There were no close neighbors. Abe got used to being alone. He did not mind because he loved the hills and the quiet hollows and the trees—especially the trees. He learned so well to tell the many kinds that many years later, on his walks around Washington, he would point out their differences. He smilingly told visitors, "I know all about trees in light of being a backwoodsman."

### Lincolns Move to Indiana

In December 1816 Thomas took his family across the Ohio River to the backwoods of Indiana. For the last few miles Thomas, probably helped by Abe, had to cut a trail out of the wilderness of trees and tangle of wild grapevines. That winter was so cold that people remembered it as the year of "eighteen hundred and froze to death." The Lincolns settled on Little Pigeon Creek in Spencer County, about 16 miles from the Ohio River.

Young Abe and Sarah helped their father build a "half-faced camp." This was a shed of poles and bark, with one side left open toward a roaring log fire. They had to keep the fire burning day and night. They needed it for warmth, cooking, and drying their snow-soaked clothes and moccasins.

**TRADITIONAL LOG-CABIN BIRTHPLACE OF ABRAHAM LINCOLN**
Abraham's father, Thomas Lincoln, built this one-room cabin near Hodgenville, Ky.
Today it is preserved in a granite and marble building on the old Lincoln farm.

While the family huddled in their lean-to through the freezing winter, Thomas and Abe worked every day building a log cabin. Abe was only eight years old, but very large for his age, and he quickly learned to swing an ax. They cut and hewed logs for a cabin 18 feet by 20, then chinked the logs with clay and grass. Once in a while the boy shot a wild turkey, for the family lived mostly on wild game, with a little corn. He never became much of a hunter, however, as he did not like to shoot to kill. With Sarah he picked berries, nuts, and wild fruits for the family and trudged a mile to a spring for water. All around them was the unbroken wilderness.

### Abraham's Fine Stepmother — Sarah

In the autumn of 1818 Nancy Hanks Lincoln died of the dread frontier disease called "milk sickness." Sarah, only 11 years old, took over the cooking and cabin chores while Thomas and young Abe cut timber to clear farm land. After a year the little family was in sorry shape. They needed a woman's help. Thomas rode back to Elizabethtown, Ky., and married a widow, Sarah Bush Johnston, whom he had known since boyhood. He brought her and her three children to the shabby little log cabin in Indiana.

Abe and his sister Sarah quickly learned to love their second mother. She was a big-boned woman, with clear skin, friendly eyes, and a quiet way of getting things done. She cleaned up the untidy cabin. She had Thomas make a wood floor and chairs and build a bed for the feather mattress she had brought from Kentucky. Young Abe and Sarah had never lived in a cabin so homelike. Thomas did better on the farm, too, and the children began to eat and dress better. Sarah Lincoln did all this without any criticism or impatient words. She knew well that the family needed her.

Best of all, she encouraged Abe to study. She was not educated, but she saw how eager he was to learn. In later years he said of her: "She was the best friend I ever had. . . . All that I am, I owe to my angel mother." Sarah Lincoln told people: "He was the best boy I ever saw. I never gave him a cross word in my life. His mind and mine, what little I had, seemed to run together."

### Abe Grows Up with Books

Sarah made Thomas send the gangling 11-year-old to school. There was no regular teacher. When some man came along who knew a little about the three R's, he might teach the boys and girls for a few weeks— usually in the winter when farm work was slack. Whenever "school kept" at Pigeon Creek, Abe hiked four miles each way, his cowhide boots sloshing in the snow. He did not mind. He was learning.

In all his life his schooling did not add up to a year, but he made up for it by reading. A cousin, Dennis Hanks, who came to live with the Lincolns, said: "I never seen Abe after he was 12 that he didn't have a book somewheres around." By the time Abe was 14 he would often read at night by the light of the log fire. His first books were the Bible, 'Aesop's Fables', and 'Robinson Crusoe'.

When he was 15 years old he was so tall and strong that he often worked as a hired hand on other farms. Usually, while he plowed or split fence rails, he kept a borrowed book tucked in his shirt to read while he lunched or rested. He could turn in a good day's work when he had to. Many neighbors, however, called him lazy, saying he was "always readin' and thinkin'."

Once Abe grinned and told his farm boss, "My father taught me to work, but he never taught me to love it."

A farmer loaned him 'The Life of George Washington', by Parson Weems, and Abe left it in the rain. To make up for his carelessness, Abe shucked corn for him for three days. All his life Abraham Lincoln made every effort to do the fair thing.

He could never get enough to read. He said: "The things I want to know are in books. My best friend is the man who'll get me a book I ain't read." Once he tramped nearly 20 miles to Rockport to borrow one.

### Storyteller, Ferryman, and Law "Listener"

After supper Abe often walked down the road to Gentryville to join the "boys" at Gentry's store. His humorous stories, sometimes told in dialect, were popular with the young men lounging against the log counter.

**AS THE INSIDE OF LINCOLN'S BIRTHPLACE APPEARED**
A replica of Lincoln's birthplace stands in the Chicago Historical Society Museum. Here we see the kinds of tools and furniture the Lincolns used.

He loved to imitate travelers and local characters and would throw back his head with a booming laugh. In his own speech he pronounced words as he had learned them on the Kentucky frontier, such as "cheer" for "chair" and "git" for "get." That was the way all Southern woodsmen talked.

Between farm chores he helped to run a ferry across the Ohio River to Kentucky. When he was 18 he built his own scow and rowed passengers over the shallows to steamers out in the river.

Always he kept teaching himself new things. He became interested in law. Borrowing a book on the laws of Indiana, he studied it long into the night. Whenever he could, he strode miles to the nearest courthouse to hear lawyers try their cases. He even crossed into Kentucky to listen in court. Every visit taught him more about the ways of lawyers and furnished him with new stories. Throughout his later life as a lawyer, politician, and statesman he shrewdly drew on this rich fund of stories to make a legal point or to win audiences.

### Down the Mississippi to New Orleans

When Abe was 19 he got his first chance to see something of the "outside world." James Gentry, the owner of the country store, hired him to take a flatboat of cargo to New Orleans, then a wealthy city of some 40,000 people. With Gentry's son, Allen, Abe cut timber, hewed great planks, and built a flatboat called a "broadhorn."

New Orleans was 1,000 miles down the twisting Mississippi River. From sunup to sundown the two brawny young men pulled the long oars—about 40 feet long at bow and stern. Often they hurriedly hauled back on the side sweeps to swing the boat from snags, clumsy flatboats, or trim steamers caught in the shifting currents. They lived on board, cooking and sleeping in a rickety lean-to on deck. At night they tied up to a tree or stump on the muddy bank.

In New Orleans Abe saw his first auction of slaves. At that time slavery was lawful in all the United States south of the Ohio River. The tall, thoughtful young man winced at the sight of slave gangs in chains being marched off to plantations. Later he said, "Slavery is a continual torment to me."

### To Illinois and Splitting Rails

Back from New Orleans, Abe clerked part time at Gentry's country store and helped his father get ready to move to Illinois. The Indiana farm had not

**ABE AND JACK ARMSTRONG STRUGGLE TO A DRAW IN NEW SALEM**
Although "thin as a rail," young Lincoln was a mighty wrestler. Here he meets the champion of the "Clary's Grove Boys." Abe was the first man Jack Armstrong could not throw. They became good friends. This scene was painted by Harold von Schmidt.

**LINCOLN-BERRY GENERAL STORE**
The New Salem State Park in Illinois has restored the village buildings as they were in Lincoln's day. The store is stocked with goods like those Lincoln sold.

been a success. Through the winter the men built wagons and chests and made yokes and harness. In March 1830 they started their 200-mile trek.

Fording rivers and creeks, the heavy wagons often broke through the ice. Lincoln later said: "Once my little dog jumped out of the wagon . . . broke through, and was struggling for life. I could not bear to lose my dog, and I jumped out of the wagon and waded waist deep in ice and water, and got hold of him."

The family settled on the Sangamon River, some ten miles southwest of Decatur, Ill. Once more Abe helped to clear a farm. With a cousin, John Hanks, he then split 3,000 rails to fence some neighbors' land. He was truly "right handy with an ax." His feats with an ax on the Illinois prairie led his political supporters to call him, later in life, the "rail splitter." Even in his last years, as president, he could hold an ax straight out at arm's length—something very few young men could do.

### Starts His Own Life at New Salem

After a winter of cold and illness Thomas Lincoln again moved, about 100 miles southeast into Coles County. This time Abe did not go. He was 21 years old and ready to live his own life. Loving the river, he again took a flatboat to New Orleans, loaded with pork, corn, and live hogs.

On his return he hired out as a clerk in the village store at New Salem, Ill. The tiny settlement stood on a bluff above the Sangamon, about 20 miles northwest of Springfield. Here he lived for six years (1831–37). For $15 a month and a sleeping room in the back, he tended store and a gristmill.

Tales sprang up fast about Lincoln in the New Salem days. People spoke about his strict honesty and his giant strength. Some told how he once walked six miles to give back a few pennies to a woman who had overpaid for dry goods. Whenever a settler bought furs, or an oxen yoke, gun, tea, or salt he knew he

would get his money's worth from "honest Abe." He would also enjoy a laugh at one of Abe's stories.

Lincoln's employer boasted of Abe's strength and wrestling ability so much that a gang of toughs in nearby Clary's Grove challenged him. Men trooped in from the neighboring villages to see the match. The Clary's Grove champion was Jack Armstrong, a thickset, powerful man. He had always thrown all comers. He rushed at Lincoln, trying to hurl him off his feet. Lincoln held Armstrong off in his long arms, then grappled and threw him to the grass where they rolled over and over.

After a panting, grunting tussle Lincoln let go of Armstrong and, according to some stories, said: "Jack, let's quit. I can't throw you. You can't throw me." Armstrong shook Lincoln's hand, saying he was the "best feller that ever broke into this settlement." They became good friends. In matches with other powerful wrestlers Lincoln often simply tossed them over his head. With his great long legs he was the fastest foot racer, and when he had to fight with his fists he did. No one challenged him a second time.

### Captain in Black Hawk War

When the Black Hawk War broke out in April 1832 Lincoln and the Clary's Grove men enlisted. The war was a series of border raids by Sauk and Fox Indians led by Chief Black Hawk. They crossed from Iowa into Illinois and attacked and scalped settlers. (*See also* Indians, American, section "Centuries of Struggle between Indians and Whites.")

The Clary's Grove men elected Lincoln captain of their rifle company. The honor pleased him, but he knew nothing about military life. Once he could not think of the order he should give to march his company through a gate in formation. Scratching his head, he finally commanded: "Halt! This company will break ranks for two minutes and form again on the other side of the gate."

When Lincoln's term of enlistment ended in 30 days he re-enlisted as a private. In all, he served three months. He never fought in a battle, but he twice saw the horror of bodies scalped by the Indians. His army experience, learned on long marches and in rough camps, taught him sympathy for soldiers' hardships in the field. In later life, when he was commander in chief in the Civil War, he treated soldiers' failings with great understanding.

### Loses in Politics; Opens a Store

Just before the outbreak of the Black Hawk War, Lincoln had decided to run for the Illinois legislature. After his war service he again started his campaign. He was 23 years old, lanky and so tall that his cheap linen pants never reached his ankles. His coarse black hair was always mussed and his dark-skinned face was already deeply lined.

In a circular he sent out to voters, he wrote: "I was born and have remained in the most humble walks of life." While he was speaking at one political rally a fight broke out. Lincoln strode up to the man who had started the brawl, seized him by the neck and seat of the pants, and hurled him out of the crowd.

Lincoln then calmly went back to his speech, saying: "My politics are short and sweet, like the old lady's dance." In just two or three sentences he told what he would vote for and ended by saying: "If elected I shall be thankful; if not, it will be all the same." He did not carry the district, but his local popularity gave him nearly every vote in New Salem.

Meanwhile the New Salem store failed. Lincoln was out of work. He thought of learning to be a blacksmith, but another New Salem store was put up for sale. Lincoln, with William Berry as partner, bought it on credit. Neither one, however, was much interested in tending to business. Lincoln preferred to visit with the few customers or to lean against the door and read. After several months Berry died, leaving Lincoln more than $1,000 in debt. Eventually he paid back every cent, but it took him years.

### Becomes Postmaster and Surveyor

Failing as a storekeeper, Lincoln again was "hard up." In May 1833 his friends got him appointed the postmaster of New Salem. The job paid only about $50 a year, but it took little of his time and gave him the chance to read all the incoming newspapers free. He read every issue and was particularly interested in the political news. To earn his board and lodging, he also split rails and worked as a mill hand and hired man. In every spare moment he read or made political talks.

In the autumn of 1833 Lincoln gladly took an appointment as deputy county surveyor. To learn the work, he plunged into books on surveying and mathematics. By studying all day, and sometimes all night, he learned surveying in six weeks. As he rode about

**"THE RAIL SPLITTER"**
An unknown artist did this oil painting about 1858, probably after Lincoln won fame in the Lincoln-Douglas debates. It shows Lincoln swinging a heavy maul as in New Salem days.

the county, laying out roads and towns, he lived with different families and made new friends.

The wife of Jack Armstrong, the Clary's Grove "champion," said: "Abe would drink milk, eat mush, corn bread and butter, and rock the cradle. . . . He would tell stories, joke people at parties . . . do anything to accommodate anybody."

### Elected to Legislature and Becomes Lawyer

In 1834 Lincoln's old friends in New Salem and his new friends throughout Sangamon County elected him to the Illinois General Assembly. They re-elected him in 1836, 1838, and 1840. Before his first term began in November 1834 he borrowed $200 to pay the most pressing of his debts and to buy a suit for his new work.

Vandalia was then the capital of Illinois. Lincoln soon became popular in the legislature. One representative said that Lincoln was "raw-boned . . . ungraceful . . . almost uncouth . . . and yet there was a magnetism about the man that made him a universal favorite." By the time he started his second term he was a skilled politician and a leader of the Whig party in Illinois. A fellow Whig declared: "We followed his lead; but he followed nobody's lead. . . . He was poverty itself, but independent."

**EARLIEST KNOWN PHOTOGRAPH**
This first photograph of Lincoln was taken in Springfield, Ill., when he was 37 years old. Notice the strong, lined features. He did not grow his beard until February of 1861.

Encouraged by friends in the legislature, he determined to become a lawyer. Between terms he borrowed law books and took them back to New Salem to study. Often he walked 20 miles to Springfield and back to return one law book and get another. He was doing what he advised a young law student to do years later: "Get the books . . . and study them till you understand them in their principal features. . . . Your own resolution to succeed is more important than any other one thing." He took some time from studying to serve as New Salem's postmaster and, as he said, "mixed in the surveying to pay board and clothing bills." On Sept. 9, 1836, he received his law license.

### Moves to Springfield, the New Capital

In 1837 Lincoln took the lead in getting the capital transferred from Vandalia to Springfield. The legislature did not meet there until 1839, but in April 1837 Lincoln left New Salem to make his home in Springfield. Putting his few belongings into saddlebags, he rode a borrowed horse to the thriving little town on the prairie (*see* Springfield, Ill.).

He was 28 years old and so poor he did not have $17 to buy furnishings for a bed. Joshua Speed, the storekeeper, recalled that when Lincoln said he could not afford it, "The tone of his voice was so melancholy that I felt for him." Speed immediately invited Lincoln to share his own lodgings. This kindness started a lifelong friendship.

### Anne Rutledge, Mary Owens, Mary Todd

When Lincoln had lived in New Salem he had boarded various times at the log inn kept by James Rutledge, a founder of the village. Rutledge's daughter Anne was tall, slim, and blue-eyed, with auburn hair. Legend says that she was Lincoln's sweetheart and that when she died in 1835, at the age of 19, he nearly lost his mind in grief. The legend grew from a lecture by William Herndon, Lincoln's last law partner, a year after Lincoln's death.

Historians today, however, are not convinced that Anne Rutledge promised to marry Lincoln. At the time of her death, from "brain fever," she was engaged to one of Lincoln's friends, John McNamar.

Two years before Anne's death Lincoln had met in New Salem a visitor from Kentucky. She was Mary Owens, daughter of a wealthy farmer. Nearly a year older than Lincoln, she was well educated. He squired her to quiltings, huskings, and other "sociables," sometimes forgetting to help her cross creeks or climb steep hills. Apparently his absent-mindedness did not suit Mary Owens. When, in the summer of 1837, he proposed to her in a rather indecisive way, she "respectfully declined" to marry him.

By 1839 Lincoln was established as a lawyer in Springfield and was taking part in the busy social life of the city. One of the society belles was Mary Todd. She had come from her home in Lexington, Ky., to live with her sister and brother-in-law, son of the governor of Illinois. Mary was 21 years old—small, plump, pretty, gay, unusually well educated, and temperamental. Lincoln first met her in the winter of 1839 at a dance. He was immediately attracted to her and said, "Miss Todd, I want to dance with you in the worst way." Later, she laughingly told friends, "And he certainly did!"

### Courtship and Marriage

Soon Lincoln was spending every free moment with Mary Todd. They both loved literature and poetry, especially Shakespeare and Robert Burns. Lincoln delighted in reciting passages from memory. He had always been, as he said, a "slow learner," but he never forgot what he learned. He was pleased too that Mary took an intelligent interest in politics.

Mary was also being courted by Stephen A. Douglas, a prominent lawyer, with whom Lincoln was later to debate dramatically. Her wealthy, aristocratic family were opposed to Lincoln—they thought him "uncouth, full of rough edges." Mary, as always, knew what she wanted. By spring she was devoted to him and told friends, "His heart is as big as his arms are long." She was also so sure of his remarkable abilities that she predicted he would some day be president of the United States. (*See also* White House, section "Hostesses of the White House.")

After a series of temperamental clashes between

**LINCOLN'S FIRST AND ONLY HOME**
This photograph was made during Lincoln's "stay-at-home" presidential campaign in 1860. He bought the house in 1843 in Springfield, Ill., for $1,500, then added the second story.

them, Mary Todd, the Kentucky belle, and Abraham Lincoln, son of the frontier, were married on Nov. 4, 1842. They were living in one room at the Globe Tavern in Springfield when their first child, Robert Todd, was born in 1843. The next year Lincoln bought a light tan frame house on the edge of town. There Edward, William, and Thomas (Tad) were born in 1846, 1850, and 1853. (*See also* White House, section "Children in the White House.")

The Lincolns' home life was often stormy. Both Mary and Lincoln were at fault. An extremely sensitive, high-strung woman, afflicted with migraine headaches, Mary frequently gave way to rages of uncontrollable temper. Sometimes they may have been justified, for Lincoln had trying habits. Most arose from his enormous power of concentration. When he became interested in a book or a problem, he forgot everything else. Once when he was pulling his baby sons in a little wagon and reading a book as he walked, one of the boys fell out. Lincoln did not notice his frightened howls until Mary rushed to pick him up, then gave the surprised father "what for."

Lincoln went to bed at all hours and got up at all hours. Often he came home two or three hours late to dinner, then was startled to find Mary upset over his tardiness. When he took off his stovepipe hat, his notes and legal papers spilled over the neat parlor floor. With a chuckle, he often said, "My hat is my walking office." If the parlor stove went out when he was lost in thought, he never noticed it. For no apparent reason he sank into black, silent moods for hours, and sometimes days, at a time.

When he thought of it, however, he would do anything to please her. Patiently, and a little humorously,

he let her teach him the "social graces." He was extremely careless about his dress and knew it bothered Mary, who wanted to be proud of him as a rising young lawyer. Every morning before walking slowly to his untidy law office, he stood in the doorway to let her inspect him. His shirt, which she made, must be fresh, his boots polished, his suit and stovepipe hat brushed. In wet weather she made him carry his baggy umbrella; on cold days, his gray shawl.

He knew she was in terror of thunder. No matter how busy he was, he would hurry from his office at the first warning of a storm. Rushing home, he would stay at her side till it ended.

Like Mary, he enjoyed entertaining. He neither drank nor smoked but loved music and people. Although he cared nothing for food and had to be prodded to eat, he liked to have friends in for supper. As he prospered in his law practice, Mary and he gave large dinner parties and became noted as generous and gracious hosts.

### Both Devoted to Their Sons

Mary and Lincoln were blindly devoted to their sons. They thought the boys could do no wrong. The lads were hopelessly spoiled and neighborhood terrors. Sundays, while Mary was at church, Lincoln took the youngsters to his law office. While he worked unheedingly on his papers, they raced, wrestled, spilled ink, and overturned furniture until Lincoln's law partner, Herndon, told friends, "I'd like to wring their necks!" He never complained to Lincoln.

Lincoln's home in Springfield is a national historic site. All the rooms are open to the public. Many pieces of Lincoln's own furniture and china are in the attractive home.

At home Lincoln gave them boisterous "romps," or read aloud to them while they climbed over him, thumping him enthusiastically. In the yard they chased around him while he curried the horse or milked the cow. When he went to market to help Mary, grocery basket in hand, they trailed along swinging from his long arms or riding his shoulders. Often the noisy procession stopped while he and the boys and neighbor children held hopping contests. Springing with his great long legs, Lincoln "in three hops could get 40 feet on a dead level."

### Elected to Congress, Retires to Resume Law

In 1847 Lincoln went to Washington, D. C., as a representative from Illinois. The Mexican War was on (*see* Mexican War). Lincoln opposed it. His antiwar speeches displeased his political supporters. He knew they would not re-elect him.

At the end of his term in 1849 he returned to Springfield. He sought an appointment as commissioner in the General Land Office in Washington, but failed to get it. Later that year he was offered the governorship of the Oregon Territory. He refused, convinced that he was now a failure in politics.

Returning to the law, he again rode the circuit, pleading cases in one county seat after another. The circuit kept him away from home nearly six months of each year. He missed his family but loved the easy comradeship of fellow lawyers staying in country inns and delighted in the sharp give-and-take in court. Wherever he went he could make the jury and court-

room weep or slap their sides with laughter. Even more important to his success was his reputation for honesty. Honest Abe would not take a case unless he believed in his client's innocence or rights. He became an outstanding lawyer.

During this period he successfully handled important cases for the Rock Island Railroad and the Illinois Central Railroad. His most famous case, perhaps, was his victorious defense of "Duff" Armstrong, who was accused of murder. Duff was the son of Jack Armstrong, Lincoln's old wrestling foe. The accusing witness said he had seen Duff bludgeon and kill a man with a "slung shot" one night in the "bright moonlight." Lincoln opened an almanac and showed it recorded that the moon on that night had set long before the scuffle.

### Returns to Politics

The threat of slavery being extended brought Lincoln back into politics in 1854. He did not suggest interfering with slavery in states where it was already lawful. The Kansas-Nebraska Act of 1854, however, enabled the people of each new territory to vote on whether the territory would be slave or free, thus threatening to extend slavery (*see* Kansas-Nebraska Act). Lincoln began a series of speeches protesting the act.

In 1856 he helped to organize the Illinois branch of the new Republican party, a political party formed by people who wanted to stop the spread of slavery (*see* Political Parties). He became the leading Republican in Illinois. When the Republicans nominated John C. Frémont for the presidency of the United States, Lincoln received 110 votes for nomination as vice-president (*see* Frémont). This brought Lincoln to the attention of the nation.

### "House Divided Against Itself Cannot Stand"

The Republicans lost, but in 1858 Lincoln won the Republican nomination for senator from Illinois. Addressing the state convention at Springfield, he gave the first of his memorable speeches.

His huge hands tensely gripping the speaker's stand, he declared slowly and firmly: "A house divided against itself cannot stand. I believe this government cannot endure permanently, half slave and half free. I do not expect the Union to be dissolved—I do not expect the house to fall—but I do expect it will cease to be divided. It will become all one thing, or all the other."

### Lincoln-Douglas Debates and Nomination

Lincoln's opponent in the senatorial election was Stephen A. Douglas, a Democrat and Lincoln's old-

**THE DEVOTED LINCOLN FAMILY**
This painting shows the Lincoln family in the White House in 1862, after the death of Willie. Tad sits at Lincoln's knee. Robert, the eldest son, stands between his father and mother.

time acquaintance in Springfield. Douglas was running for re-election and had supported the Kansas-Nebraska Act. Lincoln challenged him to a series of debates on the slavery issue (*see* Lincoln-Douglas Debates). Although he overwhelmed Douglas in the debates, Lincoln lost the election. The debates, however, enlarged the public interest in Lincoln.

Realizing his country-wide fame, Lincoln's friends sought the Republican nomination for president for him in 1860. He himself worked tirelessly to win support. He now knew what he wanted—to be president of the United States in its time of crisis. He was determined to preserve the Union.

At the Republican national convention in Chicago in 1860 he was nominated on the third ballot. When the news was telegraphed to Springfield, Lincoln was sitting in a newspaper office. As jubilant friends congratulated him, he unfolded his thin legs, stood, and said, "Well, gentlemen, there is a little woman at our house who is probably more interested in this dispatch than I. If you'll excuse me, I'll take it up and let her see it."

## Stay-Home Campaign and Election

The Democratic party was split, with the North nominating Stephen A. Douglas, and Southern Democrats naming John C. Breckinridge. Throughout the furious campaign Lincoln stayed quietly in Springfield, directing party leaders from a makeshift little office in the Capitol. He even carried his own mail back and forth from the post office. To avoid stirring up controversy and perhaps splitting the Republicans, he did not make a single political speech.

His strategy won. Lincoln was elected 16th president of the United States. He had 1,865,593 votes, Douglas had 1,382,713, and Breckinridge, 848,356. "Honest Abe, the rail splitter" was the first Republican to become president.

Alarm spread through the Southern states. They thought a Republican president would not respect their rights or property. They felt that secession was their only hope. Secession began Dec. 20, 1860, when South Carolina withdrew from the Union (*see* Confederate States of America).

As the time of Lincoln's inauguration approached, threats to kill him increased. They failed to frighten him, but no man was more aware of the danger of his position in a time of crisis. Saying farewell to friends at the Springfield railway station, he said prophetically: "I now leave, not knowing when, or whether ever, I may return, with a task before me greater than that which rested on Washington." The authorities were so fearful of a rumored assassination plot in Baltimore that they persuaded Lincoln to leave his special train at Philadelphia. He rode into Washington in a heavily guarded sleeping car. (For picture, *see* Civil War, American.)

'If' any personal description of me is thought
desirable, it may be said, I am, in height, six
feet, four inches, nearly; lean in flesh, weighing on
an average, one hundred and eighty pounds; dark
complexion, with coarse black hair, and grey eyes—
no other marks or brands recollected—

Hon J. W. Fell.                    Yours very truly
                                   A. Lincoln

284e

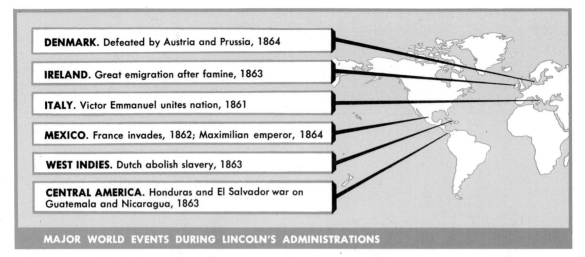

DENMARK. Defeated by Austria and Prussia, 1864

IRELAND. Great emigration after famine, 1863

ITALY. Victor Emmanuel unites nation, 1861

MEXICO. France invades, 1862; Maximilian emperor, 1864

WEST INDIES. Dutch abolish slavery, 1863

CENTRAL AMERICA. Honduras and El Salvador war on Guatemala and Nicaragua, 1863

MAJOR WORLD EVENTS DURING LINCOLN'S ADMINISTRATIONS

## Inauguration and Outbreak of Civil War

In his inaugural address Lincoln assured the South that he would respect its rights, that there was no need of war. He said: "I have no purpose . . . to interfere with the institution of slavery in states where it exists. . . . In *your* hands, my dissatisfied fellow countrymen, and not in *mine*, is the momentous issue of civil war. . . . We must not be enemies."

Less than six weeks later, on April 12, 1861, the Civil War began (*see* Civil War, American). Abraham Lincoln shouldered the giant task of bringing the rebel states back into the national family and preserving the Union. He wrote: "My paramount object in this struggle is to save the Union, and it is not either to save or to destroy slavery. If I could save the Union without freeing *any* slave, I would do it;

**LINCOLN URGES ACTION**
On Oct. 2, 1862, shortly after the Union victory at Antietam, Lincoln went to field headquarters. He faces Gen. George B. McClellan. Lincoln made many such visits during the war.

and if I could save it by freeing *all* the slaves I would do it. . . . I have here stated my purpose according to my view of *official* duty; and I intend no modification of my oft-expressed *personal* wish that all men everywhere could be free."

## Patient, Determined President

Lincoln was a strong president. At first his deliberate thinking and extraordinary patience deceived his Cabinet into thinking him uncertain. Several Cabinet members had strong political ambitions and feuded with each other. However, they all could serve the nation well, and so Lincoln patiently smoothed their differences and held them together with his great tact. He wanted their help, not their praise.

Profiting by his experience as a lawyer, he looked at every side of a question before deciding on an answer. "His mind acts slowly," said a friend, "but when it moves, it moves *forward*." When Lincoln reached a decision, he pressed his lips together firmly; then no one could change his mind. His Cabinet soon discovered this. Once every Cabinet member opposed Lincoln's plan. He smiled, said "Aye" for his own vote, and calmly announced, "The aye has it."

For months he had trouble finding capable generals to lead the Union forces. As with his Cabinet, he gave Gen. George B. McClellan and others every chance to prove themselves (*see* McClellan). When McClellan continued to delay attacking the Confederate forces, Lincoln said wryly, "He's got the slows." He kept urging McClellan to advance. Instead, McClellan childishly ignored Lincoln, his commander in chief. When Lincoln's secretary protested against McClellan's attitude, Lincoln answered quietly, "I'd hold his horse for him if only he would bring us success."

Soon Lincoln felt that he himself must take action. He read all he could on military science and made frequent inspection trips of forces in the field. Sometimes he took Mary Lincoln and his youngest son, Tad, with him to help boost the morale of the troops. Until he found competent generals, he directed much of the strategy for the Army and the Navy. He made

# Important Events

# in the Administrations

# of Abraham Lincoln

UNION STATES

CONFEDERATE STATES

TERRITORIES

STATES ADMITTED
WEST VIRGINIA (1863)
NEVADA (1864)

⊗ RICHMOND ✪ WASHINGTON

The Civil War split the nation in 1861. The Union had about 23 million people; the Confederacy, less than 10 million.

## PROCLAIMING FREEDOM AND DEDICATING A FIELD OF HONOR

On Jan. 1, 1863, Lincoln signed the Emancipation Proclamation, freeing 3 million slaves. He wrote it July 1862.

Bareheaded on a chill November day in 1863, Lincoln delivered his Gettysburg Address. It was a speech of noble humility.

## TRAGEDY OF THE CIVIL WAR

On April 12, 1861, Confederates shelled Fort Sumter. The Civil War had begun.

Union troops were routed at Bull Run in the first major battle, July 21, 1861.

On April 9, 1865, gallant Gen. R. E. Lee (left) surrendered to Gen. U. S. Grant.

## PROGRESS IN THE UNION

A Pony Express rider dashes past last link in transcontinental telegraph, 1861.

This was the first home of the Department of Agriculture, established in 1862.

The post office began free mail delivery in 1863. Only cities received the service.

Four score and seven years ago our fathers brought forth on this continent, a new nation, conceived in liberty, and dedicated to the proposition that all men are created equal.

Now we are engaged in a great civil war testing whether that nation or any nation so conceived and so dedicated, can long endure. We are met on a great battle-field of that war. We have come to dedicate a portion of that field, as a final resting place for those who here gave their lives that that nation might live. It is altogether fitting and proper that we should do this.

But, in a larger sense, we can not dedicate —we can not consecrate—we can not hallow— this ground. The brave men, living and dead, who struggled here, have consecrated it, far above our poor power to add or detract. The world will little note, nor long remember what we say here, but it can never forget what they did here. It is for us the living, rather, to be dedicated here to the unfinished work which they who fought here have thus far so nobly advanced. It is rather for us to be here dedicated to the great task remaining before us— that from these honored dead we take increased devotion to that cause for which they gave the last full measure of devotion—that we here highly resolve that these dead shall not have died in vain—that this nation, under God, shall have a new birth of freedom—and that government of the people, by the people, for the people, shall not perish from the earth.

**GETTYSBURG ADDRESS**
With this great speech Lincoln dedicated a national cemetery for soldiers at Gettysburg, Pa. One newspaper editor told readers, "Read it over, it will repay study as a model speech."

blunders but, on the whole, he was a successful commander in chief. When he found a capable general, such as Ulysses S. Grant, he supported him steadfastly despite great criticism (see Grant). For the greater part of the war most of the newspapers and people bitterly criticized Lincoln's policies. He never took the time to defend himself, convinced that he was doing what was right for the Union.

The bitter, tragic war surrounded Lincoln even in his home, the White House. Rifle companies patrolled the grounds and set up barracks in even the stately East Room. Every day secretaries brought him dispatches from the field, and his lonely mind tried to find solutions to the problems. Often he was at his desk before seven o'clock in the morning, working till Tad awakened. The lad then came down to Lincoln's office and they read the Bible together—Tad sitting in his father's lap.

## A Harassed, Gentle President

Day after day office seekers crowded up to Lincoln's desk. He was trying to win a war, trying to save the Union, yet had to spend hours making or refusing appointments to political office. The greatest strain was reading and hearing petitions for clemency for soldiers sentenced to death for desertion or failing their duty. One time, near exhaustion, he said sadly, "I've had more cases of life and death to settle in four years than all the other men who sat in this chair put together. No man knows the distress of my mind." When a mother, wife, or sister stood before him pleading a soldier's case, Lincoln felt the pain himself. His deep-set gray eyes darkened and "sorrow seemed to flow from him." Whenever he could find the slightest excuse, he ordered a pardon for the soldier.

No one felt the tragedy of the war more than he. When Harriet Beecher Stowe, author of 'Uncle Tom's Cabin', met him, he said tiredly, "Whichever way the conflict ends, I have the impression that I shan't last long after it's over."

What little relaxation he got came from his sense of humor, occasional walks and horseback rides, and his companionship with Tad. Frequently he startled his Cabinet with humorous stories, explaining, "I have to get away from myself and this tiredness in me." His beloved Tad, the impish youngster with a lisp, could always make his father smile. Nearly every night he stayed in his father's office until he fell asleep. Lincoln then carried him up to bed.

## Emancipation Proclamation

During 1862 Lincoln struggled with the problem of freeing the slaves. He knew that the slavery question must be settled if the United States, founded on the principles of liberty and equal rights for all, were to survive as a nation. He realized that the Union must be preserved, as a *free* nation—if democratic government was to succeed in the world.

With all the foresight he could muster, he worked out a plan to free the slaves. His Cabinet approved issuing the proclamation after the next Union victory. The summer passed with no victory. Then on Sept. 17, 1862, the Union forces stopped the advancing Confederate armies at Antietam.

On Sept. 22, 1862, President Lincoln issued the Emancipation Proclamation, one of the most important messages in the history of the world (see Emancipation Proclamation). He signed it Jan. 1, 1863.

## Gettysburg Address

In July 1863 the Union armies threw back the Confederate forces at Gettysburg. This was the only battle on Northern soil (see Gettysburg, Battle of).

On Nov. 19, 1863, the great, shattered battlefield was dedicated as a national cemetery. The chief speaker was Edward Everett, a noted orator. As an afterthought, President Lincoln was invited "to make a few appropriate remarks." He worked and reworked his speech, seeking—as with all his formal documents —to make it as perfect as possible.

SECOND INAUGURATION OF LINCOLN, MARCH 4, 1865
This is an early photograph of a presidential inauguration.
The Civil War was almost won. Looking ahead to peace, Lincoln
pleaded, "With malice toward none, with charity for all."

The crowd listened for two hours to Everett's extravagant oratory. Lincoln then rose slowly, put on his glasses, glanced at a slip of paper, then spoke gravely in his clear, high-pitched voice. In a little less than three minutes he finished his Gettysburg Address. He thought it a failure, as did most of the newspapers. Only a few recognized it as one of the noblest speeches ever made by any man. Everett wrote to him: "I should be glad if I could flatter myself that I came as near the central idea of the occasion in two hours as you did in two minutes."

### Fears Defeat but Is Re-elected

By November 1864 Lincoln was nearly exhausted by the burden of the war and grief at the death of his son Willie in the White House. Wherever he turned he read or heard criticism of himself and his generals. He prepared a memorandum for his Cabinet, forecasting his defeat in the coming election. The people, however, at last rallied to him and re-elected him.

When he gave his inaugural address March 4, 1865,

the end of the war was in sight. He looked forward to welcoming the Southern states back into the Union and to making their readjustment as easy as possible. He expressed that thought in these words: "With malice toward none, with charity for all, with firmness in the right as God gives us to see the right, let us strive on to finish the work we are in; to bind up the nation's wounds, to care for him who shall have borne the battle and for his widow and orphan, to do all which may achieve and cherish a just and lasting peace among ourselves and with all nations."

### Victory and Death

Little more than a month later, on April 9, 1865, Gen. Robert E. Lee surrendered his Confederate army to Gen. U. S. Grant. On April 11 the Stars and Stripes of the United States were raised over Fort Sumter, where the war had begun (see Fort Sumter).

**LINCOLN MEMORIAL IN WEST POTOMAC PARK IN WASHINGTON, D. C.**
The Memorial is built of white Colorado marble, pink Tennessee marble, and Indiana limestone. The outside columns are Doric; the inside, Ionic. A skylight lights the interior. The cornerstone was laid in 1915. Henry Bacon was the architect.

To celebrate with one of his favorite relaxations—the theater—Lincoln took Mary and two guests to Ford's Theatre on the night of April 14. Hand in hand, Lincoln and Mary were laughing at the third act of the play, 'Our American Cousin', a comedy. Noiselessly, an intoxicated, half-mad young actor, John Wilkes Booth, crept into the presidential box and shot Lincoln in the head. Booth then swung down onto the stage. Brandishing a dagger, he escaped. He died in a barn hide-out in Virginia, April 26.

Soldiers carried the unconscious president across the street to the nearest residence, a little boarding-house. There, stretched diagonally on a bed too small for his long body, he died without speaking at 7:22 in the morning. It was April 15, 1865—28 years to the day since he had left the hamlet of New Salem. As the Great Emancipator died, Secretary of War Stanton said softly in the stricken room, "Now he belongs to the ages." A funeral train carried the first assassinated president back home to Springfield, Ill., where he lies buried in Oak Ridge cemetery.

Only after his death did the world begin to realize Lincoln's greatness. He was a superb statesman, a firm idealist who would not be swayed from the right, a man of kindly and brave patience, and, above all, a believer in what he called the "family of man."

### THE "GREAT EMANCIPATOR"
This strong, sympathetic statue by Daniel Chester French is called the 'Seated Lincoln'. It is in the main chamber of the magnificent Lincoln Memorial in Washington, shown above.

### Books and Films About Abraham Lincoln

Aulaire, Ingri and E. P. d'. Abraham Lincoln (Doubleday, 1957).
Bishop, J. A. The Day Lincoln Was Shot (Harper, 1964).
The Great Debate: Lincoln vs. Douglas, film (Encyclopaedia Britannica Films).
Horgan, Paul. Citizen of New Salem (Farrar, 1961).
McNeer, M. Y. America's Abraham Lincoln (Houghton, 1957).
Meet Mr. Lincoln, film (Encyclopaedia Britannica Films).
Mitgang, Herbert. The Fiery Trial: a Life of Lincoln (Viking Press, 1974).
Roscoe, Theodore. The Lincoln Assassination, April 14, 1865 (Watts, 1971).
Sandburg, Carl. Abraham Lincoln: the Prairie Years and the War Years (Harcourt, 1954).
Thomas, B. P. Abraham Lincoln (Knopf, 1952).

THESE ARTICLES ARE IN THE FACT-INDEX

Lincoln, Benjamin
Lincoln, Robert Todd
Lincoln, England (county)

Lincoln, England (city)
Lincoln, Ill.

**LINCOLN FROM THE AIR**
This Fairchild Aerial Survey photograph shows the State Capitol at top right. On the 400-foot tower of the Capitol stands a statue, 'The Sower', symbolizing Nebraska's farms.

**LINCOLN, Neb.** The friendly, pleasant city of Lincoln is the capital of the Cornhusker State, Nebraska. It is the seat of Lancaster County, an educational center, and the trade center for a wide farming area. The city's prosperity depends to a large degree upon that of the farmers. Every spring the important question in Lincoln is, "Will the rains come in time for good crops?"

In Lincoln are the buildings housing the various departments of the city, county, and state governments, the state mental and orthopedic hospitals, the State Reformatory, and the State Penitentiary. Also in the city are a veterans' hospital and the regional headquarters of the Veterans Administration and the Department of Agriculture. The Strategic Air Command has a base here.

The state university—the University of Nebraska—opened in Lincoln in 1871. Its campus adjoins the downtown section. The College of Agriculture has a separate campus to the northeast. Also in the city are Nebraska Wesleyan University and Union College.

Lincoln is located in southeast Nebraska, about 60 miles southwest of Omaha. It lies in a shallow basin about 1,160 feet above sea level. Salt Creek and its tributaries thread through the basin.

The State Capitol, completed in 1932, is near the city's center. The state's natural history museum and Sheldon Art Gallery, dedicated in 1963, are on the state university campus. Pioneers Park, the city's most important park, has a zoo. The Nebras-

ka State Fair takes place in Lincoln in September.

Lincoln has large railroad-car repair shops and extensive grain-storage facilities. Among the city's manufactures are processed foods, gasoline engines and other machinery, metal products, cement, rubber articles, and drugs. There are a number of printing and publishing plants, and the city is the headquarters for more than 30 insurance companies.

### History and Government

Lincoln arose from a settlement established in 1856 to work salt deposits. In 1859 the settlement became the seat of Lancaster County and was named Lancaster. In 1867 Nebraska became a state and the town, renamed for the Civil War president, became its capital. William Jennings Bryan, long a leader in American politics, lived here many years (*see* Bryan).

The city is governed by a mayor and council. Lincoln owns its water and electric systems. (*See also* Nebraska.) Population (1980 census), 171,932.

**LINCOLN-DOUGLAS DEBATES.** In 1858 the Republican party nominated Abraham Lincoln for United States senator from Illinois. His Democratic opponent was Senator Stephen A. Douglas.

At that time Lincoln was well known in Illinois, but few people in the rest of the country had heard of him. Douglas, however, was noted throughout the country. As chairman of the Senate Committee on Territories, Douglas was responsible for the Kansas-Nebraska Act, a law which the whole nation discussed (*see* Kansas-Nebraska Act).

Douglas' fame did not daunt Lincoln. He was determined to make a fight for election to the Senate. On July 24, 1858, he challenged Douglas to a series of debates on the political issues of the day. The chief issue, of course, was slavery.

Both Lincoln and Douglas apparently realized that the debates would attract national interest. In a speech at Quincy, Ill., Lincoln described the debates as "the successive acts of a drama . . . to be enacted not merely in the face of audiences like this, but in the face of the nation . . ."

### The Men and Their Debates

Lincoln and Douglas were both skilled politicians. As men, however, they were very different. Douglas was short, stout, but richly dressed and suave. Lincoln was lanky, almost homely. His high, thin voice was no match for Douglas' deep tones.

Douglas often rode to the debates in a private railroad car. Lincoln traveled as best he could. Once he was riding in a caboose that was switched to a siding to let Douglas' train pass.

The first debate was at Ottawa, Ill., Aug. 21, 1858. The last of the seven was at Alton, October 15. The others were at Freeport, Jonesboro, Charleston, Galesburg, and Quincy.

At the second meeting, at Freeport, Lincoln forced from Douglas an answer that perhaps changed the course of American history. Lincoln asked Douglas

287

**LINCOLN SPEAKING IN DEBATE WITH DOUGLAS**
This informal audience is typical of crowds that gathered for the Lincoln-Douglas debates. Douglas stands behind Lincoln.

if the people of a territory could exclude slavery. According to Douglas' belief in popular sovereignty, the answer should be "yes." According to the Dred Scott Decision, which declared that Congress had no power to exclude slavery from a territory, the answer should be "no."

If Douglas answered "yes," he would displease the South. If he said "no," he would lose support in the North. Douglas answered, as Lincoln expected,

that no matter what the court might do "slavery cannot exist . . . anywhere unless it is supported by local police regulations," and that a territory could keep out slavery by "unfriendly legislation." The disappointed South called this the "Freeport doctrine."

The debates did not win Lincoln his election as senator. Douglas got the office. Although he was disappointed, Lincoln smiled slowly and said that he was "like the boy who stubbed his toe. It hurt too bad to laugh and he was too big to cry."

In the end, however, Lincoln was the winner, because Douglas' "Freeport doctrine" kept the South from nominating him for the presidency in 1860. Meanwhile the debates had brought Lincoln to the attention of the nation. Political leaders began to consider him as a candidate for the Republican nomination for president. (*See also* Douglas; Dred Scott Decision; Lincoln, Abraham.)

THESE ARTICLES ARE IN THE FACT-INDEX

| | |
|---|---|
| Lincoln Memorial University | Lincolnwood, Ill. |
| Lincoln Park, Mich. | Lind, Don L. |
| Lincoln's Inn Fields | Lind, Jenny |
| Lincoln University (Mo.) | Lindbergh, Anne Spencer |
| Lincoln University (Pa.) | Morrow |

# LINDBERGH—America's "Lone Eagle of the Sky"

**LINDBERGH, Charles Augustus** (1902–1974). On May 20–21, 1927, Charles Lindbergh flew a small silvery monoplane, the *Spirit of St. Louis*, nonstop from New York City to Paris. It was the first one-man flight across the Atlantic. Lindbergh's daring, skill, and endurance won him world acclaim. After his flight he devoted himself to aviation and science.

Charles Lindbergh was born Feb. 4, 1902, at his grandfather's home in Detroit, Mich. His father, also named Charles Augustus, had been brought from Sweden to a Minnesota farm as an infant. His mother was Evangeline Lodge Land, a teacher.

In 1906 the father was elected to Congress and became widely known for his liberal debates. Young Charles divided his time between Washington and the family's Minnesota home near Little Falls. He fished, hunted, and had a special interest in machinery. He knew every part of his bicycle and, as he grew older, of his motorcycle and car.

### Lindbergh Learns to Fly

Lindbergh graduated from Little Falls high school in 1918 and entered the University of Wisconsin. After three semesters he left and entered an aviation school at Lincoln, Neb. There he studied the theory and mechanics of flight. He also learned to make parachute jumps and to walk on the wing of a flying biplane. He made his first solo flight at Americus, Ga., in April 1923. For a time he earned his living by "barnstorming"—taking passengers for short rides

Charles Lindbergh, at eight years of age, poses with his mother. He was the only child. The Lindberghs were a very closely knit family. Charles's father was his favorite companion.

and performing in daring exhibitions of aviation.

In March 1924 he became a flying cadet in the United States Army. He trained at Brooks and Kelly fields, near San Antonio, Tex. He graduated with a pursuit pilot's rating and the rank of second lieutenant in the Army Air Corps Reserve.

He was hired as a test pilot by a St. Louis firm. This firm won a contract to fly mail between St. Louis and Chicago. Charles Lindbergh was selected to make the first flight over the route on April 15,

1926. Within a year, he flew more than 50,000 miles over this mail route. Twice he had to make parachute jumps to save his life.

### Enters Contest for the Orteig Prize

Seasoned by more than 1,500 hours of flying, Lindbergh decided to try for the Raymond Orteig prize of $25,000. This prize had been offered since 1919 for the first nonstop flight between New York City and Paris. St. Louis businessmen agreed to help pay the cost of building an airplane. Early in 1927 Lindbergh went to San Diego to superintend the building of a Ryan monoplane, which he named the *Spirit of St. Louis.*

Lindbergh put his new plane through severe tests. On May 10, 1927, he flew it from San Diego to St. Louis; and on May 12, he flew to New York, setting a new coast-to-coast record. He entered his name in the contest for the Orteig prize. Only a few days before, on May 8, the famous French aces Nungesser and Coli had perished in their attempt to fly from Paris to New York. When news spread that Lindbergh would try to fly the Atlantic *alone,* people shuddered. Few knew how carefully he had prepared.

### Off for Paris

Early in the morning of May 20 Lindbergh climbed into the *Spirit of St. Louis* at Roosevelt Field on Long Island. Down the runway the plane lurched and bounded. Heavily loaded with gasoline, it clung to the earth, bounced, dropped, and then lifted slowly. At 7:52 A.M., "We" were off, vanishing in a drizzle. Just before nightfall, Lindbergh passed over St. John's, Newfoundland, on the way to the open sea. Through fog, rain, and sleet, the plane throbbed on, true to the course. At 10:00 P.M., Paris time, May 21, a crowd at Le Bourget Field heard the faint drone of a motor. Louder and louder it grew until the searchlights played upon a silver bird. At 10:21 P.M. it alighted, having flown 3,600 miles in 33 hours and 30 minutes. (*See also* Airplane History.)

From the cabin of the plane, Lindbergh emerged a world hero. At 25 he had performed a greater feat than any other pilot in the history of aviation. He was decorated by the president of France, the king of Belgium, and the king of England. President Coolidge presented him with the Distinguished Flying Cross and made him a colonel in the Officers' Reserve Corps. Medals and gifts poured in on him from all parts of the world.

### A Career Devoted to Promoting Aviation

Lindbergh then devoted himself to inspiring confidence in the airplane as a practical means of transportation. He refused commercial offers that would have made a fortune for him. Sponsored by the Daniel Guggenheim Foundation for the Promotion of Aeronautics, he flew the *Spirit of St. Louis* to cities in every state of the Union. He made a good-will swing over Mexico, Central America, and the West Indies, which ended Feb. 13, 1928. Then he gave his plane to the

Smithsonian Institution. He was made air counsel to the Department of Commerce and adviser to commercial aviation companies.

In 1929 he married Anne Morrow, daughter of Dwight W. Morrow, then ambassador to Mexico. She accompanied him on later expeditions. In 1931 they blazed a northern air route from New York to China, and in 1933 they circled the North Atlantic coast to study air lanes and bases for commercial transatlantic flying. In 1937 they surveyed an air route from England to India.

### Lindbergh's Contributions to Science

Lindbergh also made contributions to archaeology and medical research. In 1929, flying over Yucatán, he photographed Mayan ruins. With Dr. Alexis Carrel of the Rockefeller Institute for Medical Research, he developed a method for separating red corpuscles from blood serum. With Carrel in 1935 he perfected an "artificial heart and lungs" which kept parts of the body alive with a supply of blood and air.

Along with fame, bitter tragedy came to the Lindberghs. Their first child, Charles Augustus, Jr., who was born in 1930, was kidnaped and killed in 1932. In 1935 the Lindberghs established themselves in Europe. Returning to the United States in 1939 Lindbergh publicly opposed American intervention in the

**THE FLIER WITH HIS FAMOUS AIRPLANE**
This picture of Lindbergh beside the *Spirit of St. Louis* was taken just before he took off on his historic flight.

second World War. Later, however, he served as a civilian adviser to the Army and Navy; 'The Wartime Journals of Charles A. Lindbergh' was published in 1970. He won a 1954 Pulitzer prize for his autobiographical 'The Spirit of St. Louis'. In 1968 the National Institute of Social Sciences presented distinguished service medals to the Lindberghs. He was cited for his work in conservation and she for her books, including 'North to the Orient' and 'Gift from the Sea'. Her collection of letters and diaries 'Bring Me a Unicorn' was published in 1972.

---

THESE ARTICLES ARE IN THE FACT-INDEX

| | |
|---|---|
| Lindblad, Adolf | Linde, Carl von |
| Lindblad, Otto | Linden, N. J. |

---

**LINDEN.** The American linden, also called the basswood, is the largest of the 18 species of linden native to North America. Local names applied to the various species are linn, white basswood, bee tree, lime tree, and whitewood. The basswood thrives in woods and river bottoms from Canada south to Georgia and westward. In summer its flowers, with their unusually penetrating fragrance, attract great swarms of bees. Honey from the nectar thus obtained has a distinctive flavor and is delicious. The tree may live for several hundred years, and some specimens are more than 100 feet high. (For pictures, *see* Trees.)

The southern basswood, a much smaller tree, is found from Indiana to Florida. It is distinguished by its leaves, which have a hairy, silvery-white undersurface. The European linden, often called the lime, is grown as a shade tree in Europe.

Basswood is light and white and is used chiefly for food containers, such as honey boxes and headings for flour barrels. It is also used for veneer, furniture, musical instruments, and excelsior. The fibrous inner bark (bast) is used for mats and baskets.

The scientific name of the basswood is *Tilia glabra;* of the southern basswood, *T. heterophylla.* The leaves, 4 to 7 inches long, are heart-shaped. The yellowish-white flowers droop in clusters on stalks suspended from leafy bracts. The fruit is greenish gray.

---

THESE ARTICLES ARE IN THE FACT-INDEX

| | |
|---|---|
| Linden family | Lindsay, John V(liet) |
| Lindenhurst, N. Y. | Lindsay, (Nicholas) Vachel |
| Lindenwood Colleges, The | Lindsay, Ont. |
| Lindsay, Howard | Lindsey, Benjamin Barr |

---

**LINEN.** "Purple and fine linen" was the clothing of princes in Biblical days, and fine linen is still a luxury. Lustrous table damask of linen rivals silk brocade in beauty. Snowy-white bleached linen, with its fine smooth surface, is the preferred material for handkerchiefs and embroidery fabrics. Since linen is an excellent conductor of heat, clothing made of it is cool for summer. Linen towels are preferable to cotton, for they absorb moisture more readily. Linen's great ten-

sile strength makes it desirable for sailcloth and the most delicate handmade laces. Heirlooms of lace and table linen, as well as Egyptian mummy cloths, attest to the durability of linen.

Linen does not dye as well as silk, cotton, or wool and unless specially treated is more likely to fade. Linen fabrics are traditionally given to wrinkling and creasing. Modern finishes, however, have been devised to make it "crush resistant," increasing its popularity for women's clothing. (*See also* Fabrics.)

The processes by which linen is made from the flax fiber are described in the article Flax. Combing flax preparatory to spinning produces "line" and "tow" fibers. Line fibers are the long, fine ones; tow, the short, coarse ones. Line flax makes the smoothest and most durable fabrics. Tow flax is not as strong, and threads spun from it are coarse and uneven.

---

THESE ARTICLES ARE IN THE FACT-INDEX

| | |
|---|---|
| Linfield College | Linlithgow, Victor |
| Ling, Per Henrik | Alexander John Hope, |
| Lingenberry | 2d marquess of |
| Link Foundation | Linnaea |

---

**LINNÉ, Carl von** (1707–1778). The Swedish naturalist and physician Linné brought into general use the system of naming plants and animals that is now universally employed. This is the *binomial* (two-name) system, in which each plant and each animal is assigned a name consisting of two Latin words. The first word is the name of the *genus*, and the second is the name of the *species* (see Biology). So important was Linné's work of classification that he is called the Father of Systematic Botany.

Carl von Linné, who is more often known as Linnaeus (the Latin form of his name, under which he wrote) was born at Rashult, Sweden. His father was a pastor and hoped that the boy would follow the same calling. Carl, however, was interested in plants and animals. He did so poorly at school that his father proposed to apprentice him to a shoemaker. The village physician saw, however, that the boy had unusual gifts. He encouraged the father to help care for him while he studied medicine at the University of Uppsala. Here his talents soon won him an appointment as assistant in botany. Later the Academy of Sciences of Uppsala sent him on a 5,000-mile botanical survey of Lapland. He supported himself by lecturing and tutoring but was too poor to take his degree. Aid came from his future wife. She helped provide the funds with which he obtained his doctor's degree in medicine at a university in Holland.

In Holland Linné became medical attendant to an Amsterdam banker who had a large botanic garden. Linné was made director of this garden. In the next few years he published 'Systema naturae' and 'Genera plantarum'. Into later editions of these he introduced his famous system of classification.

After scientific journeys to France and England Linné returned to Stockholm to practice medicine.

In 1742 he was appointed to the chair of botany at Uppsala. There he spent the rest of his active life. Students came to him from all quarters of the civilized world and searched the earth for specimens to contribute to his studies.

Linné's system of classification was an artificial one. He himself regarded it as a temporary convenience to be replaced by a natural system whenever the fundamental relationships of plants became known. In the 19th century the theory of evolution supplied some of the principles needed for a natural system, but the broad outlines of Linné's system were retained. (*See also* Botany.)

---

THIS ARTICLE IS IN THE FACT-INDEX

**Linnet**

---

**LINOLEUM.** Since the 1860's, when it was developed in England, linoleum has come into worldwide use. Today it covers thousands of square miles of floors in homes, offices, stores, and institutions.

The raw materials for linoleum come from widely separated sections of the globe. Jute, of which burlap is woven, comes from India and Indonesia. Portugal, Spain, France, and North Africa grow the cork oak tree. Flax, from which linseed oil is made, is grown in many countries. Resins are obtained from pine trees in the southern part of the United States. Other raw materials that go into the making of linoleum include wood, gums, chalk, and pigments.

### How Linoleum Is Made

Linseed oil *oxidizes* (combines with oxygen) when exposed to air and thickens to a rubberlike consistency. Cork and wood are ground to dusts called *flours*.

A *cement* is made of the oxidized oil, resins, and gums. These are cooked in a great kettle until they blend and thicken. The cork and wood flours, pigments, and other materials are worked into the cement; the result is called a *linoleum mixture*.

The linoleum mixture is fed to a *scratcher* machine. This has two rolls, one cold and the other hot. The hot roll softens the mixture, which then clings to the cold roll. Spikes on a rapidly revolving cylinder scratch small particles, or grains, of the mixture from the cold roll.

These grains enter a *calendering* machine. Burlap passes between the machine's two large, heated rolls. Under their pressure the grains fuse, and the fused material is squeezed into and smoothed on the burlap.

Although linoleum emerging from the calendering machine looks like the linoleum in use, it is still soft. It is *cured* (hardened) in tall, narrow stoves. The great loops of linoleum remain in the stove from a few days to a few weeks, depending upon the thickness and the quality of the linoleum.

*Plain linoleums* vary from a little more than one sixteenth to almost one quarter of an inch in thickness. *Battleship linoleum* (so called because it first was made for naval ships) is the thickest linoleum.

*Printed linoleum* is thin, plain linoleum on which an oil-paint design has been printed. The print is made before the linoleum is wholly cured, and after printing it is returned to the stove.

The colors of *inlaid linoleum* extend from the surface to the burlap backing. The linoleum for inlay is prepared without backing in variously sized blocks and strips. These are partly cured. The variously colored blocks then are fitted into a pattern or design on backing. For intricate designs, pieces are cut in desired shapes from strips. Inlaid linoleum is then passed through heated rolls so as to squeeze it into the backing and to fuse the pieces into one. The patterns of *molded inlaid linoleum* are made by sifting variously colored grain mixtures through stencils onto burlap backing. A stencil is needed for each color used. *Embossed linoleum* gives an appearance of fitted tiles. The slightly varying heights of the design are formed by the dies of a molding press. These linoleums also must be further cured.

### Linoleumlike Coverings

Manufacturers give trade names to the many linoleums and linoleumlike coverings they make. Some pieces that are to be fitted into place on walls or floors are called linotile and rubber, asphalt, and cork tiles. Tiles do not have a burlap backing.

Printed linoleums are the least expensive of the linoleum coverings. They usually have a felt rather than a burlap backing. Vinyl, a product of petroleum, now is sometimes used in place of linseed oil. Today almost all linoleums are made of mixtures of cork and wood flours. The quantities of each used depend upon the particular kind of linoleum wanted.

### How Linoleum Developed

Linoleum is the end result in the evolution of manufactured floor coverings which began with oilcloth. Practically all the development of linoleum was made in England. In 1636 the English government granted a patent for a process of applying oil paint to woolen cloth. In the 1750's a floor covering was produced by mixing India rubber with oils and resins and applying the mixture to a cloth backing.

Soon after this Nathan Smith made a floor covering by pressing a mixture of resin, Spanish brown, beeswax, and liquid linseed oil to a canvas backing. In 1844 Elijah Galloway made a floor covering by heating India rubber to a plastic softness and then mixing in cork flour.

Linoleum was developed and named by Frederick Walton, of Yorkshire. The Latin for "flax" and "oil" is *linum* and *oleum*. Walton combined these into "linoleum" as a name for his floor covering, made principally out of linseed oil. The raw materials for the first linoleum were oxidized linseed oil, resins, cork flour, and burlap. Walton's crude process has been improved, and modern manufacturers have added some materials and substituted others, but modern processes of linoleum making are essentially the same as Walton's.

# LINOTYPE—The Machine That Casts Lines of Type

Distributor

Second elevator

Distributor belt

Magazine

Escapement

Spacebands (in space-band box)

Assembler cover

Sorts tray

First elevator cam

First elevator jaw

Mold disk

Vise

Matrix delivery belt

Assembler

Assembler slide

First elevator slide

Mold disk pinion

Knife block

Assembling elevator

Copyholder

Keyboard

Galley

Waste

Base

On this modern Linotype machine, an operator can set about 10,000 characters an hour. This amounts to more than three full columns in this book. He works by lightly touching the keys on the keyboard, shown in larger view at the right. The machine responds through an intricate series of operations and produces one-piece lines of type of the desired width.

**LINOTYPE.** In the middle of the 1400's, Johannes Gutenberg developed a practical method of casting separate printing types in metal. For hundreds of years thereafter, printers used separate types to form words and lines and combined them in columns and pages. Skilled craftsmen, called *compositors*, set the type by hand. They stood at *cases* containing thousands of type characters sorted into more than a hundred small compartments. Before a book, magazine, or newspaper could be printed, compositors had to pick up and arrange into lines of even length perhaps more than a million pieces of type. A skilled compositor could set about 3,000 characters an hour—or about a column of the type in this book.

All the pieces were valuable, and after each use they were carefully distributed into their proper compartments. The distribution was slow and tedious work. Moreover, each use wore the faces of the types; and since some pieces were used more often than others, unequal wear appeared and the whole assortment, or *font*, became worthless.

Newspapers, particularly the large dailies, needed large staffs of compositors to get speedy composition. News stories were broken up into small "takes" and divided among several typesetters. The portion each man set was then assembled in proper order—again a slow and expensive process. Inventors tried many devices to satisfy the demand for speed and economy. Some of them built machines that would "compose," or bring type together, as an operator touched a keyboard. These cumbersome devices usually required two or three men to operate them.

### Line-Casting Machines Solve the Problem

Finally in 1890, after long experimenting, Ottmar Mergenthaler, a naturalized American, patented the Linotype. In 1886 Mergenthaler's first successful machine was put into use by the *New York Tribune*.

The Linotype was a revolutionary invention—one of the mechanical marvels of the age. As the name implies, the line of type is cast on a solid metal bar, called a *slug*. It contrasts with a method of individual type casting developed about the same time (*see* Monotype). With improvements contributed by numerous inventors, slug-casting, or line-casting, machines are used today to set nearly all the world's newspapers and magazines and most of the world's books. Two other line-casting machines in successful use are the Intertype and the Ludlow.

A good Linotype or Intertype operator can set 10,000 characters an hour—as much as three hand compositors. In skilled hands the quality of work done compares favorably with hand setting. Another advantage is the elimination of type distribution. The slugs are melted, and the metal is reused.

### How Line-Casting Machines Work

A modern Linotype machine is shown at the head of this article, and a modern Intertype is shown in the top picture on this page. The basic operations of both machines are similar and can be summed up as three general steps: (1) composing, or assembling the brass type molds, called *matrices* (a single mold is called a *matrix*); (2) casting the line, or slug, from the matrices; (3) distributing the matrices to their original positions. (All the working parts described can be seen in pictures throughout this article.)

The matrices are held in a large container called a *magazine*. Each magazine has nearly a hundred slots,

**THE INTERTYPE MACHINE AND ITS LINE**
This Intertype machine (top), with four auxiliary magazines, gives the operator a choice of 12 to 16 type faces. Below the machine is an assembly of Intertype matrices. Each matrix has molds for roman or italic type or both. At the bottom is a line (or slug) cast from the matrices.

or channels, one for each letter or other character. The channel contains several matrices of its particular character. When the operator presses a key, an escapement device releases the lowest matrix in the channel and moves the next one down to the low position, ready to be released at the next touch of the key. The matrix drops to a *matrix delivery belt*, which carries it to an *assembler*. At each space between words, the operator releases a special *spaceband*, or *space bar*. The distances the matrices must travel and the running speed of the belt are exactly calculated. Thus although there are nearly a hundred characters coming from different distances, they all take the same time to reach the assembler, and so they arrive in proper order.

When a full line of matrices and spacebands has been assembled, or composed, the operator presses a lever which raises the composed line in an assembly elevator. This clears the way for setting another line while the first is being cast.

### SETTING TYPE FROM A DISTANCE

On this teletypesetter, which is attached to the keyboard of a line-casting machine, the punched tape (right) operates the machine automatically. The tape may have been punched by telegraph signals from a distant city. Thus one operator can prepare tape for machines situated in widely separated places.

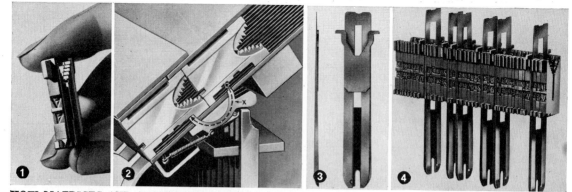

## HOW MATRICES AND SPACEBANDS FORM A LINE OF TYPE

1. This matrix can mold either a roman or an italic letter. Steps in the V-shaped slot (top) guide the matrix back into the proper magazine channel. 2. Here matrices are held in a magazine channel. The U-shaped mechanism (X) rocks to release the lower matrix, then returns to position, allowing the next matrix to slide into the "ready" spot. 3. Here are side and front views of a spaceband, used to help fill out lines. 4. Matrices and spacebands are assembled in line, ready for casting.

The line is now composed and ready for casting, except for one important detail—the automatic spacing, or *justifying*, of the line to its full width. A line of type must be set to an exact width, or *measure;* otherwise the right-hand edge of a column or page of type would appear ragged and uneven. The letter characters make up words of varying widths; and the spacebands between the words must take up all the leftover space. The adjustable spaceband is made in two parts. The smaller part looks like a matrix without a character mold. The larger part is wedge-shaped and can slide up and down the smaller part along tracks, or *gibs*. When the wedge is forced up between the matrices, it helps fill out the line.

### Casting the Line

The assembly elevator carries the assembled line of matrices and spacebands to the casting position. Here the line is held against a slot in the *molding disk*, with the matrix molds exposed to the slot. Molten type metal rises from a pot through a *spout* and fills the matrix molds to form the line. As the slug of hot metal solidifies, the molding disk revolves partway and forces the slug against knives that trim it to desired size. The slug then emerges to take its place in the galley with the lines previously cast.

The picture at the bottom of the page shows a four-position molding disk and its pot of molten metal. Molding disks are cooled by circulating water and may have as many as six molding slots. Each slot makes a slug of different width and thickness. The type metal is kept molten by gas or electric heat; and new metal is fed either automatically or by hand into the pot to keep it full.

### Distributing the Matrices

As soon as the line is cast, the matrices and spacebands are returned to their original positions to be used again. This *distributing* process begins when a long *elevator* arm swings downward. It picks up all the matrices but leaves the spacebands. These bands are pushed directly into their storage spaces. Meantime the arm carries the matrices up to the side of the magazine; and here the matrices are pushed onto a *distributor track. Distributor screws,* winding parallel to the track, push the matrices along until each matrix is positioned directly over its proper storage channel in the magazine. There it drops off automatically.

This automatic drop takes place because of the construction of the track and of the matrix itself. The track has many grooves along its length. The V-shaped notch on each matrix has a special set of projecting teeth. These teeth hook into cer-

## CASTING AND DISTRIBUTING MECHANISMS

At left is a molding disk with its pot of molten metal. A line of matrices is held against one of the molding slots. The plunger forces molten metal up the spout and into the matrices to mold a line. A piece of type metal is being dropped into the pot to renew the supply. The picture at the right shows how matrices are returned. Distributing screws push each matrix along the grooved track until it reaches its channel and drops off, as shown at X. A more exposed view is shown at Y.

tain grooves along the distributing track and so support the matrix as the screws push it along. But at the place in the track directly over the channel where a matrix belongs, the particular combination of grooves supporting the matrix is cut away. When it reaches its channel, it falls off into the magazine.

## Matrices and Slugs

A picture on a previous page shows a line of Intertype display matrices and the cast slug as it appears after trimming. The side ribs prevent one slug from sticking to the next. The letters on the matrices are cut into them and read like print. On the slug, however, the letters are raised and read backward, in order to make them read from left to right when printed. By using different fonts of matrices and different sizes of molding slots, slugs can be cast with a body size of 5 points to 60 points (in printer's measure, a point is $\frac{1}{72}$ of an inch). The slugs can be up to 5 inches (in some machines, 7 inches) long, with letters 5 to 60 points high.

The word "linotype" has come to mean line-casting machines in general. The Intertype, a later development, does practically the same work and, in fact, is virtually interchangeable with the Linotype. By an improved method of shifting from one magazine to another while in operation, the Intertype quickly casts a slug having several different type faces. Here is an extreme example of the Intertype's ability to combine different faces in one slug:

### COMpton's Encyclopedia

This line has *nine* kinds of type. From left to right they are: boldface capital, boldface italic capital, boldface small capitals, boldface lower case, boldface italics, roman lightface capital, roman lightface lower case, lightface italics, and roman lightface small capitals.

Special molding-disk equipment enables the Intertype to cast large display characters and borders. This kind of work is widely used in display advertising. Another device permits hand setting of large matrices, either with or without space bars. These hand-set lines are then cast on the machine.

A third line-casting machine in common use is the Ludlow. The matrices are assembled by hand; and the words are spaced as in hand setting. Then the line is cast as a slug. Although many books have been set by Ludlow, its chief use is in setting newspaper slugs and in job and display work. Short lines and combinations of faces are easily cast.

## Teletypesetting and Photocomposing

A semiautomatic device called the teletypesetter is used to set type by remote control. The sending operator taps out the matter on a perforating machine with a typewriter keyboard. It punches a code in a tough paper tape. If the message is to be sent by wire or radio the tape is then run through an automatic transmitter which changes the code into a series of electric impulses. In the receiving office, re-

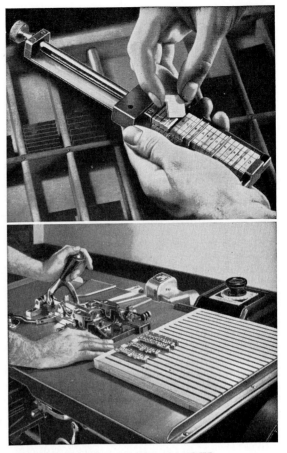

**THE LUDLOW LINE-CASTING MACHINE**
At the top, a compositor is assembling Ludlow matrices in a stick. In the bottom picture, he is locking the stick into a casting slot and forcing molten metal into the mold. Lines cast previously are stored in the slotted galley ready for use.

perforators receive the signals and convert them back into punched tapes. The tape, in turn, runs through a unit attached to the composing machine, which sets the type in galley form.

With the growth of offset printing methods came a demand for a machine to compose, or set, a line in photonegative form. Nonmetallic composing machines have been invented that operate much like slug-casting machines. They assemble a line of matrices, each containing a photographic negative of a type character. The characters are separately photographed and the lines are automatically justified. The developed film is copy for the platemaker. Another nonmetallic system has a keyboard which cuts a code on paper tape. From the tape a photographic unit makes a positive with black letters on a clear base.

THESE ARTICLES ARE IN THE FACT-INDEX

Lin Piao

Linton, Ralph

Linton, William James

Linum

Lin Yutang

Linz, Austria

# The LION—
# Feared Hunter
# and Killer

**LION.** On the plains of Africa, from South Africa to the Sahara, lions continue to thrive. They find their best hunting on the plateaus of eastern Africa and in the vast grasslands of the south. Their roar is the most terrifying voice of the veld. Lions live in rocky dens, in thorn-tree thickets, or in tall grasses at the edges of streams.

Today the only wild lions outside Africa are a few in the Gir Forest of northwestern India. Until recently, some could be found in Iraq and southern Iran. In Roman times, lions also inhabited Syria, Arabia, and southeastern Europe; still earlier, the animals roamed through western Europe.

### A Giant of the Cat Family

Except for the tiger, the lion (*Panthera leo*) is the largest member of the cat family (*see* Cat). A

The lion's huge jaws, which open a full 11 inches, can kill a medium-sized animal with one bite. The upper canine teeth measure from 2 to 2½ inches.

large male lion measures from nine to ten feet, including the tufted tail, and stands more than three feet tall at the shoulders. He weighs from 450 to more than 500 pounds. His body is covered with short yellow-brown hair, and a coarse mane grows on his head, neck, and shoulders. The female lacks the mane and usually is more slender and about a foot shorter than the male.

The lion is well fitted to live by hunting. Colored like sun-dried grass, it can slip unseen across the plains. Its jaws are so hinged that it can open its mouth 11 inches and kill a zebra or a medium-sized antelope with one bite. Its upper canine teeth measure from 2 to 2½ inches. The sickle-shaped claws, when extended from their sheaths, may be 3 inches long. The lion can span nearly 30 feet at one bound, jump over a barrier almost 6 feet tall, and dash a short distance at more than 50 miles an hour.

### The Lion's Hunting Habits

Lions usually hunt at night. Although they will eat carrion, they prefer fresh meat, particularly that of the

**ANDROCLES AND THE LION**

The lion was featured in many ancient stories and legends (*see* Fables). Among them is the following story of Androcles and the lion. One night in the first century, a Roman slave named Androcles, who had been carried to northern Africa, escaped from his master. At dawn he hid in a desert cave and fell asleep. A terrible roar awoke him, and he beheld a huge lion. The cave was the lion's den. Androcles waited to die. The lion just stood there, however, holding up one of its paws, which had been pierced by a great thorn.

Androcles bravely took the paw, drew out the thorn, and stopped the blood.

For three years he and the grateful lion shared the cave. When Androcles decided to go back among his fellow men, he was captured, sent to Rome, and thrown into the arena to fight beasts. A hungry lion sprang at him. Instead of killing him, however, it licked his hand. When Androcles recognized his friend, he leaned against the lion's mane and wept. Deeply moved, the emperor set Androcles free.

**A LION CUB**
A newborn lion cub is as big as a domestic cat. At five months it weighs about 50 pounds. At 18 months it learns to hunt.

**LION AND LIONESS**
The male lion is from nine to ten feet long and weighs about 500 pounds. The shorter, lighter female has no mane.

zebra, antelope, giraffe, and buffalo. The lion often hides beside a trail leading to a water hole and then pounces upon the shoulder or flank of a passing animal. It drives its claws deep into the flesh and kills its victim with a stabbing and crunching bite on the throat or the back of the neck. When stalking a herd, the lion creeps up from the side toward which the wind is blowing, taking advantage of cover until the moment of the last quick rush.

A pride of 4 to 12 lions sometimes hunts together, working as a team. The males roar loudly to scare up the game, while the females lie in wait along the trails to pounce on the scurrying animals. After the lionesses have had time to make a kill, the males stop roaring and come to eat.

### The Lioness and Her Cubs;
### Relations with Man

Lions usually pair for life. About 16 weeks after mating time, the young (from two to four in a litter) are born in a secluded spot selected by the mother. She guards them jealously and does not permit even the male to approach, because he is inclined to kill his offspring. The newborn cubs are about the size of large domestic cats. Their fur is frizzled and spotted. The males are marked also with stripes—several down the sides and one along the middle of the back. Although open-eyed and able to use their claws, the cubs are otherwise quite helpless. For the first two weeks they move about with their forelegs and drag the hindquarters. The mother weans them when they are about three months old.

At five months the cubs weigh about 50 pounds, but they are still as playful as kittens. At nine months most of their spots and stripes disappear. When they are about 18 months old the mother begins to teach them to hunt. She growls and snarls at their clumsy and frantic mauling when they first try to make a kill.

At three years, the male has a conspicuous mane. Lions reach their prime at eight, and then the mane is at its best. After that age, the animals tend to decline. Lions reach an average age of about 28 years, according to reports of zoos and estimates of biologists.

Usually the lion avoids man. However, old ones too slow to catch game may become man-eaters. Occasionally, a young lion that gets a taste of human blood may continue to kill humans.

For ages the lion has been a challenge to man's courage. Since the days of the Roman Empire lions have been caged for circuses and zoos. Most of those that are exhibited today have been born in captivity (*see* Circus; Zoo).

THESE ARTICLES ARE IN THE FACT-INDEX

**Lion of the North**
**Lions International**
**Lipari Islands**
**Lipchitz, Jacques**
**Lipkind, William**
**Lipmann, Fritz Albert**
**Li Po**

Lippe, Germany
Lippi, Filippino
Lippi, Fra Filippo
Lippmann, Gabriel
Lippmann, Walter
Lippold, Richard
Lipton, Sir Thomas

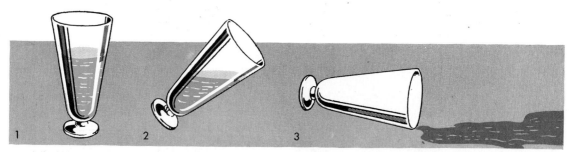

A liquid is not rigid like a solid. It changes shape to fit a container (1 and 2). If it is on a surface, it spreads into a thin film (3). In changing shape it does not change its volume. It does not expand indefinitely, as does a gas.

# LIQUID—One State of Matter

**LIQUID.** Without liquids, the earth could not have rain, rivers, and oceans. Plants and animals could not obtain nourishment or distribute it throughout their bodies. Liquids can dissolve solid materials or capture and hold gases in solution (*see* Solutions). Thus they serve as a kind of transportation system for dissolved materials.

Liquids perform these useful functions because of the way they are put together. Like gases and solids, liquids are made up of the tiny particles of matter called molecules, and an attractive force called *cohesion* exists between them. In liquids this force is not strong enough to hold the molecules together in fixed positions as it is in solid objects. It can, however, hold them in a loose group or mass, which can change shape freely and therefore flow. The molecules do not fly about separately as do those of a gas.

### Leveling Tendency and Incompressibility

Every sizable mass of liquid tends to "flatten out," with its upper surface as low as possible. This happens because the force of gravity pulls each molecule down until it can go no lower. The upper molecules tend to push lower ones aside, and these yield until they are stopped by the sides of the container. This adjustment continues until the downward pull on the upper surface of the liquid is the same everywhere, except at the very edges.

Liquids are all but incompressible, because every molecule is as "close down" against its neighbors as it can get. The only free space is that created by

### WHY A LIQUID "SEEKS ITS LEVEL"

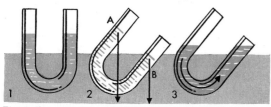

These diagrams show why the surface of a liquid is always level and as low as possible (1). If one part becomes higher than the rest (2), the higher part (A) weighs more than the lower (B). The excess liquid promptly flows downward, raising the lower part until both surfaces are even (3).

the heat vibration of each individual molecule (*see* Heat); and this vibration is energetic enough to withstand any ordinary pressure. Water is compressed only about one tenth by a pressure of 20 tons to the square inch. The only common way the volume of a liquid is altered is when a change of temperature affects the heat vibration.

### Transmission of Pressure Within Liquids

In a liquid, pressure increases with depth because at any depth the liquid bears all the weight which lies above. This weight tends to force molecules sidewise as well as downward. Hence at any point in a given level, the pressure will be the same.

These facts explain *buoyancy*. An object thrust into a liquid must overcome the liquid's internal pressure. In doing so it loses weight. According to the law of Archimedes, the loss equals the weight of the liquid which the object pushes aside or displaces. (*See also* Hydraulic Machinery; Water.)

### The Liquid Force Called Surface Tension

Many characteristics of liquids change at their surfaces, however, because of a force called *surface tension*. It consists of the inward pull exerted upon every molecule in the surface by its neighbors farther inside the liquid mass. The inward pull makes the surface act like a slightly stretched membrane, tending always to compress the underlying liquid into the most compact shape possible.

On a surface the most compact shape is a circle, and in free space it is a sphere. Hence if a drop of liquid lies on any surface to which it does not cling or stick, it tends to lie flat in a circular mass. Surface tension can draw in the edges of large drops and force the top to bulge upward. It can draw small drops into almost perfect spheres. If a liquid falls through space as rain or if it floats within another liquid, as heavy oil in water, the liquid tends to form spherical drops.

### Vaporization and Condensation

All the molecules in a liquid are constantly colliding with each other, and most of the collisions "cancel out"; that is, they tend to drive the molecules downward as often as upward and to one side as much as the other. However, some molecules receive blows which give them greater speed and drive them upward with enough energy to carry them free from the downward pull of surface tension. This process of escape is called *evaporation*, and the collection of escaped molecules becomes *vapor*. (Escape from a surface is called *evaporation* to distinguish it from the kind of escape that occurs during boiling, described later in the article.)

In an open vessel and at moderate temperature, the rate of evaporation depends upon the average speed of the liquid molecules; and the average speed constitutes the *temperature* of the liquid (*see* Heat). Since vaporized molecules have more than average speed, each escape of molecules reduces the average heat energy left in the liquid. The liquid will be cooled correspondingly, and further evaporation will be slowed. (*See also* Evaporation.)

Cooling a vapor has somewhat reverse effects. At a certain temperature, the loss of heat energy enables cohesive force to draw some molecules together into droplets, and the droplets become larger until they are heavy enough to fall back into the liquid. This process is called *condensation*.

## Vapor Pressure, Saturation, and Boiling

In a closed vessel, the rate of evaporation for any given temperature soon reaches a limit. This happens because in such a vessel the vapor molecules cannot fly away. They strike all surfaces of the confining vessel, and many of them fly back into the liquid. At length a balance is reached between the molecules that have escaped and those that have returned. The space will hold no more vapor molecules. This condition is called *saturation*, and the vapor is said to be exerting *saturated vapor pressure* upon the liquid. (Other terms for this pressure are *saturation pressure* and *vapor tension*.)

The saturation pressure in a closed vessel rises with increase of temperature because the vapor molecules fly faster and strike the walls harder and because, while the temperature is being raised, more molecules evaporate than return to the liquid. When some higher temperature is reached, the pressure in the liquid becomes equal to the saturated vapor pressure. Then molecules of sufficient speed, which happen to fly together at the same spot within the liquid, can withstand pressure from above. Thereupon they form a bubble and start pushing back the surrounding liquid. These bubbles rise to the surface and burst, letting the vapor escape.

When a liquid bubbles in this way (but not from trapped air bubbles escaping), it is said to be *boiling*, and the temperature at which this occurs is called the *boiling point*. (Another term for boiling is *ebullition*.) Thus, boiling is the vaporization of liquid *throughout the volume* of the liquid.

The boiling point depends upon the pressure exerted on the liquid. In an open vessel this pressure is exerted by the atmosphere, and applying heat be-

## EXPERIMENTS WITH SURFACE TENSION

To show the tension of a liquid film, hang a loop of thread in a wire ring and fill the ring with a film of soapy water to which the loop of thread will cling. Now break the film inside the loop with a hot pin (1). The loop will snap out into a perfect circle, drawn equally in all directions by the tension of the surrounding film (2).

To show how wetting agents (detergents) reduce surface tension, cut a boat-shaped slip from heavy paper, then cut a hole and a slit on the slip as shown (3). Lay the slip on water and place one drop of a wetting agent in the hole (4). Soon the boat starts moving ahead as though by magic (5). The diagrams below show why.

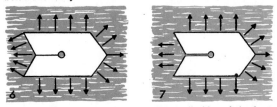

Usually surface tension pulls equally at all sides of the boat, and the boat does not move (6). Soon the wetting agent seeps back through the slit and weakens the pull on the rear edge. Then the unbalanced pull on the front draws the boat along (7).

## ARCHIMEDES' RULE

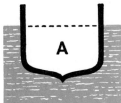

This cross section of a ship provides a simple illustration of Archimedes' law as it applies to floating objects. Water enough to fill the space (A) below the dotted line would weigh exactly as much as the whole ship.

## EXPLAINING THE NATURE OF SURFACE TENSION

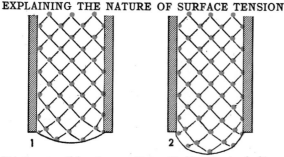

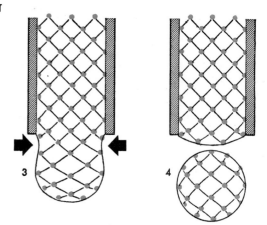

This huge medicine dropper (1) has liquid molecules inside (dots). When the bulb of the dropper is squeezed, the liquid is forced out (2). But the outside layer of molecules remains bound to those inside and to the dropper tip by force of surface tension. Squeezing the bulb further stretches the bulge of liquid to the breaking point (3); the liquid falls free as a drop (4).

yond the boiling point does not make the liquid hotter. The molecules simply escape faster and in greater number.

In a closed vessel the pressure builds up as the temperature rises, and the liquid must be correspondingly hotter before it can boil. Pressure cookers cook food faster than open vessels because the higher pressure makes water reach a higher temperature before it boils. Continued heating in a tightly closed vessel may build up pressure enough to produce an explosion unless some outlet is provided. Most vessels of this type have some device such as a safety valve to relieve dangerous pressure.

Reducing the pressure in a container by pumping off the molecules as they escape makes vaporization easier and lowers the boiling point. Vacuum pans use this principle for boiling away water from solutions of materials, such as evaporated milk, which would be injured or destroyed by the heat of ordinary boiling (*see* Sugar). Water can be boiled at 32° F. (usually the temperature of freezing) if the pressure is reduced to 4.6 mm. of mercury.

### Adhesion, "Wetting," and Mixing

When a liquid comes in contact with a solid, the reaction depends upon the attraction between the liquid and the solid. (This attraction between unlike substances is called *adhesion*.) A drop of water will spread out in a thin film over perfectly clean glass, because the force of *adhesion* between water and glass is stronger than the force of *cohesion* between the water molecules. The water is said to "wet" the glass. If water is placed on oilcloth or waxed paper it forms into drops, because there is virtually no adhesive force between oil and water. They "do not mix."

Similar results occur when the surface of a solid rises above its contact with the surface of a liquid. If the force of adhesion is greater than the force of cohesion, the liquid surface curves up at the line of contact. In a very small tube, the adhesive force is great enough to lift all the liquid in the tube above the general surrounding surface. If adhesion is weaker than cohesion, the surface curves down, as when mercury is in contact with glass.

Certain chemicals dissolved in a liquid may weaken its cohesion and reduce the surface tension. The weak forces of adhesion with normally uncongenial substances can thus make the liquid adhere to solids or

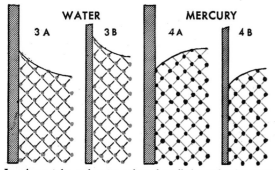

Imagine a tube and water enlarged until the molecules show as dots (3A). Some water molecules will adhere to the glass above the water level and draw others upward (3B). Mercury will not adhere to glass, so it is drawn inward and downward by surface tension (4A, 4B).

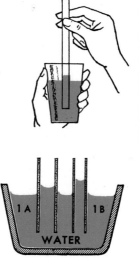

### TWO RESULTS OF CAPILLARITY

If a glass tube stands in water, the process of capillarity draws water up into the tube. The surface of the water in the tube is concave (1A). The smaller the bore of the tube, the higher the water is drawn (1B). Mercury does not wet glass, and the effects are reversed (2A, 2B).

make it mix with liquids. The chemicals which have this effect on liquids are *detergents*, or wetting agents (*see* Soap).

### Capillary Action and Osmosis

The surface tension of liquids explains the phenomenon called *capillarity*. As shown in diagrams on the preceding page, capillarity raises or depresses the level of a liquid in small tubes and at the solid edges of containers. The liquid rises if the force of adhesion is greater than cohesion within the liquid; if cohesion is stronger, the liquid is depressed. The curved surface in a tube is called a *meniscus* (*see* Capillary Action).

Another phenomenon peculiar to liquids is *osmosis*. If a strong solution of sugar, salt, or other substance is separated by a porous membrane from a weaker solution or from plain water, water will pass through the membrane into the stronger solution. The liquid particles, or molecules, on both sides of the membrane are hitting against it. But the bombardment on one side is carried on in large part by the dissolved particles which are too large to get through; on the other side the missiles are mostly or entirely water molecules, which can pass through easily. This one-way passage of molecules gives the solution more water than it loses, and its volume increases.

**LIQUID AIR.** Just as steam becomes water if its temperature falls below 212° F., so air becomes liquid when its temperature is reduced to −312° F. It looks like water, but it behaves very differently. If liquid air is poured on a block of ice it boils, sending off clouds of vapor. At −362° it becomes a solid.

Liquid air is a mixture of liquid oxygen, nitrogen, and rare elements such as helium and neon. If carbon dioxide is in the air, it crystallizes as a solid. Liquid nitrogen evaporates more readily than liquid oxygen and comes off first when liquid air starts to evaporate. The residue becomes increasingly richer in oxygen.

Air is liquefied commercially to obtain oxygen, nitrogen, and the rare gases and for use as a refrigerating agent. Liquid air also has explosive power, because as it evaporates it exerts great pressure. Air is liquefied by being forced through compressors into cooling coils at pressures of about 3,000 pounds to the square inch. Then it passes into a chamber where it suddenly expands. The acute cold caused by this expansion liquefies the air.

Liquid air can freeze and destroy a human finger in two seconds or in a few moments make an iron pan so brittle with cold that it can be broken by hand.

### BEHAVIOR THAT SEEMS TO "DEFY NATURE"

Place two straws on water. Blowing between them (1) will make them move together (2). The flow of air sets a current flowing between the straws, and as the liquid moves its pressure is reduced (the Bernoulli effect). Then the unchanged pressure of the surrounding liquid forces the straws together.

A Venturi flow meter (3) uses the same effect. When water passes from the wider to the narrower pipe, its velocity increases and its pressure is reduced. The result is shown by the different heights of water in the upright pipes.

### A POTATO REVEALS THE FORCE OF OSMOSIS

SALT SOLUTION    PLAIN WATER    TWO HOURS LATER

To show how cells and tissues exchange solutions through their walls, place a potato with its inside gouged out in a glass and fill most of the cavity with salt water (1). Next fill the glass around the potato with plain water until level with the salt water (2). Within an hour or two, the potato will have filled to overflowing (3). The force of osmosis exerted by the salt water has drawn fresh water through the potato.

At the right, a glass tube is sealed to the cut stalk of a plant and the roots are placed in water. Watery sap slowly rises in the tube, drawn up through the roots by osmotic force.

THESE ARTICLES ARE IN THE FACT-INDEX

Liquidambar                    Lisa, Manuel
Lira                           Lisboa, Antônio Francisco

**LISBON, Portugal.** The capital of Portugal is Lisbon, or *Lisboa*. It is the westernmost seaport of continental Europe. Lisbon lies seven miles from the Atlantic Ocean on the Tagus River. Immediately above the city the river broadens out into a tidal lake, 4 to 8 miles wide and 11 miles long. This lake forms one of the best harbors in the world. Beyond the harbor, the city itself rises in terraces of white houses and green parks. Behind them rise the granite mountains of Sintra.

Lisbon is almost entirely a modern city. A tidal wave in 1755 brought a death toll estimated at from 10,000 to 60,000 people. Only a small section of the town was left standing. This section contains many interesting historical buildings. The cathedral in this area was built in 1150. In it is the tomb of St. Vincent, patron saint of Lisbon. In the heart of the city is the Rossio, a colorful square. In the middle of the square is a statue of Pedro IV.

The modern part of the city makes Lisbon one of Europe's most beautiful capitals. The streets are straight and broad. The finest street is the Avenue of Liberty, a mile long and 300 feet wide, with a double row of shade trees down the middle. Its name commemorates the freeing of Portugal from Spain in 1640. Elevators carry people up and down between the terraced levels of the city. Lisbon also has one of the finest botanical gardens in Europe.

Lisbon was probably founded by the Phoenicians. It was a flourishing town before the Romans occupied it. The Moors held it from 711 to 1147. Vasco da Gama sailed from Lisbon for his voyage around Africa in 1497. The Spanish Armada started from here on its ill-fated voyage in 1588. Lisbon was the chief scene of the Revolution of 1910, when warship crews revolted and drove Manuel II from Portugal.

During World War II Portugal was neutral and Lisbon was Europe's chief outlet. It became the terminus for planes from the United States. Refugees from war-torn nations increased its normal population.

Today Lisbon is a key airline center as well as a major seaport. Manufactures include ships, chemicals, textiles, and food products. Exports are wine, fish, and cork. Spanning the Tagus is Europe's longest suspension bridge, completed in 1966. Population (1966 estimate), 822,000. (*See also* Portugal.)

THESE ARTICLES ARE IN THE FACT-INDEX

Lisgar, John Young, Baron
Lister, Joseph, Baron

**LISZT, Franz** (1811–1886). The most brilliant pianist of his day, Franz Liszt was also a distinguished composer, conductor, and teacher. He made a further contribution to music through his encouragement of younger composers.

James Press

Liszt was born Oct. 22, 1811, at Raiding, Hungary. His father, Adam Liszt, served the Esterházy family as their steward at Raiding. This family had been patrons of music for generations. Liszt's mother, Anna Lager, was an Austrian.

Adam Liszt was a talented amateur and taught his son to play the piano. At the age of nine Franz gave a concert at Oedenburg, near Raiding, and another at Prince Esterházy's palace. Liszt went to Vienna, where he studied with two well-known teachers, Karl Czerny and Antonio Salieri. He gave his first public concerts in Vienna in 1822, in Paris in 1823, and in London in 1824. His playing moved Beethoven to kiss him. In London George IV received him at Carleton House. In Paris, where he lived for 12 years, he was sensationally successful.

Liszt eloped to Geneva with the Countess d'Agoult in 1835. They had three children, Blandine, Cosima (who became the wife of Hans von Bülow and then of Richard Wagner), and Daniel. Triumphant concert tours dominated Liszt's life until October 1847, when he made his last appearance as a virtuoso.

From 1848 to 1859 he was conductor at the Court Theater at Weimar. Here he championed Wagner and produced his music dramas. He introduced and revived the works of other contemporary composers.

At 50 he retired to Rome. He received minor orders in the Roman Catholic church, with the title abbé, in 1865. In 1869 he began to visit Weimar regularly. The Hungarian government named him president of the Academy of Music at Budapest in 1870. Thereafter he divided his time between Rome, Weimar, and Budapest. After a spectacular "jubilee tour" to Paris, London, and other cities in 1886 he died at Bayreuth of pneumonia July 31.

Among Liszt's works are 13 symphonic poems, including 'Les Préludes'; two symphonies, 'Faust' and 'Dante'; 20 Hungarian rhapsodies; 55 songs; 'Transcendental Études' for piano; two oratorios, 'The Legend of St. Elizabeth' and 'Christus'; several 'Mephisto' waltzes, and many transcriptions for the piano of operas, songs, and instrumental works.

THESE ARTICLES ARE IN THE FACT-INDEX

Litany
Litchfield, Conn.
Litchi

# Awards for Writers and Illustrators

**LITERARY AWARDS.** Hundreds of literary awards are given each year throughout the world. These prizes often honor established literary figures, but they may also help relatively unknown writers and illustrators to achieve greater recognition.

Literary awards usually consist of cash prizes, medals, or citations. The sponsors include individuals, organizations, and publishing firms.

## Major Children's Book Awards

Among the many annual awards for children's literature, the most prestigious are the John Newbery and the Caldecott medals, administered by the American Library Association (ALA). They were established by Frederic G. Melcher, an American publisher.

The first John Newbery Medal—for the most distinguished contribution to literature for children published in the United States—was awarded in 1922. It was named for an 18th-century London bookseller and publisher who pioneered in children's literature. The first Caldecott Medal—for the most distinguished picture book for children published in the United States—was awarded in 1938. It was named in honor of Randolph Caldecott, a 19th-century English illustrator of children's books (*see* Caldecott; Newbery; John Newbery and Caldecott medals tables on following pages).

Library organizations also administer many of the other awards for children's books. The Laura Ingalls Wilder Award, established in 1954, honors a popular American author. Beginning in 1960, a medal has been awarded every five years by the ALA to an author or illustrator for substantial and lasting contributions to children's literature (*see* Laura Ingalls Wilder Award table on a following page).

The ALA also administers the Mildred L. Batchelder Award, established in 1966. Named for a leader in the development of library services for children, the annual citation goes to a book originally published in a foreign language in another country and subsequently published by an American publisher in the United States. The Catholic Library Association has awarded the Regina Medal since 1959 to individuals who have made distinguished contributions to literature for children (*see* Regina Medal table on a following page).

Monetary prizes include the Boston Globe-Horn Book and the American (formerly National) Book awards for children's literature. Regional, state, and religious awards honor specialized achievements.

## Awards in Other Countries

Many other countries and organizations award prizes in the field. British awards include the Carnegie and Kate Greenaway medals, both given by the Library Association. The Carnegie Medal—established in honor of the industrialist Andrew Carnegie—has been awarded annually since 1937 for an outstanding book for children (*see* Carnegie). The annual Kate Greenaway Medal—honoring the 19th-century English illustrator—was established in 1956 for distinguished illustration.

The Canadian Library Association (CLA) has presented the Book of the Year for Children Award since 1947. Beginning in 1954, individual awards were made for books in English and in French, until the French award was discontinued in 1974. Since 1971, the CLA has also awarded the Amelia Frances Howard-Gibbon Medal for outstanding illustration. The award is named for a 19th-century Canadian illustrator of children's books (*see* Canadian Library Association Awards table on a following page).

The New Zealand Library Association has presented an annual award since 1945. In 1946, national organizations in Australia began an award program that has since been expanded to include awards for picture books and for visual arts.

The Hans Christian Andersen International Children's Book Medals, established in 1956, are administered by the International Board on Books for Young People (IBBY). Honoring the 19th-century Danish author of fairy tales, the awards have been given biennially to an author and, since 1966, to an illustrator for the body of their work.

## Nobel, Pulitzer, and Other Prizes

The Nobel prize for literature is the highest international literary honor. First awarded in 1901, it is

The face of the Newbery Medal, designed by René Chambellan, depicts John Newbery's interest in children.

Both sides of the Caldecott Medal, also designed by Chambellan, have reproductions of Randolph Caldecott's illustrations.

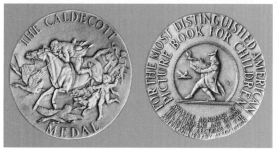

## John Newbery Medal

| Awarded | Author | Book |
|---|---|---|
| 1922 | Hendrik Willem Van Loon | The Story of Mankind |
| 1923 | Hugh Lofting | Voyages of Dr. Dolittle |
| 1924 | Charles B. Hawes | Dark Frigate |
| 1925 | Charles J. Finger | Tales from Silver Lands |
| 1926 | Arthur B. Chrisman | Shen of the Sea |
| 1927 | Will James | Smoky, the Cowhorse |
| 1928 | Dhan Gopal Mukerji | Gay-Neck |
| 1929 | Eric P. Kelly | The Trumpeter of Krakow |
| 1930 | Rachel Field | Hitty, Her First Hundred Years |
| 1931 | Elizabeth J. Coatsworth | The Cat Who Went to Heaven |
| 1932 | Laura A. Armer | Waterless Mountain |
| 1933 | Elizabeth F. Lewis | Young Fu of the Upper Yangtze |
| 1934 | Cornelia Meigs | Invincible Louisa |
| 1935 | Monica Shannon | Dobry |
| 1936 | Carol R. Brink | Caddie Woodlawn |
| 1937 | Ruth Sawyer | Roller Skates |
| 1938 | Kate Seredy | The White Stag |
| 1939 | Elizabeth Enright | Thimble Summer |
| 1940 | James Daugherty | Daniel Boone |
| 1941 | Armstrong Sperry | Call It Courage |
| 1942 | Walter D. Edmonds | The Matchlock Gun |
| 1943 | Elizabeth Janet Gray | Adam of the Road |
| 1944 | Esther Forbes | Johnny Tremain |
| 1945 | Robert Lawson | Rabbit Hill |
| 1946 | Lois Lenski | Strawberry Girl |
| 1947 | Carolyn S. Bailey | Miss Hickory |
| 1948 | William Pène Du Bois | The Twenty-One Balloons |
| 1949 | Marguerite Henry | King of the Wind |
| 1950 | Marguerite de Angeli | The Door in the Wall |
| 1951 | Elizabeth Yates | Amos Fortune: Free Man |
| 1952 | Eleanor Estes | Ginger Pye |
| 1953 | Ann Nolan Clark | Secret of the Andes |
| 1954 | Joseph Krumgold | . . . and now Miguel |
| 1955 | Meindert De Jong | The Wheel on the School |
| 1956 | Jean Lee Latham | Carry On, Mr. Bowditch |
| 1957 | Virginia Eggertsen Sorensen | Miracles on Maple Hill |
| 1958 | Harold Keith | Rifles for Watie |
| 1959 | Elizabeth George Speare | The Witch of Blackbird Pond |
| 1960 | Joseph Krumgold | Onion John |
| 1961 | Scott O'Dell | Island of the Blue Dolphins |
| 1962 | Elizabeth George Speare | The Bronze Bow |
| 1963 | Madeleine L'Engle | A Wrinkle in Time |
| 1964 | Emily Cheney Neville | It's Like This, Cat |
| 1965 | Maia Wojciechowska | Shadow of a Bull |
| 1966 | Elizabeth Borton de Treviño | I, Juan de Pareja |
| 1967 | Irene Hunt | Up a Road Slowly |
| 1968 | Elaine L. Konigsburg | From the Mixed-up Files of Mrs. Basil E. Frankweiler |
| 1969 | Lloyd Alexander | The High King |
| 1970 | William H. Armstrong | Sounder |
| 1971 | Betsy Byars | Summer of the Swans |
| 1972 | Robert C. O'Brien | Mrs. Frisby and the Rats of NIMH |
| 1973 | Jean C. George | Julie of the Wolves |
| 1974 | Paula Fox | The Slave Dancer |
| 1975 | Virginia Hamilton | M. C. Higgins, the Great |
| 1976 | Susan Cooper | The Grey King |
| 1977 | Mildred D. Taylor | Roll of Thunder, Hear My Cry |
| 1978 | Katherine Paterson | Bridge to Terabithia |
| 1979 | Ellen Raskin | The Westing Game |
| 1980 | Joan W. Blos | A Gathering of Days: a New England Girl's Journal, 1830–32 |
| 1981 | Katherine Paterson | Jacob Have I Loved |
| 1982 | Nancy Willard | A Visit to William Blake's Inn |

one of the prizes established by Alfred Bernhard Nobel, a 19th-century Swedish industrialist (*see* Nobel; Nobel Prizes). The Swedish Academy in Stockholm determines the award, which includes a gold medal and prize money of up to $90,000. Nine Americans—Sinclair Lewis, Pearl Buck, Eugene O'Neill, William Faulkner, Ernest Hemingway, John Steinbeck, Saul Bellow, Isaac Bashevis Singer, and Czeslaw Milosz—have won the prize.

Among the most important literary awards in the United States are the Pulitzer Prizes in Letters. They were established in 1917 by the will of Joseph Pulitzer, an American journalist who was the editor of the *St. Louis Post-Dispatch* and the *New York World* (*see* Pulitzer). Prizes of $1,000 each are given annually in six fields—fiction, drama, history, biography, and poetry, and for a book not eligible in any of these categories. The trustees of Columbia University award the prizes. Columbia University trustees also award the annual Bancroft Prizes, first given in 1948 under the will of Frederic Bancroft, an American historian. Three prizes of $4,000 each may be given to books in American history, diplomacy, and international relations.

The National Book Awards were established in 1950 by the American Book Publishers' Council—

## Caldecott Medal

| Awarded | Artist | Book |
|---|---|---|
| 1938 | Dorothy P. Lathrop | Animals of the Bible (Text from King James Bible) |
| 1939 | Thomas Handforth | Mei Li |
| 1940 | Ingri M. and Edgar Parin d'Aulaire | Abraham Lincoln |
| 1941 | Robert Lawson | They Were Strong and Good |
| 1942 | Robert McCloskey | Make Way for Ducklings |
| 1943 | Virginia Lee Burton | The Little House |
| 1944 | Louis Slobodkin | Many Moons (Text by James Thurber) |
| 1945 | Elizabeth Orton Jones | Prayer for a Child (Text by Rachel Field) |
| 1946 | Maud and Miska Petersham | Rooster Crows |
| 1947 | Leonard Weisgard | The Little Island (Text by Golden MacDonald) |
| 1948 | Roger Duvoisin | White Snow, Bright Snow (Text by Alvin Tresselt) |
| 1949 | Berta and Elmer Hader | The Big Snow |
| 1950 | Leo Politi | Song of the Swallows |
| 1951 | Katherine Milhous | The Egg Tree |
| 1952 | Nicolas Mordvinoff | Finders Keepers (Text by William Lipkind) |
| 1953 | Lynd Ward | The Biggest Bear |
| 1954 | Ludwig Bemelmans | Madeline's Rescue |
| 1955 | Marcia Joan Brown | Cinderella |
| 1956 | Feodor Rojankovsky | Frog Went A-Courtin' |
| 1957 | Marc Simont | A Tree Is Nice |
| 1958 | Robert McCloskey | Time of Wonder |
| 1959 | Barbara Cooney | Chanticleer and the Fox |
| 1960 | Marie Hall Ets | Nine Days to Christmas |
| 1961 | Nicolas Sidjakov | Baboushka and the Three Kings |
| 1962 | Marcia Joan Brown | Once a Mouse |
| 1963 | Ezra Jack Keats | The Snowy Day |
| 1964 | Maurice Sendak | Where the Wild Things Are |
| 1965 | Beni Montresor | May I Bring a Friend? |
| 1966 | Nonny Hogrogian | Always Room for One More |
| 1967 | Evaline Ness | Sam, Bangs & Moonshine |
| 1968 | Ed Emberley | Drummer Hoff |
| 1969 | Uri Shulevitz | The Fool of the World and the Flying Ship |
| 1970 | William Steig | Sylvester and the Magic Pebble |
| 1971 | Gail E. Haley | A Story—A Story |
| 1972 | Nonny Hogrogian | One Fine Day |
| 1973 | Blair Lent | The Funny Little Woman |
| 1974 | Margot Zemach | Duffy and the Devil |
| 1975 | Gerald McDermott | Arrow to the Sun: a Pueblo Indian Tale |
| 1976 | Leo and Diane Dillon | Why Mosquitoes Buzz in People's Ears |
| 1977 | Leo and Diane Dillon | Ashanti to Zulu |
| 1978 | Peter Spier | Noah's Ark |
| 1979 | Paul Goble | The Girl Who Loved Wild Horses |
| 1980 | Barbara Cooney | Ox-Cart Man (Text by Donald Hall) |
| 1981 | Arnold Lobel | Fables |
| 1982 | Chris Van Allsburg | Jumanji |

## Regina Medal

| | | | | |
|---|---|---|---|---|
| 1959 | Eleanor Farjeon | | 1971 | Tasha Tudor |
| 1960 | Anne Carroll Moore | | 1972 | Meindert De Jong |
| 1961 | Padraic Colum | | 1973 | Frances Clarke Sayers |
| 1962 | Frederic Gershom Melcher | | 1974 | Robert McCloskey |
| 1963 | Ann Nolan Clark | | 1975 | May McNeer and Lynd Ward |
| 1964 | May Hill Arbuthnot | | 1976 | Virginia Haviland |
| 1965 | Ruth Sawyer | | 1977 | Marcia Joan Brown |
| 1966 | Leo Politi | | 1978 | Scott O'Dell |
| 1967 | Bertha Mahony Miller | | 1979 | Morton Schindel |
| 1968 | Marguerite de Angeli | | 1980 | Beverly Cleary |
| 1969 | Lois Lenski | | 1981 | Augusta Baker |
| 1970 | Ingri and Edgar Parin d'Aulaire | | 1982 | Theodor Seuss Geisel |

now the Association of American Publishers (AAP), the American Booksellers Association, and the Book Manufacturers Institute. Until 1980 prizes of $1,000 each were given annually in six categories.

The AAP, which had been administering the National Book Awards, created the American Book Awards (TABA) as their successor. TABA was established to give recognition to a greater number of United States authors and publishers. Two monetary awards—one to a hardcover book and one to a paperback—were given in each of 13 categories, and seven additional prizes were given in special categories, including design. After the controversial TABA was boycotted by some authors and publishers, the number of categories was reduced to ten and the name was amended to ABA, beginning in 1981.

One of the most prestigious American awards is the National Medal for Literature, established in 1964. Since 1977, an annual prize of $15,000 has been given by the AAP for a writer's overall contribution.

Among the many other national, regional, and special literary awards, two of the best known have been the Bollingen Prize in Poetry and the O. Henry Memorial Awards. The Bollingen Prize was established in 1950 under the sponsorship of Yale University. The O. Henry Awards were first given in 1919.

## Canadian Library Association Awards

| Awarded | Author or Artist | Book |
|---|---|---|
| 1947 | R. L. H. Haig-Brown | Starbuck Valley Winter |
| 1948 | Bertha Mabel Dunham | Kristli's Trees |
| 1950 | R. S. Lambert | Franklin of the Arctic (U.S. title, Adventure to the Polar Sea: the Story of Sir John Franklin) |
| 1952 | Catherine Anthony Clark | The Sun Horse |
| 1954 | Emile Gervais | Monseigneur de Laval (French) |
| 1956 | Margaret Louise Riley | Train for Tiger Lily |
| 1957 | Cyrus Macmillan | Glooskap's Country, and Other Indian Tales |
| 1958 | Farley Mowat | Lost in the Barrens |
|  | Béatrice Clément | Le Chevalier du Roi (French) |
| 1959 | John Francis Hayes | The Dangerous Cove |
|  | Hélène Flamme | Un Drôle de Petit Cheval (French) |
| 1960 | Marius Barbeau | The Golden Phoenix |
|  | Paule Daveluy | L'été Enchanté (French) |
| 1961 | William Toye | The St. Lawrence |
|  | Marcelle Gauvreau | Plantes Vagabondes (French) |
| 1962 | Claude B. Aubry | Les îles du Roi Maha Maha II (French) |
| 1963 | Sheila Burnford | The Incredible Journey |
|  | Paule Daveluy | Drôle d'Automne (French) |
| 1964 | R. L. H. Haig-Brown | The Whale People |
|  | Cécile Chabot | Férie (French) |
| 1965 | Dorothy M. Reid | Tales of Nanabozho |
|  | Claude B. Aubry | Le Loup de Noël (French) |
| 1966 | James McNeill | The Double Knights |
|  | James Houston | Tikta'liktak |
|  | Monique Corriveau | Le Wapiti (French) |
|  | Andrée Maillet | Le Chêne des Tempêtes (French) |
| 1967 | Christie Harris | Raven's Cry |
| 1968 | James Houston | The White Archer: an Eskimo Legend |
|  | Claude Mélançon | Légendes Indiennes du Canada (French) |
| 1969 | Kay Hill | And Tomorrow the Stars |
| 1970 | Edith Fowke | Sally Go 'Round the Sun |
|  | Lionel Gendron | La Merveilleuse Histoire de la Naissance (French) |
| 1971 | William Toye | Cartier Discovers the Saint Lawrence |
|  | Henriette Major | La Surprise de Dame Chenille (French) |
| 1972 | Anne Blades | Mary of Mile 18 |
|  | S. Takashima | Child in Prison Camp (illustration) |
| 1973 | Ruth Nichols | The Marrow of the World |
|  | Simone Bussières | Le Petit Sapin qui a Poussé sur une Étoile (French) |
|  | Jacques de Roussan | Au delà du Soleil (illustration) |
| 1974 | Elizabeth Cleaver | The Miraculous Hind |
|  | William Kurelek | A Prairie Boy's Winter (illustration) |
| 1975 | Dennis Lee | Alligator Pie |
|  | Carlo Italiano | The Sleighs of My Childhood (illustration) |
| 1976 | Mordecai Richler | Jacob Two-Two Meets the Hooded Fang |
|  | William Kurelek | A Prairie Boy's Summer (illustration) |
| 1977 | Christie Harris | Mouse Woman and the Vanished Princesses |
|  | Pam Hall | Down By Jim Long's Stage (illustration) |
| 1978 | Dennis Lee | Garbage Delight |
|  | Elizabeth Cleaver | The Loon's Necklace (illustration) |
| 1979 | Kevin Major | Hold Fast |
|  | Ann Blades | A Salmon for Simon (illustration) |
| 1980 | James Houston | River Runners |
|  | Laszlo Gal | The Twelve Dancing Princesses (illustration) |
| 1981 | Donn Kushner | The Violin-Maker's Gift |
|  | Douglas Tait | The Trouble with Princesses (illustration) |
| 1982 | Janet Lunn | The Root Cellar |
|  | Heather Woodall | Ytek and the Arctic Orchid (illustration) |

## Laura Ingalls Wilder Award

| | | | |
|---|---|---|---|
| 1954 | Laura Ingalls Wilder | 1970 | Elwyn Brooks White |
| 1960 | Clara Ingram Judson | 1975 | Beverly Cleary |
| 1965 | Ruth Sawyer | 1980 | Theodor Seuss Geisel |

## Fellowship Awards

Fellowships are grants of money given to authors to support them while they do research and write. The John Simon Guggenheim Memorial Fellowships, established in 1925, are the most prestigious of these awards in the United States. The amounts of the grants vary. More than 8,000 Guggenheim Fellowships have been awarded, several hundred of them to poets, playwrights, novelists, and other writers. The American Academy of Arts and Letters and the American Academy in Rome collaborate to provide fellowships for study in Rome.

Grants of the National Endowment for the Arts, established in 1965, have included awards of up to $10,000 to writers for support of their work. Special programs have provided grants in varying amounts for young writers.

# LITERATURE
## A Way of Seeing, A Way of Feeling, A Way of Knowing

**LITERATURE.** Literature is more than language. It is ideas and feelings set to the music of language. And it takes the form of words—and pictures—put together with imagination.

Literature is a way of seeing, a way of feeling, a way of knowing. A listener or reader sees through the eyes of others. He feels their feelings, thinks their thoughts, dreams their dreams. In that way he escapes the limits of his own time and place. And he gets away from the narrowness of himself.

### LITERATURE—ORAL, WRITTEN, VISUAL

Some literature is oral. Stories and poems told aloud—live or on records or on tape—are examples. Stories or poems in print are examples of written literature. Both oral and written literature concentrate mostly on words.

Some literature concentrates on pictures and movement—as well as words. This is visual literature, of which films are an example. Picture books, though printed, are also a kind of visual literature.

### HOW LITERATURE MEANS

A literary work has many meanings. It means what the author meant it to say. And it means what it actually does say to different people in different times and places.

Literature is a personal experience. So its meanings are personal. To say what a story or poem means is to say only what it means for a certain listener or reader. For each new listener or reader, the meanings may be different.

### HOW LITERATURE SPEAKS

Some stories or poems speak to many people of many places and times. Chances are, such works have more value than those that speak to only a few people for a short time. But most literary works, especially

Literature is written. An old Chinese love story tells of scholar Chang and the beautiful Ying-ying. The story was also made into a play, 'The Romance of the Western Chamber'. Below, the sadness of the lovers' parting is illustrated.

From 'The Romance of the Western Chamber', reprinted by permission of Liveright Publishers, New York City

Europa Film

Literature is visual. The movie 'Elvira Madigan' tells a tragic love story of the Sweden of 1889. Here Elvira and her lover, a cavalry officer who deserts the army and his family to run off with her, share a happier moment.

new ones, are not so easily weighed. Tastes change. And what one group admires, another may not.

To the listener or reader, those works that speak to him, that move him, that stick with him are of value. He must decide for himself which those are. To do that, he must be an explorer. And that means going to old literature as well as new, to literature of other cultures as well as of his own.

## THE FORMS OF LITERATURE

Novels, short stories, plays, and poems are *fiction*. Fiction is easy to recognize as literature. Often it is about imagined people and events. And an important purpose of fiction is to entertain, not just give information.

But literature can also take other forms—the essay, the biography, and so on. Such forms are *nonfiction*. Often they are about real people and events. And an important purpose is to give information.

Nonfiction works are not always literature. And whether they are or not is sometimes hard to say. If a work has warmth and feeling, if the words are imaginatively put together, if the work comes alive, it's literature. Some histories, for instance, read like historical novels.

Literature takes many forms. The following are some of the more common.

### The Novel and the Short Story

A novel is a long story. Usually it is in prose, and often the events are imaginary. But there are exceptions. Early Japanese novels were mostly poetry connected by prose. And Truman Capote's 'In Cold Blood' is an example of a novel about real people and real events (*see* Capote).

There is no special length a novel should be. A short novel is sometimes called a *novelette*. Carson McCullers' 'Ballad of the Sad Café' is a short novel. (*See also* Novel.)

A story shorter than the novelette is a short story. Because of its length, it deals with just a few characters and events at most. A single character or event is common in many short stories. (*See also* Short Story.)

Novels and short stories are sometimes classified by types. For instance, those that deal with science in a futuristic way are called *science fiction*. Many Jules Verne novels and many Ray Bradbury short stories are science fiction. Arthur Conan Doyle's Sherlock Holmes stories are examples of *detective fiction*. In detective fiction, an investigator solves a mystery, often involving murder.

Other types of fiction include *spy fiction* and *Western fiction*. The James Bond thrillers of Ian Fleming and the novels of Len Deighton ('The Ipcress File', 'Funeral in Berlin') are typical of spy fiction. Examples of Western fiction include Jack Schaefer's 'Shane' and Charles Portis' 'True Grit'. Westerns are typically set in the Western United States—the old West often.

### The Play

A play is a story meant to be acted out. Dialogue, or conversation between the actors, often is an important part of a play. But so are movement and costume and scenery. Plays are visual literature as well as literature of words.

There are different types of plays and different ways of staging them. Two important types of plays are tragedies and comedies. A tragedy is a serious play. A comedy is less serious and often has a happy ending. (*See also* Drama; Theater.)

### The Poem

A poem often has a special, tight language. What a poem says can't usually be said as tightly in prose —or as effectively. Metaphors and other figures of speech are commonly used in poems (*see* Figures of Speech). So are rhythms of different kinds. A poem doesn't have to rhyme. Some types of poems, such as haiku, almost never rhyme.

It's sometimes hard to tell poetry from prose. Some prose uses much of the special language of poetry. (*See also* Poetry.)

### The Essay

The essay is a short prose composition. In an *informal essay*, the topic is discussed in a personal way. A *formal essay* is more impersonal. Most newspaper and magazine articles are essays.

This article was contributed by Wolfgang B. Fleischmann, Dean, School of Humanities, Montclair State College, Upper Montclair, N.J.; Margaret A. Edwards, formerly Coordinator of Work with Young Adults, Enoch Pratt Free Library, Baltimore, Md.; Emma Cohn, Assistant Coordinator, Office of Young Adult Services, New York Public Library; Sara I. Fenwick, Associate Professor, Graduate Library School, University of Chicago; and Compton's Encyclopedia Canadian Advisory Board.

Not all essays are literature. But those that move people, that speak with grace or wit or charm, can fairly be classed as such. The essays of Michel de Montaigne and those of Tom Wolfe are examples. (*See also* Essay.)

### The Biography and the Autobiography

A biography is the true story of someone's life. An autobiography is a person's own story of his life.

For a biography to be a literary work, it has to be more than facts. James Boswell's 'Life of Samuel Johnson' is a literary work. It brings the man and his time vividly to life. The same is true of Richard Wright's autobiography, 'Black Boy'. (*See also* Autobiography; Biography.)

### The Diary and the Journal

The diary is a form of the autobiography. But it usually covers a shorter period of time. And it is often a day-to-day record. Anne Frank's 'Diary of a Young Girl' is an example. (*See also* Diary.)

Diaries are sometimes called *journals*. But the term *journal* is also used for accounts of travel and other personal experiences. So there is no hard-and-fast line between *journal* and *autobiography*. Marco Polo's 'Travels', for instance, could be called either an autobiography or a journal.

### The Letter

Most letters are meant only for the eyes of the person to whom they are addressed. But sometimes personal letters have grace and interest. And many

Literature is oral. Dr. Martin Luther King, Jr.'s ideas and feelings are set to the music of language in his famous "I have a dream" speech.

Wide World

people enjoy reading them for these qualities. Such letters are literature. Examples include the letters of Madame de Sévigné, Robert Louis Stevenson, and Woodrow Wilson. (*See also* Letter Writing.)

Some letters are not personal. They are open letters, addressed to a large audience. Among such letters with the power to move people are the Epistles of Paul and Martin Luther King, Jr.'s "Letter from Birmingham Jail."

## LITERATURE IN NONBOOK FORM

Literature is not just books. There is the literature of tapes and records, the literature of film, the literature of TV. Such literature is mostly oral and visual.

Often a work is transferred from book to nonbook form with little change. 'The Stories of Franz Kafka', which is available on tape cassette, and 'The Rubáiyát of Omar Khayyám', available on record, are examples. These spoken versions of written stories and poems add another dimension to literature. Listening to them may arouse interest in the written works. And it helps listeners more fully appreciate works they have already read.

Some printed works are much changed in nonbook form. Movie versions of novels, for instance, must be rewritten and shaped to the different needs of the screen (*see* Motion Pictures, section "Creative Elements of Film").

Some nonbook literature is original in that form. Paddy Chayefsky's television plays of the 1950's— 'Marty', 'Middle of the Night', and 'The Bachelor Party'—are examples. Another example of nonbook literature original in that form is the Canadian-made 16-mm. film 'Phoebe' (1964).

Nonbook literature is sometimes transferred to book form. The film 'Phoebe', for instance, was made into a book by Patricia Dizenzo in 1970. And Driss ben Hamed Charhadi's novel 'A Life Full of Holes' (1964) began as a tape recording. Its author, who can neither read nor write, dictated it. Later it was published as a book.

## WORLD LITERATURE

Literature has no nationality, no boundaries. The poetry of Li Po was aimed at his Chinese audience to begin with. But once translated into other languages, it spoke to many people in many places and times.

The following chart is a selection of new voices in world literature. Some voices have been speaking for many years in other languages but are new to English. A few voices have been stilled. All have something to say to the young people and to the adults of today.

The voices of the past, too, have something to say to the people of today. World literature of the past is discussed in the articles on French Literature, German Literature, Russian Literature, and other literatures (*see* Reference-Outline). The following article, Literature for Children, discusses world literature that speaks to children.

# NEW VOICES IN WORLD LITERATURE

## CANADA AND UNITED STATES

**CANADA**
Sheila Burnford *The Incredible Journey* 1961 (n)
Paule Daveluy *Summer in Ville-Marie* 1962 (n)
Robertson Davies *Voice from the Attic* 1960 (e)
Gratien Gelinas *Yesterday the Children Were Dancing* 1967 (pl)
Roger Lemelin *The Town Below* 1961 (n)
Hugh MacLennan *Return of the Sphinx* 1967 (n)
Brian Moore *I Am Mary Dunne* 1968 (n)
Mordecai Richler *The Incomparable Atuk* 1963 (n)
Gabrielle Roy *The Road Past Altamont* 1966 (n)
Ethel Wilson *Mrs. Golightly, and Other Stories* 1961

**UNITED STATES**
Ray Bradbury *The Vintage Bradbury* 1965 (s)
Michael Crichton *The Andromeda Strain* 1969 (n)
Hannah Green *I Never Promised You a Rose Garden* 1964 (n)
June Jordan, poet
Harper Lee *To Kill a Mockingbird* 1960 (n)
Bernard Malamud *The Fixer* 1966 (n)
*The Autobiography of Malcolm X* 1965
N. Scott Momaday *The Way to Rainy Mountain* 1969 (l+h)
Erich Segal *Love Story* 1970 (n)
Neil Simon *The Odd Couple* 1966 (pl)
Isaac Bashevis Singer *A Day of Pleasure* 1969 (s)

## LATIN AMERICA

**ARGENTINA**
Jorge Luis Borges *The Aleph, and Other Stories* 1970
Julio Cortázar *End of the Game, and Other Stories* 1967

**BARBADOS**
Edward Brathwaite, poet

**BRAZIL**
Jorge Amado *The Two Deaths of Quincas Wateryell* 1965 (n)
João Guimarães Rosa *The Third Bank of the River, and Other Stories* 1968

**CHILE**
Pablo Neruda, poet

**COLOMBIA**
Gabriel García Márquez *No One Writes to the Colonel, and Other Stories* 1968

**CUBA**
Alejo Carpentier *War of Time* 1970 (s)

**GUATEMALA**
Miguel Angel Asturias *Strong Wind* 1968 (n)

**GUYANA**
E. R. Braithwaite *To Sir, with Love* 1959 (a)

**HAITI**
Philippe Thoby-Marcelin and Pierre Marcelin *All Men Are Mad* 1970 (n)

**JAMAICA**
Sylvia Wynter *The Hills of Hebron* 1962 (n)

**MEXICO**
Carlos Fuentes *The Death of Artemio Cruz* 1964 (n)
Gregorio López y Fuentes *El Indio* 1961 (n)

**PUERTO RICO**
Enrique La Guerre *The Labyrinth* 1960 (n)

**TRINIDAD**
V. S. Naipaul *Miguel Street* 1959 (n)

## EUROPE

| | |
|---|---|
| AUSTRIA | Fritz Habeck *Days of Danger* 1963 (n) |
| BELGIUM | Louis Boon *Chapel Road* 1972 (n) |
| | Georges Simenon *The Confessional* 1968 (n) |
| BULGARIA | Dimiter Talev *The Iron Candlestick* 1966 (n) |
| CZECHOSLOVAKIA | Václav Havel *The Memorandum* 1967 (pl) |
| | Klára Jarunková *Don't Cry for Me* 1968 (n) |
| DENMARK | Hans Christian Branner *Two Minutes of Silence* 1966 (s) |
| ENGLAND | Arthur C. Clarke *2001: A Space Odyssey* 1968 (n) |
| | Graham Greene *Twenty-One Stories* 1962 |
| | Alan Sillitoe *Loneliness of the Long-Distance Runner* 1960 (s) |
| FINLAND | Veijo Meri *The Manila Rope* 1967 (n) |
| | Mauri Sariola *The Helsinki Affair* 1971 (n) |
| FRANCE | Michel Aimé Baudouy *More Than Courage* 1961 (n) |
| | Pierre Boulle *Planet of the Apes* 1963 (n) |
| GERMANY | Margot Benary-Isbert *Under a Changing Moon* 1964 (n) |
| | Günter Grass *The Tin Drum* 1963 (n) |
| GREECE | Antonis Samarakis *The Flaw* 1969 (n) |
| | George Seferis, poet |
| HUNGARY | Tiber Déry *The Portuguese Princess, and Other Stories* 1967 |
| | Tamas Szabó *Boy on the Rooftop* 1958 (j) |
| ICELAND | Halldór Laxness *The Fish Can Sing* 1966 (n) |
| IRELAND | Bernadette Devlin *The Price of My Soul* 1969 (a) |
| | Sean O'Faolain *The Talking Trees, and Other Stories* 1970 |
| ITALY | Giovanni Guareschi *Comrade Don Camillo* 1964 (n) |
| | Ignazio Silone *Bread and Wine* 1962 (n) |
| LITHUANIA | Antanas Vaičiulaitis *Noon at a Country Inn* 1966 (s) |
| NETHERLANDS | Dola De Jong *Between Home and Horizon* 1962 (n) |
| | A. Rutgers van der Loeff *Vassilis on the Run* 1965 (n) |
| NORWAY | Agnar Mykle *Rubicon* 1966 (n) |
| | Aimée Sommerfelt *Miriam* 1963 (n) |
| POLAND | Jerzy Kosinski *The Painted Bird* 1965 (n) |
| | Monika Kotowska *The Bridge to the Other Side* 1970 (n) |
| RUMANIA | Petru Dumitriu *Family Jewels* 1961 (n) |
| RUSSIA | Mikhail Sholokhov *Fierce and Gentle Warriors* 1967 (s) |
| | Alexander Solzhenitsyn *One Day in the Life of Ivan Denisovich* 1963 (n) |
| | Andrei Voznesensky, poet |
| | Yevgeny Yevtushenko, poet |
| SCOTLAND | Gavin Maxwell *Ring of Bright Water* 1961 (j) |
| | Muriel Spark *The Prime of Miss Jean Brodie* 1961 (n) |
| SPAIN | Fernando Diaz-Plaja *Cervantes* 1970 (b) |
| | Juan Goytisolo *Fiestas* 1960 (n) |
| SWEDEN | Ann Mari Falk *A Place of Her Own* 1964 (n) |
| | Vilhelm Moberg *A Time on Earth* 1965 (n) |
| SWITZERLAND | Friedrich Dürrenmatt *The Physicists* 1964 (pl) |
| WALES | Joyce Varney *A Welsh Story* 1964 (a) |
| YUGOSLAVIA | Ivo Andrić *The Woman from Sarajevo* 1965 (n) |

## ASIA

| | |
|---|---|
| BURMA | Mi Mi Khaing *Burmese Family* 1962 (j) |
| CHINA | Lai Ying *The Thirty-Sixth Way* 1969 (j) |
| | Sansan *Eighth Moon* 1964 (a) |
| INDIA | Kamala Markandaya *A Handful of Rice* 1966 (n) |
| | Ved Mehta *Walking the Indian Streets* 1960 (j) |
| | R. K. Narayan *The Man-Eater of Malgudi* 1961 (n) |
| | Santha Rama Rau *Gifts of Passage* 1961 (a) |
| IRAN | Fereidoun M. Esfandiary *Identity Card* 1966 (n) |
| | Najmeh Najafi *A Wall and Three Willows* 1967 (a) |
| ISRAEL | S. Y. Agnon *Twenty-One Stories* 1970 |
| | Isaak Diqs *A Bedouin Boyhood* 1969 (a) |
| | Ephraim Kishon *Noah's Ark, Tourist Class* 1962 (e) |
| JAPAN | Kobo Abe *Inter Ice Age 4* 1970 (n) |
| | Masashi Ito *The Emperor's Last Soldiers* 1967 (n) |
| | Yasunari Kawabata *Thousand Cranes* 1959 (n) |
| | Yukio Mishima *The Sailor Who Fell from Grace with the Sea* 1965 (n) |
| | Yuki *Leaves in the Sun* 1968 (p+d) |
| KOREA | Richard Kim *Lost Names* 1970 (a) |
| | Kim Yong Ik *Love in Winter* 1969 (s) |
| MALAYA | Chin Kee Onn *The Grand Illusion* 1961 (n) |
| PAKISTAN | Mohammad Ata-Ullah *Citizen of Two Worlds* 1960 (a) |
| | Zulfikar Ghose *The Murder of Aziz Khan* 1969 (n) |
| PHILIPPINES | N. V. M. Gonzalez *Selected Stories* 1964 |
| | Carlos Romulo *I Walked with Heroes* 1961 (a) |
| THAILAND | Kukrit Pramoj *Red Bamboo* 1961 (n) |
| TURKEY | Yashar Kemal *Memed, My Hawk* 1961 (n) |
| VIETNAM | Ly-Qui-Chung, ed. *Between Two Fires* 1970 (s) |

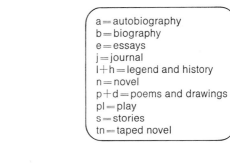

a = autobiography
b = biography
e = essays
j = journal
l+h = legend and history
n = novel
p+d = poems and drawings
pl = play
s = stories
tn = taped novel

## AUSTRALIA AND NEW ZEALAND

AUSTRALIA
Morris West *The Shoes of the Fisherman* 1963 (n)
Patrick White *The Vivisector* 1970 (n)
Judith Wright, poet

NEW ZEALAND
Sylvia Ashton-Warner *Teacher* 1963 (j)
Joy Cowley *Man of Straw* 1970 (n)
Janet Frame *Scented Gardens for the Blind* 1963 (n)

## AFRICA

ALGERIA
Driss Charhadi *A Life Full of Holes* 1964 (tn)

CAMEROON
Mongo Beti *King Lazarus* 1961 (n)

ETHIOPIA
Sahle Sellassie *Shinega's Village* 1964 (n)

GAMBIA
Lenrie Peters, poet

GHANA
Akosua Abbs *Ashanti Boy* 1959 (n)
Kofi Awoonor *This Earth, My Brother* 1971 (n)

GUINEA
Camara Laye *The Dark Child* 1969 (a)

KENYA
James Ngugi *Weep Not, Child* 1967 (n)

MALAWI
Legson Kayira *I Will Try* 1965 (a)

NIGERIA
Chinua Achebe *Arrow of God* 1964 (n)
Cyprian Ekwensi *Jagua Nana* 1961 (n)
Dilim Okafor-Omali *A Nigerian Villager in Two Worlds* 1965 (b)
Wole Soyinka *Five Plays* 1964

RHODESIA
Doris Lessing *African Stories* 1965

SENEGAL
Léopold Senghor, poet

SIERRA LEONE
R. Sarif Easmon *Dear Parent and Ogre* 1964 (pl)

SOUTH AFRICA
Bessie Head *Maru* 1971 (n)
Albert Luthuli *Let My People Go* 1962 (a)
Alan Paton *Tales from a Troubled Land* 1961

TUNISIA
Albert Memmi *Strangers* 1960 (n)

UGANDA
Okot p'Bitek, poet

# REFERENCE-OUTLINE FOR STUDY OF LITERATURE

## LITERATURE AND LITERARY FORMS

I. The scope of literature L-305–306e, L-309–12, A-429–30, F-291–306, M-573–80, R-104–11e, R-111f–12f, V-248. See also Literature and Literature for children in Fact-Index
  A. Oral L-305, 306a: storytelling S-460–82
  B. Written L-305, A-608–9: creative writing W-310–12. See also Reference-Outline for Language
  C. Visual L-305, 306a, A-606–7, 610: cartoons C-145a–6, D-131; drama D-169–77; motion pictures M-507–8

II. Literature and its meanings are personal experiences L-305–6, A-599–601, F-304–5

III. The forms of literature are many L-306–306a, L-309–10g
  A. Fiction L-306, A-609: novel N-375–7; short story S-183–4; romance R-239; fables F-1–3; drama D-169–77, T-148, A-610; poetry P-403–7 (nursery rhymes N-381a–d, M-502). See also Allegory, Epic poetry, Science fiction, and Stories in Fact-Index
  B. Nonfiction L-306–306a, A-609: essay E-289–90; autobiography A-774; biography B-162–3; diary D-104; journal L-306a; letter L-197, L-306a; history H-159–60
  C. Nonbook forms of literature L-306a, L-309, 310g

## HERITAGE OF MODERN LITERATURE

I. The beginnings of literature C-368, 369, C-490, L-309: mythology M-573–80; fables F-1–3, A-66; folklore F-291–3, F-16–17; storytelling S-460. See also Reference-Outline for Mythology

II. Literature of ancient peoples
  A. Sumerian B-8–9, 11, A-15, S-469, 480
  B. Egyptian E-125, S-469, 480
  C. Hebrew: the Bible B-145, 146, B-163, D-41a (Adam and Eve A-14–15, Esther E-291, Job J-460, Ruth R-365)
  D. Far East S-467: Indian I-78; Chinese C-295d

III. Literary contributions of the Greeks and Romans
  A. Greek G-232–6, S-473–4. See also Greek literature and Greek mythology in Fact-Index
    1. Drama D-170, T-154, pictures T-152. See also Drama, subhead Greek in Fact-Index
    2. Poets, writers, dramatists: Aesop A-66; Aristotle A-528; Herodotus H-146; Homer H-211, G-233, O-406–9, T-265–7; Plato P-384; Plutarch P-394; Xenophon X-329; Aeschylus, Aristophanes, Euripedes, Pindar, Sappho, Sophocles, Thucydides (Fact-Index)
  B. Roman (Latin) L-154–5, B-163. See also Latin literature and Roman mythology in Fact-Index
    1. Drama D-170, T-154
    2. Poets, writers, dramatists: Caesar C-14; Cicero C-341; Seneca S-108a; Tacitus T-3; Virgil V-328; Horace, Lucretius, Livy, Ovid, Pliny the Younger (Fact-Index)

IV. The Middle Ages in Western Europe N-375–6, B-163, F-75f, A-467, L-309, R-239, C-225–6, N-282, R-238: drama D-170–1, T-154–5 (miracle plays M-369, picture T-153). See also Middle Ages, subheads drama and literature in Fact-Index

V. The Renaissance in Western Europe R-145–6, 148, I-321, D-30–1: drama D-171, T-155, S-135–7

## LITERATURE AROUND THE WORLD

I. Literature of Asia S-467–9, L-310f, lists L-306d, L-310j–11, S-478–80
  A. Chinese C-295d–e, S-467, L-310f, list S-478: Confucius C-511
  B. Indian I-78, S-461, 467, F-3, list S-478
  C. Persian (Iranian) and Turkish P-213–14, S-469, L-310f, list S-480
  D. Hebrew (Israeli) H-120–1, B-146–7, B-163, L-310f, S-481: Saadia ben Joseph S-1
  E. Japanese J-391, S-467, L-310f, list S-478–9
  F. Korean K-76b, S-468, 479, L-310f
  G. Philippine P-257c–d, S-468, 479, L-310f: Jose Rizal R-211
  H. Arabian M-421, S-468–9, list S-480: the Koran K-74; 'Arabian Nights' A-472–3

II. Literature of Europe S-469–76, L-309–310b, lists L-306c, L-310i–j, S-480–481c
  A. Belgian B-125, L-310a: Maurice Maeterlink M-32
  B. English E-253–72, S-472–3, L-309–310b, lists E-273–6, S-481a–b. See also English literature and Drama, subhead English in Fact-Index
    1. Old and Middle English E-253–5, list E-273: drama D-171 (miracle plays M-369)
      a. Legends and folklore S-472–3, R-239: 'Beowulf' B-136b; King Arthur A-593–4 (Galahad G-3, Round Table R-299a); Robin Hood R-224–6
      b. Writers: Caedmon C-13; Chaucer C-222
    2. From the Renaissance through the 17th century E-256–9, N-376, lists E-273: drama D-171–2, T-155–6, S-135–7
      a. The Renaissance (including the Elizabethan Age) E-256–7, E-185: Francis Bacon B-12; Richard Hakluyt H-8; Ben Jonson J-478; Thomas More M-487, U-235; Walter Raleigh R-90; William Shakespeare S-129, A-663, H-15, K-57, M-3, M-225, M-306, O-506, R-258, T-76, W-188–9; Edmund Spenser S-378
      b. The 17th century E-258–9: John Bunyan B-376; John Dryden D-201; Robert Herrick H-148; John Locke L-324; John Milton M-326; Samuel Pepys P-197b
    3. The 18th century E-260–3, N-376, N-161, list E-273–4: biography B-162; drama D-172–3
      a. Samuel Johnson and his circle E-262, pictures C-551, B-163: Edmund Burke B-380; Oliver Goldsmith G-153; Samuel Johnson J-477; James Boswell, Edward Gibbon, Richard Brinsley Sheridan (Fact-Index)
      b. Other writers E-260–2: Joseph Addison A-26; William Cowper C-597; Daniel Defoe D-61, C-619–20; Thomas Gray G-197; David Hume H-269; Alexander Pope P-445; Jonathan Swift S-530, G-260
    4. The Romantic movement E-263–5, N-376, list E-274: Jane Austen A-708; William Blake B-219; Robert Burns B-383; George Gordon, Lord Byron B-401; Samuel Taylor Coleridge C-431; William Hazlitt H-83; John Keats K-23; Charles Lamb L-103; Sir Walter Scott S-72; Percy Bysshe Shelley S-154; William Wordsworth W-234

5. The Victorian Age E-265–9, N-376, B-162, list E-274–5: drama D-174, E-268–9
    a. Poets E-265–7: Matthew Arnold A-585; Elizabeth Barrett Browning B-347; Robert Browning B-347; Rudyard Kipling K-59; Edward Lear L-168; William Morris M-491; Christina Rossetti R-298; Dante Gabriel Rossetti R-298; Algernon Charles Swinburne S-535; Alfred Tennyson T-104; Francis Thompson T-163
    b. Writers and dramatists E-267–8, 269: Richard Blackmore B-216; Brontë family B-344; Thomas Carlyle C-136; Lewis Carroll C-141; Charles Darwin D-34; Charles Dickens D-105; Benjamin Disraeli D-132; Arthur Conan Doyle D-165; George Eliot E-182; Thomas Hardy H-32; Thomas Henry Huxley H-281; Charles Kingsley K-58; Rudyard Kipling K-59; Thomas Macaulay M-2; John Henry Newman N-205; Charles Reade R-99; John Ruskin R-319; George Bernard Shaw S-145; Herbert Spencer S-377; Robert Louis Stevenson S-446; William Makepeace Thackeray T-141; Anthony Trollope T-267
6. Modern English literature E-269–72, list E-275–6: drama D-174–5. See also Irish literature on this page
    a. Poets E-270, 271–2: Walter de la Mare D-63; T. S. Eliot E-183; A. E. Housman H-258; John Masefield M-142; Dylan Thomas T-161
    b. Writers and dramatists E-269–71, 272: James M. Barrie B-70; Hilaire Belloc B-134; Arnold Bennett B-135; Winston Churchill C-338; Joseph Conrad C-535; Norman Douglas D-164c; Eleanor Farjeon F-35; John Galsworthy G-6; Kenneth Grahame G-165; T. E. Lawrence L-166; Katherine Mansfield M-91a; W. Somerset Maugham M-176; A. A. Milne M-326; H. G. Wells W-99; Aldous Huxley, Lytton Strachey, Virginia Woolf (Fact-Index)

C. French F-436–41, S-475–6, L-310, 310a, 310b, lists F-440–1, S-481b–c. See also French literature in Fact-Index
  1. Early romances and fairy tales R-239, F-436, S-475–6, L-310: 'Song of Roland' R-238
  2. Writers, list F-440–1: Honoré de Balzac B-48; Auguste Comte C-502f; Alexandre Dumas D-208 (Dumas the Younger D-209); Jean Henri Fabre F-3; Gustave Flaubert F-217; Anatole France F-379; Jean Froissart F-463; Victor Hugo H-267; Jean de la Fontaine L-102; Guy de Maupassant M-177; Michel de Montaigne M-457; François Rabelais R-23; Jean Jacques Rousseau R-299b; Madame de Sévigné S-118; Jules Verne V-303; Voltaire V-385; Émile Zola Z-356; André Gide, George Sand (Fact-Index)
  3. Drama D-172, 173, 175, F-437: Pierre Corneille C-579; Victor Hugo H-267; Molière M-422; Jean Baptiste Racine R-28

D. German (including Austrian writers) G-96a–8, A-768, S-470–1, L-310, 310a, 310b, lists G-97–8, S-481–481a: drama D-173–4, G-96a, 96b, 97 (Passion play in Oberammergau O-390–1). See also German literature in Fact-Index

1. Legends: 'Song of the Nibelungs' N-282, S-192a; Faust F-78; Lohengrin L-334
2. Folktales and fairy tales F-292, G-241–2
3. Poets, writers, and dramatists, list G-97–8: Johann Goethe G-147; Jakob and Wilhelm Grimm G-240; Georg Hegel H-124; Heinrich Heine H-124; Immanuel Kant K-20; Martin Luther L-396; Thomas Mann M-91; Karl Marx M-121; Johann Schiller S-53; Oswald Spengler S-377; Heinrich Böll, Friedrich Nietzsche, Erich Maria Remarque, Arthur Schopenhauer, Theodor Storm, Franz Werfel, Stefan Zweig (Fact-Index)

E. Greek G-216, G-233–5, L-310b, S-473–4, list S-481b. See also in this outline "Heritage of Modern Literature"

F. Irish I-291–2, C-185: drama D-174, E-270
  1. Folktales S-473, L-310a, list S-481b: Ossian (Fact-Index)
  2. Poets, writers, and dramatists: Samuel Beckett B-102; James Joyce J-480; William Butler Yeats Y-339; Padraic Colum, Lord Dunsany, Sean O'Casey, Liam O'Flaherty, James Stephens, John M. Synge (Fact-Index)

G. Italian I-321–2, N-376, L-309, 310a, list I-322: drama I-322. See also in this outline "Heritage of Modern Literature"
  1. Folktales S-474–5, list S-481b
  2. Poets, writers, and dramatists, list I-322: Dante Alighieri D-30; Giovanni Papini P-108; Luigi Pirandello P-341; Torquato Tasso T-28; Giovanni Boccaccio, Francesco Petrarch (Fact-Index)

H. Polish P-413: Ladislas Reymont R-174

I. Russian R-359–62, L-310, 310a, 310b, list R-361–2: drama D-174
  1. Folktales R-359, S-469–70, list S-480–1
  2. Poets, writers, and dramatists, list R-361–2: Fedor Dostoevski D-164b; Nikolai Gogol G-149; Vladimir Nabokov N-1; Leo Tolstoi T-196; Ivan Turgenev T-296; Anton Chekhov, Mikhail Lomonosov, Boris Pasternak, Aleksander Pushkin, Mikhail Sholokhov, Alexander I. Solzhenitsyn (Fact-Index)

J. Scandinavian S-52g, N-361, S-471, L-310a, 310b: drama D-173
  1. Danish S-472, L-310a, 310b, list S-481a: Hans Christian Andersen A-391
  2. Icelandic I-13, N-361, S-471–2, list S-481a
  3. Norwegian N-367, S-472, L-310a, 310b, list S-481a: Björnstjerne Björnson B-214; Henrik Ibsen I-3; Sigrid Undset U-4; Johan Bojer, Knut Hamsun (Fact-Index)
  4. Swedish S-472, 481a, L-310a, 310b: Selma Lagerlöf L-102; August Strindberg S-490

K. Spanish S-365–8, N-376, L-310, 310b, list S-366–8: drama D-171, S-365a, 365b, 366
  1. Folktales S-476, list S-481c
  2. Writers, list S-366–8: Pedro Calderón de la Barca C-27; Miguel de Cervantes C-201

L. Swiss L-309–10, 310a: Johanna Spyri S-398

III. Literature of Canada and the United States
A. Canadian C-113–17, L-310d–e, lists C-115–17, L-306b, L-310h: drama C-115
  1. Legends and folklore S-477, list S-481d
  2. Poets, writers, and dramatists, list C-115–17: William Drummond D-200e; Bliss Carman, Stephen Leacock (Fact-Index)

B. **American** A-342-67, L-310b-d, M-8, lists A-363-6, L-306b, L-310h: legends and folklore F-292-302, I-114, S-477, lists F-306, S-481c-d; drama D-175-7, A-358-9. See also American literature in Fact-Index
1. Colonial times in America A-342-5, list A-363: John Winthrop W-189
2. The shaping of a new nation A-345-7, list A-363: Benjamin Franklin F-422; Thomas Jefferson J-427; Thomas Paine P-21; Noah Webster W-91
3. Literature of the early republic A-347-9, list A-363: William Cullen Bryant B-351; James Fenimore Cooper C-562; Washington Irving I-315
4. The flowering of American literature A-349-52, list A-364: Ralph Waldo Emerson E-196; Nathaniel Hawthorne H-76; Oliver Wendell Holmes H-202; Henry Wadsworth Longfellow L-346; James Russell Lowell L-385; Herman Melville M-218b; Francis Parkman P-124; Edgar Allan Poe P-401; Henry David Thoreau T-165; Walt Whitman W-157; John Greenleaf Whittier W-158
5. Transition to the Modern Age A-352-5, N-126a, list A-364-5: Henry Adams A-15; Louisa May Alcott A-255; John Burroughs B-384; Emily Dickinson D-110; Eugene Field F-106; Edward Everett Hale H-9; Joel Chandler Harris H-35; Francis Brett Harte H-44; William Dean Howells H-263; Henry James J-360; William James J-361; Joyce Kilmer K-50; Sidney Lanier L-124; Jack London L-335; John Muir M-541; O. Henry (William Sydney Porter) P-451; Howard Pyle P-541; James Whitcomb Riley R-208; Harriet Beecher Stowe S-483; Mark Twain T-310
6. Modern American literature A-355-62, N-126b, 126c, 126f, lists A-365-6, N-126i-j
   a. Drama D-176-7, A-358-9: Maxwell Anderson A-393; Lillian Hellman H-131; Eugene O'Neill O-455
   b. Poets and writers A-355-8, 360-2: George Ade A-31; Sherwood Anderson A-393; James Baldwin B-22; Saul Bellow B-134; Gwendolyn Brooks B-345; Pearl Buck B-356; Truman Capote C-130b; Willa Cather C-158; John Dos Passos D-164b; William Faulkner F-77; Rachel Field F-106; F. Scott Fitzgerald F-181; Robert Frost F-464; Ernest Hemingway H-132; Langston Hughes H-266; Sinclair Lewis L-202; Amy Lowell L-385; Carson McCullers M-5; Edna St. Vincent Millay M-324; Harriet Monroe M-453; Vladimir Nabokov N-1; Ogden Nash N-15; Kenneth Roberts R-223; Edwin Arlington Robinson R-226; Carl Sandburg S-38; John Steinbeck S-442; Booth Tarkington T-25; Thomas Wolfe W-211; Richard Wright W-304

IV. **Literature of Latin America** L-148-53, L-310e-f, S-476-7, lists L-149a-53, L-306b, L-310h-i, S-481c, 481d-2: Jorges Luis Borges B-268; Las Casas L-129

V. **Literature of Australia and New Zealand** A-741-2, L-310f-g, S-468, 479, lists L-306e, L-311

VI. **Literature of Africa** L-310g, S-478, lists L-306e, L-311, S-482: Chinua Achebe A-10

## BIBLIOGRAPHY FOR LITERATURE

**Abrams, M. H.** A Glossary of Literary Terms, 3d ed. (Holt, 1971).

**Appel, Benjamin.** The Fantastic Mirror (Pantheon, 1969). A survey of science fiction writing.

**Arbuthnot, M. H. and others, comps.** The Arbuthnot Anthology of Children's Literature, 4th ed. rev. (Scott, Foresman, 1976). Includes 'Time for Poetry', 'Time for Fairy Tales', and 'Time for True Tales'.

**Benét, W. R., ed.** The Reader's Encyclopedia, 2d ed. (Crowell, 1965). Alphabetically arranged short articles on plots, themes, characters, titles, and authors.

**Bowen, C. D.** Biography: the Craft and the Calling (Little, 1969). A discussion of the techniques and literary problems of writing full-length biographies.

**Brewer, E. C.** Brewer's Dictionary of Phrase and Fable, rev. ed. (Harper, 1971). Authors, proverbs, and mythological and fictitious characters of the world's literature.

**Ellmann, Richard and Feidelson, Charles, Jr., eds.** The Modern Tradition (Oxford, 1965). An anthology of modern poems, essays, and stories.

**Foley, Martha and Burnett, David, eds.** Best American Short Stories (Houghton, annual).

**Peterson, Houston, ed.** A Treasury of the World's Great Speeches, rev. ed. (Simon & Schuster, 1965).

**Rosenheim, E. M.** What Happens in Literature (Univ. of Chicago Press, 1960). A guide to the techniques and enjoyment of reading poems, plays, and novels.

**Stevick, Philip, comp.** The Theory of the Novel (Free Press, 1967). Noted authors discuss the art of the novel.

**Trilling, Lionel.** The Experience of Literature (Doubleday, 1967). Anthology of classical and modern literature.

### DRAMA

**Burack, A. S., ed.** One Hundred Plays for Children (Plays, 1970). An anthology of easy-to-produce one-act plays.

**Howard, Vernon.** The Complete Book of Children's Theater (Doubleday, 1969). Theatrical techniques and material for pantomimes, puppet shows, and plays.

**Kline, Peter.** The Theatre Student: Playwriting (Rosen, 1970). How to create characters, write dialogues, and build plots.

**Priestley, J. B.** The Wonderful World of the Theatre (Doubleday, 1969). Discusses theater types and history.

**Williams, Raymond.** Drama from Ibsen to Brecht (Oxford, 1969). A century of plays and playwrights.

### POETRY

**Adoff, Arnold, ed.** Black Out Loud: an Anthology of Modern Poems by Black Americans (Macmillan, 1970).

**Auslander, Joseph and Hill, F. E.** The Winged Horse (Haskell, 1969). A classic book for young readers tells the history of poetry through biographies of poets.

**Behn, Harry, comp. and tr.** Cricket Songs (Harcourt, 1964); More Cricket Songs (Harcourt, 1971). Haiku for younger readers.

**Bierhorst, John, ed.** In the Trail of the Wind: American Indian Poems and Ritual Orations (Farrar, 1971).

**Ciardi, John and Williams, Miller.** How Does a Poem Mean?, 2d ed. (Houghton, 1975). Two poets describe the techniques of poetry.

**Cole, William, comp.** Oh, How Silly! (Viking Press, 1970). Amusing nonsense verse by Nash, Lear, Carroll, and others.

**Deutsch, Babette.** Poetry Handbook, 4th ed. (Funk, 1974).

**Hughes, Ted.** Poetry Is (Doubleday, 1967). An introduction to poetic forms and themes and how to listen to poetry.

**Sechrist, E. H., comp.** One Thousand Poems for Children, rev. ed. (Macrae, 1946). Familiar poetry grouped by subject.

(*See also* bibliographies for **American Literature; Canadian Literature; Drama; English Literature; Fables; Folklore; Latin American Literature; Letter Writing; Literature for Children; Mythology; Reading/Books for Children; Reading/Books for Young Adults; Russian Literature; Storytelling,** subheads "Books About Storytelling" and "Books of Stories" and section "Folktales from Many Lands"; **Writing, Creative.**

# LITERATURE THAT SPEAKS TO CHILDREN

**LITERATURE FOR CHILDREN.** Children's literature is literature that speaks to children. Many stories, poems, and other types of literature were made especially for the young. But a large number of children's favorites were originally aimed at grown-ups. These include 'The Panchatantra', Aesop's fables, 'Arabian Nights', and 'The Pilgrim's Progress'.

Books are an important part of children's literature. But children's literature is more than books. It is magazines, newspapers, tapes, records, TV, films. It is folktales and storytellers, writers and artists and publishers, libraries and librarians—all the things and all the people that bring children and literature together.

## THE BACKGROUND

In the beginning there was little literature for children. But there was literature children liked.

All literature began with folklore. Much folklore was probably aimed at a general audience, but children were sometimes a part of that audience. And they adopted many of the stories and songs for their excitement and action and rhythm (*see* Storytelling).

Early books aimed at grown-ups generally. The first books actually aimed at children, or for use with children, were often lesson books. There were also conduct books, which taught manners and morals. These were not typically literature (*see* Literature).

In England of the 600's and 700's, churchmen such as Bede and Alcuin wrote lesson books for students. In Moravia (now Czechoslovakia) in about 1648, Johann Comenius wrote 'Orbis Sensualium Pictus'. 'Orbis Pictus' (The World in Pictures) was a textbook with lots of pictures. Comenius felt these would make it easier for children to learn.

The hornbooks of England and the United States were lesson books. A *hornbook* was not really a book. It was a printed page pasted on a paddle-shaped piece of wood. The page was protected by a see-through sheet of horn, which looked like a clear plastic. On the page were the alphabet, a short prayer, and other material for learning to read.

Primers and battledores followed hornbooks in England. The *battledore* was a sheet of cardboard-like paper folded into several panels.

The first book printed in Burmese, 'First Burmese Reader' (1776), was a lesson book. So was Peter Beron's 'Primer with a Fish' (1824), Bulgaria's first book for children.

## CHILDREN'S LITERATURE OF EUROPE

In Europe, written literature for children began in the 1600's. There was little of it at first, and children often turned, as always, to adult literature for adventure.

### Scattered Beginnings

In Italy Giambattista Basile's collection of folktales, 'Lo Cunto de li Cunti' (The Tale of Tales), was not written for children. But many of the stories, such as "Sleeping Beauty" and "Cinderella," came to be children's favorites. In Zürich, Switzerland, children who delivered money on New Year's Day were used to getting a treat. But in 1645, each child

More than 800 years ago, the Japanese artist Toba Sojo drew a comic picture story that spoke to children, though it was not intended for them. His scroll showed animals frolicking at a picnic and having such contests as an archery shoot.

Reprinted by permission of G. P. Putnam's Sons from Toba Sojo, 'The Animal Frolic' (© 1954 Temple of Kazanji)

# LITERATURE FOR CHILDREN

Like the hornbook, the battledore was a beginning lesson book, but it was in the form of a sheet of stiff paper, folded.

received a sheet of paper instead. On it was a picture, with some verse underneath. These *Zürcherischen Neujahrsblätter* (Zürich New Year's Sheets) were the beginning of Swiss literature for children.

Children's books of the 1600's were often preachy and dull. But there were exceptions. One of them was Jean de La Fontaine's 'Fables' (1668) (*see* La Fontaine). Another exception was John Bunyan's 'Pilgrim's Progress' (1678) (*see* Bunyan). A third exception was Charles Perrault's French fairy tales, sometimes known as 'Tales of Mother Goose'. Perrault actually rewrote the stories of "Red Riding Hood," "Bluebeard," and others for children.

Another exception to preachy and dull books were the *chapbooks*. They were little paperbacks sold by peddlers, or chapmen, and commonly written for grown-ups. Earlier chapbooks were often sensational versions of medieval romances and other stories. Later chapbooks also contained fairy tales, and many of these appealed to children.

## More Children's Books, with Morals

Two outstanding English books of the early 1700's were written for grown-ups. But children claimed the stories as their own—Daniel Defoe's 'Robinson Crusoe' and Jonathan Swift's 'Gulliver's Travels' (*see* Defoe; Swift). In England, publisher John Newbery began to put out a large number of books for children. The first of them was 'A Little Pretty Pocket-Book' (1744). Two of Newbery's most famous books are 'The History of Little Goody Two-Shoes' and 'Mother Goose's Melody'. His Mother Goose book was the first collection of Mother Goose rhymes in English (*see* Mother Goose; Newbery).

Jean Jacques Rousseau's 'Émile' (1762) is about a boy whose learning was based on his interests. Many children's books of the time adopted Rousseau's main

This article was contributed by Augusta Baker, Coordinator of Children's Services, New York Public Library, and by Compton's Encyclopedia Canadian Advisory Board.

characters—the boy and his teacher. In the imitations, however, everything the two did was made to teach a lesson. English engraver Thomas Bewick began to illustrate fine picture books for children. Children's magazines and newspapers appeared. These included Germany's *Leipziger Wochenblatt für Kinder* (Leipzig Children's Weekly) (1772) and Spain's *Gaceta de los Niños* (Children's Magazine) (1798).

## Books Get Better

With the 1800's, writing for children became more respectable in Europe. And the quality of both children's writers and children's books improved.

An early book of poems for children was 'Original Poems for Infant Minds' (1804), by Ann and Jane Taylor of England. Jane wrote the famous "Twinkle, Twinkle, Little Star." Charles Lamb and his sister Mary began the retelling of classics for children with their 'Tales from Shakespeare', a version of Shakespeare's plays. Jakob and Wilhelm Grimm collected German folktales (*see* Grimm). In Switzerland, Johann Wyss' 'Swiss Family Robinson' appeared.

Russia's Ivan A. Krylov published his fables in 1825. Sir Walter Scott's 'Tales of a Grandfather'

The English artist John Tenniel gave the Jabberwock horrifying shape and form in Lewis Carroll's 'Alice in Wonderland'.

marked the beginning of Scottish children's literature. Petr P. Ershov's story of a magic horse, 'The Little Humpbacked Horse' (1834), was printed in Russia. In Denmark appeared the first fairy tales by one of the world's great storytellers, Hans Christian Andersen (*see* Andersen).

Charles Dickens' 'Christmas Carol' (1843) gave children Scrooge and Tiny Tim. Peter Asbjörnsen and Jörgen Moe collected Norwegian folktales. Many of these were later retold by a noted Norwegian storyteller, Gudrun Thorne-Thomsen, in 'East o' the Sun and West o' the Moon'. Heinrich Hoffman, a doctor of Frankfurt, Germany, drew humorous pictures for children in his waiting room. The result was 'Struwwelpeter' (Strawhead Peter), later translated as 'Slovenly Peter'. Edward Lear's 'Book of Nonsense' (1846) was pure fun—a taste of things to come in children's literature (*see* Lear).

### More Types and Masterpieces

From about the 1850's, children's literature aimed more and more to please rather than teach. Story characters were pictured more like real people. And more types of children's books began to appear.

Aleksandr Afanas'ev collected Russian folktales. Thomas Hughes' 'Tom Brown's School Days' (1857) became one of the best-known school stories in English. 'Cinq Semaines en Ballon' (Five Weeks in a Balloon) (1863) was the first of the Jules Verne science fiction books.

Karel Erben of Czechoslovakia collected folktales, later translated as 'Panslavonic Folk-Lore'. In Germany Wilhelm Busch came out with a picture story, 'Max and Moritz' (1865). It was an ancestor of the comic strip. The outstanding literary event of the time was Lewis Carroll's 'Alice's Adventures in Wonderland' (1865), with illustrations by John Tenniel. It is one of the great fantasies of world literature for children (*see* Carroll).

Among the most important illustrators of the period were Walter Crane, Randolph Caldecott, and Kate Greenaway. These English artists helped develop the colored picture book for the very young.

One children's masterpiece after another began to appear. George MacDonald of Scotland wrote his fantasy 'At the Back of the North Wind' (1871). In 1875 appeared 'Broučci' (The Fireflies) by Jan Karafiát of Czechoslovakia. Retold by Max Bolliger, the book was later translated into English as 'The Fireflies'. Johanna Spyri's 'Heidi' (1880) was written in Switzerland (*see* Spyri). 'Pinocchio', the story of a wooden boy, was written in Italy by Carlo Lorenzini, who used the name Carlo Collodi. Robert Louis Stevenson of Scotland wrote 'Treasure Island' (*see* Stevenson). 'The Heart of a Boy' was written by Edmondo de Amicis of Italy. And Rudyard Kipling wrote 'The Jungle Book' (1894) (*see* Kipling).

### Children's Literature Takes a Giant Step

Good books are important. But it's also important to get them into the hands of children. In the early

MGM-EMI Distributors Ltd.

**The frog called Mr. Jeremy Fisher leaps out of the pages of Beatrix Potter to dance in the 'Beatrix Potter Ballet'.**

1900's, children's libraries opened in many countries of Europe. So did training centers for children's librarians. Children's book councils, book weeks, book reviews, and book awards were organized.

Outstanding children's books appeared in rapid succession. Seumas MacManus' 'Donegal Fairy Stories' (1900) retold Irish tales. Out of England came Beatrix Potter's 'Tale of Peter Rabbit' (1901) and Walter de la Mare's 'Songs of Childhood' (1902). 'Peter Pan', a play by James Barrie of Scotland, was first staged in 1904 (*see* Barrie). From Sweden came Selma Lagerlöf's 'Wonderful Adventures of Nils'. Kenneth Grahame, a Scot, wrote 'The Wind in the Willows' (1908) (*see* Grahame). 'The Blue Bird', by Maurice Maeterlinck of Belgium, was staged in 1908, published 1909 (*see* Maeterlinck). From Sweden came Elsa Beskow's 'Pelle's New Suit'; from Yugoslavia, Ivana Brlić-Mazuranić's 'Brave Adventures of Lapitch'; from Spain, 'Platero and I', by Juan Ramón Jiménez; from Ireland, Padraic Colum's 'King of Ireland's Son'; from England, Hugh Lofting's 'Story of Dr. Dolittle'. In England A. A. Milne's 'Winnie-the-Pooh' (1926) was illustrated by Ernest H. Shepard.

Germany's Erich Kästner wrote 'Emil and the Detectives'. The first of the Babar the elephant series, 'The Story of Babar', was written by Jean de Brunhoff of France. From England came 'Mary Poppins' (1934), by Australian-born Pamela L. Travers; from Russia,

310a

Illustration © 1958 Tove Jansson, used by permission of Henry Z. Walck, Inc., publishers

**A plate of fish soup glides toward an astonished Moomintroll in Tove Jansson's 'Moominland Midwinter'.**

Sergei Prokofiev's musical fairy tale 'Peter and the Wolf' (1936) (*see* Prokofiev). Antoine de Saint-Exupéry of France wrote 'The Little Prince'. In Sweden appeared Astrid Lindgren's 'Pippi Longstocking'. Tove Jansson of Finland wrote her first book about the Moomins, 'Comet in Moominland'.

### Books Seamy Side Up

From about the 1950's, more and more children's books were realistic. Some began to show the ugly and distasteful side of life. 'Marcelino' by José M. Sanchez-Silva of Spain, is about an orphan boy who kept and killed small animals. 'The Ark', by Margot Benary-Isbert, shows the aftereffects of war on the people of Germany.

But fantasy and folktales continued to flourish. 'The Borrowers' was the first of a charming fantasy series by Mary Norton of England. Gwyn Jones retold 'Welsh Legends and Folk-Tales' (1955). Karl Bruckner of Austria retold the story of Tutankhamen in 'The Golden Pharaoh'. The Scottish folktales of 'Heather and Broom' (1960) were retold from the Gaelic by Leclaire G. Alger, who used the name Sorche Nic Leodhas. She also did 'Always Room for One More'.

More children's literature of Eastern Europe became available in English in the 1960's and 1970's. Stefan Dichev of Bulgaria wrote 'Rali' (1960), a realistic story about Bulgaria when it was ruled by the Turks. 'The Golden Seed' by Poland's Maria Konopnicka was translated in 1962.

Babbis Friis-Baastad, who did her first radio play for Norwegian children in 1957, wrote 'Kristy's Courage', followed by 'Don't Take Teddy'. The first is about a disfigured girl, the second about a retarded child. In England Rosemary Sutcliff wrote 'Dawn Wind', one of the best of her historical novels.

Nada Ćurčija-Prodanović retold Yugoslavian folktales in 'Heroes of Serbia' (1963). 'Koko and the

Ghosts', a mystery story from Yugoslavia by Ivan Kušan, was retold in English. 'The Three Poor Tailors' (1965), a picture book version of a Hungarian folktale, was done by Hungarian-born Victor Ambrus. Alki Zei's 'Wildcat Under Glass', a realistic story of the Greece of the 1930's, was translated in 1968.

Among notable books of the 1970's was 'The Little Chalk Man', by Czechoslovakia's Václav Ctvrtek, the story of a chalk drawing come to life. Denmark's Ib Spang Olsen wrote 'Smoke', about an unorthodox fight against air pollution. Estonian-born Selve Maas retold 'The Moon Painters and Other Estonian Folk Tales' (1971). S. R. van Iterson of the Netherlands wrote 'Pulga', the realistic story of a street child of Bogotá, Colombia. Ioana Sturdza translated 'Fairy Tales and Legends from Romania' (1972).

## CHILDREN'S LITERATURE OF THE UNITED STATES

During the colonial period, few children's books were written in the United States. And these were commonly preachy and dull. Not until the 1800's did notable children's writers begin to appear.

### The Beginnings

Washington Irving's 'Sketch Book' was not written for children. But the stories "Rip Van Winkle" and "The Legend of Sleepy Hollow" became children's favorites (*see* Irving). In 1822 Clement Moore's 'Visit from St. Nicholas' began a Christmas tradition in the United States. It is commonly known as 'The Night Before Christmas'.

From about the 1850's, story characters were drawn in a more lifelike, less wooden way. An example is

**Yesterday's children discover books that speak to them in the children's department of the Cleveland Public Library.**

Cleveland Public Library

Peter meets the wolf in Walt Disney's 'Peter and the Wolf', a movie based on Sergei Prokofiev's musical fairy tale.

Mary Mapes Dodge's 'Hans Brinker, or the Silver Skates' (1865). 'Hans Brinker' was also a forerunner of a popular type—stories about other lands. 'Ragged Dick' (1867) was Horatio Alger's first of a series of popular rags-to-riches stories, with morals. Louisa May Alcott's 'Little Women' is a family story with lifelike characters (see Alcott). In 1873 *St. Nicholas* magazine was founded. It greatly influenced writing for children in the United States. Mark Twain's 'Adventures of Tom Sawyer' (1876) shows the seamy side of life and human nature—with humor and understanding (see Twain).

In 1877 Minerva Saunders set aside a corner for children's books at the Pawtucket, R.I., library. It was a giant step for children's literature. Joel Chandler Harris' 'Uncle Remus' (1880) was one of the first folktale collections in the United States (see Harris).

One of the first fine illustrators for children in the United States was Howard Pyle. He wrote and illustrated 'The Merry Adventures of Robin Hood' (1883) (see Pyle). Pratt Institute in Brooklyn, N.Y., began training children's librarians in 1898. A training school for children's librarians was also set up at Carnegie Library in Pittsburgh, Pa. In 1899, story hours began at Carnegie Library. These were crucial steps in the development of children's literature.

### Growth in Libraries and Books

The 20th century opened promisingly for children's literature in the United States. L. Frank Baum wrote 'The Wonderful Wizard of Oz' (1900). That same year the American Library Association opened a children's section. A few years later, Effie L. Power set up a children's department in the Cleveland Public Library. And Anne Carroll Moore did the same in the New York Public Library.

In Boston, Mass., Bertha Mahony Miller opened a Bookshop for Boys and Girls in 1916. It was the first bookshop of its kind in the United States. Frederic G.

Melcher helped found Children's Book Week in 1919. Later Melcher and the American Library Association inaugurated the Newbery and Caldecott awards (see Literary Awards). The Macmillan Publishing Company opened the first children's book department in the United States, with Louise Seaman Bechtel as editor.

In 1924 Anne Carroll Moore began reviewing children's books in the *New York Herald Tribune* book section. Her column was called "The Three Owls." *The Horn Book Magazine*, a review of children's books, began the same year. Wanda Gág's 'Millions of Cats' (1928) was one of the first fine picture books for the very young in the United States. In 1928 Walt Disney created Mickey Mouse in a movie cartoon, 'Steamboat Willie' (see Disney).

### Types of Books Multiply

From about 1930 to the end of World War II, good children's books of many types became plentiful. In 1932 appeared 'The Dream Keeper and Other Poems', by Langston Hughes (see Hughes). Marjorie Flack's 'Story About Ping' (1933), set in China, was a sign of growing interest in books about other lands. So was Monica Shannon's 'Dobry' (1934), about a Bulgarian peasant boy. Ellis Credle wrote 'Down, Down the Mountain' (1934), a regional story of two Southern mountain children. 'The Good Master' (1934), by Kate Seredy, is set in her native Hungary. Carol Ryrie Brink's 'Caddie Woodlawn' (1935) is historical fiction.

Theodore Seuss Geisel wrote and illustrated his first fantasy for children, 'And to Think That I Saw It on Mulberry Street' in 1937. Geisel used the name Dr. Seuss. In 1938 Augusta Baker compiled 'Books About Negro Life for Children', the first of a series of book lists about the black experience.

Outstanding author-illustrated books of 1939 included Robert Lawson's fantasy 'Ben and Me' and James Daugherty's biography 'Daniel Boone'. Ann Nolan Clark's 'In My Mother's House' (1941) is one of a series of her books about American Indians. A high point in historical fiction for children was Esther Forbes's 'Johnny Tremaine' (1943). Richard Chase's 'Jack Tales' is a collection of Southern mountain legends. Lois Lenski's 'Strawberry Girl' (1945) is one of the best of her regional stories. 'Misty of Chincoteague' (1947), by Marguerite Henry, is an outstanding horse story.

### Books About Many Groups—And Some Starkness

From about the 1950's, more and more books about minority-group children and children of other lands began to appear. 'Amos Fortune, Free Man' (1950), by Elizabeth Yates, is the biography of an African prince sold as a slave in the New World. In 1952 appeared E. B. White's outstanding fantasy, 'Charlotte's Web'. 'The Wheel on the School' (1954), by Meindert de Jong, is set in the Netherlands; Taro Yashima's 'Crow Boy' (1955), in Japan. 'Bronzeville Boys and Girls' (1956), by Gwendolyn Brooks, is an outstanding collection of children's poems in a black setting (*see* Brooks).

In the 1960's and 1970's, realism in children's books was sometimes stark. Paperback books for children appeared, many of them reprints of children's favorites. And there was rapid growth of children's literature in nonbook form—records, films, tapes, and other materials.

Scott O'Dell's 'Island of the Blue Dolphins' (1960) is about an American Indian girl. The author–illustrator Ezra Jack Keats did a series of picture books about a little black boy, beginning with 'The Snowy Day' (1962). 'City Rhythms' (1965), by the author–illustrator Ann Grifalconi, was one of a growing number of books about city life. Isaac Bashevis Singer's 'Zlateh the Goat and Other Stories' (1966) is a collection of Jewish tales filled with humor and wisdom. Realistic stories of ghetto life included "How Many Miles to Babylon?', by Paula Fox, and 'The Jazz Man', by Mary Hays Weik.

Jane Wagner's 'J. T.' (1969) is one of a number of children's books to use photos instead of drawings. 'Who Look at Me' (1969), by the poet June Jordan, expresses the black experience through paintings and poetry. Pura Belpré's 'Santiago' (1969) is about a little Puerto Rican boy in the United States. Traveller Bird's 'Path to Snowbird Mountain' (1972) contains Cherokee legends he heard from his grandmother.

## CHILDREN'S LITERATURE OF CANADA

Early Canadian children's literature aimed at "pious feelings and moral lessons." Examples can be found in the first Canadian children's magazine, *The Snow Drop* (1847).

Early writers who put their stories in a Canadian setting include Catherine Parr Traill. Her 'Canadian Crusoes' (1852) was later republished as 'Lost in the Backwoods'. James de Mille wrote the first Canadian series, the Brethren of the White Cross schoolboy stories (1869–73).

'Beautiful Joe' (1894), by Margaret Marshall Saunders, is a sentimental—and very popular—dog story. But Ernest Thompson Seton and Sir Charles G. D. Roberts created the realistic animal story, a unique Canadian contribution to children's literature. 'Wild Animals I Have Known' (1898) was Seton's first collection of animal tales. One of Robert's best is 'The Kindred of the Wild' (1902).

A Canadian regional story, Lucy Maud Montgomery's 'Anne of Green Gables' (1908) became an international best-seller. In 1912 Lillian H. Smith began her work in Boys and Girls Services at the Toronto Public Library. During her almost 40 years there, she greatly influenced selection of children's books in Canada and elsewhere. The year 1922 marked a giant step for Canadian children's books. The Toronto Public Library built Boys and Girls House, the first library building for children in Canada. 'Silver: The Life of an Atlantic Salmon' (1931) is a realistic animal story by one of Canada's outstanding writers for children, Roderick L. Haig-Brown.

There are many romantic stories about the North West Mounted Police (now the Royal Canadian Mounted Police). One of the best known is Muriel Denison's 'Susannah: A Little Girl with the Mounties' (1936). In 1936 *La Bibliothèque des Enfants* (The Children's Library) opened in Montreal to serve the needs of the area's French-speaking children.

The best-illustrated Canadian books of the 1940's are by the author-illustrator Clare Bice. His 'Jory's Cove' (1941) captures the flavor of fishing life in Nova Scotia. In 1941 Mary Grannan's fantasy 'Just Mary' was broadcast over the radio. It was the first of a series, later published in book form. Two of Haig-Brown's best stories of outdoor life are 'Starbuck Valley Winter' (1943) and 'Saltwater Summer' (1948), set in British Columbia.

Bertha Mabel Dunham's 'Kristli's Trees' (1948) is a warm picture of Mennonite farm life in Ontario. In 1948 the Canadian Association of Children's Librarians sponsored the first Young Canada's Book Week. The Canadian Library Association had begun awarding prizes for the best Canadian children's books in 1946. But the awards were confined to books in English. Several years later awards were also established for books in French.

'The Talking Cat' (1952) is a delightful collection of French Canadian folktales retold by Natalie Savage Carlson. A first-class example of history for

**The sly thief of Valenciennes outsmarts the people trying to catch him in Marius Barbeau's 'Golden Phoenix'.**

Illustration by Arthur Price, reproduced by permission of Oxford University Press, Canadian Branch, from Marius Barbeau, 'The Golden Phoenix', retold by Michael Hornyansky

children is Pierre Berton's 'Golden Trail' (1954), the story of the Klondike Gold Rush. Farley Mowat's prizewinning 'Lost in the Barrens' (1956) was later republished as 'Two Against the North'. Another popular Mowat story is 'The Dog Who Wouldn't Be' (1957).

An outstanding book of 1958 was Marius Barbeau's 'Golden Phoenix, and Other French-Canadian Fairy Tales', a retelling of stories from his 'Contes du Grand-Père Sept-Heures' (Tales of Grandfather Seven O'Clock). Sheila Burnford's 'Incredible Journey' (1960) was made into a movie. Claude Aubry's fantasy 'Les Îles du Roi Maha Maha II' (The Islands of King Maha Maha II) tells the story of how the Thousand Islands came to be. In 1963 it was translated as 'The King of the Thousand Islands'.

Christie Harris' 'Once Upon a Totem' (1963) is a noteworthy retelling of Indian legends. A memorable book based on Eskimo legend is James Houston's 'Tikta'liktak' (1965). Later books by the same author-illustrator include 'The White Archer'.

Claude Aubry's 'Christmas Wolf' (1965), the fanciful story of a Christmas Eve conversion, was translated from 'Le Loup de Noël'. Another outstanding 1965 book is William Stevenson's 'Bushbabies', a story of friendship and adventure set in Kenya. In 1971 the Amelia Frances Howard-Gibbon Medal for illustration was given for the first time. It was awarded to Elizabeth Cleaver, illustrator of the poetry collection 'The Wind Has Wings' (1968).

## CHILDREN'S LITERATURE OF LATIN AMERICA

Latin American literature for children began in the late 1800's. It was often moralistic and still is.

Domingo Faustino Sarmiento, president of Argentina, laid the foundation for children's libraries in that country. The Sarmiento Law of 1870 provided for a national library commission and for books. Through his writings, Sarmiento also influenced the development of children's libraries in many other countries of Latin America.

In 1889 José Martí, the Cuban liberator, founded an early children's magazine, *La Edad de Oro* (The Golden Age). Several years later, 'Contos da Carochinha' was published in Brazil. A collection of folktales from several countries, it was the first known book written to entertain children in Latin America. The Biblioteca de Chapulín series of children's books began to appear in Mexico in 1904. Each book was chosen for its literary quality and was illustrated by a noted Mexican artist.

Rafael Pombo of Colombia, one of the first fine children's poets of Latin America, wrote 'Fábulas y verdades' (Fables and True Stories) (1916). 'South American Jungle Tales', by Horacio Quiroga of Uruguay, was translated in 1922. Antonio Robles Soler, who wrote under the name Antoniorrobles, went to Mexico from Spain. His popular children's stories include the books later translated as 'Tales of Living Playthings' and 'Merry Tales from Spain'. 'Perez and Martina' (1932), a Puerto Rican folktale, was

From José Martí, *The Golden Age*

*La Edad de Oro*, an early Cuban children's magazine, was dedicated to the children of America.

written down by Pura Belpré as she heard it from her grandmother.

In 1936 the National Commission for Children's Literature was founded in Brazil. Two years later, one of Venezuela's outstanding children's magazines came out. It was *Onza, Tigre y Leon*. A later Venezuelan magazine was *Tricolor*. 'Cuentos para Mari-Sol' (Tales for Mari-Sol) (1938), by Chile's Marta Brunet, was a collection of nursery stories. Constancio C. Vigil of Argentina was famous for his animal fantasies. One of his best-loved stories was translated as 'La Hormiguita Viajera/The Adventures of Hormiguita'.

In 1940 Margarida Bandeira Duarte published a Brazilian "why" story, later translated as 'The Legend of the Palm Tree'. Philip M. Sherlock wrote 'Anansi, the Spider Man' (1954), one of the best collections of Jamaican folktales. Costa Rica's María Isabel Carvajal wrote under the name Carmen Lira. Her 'Los Cuentos de mi tía Panchita' (Tales Told by My Aunt Panchita), was published in 1956. 'The Snow and the Sun/La Nieve y el Sol' (1961), a South American folk rhyme in English and Spanish, was done by the author-illustrator Antonio Frasconi, who was born in Uruguay.

Andrew Salkey, a leading Jamaican writer, wrote several exciting children's stories, among them 'The Shark Hunters' (1966). 'Crick-Crack!' (1966), folktales from Trinidad and Tobago, were retold by Eaulin Ashtine. Ricardo E. Alegría of Puerto Rico retold

310e

'The Three Wishes' (1969), a collection of Puerto Rican folktales.

## CHILDREN'S LITERATURE OF ASIA

In much of Asia, children's literature has been at least partly to teach. The idea of children's literature for pure fun is not generally accepted.

One of the first to write for children in Asia was Sazanami Iwaya of Japan. In the late 1800's he rewrote old stories, later translated as 'Japanese Fairy Tales'. In 1909 *Phool*, the leading children's magazine in Urdu, appeared in Pakistan. Lu Hsün of China collected old Chinese fairy tales and wrote stories for children. *Akai Tori* (Red Bird), the most important children's magazine in Japan, first came out in 1918. Dhan Gopal Mukerji of India wrote the prizewinning 'Gayneck: The Story of a Pigeon' (1927).

In 1939 a Lahore, Pakistan, publisher began a sort of children's book-of-the-month club called the Paisa Library. For a paisa (about 1½ cents) a day, a member received one children's book at the end of the month. Ch'eng-en Wu's 'Monkey', a popular Chinese story of about 1550, was retold in English for children in 1943. Htin Aung retold 'Burmese Folk-Tales' (1948). In 1949 the Tondo Children's Library opened in Manila. It was the first of its kind in the Philippines.

'The Animal Frolic' (1954) was a reprint, with a few words added, of Toba Sojo's Scroll of Animals. The Japanese artist drew the picture scroll about 1100. So-Un Kim's 'Story Bag' is a collection of Korean folktales. Ashraf Siddiqui of Pakistan wrote 'Bhombal Dass: The Uncle of Lion' (1959).

In the 1960's and 1970's especially, more children's literature of Asia became available in English. This reflected, in part, a growing interest among English speakers in children of other lands. Janice Holland retold a story from 'The Book of Huai Nan Tzu' in 'You Never Can Tell' (1963). The original was written in China before 122 B.C. Miyoko Matsutani's 'Fox Wedding' is a Japanese folktale retold. Mom Dusdi Paribatra retold a Thai legend of love, 'The Reluctant Princess'. 'Blue in the Seed' (1964), by Korea's Yong Ik Kim, is a realistic story about a tormented blue-eyed boy. In 1964 Eliezer Smoli's 'Frontiersmen of Israel' appeared in English. Selma Ekrem retold 'Turkish Fairy Tales' (1964).

Among many excellent translations from Japanese are Momoko Ishii's 'Issun Boshi, the Inchling', a Japanese Tom Thumb story, and Kenji Miyazawa's 'Winds and Wildcat Places' (1967). 'Gilgamesh: Man's First Story' (1967) was retold by Bernarda Bryson. An outstanding book from Iran is Faridah Fardjam's 'Crystal Flower and the Sun'. Devorah Omer's 'Gideonites' is an outstanding book from Israel.

Yasuo Segawa, a top Japanese artist, illustrated Miyoko Matsutani's 'Witch's Magic Cloth' (1969). Vo-Dinh wrote and illustrated 'The Toad Is the Emperor's Uncle' (1970), a collection of animal folktales from Vietnam. 'Juan and the Asuangs' (1970), the story of a little boy and jungle spirits, was done by the author-illustrator José Aruego of the Philippines. Later picture books by Aruego include 'Look What I Can Do' (1971), about two carabaos who are always trying to outdo each other.

## CHILDREN'S LITERATURE OF AUSTRALIA AND NEW ZEALAND

Few books for children were written in Australia until the late 1800's. And there has been very little children's literature of New Zealand.

One of the best-known children's writers of Australia, Ethel Sibyl Turner, wrote 'Seven Little Australians' (1894). K. Langloh Parker retold the folktales of the Australian aborigines in 'Australian Legendary Tales' (1896).

Children's services began in the Dunedin Public Library of New Zealand in 1910. That same year, Mary Grant Bruce wrote 'A Little Bush Maid', the first of a popular series about a family who lived on a place called "Billabong." In 1915 the Public Library of South Australia opened a children's department.

May Gibbs's 'Gumnut Babies' (1916) later appeared as a comic strip. Esther Glen, who wrote 'Six Little New Zealanders' (1917), set the standards for children's writing in New Zealand. The author-illustrator Norman Lindsay wrote 'The Magic Pudding' (1918), one of Australia's first fine picture books.

Dorothy Wall's 'Blinky Bill, the Quaint Little Aus-

The Witch of the Mountain tells the villagers to bring her rice cakes in Miyoko Matsutani's 'Witch's Magic Cloth'.

Illustration by Yasuo Segawa, reprinted with the permission of Parents' Magazine Press (© 1969)

tralian' (1933) was the first of a popular series. 'Whalers of the Midnight Sun' (1934), by the Australian Alan John Villiers, is one of the best adventure stories of its time. Mary and Elizabeth Durack wrote 'The Way of the Whirlwind' (1941), a fantasy. 'The Book of Wiremu' (1944), by New Zealand's Stella M. Morice, is a story of Maori life.

The first Children's Book Week in New Zealand was held in 1944. In 1945 the first Children's Book Council was organized in Australia. The Esther Glen awards for the best children's books began in New Zealand in 1945. The following year the Australian Children's Book of the Year awards began. All these helped bring children and good books together.

Recent outstanding books from Australia include Nan Chauncy's 'Tangara' (1960) and Ivan Southall's 'Hills End' (1962) and his dramatic 'To the Wild Sky' (1967). Patricia Wrightson's realistic 'I Own the Racecourse' (1968) is another excellent book.

## CHILDREN'S LITERATURE OF AFRICA

Children's literature of Africa is fairly new—from the 1960's and 1970's mostly. Often only small numbers of books by African writers were printed, so that there were few available in United States libraries.

In 1913 the Durban Public Library, South Africa, set aside a children's book section. Six years later the first children's librarian was appointed there. Abayomi Fuja began collecting Yoruba folktales in Nigeria in 1938. There were later published as 'Fourteen Hundred Cowries'. In 1959 the Sierra Leone Library Board began services to children. The Kenya Children's Library opened in Nairobi in 1960.

In 1962 the African Universities Press of Lagos, Nigeria, began to publish a series of children's books called the African Reader's Library. Among these stories by outstanding writers is Cyprian Ekwensi's 'African Night's Entertainment' (1962), set in Moslem Nigeria. J. H. Kwabena Nketia's 'Folk Songs of Ghana' (1963) includes songs about Ananse the spider. In Kola Onadipe's 'Adventures of Souza' (1963), he recalled his childhood adventures in a rural Nigerian village. His 'Sugar Girl' (1964) is a lively fairy tale. In 1964 the Juvenile Book Writers' Group was founded in Nigeria, a giant step in providing more and better books for children.

Ngumbu Njururi's 'Agikuyu Folk Tales' (1966) retells stories from Kenya. 'The Adventures of Coalpot' (1966), about a clay stove and coalpot replaced by an electric stove, was written by Ghana's Nana Adoma. Birago Diop retold Senegal folktales in 'Tales of Amadou Koumba'. J. K. Njoroge's 'Tit for Tat and Other Stories' (1966) is a collection of Kenyan folktales.

'Chike and the River' (1966) was written by Chinua Achebe, one of Nigeria's—and Africa's—best novelists. Nigerian Solomon Irein Wangboje illustrated 'A Crocodile Has Me by the Leg' (1967), a collection of African poems. Mesfin Habte-Mariam's 'Rich Man and the Singer' (1971) is a collection of folktales from Ethiopia.

Illustration © 1967 by Solomon Irein Wangboje, reproduced by permission of the publisher, Walker & Co., Inc. (© 1966, 1967 Leonard W. Doob).

**An unlucky man sings a song of problems in 'A Crocodile Has Me by the Leg', a book of African poems.**

## A PICTURE BOOK

A picture book is not just a book with pictures. Nor is it just a story with pictures added. In a picture book, words and pictures are like peanut butter and jelly. They go well together, and they add to each other. In a picture book, pictures are at least as important as the words.

Some picture books have no words, but they still tell a story. Then the pictures and the unspoken story must do something for each other. Films without words are picture books in a different form.

## A GOOD BOOK

A good book is a grabber. It latches onto a child and won't let go. What a child needs is lots of books around to talk to him. And he needs lots of books around to choose from. What he doesn't need is a grown-up forcing a book on him and telling him it's a good book.

Just the same, many adults want to know how to help children find good books. Or how to find good books with which to surround children. There are no sure-fire formulas. Every child is different, and every child is always changing. But a few general guidelines might be of help.

**A good book is easy to hold.**

**A good book is easy to read.** Type is large enough, with not too many words on a page. Children from about grade 4 shy away from what looks like a baby book—type that's too large. But most children of any age dislike what looks like a reading chore.

**A good book is easy to understand.** In a storybook, the plot is clear and easy to follow. As for reading levels of books, children's librarians and children's teachers can offer suggestions, especially if they know the child (see Reading.)

**A good book is excitement.** Children like interesting characters, lots of action, lively writing. They also appreciate good illustrations (see Reading/Books for Children).

## A GIANT STEP

In the history of children's literature, there are many giant steps. The following chart is a selection

*Continued on page 312*

**310g**

# Giant Steps in Children's Literature

### CANADA AND UNITED STATES

CANADA    *The Snow Drop,* children's magazine 1847
Ernest Thompson Seton *Wild Animals I Have Known* 1898
Lucy Maud Montgomery *Anne of Green Gables* 1908
Boys and Girls House, Toronto, Ont. 1922
Muriel Denison *Susannah, a Little Girl with the Mounties* 1936
Mary Grannan, radio broadcasts for children 1941
Young Canada's Book Week 1948
Farley Mowat *Lost in the Barrens* 1956
Marius Barbeau *The Golden Phoenix* tr. 1958
Claude Aubry *The King of the Thousand Islands* 1960
James Houston *Tikta'liktak* 1965
Elizabeth Cleaver, ill. *The Wind Has Wings* 1968

UNITED STATES    Clement Moore *A Visit from St. Nicholas* 1822
Mary Mapes Dodge *Hans Brinker; or, The Silver Skates* 1865
Louisa May Alcott *Little Women* 1868
*St. Nicholas,* children's magazine 1873
Mark Twain *The Adventures of Tom Sawyer* 1876
Children's corner, Pawtucket, R.I., library 1877
Pratt Institute, New York City, trains children's librarians 1898
Story hours, Carnegie Library, Pittsburgh, Pa. 1899
L. Frank Baum *The Wonderful Wizard of Oz* 1900
Children's Book Week 1919
Newbery Medal 1922
Anne Carroll Moore, first newspaper column on children's books 1924
Walt Disney creates Mickey Mouse 1928
Caldecott Medal 1938
Gwendolyn Brooks *Bronzeville Boys and Girls* 1956

### LATIN AMERICA

ARGENTINA    Sarmiento Law lays foundation for children's libraries 1870
Constancio C. Vigil *La Hormiguita Viajera/The Adventures of Hormiguita* 1940

BRAZIL    Margarida Bandeira Duarte *The Legend of the Palm Tree* 1940

CHILE    Marta Brunet *Cuentos para Mari-Sol* (Tales for Mari-Sol) 1938

COLOMBIA    Rafael Pombo *Fábulas y verdades* (Fables and True Stories) 1916

COSTA RICA    Carmen Lira *Los Cuentos de mi tía Panchita* (Tales Told by My Aunt Panchita) 1956

| | |
|---|---|
| CUBA | José Martí founds *La Edad de Oro,* children's magazine 1889 |
| JAMAICA | Philip M. Sherlock *Anansi, the Spider Man* 1954 |
| MEXICO | Biblioteca de Chapulín series 1904<br>Antonio Robles *Tales of Living Playthings* 1931 |
| PUERTO RICO | Pura Belpré *Perez and Martina* 1932<br>Ricardo E. Alegría *The Three Wishes* 1969 |
| TRINIDAD AND TOBAGO | Eaulin Ashtine *Crick-Crack!* 1966 |
| URUGUAY | Horacio Quiroga *South American Jungle Tales* tr. 1922<br>Antonio Frasconi *The Snow and the Sun / La Nieve y el Sol* 1961 |

**EUROPE**

| | |
|---|---|
| AUSTRIA | Karl Bruckner *The Golden Pharaoh* 1957 |
| BELGIUM | Maurice Maeterlinck *The Blue Bird* 1908 |
| BULGARIA | Stefan Dichev *Rali* 1960 |
| CZECHOSLOVAKIA | Karel Erben *Panslavonic Folk-Lore* 1865<br>Jan Karafiát *The Fireflies* 1875<br>Václav Ctvrtek *The Little Chalk Man* tr. 1970 |
| DENMARK | Hans Christian Andersen *Fairy Tales* 1835<br>Ib Spang Olsen *Smoke* 1970 |
| ENGLAND | John Newbery, publ. *A Little Pretty Pocket-Book* 1744<br>Charles Dickens *A Christmas Carol* 1843<br>Lewis Carroll *Alice's Adventures in Wonderland* 1865<br>Rudyard Kipling *The Jungle Book* 1894<br>Beatrix Potter *The Tale of Peter Rabbit* 1901<br>A. A. Milne *Winnie-the-Pooh* 1926<br>Pamela L. Travers *Mary Poppins* 1934 |
| ESTONIA | Selve Maas *The Moon Painters, and Other Estonian Folk Tales* 1971 |
| FINLAND | Tove Jansson *Finn Family Moomintroll* 1949 |
| FRANCE | Charles Perrault *Histories or Tales of Past Times* about 1697<br>Jules Verne *Five Weeks in a Balloon* 1863<br>Jean de Brunhoff *The Story of Babar* 1931<br>Antoine de Saint-Exupéry *The Little Prince* 1943 |
| GERMANY | Jakob and Wilhelm Grimm *Household Stories* 1812<br>Wilhelm Busch *Max and Moritz* 1865<br>Erich Kästner *Emil and the Detectives* 1929 |
| GREECE | Aesop, fables about 600 B.C.<br>Alki Zei *Wildcat Under Glass* tr. 1968 |

HUNGARY      Victor Ambrus, ill. *The Three Poor Tailors* 1965

IRELAND      Padraic Colum *The King of Ireland's Son* 1916

ITALY        Giambattista Basile *Il Pentamerone; or, The Tale of Tales* 1634
Carlo Collodi *The Adventures of Pinocchio* about 1881
Edmondo de Amicis *The Heart of a Boy* 1886

NETHERLANDS  S. R. van Iterson *Pulga* tr. 1971

NORWAY       Peter Asbjörnsen and Jörgen Moe *Norwegian Fairy Tales* about 1843
Babbis Friis-Baastad, radio plays for children 1957

POLAND       Maria Konopnicka *The Golden Seed* tr. 1962

RUMANIA      Ioana Sturdza, tr. *Fairy Tales and Legends from Romania* 1972

RUSSIA       Ivan A. Krylov, fables 1825
Alexandr Afanas'ev *Russian Folk-Tales* 1855
Sergei Prokofiev *Peter and the Wolf,* musical fairy tale 1936

SCOTLAND     George MacDonald *At the Back of the North Wind* 1871
Robert Louis Stevenson *Treasure Island* 1883
James Barrie *Peter Pan* 1904
Kenneth Grahame *The Wind in the Willows* 1908

SPAIN        Juan R. Jiménez *Platero and I* 1914
José M. Sanchez-Silva *Marcelino* 1952

SWEDEN       Selma Lagerlöf *The Wonderful Adventures of Nils* 1906
Elsa Beskow *Pelle's New Suit* 1912
Astrid Lindgren *Pippi Longstocking* 1945

SWITZERLAND  *Zürcherischen Neujahrsblätter,* picture-poetry sheets 1645
Johann Wyss *Swiss Family Robinson* 1812
Johanna Spyri *Heidi* 1880

WALES        Gwyn Jones *Welsh Legends and Folk-Tales* 1955

YUGOSLAVIA   Ivana Brlić-Mazuranić *The Brave Adventures of Lapitch* 1913
Ivan Kušan *Koko and the Ghosts* tr. 1966

**ASIA**

BURMA        Htin Aung *Burmese Folk-Tales* 1948

CHINA        Ch'eng-en Wu *Monkey* about 1550

INDIA        *The Panchatantra* is written down  about 200 B.C.
Dhan G. Mukerji *Gayneck: The Story of a Pigeon* 1927

IRAN         Faridah Fardjam *Crystal Flower and the Sun* 1968

IRAQ         Sumerians write down Gilgamesh legend  about 3000 B.C.

| ISRAEL | Devorah Omer *The Gideonites* 1968 |
|---|---|
| JAPAN | Toba Sojo, ill. *The Animal Frolic* about 1100<br>Sazanami Iwaya *Japanese Fairy Tales* about 1895<br>*Akai Tori,* children's magazine 1918<br>Kenji Miyazawa *Winds and Wildcat Places* tr. 1967 |
| KOREA | So-Un Kim *The Story Bag* tr. 1955<br>Yong Ik Kim *Blue in the Seed* 1964 |
| PAKISTAN | Paisa Library series 1939<br>Ashraf Siddiqui *Bhombal Dass* 1959 |
| PHILIPPINES | José Aruego *Juan and the Asuangs* 1970 |
| THAILAND | Mom Dusdi Paribatra *The Reluctant Princess* 1963 |
| TURKEY | Selma Ekrem *Turkish Fairy Tales* 1964 |
| VIETNAM | Vo-Dinh *The Toad Is the Emperor's Uncle* 1970 |

## AUSTRALIA AND NEW ZEALAND

| AUSTRALIA | Ethel Turner *Seven Little Australians* 1894<br>K. Langloh Parker *Australian Legendary Tales* 1896<br>Nan Chauncy *Tangara* 1960<br>Ivan Southall *Hills End* 1962 |
|---|---|
| NEW ZEALAND | Esther Glen *Six Little New Zealanders* 1917<br>Stella Morice *The Book of Wiremu* 1944 |

## AFRICA

| ETHIOPIA | Mesfin Habte-Mariam *The Rich Man and the Singer* 1971 |
|---|---|
| GHANA | J. H. Kwabena Nketia *Folk Songs of Ghana* 1963<br>Nana Adoma *The Adventures of Coalpot* 1966 |
| KENYA | J. K. Njoroge *Tit for Tat, and Other Stories* 1966<br>Ngumbu Njururi *Agikuyu Folk Tales* 1966 |
| NIGERIA | Abayomi Fuja collects Yoruba folktales 1938<br>Juvenile Book Writers' Group 1964<br>Chinua Achebe *Chike and the River* 1966 |
| SENEGAL | Birago Diop *Tales of Amadou Koumba* 1966 |
| SOUTH AFRICA | Children's book section, Durban Public Library 1913 |

Except where preceded by *tr.,* dates give year of publication in the original language. Dates preceded by *tr.* give year translated into English.

eds. = editors        publ. = publisher
ill. = illustrator        tr. = translated into English; translator

only. All titles in English are as published in English. Titles in parentheses are free translations of titles not published in English.

## Books About Literature for Children

**Summoned by Books: Essays and Speeches by Frances Clarke Sayers.** Compiled by Marjeanne Jensen Blinn. (Penguin, 1968.) A collection of the writings and speeches of a distinguished children's librarian and writer.

**The Green and Burning Tree.** By Eleanor Cameron. (Little, 1969.) A personal approach to the writing of children's books by a well-known writer for children.

**Only Connect: Readings on Children's Literature.** Edited by Sheila Egoff, G. T. Stubbs, and L. F. Ashley. (Oxford, 1969.) A compilation of critical essays.

**Your Child's Reading Today.** By Josette Frank. (Doubleday, 1969.) A unique parents' guide to children's reading.

**Books in Search of Children: Speeches and Essays by Louise Seaman Bechtel.** Selected by Virginia Haviland. (Macmillan, 1969.) Articles and speeches by the editor of the first children's department in a publishing company in the United States.

**Books, Children and Men.** By Paul Hazard. (Horn Book, 1960.) Universal truths of childhood set forth with wit and wisdom by an eminent French scholar.

**Illustrators of Children's Books, 1744–1945.** Compiled by Bertha E. Mahony, Louise P. Latimer, Beulah Folmsbee. (Horn Book, 1947.) Essays about illustrators and the graphic arts. Supplemented by **Illustrators of Children's Books, 1946–1956** (Horn Book, 1958) and by **Illustrators of Children's Books, 1957–1966** (Horn Book, 1968).

**From Rollo to Tom Sawyer and Other Papers.** By Alice M. Jordan. (Horn Book, 1948.) An illuminating discussion of children's books and magazines published in the United States during the 19th century.

**A Critical History of Children's Literature.** By Cornelia Meigs, Anne Eaton, Elizabeth Nesbitt, and Ruth Hill Viguers. (Macmillan, 1969.) A survey of children's books in English from earliest times to 1968.

**My Roads to Childhood.** By Anne Carroll Moore. (Horn Book, 1961.) Autobiographical essays with appraisals of children's books and their illustrations.

**A Harvest of Russian Children's Literature.** Edited by Miriam Morton. Foreword by Ruth Hill Viguers. (Univ. of Calif. Press, 1967.) An anthology in English of Russian children's literature of the past 150 years.

**The World of Children's Literature.** By Anne Pellowski. (Bowker, 1968.) An outstanding bibliography on children's literature and libraries in 106 countries, compiled by the Director/Librarian of the UNICEF Information Center on Children's Cultures.

**The Unreluctant Years: A Critical Approach to Children's Literature.** By Lillian H. Smith. (ALA, 1953.) An inspiring guide to the selection of children's books.

**A Sense of Story: Essays on Contemporary Writers for Children.** By John Rowe Townsend. (Lippincott, 1971.) Critical essays by a well-known British writer.

**Margin for Surprise: About Books, Children, and Librarians.** By Ruth Hill Viguers. (Little, 1964.) Articles and lectures by a distinguished librarian.

**That Eager Zest: First Discoveries in the Magic World of Books.** Selected by Frances Walsh. (Lippincott, 1961.) The reminiscences of different people about their first discoveries as children of the wonderful world that books provide.

**LITHOGRAPHY.** Most printing is done from type or from designs which project above their background. Thus they alone receive the ink or touch the paper on which the printing is done. In lithography, however, the printing is done from a smooth surface on which the writing or design is drawn with a greasy substance, or it is produced by photography. This form of lithography is called photolithography.

The lithographic method of printing was invented about 1796 by a Bavarian playwright, Alois Senefelder (1771–1834). It got its name from the Greek words meaning "stone" and "writing," because stone was for long the only satisfactory surface. Today specially prepared plates of zinc or aluminum are often preferred.

The design may either be made directly on the plate with oily crayons, or it may be drawn on paper and transferred to the plate by pressure. A mixture of gum arabic and acid is then applied. This fixes the design and cleans all grease from the other parts of the plate, etching them slightly. To print from this plate, water and then a special greasy ink are applied in succession. The water moistens the etched or "empty" parts of the plate but is repelled by the oily design. The ink, however, clings to the design but is repelled by the remainder of the plate.

By using a separate plate or stone for each color, *chromolithographs* of colored designs can be made. In *photolithography* the design is photographically reproduced on the sensitized surface of the plate. The *offset* method of printing lithographs consists of impressing the design from the plate to the surface of a rubber-covered cylinder, which in turn transfers it to the paper. This permits printing on many different textures of paper instead of only the smooth paper required for *direct* lithography. (*See also* Photoengraving and Photolithography; Printing.)

Lithography, like engraving, is also a medium for artistic expression. Adolph Menzel, in Germany, kept it alive for illustrating books into the late 1860's. In France it was used by Honoré Daumier. Ignace Fantin-Latour produced a famous series of lithographs. Francisco Goya's grim subjects are masterpieces of the art. In England Samuel Prout did superb lithography. James Whistler helped in its revival. The lithographic process has been used for posters by many artists, including Henry Bone, Louis Raemakers, Joseph Pennell, and George Bellows.

**LITHUANIAN SOVIET SOCIALIST REPUBLIC.** From 1918 to 1940 Lithuania was an independent republic. Russian troops occupied it in June 1940; and in August it was proclaimed a republic of the Soviet Union.

Lithuania is the southernmost of the three Baltic States. Unlike the Latvian and Estonian Soviet republics, it has only a short coastline on the Baltic Sea.

The chief port is Klaipeda (Memel). The capital is Vilna (or Vilnius). The land is a rolling plain of fertile soil, partly covered with forests and marshes. The chief crops are potatoes, rye, barley, oats, wheat, and flax. Industry is little developed.

### Early History

The Lithuanians have lived on the shore of the Baltic since the dawn of history, and they have preserved their early traditions in hundreds of folk songs and folk stories. Their language is an ancient Indo-European tongue. Before the Russian conquest, the majority were Roman Catholics. Primary education was widespread, and higher education was provided in the University of Vilna and technical colleges.

During the Middle Ages Lithuania rose from a small duchy to the largest state in Europe, spreading from the Baltic to the Black Sea. In 1386 it was joined to Poland by the marriage of the countries' rulers. In the 18th century it was divided between Russia and Prussia through the partition of Poland (*see* Poland). After the Russian Bolshevik revolution (1917), Lithuania gained its independence. Russia seized the Baltic States following its 1939 pact with Hitler; but Germany occupied them from 1941 to 1944, when they were reconquered by Russia. Russia forced the peasants to merge their farms into "collectives" (state-owned farms). (*See also* Russia; Union of Soviet Socialist Republics.) Area, about 25,100 square miles; population (1970 preliminary census), 3,129,000.

THESE ARTICLES ARE IN THE FACT-INDEX

Litmus
Little, Arthur Dehon
Little Belt
'Little Brown Church in the Vale, The'
"Little Church Around the Corner"

Little Falls, Minn.
Little Falls, N. Y.
Littlefield, Catherine
Little Khingan Mountains
'Little Lord Fauntleroy'
'Little Minister, The'

**LITTLE ROCK, Ark.** Arkansas's capital and largest city, Little Rock, draws its prosperity from an area rich in farmlands, minerals, and timber. On the farmlands cotton, alfalfa, rice, fruits, vegetables, and livestock are raised. Mineral deposits yield coal, oil, natural gas, marble, granite, and bauxite (aluminum ore). High-grade timber is cut nearby.

The city is an industrial and agricultural center. Its factories process meats and manufacture cotton goods, furniture and other wood products, fertilizers and insecticides, bicycles, electrical and electronic apparatus, watches, clocks, and roofing materials. The separately incorporated city of North Little Rock, on the opposite bank of the Arkansas River, has large railroad workshops.

Little Rock is on the south bank of the river. It is set on the edge of the Gulf Coastal Plain; the foothills of the Ozark Mountains lie to the west. The business district spreads back from the riverbank.

The Capitol, completed in 1915, is surrounded by a 12-acre park. Two former Arkansas capitols have been restored—the Old State House and the Territorial Capitol. MacArthur Park contains the Arkansas Arts Center and the birthplace of Gen. Douglas MacArthur, which houses the Museum of Natural History. In Little Rock are also the State History Museum, the Joseph T. Robinson Memorial Auditorium, state schools for the deaf and blind, and state and federal hospitals. The city is the site of the University of Arkansas at Little Rock and the University of Arkansas Medical Center. Little Rock is also the home of Philander Smith College and Arkansas Baptist College.

A large rock on the riverbank was called "Little Rock" by an early French explorer to distinguish the site from a high stone bluff two miles farther up the river. Little Rock's first house was built in 1812 by William Lewis. After the site was surveyed for the territorial capital, the government moved from Arkansas Post in 1821 (*see* Arkansas). In early days the town was a busy river port and frontier post. During the Civil War it was taken by Federal forces in 1863. Little Rock was incorporated as a town in 1831 and chartered a city in 1836. It is the seat of Pulaski County and has a city-manager form of government. Population (1980 census), 158,461.

THESE ARTICLES ARE IN THE FACT-INDEX

Little St. Bernard Pass
Little Sisters of the Poor
Little Steel formula
Littleton, Sir Thomas
Littleton, Colo.

Little Turtle
Liturgy
Litvinov, Maxim Maximovich
Liu Shao-ch'i
Live-forever

**LIVER.** In all animals that have a backbone, as well as in some that do not, there is a large gland called the liver, which serves as one of the digestive organs. The liver in man is situated in the abdominal cavity, on the right side slightly above and behind the stomach. It is the largest gland organ of the body, weighing from three to four pounds. It measures about six or seven inches from front to back, and about twelve inches from right to left.

The liver has four main functions: (1) It produces bile, which aids in the digestion and absorption of fats, and is the vehicle that carries some waste material from the body. (2) Glycogen (or animal starch) is formed from the sugar in the blood and stored away in the liver cells, to be given out again as sugar when it is needed. (3) The liver forms *urea* and other substances. Urea is one of the wastes of the human body, which must be thrown off (*see* Kidneys). (4) The liver also has an important duty in preparing fats for oxidation in the body.

Blood flows into the liver from two main sources. The small hepatic artery brings blood directly from the heart to feed the liver itself; the large portal vein brings all the venous blood from the stomach and intestine to the liver before it goes back to the heart. The liver makes important changes in this blood before it passes on to the general circulation.

Just below the liver is the gall bladder, a small pear-shaped sac used as a storeroom for the bile. The common bile duct carries bile to the intestine just beyond the stomach. (*See also* Anatomy.)

---

THESE ARTICLES ARE IN THE FACT-INDEX
**Livermore, Mary Ashton Rice**
**Livermore, Calif.**

---

**LIVERPOOL, England.** The "city of ships," Liverpool, is England's second greatest port, ranking after London. Liverpool is in Lancashire on the Mersey River, three miles inland from the Irish Sea. It is the natural outlet for the Lancashire industrial region's textiles and machinery. The chief imports are grain, meat, tobacco, and the raw materials for Lancashire industries—cotton, wool, hides, rubber, and timber.

The most interesting sight in Liverpool is the docks. They occupy a river frontage of seven miles. The quays are about 40 miles long. Passenger ships dock at a landing stage in the river—a floating structure half a mile long. Hinged bridges connect the landing stage with the river wall. The west side of the river is lined with the docks and quays of the busy port of Birkenhead, in Cheshire.

### Constant Dredging

Liverpool's great port owes little to natural advantages. The Mersey estuary has shifting sand bars across the channel and a tide with a range of 26 feet. To remove the sand the Dock Board keeps a fleet of dredges constantly at work maintaining a 30-foot low-water channel. The advantages of a tideless harbor have been secured by a wonderful system of wet docks operated like the locks of a canal.

Behind the teeming water front, the city stretches in a rough semicircle about nine miles long. The land rises gradually from the river bank. The commercial section of the city has impressive business buildings. In the residential sections are many well-preserved Georgian houses. The University of Liverpool, established in 1903, is noted for its School of Tropical Medicine. The Walker Art Gallery has many famous pictures. The most famous building is St. George's Hall, completed in 1854, which was built after the style of the Parthenon in Athens.

Two great cathedrals were long in building. The foundation stone of Liverpool Cathedral was laid in 1904, and its central door was opened by Princess Elizabeth, later to become Elizabeth II, in 1949. It is in the new Gothic style. It is the largest Anglican church in the country. A modern Roman Catholic church, the Metropolitan Cathedral of Christ the King, was consecrated in 1967.

Britain's heavy chemical industry is concentrated in and near Liverpool. The Merseyside region is also the greatest flour-milling center in the country. Other industries are shipbuilding, ship repairing, engineering works, oil- and seed-crushing mills, tobacco, sugar refining, tanning, rubber, food processing, and clothing. At Birkenhead are the noted Laird shipbuilding yards, which have produced many of Britain's famous battleships and large passenger liners. Birkenhead is connected with Liverpool by the Queensway Road Tunnel.

Liverpool's commercial importance began in the 17th century. In the 18th century the power loom began to make Lancashire the world's greatest cotton-manufacturing center and Liverpool its chief port. The city suffered heavy damage from German air attacks in World War II. Population (1969 estimate), 677,450.

---

THIS ARTICLE IS IN THE FACT-INDEX
**Liverpool, N. S.**

---

**LIVERWORT.** The liverworts look like flat green leaves with rounded lobes. They grow in wet places—on rocks, logs, or damp earth. Their name comes from their shape, which in some varieties looks like that of the human liver. "Wort" comes from an Anglo-Saxon word meaning "plant."

The liverwort is a simple, flowerless plant, one of the first in the earth's history to grow on land. The plant body, called a *thallus*, is not differentiated into leaves, stem, and root. On the under surface are fine white hairs (*rhizoids*). These anchor the plant and absorb food materials. The organs of reproduction are on the upper surface.

Liverworts have three different ways of reproducing. The most common genus, *Marchantia*, is a typical

The most common genus of liverworts is the Marchantia, shown here. Its cupules ("little cups") are too tiny to be seen.

Gottscho-Schleisner

example. On its upper surface it bears little green cuplike organs called *cupules* (Latin for "little cups"). Within the cups are tiny greenish balls known as *gemmae* (Latin for "twins"). Notches at opposite sides make them look like joined twins. When gemmae fall to moist ground, they grow into new plants. This is a form of asexual (without sex) reproduction.

Marchantia may also reproduce by male and female sex organs and by spores (asexual). The sex organs are borne on upright umbrellalike stalks that grow from a notch in the upper side of the thallus. At the top of one stalk is the archegonium, which bears egg cells. At the top of another is the antheridium, which contains sperm cells. The two sexes are borne on different plants. During wet weather the sperms swim to the archegonium of a nearby plant to fertilize the eggs. A fertilized egg (*zygote*) grows into a spore-bearing plant (*sporophyte*). The ripe spores are scattered by wind and water. A germinating spore develops into a new thallus, known as the *gametophyte*, from which new sex organs grow. Such a life history, in which a plant producing spores alternates with a plant producing sex cells, is called "alternation of generations." (*See also* Spore.)

Liverworts form the group *Hepaticae* in the *Bryophyta* division of the plant kingdom.

**LIVING COSTS.** Wage rates of millions of people in free nations today are based largely on the cost of living. When living costs go up, workers receive higher wages to meet the higher prices. When living costs drop, employers tend to cut wages. In the United States some labor union contracts have *escalator clauses*. Under such a clause, wages automatically increase when living costs rise and decrease when costs fall.

Changes in the cost of living in the United States are shown by a report published by the Bureau of Labor Statistics of the United States Department of Labor. The official name of the report is *Consumer Price Index for Urban Wage Earners and Clerical Workers*. It is often called the *Consumer Price Index*. It is published monthly.

**CHANGING LIVING COSTS IN THE UNITED STATES**

Consumer Price Index for moderate-income families in U.S. cities
1967 average = 100
Source: Bureau of Labor Statistics, U.S. Dept. of Labor

WORLD WAR I — WORLD WAR II — KOREAN WAR — VIETNAM CONFLICT

Index line 100 represents the base. Prices rise during and after wars (shaded areas), when goods are scarce and the government borrows heavily.

The bureau gathered data about the goods and services bought in 1972 and 1973 by average urban working families and by single workers living alone. Trained investigators questioned 20,000 families in 85 urban areas; another 20,000 families were asked to keep a two-week diary of small, frequent purchases. In 1972–73 the average *Index* family income after taxes was about $9,731 a year.

The investigators noted the kind, quality, and amount of items and services purchased during the year. These included food, clothing, rent or home payment, and utilities. From the many hundreds of items and services listed, the bureau chose 357 as the most representative. Among them were 92 foods, 53 articles of clothing, and 94 housing items (including rent, home purchase, fuel, utilities, and housewares). The 118 other items included medical and dental care, personal care, transportation, tobacco, alcoholic beverages, and reading and recreation. The bureau averaged these records to make up a representative "market basket."

The price of every item in the "market basket" is checked periodically. Part-time investigators, many of them housewives, note the prices of food, fuel, and a few other items every month in all 85 locations. Most other prices are checked monthly in the 5 largest cities and every other month in the rest.

The bureau's statisticians find the average cost of each item. They then multiply the average cost by the quantity shown in the "market basket." This is called *weighting*. A change in the price of food (which accounts for about 22 percent of the average "basket") has roughly twice as much effect on the *Index* as a change in the price of clothing, which accounts for some 10 percent.

The statisticians then figure the *degree* of change in living costs. For a standard of comparison, they use the year 1967. This *base* is assigned a value of 100. If current living costs are 15 percent above the base, the *index number* is 115. If costs are 5 percent lower than the base, the *index number* is 95. The bureau began the *Index* in 1918 and has revised it periodically. In 1964 the *Index* began to reflect the living costs of single workers. Their lower expenses had been expected to reduce consumer price estimates slightly.

THESE ARTICLES ARE IN THE FACT-INDEX

Livingston, Edward      Livingston, William
Livingston, Robert R.     Livingston, Mont.

# DAVID LIVINGSTONE, British Explorer of Africa

**LIVINGSTONE, David** (1813–1873). How does it feel to be crunched in the jaws of a lion? Dr. Livingstone, the noted British missionary and African explorer, was one of the few men who knew from personal experience and lived to tell the tale.

Soon after he began his work in South Africa he was sent to establish an advanced station in the heart of the wilderness some 800 miles northeast of Capetown. The "charming valley" which he and his white companion chose proved to be infested with lions, which attacked the herds by day and leaped into the cattle pens at night. At a distance of 30 yards Dr. Livingstone fired two bullets into one of these ferocious beasts, severely wounding it. Then with a roar it hurled itself upon him, crushing his left shoulder in its jaws, and bearing him to the ground.

"Growling horribly close to my ear," wrote Livingstone, "he shook me as a terrier dog does a rat. The shock produced a stupor similar to that which seems to be felt by a mouse after the first shake of a cat. It caused a sort of dreaminess, in which there was no sense of pain nor feeling of terror, though I was quite conscious of all that was happening."

Fortunately the lion soon left Livingstone to attack his companion and presently fell dead of its wound. Livingstone's shoulder was so badly crushed that it troubled him the rest of his life.

But no dangers of this sort, nor hunger, fever, attacks by hostile Boers or native cannibals, the perfidy of Arab slave traders, nor any of the countless perils that beset him could dampen his ardor or make him abandon his chosen field. His patient resourcefulness, courage, fair dealing, and Christian character laid the basis for missionary work over a large part of South and Central Africa. In addition, no other explorer ever did so much for African geography as Livingstone during his 30 years' work. He remade much of the map of Africa and laid the basis for Britain's claim to the area now comprising Botswana, Rhodesia, Zambia, and Malawi.

A poor Scottish lad, Livingstone had to go to work in a cotton mill at the age of ten. With the first money that he earned he bought a beginning Latin book. Although work at the factory started at six in the morning and lasted ten hours or more, he attended night school and studied at home until he had read Vergil and Horace. At the factory he kept a book open where he could read a sentence now and then as he went about his work.

In his 20th year he was thrilled by reading an account of a missionary's labors in Asia, and as he says, "resolved to devote my life to the alleviation of human misery." Then followed college classes in Glasgow, examination and acceptance by the London Missionary Society in the great English metropolis, the completion of his medical education, with studies of theology, botany, zoology, geology, chemistry, and astronomy—all with a view to his work. At last came his arrival at Algoa Bay in South Africa in 1841 and a 700-mile trip by oxcart to begin his ministry among the natives of what is now Botswana.

**MEETING OF LIVINGSTONE AND STANLEY IN CENTRAL AFRICA**

Henry Stanley searched for eight months through trackless African jungles before he found the missionary-explorer ill and almost destitute in the village of an Arab slave trader. Yet under the hostile eyes of the Arabs, he restrained his joy. "Dr. Livingstone, I presume," was his greeting. This sketch was made for the Aug. 31, 1872, issue of *Harper's Weekly*.

For over 30 years Dr. Livingstone traveled up and down Africa, from the Cape nearly to the equator and from the Atlantic to the Indian Ocean. He discovered the Victoria Falls of the Zambezi River, Lakes Nyasa and Mweru, and Lake Bangweulu, where he afterward died. He also discovered the upper course of the Congo, called the Lualaba, but he believed it to be the upper Nile. His wife went with him on many of his expeditions. She was the daughter of a missionary and was born in South Africa. His children were also born in Africa. During the last 15 years of his life he was aided by the British government, from which he held an appointment as roving consul.

In addition to his missionary work, Livingstone wanted to discover the source of the Nile and to see an end to the Arab slave trade in Africa. He called this trade the "great open sore of the world" and sent home many descriptions of horrible slave raids. In time these reports helped to bring action which ended the trade. Livingstone never found the sources of the Nile, although he died in the attempt.

About a year and a half before he died, an expedition sent by the *New York Herald* under Henry M. Stanley found him at Ujiji on Lake Tanganyika (*see* Stanley). Livingstone was without many necessities and was weakened by fever. Some of his carriers had deserted with supplies and his precious medicine chest. Stanley tried to persuade him to return to civilization, but he refused.

After the relief party had left, Livingstone again started west, looking for the sources of the Nile. Dysentery, complicated by his weakened condition, attacked him. He grew steadily worse. On the morning of May 1, 1873, his men found him kneeling beside his cot, dead. His attendants preserved the body in salt and carried it to Zanzibar. It was taken to England and buried in Westminster Abbey. A monument stands on the spot where he died.

Livingstone's books included 'Missionary Travels and Researches in South Africa', 'The Zambesi and Its Tributaries', and 'Letters, 1840–1872'. Good books about him are 'David Livingstone, Foe of Darkness', by Jeanette Eaton (Morrow, 1947); 'David Livingstone: His Life and Letters', by George Seaver (Harper, 1957); and 'Livingstone and Africa', by Jack Simmons (Collier Books, 1955).

THESE ARTICLES ARE IN THE FACT-INDEX

Livingstone College
Livingstone Mountains
Livingston University
Livius Andronicus

Livonia, Estonian S.S.R. and Latvian S.S.R.
Livonia, Mich.
Livre
Livy

# The Scaly Dragons of Modern Times

**LIZARDS.** Almost everyone thinks he can recognize a lizard. Yet the 3,000 different kinds in the world differ amazingly in shape, size, color, and habits. There are tiny creatures two or three inches long and giants measuring 12 feet. Most lizards have sturdy legs, with long toes and claws; but some have only front legs, some only back legs, and some no legs at all. They may be green, blue, red, gray, brown, or black. They may live in trees, on the ground, underground, or in the water. Some dart about with lightning speed. Some glide through the air on "wings" of skin. Some lie sluggish and still.

Lizards may be sleek, slender, and graceful; or they may be fantastically ugly, with grotesque horns, spines, and frilly collars. They have startling habits. They may snap off their tails when they are seized. Some may rear up and run away on their hind legs. Certainly there is nothing commonplace about lizards.

Although there are many superstitions about lizards, only two kinds are poisonous. Most of the others benefit mankind by their preference for insect food.

The land iguana of the Galápagos Islands reminds one of a prehistoric dinosaur. It reaches a length of four feet.

Lizards are reptiles. Together with their close relatives the snakes, they constitute the order *Squamata* of the class *Reptilia*. Many people confuse lizards with salamanders. Like all reptiles, lizards are cold-blooded. They have dry, scaly skin, and claws on their toes. Salamanders are amphibians, related

317

# LIZARDS

to frogs and toads. They have smooth, thin, moist skin, and they never have scales or claws. Legless lizards, such as the glass snake, may be mistaken for true snakes. Unlike snakes, however, these lizards have eyelids which they can open and close and ear openings on the sides of the head.

Even more unlike the typical lizards are the wormlike amphisbaenae of tropical America and Africa, known also as worm lizards, blindworms, and blind snakes. They burrow into loose soil and can move backward or forward with equal ease by moving the narrow rings which encircle the body, just as an earthworm does. The eyes and ears are hidden under thin growths of skin. The body, however, is marked off into small, scaly squares, and the head is scaly.

Lizards, therefore, may commonly be distinguished from other animals which they resemble. They will differ in one or more of four external features—scales, claws, movable eyelids, and ear openings.

Most lizards lay eggs with tough, leathery shells. Some bring forth living young. Some help to incubate the eggs with their bodies, but most of them leave

the eggs to be warmed by the sun, and no care is taken of the young after they have hatched. Lizards are cold-blooded and cannot maintain a constant body temperature. Hence they cannot stand extremes of heat or cold. In temperate climates they hibernate in the winter. In warm climates they bask in the sun for short periods but take shelter during the heat of the day. The smaller lizards feed on worms, insects, and larvae. Some of the large species are plant eaters, and some eat other lizards and their own young.

## Some American Lizards

Warmer portions of the earth have the greatest number and variety of lizards, but they are also found in temperate latitudes. There are about 125 different kinds in the United States. One of the most familiar is the little chameleon, also called anolis. It belongs to the iguana family, *Iguanidae*, and is quite different from the true chameleon family of Africa. Both families are interesting for their ability to change color (*see* Chameleon). The chameleons' large, powerful relatives, the iguanas, dwell in the jungles of Mexico, Central and South America, the West Indies, and the Galápagos Islands (*see* Iguana).

The fence lizard, or common swift, is abundant in the eastern United States in dry pine woods from New Jersey southward. It is brown or gray, with scales that blend perfectly with stones, logs, and the bark of trees. The usual length is about five inches.

## Skinks and Race Runners

The skinks are slender, snakelike animals, but with well-developed legs on which they run swiftly. They have smooth, glassy scales. Most of them have light stripes against a brown or black background. Most widely distributed, from Texas eastward through the central and southern states, is the five-lined skink.

## LIZARDS OF ALL SIZES AND SHAPES

The common lizard of northern and central Europe is a graceful, quick little creature, only six or seven inches long. It is found in hedges, gardens, and woodlands everywhere.

The dragon lizard of Komodo (left), in the East Indies, is the largest of all. It is twelve feet long and weighs 250 pounds.

The Australian frilled lizard (right) is three feet long. That great collar stands up when the animal is angry or frightened.

318

The young have blue tails and five yellowish stripes on a black background. As they grow older their tails become gray, the heads reddish, and the bodies a uniform olive-brown. They grow to be about $7\frac{1}{2}$ inches long. These skinks usually live in woods. They are almost impossible to catch. The glassy scales and quick movements make them difficult to grasp, and the tails break off with only a pinch. While the tail wriggles furiously and distracts the attention of the "enemy," the skink makes a hasty escape. Skinks are called scorpions in some regions, probably because they can bite and pinch painfully. They are in no way related to true scorpions.

The six-lined race runner lives in open sandy places in the Southern states. It may be recognized by the tiny scales and six stripes down the back. It grows to be nine inches long.

The glass snake of the southeastern and south-central United States has no legs except two tiny spikes at the rear of the body. Over half its length of nearly two feet consists of tail. The tail is extremely brittle and the highly polished scales make the animal appear truly glassy. The popular belief that a glass snake will try to seek its lost tail and rejoin the broken pieces is untrue. It soon grows a new tail, however, to replace the missing member.

## Lizards of the Western Deserts

In the Western states and Mexico are several different kinds of swifts closely related to the eastern fence lizard. Some have coarse, spiny-tipped scales.

Only two species of lizards are poisonous. These are the Gila monster of Arizona and Mexico, and its cousin, the horrid heloderm of Mexico and Central America. Each has a fat, sluggish body, about two feet long. The short tail is a storage reservoir of fat on which the animal can live for months if it is deprived of food. The Gila monster is pink or orange, marked with black. The surface of the body is warty or beady, and the effect combined with the gaudy color and pattern looks like Indian beadwork. The horrid heloderm is yellow and black.

The Gila monster moves in a sprawling manner, dragging its chunky body on the ground. When it is angry it leaps and twists in a flash, snapping its fangs into the attacker. It keeps a bulldog grip for as long as ten minutes, chewing with its grooved teeth and working the poison into the wound. The poison sacs lie in the base of the mouth. Small animals die quickly when bitten by the vicious creature, and it is extremely dangerous to man. It feeds chiefly on the eggs of snakes and other lizards.

The horned toad, so called because of its flat, toadlike body, dwells throughout the dry plains and deserts of western America. It is covered with short sharp spines, particularly about the head, which protect it from being swallowed by snakes. (For a picture, *see* Protective Coloration.) New Mexico forbids the killing of this lizard because of its value in destroying insects. The chuckwalla, or chuckawalla, is a plant-eating lizard highly esteemed as a food by the Indians. It lives on tender leaves and flowers.

The collared lizard ranges from Kansas to Arizona. It is one of the handsomest and most amusing of the lizards. The male in the breeding season is green, dotted with yellow spots. It has a black collar, an orange throat, and red spots on the hind legs. The female is slaty gray, but just before the eggs are laid its sides turn brick red. These lizards hop and jump nimbly over the rocky places where they prefer to live. They run swiftly on their long hind legs, their bodies erect.

Geckos form an interesting group that breaks most of the rules for lizard appearance and behavior. Al-

### A "MONSTER" AND A "DRAGON"

The Gila monster of the southwestern United States (above) and the horrid heloderm are the only poisonous lizards in the world. The Gila monster, lying beside its egg, looks like Indian beadwork in a gaudy pattern of pink and black. The little flying dragon of Malaysia (right) has "wings" of skin. The undersides are colored a brilliant orange or yellow with blotches of black. Thus by means of protective coloration the lizard conceals itself among the brilliant flowers of the jungle treetops where it lives and feeds.

though most kinds of lizards have no voice, the gecko produces a variety of clicking sounds. The gecko has wide-spreading toes on its feet. On each toe is a pad covered with hairlike hooks that can be seen only under a microscope. These hooks grasp tiny irregularities that occur on any surface, even glass, so the gecko can scamper over walls, ceilings, and windows in pursuit of insects. It hunts at night and often enters dwellings in search of prey. Its eyes have elliptical pupils, typical of night-roaming animals. Most geckos live in trees, but one kind makes its home in the desert. It has a lighter, more slender body than the tree-dwelling kind. Its toes are surrounded by a fringe of scales that help prevent the feet from sinking deeply into the sand.

### "Dragons" of Faraway Lands

The nearest thing to flying found among the lizards is the sailing leap from tree to tree performed by the small "flying dragons" of Malaysia. The "wings" are thin membranes of skin stretched over an outward extension of the ribs. They support the lizard like a

### SKINK, "SNAKE," GECKO, AND SWIFT

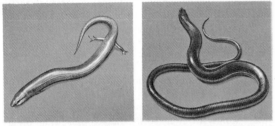

The sand skink (left) of the Sahara and Arabian deserts and the American glass snake (right) are both snakelike lizards.

The little gecko has hairlike hooks on pads on each of its toes by which it can climb smooth surfaces or walk upside down.

The collared swift of Mexico has coarsely overlapping, spine-tipped scales and a broad, scaly collar.

parachute as it glides through the air. The underside is brightly colored and so helps conceal the animal as it lies among the colorful blossoms in the jungle treetops (protective coloration).

The frilled lizard of Australia runs swiftly for great distances on its hind legs. The "frill" is a broad collar of loose skin around the neck. It spreads out like an umbrella when the animal is frightened or angry. The hooded basilisk of Central America, named after the fabled monster that was supposed to strike men dead with its glance, is a good example of such "frightfulness." It is about three feet long and has jagged crests which it can raise at will on its head, back, and tail. It is quite harmless.

Not all lizards depend on frightfulness or flight to defend themselves. Some are fierce fighters and biters. This is particularly true of the monitor family, whose members are scattered through Africa, Arabia, southern Asia, and Australia. The largest lizard of all is the dragon lizard of Komodo (in the East Indies), which reaches a length of 12 feet and may weigh 250 pounds. It has a long whiplike tail with which it lashes its assailants when it is unable to reach them with its sharp teeth. It is one of the few lizards that feed on small mammals.

### Lizards as Pets

Lizards make attractive pets. They should be kept in a terrarium with dry soil, sand, or moss on the bottom. (For instructions on how to make a desert terrarium, *see* Nature Study.) Lizards need direct sunlight for a part of the day, but they must have a place to seek shade if they become too warm. A hiding place, made of plants, stones, or bits of wood, should be provided in a corner.

Most lizards should be fed insects. Mealworms and roaches, flies, crickets, and grasshoppers are relished. Some will learn to eat raw ground beef and eggs. As a rule they will not drink from a pan. Water for them must be sprinkled on leaves, stones, and other objects. Since their habits vary, it is wise to study the exact species that is to be caged.

### Scientific Classification

Lizards belong to the suborder *Lacertilia*. It is divided into many different families: *Gekkonidae*, the geckos; *Agamidae*, frilled lizard and flying dragon; *Iguanidae*, iguanas, anolis or American chameleon, basilisk, chuckwalla, collared lizard, swift, horned toad; *Anguidae*, glass snake; *Helodermatidae*, Gila monster and horrid heloderm; *Varanidae*, monitor lizard; *Teiidae*, race runner; *Amphisbaenidae*, worm lizard, or blind snake; *Lacertidae*, European common lizard; *Scincidae*, skink; and *Chamaeleontidae*, African chameleon.

THESE ARTICLES ARE IN THE FACT-INDEX

Lizard, The
Ljubljana, Yugoslavia
Ljusne River

**LLAMA** (läm'ä). The Americas have no camels, but South America has a close relative in the llama of the Andes. Unlike the camel, the llama has no hump, and a grown llama is only about three feet high at the shoulder. However, it has the camel's peculiar bone structure and teeth, the same kind of cloven, padded hooves, and a water-storing stomach.

When the Spaniards conquered Peru in the 16th century, they found the Incas using llamas as beasts of burden. Earlier Indians had domesticated them from the guanaco, an animal which still lives wild in remote parts of the Andes. In all the New World llamas and dogs were the only domesticated animals.

The Spanish conquerors continued to use llamas with Indian drivers, particularly to carry silver over the narrow mountain trails from the mines to the coast. Until the middle of the 19th century, no other means of transportation was developed in the rugged, mountainous regions of the South American continent.

Llamas can carry 120 pounds at the rate of 12 miles a day. They can stand the cold of high altitudes and can travel over places too rough and steep for any other burden-bearing animal. When disturbed, they spit a ball of food and saliva at their tormentor.

Llama wool is not valuable, as is the wool of its near relatives the alpaca and vicuña. Coarse and rough, llama wool is usually brown, with shades or speckles of yellow and black. Occasionally a llama will be pure white or pure black. The male llama is chiefly valued as a beast of burden. The females are useful for their milk and meat, which resembles mutton. They bear single young once a year. The scientific name of the llama is *Lama peruana*.

THESE ARTICLES ARE IN THE FACT-INDEX

Llano Estacado
Llanquihue, Lake
Llewellyn, Richard
Lloyd, Harold (Clayton)

Lloyd, (John) Selwyn (Brooke)
Lloyd Barrage

**LLOYD GEORGE, David** (1863–1945). At the age of 17, a small slender Welshman visited the British House of Commons. Afterward he recorded in his diary his hope for a political career. The young Welshman was David Lloyd George. In time he became the prime minister who guided Britain to victory over Germany in World War I.

James Press

Lloyd George was born on Jan. 17, 1863, in Manchester, England, where his Welsh father, William George, had gone to teach school. Soon after David's birth the family returned to Wales. His father died two years later. David was educated by his uncle, Richard Lloyd, the village cobbler. In his honor the boy took the name Lloyd.

At the age of 14 he began to study law and at 21 was admitted to practice as a solicitor. In 1890 he was elected to Parliament as a Liberal from the Welsh district of Carnarvon. "The great little Welshman" held his seat in the Commons for more than 50 years. At no time could public opinion turn him from what he thought was just. He denounced the British campaign in the Boer War (1899) as an act of aggression against a struggling young republic. Crowds in Birmingham mobbed him.

In 1905 he accepted a minor office in the Cabinet as head of the Board of Trade. There he put through a shipping act to aid seamen and settled a critical railway strike. Conciliation combined with aggressiveness marked the rest of his political life.

He advanced to the second highest Cabinet post in 1908 when he became chancellor of the exchequer, with Herbert Asquith as prime minister. As man-

Philip D. Gendreau

The llama of the Andes is a small relative of the camel. Like its Old World cousin, it has a mean and ugly disposition, but it is the best beast of burden for its homeland.

ager of British finances, Lloyd George determined to ease the tax burden on the poor. He also planned an Old Age Pension Act. To provide funds for it, he drew up a national budget that put new taxes on the wealthy. These taxes threatened to break up the old landed estates.

The conservative House of Lords rejected Lloyd George's budget. But a general election showed that the mass of British people favored it. So strong was public support that in 1911 an act of Parliament abolished the power of the House of Lords to reject a money bill such as the budget. Lloyd George at once launched a more extended program of social reform. Laws were passed to give workers cheap insurance against sickness and unemployment, free medical service, and maternity benefits.

When World War I broke out in 1914, many people expected him to resign, as he had long been regarded as a pacifist. The moment Germany invaded Belgium, however, he denounced the aggression. He was put in charge of the new Ministry of Munitions in 1915. In 1916 he became head of the war office.

The Liberal party at this time was divided. In December 1916 Lloyd George forced Asquith's resignation and became prime minister, heading a coalition government. Before going to the peace conference at Versailles, France, he strengthened his position by winning the "khaki election" of November 1918. At the peace conference he seemed uncertain. Sometimes he sided with France's efforts to destroy Germany. At other times he sided with the United States efforts for a peace based on reconciliation and the rights of nations and people.

After 1919 Lloyd George's leadership weakened, largely as a result of a slump in business that brought on strikes and unemployment. In 1922 the Conservatives withdrew from the coalition and Lloyd George at once resigned. He remained in the Commons for the rest of his life, but the influence of the divided Liberal party grew weaker and weaker. His last great effort to return to office came in the general election of 1929, when he made glittering promises to "conquer unemployment." Unimpressed, the voters returned the rising Labor party instead. Lloyd George's later years were given to the writing of his 'War Memoirs'. In 1944 he was made first Earl Lloyd George of Dwyfor. He died just as World War II was coming to an end. (*See also* English History.)

THESE ARTICLES ARE IN THE FACT-INDEX

Lloydminster, Alta.
Lobachevski, Nikolai
  Ivanovich
Lobbying

Lobelia
Lobengula
Lobito, Angola

**LOBSTER.** At the bottom of shallow waters along many seacoasts, lobsters may be found. Big cousins of the common crayfishes, they are distantly related to shrimps and crabs. Like all crustaceans, they have tough shells and breathe through gills.

The American lobster (*Homarus americanus*) lives along the Atlantic coast from North Carolina to Labrador. In warm weather it stays near shore in water from 60 to 100 feet deep. With the approach of cold weather it moves out to depths of more than 200 ft.

Most lobsters caught by fishermen weigh less than two pounds, but giant specimens are sometimes taken. Lobsters are blue-green in color, spotted with green-black. The pincers are marked with orange. These colors come from pigments in the blood and in the thin skin. The shell is colorless. Made of the same substance (chitin) as the outer covering of insects, it is stiffened with calcium salts.

The shell covers the lobster's body and limbs. It is jointed in many places to allow freedom of movement. A single expanse called the *carapace* covers the head and thorax. Six overlapping rings enclose the abdomen. To the sixth ring is joined a fan-shaped tailpiece which serves as both rudder and oar. The lobster can move forward, but its fastest motion is in reverse. A single flip of its tail may drive it 25 feet backward.

The lobster's head bears a pair of large compound eyes, set on freely moving stalks, and two pairs of antennae. On the underside of the head lies the mouth. Food is chewed by toothed appendages set around the opening.

From the thorax extend five pairs of legs. Each of the first pair has a pincerlike claw. One of these—either right or left—grows larger than the other. It is called the club claw and is used for crushing. The

**HOW THE LOBSTER EATS**
The antennae help locate food. The smaller (quick) claw seizes and cuts food. The heavier (club) claw is used for crushing.

smaller claw (quick claw), set with sharp teeth, is used for seizing and tearing prey. The lobster's other legs are used for walking. From the abdomen dangle five pairs of fringed paddles, the swimmerets.

**Why the Lobster Thrives in the Deep**

The lobster is well equipped for life in the ocean. It has 20 pairs of gills to extract from water the oxygen it needs. Antennae, body, and limbs are covered with thousands of sensory hairs that inform the lobster of food and enemies which its eyes fail to detect. Some of these hairs combine the senses of taste and smell.

By day the lobster lurks in its burrow in the bottom of the sea. At night it goes hunting. It whips the water with its small antennae and with its large ones probes every crevice. Suddenly the small claw seizes a fish, snail, sea urchin, or starfish. When the keen antennae detect a clam buried deep in the sand, the large claw digs it out and crushes its shell. Then the small claw passes bits of the flesh along to the mouth.

Soon the lobster grows too big for its shell and must get rid of it. The shell splits across the back, and the lobster draws itself out of it, shedding not only the shell and its hairs, but also the lining of the mouth, throat, and forestomach. For three weeks after molting, until its skin hardens into a new shell, the lobster is weak and helpless. It may then be eaten by one of its many enemies, especially the codfish, skate, and dogfish. Adult males often have two new suits a year; the females, only one. If a lobster happens to break off a limb, the bud of a new one begins to form at once.

### How Lobsters Multiply

Lobsters spawn in spring or summer (June in the South, September in the North). The female produces from 3,000 to more than 70,000 eggs, according to its size and age, and secretes a glue which fastens them to its swimmerets. Called a "berry lobster" in this state, the female carries the eggs for 10 to 11 months, flexing its tail to enclose them in a kind of pocket when eels or other hungry enemies draw near. During the hatching period of about seven nights, switches of the tail disperse the young (larvae) in clouds as they emerge from the eggs. Not until spring or summer of the following year will the female spawn again.

The new larvae are only one third of an inch long, with big green eyes. They lack swimmerets, and paddle along the surface with hair-fringed legs, snapping up drifting food particles. Many are eaten by herring, menhaden, and other fishes. The larvae molt three times in their first 15 to 18 days. By this time they are half an inch long and resemble small adults. When they are a year old, they are two to three inches long and have molted 14 to 17 times. They mature when they are three to five years old.

### Catching Lobsters for the Market

American lobsters seldom grow old, for they have been a favorite food ever since the Pilgrims first tasted them. To capture them, a slatted box called a "lobster pot" is baited with fish, weighted with a flat stone, and sunk to the bottom on a quarter-inch line. On the other end of the line is a buoy which carries the lobsterman's private mark, name, and license number. At one end of the lobster pot is a funnel-shaped opening made of coarse netting. The funnel points invitingly inward, and the lobster finds it easy to enter the pot. However, it is not bright enough to find its way out. In good weather,

**HOW LOBSTERS ARE TRAPPED**
The man is taking a lobster from the trap, or "lobster pot," in which it was caught at the bottom of the sea. The lobster entered through a funnel of netting to get the bait inside.

the lobsterman visits his pots once a day to remove the lobsters and replenish the bait.

The chief lobster fisheries of the United States lie along the coast of Maine. From Maine north to Gaspé, Québec, extend the principal lobster fisheries of Canada, which are the greatest in the world. To keep the lobsters from being exterminated, spawning females are protected, and lobsters below a minimum size may not be taken. In Maine there is also a maximum-size limit to protect large spawners. The United States catch is marketed fresh. In Canada a portion of the catch is canned. The claws furnish the tenderest meat. When the lobster is cooked, its shell turns a brilliant red.

The lobster belongs to the family *Homaridae* of the crustaceans. The family includes the European lob-

**A CARGO OF EGGS**
For 10 to 11 months the female lobster carries its eggs glued to the swimmerets beneath its abdomen.

ster (*Homarus gammarus*) and the small Norway lobster (*Nephrops norvegicus*). Both species inhabit Europe's coastal waters from Norway to the Mediterranean.

In the warmer seas of the world live the *spiny lobsters* (family *Palinuridae*). They lack the large pincers of the true lobsters. Many species compare with the American lobster in size and flavor. Among these are the sea crawfish (*Palinurus*, or *Panulirus*, *argus*), along the Atlantic coast from North Carolina to Florida. The California spiny lobster (*P. interruptus*) is found along the Pacific coast from Point Conception, Calif., to Mexico.

THESE ARTICLES ARE IN THE FACT-INDEX

| | |
|---|---|
| Lobworm | Lochinvar |
| Locarno, Switzerland | Lochner, Stephan |

**LOCKE, Alain LeRoy** (1886-1954). As a writer and teacher, Alain Locke was one of the first to tell Americans how much his fellow Negroes have contributed to music, art, and literature. He has been equally influential in encouraging other Negroes to add their accomplishments to the record.

Locke was born in Philadelphia, Pa. Both his parents were schoolteachers. They wanted their son to enter one of the professions, perhaps medicine, as a means of rising above some of the restrictions placed upon his race. But sickness made a career as a doctor impossible, and the parents helped young Locke to prepare himself as a teacher.

After graduating from the Philadelphia School of Pedagogy in 1904, he entered Harvard University. There he studied under such great teachers as Barrett Wendell and Charles T. Copeland. His major study, philosophy, also brought him under the influence of Josiah Royce, William James, and George Santayana.

Locke won a Rhodes scholarship after graduation from Harvard in 1907. He studied in England at Oxford University for the next three years. After another year, at the University of Berlin, he returned home in 1912. He began teaching at Howard University in Washington, D. C.

His books stressed Negro culture, but he always tried to show how this fitted into the whole of American life. His first book was 'The New Negro' (1925). He acted either as author or editor for a number of others. Among these were 'The Negro in America' (1933), 'The Negro and His Music' (1936), and 'The Negro in Art' (1941). With Bernhard J. Stern he edited 'When Peoples Meet: a Study in Race and Culture Contacts' (1942).

**LOCKE, John** (1632-1704). One of the pioneers in modern thinking was the English philosopher John Locke. He made great contributions in studies of politics, government, and psychology.

John Locke was the son of another John Locke, a well-to-do Puritan lawyer who fought for Cromwell in the English Civil War. The father was a devout,

even-tempered man, and the boy was devoted to him. There is a story that the elder Locke once struck young John in anger, and the act weighed on him for many years. Long afterward, when John had grown to manhood, his father reminded him of the incident and asked his forgiveness.

The boy was educated at Westminster School and Oxford, and later became a tutor at the university. His friends urged him to enter the Church of England, but he decided that he was not fitted for the calling. He had long been interested in meteorology and the experimental sciences, especially chemistry. He turned to medicine and by adopting new methods of treatment he became one of the most skilled practitioners of his day.

**JOHN LOCKE**
Locke's ideas are reflected in the Declaration of Independence.

In 1667 Locke became confidential secretary and personal physician to Anthony Ashley Cooper, later lord chancellor and first earl of Shaftesbury. Locke's association with Shaftesbury enabled him to meet many of the great men of England, but it also caused him a great deal of trouble. Shaftesbury was indicted for high treason. He was acquitted, but Locke was suspected of disloyalty. In 1683 he left England for Holland and returned only after the revolution of 1688.

### Ideas About Government, Psychology

Locke is remembered today largely as a political philosopher. He preached the doctrine that men naturally possess certain large rights, the chief being life, liberty, and property. Rulers, he said, derived their power only from the consent of the people. He thought that government should be like a contract between the rulers and his subjects. The people give up certain of their rights in return for just rule. And the ruler should hold his power only so long as he uses it justly. These ideas had a tremendous effect on all future political thinking. The American Declaration of Independence clearly reflects Locke's teachings.

Locke was always much interested in psychology. About 1670, friends urged him to write a paper on the limitations of human judgment. He started to write a few paragraphs, but 20 years passed before he finished. The result was his great and famous 'Essay Concerning Human Understanding'. In this work he stressed the theory that the human mind starts as a *tabula rasa* (smoothed tablet)—that is, a waxed tablet ready to be used for writing. The mind has no inborn ideas, as most men of the time believed. Throughout life it forms its ideas only from impressions (sense experiences) which are made upon its surface. Because he stressed the role of experience, Locke is called the "father of English empiricism."

In discussing education Locke urged the view that character formation is far more important than information and that learning should be pleasant. In later years he turned more and more to writing about religion. He favored simplicity and considered primitive Christianity as the best of all forms of religion. It may seem strange in modern times that Locke favored outlawing atheists and Roman Catholics in England. In his day, however, England was engaged in one of its bitterest religious controversies. For the times he lived in Locke was tolerant in matters of religion.

Locke's principal works are letters—'On Toleration' (1689, 1690, 1692); 'An Essay Concerning Human Understanding' (1690); two treatises—'On Civil Government' (1690), 'Some Thoughts Concerning Education' (1693); and 'The Reasonableness of Christianity' (1695).

THESE ARTICLES ARE IN THE FACT-INDEX

Locke, William John
Lockhart, John Gibson
Lock Haven, Pa.

Lock Haven State College
Lockport, N. Y.

**LOCKS AND KEYS.** Locks are special kinds of fastening devices. They are used on doors, drawers, and trunks and in homes, jails, automobiles, and many other places. They help prevent unauthorized entry, exit, or operation of equipment and machinery. A lock may be opened by a key which is shaped to fit it.

Two types of locks are used today—*warded* locks and *tumbler* locks. Warded locks are simple and inexpensive but are easily opened by means of master, or "skeleton", keys. Warded locks are ordinarily used in desk drawers, closet doors, and other places where great security is unnecessary.

A warded lock has a number of projections, called *wards*, inside its case. The key for a warded lock resembles a flag on a pole. The "flag" part is notched to permit the key to turn past the wards when it is pivoted on its "pole" part. Turning the key slides the bolt which secures the door.

Tumbler locks are used where greater precautions are needed. Tumbler locks employ a number of small levers, or pins. Each of these *tumblers* must be raised to a predetermined height before a key can turn to work the bolt. The tumblers are raised to operating position by notches on the edge of the key. The earliest of modern tumbler locks was developed by an Englishman, Robert Barron, about 1778. In 1784 another Englishman, Joseph Bramah, devised an improved version. The Bramah lock was widely used.

An American, Linus Yale, Jr., invented the pin-tumbler cylinder lock in 1860. This is the Yale lock that guards the doors of many homes today. The Yale lock consists of an outer case, the *shell*, and an inner cylinder, or plug. The cylinder revolves to slide the bolt when the key is twisted in the lock. The shell and the cylinder are bored with matching tunnels, which contain spring-loaded tumbler pins. Each pin is in two pieces. The inner cylinder can

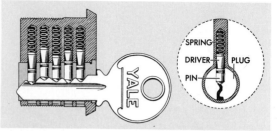

**WRONG KEY**
With the wrong key, some tumblers project into the cylinder, or plug, of a pin-tumbler lock. The plug will not turn.

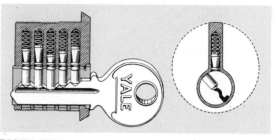

**RIGHT KEY**
When the right key is used, the tops of the tumbler pins line up with the top of the plug, and the latter will turn.

be twisted only when the tops of all the pins line up with the outside of the cylinder. If the pins are too high or too low, the cylinder will not turn.

*Combination*, or dial, locks are operated by a pattern of movements of a knob or handle over predetermined sets of numbers. These locks are used where extreme precautions are needed. Since they have no keyholes, the lock mechanisms are inaccessible.

*Time* locks are equipped with clockwork devices. These make it impossible to open the lock except during the particular hours for which the timepiece is set.

### Locks in History

The use of locks for protection and privacy is not new. There is evidence that the ancient Egyptians used intricate locks 4,000 years ago. The first lock for a hinged door was probably a wooden bar placed in L-shaped cleats. A locking bar can easily be made to pivot or to slide in its cleats. A sliding locking bar is called a *bolt*.

The ancient Greeks developed several refinements of the basic bar-and-bolt locks. These permitted a door to be unbarred from the outside as well as from the inside. One improvement consisted of a rope attached to a pivoted bar and passed through a hole in the door. A tug on the rope lifted the bar from its cleats. Another refinement was the use of a shaped hook (the "key") which was passed through a hole (the "keyhole") to lift or slide the bar.

THESE ARTICLES ARE IN THE FACT-INDEX

Lockwood, Belva Ann Bennett
Lockyer, Sir (Joseph) Norman
Loco-foco

The Four Power Units of This Sleek Diesel-Electric Locomotive Can Generate 6,000 Horsepower

# LOCOMOTIVE—A Power Plant on Wheels

**LOCOMOTIVE.** At the head of every railroad train is a power plant on wheels. Many a locomotive actually develops enough power to supply a small city. Most of the time, however, the "iron horse" does not use its full power. When a train is rolling along on level track, only a few pounds of tractive effort (pulling power) will keep one ton of the train's weight in motion. Full power is needed principally for starting a long train or for pulling up a steep grade.

Three major types of locomotives are in general use today. They are the *reciprocating steam locomotive*, the *diesel-electric*, and the *electric locomotive*.

### The Steam-Powered Locomotives

The old reciprocating steam locomotive is a steam engine that moves itself (*see* Steam Engine). Steam from the boiler is fed to the cylinders to move pistons in a back-and-forth (reciprocating) motion. Connecting rods from the pistons move the driving wheels.

The firebox at the rear of the boiler is fed with coal or oil. Exhaust steam from the cylinders is directed up the smokestack to create a heavy draft for the boiler fire. This accounts for a locomotive's puffing. The pistons and connecting rods supply power to the wheels on one side a quarter turn ahead of the wheels on the other side. Thus the locomotive is never caught "on dead center"—that is, with all connecting rods straight forward or back and unable to turn the wheels.

Some reciprocating steam locomotives weigh 500 tons or more and develop more than 6,000 horsepower. They can pull a freight train a mile long or pull a passenger train at about a hundred miles an hour. For extremely heavy loads or steep grades, two or more locomotives may be coupled to a train.

### Other Types of Locomotives

Diesel-electric locomotives are comparable to the reciprocating type in size, power, and speed. In them, oil-burning diesel engines generate current for the electric motors which drive the wheels. After World War II the diesel-electric locomotive began replacing the reciprocating steam types on most American railroads (*see* Diesel Engine). Variations of this type

326

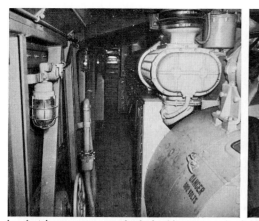

An electric generator on wheels is this power unit of a large diesel-electric locomotive. It can produce 2,000 horsepower.

The engineer (right) and fireman (left) of this fast-moving diesel-electric locomotive see the once-formidable Rockies ahead.

include the *gas turbine* electric locomotives which burn natural gas, oil, or powdered coal. In these types a blast of hot gas drives a turbine which operates the electric generators. (*See also* Electricity; Internal Combustion Engine; Turbine.)

These types of locomotives are all *self-contained;* that is, they carry their power source with them, like a ship at sea. The *electric locomotive*, however, gets its power from the outside, through an overhead wire or third rail. A few main lines use this type of locomotive; but most of them are used in suburban service and in handling through trains near terminals. Another type of electric locomotive, powered by storage batteries, is frequently used in mines.

### History of the Locomotive

Like all great inventions, the locomotive grew through the slow accumulation of improvements made by different inventors. Men in England worked on the idea as early as the 1700's. Most of their devices were designed to run on ordinary highways, and so were forerunners of the automobile (*see* Automobile History). In 1804 Richard Trevithick ran one of his road engines on rails at Pen-y-darran, in Wales, at five miles an hour. William Hedley improved on this in 1813 with his *Puffing Billy*, so called because it used exhaust steam in the smokestack, as many locomotives do today. This was the first engine to use smooth wheels on smooth track.

George Stephenson built a workable locomotive for the Killingworth colliery in 1815. In 1825 his locomotives ran at the rate of 16 miles an hour on the newly opened Stockton and Darlington Railway. In 1829 Stephenson and his son Robert devised a multitubular boiler for the locomotive *Rocket*. This boiler gave power enough to maintain a speed of 25 to 30 miles an hour, and the *Rocket* won a speed, pulling, and endurance contest held by the Liverpool and Manchester Railway. This event is considered the birth of the modern railroad.

The first American-built locomotive was the *Tom Thumb*, constructed by Peter Cooper. In 1830 this locomotive lost a famous race with a horse-drawn

### "WORKING ON THE RAILROAD"

The engineer in this diesel switcher talks to the traffic control tower by means of a two-way radio in his cab.

An electric freight locomotive uses a rectifier to convert the alternating current of the overhead line to direct current.

An 8,500-horsepower gas turbine pulls this freight train. The turbine generates its own electric power.

By courtesy of the Union Pacific Railroad (bottom photo only)

One of the basic types of steam locomotives is this *American*, which has a four-wheel leading truck and two pairs of driving wheels. This arrangement is called 4–4–0 (the "0" meaning no trailing axle). It was the ancestor of many later types.

For freight service the four-wheel leading truck was replaced by a two-wheel axle and another pair of driving wheels was added. This made the *Mogul* a 2–6–0 type. The locomotive above is the *Show-wa-no*, first placed in service in 1871.

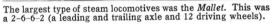

The largest type of steam locomotives was the *Mallet*. This was a 2–6–6–2 (a leading and trailing axle and 12 driving wheels).

An early electric locomotive was this 0–4–4–0. Electric locomotives may also be classified by idle and driving axles.

This 4–8–4 steam locomotive is the *Northern, Niagara,* or *Pocono* type. The identification of steam locomotives by counting the wheels in a truck is known as the Whyte system, which may also be illustrated symbolically as oo0000oo for the 4–8–4.

## FIVE PIONEERS AMONG THE STEAM LOCOMOTIVES

The first locomotive in the world to do actual work was this one built by Richard Trevithick in 1804. It pulled a short train of cars uphill on a coal-mine railway in Wales.

The British *Rocket*, built by George and Robert Stephenson, demonstrated the first really successful use of steam power in the famous locomotive trials at Rainhill, England, in 1829.

The first steam locomotive to operate in America was this British-built *Stourbridge Lion*. It made a trial run in Pennsylvania, but proved to be too heavy for the tracks.

Peter Cooper's *Tom Thumb* was the first American-built locomotive to operate in the United States. Weighing only one ton, it lost a famous race with a horse-drawn car on Aug. 28, 1830.

car on the newly laid tracks of the Baltimore and Ohio Railroad. American-built locomotives that were placed in operation in 1830-31 were the *Best Friend of Charleston*, *West Point*, *York*, and *DeWitt Clinton*. (*See also* Railroads.)

### LOCOMOTIVE WHISTLE AND HORN SIGNALS

o indicates short sounds, — longer sounds.

| | |
|---|---|
| o . . . . . . . . . | Apply brakes. Stop. |
| oo . . . . . . . . | Engineer's answer to signal. |
| ooo . . . . . . . | When standing, back. |
| ooo . . . . . . . | When running, stop at next station. |
| oooo . . . . . . | Call for signals. |
| oooooooooo . . | Alarm for persons or livestock on track. |
| ——————— | Approaching station or junction at grade. |
| —oo . . . . . . . | A second section is following. |
| —ooo . . . . | Flagman protect rear of train. |
| — — . . . . . . . | Release brakes. Proceed. |
| — — o — — | Approaching public crossings at grade. |

The American-built *Best Friend of Charleston*, operating on the South Carolina Railroad, opened regular service in 1831.

329

# LOCUST

THIS ARTICLE IS IN THE FACT-INDEX
**Locris**

**LOCUST.** The name locust is popularly given to two different kinds of insects—the short-horned grasshopper and the cicada. Both kinds do great damage to trees and crops when they swarm in huge numbers.

The locusts mentioned in the Bible are short-horned grasshoppers. They belong to the family *Locustidae* (*Acrididae*). There is at least one species of these insects on each of the major continents of the earth. Vast numbers of them, flying in swarms, appear periodically in countries in the Far East and in the Western United States. A column of flying locusts seen in India was estimated to be several hundred miles long. The column was so dense that it blocked out the light of the sun. (*See also* Grasshopper.)

The "17-year locust" is a cicada. It belongs to the family *Cicadidae*, which has many species. The cicada was called a "locust" by early settlers of the United States, because the destruction caused by the swarming females resembled that caused during the locust plagues noted in the Bible. (*See also* Cicada.)

**THE CICADA, WRONGLY CALLED A "LOCUST"**
Female 17-year cicadas were mistakenly thought by early American settlers to be locusts. They do great damage to plant life.

**LOCUST TREE.** The hardy locust tree thrives in most northern temperate regions. It is native, however, only to North America. The creamy white, purple, or reddish flowers of locust trees scent the air with a fragrant odor when they bloom in the spring. The lovely flowers grow in plumelike clusters, called *racemes* (*see* Flower). In September, long, hairy pods containing from four to six seeds grow from the flower stalks. The pods remain on the trees through the winter.

A number of *species* make up the group of true locusts. There are other trees called "locusts" which, although related, are not true locusts. All locust trees, true or otherwise, belong to the pea family of plants—*Leguminosae*.

**THE BLACK LOCUST TREE
WITH ITS LEAVES AND PODS**
This branch of the black locust (left) shows the leaves and sweet-pulped pods. The tree itself (right) is among the most beautiful to be found in parks and forests.

The *black locust*, or *yellow locust*, grows from Pennsylvania southward to Georgia and westward. Often planted as an ornamental tree, the black locust grows up to 80 feet high. It has fragrant white flowers. The black locust is thought to be the only American tree that has become widely naturalized in Europe. The *clammy locust*, so called because of its sticky, clammy buds and branchlets, thrives in the Southern United States. It bears showy pink flowers. The *rose locust*, or *moss locust*, is a shrub. Its rose-colored flowers are especially large.

Several trees commonly called "locust" belong to a different *genus* than these true locusts. One, the *honey locust*, common from New York State southward and westward, is distinguished by a mass of feathery leaves and unusually long, flat pods. Its greenish-white flowers are less showy than those of the true locusts. The *carob*, or *Saint-John's-bread*, flourishes in the area of the Mediterranean Sea.

The scientific name of the black locust is *Robinia pseudoacacia;* of the clammy locust, *R. vicosa;* and of the rose locust, *R. hispida*. Honey locusts belong to the genus *Gleditsia*. The scientific name of the carob is *Ceratonia siliqua*.

THESE ARTICLES ARE IN THE FACT-INDEX

Lodge, Henry Cabot
Lodge, Henry Cabot, Jr.
Lodge, Sir Oliver Joseph
Lodge, Thomas
Lodgepole pine
Lodi, Calif.
Lodi, Italy
Lodi, N. J.
Lodz, Poland
Loeb, Jacques
Loeffler, Charles Martin

Loening, Grover
Loesser, Frank
Loewe, Johann Karl
　Gottfried
Loewi, Otto
Loewy, Raymond Fernand
Löffler, Friedrich August
　Johannes
Lofoten Islands
Lofting, Hugh

## LOG, SHIP'S.

**LOG, SHIP'S.** The devices employed through the years to calculate the speed of a ship through the water have been called logs. In the years when sails powered ships, the *Dutchman's log* was the first method of calculating ship speed. An object that would float was thrown into the water near the forward (front) part of a ship. In the after (rear) section, a sailor with a sandglass noted the time taken for the ship to pass the object floating in the water. From the time and the known distance between the two points on the ship, a rough calculation could be made of the ship's speed.

### Chip Log and Patent Log

Subsequently, the *chip log* (ship log, or common log) came into use. The "chip" was a flat quarter-circle of wood, perhaps five inches in radius, with a lead weight on the rounded edge. To it was tied a *log line* about 150 fathoms (900 feet) long. Knots were tied in the line at $47\frac{1}{4}$-foot intervals. One sailor cast the chip log into the water; another paid out the log line from a reel. A third noted the number of knots paid out in the 28-second interval shown by a special sandglass called the *log glass.* The term *knot,* meaning "one nautical mile per hour," comes from the knots in the log line.

By the end of the 18th century the *taffrail log,* or *patent log,* had been invented. A finned *rotator,* attached by a special line to a meter, was towed behind the ship. The rotator spun in the water at a rate proportional to the ship's speed, twisting the line and thus turning gears in the meter. The meter registered the distance covered by the ship. Its speed could be calculated by dividing the time traveled into the distance.

### Modern Methods of Measuring Ship Speed

Today the counting of propeller revolutions is a widely used method of determining speed. During its early trials a new ship is tested over a measured mile. The number of propeller revolutions needed to drive it a mile is determined, as are the revolutions per minute required for various speeds. In service, the speed indicated by the revolution counter is corrected for such factors as the draft and trim of the vessel, the state of the sea, and the condition of the ship's bottom.

Most large ships use a *Pitot-static log* to measure speed. Such a log is actuated by the difference between static and dynamic water pressures. *Static* pressure is due solely to the depth and density of water; *dynamic* pressure is proportional to speed.

The Pitot apparatus consists of an inner tube with a hole at its forward end and an outer tube with holes along its sides. The holes in the outer tube are exposed only to static pressure. The hole at the forward end of the Pitot tube is subject only to static pressure when the ship is motionless, but it receives the sum of static and dynamic pressures when the ship is moving. This pressure is called the *Pitot,* or *total,* pressure.

**MEASURING SPEED WITH A CHIP LOG**
The top picture shows how the men on sailing vessels used the chip log (bottom) to measure their ship's speed.

Pitot pressure and static pressure are transmitted to separate bellows in the ship. Responding to the different pressures, the bellows actuate an electric pump which equalizes the pressures upon them. The greater the ship's speed, the greater the difference between pressures, and the harder the pump must work to equalize them. Thus the speed of the pump is proportional to the speed of the ship.

The speed of the pump shaft is electrically transmitted to a timing device and then to one or more indicators which register speed and distance traveled. Airplane airspeed indicators also operate on the Pitot-static principle.

Generally, logs only indicate speed through the water, which must be corrected for tide and current to obtain the distance traveled.

### Logbooks

Written accounts of ship voyages are kept in *logbooks,* or *logs.* Entries commonly include such navigational data as the ship's course, speed, and distance traveled, as well as weather information. Carefully prepared logbooks may be sources for data used in preparing navigational charts. Dramatic stories of casualties and emergency operations are sometimes found written in the sober language of the logbook.

THESE ARTICLES ARE IN THE FACT-INDEX

| | |
|---|---|
| Logan, George | Logan, Rayford |
| Logan, James | W(hittingham) |
| Logan, John | Logan, Stephen Trigg |
| Logan, John Alexander | Logan, Sir William Edmond |
| Logan, Joshua | Logan, Utah |

**LOGANBERRY.** The loganberry is among the finest of the table berries grown in the United States. It is a comparatively recent product, but its origin is uncertain. The berry first appeared in 1881 at Santa Cruz, Calif., in the garden of Judge J. H. Logan. Also called the Logan and the Logan blackberry, it is believed to be a hybrid between a wild

**THE LOGANBERRY PLANT**
An average acre of loganberry plants yields about 2,000 quarts of the berries during a ten-year period.

blackberry of the Pacific coast and a red raspberry.

The fruit of the loganberry is purplish red and quite large. Its flavor is between that of a wild blackberry and a raspberry. The berry is used as a dessert fruit and is extensively canned or dried. The juice is also a popular beverage.

The loganberry is extensively cultivated on the Pacific coast from southern California to British Columbia. When it is protected in the winter it can also be grown in other parts of the United States.

Loganberries thrive in well-drained loamy soil. The plants have trailing *canes* (stems) that may grow more than 20 feet in length. New loganberry plants form when the tips of the canes send roots into the ground.

The loganberry plant is a biennial—the canes grow one year, bear fruit the second year, and then die. Planting is done in the early spring. Wire trellises are usually strung along the rows to support the berries. (*See also* Berry.)

THESE ARTICLES ARE IN THE FACT-INDEX
**Logania family**
**Logansport, Ind.**

**LOGARITHMS.** Lengthy multiplication and division problems can be solved through simple addition and subtraction by using logarithms. To further illustrate the simplicity of this mathematical system, the square root of a number can be found by dividing its logarithm by two. Logarithms, especially as applied in the slide rule, are one of the greatest mathematical aids ever invented.

### What Logarithms Are

A logarithm is an *exponent* applied to a number, commonly 10 (*see* Algebra). Thus the logarithm 2 stands for $10^2$, or 100; the logarithm 3 stands for $10^3$, or 1,000; and so on. To multiply 100 by 1,000, it is necessary only to add the logarithms 2 and 3. The sum of this addition, 5, is the logarithm of 100,000, or $10^5$—the desired answer. To divide 100,000 by 1,000, the logarithm 3 ($10^3$, or 1,000) is subtracted from the logarithm 5 ($10^5$, or 100,000). The remainder, 2, is the logarithm of 100, which is the answer to the problem.

Most numbers, of course, do not happen to be even powers of 10. However, logarithms can be written for them by using decimal fractions. For example, the logarithm of 1,074 must be slightly greater than 3 because 1,074 is greater than 1,000. Calculations show the logarithm to be 3.0311; that is, $10^{3.0311}$ equals 1,074.

### Using Logarithmic Tables

Logarithms for the entire series of numbers have been calculated and printed in tables for easy reference. In these tables only the fractional part of the logarithm, called the *mantissa*, is printed. The user supplies the whole part, called the *characteristic*. For example, since the logarithm of 100 is 2 and the logarithm of 1,000 is 3, the user reasons that all numbers between 100 and 1,000 will have the characteristic 2. The logarithm of 1,074 was already shown to be 3.0311. This logarithm's mantissa is .0311; its characteristic is 3. Logarithms of numbers less than 1 have negative characteristics.

To raise a number to a power, its logarithm is multiplied by the desired power. To cube 1,074, for example, the logarithm is multiplied by 3. Thus, 3 times 3.0311 equals 9.0933. The table on the next page shows that the mantissa (.0933) corresponds to the number 1.239. Because of the characteristic 9, the number must be written with 10 places to the left of the decimal point—1,239,000,000. Computation shows this to be very close to the full answer— 1,238,833,224. To find the square root of 1,074, simply divide its logarithm by 2, then find the corresponding mantissa and number. To find the cube root of a number, divide its logarithm by 3. For further examples of the use of logarithms, *see* the instructions below the table on the next page.

A logarithmic system was invented by John Napier in 1614. By 1624, however, Henry Briggs had devised the standard system described in this article. (*See also* Slide Rule.)

# TABLE OF LOGARITHMS

| N | 0 | 1 | 2 | 3 | 4 | 5 | 6 | 7 | 8 | 9 | D |
|---|---|---|---|---|---|---|---|---|---|---|---|
| 1.0 | 0000 | 0043 | 0086 | 0128 | 0170 | 0212 | 0253 | 0294 | 0334 | 0374 | 42 |
| 1.1 | 0414 | 0453 | 0492 | 0531 | 0569 | 0607 | 0645 | 0682 | 0719 | 0755 | 38 |
| 1.2 | 0792 | 0828 | 0864 | 0899 | 0934 | 0969 | 1004 | 1038 | 1072 | 1106 | 35 |
| 1.3 | 1139 | 1173 | 1206 | 1239 | 1271 | 1303 | 1335 | 1367 | 1399 | 1430 | 32 |
| 1.4 | 1461 | 1492 | 1523 | 1553 | 1584 | 1614 | 1644 | 1673 | 1703 | 1732 | 30 |
| 1.5 | 1761 | 1790 | 1818 | 1847 | 1875 | 1903 | 1931 | 1959 | 1987 | 2014 | 28 |
| 1.6 | 2041 | 2068 | 2095 | 2122 | 2148 | 2175 | 2201 | 2227 | 2253 | 2279 | 26 |
| 1.7 | 2304 | 2330 | 2355 | 2380 | 2405 | 2430 | 2455 | 2480 | 2504 | 2529 | 25 |
| 1.8 | 2553 | 2577 | 2601 | 2625 | 2648 | 2672 | 2695 | 2718 | 2742 | 2765 | 24 |
| 1.9 | 2788 | 2810 | 2833 | 2856 | 2878 | 2900 | 2923 | 2945 | 2967 | 2989 | 22 |
| 2.0 | 3010 | 3032 | 3054 | 3075 | 3096 | 3118 | 3139 | 3160 | 3181 | 3201 | 21 |
| 2.1 | 3222 | 3243 | 3263 | 3284 | 3304 | 3324 | 3345 | 3365 | 3385 | 3404 | 20 |
| 2.2 | 3424 | 3444 | 3464 | 3483 | 3502 | 3522 | 3541 | 3560 | 3579 | 3598 | 19 |
| 2.3 | 3617 | 3636 | 3655 | 3674 | 3692 | 3711 | 3729 | 3747 | 3766 | 3784 | 18 |
| 2.4 | 3802 | 3820 | 3838 | 3856 | 3874 | 3892 | 3909 | 3927 | 3945 | 3962 | 18 |
| 2.5 | 3979 | 3997 | 4014 | 4031 | 4048 | 4065 | 4082 | 4099 | 4116 | 4133 | 17 |
| 2.6 | 4150 | 4166 | 4183 | 4200 | 4216 | 4232 | 4249 | 4265 | 4281 | 4298 | 16 |
| 2.7 | 4314 | 4330 | 4346 | 4362 | 4378 | 4393 | 4409 | 4425 | 4440 | 4456 | 16 |
| 2.8 | 4472 | 4487 | 4502 | 4518 | 4533 | 4548 | 4564 | 4579 | 4594 | 4609 | 15 |
| 2.9 | 4624 | 4639 | 4654 | 4669 | 4683 | 4698 | 4713 | 4728 | 4742 | 4757 | 15 |
| 3.0 | 4771 | 4786 | 4800 | 4814 | 4829 | 4843 | 4857 | 4871 | 4886 | 4900 | 14 |
| 3.1 | 4914 | 4928 | 4942 | 4955 | 4969 | 4983 | 4997 | 5011 | 5024 | 5038 | 14 |
| 3.2 | 5051 | 5065 | 5079 | 5092 | 5105 | 5119 | 5132 | 5145 | 5159 | 5172 | 13 |
| 3.3 | 5185 | 5198 | 5211 | 5224 | 5237 | 5250 | 5263 | 5276 | 5289 | 5302 | 13 |
| 3.4 | 5315 | 5328 | 5340 | 5353 | 5366 | 5378 | 5391 | 5403 | 5416 | 5428 | 13 |
| 3.5 | 5441 | 5453 | 5465 | 5478 | 5490 | 5502 | 5514 | 5527 | 5539 | 5551 | 12 |
| 3.6 | 5563 | 5575 | 5587 | 5599 | 5611 | 5623 | 5635 | 5647 | 5658 | 5670 | 12 |
| 3.7 | 5682 | 5694 | 5705 | 5717 | 5729 | 5740 | 5752 | 5763 | 5775 | 5786 | 12 |
| 3.8 | 5798 | 5809 | 5821 | 5832 | 5843 | 5855 | 5866 | 5877 | 5888 | 5899 | 11 |
| 3.9 | 5911 | 5922 | 5933 | 5944 | 5955 | 5966 | 5977 | 5988 | 5999 | 6010 | 11 |
| 4.0 | 6021 | 6031 | 6042 | 6053 | 6064 | 6075 | 6085 | 6096 | 6107 | 6117 | 11 |
| 4.1 | 6128 | 6138 | 6149 | 6160 | 6170 | 6180 | 6191 | 6201 | 6212 | 6222 | 10 |
| 4.2 | 6232 | 6243 | 6253 | 6263 | 6274 | 6284 | 6294 | 6304 | 6314 | 6325 | 10 |
| 4.3 | 6335 | 6345 | 6355 | 6365 | 6375 | 6385 | 6395 | 6405 | 6415 | 6425 | 10 |
| 4.4 | 6435 | 6444 | 6454 | 6464 | 6474 | 6484 | 6493 | 6503 | 6513 | 6522 | 10 |
| 4.5 | 6532 | 6542 | 6551 | 6561 | 6571 | 6580 | 6590 | 6599 | 6609 | 6618 | 10 |
| 4.6 | 6628 | 6637 | 6646 | 6656 | 6665 | 6675 | 6684 | 6693 | 6702 | 6712 | 9 |
| 4.7 | 6721 | 6730 | 6739 | 6749 | 6758 | 6767 | 6776 | 6785 | 6794 | 6803 | 9 |
| 4.8 | 6812 | 6821 | 6830 | 6839 | 6848 | 6857 | 6866 | 6875 | 6884 | 6893 | 9 |
| 4.9 | 6902 | 6911 | 6920 | 6928 | 6937 | 6946 | 6955 | 6964 | 6972 | 6981 | 9 |
| 5.0 | 6990 | 6998 | 7007 | 7016 | 7024 | 7033 | 7042 | 7050 | 7059 | 7067 | 9 |
| 5.1 | 7076 | 7084 | 7093 | 7101 | 7110 | 7118 | 7126 | 7135 | 7143 | 7152 | 8 |
| 5.2 | 7160 | 7168 | 7177 | 7185 | 7193 | 7202 | 7210 | 7218 | 7226 | 7235 | 8 |
| 5.3 | 7243 | 7251 | 7259 | 7267 | 7275 | 7284 | 7292 | 7300 | 7308 | 7316 | 8 |
| 5.4 | 7324 | 7332 | 7340 | 7348 | 7356 | 7364 | 7372 | 7380 | 7388 | 7396 | 8 |

| N | 0 | 1 | 2 | 3 | 4 | 5 | 6 | 7 | 8 | 9 | D |
|---|---|---|---|---|---|---|---|---|---|---|---|
| 5.5 | 7404 | 7412 | 7419 | 7427 | 7435 | 7443 | 7451 | 7459 | 7466 | 7474 | 8 |
| 5.6 | 7482 | 7490 | 7497 | 7505 | 7513 | 7520 | 7528 | 7536 | 7543 | 7551 | 8 |
| 5.7 | 7559 | 7566 | 7574 | 7582 | 7589 | 7597 | 7604 | 7612 | 7619 | 7627 | 8 |
| 5.8 | 7634 | 7642 | 7649 | 7657 | 7664 | 7672 | 7679 | 7686 | 7694 | 7701 | 7 |
| 5.9 | 7709 | 7716 | 7723 | 7731 | 7738 | 7745 | 7752 | 7760 | 7767 | 7774 | 7 |
| 6.0 | 7782 | 7789 | 7796 | 7803 | 7810 | 7818 | 7825 | 7832 | 7839 | 7846 | 7 |
| 6.1 | 7853 | 7860 | 7868 | 7875 | 7882 | 7889 | 7896 | 7903 | 7910 | 7917 | 7 |
| 6.2 | 7924 | 7931 | 7938 | 7945 | 7952 | 7959 | 7966 | 7973 | 7980 | 7987 | 7 |
| 6.3 | 7993 | 8000 | 8007 | 8014 | 8021 | 8028 | 8035 | 8041 | 8048 | 8055 | 7 |
| 6.4 | 8062 | 8069 | 8075 | 8082 | 8089 | 8096 | 8102 | 8109 | 8116 | 8122 | 7 |
| 6.5 | 8129 | 8136 | 8142 | 8149 | 8156 | 8162 | 8169 | 8176 | 8182 | 8189 | 7 |
| 6.6 | 8195 | 8202 | 8209 | 8215 | 8222 | 8228 | 8235 | 8241 | 8248 | 8254 | 7 |
| 6.7 | 8261 | 8267 | 8274 | 8280 | 8287 | 8293 | 8299 | 8306 | 8312 | 8319 | 6 |
| 6.8 | 8325 | 8331 | 8338 | 8344 | 8351 | 8357 | 8363 | 8370 | 8376 | 8382 | 6 |
| 6.9 | 8388 | 8395 | 8401 | 8407 | 8414 | 8420 | 8426 | 8432 | 8439 | 8445 | 6 |
| 7.0 | 8451 | 8457 | 8463 | 8470 | 8476 | 8482 | 8488 | 8494 | 8500 | 8506 | 6 |
| 7.1 | 8513 | 8519 | 8525 | 8531 | 8537 | 8543 | 8549 | 8555 | 8561 | 8567 | 6 |
| 7.2 | 8573 | 8579 | 8585 | 8591 | 8597 | 8603 | 8609 | 8615 | 8621 | 8627 | 6 |
| 7.3 | 8633 | 8639 | 8645 | 8651 | 8657 | 8663 | 8669 | 8675 | 8681 | 8686 | 6 |
| 7.4 | 8692 | 8698 | 8704 | 8710 | 8716 | 8722 | 8727 | 8733 | 8739 | 8745 | 6 |
| 7.5 | 8751 | 8756 | 8762 | 8768 | 8774 | 8779 | 8785 | 8791 | 8797 | 8802 | 6 |
| 7.6 | 8808 | 8814 | 8820 | 8825 | 8831 | 8837 | 8842 | 8848 | 8854 | 8859 | 6 |
| 7.7 | 8865 | 8871 | 8876 | 8882 | 8887 | 8893 | 8899 | 8904 | 8910 | 8915 | 6 |
| 7.8 | 8921 | 8927 | 8932 | 8938 | 8943 | 8949 | 8954 | 8960 | 8965 | 8971 | 6 |
| 7.9 | 8976 | 8982 | 8987 | 8993 | 8998 | 9004 | 9009 | 9015 | 9020 | 9025 | 5 |
| 8.0 | 9031 | 9036 | 9042 | 9047 | 9053 | 9058 | 9063 | 9069 | 9074 | 9079 | 5 |
| 8.1 | 9085 | 9090 | 9096 | 9101 | 9106 | 9112 | 9117 | 9122 | 9128 | 9133 | 5 |
| 8.2 | 9138 | 9143 | 9149 | 9154 | 9159 | 9165 | 9170 | 9175 | 9180 | 9186 | 5 |
| 8.3 | 9191 | 9196 | 9201 | 9206 | 9212 | 9217 | 9222 | 9227 | 9232 | 9238 | 5 |
| 8.4 | 9243 | 9248 | 9253 | 9258 | 9263 | 9269 | 9274 | 9279 | 9284 | 9289 | 5 |
| 8.5 | 9294 | 9299 | 9304 | 9309 | 9315 | 9320 | 9325 | 9330 | 9335 | 9340 | 5 |
| 8.6 | 9345 | 9350 | 9355 | 9360 | 9365 | 9370 | 9375 | 9380 | 9385 | 9390 | 5 |
| 8.7 | 9395 | 9400 | 9405 | 9410 | 9415 | 9420 | 9425 | 9430 | 9435 | 9440 | 5 |
| 8.8 | 9445 | 9450 | 9455 | 9460 | 9465 | 9469 | 9474 | 9479 | 9484 | 9489 | 5 |
| 8.9 | 9494 | 9499 | 9504 | 9509 | 9513 | 9518 | 9523 | 9528 | 9533 | 9538 | 5 |
| 9.0 | 9542 | 9547 | 9552 | 9557 | 9562 | 9566 | 9571 | 9576 | 9581 | 9586 | 5 |
| 9.1 | 9590 | 9595 | 9600 | 9605 | 9609 | 9614 | 9619 | 9624 | 9628 | 9633 | 5 |
| 9.2 | 9638 | 9643 | 9647 | 9652 | 9657 | 9661 | 9666 | 9671 | 9675 | 9680 | 5 |
| 9.3 | 9685 | 9689 | 9694 | 9699 | 9703 | 9708 | 9713 | 9717 | 9722 | 9727 | 5 |
| 9.4 | 9731 | 9736 | 9741 | 9745 | 9750 | 9754 | 9759 | 9763 | 9768 | 9773 | 5 |
| 9.5 | 9777 | 9782 | 9786 | 9791 | 9795 | 9800 | 9805 | 9809 | 9814 | 9818 | 5 |
| 9.6 | 9823 | 9827 | 9832 | 9836 | 9841 | 9845 | 9850 | 9854 | 9859 | 9863 | 5 |
| 9.7 | 9868 | 9872 | 9877 | 9881 | 9886 | 9890 | 9894 | 9899 | 9903 | 9908 | 4 |
| 9.8 | 9912 | 9917 | 9921 | 9926 | 9930 | 9934 | 9939 | 9943 | 9948 | 9952 | 4 |
| 9.9 | 9956 | 9961 | 9965 | 9969 | 9974 | 9978 | 9983 | 9987 | 9991 | 9996 | 4 |

The general principles that underlie the use of logarithms, especially those of the mantissa and characteristic, are explained in the text on the preceding page.

**Finding logarithms of numbers.** Locate the first two figures in the left-hand column and the third at the top. The corresponding four numbers in the table are the mantissa (mantissa of 1.51 is 1790). The characteristic is one **less** than the number of digits **left** of the decimal point. Thus the logarithm of 1.51 (usually written log 1.51)=0.1790; log 15.1=1.1790; log 151=2.1790; and so on.

For decimal fractions, the characteristic is one **greater** than the number of zeros between the decimal point and the first significant digit, and has a **negative sign above** the characteristic, with the mantissa in the table (log 0.151 = $\overline{1}$.1790; log 0.0151 = $\overline{2}$.1790; and so on).

With a number having four significant digits, proceed by interpolation as follows: obtain the difference between the mantissas for the next smaller and next larger three-digit numbers; multiply this by the last digit of your number, divide by 10, and add the result to the logarithm for the first three digits of the number. Thus, to find log 15.13. Log 15.2 (=1.1818)−log 15.1 (=1.1790) =.0028. $\frac{3}{10}\times$.0028=.00084. Adding: 1.1790+.00084= 1.17984 (=log 15.13 approx.). The column marked D at the right gives the average value for the difference between any two mantissas on the line and may be used (remembering to multiply, then divide by 10 as above)

if less accurate results are sufficient for your purposes.

**To find a number from its logarithm.** Locate in the table the mantissa next below the one you have, write the three corresponding digits from the side and top, and point off decimally as the characteristic requires. For remaining digits, reverse the interpolation process given above. Thus, to find the number for the logarithm 1.17984. The next lowest mantissa is .1790, and the number (pointed off for characteristic 1) is 15.1. The difference between mantissas .1790 and .1818 is .0028. The given mantissa is .00084 greater than .1790. Divide: $\frac{.00084}{.0028}$ = .3; therefore the corresponding number lies $\frac{3}{10}$ of the way between 15.1 and 15.2: 15.13.

**Computing with logarithms.** When all characteristics are positive, computations proceed as explained in the article. When negative characteristics appear, treat the characteristics and mantissas separately, and at the end combine any characteristic resulting from combination of the mantissas with the other characteristics. Thus, to find 151×0.151. To log 151 (=2.1790) add log 0.151 (=$\overline{1}$.1790). Result: 1.3580 (=log of 22.8 approx.). To divide 0.151 by 151: from log 0.151 (=$\overline{1}$.1790) subtract log 151 (=2.1790). Result $\overline{3}$.000 (=log of .001). To find the 7th power of 0.151: multiply log 0.151 (=$\overline{1}$.1790) by 7. Answer: $\overline{7}$+7×.1790=$\overline{7}$+1.2530=$\overline{6}$.2530 (=log of 0.00000179 approx.).

**LOGIC.** The study of the various steps and processes involved in reasoning is called *logic*. A person does not have to study logic in order to think correctly or to argue persuasively. But the study of logic will provide a means for testing the accuracy of his own conclusions and those of others. There are two general kinds of reasoning—*deductive* and *inductive*.

### Deductive Reasoning

When a person uses a general principle to draw a specific conclusion, he is using deductive reasoning. A deductive argument is frequently stated in the form of a *syllogism*, invented by the ancient Greeks. A syllogism consists of three parts—*major premise, minor premise,* and *conclusion.* The following example shows the order of the parts:

> Honest men do not lie;
> Jones is an honest man;
> Therefore Jones does not lie.

Broken down in this way, an argument is far easier to test for *fallacies* (errors) than when stated in an ordinary conversational form. The conclusion of a deductive argument *must* be valid if the premises are true and the conclusion is properly drawn.

### Inductive Reasoning

When a person uses a number of established facts to draw a general conclusion, he uses inductive reasoning. For example, a scientist may gather all the facts he can about a certain disease from observations and experiments. Then he draws his inductive conclusion that a certain microbe causes the disease. An inductive argument, however, is never final. It is based upon known facts and is always subject to revision if new facts are discovered.

The principles of inductive reasoning were stated by the Greek philosopher Aristotle. They were little used, however, until the time of Sir Francis Bacon in the 17th century. (*See also* Philosophy.)

---

THESE ARTICLES ARE IN THE FACT-INDEX

**Logistics**
**Logroño, Spain**

---

**LOGWOOD.** The heartwood (strong, inner wood) of the logwood tree is commercially important because it contains a chemical that is used for making dyes. The logwood tree is native to the West Indies, Mexico, and Central America. It grows from 30 to 50 feet high. When it is about 10 years old it is ready for cutting. It is then stripped of the bark and sapwood, which have no commercial value, and cut into three- and four-foot lengths.

The logwood tree's heartwood, which is very hard and heavy, takes on a beautiful brownish-red color when exposed to the air. This is caused by the chemical reaction of a crystalline substance, *hematoxylin*, in the wood. The hematoxylin is extracted from the wood and is used in making dyes for cotton,

wool, silk, and leather. It is also used in making ink, for staining biological specimens to be studied microscopically, and in drug manufacturing.

The finest and greatest quantity of logwood comes from Campeche in Mexico. Because of this the wood is sometimes called "campeachy wood." The tree's scientific name is *Haematoxylon campechianum*.

**LOHENGRIN** (*lō'ĕn-ḡrĭn*). This "Knight of the Swan" is the hero of a beautiful medieval German legend. According to the story, Elsa, a lovely young duchess of Brabant, was in distress and longed for help. At last a knight appeared in a boat drawn by a silver swan. This was Lohengrin, the son of Parsifal (Percivale). King Arthur had sent him from the castle of the Holy Grail to fight as her champion. Having won her cause, Lohengrin married Elsa. But he made her promise that she would never ask his name or from where he had come. They lived happily until Elsa could no longer keep from asking the fatal question. Then Lohengrin was forced to bid her farewell. The swan boat reappeared on the river and carried him away, never to return. Wagner made this legend the subject of one of his beautiful operas.

**LOIRE** (*lŏ-wär'*) **RIVER.** The longest river in France is the Loire. Its whole course covers about 629 miles. The Loire rises in southeastern France, only 85 miles north of the Mediterranean Sea, and flows northward for more than half its course. Then it sweeps with a great curve to the southwest and flows into the Bay of Biscay.

The Loire rises in a spur of the Cevennes range some 4,500 feet above sea level. Its headwaters are fed by melting snows from mountain peaks. As it races through narrow gorges it carries remains of old volcanic eruptions. Below the mountains it flows through gentle lowlands and through the Paris Basin, the chief agricultural region of France.

With its many tributaries, the Loire Valley has been called the heartland of France. The Loire uplands produce rye and buckwheat. The great bend of the river near Orléans supports grazing lands. Broad stretches of the valley are planted with vegetables and fruit, especially grapes. In some places the land is worked so intensively that farmers leave fields unfenced to make more room for crops.

The Loire is of little use for navigation, except by rafts. Rocks and gravel choke its mountain course, and sediment from the Paris Basin clogs its lower channel. In summer the Loire shrinks to a maze of sandbars and shallows. But many canals have been built to aid navigation through its valley and connect it with the Seine and the Saône. In the rainy season tributaries increase the volume of the Loire, and it floods wide stretches along its banks. Some cities, such as Tours, have built large protecting dikes.

THESE ARTICLES ARE IN THE FACT-INDEX

Lolland

Lollards

Lomax, John Avery

Lombard College

Lombardo, Guy (Albert)

**LOMBARDS.** The most productive region of Italy is Lombardy, the great fertile valley of the Po River. It takes its name from the barbarian Lombard hordes who overran it in the 6th century. These people were the last Germanic invaders of Italy. They pressed down from the north in A.D. 568 within 15 years after the emperor Justinian had expelled the East Goths (*see* Goths). The Lombards soon held most of the peninsula, though Rome, Ravenna, and a few other fortified cities successfully resisted their attack. But the Lombards failed to establish a strong central government. Many small dukedoms grew up and cut Italy into small divisions.

The Lombard kingdom in the valley of the Po existed a little more than two centuries. It was overthrown by Charlemagne in 773. He invaded Italy at the request of the pope, dethroned the king, and was himself crowned with the "iron crown" of Lombardy. The crown was so called because beneath the gold was a circlet of iron, said to be made from one of the nails with which Christ was crucified. After the breakup of Charlemagne's empire the Lombards gradually merged with the other peoples of Italy.

The energetic people which grew from this fusion of Latin and Teuton became famous from the 13th to the 16th centuries for their success as merchants and moneylenders. So many of them came to London and other European cities that all Italians north of the Alps came to be known as Lombards. Finally the name became synonymous with "money-lender."

THESE ARTICLES ARE IN THE FACT-INDEX

Lombok Island

Lombroso, Cesare

Lomond, Loch

Lomonosov, Mikhail
  Vasilievich

Lompoc, Calif.

London, George

**LONDON, John Griffith** (1876–1916). No tale that Jack London wrote is more exciting than his own life story. From his adventurous years as a sailor and gold prospector, he drew dozens of books and short stories. But like many of his heroes he died unsatisfied and short of his goal.

His father, William Chaney, a traveling astrologer, met Jack's mother, Flora Wellman, in Seattle. Jack was born in San Francisco, Calif. Eight months after his birth, his mother married John London.

Jack London's boyhood was grim. His foster father drifted from job to job around Oakland and San Francisco. His mother's elaborate schemes for making money failed. Jack began early to help support the family by carrying papers, delivering ice, and working in a mill and canneries. Fascinated by books about the sea, he learned sailing while robbing oyster beds in San Francisco Bay. Later he worked in the fish patrol that policed the oyster beds. At 17 he sailed on a seal-hunting voyage to Siberia and Japan.

Home again, London worked briefly and then traveled across the country as a tramp on freight trains. He became interested in socialism and made "soapbox" speeches on street corners.

A growing determination to live by his head rather than his hands led him to finish a year of high school. A brilliant, determined student, he then "crammed" furiously to enter the University of California. But after one semester he had to go to work again. In 1897 he joined the Alaskan gold rush. He did not find gold, but Alaska gave him his best story material. Perhaps the most popular of London's many stories about Alaskan life is 'Call of the Wild' (1903), a tale of a giant sled dog that goes wild after its master dies.

A great reader himself, London sometimes tried to make his characters both adventurers and scholars. 'The Sea Wolf' (1904) is a curious story of a brutal sea captain devoted to poetry and philosophy.

London's writing schedule of a thousand words a day brought him wealth, but he spent or gave away all of it. Two marriages turned out unhappily. He spent his later life at his Beauty Ranch in California. After Wolf House, his "dream castle," burned before completion in 1913, he was a tired, sick man. He renounced socialism, just as the hero of his 'Martin Eden' (1909) did, and died in 1916.

**SAILOR AS WELL AS AUTHOR**
As daring as any of his heroes, Jack London sailed the Pacific Ocean in quest of adventure.

# LONDON—Capital of the United Kingdom

No spot in London calls up more memories of historical names and events than the ancient Tower of London. Tower Bridge, across the Thames, was built in the 19th century.

point at which the river could be easily forded or bridged. On Lud Hill the Romans built Londinium, "the City," and ringed it with massive walls reaching down to the Thames. They also built the first London Bridge and laid six roads radiating from it to the north and the south. The City was soon crowded with merchants dealing in tin, cattle, hides, and slaves.

About a mile west of the old walled City of London there grew up on the Thames the City of Westminster. Here the king lived and Parliament met, and here also was Westminster Abbey, the coronation church. The riverside street between the two cities—called the Strand (shore)—became lined with palaces and gardens. Houses spread over the high ground

**LONDON, England.** London is the capital of Great Britain and the mother city of the British Commonwealth of Nations. It is the seat of one of the world's oldest parliamentary governments, yet it retains all the pomp and ceremony of a medieval kingdom. It is a great industrial city, an international center of finance, and a huge port. Greater London is the world's third largest city, ranking after Tokyo and New York City.

The visitor to London usually sees little of its great port and factories. He is more interested in its historic palaces and churches, which link the present with the past. Even the streets of London are memorable. They are well known through English fiction and biographies of great men of the past who lived and walked on them.

London owed its rise to its location on the Thames River (see Thames River). This river is the outlet for the English plain and the principal gateway into England from the continent of Europe. When the Romans occupied England—in the 1st century A.D.—there was already a small village on Lud Hill, about 60 miles above the mouth of the Thames. Below this point the shores were swampy. At Lud Hill was firm ground on which ships could unload. Here also was the lowest

north of the Thames and later over the low ground in Southwark, at the south end of London Bridge.

The City of London became the home of great craft and merchant companies (see Guilds). It preserved a degree of independence from the king in Westminster and jealously guarded its privileges. William the Conqueror was compelled to treat with it as with a separate state. He built a strong fortress—the famous Tower of London—to overawe its citizens; but he had to place it outside the city walls.

Throughout the Middle Ages the City kept within the Roman wall. Only a remnant of that wall remains today, but the names of its gates survive in such streets as Newgate, Aldgate, Cripplegate, and Ludgate, as well as in the fish market of Billingsgate. Gradually the City spread west to Temple Bar, at the eastern end of the Strand.

In 1665 the Great Plague ran its course in London. The next year the Great Fire destroyed the City. London quickly recovered from both calamities. Sir Christopher Wren, genius of church architecture, rebuilt many of the City's ancient churches. His masterpiece was the new St. Paul's Cathedral on Ludgate Hill (the ancient Lud Hill). The dome of this great church is still one of the highest points in London.

In the 18th century London grew from 500,000 to 1,000,000 inhabitants. In the 19th century it became the largest and wealthiest city in the world. Beautiful homes spread over the West End, the area around

Westminster. The old City became a world center of finance. Up the muddy waters of the Thames came ships of all nations, with all kinds of cargo. Most English railways made London their terminal. Highways also radiated from it in all directions. While London owes its importance principally to commerce, it is also a great manufacturing center, turning out clothing, foodstuffs, furniture, machinery, and miscellaneous products.

In World War II London suffered heavily from bombing. From August 1940 to May 1941, German bombers came over night after night. The heaviest attack took place on Dec. 29, 1940, when incendiary bombs ignited London's second Great Fire. In 1944 came the deadly V-bombs, launched from German bases in France. Many Londoners slept in subway stations. Thousands were killed. In the mile-square City, 134 acres were leveled.

## Streets, Squares, and Houses

As London grew, it swallowed up more than a hundred towns, villages, and parishes. Many of these communities retained their names and their individual character, along with their irregular street systems. The main east-west thoroughfares follow the windings of the Thames. Others cut across them, making a beeline for one of London's 15 bridges. A wide boulevard, called the Embankment, now borders the north bank of the Thames, hiding London's historic waterfront street, the Strand.

The clay soil made difficult the construction of tall buildings, and the development of transportation encouraged the growth of suburbs. London therefore spread out horizontally and now covers an area about

**TRAFALGAR SQUARE IN THE HEART OF LONDON**
The Nelson Monument, 185 feet high, towers above this famed traffic center and meeting place. The church to the right is St. Martin's-in-the-Fields.

half the size of Rhode Island. Even in central London most of the buildings are less than six stories high. Blocks of apartment houses are beginning to replace private dwellings; however, the typical London street is still lined with narrow-fronted stone or brick residences that date back to the 18th or 19th

**GREATER LONDON**

HERTFORD · BUCKINGHAM · ESSEX · KENT · SURREY

Thames R.

SCALE OF MILES 0 5

N

## LONDON BOROUGHS

| | |
|---|---|
| 16. Barking | 25. Hounslow |
| 30. Barnet | 3. Islington |
| 18. Bexley | 12. Kensington and Chelsea |
| 28. Brent | 23. Kingston upon Thames |
| 19. Bromley | 9. Lambeth |
| 2. Camden | 7. Lewisham |
| 20. Croydon | 22. Merton |
| 27. Ealing | 17. Newham |
| 32. Enfield | 14. Redbridge |
| 6. Greenwich | 24. Richmond upon Thames |
| 4. Hackney | 8. Southwark |
| 11. Hammersmith | 21. Sutton |
| 31. Haringey | 5. Tower Hamlets |
| 29. Harrow | 13. Waltham Forest |
| 15. Havering | 10. Wandsworth |
| 26. Hillingdon | 1. Westminster |

**Area:** Greater London, 616 square miles; City of London, 1.06 square miles.
**Population** (1969 estimate): Greater London, 7,703,410; City of London, 4,350.

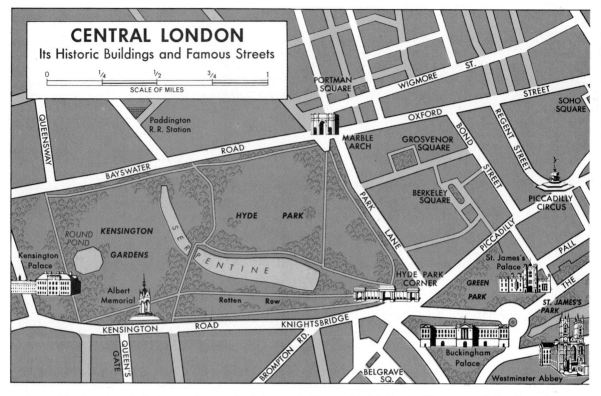

## CENTRAL LONDON
### Its Historic Buildings and Famous Streets

SCALE OF MILES

century. The houses gain in impressiveness by being built in an unbroken row. From every roof rises a cluster of chimney pots. Each chimney pot is the flue of an open fireplace that heats a single room.

The Londoner is seldom far from grass and flowers. Scattered over the city—particularly in the West End —are great parks and dozens of small green squares. The parks are open to the public, but the squares belong to residents of the district and are private.

The open spaces where several streets come together are also called squares, or sometimes circuses. They may be any shape. (Piccadilly Circus is almost a triangle.) When a thoroughfare crosses a square it usually changes its name. Most of London's best-known streets are therefore less than a mile long.

### Charing Cross and Trafalgar Square

The center of London is usually regarded as Charing Cross, a small traffic square near the river. Here, until 1647, stood one of the 13 crosses erected in 1291 by Edward I to his queen, Eleanor, marking the stopping places in her funeral procession. A line north from Charing Cross roughly divides the residential West End from the commercial East End.

On the north, Charing Cross opens into Trafalgar Square, named for Lord Nelson's great naval victory (*see* Nelson). From the double open space formed by these two squares, important streets radiate in all directions. Here one may board a bright red two-story bus for any part of London; and here also are three stations of London's extensive subway system, called the Underground. The older subway lines are

shallow and brick-lined. The newer "tubes" are deep metal-lined tunnels.

### The Strand Leads to the City

From Charing Cross the wide Strand runs northeast to the old City of London, following the line of the river. This short thoroughfare was once the center of London's night life, and it still has many theaters and restaurants as well as office buildings. Just north of the Strand, on Drury Lane, is the Drury Lane Theater, long famous as the home of drama. Near it, on Bow Street (which runs in the shape of a bent bow), stands Covent Garden, the huge Royal Opera House built more than 200 years ago. The theater takes its name from an open space nearby, which was once a quiet convent garden. This open space is now London's market for fruit, vegetables, and flowers.

The Strand ends at Temple Bar and enters the City as Fleet Street. In old times Temple Bar was actually a stout wooden bar placed across the street to keep the king and his followers out of the City of London. The last barrier was removed in 1787.

### The Temple and Fleet Street

Temple Bar takes its name from the Temple, which lies between Fleet Street and the Embankment. The entrance is a gateway designed by Wren. Inside is a quiet courtyard that takes us back to the Middle Ages. Then the Temple was the headquarters of the Knights Templars, a military religious order dedicated to the protection of the Holy Sepulchre. The Temple Church, dating from the 12th century, is one

338

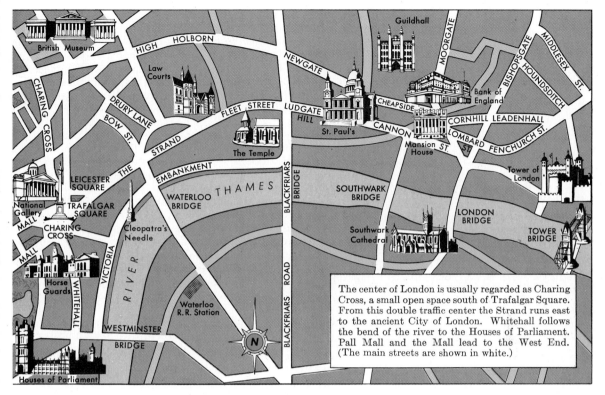

The center of London is usually regarded as Charing Cross, a small open space south of Trafalgar Square. From this double traffic center the Strand runs east to the ancient City of London. Whitehall follows the bend of the river to the Houses of Parliament. Pall Mall and the Mall lead to the West End. (The main streets are shown in white.)

of the finest ancient "round" churches of England.

The Temple has long been part of "legal London." The Inner Temple and the Middle Temple are two of London's "inns of court," which serve as universities for law students. They are called inns because they once furnished permanent residence for their members. They still include dining halls, libraries, chapels, and gardens as well as offices of leading lawyers. The other two inns of court—Lincoln's Inn Fields and Gray's Inn—lie north of Fleet Street. They are reached by Chancery Lane, a curving street on which many lawyers have their offices.

Fleet Street, a narrow, busy thoroughfare, was named for Fleet River (now a sewer). Here newspapers have had their headquarters since newspapers began. On the street are the offices of great London dailies. Printing is done in the maze of small courts and alleys on either side.

### St. Paul's and the Bells of Bow

Fleet Street ends at Ludgate Circus, where the east-west thoroughfare changes its name to Ludgate Hill. This short street leads up to St. Paul's Cathedral, the "parish church" of the British Commonwealth and the cathedral of the bishop of London. The church is in the form of a Latin cross, 515 feet in length and 250 feet across the two arms (transepts). The diameter of the dome is 102 feet. The cross on top of the dome is 366 feet above the pavement. The vast interior is crowded with monuments, chiefly of naval and military officers. Tombs lie in the crypt below. In the center of the crypt is the tomb of Admiral Nelson, Britain's great naval hero.

From St. Paul's, Cheapside runs east to the "Wall Street" section of the City. This area suffered heavily in World War II and many of its famous old guild-halls were destroyed. Wren's Bow Church (St. Mary-le-Bow) and its famous bells were badly damaged. According to an old story, the bells called back Dick Whittington to be three times lord mayor of London. Anyone born within the sound of the Bow Bells was said to be a true Cockney—that is, a real Londoner. The bells were restored in 1961.

### The Bank of England

Cheapside, after changing its name to Poultry, leads to a small triangular "square" where eight streets meet. Facing this square stands the Bank of England, "the Old Lady of Threadneedle Street." Low, solid, and windowless (for greater security), the bank covers four acres. For centuries it has served the central banks of other countries throughout the world. Though nationalized by the government (in 1946), it still keeps its traditions. Its messengers are known by their pink tail coats and scarlet waistcoats.

East of the bank is the Stock Exchange and close by, on Leadenhall and Lime Streets, is Lloyd's, the world's largest and most famous insurance company. Lloyd's specializes in marine insurance, but it will insure against almost any calamity except death.

### The Lord Mayor of the Mile-Square City

Across from the bank stands Mansion House, the residence of the lord mayor, chief magistrate of the

**ST. PAUL'S CATHEDRAL**
Wren's greatest church miraculously escaped serious damage in the second World War, when buildings near it were destroyed.

**City of London.** The lord mayor is elected yearly by the guilds and corporations of the City, some of which date back to the Middle Ages. The election takes place in the nearby Guildhall, a magnificent 15th-century building. After his election, tradition decrees that the lord mayor must present himself for royal approval. On November 9 he sets out in his lavishly carved and gilded coach, drawn by six horses, to the law courts in the Strand to take his oath before the lord chief justice. The citizens show their approval of their new mayor by accompanying him in gaily decorated trucks or horse-drawn carts. The mayor is always approved. Then he returns to the Guildhall for a banquet that is usually attended by the prime minister and his cabinet.

The king or queen still may not enter the City without permission of the lord mayor. Whenever the sovereign wishes to come, the lord mayor meets him at one of the gates—usually Temple Bar—and hands over a ponderous "key to the City" to open an imaginary gate. Then the sovereign enters and is welcomed by cheering crowds.

### The Tower of London

Just east of the City, on the Thames, stands the Tower of London. The ancient fortress is England's most famous historic monument. For centuries it served as a state prison. It is now a museum; but visitors are drawn to it chiefly by the memories it evokes of illustrious prisoners who were confined or executed here.

The Tower of London covers 13 acres and has all the parts of a medieval castle (*see* Castle). The moat, formerly fed by the Thames, is now dry. Inside the moat an outer wall encloses a narrow outer ward. From the inner wall 13 towers rise at intervals. This inner wall surrounds the inner ward, or "bail." In the center stands the White Tower, or Keep, the oldest part of the fortress, which was begun by William the Conqueror in 1078. It is now a museum, in which are displayed old arms, armor, and instruments of torture.

In the outer wall, facing the Thames, is Traitors' Gate, through which state prisoners, brought by way of the river from Westminster, were conveyed to the Tower. Beauchamp Tower, in the west wall, was long the principal prison for persons of rank, but the Bell Tower, the Bloody Tower, the Salt Tower, and the Broad Arrow Tower also have dungeons and other prison chambers in which historic personages were confined. Executions took place both within the Tower and outside the walls on Tower Hill. Many of those executed were buried in the Tower chapel. They included Sir Thomas More; Anne Boleyn; Catherine Howard; and Lady Jane Grey and her husband, Guildford Dudley. Elizabeth I, when a princess, was a prisoner here. Here also Sir Walter Raleigh wrote a history of the world while awaiting his tragic end.

### The Crown Jewels

In Wakefield Tower, close to Traitors' Gate, the public may view, glittering under bright lights, the crown jewels, or regalia, of Great Britain. The coronation crown, made for Charles II in 1662, is a copy

**ST. CLEMENT DANES IN THE STRAND**
This Wren church, badly damaged by bombs, is famous for the rhyme, "Oranges and lemons, say the bells of St. Clement's."

Ewing Galloway

The Houses of Parliament (center) overlook the Thames. The church is Westminster Abbey. In the foreground is Parliament Street, the lower end of Whitehall, lined with government offices. Across the river is London County Hall.

of the ancient crown of Edward the Confessor, which was destroyed by Cromwell. The imperial state crown, made for Victoria's coronation, contains more than 2,700 diamonds, 300 pearls, and the Black Prince's ruby, which is almost as large as a hen's egg.

The guardians of the jewels and other attendants in the Tower are familiarly known as "beefeaters." They have close-cropped beards and wear scarlet doublets and knee breeches, a quaint costume that dates from Tudor times. They are all old soldiers, honorary members of the Yeomen of the Guard.

### Whitehall—Heart of the Commonwealth

From Charing Cross, a short, wide street, called Whitehall, follows a bend in the Thames south to the Houses of Parliament. At the north end of Whitehall are the War Office, the Admiralty, the Scottish Office, and the Treasury. Around the corner from the Treasury is No. 10 Downing Street, the modest official residence of the British prime minister. At the south end, called Parliament Street, are huge blocks of government buildings. In the center of Whitehall rises the Cenotaph, a simple square shaft of stone commemorating the "glorious dead" of two world wars.

Whitehall takes its name from the royal palace of Whitehall, formerly the residence of the sovereign. The palace's main buildings burned down in 1698 except for the Banqueting House. This building, erected by Inigo Jones in 1622, houses the Royal United Service Museum.

Opposite the Banqueting House stands the Horse Guards, once a guardhouse for Whitehall Palace and now a military headquarters. Two troopers, in huge sentry boxes, guard the passage to the Horse Guards Parade, a wide graveled space. Every morning a small crowd gathers to watch the half-hour ceremony of the Changing of the Guard. A more elaborate ceremony, Trooping the Color, takes place here on the sovereign's official birthday.

Old Scotland Yard, a short street running east from the north end of Whitehall, was the site of a palace in which the Scottish kings lived when in London. In 1829

Ewing Galloway

No. 10 Downing Street, a modest house on a narrow street, has long been the official residence of British prime ministers.

the street became the headquarters of the Metropolitan Police. In 1890 "Scotland Yard" was moved to new buildings, called New Scotland Yard, on the Embankment. In 1966 it was scheduled to be moved again, into new quarters near Westminster Abbey.

## Parliament and Westminster Abbey

Parliament Street, at the south end of Whitehall, opens into Parliament Square, one of London's busiest traffic whirlpools. Westminster Abbey and the Houses of Parliament (on the Thames) face this square.

The official name of the Houses of Parliament is the New Palace of Westminster. The old Palace of Westminster was destroyed by fire in 1834 except for Westminster Hall. This beautiful building was the seat of the chief English law courts after the 13th century. Here Richard II was deposed, and here Charles I was condemned to death. Westminster Hall now serves as a spacious vestibule to the Houses of Parliament.

Parliament's "new palace," completed in 1850, was designed by Sir Charles Barry. It covers eight acres and has 1,100 rooms and two miles of passages. The House of Lords is in the southern half. The chamber of the House of Commons, in the northern half, was destroyed during World War II and rebuilt after the war with little change (see Parliament, British).

At the north end of the Parliament building rises the Clock Tower, 320 feet high. This is the home of the great bell called Big Ben. The bell weighs $13\frac{1}{2}$ tons; it is $7\frac{1}{2}$ feet high and 9 feet in diameter at its mouth. It was cast in 1858 to replace an earlier bell that cracked (1852) while being tested. The pres-

ent bell also cracked shortly after it was hung, causing a shrill note, but after the crack had been filed open and smoothed the tone became quite pure. The note is E sharp. The great bell, which rings the hours, is flanked by smaller bells that ring the quarter hours. Big Ben takes its name from Sir Benjamin Hall, who had charge of the work on the first bell. The name is also commonly applied to the tower clock. This has four faces, one on each side of the tower, with dials 23 feet in diameter.

Westminster Abbey, a great Gothic church, is the most historic building in the West End. Here England's kings and queens are crowned and some are buried; and here are tombs, monuments, and tablets commemorating statesmen and priests, scientists and artists, warriors and poets. A slab in the floor marks the tomb of an Unknown Warrior of the first World War. (See also Westminster Abbey.)

From Westminster Abbey, Victoria Street leads west to Westminster Cathedral, near the Victoria station. Westminster Cathedral is the most important Roman Catholic church in England. Erected in 1895–1903, it is a huge edifice in Christian Byzantine style.

## London's Parks and Palaces

From Charing Cross the Mall runs southwest to Buckingham Palace, the residence of the royal family. The Mall is a wide, tree-lined avenue, about a mile long, used for ceremonial processions. At the Charing Cross end stands Admiralty Arch. In front of Buckingham Palace rises the Queen Victoria Memorial, a white marble statuary group.

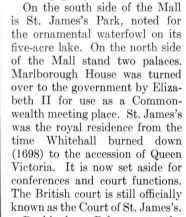

On the south side of the Mall is St. James's Park, noted for the ornamental waterfowl on its five-acre lake. On the north side of the Mall stand two palaces. Marlborough House was turned over to the government by Elizabeth II for use as a Commonwealth meeting place. St. James's was the royal residence from the time Whitehall burned down (1698) to the accession of Queen Victoria. It is now set aside for conferences and court functions. The British court is still officially known as the Court of St. James's.

Buckingham Palace, once the residence of the duke of Buckingham, was purchased by George III and rebuilt by John Nash before Queen Victoria chose it for her home in 1837. When the sovereign is in residence the guard at the entrance is changed every day at 10:30 A.M., while a guard's band plays. The palace and its 40-acre gardens are not open to the public. Constitution Hill, a beautiful avenue, runs between the palace

**POETS' CORNER, WESTMINSTER ABBEY**
At the left, next to the bust of Longfellow, is the Gothic tomb of Chaucer. Spenser also is buried here. Tombs and memorials of writers have overflowed from this original Poets' Corner, in the south transept, into the central aisle.

gardens and Green Park, on the north.

Constitution Hill ends with a great arch at Hyde Park Corner, London's busiest traffic center. On the north side of Hyde Park Corner stands a triple archway that is the principal entrance to Hyde Park.

Hyde Park was once a royal pleasure and hunting ground. After it was opened to the public, crowds used to gather to watch people of fashion ride on horseback or in elegant carriages around the Ring and along Rotten Row. Today the crowds gather near Marble Arch, at the northeast corner of the park, where impromptu orators speak freely on almost every subject.

Only a driveway separates Hyde Park from Kensington Gardens, to the west. Together they form a continuous park of over 600 acres. Kensington Gardens was once the private gardens of Kensington Palace, which stands at the west end of the park.

J. Allan Cash

Buckingham Palace has been the London residence of the reigning monarch of England since Victoria became queen in 1837. Westminster, Whitehall, and St. James's palaces were London homes of England's monarchs in earlier years.

### Streets and Districts of the West End

East of Hyde Park lies Mayfair, the traditional home of the English aristocracy. Its western boundary, Park Lane, faces the park. The eastern boundary is Bond Street, famous for its fine shops. Near Bond Street is Savile Row, street of fashionable tailors. High income taxes have driven out many of the former residents of Mayfair. Their stately mansions are being replaced by hotels, shops, and business offices.

Piccadilly, a world-famous street about a mile long, bounds Mayfair on the south. At its western end luxurious clubs overlook Green Park. Farther east are fashionable shops and hotels. Piccadilly ends at Piccadilly Circus, the center of London for the pleasure seeker. To the east is Leicester Square, heart of the theater district. To the north lies Soho, a foreign island in the West End, famous for its restaurants— French, Italian, Spanish, and Chinese.

Mayfair and Soho extend north to Oxford Street, a main east-west thoroughfare, lined with shops and department stores. North of Oxford Street is Bloomsbury, London's intellectual center, site of the British Museum and of the University of London.

South of Mayfair, between Piccadilly and Pall Mall, is a small district called St. James's, after the palace. This is the traditional home of the wealthy bachelor and the center of London's famous clubs, which have played an important part in English social and political life. Pall Mall, lined with palatial clubs, is one of London's finest streets. Both Pall Mall and the Mall take their names from the old French game "paille maille," a kind of croquet, played here in the 17th century.

Belgravia, another fashionable district, lies south of Hyde Park. On the river is Pimlico, a busy working-class neighborhood. West of Kensington Gardens is the well-to-do residential district of Kensington. Chelsea spreads west from Pimlico along the river. It is a charming residential district, the home of artists and writers since the 16th century.

### Museums, Art Galleries, and Universities

The British Museum at Bloomsbury is the oldest of national museums and is unrivaled for the richness and variety of its collections. Its exhibits represent the art of all ages. Among its most famous treasures are the beautiful sculptures called the Elgin marbles, which once adorned the Parthenon and other temples in Athens. The museum contains also one of the world's largest libraries (see Libraries).

The National Gallery, on Trafalgar Square, aims to cover the whole range of classical European painting. Here all the important old masters are represented, many of them in great works. Part of the collection is housed in the Tate Gallery, on the Thames, north of the Houses of Parliament. This gallery was originally intended to show only British art, but its scope has been widened, and it is now the National Gallery of British Paintings and of Modern Foreign Art.

The National Portrait Gallery adjoins the National Gallery. Here one may see how the nation's famous men and women looked. Portraits are chosen on the basis of genuine likeness rather than for artistic merit.

In Kensington is the vast Victoria and Albert Museum. It is concerned with arts and crafts of all

343

Fox Photos, London

**PICCADILLY CIRCUS, FAMOUS TRAFFIC CENTER**

A half dozen important streets meet at Piccadilly Circus, in the heart of London's West End. In the center rises a bronze fountain topped by a winged figure of Eros.

London south of the Thames—the Surrey side—is largely industrial and offers little of historic interest to the tourist. Facing the Houses of Parliament, in Lambeth, is Lambeth Palace, the London residence of the archbishop of Canterbury. Near it, at the end of Westminster Bridge, stands the huge building of the Greater London Council, which governs Greater London. Close to the south end of London Bridge stands Southwark Cathedral, one of London's oldest churches. Southwark was the center of stage life in Shakespeare's time. Now it is an area of drab streets. Theatergoers, however, still go to the Surrey side to see classic drama in the Old Vic repertory theater. This theater stands opposite Waterloo station, the largest railway station in England.

A little farther down the river is the borough of Greenwich. Through Greenwich runs the meridian from which longitude and standard time zones are reckoned around the world. Its National Maritime Museum contains portraits and relics of England's great sailors.

peoples. Furniture, embroidery, jewels, miniatures, ceramics, and textiles of various periods are displayed. Also in Kensington are the Natural History Museum and the Science Museum.

The huge headquarters building of the University of London is located near the British Museum. This university administers, directly or indirectly, more than 60 colleges, specialized schools, and departments scattered over Greater London. The best known of these are University College, which is near the British Museum, and King's College, in Somerset House, on the Strand.

### The East End and the Surrey Side

East of the City and the Tower spreads the East End. It has more slums than any other part of London. The district suffered heavily from bombing in World War II and rebuilding has been extensive. Back from the wide main thoroughfares are narrow, twisting alleys lined with rows of attached boxlike little houses, each with a door and window on the ground floor and two windows above. The newer buildings are blocks of flats. Whitechapel, one of London's oldest slum districts, is the hub of the clothing industry. Along the water front, the life and activity of the people center on the docks. The waterside district of Limehouse, London's Chinatown, once notorious, is now quiet and respectable.

### Dockland—London's Great Port

The best way to see London's great port is from one of the water-buses that in summer run up and down the Thames. The best time is at high tide, when ocean vessels ascend the river. Most of them quickly disappear below Tower Bridge into the maze of waterways of the inner docks. A few come up as far as the Pool, between Tower Bridge and London Bridge. There the cargo is lowered quickly onto barges because the ships must go downstream as the tide ebbs.

The heart of dockland is the Isle of Dogs, a small peninsula on the north bank formed by a loop in the river. Here are the West India Docks, the oldest docks in London. Some docks specialize in handling timber, others grain or meat. Surrounding the London docks near Tower Bridge are warehouses for storing ivory, spices, gums, and rubber. Tilbury Docks, 26 miles below London Bridge by water, can receive the largest vessels afloat.

Every ebb of the tide sees ships going downstream loaded with products of British industries. London imports much more than it exports, however, because most of its factories supply the home market.

**LONDON, Ontario.** Like the famous city of England from which it takes its name, London, Ont., is situated on a river named the Thames. It is in southwestern Ontario—115 miles southwest of Toronto and 23 miles north of Port Stanley, a harbor on Lake Erie.

Lieutenant governor John Graves Simcoe in 1792 chose this location as the future capital of Upper Canada. His plans miscarried, however, and no building was completed until 1826. When London was made the judicial center of the district soon after 1826, its growth was rapid. In 1855 it became a city.

London is now the financial, industrial, marketing, and distributing center for a rich and thickly settled agricultural section. Electric power from Niagara Falls adds to the city's advantages as a manufacturing center. Among its products are adhesives and abrasives, electrical equipment, chemicals, brass goods, iron, steel, textiles, paper boxes, and cereals.

The University of Western Ontario, founded in 1878, is in London. There is also a provincial teachers college. London's little theater has achieved a wide reputation, and the city has its own Conservatory of Music. (*See also* Ontario.) Population of city (1971 census), 223,222; metropolitan area, 286,011.

---

THESE ARTICLES ARE IN THE FACT-INDEX

London, University of London Bridge London Company

Londonderry, Northern Ireland Lone Mountain College

---

**LONG, Crawford Williamson** (1815–1878). On March 30, 1842, Dr. Crawford Long, a young surgeon of Jefferson, Ga., performed the first recorded operation on an anesthetized patient. He administered sulfuric ether before removing a tumor from the neck of James Venable, who felt no pain during the operation. The experiment was a complete success, but Long did not make his work public until 1849, after he had used ether in more operations. Meanwhile the benefits of surgical anesthesia had been proved by others, and Long's delay in reporting his discovery kept him for many years from being recognized as the pioneer anesthetist.

Crawford Williamson Long was born on Nov. 1, 1815, in Danielsville, Ga. He entered Franklin College (now the University of Georgia) at the age of 14 and took his medical degree at the University of Pennsylvania in 1839.

Strangely enough, Long's discovery of anesthesia was made as the result of a prank. A few weeks before the famous operation, some gay young friends of his saw a traveling medicine vendor demonstrate a new curiosity, laughing gas (nitrous oxide). Volunteers who inhaled this gas felt extremely exhilarated. Long's friends then asked him for permission to hold a "nitrous oxide frolic" in his room. Since he had no nitrous oxide, he gave them sulfuric ether. Excited by the gas the young men became hilariously rowdy and pommeled one another severely. Long noticed that none of them seemed to feel pain. He decided to experiment with ether in his surgical work.

After his achievement Long continued to live the quiet life of a country doctor. In 1850 he moved to Athens, Ga., where he died on June 16, 1878. In 1910 an obelisk was erected in Athens to his memory.

---

THESE ARTICLES ARE IN THE FACT-INDEX

Long, Huey Pierce Long, John Davis Long, John Luther

Long, Russell B(illiu) Long, Stephen Harriman

---

**LONG BEACH, Calif.** Because of farsighted industrial and civic planning and the discovery of large oil fields, beautiful Long Beach has grown from a small fishing village and seaside resort into one of California's chief cities. It lies 20 miles south of Los Angeles on a strip of coastal plain between San Pedro Bay and the snow-crested Sierra Madre range. The city is built on a terrace along the miles of white bathing beach, making it a favorite ocean resort. However, right in its "backyard" are thousands of oil derricks.

The amazing development of Long Beach began in 1921 with the discovery of petroleum on nearby Signal Hill. This great oil field of the Long Beach region soon became one of the nation's chief producers of petroleum. Another oil field was discovered in 1940 along the tidelands of the Port of Long Beach. The city receives large royalties from wells in this field.

Many industries soon came to Long Beach to use the cheap fuel provided by the Signal Hill field. They include oil refineries; aeronautical, shipbuilding, and automobile plants; gypsum works; soap factories; vegetable-oil plants; canneries; and packinghouses.

The Los Angeles-Long Beach Harbor is one of the greatest on the coast. It has two ports, one operated by Los Angeles, the other by Long Beach.

Long Beach was founded in 1881 by W. E. Willmore, an Englishman, and named Willmore City. It was incorporated as a city under its present name in 1888. The city is governed on the council-manager plan. It has a 3-million-dollar Civic Auditorium on the oceanfront, a Marine Stadium on Alamitos Bay, and a 740-acre municipal airport. There are fine parks, libraries, a city college, and a state college. (*See also* California.) Population (1980 census), 361,334.

---

THESE ARTICLES ARE IN THE FACT-INDEX

Long Beach, N. Y. Long Branch, N. J.

Longchamps Longcloth

---

# LONGFELLOW—
# Best Loved
# of American Poets

LONGFELLOW, Henry Wadsworth (1807–1882). Probably the best loved of American poets the world over is Henry Wadsworth Longfellow. Many of his lines are as familiar to us as rhymes from Mother Goose or the words of nursery songs learned in early childhood. Like these rhymes and melodies, they remain in the memory and accompany us through life.

There are two reasons for the popularity and significance of Longfellow's poetry. First, he had the gift of easy rhyme. He wrote poetry as a bird sings, with natural grace and melody. Read or heard once or twice, his rhyme and meters cling to the mind long after the sense may be forgotten.

Second, Longfellow wrote on obvious themes which appeal to all kinds of people. His poems are easily understood; they sing their way into the consciousness of those who read them. Above all, there is a joyousness in them, a spirit of optimism and faith in the goodness of life which evokes immediate response in the emotions of his readers.

Americans owe a great debt to Longfellow because he was among the first of American writers to use native themes. He wrote about the American scene and landscape, the American Indian ('Song of Hiawatha'), and American history and tradition ('The Courtship of Miles Standish', 'Evangeline'). At the beginning of the 19th century, America was a stumbling babe as far as a culture of its own was concerned. The people of America had spent their years and their energies in carving a habitation out of the wilderness and in fighting for independence. Literature, art, and music came mainly from Europe and especially from England. Nothing was considered worthy of attention unless it came from Europe.

But "the flowering of New England," as Van Wyck Brooks terms the period from 1815 to 1865, took place in Longfellow's day, and he made a great contribution to it. He lived when giants walked the New England earth, giants of intellect and feeling who established the New Land as a source of greatness. Nathaniel Hawthorne, Ralph Waldo Emerson, Henry David Thoreau, Oliver Wendell Holmes, and William Prescott were a few of the great minds and spirits among whom Longfellow took his place as a singer and as a representative of America.

## Family and Boyhood

The first Longfellow came to America in 1676 from Yorkshire, England. Among the ancestors of the poet

Longfellow was a striking figure, especially in later life. His flowing white hair and beard emphasized strong, peaceful features. In dress and manner he was simple and dignified.

on his mother's side were John and Priscilla Alden, of whom he wrote in 'The Courtship of Miles Standish'. His mother's father, Peleg Wadsworth, had been a general in the Revolutionary War. His own father was a lawyer. The Longfellow home represented the graceful living which was beginning to characterize the age.

Henry was the son of Stephen Longfellow and Zilpah Wadsworth Longfellow. He was born Feb. 27, 1807, in Portland, Me. Portland was a seaport, and this gave its citizens a breadth of view lacking in the more insular New England towns. The variety of people and the activity of the harbors stirred the mind of the boy and gave him a curiosity about life beyond his own immediate experience. He was sent to school when he was only three years old. When he was six, the following report of him was received at home: "Master Henry Longfellow is one of the best boys we have in school. He spells and reads very well. He can also add and multiply numbers. His conduct last quarter was very correct and amiable."

From the beginning it was evident that this boy was to be drawn to writing and the sound of words. His mother read aloud to him and his brothers and sisters the high romance of Ossian, the legendary Gaelic hero. Cervantes' 'Don Quixote' was a favorite among the books he read. But the book which influenced him most was Washington Irving's 'Sketch Book'. Irving was another American author for whom the native legend and landscape were sources of inspiration.

"Every reader has his first book," wrote Longfellow later. "I mean to say, one book among all others which in early youth first fascinates his imagination, and at once excites and satisfies the desires of his mind. To me the first book was the 'Sketch Book' of Washington Irving."

Longfellow's father was eager to have his son become a lawyer. But when Henry was a senior at Bowdoin College at Brunswick, Me., he gently asserted himself. He wrote his father, "I most eagerly aspire after future eminence in literature." It is significant that his graduation oration was on the topic "Our Native Writers."

### His Career Starts

Fortunately for Henry, when he was graduated from Bowdoin College at 19, the college established a chair of modern languages. The recent graduate was asked to become the first professor, with the understanding that he should be given a period of time in which to travel and study in Europe.

In May of 1826 the fair-haired youth with the azure blue eyes set out for Europe to turn himself into a scholar and a linguist. He had letters of introduction to men of note in England and France, but he had his own idea of how to travel. Between conferences with important people and courses in the universities, Longfellow walked through the countries. He stopped at small inns and cottages, talking to peasants, farmers, traders, his silver flute in his pocket as passport to friendship. He traveled in Spain, Italy, France, Germany, and England, and returned to America in 1829. At 22 he was launched upon his career as a college professor. He had to prepare his own texts, because at that time none were available.

Much tribute is due him as a teacher. Just as he served America in making the world conscious of its legend and tradition, so he opened to his students and to the American people the literary heritage of Europe. He created in them a new consciousness of the literature of Spain, France, Italy, and especially writings from the German, Nordic, and Icelandic cultures.

In 1831 he married Mary Storer Potter, whom he had known as a schoolmate. When he saw her at church upon his return to Portland, he was so struck with her beauty that he followed her home without courage enough to speak to her. With his wife he settled down in a house surrounded by elm trees. He expended his energies on translations from Old World literature and contributed travel sketches to the *New England Magazine,* in addition to serving as a professor and a librarian at Bowdoin.

### Tragedy and a New Life

In 1834 he was appointed to a professorship at Harvard and once more set out for Europe by way of preparation. This time his young wife accompanied him. The journey ended in tragedy. In Rotterdam his wife died, and Longfellow came alone to Cambridge and the new professorship. The lonely poet took a room at historic Craigie House, an old house overlooking the Charles River. It was owned by Mrs. Craigie, an eccentric woman who kept much to herself and was somewhat scornful of the young men to whom she let rooms. But she read widely and well, and her library contained complete sets of Voltaire and other French masters. Longfellow entered the beautiful old elm-encircled house as a lodger, not knowing that this was to be his home for the rest of his life. In time it passed into the possession of Nathan Appleton. Seven years after he came to Cambridge, Longfellow married Frances Appleton, daughter of Nathan Appleton, and Craigie House was given to the Longfellows as a wedding gift.

Meantime, in the seven intervening years, he remained a rather romantic figure in Cambridge, with his flowing hair and his yellow gloves and flowered waistcoats. He worked, however, with great determination and industry, publishing 'Hyperion', a prose romance that foreshadowed his love for Frances Appleton, and 'Voices of the Night', his first book

**CRAIGIE HOUSE, LONGFELLOW'S HOME**
Longfellow rented a room at Craigie House, once Gen. George Washington's headquarters, in 1836. Longfellow received the house, in Cambridge, Mass., as a wedding gift in 1843.

of poems. He journeyed again to Europe, wrote 'The Spanish Student', and took his stand with the abolitionists, returning to be married in 1843.

The marriage was a happy one, and the Longfellow house became the center of life in the university town. The old Craigie House was a shrine of hospitality and gracious living. The young people of Cambridge flocked there to play with the five Longfellow children—two boys and the three girls whom the poet describes in 'The Children's Hour' as "grave Alice and laughing Allegra and Edith with golden hair."

### Great Poems and a Second Tragedy

From his friend Nathaniel Hawthorne, Longfellow got the brief outline of a story from which he composed one of his most famous poems, 'Evangeline'. The original story had Evangeline wandering about New England in search of her bridegroom. Longfellow extended her journey through Louisiana and the western wilderness. She finds Gabriel at last, dying in Philadelphia.

'Evangeline' was published in 1847 and was widely acclaimed. Longfellow began to feel that his work as a teacher was a hindrance to his own writing. In 1854 he resigned from Harvard and with a great sense of freedom gave himself entirely to the joyous task of his own poetic writing. In June of that year he began 'The Song of Hiawatha'.

Henry Schoolcraft's book on Indians and several meetings with an Ojibway chief provided the background for 'Hiawatha'. The long poem begins with Gitche Manito, the Great Spirit, commanding his people to live in peace and tells how Hiawatha is born. It ends with the coming of the white man and Hiawatha's death.

The publication of 'Hiawatha' caused the greatest excitement. For the first time in American literature Indian themes gained recognition as sources of imagination, power, and originality. The appeal of 'Hiawatha' for generations of children and young people gives it an enduring place in world literature.

The gracious tale of John Alden and Priscilla came next to the poet's mind, and 'The Courtship of Miles Standish' was published in 1858. It is a work which reflects the ease with which he wrote and the pleasure and enjoyment he derived from his skill. Twenty-five thousand copies were sold during the first week of its publication, and 10,000 were ordered in London on the first day of publication.

In 1861 the happy life of the family came to an end. Longfellow's wife died of burns she received when packages of her children's curls, which she was sealing with matches and wax, burst into flame. Longfellow faced the bitterest tragedy of his life. He found some solace in the task of translating Dante into English and went to Europe for a change of scene.

### Longfellow's Last Years

The years following were filled with honors. He was given honorary degrees at the great universities of Oxford and Cambridge, invited to Windsor by Queen

**THE POINTED QUESTION**
As John Alden courts Priscilla Mullins on behalf of his friend, she asks him why he is not speaking for himself. Her question is the subject of Newell Convers Wyeth's illustration for Longfellow's 'The Courtship of Miles Standish'.
©Houghton Mifflin Company

Victoria, and called by request upon the Prince of Wales. He was chosen a member of the Russian Academy of Sciences and of the Spanish Academy.

When it became necessary to remove "the spreading chestnut tree" of Brattle Street, which Longfellow had written about in his 'Village Blacksmith', the children of Cambridge gave their pennies to build a chair out of the tree and gave it to Longfellow. He died on March 24, 1882. "Of all the sons of the New England morning," says Van Wyck Brooks, "he was the largest in his golden sweetness."

### Books by Longfellow

Longfellow's works include 'Outre-Mer' (travel sketches, 1835); 'Hyperion' (a romance in prose, 1839); 'Voices of the Night' (the first book of poems, 1839); 'Ballads and Other Poems' (1842); 'The Spanish Student' (a play, 1843); 'The Belfry of Bruges' (1846); 'Evangeline' (1847); 'Kavanagh' (a tale in prose, 1849); 'The Seaside and the Fireside' (1850); 'The Golden Legend' (1851); 'The Song of Hiawatha' (1855); 'The Courtship of Miles Standish' (1858); 'Tales of a Wayside Inn' (1863); 'The Divine Comedy of Dante Alighieri' (a translation, 1865–67); 'The Masque of Pandora' (1875); 'Kéramos and Other Poems' (1878); 'Ultima Thule' (1880); and 'In the Harbor' (1882).

THIS ARTICLE IS IN THE FACT-INDEX
**Longford, Ireland**

**JONES BEACH ON LONG ISLAND'S SOUTH SHORE**
With six miles of sand, Jones Beach can accommodate some 140,000 swimmers and sunbathers. They may swim in the ocean, a sheltered bay, or a heated pool. The resort, a state park, contains playfields, restaurants, and other facilities.

**LONG ISLAND.** Only nine states have larger populations than Long Island in New York State. Its great center, Brooklyn, is a borough of New York City. Most other places on the island are suburbs, growing swiftly to ease the pressure of population within the city. In one town, more than 15,000 homes were built between July 1947 and March 1951. Elsewhere huge apartment blocks sprang up to house as many as 12,000 people. (*See also* Brooklyn; New York, N. Y.)

The island extends from the lower Hudson River about 118 miles northeast. It roughly parallels the Connecticut coast, from which it is separated by Long Island Sound. It is from 15 to 23 miles wide and has an area of 1,401 square miles and a population (1980 census) of 6,728,074. (For map, *see* New York.)

A century and a half ago Long Island was a region of farms, pastures, dunes, and fishing villages, except at the Brooklyn end. Sag Harbor and the towns called The Hamptons were whaling ports. Blue Point was an oyster center.

The construction of rail lines, begun in the 1830's, led to rapid changes in the island. The western counties, Kings (coextensive with Brooklyn) and Queens, were absorbed into New York City and became a great industrial center (*see* Brooklyn). Nassau County grew to be a region of suburban homes. Suffolk County came to be noted for its summer resorts and its farms where vegetables and poultry—notably potatoes, cauliflower, and Long Island ducklings—are raised.

In recent decades a network of highways, bridges, and tunnels to New York City has speeded the huge flow of traffic and stimulated the island's growth. New York City's two huge airports, La Guardia and John F. Kennedy International, are both situated on Long Island.

The island was formed in the Ice Age, when the glacier that covered New England pushed a moraine into the ocean to rest on an underwater rocky ridge (*see* Ice Age). Many of the scenic areas on the island have been preserved in the state parks. Another tourist attraction is Sagamore Hill, President Theodore Roosevelt's home in Oyster Bay, Long Island. It was established as a national historic site in 1963. President Roosevelt lived at Sagamore Hill from 1886 until his death in 1919. He is buried in the cemetery nearby.

The early inhabitants were Delaware Indians, whose names remain in many geographical features of the region. Giovanni da Verrazzano, an Italian navigator exploring for France, saw the island in 1524, and Henry Hudson, an Englishman sailing for the Dutch, landed on it in 1609. Four years later the Dutch navigator Adriaen Block explored the north shore. The Dutch named the island and claimed it. When the English captured New Amsterdam in 1664, renaming it New York, the island became part of the city.

The battle of Long Island, Aug. 27, 1776, was fought on Brooklyn Heights. The British under Gen. William Howe outflanked the colonial troops and drove them from the field. Long Island remained in British hands until 1783.

---

THESE ARTICLES ARE IN THE FACT-INDEX

Long Island University
Longman, (Mary) Evelyn
  Beatrice
Longmont, Colo.
Longs Peak, Colo.
Longstreet, Augustus
  Baldwin

Longstreet, James
Longview, Tex.
Longview, Wash.
Longwood College
Longworth,
  Nicholas
Lönnrot, Elias

---

**LOON.** "As crazy as a loon" is an expression that comes from the strange laughterlike notes which the common loon sends ringing across the waters of North American inland lakes. This bird and three other species make up the family *Gaviidae*.

During the nesting season loons live near freshwater lakes and ponds. In winter they cruise the seas and large lakes, often living 50 or more miles from land. Because their webbed feet are set far back on the body, they are clumsy creatures on land, wobbling along with the assistance of their wings and bill. Although they have some difficulty in rising from the water, they are strong fliers. Fishes, frogs, and aquatic insects are their chief food. Their nests, with two brown eggs, are usually roughly fashioned near the water. The parents are remarkably affectionate, swimming about in company with their young and carrying them on their backs when they grow tired.

The common loon is about 32 inches in length. In summer its plumage is a beautiful black spotted and barred with white, shading to pure white beneath. In winter the upper parts are blackish without white spots. It breeds from Labrador to Maine and west to northern Illinois and winters from the Great Lakes south. (For picture in color, *see* Birds.)

The red-throated loon, a smaller species about 25 inches in length, visits the United States only during winter, when it frequents both the Atlantic and Pacific coasts. The plumage of the back, wings, and tail is a dusky brown slightly spotted with white.

Its name is derived from its chestnut-colored foreneck. The Pacific loon has black upper parts with a band of white streaks on the throat. It is found in the United States mainly in winter, when it ranges along the Pacific coast from Alaska to Lower California. The loon is the state bird of Minnesota.

The loons form the order *Gaviiformes* or birds of diving type. The scientific name of the common loon is *Gavia immer immer;* of Pacific loon, *Gavia arctica pacifica;* of red-throated loon, *Gavia stellata.* Some classifications use the generic name *Colymbus*, of the grebes, for loons.

---

THESE ARTICLES ARE IN THE FACT-INDEX

Loos, Anita
Loos-en-Gohelle, France
Loosestrife
Loosestrife family
López, Carlos Antonio
López de Legaspi, Miguel
López de Villalobos, Ruy
López Mateos, Adolfo
Lop Nor
Loquat
Lorain, Ohio
Loras College
Lorca, Spain
Lord
Lord Dunmore's War
Lord Howe Island
Lord's Prayer, The
Lord's Supper

Lorelei
Lorentz, Hendrik Antoon
Lorentz, Pare
Lorenz, Adolf
Lorenz, Konrad Zacharias
Lorenzetti, Ambrogio and Pietro
Lorenzo de' Medici
Loretto Heights College
Lorient, France
Lorimer, George Horace
Loring, Eugene
Loris
'Lorna Doone'
Lorrain. Claude
Lory
Los Altos, Calif.
Los Angeles, Victoria de

---

# LOS ANGELES—City of Sunshine and Industry

**LOS ANGELES, Calif.** On the Pacific coast of southern California lies an urban area that some people expect to become the largest in the world. The heart of this swelling community is the city of Los Angeles.

Within its limits live about 3 million people. Another 4.5 million reside outside the city proper but within the Los Angeles-Long Beach Standard Metropolitan Statistical Area, which includes all of Los Angeles County. Between 1960 and 1980 the population of this metropolitan area increased by almost 1.5 million persons.

### Sprawling Giant of a City

Los Angeles lies on a sun-drenched plain between the San Gabriel Mountains and the Pacific Ocean. The nation's third largest city in population, it covers an area of 464 square miles. This is one of the largest land areas of any city in the world.

The 32-story City Hall dominates the Civic Center in downtown Los Angeles. It was completed in 1928.

The city thrusts a finger nine miles long and half a mile wide down to the coast to include within its corporate limits the communities of San Pedro and Wilmington. Here is Los Angeles Harbor, one of the nation's leading seaports, with a busy Oriental and coastwise trade. From the shore line it stretches 44 miles inland to residential districts in the foothills of the mountains.

Included within its limits are the fertile acres of the San Fernando Valley; Mount Lukens (Sister Elsie Peak), which towers 5,081 feet above sea level; and some of the richest oil fields in the world. In its swift expansion Los Angeles has overtaken and surrounded the independent cities of Santa Monica, Culver City, San Fernando, and Beverly Hills. Others, such as Pasadena, Glendale, Burbank, Inglewood, and Long Beach, fit into the borders of its uneven outline like the pieces of a jigsaw puzzle. (*See* Glendale; Long Beach; Pasadena.)

### Entertainment a Major Industry

The motion-picture industry settled in Los Angeles about 1910. It was attracted by the variety of scenery and the clear, mild weather. With most films now being made in soundproof enclosures, scenery and climate are no longer so important. Nevertheless, the industry has continued to grow and now produces almost 90 per cent of the nation's motion pictures.

Hollywood, the traditional name of movieland, is not a suburb but a section of Los Angeles. The suburbs of Culver City, Burbank, Beverly Hills, and

**Population:** 2,966,763 (1980 census); metropolitan area, 7,477,657. Growth of city: *1850,* 1,610; *1890,* 50,395; *1900,* 102,479; *1910,* 319,198; *1920,* 576,673; *1930,* 1,238,048; *1940,* 1,504,277; *1950,* 1,970,358; *1960,* 2,479,015.

**Area (Land):** 464 sq. mi.; of county, 4,060 sq. mi.; of metropolitan area, 4,060 sq. mi.

**Climate:** *Average Temperatures*—monthly average, 73.0° F (July); monthly average, 55.8° (January); annual average, 64.4°. *Precipitation*—annual average, 14.68 inches; monthly high, 3.27 inches (February); monthly low, .01 inch (July). *Sunshine*—Percentage of possible sunshine, 72.

**Principal Water Shipments:** *Exports*—Crude petroleum and refined petroleum products, aircraft, raw cotton, canned fish, citrus fruits. *Imports*—Sugar, bananas, tin, coffee, rubber, raw silk, lumber. *Coastwise*—Fish, lumber, crude petroleum, canned goods, cotton.

**Principal Manufactures:** Refined petroleum, oil-well machinery and tools; aircraft, parts, and engines; canned fish, meats; motion pictures, ships, automobiles, tires and tubes, furniture, women's clothing, chemicals, metal products.

Universal City (unincorporated) also have large studios. Radio broadcasting, television, and phonograph recording have also flourished in this great center of entertainment.

The motion-picture industry, together with the mild climate and other attractions, has made Los Angeles an important tourist center. In one year during the

California Department of Public Works

To ease its transportation problem Los Angeles has constructed a network of high-speed freeways. The "Stack" is the transfer point for four freeways which intersect near the City Hall.

Earl Dotter—B.B.M. Associates

The heavily populated, sprawling area of Los Angeles includes a wide variety of neighborhoods. Mobile homes in fixed position make up this residential neighborhood near a freeway.

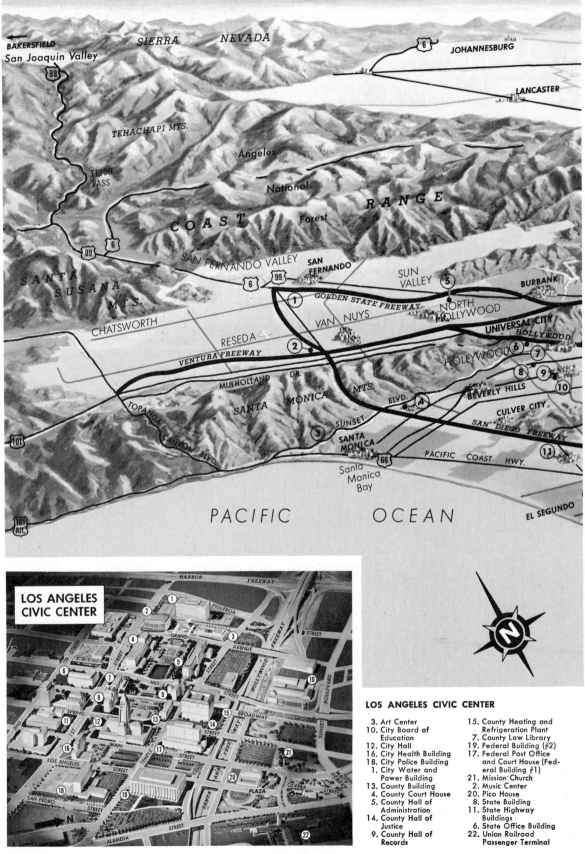

BAKERSFIELD
San Joaquin Valley

SIERRA     NEVADA

JOHANNESBURG

LANCASTER

TEHACHAPI MTS.

Angeles

TEJON
PASS

National

COAST     RANGE

Forest

SAN FERNANDO VALLEY

SANTA
SUSANA
MTS.

SAN
FERNANDO

SUN
VALLEY

BURBANK

CHATSWORTH

GOLDEN STATE FREEWAY

NORTH
HOLLYWOOD

VAN NUYS

UNIVERSAL CITY
HOLLYWOOD

RESEDA

HOLLYWOOD

VENTURA FREEWAY

MULHOLLAND     DR.

BEVERLY HILLS

SANTA     MONICA     MTS.

BLVD.

CULVER CITY

SUNSET

SAN DIEGO FREEWAY

TOPANGA CANYON BLVD.

SANTA
MONICA

Santa
Monica
Bay

PACIFIC COAST HWY.

EL SEGUNDO

PACIFIC     OCEAN

## LOS ANGELES CIVIC CENTER

HARBOR     FREEWAY

FIGUEROA

GRAND     AVENUE

STREET

HOLLYWOOD     FREEWAY

BOULEVARD

SPRING

HILL

BROADWAY

SUNSET

2ND

1ST

MAIN

TEMPLE

STREET

LOS ANGELES

SANTA     ANA     FREEWAY

OLVERA

PLAZA

SAN PEDRO

ALAMEDA

N

### LOS ANGELES CIVIC CENTER

3. Art Center
10. City Board of Education
12. City Hall
16. City Health Building
18. City Police Building
1. City Water and Power Building
13. County Building
4. County Court House
5. County Hall of Administration
14. County Hall of Justice
9. County Hall of Records
15. County Heating and Refrigeration Plant
7. County Law Library
19. Federal Building (#2)
17. Federal Post Office and Court House (Federal Building #1)
21. Mission Church
2. Music Center
20. Pico House
8. State Building
11. State Highway Buildings
6. State Office Building
22. Union Railroad Passenger Terminal

352

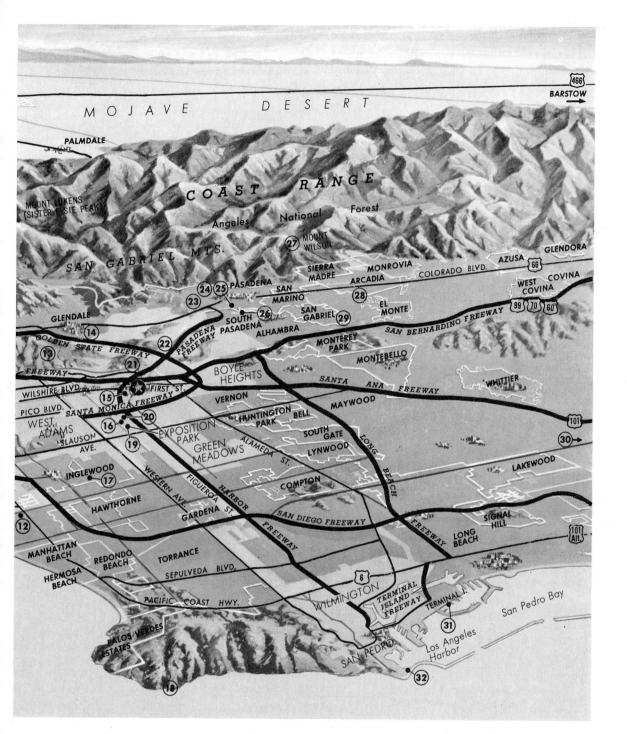

Places of Interest in
# LOS ANGELES
and Vicinity

⭐ CIVIC CENTER

25. California Institute of Technology
24. Christmas Tree Lane (Santa Rosa Ave.)
30. Disneyland
21. Dodger Stadium (Dodgers' Baseball Park)
19. Exposition Park: County Museum; Memorial
    Coliseum; Memorial Sports Arena; State
    Exposition Building
 8. Farmers Market
14. Forest Lawn Memorial Park
 7. Grauman's Chinese Theater
13. Griffith Park: Greek Theatre; Zoo;
    Observatory and Planetarium
 6. Hollywood Bowl
17. Hollywood Park Race Track
26. Huntington Library and Art Gallery
 9. La Brea Tar Pits (Hancock Park)
 5. Lockheed Air Terminal
12. Los Angeles International Airport

11. Loyola University
18. Marineland of the Pacific
32. Marine Museum
10. Miracle Mile
27. Mount Wilson Observatory
15. Public Library
23. Rose Bowl
 1. San Fernando Mission
29. San Gabriel Mission
28. Santa Anita Park Race Track
 2. Sepulveda Dam Recreation Area
20. Shrine Civic Auditorium
22. Southwest Museum
31. United States Naval Station
 4. University of California at Los Angeles
    (U.C.L.A.)
16. University of Southern California
 3. Will Rogers State Park

353

## HIGH LIGHTS IN THE LOS ANGELES AREA

### Places of Business

Aircraft manufacturing plants: Douglas, in Santa Monica; Lockheed, in Burbank; North American, in Los Angeles; Northrop, in Hawthorne.

Lockheed Air Terminal (opened 1928), at Burbank.

Los Angeles International Airport (opened 1927): one of the largest air terminals in the United States.

Miracle Mile, along Wilshire Boulevard: noted for its supermodern retail and service establishments.

Motion-picture studios: Columbia, Paramount, and United Artists, all in Hollywood; Warner Brothers and Disney, in Burbank; MGM, in Culver City; 20th Century-Fox, in Beverly Hills; Universal-International, in Universal City.

Wilmington Oil Field (opened 1936): greatest producing oil field in nation except East Texas.

### Places of Culture

Griffith Observatory and Planetarium (built 1935): museum of astronomy, physics, chemistry, and geology.

Huntington Library and Art Gallery (opened 1928), in San Marino: rare books, manuscripts, art collection.

Los Angeles County Museum of Art (opened 1965).

Los Angeles County Museum of Natural History (opened 1913): includes relics from La Brea pits.

Los Angeles Music Center for the Performing Arts (opened 1964): music, opera, ballet, and theater.

Los Angeles Public Library (central building opened 1926): 52 branches, 4 bookmobiles.

Mount Wilson Observatory (established 1904): eight large telescopes, exhibit hall, and technical library.

### Places of Education

California Institute of Technology, at Pasadena (founded 1891).

California State College at Los Angeles (founded 1949).

Claremont Graduate School and University Center, at Claremont (incorporated 1925).

Immaculate Heart College (founded 1916).

Los Angeles City College (founded 1929).

Loyola University of Los Angeles (founded 1929).

Mount St. Mary's College (founded 1925).

Occidental College (founded 1887).

Pepperdine University (founded 1937).

University of California at Los Angeles (opened 1919).

University of Redlands, at Redlands (founded 1907).

University of Southern California (opened 1880).

Whittier College, at Whittier (founded 1901).

### Other Places of Interest

Angeles National Forest, northeast of city: has about 700,000 acres of mountainous recreational area.

Brookside Park, in Pasadena: home of the Rose Bowl.

Disneyland, amusement park (opened 1955) in Anaheim: has educational exhibits (Frontierland, Tomorrowland).

Forest Lawn Memorial Park (founded 1917), at Glendale: elaborately maintained cemetery.

Griffith Park, 4,253 acres (opened 1912): zoo.

Hancock Park: La Brea tar pits; prehistoric bones.

Hollywood Bowl (organized 1922): natural amphitheater in Beachwood Canyon; seats 20,000.

Los Angeles Dodger Stadium (opened 1962): baseball park in Chavez Ravine; seats 56,000.

Los Angeles Memorial Coliseum (completed 1923): stadium seating 105,000; adjacent Memorial Sports Arena (1960) seats 17,500 for sports events.

Olvera Street, or Walk of the Angels: preserves the markets and cafés of "Old Mexico."

San Fernando Mission (founded 1797): restored convent.

San Gabriel Mission (founded 1794), at San Gabriel: first Los Angeles County settlement (1771).

Santa Catalina Island: resort 25 miles off the coast.

Los Angeles Chamber of Commerce

One of the city's oil fields—the Venice-Playa Del Rey, first drilled in 1930—stands along Santa Monica Bay.

1950's almost 4 million out-of-state vacationists spent more than $600,000,000 in the Los Angeles area.

### The Nation's Third City in Industry

The economic base of Los Angeles is diversified. Although manufacturing is the dominant industry, it employs less than half of all the workers in the area. The others are engaged in small businesses, services, trades, and fishing. Farming is also an important occupation in the outlying sections.

In the manufacture of aircraft, the Los Angeles area leads the world. Like the "movies," this industry was first attracted to southern California by the high percentage of clear days—"350 flying days a year." During World War II the manufacture of aircraft grew enormously.

Los Angeles assembles more automobiles than any other city except Detroit. It makes almost as many rubber tires and inner tubes as Akron and more furniture than Grand Rapids. It is a leader in food processing and in oil refining. It makes more oil-well machinery than any other city except Houston. In the manufacture of women's clothing it is second only to New York City. The city ranks high in fabricated metal products and as an insurance and banking center.

### The Water Front and Fisheries

The harbor, 20 miles from "downtown" Los Angeles, was originally an unprotected seaway rimmed by mud flats. In 1909 the city annexed the sleepy little coastal villages of San Pedro and Wilmington. With the aid of the federal government, it then built one of the world's largest man-made harbors.

A great breakwater enclosed a roadstead where ships safely rode at anchor. The dredging of channels and slips made an inner harbor with 46 miles of water front (with Long Beach) and hundreds of acres of re-

Ewing Galloway

This view looks across the East Basin Channel to oil-storage tanks jutting into the Main Channel of Los Angeles Harbor.

Ewing Galloway

Almost deserted during the day the famous Grauman's Chinese Theater in Hollywood is a popular recreation center at night.

claimed land for terminals, warehouses, and shipyards. Here is one of the nation's "free ports" where imports may be stored duty free. Each year the port handles about 6,000 ships carrying hundreds of millions of dollars in cargo.

The harbor is also the home port of one of the world's largest fisheries. The annual commercial catch is about 500,000,000 pounds, with tuna and mackerel the most important.

## The People of the Los Angeles Area

The Los Angeles-Long Beach metropolitan area (population, 1980 census, 7,477,657) is the second largest in the United States, ranking only behind New York City. The metropolitan area, redefined in 1963, consists only of Los Angeles County. The city

of Los Angeles is the third largest in the nation.

Within the city are many distinct communities. They vary in size from Hollywood, which has a population of about 129,000, to Del Rey Palisades, which has less than 5,000 inhabitants. Other large communities are Van Nuys, North Hollywood, Green Meadows, and Boyle Heights.

In 1980 there were over 1,600,000 foreign-born inhabitants in the Los Angeles area. The largest single group is from Mexico. Canada, England (and Wales), Germany, Russia, and Cuba are the countries of origin of other large groups.

### Arrangement of the City

The sprawling area covered by Los Angeles and its decentralization into many separate communities make it a true city of the motor age. There are some 4.3 million passenger cars registered in Los Angeles, Orange, and Ventura counties. These have the highest ratio of cars to people in the United States. The resulting heavy traffic is carried by the world's most extensive network of freeways and expressways. These high-speed, limited-access roads already total about 400 miles. Ultimately, the system is planned to comprise more than 1,300 miles.

In the city the numbered streets run approximately east and west, with Main Street as the base line. North and south streets have First Street as the base.

The original heart of Los Angeles was near the present Plaza. It was a Mexican pueblo laid out in 1781. Still the center of the Mexican population, this section is gay with shops and restaurants. Almost as colorful is New Chinatown, a few blocks to the northwest. Of modern oriental architecture, with landscaped courts and narrow arcades, it grew up when old Chinatown was razed to make room for the giant Union Station east of the Plaza.

The Civic Center is south of the Plaza. The plan for its construction was adopted in 1941, with some later revisions. The Center includes the 32-story City Hall and several other government buildings (see the map of the Civic Center on page 352). The Civic Center when completed will also include a state historical park and landscaped parkways. Some parts of the city government are being decentralized to branch administrative centers such as those in Van Nuys and Hollywood.

Northwest of the Civic Center is the community of

A lithograph in 'Reports of Explorations and Surveys' in the collection of the Library of Congress shows Los Angeles as it appeared shortly after receiving a city charter in 1850. The area soon began to grow and is still expanding.

Hollywood, with its world-famous crossroads of Hollywood and Vine streets. Here are the western headquarters of the national radio and television networks, Hollywood Bowl, and Grauman's Chinese Theater.

The specialty shops, restaurants, and night clubs along Sunset Boulevard from Hollywood to Beverly Hills make up the Sunset Strip. Another famous section is the Miracle Mile along Wilshire Boulevard, which runs west to the ocean at Santa Monica. Here are many large shops and department stores.

### Education, Culture, Recreation

Young people in Los Angeles have every educational opportunity. They may take their choice of one of the many colleges and universities in the area (*see* table on a preceding page). The California Institute of the Arts, in Burbank, and Otis Art Institute offer courses in fine and commercial arts.

In 1964 the Philharmonic Orchestra took up residence in the new Los Angeles Music Center for the Performing Arts. Two opera companies, a chorus, and a theater group are also in residence at the center. The city supports two major daily newspapers, nine television stations, and over 30 radio stations.

Los Angeles has more than 200 public parks and playgrounds, totaling about 8,800 acres. Within easy driving distance are miles of ocean beaches. The nearby mountains are the site of many winter sports. The recreational island of Santa Catalina is only 25 miles out from Los Angeles harbor. The old Spanish missions attract many visitors. Nearby are two of the world's largest telescopes at the Hale Observatories (Palomar and Mount Wilson).

Pasadena's Tournament of Roses on New Year's Day is a spectacular flower festival. Its climax is the intersectional Rose Bowl football game. Memorial Coliseum is the home football field of the University of Southern California, the University of California at Los Angeles, and the Los Angeles Rams, a professional team. The Los Angeles Dodger Stadium was carved out of a mountainous Chavez Ravine site.

### The Government of Los Angeles

Since 1925 the city has had a mayor-council type of government. The mayor is popularly elected for a four-year term. The city council consists of 15 members, each representing a separate district. Councilmen serve four-year terms.

Much of the work is done by boards of commissioners, who are appointed by the mayor subject to approval of the council. There are more than 20 such boards, including those for city planning, police, fire, health, parks, municipal housing, and the harbor. The city also serves as the county seat of Los Angeles County. Within the county are special governmental units for flood control, lighting, sanitation, and fire protection. The Metropolitan Water District administers the water supply of 48 cities in Southern California.

### History of the City

Los Angeles was founded in 1781 by the Spanish governor of California, Felipe de Neve, near the site of the Indian village of Yang-na. It was named *El Pueblo de Nuestra Señora la Reina de Los Angeles de Porciuncula*—the Town of Our Lady Queen of the Angels of Porciuncula (a chapel in Italy). At that time it was a sleepy settlement of 44 people.

Under later Mexican rule it alternated with Monterey as the capital of California. During the Mexican War, the village was taken by Americans in 1847. It received a city charter in 1850.

Adventurers from the San Francisco gold rush moved to Los Angeles and made it a lawless cow town popularly called "Los Diablos." The Southern Pacific railroad arrived in 1876 from San Francisco. The Santa Fe line arrived in 1885 and began a rate war with the Southern Pacific. Middle Westerners poured

The Los Angeles Dodger Stadium, opened in Chavez Ravine in the spring of 1962, can seat 56,000 people. Notable among its many luxurious features are its ample parking facilities.

into the city. When the boom collapsed in 1888, many of them returned home, paying full fare. Two years later the population was more than 50,000.

In 1892 oil was discovered and a new boom began. By now irrigation was beginning to turn the semiarid plain into the richest agricultural county in the United States. In 1914 the great harbor on the Pacific was opened. Meanwhile an aqueduct 233 miles long was piping the entire flow of the Owens River into the county. Still the city and its need of water grew. In 1941 the Colorado River Aqueduct was completed. The system was expanded in 1951–59 (see Aqueducts). In the mid-1960's new systems were being built.

The city gained almost half a million in population between 1910 and 1920. Motion pictures, oil, and new manufacturing industries added more than half a million in the next decade. During World War II the city grew by another 300,000. The 1970 census showed an increase of 330,581 over the 1960 census.

Among the city's recent achievements are the expansion and improvement of the 265-acre Los Angeles International Airport and the construction of a new 16-million-dollar passenger and cargo terminal in the harbor area. The Vincent Thomas Bridge was opened in 1963. In 1971 Los Angeles was hit by a devastating earthquake. Smog is still a problem in the city, and efforts are being made to eliminate this nuisance. (See also California.)

---

THESE ARTICLES ARE IN THE FACT-INDEX

Lossing, Benson John
"Lost Battalion, The"
Lost Colony of Virginia
Lota, Chile
Lothair I (Holy Roman emperor)
Lothair II

Lothair II (king of Lorraine)
Lothian, Philip Henry Kerr, 11th marquis of
Loti, Pierre
Lottery

---

**LOTUS.** In the Odyssey, Homer tells about the magical lotus fruit that caused those who ate it to forget country, home, and friends. Through the centuries the expression "lotus-eater" has meant a dreamy, lazy person who has lost contact with reality. In ancient Greece, the lotus was probably a prickly shrub (*Zizyphus lotus*) with a sweet, mealy fruit. This is still eaten in some Mediterranean districts. Today, however, the word is usually associated with the blue Egyptian lotus or the sacred pink lotus of the Chinese, Japanese, and Hindus.

The American lotus (also called the yellow water lily, water chinquapin, or nelumbo) is a magnificent water lily found from southern Ontario to Texas and Louisiana. It is especially abundant in the Mississippi and Missouri rivers, and at Grass Lake, in northern Illinois. The plants form a dense tangle of giant circular leaves up to 30 inches across, raised on strong stems 2 to 6 feet above the water. The Indians ate the rootstocks and seeds.

In art and architecture the lotus, in conventionalized designs, is a common ornament. This design

The American lotus, or nelumbo, spreads a luxuriant carpet of glossy green leaves and large yellow blossoms over ponds and lakes of the eastern United States. It is a water lily.

originated in Egypt, where it was used on the capitals of columns, and in India and China. It still appears in modern European and American art.

The lotuses belong to the water-lily family *Nymphaeaceae*. The American lotus (*Nelumbo lutea*) is closely related to the pink East Indian lotus (*Nelumbo nucifera*). The Egyptian lotus of the Nile River belongs to a related genus—*Nymphaea*. *Nymphaea lotus* has white or rose petals. *Nymphaea coerulea* has blue petals. Lotus is also the name of a genus of the pea family (*Leguminosae*), of which the bird's-foot trefoil (*Lotus corniculatus*), a small perennial herb, is the most widespread.

---

THESE ARTICLES ARE IN THE FACT-INDEX

Lotze, Rudolf Hermann
Loubet, Émile
Loucks, Henry Langford
Lougheed, Peter

Louis II (Holy Roman emperor)
Louis III, the Blind
Louis IV, the Bavarian
Louis II, the German

---

# LOUIS—
## Kings of France

THE FIRST of the many French kings to bear the name Louis was actually Clovis (ruled 481–511), founder of the kingdom of the Franks (*see* Clovis). In after years the "C" was dropped and the "v" was written as "u," thus making the name Louis. It is the same as the English Lewis and the German Ludwig.

**LOUIS THE PIOUS** (ruled 814–840) is usually reckoned as Louis I. He was the son of Charlemagne, and he succeeded his father both as king of the Franks and as Holy Roman Emperor (*see* Charlemagne). The great empire built up by Charlemagne was divided after Louis I died, and the next four rulers of this name left too little mark on the course of history to deserve mention here.

Pious St. Louis (Louis IX) led one of the last Crusades. The Saracens took him prisoner in Egypt and held him for a large ransom. During his captivity he won the admiration of the Saracen chiefs.

**LOUIS VI,** "the Fat" (ruled 1108–1137), was the first important king of the Capetian line. This line sprang from Hugh Capet, who became king in 987. Louis the Fat was a great fighter, a great hunter, and a great eater. At 46 he became too fat to mount a horse, but he remained the embodiment of warlike energy. His great task was to reduce to order the petty nobles of the royal domain, who were truly "robber barons." When Louis came to the throne every lord of a castle robbed at will, and it was not safe for even the king to pass along the road. Twenty years of hard fighting were necessary to remedy this condition, but in the end the king triumphed, and law and order prevailed. So that such evils might not recur, every castle that was captured was destroyed or given to faithful followers.

**LOUIS VII** (ruled 1137–1180) was the eldest son of Louis VI. Shortly before his death, Louis VI arranged for his son's marriage to Eleanor of Aquitaine. By this marriage southwest France was added to the domains of the new French king. Unfortunately Louis soon discovered that his beautiful queen was something of a flirt. He himself was very religious.

In 1147 Louis departed for the Holy Land on the Second Crusade, taking his queen with him. This Crusade was a miserable failure (*see* Crusades). After they returned, Louis had his marriage annulled

(1152). Eleanor at once sent an embassy to Henry, Count of Anjou and Duke of Normandy, proposing marriage. Henry was overjoyed because the alliance transferred to him the great duchy of Guienne. Two years later Henry and Eleanor were crowned king and queen of England. (*See* Henry, Kings of England, Henry II.) France thus lost a rich territory to England, its greatest rival.

**LOUIS VIII** (ruled 1223–1226), the son of Philip Augustus, reigned too short a time to accomplish anything of real importance.

**LOUIS IX** (born 1214, ruled 1226–1270), called Saint Louis, was one of the most virtuous and heroic kings of France. He was the dutiful son of Louis VIII and his queen, Blanche of Castile. Blanche was a remarkable woman. During her son's minority she bravely faced numerous revolts of powerful feudal nobles. In her son she was fortunate, for he had all the good qualities and few of the bad ones of the age in which he lived. Indeed, his virtues were so remarkable that after his death the Roman Catholic church declared him a saint.

Louis's acts of piety, such as wearing a haircloth shirt, fasting, and waiting on lepers, were usually performed in private. To the world he was a fearless knight, thoroughly trained in the art of war; a conscientious, just, and able king, usually good-humored and kindly, but at times impatient and angry. He was a strong ruler, who greatly strengthened the royal power. He improved the government by appointing local officials who were responsible to him for the administration of justice, the collection of taxes, and the government of their districts. He encouraged the people to appeal to him if the nobles oppressed them or if his officials were unjust. He improved the administration of justice by abolishing trials by combat and by using in his courts the new lawyers trained in the Roman law, in place of the churchmen who, formerly, alone could read and write. These reforms not only benefited the people but they checked the power of the nobles, who, according to a writer of the time, "undertook nothing against their king, seeing clearly that the hand of the Lord was with him."

Saint Louis made two crusades—one to Egypt and the Holy Land (1248–54), on which he was captured and held for ransom by the Mohammedans; and the other to Tunis, in 1270, where he died of the plague.

**LOUIS X** (born 1289), ruled for only two years, 1314–1316.

**LOUIS XI** (born 1423, ruled 1461–1483) presents a striking contrast to Louis IX. In appearance Louis XI was ugly and unkingly; in character he was unscrupulous and underhanded. Like his contemporaries, Caesar Borgia and Richard III, he was an embodiment of the principle which we call Machiavellian. He believed that "he who has success has honor" and cared nothing for the way in which he attained success. He made promises only to break them, unless he had sworn by one particular saint; then his word was good. His one ambition seemed to be to extend the boundaries of France. Although he was too stingy to buy a hat to replace the shabby one he wore, he spent large sums in buying back border cities. In his conflicts with the nobles, especially with Charles the Bold, Duke of Burgundy, he also acquired much territory, so that by the time of his death most of the land of France was under the direct control of the king. The power of the crown in the latter part of his reign was truly absolute over the territory it held.

Sir Walter Scott, in his novel 'Quentin Durward', gives a very fine description of Louis XI, as well as an excellent survey of the customs and traditions of the period.

**LOUIS XII** (born 1462, ruled 1498–1515) is chiefly noted for the Italian wars, begun by his predecessor Charles VIII, and continued after Louis XII by Francis I.

**LOUIS XIII** (born 1601, ruled 1610–1643) is chiefly important for the fact that, in spite of all opposition, for 18 years he kept in power his able minister, Richelieu (*see* Richelieu, Cardinal). The first years of the reign were filled with anarchy and disorder. The king was a child, and his mother, who ruled for him, was weak and selfish. When Richelieu came into

**LOUIS XI, A MASTER OF INTRIGUE**
This king was physically weak and ugly, but he was very intelligent, and relentless in gaining his ends. Around his shabby hat he wore images of saints—for he was pious, in his way.

power, however, all this was changed. The Huguenots were reduced from a powerful political party to a mere religious body, and the nobles were humbled (*see* Huguenots). National unity and religious peace were secured at home, and France was raised to the first position among the powers of Europe.

**LOUIS XIV** (born 1638, ruled 1643–1715) inherited this power from his father and carried it further. He was styled the Grand Monarch, and his brilliant court at Versailles became the model and the despair of other less rich and powerful princes, who accepted his theory of absolute monarchy (*L'état c'est moi,* "I am the state"). Until 1661 the government was largely in the hands of the wily Italian Cardinal Mazarin. At the cardinal's death Louis declared that he would be his own prime minister. From then on he worked faithfully at "his trade of a king."

A passion for fame and the desire to increase French territory in Europe were the leading motives of Louis XIV. He neglected the opportunities to gain an empire in America and India and involved France in wars which ruined the country financially and paved the way for the outbreak of the French Revolution.

His first war (1667–68) was an attempt to enforce flimsy claims to part of the Spanish Netherlands (Belgium). His second (1672–78) was directed against "their High Mightinesses," the States-General of Holland, who had balked him of his prey in the first contest. In spite of the great military power of France, the Dutch admiral De Ruyter twice defeated the fleets of the French and their English allies, and Louis XIV failed ingloriously in his attempt to conquer Holland. The third war (1689–97) also was directed chiefly against Holland, whose "Stadholder" had now become King William III of England. The German province of the Palatinate was terribly wasted, but the Peace of Ryswick brought only slight gains for France. Louis's last and greatest effort was the War of the Spanish Succession (1701–13). In this conflict the English Duke of Marlborough (*see* Marlborough) was the principal leader of the opposing European coalition. The right to seat his grandson Philip V on the throne of Spain was small compensation for the thousands of lives and the millions of treasure which the French king wasted in the struggle.

Millions more were spent by Louis in building the beautiful palace at Versailles, near Paris, and in maintaining his brilliant court. There etiquette "became the real constitution of France." It required seven persons, some of them the highest princes of the realm, to put the king's shirt on him at his getting up (*levée*) in the morning. A French historian says of Louis XIV: "He was a god in his temple, celebrating his own worship in the midst of his host of priests and faithful." This extravagance of the court meant a heavy burden of taxation for the common people, who were thereby reduced to a misery so great that three quarters of a century later they rose up in rebellion and drove the Bourbons from the throne.

Louis XIV has the distinction of ruling longer than any other European king; for it was 72 years from the time when he ascended the throne, as a child of less than five, until his death in 1715. The Grand Monarch had outlived both his son and his son's son, so that he was succeeded by his five-year-old great-grandson, Louis XV.

**LOUIS XV** (born 1710, ruled 1715–1774). The luxurious court of Louis XIV was continued under

**THE GRAND MONARCH OF FRANCE**

Louis XIV, the Grand Monarch, is shown here in all the pomp of his royal robes. The common people of France had to pay for all his magnificence in frightful burdens of taxation. Three quarters of a century later another Louis paid with his life for the follies of his luxury-loving ancestors.

Louis XV, who came to the throne at the age of five. The evils from which the country suffered were clearly recognized, but the king when he grew up was too lazy and selfish to try to remedy them. Misgovernment was common at home, and the position of France abroad was lowered by the loss of its colonial possessions in India and America. These misfortunes, however, made little impression on the king or his courtiers, whose attitude was expressed in the phrase, "After us the deluge."

**LOUIS XVI** (born 1754, ruled 1774–1792). The storm broke in the reign of Louis XVI. Awkward and timid, no man could have appeared less like a king than did Louis XVI, who was 20 years old when he came to the throne; and none could have seemed more out of place in the brilliant and polished court of which he was the center. Louis realized this himself and often wished, even before the Revolution, that he were only a common man. He was a good horseman, fond of hunting, and delighted in making and mending locks. His greatest fault was that he was always ready to listen to and follow the advice of others. When this advice was good all went well; but in the latter part of Louis's reign the advice was bad and it cost the king his life.

When he first came to the throne he entrusted the management of the finances of the kingdom to Turgot, one of the greatest of statesmen. As long as the king followed his minister's advice, the state of the kingdom was improved. But he was more often under the influence of the beautiful but frivolous and extravagant queen, Marie Antoinette, and of the selfish courtiers. They opposed any financial reforms which would threaten their "graft" and pensions and life of ease, and they soon persuaded the king to dismiss his able minister.

### The Beginning of the French Revolution

From this time on the situation gradually grew worse, and finally Louis XVI was forced to call the Estates-General, a body which had not met since 1614. Its meeting was the first step in the French Revolution (*see* French Revolution). The members of the Third

Estate refused to follow the old method of voting and finally declared themselves a national assembly.

At first the king seemed inclined to work with the revolution and to try to remedy conditions in the country. But the influence of the queen and of the courtiers proved too strong for his weak will. Encouraged by them, he disregarded the promises he had made and sought to flee from France in order to obtain aid against the revolution from Austria.

This attempted flight was the beginning of the end. The people saw that they could not trust the king and the "Austrian woman," as they called the queen. His disregard of his promises to abide by the constitution led to the storming of the royal palace of the Tuileries on Aug. 10, 1792. The king and his family escaped before the mob arrived and took refuge in the hall of the Legislative Assembly. The assembly declared that the king was suspended from office and ordered that he and his family should be imprisoned. They then called a new assembly (the Convention) to decide whether France should continue to be a monarchy.

**THE LOST DAUPHIN**

When Louis XVI was executed, his son, Louis Charles, was placed in solitary confinement. The authorities claimed he died there, but many royalists believed the dead child was a substitute and the real prince, or dauphin, had been spirited away. Although he never reigned he is known as Louis XVII.

The convention first decided against a monarchy and declared the king deposed. They then brought Louis XVI to trial on the charge of combining with foreign countries for the invasion of France. Almost unanimously Louis Capet, as he was now called, was declared guilty and was sentenced to death. The next day he was beheaded, meeting his fate with a steadfast courage, and proving greater in death than he had ever been in life. His execution had important consequences for France, because it aroused opinion in other countries against the French Revolution.

**LOUIS XVII,** the Dauphin (born 1785), never ruled. He was imprisoned with his parents, Louis XVI and Marie Antoinette, when he was seven. According to the French government, he died at the age of ten.

**LOUIS XVIII** (born 1755, ruled 1814–1824). When the Bourbons returned to the throne of France in 1814, the younger brother of Louis XVI assumed the crown as Louis XVIII. The difficult task of reconstruction was before the king, but he seemed admirably adapted to meet the situation. He was cold-blooded and cared nothing for revenge; therefore he was satisfied to leave alone those who had driven his family from France. He was a lazy man, and his one ambition was to keep his throne. This ambition seemed likely at first to go unfulfilled, for in 1815 Napoleon returned from the island of Elba, and Louis XVIII fled in a panic from France. At the end of the Hundred Days, however, Napoleon was again overthrown, at Waterloo, and the Allies entered Paris, "bringing Louis XVIII in their baggage."

Until 1820 the king was able to resist the demands of the extreme royalists for vengeance and to build up his kingdom, but finally under the leadership of his brother they became too strong for him. He yielded to their demands for a reactionary government. This marked the beginning of the end of the Bourbons, for 10 years later, under his brother, Charles X, they were finally driven from the throne of France.

**LOUIS PHILIPPE** (born 1773, ruled 1830–1848). Having disposed of the old Bourbons, the French had to set up a new government. Influenced by Lafayette (*see* Lafayette, Marquis de), they decided to keep France a monarchy, with Louis Philippe, a member of the Orléans family, as king.

Louis Philippe was known for his democratic ideas, but his government was undemocratic. Demands for a more liberal government were not met.

When the government forbade a banquet organized by supporters of political reform, which was to be held on Feb. 22, 1848, the Republicans of Paris revolted. Guizot was forced to resign. This did not satisfy the rioters, however, and Louis Philippe abdicated on February 24. He fled to England, where he died two years later.

THESE ARTICLES ARE IN THE FACT-INDEX

Louis I (king of
    Portugal)
Louis II (prince of
    Monaco)

Louise
Louisiade
    Archipelago

In the coastal marshes of Louisiana, where the bayous wind past trees draped with Spanish moss, are the homes of the hardy fishermen and fur trappers who ply their trades here.

# LOUISIANA—Gateway to the Mississippi Valley

**LOUISIANA.** One of the most favorably located states in the Union is Louisiana. It stands on the Gulf of Mexico astride the mouth of the mighty Mississippi River. To the north lies the vast basin of the Mississippi, the richest river valley in the world. To the south, across the Gulf, are the growing markets of Latin America.

This location has made Louisiana one of the great commercial states. Its chief city, New Orleans, is one of the three leading United States ports in value of foreign trade (*see* New Orleans). In addition to trade Louisiana ranks high in minerals, fish, lumber, furs, and tourism. Its manufactures—of which the most important are chemicals and food products—are worth about 2 billion dollars a year. Its farms produce much rice and cotton and lead in sweet potatoes. The state ranks second to Hawaii in sugarcane.

For almost a hundred years Louisiana was settled and controlled by France and Spain. This early history is shown in the many French and Spanish names on its map and in the term "parish," used instead of "county." The state also has a strong French and Spanish heritage in its population, customs, and architecture. Louisiana's civil law is based on that of France and Spain rather than on English common law as in the other states.

**Population** (1980): 4,203,972—rank, 19th state. Urban, 68.6%; rural, 31.4%. Persons per square mile, 94.4—rank, 21st state.

**Extent:** Area, 48,523 square miles, including 3,593 square miles of water surface (31st state in size).

**Elevation:** Highest, Driskill Mountain, 535 feet, near Bienville; lowest, New Orleans, 5 feet below sea level; average, 100 feet.

**Geographic Center:** 3 miles southeast of Marksville.

**Temperature** (° F): Extremes—lowest, −16° (Minden, Feb. 13, 1899); highest, 114° (Plain Dealing, Aug. 10, 1936). Averages at Alexandria—January, 50.3°; July, 82.2°; annual, 66.4°. Averages at New Orleans—January, 54.6°; July, 81.6°; annual, 68.6°. Averages at Shreveport—January, 47.5°; July, 83.7°; annual, 66.1°.

**Precipitation** (inches): At Alexandria—annual average, 56.69 (including 0.3 snowfall). At New Orleans—annual average, 53.90 (including 0.2 snowfall). At Shreveport—annual average, 46.28 (including 1.5 snowfall).

**Land Use:** Crops, 17%; pasture, 12%; forest, 55%; other, 16%.

**For statistical information about Agriculture, Communication, Education, Employment, Finance, Fishing, Forests, Government, Health Care, Manufacturing, Mining, Population Trends, Trade, Transportation, Vital Statistics, and Welfare, see LOUISIANA FACT SUMMARY.**

362

Louisiana, meaning "land of Louis," was named by the explorer La Salle in honor of King Louis XIV of France. The nickname Pelican State comes from the pelicans that live along the Gulf coast.

## Survey of the Pelican State

Louisiana lies in the southern part of the United States. To the east is the state of Mississippi, separated by three boundaries—the Mississippi River, the 31st parallel, and the Pearl River. Arkansas is to the north. To the west is Texas, separated from Louisiana in part by the Sabine River. Louisiana's southern border, 397 miles in length, is on the Gulf of Mexico.

The state is shaped somewhat like a boot, with its toe pointing eastward along the Gulf of Mexico. Its greatest length is, from east to west, 300 miles. Its greatest width is 275 miles, from north to south. Louisiana's area is 48,523 square miles, including 3,593 miles of inland water surface.

## Louisiana's Three Natural Regions

With an average elevation of about 100 feet, Louisiana is one of the lowest and flattest states in the Union. Its surface rises from sea level along the coast to only 400 to 500 feet in the northwest. The highest point in the state is Driskill Mountain (535 feet), in Bienville Parish. The lowest point is at New Orleans, 5 feet below sea level. The state is divided into three distinct natural regions.

**The West Gulf Coastal Plain** occupies all western Louisiana. Its eastern boundary is an irregular north-south line running near Monroe, Alexandria, and Lafayette. The plain is wooded with many pine trees. Along the coast is a wide fringe of marshland.

**The Mississippi Flood Plain** covers a 50-mile belt west from the river and some 12,000 square miles of swamps in the delta of the Mississippi. The soil is a mixture of clay and fertile silt left by floodwaters of the river. Where the river flows between low ridges it is often higher than the surrounding floodplain. The plain has many oxbow lakes, formed as cutoffs when the Mississippi changed its course.

**The East Gulf Coastal Plain** occupies most of the area between the Mississippi and Pearl rivers. It is a low, level region similar to the West Gulf Coastal Plain. On the east bank of the Mississippi are bluffs that reach heights of about 300 feet in the Tunica Hills of West Feliciana Parish.

The chief river of Louisiana is the Mississippi (*see* Mississippi River). Its principal tributary is the Red, which receives the waters of the Ouachita. At the junction of the Red and the Mississippi is a short channel called Old River, which connects the Mississippi with the Atchafalaya River. Much of southwestern Louisiana is drained by the Calcasieu River.

## Climate and Weather

Louisiana has a moist, near-tropical climate. Warm winds from the Gulf of Mexico keep the temperature fairly even the year around. Average January temperatures range from a low of 47° F. in the northwest to a high of 57° in the southeast. July temperatures average 82° throughout the state.

The average precipitation (rain and melted snow) varies from 66 inches a year near Grand Lake to 46 inches in Caddo and De Soto parishes. The extreme southeast has about 350 growing days a year; the northeast and northwest, over 220 days.

## Natural Resources and Conservation

Louisiana's chief agricultural resources are fertile soil, plenty of rainfall, and a long growing season. More than half the state is forested. The chief commercial trees are longleaf pine in the east and southwest, shortleaf pine in the northwest, cypress in the south swamps, and hardwoods in the river bottoms. In the damp forests Spanish moss is gathered for mattresses, pillows, and upholstery.

Mineral resources include sulfur and such fuels as petroleum and natural gas. Waterways on the Mississippi and Red rivers and outlets to the Gulf of Mexico aid commerce. The climate and such festivals as Mardi Gras attract tourists.

Conservation work has been aimed at controlling the floodwaters of the Mississippi and its tributaries. There are extensive levee systems along the Mississippi and along the Red and the upper Atchafalaya. In 1927 the Mississippi overflowed hundreds of

Pix

The New Orleans City Hall is part of the Civic Center, which was completed in 1959. The large building at the left is Charity Hospital.

This map shows the three natural regions and the surface features of Louisiana. The use that can be made of the land is related to the physical features of each region.

square miles. Since that time three runoffs have been provided for high water. On the Sabine River is Toledo Bend Dam, a project of Texas and Louisiana. The dam's reservoir supplies municipal, industrial, and irrigation water to the Sabine River basin.

Much of the conservation work is handled by the Department of Conservation. Forests are protected by a forestry commission. The Department of Commerce and Industry directs industrial development.

## People of the Pelican State

Louisiana's largest tribe of American Indians was the Caddo. A few Choctaw lived north of Lake Pontchartrain. In 1835 the Caddo ceded their remaining land in the northwest for $80,000. Most Indians had left the state by 1859. (*See also* Indians, American.)

The first white settlers were French, followed by Spaniards. Today the descendants of these colonists are called Creoles. Most of them belong to the Roman Catholic church. From 1760 to 1800 about 5,000 French from Acadia (Nova Scotia) settled in south-central Louisiana (*see* Acadia).

After the Louisiana Purchase of 1803 the center and north were settled by English, Irish, and Scottish from the southeastern United States. Many blacks were brought in as slaves. Today 2.1 percent of the people are foreign born. Of the total foreign stock, Italians are the largest group. Blacks make up one third of the population.

## Manufacturing and Cities

From 1939 to 1947 the value of manufacturing in Louisiana more than tripled. Between 1947 and 1963 it tripled again, reaching almost 2 billion dollars. New and expanding industries are aided by a ten-year exemption from certain taxes. The Industry Inducement Plan of 1952 permits local governments to construct and lease industrial plants.

The chief industry is the production of chemicals and allied products. Next in importance is the preparation of food products, such as cane sugar, beverages, and bakery products. The third largest industry is petroleum refining. Louisiana's forests provide the basis of the state's fourth most valuable industry—paper and allied products. Each year the state produces about $1\frac{1}{2}$ billion board feet of lumber.

Louisiana's largest city is New Orleans, 117 miles upstream from the mouth of the Mississippi River. It ships much cotton, sugar, grain, and oil (*see* New Orleans. The second city in size is Baton Rouge, which is the capital of the state (*see* Baton Rouge).

Shreveport, the third largest city, is a port on the Red River and the commercial center of the oil-rich northwest (*see* Shreveport). Fourth in population is Lafayette. Lake Charles, the fifth largest, is the chief city of the southwest and a source of chemicals and petroleum products. Monroe, a trade center, lies in a gas-producing region in the northeast. Alexandria is a lumbering center on the Red River.

## Agriculture in Louisiana

About a fourth of the land is in crops and non-forested pasture. Most farms are operated by their owners. About one sixth of the commercial farms are occupied by tenants, who rent or sharecrop the land.

The most valuable field crops are rice and cotton. Most leading cotton-producing parishes are in the north. The crop is grown in the valleys of the Mississippi, Ouachita, and Red rivers. Rice is grown chiefly in marshy lowlands of the southwest. Louisiana is one of the three leading states in rice production. It ranks second in the production of sugarcane.

For many years the only sugar produced from the cane was a brownish, milky liquid suitable for rum making. Then in 1795 Étienne de Boré, on his plantation near New Orleans, succeeded in refining sugar by boiling the cane juice until it reached the gran-

364

ulation point. From that time on the sugar industry became increasingly important.

Louisiana also leads the states in sweet potatoes. It is one of the top five states in pecans, tung nuts, and oranges. Other important agricultural products are cattle, milk, soybeans, eggs, chickens, hay, corn, hogs, and truck crops.

## Minerals, Fish, and Fur

Louisiana is second only to Texas in mineral production. The most valuable mineral by far is petroleum. Next in importance are natural gas and natural-gas liquids. The chief sources for these minerals are the parishes on the Gulf of Mexico and the adjacent offshore areas. The fourth-ranking mineral is sulfur, which is obtained from sources in Jefferson, Plaquemines, and Terrebonne parishes. Louisiana and Texas produce most of the nation's sulfur.

Louisiana's fishing industry is usually surpassed only by those of Alaska, California, and Massachusetts. Most of the catch comes from the Gulf of Mexico, which yields shrimps, menhaden, oysters, and crabs. Inland waterways supply valuable catches of crayfish, catfish and bullheads, and buffalofish. Louisiana ranks second to Texas in its shrimp catch.

Louisiana is the leading fur-producing state, followed by Alaska. Nutria provides the bulk of the income. Muskrat, mink, and raccoon are also important.

## The Development of Transportation

Flatboats were the first important vessels on the Mississippi River. The steamboat era began in 1812

**HARVESTING SUGARCANE**
Sugarcane has been grown in Louisiana since 1742. Cane for sugar is grown in the south; cane for syrup, in the north.

when the *New Orleans* made the first trip downriver from Pittsburgh, Pa. Today the river still carries much barge traffic. Louisiana has more than 5,000 miles of commercial waterways. New Orleans, Baton Rouge, and Lake Charles are deepwater ports.

The first railroad in the state was completed between New Orleans and Lake Pontchartrain in 1831. By 1858 New Orleans was linked to Jackson, Miss., by

**MAKING GASOLINE FROM PETROLEUM**
Lighting the night sky at Baton Rouge is a huge oil refinery. Here crude oil is refined by a special process called alkylation.

A major refinery center, Baton Rouge ships much of its processed petroleum down the Mississippi to the Gulf.

Photographs, Louisiana State Department of Commerce and Industry

Many fur-bearing animals live in the state's swamps and marshes. Here muskrat are skinned and the furs hung up to cure (left). Lumbering is important in many parts of the state. This mill (right) at Bogalusa uses logs to make wooden boxes.

rail. Through trains began operating between New Orleans and Chicago in 1873. Ten years later a transcontinental line led to the Pacific coast. Today the state is served by some 20 railroads.

An important part of Louisiana's transportation network is the system of state primary and secondary roads. The major north-south routes are US 71, 171, 167, 165, and 61 and Interstate 55 and 59. The chief east-west highways are US 80, 84, 190, and 90 and Interstate 10 and 20. The state is also served by national and international airlines.

## Recreation and Tourist Attractions

The chief tourist attraction is New Orleans. This city is the site of the annual Mardi Gras and of the Mid-Winter Sports Carnival, climaxed by the Sugar Bowl football game. A few miles to the east is Chalmette National Historical Park, the site of Gen. Andrew Jackson's victory over the British in 1815.

The Louisiana Shrimp Festival draws many visitors to Morgan City. Shreveport is the site of the annual state fair. Old plantation homes along the Mississippi River are popular attractions. The state is also noted for its fishing and hunting.

## Louisiana's Schools

The first school in the Louisiana Territory was established in New Orleans in 1725 by Father Raphael. It had seven students. Education for girls began in 1727 with the opening of a convent in New Orleans.

Education was hampered by poor transportation, the Civil War, and reconstruction. The modern school system began in 1898, when parish districts were authorized to issue school bonds. Since then the school system has been greatly improved and now includes more than 60 vocational centers throughout the state.

The largest school of higher learning is Louisiana State University, at Baton Rouge, with campuses at Alexandria, Eunice, New Orleans, and Shreveport and a medical center at New Orleans. Other state schools

Louisiana State Department of Commerce and Industry

In August the vessels of the shrimp fishermen are blessed by Roman Catholic priests at bayous near Houma, Morgan City, and Golden Meadow.

include Grambling College, at Grambling; Louisiana Tech University, at Ruston; McNeese State University, at Lake Charles; Nicholls State University, at Thibodaux; Northeast Louisiana University, at Monroe; Northwestern State University of Louisiana, at Natchitoches; Southeastern Louisiana University, at Hammond; Southern University and Agricultural and Mechanical College, at Baton Rouge, with branches at New Orleans and Shreveport; and The University of Southwestern Louisiana, at Lafayette.

Tulane University of Louisiana and Loyola University, both at New Orleans, are large private schools. Others are Centenary College, at Shreveport; Xavier University and Dillard University, both at New Orleans; and Louisiana College, at Pineville.

## Government and Politics

New Orleans served as the seat of government from 1722 until 1849, except for the year 1830, when Donaldsonville served as the capital. Baton Rouge has been the capital since 1849. The state is governed under a constitution adopted in 1974. Louisiana's chief executive officer is the governor. Lawmaking is in the hands of the Senate and the House of Representatives. The Supreme Court heads the judiciary.

The Democratic party dominates Louisiana politics. The state has supported the Democratic candidate in most presidential elections since 1876. The exceptions were the elections of 1948, when it voted States' Rights Democratic; 1956, 1964, and 1972, Republican; and 1968, American Independent.

## HISTORY OF LOUISIANA

What is now the Pelican State was part of the Louisiana Purchase of 1803. Its northern boundary, along the 33d parallel, was fixed by Congress in 1804. Its original eastern boundary followed the Mississippi River and then the 31st parallel as far east as the Perdido River. In 1812 Louisiana's southeastern boundary was cut back to the Pearl River. The western border was in dispute until 1819, when Spain accepted the Sabine River as the basis of the Loui-

Louisiana State Department of Commerce and Industry

**A Creole landmark, the Acadian House Museum, in Longfellow-Evangeline State Park, displays relics of Acadian life.**

siana-Texas line. The following sections tell the story of Louisiana's development into a modern state.

## Exploration and Settlement

The early history of Louisiana was made by three bold explorers. La Salle descended the Mississippi River to its mouth in 1682 and claimed the entire basin for France. The Canadian Iberville made the first thorough exploration of the present New Orleans-Baton Rouge area in 1699. His brother Bienville founded New Orleans in 1718. (*See also* La Salle; Iberville; Bienville.)

In 1762 France ceded the Louisiana region to its ally Spain (*see* French and Indian War). After the Revolutionary War hardy Western boatmen and traders began shipping produce into New Orleans.

**Couples stroll on the lawn of 'The Olivier Plantation'. The watercolor was painted by Adrian Persac in about 1861.**

By courtesy of the Louisiana State Museum; photograph, Jack Beech

High customs duties and Spanish threats to close the port angered the Americans.

Spain returned the Louisiana Territory to France by secret treaty in 1800. At that time most of the Louisianans lived along the Red and Mississippi rivers. New Orleans was the chief settlement, with a population of about 10,000.

### Louisiana Purchase to the Civil War

The growing tension over trading rights in New Orleans led to the American purchase of Louisiana from France in 1803 (*see* Louisiana Purchase). The following year Congress divided the region into the District of Louisiana (later Missouri Territory), north of latitude 33°, and the Territory of Orleans, south of that parallel. In 1812 the southern section, renamed Louisiana, became the 18th state. In 1815 the British lost the battle of New Orleans near the city (*see* War of 1812). The first street parade of the Mardi Gras in New Orleans was held in 1838.

Louisiana seceded from the Union and joined the Confederacy in 1861. Its control of the mouth of the Mississippi was lost in 1862 when a Federal fleet under David G. Farragut captured New Orleans and Baton Rouge (*see* Farragut; Civil War, American).

Louisiana was readmitted to the Union in 1868 after it had drawn up a new constitution granting equal rights to its black population. P. B. S. Pinchback was one of three blacks who served as lieutenant governor during Reconstruction; he also served for a short time as acting governor. The Reconstruction government was toppled in 1877, when Federal troops were withdrawn (*see* Reconstruction Period).

### The Modern State

Louisiana's present commercial importance owes much to the work of two 19th-century men. In the 1830's Capt. Henry M. Shreve opened the Red River to navigation (*see* Shreveport). Another riverman, James B. Eads, completed a system of jetties in the mouth of the Mississippi in 1879 (*see* Jetty).

Much of the state's progress in the 1900's has been due to the development of its rich mineral resources and manufacturing industries. Louisiana's politics were dominated by Huey P. Long, called the Kingfish, from 1928 until his assassination in 1935.

Since 1970 the state's population has increased by about 560,000 persons. (*See also* United States, section "The South"; individual entries in the Fact-Index on Louisiana persons, places, products, and events.)

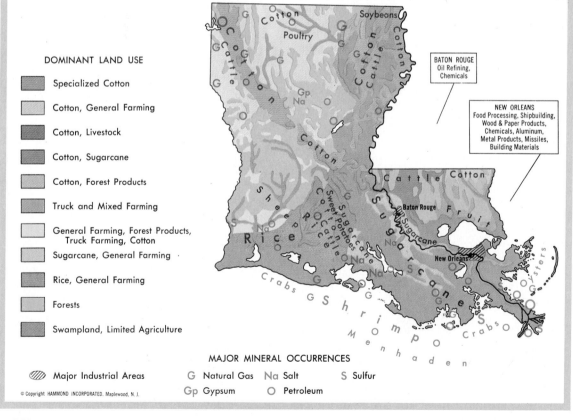

## AGRICULTURE, INDUSTRY and RESOURCES

**DOMINANT LAND USE**

- Specialized Cotton
- Cotton, General Farming
- Cotton, Livestock
- Cotton, Sugarcane
- Cotton, Forest Products
- Truck and Mixed Farming
- General Farming, Forest Products, Truck Farming, Cotton
- Sugarcane, General Farming
- Rice, General Farming
- Forests
- Swampland, Limited Agriculture

Major Industrial Areas

© Copyright HAMMOND INCORPORATED, Maplewood, N. J.

**MAJOR MINERAL OCCURRENCES**

G Natural Gas  Na Salt  S Sulfur
Gp Gypsum  O Petroleum

BATON ROUGE
Oil Refining, Chemicals

NEW ORLEANS
Food Processing, Shipbuilding, Wood & Paper Products, Chemicals, Aluminum, Metal Products, Missiles, Building Materials

# Notable Events ·in Louisiana History

1541—De Soto explores northern Louisiana.

1682—**La Salle descends Mississippi River; names territory Louisiana.**

1713–14—Louis St. Denis builds Fort St. Jean Baptiste on site of Natchitoches.

1717—Spaniards establish mission near Natchitoches.

1718—Bienville founds New Orleans; names it for duke of Orléans. Cotton planted near Natchitoches.

1760—Acadians begin arriving from Nova Scotia.

1762—Louis XV gives all Louisiana west of Mississippi River plus "island of New Orleans" to Spain; rest of Louisiana ceded to Britain in 1763.

1768–69—New Orleans revolt against Spain put down.

1779—Spain and Britain at war; Bernardo de Galvez seizes Baton Rouge from British.

1795—Boundary between Louisiana and West Florida set at 31st parallel. Spanish-U. S. treaty permits U. S. navigation on the Mississippi. **Étienne de Boré perfects sugarcane refining.**

1800—Spain cedes Louisiana Territory to France.

1803—U. S. purchases Louisiana from France.

1804—Territory of Orleans created south of 33d parallel; capital, New Orleans; governor, William Claiborne.

1810—West Floridians rebel; seize Baton Rouge.

1812—Louisiana becomes 18th state, April 30; capital, New Orleans; governor, William Claiborne. **First steamboat, 'New Orleans', navigates the Mississippi River from Pittsburgh, Pa., to New Orleans.**

1815—Andrew Jackson defeats British at New Orleans.

1819—Spain cedes claim to areas west of Sabine River.

1823—First gas well in state drilled near Natchitoches.

1830—Capital moved to Donaldsonville; New Orleans, in 1831; Baton Rouge, 1849–62 and after 1882.

1835—Caddo Indians cede lands in Louisiana. Capt. Henry M. Shreve founds Shreveport.

1838—**First Mardi Gras parade in New Orleans held.**

1853—Thousands die in yellow fever epidemic in New Orleans.

1860—Louisiana State University is founded at Baton Rouge.

1861—Louisiana secedes from Union; joins Confederacy.

1862—David G. Farragut takes New Orleans and Baton Rouge.

1864—Confederates retain hold on western Louisiana.

1868—Louisiana readmitted to Union.

1879—James B. Eads builds jetties on Mississippi River.

1894—Federal leprosarium opened at Carville.

1901—Oil discovered near Jennings.

1905—Mining of sulfur begins in Calcasieu Parish.

1927—Mississippi flood causes immense damage.

1928—Huey P. Long, born 1893 in Winnfield, elected governor; elected U. S. senator in 1930; assassinated in 1935.

1932—Present State Capitol completed.

1935—Huey P. Long Bridge across Mississippi River dedicated; Bonnet Carré Spillway constructed.

1946—Second free port in U. S. opened at New Orleans.

1952—Louisiana's Industry Inducement Plan established.

1956—Causeway over Lake Pontchartrain completed.

1958—Longest cantilever bridge in U. S. completed across Mississippi River at New Orleans.

1963—Pontchartrain Expressway completed. Mississippi River-Gulf Outlet completed.

1965—Hurricane Betsy causes 500 million dollars' property damage; 81 persons die in wake of storm.

1974—Present state constitution adopted.

1975—Louisiana Superdome, world's largest indoor stadium, opened in New Orleans.

1682

1795

1812

1838

**STATE FLOWER:**
Magnolia

**STATE TREE:**
Bald Cypress

**STATE BIRD:**
Brown Pelican

**STATE SEAL: A pelican feeds its
young; surrounding birds is
state motto.**

# Louisiana Profile

**FLAG:** *See* **Flags of the United States.**
**MOTTO: Union, Justice, Confidence.**
**SONG: 'Give Me Louisiana'—words and
music by Doralice Fontane.**

Louisiana is a state in transition—from a rural, agricultural economy to an urban, industrial one. This transition holds great promise for the future of the Pelican State, but it has also created many of the problems and peculiar contrasts that mark Louisiana life today. In colorful New Orleans, a huge facility for the manufacture of Saturn rockets bears witness to Louisiana's commitment to the Space Age. The production of these rockets has made Louisiana vital to the United States space program. Nearby, Cajun trappers still ply the bayous in dugout canoes, hunting fur-bearing animals much as their ancestors did. Agriculture accounts for only about a tenth of the value of the state's annual production, and only 3 percent of the labor force work on farms. Tenant farmers still operate about one sixth of Louisiana's farms, but they are being displaced by the use of modern machinery.

Increasingly, the state's population has come to center upon its cities. New Orleans, perhaps the most genuinely international of United States cities, ranks close to New York City in the value of its foreign trade. The millions of tourists who visit it each year are attracted mainly by the traditional—Mardi Gras, New Orleans jazz, fine antebellum mansions, and Cajun and Creole cooking.

Louisiana has made great progress in attracting new industries, particularly those capable of effectively utilizing the rich mineral resources that are the state's chief source of wealth. Personal income has risen steadily in recent years, and so has the number of available jobs. At the same time Louisiana, like many Northern and Southern states, has suffered serious racial difficulties as school desegregation has extended from the cities into the rural areas and as other branches of Louisiana life have gradually become integrated.

# Louisiana picture profile

Louisiana has the tallest State Capitol. Its 34 stories rise high over the city of Baton Rouge. Built in 1932, the Capitol stands in a handsome 27-acre park.

Built before the Civil War, The Shadows is one of the South's many handsome plantation homes. The mansion, in New Iberia, is now owned by the National Trust for Historical Preservation.

The War Memorial Tower, a campanile 175 feet high, dominates the Louisiana State University campus at Baton Rouge. The university opened in 1860 as a seminary and military academy and was given its present name in 1870. For educational statistics, *see* LOUISIANA FACT SUMMARY.

The Old State Capitol at Baton Rouge was originally completed in the late 1840's. It was designed in a mixture of styles—Norman, Gothic, and Moorish. The building was reconstructed in 1882.

The facade of St. Louis Cathedral is seen from the lawns of Jackson Square in the French Quarter of New Orleans, Louisiana's largest city. In the foreground is a bronze statue of Gen. Andrew Jackson.

# Louisiana picture profile

These Southern belles have gathered at Chalmette National Historical Park to celebrate the anniversary of General Jackson's victory against the British in the battle of New Orleans. The obelisk marks his battle position.

Graceful egrets are characteristic of the varied wildlife of Louisiana. The Jungle Gardens at Avery Island, one of the Salt "islands" of Iberia Parish, is a sanctuary for these and other birds as well as a preserve for rare plants.

Fontainebleau State Park is near Mandeville on Lake Pontchartrain. It is one of nearly 20 picturesque sites that are maintained by the Louisiana State Parks and Recreation Commission.

In the portions of New Orleans that are below sea level, bodies are interred aboveground. In this corner of a New Orleans cemetery, it has not been possible to dig conventional graves.

The Mississippi, which flows through Louisiana and empties into the Gulf of Mexico, is not only one of the great continental waterways but also an inspiration to artists and writers.

Surrounded by the bustle of modern New Orleans, the old French Quarter of the city still preserves a European look. Iron lace, adorned with plants and flowers, is typical of the balconies in the French Quarter.

The Spanish influence on southern Louisiana is noticeable in the St. Joseph Abbey at St. Benedict, a small town 15 miles north of Lake Pontchartrain. The Spanish ruled Louisiana from 1762 to 1800.

At the Cotton Festival, held annually in Ville Platte, Le Tournoi (The Tourney) combines the spirit of a modern American rodeo with that of a medieval joust. The cowboy shown here is riding at full gallop in an attempt to spear a small, dangling ring.

The festival of Mardi Gras, or Shrove Tuesday, is the occasion of a spectacular carnival parade every year in the streets of New Orleans. The festival attracts visitors from all parts of the country.

JEAN LAFITTE

MAHALIA JACKSON

some famous people*

LOUISIANA
PROFILE

HUEY P. LONG

ZACHARY TAYLOR

MINNIE MADDERN FISKE

LEONIDAS POLK

GEORGE WASHINGTON CABLE

LOUIS (SATCHMO) ARMSTRONG

TRUMAN CAPOTE

JUDAH P. BENJAMIN

P. G. T. BEAUREGARD

*Only a few of Louisiana's famous people are shown here. The persons de-
picted are generally associated with the state, though not all of them were
born there. For biographical information, see entries in the Fact-Index.

# LOUISIANA FACT SUMMARY

## POPULATION TRENDS

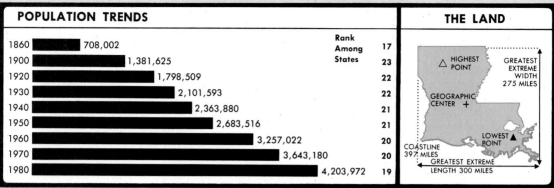

| Year | Population | Rank Among States |
|------|-----------|------|
| 1860 | 708,002 | 17 |
| 1900 | 1,381,625 | 23 |
| 1920 | 1,798,509 | 22 |
| 1930 | 2,101,593 | 22 |
| 1940 | 2,363,880 | 21 |
| 1950 | 2,683,516 | 21 |
| 1960 | 3,257,022 | 20 |
| 1970 | 3,643,180 | 20 |
| 1980 | 4,203,972 | 19 |

## THE LAND

HIGHEST POINT △
GREATEST EXTREME WIDTH 275 MILES
GEOGRAPHIC CENTER +
LOWEST POINT ▲
COASTLINE 397 MILES
GREATEST EXTREME LENGTH 300 MILES

## GOVERNMENT

**Capital:** Baton Rouge (since 1849).

**Statehood:** Became 18th state in the Union on April 30, 1812.

**Constitution:** Adopted 1974. Amendment may be passed by two-thirds vote of Legislature; ratified by majority voting on it in an election.

**Representation in U. S. Congress:** Senate—2. House of Representatives—8. Electoral votes—10.

**Legislature:** Senators—39; term, 4 years. Representatives—105; term, 4 years.
  Convenes 3d Monday in April annually. Session limit—60 calendar days. Special session limit—30 calendar days. Special session convened by petition of two thirds of the elected members of each house or may be called by governor.

**Executive Officers**
  Governor—term, 4 years. May succeed himself once.
  Other officials—lieutenant governor, secretary of state, attorney general, and treasurer; all elected; terms, 4 years.

**Judiciary:** Supreme Court—7 justices; elected; term, 10 years. Appellate courts—29 judges; elected; term, 10 years. District courts—125 judges; elected; term, 6 years.

**Parish:** 64 parishes. Governed by a police jury of 5 to 16 members; 2 parishes (Orleans and East Baton Rouge) governed by city-parish council and mayor; all officials elected; terms, 4 years.

**Municipal:** Mayor-council plan most common; some cities have commission form of government.

**Voting**
  Residency requirements—none.
  General election—1st Tuesday after 1st Monday in November.
  Primary elections—gubernatorial, last Saturday in October; congressional, 3d Saturday in September.
  Preferential presidential primary—none.

## EDUCATION

**Private Elementary and Secondary Day Schools**
  Enrollment—elementary, 130,400; secondary, 35,500.
  Classroom teachers—6,940.

**Public Elementary and Secondary Schools***
  Operating school districts—66.
  Compulsory school age—7 to 16.
  Enrollment—elementary, 507,450; secondary, 338,800.
  Average daily attendance—759,086.
  High school graduates—48,378.
  Administrative officials
    Superintendent of education; elected; term, 4 years.
    Parish superintendents; appointed or elected; term, 4 years.

Superintendents of schools; appointed by elected city boards; term, 4 years.

Instructional staff—total, 44,835; principals and supervisors, 2,243; elementary teachers, 23,936; secondary teachers, 18,656.

Teachers' average annual salaries—elementary, $10,083; secondary, $10,663.

Revenue receipts—$957,500,000.
  Source of receipts (% of total)—federal, 17.5; state, 55.9; local, 26.5.

Nonrevenue receipts†—$118,000,000.

Current expenditures
  For day schools—$852,800,000.
  For other programs—$4,200,000.

State expenditure on education—$1,031 per pupil.

Head Start programs—participants, 9,584; funds allocated, $11,776,042.

**Universities and Colleges‡**
  Number of institutions—total, 31; public, 20; private, 11.
  Degree-credit enrollment—154,000.
  Earned degrees conferred—bachelor's and first professional, 17,195; master's except first professional, 4,326; doctor's, 386.

**Special Institutions** (for the handicapped): Belle Chasse State School; Evergreen Presbyterian Vocational School, Minden; Leesville State School; Louisiana State School for Spastic Children, Alexandria; Louisiana State School for the Blind and Louisiana State School for the Deaf, both in Baton Rouge; Pinecrest State School, Pineville; Ruston State School.

**Libraries:** City and town public libraries—4; parish libraries—57; bicity library—1. State library aids in developing public libraries. State Department of Education aids in developing school libraries.

**Outstanding Museums:** Louisiana Art Commission, Anglo-American Art Museum at Louisiana State University, and Louisiana Arts and Science Center, all in Baton Rouge; New Orleans Museum of Art, Louisiana State Museum, and New Orleans Jazz Museum, all in New Orleans; Louisiana State Exhibit Museum and R. W. Norton Art Gallery, both in Shreveport.

## CORRECTIONAL AND PENAL INSTITUTIONS

**State**
  Adult—Louisiana State Penitentiary, Angola; Louisiana Correctional Institute for Women, St. Gabriel; Corrections Special Treatment Unit, New Orleans; Dixon Correctional Institute, Jackson.
  Adult-juvenile—Louisiana Correctional and Industrial School, De Quincy.
  Juvenile—Louisiana Training Institutes, Baton Rouge, Pineville, Bridge City, and Monroe.

**Federal**
  None.

All Fact Summary data, including estimates, are based on current government reports.
*Kindergartens are included in the elementary schools; junior high schools, in the secondary schools.
†Money received from loans, sales of bonds, sales of property, and insurance adjustments.
‡Excludes data for service academies.

# LOUISIANA FACT SUMMARY

## PRODUCTION—YEARLY VALUE: $5,293,740,000

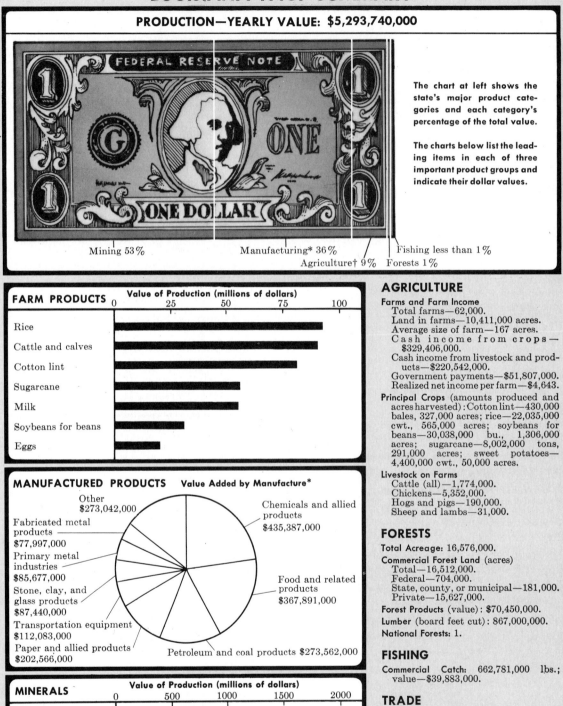

The chart at left shows the state's major product categories and each category's percentage of the total value.

The charts below list the leading items in each of three important product groups and indicate their dollar values.

Mining 53%  Manufacturing* 36%  Fishing less than 1%
Agriculture† 9%  Forests 1%

## FARM PRODUCTS
Value of Production (millions of dollars)
0  25  50  75  100

- Rice
- Cattle and calves
- Cotton lint
- Sugarcane
- Milk
- Soybeans for beans
- Eggs

## MANUFACTURED PRODUCTS   Value Added by Manufacture*

- Other $273,042,000
- Fabricated metal products $77,997,000
- Primary metal industries $85,677,000
- Stone, clay, and glass products $87,440,000
- Transportation equipment $112,083,000
- Paper and allied products $202,566,000
- Chemicals and allied products $435,387,000
- Food and related products $367,891,000
- Petroleum and coal products $273,562,000

## MINERALS
Value of Production (millions of dollars)
0  500  1000  1500  2000

- Petroleum
- Natural gas
- Natural-gas liquids
- Sulfur

## AGRICULTURE

**Farms and Farm Income**
Total farms—62,000.
Land in farms—10,411,000 acres.
Average size of farm—167 acres.
Cash income from crops—$329,406,000.
Cash income from livestock and products—$220,542,000.
Government payments—$51,807,000.
Realized net income per farm—$4,643.

**Principal Crops** (amounts produced and acres harvested): Cotton lint—430,000 bales, 327,000 acres; rice—22,035,000 cwt., 565,000 acres; soybeans for beans—30,038,000 bu., 1,306,000 acres; sugarcane—8,002,000 tons, 291,000 acres; sweet potatoes—4,400,000 cwt., 50,000 acres.

**Livestock on Farms**
Cattle (all)—1,774,000.
Chickens—5,352,000.
Hogs and pigs—190,000.
Sheep and lambs—31,000.

## FORESTS

Total Acreage: 16,576,000.
**Commercial Forest Land** (acres)
Total—16,512,000.
Federal—704,000.
State, county, or municipal—181,000.
Private—15,627,000.
**Forest Products** (value): $70,450,000.
**Lumber** (board feet cut): 867,000,000.
**National Forests:** 1.

## FISHING

Commercial Catch: 662,781,000 lbs.; value—$39,883,000.

## TRADE

Wholesale: $4,598,199,000.
Retail: $3,391,184,000.
Service: $476,073,000.

## ELECTRIC UTILITIES

Number of Utilities: 30.
Total Capacity: 4,751,171 kw.

All Fact Summary data are based on current government reports.
*Value Added by Manufacture—value of manufactured products as they leave the factory, less the cost of materials, supplies, fuel, etc. For complete definition, see Fact-Index.
†Cash receipts.

# LOUISIANA FACT SUMMARY

## TRANSPORTATION

**Roads and Streets**
Total state mileage—54,700.
Municipal mileage—11,800.
Rural mileage—42,900.
National Interstate Highway System
Total designated mileage—718.
Mileage open to traffic—606.
Mileage under construction or projected—112.
**Automobiles, Trucks, and Buses** (registrations)*
Total motor vehicles—2,277,000.
Automobiles—1,731,000.
Trucks and buses—546,000.
**Motorcycles** (registrations): 54,000.
**Railroads**
Total mileage owned—3,710.
First railroad—New Orleans to Lake Pontchartrain, 1831.
**Airports:** 280.
**Pipelines** (mileage)†: 9,460.

## COMMUNICATION

**Post Offices:** 535.
**Radio Stations** (commercial): AM—94; FM—55. First station —WWL, New Orleans, licensed March 31, 1922.
**TV Stations:** Commercial—16; educational—3. First station—WDSU-TV, New Orleans, began operation Dec. 18, 1948.
**Telephones:** Total—2,293,000; residence—1,731,000; business —562,000.
**Newspapers**
Daily—27; circulation—839,000.
Weekly—83.
Sunday—14; circulation—765,000.
First newspaper—*Le Moniteur de la Louisiane* (*The Louisiana Monitor*), New Orleans, 1794.
**Periodicals:** 57.

## FINANCE‡

**Revenue:** $3,092,100,000.
**Expenditures:** Total—$3,088,351,000; education—$1,157,774,-000; highways—$554,963,000; public welfare—$404,847,-000; hospitals—$193,120,000.
**Debt:** Total—$1,457,976,000; issued (long term only)—$287,440,000; retired (long term only)—$50,845,000.
**Taxation**
State tax collections—$1,655,576,000; general sales—$421,278,000; individual income—$117,641,000.
Intergovernmental—$828,092,000.
**Personal Income per Capita:** $5,386.
**Banks:** 254; total assets or liabilities—$15,369,000,000.
**Savings and Loan Associations:** 112; total assets—$5,167,000,000; per capita assets—$1,345.
**Life Insurance Policies:** 8,985,000; value—$38,225,000,000.

## VITAL STATISTICS§

**Birthrate:** 17.9.
**Death Rate:** 8.9.
**Marriage Rate:** 9.8.

## HEALTH CARE

**Hospitals:** 154; beds—24,726.
**Nursing Homes:** 212; beds—17,004.
**Physicians:** 5,266.
**Dentists:** 1,499.
**Licensed Practical Nurses:** 9,416.

## EMPLOYMENT

**Total Number of Persons Employed:** 1,166,668.

THOUSANDS OF WORKERS — bar chart with scale 0, 50, 100, 150, 200, 250
Trade
Professional services
Manufacturing
Transportation, communication, and utilities
Construction
Personal services
Government
Finance, insurance, and real estate
Agriculture, forestry, and fisheries
Mining
Business and repair services
Recreation services
Not accounted for

## WELFARE‡

**Old-Age and Survivors Insurance:** Beneficiaries—440,048; benefits—$881,416,000.
**Disability Insurance:** Beneficiaries—114,067; benefits—$209,492,000.
**Unemployment Insurance:** Beneficiaries (weekly average)—28,965; benefits—$10,715,332.
**Workmen's Compensation Benefits:** $138,014,000.
**Vocational Rehabilitation**
Disabled persons rehabilitated—6,693; in process of rehabilitation—21,845.
Total federal and state funds—$22,677,000.
**Public Assistance**
Dependent children—recipients, 211,955; average payment, $36.92.
General assistance—recipients, 2,967; average payment, $57.06.
**Supplementary Security Income**
Old age—recipients, 79,992; total, $7,185,000.
Permanently and totally disabled—recipients, 65,912; total, $8,437,000.
Blind—recipients, 2,201; total, $296,000.
**Maternal and Child Health Services**
Federal grants—maternal and child health services, $5,041,000; crippled children, $1,946,500.
**United Way Campaigns◆:** 11; amount raised—$13,712,869.

All Fact Summary data are based on current government reports.
*Excludes vehicles owned by military services.
†Petroleum and products only.
‡Figures for one-year periods.
§Rates per 1,000 population.
◆Data based on state reports to United Way of America.

# LOUISIANA FACT SUMMARY

## LARGEST CITIES AND OTHER PLACES*

**New Orleans** (557,482): a major U.S. port on the Mississippi River; the commercial center of the South; cotton market; International Trade Mart; New Orleans Museum of Art; Tulane and Loyola universities; Mardi Gras; annual Sugar Bowl football classic; Cabildo, St. Louis Cathedral, and French Market in the French Quarter (*see* New Orleans).

**Baton Rouge** (219,419): state capital; Mississippi River port and industrial center; petrochemical products; sugar plantations nearby; Louisiana State University; Southern University (*see* Baton Rouge).

**Shreveport** (205,820): on Red River; oil and natural-gas center; cotton; fabricated metal and lumber products; Louisiana State Fair; Barksdale Air Force Base nearby (*see* Shreveport).

**Metairie** (164,160): residential area west of New Orleans; Phillips College of Greater New Orleans.

**Lafayette** (81,961): industrial city; sugar factories, cotton gins; The University of Southwestern Louisiana.

**Lake Charles** (75,226): port; oil refineries; rice; McNeese State University.

**Kenner** (66,382): suburb of New Orleans; Jefferson Downs Racetrack.

**Monroe** (57,597): natural-gas field, chemicals, paper, furniture manufactures; Northeast Louisiana University.

**Alexandria** (51,565): located on Red River; lumbering and trade center; cotton; livestock; state university.

**Bossier City** (50,817): located on Red River; oil; cotton; cattle; site of Fort Smith memorial park.

## PLACES OF INTEREST

**Abbeville:** annual Louisiana Dairy Festival.

**Abita Springs State Park:** in Abita Springs; mineral springs.

**Audubon Memorial State Monument:** near St. Francisville; museum in Oakley Plantation House; picnicking.

**Avery Island:** near New Iberia; Jungle Gardens; rock-salt mine; tabasco-sauce factory.

**Chalmette National Historical Park:** near New Orleans; here Gen. Andrew Jackson defeated British in battle of New Orleans (1815) in War of 1812; cemetery.

**Chemin-A-Haut State Park:** near Bastrop; cabins; fishing.

**Crowley:** annual International Rice Festival; Frog Derby; International Duck Calling contest.

**Edward D. White State Monument:** near Thibodaux; home of chief justice of U. S.

**Evergreen:** near Edgard; restored antebellum home (1840) in Greek Revival style.

**Fort Jesup State Monument:** near Many; museum; relics of Mexican campaign.

**Fort Macomb State Monument:** Chef Menteur Pass; built to defend New Orleans (1819–28).

**Fort Pike State Monument:** Rigolets Pass; built to defend New Orleans (1819–28).

**Jefferson Island:** near New Iberia; salt mine; Jean Lafitte's secret headquarters; home of famous 19th-century actor and artist Joseph Jefferson.

*1980 census.

**Lake Bistineau State Park:** near Shreveport; fishing.

**Lake Pontchartrain Causeway:** 24-mile causeway across Lake Pontchartrain.

**Les Jardins de Mouton:** near Lafayette; rose, sunken, and cypress gardens; outdoor theater.

**Longfellow-Evangeline State Park:** near St. Martinville; in Acadian country; Acadian House Museum.

**Mansfield Battle Park State Monument:** near Mansfield; site of Confederate victory in Civil War (1864); museum.

**Marksville Prehistoric Indian Park State Monument:** in Marksville; Indian mounds; natural history museum.

**Morgan City:** annual Blessing of Shrimp Fleet.

**Napoleonville:** antebellum homes; Madewood; Christ Episcopal church.

**Natchitoches:** oldest town in Louisiana Purchase (1713–14); Los Adais nearby, capital of Spanish Province of Texas to 1773; plantation homes.

**Oak Alley:** near Vacherie; beautiful antebellum home (1836); avenue of oaks.

**Opelousas:** former state capital (1862–63); Chrétien Point Plantation; Yambilee Festival.

**Sabine National Wildlife Refuge:** near Hackberry; migratory waterfowl; blue and snow goose winter grounds.

**St. Francisville:** Afton Villa, Greenwood, Waverly, Oakley, other antebellum homes nearby.

**St. Martinville:** Acadian center; St. Martin Catholic Church (1765); grave of Emmeline la Biche, heroine of Longfellow's 'Evangeline'.

**San Francisco Plantation:** near Garyville; house in "Steamboat Gothic" style.

## BOOKS AND FILMS ABOUT LOUISIANA

**Bailey, B. F.** Picture Book of Louisiana, rev. ed. (Whitman, 1967).

**Bougere, M. B.,** ed. Louisiana Stories for Boys and Girls (La. State Univ. Press, 1966) o.p.

**Bristow, Gwen.** Plantation Trilogy (Crowell, 1962).

**Carpenter, Allan.** Enchantment of Louisiana (Childrens, 1967) o.p.

**Davis, E. A.** Louisiana: the Pelican State (La. State Univ. Press, 1975).

**Dufour, C. L.** Ten Flags in the Wind (Harper, 1967).

**Feibleman, Peter.** The Bayous (Time-Life, 1973).

**Hall-Quest, Olga.** Old New Orleans: the Creole City (Dutton, 1968).

**Kniffen, F. B.** Louisiana: Its Land and People (La. State Univ. Press, 1968).

**Lenski, Lois.** Bayou Suzette (Lippincott, 1943) o.p.

**Life in Old Louisiana,** film (Encyclopaedia Britannica Films).

**Saxon, Lyle,** ed. Gumbo Ya-Ya (Johnson Reprint, 1970).

**Scroggs, W. O.** Story of Louisiana (Bobbs, 1953) o.p.

**Taylor, J. G.** Louisiana: a Bicentennial History (Norton, 1976).

**Williams, T. H.** Huey Long (Knopf, 1969).

**Writers' Program.** Louisiana: a Guide to the State (Somerset, 1941).

## PARISHES

| Name | Pop. | Ref. |
|---|---|---|
| Acadia | 52,109 | F 6 |
| Allen | 20,794 | E 5 |
| Ascension | 37,086 | J 6 |
| Assumption | 19,654 | H 7 |
| Avoyelles | 37,751 | G 4 |
| Beauregard | 22,888 | D 5 |
| Bienville | 16,024 | D 2 |
| Bossier | 63,703 | C 1 |
| Caddo | 230,184 | C 1 |
| Calcasieu | 145,415 | D 6 |
| Caldwell | 9,354 | F 2 |
| Cameron | 8,194 | D 7 |
| Catahoula | 11,769 | G 3 |
| Claiborne | 17,024 | D 1 |
| Concordia | 22,578 | G 4 |
| De Soto | 22,764 | C 2 |
| East Baton Rouge | 285,167 | K 1 |
| East Carroll | 12,884 | H 1 |
| East Feliciana | 17,657 | H 5 |
| Evangeline | 31,932 | F 5 |
| Franklin | 23,946 | G 2 |
| Grant | 13,671 | E 3 |
| Iberia | 57,397 | G 7 |
| Iberville | 30,746 | H 6 |
| Jackson | 15,963 | E 2 |
| Jefferson | 338,229 | K 7 |
| Jefferson Davis | 29,554 | E 6 |
| Lafayette | 111,745 | F 6 |
| Lafourche | 68,941 | K 7 |
| La Salle | 13,295 | F 3 |
| Lincoln | 33,800 | E 1 |
| Livingston | 36,511 | L 2 |
| Madison | 15,065 | H 2 |
| Morehouse | 32,463 | G 1 |
| Natchitoches | 35,219 | D 3 |
| Orleans | 593,471 | L 6 |
| Ouachita | 115,387 | F 2 |
| Plaquemines | 25,225 | L 8 |
| Pointe Coupee | 22,002 | G 5 |
| Rapides | 118,078 | E 4 |
| Red River | 9,226 | D 2 |
| Richland | 21,774 | G 2 |
| Sabine | 18,638 | C 3 |
| St. Bernard | 51,185 | L 7 |
| St. Charles | 29,550 | K 7 |
| St. Helena | 9,937 | J 5 |
| St. James | 19,733 | L 3 |
| St. John the Baptist | 23,813 | M 3 |
| St. Landry | 80,364 | F 5 |
| St. Martin | 32,453 | G 6 |
| St. Mary | 60,752 | H 7 |
| St. Tammany | 63,585 | L 6 |
| Tangipahoa | 65,875 | K 5 |
| Tensas | 9,732 | H 2 |
| Terrebonne | 76,049 | J 8 |
| Union | 18,447 | F 1 |
| Vermilion | 43,071 | F 7 |
| Vernon | 53,794 | D 4 |
| Washington | 41,987 | K 5 |
| Webster | 39,939 | D 1 |
| West Baton Rouge | 16,864 | H 6 |
| West Carroll | 13,028 | H 1 |
| West Feliciana | 11,376 | H 5 |
| Winn | 16,369 | E 3 |

## CITIES AND TOWNS

| Name | Pop. | Ref. |
|---|---|---|
| Abbeville | 10,996 | F 7 |
| Abita Springs | 839 | L 6 |
| Acme | 212 | G 4 |
| Acy | 570 | L 3 |
| Addis | 724 | J 2 |
| Adeline | 200 | G 7 |
| Ajax | 75 | D 3 |
| Akers | 140 | N 2 |
| Albany | 700 | M 1 |
| Alberta | 300 | D 2 |
| Alexandria | 41,557 | E 4 |
| Allen | 75 | D 3 |
| Amelia | 2,292 | H 7 |
| Amite | 3,593 | K 5 |
| Anacoco | 575 | D 4 |
| Anandale | 1,779 | F 4 |
| Andrew | 100 | F 6 |
| Angie | 317 | L 5 |
| Angola | 550 | G 5 |
| Ansley | 100 | E 2 |
| Arabi | 12,854 | K 7 |
| Arcadia | 2,970 | E 1 |
| Archibald | 300 | G 2 |
| Archie | 280 | G 3 |
| Arcola | 200 | K 5 |
| Arnaudville | 1,673 | G 6 |
| Ashland | 211 | D 2 |
| Athens | 387 | E 1 |
| Atlanta | 342 | E 3 |
| Avery Island | 591 | G 7 |
| Bains | 400 | H 5 |
| Baker | 8,281 | K 1 |
| Baldwin | 2,117 | H 7 |
| Ball | 500 | F 4 |
| Bancroft | 114 | C 5 |
| Baptist | 150 | M 1 |
| Barataria | 950 | K 7 |
| Basile | 1,779 | E 5 |
| Baskin | 177 | G 2 |
| Bastrop | 14,713 | G 1 |
| Batchelor | 100 | G 5 |
| BATON ROUGE | 165,963 | K 2 |
| Baton Rouge | †285,167 | K 2 |
| Bayou Barbary | 200 | M 2 |
| Bayou Cane | 9,077 | J 7 |
| Bayou Chicot | 60 | F 5 |
| Bayou Goula | 850 | J 3 |
| Bayou Vista | 5,121 | H 7 |
| Baywood | 100 | K 1 |
| Beaver | 60 | E 5 |
| Beekman | 300 | G 1 |
| Bel | 150 | D 6 |
| Belcher | 482 | C 1 |
| Bell City | 350 | D 6 |
| Belle Alliance | 350 | K 3 |
| Belle Chasse | 950 | O 4 |
| Belle Rose | 900 | K 3 |
| Belledeau | 450 | F 4 |
| Bellwood | 150 | D 3 |
| Belmont | 150 | C 3 |
| Benson | 200 | C 3 |
| Bentley | 300 | E 3 |
| Benton | 1,493 | C 1 |
| Bermuda | 100 | D 3 |
| Bernice | 1,794 | E 1 |
| Bertrandville | 175 | L 7 |
| Berwick | 4,168 | H 7 |
| Bethany | 250 | B 2 |
| Bienville | 287 | D 2 |
| Blanchard | 806 | C 1 |
| Bogalusa | 18,412 | L 5 |
| Bolinger | 250 | C 1 |
| Bonita | 533 | G 1 |
| Boothville | 300 | M 8 |
| Bordelonville | 450 | G 4 |
| Bosco | 780 | F 2 |
| Bossier City | 41,595 | C 1 |
| Boudreaux | 275 | J 8 |
| Bourg | 900 | J 7 |
| Boutte | 950 | N 4 |
| Boyce | 1,240 | E 4 |
| Braithwaite | 550 | P 4 |
| Branch | 125 | F 6 |
| Breaux Bridge | 4,942 | G 6 |
| Brittany | 290 | L 3 |
| Broussard | 1,707 | F 6 |
| Brusly | 1,282 | J 2 |
| Bryceland | 65 | E 2 |
| Buckeye | 75 | F 4 |
| Bunkie | 5,395 | F 5 |
| Buras-Triumph | 4,113 | L 8 |
| Burnside | 500 | L 3 |
| Bush | 275 | L 5 |
| Cade | 800 | G 6 |
| Calcasieu | 400 | E 4 |
| Calhoun | 653 | F 2 |
| Calumet | 100 | H 7 |
| Calvin | 286 | E 3 |
| Cameron | 975 | D 7 |
| Campti | 1,078 | D 3 |
| Cankton | 260 | F 6 |
| Carencro | 2,302 | G 6 |
| Carlisle | 975 | L 7 |
| Carville | 950 | K 3 |
| Castor | 183 | D 2 |
| Cecelia | 550 | G 6 |
| Center Point | 850 | F 4 |
| Centerville | 500 | H 7 |
| Central | 546 | L 3 |
| Chacahoula | 150 | J 7 |
| Chalmette | 14,220 | P 4 |
| Charenton | 950 | H 7 |
| Charlieville | 60 | G 2 |
| Chase | 150 | G 2 |
| Chataignier | 725 | F 5 |
| Chatham | 827 | F 2 |
| Chauvin | 900 | J 8 |
| Cheneyville | 1,082 | F 4 |
| Chopin | 75 | E 4 |
| Choudrant | 555 | F 1 |
| Church Point | 3,865 | F 6 |
| Clarence | 448 | E 3 |
| Clarks | 889 | F 2 |
| Clay | 400 | E 2 |
| Clayton | 1,103 | H 3 |
| Clear Lake | 100 | E 3 |
| Clifton | 80 | K 5 |
| Clinton | 1,884 | J 5 |
| Cloutierville | 250 | E 3 |
| Colfax | 1,892 | E 3 |
| Collinston | 397 | G 1 |
| Columbia | 1,000 | F 2 |
| Convent | 650 | L 3 |
| Converse | 375 | C 3 |
| Cooper Road | 9,034 | *C 2 |
| Corbin | 189 | L 1 |
| Corey | 110 | F 2 |
| Cotton Valley | 1,261 | D 1 |
| Cottonport | 1,924 | F 5 |
| Couchwood | 150 | D 1 |
| Coushatta | 1,492 | D 2 |
| Covington | 7,170 | K 5 |
| Cow Island | 100 | F 7 |
| Cravens | 475 | E 5 |
| Creole | 175 | D 7 |
| Crescent | 300 | J 2 |
| Creston | 150 | E 3 |
| Crowley | 16,104 | F 6 |
| Crowville | 400 | G 2 |
| Cullen | 1,956 | D 1 |
| Curtis | 110 | C 2 |
| Cut Off | 750 | K 7 |
| Cypress | 75 | D 3 |
| Dalcour | 275 | P 4 |
| Danville | 100 | E 2 |
| Darrow | 500 | K 3 |
| Davant | 650 | L 7 |
| De Quincy | 3,448 | D 6 |
| De Ridder | 8,030 | D 5 |
| Deerford | 100 | K 1 |
| Delcambre | 1,975 | F 7 |
| Delhi | 2,887 | H 2 |
| Delta | 153 | J 2 |
| Denham Springs | 6,752 | L 1 |
| Derry | 75 | E 3 |
| Des Allemands | 2,318 | N 4 |
| Destrehan | 800 | N 4 |
| Deville | 500 | F 4 |
| Diamond | 370 | L 7 |
| Dixie | 330 | C 1 |
| Dixie Inn | 456 | D 1 |
| Dodson | 457 | E 2 |
| Donaldsonville | 7,367 | K 3 |
| Donner | 500 | J 7 |
| Downsville | 250 | F 1 |
| Doyline | 716 | D 1 |
| Dry Creek | 480 | D 5 |
| Dry Prong | 352 | E 3 |
| Dubach | 1,096 | E 1 |
| Dubberly | 212 | D 1 |
| Dulac | 225 | J 8 |
| Dunn | 225 | G 2 |
| Duplessis | 700 | K 2 |
| Duson | 1,199 | F 6 |
| East Hodge | 363 | E 2 |
| East Point | 200 | D 2 |
| Easton | 365 | F 5 |
| Echo | 450 | F 4 |
| Edgard | 300 | M 3 |
| Edgefield | 201 | D 2 |
| Edgerly | 250 | C 6 |
| Effie | 950 | F 4 |
| Elizabeth | 504 | E 5 |
| Elm Grove | 350 | C 2 |
| Elm Park | 200 | H 5 |
| Elmer | 445 | E 4 |
| Elton | 1,598 | E 6 |
| Empire | 700 | L 8 |
| Enterprise | 300 | G 3 |
| Eola | 100 | F 5 |
| Epps | 448 | G 1 |
| Erath | 2,024 | F 7 |
| Eros | 164 | F 2 |
| Erwinville | 790 | H 5 |
| Esther | 90 | F 7 |
| Estherwood | 661 | F 6 |
| Ethel | 350 | H 5 |
| Eunice | 11,390 | F 6 |
| Eva | 100 | G 4 |
| Evangeline | 400 | F 6 |
| Evans | 400 | D 5 |
| Evergreen | 307 | F 5 |
| Extension | 950 | G 2 |
| Fairbanks | 150 | F 1 |
| Farmerville | 3,416 | F 1 |
| Fenton | 404 | E 6 |
| Ferriday | 5,239 | G 3 |
| Fields | 125 | C 5 |
| Fisher | 300 | D 4 |
| Flatwoods | 450 | E 4 |
| Flora | 200 | D 3 |
| Florien | 639 | D 4 |
| Floyd | 53 | H 1 |
| Fluker | 400 | K 5 |
| Folsom | 249 | K 5 |
| Forbing | 100 | C 2 |
| Fordoche | 488 | G 5 |
| Forest | 221 | H 1 |
| Forest Hill | 370 | E 4 |
| Fort Jesup | 950 | C 3 |
| Fort Necessity | 150 | G 2 |
| Franklin | 9,325 | G 7 |
| Franklinton | 3,562 | K 5 |
| French Settlement | 800 | L 2 |
| Frierson | 700 | C 2 |
| Frost | 500 | L 2 |
| Fryeburg | 150 | D 2 |
| Fullerton | 120 | D 4 |
| Galbraith | 75 | E 4 |
| Galliano | 950 | K 8 |
| Gallion | 100 | G 1 |
| Galvez | 200 | L 2 |
| Gansville | 55 | E 2 |
| Garden City | 515 | H 7 |
| Garyville | 2,474 | M 3 |
| Geismar | 300 | K 3 |
| Georgetown | 306 | F 3 |
| Gheens | 116 | K 7 |
| Gibsland | 1,380 | D 2 |
| Gibson | 950 | J 7 |
| Gilbert | 746 | G 2 |
| Gilliam | 211 | C 1 |
| Girard | 250 | G 2 |
| Glencoe | 200 | G 7 |
| Glenmora | 1,651 | E 5 |
| Gloster | 975 | C 2 |
| Glynn | 400 | H 5 |
| Golden Meadow | 2,681 | K 8 |
| Goldonna | 337 | D 2 |
| Gonzales | 4,512 | L 2 |
| Good Hope | 950 | N 4 |
| Good Pine | 535 | F 3 |
| Goodbee | 75 | K 6 |
| Goudeau | 79 | G 5 |
| Grambling | 4,407 | E 1 |
| Gramercy | 2,567 | M 3 |
| Grand Cane | 284 | C 2 |
| Grand Chenier | 710 | E 7 |
| Grand Coteau | 1,301 | G 6 |
| Grand Isle | 2,236 | L 8 |
| Grand Lake | 400 | D 6 |
| Grant | 225 | E 5 |
| Gray | 750 | J 7 |
| Grayson | 516 | F 2 |
| Greensburg | 652 | J 5 |
| Greenwell Springs | 225 | K 1 |
| Greenwood | 212 | B 2 |
| Gretna | 24,875 | O 4 |
| Grosse Tete | 710 | G 6 |
| Gueydan | 1,984 | E 6 |
| Gurley | 150 | H 5 |
| Hackberry | 750 | D 7 |
| Hahnville | 2,362 | N 4 |
| Haile | 300 | F 1 |
| Hall Summit | 190 | D 2 |
| Hammond | 12,487 | N 1 |
| Hanna | 125 | D 3 |
| Happy Jack | 800 | L 7 |
| Harahan | 13,037 | O 4 |
| Harrisonburg | 626 | G 3 |
| Harvey | 6,347 | O 4 |
| Haughton | 885 | C 1 |
| Hayes | 800 | E 6 |
| Haynesville | 3,055 | D 1 |
| Head of Island | 420 | L 2 |
| Hebert | 150 | G 2 |
| Heflin | 314 | D 2 |
| Hessmer | 454 | F 4 |
| Hester | 280 | L 3 |
| Hicks | 369 | E 4 |
| Hico | 125 | E 1 |
| Hineston | 125 | E 4 |
| Hodge | 818 | E 2 |
| Hohen Solms | 125 | K 3 |
| Holden | 750 | M 1 |
| Holly Ridge | 200 | G 2 |
| Hollywood | 1,794 | D 6 |
| Holmwood | 60 | D 6 |
| Homeplace | 600 | L 8 |
| Homer | 4,483 | D 1 |
| Hornbeck | 525 | D 4 |
| Hosston | 428 | C 1 |
| Houma | 30,922 | J 7 |
| Humphreys | 900 | J 7 |
| Hutton | 75 | D 4 |
| Iberville | 221 | K 2 |
| Ida | 370 | C 1 |
| Independence | 1,770 | M 1 |
| Indian Village | 106 | H 6 |
| Innis | 300 | G 5 |
| Iota | 1,271 | E 6 |
| Iowa | 1,944 | D 6 |
| Isabel | 365 | K 5 |
| Ivan | 125 | C 1 |
| Jackson | 4,697 | H 5 |
| Jamestown | 153 | D 2 |
| Jeanerette | 6,322 | G 7 |
| Jefferson Heights | 16,489 | O 4 |
| Jena | 2,431 | F 3 |
| Jennings | 11,783 | E 6 |
| Jesuit Bend | 100 | K 7 |
| Jigger | 400 | G 2 |
| Johnsons Bayou | 300 | C 7 |
| Jones | 200 | G 1 |
| Jonesboro | 5,072 | E 2 |
| Jonesville | 2,761 | G 3 |
| Joyce | 700 | E 3 |
| Junction City | 733 | E 1 |
| Kaplan | 5,540 | F 6 |
| Keatchie | 328 | C 2 |
| Keithville | 500 | C 2 |
| Kelly | 250 | F 3 |
| Kenner | 29,858 | O 4 |
| Kentwood | 2,736 | J 5 |
| Kilbourne | 370 | H 1 |
| Killian | 275 | M 2 |
| Killona | 600 | M 3 |
| Kinder | 2,307 | E 6 |
| Kisatchie | 105 | D 4 |
| Klotzville | 248 | K 3 |
| Kraemer | 510 | M 4 |
| Krotz Sprs. | 1,435 | G 5 |
| Kurthwood | 50 | D 4 |
| Labadieville | 700 | K 4 |
| Lacamp | 100 | E 4 |
| Lacassine | 494 | E 6 |
| Lacombe | 750 | L 6 |
| Lafayette | 68,908 | F 6 |
| Lafayette | †111,745 | F 6 |
| Lafitte | 1,223 | K 7 |
| Lafourche | 200 | J 7 |
| Lagan | 90 | L 4 |

*No room on map for name.  †Population of metropolitan area.

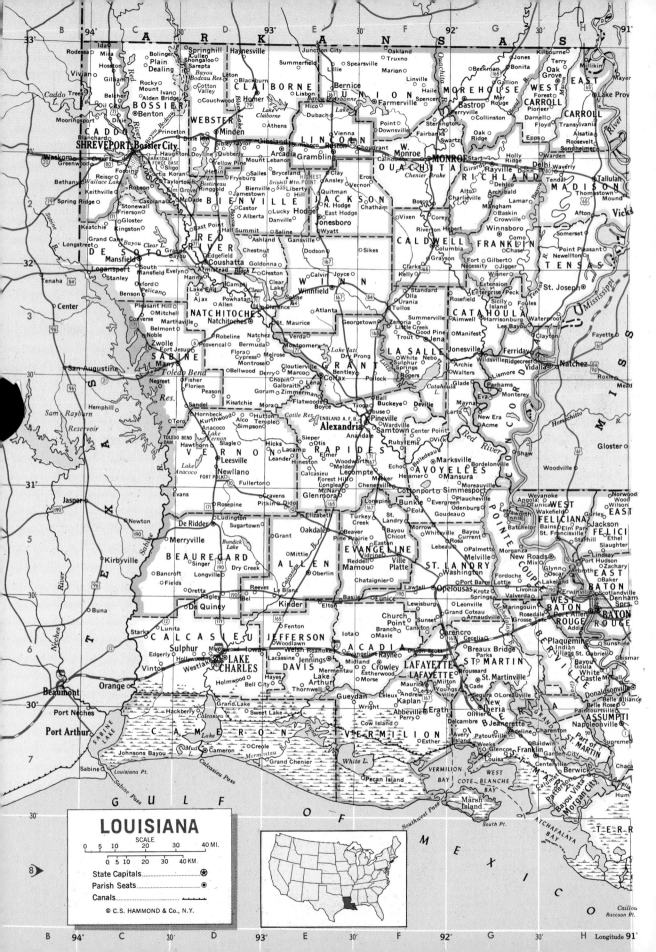

# LOUISIANA

SCALE
0 5 10 20 30 40 MI.
0 5 10 20 30 40 KM.

State Capitals..........⊛
Parish Seats............◉
Canals.................

© C.S. HAMMOND & Co., N.Y.

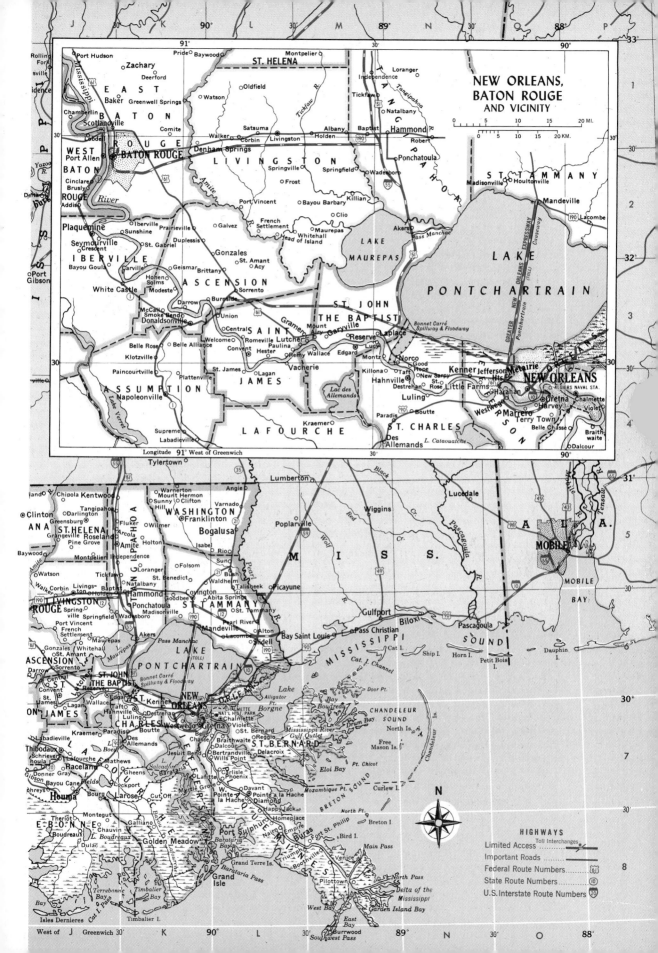

| Name | Pop. | Ref. |
|---|---|---|
| Lake Arthur | 3,551 | E 6 |
| Lake Charles | 77,998 | D 6 |
| Lake Charles | †145,415 | D 6 |
| Lake End | 75 | D 3 |
| Lake Providence | 6,183 | H 1 |
| Lakeland | 400 | H 5 |
| Lamar | 60 | G 2 |
| Laplace | 5,953 | N 3 |
| Larose | 4,267 | K 7 |
| Larto | 500 | G 4 |
| Lawtell | 600 | F 5 |
| Le Blanc | 102 | E 5 |
| Leander | 125 | E 4 |
| Lebeau | 270 | F 5 |
| Lecompte | 1,518 | F 4 |
| Leesville | 8,928 | D 4 |
| Leleux | 100 | F 6 |
| Lena | 250 | E 4 |
| Leonville | 512 | G 6 |
| Leroy | 75 | F 6 |
| Leton | 125 | D 1 |
| Lettsworth | 200 | G 5 |
| Lewisburg | 265 | F 6 |
| Liberty Hill | 75 | E 2 |
| Libuse | 500 | F 4 |
| Lillie | 160 | E 1 |
| Linville | 100 | F 1 |
| Lisbon | 151 | E 1 |
| Lismore | 380 | G 3 |
| Little Creek | 110 | F 3 |
| Little Farms | 15,713 | N 4 |
| Livingston | 1,398 | L 1 |
| Livonia | 611 | G 5 |
| Lockport | 2,398 | K 7 |
| Logansport | 1,330 | C 3 |
| Lonepine | 850 | F 5 |
| Longleaf | 250 | E 4 |
| Longstreet | 182 | B 2 |
| Longville | 250 | D 5 |
| Loranger | 200 | N 1 |
| Loreauville | 728 | G 6 |
| Lottie | 350 | G 5 |
| Lucky | 50 | E 2 |
| Lucy | 825 | M 3 |
| Luling | 3,255 | N 4 |
| Lunita | 75 | C 6 |
| Lutcher | 3,911 | L 3 |
| Madisonville | 801 | K 6 |
| Mamou | 3,275 | F 5 |
| Mandeville | 2,571 | L 6 |
| Mangham | 544 | G 2 |
| Manifest | 75 | G 3 |
| Mansfield | 6,432 | C 2 |
| Mansura | 1,699 | G 4 |
| Many | 3,112 | C 3 |
| Maplewood | 900 | D 6 |
| Marco | 125 | E 3 |
| Maringouin | 1,365 | G 6 |
| Marion | 796 | F 1 |
| Marksville | 4,519 | G 4 |
| Marrero | 29,015 | O 4 |
| Marthaville | 150 | D 3 |
| Mathews | 600 | J 7 |
| Maurepas | 200 | M 2 |
| Maurice | 476 | F 6 |
| Maxie | 65 | F 6 |
| Mayna | 122 | G 4 |
| McCall | 150 | K 3 |
| McDade | 100 | D 2 |
| McNary | 220 | E 5 |
| Meeker | 150 | F 4 |
| Melder | 200 | E 4 |
| Melrose | 150 | E 3 |
| Melville | 2,076 | G 5 |
| Mer Rouge | 819 | G 1 |
| Mermentau | 756 | E 6 |
| Merryville | 1,286 | D 5 |
| Metairie | 136,477 | O 4 |
| Midland | 500 | F 6 |
| Milton | 500 | F 6 |
| Mimosa Park | 1,624 | *N 4 |
| Minden | 13,996 | D 1 |
| Mira | 137 | C 1 |
| Mitchell | 125 | C 3 |
| Mix | 150 | G 5 |
| Modeste | 230 | K 3 |
| Monroe | 56,374 | F 1 |
| Monroe | †115,387 | F 1 |
| Montegut | 950 | J 8 |
| Monterey | 800 | G 4 |
| Montgomery | 923 | E 3 |
| Montpelier | 211 | M 1 |
| Montrose | 95 | D 3 |
| Montz | 200 | M 3 |
| Mooringsport | 830 | B 1 |
| Mora | 378 | E 4 |
| Moreauville | 807 | G 4 |
| Morgan City | 16,586 | H 7 |
| Morganza | 836 | G 5 |
| Morrow | 350 | F 5 |
| Morse | 759 | F 6 |
| Mound | 78 | H 2 |
| Mount Airy | 700 | M 3 |
| Mt. Hermon | 110 | K 5 |
| Mt. Lebanon | 102 | D 2 |
| Myrtle Grove | 100 | K 7 |
| Nairn | 500 | L 8 |
| Napoleonville | 1,008 | K 4 |
| Natalbany | 900 | N 1 |
| Natchez | 600 | D 3 |
| Natchitoches | 15,974 | D 3 |
| Nebo | 200 | F 3 |
| Negreet | 200 | C 4 |
| New Era | 200 | G 4 |
| New Iberia | 30,147 | G 6 |
| New Orleans | 593,471 | O 4 |
| New Orleans | †1,046,470 | O 4 |
| New Roads | 3,945 | G 5 |
| New Sarpy | 1,643 | N 4 |
| Newellton | 1,403 | H 2 |
| Newllano | 1,800 | D 4 |
| Noble | 209 | C 3 |
| Norco | 4,773 | N 3 |
| North Hodge | 640 | E 2 |
| Norwood | 348 | H 5 |
| Oak Grove | 1,980 | H 1 |
| Oak Ridge | 276 | G 1 |
| Oakdale | 7,301 | E 5 |
| Oberlin | 1,857 | E 5 |
| Odenburg | 175 | H 5 |
| Oil City | 907 | C 1 |
| Olivier | 300 | G 7 |
| Olla | 1,387 | F 3 |
| Opelousas | 20,387 | G 5 |
| Oretta | 110 | D 5 |
| Oscar | 700 | H 5 |
| Otis | 64 | E 4 |
| Oxford | 125 | C 3 |
| Palmetto | 312 | G 5 |
| Paincourtville | 600 | K 3 |
| Parhams | 100 | G 4 |
| Parks | 491 | G 6 |
| Patoutville | 230 | G 7 |
| Patterson | 4,409 | H 7 |
| Paulina | 500 | L 3 |
| Pearl River | 1,361 | L 6 |
| Pecan Island | 480 | F 7 |
| Pelican | 150 | C 3 |
| Perry | 225 | F 7 |
| Perryville | 100 | G 1 |
| Phoenix | 525 | L 7 |
| Pilottown | 150 | M 8 |
| Pine Grove | 500 | J 5 |
| Pine Prairie | 515 | E 5 |
| Pineville | 8,951 | F 4 |
| Pioneer | 188 | H 1 |
| Pitkin | 700 | E 5 |
| Plain Dealing | 1,300 | C 1 |
| Plaquemine | 7,739 | J 2 |
| Plattenville | 400 | K 4 |
| Plaucheville | 224 | G 4 |
| Pleasant Hill | 826 | C 3 |
| Pointe a la Hache | 750 | L 7 |
| Pollock | 341 | F 4 |
| Ponchatoula | 4,545 | N 2 |
| Port Allen | 5,728 | J 2 |
| Port Barre | 2,133 | G 5 |
| Port Hudson | 200 | J 1 |
| Port Sulphur | 3,022 | L 8 |
| Port Vincent | 387 | L 2 |
| Powhatan | 277 | D 3 |
| Prairieville | 500 | K 2 |
| Pride | 100 | K 1 |
| Princeton | 350 | C 1 |
| Provencal | 530 | D 3 |
| Quitman | 169 | E 2 |
| Raceland | 4,880 | J 7 |
| Ragley | 82 | D 5 |
| Rayne | 9,510 | F 6 |
| Rayville | 3,962 | G 2 |
| Reddell | 800 | F 5 |
| Reeves | 214 | D 5 |
| Reggio | 400 | L 7 |
| Remy | 850 | L 3 |
| Reserve | 6,381 | M 3 |
| Ridgecrest | 1,076 | G 3 |
| Ringgold | 1,731 | D 2 |
| Rio | 250 | L 5 |
| Riverton | 100 | F 2 |
| Roanoke | 640 | E 6 |
| Robeline | 274 | D 3 |
| Robert | 600 | N 1 |
| Robson | 50 | C 2 |
| Rocky Mount | 100 | C 1 |
| Rodessa | 273 | B 1 |
| Rogers | 150 | F 3 |
| Romeville | 133 | L 3 |
| Rosa | 150 | G 5 |
| Rosedale | 621 | G 6 |
| Roseland | 1,273 | J 5 |
| Rosepine | 587 | D 5 |
| Ruby | 350 | F 4 |
| Ruston | 17,365 | E 1 |
| Saint Amant | 900 | L 2 |
| Saint Benedict | 200 | K 5 |
| Saint Bernard | 750 | L 7 |
| Saint Francisville | 1,603 | H 5 |
| Saint Gabriel | 975 | K 2 |
| Saint James | 600 | L 3 |
| Saint Joseph | 1,864 | H 3 |
| Saint Landry | 950 | F 5 |
| Saint Martinville | 7,153 | G 6 |
| Saint Maurice | 650 | E 3 |
| Saint Rose | 2,106 | N 4 |
| St. Tammany | 150 | L 6 |
| Saline | 307 | E 2 |
| Samtown | 4,210 | F 4 |
| Sarepta | 882 | D 1 |
| Schriever | 700 | J 7 |
| Scotlandville | 22,557 | J 1 |
| Scott | 1,334 | F 6 |
| Segura | 200 | G 6 |
| Seymourville | 2,506 | J 2 |
| Shaw | 125 | D 4 |
| Shongaloo | 173 | D 1 |
| Shreveport | 182,064 | C 1 |
| Shreveport | †293,887 | C 1 |
| Sibley | 869 | D 1 |
| Sicily Island | 630 | G 3 |
| Sieper | 200 | E 4 |
| Sikes | 237 | F 2 |
| Simmesport | 2,027 | G 5 |
| Simpson | 491 | D 4 |
| Simsboro | 412 | E 1 |
| Singer | 400 | D 5 |
| Slagle | 200 | D 4 |
| Slaughter | 580 | H 5 |
| Slidell | 16,101 | L 6 |
| Sligo | 75 | C 2 |
| Smoke Bend | 300 | K 3 |
| Somerset | 75 | H 2 |
| Sondheimer | 325 | H 1 |
| Sorrento | 1,182 | L 3 |
| S. Mansfield | 439 | C 3 |
| Spearsville | 197 | E 1 |
| Spencer | 80 | F 1 |
| Springfield | 423 | M 2 |
| Springhill | 6,496 | D 1 |
| Standard | 190 | H 3 |
| Stanley | 145 | C 3 |
| Starks | 750 | C 6 |
| Start | 200 | G 2 |
| Sterlington | 1,118 | F 1 |
| Stonewall | 500 | C 2 |
| Sugartown | 86 | D 5 |
| Sulphur | 15,247 | D 6 |
| Summerfield | 170 | E 1 |
| Summerville | 80 | F 3 |
| Sun | 288 | L 5 |
| Sunset | 1,675 | F 6 |
| Sunshine | 900 | K 2 |
| Supreme | 617 | K 4 |
| Swartz | 650 | G 1 |
| Sweet Lake | 300 | D 7 |
| Taft | 90 | N 4 |
| Talisheek | 292 | L 5 |
| Tallulah | 9,643 | H 2 |
| Tangipahoa | 469 | J 5 |
| Taylor | 500 | D 1 |
| Taylortown | 150 | C 2 |
| Tendal | 200 | H 2 |
| Terry | 100 | H 1 |
| Terry Town | 13,832 | O 4 |
| Theriot | 950 | J 8 |
| Thibodaux | 15,028 | J 7 |
| Thomastown | 65 | H 2 |
| Thornwell | 116 | E 6 |
| Tickfaw | 370 | M 1 |
| Tioga | 457 | F 4 |
| Toro | 75 | C 4 |
| Transylvania | 400 | H 1 |
| Trees | 247 | B 1 |
| Triumph-Buras | 4,113 | L 8 |
| Trout | 500 | F 3 |
| Tullos | 600 | F 3 |
| Tunica | 475 | G 5 |
| Turkey Creek | 280 | F 5 |
| Union | 665 | L 3 |
| Urania | 874 | F 3 |
| Vacherie | 2,145 | L 3 |
| Valverda | 200 | G 5 |
| Varnado | 320 | L 5 |
| Venice | 900 | M 8 |
| Verda | 100 | E 3 |
| Vernon | 150 | E 2 |
| Vick | 500 | F 4 |
| Vidalia | 5,538 | G 3 |
| Vidrine | 100 | F 5 |
| Vienna | 250 | E 1 |
| Ville Platte | 9,692 | F 5 |
| Vinton | 3,454 | C 6 |
| Violet | 975 | P 4 |
| Vivian | 4,046 | B 1 |
| Wadesboro | 125 | M 2 |
| Wakefield | 200 | H 5 |
| Waldheim | 75 | L 5 |
| Walker | 1,363 | L 1 |
| Wallace | 200 | M 3 |
| Walters | 500 | G 3 |
| Warden | 350 | H 1 |
| Wardville | 1,087 | F 4 |
| Washington | 1,473 | G 5 |
| Waterproof | 1,438 | H 3 |
| Watson | 700 | L 1 |
| Waverly | 350 | H 2 |
| Weeks | 400 | G 7 |
| Welcome | 450 | L 3 |
| Welsh | 3,203 | E 6 |
| West Monroe | 14,868 | F 1 |
| West Pointe a la Hache | 250 | L 7 |
| Westlake | 4,082 | D 6 |
| Westwego | 11,402 | O 4 |
| Weyanoke | 500 | H 5 |
| White Castle | 2,206 | J 2 |
| Whitehall | 380 | M 2 |
| Whiteville | 450 | F 5 |
| Wildsville | 650 | G 3 |
| Wills Point | 175 | L 7 |
| Wilson | 606 | H 5 |
| Winnfield | 7,142 | E 3 |
| Winnsboro | 5,349 | G 2 |
| Wisner | 1,339 | G 3 |
| Woodland | 64 | J 5 |
| Woodlawn | 150 | E 6 |
| Woodworth | 409 | E 4 |
| Wright | 100 | F 6 |
| Wyatt | 100 | E 2 |
| Yellow Pine | 100 | D 2 |
| Youngsville | 1,002 | G 6 |
| Zachary | 4,964 | K 1 |
| Zenoria | 95 | F 3 |
| Zwolle | 2,169 | C 3 |

## OTHER FEATURES

| Feature | Ref. |
|---|---|
| Algiers Naval Sta. | O 4 |
| Allemands (lake) | M 4 |
| Amite (riv.) | L 2 |
| Anacoco (lake) | D 4 |
| Atchafalaya (bay) | H 8 |
| Atchafalaya (riv.) | G 6 |
| Barataria (bay) | L 8 |
| Barksdale A.F.B. | C 2 |
| Bayou Bodcau (res.) | D 1 |
| Bayou D'Arbonne (lake) | F 1 |
| Bistineau (lake) | D 2 |
| Black (lake) | D 3 |
| Bodcau (bayou) | C 1 |
| Boeuf (riv.) | G 1 |
| Borgne (lake) | L 7 |
| Bonnet Carré Spillway | N 3 |
| Breton (sound) | M 7 |
| Bundick (lake) | D 5 |
| Caddo (lake) | B 1 |
| Calcasieu (lake) | D 7 |
| Calcasieu (riv.) | E 5 |
| Cat I. (chan.) | M 6 |
| Catahoula (lake) | F 4 |
| Cataouatche (lake) | N 4 |
| Chalmette Nat'l Hist. Park | L 7 |
| Chandeleur (isls.) | N 7 |
| Chandeleur (sound) | M 7 |
| Chenier Brake (res.) | F 2 |
| Claiborne (lake) | E 1 |
| Clear (lake) | C 2 |
| Clear (lake) | D 3 |
| Cotile (res.) | E 4 |
| Cross (lake) | C 2 |
| Driskill (mt.) | F 1 |
| East (bay) | M 8 |
| England A.F.B. | 3,715 E 4 |
| Fields (lake) | J 7 |
| Fort Polk | 23,555 D 4 |
| Garden I. (bay) | M 8 |
| Grand (lake) | E 7 |
| Grand (lake) | H 7 |
| Grand (riv.) | H 6 |
| Iatt (lake) | E 3 |
| Lafourche (bayou) | K 8 |
| Little (riv.) | F 3 |
| Louisiana (pt.) | C 7 |
| Macon (bayou) | H 1 |
| Main (pass.) | M 8 |
| Manchac (passage) | N 2 |
| Marsh (isl.) | G 7 |
| Maurepas (lake) | N 2 |
| Mexico (gulf) | F 8 |
| Mississippi (delta) | M 8 |
| Mississippi (riv.) | H 3 |
| Mississippi (sound) | M 6 |
| North (pass.) | M 8 |
| Ouachita (riv.) | F 1 |
| Pearl (riv.) | L 5 |
| Pontchartrain (lake) | O 3 |
| Red (riv.) | G 4 |
| Sabine (lake) | C 7 |
| Sabine (pass.) | C 7 |
| Sabine (riv.) | C 5 |
| Saline (lake) | E 3 |
| Salvador (lake) | K 7 |
| Southwest (pass.) | M 8 |
| Tangipahoa (riv.) | N 1 |
| Tensas (riv.) | G 3 |
| Terrebonne (bay) | J 8 |
| Tickfaw (riv.) | M 1 |
| Timbalier (bay) | K 8 |
| Toledo Bend (res.) | C 3 |
| Vermilion (bay) | F 7 |
| Vernon (lake) | D 4 |
| Verret (lake) | K 4 |
| Wallace (lake) | C 2 |
| West (bay) | M 8 |
| West Cote Blanche (bay) | G 7 |
| White (lake) | E 7 |

THIS ARTICLE IS IN THE FACT-INDEX
Louisiana College

**LOUISIANA PURCHASE.** In 1803 President Jefferson set the example of getting new territory by purchase rather than by war. He did so by buying from France the vast tract of land known as Louisiana. The United States did not differ from Old World countries in wanting to reach its "natural boundaries." It did differ in the method it used.

The city of New Orleans was wanted very much by all the people west of the Alleghenies. The nation that controlled New Orleans could control the Mississippi River. Western farmers were eager for this control to be in the hands of the United States. Their grain, hogs, cattle, and other produce were sent to market by flatboats which floated down the great "father of waters."

Spain had held this important gateway to the West ever since 1762. It was given to Spain by treaty from France. Then suddenly, in 1802, news came that two years earlier Napoleon had forced weak Spain to give New Orleans and the whole Louisiana territory to the all-conquering French. This was bad news for the Western farmer. France was then the most powerful country in the world, and there was no hope of forcing any privileges from it.

Napoleon's dream of a vast colonial empire vanished almost as suddenly as it had come. England in its war against France defeated the French navy. France could hardly hold territory across the Atlantic Ocean while England controlled the seas. Robert Livingston, the American minister to France, pointed out this fact to Napoleon. Napoleon then decided to sell the Louisiana territory.

### Cost of Purchase

When James Monroe arrived in France with power from President Jefferson to buy New Orleans and West Florida for not more than 10 million dollars, he was offered the *whole* of the French territory for approximately 15 million dollars. Although the American agents had no authority to spend such a large sum, they signed the treaty of purchase on April 30, 1803. The area involved was a vast 529,911,680 acres. In December the Stars and Stripes was raised over New Orleans.

Thus at one stroke the area of the United States was doubled. President Jefferson believed that the annexation and government of so vast a territory was unconstitutional. He wanted an amendment to the Constitution to ratify it. The members of his Cabinet did not think this necessary, and their views prevailed. The New England Federalists were enraged at the prospect of the admission of numerous new states, whose votes in Senate and House would reinforce those of the South and West. Some, such as Josiah Quincy, advocated secession—"amicably, if they can; violently if they must." Thirteen states, either in whole or in part, were carved out of this land between the Mississippi River and the Rockies. The price of the Louisiana Purchase was only a tiny fraction of its value today. (For map, *see* United States History, Section 4, "The Nation's Westward Advance.")

THESE ARTICLES ARE IN THE FACT-INDEX
Louisiana Purchase Exposition
Louisiana State University
Louisiana Tech University

**LOUISVILLE, Ky.** The Falls of the Ohio River determined the location of Louisville, the largest city in Kentucky. Actually the falls are great rapids. In pioneer days these treacherous rocks interrupted river traffic and forced upstream and downstream vessels to exchange cargoes over a portage. This transfer point soon became a trading center, which was chartered as a city in 1828.

The completion of the Louisville and Portland Canal in 1830 ended the portaging business. The Ohio River was now open to through traffic from Pittsburgh, Pa., to the Mississippi. As a result the port of Louisville grew in commercial importance.

Louisville's industrial growth started soon after the Civil War. Its strategic location was important. To the north and west lay the great grain regions of the United States. To the south were abundant supplies of tobacco, cotton, and minerals. All these raw materials fed the many busy factories which spread to both sides of the river.

A hydroelectric plant at the falls and steam-electric plants provide abundant power. Coal, oil, and gas fields nearby supply much of the city's fuel, but some natural gas and petroleum are piped from West Virginia and Texas. Louisville's factories make electrical appliances, tobacco products, distilled spirits, chemicals, processed foods, farm machinery and other metal goods, plumbing fixtures, synthetic rubber, paints, and textiles.

Eight trunk-line railroads serve the city, which also contains large railroad headquarters and repair

The Sherman Minton Bridge in the foreground is one of Louisville's three highway bridges over the Ohio River to Indiana. There are also three railroad bridges.

Free Publications Photo

shops. Several air-transport lines use the two airports. Louisville is a major center for livestock and tobacco transactions.

Louisville's parks and playgrounds cover more than 3,300 acres. The city is the seat of the University of Louisville, two accredited colleges, and two theological seminaries. The J. B. Speed Art Museum has notable collections. In 1962 the Rauch Memorial Planetarium was opened. The Kentucky Derby is run every May at Churchill Downs, the city's famous racetrack. The state fair is held annually in September at the Kentucky Fair and Exhibition Center.

### The City's History

Louisville was first called Beargrass Settlement. It was founded in 1778 by George Rogers Clark as a frontier outpost. When it was incorporated as a town in 1780, Clark named it Louisville in honor of Louis XVI of France. Many of its early settlers came from France, and later a number from Germany.

Among the city's famous residents was the noted journalist Henry Watterson, editor of the Louisville *Courier-Journal*. Others included Louis Philippe, later the Citizen King of France, and Louis D. Brandeis, Supreme Court justice (*see* Brandeis).

The city was incorporated in 1828. It is governed by a mayor and board of 12 aldermen. Population (1980 census), 298,840.

---

THESE ARTICLES ARE IN THE FACT-INDEX
**Louisville, University of**
**Lounsbury, Thomas Raynesford**

---

**LOURDES** (*lụr d*), **France.** Almost 3 million pilgrims—many of them sick or disabled—visit Lourdes each year. Located in southwestern France, the town is primarily important for its religious history.

At Lourdes in 1858 in a grotto beside a mountain stream called the Gave de Pau, a young girl, Bernadette Soubirous (*sọ-bē-rọ'*), saw visions of the Virgin Mary. She also found a spring said to have healing powers. Today Roman Catholics from all over the world visit the shrine at Lourdes and receive water from the spring.

### Bernadette's Vision

Bernadette, christened Marie Bernard, was born Jan. 7, 1844, in Lourdes. She was the oldest child in the large Soubirous family. At that time Lourdes was a market town of about 5,000 people.

Bernadette's parents, François and Louise, owned a mill inherited from Louise's father. They lost it, however, a year after Bernadette's birth. Then both François and Louise worked at odd jobs. When Bernadette was 12, the family went to live in a cell of an unused jail that was known as "the dungeon."

On Feb. 11, 1858, Bernadette, her sister Marie, and a friend, Jeanne Abadie, went to gather twigs for firewood by the banks of the Gave. A delicate girl, Bernadette lagged behind her companions. They had waded across a shallow part of the stream that separated them from a grotto on the other side. As she was preparing to cross, Bernadette heard the roar of a great wind; yet the poplars were still. Looking up, she saw in the grotto a vision she later described as "a lady, young and beautiful."

Bernadette continued to have visions, always in the grotto. During the ninth vision she uncovered a trickle of water which proved to be a spring. A few days later a blind stonecutter bathed his eyes in the water and reported a miraculous cure.

Twenty thousand people gathered at Lourdes the day of Bernadette's 16th vision. According to various historians, she saw 18 or 19 visions.

### Bernadette Becomes a Nun

The grotto became a popular shrine. Police tried several times to close it, but Napoleon III ordered it left open. Bernadette was so famous that privacy was impossible. For two years she had a daily stream of visitors. Then she went as a boarder to the Convent of the Sisters of Charity at Nevers.

She took final vows with the order in 1878. On April 16, 1879, Bernadette died of tuberculosis. She was buried in the convent chapel at Nevers. She was beatified in 1925 and canonized on Dec. 8, 1933. Her feast day is February 18.

### The Grotto at Modern Lourdes

Today there are three churches near the site of Bernadette's visions. The first church, which was opened in 1866, is the Crypt, hewn out of the great rock. Above it rises a spired basilica, Notre Dame de Lourdes. Below it is the great round Romanesque Church of the Rosary.

A Way of the Cross with life-size figures mounts the tree-covered hill to the left of the basilica. Down by the grotto are three low buildings where the sick can bathe in water from the spring. Twelve bronze hydrants also supply water.

Inside the grotto is an altar. Hundreds of votive candles left by pilgrims burn in and around the grotto. In the grotto and around it hang crutches left by cripples who have visited the shrine.

Lourdes is in the Pyrenees Mountains in the department of Hautes-Pyrénées. It is divided into an old town and a new town by the Gave de Pau. The new quarter, of which the grotto is a part, is on the left bank. The old quarter, on the right bank, is famous for its ancient fortress. Population (1968 census), 17,627.

---

THESE ARTICLES ARE IN THE FACT-INDEX
**Louse**                    **Lousma, Jack R.**
**Louse fly**                **Louth, Ireland**

---

**LOUVAIN** (*lo͞o-văn'*, Flemish *Leuven*), **Belgium.** In the 14th century the charming town of Louvain on the Dyle River was the capital of the duchy of Brabant. It was also a leading cloth-weaving center of Europe. A feud between citizens and patricians toward the end of the century led to the decline of its wool trade and to the rise of Brussels, 18 miles to the west. After the founding of its famous Roman Catholic university in 1425, Louvain became a noted seat of learning.

. Of the town's many beautiful old buildings, two are outstanding. The Gothic Town Hall and the Church of St. Pierre, both built in the 15th century, are among the finest medieval structures in Europe.

One of the town's chief treasures was the university library, which contained many priceless old manuscripts. It was destroyed in 1914, when the Germans set fire to the town. A new library, built and endowed with a fund contributed by Americans, was opened in 1928. Destroyed again by the Germans in 1940, the library has since been rebuilt. Population (1961 census), 32,524.

---

THESE ARTICLES ARE IN THE FACT-INDEX

| | |
|---|---|
| Louvois, François Michel Le Tellier, marquis de | Lover, Samuel |
| Louÿs, Pierre | 'Love's Labour's Lost' |
| Lovejoy, Elijah Parish | Lovett, Robert Abercrombie |
| Lovelace, Maud Hart | Lovett, Robert Morss |
| Lovelace, Richard | Lovington, N. M. |
| Love-lies-bleeding | Low, Archibald Montgomery |
| Lovell, James Arthur, Jr. | Low, Sir David |
| Loveman, Robert | |

---

**LOW, Juliette Gordon** (1860–1927). Girl Scouts in the United States celebrate October 31 as Founder's Day. It is the birthday of Juliette Low, who organized the first Girl Guides in the United States at her home in Savannah, Ga., March 12, 1912. The Girl Guides soon took the name of Girl Scouts. Mrs. Low became their first president.

Juliette Gordon Low was born in Savannah Oct. 31, 1860. Her father was Gen. William Washington Gordon. Her mother, Eleanor Kinzie Gordon, is said to have been the first white child born in Chicago. Juliette went to private schools in Virginia and New York City. In 1886 she married William Low of Warwickshire, England.

The Lows had houses in England, in Scotland, and in the United States. They were friends of Lord Robert Baden-Powell and of his sister, Agnes. Baden-Powell had founded the Boy Scouts and, with his sister, in 1911 established the Girl Guides.

Juliette Low was a talented artist and helped organize the Savannah Art Club. Her chief interest, however, was the Girl Scouts. Although deaf, she overcame the handicap and traveled widely to in-

terest people in the Girl Scout movement. After retiring as president, she received the title of Founder. She died Jan. 17, 1927, in England.

---

THESE ARTICLES ARE IN THE FACT-INDEX

| | |
|---|---|
| Low, Seth | Lowe, Thaddeus Sobieski |
| Low, Will Hicok | Coulincourt |
| Lowden, Frank O(rren) | Lowell, Abbott Lawrence |
| Lowe, Sir Hudson | |

---

**LOWELL, Amy** (1874–1925). The American poet Amy Lowell was a contradictory person, radical in her behavior but conservative in her background and in many of her attitudes. She is most famous for her effective use of free verse.

Amy Lowell was born Feb. 9, 1874, in Brookline, Mass. She was the youngest of five children and came from a distinguished family.

In 1912 Amy Lowell's first book of poems, 'A Dome of Many-Coloured Glass', was published. In 1913 in England she met the imagist poets and was greatly influenced by them.

From 1915 until her death Amy Lowell read and lectured at universities and clubs throughout the United States. She had a vivid personality and a striking appearance. She attracted public attention by her outspokenness and her unusual habits. She smoked cigars most of her life and chose to work at night and sleep during the day. Amy Lowell died May 12, 1925, at Brookline, Mass., in the house where she was born.

Amy Lowell wrote more than 650 poems, few of which are read today. Much of her poetry seems to have suffered from lack of restraint. However, her work has beauty. Perhaps her most famous poem is 'Patterns'. Her books include 'Men, Women, and Ghosts', 'What's O'Clock' (awarded a Pulitzer prize), and 'John Keats', a biography.

---

THIS ARTICLE IS IN THE FACT-INDEX
Lowell, Francis Cabot

---

**LOWELL, James Russell** (1819–1891). One of the most famous American writers of his time was James Russell Lowell. His reputation has now declined, and he is remembered chiefly for a few poems and essays.

James Russell Lowell was born Feb. 22, 1819, in Cambridge, Mass. After attending classical school in Cambridge, James entered Harvard College. He read a great deal but neglected his formal studies. He was graduated in 1838. Although he did not like it, he studied law at Harvard Law School and was admitted to the bar in 1840.

By 1844 Lowell had made his start as a poet, editor, critic, and reformer. His literary work had gained him fame, and in 1855 he was asked to give a series of lectures in Boston. His success led to the offer of a professorship at Harvard. Lowell accepted but asked to go to Europe for a year to renew his knowledge of modern languages. On his return he married Frances Dunlap, who had been a governess for his daughter. He then settled down to a life devoted to teaching and writing.

In 1857 he became editor of the *Atlantic Monthly*. Although he resigned four years later, he continued to contribute most of his poems to that magazine. His prose writings went to the *North American Review*. During the time he was on the Harvard faculty, prose was his usual method of expression. He wrote largely travels, criticisms, and literary and political essays. He also wrote some poems.

In 1877 Lowell was called by the government from his university work to become the United States minister to Spain. He later exchanged this post for that of minister to England. The last years of his life were spent in Cambridge. He died Aug. 12, 1891, at his family home, Elmwood, in Cambridge. Lowell's prose works include 'Among My Books' (1870); 'My Study Windows' (1871); and 'Among My Books, Second Series' (1876).

THESE ARTICLES ARE IN THE FACT-INDEX

Lowell, John
Lowell, Percival
Lowell, Robert (Traill Spence, Jr.)

**LOWELL, Mass.** One of the oldest of the great American industrial cities is Lowell. It was founded in 1822 by the Merrimack Manufacturing Company and was named for Francis Cabot Lowell, who originated cotton manufactur-

ing in the United States. The corporation bought a site at the junction of the Concord and Merrimack rivers and set about harnessing the 32-foot falls of the Merrimack, drawing the water through five miles of canals to various mills. Later, water power was supplemented by steam power.

Today the city's factories are operated mainly by power from hydroelectric and steam-electric plants. Lowell is no longer a one-industry city. It lost textile mills to the South in the 1920's. Others closed after World War II. New industries, however, have come to the city. Among the city's leading manufactures today are electronic apparatus, printing, biscuits and crackers, shoes, and shirts. Also manufactured in Lowell are electric wire, textile machinery, and plastic products.

Educational institutions include Lowell Technological Institute. The artist James Whistler was born in Lowell, and his home is now an art museum.

Lowell was chartered as a town in 1826 and as a city in 1836. It has the city-manager form of government. Population (1980 census), 92,418.

THESE ARTICLES ARE IN THE FACT-INDEX

Lowell State College,
  at Lowell, Mass.
Lowell Technological
  Institute
Lower Austria
Lower Burrell, Pa.
Lower Merion, Pa.
Lower Saxony, West
  Germany
Lower Southampton, Pa.

Lowes, John Livingston
Lowestoft, England
Lownsbery, Eloise
Loyal Legion, Military
  Order of the
Loyalty Day
Loyalty Islands
Loyang, People's Republic
  of China

**LOYOLA, ST. IGNATIUS OF** (1491?–1556). The founder of the Society of Jesus (Jesuits), St. Ignatius spent the early part of his life as a worldly man.

The Bettmann Archive

Iñigo de Oñez y Loyola (Ignatius' real name) was born about 1491 at the castle of Loyola, near Azpeitia in Guipúzcoa province in northern Spain. He was the youngest of 11 children of an ancient noble family. He received only a sketchy education, being more interested in games and military matters. He was trained as a soldier. During the siege of Pampeluna in 1521, Ignatius broke his leg, thus ending his military career. While convalescing, he had only the lives of the saints to read. This reading converted him from his former ways and filled him with the desire to serve God. He went in 1522 to Our Lady's shrine at Montserrat and returned to pray and do penance in a cave near Manresa. He gave his worldly garments to the poor and wore a pilgrim's dress of sackcloth and hempen shoes. He spent seven hours a day in prayer.

With difficulty Ignatius reached Jerusalem, but he was not allowed by the authorities to remain. Back in Spain, at the age of 32, he again became a student. He was suspected of heresy, however, and was imprisoned by the Inquisition for teaching before he had completed the prescribed studies.

Meanwhile his plans were taking more definite form. He would found a "Society of Jesus"—spiritually drilled and disciplined like a military company —to combat heresy and to do missionary work in heathen countries. The members should be bound by the monastic vows of poverty, chastity, and obedience. They should wear no distinctive dress and should not be tied down by minute monastic rules or unusual forms of discipline.

In 1534 in Paris, France, Ignatius and six companions formed the beginning of this organization. In 1540 its members received at Rome the sanction of the pope, and Ignatius became its first "general." The remainder of his life was spent devising the constitution of his order. He also prepared the order for its work in the Counter Reformation, in which the Roman Catholic church was to win back half the lands it had lost through Luther's revolt (*see* Reformation). He died at Rome July 31, 1556. In 1628 he was canonized.

THESE ARTICLES ARE IN THE FACT-INDEX

Loyola Marymount
  University
Loyola University in
  New Orleans
Loyola University of
  Chicago
Loyson, Charles
Lozeau, Albert
LSD

Luanda, Angola
Luang Prabang, Laos
Lubang Islands
Lubbock, Tex.
Lübeck, West Germany
Lubin, David
Lubitsch, Ernst
Lübke, Heinrich
Lublin, Poland

**LUBRICANTS.** Friction is the worst enemy of machinery. It wears out the metal, wastes power, and generates heat. To combat friction, substances called lubricants are applied to the bearing surfaces of machinery; that is, the surfaces that rub against each other (*see* Friction). The word lubricant comes from the Latin *lubricus*, meaning "slippery."

Several qualities are essential to a good lubricant. It must have "wetting power" so it will spread easily over metal and penetrate between surfaces in close contact with each other. It must cling to the surfaces in order that rapid friction will not rub it off. It must not evaporate or in any other way change its essential greasiness. Freedom from acid and grit is important, for these corrode or scratch the bearings. A lubricant must not catch fire easily or become gummy at low temperatures.

The quality of a lubricant which makes it cling together and resist being squeezed out of a bearing is called its *viscosity*. This is opposed to freedom of flow. The two qualities must be balanced to suit the purpose for which the lubricant is used. For heavy loads more viscosity is needed; for high speeds, more freedom of flow. Cold increases viscosity. Most lubricants come from petroleum (*see* Petroleum). These range from light oils to heavy greases. For very heavy machinery, greases are often mixed with graphite (*see* Graphite).

Animal and vegetable oils have served as lubricants since long before the discovery of petroleum oils and greases. Oil from the head of porpoises and from dolphins is used in watches. Sperm oil, a liquid wax from the head of the whale, lubricates fine machinery. Tallow, lard, and neat's-foot (obtained by boiling the feet of cattle) oils are often blended with mineral oils. Among the more important vegetable oils used as lubricants are castor, olive, cottonseed, corn, and rapeseed.

THESE ARTICLES ARE IN THE FACT-INDEX

Lubumbashi, Zaire
Lucan
Lucas, Anthony Francis
Lucas, Edward Verrall
Lucas, Jerry
Lucas Van Leyden
Lucca, Italy
Luce, Clare Boothe

Luce, Henry Robinson
Lucerne, Switzerland
Lucerne, Lake
Lucifer
Luciferase
Luckhardt, Arno Benedict
Luckman, Sid(ney)
Luckner, Felix von, Count

**LUCKNOW** (*lŭk'nou*), India. The city of Lucknow is situated in the northern part of the republic of India, 540 miles northwest of Calcutta. It lies on the Gumti River, a tributary of the Ganges. It presents a striking appearance with  its beautiful domes, cupolas, and minarets. There are many parks, gardens, and monuments.

Lucknow has a fine medical school and hospital, a university, and several colleges. Skilled craftsmen make gold and silver brocades, embroidery, brass and copper objects, pottery, and beaten silver ornaments. The chief industrial establishments are paper mills, printing plants, and metalworks.

The British withstood a famous siege in Lucknow in 1857 during a rebellion of native soldiers (called *sepoys*) against rule by the British East India Company. At Lucknow on July 1 the rebellious sepoys forced a regiment of British troops under Sir Henry Lawrence to take refuge in the Residency and adjoining grounds of the company's chief commissioner. They were joined by British civilians.

Lawrence died from a wound a few days later. The small garrison, numbering only a few thousand men, held out against 10,000 sepoys for more than four months. At last the defenders saw the signals of Sir Colin Campbell, commander in chief of a strong relief force. The sepoys lifted the siege immediately, and survivors and rescuers quietly withdrew from the town November 17. Lucknow's population is 750,512 (1971 preliminary census). (*See also* India.)

THESE ARTICLES ARE IN THE FACT-INDEX

Lucretia
Lucretius
Lucullus, Lucius Licinius
Lucy, Saint
Lucy, Sir Thomas
Luddites
Ludendorff, Erich von
Lüderitz, South-West
  Africa
Ludington, Sybil
Ludington, Mich.
Ludwig I
Ludwig II
Ludwig III
Ludwig, Emil
Ludwig, Otto

Ludwigia
Ludwigshafen, West
  Germany
Lufbery, Raoul
Lufkin, Tex.
Luftwaffe
Lugano, Lake
Luini, Bernardino
Luke, Saint
Luke, Frank
Lukeman, (Henry) Augustus
Luks, George Benjamin
Luleå, Sweden
Lulli, Giovanni Battista
Lully, Raymond

The first step in felling a tree is to saw a notch, or undercut, on one side of the tree. The tree will fall in the direction of the notch when the faller saws straight through the trunk from the other side.

# LUMBER—The Major Forest Product

**LUMBER.** Wood is used to make many things—from homes to furniture to toothpicks. The lumber industry transforms the trees of the forests into the lumber from which other products are made. Its tasks include logging—cutting trees down, sawing them into logs, and carrying the logs to the sawmill to be sawed into boards and timbers, or lumber.

In earlier years the lumber industry of the United States was unable to make use of more than 30 percent of most trees. Small and crooked logs, treetops, branches, limbs, and high stumps were left in the woods to rot. In the sawmill the first slices from logs and the trimmings from sawed planks were burned as fuel or as waste. The present-day lumber industry converts about 70 percent of each tree harvested into useful products. Better equipment permits less wasteful cutting. Thinner saws, for example, reduce the amount of sawdust. Chips that were formerly scrapped are now sold to paper mills.

Improvements in the lumber industry have not been limited to cutting methods. In the United States loggers once stripped forests with no regard for their future regrowth. The men would enter a wooded area, cut down all the valuable trees, and then move on to repeat the performance elsewhere. The early loggers were almost as great a threat to the forests as fire. They destroyed much of America's vast and beautiful virgin forests. Their methods were abandoned only when lumbermen came to realize that America's forests were not inexhaustible and that their industry would eventually run out of trees if the forests were not replanted.

The concept of *forest management* was adopted by the United States lumber industry. The industry now regards forests as farms and trees as crops. Its foresters protect trees from fire, insects, and disease. Many lumber companies maintain tree nurseries. The young trees from these nurseries are transplanted to replace trees that die or are cut down in forest areas. In an effort to keep pace with the growing need for wood, by 1970 the lumber industry was planting 30 percent more trees than were logged or destroyed by fire, insects, disease, and wind.

Modern forest management employs the sustained-yield system. Under this system a forester chooses certain valuable trees for harvest. He also has poor-quality trees removed to improve the composition of the forest. He makes sure that enough valuable trees remain to reseed the forest and may also have nursery seedlings transplanted in it. The forest is never destroyed. It continues to be used for recreation. Wild animals continue to find shelter in it. The roots of the remaining trees continue to retain water and prevent erosion. The management of forests to serve all of these purposes is called the multiple-use system. This approach proved so successful that in 1941 the wood-using industries started the American Tree Farm System, a voluntary program which encourages private owners to use a sustained-yield system. (*See also* Forests and Forestry.)

## LOGGING

Before a tree can be sawed or chopped into useful wood, loggers must cut it down and transport it to

**BUCKING THE FALLEN TREE**
Large trees are bucked, or cut into shorter logs, so they can be dragged away easily. Only the tops and branches of small trees are removed.

the sawmill. Logging is still rugged work, though power tools and power-driven lifting equipment have eliminated much of the drudgery.

## Felling the Tree

Once a tree has been marked for cutting, logging can begin. The person who cuts the tree down is the faller. First he decides the direction in which the tree should fall. He makes sure that other trees will not be damaged when it falls and that it will be easy to move the fallen tree to the loading area.

Having decided the direction of the fall, the faller cuts a large notch, or undercut, on that side of the tree. The undercut is located opposite and below the point where he plans to make the main cut. The exact position of the undercut and the depth to which it is made depend upon the size and the shape of the tree, wind conditions, and other factors. Planning the undercut takes great skill and experience.

When the undercut has been made, the faller makes the main cut on the opposite side. As the saw bites deeper into the trunk, wedges may be driven into the cut behind the saw. The wedges keep the tree from squeezing down on the saw.

Today's loggers use engine-driven chain saws that can be carried by hand. These saws have taken much of the hard labor out of felling. They have helped make the work safer both by reducing fatigue and because they are equipped with protective devices.

## Sawing and Assembling the Logs

After a tree is down, the limbs must be removed. A chain saw is generally used to cut off the big limbs. The practice of chopping off smaller limbs with an ax is dying out.

The next step is bucking, or cutting the tree into shorter logs. The length of these logs depends upon the use that will be made of the wood and upon the capability of the equipment that will carry the logs to the sawmill. Ordinarily, small trees are not cut into logs. Only the top is cut off, at the point where the diameter grows too small to be usable.

Whatever their length, the logs must be yarded, or moved to a central collection point called the landing.

**AT THE LANDING**
Cables run from this 110-foot-tall spar pole (left) to the sites where trees have been cut down. Logs are attached to these cables and reeled in. When the logs arrive at the landing, mechanical loaders (below) hoist them onto the trucks that will transport them to the sawmill.

Yarding is done either with cables that lead from the landing or with tractor-type vehicles. Factors that determine which method is used include the size of the timber, the steepness of the terrain, and the need to protect soil, streams, and younger trees.

One frequent cable arrangement is the high-lead system. A tall spar pole is erected at the landing. Cables lead from the pole to the felling areas. Logs are attached to the cables, and an engine reels the cables in. The spar poles are now often made of steel, but very tall trees still serve this purpose.

Helium balloons have been used experimentally to replace the spar pole. They lift the logs completely off the ground and carry them to the landing. Tractors are the most common method of yarding in most

### INTO THE MILL
Logs are carried from the storage pond to the upper level of the sawmill on a bull chain, or jack ladder. Jets of water wash dirt and grit from the logs before they are sawed.

parts of the United States. Crawler treads or large tires enable them to operate in rugged logging terrain. They drag, or skid, the logs to the landing.

### Moving the Logs to the Sawmill

The landing is the center of logging activity. It receives logs from many directions. The logs are then transported from the landing to the sawmill.

Formerly, logs were brought to the mill by railway or were floated downstream in river drives. Today most logs are transported by large trucks, though the other methods are still used. Mechanical loaders at the landing lift the logs onto the trucks.

Road building has become an important task of the lumber industry. The industry constructs its own roads from the forest logging areas to sawmills or public highways. These roads must be able to support heavy cargoes. They may be relatively simple to build in level country. In rough terrain, however, their construction is very difficult, since steep grades, sharp curves, and narrow roadbeds must be avoided.

After the trip over the forest road, the trucks may still travel many miles by public highway. Sometimes, however, the forest road leads directly to the sawmill. In such cases, vehicles that are too large for public highways can be used to haul the logs.

### MILLING

Logs are usually stored at the mill for some time before being sawed up. Often they are sorted by size or species. Some storage areas are on dry land, but frequently the logs are left in ponds. Specialized equipment may be used to unload the trucks and stack the logs. Logs stored in a pond may be moved about by a special boom boat.

### Sawing the Logs

When a log is selected for sawing, an endless conveyor, called a bull chain or jack ladder, carries it from the water to the upper levels of the sawmill. The log may be washed clean on the jack ladder, or the bark may be entirely removed before sawing.

One type of debarking equipment works something like a pencil sharpener. It follows the configuration of the log and does not cut deeper than the thickness of the bark. In another debarking method, water jets under extreme pressure blast the bark from the log.

Debarking protects the sawing equipment by removing grit and other foreign objects that might damage the saw teeth or cause excessive wear. When the log is sawed into boards, debarked outer pieces can be chopped up into small, clean chips, which are sold to pulp and paper mills. Previously, the outer pieces were burned as fuel or as waste.

After washing or debarking, the log is rolled onto the carriage, a special wheeled platform that rolls on tracks. The carriage has a framework that holds the log securely. The head sawyer, one of the most important men in the mill, controls the carriage. He maneuvers it to the head saw, a high-speed saw that slices the log from end to end.

Small mills usually have a circular head saw. Most large mills, however, use an enormous band saw. The blade may extend from floor to ceiling. The first pass of the saw through the length of the log removes a slab which is flat on one side and round from the curvature of the log on the other. Succeeding passes produce rough-edged boards, some of them enormous because the log is so thick. After each pass, the head sawyer manipulates the controls that move the log into position for the next cut.

### Handling the Boards

When the log has been reduced to boards and other wood products, the boards travel to the edger, whose parallel saws remove any irregular shapes and square the edges. Trimmer saws then cut each board to its proper length and square the ends.

The boards then move to the green chain, a conveyor which passes in front of men who grade each piece of lumber. "Green" refers to the moisture in the freshly cut lumber, not to the conveyor color.

The pieces are sorted by grade and by species. Most of them are then dried, or seasoned. Some are stacked in the yard for air-drying. Others are placed in oven-type structures called dry kilns. The heat and humidity control in these kilns permits faster and more precise drying. Many of the larger sawmills have additional equipment, such as the planers which are used to smooth the surface of boards.

Some sawmills have equipment for remanufacturing, or reshaping wood to make specific products. The wood may be converted into a variety of forms. Typical products of remanufacturing include furniture frames, tool handles, wooden dishes, and baseball bats.

### Laminated Woods and Plywoods

Logs are sometimes cut into thin sheets of wood. A decorative veneer is a sheet that comes from a valuable wood and is used as the surface of a wood product because of its attractiveness. Other woods are also cut into thin layers. A log may be sliced or sawed into sheets, or sheets may be obtained by a process called rotary cutting. In rotary cutting the log is turned on a lathe against a long, stationary knife.

The sheets are usually glued together to make laminated wood or plywood. Laminated wood consists of thin sheets of wood whose grains run roughly parallel. It can be constructed from lower grades of lumber with a surface layer of decorative veneer. Laminated wood can be made in any size or shape. Its component sheets can be impregnated with a fire retardant and a decay preventive.

The wood in plywood is usually rotary cut. Thin sheets of this wood are glued together at right angles to each other. Plywood does not split and is very strong. (*See also* Plywood.)

**FROM LOG TO LUMBER**
A mechanical debarker (left) may be used to remove bark from the log. A wheeled platform then carries the log to the head saw, which slices it into boards or other forms of lumber. In most large mills the head saw is a band saw (below). The band saw may be a full story tall.

**PROCESSING LUMBER**
Trimmer saws (top) cut lumber into appropriate lengths and square off the ends. The boards are then carried to the green chain (bottom), where they pass in front of men who grade each piece. The green chain gets its name from the newly cut "green" lumber, which has a high moisture content. Seasoning, or drying, reduces the moisture content.

## Lumber Users

Rough lumber may be shipped from the sawmill to mills which finish and shape the boards and make other lumber products. Wholesalers may purchase lumber to sell to large users or to retail lumber yards from which individuals buy it in small amounts.

The construction industry, which makes homes and other kinds of buildings, consumes about three fourths of the lumber produced in the United States. The next largest consumer is the shipping-container industry, which uses about one tenth of the lumber produced. Shipping containers are boxes in which merchandise is shipped or stored. The shipping-container industry also makes pallets, the wooden platforms used to carry materials or merchandise, particularly in the food industry. Somewhat over a twentieth of United States lumber production goes to the furniture industry, the third largest consumer.

## THE LUMBER INDUSTRY

Lumber is produced in every section of the United States. Output is measured in board feet. One board foot is represented by a board one foot long, one foot wide, and one inch thick. The peak year for lumber production in the United States was 1909, when about 45 billion board feet were produced. The demand for lumber lessened when the construction industry began to substitute steel, brick, and concrete for wood and as improved preservatives lengthened the life of wood products. Annual lumber production now hovers at about 35 billion board feet.

The nation's lumber production comes from its commercial forest land. This is land that can grow trees of marketable quality which are available to the lumber industry. Noncommercial forest land includes land too poor to grow good timber, land with too few trees for lumbering to be profitable, and land that has been withdrawn from commercial use to be used for parks, wildlife refuges, and wilderness areas.

The half-billion acres of commercial forest land in the United States provide more than nine tenths of the nation's lumber needs. About three fourths of the domestic output is harvested from land owned by private concerns and individuals.

Government-owned commercial forests—about one fourth of the total commercial acreage—produce approximately one fourth of the nation's lumber. Most of these woodlands are in some 150 national forests located in 41 states and Puerto Rico. They are administered by the United States Forest Service of the Department of Agriculture. Over one half of the government-owned commercial acreage is concentrated in 11 Western states.

National forests are managed under the multiple-use system to provide watershed protection, lands for recreation, food and shelter for wildlife, and a continued supply of timber. Private companies bid competitively for timber located on government lands. Logging is done by the companies under the careful supervision of government foresters.

**CONSTRUCTION USES OF PLYWOOD AND BOARDS**
Sheets of plywood are nailed to the framework of this barn to form the walls. The framework is made of rough boards. Even rougher boards were used to make the scaffold.

Over 1,000 species of trees grow in the commercial forests of the United States. About 180 of these have commercial value, and 35 species provide most of the lumber. From the earliest days of American lumbering, the softwoods—pine, spruce, fir, hemlock, cedar, and other conifers—have been harvested in greatest quantities. The hardwoods—oak, poplar, gum, ash, beech, birch, and other deciduous trees—account for about one fifth of the total harvest.

The Western states are the source of over half of the nation's lumber production. Oregon has led the country since 1938. In the late 1960's its annual output was about 8 billion board feet. California and Washington followed, with annual outputs of about 5 billion and $3\frac{1}{2}$ billion board feet, respectively. Two Rocky Mountain states, Idaho and Montana, were next. Softwoods—Douglas fir, the Western pines (Ponderosa, Idaho white, and sugar), and the Coast redwoods—form the bulk of Western production.

The great forest of the Southern coastal plain, which includes South Atlantic and Gulf coast states, accounts for almost one third of United States production. Much of this is softwood. Important hardwood stands are also scattered through the area. Arkansas, North Carolina, and Alabama are major producers.

## Patterns of World Lumber Production

Russia and the United States account for over half the world's annual production of about 160 billion board feet of lumber. Russia alone produces some 45 billion board feet per year. Other major producers are Japan, Canada, the People's Republic of China, Sweden, West Germany, France, Poland, and Brazil. Northern countries have large softwood forests. Countries nearer the equator contain a greater proportion of deciduous trees. Over a third of the

**VERSATILE LAMINATED WOOD**
A single piece of laminated wood can be made in any length and can be given many shapes. Structural supports of boats and of modern, curved roofs may be made of laminated wood.

lumber production in both the People's Republic of China and Brazil is hardwood. As the climate becomes hotter and more humid, the trees become more varied. Some tropical countries whose lumber output is small are important sources of rare hardwoods: Burma, for example, exports teak.

## LOGGING'S ROUGH AND EXCITING PAST

Most of the early American settlers did some logging. The land they were opening up was covered with forests. Each settler had to begin by cutting down enough trees to make a clearing for his house and farm. Some of the timber was used to erect buildings. The rest was burned.

As communities grew, local sawmills supplied their needs with wood logged from nearby forests. As long as transportation of logs and lumber over long distances was unprofitable, lumbering remained a local business. New England was the center of this type of lumbering activity during colonial days. The expansion of the United States created greater demands for lumber. At the same time, long-distance transportation was improved to serve the new settlers. Increased demand and improved and cheaper transportation encouraged the nationwide development of the industry.

In the second half of the 19th century the industry's center moved westward. About 1850 New York was the hub of the lumber industry. Ten years later Pennsylvania dominated lumber production. From about 1870 to 1890 the Great Lakes states Michigan, Minnesota, and Wisconsin were the major lumber producers. The South took the lead around 1895, while production rose steadily in the Far West. This was the situation during the peak production years 1907 to 1910. By 1920 the lead had shifted from the South to the West, where it remained.

**SEASONING LUMBER**
Most lumber must be seasoned, or dried, before it can be used. A common method of seasoning is to stack the green lumber in an outside yard to be air-dried.

**LIFE OF THE OLD-TIME LOGGERS**
The old-time loggers ate at long tables in a common dining room. They slept in double-deck bunk beds in a one-room bunkhouse. Their tools included a two-man saw, a large wedge, and double-bladed axes. The logs were often floated downriver to the sawmill. A log might get caught and cause a jam. Men were drowned trying to break logjams.

## Life in the Logging Camps

The early logging companies usually established a logging camp on the land to be worked. The men hired by a company lived in the camp and worked in the surrounding forest. The early loggers led an unsettled life, wandering freely from one job to another. Many stayed at a camp for only a few days or weeks. Their work was hard and long. They were free only Sundays and evenings. Before 1910, the loggers worked 11 hours a day. Then their workday was reduced to 10 hours. After 1920, loggers worked 8 hours a day, five days a week. Usually, they worked even in rain, snow, and freezing cold. If bad weather did stop work, they were not paid for lost time.

A typical logging camp contained a bunkhouse, a cook house, and a dining room; an office; stables and a blacksmith's shop; and perhaps a store, a meat house, and storage sheds. The number of buildings depended on how many men were working at a camp and on the kind of equipment that had to be stored and maintained.

The bunkhouses were rude buildings that had tiers of bunks nailed to the walls. There was just room enough between a bunk and the one above it for the men to crawl into bed and roll over. Often double bunks were used. One man would be assigned to each side. Blankets were furnished, and sometimes a straw mattress came with the bunk. Otherwise, the men made do with spruce boughs. Bedbugs were a common complaint.

Heat was provided by a stove in the middle of the room. After working in the rain or snow, or when they had done their laundry, the loggers hung their clothes around the stove to dry. Smoke from the stove mixed with steam from the wet clothes.

The day began at 5:00 A.M. when the bull cook (the camp odd-jobs man) woke the loggers. At 5:30 the gong sounded for the huge breakfast that prepared them for the day's work. The cook was one of the most important and best-paid men in the camp. His meals had to satisfy the ravenous appetites of the hardworking loggers. If they did not like their food,

they might refuse to work until the foreman agreed to replace the cook.

At 9:00 P.M. the lights were turned out. The men immediately went to bed and were quiet. Plenty of rest was as necessary as plenty of food.

Men whose homes were near the camp could leave it on Saturday evening and return on Sunday. The others might not leave the camp until payday. Most evenings were spent talking or playing cards. Occasionally, someone might haul out his fiddle, or guitar, or harmonica. A favorite occupation was spinning yarns. The Paul Bunyan legend grew out of these tales (see Folklore).

## In the Woods

Felling and bucking were far more difficult before power tools came into use. The trees had to fall near a roadway so the logs could be skidded to the landing. Many younger trees were crushed in the process.

At first, oxen were generally used to drag logs to the landing. When wheeled platforms to carry the logs were introduced, horses were used more frequently. The job of driving a team of oxen or horses could be dangerous. The teamster had to keep control of the logs while they were being dragged downhill. If they started rolling, the heavy logs could crush a team to death. Another danger was the possibility that a log rolling sideways might catch the driver in the legs. The teamsters were well paid to do their dangerous work. Later, when tall trees were used as spar poles, the most dangerous job was done by the men who climbed 200 feet up the trunk to cut the top off and to attach the block and tackle.

THESE ARTICLES ARE IN THE FACT-INDEX

Lumberton, N. C.
Lumière, Auguste Marie
 Louis Nicolas
Lumière, Louis Jean
Lummis, Charles Fletcher
Lumpsucker
Lumumba, Patrice (Emergy)

Luna
Lunacharsky, Anatoly
 Vasilievich
Lunaria
Lundy, Benjamin
Lüneburg, West Germany
Lunéville, France

**LUNGS.** All living animals must absorb oxygen and eliminate the waste gas carbon dioxide. In many of the highly developed air-breathing animals, including man, the two processes are performed in special organs called the lungs. From species to species, lungs vary in size and shape but are strikingly similar in structure.

The function of the lungs is to provide a place where oxygen can reach the blood and carbon dioxide be removed. They are so constructed that a very large surface is available for the transfer. It has been estimated that the total surface area in adult human lungs is equal to approximately 100 square yards—an area larger than a badminton court. Beyond providing this surface and tubes for air to reach it, the lungs themselves do not actually contribute to the act of respiration. They are passive.

The pair of lungs is in the chest cavity, or *thorax*, one lung on each side. Each lung is shaped somewhat like a cone with its broad base resting upon the surface of the diaphragm. Thin membranes, called *pleurae*, cover each lung. Lung tissue is soft, light, spongy in texture, and remarkable for its elasticity.

About halfway down the chest, the windpipe (trachea) divides into a right and a left *bronchus*. Each enters a lung, where it divides into smaller and smaller air passageways. The trachea, bronchi, and smaller bronchi make up the *bronchial tree*.

The smallest bronchi end in tiny balloonlike air sacs called *alveoli*. There are many millions of alveoli. *Pulmonary capillaries*, the smallest blood vessels of the lungs, are wrapped around each tiny alveolus. Oxygen is absorbed, and carbon dioxide is expelled from the blood through the thin-walled alveoli and the equally thin-walled surrounding capillaries.

Air on its way to the lungs is first warmed, moistened, and cleansed in the nose and pharynx before reaching the bronchi. All the bronchi are lined with special cells that have tiny oarlike projections called *cilia*. The many millions of cilia move constantly in unison, fanning dust and dirt that are inhaled back to the nose and mouth. Some dust and dirt, however, remain permanently in the lungs and darken them. Children's lungs are always very pink. Adults' lungs vary in the degree

of darkening, depending upon the cleanness of air usually breathed. This apparently harmless color change is most pronounced in persons who smoke and who live or work in dusty places. The color change is called *anthracosis*.

The main muscle for breathing is the diaphragm. Its motion as a whole is almost as much forward as downward and is most effective in ventilating the inferior, or lower, lobes of the lungs. This method of breathing is called *abdominal*. The ribs also contribute to breathing by rising and increasing the chest area. This method of breathing is called *costal*. Both methods are normally operative at all times.

Adult lungs hold from three to four quarts of air. In quiet breathing, a person inhales about one pint of air with each breath. When very active, one may inhale six times as much air with each breath and breathe much more rapidly to provide the needed oxygen.

(For a description of the mechanical and chemical processes of the interchange of oxygen and carbon dioxide, *see* Respiration. *See also* Blood.)

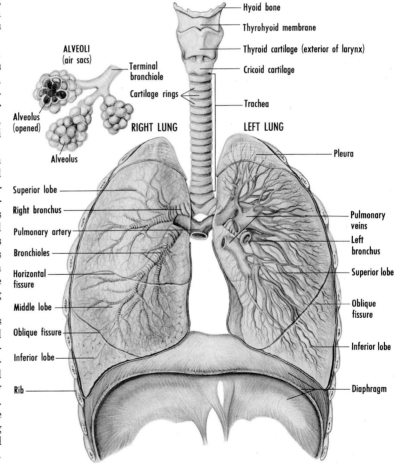

**THE HUMAN LUNGS**
The ribs have been removed to show the position and parts of each lung. Each lung is drawn to appear transparent. The right lung shows how the bronchi divide again and again before they end in thin-walled sacs, called alveoli. There are more than 700 million alveoli. Two pulmonary veins from each lung carry oxygen-laden blood to the heart. The pulmonary artery carries venous blood from the heart to the lungs.

THESE ARTICLES ARE IN THE FACT-INDEX

Lungwort
Lunt, Alfred
Lupines
Lurçat, Jean
Luria, Salvador E(dward)

'Lusiads, The'
Lusitania
Lüta, People's Republic
   of China
Luther, Hans

**LUTHER, Martin** (1483–1546). The leader of the Protestant Reformation in Germany was Martin Luther. This religious movement divided Western European Christians into Roman Catholics and Protestants.

Luther's defiance of the Catholic church was one of the most important factors in the success of the Reformation. There was little in Luther's background to indicate that he would be a religious man, much less to hint that he would become a famous innovator who would affect the course of history.

Martin Luther was born Nov. 10, 1483, in the village of Eisleben in Saxony. His parents, Hans and Margaret Ziegler Luther, were peasants. Shortly after Martin was born they moved to Mansfeld, an iron industry center. There Hans was a miner.

The Luther home was poor but pious. Martin was reared in a conventional religious atmosphere. When he was seven he attended the local Latin school. He was a good student. At 14 he went to Magdeburg for further education. He sang in the streets for bread, as was the custom of poor students. At the end of the school year he went to Eisenach. There a wealthy merchant took an interest in him and supported him for the next three years while he studied under local schoolmasters.

In 1501 Martin Luther entered the University of Erfurt, one of the most famous German universities of the time. During four years of study there he distinguished himself as one of the university's most outstanding students.

His course of study included grammar, logic, rhetoric, physics, philosophy, mathematics, metaphysics, and ethics. Under the urging of his father, Martin Luther began the study of law in 1505. Only two months later, however, he gave this up and turned to a religious life.

### Luther Becomes a Monk

Luther's decision to take up a religious life was sudden. One evening, while he was walking on the road near Erfurt during a storm, a flash of lightning knocked him down. He was filled with a fear of death and a consciousness of sin. He renounced the world and entered the monastery of the Augustinian Eremites at Erfurt.

His father and his friends were upset at his decision. Luther, however, entered his new life in religious seriousness. After a year he took the vows of obedience, poverty, and chastity. The order was a strict one, and he was forced to do hard labor in addition to his studies.

After a course of instruction, Luther was ordained a priest in 1507. He then continued his theological studies. Luther was such an able scholar that he was sent to Wittenberg to spend a year as a lecturer. In 1509 he returned to Erfurt to accept an advanced degree and to give a series of lectures on religious subjects.

Luther was transferred to the monastery at Wittenberg in 1511. Soon he was made subprior of the monastery and took the degree of doctor of theology. He was made professor of biblical literature.

In 1510 Luther had visited Rome on business for his order. While there he became greatly upset with the low moral standards of the church in Rome.

A few years later Pope Leo X, in order to raise money for the rebuilding of the church of St. Peter's at Rome, had offered indulgences for sale to the people. These were promises of forgiveness of sin which were made to all who donated money. Luther felt he had to protest against this practice.

### The Ninety-five Theses

Luther made his objections public in 1517 by nailing to the door of the Wittenberg church a list of 95 propositions, or theses. They denied the right of the pope to give forgiveness for sins by indulgences. He sent a copy of the theses to the archbishop and offered to debate his ideas in public.

No debate took place, but Luther's theses were circulated widely. Within a year many people had read them and they were being heatedly discussed throughout Germany. Great controversy arose. Luthér made addresses and wrote essays calling for a thorough reform of the church, especially in regard to the sacraments. He defended his idea of "justification by faith." Luther believed salvation is possible through trust in God's mercy rather than through penances and other works of righteousness.

The pope ordered Luther to appear before Cardinal Cajetan in Augsburg. The cardinal demanded that Luther retract all he had said. Luther refused to do this unless it could be proved to him from the Bible that he was wrong.

In his pamphlets 'Address to the German Nobility' and 'The Babylonian Captivity of the Church' Luther broke completely with the Roman Catholic church. In a debate in 1519 with John Eck he denied the divine right of the papacy and said that the Scriptures were the supreme authority.

In 1520 the pope issued a proclamation, or bull, condemning many errors in Luther's teachings. He demanded that Luther retract his sayings within 60 days or suffer excommunication. Luther publicly burned the bull in Wittenberg. He continued his teaching and his writing.

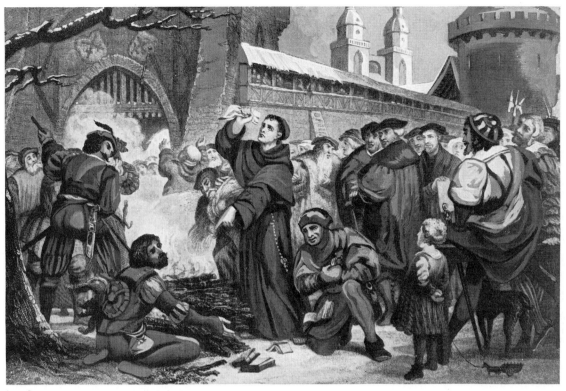

James Press

This dramatic moment took place in Wittenberg on Dec. 10, 1520. The pope had sent a proclamation, or bull, condemning Luther's teachings. Luther called his students together and when the bull was delivered cast it into the flames.

Early in 1521 the pope issued a Bull of Excommunication against Luther and ordered Emperor Charles V to execute it. Instead, the emperor called a "diet," or council, at Worms and summoned Luther for examination. The diet demanded that Luther recant, but he refused and was outlawed.

While returning from the Diet of Worms Luther was seized with the help of his friend, the elector of Saxony. He was hidden in the castle of Wartburg, near Eisenach. There he remained in disguise. During his time at Wartburg he began to translate the New Testament into German.

Finally the emperor's preoccupation with the wars he was waging with France made it safe for Luther to return to his work at Wittenberg. While Luther was in concealment some of his followers had carried the reform movement further than he had intended. On Luther's return he tried to check these excesses but was not successful. In 1524 many of the German peasants used his teachings as a reason for revolting.

In 1525 Luther married a former nun, Katharina von Bora. This emphasized his rejection of monasticism and celibacy for the clergy. The remainder of Luther's life was spent in writing, preaching, and organizing the reformed church in Saxony. He replaced the Latin service of the mass with a service in the German language and wrote many hymns which are still in use, notably the famous *Ein feste Burg ist unser Gott* ('A Mighty Fortress Is Our God').

Luther died Feb. 18, 1546, at Eisleben, his birthplace, just as the long-deferred war to put down his teachings was to break over Europe (*see* Thirty Years' War). His body was carried in state to Wittenberg, attended by throngs of mourners, and buried in the castle church to whose door he had nailed the Ninety-five Theses. (*See also* Reformation.)

THESE ARTICLES ARE IN THE FACT-INDEX

Luther College
Luther League of America
Luthuli, Albert John
Lutine Bell
Luton, England

Lutyens, Sir Edwin
Landseer
Lutz, Frank Eugene
Luxemburg, Rosa

**LUXEMBURG;** French, **LUXEMBOURG.** The grand duchy of Luxemburg is only 998 square miles in area. Shaped like a shield, it is 55 miles from north to south and 35 miles from east to west. Its population is 334,790 (1966 census).

Tiny Luxemburg is one of the leading iron and steel producers in the world. Its ore comes from the Luxemburg-Lorraine basin. The producing center is Esch-sur-Alzette. In 1953 its capital, also named Luxemburg, became headquarters for the European

**LUXEMBURG, THE CAPITAL CITY OF THE GRAND DUCHY**

The picturesque little city of Luxemburg rests on a crag 200 feet above the valleys of the Alzette and Petrusse rivers, tribu- taries of the Moselle. Thick walls and remnants of towers recall the feudal days when it was a mighty fortress.

Coal and Steel Community (ECSC). When the executive body of the ECSC merged with those of the European Economic Community (EEC), or Common Market, and the European Atomic Energy Community (Euratom), Brussels, Belgium, became the seat of the fused commission. The EEC Court of Justice convenes in Luxemburg, and certain meetings of the Council of Ministers are also held there.

Other important cities are Differdange, Dudelange, and Pétange. In addition to steel production, the chief industries include the manufacture of chemicals, rubber, and fertilizers. The leading crops are wheat, oats, and potatoes. The vineyards yield grapes for Moselle wines. Luxemburgers also engage in lumbering, dairying, and stock raising.

This constitutional monarchy is ruled by the House of Nassau. Grand Duchess Charlotte, ruler of Luxemburg since 1919, abdicated in 1964 in favor of her son Jean. The constitution of 1868 was revised in 1919, 1948, and 1956. An advisory Council of State is appointed; the Chamber of Deputies is elected.

In 1944 Allied armies drove out the Germans after destructive battles. With Belgium and the Netherlands, Luxemburg established the Benelux customs union in 1947. In 1949 it joined the North Atlantic Treaty Organization. In 1958 Italy, West Germany, France, and the Benelux nations formed the EEC.

THESE ARTICLES ARE IN THE FACT-INDEX

| | |
|---|---|
| Luzon | Lycia, Asia Minor |
| L'vov, Russia | 'Lycidas' |
| Lwoff, André | Lycoming College |
| Lyallpur, Pakistan | Lycopodium |
| Lyautey, Louis Hubert | Lycoris |
| Lycabettus, Mount | |

**LYCUR'GUS.** The life of Lycurgus, as told by Plutarch, is one of the most fascinating in the times of ancient Greece. No one, however, knows how much of the account is truth and how much is fancy (see Plutarch). Many scholars believe that Lycurgus was a real person who lived in the late 9th or early 8th century B.C.

According to Plutarch, Lycurgus had not only the gift of wisdom but also the superb attribute of unselfishness. At one time a lawless youth struck at him with a staff and put out an eye. Instead of taking revenge on the lad, Lycurgus brought him into his own home to live. There the young man, seeing how Lycurgus lived, learned the nobility of his host's attitude toward his fellow men. Appreciatively, the lad turned from his wild ways and became a good citizen of Sparta—the Greek state loved by Lycurgus.

Some scholars believe Lycurgus was the son of Eunomos, king of Sparta. His brother inherited the throne, then died before his heir was born. Lycurgus became regent but soon left Sparta to travel abroad.

Years later he returned to find Sparta in disorder. Lycurgus is said to have made himself master of the city-state and to have drawn up a new body of laws. He designed the new code to place the citizens under complete control of the state and to build Sparta into a military power. His laws, in fact, created a new way of life in Greece. From that stern, regimented, courageous life comes the word "Spartan" (see Sparta).

After his fellow citizens pledged that they would obey the laws and not change them until he returned, Lycurgus again went abroad. He heard from an oracle that the Spartans would enjoy prosperity as long as they kept their vow. In an effort to insure their good fortune, he decided never to return.

THESE ARTICLES ARE IN THE FACT-INDEX

| | |
|---|---|
| Lydda, Israel | Lyme grass |
| Lydgate, John | Lyme Regis, England |
| Lydia, Asia Minor | Lymphatic glands |
| Lyell, Sir Charles | Lynbrook, N. Y. |
| Lyle, David Alexander | Lynchburg, Va. |
| Lyly, John | Lynchburg College |

**LYNCHING.** The word "lynching" has come to mean mob violence that deprives a person of his life for some presumed crime or offense. It usually occurs without a trial in a regular court of law.

The term probably originated during the Revolutionary War, when Col. Charles Lynch, a Virginia magistrate, formed an extralegal court to try and to punish outlaws and Loyalists. In frontier days "lynch law" was practiced by vigilantes in the West, where courts and policemen were either scarce or corrupt. Settlers developed their own police and trial procedures to keep order. Those who committed grave offenses were lynched, usually by hanging.

In the South after the Civil War a secret, antiblack terrorist group, the Ku Klux Klan, was created by former Confederate officers. They tried to frighten newly freed slaves back into submission to their former owners. They also attacked whites who sympathized with the plight of the blacks.

The more violent bands flogged, tarred and feathered, or sometimes hanged their victims. From these illegal acts the practice of lynching black people grew. Sometimes blacks were lynched for such trivial offenses as appearing to insult white people.

Over the years a strong sentiment against lynching developed throughout the country, and the number of such crimes decreased. According to figures published by the Tuskegee Institute, the worst year was 1892, when 161 lynchings of blacks were reported. In that year 69 whites were also lynched. In many recent years there have been no lynchings.

Many states have antilynching laws. Efforts have been made by civil rights groups to secure federal legislation specifically prohibiting lynching.

THESE ARTICLES ARE IN THE FACT-INDEX

Lynd, Robert Staughton     Lyndon State College
Lyndhurst. N. J.     Lynen, Feodor
Lyndhurst, Ohio     Lynn, James Thomas

**LYNN, Mass.** Since early colonial days Lynn has been a shoemaking city. It was founded on Massachusetts Bay, ten miles northeast of Boston, in 1629, under the Indian name Saugus. It was renamed in 1632 for King's Lynn in England. By 1700 almost every household had a shoeshop. Lynn made shoes for most of Boston. When shoemaking machinery was introduced in 1848, Lynn became the nation's footwear center.

A half century later the industry spread to other cities, but Lynn still ranks high in the production of footwear. It has added many new manufactures, such as electrical equipment, turbine and jet engines, clothing, and medicines.

Lynn has over 2,500 acres of parks, playgrounds, and beaches, including Lynn Woods, Flax Pond, and Lynn Beach on Nahant Bay. The Mary Baker Eddy House marks the birthplace of Christian Science (*see* Eddy). At nearby Saugus one of America's first ironworks was built in 1643. Lynn was incorporated as a city in 1850. It is governed by a mayor and council. Population (1980 census), 78,471.

THESE ARTICLES ARE IN THE FACT-INDEX
**Lynnwood, Wash.**
**Lynwood, Calif.**

**LYNX.** So acute is the sight of the lynx that the people of ancient times believed it could see even through a stone wall. That is why sharp-sighted people are still referred to as "lynx-eyed."

A member of the cat family, the lynx is found in the northern regions of both the New and the Old World. It is smaller than the leopard and larger than the true wildcat, which exists only in Europe. The name wildcat is, however, applied in North America to various species of lynx. All have stumpy tails, long limbs, tufted ears, and eyes which contract in the daytime to narrow slits. They live in forests and rocky places and are fond of resting stretched out on a tree limb in the sun. By night they hunt their food, which consists of birds and small animals.

The sudden cry of a lynx at night is one of the most frightful sounds known to woodsmen. Usually it consists of a single sharp howl. Then there is silence. The creatures on which the animal preys, such as rabbits or quail, seek to escape notice by lying perfectly still. The lynx, unable to distinguish the exact position, crouches down ready for a leap, then emits its piercing cry. The timid victim, startled by the fearful sound, cannot help jumping convulsively. At that instant the lynx strikes and kills.

The Canada lynx has heavy gray fur mottled with brown. The bobcat, also known as the red, or bay, lynx, is common to many parts of the United States and has yellowish-brown fur tinged with red. The European lynx has a restricted range in parts of Europe. The scientific name of the Canada lynx is *Lynx*

The lynx, looking like an overgrown cat, faces a huntsman's dog. This wary dog perhaps knows that no dog is a match for a full-grown lynx if the lynx should decide to fight.

Paul Hosmer

*canadensis;* of the bobcat, *Lynx rufus;* and of the European lynx, *Lynx lynx.* (*See* Cat.)

THESE ARTICLES ARE IN THE FACT-INDEX

Lyon, Mary
Lyon, Nathaniel
Lyonesse
Lyons, Joseph Aloysius

**LYONS** (*lī'ŭnz*); French, **LYON** (*lē-ôṅ*), **France.** The third largest city in France, Lyons became famous as a silk-manufacturing center. Today it has many industries and is a financial and cultural hub.

It stands where two great rivers, the Rhone and the Saône, meet. The city spreads back from the slender point between the rivers onto steep hills on both banks. The Rhone and the Saône are bordered by quays and crossed by fine bridges.

The silk industry was introduced in the 15th century. At first, hand looms in the weavers' homes turned out the silks, and a few special fabrics are still hand-woven. Water power from plunging streams in the nearby Jura Mountains permitted the spread of factories here and in neighboring villages. Today huge hydroelectric plants furnish power. Lyons has become important in chemical and metal manufacturing. It has a large automobile assembly plant; numerous foundries and machine shops; tanneries; distilleries; and clothing, paper, and clock factories.

Each spring an international fair is held. Almost every branch of industry is represented. Exhibitors and visitors come from all Europe.

The University of Lyons has schools of letters, law, science, medicine, and pharmacy. There are other notable colleges, schools, and museums. The Museum of Textiles has collections of materials of all periods and regions. The old Cathedral of St. John is outstanding among the city's beautiful buildings.

The town, then called Lugdunum, was founded by the Romans before the Christian era. Augustus made it the capital of Celtic Gaul. Later the town was ravaged by barbarians and abandoned by the Romans. Late in the 5th century it was made the capital of the Burgundians. In 1312 it became part of France.

During the French Revolution a counterrevolutionary uprising did great damage to the city. Napoleon, however, took an interest in its rebuilding and improvement. The invention here of the Jacquard loom in 1802 led to increased prosperity in the silk industry. Lyons was a center of the resistance movement during World War II and again suffered considerable damage. Population (1968 census), 524,500.

THIS ARTICLE IS IN THE FACT-INDEX

Lyra

Australian News and Information Bureau

Here the male lyrebird sings on his mound. When his tail is erect the broad, curved side plumes look like the frame of a lyre and the inner feathers like the strings.

**LYREBIRD.** The bird whose tail has brought it renown is the lyrebird of Australia. Except for the 16 strange tail feathers of the male, this bird is not unusual. Both male and female are of ordinary form, about the size of a hen, and of a sooty-brown color with a few red markings. The tail feathers are about two feet long. They droop like a peacock's train. When they are raised, however, they take the shape of a lyre. The tail does not reach perfection until the bird is about four years old. It is shed in the fall and renewed in spring.

### Courtship Behavior

The male bird seems very proud of his fine feathers. When he is courting his mate, he scratches together a little mound of soil and leaves on which he stands. First he breaks forth into a tuneful song. Then he struts about in a dance, lifting and spreading his gorgeous tail feathers. (For picture in color, (*see* Paradise, Birds of.)

The lyrebird is the largest of the singing birds. It has a mellow, liquid note and imitates the songs of birds and other sounds. The female builds a dome-shaped nest on the ground or at the fork of a tree. She makes a frame of sticks and a soft lining of fern roots and feathers. A side entrance protects the single dark egg she lays.

The birds are very shy. When molested they escape by running rapidly through the underbrush. They are poor fliers, so they reach nests in trees by jumping from limb to limb. The scientific name of the best-known species is *Menura superba.*

THESE ARTICLES ARE IN THE FACT-INDEX

Lysander
Lysias
Lys River
Lyte, Henry Francis
Lythrum
Lytton, Edward George
Earle Bulwer-Lytton,
first Baron
Lytton, Edward Robert
Bulwer-Lytton, first
earl of

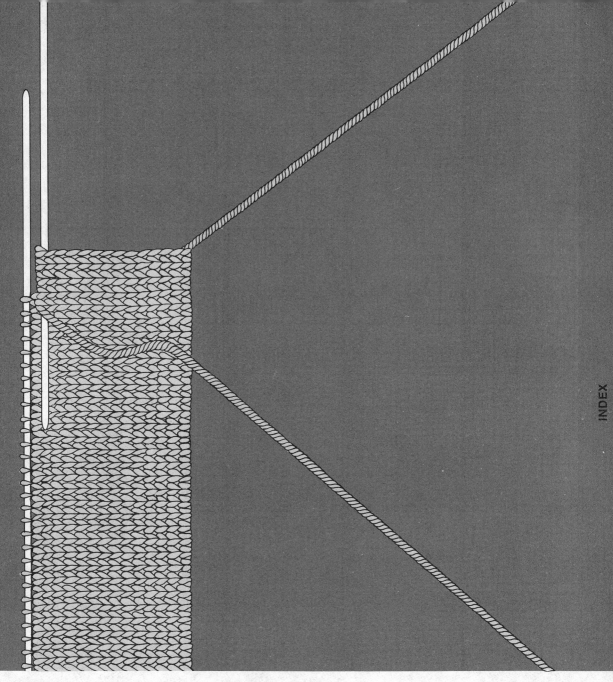

# The letter K

may have started as a picture sign of the palm of the hand, as in Egyptian hieroglyphic writing (1) and in a very early Semitic writing used about 1500 B.C. on the Sinai Peninsula (2). About 1000 B.C., in Byblos and other Phoenician and Canaanite centers, the sign was given a linear form (3), the source of all later forms. In the Semitic languages the sign was called *kaph,* meaning "palm."

The Greeks changed the Semitic name to *kappa*. They also turned the letter around to suit the left-to-right direction of their writing (4).

The Romans took the sign over into Latin, but they used it sparingly. From Latin the capital letter K came into English unchanged.

The English small handwritten "k" is simply a capital K with small, straight strokes, which were gradually rounded. The printed "k" is similar to the handwritten form.

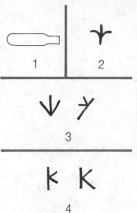

**K2,** or **Godwin Austen,** peak in Karakoram Range, n. Kashmir; altitude 28,250 ft (8610 m); 2d highest mountain in world: K-1, *maps* I-66, C-312
■ height, comparative. *see in index* Mountain, *table*

**Kaaba,** or **Caaba** [*kä′a-ba* or *kä′ba*], or **Kaabeh** [*kä′a-bè*], Mohammedan shrine at Mecca: M-195, *picture* M-195

**Kabbala,** or **Cabala,** mystical interpretation of Scriptures H-121

**Kabinda,** Angola. *see in index* Cabinda

**Kabotie, Fred** (born 1900), American Indian artist and author, born Shungopavy, Ariz.; author of 'Designs from the Ancient Mimbrenos'
■ Hopi snake dance, painting, *picture* I-128

**Kabuki** [*ka-bu′kē*], Japanese dance drama J-398, 391, D-23, *pictures* D-22, J-398

**Kabul** [*kä′bμl* or *ka-bμl′*], Afghanistan, capital, in province of Kabul; pop. 488,844: A-89
■ earthquake (1956) E-32
■ Salang Tunnel, *table* T-292

**Kabul University,** in Kabul, Afghanistan A-90

**Kachina** [*kä-chē′na*], Indian name for spirit of an ancestor, also a portrayal of the spirit: I-113
■ dolls D-162, I-113, *picture* I-113

**Kachin** [*ka-chīn′*] **Hills,** in Burma, *map* I-162

**Kachins,** a marauding people of Indo-Chinese origin living along border of upper Burma: I-161

**Kadar** [*kä′där*], **Janos** (born 1912), Hungarian political leader, born Kapoly, s. of Lake Balaton; active Communist 1932–; first secretary Hungarian Communist party 1956–; premier 1956–58, 1961–65.

**Kadiak Island,** Alaska. *see in index* Kodiak Island

**Kaesong** [*kä-sông*], North Korea, city 5 mi (8 km) n.w. of Panmunjom; pop. 139,900; commercial center; ginseng grown in area; fine porcelain ware; capital of Korea 915–1392; first city occupied by North Koreans in 1950 invasion: K-76f, 78, *map* K-77d
■ ancient Korean capital K-76f

**Kafir** [*kǎf′ēr*], or **kafir corn,** variety of sorghum introduced from South Africa; grown in southwestern U.S.; grain used for livestock feed
■ millet, variety of M-325

**Kafka** [*kǎf′kä*], **Franz** (1883–1924), writer, born Prague, Bohemia; his psychological stories penetratingly treat futile struggles of the individual against the sense of guilt and frustration: G-97, 98, *picture* G-97

**Kagame, Abbe,** Rwandan priest A-121

**Kaganovich** [*ka-gͧ-nô′vyïch*], **Lazar Moiseevich** (born 1893), Russian government official, born in the Ukraine; joined Central Committee of Communist party 1924, Politburo 1926; as secretary of Ukrainian Central Committee 1925–28 built Dnieper Dam; as Communist party boss of Moscow 1930–35 reconstructed city and began subway; member of Presidium 1952–57; a first deputy premier 1953–57; expelled from Communist party 1964.

**Kagawa, Toyohiko** (1888–1960), Japanese preacher and social reformer, born Kobe, Japan; converted to Christianity in his teens; author of poetry, essays, religious studies, stories for children, and novels.

**Kagera** [*kä-gā′rä*] **River,** in e.-central Africa, flows into Lake Victoria; about 450 mi (725 km) long; courses through marshlands and lake regions; navigable in lower section; supplies hydroelectric power.

**Kagoshima** [*kä-gō-shē-mä*], Japan, one of chief cities of Kyushu Island; pop. 1,729,150; home of crackled Satsuma ware; space-industries center: *map* J-418

**Kahanamoku, Duke** (1890–1968), swimming champion, born Honolulu, Hawaii; won 100-meter free-style race in 1912 and 1920 Olympics; revolutionized swimming by introducing flutter kick; called "greatest swimmer of his time": *picture* H-66

**Kahn, Louis** (1901–74), architect A-566

**Kahn, Otto Hermann** (1867–1934), American banker and patron of music and art, born Mannheim, Germany; came to U.S. 1893; member firm Kuhn, Loeb & Co., New York City, after 1897 ('Of Many Things')

**Kahn test,** for syphilis V-272

**Kahoolawe** [*kä-hō-lä′vē*], island of Hawaii; 45 sq mi (115 sq km): H-53, *maps* H-52, 71, U-117, P-5

**Kahului** [*kä-hμ-lμ′ē*], Hawaii, port town set in beautiful Iao valley on n. coast of Maui; pop. 8280; sugar, pineapples; Hawaii's first telephone line installed 1876 between Kahului and Wailuku: *map* H-71

**Kaibab** [*kī′bäb*] **National Forest,** in Arizona, adjoining Grand Canyon National Park; 1,780,475 acres (691,395 hectares); forest headquarters Williams, Ariz.
■ deer and cougars in E-54, N-77

**Kaieteur** [*kī-ē-tμr′*] **Falls,** in central Guyana W-73c, *pictures* S-276, W-73b

**Kaifeng** [*kī′fμng′*], People's Republic of China, city in Honan Province; pop. 318,000;

flour, oilseed processing: C-293b, *map* C-313

**Kailua** [*kī-lμ′a*], Hawaii, residential center on Kailua Bay on s.e. coast of island of Oahu; pop. 35,812; in livestock-raising region about 11 mi (18 km) n.e. of Honolulu: *map* H-71

**Kailyard** [*kāl′yärd*] (meaning kitchen, or cabbage, garden) **school,** term applied to group of Scottish novelists who wrote of life of common people with copious use of dialect; best represented by Ian MacLaren and Sir James M. Barrie.

**Kainite,** a mineral salt M-335

**Kairouan** [*kěr-wän′*], also **Kairwan** [*kīr-wän′*], Tunisia, sacred city of Mohammedans; Ukbah mosque, rebuilt in 827; pop. 46,200: T-289

**Kaisaria,** Turkey. *see in index* Kayseri

**Kaiser** [*kī′zēr*], official title of German and Holy Roman emperors. *see also in index* Holy Roman Empire, *table*
■ Germany. *see in index* William I, first German emperor; William II
■ origin C-14

**Kaiser, Georg** (1878–1945), German dramatist and critic, born Magdeburg, Germany; a leader of expressionist school; his plays focus on various social problems: G-98

**Kaiser, Henry J(ohn)** (1882–1967), industrialist, born near Canajoharie, N.Y.; constructed piers for San Francisco-Oakland Bay Bridge; built Hoover, Bonneville, and Grand Coulee dams; shipbuilder, World War II; industries include cement, sand and gravel, aluminum, steel, chemicals, automobiles, electronics, aircraft components, real-estate development.

**Kaiser-Permanente health-care plan** M-213

**Kaiserslautern** [*kī′zērz-lou-tērn*], West Germany, industrial city 55 km (35 mi) w. of Mannheim; pop. 99,617; Frederick Barbarossa built castle here about 1152: *map* G-115

**Kaiser Wilhelm Memorial Church,** West Berlin B-168, *map* B-170, *picture* B-169

**Kaiser Wilhelm's Land,** New Guinea N-168

**Kajima** [*kä-gē-ma*] **Peace Award,** gold medal and engraved certificate presented annually by Kajima Institute of International Peace, in Tokyo, "to the person or persons who have contributed toward peace in various fields of endeavor"; institute founded by Dr. Morinosuke Kajima, Japanese industrialist; 1969 peace award received by Americans William Benton and Hubert H. Humphrey.

**Kakemono** [*käk-ī-mō′nō*], Japanese scroll painting J-392, *picture* J-392

**Kala azar** [*kä′lä ä-zär′*], a fatal malarialike fever common in certain parts of India, transmitted by the bite of a sand fly.

**Kalah,** also **Nimrud,** ancient Assyrian city, near Nineveh, built 1300 B.C. by Shalmaneser I; abandoned, then rebuilt as royal residence city about 880 B.C.: *map* I-280
■ archaeological excavations A-532

**Kalahari** [*kä-lä-hä′rē*] **Desert,** in s. Africa, lying chiefly in Botswana; about 240,000 sq mi (620,000 sq km): S-263, 264, *maps* S-264, D-93

**Kalakaua** [*kä-lä′kä′u-ä*], **David** (1836–91), king of Hawaii 1874–91; because of his extravagant and disorderly rule was forced to grant a new constitution (1887) which restricted royal power: H-58, D-154d

**Kalamazoo,** Mich., industrial city in s.w. on Kalamazoo River, about 40 mi (65 km) e. of Lake Michigan; pop. 79,722; celery and fruits; paper, pharmaceuticals, chemicals, metal products; Western Michigan University, Kalamazoo

College, Nazareth College: *maps* M-285, 276, 273, U-41

**Kalamazoo Case, The,** in history of education; citizens of Kalamazoo, Mich., challenged (1872) collection of taxes for support of a public high school; the Michigan Supreme Court decided (1874) state had right to levy taxes for support of complete system of public education, including high schools and universities; case set a precedent for other states.

**Kalamazoo College,** at Kalamazoo, Mich.; Baptist; chartered 1833 as Michigan and Huron Institute, as college 1855; arts and sciences, education; quarter system; programs in France, Spain, and West Germany.

**Kalanianaole, Prince Jonah Kuhio.** *see in index* Kuhio, Prince

**Kalantiaw, Code of,** ancient Filipino legal code written by Lakan (Prince) Kalantiaw; admired by juridical scholars for its simple language, common sense, and clarity; consists of 18 orders.

**Kalat,** or **Khelat** [*kạ-lät'*], in Pakistan, division of Baluchistan Province; formerly a princely state of India; joined Pakistan 1948: *map* I-81
■ earthquake (1935) E-32

**Kalaupapa** [*kä-lä'ụ-pä'pä*], Hawaii, leper settlement (established 1860) on Molokai: *map* H-71

**Kalb, Baron de.** *see in index* De Kalb

**Kale,** vegetable of mustard family C-1, 2

**Kaleidoscope** [*kạ-lī'dō-skōp*], scientific toy invented by Sir David Brewster 1817; tube that encloses angled mirrors and colored bits of glass between two flat plates.

**Kalends,** or **Calends,** in Roman calendar C-28

**'Kalevala'** [*kä'lä-vä-lä*], ancient Finnish epic S-4708 481
■ Sibelius' 'Kullervo' based on S-187

**Kalgan** [*käl'gän'*], People's Republic of China, city at gate in Great Wall, in Hopei Province, 100 mi. (160 km) n.w. of Peking; pop. 1,000,000; historic trade and transportation center: *maps* M-433, C-313

**Kalgoorlie,** mining town, Australia A-788

**Kali.** *see in index* Devi

**Kalidasa** [*kä-lĭ-dä'sạ*] (5th century?), greatest dramatic and lyric poet of India; believed to have been court poet for rulers of Gupta dynasty, works translated into modern languages ('Sakuntala').

**Kalimantan.** *see in index* Borneo, Indonesian

**Kaline, Albert William** (Al) (born 1934), baseball player, born Baltimore, Md.; outfielder with Detroit, A.L., 1953–74; career batting average .297

**Kalinin** [*kạ-lē'nĭn*], **Mikhail Ivanovich** (1875–1946), Russian statesman, born near Tver, later named Kalinin in his honor; a peasant himself, represented peasants in Soviet government in which he became president of central executive committee 1919, chairman 1923; chairman of Supreme Soviet of U.S.S.R. 1938–46.

**Kalinin,** formerly **Tver** [*tạ-vĕr'*], Russia, city on Volga River, 160 km (100 mi) n.w. of Moscow; pop. 345,000; capital of independent principality 13th to 15th century: *maps* R-344, 348, E-335

**Kaliningrad** [*kạ-lē'nĭn-grăd*], German **Königsberg** [*kū'nĭks-bĕrk*], Russia, fortified seaport, former capital of East Prussia, on Pregel River, 6 km (4 mi) from mouth; included in Russia since 1945; pop. 297,000; university, castle: *maps* R-344, 348, E-335, P-414, W-253

**Kalispell,** Mont., city in Flathead Valley near Glacier National Park; pop. 10,648; tourist center in farm region; aluminum, lumber products; settled 1883: M-460, *maps* M-470, U-40

**Kalium,** Latin name for potassium, *table* C-233

**Kalix River,** Sweden, flows s.e. 335 km (208 mi) to Gulf of Bothnia, *maps* S-524, F-119

**Kallikak,** fictitious name of a two-branch family dating from Revolutionary War days, investigated by H. H. Goddard in his studies of heredity; of 480 descendants of a feeble-minded mother and a sound father 282 were mental, moral, or physical defectives; all below normal in intelligence; of 496 descendants of same father and a mother of good stock only 4 were defective; all were of sound mentality. *see also in index* Jukes

**Kallima butterfly.** *see in index* Oriental leaf butterfly

**Kalm, Peter** or **Per** (1715–79), Swedish botanist, born Finland; visited North America to make survey of natural history 1748–51 ('Travels into North America'): F-260

**Kalmar,** formerly **Calmar,** Sweden, port and cathedral town 320 km (200 mi) s. of Stockholm; pop. 34,918; historic castle dating from 12th century.

**Kalmar, Union of** (1397) D-91, N-369, S-527, S-52g

**Kalmia,** genus of plants of the heath family, best-known species being mountain laurel (*Kalmia latifolia*). *see in index* Mountain laurel

**Kalmucks,** branch of Mongols M-436

**Kalmus, Herbert Thomas** (1881–1963), chemical engineer, born Chelsea, Mass.; director Research Laboratory of Electrochemistry and Metallurgy, Canadian government 1913–15; invented Technicolor in motion pictures with wife, Natalie.

**Kalthoeber, Charles,** one of best of colony of German bookbinders who lived in London at end of 18th century; influenced by Roger Payne; style recognizable by ornaments in the panels of the back.

**Kamakura** [*kä-mä'kọ-rä*], Japan, seacoast city on Honshu s. of Yokohama; pop. 165,552; seat of shogunate 1192 to 1333: J-405, *map, inset* J-419
■ Great Buddha, *picture* J-389

**Kama** [*kä'mä*] **River,** in e. European Russia, largest tributary of Volga River; over 1600 km (1000 mi) long; timber trade: *maps* R-348, E-335

**Kambalda,** Western Australia A-814

**Kamchatka** [*kăm-chăt'kạ*, Russian *käm-chät'kạ*], peninsula of e. Siberia; 270,000 sq km (105,000 sq mi); pop. 280,000: K-1, *maps* R-322, 345

**Kamehameha** [*kä-mā'hä-mā'hä*] **I** (1758?–1819), Hawaiian king (1795–1819); promoted European commerce; thwarted Russian colonization (1815–16); stopped Spanish piracy (1818): H-59, *pictures* H-66, 61
■ Kamehameha Day F-93
■ Statuary Hall, *table* S-437a
■ statue, *picture* H-63

**Kamel,** or **Camel, George Joseph** (1661–1706), Moravian botanist, Jesuit missionary to Philippines; made study of plant and animal life and minerals on islands
■ camellia named for C-58

**Kamerlingh Onnes, Heike** (1853–1926), Dutch physicist, born Groningen, Netherlands; discovered method of liquefying helium; professor of physics, Leiden University in Netherlands
■ Nobel prize, *table* N-294a

**Kamerun.** *see in index* Cameroons

**Kamik** [*kä'mĭk*], sealskin boot worn by Eskimos, *picture* S-178

**Kamikaze** [*kä-mĭ-kä'zē*], Japanese for "divine wind"; applied to typhoon that swept away Kublai Khan's fleet during attempt to invade Japan 1281: A-159

**Kamikaze,** term used for suicidal Japanese air force units in World War II: W-278, 297

**Kamimura** [*kä-mē-mụ-rä*], **Hikonojo, Baron** (1850–1916), Japanese admiral; notable victory over Russian cruiser squadron off coast of Korea in Russo-Japanese War.

**Kamloops,** B.C., Canada, city at junction of North and South Thompson rivers 250 km (155 mi) n.e. of Vancouver; pop. 26,168; railway divisional point; oil refinery; lumber, cattle, fruit, vegetables: *map* C-98

**Kampala** [*käm-pä'lä*], Uganda, capital and chief commercial center; pop. 330,700: U-2, K-45, *map* A-94
■ university L-243, *picture* L-227

**Kampen** [*käm'pĕn*], Netherlands, city near mouth of IJssel River; pop. 25,464; formerly a Hanseatic town; 14th-century town hall, church.

**Kampong** [*käm-pŏng'*], in s.e. Asia, a compound
■ Cambodia C-56
■ Indonesia D-135c
■ Malaysia M-67b

**Kampuchea, Democratic.** *see in index* Cambodia

**Kana** [*kä'nạ*], in Japanese language J-390, *picture* J-390

**Kanagawa, Treaty of,** name of Perry's treaty with Japan (1854). *see in index* Perry, Matthew Calbraith

**Kanakas,** Polynesians P-8, A-785, *pictures* P-7–8

**Kan-ami Kiyotsugu** (1333–1384), creator of drama A-27

**Kananga,** formerly **Luluabourg,** Zaire, city 500 mi (800 km) s.e. of Kinshasa; pop. 601,239: *picture* Z-353a

**Kanawha** [*kạ-nô'wạ*] **River,** in West Virginia; formed in w.-central part of state by junction of New and Gauley rivers; flows n.w. and joins Ohio River at Point Pleasant; length about 100 mi (160 km); Little Kanawha rises in central West Virginia and flows w. and n.w. about 100 mi (160 km) into Ohio River at Parkersburg: *maps* W-112, 124, *pictures* W-119
■ chemical plants in valley W-112–13
■ South Charleston on, *picture* W-113

**Kanazawa** [*kä-nä-zä-wä*], Japan, city on w. coast of Honshu Island; pop. 395,263; bronze and lacquer work, silk; fine public gardens: *maps* J-418

**Kanchenjunga** [*kŭn-chĕn-gụng'gä*], or **Kinchinjunga** [*kĭn-chĭn-gụng'gạ*], 3d highest mountain in world (28,146 ft; 8579 m); one of the e. Himalayas; on boundary between Nepal and India; first successfully climbed 1955: *picture* I-65

**Kandahar** [*kän'dạ-här*], also **Qandahar,** Afghanistan, trade center in province of Kandahar, 300 mi (480 km) s.w. of Kabul; pop. 160,684; captured by Genghis Khan, Timur Leng, and others; prominent in wars between British and Afghans

**Kandinski, Vasili** (1866–1944), Russian painter, born Moscow; identified with the German modern movement; one of leaders among nonobjective painters; splendid colorist; author of 'Upon the Spiritual in Art'.

**Kändler** [*kĕnt'lĕr*], **Johann Joachim** (1706–75), German potter, born Saxony: P-475

**Kandy** [*kăn'dĭ*], Sri Lanka, highland city in s.-central part of island on artificial lake; pop. 93,602; capital of former kingdom of Kandy; Buddhist and Brahman temples

**Kane** [*kān*], **Elisha Kent** (1820–57), Arctic explorer and scientist, born Philadelphia, Pa.; accompanied Grinnell expeditions (commanded 2d) searching for Sir John Franklin; attained Kane Basin (1853) and the then farthest north.

**Kane, Harnett Thomas** (born 1910), author, born New Orleans, La. ('Queen New Orleans'; historical novels: 'Bride of Fortune' on Mrs. Jefferson Davis, 'The Lady of Arlington' on Mrs. Robert E. Lee, 'The Smiling Rebel' on Belle Boyd, Confederate spy; 'Gone Are the Days', pictorial history of the South).

**Kane, Paul** (1810–71), Canadian painter, born Mallow, Ireland; large collections in Royal Ontario Museum, Toronto, and Parliament buildings, Ottawa: C-85

**Kaneohe** [*kän'ē-ō'ē*], Hawaii, residential center on s.e. coast of island of Oahu; pop. 29,919; noted for coral gardens; Hawaii Loa College; missile-tracking station: *map* H-71

**Kanev Dam,** in Russia, on Dnieper River, *table* D-12

**K'ang** [*käng*], a Chinese bed C-291c

**Kangaroo** K-1–2, A-778, *pictures* K-1–2
■ foot K-2, *picture* F-329
■ fossil remains K-2
■ jumping, *picture* K-2
■ leather L-175
■ tree kangaroo K-2

**Kangaroo paw,** an Australian plant A-783

**Kangaroo rat** A-429, *picture* A-428

**Kangen** [*kän-gĕn*], Japanese music J-396

**K'ang Hsi** [*käng'shē'*], or **K'ang Hi** (1655–1722), Chinese emperor (1662–1722); encouraged arts and literature; consolidated empire
■ pottery of period P-473, *picture* P-472

**K'ang te.** *see in index* Pu-yi

**Kania, Stanislaw,** political leader P-415

**Kanji** [*kän'gē*], in Japanese language J-390, *picture* J-390

**Kankakee,** Ill., city about 50 mi (80 km) s. of Chicago; pop. 30,141; agricultural area; furniture and home appliances, farm implements, food processing; mental hospital; Olivet Nazarene College: *maps* I-50, U-41

**Kankakee River,** rises in n.w. Indiana and flows s.w. into Illinois; headstream of Illinois River: *maps* I-50, I-87, 100

**Kannapolis,** N.C., community in Cabarrus and Rowan counties, 23 mi (37 km) n.e. of Charlotte; pop. 36,293; home of Cannon Mills, Inc., manufacturer of household textiles, including towels and bedsheets; mills established 1877, community founded 1905: N-325, *maps* N-336, 323

**Kanpur** [*kän'pụr*], or **Cawnpore** [*kạn'pōr*], India, industrial city on Ganges River; pop. 1,154,388: I-76, G-16, *maps* I-84b, 66

**Kansa,** or **Kaw,** a Siouan Indian tribe formerly living along Kansas River, now in Oklahoma: K-4–5, *map* I-145
■ name K-3

**Kansan Ice Sheet** I-5, *map* I-5

**Kansas,** a central state of U.S.; 82,264 sq mi (213,063 sq km); pop. 2,363,208; cap. Topeka: K-3–18, *Fact Summary* K-14a–d, *maps* K-16–17, 5, 8, 14a, U-40–1, 70, *pictures* K-3–4, 6–7, 9–14
■ agriculture K-5, 14b, 3, 4, 8, 10, *charts* K-14b, *map* K-8, *picture* K-6
□ wheat K-5, 3, *pictures* K-3, 9, 13: flour production, *chart* F-252
■ antiliquor efforts P-507, K-9: Nation, Carry K-8, *picture* K-14
■ bibliography K-14d
■ bird, state, western meadowlark M-184, *picture* K-10
■ Capitol, State T-208, *picture* K-11
■ cities K-5–6, 14d, *map index* K-15, 18. *see also in index* cities listed below and other cities by name
□ Kansas City K-19, *picture* K-19
□ Topeka T-208
□ Wichita W-159
■ climate K-4, *list* K-3
■ communication K-14c
■ conservation K-4
■ counties, *map index* K-15
■ education K-7, 14a, *picture* K-11
□ missions K-7: Shawnee Methodist Mission, *picture* K-7
■ elevation K-4, *list* K-3, *map* K-14a
■ employment, *chart* K-14c
■ extent K-4, *list* K-3, *map* K-14a
■ fisheries K-14b, *chart* K-10
■ flag F-194, *picture* F-195
■ flower, state, sunflower S-518, *pictures* K-10, S-427
■ forests K-14b
■ geodetic center of North America K-3
■ geographic center, *list* K-3, *map* K-14a
■ geographic regions, *maps* U-36, 70: Great Plains U-75–7, *maps* U-36, 70, 80–1, *pictures* U-75, U-77, *Reference-Outline* U-135; North Central Plains U-68–74, *map* U-70, *pictures* U-68–9, *Reference-Outline* U-135
■ government K-7, 14a
□ elections K-14a, 7
■ history K-4–5, M-8, 9, 10, *pictures* K-7, 9
□ cattle ranges and trails K-8, W-159, C-177, *map* F-71
□ Hickok, Wild Bill H-153, *picture* H-153
□ Kansas-Nebraska Act K-20, K-5, 7–8, *picture* P-321
□ Santa Fe Trail F-69
■ industries K-5–6, 10, *charts* K-14b, *map* K-8, *pictures* K-6, K-13: wheat flour, *chart* F-252
■ irrigation and dams K-4, *map* M-414–15
■ land use, *list* K-3, *map* K-8
■ libraries K-14a: Eisenhower E-137, K-7, *picture* N-12
■ location K-3, 4, *locator map* K-3
■ minerals K-5, *chart* K-14b, *map* K-8, *picture* K-6
■ motto K-10
■ name K-3
■ natural regions K-4, 14b, *map* K-5
■ natural resources K-4, 5, 9, *charts* K-14b, *map* K-8
■ parks and other areas K-6–7, 14d, *map* K-16–17: Fort Larned N.H.S. N-36; Fort Scott Historic Area and Other Kansas Historic Areas N-37
■ people K-4–5: famous, *pictures* K-14

■ places of interest K-14d: Eisenhower memorials E-137, 127, K-7, *pictures* K-12
■ population K-5, 8, 7, *chart* K-14a, *list* K-3
■ products K-5–6, *charts* K-14b, *map* K-8, *picture* K-6
■ profile K-10–14, *pictures* K-10–14
■ recreation K-6–7, *picture* K-12
■ rivers K-4, 9, *map* K-5, 16–17
■ seal, state, *picture* K-10
■ sea lily fossils, *picture* G-63
■ song, state K-10
■ Statuary Hall, *table* S-437a
■ trade K-14b
■ transportation K-6, 14c: roads K-6, K-14, *map* K-16–17
■ tree, state, cottonwood P-446, *pictures* T-257, K-10

**Kansas, University of,** at Lawrence, Kan.; state control; founded 1865; liberal arts and sciences, architecture and urban design, business, education, engineering, fine arts, journalism, law, pharmacy, and social work; graduate school; medical school at Kansas City: *picture* K-11

**Kansas City,** Kan., 2d city of state, on Kansas River; pop. 161,148: K-19, *maps* K-17, 5, 8, U-41, *picture* K-19
■ location, *locator map* K-19
■ Shawnee Methodist Mission nearby, *picture* K-7

**Kansas City,** Mo., 2d city of state, at confluence of Kansas and Missouri rivers; pop. 448,159: K-19–20, *maps* M-395, 400, U-41, *inset* M-409, *pictures* K-19, M-405
■ cattle trail from, *map* F-71
■ Federal Reserve Bank (10th) and district, *map* F-82
■ jazz style developed J-426
■ location, *locator map* K-19
■ museums K-20. *see also in index* William Rockhill Nelson Gallery of Art
■ radar weather station W-88

**Kansas-Nebraska Act** (1854) K-20, *pictures* P-321
■ Douglas and D-164c
■ effect on Kansas K-5, M-7–8
■ Lincoln opposes L-284c
■ Pierce and P-322
■ slavery territorial issue B-291
■ Sumner opposes S-511

**Kansas Newman College.** *see in index* Sacred Heart College, Kansas

**Kansas River,** Kan., formed by junction of Smoky Hill and Republican rivers, Geary County, Kan.; often called Kaw River; flows 169 mi (272 km) across state to Missouri River: *maps* K-5, 17, U-70

**Kansas State College at Pittsburg,** at Pittsburg, Kan.; founded 1903; formerly a teachers college; arts and sciences, education, and technology; graduate studies.

**Kansas State Teachers College,** renamed **Emporia Kansas State College** 1974, at Emporia, Kan.; founded 1863; liberal arts; graduate studies.

**Kansas State University of Agriculture and Applied Science,** at Manhattan, Kan.; founded 1863; arts and sciences, agriculture, architecture, commerce, education, engineering, home economics, veterinary medicine; graduate school.

**Kansas Turnpike** K-6, *map* K-17

**Kansas Wesleyan,** at Salina, Kan.; affiliated with United Methodist church; established in 1886; liberal arts.

**Kansu** [*kän'sụ'*], province in n. People's Republic of China; area 137,000 sq mi (355,000 sq km); pop. 18,978,000; cap. Lanchow: C-293b, *maps* C-293, C-312
■ Buddhist caves, *picture* C-295b
■ earthquake (1920) E-32

**Kant** [*känt*], **Immanuel** (1724–1804), German philosopher: K-20–1, P-266, *picture* K-20
■ political theories P-434
■ universe, views of U-199

**Kanto** [*kän-tō*] **Plain,** or **Kwanto** [*kwän-tō*] **Plain,** lowland in Japan: J-401, 367, 382, T-193, 194

**Kantor, MacKinlay** (1904–77), novelist, short-story writer, and poet, born Webster City, Iowa; awarded 1956 Pulitzer prize for 'Andersonville', Civil War novel ('Turkey in the Straw', 'Glory for Me', poetry; 'Long Remember', 'God and My Country', 'Spirit Lake', novels; 'The Voice of Bugle Ann', 'The Daughter of Bugle Ann', dog stories).

**Kantorovich, Leonid** (born 1912), Russian economist, born Leningrad (then St. Petersburg); head of mathematical economics laboratory at Institute of Economic Management, Moscow
■ Nobel prize, *table* N-294h

**Kantrowitz, Adrian** (born 1918), heart surgeon, born New York, N.Y.; director of surgery Maimonides Medical Center, Brooklyn, 1964–70; chairman department of surgery Sinai Hospital, Detroit 1970–; pioneer research in motion pictures inside the heart, pump oxygenators, and mechanical hearts; first permanent partial mechanical heart surgery 1966; first U.S. heart transplant 1967; Max Berg Award 1966.

**Kantrowitz, Arthur (Robert)** (born 1913), physicist, born New York, N.Y.; collaborated with brother Adrian in heart research projects; professor Cornell University 1946–56; director Avco-Everett Research Laboratories 1955–72, chairman 1972–.

**Kaohsiung** [*gou'shyụng'*], Republic of China, seaport of s. Formosa; pop. 1,000,000; shipyards; refineries for petroleum and metals; food processing: *maps* C-316, C-313

**Kao K'o-kung** (fl. 13th century), Chinese painter, one of six great masters of Mongol period; took up painting after retiring from government service under Kublai Khan.

**Kaoliang** [*kä-ō-lē-äng'*], grain sorghum M-84

**Kaolin** [*kā'ō-lĭn*], or **China clay**
■ Georgia, source G-80
■ ink I-191
■ pottery C-383, P-470

**Kaolinite,** principal mineral of kaolin M-337

**Kapa cloth.** *see in index* Tapa cloth

**Kapidagi,** peninsula of Turkey. *see in index* Cyzicus

**Kapitza, Peter Leonidovich** (born 1894), Russian physicist, born Kronshtadt, Russia; director Institute for Physical Problems, Moscow, 1935–46, 1955–; noted for work with intense magnetic fields and low temperatures, also for atomic researches; a key figure in development of Sputniks
■ Nobel prize, *table* N-294b

**Kaplan, Joseph** (born 1902), American physicist, born Hungary; became U.S. citizen 1920; professor University of California at Los Angeles 1940–70; head of U.S. program, I.G.Y., 1957–58.

**Kapok** [*kā'päk*] K-21, F-105, *table* F-105
■ Guatemala produces G-248b
■ milkweed substitutes M-323

**Kapp** [*käp*], **Wolfgang von** (1858–1922), German monarchist, leader of revolt, March 1920, in which Berlin republican government was seized, but which failed because of a general strike; fled to Sweden; arrested for treason on return to Germany 1922; died before trial.

**Kappa Delta Pi,** national college honor society in education, founded at University of Illinois, Urbana, 1909, for high-ranking junior, senior, and graduate students.

**Kappel,** or **Cappel,** Switzerland, village in canton of Zurich; pop. 648: Z-370

**Kapteyn** [*käp-tīn'*], **Jacobus** (1851–1922), Dutch astronomer; directed work of computing positions of stars on Sir David Gill's photographic plates of s. heavens; pioneered in modern study of Milky Way.

**Karachi** [*kạ-rä'chĭ*], Pakistan, capital of Sind Province; port on Arabian Sea; pop. 4,465,000 (1975 est., metropolitan area); was also capital of province under Indian Empire: K-21, *maps* I-66, *pictures* P-77–8
■ Ford Foundation project, *picture* F-363
■ library L-241
■ location, *locator map* K-21
■ policeman, *picture* P-430b
■ silk mill, *picture* P-78

**Karafuto,** Russia. *see in index* Sakhalin

**Karaganda,** Russia, city in e.-central Kazakh S.S.R.; pop. 522,000; center of Karaganda coal basin; mining machinery, boots, candy, soft drinks; technical institutes, including medicine and mining: *map* R-344

**Karageorge** ("Black George") (1766?–1817), nickname given by Turks to George Petrovitch, or George Czerny, Serbian peasant, leader of first Serbian war of independence (1804–8) and founder of Karageorge dynasty: S-113

**Karaite** [*kăr'ạ-īt*] **sect,** in Japan S-1

**Karajan** [*kä'rä-yän*], **Herbert von** (born 1908), Austrian conductor, born Salzburg; prominently associated with London Philharmonia, Berlin and Vienna Philharmonic, La Scala, and Vienna State Opera orchestras; won 1970 Grammy award for work with Berlin Philharmonic; toured widely.

**Karajich** [*kä-rä'ġich*], **Vuk Stefanovich** (1787–1864), Serbian writer, called father of modern Serbian literature; bent efforts toward adoption of Serbian mother tongue as literary language; wrote grammar and dictionary, published Serbian folk songs.

**Karakoram Range,** or **Karakorum Range,** system of mountains in n. Kashmir (Jammu and Kashmir); highest peak K2, or Godwin Austen, 28,250 ft (8610 m): K-22, *map* C-312. *see also in index* K2

**Karakorum** [*kăr-ạ-kō'rŭm*], Mongolian People's Republic, ruined city 200 mi (320 km) s.w. of Ulan Bator; capital of Mongol Empire; established by Genghis Khan in early 13th century; capital moved to Peking by Kublai Khan in 1267: G-45, *maps* C-312

**Karakul,** also **Caracul** [*kăr'ạ-kŭl*], a breed of sheep S-146, *pictures* S-146
■ Caracul fur S-146

**Kara-Kum,** a desert in Russia, e. of Caspian Sea R-324, *maps* R-344, D-93

**Karamanlis, Konstantinos.** *see in index* Caramanlis, Constantine

**Karamzin** [*kŭ-rŭm-zyĕn'*], **Nikolai Mikhailovich** (1765–1826), Russian historian, novelist, and critic; born Mikhaylovka: R-361

**Karankawa** [*kä-rän'kä-wä*], Indian tribe that formerly lived in Texas: *map* I-134, *table* I-136
■ Cabeza de Vaca C-3

**Kara Sea,** also **Karskoe More,** arm of Arctic Ocean between Novaya Zemlya and n.w. coast of Siberia: *maps* R-322, R-344–5, 348

**Karat.** *see in index* Carat

**Karate** [*kạ-rät'ē*], method of weaponless self-defense developed in the Orient in early times; hands, elbows, feet, and knees are used to strike various areas of the body; can maim or kill opponent: J-399

**Karawanken Tunnel,** crosses Austria-Yugoslavia border, *table* T-292

**Karbala,** or **Kerbela,** Iraq, town 60 mi (95 km) s.w. of Baghdad; pop. 211,214; sacred city and place of pilgrimage of Shiite Moslems; tomb of martyr Husein: *map* I-280

**Karelian Isthmus,** land between Lake Ladoga and Gulf of Finland; in Russian Soviet Federated Socialist Republic.

**Kariba** [*kạ-rē'bạ*] **Gorge Dam,** between Zambia and Rhodesia, on Zambezi River: *table* D-12
■ Africa's natural resources A-106

**Karikal** [*kăr-ĭ-käl'*], India, former French settlement in s.e. on Coromandel coast; 52 sq mi (135 sq km); became part of India in 1954; town of Karikal (pop. 26,080) in former settlement: *maps* I-81, 84c

**Karim el-Huseini.** *see in index* Aga Khan IV

**Karlfeldt** [*kärl'fĕlt*], **Erik Axel** (1864–1931), Swedish poet; wrote of life of peasants in Dalecarlia, his native region
■ Nobel prize, *table* N-294f

**Karl Johansgate,** in Oslo, Norway O-505c

**Karl-Marx-Stadt** [*kärl'märks'-shtät*], formerly **Chemnitz** [*kĕm'nĭts*], East Germany, city 61 km (38 mi) s.w. of Dresden; pop. 299,312; textiles, machinery, chemicals, food products: *maps* G-115, 99a

**Karl Marx University.** *see in index* Leipzig, University of

**Karloff, Boris,** real name William Henry Pratt (1887–1969), stage, motion-picture, and television actor; born London, England; to U.S. 1909; in 'Frankenstein' (released 1931), began career as "menace" in horror films.

**Karlovy Vary** [*kär'lo-vē vä'rē*], also **Karlsbad,** or **Carlsbad,** Czechoslovakia, resort in Bohemia; pop. 43,091; ceded to Germany 1938, restored to Czechoslovakia 1945; Karlsbad decrees issued here at conference of German states (1819)
■ Glauber's salt in waters S-31

**Karlowitz,** or **Carlowitz** [*kär'lō-vĭts*], Yugoslavia, modern **Sremski Karlovci** [*srĕm'skĭ kär'lōv-tsĭ*], town on Danube River, 65 km (40 mi) n.w. of Belgrade; peace between Turkey, Austria, Poland, Venice, and Russia signed here (1699).

**Karlsbad,** Czechoslovakia. *see in index* Karlovy Vary

**Karlsefni, Thorfinn** [*thôr'fĭn kärl-sĕf'nē*], Norse navigator of the 11th century: E-283
■ Vinland colony, *picture* N-358

**Karlskrona,** or **Carlscrona** [*kärls-krọ'nạ*], Sweden, port on Baltic Sea, 383 km (238 mi) s.w. of Stockholm; pop. 33,010; Swedish naval headquarters; exports fish and lumber: *map* E-334

**Karlsruhe,** or **Carlsruhe** [*kärls'rụ-ē*], West Germany, city 63 km (39 mi) n.w. of Stuttgart; pop. 249,528; mineral springs: *maps* G-115, E-334

**Karma,** in Hinduism H-158

**Kármán, Theodore von.** *see in index* Von Kármán

**Karnak, El,** Egypt, village beside Nile River on n. part of site of ancient Thebes: T-157, *map* E-109
■ temple T-157, E-119, *picture* E-124: "Avenue of Sphinxes" S-379

**Karnataka,** formerly **Mysore,** state in s. India; area 74,122 sq mi (191,975 sq km); pop. 29,299,014; cap. Bangalore; gold, manganese, iron ore; coffee, tea, rice, cotton; early a Hindu kingdom; in mid-1700's taken by Moslem, Hyder Ail, and maintained as princely state until 1947: B-58, I-79, *maps* I-81, 84c

**Kärnten,** Austria. *see in index* Carinthia

**Karok,** an Indian tribe that lived in the Klamath River valley in n.w. California; a Quoratean division of Hokan language family.

**Károlyi** [*kä'rō-lyĭ*], **Mihály, Count** (1875–1955), Hungarian statesman, born Budapest; although from wealthy family was early influenced by Marxian socialism; president of Hungarian People's Republic 1918–19; resigned when Bolshevists seized government, lived in exile ('The Struggle for Peace'; 'Memoirs').

**Kárpathos** [*kär'pạ-thŏs*], Italian **Scarpanto** [*skär'pän-tō*], island of Dodecanese in Aegean Sea; area 287 sq km (111 sq mi): D-135d, *map* G-213

**Karrer, Paul** (1889–1971), Swiss chemist, born Moscow, Russia; research on vitamins A and $B_2$, carotenids, and flavins
■ Nobel prize, *table* N-294c

**Karroo,** or **karoo,** barren tableland in South Africa S-263, 264
■ Great Karroo, *map* S-264

**Kars,** Turkey, town 110 mi (175 km) n.e. of Erzurum; pop. 32,141; Mohammedan holy city, with 11th-century Cathedral of the 12 Apostles; capital of a medieval Armenian principality.

**Karsavina** [*kŭr-sä'vyĭ-nŭ*], **Tamara** (1885–1978), Russian dancer; ballerina of the Maryinsky Theater, the Russian Imperial theater, at St. Petersburg (now Leningrad), and of Diaghilev's company: B-34

**Karsh, Yousuf** (born 1908), Canadian photographer, born Armenia; to Canada 1924; known for sensitive portraits of the famous ('Faces of Destiny'; 'Portraits of Greatness'; autobiography, 'In Search of Greatness').

**Karun** [*kä-rụn'*] **River,** only navigable river in Iran; rises in western mountains and flows into the Shatt-al-'Arab; 400–500 mi (650–800 km) long: *map* I-280

**Kasai** [*kä-sī'*] **River,** rises in n.e. Angola and flows n.w. 1000 mi (1600 km) to Congo River; important for transportation; diamonds found in Tshikapa area, lower section known as Kwa River

**Kasavubu, Joseph** (1910?–69), Congolese political leader, born near Léopoldville; president of Democratic Republic of the Congo (now Zaire) 1960–65: Z-353a, b

**Kasbah.** *see in index* Casbah

**Kaschau,** Czechoslovakia. *see in index* Kosice

**Kashgar,** Chinese **Shufu,** People's Republic of China, city in w. Sinkiang-Uigur Autonomous Region; pop. 175,000; trade in silk, cotton, sheepskins: *maps* C-312
- climatic region, *map* C-304: temperature and precipitation, *graph* C-304

**Kashmir** [*kăsh'mĭr*], also called **Jammu and Kashmir** (sometimes **Kashmir and Jammu**), mountainous state n. of peninsula of India; 86,024 sq mi (222,801 sq km); pop. 4,616,632: K-22, I-82, *maps* I-81, 84b, *picture* K-22
- Himalayas H-156–7
- K2, peak. *see in index K2*
- language L-116, *diagram* L-115i
- Pakistan-India dispute K-22, P-79

**Kashmir, Vale of** K-22, *picture* K-22

**Kaskaskia,** tribe of Indians of Algonquian family, one of leading tribes of Illinois confederacy; remnants of tribe removed to Indian Territory in 1867. *see also in index* Illinois, a confederacy

**Kaskaskia,** Ill., village in s.w. part of state, on Kaskaskia Island in Mississippi River; pop. 33; site of French Jesuit mission (1703), later a trading post, nearby; Fort Kaskaskia built on bluffs (1733); capital of Illinois Territory (1809–18); old town destroyed and island of present village created by floods in late 1800's: *map* I-51
- capital of Illinois (1818–20) I-40
- captured by George Rogers Clark (1778) C-381

**Kaskaskia River,** in s. Illinois; about 300 mi (480 km) long; rises in Champaign County; flowing s.w. enters the Mississippi in Randolph County just n.w. of Chester: *maps* I-34, 50–1

**Kaso no zu** [*ká-sō nō zụ*], Japanese zodiacal wheel J-373, *diagram* J-373

**Kassa,** Czechoslovakia. *see in index* Kosice

**Kassebaum, Nancy Landon** (born 1932), political leader; daughter of 1936 presidential candidate and former Kansas governor Alf Landon; radio station executive 1975–76; U.S. senator (Republican) from Kansas 1979–: W-215b

**Kassel,** or **Cassel** [*käs'ĕl*], West Germany, city on Fulda River 145 km (90 mi) n.e. of Frankfurt; pop. 211,773; locomotives, machinery, scientific instruments: *maps* G-115, E-334

**Kassites** [*kăs'īts*], Elamite tribe; overran Babylonia and founded dynasty (about 1600–1200 B.C.): B-8, *map* B-4

**Kastler, Alfred** (born 1902), French physicist, born Guebwiller; professor l'École Normale Supérieure, Paris
- Nobel prize, *table* N-294b

**Kästner** [*kĕst' nĕr*], **Erich** (born 1899), German poet, journalist, and author, born Dresden; children's book 'Emil and the Detectives' translated into many languages and used as text to teach German in various countries ('Lisa and Lottie'; 'Little Man'; 'Little Man and the Big Thief'): R-111a

**Kat** [*kät*], also **khat,** or **cafta** (*Catha edulis*), evergreen shrub with clusters of small white flowers, native to Arabia and Egypt; leaves used to make stimulating beverage and are also chewed by Arabs.

**Kataev** [*kạ-tä'yĕf*], **Valentin** (born 1897), Russian novelist, short-story writer, and playwright, born Odessa; won Stalin prize: R-361

**Katahdin** [*kạ-tä'dĭn*], **Mount** (Indian "big mountain"), bare granite peak in e. Piscataquis County, n.-central Maine, highest point in state 5268 ft (1606 m); situated in Baxter State Park: N-29, *maps* M-53, 64, U-44
- painting by Marsden Hartley P-26, *picture* P-26

**Katanga** [*kạ-täng'gạ*], officially **Shaba,** former province in south of Zaire; about 192,000 sq mi (497,000 sq km); pop. 2,753,714: Z-353a

**Katayama** [*kä-tä-yä-mä*], **Tetsu** (1887–1978), Japanese statesman, born near Wakayama; leader in labor groups; prime minister 1947–48: *table* J-410

**Kate Greenaway Medal** L-303

**Kater, Henry** (1777–1835), English physicist, born Bristol; invented floating collimator; determined length of seconds pendulum; constructed standards of weights and measures for Russia.

**Kathak,** school of dance in India D-22

**Kathakali,** school of dance in India D-22; *picture* D-22

**Katherine,** or **Katharina,** daughter of Baptista of Padua in Shakespeare's 'Taming of the Shrew'; because of temper was called "the shrew."

**Kathmandu,** also **Katmandu** [*kät-män-dụ'*], Nepal, capital, situated near junction of Baghmati and Vishnumati rivers; pop. 150,402; noted for palaces and pagoda-shaped temples; founded in 723: N-128, *map* I-66

**Katipunan revolt,** in Philippine history P-259d, A-144, R-211

**Katmai** [*kăt'mī*], **Mount,** volcano of Aleutian Range, in Katmai National Monument, near head of Alaska Peninsula; height 7000 ft (1150 m).

**Katmai National Monument,** in s. Alaska N-40–40a, *maps* U-39, 94, *inset* N-30 *picture* A-251

**Katmandu,** Nepal. *see in index* Kathmandu

**Kato** [*kä'tō*], **Takaakira, Viscount** (1859–1926), Japanese statesman, born Nagoya; ambassador to Great Britain 1894–99, 1908–13; four times foreign minister; leader of the Constitutionalist party.

**Katowice** [*kä-tô-vē' tsĕ*], German **Kattowitz** [*kät'ō-vĭts*], Poland, city, 165 mi (265 km) s.w. of Warsaw; pop. 282,500; ironworks, foundries; in zinc and coal area: *map* E-334–5

**Katrine, Loch,** lake near Glasgow, Scotland; 13 sq km (5 sq mi); its Ellen Isle immortalized by Scott in 'The Lady of the Lake'; furnishes water supply to city of Glasgow.

**Katsura** [*kä-tsụ-rä*], **Taro, Prince** (1847–1913), Japanese statesman, governor of Formosa, minister of war, then premier 1901–6; again premier 1908–11 and 1912–13; accomplished commercial and financial reforms, annexation of Korea: J-407

**Katsushika, Hokusai.** *see in index* Hokusai Katsushika

**Kattegat,** or **Cattegat,** strait between Denmark and Sweden N-362, *maps* D-91, E-334, S-524
- Baltic Sea B-46

**Katydid,** green insect of the grasshopper family K-23

**Katyn** [*kä'tĭn*], Russia, village 19 km (12 mi) s.w. of Smolensk; near Katyn Forest, scene of massacre of thousands of Polish officers captured by Russians in 1939 invasion.

**Katz, Sir Bernard** (born 1911), British biophysicist, born Leipzig, Germany; professor of biophysics University College, London, 1952–78
- Nobel prize, *table* N-294e

**Katzenbach, Nicholas deBelleville** (born 1922), lawyer, born Philadelphia, Pa.; associate professor of law Yale University 1952–56; professor University of Chicago 1956–60; deputy U.S. attorney general 1962–64, acting attorney general Sept. 1964–Jan. 1965, attorney general 1965–66; undersecretary of state 1966–69; vice-president, general counsel IBM 1969–.

**Kauai** [*kou'ī*], island of Hawaii; 553.3 sq mi (1,433.0 sq km); pop. 29,524: H-53, 54, 55, *maps* H-52, 71, U-98, 117, P-5
- barking sands S-38
- precipitation extremes, *list* W-88

**Kauffer, E. McKnight,** English artist, *picture* A-665

**Kauffmann** [*kouf'män*], **Angelica** (1741–1807), Swiss portrait painter, born Chur, Switzerland; graceful but poorly drawn pictures; friend of Goethe and Reynolds.

**Kaufman** [*kôf'mạn*], **George S(imon)** (1889–1961), playwright, director, and producer, born Pittsburgh, Pa.; began as newspaperman; with Marc Connelly wrote 'Dulcy', 'Merton of the Movies', 'Beggar on Horseback'; with Edna Ferber 'Royal Family', 'Dinner at Eight'; with Morris Ryskind 'Of Thee I Sing' (Pulitzer prize 1932); with Moss Hart 'You Can't Take It with You' (Pulitzer prize 1937), 'The Man Who Came to Dinner'; with Howard Teichmann 'The Solid Gold Cadillac': A-356, D-176

**Kaufman, Sue** (1926–1977), American author A-363

**Kaukauna** [*kạ-kạ'nạ*], Wis., agricultural city 21 mi (34 km) e. of Appleton; pop. 11,292; paper, farm equipment; incorporated 1885: *map* W-207

**Kaulbach** [*koul'băk*], **Wilhelm von** (1805–74), German fresco and historical painter and book illustrator, first and most celebrated of a family of painters; born Arolsen, Hesse-Nassau, w. Germany; illustrated 'Reynard the Fox'.

**Kaunas** [*kou'näs*], also **Kovno** [*kôv'nŭ*], Lithuanian S.S.R., trade center on Niemen River; pop. 306,000; provisional capital of Lithuania 1918–40: *maps* R-344, 348–9

**Kaunitz** [*kou'nĭts*], **Prince Wenzel Anton von** (1711–94), Austrian statesman, born Vienna; minister of Maria Theresa: S-117

**Kauri** [*kou'rĭ*] **gum,** a resin G-263

**Kauri pine** N-276b, G-263

**Kava** [*kä'vä*], or **ava,** name of a shrub and of an intoxicating drink prepared from its root; plant belongs to pepper family; native to Pacific islands.

**Kaw,** Indian tribe. *see in index* Kansa

**Kawabata** [*kä-wạ-bät'ạ*], **Yasunari** (1899–1972), Japanese novelist, born Osaka; first Japanese to win Nobel prize in literature (1968) ('Snow Country'; 'Thousand Cranes'; 'The Sound of the Mountain'; 'The Master of Go'): *pictures* J-391, N-294e
- Nobel prize, *table* N-294f

**Kawasaki** [*kä-wạ-säk'ē*], Japan, city on Tokyo Bay, island of Honshu; pop. 1,032,852 (1977 est.); shipbuilding; textiles, machinery: J-382, 367, *map* J-367, *inset* J-419

**Kawm al Dikka,** Roman amphitheater, Alexandria A-281

**Kaw River.** *see in index* Kansas River

**Kay, John** (1704–64), English inventor, born near Bury, England; invented flying shuttle 1733; device considered a menace to labor; was mobbed by weavers and model destroyed; resumed work in France where he died in poverty: I-170, I-250

**Kay, Ulysses (Simpson)** (born 1917), composer, born Tucson, Ariz.; studied with Hindemith; composed suite for orchestra and music for film 'The Quiet One'; won many awards and prizes

**Kayageum,** Korean harp K-76c

**Kayak** [*kī'ăk*], Eskimo canoe C-126, *pictures* E-288, U-224

**Kayans** [*kī'ănz*], a tribe in Borneo, distinguished by industry, warlike qualities, and skill at handicrafts; live on river banks in long houses containing many apartments.

**Kaye, Danny,** real name David Daniel Kominski (born 1913), comedian of stage, screen, radio, and television; born Brooklyn, N.Y.; known for rapid patter songs and mimicry; much of his material written by wife, Sylvia Fine; starred in motion pictures: 'Up in Arms', 'The Secret Life of Walter Mitty', and 'Hans Christian Andersen'; named "Big Brother of 1956" by President Eisenhower for making world tour and motion picture for UNICEF.

**Kaye, Nora,** real name Nora Koreff (born 1920), ballerina, born New York, N.Y., of Russian parents; ballerina with Ballet Theatre and New York City Ballet ('Pillar of Fire'; 'Lilac Garden'): B-36

**Kaye-Smith** [*kā'smĭth'*], **Sheila** (Mrs. Theodore Penrose Fry) (1887–1956), English novelist, born St. Leonards-on-Sea; wrote chiefly of country life ('Sussex Gorse'; 'Joanna Godden'; 'Mrs. Gailey'; 'The View from the Parsonage').

**Kayseri** [*kī-sĕ-rē'*], or **Kaisaria** [*kī-sä-rē-yä'*], ancient **Caesarea Mazaca** [*sē-zạ-rē'ạ măz'ạ-kạ*], Turkey, city in Asia Minor, 160 mi (260 km) s.e. of Ankara; pop. 207,037; rugs, tile, meat: *maps* T-299, I-280
- cotton mill, *picture* T-302

**Kaysville,** Utah, city 14 mi (22 km) s. of Ogden; pop. 9811; in agricultural region; food products; annual rodeo: *map* U-232

**Kazakh** [*kä-zäk'*], one of a Turkic people living in n.e. part of Aral-Caspian basin and related to the Kirghiz.

**Kazakh Soviet Socialist Republic,** of Russia, e. and n. of Caspian Sea and w. of China; area 2,765,980 sq km (1,067,950 sq mi); pop. 12,850,000; cap. Alma-ata: U-14, *maps* U-14, R-325, 344
- agriculture, *picture* R-324
- folktales, *list* S-481
- people R-325
- Tyuratam S-342b–c

**Kazan** [*kạ-zăn'*], **Elia,** real name Elia Kazanjoglous (born 1909), theater and motion-picture director, born Constantinople (now Istanbul), Turkey; directed stage plays ('Skin of Our Teeth', 'A Streetcar Named Desire', 'Tea and Sympathy', 'Cat on a Hot Tin Roof'); motion pictures ('A Streetcar Named Desire', 'East of Eden'); won Academy awards for 'Gentleman's Agreement' (1947), 'On the Waterfront' (1954); helped found Actors' Studio, a theater workshop; wrote novels ('America, America', 'The Arrangement', and 'The Assassins').

**Kazan'** [*kạ-zăn'*], Russia, city 725 km (450 mi) e. of Moscow; pop. 869,000; industrial and cultural center; made capital of Tatar kingdom in 15th century: *maps* R-344, 348–9, E-335

**Kazan defile,** on Danube River D-32

**Kazantzakis** [*kä-zän-tzä'kĭs*], **Nikos** (1885–1957), Greek author and philosopher, born Candia, Crete; director UNESCO translation bureau 1947–48 (novels: 'Zorba the Greek', 'The Greek Passion'; poem: 'The Odyssey'; autobiography: 'Report to Greco').

**Kazbek** [*kŭz-byĕk'*], **Mount,** one of the highest peaks of the Caucasus Mountains (5047 m; 16,558 ft); situated above Daryal Pass; noted in mythology as site of Prometheus' torture: *diagram* E-329, *map* R-349

**Kazvin** [*kăz-vēn'*], Iran, town 100 mi (160 km) n.w. of Tehran; pop. 110,000; rugs, cotton and wool weaving, flour; has suffered several earthquakes: *map* I-280

**Kea,** a sheep-killing parrot P-135

**Kean** [*kēn*], **Charles John** (1811–68), English actor, born Waterford, Ireland; not as great as his father, Edmund Kean, but noted as actor in 'Hamlet' and other Shakespearean plays, and as theatrical manager; married Ellen Tree.

**Kean, Edmund** (1787–1833), English Shakespearean tragedian, born London; father of Charles J. Kean; Coleridge said, "Seeing him act was like reading Shakespeare by flashes of lightning" ('Shylock'; 'Othello'; 'Richard III').

**Kean, Ellen,** born Ellen Tree (1805–80), English actress, born s. Ireland; played leads with husband, Charles J. Kean.

**Kean College of New Jersey.** *see in index* Newark State College

**Keane, John Joseph** (1839–1918), American Roman Catholic archbishop and educator, born Ireland; founded churches and schools for Negroes in South; rector Catholic University of America 1886–97; archbishop Dubuque, Iowa, 1900–1911.

**Kearney** [*kär'nĭ*], **Denis** (1847–1907), American labor organizer, born County Cork, Ireland; in 1868 emigrated to San Francisco, Calif.; helped organize the Workingmen's party of California in 1877.

**Kearney,** Neb., city on Platte River, 125 mi (200 km) w. of Lincoln; pop. 21,158; livestock raising, metal products; Kearney State College, city was named for Fort Kearney (sometimes spelled Fort Kearny), built nearby in 1848 to protect emigrants on Oregon Trail but abandoned in 1871: *maps* N-121, U-40
■ Fort Kearney, *map* O-495

**Kearney State College,** at Kearney, Neb.; founded 1905; fine arts and humanities, business and technology, education, and natural and social sciences; graduate school.

**Kearns,** Utah, community s.w. of Salt Lake City; pop. 17,071: *map* U-232

**Kearny, Philip** (1814–62), American brigadier general and cavalry leader, born New York City; served in Mexican War, French cavalry, and Civil War; killed at Chantilly; nephew of Gen. S. W. Kearny
■ Statuary Hall, *table* S-437b

**Kearny, Stephen Watts** (1794–1848), major general, born Newark, N.J.; served in War of 1812; in war with Mexico occupied New Mexico; civil governor of California March–June 1847, of Veracruz and Mexico City brief periods in 1848: C-41, *picture* N-218
■ Carson and F-69, C-143–4
■ Frémont and F-434
■ Mexican War M-238, *map* M-238

**Kearny,** N.J., town on Passaic River opposite Newark; pop. 35,735; shipyards, twine, plastics, linoleum, telephones, metal products; named for Gen. Philip Kearny: *map, inset* N-202

**Keating, Kenneth B.** (1900–75), public official, born Lima, N.Y.; Republican congressman from New York 1946–58; senator from New York 1958–65; associate justice New York State Court of Appeals 1965–69; ambassador to India 1969–72.

**Keaton, Buster** (1895–1966), American actor A-27

**Keaton, Diane,** U.S. actress A-309

**Keats, Ezra Jack** (born 1916), author and illustrator, born Brooklyn, N.Y.; awarded Caldecott medal 1963 for 'The Snowy Day'; 'Whistle for Willie'; 'John Henry'; 'God Is in the Mountain': N-126i, R-106

**Keats, John** (1795–1821), English poet K-23, E-265, *picture* K-23
■ memorial in Rome R-255
■ quoted E-265, K-23, W-310b
■ Shelley's elegy, 'Adonais' S-154

**Keban Dam,** in Turkey, on Euphrates River, *table* D-12

**Keble** [*kē'b'l*], **John** (1792–1866), English poet and clergyman, born Fairford, near Swindon, England; professor of poetry at Oxford University for 10 years; Keble College built as a memorial ('The Christian Year').

**Keble College,** Oxford University, England O-515

**Kebnekaise** [*kĕb'nŭ-kī-sŭ*], highest peak in Sweden, in Kjölen Mountains (2123 mi; 6965 ft); in n. 40 km (25 mi) from Norwegian border; glaciers: *map* S-524

**Kecskemét** [*kĕch'kĕ-māt*], Hungary, city 80 km (50 mi) s.e. of Budapest; pop. 68,327; center of fruit, cattle, grain area; farm implements, chemicals, shoes, fruit preserves, wine, flour: *map* E-335

**Kedah** [*kā'dä*], state in former Federation of Malaya; 3660 sq mi (9480 sq km); pop. 955,374; rice, rubber, tapioca; tin, tungsten; became part of Malaysia 1963. *see also in index* Malay State, Unfederated

**Keddah** [*kĕd'ạ*], corral for trapping elephants in s.e. Asia E-179, *picture* E-178

**Kedron** [*kē'drȯn*], **Valley of,** also **Cedron,** or **Kidron,** deep depression e. of Jerusalem where brook flowed in Bible times: *map* J-439

**Keefe, Tim(othy J.),** (1856–1933), baseball pitcher, born Cambridge, Mass.; began career 1880, Troy, N.L., finished Philadelphia, N.L., 1893; won 346 games (19 in row 1888), lost 225

**Keel,** muscular structure in birds B-276

**Keel** S-171, B-328, *diagram* B-326
■ development S-164

**Keeler, William H.** (Wee Willie) (1872–1923), baseball outfielder, born Brooklyn, N.Y.; outfielder with 3 N.L. teams and 1 A.L. team 1892–1910; famed for his batting philosophy "Hit 'em where they ain't!"; hit safely in 44 consecutive games 1897

**Keeley, Leslie E.** (1832–1900), physician, born Saint Lawrence County, N.Y.; originator of Keeley Cure, treatment for alcoholics and drug addicts; first sanitarium Dwight, Ill., 1879–1966; many branches.

**Keeling Islands,** in Indian Ocean. *see in index* Cocos Islands

**Keelung** [*kē'lụng'*], Republic of China, seaport and naval base in n. Formosa, 15 mi (25 km) n.e. of Taipei; pop. 248,799; shipbuilding; chemicals, food products: *maps* C-316, C-313

**Keen, William Williams** (1837–1932), surgeon, born Philadelphia, Pa.; professor surgery Jefferson Medical College 1889–1907; pioneer work in delicate operations of brain and nervous system; wrote and edited books on surgery and anatomy.

**Keene, Charles Samuel** (1823–91), English pen-and-ink artist, born Hornsey, England; for 40 years a contributor to *Punch;* foremost among English craftsmen in black and white; work unconventional.

**Keene, Laura** (1826?–73), Anglo-American actress and manager; her company was playing 'Our American Cousin' at Ford's Theater, Washington, D.C., when Lincoln was shot.

**Keene,** N.H., city on Ashuelot River, 42 mi (68 km) s.w. of Concord; pop. 21,449; ball bearings, machinery, textiles, furniture, leather products; Keene State College: *maps* N-183, 170

**Keene State College,** at Keene, N.H.; part of University of New Hampshire; state control; founded 1909; liberal arts, teacher education, and vocational courses; graduate study.

**Keep,** of castle C-149, *picture* C-149

**Keep America Green** F-342

**Keeshond** [*kās'hŏnd*], dog, *picture* D-150

**Keewatin** [*kē-wä't'n*], **District of,** in e. Canada, part of Northwest Territories in Canadian Shield; 590,930 sq km (228,160 sq mi); pop. 3403; tundras: N-362, *maps* C-73, 98–9

**Keewatin ice sheet** I-5, *map* I-6

**Kefauver** [*kē'fạ-vẽr*], **Estes,** real name Carey Estes Kefauver (1903–63), political leader, born near Madisonville, Tenn.; five terms in U.S. House of Representatives; U.S. senator 1948–63; chairman Senate Crime Investigating Committee 1950–51 ('Crime in America'); Democratic vice-presidential nominee 1956: K-24e

**Kegon** [*kā'gȯn*] **Falls,** in Nikko National Park, Japan, *picture* J-388

**Keighley** [*kēth'lĭ* or *kē'lĭ*], England, town in Yorkshire, 90 km (55 mi) n.e. of Liverpool; Leeds-Liverpool Canal connects it with Hull; pop. 55,400; worsted, tools, machines, paper: *map* G-199h

**Keihin** [*kā-hĭn*], industrial area J-382, Y-342, *map* J-382

**Keijo,** South Korea. *see in index* Seoul

**Keitel** [*kī'tĕl*], **Wihelm** (1882–1946), German army officer, born Helmscherode, near Brunswick, Germany; made commander in chief of German armed forces 1938; signed World War II surrender 1945; hanged for war crimes 1946: *picture* W-270

**Keith, Sir Arthur** (1866–1955), British anatomist and anthropologist, born Aberdeen, Scotland; a leading authority in study of human race and its antiquity and expert on reconstruction of prehistoric man from fragments of fossil remains ('The Antiquity of Man'; 'A New Theory of Human Evolution'; 'An Autobiography').

**Keith, Harold** (born 1903), children's author, born Watonga, Okla. ('Boy's Life of Will Rogers'; 'A Pair of Captains'; 'Sports and Games'; 'Rifles for Watie', awarded Newbery Medal 1958).

**Keith, James Francis Edward** (1696–1758), Scottish soldier, born near Peterhead, Scotland; Jacobite adherent, field marshal under Frederick the Great in Seven Years' War.

**Kejimkujik National Park,** in Nova Scotia, Canada N-24c *map, inset* N-24b

**Kekulé** [*kā'kụ-lā*], or **Kekulé von Stradonitz, Friedrich August** (1829–96), German chemist, born Darmstadt; chemistry of explosives, dyestuffs, and coal-tar products based largely upon his researches.

**Kelantan** [*kĕ-lăn'tăn*], state in former Federation of Malaya; 5746 sq mi (14,882 sq km); pop. 680,626; rice, coconuts, rubber; tin, iron ore, gold. *see also in index* Malay States, Unfederated

**Kelland, Clarence Budington** (1881–1964), writer of novels and short stories, born Portland, Mich.; created fictional characters Mark Tidd and Scattergood Baines; story 'Opera Hat' basis for movie 'Mr. Deeds Goes to Town'.

**Keller, Friedrich Gottlob** (1816–95), German weaver of Saxony, patented a machine to make wood pulp: P-104

**Keller, Gottfried** (1819–90), German poet and novelist, born Zurich, Switzerland; combined realism with imagination and sincerity: G-96b, 98

**Keller, Helen Adams** (1880–1968), American blind and deaf woman of remarkable ability: K-24
■ bibliography K-24

**Kellermann** [*kĕl'ẽr-măn*], **Bernhard** (1879–1951), German novelist, born Fürth; early novels subjective ('The Fool'); later work on social problems ('The Ninth November'; 'The Tunnel').

**Kellermann** [*kĕ-lĕr-mȧn'*], **François Christophe de** (1735–1820), French Revolutionary general, marshal of France, victor at Valmy (1792); father of François Étienne de Kellermann, one of Napoleon's ablest generals.

**Keller milling machine,** industry
■ automobile manufacture A-872

**Kelley, Florence** (1859–1932), social worker, born Philadelphia, Pa.; resident Hull House 1891–99, Henry Street Settlement 1899–1924; secretary National Consumers League 1899.

**Kelley, Joseph James** (1871–1943), baseball outfielder, born Cambridge, Mass.; began career with Boston 1891, finished with Cincinnati 1906.

**Kelley, Oliver H(udson)** (1826–1913), farmer and agrarian reformer, born Boston, Mass.; founded National Grange of the Patrons of Husbandry 1867: *picture* M-360

**Kellgren** [*chĕl'grān*], **Johan Henrik** (1751–95), Swedish poet and critic, born Floby, near Falköping; cofounder and editor *Stockholmsposten;* librarian and private secretary to Gustavus III.

**Kellogg, Frank Billings** (1856–1937), lawyer and diplomat, born Potsdam, N.Y.; U.S. senator from Minnesota 1917–23; ambassador to Great Britain 1923–24; secretary of state 1925–29; coauthor of Kellogg-Briand Pact to outlaw war; elected World Court Judge 1930, resigned 1935: C-560, *picture* M-360
■ Nobel prize, *table* N-294g

**Kellogg, Vernon Lyman** (1867–1937), zoologist, born Emporia, Kan.; professor entomology, Stanford University, 1894–1920; secretary National Research Council 1919–31; wrote on zoology, entomology, heredity.

**Kellogg, W(ill) K(eith)** (1860–1951), industrialist and philanthropist, born Battle Creek, Mich.; in 1906 founded giant cereal industry: *picture* M-282
■ Kellogg Foundation F-363, *table* F-362
■ breakfast cereals B-433

**Kellogg,** Idaho, city 33 mi (53 km) s.e. of Coeur d'Alene; pop. 3417; center for important mining and smelting district producing lead, zinc, silver, cadmium, antimony: *map* I-28
■ mine nearby, *picture* I-18

**Kellogg-Briand Pact,** or **Pact of Paris** (Treaty for the Renunciation of War, 1928): C-560

**Kellogg Foundation, W. K.,** established 1930 F-363, *table* F-362

**Kells,** or **Ceanannus Mór,** Ireland, market town of County Meath in e.; of ancient origin; pop. 2274: *map* G-199h
■ cross, *picture* I-287

**Kelly, Colin P(urdie), Jr.** (1915–41), U.S. Army aviator ("America's first hero of World War II"), born Madison, Fla.; in B-17 bomber, Dec. 10, 1941, he attacked Japanese heavy cruiser *Ashigara;* killed when his bomber crashed on Mt. Arayat on Luzon: *picture* F-244

**Kelly, Ellsworth** (born 1923), artist, born Newburgh, N.Y.; noted for bright geometrics on large canvas, also ink and pencil drawings, sculpture, and lithographs; numerous awards
■ 'Blue, Black, Red' P-67, *picture* P-67

**Kelly, Emmett** (1898–1979), clown, born Sedan, Kan. C-410d, *pictures* C-410d, K-14

**Kelly, Eric Philbrook** (1884–1960), writer of children's books and educator, born Amesbury, Mass.; lectured at University of Cracow (Poland) 1925–26 and wrote 'The Trumpeter of Krakow', awarded 1929 Newbery Medal; professor of journalism at Dartmouth College 1929–54 ('The Land of the Polish People'; 'In Clean Hay'): R-111d

**Kelly, George** (1887–1974), playwright, born Philadelphia, Pa.; uncle of Grace Kelly; author of penetrating plays tinged with satire ('Craig's Wife', won Pulitzer prize 1926; 'The Showoff'): D-176

**Kelly, George Lange** (High Pockets) (born 1896), baseball player, born San Francisco, Calif.; first baseman with New York, N.L., 1915–17, 1919–26, Pittsburgh, N.L., 1917, Cincinnati, N.L., 1927–30, Chicago, N.L., 1930, Brooklyn, N.L., 1932; batted .331 with Chicago 1930

**Kelly, Grace.** *see in index* Grace, princess of Monaco

**Kelly, John** (1822–86), political leader, born New York City; joined Tammany organization 1853; U.S. congressman 1855–59; sheriff of New York County 1859–61 and 1865–67; opposed "Tweed Ring" and controlled Tammany 1874–82.

**Kelly, Michael Joseph** (King) (1857–94), baseball player, born Troy, N.Y.; colorful catcher and outfielder with 4 N.L. teams 1878–93; batted .394 and stole 84 bases for Boston, 1887

**Kelly, Lieut. Oakley,** aviator A-204

**Kelly, Walt(er)** (1913–73). cartoonist, born Philadelphia, Pa.; animator Walt Disney Studio 1935–41; commercial artist New York, N.Y., 1941–48; political cartoonist *New York Star* 1948–49
■ 'Pogo' C-145e, F-2, *picture* C-145e

**Kelly, William** (1811–88), inventor, born Pittsburgh, Pa.; invented process for making steel now known as Bessemer process; designated (1857) by

U.S. Patent Office as originator of the invention: I-297b
■ converter I-297b, *picture* I-298

**Kelmscott Press** M-491

**Kelowna** [*kē-lō'na*], B.C., Canada, city on Okanagan Lake 265 km (165 mi) n.e. of Vancouver; pop. 51,955 (1976 census); center for growing and processing of fruits, vegetables; lumbering, resort: *maps* 331, C-98

**Kelp,** a large coarse seaweed S-104, A-283, *picture* P-361

**Kelpies,** water fairies F-17, S-473

**Kelsey, Henry** (1670?–1724?), English explorer, born London; with Hudson's Bay Company 1684–1722, led expedition to northern Saskatchewan 1690–92, governor of posts 1718–22: C-108
■ route, *map* C-109

**Kelso,** Wash., city on Cowlitz River at Oregon border, 74 mi (119 km) s.e. of Aberdeen; pop. 11,129; boat building; incorporated 1889: *map* W-52

**Keltie, Sir John Scott** (1840–1927), British geographer, born Dundee, Scotland; editor *Statesman's Year Book* for 43 years ('History of the Scottish Highlands and Clans'; 'The Partition of Africa').

**Kelts.** *see in index* Celts

**Kelvin, William Thomson,** first **Baron** (1824–1907), British scientist and inventor; estimated earth's age: K-24, *pictures* K-24, E-154
■ absolute Celsius (centigrade) scale C-620a, H-111, K-24, S-512, *diagrams* C-620a, H-111
■ Atlantic cable C-8, K-24

**Kelvin scale,** of absolute temperature, devised by William Thomson, first Baron Kelvin: C-620a, H-111, K-24, M-236, S-512, *diagrams* C-620a, H-111

**Kemal** [*kĕ-mäl'*], **Yashar** (born 1922), Turkish novelist and journalist; self-taught ('Memed, My Hawk'; 'The Wind from the Plain'; 'Anatolian Tales').

**Kemal Atatürk** [*ăt'a-tŭrk*]. *see in index* Atatürk, Kemal

**Kemble,** famous family of English actors (18th and 19th centuries); most celebrated members were Mrs. Sarah Siddons, her brothers John Philip and Charles, and her niece Fanny.

**Kemble, Fanny** (Frances Anne) (1809–93), English actress and author, born London; daughter of Charles Kemble; married Pierce Butler, an American, and lived in U.S. 1834–48 ('Journals', interesting picture of American life).

**Kemerovo,** Russia, city in s. Siberia, on Tom' River; pop. 385,000; coal mining; fertilizers, paint, plastics, pharmaceuticals, coke by-products, machinery; sawmilling: *maps* R-344

**Kemmel, Mont,** isolated rocky hill 10 km (6 mi) s.w. of Ypres, Belgium; overlooks Flanders plain to n.e. and s.e.; taken by Germans in World War I, 1918.

**Kemmerer, Edwin Walter** (1875–1945), economist, born Scranton, Pa.; professor economics and finance, Cornell University, 1909–12, Princeton University 1912–43, professor emeritus after 1943; financial adviser to U.S. Philippine Commission, to Mexico, Guatemala, Colombia, South Africa, Chile, Poland, Ecuador, Bolivia, China; author of works on economics.

**Kemp Coast,** district in Antarctica between 56° and about 59°40' e.; discovered 1833 by Peter Kemp, a British sealing captain.

**Kempis, Thomas à** (1380?–1471), German monk and mystic, born Kempen, near Krefeld, Germany; remembered for one book, 'Imitation of Christ', a classic of devotional literature.

**Ken, Thomas** (1637–1711), English bishop, born Great or Little Berkhamstead, near St. Albans, England; one of seven imprisoned for refusing to read Declaration of Indulgences issued by James II; following the revolution, lost bishopric rather than transfer loyalty from James II to William of Orange; remembered today for his hymns ('Praise God from Whom All Blessings Flow'; 'Awake, My Soul, and with the Sun').

**Kenaf,** a fiber plant, botanically known as *Hibiscus cannabinus;* original home in India, grown now in Cuba and other Latin American countries, also in Florida; from 2½ to 3½ m (8 to 12 ft) high; fiber, which is in bark, used as substitute for jute.

**Kenai Mountains,** Alaska A-242

**Kenai Peninsula,** in s. Alaska; 150 mi (240 km) long; farmlands, coal deposits; includes city Kenai (pop. 4324), on Cook Inlet, and ice-free seaports Seward and Whittier; severe earthquake 1964: *maps* U-94, 39

**Kendall, Amos** (1789–1869), newspaper editor and public official, born Dunstable, Mass.; auditor in Treasury Department under Jackson 1829–35; postmaster general 1835–40; reorganized Post Office Department and paid off debt; S.F.B. Morse's agent in development of telegraph systems; helped found Columbia Institute for Deaf.

**Kendall, Edward C(alvin)** (1886–1972), biochemist, born South Norwalk, Conn.; isolated thyroxin 1914; professor of physiological chemistry Mayo Foundation for Medical Education and Research, Rochester, Minn., 1914–51
■ Nobel prize, *table* N-294d

**Kendall, Henry Clarence** (1841–82), Australian poet, born New South Wales; son of missionary; held government posts at Sydney; journalist at Melbourne 1869–73: A-797

**Kendo** [*kĕn'dō*], Japanese fencing J-399, *picture* J-399

**Kendrew, John C(owdery)** (born 1917), English biochemist, born Oxford; deputy chairman Medical Research Council Laboratory for Molecular Biology, Cavendish Laboratory, Cambridge 1946–75; director general European Molecular Biology Laboratory
■ Nobel prize, *table* N-294c
■ protein study B-237

**Kendrick, John** (1745?–1800), navigator, born Boston, Mass., died Hawaii; commanded privateer during Revolution; explored n.w. coast of America and Pacific islands.

**Kendrick, John Benjamin** (1857–1933), cattleman and political leader, born Cherokee County, Tex.; governor of Wyoming 1915–17; U.S. senator (Democrat) 1917–33: *picture* W-324

**Kenilworth,** England, town in Warwickshire; pop. 21,000; ruins of castle given by Queen Elizabeth I to earl of Leicester; scene of Sir Walter Scott's novel 'Kenilworth': *map* G-199h

**'Kenilworth',** novel by Scott S-74

**Kenilworth ivy,** a creeping perennial plant (*Cymbalaria muralis*) of the figwort family, native to Europe; trailing stems root at nodes (joints); leaves lobed; flowers lilac with yellow throat, tiny.

**Kenmore,** N.Y., village 5 mi (8 km) n. of Buffalo; pop. 18,474; chemicals, machinery, silk, electrical appliances: incorporated 1899: *map* N-260

**Kenna, John Edward** (1848–93), statesman, born Valcoulan, W. Va. (then Virginia); entered Confederate army at 16; admitted to bar 1870; served in House of Representatives and in U.S. Senate; Democrat
■ Statuary Hall, *table* S-437b

**Kennan, George Frost** (born 1904), diplomat, born Milwaukee, Wis.; in foreign service 1926–53, ambassador to Soviet Union 1952–53; professor Institute for Advanced Study, Princeton University 1956–61, 1963–74; ambassador to Yugoslavia 1961–63; won two Pulitzer prizes, one in history 1956 for first volume of 'Soviet-American Relations, 1917–1920', the other in biography 1968 for 'Memoirs, 1925–1950': R-358

**Kennebec** [*kĕn'ĕ-bĕk*] **River,** 2d largest river of Maine; rises in Moosehead Lake, flows s. 190 mi (305 km) to Atlantic: *maps* M-53, 64–5, *picture* M-60

**Kennedy, David M(atthew)** (born 1905), public official, born Randolph, Utah; president Continental Illinois National Bank and Trust Company of Chicago 1956–59, chairman 1959–69; special assistant to U.S. secretary of the treasury 1953–54, secretary 1969–71; ambassador at large, state department, 1971–72; ambassador to NATO 1972–73.

**Kennedy, Edward Moore** (Ted) (born 1932), political leader, born Brookline, Mass.; U.S. senator (Democrat) from Massachusetts 1962–; assistant majority leader (majority whip) 1969–70; author of 'In Critical Condition: the Crisis in American Health Care': K-24b, e, *picture* K-24d

**Kennedy, Jacqueline Bouvier.** *see in index* Onassis, Jacqueline Bouvier Kennedy

**Kennedy, John E.,** U.S. advertiser A-59

**Kennedy, John F(itzgerald)** (1917–63), 35th president of United States: K-24a–5c, *pictures* K-24a–b, d–f, 25b, M-158
■ administration (1961–63), major events K-24e–5, U-195, *list* K-24b, *pictures* K-25b
□ Alliance for Progress S-292, L-147, *picture* K-25b
□ civil rights K-24f: employment F-15; March on Washington N-126d, *picture* K-55
□ Cuban crisis C-628a–b, *pictures* K-25b, C-628b
□ Mercury space flights S-346f, *pictures* S-346a, *table* S-348: animals S-345, *picture* S-345
□ Mexican border settlement M-256, T-119, N-33
□ Peace Corps P-143–143a, L-147, *pictures* P-143–143a
□ silver certificate retired S-204
□ tariff proposal I-243
□ test ban treaty P-144, T-251, K-25, *picture* K-25b
□ Trade Expansion Act T-25, K-24f
□ 23d Amendment U-146, 153, K-24f
□ Vietnam conflict V-321–2
□ world events, *map* K-24c
■ ancestors K-24a
■ assassination A-703, K-25–25c, *pictures* K-25–25a: Warren Report K-25c, *picture* K-25c
■ bibliography K-25d
■ birthplace, John Fitzgerald Kennedy N.H.S. N-40
■ early political career K-24c–d
■ funeral K-25a–c, *pictures* K-25–25b
■ Nixon, Richard N-293d, K-24e
■ portrait on half-dollar, *picture* M-425b
■ 'Profiles in Courage' R-112, K-24e
■ quoted K-25c
■ signature reproduced K-24a
■ summer homes, *picture* K-24c
■ time line, *chart* K-24a
■ wife and family W-150–1, 155, K-24d–e, 25, *pictures* W-150, 155, K-24d–e
■ World War II service K-24c, *picture* K-24b

**Kennedy, John Pendleton** (1795–1870), pen name Mark Littleton, author and statesman, born Baltimore, Md.; fought in War of 1812; Whig representative from Maryland 1838, 1840, 1842; secretary of the navy 1852–53: A-346

**Kennedy, Joseph P(atrick)** (1888–1969), banker, business executive, and statesman, born Boston, Mass.; father of John F., Robert, and Edward; chairman, Securities and Exchange Commission 1934–35; chairman, U.S. Maritime Commission 1937; ambassador to England 1937–40: K-24a–b, b–c
■ summer home, *picture* K-24c

**Kennedy, Margaret** (Mrs. David Davies) (1896–1967), English novelist, born London: E-276

**Kennedy, Robert F(rancis)** (1925–68), lawyer and government official, born Brookline, Mass.; brother of President John F. Kennedy; U.S. attorney general 1961–64; U.S. senator (Democratic) from New York 1965–68; author, 'Just Friends and Brave Enemies', 'Rights for Americans': K-24d, e, 25a, U-196, N-20, *picture* K-24d
■ assassination, *list* A-704
■ memorial stadium W-35, *map, inset* W-32

**Kennedy, Rose (Fitzgerald)** (born 1890), civic leader, born Boston, Mass.; wife of Joseph P.; mother of John F., Robert F., and Edward: K-24a–b

**Kennedy, Ted.** *see in index* Kennedy, Edward Moore

**Kennedy, Cape.** *see in index* Canaveral, Cape

**Kennedy, Mount,** in St. Elias Mountains, Yukon Territory; height about 4300 m (14,000 ft); named by Canadian government in memory of President John F. Kennedy; Robert Kennedy first to climb.

**Kennedy International Airport.** *see in index* John F. Kennedy International Airport

**Kennedy Space Center.** *see in index* Canaveral, Cape

**Kennel,** for dog D-152, *list* D-137

**Kennel clubs** D-141, 154b
■ dog shows D-154, *pictures* D-154

**Kennelly, Arthur Edwin** (1861–1939), American electrical engineer, born Bombay, India; principal electrical assistant to Thomas Edison 1887–94; professor at Harvard 1902–39.

**Kennelly-Heaviside layer,** of upper atmosphere; suggested by Oliver Heaviside and A. E. Kennelly: R-36

**Kenner,** La., city 9 mi (14 km) w. of New Orleans, on Mississippi River; pop. 66,382; trading and shipping center; sheet metal, concrete and wood products: *map, inset* L-381

**Kennesaw Mountain,** a height 25 mi (40 km) n.w. of Atlanta, Ga., where Confederates repulsed Sherman's army inflicting heavy losses June 27, 1864: *map* C-376
■ Kennesaw Mountain N.B.P. N-40a, *map* G-92

**Kenneth I, MacAlpine** (died 860?), king of the Scots and conqueror of Picts, called first king of Scotland: S-70

**Kennett Square,** Penn., Longwood Geadens *table* B-379

**Kennewick,** Wash., city in s.e. part of state, on Columbia River opposite Pasco; pop. 34,397; river port; fruit and vegetable farming; chemicals, metals, cement: *map* W-53

**Kenney, George Churchill** (1889–1977), U.S. Air Force officer, born Yarmouth, N.S., Canada, of American parents; commander of Allied air forces in Southwest Pacific during World War II.

**Kenny, Elizabeth** (1886–1952), Australian nurse (called Sister), born Warrialda, New South Wales; developed method for treating polio introduced into U.S. 1940.

**Kennywood Park,** Pittsburgh's amusement park A-386

**Kenora,** Ont., Canada, manufacturing town and summer resort on Lake of the Woods, 195 km (120 mi) e. of Winnipeg, Manitoba; pop. 10,952; flour, lumber, pulp and paper mills, boat factories, fisheries; gold, silver, copper, mica nearby: *map* C-98, *inset* O-457

**Kenosha,** Wis., manufacturing city and port on s.w. shore of Lake Michigan, 33 mi (53 km) s. of Milwaukee; pop. 77,685; automobiles, metal products, industrial tools, wire rope, cranberries; Carthage College, Gateway Technical Institute: *maps* W-198, *inset* W-206

**Kensington,** P.E.I., Canada, town 13 km (8 mi) n.e. of Summerside; near Malpeque Bay; pop. 1150 (1976 census); agricultural market and shipping center; butter and cheese: P-497f, *map* P-497h

**Kensington and Chelsea,** borough in w.-central section of Greater London, England; pop. 208,480; Kensington district has Kensington Palace (birthplace of Queen Victoria) and Gardens: L-343–4, *maps* L-337–8, *inset* G-199h

**Kent, Edward Augustus, duke of** (1767–1820), English prince, 4th son of George III; father of Queen Victoria; born London
■ Prince Edward Island P-497e

**Kent, James** (1763–1847), jurist and author, born Fredericksburg, Putnam County N.Y.; his 'Commentaries upon American Law' is a legal classic
■ Hall of Fame, *table* H-11

**Kent, Rockwell** (1882–1971), American artist K-25d, *picture* K-25d
■ illustrations: 'Moby-Dick', *picture* W-128
■ Mount Equinox in Vermont, *picture* K-25d
■ wood engraving E-278

**Kent,** ancient kingdom of Anglo-Saxons in England; settled by Jutes; conquered by Egbert, king of Wessex, made part of Wessex: *map* E-230

**Kent,** county of s.e. England; 3950 sq km (1525 sq mi); pop. 1,388,820: K-25d, *map* E-218
■ Canterbury and early kingdom C-127
■ Conrad in C-535
■ Penshurst Place, *picture* F-487

**Kent,** Ohio, city 11 mi (18 km) n.e. of Akron; pop. 26,164; electric motors, motor vehicles, machine parts, school blackboards, plastic products; Kent State University: *map* O-428

**Kent,** Wash., city 16 mi (26 km) s. of Seattle; pop. 23,152; aerospace research and products, fiberglass, telephone equipment: *map* W-52

**Kente cloth,** for ritual garments in Africa A-101

**Kent Island,** largest island in Chesapeake Bay, Md., 7 mi (11 km) e. of Annapolis; oyster fisheries: *maps* M-127, 139
■ Chesapeake Bay Bridge M-128, *picture* C-246
■ early settlement M-129

**Kenton, Simon** (1755–1836), frontiersman and Indian fighter; birthplace probably Fauquier County, Va.; scout for Daniel Boone 1775–78; with George Rogers Clark in capture of Kaskaskia and Vincennes; became brigadier general of militia 1805; in War of 1812.

**Kenton, Stan(ley Newcomb)** (1912–79), bandleader, born Wichita, Kan.; band noted for progressive jazz; introduced new compositions and arrangements after mid-1940's.

**Kent State University,** at Kent, Ohio; founded 1910; arts and sciences, business administration, education, fine and professional arts, library science, and nursing; graduate school; regional campuses at Ashtabula, East Liverpool, New Philadelphia, North Canton, Salem, and Warren.

**Kentucky,** an e.-central state of U.S.; 40,395 sq mi (104,625 sq km); pop. 3,661,433; cap. Frankfort: K-26–43, *Fact Summary* K-38a–d, *maps* K-40–1, 28, 32, 38a, U-41, 58–9, *pictures* K-26–31, 33–8
■ agriculture K-29, 38b, 27–8, 34, *charts* K-38b, *map* K-32, *pictures* K-30, 37, U-56
■ bibliography K-38d
■ bird, state, cardinal C-134–5, *pictures* K-34, F-114. *see also in index* Cardinal
■ Capitol, State F-421, *picture* K-35
■ cities K-29, 38d, *map index* K-39, 42–3. *see also in index* cities listed below and other cities by name
□ Frankfort F-420–1
□ Louisville L-383–4, *picture* L-383
■ climate K-27–8, *list* K-26
■ communication K-38c
■ Confederate Memorial Day F-93
■ conservation K-28
■ counties, *map index* K-39
■ dams K-28, *map* K-28, *inset* K-40. *see also in index* Kentucky Dam
■ education K-30–1, 38a, *picture* K-35
■ elevation K-27, *list* K-26, *map* K-38a
■ employment, *chart* K-38c
■ extent K-27, *list* K-26, *map* K-38a
■ flag F-194, *picture* F-195
■ flower, state, goldenrod G-152, *pictures* F-255, K-34, S-427, F-277c
■ forests K-28, 38b, *chart* K-38b, *map* K-32
■ geographic center, *list* K-26, *map* K-38a
■ geographic region: South, the U-56–67, *map* U-58–9, *pictures* U-60, 57, *Reference-Outline* U-133–4
■ government K-31, 38a
□ elections K-31, 38a
■ history K-31–2, 28–9, 30, 33, *pictures* K-33: Boone, Daniel B-365; Civil War K-32, C-376, 377, 378, *map* C-376; Clark, George Rogers C-381; nullification resolutions S-429d; pioneer life P-331–4
■ horses K-29, *picture* K-26: Kentucky Derby L-384, *pictures* K-27, 33
■ industries K-29, *charts* K-38b, *map* K-32, *picture* K-30
■ land use, *list* K-26, *map* K-32
■ libraries K-38a
■ location K-27, *locator map* K-26
■ minerals K-28, 29, *charts* K-38b, *map* K-32, *picture* K-30
■ motto K-34
■ name K-26–7
■ natural features K-26–7, *map* K-28, *picture* K-29
■ natural regions K-27, *map* K-28
■ natural resources K-28, 29, 38b, *charts* K-38b, *map* K-32
■ parks and other areas K-38d, 30, *maps* K-40–1, N-30, *pictures* K-30, 35–7
□ Abraham Lincoln Birthplace N.H.S. N-29, *pictures* K-31, L-280
□ Cumberland Gap N.H.P. N-34, *picture* K-35
□ Mammoth Cave N.P. N-40a–b, C-178a, *pictures* N-40a, C-178b, K-36
■ people K-28–9: famous K-26, 32, L-384, *pictures* K-38; mountaineers K-29
■ places of interest K-38d
■ population K-26, 29, *chart* K-38a, *list* K-26
■ products K-29, *charts* K-38b, *map* K-32, *pictures* K-30
■ profile K-34–8, *pictures* K-34–8
■ recreation K-30, *pictures* K-27, 29–30, 35–7
■ rivers K-27, *maps* K-28, 40–1, *pictures* K-30, 36: Ohio O-432, *map* O-432
■ seal, state, *picture* K-34
■ song, state K-34, F-357
■ Statuary Hall, *table* S-437a
■ trade K-38b
■ transportation K-29–30, 38c: roads K-30, 29, 38c, *map* K-40–1: bridges, *picture* L-383
■ tree, state, Kentucky coffee tree, *picture* K-34. *see also in index* Kentucky coffee tree

**Kentucky, University of,** at Lexington, Ky.; state control; founded 1865; arts and sciences, agriculture, allied health professions, architecture, business and economics, dentistry, education, engineering, home economics, law, library sciences, medicine, nursing, pharmacy, and social professions; graduate school; Lexington Technical Institute; 14 community colleges: *picture* K-35

**Kentucky coffee tree,** a medium-sized tree (*Gymnocladus dioicus*) of the pea, or pulse, family; so called because its seeds resemble coffee beans; grows w. of Appalachian Mountains to Great Plains; state tree of Kentucky, *picture* K-34

**Kentucky Dam,** in Kentucky, on Tennessee River, *maps* K-28, T-100, *inset* K-40, *picture* K-33
■ height compared, *diagram* T-100
■ Kentucky Lake T-100, *picture* K-36

**Kentucky Derby** L-384, *pictures* K-27, 33

**Kentucky Resolutions** J-431, S-429d

**Kentucky rifle,** *picture* F-127

**Kentucky River,** in Kentucky, formed by several forks, rising in Cumberland Mts. of s.e.; flows 250 mi (400 km) n.w. to Ohio River: *maps* K-28, 40–1

**Kentucky State University,** at Frankfort, Ky.; founded as normal school 1886; arts and sciences, applied sciences, and teacher education; graduate studies.

**Kentucky Wesleyan College,** at Owensboro, Ky.; Methodist; founded 1858; opened 1866; arts and sciences, education.

**Kentwood,** Mich., city 5 mi (8 km) s.e. of Grand Rapids; pop. 30,438; residential; incorporated 1967: *map* M-285

**Kenya** [*kĕn'yạ*, also *kēn'yạ*], nation on Indian Ocean s. of Ethiopia; area 224,960 sq mi (582,645 sq km); pop. 10,942,705 (1969 census); cap. Nairobi: K-44–5, *pictures* K-44–5
■ Africanization A-105
■ cities K-45. *see also in index* cities by name
■ clothing K-44
■ education L-243, *picture* K-45
■ elephants, *picture* A-95
■ flag F-207, *picture* F-205
■ history K-45
■ Lake Victoria borders V-314
■ libraries L-243, L-310g, *picture* L-238
■ literature, *list* L-306e: children's L-310g, *list* L-311
■ location K-44, *locator map* K-44
■ money, *table* M-428
■ national anthem, *table* N-52
■ natural features K-44, *picture* K-44
■ parks N-23
■ Peace Corps aid, *picture* P-143a
■ people K-44–5
■ pyrethrum harvest, *picture* I-195
■ railroad mileage, *table* R-85
■ remains of early animals M-76, 79, F-356
■ shelter K-44, 45
■ transportation K-45

**Kenya, Mount,** volcanic peak (17,058 ft; 5199 m) in central Kenya, Africa, near equator; discovered 1849; first ascended 1899: K-44, *picture* K-44

**Kenyahs,** tribe in Borneo, of good physique and intelligence; traditionally rice growers; entire village often lives in one huge communal house.

**Kenyatta** [*kĕn-yä'tạ*], **Jomo** (1893?–1978), African political leader, born near Nairobi, Kenya; imprisoned 1953–59 for Mau Mau leadership; prime minister of Kenya 1963–64, president from 1964: K-45

**Kenyon, Dame Kathleen (Mary)** (1906–78), English archaeologist
■ Jericho finds A-532

**Kenyon College,** at Gambier, Ohio; Protestant Episcopal; founded 1824 (at Worthington, moved 1827 to Gambier); arts and sciences.

**Keogh, James** (born 1916), journalist and government official, born Platte County, Neb.; on staff of *Time* 1951–68, assistant managing editor 1961–68, executive editor 1968; chief writer and researcher Nixon for President campaign 1968; special presidential assistant 1969–70; director U.S. Information Agency 1973–76 ('This Is Nixon'; 'President Nixon and the Press').

**Keogh plan** individual retirement plan: P-189

**Keokuk** ("one who moves alertly") (1780?–1848), American Indian of the Fox clan; became leader of Sauks and Foxes and secured for them the territory of Iowa from the government; buried in Keokuk, Iowa, which was named for him. His son, **Moses Keokuk** (1818?–1903), was a famous orator

**Keokuk,** Iowa, city on Mississippi and Des Moines rivers at s.e. corner of state; pop. 13,536; metal products, corn and cereal products, carbides: *maps* I-275, U-41
■ dam I-261, *picture* I-267
■ temperature record, *list* I-259

**Kephallenia** [*kyĕ-fä-lyĕ-nyē'ä*], or **Cephalonia** [*sĕf-ạ-lō'nĭ-ạ*], mountainous Greek island w. of mainland; largest of Ionian group; about 750 sq km (290 sq mi); pop. 31,787; currants and olives: G-213, *map* G-213

**Kepler, Johannes** (1571–1630), German astronomer K-45–6, S-57g, A-713, *picture* S-62b
■ improves telescope T-62, K-46
■ story of trip to moon S-341d

**Kepler's laws of planetary motion** K-46, S-57g, A-713

**Kepone,** an insecticide, *table* I-194

**Keppel, Frederick Paul** (1875–1943), educator, born Staten Island, N.Y.; assistant secretary of war 1918–19; president Carnegie Corporation 1923–41.

**Kerala** [*kĕr'ạ-lạ*], state in s.w. India; area 14,980 sq mi (38,800 sq km); pop. 21,347,375; cap. Trivandrum; formed 1956 from parts of former Travancore-Cochin and Madras states: I-82, *maps* I-81, 84c

**Kerazeh,** Palestine. *see in index* Chorazin

**Kerbela,** Iraq. *see in index* Karbala

**Kerch'** [*kĕrch*], Russia, port of Crimea, on Kerch' Peninsula; pop. 128,000; steel mills: *maps* R-349, E-335

**Kerchief,** head covering D-190

**Keren Hayesod,** German Jewish organization B-17

**Kerensky, Alexander Feodorovich** (1881–1970), Russian revolutionary statesman, born Simbirsk (now Ul'yanovsk); fled to Paris, France, when Bolsheviks overthrew his government Oct. 1917; moved to U.S. 1940; author of 'Russia and History's Turning Point': R-354

**Keres,** or **Queres** [*kā'rĕs*], a linguistic stock of North American Indians living in pueblos on the Rio Grande and Rio Jemez and New Mexico.

**Kerf,** in mining C-414

**Kerguelen** [*kûr'gĕ-lĕn*] **Island,** volcanic island 100 mi (160 km) long in s. Indian Ocean; French possession; whaling, seal hunting base; discovered 1772 by Yves Joseph de Kerguélen-Trémarec: *map* W-243

**Kerguélen-Trémarec** [*kĕr-gā-lĕn' trā-mȧ-rĕk'*], **Yves Joseph de** (1734–97), French explorer, born Quimper, France; discovered (1772) what he thought was rich continent in Antarctic and named it south France; realizing it was only a barren island, renamed it Isle of Desolation; later called Kerguelen Island.

**Kérkyra,** island. *see in index* Corfu

**Kermadec** [*kẽr-măd'ĕk*] **Islands,** group in Pacific about 950 km (600 mi) n.e. of New Zealand, to which it was annexed in 1887; total area, 34 sq km (13 sq mi); pop. 9; Raoul, or Sunday Island, largest: *map* P-5

**Kerman,** or **Kirman** [*kĕr-män'*], ancient **Carmana,** Iran, city in s.e.; capital of province of Kerman; pop. 110,000; Iran's chief rug exporter; 11th-century mosque, now restored: *maps* I-280, P-212
■ rugs, *picture* R-312

**Kermanshah** [*kĕr-män'shä*], Iran, city in w.; pop. 250,000; on road between Baghdad and Tehran; trade in grain, rugs: *map* I-280

**Kermit,** Tex., city 40 mi (65 km) w. of Odessa; pop. 8015; in area producing oil and natural gas; cattle ranching; incorporated 1938: *map* T-128

**Kern, Jerome** (1885–1945), composer, born New York City M-567b
■ 'Show Boat' M-567b

**Kernel clause** S-110–11

**Kernite,** or **rasorite,** mineral yielding borax M-335

**Kern River,** stream rising in mountains of s.e. California; flows s.w. and n. to Lake Tulare: *map* C-53

**Kerogen,** a substance in oil shale P-230

**Kerosene,** or **kerosine,** also **coal oil,** an oil distilled from petroleum; ending "ine" adopted 1957 by petroleum chemists because "ene" suggests falsely that oil consists of unsaturated compounds: P-232, *charts* P-241–241b
■ asphalt distilled A-702
■ fire prevention, *picture* F-143
■ first used P-232
■ jet fuel A-74, J-446
■ lamps and lighting L-106, *picture* L-105
■ rocket fuel S-342a, 346d
■ soaps contain S-231

**Kerr, Jean (Collins)** (born 1924), writer, born Scranton, Pa.; married Walter F. Kerr 1943 ('Please Don't Eat the Daisies', 'The Snake Has All the Lines', humorous pieces; 'Mary, Mary', play and movie).

**Kerr, Robert Samuel** (1896–1963), lawyer, oil producer, and political leader; born Ada, Okla.; governor of Oklahoma 1943–47; U.S. senator (Democrat) 1949–63: *picture* O-444

**Kerr, Walter F(rancis)** (born 1913), drama critic and playwright, born Evanston, Ill.; on faculty Catholic University of America (drama department) 1938–49; drama critic *New York Herald Tribune* 1951–66; *The New York Times* after 1966; husband of Jean Kerr (play: 'Sing Out, Sweet Land'; criticism: 'How Not to Write a Play', 'The Theater in Spite of Itself', 'Tragedy and Comedy').

**Kerrville,** Tex., city 55 mi (90 km) n.w. of San Antonio, at mouth of Guadalupe River; pop. 15,276; wool processing, ranching, incorporated 1942: *map* T-129

**Kerry,** county of s.w. Ireland in province of Munster; 4700 sq km (1815 sq mi); pop. 112,785; beautiful mountain scenery; lakes of Killarney: *map* I-283

**Kerry blue terrier,** *picture* D-148

**Kerry cattle** C-167

**Kersey,** a thick, coarse woolen cloth used to make clothing; woven first in medieval England.

**Kerst, Donald William** (born 1911), physicist, born Galena, Ill.; joined faculty of University of Illinois 1938, professor of physics 1943–57; invented betatron there.

**Kerulen River,** 780 mi (1255 km) long, rises in n.e. Mongolian People's Republic, flows into Hulun Nor (lake) in People's Republic of China: *maps* C-291, C-313

**Kerwin, Joseph P.** (born 1932), astronaut, physician, born Oak Park, Ill.; flight surgeon with U.S. Marine Corps 1956–58, with U.S. Navy 1958–; scientist-astronaut 1965–; member Skylab crew 1973: *table* S-348

**Kerwin, Patrick** (1889–1963), Canadian jurist, born Sarnia, Ont.; created king's counsel 1928; appointed judge of the Supreme Court of Canada 1935, chief justice 1954–63.

**Kesselring, Albert** (1885–1960), German army officer; led air attacks on Poland 1939, on Netherlands, Belgium, Britain 1940, on Russia 1941–42; became commander in Italy 1943, in west 1945; death sentence for war crimes in Italy commuted to life imprisonment, later to 21 years; freed by British 1952; wrote 'Kesselring: a Soldier's Record'.

**Kestrel,** or **windhover,** a bird of prey, one of smallest of true falcons (*Falco tinnunculus*) found throughout Old World; resembles common sparrow hawk of America, to which it is related; strong flier, hovers for minute or two in one spot.

**Keta salmon, dog salmon,** or **chum salmon** S-28

**Ketch,** sailing craft, *pictures* B-327, S-166

**Ketchel, Stanley,** real name Stanislaus Kiecal (1887–1910), middleweight boxer, born Grand Rapids, Mich.; scored 46 knockouts, 14 in succession; was shot to death.

**Ketchikan,** Alaska, city and port of entry in s.e. Alaska 235 mi (380 km) s.e. of Juneau; pop. 7198; pulp mill; salmon canning, halibut processing, lumbering; totem pole collection; Ketchikan King Salmon Derby: A-242, *maps* U-39, N-308
■ cable connections, *map* C-5, *table* C-8

**Ketchup,** or **catsup** T-197
■ calories, *chart* F-310

**Ketchwayo.** *see in index* Cetewayo

**Ketones,** in chemistry O-502–3
■ formula O-502

**Ket's Rebellion.** *see in index* Kett's Rebellion

**Kettering, Charles F(ranklin)** (1876–1958), engineer and inventor, born near Loudonville, Ohio; originated Delco electric power and light generating unit for farmhouses; president and general manager General Motors Research Corporation 1920–47, research consultant 1947–58; founded Charles F. Kettering Foundation 1927, board chairman 1927–58
■ automobile self-starter A-856, 859
■ guided missiles G-252

**Kettering,** Ohio, residential city just s.e. of Dayton; pop. 61,186; electric motors; Defense Electronics Center; incorporated 1955: *map* O-429

**Kettledrums, timpani,** or **tympani** D-200e, M-568, *picture* M-569
■ place in orchestra, *picture* O-476

**Kettle Hill,** Cuba. *see in index* San Juan Hill

**Kett's,** or **Ket's, Rebellion,** a revolt in Norfolk, England (1549), led by William and Robert Kett against the unlawful closing off from the people of common land; suppressed, at great loss to rebels, by forces under leadership of earl of Warwick; Kett brothers executed.

**Keuka College,** at Keuka Park, N.Y.; private control; operated 1890–1915 as coeducational institution, reopened as college for women 1921; arts and sciences, education; quarter system.

**Kew** [kū], residential suburb of London, England; famous for its extensive botanical gardens: B-377, *table* 379

**Kewanee** [kē-wŏn'ē], Ill., city about 42 mi (60 km) n.w. of Peoria; pop. 14,508; center of corn and hog area; trailers, lift trucks; boilers, farm machinery: *map* I-50

**Kewaunee,** Wis., port city on Lake Michigan 25 mi (40 km) e. of Green Bay; pop. 2801; metal products; fur-trade post set up 1795: *map* W-207
■ car ferry M-287

**Kew barometer,** or **marine barometer** B-82

**Keweenaw** [kē'wē-na] **Bay,** inlet of Lake Superior in n. peninsula of Michigan, *maps* M-270, 284

**Keweenaw Peninsula,** in Lake Superior, northernmost projection of Michigan C-567, *map* M-284
■ copper mining S-518

**Kew Gardens,** officially **Royal Botanic Gardens,** near London, England; 117 hectares (288 acres): B-377
■ replica, *picture* P-128

**Kewpie,** doll D-156

**Key** [kĕ'ĭ], **Ellen** (1849–1926), Swedish social writer and feminist, born Småland, s. Sweden ('The Century of the Child'; 'The Woman Movement').

**Key** [kē], **Francis Scott** (1779–1843), American lawyer K-46–7, *pictures* K-46, M-131, 136
■ ancestor of F. Scott Fitzgerald F-181
■ grave, *picture* F-186
■ Polk and P-437
■ writes 'The Star-Spangled Banner' N-50, K-46–7, *pictures* N-50, M-27: inspired by Fort McHenry flag F-190, *pictures* W-12, F-189; words N-50

**Key,** in ciphers and codes C-342a, b, c, *list* C-343, *picture* C-342a

**Key,** in music, *table* M-566a

**Key,** of chart G-180

**Key,** sending instrument in telegraphy T-52

**Keyboard operator,** computer career C-504

**Keyes** [kīz], **Frances Parkinson** (1885–1970), novelist, born Charlottesville, Va. ('Queen Anne's Lace'; 'The Great Tradition'; 'All That Glitters'; 'Dinner at Antoine's'; 'Joy Street'; 'Steamboat Gothic').

**Keynes** [kānz], **John Maynard** (1883–1946), first **Baron,** English economist, born Cambridge; advocated government spending in time of economic crisis to create mass purchasing power; influenced economic policies of "New Deal" in U.S.; started compulsory savings plan ('The Economic Consequences of the Peace'; 'The General Theory of Employment, Interest and Money'): *picture* E-62

**Keys, Florida.** *see in index* Florida Keys

**Keys and locks** L-325, *diagrams* L-325

**Keyserling** [kī'zẽr-lĭng], **Hermann, Count** (1880–1946), German philosopher, born Könno, near Reval, Livonia (now Estonian S.S.R.), of wealthy German-speaking nobility; inspired by Eastern thought; founded School of Wisdom at Darmstadt ('The Travel Diary of a Philosopher'; 'Europe'; 'The Recovery of Truth'; 'America Set Free').

**Key signature,** in music M-566, *picture* M-566

**Keystone,** in arch, *diagram* M-205

**Keystone Kops,** *picture* M-522

**Keystone Province** (Manitoba, Canada) M-89, 88

**Keystone State,** popular name for Pennsylvania P-163

**Key West,** Fla., winter and health resort on island about 100 mi (160 km) n. of Havana, Cuba; pop. 24,382: K-47, *maps* F-247, U-41, *picture* K-47
■ cable connections C-8
■ shrimp boats, *picture* F-235

**KGB,** Russian secret police P-430a, R-328

**Kha,** hill people of Laos L-125a

**Khabarovsk** [kŭ-bä'rŭfsk], Russia, city in e. Siberia, about 650 km (400 mi) n.e. of Vladivostok, near junction of Amur and Ussuri rivers; on Trans-Siberian Railroad; pop. 500,000; trade, industrial, and educational center: *maps* R-322, 345, *picture* R-330a

**Khachaturian** [kä-chä-tụ'rĭ-än], **Aram** (1903–78), Armenian composer, born Tiflis, Russia; work shows influence of Eastern folk music ('Gayne', a ballet; 'Concerto for Pianoforte and Orchestra'): M-561

**Khadija** [kä-dē'ġa], wife of Mohammed M-419

**Khafre** [käf'rā], or **Chephren,** king of Egypt (2560 B.C.)
■ pyramid P-542, *picture* P-542
■ Sphinx, a portrait of S-378–9

**Khairpur** [kīr'pụr], in Pakistan; division of Sind Province; before joining Pakistan in 1948, Khairpur was a princely state affiliated with India.

**Khaki** [kăk'ē] U-5, 6, 12

**Khalid ibn Abd al-Aziz Al Saud** (born 1913), king of Saudi Arabia; son of Ibn Saud; crown prince 1964–75; succeeded brother Faisal after his assassination 1975.

**Khalkidike,** peninsula, Greece. *see in index* Chalcidice

**Khalkis,** or **Chalcis** [kăl'kĭs], Greece, chief town of island of Evvoia; pop. 24,745

**Khamsin** [kăm'sĭn or kăm-sēn'], hot, sand- or dust-laden wind blowing in Egypt in late spring; it is supposed to continue about 50 days, *khamsin* being the Arabic word for "fifty": S-15, E-109

**Khan,** in Orient, large unfurnished inn, generally surrounding a court, for traders and their caravans, a resthouse
■ Damascus D-14

**Khan,** title applied to rulers among Tatars, also to persons of various ranks in Iran, Turkey, India, Pakistan, and other Eastern countries.

**Khaniá** [kä-nyä'], also **Canea** [ka-nē'a], Crete, seaport and capital (since 1841), on n.w. shore; pop. 38,467: C-605, *maps* G-213, T-299, E-335

**Khan Tengri** [tĕng'rē], a peak of the Tien Shan, in Russia near border of People's Republic of China; height 6953 m (22,812 ft)

**Khârga** [kär'gä], Egypt, oasis in Libyan Desert, *map* E-109

**Khar'kov** [kär'kôf], Russia, city of Ukrainian S.S.R.; pop. 1,223,000: K-48, *maps* R-322, 344, 349, E-335, W-253, *picture* K-48
■ Lenin memorial, *picture* R-328
■ location K-48, *locator map* K-48
■ woman, *picture* R-321

**Khartoum,** also **Khartum** [kär-tọm'], Republic of the Sudan, capital, at union of Blue Nile and White Nile rivers; pop. 321,666; trade center on Cape-to-Cairo route; Gordon College: S-501, 502, 503, *picture* S-501
■ Kitchener captures K-62
■ library L-242
■ siege of G-159

**Khattushash,** Hittite capital H-180

**Khaya** [kā'ya], a genus of tropical trees of the mahogany family native to Africa from Gambia to Madagascar. Grows to 45 m (150 ft) with a trunk 24 m to 30 m (80 ft to 100 ft) high; trees reach maturity at 100 yrs.; wood, often called Africa mahogany, has pale rose to dark red-brown heartwood, gray-white to red-brown sapwood; 4 species, dry-zone, red, white, and bigleaf khaya, make up bulk of this wood and they often appear in trade under name of port from which shipped, as "Benin mahogany"; used as veneer for furniture; lumber used for ships, boats, and caskets.

**Khayyám, Omar.** *see in index* Omar Khayyám

**Khelat,** Pakistan. *see in index* Kalat

**Kherson** [kĕr-sôn'], Russia, port on Dnieper River in s., 160 km (100 mi) e. of Odessa; pop. 261,000; grain and woolen mills, tobacco manufactures: *maps* R-344, 349

**Khingan.** *see in index* Great Khingan Mountains; Little Khingan Mountains

**Khios** [kē'ôs], **Chios** [kī'ŏs], or **Scio** [shē'ō], fertile island in Aegean Sea w. of Izmir; 830 sq km (320 sq mi); pop. 60,061; ancient Greek colony; reputed birthplace of Homer; ceded to Greece by Turkey 1913: *maps* G-213, E-335

**Khirbet Qumran,** ruin D-41b, *picture* D-41

**Khmer Empire,** Indochina
■ Angkor Wat A-415

**Khmer Republic.** *see in index* Cambodia

**Khmer Rouge,** Communist military force in Cambodia C-56a

**Khmers** [k'mĕrz], people inhabiting Cambodia, parts of Thailand, and southern Vietnam; tall and muscular with large, dark eyes; remnants of cultured ancient race; according to tradition came from India: C-56a, 56, I-161, 162, 163, V-318. *see also in index* Angkor
■ language, *diagram* L-118

**Khnemu** [k'nĕ'mụ], ancient Egyptian god E-122, 123

**Khoisan language family** L-116, *map* A-89
■ African languages spoken A-119

**Khomeini, Ruhollah Ayatollah,** (born 1902), Iranian religious and political leader, born Khomeyn; a leader of Shiite branch of Islam; banished 1964 for criticism of shah; lived in Iraq 1964–78, in France 1978–79; returned to Iran 1979 following successful overthrow of shah; established Iran as an Islamic republic: I-280, I-281

**Khone** [kō-nä'] **Falls,** in Mekong River at Cambodia-Laos boundary M-217, *table* W-73c

**Khons,** ancient Egyptian temple A-729

**Khor-al-Amaya,** man-made island in Persian Gulf off Iraq H-26

**Khorana, Har Gobind** (born 1922), American biochemist, born Raipur, in present state of Madhya Pradesh, India; professor University of Wisconsin 1960–71, Massachusetts Institute of Technology 1971–
■ Nobel prize, *table* N-294e

**Khorasan** [kō'ra-sän], or **Khurasan** [kụr'a-sän], province, n.e. Iran; 121,000 sq mi (313,000 sq km); pop. 2,497,381; cap. Meshed; salt deserts; turquoise, iron, copper, and lead mines; agricultural products and livestock
■ rainfall R-89

**Khorsabad,** Iraq. *see in index* Dur Sharrukin, Assyria

**Khotan** [kō'tän'], Chinese **Hotien** [hō'tyĕn'], People's Republic of China, town and oasis in s.w. part of Sinkiang-Uigur Autonomous Region; farming; silk and cotton growing; textiles, metalwork: *map* C-312

**Khotana** [kō-tä-nä'], Indian tribe that lives in Alaska, *map* I-134, *table* I-136

**Khrunov, Yevgeni Vasilyevich** (born 1933), Russian cosmonaut, research engineer: *table* S-348

**Khrushchev** [krush-chôf'], **Nikita Sergeevich** (1894–1971), Russian dictator: K-48–48a, R-357–8, C-497b, *pictures* K-48–48a, U-15
■ Brezhnev's association with B-435
■ Cuba C-628b: Castro, *picture* C-628a
■ economic policy R-330
■ Stalin discredited S-404
■ visits United States E-136

**Khufu** [kụ'fụ], or **Cheops** [kē'ŏps], king of Egypt (2600 B.C.)
■ Great Pyramid P-542, *picture* P-542

**Khulna** [kụl'na], Bangladesh, town on river branch in Ganges Delta 77 mi (124 km) n.e. of Calcutta, India; pop. 403,000;

river port, shipbuilding; exports timber and forest products: *map* I-84b

**Khurasan,** Iran. *see in index* Khorasan

**Khus-khus.** *see in index* Vetiver

**Khwarizmi, al-** [*ăl-kwä'rĭz-mē*], in Arabic, Muhammad ibn-Musa al-Khwarizmi (780–850?), Arab mathematician, born Khwarizm (now Khiva), Russia; Europe learned the decimal system from his book on Hindu (Arabic) numerals and use of zero

**Khyber** [*kī'bẽr*] **Pass,** narrow mountain pass between Pakistan and Afghanistan; length 33 mi (53 km); great strategic importance for 2000 years: *map* I-66

**Kiang** [*kĭ-ăng'*], wild ass A-702

**Kiangsi** [*ġĭ-äng'sē'*], an inland province of People's Republic of China; 67,000 sq mi (173,500 sq km); pop. 18,610,000; cap. Nanchang: C-293d, *maps* C-293, C-313
■ early porcelain making P-470, 473

**Kiangsu** [*ġĭ-äng'sụ'*], province on e. coast of People's Republic of China; area (excluding Shanghai) 39,460 sq mi (102,200 sq km); pop. 45,230,000; cap. Nanking: C-293d–e, *maps* C-293, C-313

**Kiaochow** [*ġĭ-ou'ġō'*], former coastal district of Shantung Province; territory leased by Germany 1898; taken by Japanese 1914; returned to Chinese rule 1922.

**Kibbutz** [*kĭb-ŭtz'*], a communal settlement in Israel I-318, *picture* I-319

**Kibera, Leonard,** Anglophone novelist A-128

**Kibo, Mount,** in Tanganyika. *see in index* Kilimanjaro

**Kickapoo Indians,** tribe of Algonquian stock; closely related to Sauk and Fox; first known in central Wisconsin; moved s. into Wabash River region of Indiana and Illinois, some as far s. as Mexico; later parts of tribe removed to Indian Territory: *map* I-145

**Kickinghorse Pass,** in Rocky Mts. of British Columbia and Alberta, Canada; at Banff National Park; 1614 m (5296 ft) high; traversed by Kickinghorse River; magnificent scenery.

**Kid,** goatskin leather L-174, G-144d
■ imitation G-147

**Kidd, Benjamin** (1858–1916), English sociologist; his 'Social Evolution' (1894) is one of the most widely read books in its field, having been translated into many languages.

**Kidd, Michael** (born 1919), dancer and choreographer, born New York City; has danced with leading ballet companies in U.S.; created ballet 'On Stage!', also has staged dances and musical numbers for musical plays and for motion pictures.

**Kidd, William, Captain** (1645?–1701), British pirate K-48b, *picture* K-48b

**Kidderminster,** England, town in Worcestershire on Stour River; pop. 46,740; noted for manufacture of carpets: *map* G-199h

**"Kiddieland,"** amusement park development A-386

**'Kidnapped',** a tale of adventure by Robert Louis Stevenson (1886) in which the hero, David Balfour, after being kidnapped and cast away on a desert island, meets the Jacobite, Alan Breck Stewart. 'David Balfour', a sequel, completes their adventures.

**Kidnapping** F-80, U-160
■ ancient Greeks for slave labor G-224
■ Lindbergh case L-289
■ Pacific islanders P-15. *see also in index* Blackbirding

**Kidney,** animal
■ polio vaccine source, *pictures* V-251–2

**Kidney,** human K-48b–9, *diagrams* K-49
■ anatomy A-391
■ artificial B-211
■ diseases D-130, K-49, *picture* D-130
■ hormone affects H-225
■ transplant S-519d
■ watermelon juice W-74

**Kidney diseases,** commonly the result of inflammation or damage to the blood vessels of the kidneys; severe forms lead to breakdown of normal elimination of waste products: D-130, K-49, W-74, *picture* D-130
■ poisoning M-226

**Kido** [*kē'dō*], **Takayoshi** (1832–77), Japanese statesman, plotted and carried through the coup d'état of 1868; advocate of Western civilization and constitutional government; founder of first real Japanese newspaper.

**Kidron, Valley of.** *see in index* Kedron

**Kidskin** L-174, G-144d

**Kieffer pear** P-147

**Kieft** [*kēft*], **William (Wilhelmus)** (1597–1647), director general of Dutch colony of New Netherland 1638–47; unpopular for his tyrannical methods; held responsible for massacre of River Indians 1643 and beginning of disastrous wars between colonists and Indians
■ prohibits smoking, *picture* I-316

**Kiel** [*kēl*], West Germany, former naval port on Baltic; pop. 271,719; shipbuilding; university; terminus of Kiel Canal; scene of German naval mutiny in 1918: *maps* G-114, E-334

**Kiel, Peace of,** treaty by which Denmark ceded Norway to Sweden in 1814, as compensation for Sweden's having lost Finland to Russia. By an Act of Union (1815) Norway was to be independent of Sweden, but with same king.

**Kiel Canal,** West Germany, strategic and commercial canal in Schleswig-Holstein, s. of Denmark; connects the Baltic and the North seas; runs from Holtenau on the Baltic to Brunsbüttelkoog at estuary of the Elbe River: C-118, H-125, *maps* G-99a, 114
■ Baltic Sea B-46

**Kielce** [*kyĕl'tsĕ*], Poland, city in mountains 155 km (95 mi) s. of Warsaw; pop. 83,000; manufactures hemp, brick, paint: *map* E-335

**Kielland** [*kĕl'län*], **Alexander** (1849–1906), Norwegian novelist, born Stavanger, Norway; keen psychologist and critic of society in charming, witty manner ('Garman and Worse'; 'Skipper Worse'; 'Snow'; 'Jacob').

**Kienzl** [*kĕn'ts'l*], **Wilhelm** (1857–1941), Austrian composer, born Waizenkirchen, near Linz, Austria; songs, instrumental pieces, and operas; wrote music for 'Oesterreichische Bundeshymne', patriotic song of Austrian republic 1920–29.

**Kiepura** [*kyĕ-pụ'rä*], **Jan** (1902–66), American operatic tenor, born Sosnowiec, Poland; European debut, Warsaw, 1925; American debut, Chicago Civic Opera House, 1931; often called "Polish Caruso"; also popular as motion-picture star.

**Kierkegaard** [*kĭr'kĕ-ġär*], **Sören** (1813–55), Danish philosopher and theologian, born Copenhagen; influenced religious thought and literary style in Denmark; some of his principles and ideas adopted by existentialists ('A Kierkegaard Anthology'; 'The Living Thoughts of Kierkegaard', edited by W. H. Auden): P-266, 267

**Kieselguhr** M-332, D-104, F-357

**Kiesinger** [*kē'zĭng-ẽr*], **Kurt Georg** (born 1904), German public official, born Ebingen; Nazi 1933–45, Christian Democrat 1948–; member Bundestag 1949–58; governor of Baden-Württemberg 1958–66; chancellor West Germany 1966–69: G-112, *picture* I-239h

**Kiesling, Walt(er)** (1903–62), football coach and guard, born St. Paul, Minn.; guard 1926–36 for Duluth Eskimos, Pottsville Maroons, Chicago Cardinals, Chicago Bears, Green Bay Packers; coach 1939–61 for Pittsburgh Steelers, Philadelphia-Pittsburgh, and Chicago-Pittsburgh: *list* F-337

**Kiev** [*kē'yĕf*], Russia, capital of Ukrainian S.S.R.; pop. 1,632,000: K-49, U-2, *maps* R-322, 344, 349, E-335, W-253, *picture* U-2
■ Christianity introduced R-351
■ dam, *table* D-12
■ early history R-351
■ location, *locator map* K-49
■ summer camp, *picture* C-359
■ World War II K-49, W-270

**Kiev Dam,** in Russia, on Dnieper River, *table* D-12

**Kigali** [*kē-ġä'lē*], Rwanda, capital; pop. 14,000: R-366a

**Kigoma-Ujiji** [*kē-ġō'mạ-ụ-ġē'ġē*], Tanzania, port town in Tanganyika on Lake Tanganyika; pop. 21,369; serves as headquarters for Kigoma Region (area about 17,400 sq mi; 45,100 sq km)

**Kikuyu,** Negro people of east Africa dwelling in highlands w. of Mt. Kenya; rather small but strong and muscular: K-44, *picture* K-45

**Kilauea** [*kē-lou-ā'ạ*] **Crater,** volcano on island of Hawaii, part of Hawaii Volcanoes National Park: N-39, H-52, *maps* H-52, 71

**Kilbane, John (Johnny) Patrick** (1889–1957), featherweight champion boxer B-392

**Kildare** [*kĭl-dâr'*], county of e.-central Ireland in province of Leinster; 1694 sq km (654 sq mi); pop. 66,404; agricultural; Kildare is county seat: *map* I-283

**Kildare,** Ireland, old town in County Kildare, 50 sq km (30 mi) s.w. of Dublin; pop. 2731; originated in nunnery founded 5th century by St. Bridget: *map* G-199h

**Kilgore,** Tex., city 10 mi (16 km) s.w. of Longview; pop 10,968; livestock; oil refining; varied manufactures, including tools and ceramic goods; incorporated 1931 after 1930 boom in oil: *map* T-128

**Kilimanjaro** [*kĭl-ē-män-ġä'rō*], volcanic mountain, in n. Tanganyika, Tanzania; two main peaks linked by saddle 7 mi. long: Mt. Kibo (19,340 ft; 5895 m), highest peak of Africa, and Mt. Mawenzi (17,564 ft; 5353 m) A-94, *picture* T-16
■ height, comparative. *see in index* Mountain, *table*

**Kilim rugs** R-314

**Kilindini,** Kenya. *see in index* Mombasa

**Kilkenny,** Ireland, town 105 km (65 mi) s.w. of Dublin; pop. 10,052; has great 13th-century cathedral; capital of Kilkenny County (2062 sq km [796 sq mi]; pop. 60,463); the story of the Kilkenny cats which fought until nothing was left but their tails is said to be a satire on the long-standing boundary dispute between Kilkenny and its neighbor, Irishtown: *maps* G-199h, I-283, *picture* I-285

**Killarney** [*kĭ-lär'nĭ*], Ireland, market town in s.w.; pop. 6877: K-50, *map* G-199h, *picture* K-50
■ jaunting car, *picture* I-284

**Killarney Lakes,** Ireland K-50, *map* G-199h, *picture* K-50

**Killdeer,** or **killdee,** a North American plover P-391
■ egg, *picture* E-105

**Kill Devil Hills,** N.C. *see in index* Wright Brothers National Memorial

**Killeen,** Tex., city 45 mi (72 km) s.w. of Waco; pop. 46,296; in area of sheep and cattle ranching; construction industries; doors, windows, and screens; computer science center; adjacent to Fort Hood; founded 1882: *map* T-128

**Killer whale.** *see in index* Grampus

**Killian, James R(hyne), Jr.** (born 1904), educator, born Blacksburg, S.C.; joined executive staff Massachusetts Institute of Technology 1939, vice-president 1945–48, president 1949–59, corporation chairman 1959–71; special assistant to President Eisenhower for science and technology 1957–59.

**Killiecrankie** [*kĭl-ĭ-krăng'kĭ*], pass in Perthshire, Scotland; Viscount Dundee, leader of Jacobite Highlanders, killed in victory over royal forces 1689.

**Killingly** [*kĭl'ng-lē*], Conn., 24 mi (39 km) n.e. of Norwich; pop. of township 13,573; settled 1693, incorporated 1708: *map* C-533

**Kill van Kull** [*kĭl văn kŭl*], strait connecting Upper New York Bay and Newark Bay, between Staten Island, N.Y., and Bayonne, N.J.: N-187, *map* N-272

**Killy** [*kē-lē*], **Jean Claude** (born 1943), French ski champion, born Saint-Cloud, suburb of Paris; international downhill and combined championships 1966–67, 1967–68; in 1968 became second in history to win Olympic triple crown, competition at Grenoble, France; starred in motion picture, 'Snow Job'.

**Kilmainham Treaty,** agreement between William Gladstone and Charles Stewart Parnell, signed at Kilmainham, w. suburb of Dublin, Ireland.

**Kilmarnock** [*kĭl-mär'nŏk*], Scotland, town on Kilmarnock Water, in Ayrshire 30 km (20 mi) s.w. of Glasgow; pop. 47,631; textiles, machinery; first edition of Robert Burns's poems published here 1786: *map* G-199g

**Kilmer, Joyce** (Alfred Joyce Kilmer) (1886–1918), American poet, essayist, journalist K-50, *pictures* K-50, N-200

**Kiln** [*kĭln*], oven for burning or baking industrial products
■ brick B-436
■ cementmaking C-188, *pictures* C-186–7: early types C-189
■ pottery P-478, *picture* P-477

**Kilocalorie** F-309

**Kilocycle,** in radio R-45, *tables* R-50, 54, R-34

**Kilogram,** a unit of weight in the metric system (2.204 lbs.) M-236, W-95, *diagram* W-95
■ international, *picture* W-94

**Kiloliter,** a unit of volume in the metric system (264.17 gals.)

**Kilometer,** a metric unit of length (3280 ft.) M-236, *table* W-97
■ astronomy A-714

**Kilowatt** E-141

**Kilpatrick, Hugh Judson** (1836–81), Union general in Civil War, born near Newton, N.J.; brilliant cavalry leader; commanded cavalry of Sherman's army (1864) in march from Atlanta to Savannah.

**Kilpatrick, William Heard** (1871–1965), educator, born White Plains, Ga.; professor philosophy of education, Teachers College, Columbia University, 1918–38: *table* E-90

**Kilt** S-68, *pictures* S-70, C-398
■ Scottish regiments wear U-12

**Kilwa Kivinje,** Tanzania, seaport in Tanganyika on Indian Ocean; pop. 2828; Kilwa Kisiwani, an early town, is on island to the s.

**Kim,** Korean surname K-75b

**'Kim',** novel by Kipling in which the hero, Kimball O'Hara, nicknamed "Kim," roams through India with a Tibetan priest: K-60, R-111d

**Kimberley,** B.C., Canada, city in s.e. 26 km (16 mi) n.w. of Cranbrook; pop. 7641; mining region.

**Kimberley,** South Africa, diamond-mining center, Cape of Good Hope Province; pop. 105,258: *maps* S-264
■ diamond mines D-100, S-267
■ Rhodes at R-193

**Kimberlite,** a blue rock D-100, *diagram* D-102

**Kimbrough, Emily** (born 1899), author and editor, born Muncie, Ind. ('How Dear to My Heart'; 'Water, Water Everywhere'; 'Forever Old, Forever New').

**Kimchi** [*kĭm'chē*], Korean food K-75c

**Kimigayo** [*kĭ-mĭ-ġä-yō*], national anthem of Japan
■ reproduced J-376

**Kim Il Sung** [*sụng*] (born 1912), North Korean political and military leader, born Pyongyang, present North Korea; a founder of Communist Youth League 1927; commander-in-chief of North Korean People's Army 1950–53; chief secretary Communist Party of Korea 1945–; chairman North Korean provisional government 1946–47; premier North Korea 1948–72; president 1972–: K-77, 76h

**Kim Koo** (1875–1949), Korean political leader, born Haeju; anti-Japanese nationalist; committed life to independence movement; assassinated by political enemy.

**Kimmel, Husband E(dward)** (1882–1968), U.S. Navy officer, born Henderson, Ky.; commander in chief of U.S. Fleet, in Hawaii at time of Japanese attack on Pearl Harbor 1941; relieved of command; found derelict of duty 1942 by presidential inquiry board, charges minimized to errors of judgment in 1946 Congressional investigation.

**Kimono** [*kĭ-mō'nŏ*], Japanese garment J-374, 371, D-194, *pictures* J-371, C-398, T-44

**Kim Sowol** (1903–34), Korean poet, born Kwaksan; typifies the simple beauty of Korean literature: K-76b

**Kim Yong Ik** (born 1920), Korean writer, educated in Japan and U.S. (nonfiction: 'Moons of Korea'; children's books: 'The Happy Days' 'Blue in the Seed'; novel: 'The Diving Gourd'; short stories: 'Love in Winter').

**Kim Yusin** (595–673), Korean general and political leader of Silla dynasty; led wars for unification of Korean peninsula.

**Kina,** monetary unit of Papua New Guinea: *table* M-428

**Kinard, Frank** (Bruiser) (born 1914), football tackle, born Pelahatchie, Miss.: *list* F-337

**Kinases,** enzymes B-202

**Kinchinjunga,** mountain. *see in index* Kanchenjunga

**Kinck** [*kĭngk*], **Hans** (1865–1926), Norwegian writer, born Oksfjord, n. Norway ('The Avalanche', a novel; 'The Cattle Dealer', a play).

**Kindergarten** K-51–3, E-96, *pictures* K-51–3. *see also in index* Nursery school
■ first in U.S. W-196, K-53
■ Froebel F-447, E-86, K-53
■ Italy, *picture* I-332
■ language arts, *picture* L-121
■ Montessori Method M-474, *pictures* K-51–2
■ physical education K-53, H-103, *picture* K-51
■ Russia R-332c

**Kindling** C-66, *picture* C-65

**Kindling point,** or **ignition point** F-122–3, *table* F-123

**Kinematics** S-61d

**Kiner, Ralph** (born 1922), baseball player, born Santa Rita, N.M.; outfielder, N.L. 1946–54, A.L. 1955.

**Kinescope,** or **picture tube,** in television T-71, 74, C-451, *diagrams* T-72–3
■ production G-139

**Kinesics** [*kĭ-nē'sĭks*], the scientific study of body language such as a wink, a blush, used in place of verbal communication: L-115c, d, *pictures* L-115d–e
■ acting techniques A-25

**Kinesthetic sense,** S-109
■ learning and L-170

**Kinetic energy,** in physics E-204, 207–8, 210, M-210, H-109, G-61, *pictures* E-204, 206

**Kinetics** S-61d

**Kinetic theory of matter** H-109

**Kinetograph,** early motion-picture camera M-518, E-72, *picture* E-71

**Kinetoscope,** movie projector M-518, E-72, *picture* M-519

**King, Basil (William Benjamin)** (1859–1928), Canadian poet and novelist; born Charlottetown, P. E. I. ('The Inner Shrine'; 'Wild Olive'; 'The Street Called Straight').

**King, Clarence** (1842–1901), geologist, born Newport, R.I.; led survey of 40th parallel across Rockies; first director U.S. Geological Survey 1879.

**King, Coretta (Scott)** (born 1925), lecturer and writer, born Marion, Ala.; noted for her work with civil rights and peace organizations; wife of Martin Luther King, Jr.: K-54, 55

**King, Ernest Joseph** (1878–1956), U.S. Navy officer, born Lorain, Ohio; commander in chief of Atlantic Fleet 1940–41; commander in chief of the U.S. Fleet 1941; chief of naval operations 1942–45; appointed fleet (5-star) admiral 1944; coauthor of 'Fleet Admiral King, a Naval Record': W-273

**King, Martin Luther, Jr.** (1929–68), American integration leader and clergyman K-54–5, P-143d, *pictures* K-54–5, G-90
■ assassination A-704
■ Baptist ministers B-76
■ bibliography K-55
■ birthday celebrated F-91, 92
■ civil rights movement A-742, B-76
■ grave K-55
■ "I Have a Dream" speech K-55, L-207, *pictures* K-55, L-306a
■ Nobel prize, *table* N-294h
■ Selma march K-54, *picture* U-195
■ 'Stride Toward Freedom' R-111i

**King, Rufus** (1755–1827), statesman, born Scarboro, Me., then part of Massachusetts; member Constitutional Convention; signed United States Constitution for Massachusetts; U.S. senator 1789–96, and minister to England: M-456

**King, Thomas Starr** (1824–64), Unitarian clergyman, born New York City; popular lyceum lecturer; helped keep California in Union
■ Statuary Hall, *table* S-437a

**King, Wayne** (born 1901), saxophonist and orchestra leader, born Savanna, Ill.; exponent of "sweet" music.

**King, William** (1768–1852), statesman, born Scarboro, Me., then part of Massachusetts; first governor of Maine (1820–21); shipbuilder and owner, leading citizen of Bath; led 7-year struggle for separation of Maine from Massachusetts
■ Statuary Hall, *table* S-437a

**King, William Lyon Mackenzie** (1874–1950), Canadian statesman K-56, C-112e, f, *picture* K-56
■ boyhood home, Woodside N.H.P. N-24d, *map* N-24b

**King, William Rufus** (1786–1853), statesman, born Sampson County, N.C.; House of Representatives 1810–16; U.S. Senate 1819–44; *picture* N-334
■ vice-president, *table* V-310

**King,** a male sovereign of a nation, tribe, or territory; title usually hereditary and for life; comes from Anglo-Saxon *cyning* meaning "belonging to the tribe": G-164, D-82. *see also in index* kings by name; for tables, *see* Denmark; England; France, history of
■ abdications. *see in index* Abdications, *table*
■ constitutional monarchy D-85, U-17, *picture* D-85
■ divine right. *see in index* Divine right of kings
■ Egypt E-115. *see also in index* Pharaohs
■ Greece G-217, 218, 219
□ ancient G-221–2, 223, 225, S-369, T-159, *see also in index* Alexander the Great
■ Jews, ancient J-456–7. *see also in index* David; Solomon
■ Norway N-367–8, 369, 366, O-505c–d, H-1, *picture* D-85: Saur, dog "king," *list* D-137
■ origin of G-163
■ Persia (Iran): ancient P-211–12, 213, P-214, 215, D-34, *picture* P-213; shah I-279–80, P-214
■ Rome R-240–1, E-303, N-13

**'King and I, The',** musical comedy by Rodgers and Hammerstein O-464a

**Kingbird** K-56, F-282, *picture* F-282
■ western, or Arkansas, kingbird K-56

**King bird of paradise,** *picture* P-110

**King cobra,** or **hamadryad,** a large, venomous snake C-422, *pictures* C-422

**King College,** at Bristol, Tenn.; affiliated with Presbyterian church, U.S.; opened 1867; arts and sciences, teacher education.

**King crab,** also called **spider,** or **Japanese, crab** C-599. *see also in index* Horseshoe crab

**Kingdom,** in plant and animal classification L-259, *diagram* Z-366, *pictures* L-258

**King Edward's School,** Birmingham B-282

**Kingfish,** excellent food fish (*Menticirrhus*); dull in color; abundant in shallow water from Cape Ann, n.e. Massachusetts; name also for large Spanish mackerel (*Scomberomorus*) of West Indies.

**Kingfisher** (ancient name **halcyon**), a fish-eating bird K-56

**King George VI Falls,** in branch of Mazaruni River, n.w. Guyana, near Mount Roraima: *table* W-73c

**King George's War,** name given by English colonists to conflict in America between French and English 1744–48: K-57

**'King Henry IV',** one of best of Shakespeare's historical plays; in two parts; concerns life of Henry IV, featuring Prince Hal, Henry's son, and Falstaff, comic character
■ chronology of play S-133
■ rank of play S-139

**'King Henry V',** historical drama by Shakespeare; concerns Prince Hal, now wise King Henry V, up to marriage with Katherine of France
■ chronology of play S-133
■ rank of play S-139

**'King Henry VI',** historical drama in three divisions, most of which Shakespeare wrote or revised
■ chronology of play S-133
■ rank of play S-139

**'King Henry VIII',** historical drama by Shakespeare; concerns life of Henry with Queen Katherine and with Anne Boleyn, ending with christening of Elizabeth
■ chronology of play S-133
■ quoted W-212
■ rank of play S-139

**King James Version,** of Bible E-257

**'King John',** Shakespeare's earliest historical play, concerns John, usurper of English throne, and his struggle to keep power from his nephew Arthur, rightful heir
■ chronology of play S-133
■ rank of play S-139

**'King Lear',** tragedy by Shakespeare K-57, *picture* E-257
■ appreciation S-139–40
■ chronology of play S-133
■ rank of play S-139

**Kinglets,** birds K-57

**Kingmaker, The.** *see in index* Warwick, Richard Neville, earl of

**Kingman, Dong (Moy Shu)** (born 1911), watercolorist, illustrator, and teacher; born Oakland, Calif.; Chinese parentage; background scenes for movie 'Flower Drum Song'; his skill and integrity of style have earned him many awards.

**Kingman,** Ariz., city 65 mi (105 km) s.e. of Hoover Dam; pop. 9257; mining, livestock, light industry; tourist center; incorporated 1952.

**Kingman Reef,** U.S. naval base in Pacific, 1770 km (1100 mi) s. of Honolulu; 1 sq. mi.: *map* H-71

**King of beasts,** title usually given to the lion L-296–7, *pictures* L-296–7

**'King of the Golden River, The',** fairy tale by John Ruskin (1851); a dwarf king rewards Gluck for his kindness and punishes his brothers Hans and Schwartz for their cruelty.

**'King of the Wind',** story by Marguerite Henry H-238, *picture* H-238

**King penguin** P-160, 162

**King Philip's War** (1675–76), led by King Philip, chief of Wampanoag Indians, against New England colonists: K-57, I-144b
■ Great Swamp Fight, *picture* R-185
■ Springfield burned S-398

**King rail** R-71, *picture* R-71

**'King Rat',** work by Clavell A-361

**'King Richard II',** historical drama by Shakespeare in which King Richard's insincerity leads to his murder
■ chronology of play S-133
■ rank of play S-139

**'King Richard III',** historical tragedy by Shakespeare; ruthless king is slain in battle: R-203
■ chronology of play S-133
■ Olivier as Richard III, *picture* S-141
■ rank of play S-139

**Kings,** eleventh and twelfth books of the Old Testament, usually written I Kings and II Kings, dealing with the period that embraces the reigns of all the kings of Israel except Saul and David.

**King salmon, Chinook salmon,** or **tyee salmon** S-28, *picture* F-172

**King's Bench** (or **Queen's Bench**), **Court of,** in England C-594

**Kings Canyon National Park,** in California N-40a, *maps* C-53, N-30

**King's College,** at Briarcliff Manor, N.Y.; private control; founded 1938; liberal arts, teacher education.

**King's College,** at Toronto, Canada, now University of Toronto: T-211

**King's College,** at Wilkes-Barre, Pa.; private control; chartered 1946; arts and sciences, teacher education.

**King's College, University of,** at Halifax, N.S., Canada; Anglican; founded 1789 at Windsor; royal charter 1802; moved to Halifax 1923; arts and sciences, journalism, theology: N-373f, U-210–11, *picture* N-373e

**King's evil.** *see in index* Scrofula

**Kingsford, William** (1819–98), Canadian engineer and historian, born London, England; surveyed Lachine Canal; helped build Hudson River Railroad and Panama Railroad; was Dominion engineer in charge of St. Lawrence River and the Great Lakes ('History of Canada').

**Kingsford-Smith.** *see in index* Smith, Sir Charles Edward Kingsford

**'King's Henchman, The',** work by Millay, M-325

**King's Highway,** or **King's Way,** historical road in United States R-221, P-169

**King's Highway,** or **Royal Road,** in California. *see in index* Camino Real

**Kingsley, Charles** (1819–75), English clergyman and author K-58, S-481b

**Kingsley, Henry** (1830–76), English novelist, born Barnack, Northamptonshire; brother of Charles Kingsley ('Ravenshoe'): A-797

**Kingsley, Mary Henrietta** (1862–1900), English author and ethnologist, born London; niece of Charles Kingsley; wrote on w. Africa.

**Kingsley, Sidney** (real name Kirshner) (born 1906), playwright, born New York City; 'Men in White', Pulitzer prize play (1934), about a city hospital; 'Dead End', pungent drama of a tough gang of New York City boys; 'The Patriots', about Thomas Jefferson and Alexander Hamilton, written with wife **Madge (Evans) Kingsley** (1909–81), actress: D-176, A-356

**Kingsley Dam,** in Nebraska, on North Platte River N-109, *map* N-120, 108

**Kings Mountain,** 8-mile (13-kilometer) ridge extending from near Kings Mountain (city), N.C., into South Carolina; a spur of the ridge in South Carolina, where Americans defeated British October 1780: S-118, S-306, T-83, *maps* S-318, N-336
■ Kings Mountain N. Mil. P. N-40a, *map* S-318

**King snake** S-226a, c, *pictures* S-224, 225

**Kings Park,** N.Y., village 35 mi (55 km) n.e. of New York City on Long Island; pop. 5555; Sunken Meadow State Park nearby: *map, inset* N-260

**Kings Peak,** Utah, in Uinta range of Rocky Mountains; highest point in state (13,498 ft; 4114 m): *maps* U-232, 217

**Kings Point,** N.Y., village on n.w. Long Island 8 mi (13 km) n. of Jamaica; pop. 5234; United States Merchant Marine Academy: *map, inset* N-260. *see also in index* United States Merchant Marine Academy

**Kingsport,** Tenn., city on Holston River 88 mi (142 km) n.e. of Knoxville; pop. 32,027; book manufacturing, chemicals, plastics, synthetic yarn, glass, paper, textiles: *map* T-97

**King's Rangers.** *see in index* Rogers, Robert

**Kingston, Charles Cameron** (1850–1908), Australian statesman; premier of South Australia 1893–99; helped to pass radical laws.

**Kingston,** Jamaica, capital and chief port, on s.e. coast; pop. 117,900; noted for excellent harbor; resort; coffee center; food processing; oil refining: J-358, *maps* W-104, C-628
■ Round Hill, *picture* J-359
■ U.S. naval and air base nearby J-358

**Kingston,** N.Y., city on Hudson River, about 52 mi (84 km) s. of Albany; pop. 24,481; electronics, clothing, cement, boats, brick, wood and metal products; founded by Dutch 1652; first state constitutional convention temporary capital 1777; burned by British same year: *map* N-261

**Kingston,** Ont., Canada, at n.e. end of Lake Ontario, historic city commanding entrance to St. Lawrence River; pop. 59,047: K-58, *maps* O-457, C-99
■ beach, *picture* G-206
■ Bellevue House N.H.P. N-24b, O-456i, *map* N-24b
■ location K-58, *locator map* K-58
■ Royal Military College C-100d

**Kingston,** Pa., borough on Susquehanna River opposite Wilkes-Barre; pop. 15,681; coal, cigars, rayon and nylon textiles; site of Forty Fort (built 1772) nearby: *map* P-185

**Kingston-upon-Hull,** England. *see in index* Hull

**Kingstown,** Ireland. *see in index* Dun Laoghaire

**Kingsville,** Tex., city 35 mi (55 km) s.w. of Corpus Christi; pop. 28,808; dairying, ranching; oil center; railroad shops; chemicals; Texas College of Arts and Industries; nearby is the headquarters of famous King Ranch (about 823,400 acres; 333,200 hectares acquired by Richard King, a Rio Grande steamboat captain); first unit of ranch established 1854; Kingsville Naval Air Station near city: *map* T-129

**Kingtehchen** [*gĭng'dŭ'gŭn'*], or **Ching-te-chen,** also **Fowliang,** People's Republic of China, city in n.e. Kiangsi Province, just e. of Poyang Lake; pop. 300,000: *map* C-313
■ porcelain center P-470

**King vulture** V-388, B-280

**King Wilhelm Land,** in n.e. Greenland

**King William Island,** in District of Franklin, Northwest Territories, Canada, s.e. of Victoria Island; area 12,615 sq km (4870 sq mi): *map* C-98
■ Franklin's expedition perished P-419

**King William's War** (1689–97), colonial war in North America K-58
■ Frontenac F-463
■ Kidd, Captain, privateer K-48b
■ Schenectady massacre S-52h

**Kinkajou** (*Cercoleptes caudivolvulus*), small mammal of the raccoon family; common in tropical regions of Americas; eats honey, eggs, small mammals; sometimes called a "honey bear"; often a pet; fur used commercially

**Kinley, David** (1861–1944), American educator and economist, born Scotland; to U.S. 1872; taught at Goucher College and University of Wisconsin; at University of Illinois after 1893, president 1920–30.

**Kinnaird, Mary Jane** (Mrs. Arthur F. Kinnaird) (1816–88), English philanthropist, born Blatherwick Park, Northamptonshire; one of founders of YWCA.

**Kinneret, Lake.** *see in index* Tiberias, Lake

**Kino** [*kē'nō*], **Eusebio** (1645?–1711), Jesuit missionary, born Segno, n. Italy; founder of missions in American Southwest: S-338, A-602
■ Casa Grande Ruins N. Mon. N-33, *maps* N-30, *picture* N-33
■ Organ Pipe Cactus N. Mon. N-42, *maps* A-547, N-30
■ Statuary Hall, *table* S-437a
■ Tumacacori N. Mon. N-46, *map* N-30

**Kinsey, Alfred Charles** (1894–1956), zoologist, born Hoboken, N.J.; on faculty Indiana University 1920–56, professor of zoology 1929–56; directed studies on human sex behavior supported by Indiana University and by Rockefeller Foundation (through National Research Council) 1938–56; with others, author of 'Sexual Behavior in the Human Male' and 'Sexual Behavior in the Human Female'; authority on gall wasps.

**Kinshasa** [*kĭn-shäs'a*], formerly **Léopoldville,** Republic of Zaire, capital, along s. bank of the Congo River; pop. 2,710,300 (1977 est.): K-59, Z-353a, C-513, 514
■ location K-59, *locator map* K-59
■ schoolroom, *picture* Z-353
■ university L-243

**Kinston,** N.C., city on Neuse River, 70 mi (115 km) s.e. of Raleigh; pop. 25,234; tobacco marketing and processing, textiles, apparel, fertilizer, concrete products, lumber; state school for mentally retarded children; Dobbs Farm (state correctional institution): *map* N-337

**Kinzie, John** (1763–1828), American pioneer fur trader, born Quebec, Canada; first white settler of Chicago, Ill.; grandfather of Juliette Low: C-262

**Kioga, Lake,** in Uganda

**Kioto,** Japan. *see in index* Kyoto

**Kiowa,** Indian tribe, formerly ranging in Oklahoma, Colorado, and Texas; now chiefly on reservation in Oklahoma: O-435, *map* I-134, *picture* I-113, *table* I-136
■ buffalo dance, *picture* I-115
■ calendar, *picture* I-138
■ 'Winter-Telling Stories' S-481d

**Kipchaks** [*kĭp-chäks'*], branch of the Mongols M-435

**Kipling, John Lockwood** (1837–1911), British artist and educator; father of Rudyard Kipling: K-59, 60

**Kipling, Rudyard** (1865–1936), English writer, famous for stories of India: K-59–61, E-268, *picture* K-59
■ bibliography K-61
■ 'Captains Courageous' K-60
■ 'Jungle Books, The' K-59, 60, R-111a: 'All the Mowgli Stories', *picture* K-60
■ 'Just So Stories' R-110a, K-59, S-464
■ 'Kim'. *see in index* 'Kim'
■ Nobel prize K-61, *table* N-294f
■ verse, quoted R-130

**Kiplinger, W(illard) M(onroe)** (1891–1967), journalist and publisher, born Bellefontaine, Ohio; editor *Kiplinger Washington Letter* 1923–67 and *Changing Times* 1947–67; author 'Washington Is Like That'.

**Kipnis, Alexander** (1896–1978), American operatic bass, born Zhitomir, Russia; studied in Berlin, Germany; member, Metropolitan Opera Company, New York City, 1939–46.

**Kippered herring,** a herring which has been split, salted, dried, and smoked: H-148

**Kirby, Rollin** (1875–1952), cartoonist, born Galva, Ill.; cartoonist on *New York Mail, New York Sun;* political cartoonist, *New York World* 1914–31, *New York World Telegram* 1931–39, New York Post 1939–42; did cartoons for *Look* and *New York Times Magazine;* won Pulitzer prize three times: C-145c

**Kirby, William** (1817–1906), Canadian novelist, born Kingston-upon-Hull, England; edited *Niagara* (Ontario) *Mail* for 20 years; collector of customs, Niagara 1871–95 ('The Golden Dog'; 'U.E.', an epic poem; 'Canadian Idylls'): C-113b, *picture* C-113a

**Kirby-Smith, Edmund.** *see in index* Smith, Edmund Kirby

**Kirchhoff** [*kĭrk'hôf*], **Gustav Robert** (1824–87), German physicist, born Königsberg, East Prussia (now Kaliningrad, Russia); developed spectrum analysis and discovered cesium and rubidium (with Bunsen); explained the Fraunhofer lines; professor of physics at Heidelberg 1854–74, at Berlin 1874–87
■ spectroscopic discoveries S-371, P-303

**Kirghiz** [*kĭr-gēz'*], one of a nomadic people of central Asia, of Turko-Tataric (Mongolian) race, ranging from borders of European Russia to w. China: *picture* A-680

**Kirghiz Soviet Socialist Republic,** of Russia, in central Asia; area 198,000 sq km (76,450 sq mi); pop. 2,933,000; cap. Frunze: U-14, *maps* U-14, R-325, 344

**Kiribati,** formerly Gilbert Islands, nation in Pacific; consists of Gilbert Islands, Ocean Island, Phoenix Islands, and eight of the Line Islands including Washington Island, Fanning Island, and Christmas Island; 710 sq km (275 sq mi); pop. 55,000; cap. Bairiki; most of area under British protection 1892–1979; self-governing since 1977; independent since 1979: *map* P-4–5. *see also in index* names of islands

**Kirin** [*kē'rĭn'*], a province in n.e. part of People's Republic of China; area 73,000 sq mi (189,000 sq km); pop. 20,412,000; cap. Changchun: M-83, C-293a, *maps* M-84, C-293, C-313, *picture* C-299
■ minerals M-84

**Kirin,** People's Republic of China, city on Sungari River in Kirin Province; pop. 720,000; chemical industries powered by Sungari hydroelectric plant: M-84, *maps* M-84, C-313

**Kirizuma** [*kĭr-ĭ-zu-mä*], Japanese roof style, *diagram* J-373

**Kirk, Grayson (Louis)** (born 1903), educator, born near Jeffersonville, Ohio; joined faculty of Columbia University 1940, became professor of government 1943, provost 1949–53, vice-president 1950–53, acting head during Dwight D. Eisenhower's leave of absence 1951–53, president 1953–68.

**Kirkland,** Wash., city on inlet of Puget Sound 10 mi (16 km) n.e. of Seattle; pop. 18,779; furniture, paint, feed mill; *map, inset* W-52

**Kirklareli** [*kĭrk-lär-ĕ-lē'*], formerly **Kirk-Kilissa,** European Turkey, town: pop. 20,196; mosques and Greek churches; scene of first important Bulgarian victory over Turks in Balkan War of 1912.

**Kirkpatrick, Jeane J.** (born 1926), political scientist and diplomat, born Duncan, Okla.; associate professor of political science Georgetown University 1967–73, professor after 1973; member Democratic National Committee after 1972; campaigned for Ronald Reagan in 1980 presidential race; chief U.S. delegate to UN 1981–: R-112j

**Kirkstall Abbey,** at Leeds, England L-184

**Kirksville,** Mo., city about 75 mi (120 km) n.w. of Hannibal; pop. 17,167; shoes, gloves, dairy products, printing; Northeast Missouri State University: *map* M-408
■ American School of Osteopathy O-505d

**Kirkuk** [*kĭr-kuk'*], Iraq, city 150 mi (240 km) n. of Baghdad; pop. 187,509; oil center; in dry-farming region; distributing point for grains, fruit, cotton, wool, cattle, gallnuts, and tragacanth: *map* I-280

**Kirkwall,** Orkney Islands, capital; important British base during World War I; pop. 4688; fine Norman-Gothic cathedral begun in 1138: O-505a, *map* G-199g

**Kirkwood, Samuel Jordan** (1813–94), political leader, born Harford County, Md.; Civil War governor of Iowa; U.S. senator; secretary of interior under President Garfield: *picture* I-272
■ Statuary Hall, *table* S-437a

**Kirkwood,** Mo., city 12 mi (19 km) w. of St. Louis; pop. 27,987; residential suburb with varied manufactures including cement and wood products; horticulture; founded 1853, incorporated 1865: *map, inset* M-409

**Kirman,** Iran. *see in index* Kerman

**Kirsten, Dorothy** (born 1917) (Mrs. John Douglas French), concert and operatic soprano, born Montclair, N.J.; United States debut 1940; member of Metropolitan Opera Co., New York City, from 1945.

**Kirstein, Lincoln** (born 1907), U.S. businessman and dance authority B-22

**Kiruna,** Sweden, city n. of Arctic Circle; pop. 23,279; iron mining: S-523, *maps* S-524, N-365, F-119, *pictures* S-526, E-316

**Kisaeng** [*kē'săng*], traditional Korean female singer and dancer at the feast; some famed for interest in poetry, calligraphy, and painting; originally a low caste serving ruling aristocracy.

**Kisangani** [*kē-san-gän'ē*], formerly **Stanleyville,** Zaire, city on Congo River below Stanley Falls; railroad around falls; pop. 362,009: Z-353a, C-513, 514

**Kish,** Mesopotamia (Iraq), ancient city near the Euphrates River, 8 mi (13 km) e. of Babylon: K-61

**Kishi, Nobusuke** (born 1896), Japanese statesman, born Yamaguchi, s.w. Honshu; prime minister 1957–60; president Liberal-Democratic party 1957–60; pro-Western: J-411

**Kishinev** [*kĭsh'ĭ-nĕf*], Rumanian **Chisinau** [*kē-shē-nü'u*], Russia, capital of Moldavian S.S.R., 155 km (95 mi) n.w. of Odessa; pop. 357,000; agricultural center; ceded by Russia to Rumania after World War I; returned to Russia 1940; terrible pogroms (1903, 1905): *maps* R-344, 349, E-335

**Kiska Island,** largest of Rat Islands in Aleutians: *map, inset* U-39
■ World War II W-272, 294

**Kismayu** [*kĭs-mä'yu*], or **Chisimaio** [*kē-zē-mä'yō*], Somalia, port on Indian Ocean; pop. 17,872; fish, hides, livestock

**Kiss** [*kĭs*], **August** (1802–65), German sculptor, born near present Katowice, Poland; well known for studies of animals ('Mounted Amazon Attacked by a Tiger').

**Kissimmee River,** Florida, rises in lake of same name; flows s.e. 90 mi (145 km) to Lake Okeechobee: *maps* F-233, 247

**Kissingen, Bad,** West Germany. *see in index* Bad Kissingen

**Kissinger** [*kĭs'ĭn-gĕr*], **Henry A(lfred)** (born 1923), American political scientist, born Fürth, Germany; to U.S. 1938, citizen 1943; associate professor of government Harvard University 1959–62, professor 1962–68; assistant to U.S. president for national security affairs 1969–75; secretary of state 1973–77: N-293g
■ Nobel prize, *table* N-294h

**Kistiakowsky** [*kĭs-tăk-ôf'skĭ*], **George B(ogdan)** (born 1900), American chemist, born Kiev, Russia; to U.S. 1926, became citizen 1933; professor of chemistry Harvard University after 1937; presidential special assistant for science and technology 1959–61.

**Kistna River,** or **Krishna River,** in s. India, rises in Western Ghats and flows e. to Bay of Bengal; 800 mi (1300 km) long: *map* I-66

**Kisumu** [*kē-su'mu*], Kenya, port on Lake Victoria, just s. of equator; pop. 46,700; terminus of railroad; commercial center; fisheries; processing of cotton, peanuts, coffee, and sesame.

**Kitakyushu** [*kē-ta-kyu'shu*], Japan, seaport city on n. Kyushu; pop. 1,067,915 (1977 est.); formed 1963 by merger of cities Yawata, Wakamatsu, Moji, Tobata, and Kokura: J-367, 383, *map* J-418, *picture* J-384

**Kitazato** [*kē-tä-zä-tō*], **Shibasaburo** (1852–1931), Japanese bacteriologist, born Kumamoto; pupil of Robert Koch; isolated tetanus bacillus 1889; helped develop diphtheria antitoxin 1890; a discoverer of bubonic plague bacillus 1894.

**Kit Carson.** *see in index* Carson, Christopher

**Kit Carson Memorial State Park,** in Taos, N.M., *picture* N-216

**Kit-Cat Club,** famous 18th-century club in London including among members Addison, Steele, and other prominent writers and political leaders, all Whigs; named for tavern of Christopher Cat where meetings were held.

**Kitchen** H-244, S-160
■ changes in, *picture* D-94d
■ colonial, *pictures* D-75, F-488
■ demonstration, *picture* F-51
■ equipment C-556, *pictures* C-555–6b, F-314
■ fans F-32
■ farm, *picture* F-40
■ Japan J-371, *diagrams* J-372
■ Korean K-75c
■ medieval castle, *picture* M-297
■ test kitchen research H-206, *picture* H-204

**"Kitchen Cabinet,"** popular name applied to a group of friends and advisers who (although they held no important offices) influenced President Jackson: J-356

**Kitchener, Horatio Herbert,** first **Earl Kitchener of Khartoum** (1850–1916), British general: K-62, B-331, S-503, *picture* K-62

**Kitchener,** formerly **Berlin,** Ont., Canada, city 90 km (55 mi) s.w. of Toronto; pop. 111,804; meat-packing; furniture, electrical products, textiles, rubber products, shoes, machinery, chemicals: O-456i, *maps* O-4561, b, *inset* C-98
■ Woodside N.H.P. N-24d, *map* N-24b

**Kitchener wheat,** *picture* W-134

**Kitchen middens,** refuse heaps of prehistoric settlements, containing bones, shells, debris, and relics of industry and art; valuable to archaeological studies.

**Kite** K-62–4, *diagrams* K-62–3
■ Asia K-63–4, C-291f
■ Bangkok recreation B-59
■ bibliography H-194, S-65
■ flying, *picture* H-181
■ Franklin, Benjamin F-425, *picture* F-426
■ safety in flying S-8, K-63, A-65

**Kite,** a bird of prey K-62
■ classification B-278, H-75
■ swallow-tailed K-62, H-75.

**Kite,** in geometry G-67, *diagram* G-68

**Kitimat,** B.C., Canada, city with deepwater harbor at head of inlet of the Pacific, 120 km (75 mi) s.e. of Prince Rupert; pop. 9782; a thoroughly planned city (incorporated 1953) based on aluminum smelting
■ dock, *picture* C-79

**Kitksan** [*kĭt-ksăn'*], a Tsimshian Indian tribe living on upper Skeena River, British Columbia, Canada; term also applied to individual members of the tribe and the dialect.

**Kitson, Henry Hudson** (1863–1947), American sculptor, born Huddersfield, England; husband of sculptor, **Theo (Ruggles) Kitson** (1871–1932); his many monuments to national and historic figures include 'The Pilgrim Maiden' at Plymouth, Mass.
■ 'Minute Man at Lexington', statue, *picture* M-150

**Kittatinny Mountain,** a ridge of the Appalachians, mainly in n.w. New Jersey along Delaware River; extends from Shawangunk Mountains in s.e. New York to Blue Mountain in e. Pennsylvania
■ Delaware Water Gap D-79, N-187, *map* P-185
■ New Jersey N-187, *maps* N-188, 202, *picture* N-189

**Kitten** C-153e, N-61, *picture* C-153e
■ birth C-153e

**Kitten ball** S-248

**"Kittens, Three Little,"** nursery rhyme, *picture* N-381a

**Kittery,** Me., community across bay from Portsmouth, N.H.; pop. of township 11,028; site of Portsmouth Navy Yard; incorporated 1647: *map* M-65

**Kittim,** Cyprus. *see in index* Citium

**Kittinger, Joseph William, Jr.** (born 1928), U.S. Air Force officer, born Tampa, Fla.; broke many records as high altitude test parachutist: P-109b

**Kittiwake,** a gull (*Rissa tridactyla*) which breeds in the Arctic regions and winters as far south as the Atlantic and Pacific coasts of the United States; about 46 centimeters (18 inches) long and has white plumage with a pale bluish-gray mantle; hind toe is entirely absent or rudimentary: G-262

**Kitt Peak National Observatory,** 45 mi (72 km) s.w. of Tucson, Ariz., on Papago Indian reservation; dedicated 1960; maintained by National Science Foundation, coordinated with NASA astronomy in space program; world's largest solar telescope; 213-centimeter (84-inch) reflecting telescope.

**Kittredge, George Lyman** (1860–1941), educator and philologist, born Boston, Mass.; professor of English at Harvard University 1894–1936; author of standard works on English grammar and philology; authority on Shakespeare.

**Kittson, Norman Wolfred** (1814–88), Canadian fur trader; born Chambly, Lower Canada; 1830 joined American Fur Company; 1844–54 ran trading post at Pembina on Red River and helped break Hudson Bay Company monopoly.

**Kitty Hawk,** N.C., village in n.e. on strip of land between Albemarle Sound and Atlantic Ocean; pop. 600; Wright Brothers National Memorial nearby: *map* N-337
■ first airplane flight W-305, A-202, *table* A-206, N-329

**Kiushu,** Japan. *see in index* Kyushu

**Kiva** [*kē'vạ*], ceremonial room of Indians in s.w. U.S. I-126

**Kivu, Lake,** in e.-central Africa on e. border of Zaire; 60 mi (95 km) long, 30 mi (50 km) wide; tourist center: Z-353a

**Kiwanis clubs,** organizations of business, professional, and agricultural men for the rendering of civic and social service to their communities; the first Kiwanis club was formed in Detroit in 1915, and Kiwanis International was organized in 1917; clubs have two members of each business or profession in the community; motto, "We build"
■ Casa Loma, Toronto, *picture* T-212

**Kiwi** [*kē'wē*], or **apteryx** [*ăp'tēr-ĭks*], a flightless bird native to New Zealand; about size of domestic fowl; nocturnal: B-277, N-276b, *picture* N-276b
■ ostrich related O-506

**Kizilirmak** [*kĭz-ĭl-ĭr-măk'*] (ancient **Halys** [*hā'lĭs*]), river in Turkey, rises near border of Armenia; flows n. and w. into Black Sea; 600 mi (950 km) long: *maps* T-299, P-212, M-7

**Kjelgaard, James Arthur** (1910–59), author of children's books, born New York City; American history and the outdoors ('Big Red'; 'Snow Dog'; 'Explorations of Père Marquette'; 'Haunt Fox'; 'Desert Dog'; 'Rescue Dog of the High Pass'; 'The Black Faun'; 'Boomerang Hunter'): D-154c

**Kjölen Mountains,** or **Kjølen Mountains** [*chŏ'lĕn*], formerly **Keel,** between Sweden and Norway: N-363, S-523, *maps* S-524, N-365, E-334

**Klabund** [*klä-bụnt'*], pen name of Alfred Henschke (1890–1928), German author of lyrics, novels, and dramas; born Crossen on the Oder; in his short life made important contribution to German literature; among his plays are 'Kirchblütenfest' with Japanese setting and Chinese play 'Kreidekreis'; novels, mainly historical, include 'Mohammed', 'Pjotr', and 'Borgia'.

**Klagenfurt** [*klä'gĕn-fụrt*], Austria, city in s., capital of province of Carinthia; pop. 69,218; in manufacturing area; tourist center.

**Klaipeda.** *see in index* Memel

**Klamath** [*klăm'ăth*] **Falls,** Ore., city at s. tip of Upper Klamath Lake, about 15 mi (25 km) n. of California line; pop. 16,661; railroad and tourist center in lumbering, farming (barley, potatoes), and livestock-raising area; farm machinery; Kingsley Field; annual rodeo: O-483, *maps* O-492–3, 480, U-40

**Klamath Indians,** a tribe in s. Oregon O-481, I-147. *see also in index* Modoc Indians

**Klamath River,** 180 mi (290 km) long rising in Upper Klamath Lake in s. Oregon and flowing through n. California into Pacific: *maps* C-52, O-492

**Klaproth** [*kläp'rōt*], **Martin Heinrich** (1743–1817), German chemist and mineralogist, born Wernigerode, Prussia; his research led to discovery of uranium and zirconium: U-212, T-182

**Klar River,** short stream in s. of Scandinavian peninsula; flows into Lake Vänern: *map* S-524

**Klassen, Elmer Theodore** (born 1908), public official, born Hillsboro, Kan.; with American Can Company 1925–68, president 1965–68; deputy postmaster general 1969–71, postmaster general 1972–75.

**Klaus, Karl Karlovich** (1796–1864), Russian chemist and biologist, known as the discoverer of ruthenium; also investigated flora and fauna of Volga steppes
■ ruthenium R-366

**Klausenburg,** Rumania. *see in index* Cluj

**Kléber** [*klā-bĕr'*], **Jean Baptiste** (1753–1800), French Revolutionary general, one of greatest of epoch; born Strasbourg; assassinated while subjugating Egypt.

**Klebs** [*klāps*], **Edwin** (1834–1913), pathologist, born Königsberg, Germany; professor at Bern, Würzburg, Prague, Zurich, and Rush Medical College, Chicago; known for work in pathology of infectious diseases; with Friedrich Löffler discovered diphtheria bacillus.

**Klee** [*klā*], **Paul** (1879–1940), Swiss surrealist painter: K-64, *picture* K-64
■ 'Intention' P-27, *picture* P-27
■ 'Old Man Figuring' D-183–4, *picture* D-183

**Kleiber** [*klī'bĕr*], **Erich** (1890–1956), Austrian opera conductor, born Vienna; general director Berlin Staatsoper 1923–35; guest conductor New York Philharmonic Orchestra.

**Klein, A(braham) M(oses)** (1909–72), Canadian poet, born Montreal, Que.: C-114, 116

**Klein, Charles Herbert** (Chuck), (1904–58), baseball player, born Indianapolis, Ind.; N.L. outfielder for Philadelphia 1928–33, Chicago 1934–36, Philadelphia 1936–39, Pittsburgh 1939, Philadelphia 1940–44; career batting average .320.

**Klein, Herbert G(eorge)** (born 1918), newspaper editor, born Los Angeles, Calif.; editor *The San Diego Union* 1959–68; manager of communications for Richard M. Nixon's presidential campaign 1968; U.S. director of communications for the executive branch 1969–73.

**Kleindienst, Richard Gordon** (born 1923), public official and lawyer, born Winslow, Ariz.; deputy attorney general 1969–72; attorney general 1972–73: N-293f, g

**Kleist** [*klīst*], **Heinrich von** (1777–1811), German romantic dramatist and poet, born Frankfurt-an-der-Oder ('Penthesilea', tragedy; 'The Broken Pitcher', comedy): G-98

**Klem, William J.** (Bill) (1874–1951), baseball umpire, born Rochester, N.Y.; N.L. umpires 1941–51; worked in 18 world series for all-time record for umpires.

**Klemperer, Otto** (1885–1973), German conductor, born Breslau; conductor Kroll Opera, Berlin, 1927–33, Los Angeles Philharmonic 1933–39, Budapest Opera 1947–50, named conductor of Philharmonia Orchestra of England 1959 and of its successor, New Philharmonia, 1964–72; appeared worldwide; interpreter of Beethoven.

**Kleppe, Thomas S.** (born 1919), public official, born Kintyre, N.D.; member U.S. Congress (Republican) 1967–70; administrator Small Business Administration 1971–75; secretary U.S. Department of Interior 1975–77.

**Kleptomania,** neurotic impulse to steal, especially when there is no economic need; articles often useless but symbolic.

**Klerk, Michel de** (1884–1923), Dutch architect, identified with modern movement in the Netherlands; obtained decorative effects with brick and tile; especially noted for municipal buildings and a housing project in Amsterdam.

**Kleve** [*klā'vĕ*], also **Cleves,** West Germany, town in n.w. near frontier of the Netherlands; pop. 22,100; formerly capital of duchy; castle associated with the legend 'Knights of the Swan', in Wagner's 'Lohengrin': *map* G-114

**Klima,** ancient Greek climate zones C-395

**Klinger** [*klĭng'ĕr*], **Friedrich Maximilian von** (1752–1831), German dramatist, born Frankfurt; leading figure of the 'Storm and Stress' (*Sturm und Drang*) period of German romanticism named after his drama of that title; other works: 'Die Zwillinge' (The Twins) and 'Fausts Leben, Taten und Höllenfahrt' (Faust's Life, Deeds, and Journey to Hell).

**Klinger, Max** (1857–1920), German painter, sculptor, and etcher, born Leipzig; his works are highly personal, subjective, morbidly imaginative; sculptures 'Salome' and 'Cassandra' are typical; renowned is a statue of Beethoven, in marble, ivory, fine metals, and bronze: S-90

**Klinokinesis,** orienting behavior A-441

**Klipfish,** salted, dried cod N-365

**KLM.** *see in index* Royal Dutch Airlines

**Klondike,** a gold-mining district in Yukon Territory, Canada: K-65, Y-352, *picture* C-112d
■ gold discovered M-19, *picture* M-21: gold rush G-151, *pictures* M-18, G-150d

**Klondike River,** Yukon Territory, Canada K-65

**Klong,** a Thailand canal T-143, *picture* T-143

**Klopstock** [*klŏp'shtŏk*], **Friedrich Gottlieb** (1724–1803), German epic, lyric, and dramatic poet, born Quedlinburg, Prussian Saxony; deeply religious and patriotic; sought to restore ancient German spirit: G-96b, 98

**Kluane National Park,** in Yukon Territory, Canada N-24c, *map* N-24b

**Kluck** [*klụk*], **Alexander von** (1846–1934), Prussian general and field marshal of World War I, born Münster, Germany; forced to retire 1916 because of wounds suffered in 1915
■ first battle of Marne M-112

**Klutland Glacier,** Alaska, *picture* G-131

**Klutznick, Philip M.** (born 1907), executive and public official, born Kansas City, Mo.; U.S. representative to UN Economic and Social Council 1961–63; founder and former head Urban Investment and Development Co.; president World Jewish Congress 1977–79; secretary of commerce 1979–81.

**Klystron,** an electron tube E-173

**Klyuchevskaya** [*klyọ-chĕf'skạ-yạ*], or **Kluchev,** active volcano in Kamchatka, Siberia: K-1

**Knapweed** [*năp'wēd*], a perennial plant (*Centaurea nigra*) of composite family, native to Europe but now common to North America; the plant grows to 0.6 m (2 ft); leaves lance-shaped, to 15 cm (6 in.) long; small flowers rose-purple; also called hardheads.

**Knee**
■ patella, *diagram* S-210

**Knee jerk,** a simple reflex R-132, *diagram* N-130a

**Kneisel** [*k'nī'zĕl*], **Franz** (1865–1926), violinist and musical conductor, born Bucharest, Rumania, of German parents; founder and first violinist of Kneisel Quartet.

**Kneller** [*nĕl'ĕr*], **Sir Godfrey** (1646–1723), court painter to Charles II and succeeding English sovereigns to time of George I; born Germany.

**Knesset,** Israeli parliament I-319

**Knickerbocker, Diedrich,** pretended author of Washington Irving's burlesque history of New York City; the

Knickerbockers were an old Dutch family; name now applied to descendants of the original Dutch settlers of New York, more widely to any New Yorker: A-345

**Knickerbocker Baseball Club of New York City** (1845)

**Knife,** a tool, *pictures* T-199
■ electric, *picture* D-198
■ Indian knife, *picture* I-110
■ Indian sheath, *picture* I-124
■ use in camping C-67

**Knife, fork, and spoon** K-69
■ etiquette E-299, *pictures* E-300–1: table setting E-299, *pictures* E-300–1

**Knife edge,** in weighing machines W-93

**Knight, Charles Robert** (1874–1953), painter, illustrator, sculptor, and muralist; born Brooklyn, N.Y.; favorite subjects animals and birds, prehistoric men and animals
■ paintings, *pictures* R-153–7, S-1

**Knight, Eric Mowbray** (1897–1943), author, born Yorkshire, England; to U.S. 1912; in British Army in World War I; major, U.S. Army, World War II; killed in airplane crash
■ 'Lassie Come-Home' D-154c, *picture* D-154c

**Knight, Frank H(yneman)** (1885–1972), economist and author, born McLean County, Ill.; professor of economics University of Chicago 1928–52.

**Knight, John Shively** (born 1894), journalist and publisher, born Bluefield, W.Va.; publisher of many daily newspapers including *Miami Herald, Detroit Free Press, Akron Beacon Journal, Philadelphia Inquirer,* and *Philadelphia Daily News;* owner-editor-publisher of *Chicago Daily News* 1944–59; won Pulitzer prize for editorial writing 1968, many other awards: *picture* W-122

**Knight, Dame Laura** (1877–1970), English painter, chiefly of life of the stage and circus; born Long Eaton, near Derby, England; wife of **Harold Knight** (1874–1961), a portrait painter, born Nottingham.

**Knight, William J.** (born 1929), U.S. Air Force test pilot, born Noblesville, Ind.; chosen for NASA-USAF X-15 research program 1965.

**Knight,** a British title T-185
■ armor and training A-639

**'Knight, Death, and the Devil, The,'** engraving by Dürer D-210, *picture* D-210

**Knighthood** K-65–7, *pictures* K-65–6
■ armor. *see in index* Armor, *subhead* knights
■ Arthurian legend portrays A-655
■ castle C-149–50, *picture* C-149
■ crusading orders C-618–19, C-616
■ Froissart's 'Chronicles' F-463
■ heraldry H-141–2, *pictures* H-141–2
■ honorary orders K-67. *see also in index* chief orders by name
■ horses H-232e, 234j–5, *pictures* H-234j, 236
■ romances R-239
■ tournaments A-383, K-66–7, M-299, *pictures* K-65, H-234j, M-298

**'Knights, The',** play by Aristophanes A-588

**Knights Hospitalers of St. John** (crusading order) C-618–19
■ Malta, Knights of M-70, C-619
■ medieval ambulance service A-326
■ Rhodes, Knights of R-194
■ Tripoli L-249

**Knights of Columbus,** Roman Catholic fraternal organization K-67

**Knights of Labor,** United States L-86
■ Labor Day L-91

**Knights of Malta,** crusading order, originally Knights Hospitalers of St. John: M-70, C-619

**Knights of Pythias** D-15

**Knights of Rhodes** R-194

**Knights of St. Gregory,** order of knighthood under patronage of St. Gregory I, founded 1831 by Pope Gregory XVI, originally to reward service of citizens of church states; now granted to members of any faith or country whose services benefit the Vatican and religion.

**Knights of St. John,** or **Hospitalers.** *see in index* Knights Hospitalers of St. John

**Knights of the Golden Circle.** C-379

**Knights of the Round Table.** *see in index* Arthurian legends

**Knights of the White Camelia,** secret society in South during Reconstruction period: R-116

**Knight's Tale,** in Chaucer's 'Canterbury Tales' C-225. *see also in index* Palamon and Arcite

**Knights Templar,** a Masonic order; based on traditions of crusading order; open only to Masons who have taken Royal Arch degree: F-432

**Knights Templars,** a crusading order C-618, C-616
■ Temple in London L-338

**Kniphofia** [*nĭp-hō'fĭ-ạ*], a genus of perennial plants of the lily family, native to Africa; root is a bulb; leaves long, grasslike; flowers small, tubular, densely clustered at top of smooth, tall stem, shading from yellow to orange, or coral, rarely white; also called tritoma, red-hot-poker plant, torch lily, or flame flower.

**Knitted goods** K-67–9, F-6, *picture* K-68

**Knitting, hand** K-67
■ stockings S-449

**Knitting machines** K-67–9, *pictures* K-68, R-329

**Knitting process,** in rugmaking R-313, 316

**Knobs**
■ area in Indiana I-86
■ area in Kentucky K-27

**Knock,** in automobile engine G-42, A-73, A-848

**Knockout,** in boxing B-388

**Knolls Atomic Power Laboratory,** in Schenectady, N.Y., *picture* N-243

**Knopf, Alfred A(braham)** (born 1892), publisher, born New York, N.Y.; started own publishing firm in 1915; pioneered in translating works of European authors; books known for quality of content and excellent manufacture.

**Knossus,** Crete. *see in index* Cnossus

**Knot,** shorebird of family *Scolopacidae;* the American knot (*Calidris canutus*) is about 27 centimeter (10½ inches) long; ranges from Arctic regions of North America to Patagonia in South America; breast is reddish in summer, but barred with black in winter; another species, the eastern Asiatic knot (*Calidris tenuirostris*), ranges from Siberia, China, and Japan to Australia and India.

**Knot,** a speed of one nautical mile per hour L-331, *table* W-96

**Knotroot.** *see in index* Stachys

**Knots, hitches, and splices** K-70–2, *pictures* K-70–2
■ bibliography H-186
■ fishermen's knots, *pictures* F-177
■ rugmaking R-313–14, 315, *diagrams* R-313
■ square knot in sewing, *picture* S-122

**Knotty pine.** *see in index* Lodgepole pine

**Knotweed, jointweed,** or **smartweed,** common trailing weeds comprising the genus *Polygonum* of the buckwheat family; jointed stems, long grasslike leaves, and small white, rose, or green flowers.

**Know-how,** in American industry I-177

**Knowland, William F(ife)** (1908–74), political leader and publisher, born Alameda, Calif.; member Republican National Committee 1938–42, chairman of executive committee 1940–42; in World War II 1942–45; U.S. senator 1945–58, majority leader 1953–55; minority leader 1955–58.

**Knowledge** P-266, 264, *list* P-265
■ Aristotle's classification A-589

**Knowles, Lucius James** (1819–84), inventor, born Worcester, Mass.; devised a safety steam boiler feed regulator, several models of steam engines, and many loom improvements.

**Know Nothing Party.** *see in index* American party

**"Know then thyself, presume not God to scan"** (Alexander Pope) P-445

**"Know thyself,"** the motto of Socrates S-246

**Knox, Frank,** full name William Franklin Knox (1874–1944), newspaper publisher, born Boston, Mass.; editor and publisher of the *Chicago Daily News* after 1931; Republican nominee for vice-president of U.S., 1936; appointed secretary of the navy in F. D. Roosevelt's Cabinet 1940: *picture* R-272

**Knox, Henry** (1750–1806), Revolutionary War general, born Boston, Mass., commander of artillery forces; trusted adviser of Washington, and directed many successful operations for him; started military school which later became West Point; secretary of war (1785–94), first under Continental Congress, later under Washington as first president; retired to Thomaston, Me.; *pictures* M-62, C-3
■ reproduction of home, *picture* M-55

**Knox, John** (1505?–72), Scottish Protestant leader K-73, S-70–1, *picture* K-73
■ Edinburgh church E-68
■ "Knoxian" Puritans P-539

**Knox, John Jay** (1828–92), financier, born Augusta, N.Y.; author of Coinage Act of 1873 which dropped silver dollar from coinage; had been comptroller of the treasury and president National Bank of the Republic.

**Knox, Philander Chase** (1853–1921), lawyer and statesman, born Brownsville, Pa.; United States attorney general 1901–4 under McKinley and Theodore Roosevelt; secretary of state 1909–13 under Taft; senator from Pennsylvania after 1913
■ Roosevelt and the trusts R-285

**Knox College,** at Galesburg, Ill.; private control; established in 1837; arts and sciences, music, and teacher education; quarter system.

**Knoxville,** Tenn., city in e. on Tennessee River; pop. 175,030: K-73–4, T-81, *maps* T-97, 79, 84, U-41, *picture* K-73
■ Farragut's birthplace F-64
■ location K-73, *locator map* K-73
■ Tennessee, University of, *picture* T-87

**Knoxville College,** at Knoxville, Tenn.; controlled by United Presbyterian church; founded 1863 as McKee School in Nashville, Tenn.; arts and sciences, education.

**Knubel, Frederick Hermann** (1870–1945), clergyman, born New York City; founder and pastor, Church of Atonement, New York City; president United Lutheran Church in America.

**Knudsen, William S(ignius)** (1879–1948), American industrial executive, born Copenhagen, Denmark; president General Motors 1937–40; member National Defense Advisory Commission 1940; director Office of Production Management 1941–45; in charge of production for War Department 1942–44, also 1945; head of Air Forces Matériel and Services Command July 1944–April 1945; returned to General Motors board.

**Knut.** *see in index* Canute

**Koa** [*kō'ạ*], a tree (*Acacia koa*) found in Hawaii; timber valuable for building and cabinetwork; bark used in tanning.

**Koala** [*kō-ä'lạ*], a tree-dwelling Australian marsupial about 0.6 m (2 ft) long A-779, K-2
■ bear's characteristics B-116
■ San Francisco zoo Z-359

**Kobe** [*kō'bĕ*], or **Hiogo-Kobe,** Japan, seaport in s. of island of Honshu, 20 mi (30 km) w. of Osaka; twin port with Osaka; pop. 1,366,397 (1977 est.); silk trade; shipbuilding, metal and rubber manufactures; half destroyed in World War II: J-383, 385, 386, 367, *maps* J-367, *inset* J-418
■ Rokko Tunnel, *table* T-292

**København,** Danish name of Copenhagen. *see in index* Copenhagen

**Koberger,** or **Koburger, Anton** (1440?–1513), German printer-publisher; introduced printing in Nuremberg; established agencies in all parts of Europe to sell books; developed a style of bookbinding which is still associated with name: T-317
■ bookbinding style B-354

**Koblenz,** West Germany. *see in index* Coblenz

**Kobold,** or **gnome,** in German folklore, a teasing, mischievous elf: F-16

**Koburg,** West Germany. *see in index* Coburg

**Kocaeli,** Turkey. *see in index* Nicomedia

**Koch, Karl** (1809–79), German botanist and traveler, born Ettersberg, near Weimar; professor of botany University of Jena; made scientific researches in Russia, also in the Orient.

**Koch, Lauge** (1892–1964), Danish geologist, born near Kalundborg; noted as explorer of Greenland.

**Koch, Robert** (1843–1910), German physician and bacteriologist: K-74, *picture* K-74
■ Nobel prize, *table* N-294d

**Kochanowski** [*kō-kä-nôf'skē*], **Jan** (1530–84), Polish humanistic poet; wrote in Latin and Polish, contributed greatly to development of his native language; fine translation of Psalms in verse.

**Kocher** [*kō'kẽr*], **Emil Theodor** (1841–1917), Swiss surgeon, born Bern; noted for work on thyroid gland; first to operate successfully for exophthalmic goiter
■ Nobel prize, *table* N-294d

**Kochi** [*kō'chē*], Japan, seaport city on s. coast of Shikoku on Tosa Bay 23 mi (37 km) n.w. of Nangoku; pop. 280,962: *map* J-418

**Kochia** [*kō'kĭ-ạ*], an annual plant of the goosefoot family, native to Eurasia. Grows 0.3 to 1.5 m (1 to 5 ft) high, forming an oval or pyramidal plant of bright green which turns, in one variety, to brilliant scarlet in autumn; leaves and flowers tiny; also called burning bush, belvedere, and summer cypress but not to be confused with the true burning bush, a spindle tree. *see also in index* Spindle tree

**Kodak,** camera P-299

**Kodály** [*kō'dī*], **Zoltán** (1882–1967), Hungarian composer, born Kecskemét; intense interest in Hungarian and Slovak folk songs; own works, modern and original, often contain folk-song material; stage, choral, and orchestral works, church and chamber music, songs, piano pieces; author, 'Folk Music of Hungary': M-561

**Kodiak Island,** or **Kadiak Island,** off coast of Alaska, s. of Cook Inlet; 100 mi (160 km) long and 50 mi (80 km) wide; hills, forests, grasslands; home of Kodiak bear; salmon fisheries; growing agricultural and grazing industries; U.S. Coast Guard base; chief city Kodiak (pop. 3798); severely damaged by earthquake 1964: A-242, *picture* A-249, *maps* U-94, 39, N-308

**Kodkod,** a member of the cat family, *picture* C-154d

**Kodok** [*kō'dŏk*], formerly **Fashoda** [*fạ-shō'dạ*], Sudan, town on the White Nile; occupation by French 1898 (the Fashoda Incident) caused an Anglo-French crisis; under an agreement (March 21, 1899) France surrendered Sudan claims to Great Britain.

**Koenig** [*kû'nĭk*], **Frederick** (1774–1833), German inventor, born Eisleben, near Halle: P-504

**Koerner, Theodor** (1873–1957), Austrian statesman and general inspector of army, born Komárno; mayor of Vienna 1945–51; president of Austria 1951–57.

**Koestler** [*kĕst'lẽr*], **Arthur** (born 1905), British writer and foreign correspondent, born Budapest, Hungary; became British citizen 1948 (novels:

'Darkness at Noon', 'The Age of Longing'; history: 'Promise and Fulfilment, Palestine 1917–1949'; autobiographies: 'Arrow in the Blue', 'The Invisible Writing')
■ 'Darkness at Noon' R-111i

**Koffka** [*kôf'kạ*], **Kurt** (1886–1941), German psychologist, born Berlin; in U.S. after 1927; professor of psychology Smith College 1932–41 ('The Growth of the Mind'; 'Principles of Gestalt Psychology').

**Koga, Mineichi** (1885–1944), Japanese admiral; succeeded Isoroku Yamamoto as commander in chief of Japanese Combined Fleet 1943; had important role in seizure of Hong Kong and the Philippines; killed in airplane crash.

**Koguryo,** historic Korean kingdom K-76f

**Koh-i-noor** [*kō-ĭ-nụr'*], a famous diamond D-102, *pictures* D-101

**Köhler** [*kû'lẽr*], **Wolfgang** (1887–1967), American psychologist, born Tallinn, Estonia; to U.S. 1935, became citizen 1946; professor of psychology Swarthmore College 1935–55; chief exponent of Gestalt theory and investigator into animal behavior: P-520, 521

**Kohlrabi** [*kōl'rä'bĭ*], vegetable of the cabbage type C-1, 2, *picture* C-2

**Koiso, Kuniaki** (1880–1950), Japanese statesman and general, born island of Honshu; in July 1944 succeeded Tojo as prime minister of Japan, resigned April 1945; convicted as war criminal Nov. 1948, sentenced to life imprisonment.

**Kokomo,** Ind., city 50 mi (80 km) n. of Indianapolis in agricultural area; pop. 44,042; automobile radios and transmissions, metal products, plumbing fixtures, printing; regional campus of Indiana University: *maps* I-100, 92, U-41

**Koko Nor,** salt lake in People's Republic of China, in n.e. Tsinghai Province, w. of Sining: *map* C-291

**Kokoschka** [*kō-kŏsh'kä*], **Oskar** (1886–1980), Czech painter, born Pöchlarn, near Sankt Pölten, Austria; identified with German expressionists.

**Kok-saghyz,** Russian dandelion D-30, U-2

**Koksoak River,** in n.e. Quebec, Canada; flows into Ungava Bay: *maps* Q-9a, C-99, N-165k

**Kokutai** [*kō-kụ-tī*], former Japanese ideology J-378

**Kola nut,** or **cola nut,** the seed of several trees (genus *Cola*), native to Africa and cultivated elsewhere in tropics; also called goora nut
■ drinks made from P-376

**Kola Peninsula,** a mountainous peninsula of Russia between the Arctic Ocean and the White Sea; 130,000 sq km (50,000 sq mi) n. coast (Murman Coast) has several ice-free ports: *maps* R-344, 348

**Kolbe** [*kōl'bĕ*], **Adolf Wilhelm Hermann** (1818–84), German chemist, born Elliehausen, near Göttingen; noted for his theory of radicals; often regarded as discoverer of method for making salicylic acid from carbolic and carbonic acids.

**Kolbe, Georg** (1877–1947), German sculptor; best known for small bronze figures, simple and severe in design.

**Kolin** [*kō'lēn*], Czechoslovakia, Bohemian town on Elbe River, 50 km (30 mi) e. of Prague; pop. 23,225; Austrians defeated Frederick II of Prussia (1757), securing evacuation of Bohemia
■ Frederick the Great after battle, *picture* G-104

**Kolkhoz,** Russian collective farm R-330c–1, *picture* R-330d

**Kölln** [*kûln*], medieval German city, now a part of Berlin B-171

**Kollwitz, Käthe** (1867–1945), German artist, born Königsberg, East Prussia (now Kaliningrad, Russia); a socialist, whose husband practiced medicine in Berlin slums, she was noted for realism; first woman member Prussian Academy; author of 'Diary and Letters'.

**Kolmer test,** for syphilis V-272

**Köln,** West Germany. *see in index* Cologne

**Kölnbrein Dam,** in Austria, on Malta River, *table* D-12

**Kol Nidre** [*kôl nĭd'rā*], prayer of the Jewish religious ritual, sung at evening service on the Day of Atonement (Yom Kippur); written in Aramaic; opening words, Kol Nidre, mean "All vows."

**Kolokol, Czar,** bell B-154

**Kolozsvar,** Rumania. *see in index* Cluj

**Koltsov** [*kôlt-sôf'*], **Alexis Vasilevich** (1809–42), Russian lyric poet, born Voronezh; called the "Russian Burns"; author of numerous songs and ballads.

**Komandorskiye Islands,** or **Commander Islands,** in Bering Sea; belong to Russia: *map* R-345
■ fur seals S-99

**Komárno** [*kô'mär-nō*], also **Komárom** or **Komorn,** Czechoslovakia, town on Danube River 80 km (50 mi) s.e. of Bratislava; pop. 24,009; surrendered to Austrians (1849) after brilliant defense in Hungarian revolution.

**Komarov, Vladimir Mihailovich** (1927–67), Russian cosmonaut, born near Moscow: S-346f, *table* S-348

**Komatik,** Eskimo dog sledge E-287

**Komeito** [*kō-mā-tō*] **party,** Japan J-377, *table* J-378

**Komensky, Johann Amos.** *see in index* Comenius

**Komodo** [*kō-mō'dō*], hilly island in Indonesia e. of Sumbawa and w. of Flores; area about 184 sq mi (477 sq km); fish
■ dragon, or giant, lizard L-320, *picture* L-318

**Komondor** [*kō'mŏn-dôr*], a working dog native to sheep and cattle regions of Hungary: *picture* D-146

**Komsomol.** *see in index* Young Communist League

**Komsomol'sk,** Russia, city in e. Siberia on Amur River; pop. 240,000; coal, iron, steel: S-188, 189, *maps* R-322, 345, *picture* S-188

**Konakry.** *see in index* Conakry

**Kondylis** [*kôn-thē'lyĕs*], **George** (1879–1936), Greek general and political leader; overthrew Pangalos government by coup, 1926, but resigned in same year.

**Konev** [*kôn'yĕf*], **Ivan Stepanovich** (1897–1973), Russian marshal, born near Nikolsh; alternate member Central Committee of Communist party 1939–52, became full member 1952; a Soviet hero World War II; chief of East European satellite forces 1955–60; commander Soviet troops in East Germany 1961–62.

**Königgrätz,** Czechoslovakia. *see in index* Hradec Kralove

**Königsberg,** Russia. *see in index* Kaliningrad

**Konigsburg, Elaine L.** (born 1930), children's author and illustrator, born New York, N.Y. ('Jennifer, Hecate, Macbeth, William McKinley and Me, Elizabeth'; 'From the Mixed-up Files of Mrs. Basil E. Frankweiler' awarded 1968 Newbery Medal): R-110a

**Konoye** [*kō-nō-yĕ*], **Fumimaro, Prince** (1891–1945), Japanese statesman, born Tokyo; as prime minister of Japan 1937–39 and 1940–41, largely responsible for nation's war policies; committed suicide.

**Konstanz** [*kōn'shtänts*], or **Constance,** West Germany, city on Lake Constance at efflux of Rhine; pop. 55,100; one of the oldest towns in Germany: *map* G-115
■ Council of Constance H-280

**Konti, Isidore** (1862–1938), American sculptor, born Vienna, Austria; monumental decorative work for Chicago World's Fair (1893) and various other expositions.

**'Kon-Tiki',** Thor Heyerdahl's raft, *picture* E-355. *see also in index* Heyerdahl, Thor
■ in museum at Oslo O-505c

**Konya** [*kôn-yä'*], Turkey, city in Asia Minor about 150 mi (240 km) s. of Ankara; pop. 246,727; ancient **Iconium** [*ī-kō'nĭ-ŭm*]; became Seljuk capital 1097; taken by Frederick Barbarossa 1190; annexed to Turkey in 15th century; orchards famous since Middle Ages; carpets, textiles: *maps* T-299, P-212

**Koo, V(i) K(yuin) Wellington** (born 1887), Chinese diplomat, born Shanghai; educated at Columbia University; Chinese ambassador to France 1936–40, Great Britain 1941–46, U.S. 1946–56; judge International Court of Justice 1957–66.

**Koodoo.** *see in index* Kudu

**Kookaburra,** or **"laughing jackass,"** an Australian bird A-782

**Koopmans, Tjalling C.** (born 1910), American economist, born s'Graveland, Netherlands; came to U.S. 1940, naturalized 1946; director Cowles Commission for Research in Economics and professor Yale University 1955–
■ Nobel prize, *table* N-294h

**Kootenay Indians.** *see in index* Kutenai Indians

**Kootenay Lake,** in Rocky Mts., s.e. British Columbia, Canada; 221 sq. mi.: *map* C-98

**Kootenay National Park,** in British Columbia, Canada N-24c, *map* N-24b, C-98

**Kootenay River** (in U.S. known as **Kootenai**), tributary of Columbia River; 650 km (400 mi) long, rises in Canadian Rockies, British Columbia, Canada, flows s. into Montana and Idaho and back into British Columbia: M-459, *maps* I-17, 28
■ flood F-223

**Köppen, Vladimir Peter** (1846–1940), Russian-German climatologist, born St. Petersburg (now Leningrad); meteorologist German Naval Observatory, Hamburg, 1875–1918; in 1900 introduced climatic classifications on which present systems are based: C-395, 395a

**Korab,** highest mountain in Albania A-257

**Koran,** sacred book of Mohammedans K-74
■ angel and demon roles A-414
■ birth control views B-284
■ children learning, *picture* M-419

**Korat,** a breed of cat, *picture* C-153c

**Korçë,** Albania. *see in index* Koritsa

**Korcula** [*kôr'chọ-lä*], or **Curzola** [*kọrt-sō'lä*], island of Yugoslavia in Adriatic: *map* I-325

**Kordofan** [*kôr-dō-fän'*], region in central part of Republic of the Sudan; on plateau about 2000 ft (600 m) with scattered ranges reaching 4000 ft (1200 m); chief settlements El Obeid and Nahud; gum arabic.

**Korea** or **Chosen** [*chō'sĕn'*], peninsula of e. Asia between Sea of Japan and Yellow Sea; divided into North Korea (area 46,800 sq mi; 121,200 sq km; pop. 17,078,000, 1978 est.; cap. Pyongyang) and South Korea (area 38,169 sq mi [98,857 sq km]; pop. 37,018,932, 1978 est.; cap. Seoul); separating the two is demilitarized zone (area 487 sq mi; 1261 sq km): K-75–7e, *charts* K-75b, 75f–6, *Fact Summary* K-77b, *graphs* K-75g, 76e, *maps* K-77d, 75a, c, d–e, K-77h, J-418, M-84, *pictures* K-75, 75d–e, 76g–7a, 75h–6c, 76g, 77c, *Reference-Outline* K-77c, *tables* K-75h, 76b
■ agriculture K-75g, 75h–6, 76d, f, 77, *table* K-75h: farm life K-75c, *picture* K-75d
■ animals K-76e
■ architecture K-76c, *pictures* K-75, 75e, 76a
■ area K-75a, *list* K-75a, *map* K-77b
■ arts K-76b–c: sculpture K-76c, *pictures* K-76a, g
■ assassination A-704
■ bibliography K-77c
■ Buddhism B-483
■ cities K-75b, h, 76, 76d, *map index* K-77e. *see also in index* Seoul and other cities by name
■ climate K-76d–e, A-675, *graph* K-76e, *list* K-75a, *maps* K-76e
■ clothing K-75c, *pictures* K-75d, 75h–6, 76c
■ communication K-75h
■ customs K-75b–c, d
■ dance K-76c, *picture* K-76c
■ dolls D-156
■ drama K-76c
■ education K-75d, *picture* K-75d
■ extent K-75a, *list* K-75a
■ festivals K-75d
■ fisheries K-75g, 76, *picture* K-75h
■ flags F-210, *pictures* F-209
■ food K-75c
■ forests K-75g–h, 76, 76e, *chart* K-75g
■ governments, South and North K-75e–f, 77, 76h, K-77g, *chart* K-75f, *pictures* K-75e, 77a
■ history K-76f–7a, K-77g, S-111, *pictures* K-76g–7a, *Reference-Outline* K-77c
□ alphabet developed (1446) K-76f, b
□ Japanese invasions (1592–98) K-76f, J-406, *pictures* K-77a, 76g
□ Japanese occupation (1910–45) K-76g, 77, 75g, 76b, c, *picture* K-77a
□ Korean War. *see in index* Korean War
□ Mongol invasions and domination (1231–1368) K-76f
□ notable events K-77a, *pictures* K-77a
□ partition after World War II K-77, 76h, 75g, K-77g
□ prehistoric times K-76f
□ Russo-Japanese War (1904–5) R-362
□ since Korean War K-77, 76h, K-78a, *pictures* K-76h, 77a, K-78a
□ Sino-Japanese War (1894–95) K-75g, *picture* K-76g
□ Three Kingdoms (1st century B.C.–A.D. 935) K-76f
△ cultural influence on Japan K-76c: religion J-400; silk S-202
□ time line, *chart* K-77a
□ Yi Dynasty established (1392) K-76f
■ holidays F-96
■ hydroelectric power K-75h, 76, 76d
■ industries K-75h, 76, *picture* K-76, *table* K-75h
■ kite flying K-64
■ land use, *chart* K-75g
■ language and literature K-76b, f, L-116, *diagram* L-118, *list* L-306d, *table* K-76b: children's L-310f, *list* L-311; everyday expressions, *list* K-75c; folktales S-468, *list* S-479, *picture* S-469
■ libraries L-238, 241, 242, 245
■ location K-75–75a, *locator map* K-75a
■ metalwork, *picture* M-231
■ minerals K-75h, 76, *table* K-75h
■ money, *list* K-75a, *table* M-428
■ mountains K-76d, *maps* K-76d, 77d, *picture* K-76a
■ national anthem reproduced K-75e
■ natural features K-76d, *map* K-76d, *pictures* K-76a
■ people K-75b: children K-75b, d; how the people live K-75b–c, d, *chart* K-75h, *pictures* K-75d, 75h–6, 76c; women K-75b, c, *pictures* K-75d, 76c; workers, *chart* K-75g
■ plants K-76e
■ population K-75b, *charts* K-75b, 77b, *list* K-75a: birth and death rates K-75b; density K-75b, *chart* K-77b, *list* K-75a, *map* K-75c: compared with other countries, *chart* J-414
■ pottery P-473, K-76c, f, *picture* K-76b
■ products K-77b, 75g, 75h–6, *list* K-75a, *picture* K-75h, *table* K-75h: ginseng G-126
■ railroad mileage, *table* R-85
■ religion K-75d, 76f, c, *pictures* K-76a
■ rivers K-76d, *maps* K-76d, 77d
■ shelter K-75c, 76c, H-249, 254, *pictures* K-75d, 76a
■ social welfare K-75d
■ sports K-75d
■ 38th parallel K-77f, g, h, 78, K-77, 76h, *maps* K-77h, K-77d, J-418
■ trade K-75h, 76, *charts* K-76: 19th century K-76g
■ transportation K-75h, 76

**Korean War** K-77f–8b, *map* 77h, *pictures* K-77f–8a, T-277, *tables* K-77g, 78b
■ aerospace industry A-69
■ American Red Cross R-119, *picture* R-119
■ armor use in A-631
■ Asian post-colonial history A-693
■ brainwashing B-404
■ Canadian action C-100h
■ casualties, *table* K-77g
□ compared with American Civil War, *chart* C-378
■ Chinese Communists K-77h–8a, U-193, *map* K-77h, *picture* C-309, *table* K-78b
■ chronology, *table* K-78b
■ decorations D-58, U-6, M-110

■ firearms, types used M-9
■ helicopters H-127, *picture* K-78a
■ military cemeteries, *pictures* H-59, N-20
■ racial integration B-295
■ slang words coined S-212
■ tanks T-16
■ truce K-78a, U-193–4, *map* K-77h, *picture* E-131: talks K-78–78a, U-193
■ United Nations measures U-24, U-193, K-77f
■ U.S. Air Force A-159
■ U.S. Marines M-110, *pictures* K-77g–h, M-111: Inchon landing K-77h, N-106, *pictures* K-77h, N-106
■ veterans: Canadian V-308; United States V-306, *table* V-307

**Korea Strait,** channel separating Korea from Japan and connecting Sea of Japan with East China Sea; Russian naval power destroyed here by Japanese in 1905: *maps* K-77d, J-418, P-4

**Korinthos,** Greece. *see in index* Corinth

**Koritsa** [*kô-rē-tsä'*], Albanian **Korçë** [*kôr'chĕ*], Albania, town in s.e.; pop. 39,386: *map* G-213

**Kornberg, Arthur** (born 1918), biochemist, born Brooklyn, N.Y.; professor, Washington University 1953–59, Stanford University 1959–; won Max Berg Award 1968
■ Nobel prize, *table* N-294e

**Körner** [*kûr'nēr*], **Karl Theodor** (1791–1813), German poet and patriot, born Dresden, Germany; wrote patriotic songs; died fighting against Napoleon.

**Korngold** [*kôrn'gōlt*], **Erich Wolfgang** (1897–1957), Austrian composer, born at Brünn, in Moravia; was child prodigy; at age of 11 composed pantomime, 'The Snowman', produced in Vienna; to U.S. 1934, became citizen 1943; won Academy award for motion-picture scores of 'Anthony Adverse' 1936 and 'The Adventures of Robin Hood' 1938 (opera, 'The Dead City').

**Kornilov, Lavr Georgievich** (1870–1918), Russian general, commanded in Galician campaign during World War I; his unsuccessful mutiny against Kerensky's provisional government (1917) prepared way for later Bolshevik victory; killed in battle against Red army while leading Volunteer army in the Kuban region.

**Korolenko** [*kŏ-rŏ-lyĕn'kŏ*], **Vladimir** (1853–1921), Russian fiction writer and publicist; born Zhitomir, Russia, of Russian-Polish family; opposed czarism and Communism ('Makar's Dream and Other Stories'; 'The Blind Musician'; 'The Day of Atonement'; autobiography, 'The History of My Contemporary'): R-361

**Kortrijk,** Belgium. *see in index* Courtrai

**Koruna,** monetary unit of Czechoslovakia: *table* M-428

**Koryo period,** in Korean history K-76f
■ poetry K-76b
■ pottery P-473, K-76c

**Korzeniowski, Teodor Josef Konrad.** *see in index* Conrad, Joseph

**Korzybski, Alfred Habdank** (1879–1950), American scientist, born Warsaw, Poland; secretary Polish Commission to League of Nations, 1920; in 1938 became president and director of the Institute of General Semantics ('Manhood of Humanity—The Science and Art of Human Engineering'; 'Science and Sanity, an Introduction to Non-Aristotelian Systems and General Semantics').

**Kos** [*kŏs*], Italian **Coo** [*kô'ō*], island of Dodecanese in Aegean Sea; area 288.5 sq km (111.4 sq mi): D-135d, *map* G-213

**Kosciusko** [*käs-ē-ŭs'kō*], or **Kosciuszko, Thaddeus** (1746–1817), Polish general K-78c, *picture* K-78c
■ burial place at Cracow C-600

**Kosciusko, Mount,** in Australian Alps, New South Wales, highest peak in Australia (2230 m; 7310 ft): A-769
■ height, comparative. *see in index* Mountain, *table*

**Koshare,** a Pueblo Indian priest who acts as holy clown at public religious ceremonies, *picture* I-115

**Kosher** [*kō'shēr*], Jewish term meaning "fit" or "proper"; applies especially to food made ceremonially clean according to Mosaic law.

**Kosice** [*kō-shē'tsĕ*], Hungarian **Kassa** [*kŏsh'shŏ*], German **Kaschau** [*käsh'ou*], Czechoslovakia, city in e. part; pop. 82,885; held by Hungary 1938–45; wool center; 14th-century Gothic cathedral: *map* C-635

**Kosinski, Jerzy Nikodem** (born 1933), author, born Lodz, Poland; to U.S. 1957, citizen 1965; won National Book Award for 'Steps' 1969, literary award from American Academy of Arts and Letters 1970 ('No Third Path'; 'The Painted Bird'; 'Being There').

**Koslov, Peter Kuzmich** (1863–1935), Russian archaeologist; made important discoveries in Mongolia; including Genghis Khan's capital Karakorum (1899).

**Kosovo,** or **Kossovo** [*kō'sō-vō*], plain in s.w. Yugoslavia near Prizren
■ battle (1389) S-113, T-303

**Kossel** [*kŏs'ĕl*], **Albrecht** (1853–1927), German physiologist, born Rostock; research on chemistry of the cell and proteins
■ Nobel prize, *table* N-294d

**Kossuth, Louis** (Hungarian **Lajos**) (1802–94), Hungarian patriot K-78c, H-276, *picture* K-78c

**Kostelanetz, André** (1901–80), American orchestra conductor, born in Russia; to U.S. 1922; married Lily Pons 1938, divorced 1958; won popularity on radio.

**Koster, Laurens Janszoon.** *see in index* Coster

**Kosygin, Aleksei Nikolaevich** (1904–80), Russian government official K-78c–d, R-358, *picture* K-78c
■ Johnson. L. B. J-476, *picture* J-476
■ Nixon, *picture* N-293h

**Kotatsu** [*kō-tá-ts'*], Japanese burner J-371

**Koto** [*kō'tō*], a Japanese harp consisting of a long box over which are stretched 13 strings, each with a bridge; played with both hands and tuned by shifting the bridges: J-396

**Kotor** [*kō'tôr*], or **Cattaro** [*kät'tä-rō*], Yugoslavia, fortified town on Gulf of Kotor, inlet of Adriatic; pop. 8572; excellent harbor.

**Kotzebue** [*kôt'sĕ-bụ*], **August Friedrich von** (1761–1819), German playwright, born Weimar; prolific; popular all over Europe; best-known play 'The Stranger'.

**Kouchibouguac National Park,** in New Brunswick, Canada N-24d, N-162g, *map, inset* N-24b

**Koufax** [*kō'făks*], **Sanford** (Sandy) (born 1935), left-handed baseball pitcher, born Brooklyn, N.Y.; with Brooklyn Dodgers 1955–57, Los Angeles Dodgers 1958–66; set many pitching records; TV sportscaster 1967–73: *profile* B-95

**Koussevitzky** [*kọ-sĕ-vĭts'kĭ*], **Serge** (1874–1951), musical conductor, born Tver, Russia; double-bass soloist in Imperial Theatre Orchestra; organized own orchestra; conducted orchestras in most European countries; conductor Boston Symphony Orchestra 1924–49; director Berkshire Music Center at Lenox, Mass., 1940–51.

**Kovalevsky** [*kŏv'ạ-lĕf'skĭ*], **Sonya,** or **Sophie** (1850–91), Russian mathematician, genius in mathematical treatment of mechanical problems; professor University of Stockholm 1884–91.

**Kovno,** Lithuania. *see in index* Kaunas

**Kowait,** monarchy in Arabia. *see in index* Kuwait

**Kowloon,** peninsula and port of Hong Kong colony, on Chinese mainland opposite island of Hong Kong; pop. 716,272: H-215, *map* C-313, *picture* H-215

**Koxinga,** Chinese **Cheng Ch'eng-kung** [*gŭng' chŭng' gụng'*] (1623–63), Chinese pirate-patriot F-349

**Kozhikode** [*kō'zhĭ-kōd*], formerly **Calicut,** India, city and port on s.w. coast, in Kerala state; pop. 333,979; exports copra, coffee, ginger, tea, rubber: *map* I-84c
■ Gama, Vasco da G-8

**Kozlov** [*kŭs-lôf'*], **Frol Romanovich** (1908–65), Russian government official, born near Kasimov; member of Communist party 1926–65, of Presidium 1957–65; a first deputy premier 1958–60; member of Central Committee secretariat 1960–64.

**Kra, Isthmus of,** Thailand *map* I-162

**Kraal** [*kräl*], a native village in Africa K-44

**Kraepelin** [*krĕ-pĕ-lēn'*], **Emil** (1856–1926), German psychiatrist, born Neustrelitz; professor at University of Munich; revised classification of mental diseases; analyzed fatigue process and studied effect of alcohol on the mind.

**Kraftt,** or **Kraft** [*kräft*], **Adam** (1455?–1509), principal German sculptor of late Gothic period; birthplace probably Nuremberg, Germany; executed tabernacles, tombs, reliefs, and religious figures.

**Kraft** [*kráft*] **paper** P-105, P-328

**Krakatoa** [*krä-kạ-tō'ạ*], volcanic island in Indonesia between Java and Sumatra
■ eruption of 1883 V-378, 380, F-222

**Krakow,** Poland. *see in index* Cracow

**Kramer, Jack** (John Albert Kramer) (born 1921), tennis player, born Las Vegas, Nev.; won U.S. singles 1946–47; Wimbledon champion 1947; turned professional 1947; promoter 1952–62; first executive director Association of Tennis Professionals: *picture* N-154

**Kranach, Lucas.** *see in index* Cranach

**Krasnodar** [*kräs'nō-där*], formerly **Ekaterinodar** [*ē-kät-ēr-ē'nō-där*], Russia, city of n. Caucasia on Kuban' River in farm area e. of Black Sea; pop. 465,000; food products, machinery; petroleum refining: *maps* R-344, 349, E-355

**Krasnoyarsk** [*kräs'nō-yärsk*], Russia, Siberian city on Yenisey River and Trans-Siberian Railroad; pop. 748,000; machinery; lumber, paper, and cement industries; flour milling; world's largest hydroelectric plant nearby: *maps* R-345

**Krasnoyarsk Dam,** in Russia, on Yenisey River; *table* D-12

**Kratzer, Nicholas** (1487–1550?), astronomer to Henry VIII of England, born Munich, Germany
■ portrait by Holbein, *picture* H-201

**'Krazy Kat',** comic strip C-145d, *picture* C-145c

**Krebs, Sir Hans Adolf** (1900–81), British scientist, born Hildesheim, Germany; professor of biochemistry Oxford University 1954–67
■ Krebs cycle B-202 *diagram* B-200
■ Nobel prize, *table* N-294e

**Krebs cycle,** biochemistry
■ cellular activity B-202, *diagram* B-200

**Kredel, Fritz** (1900–1973), artist and illustrator, born Michelstadt, Germany; taught art in Germany; to U.S. 1938; illustrated for children: Andersen's 'Fairy Tales'; Grimm's 'Fairy Tales'; 'Pinocchio', by Carlo Lorenzini.

**Krefeld** [*krä'fĕlt*], West Germany, manufacturing town 50 km (30 mi) n.w. of Cologne; pop. 216,871; famous textile institute: *maps* G-114, 110

**Krehbiel** [*krā'bēl*], **Henry Edward** (1854–1923), music critic and writer, born Ann Arbor, Mich.; music critic *Cincinnati Gazette* 1874–80, *New York Tribune,* 1880–1923; known as "dean of American critics" ('How to Listen to Music'; 'Chapters of Opera').

**Kreisel, Henry** (born 1923), Canadian novelist C-116

**Kreisler** [*krīs'lēr*], **Fritz** (1875–1962), American violinist and composer, born Vienna, Austria; through artistry and musical grace became worldwide favorite; served in Austrian army in World War I and was wounded at Lemberg; returned to concert stage; composed songs, violin pieces ('Caprice Viennois'), and an operetta ('Apple Blossoms'); became U.S. citizen 1943.

**Kremlin,** citadel of a Russian city
■ Kiev R-351
■ Moscow M-493, 493a, b, R-333, *diagrams* M-493b, *map* M-493a, *pictures* M-493, R-320, 333: Palace of Congresses, *picture* R-326

**Krenek, Ernst** (born 1900), American composer, born Vienna, Austria; to U.S. 1938, became citizen 1945; extreme modernist in style; won first widespread fame with 'Jonny spielt auf', jazz opera; other operas include 'The Life of Orestes'.

**Kreps, Juanita M.** (born 1921), educator and public official, born Lynch, Ky.; member faculty Duke University 1955–77, professor 1968–77, vice-president 1973–77; U.S. secretary of commerce 1977–79: W-215b

**Kresge, Sebastian Spering** (1867–1966), merchant and philanthropist, born Bald Mount, Pa.; partner Kresge and Wilson, Detroit, 1907, incorporated as S. S. Kresge Company 1912: C-204
■ Kresge Foundation, *table* F-362

**Kresge Foundation,** established 1924, *table* F-362

**Kress, Samuel Henry** (1863–1955), merchant and art patron, born Cherryville, Northampton County, Pa.; founded S. H. Kress & Co. (chain of 5-, 10-, and 25-cent stores) at Memphis, Tenn., 1896; established Samuel H. Kress Foundation 1929; donated many art treasures to National Gallery of Art and other leading museums.

**Krete,** island. *see in index* Crete

**Kreuger, Ivar** (1880–1932), Swedish "match king" and financial wizard, born Kalmar; built a huge international match trust; committed suicide when faced with bankruptcy.

**Kreutzer** [*kroi'tsēr*], **Konradin** (1780–1849), German pianist, conductor, and composer of operas, church music, and chamber music; born near Konstanz; among best-known works is light opera, 'Nachtlager von Granada'.

**Kreutzer, Rodolphe** (1766–1831), French violinist of German extraction, born Versailles; wrote many operas and instrumental works; Beethoven dedicated to him the sonata for violin and piano known as the Kreutzer sonata.

**'Kreutzer',** work by Beethoven B-136

**Kreuzotter** [*kroit'sôt-ēr*], a viper V-328

**Krieghoff, Cornelius** (1812–72), Canadian painter, born Düsseldorf, Germany; with U.S. Army in Seminole Wars 1837–40; known for landscapes, portraits, and portrayals of early French-Canadian life: C-85

**Kriegsakademie,** German academy
■ military education and training M-319

**Kriemhild** [*krēm'hĭlt*], in the Nibelungenlied, wife of the hero Siegfried: S-192a, N-282

**Kriemhilde Line** (in World War I), German defensive position in Meuse-Argonne region M-237, *map* M-237

**Krill,** animal
■ Antarctic food chain A-473

**Krim, Mohammed ben Abd el.** *see in index* Abd el Krim, Mohammed ben

**Krim,** Russia. *see in index* Crimea

**Krimml Falls,** in Krimml River, s.w. Austria, *table* W-73c

**Kris,** Malay dagger, *picture* S-546

**Krishna,** a Hindu god H-158
■ Jagannath celebration, *picture* I-69
■ 'Krishna Holding Mount Govardhan', miniature painting P-67f, *picture* P-67f
■ pearl myth P-149

**Krishna Menon, V(engalil) K(rishnan)** (1897–1974), Indian diplomat, born Calicut, now Kozhikode; worked for Indian independence; delegate to UN

1946–47, 1952–62; high commissioner of India in London 1947–52; minister for defense 1957–62.

**Krishna River,** in India. *see in index* Kistna River

**Kriss Kringle,** German name for Santa Claus S-45

**Kristensen, Leonard,** Norwegian whaling captain; member of small party, the first persons to land on Antarctic Continent (1895): *table* P-422

**Kristiansand,** Norway, seaport on s. coast; pop. 50,217; exports wood pulp, lumber, nickel, fish; has 17th-century Gothic cathedral; founded 1641: *maps* N-365, E-334

**'Kristin Lavransdatter',** trilogy by Sigrid Undset U-4

**Krivoy Rog,** or **Krivoi Rog** [*kriv' oi rōḡ'*], Russia, city in s. Ukrainian S.S.R.; pop. 573,000: K-48, *maps* R-344, 349, E-335

**KRM.** *see in index* Kurzweil Reading Machine

**Kroeber, Alfred Louis** (1876–1960), anthropologist, born Hoboken, N.J.; taught anthropology at University of California 1901–46; expert on North American Indians and archaeology of Mexico and Peru; wrote textbook, 'Anthropology'.

**Kroger, Bernard Henry** (1860–1938), banker and grocer, born Cincinnati, Ohio; founded Kroger Grocery and Baking Co. (1882) which became a grocery chain: C-204

**Krogh** [*krôḡ*], **(Schack) August (Steenberg)** (1874–1949), Danish physiologist, born Grenaa; noted for experiments in respiration and for researches in capillaries and the blood
■ Nobel prize, *table* N-294d

**Krohg, Christian** (1852–1925), Norwegian painter and author, born Oslo; depicted sea and seamen with realism and strength; wrote novels and books on art
■ painting, *picture* A-328

**Krol, John Joseph, Cardinal** (born 1910), Roman Catholic prelate, born Cleveland, Ohio; auxiliary bishop of Cleveland 1953–61; archbishop of Philadelphia 1961–; created cardinal 1967; president National Conference of Catholic Bishops 1972–74.

**Kroll, Leon** (1884–1974), painter, born New York City; simple, strong, and highly individual in landscape, still life, and figure work.

**Kroll process,** of titanium T-182

**Krona** [*krō'na*], monetary unit of Sweden and Iceland; historic value about 27 cents: *table* M-428

**Kronborg Castle,** Denmark, *picture* D-90

**Krone** [*krō'ně*], monetary unit of Denmark and Norway; also various former gold coins of central Europe; Austrian was worth about $6.64, German about $2.38: *table* M-428

**Kronshtadt,** or **Kronstadt** [*krōn'shtät*], Russia, port and naval base on island of Kotlin in Gulf of Finland 30 km (20 mi) w. of Leningrad; founded 1710 by Peter the Great: *maps* P-348, W-253

**Kroo,** African tribe. *see in index* Kru

**Kropotkin, Peter, Prince** (1842–1921), Russian geographer and anarchist, born Moscow; first to show that structural lines of the Asiatic continent run s.w.–n.e.; exiled and imprisoned for advocating peaceful anarchy: A-388

**Kru,** also **Kroo,** or **Croo,** a Negro people of Liberia and adjacent parts of w. Africa; famous as canoe men and sailors; tribal mark (black or blue line) tattooed on forehead.

**Krueger, Karl** (1894–1979), orchestral conductor, born Atchison, Kan.; studied at Heidelberg, Germany, and Vienna, Austria; conductor Seattle Symphony Orchestra, Kansas City Philharmonic; Conductor Detroit Symphony Orchestra 1943–49.

**Krug, J(ulius) A(lbert)** (1907–70), public power expert and government official, born Madison, Wis.; with Tennessee Valley Authority 1938–40, War Production Board 1942–45, chairman after Sept. 1944; U.S. secretary of the interior 1946–49.

**Kruger** [*krụ'ḡẽr*], **Paul** (1825–1904), Boer patriot, known as "Oom Paul" (Uncle Paul); born Colesburg, Cape Colony; president of South African Republic (Transvaal) 1883–1901: S-267
■ Rhodes R-193
■ Smuts S-220

**Kruger National Park,** in South Africa S-264, N-23, *map* S-264

**Kruglov, Sergei Nikiforovich** (born 1900?), Russian government official; deputy commissar for internal affairs during World War II; minister of internal affairs 1946–56.

**Krumgold, Joseph** (1908–80), author and motion-picture producer, born Jersey City, N.J.; writer and producer for major motion-picture companies 1931–41, for Office of War Information during World War II, operated own company in Israel 1946–50 ('. . . and now Miguel', awarded 1954 Newbery Medal; 'Onion John', awarded 1960 Newbery Medal): R-111a

**Krung Thep,** Thailand. *see in index* Bangkok

**Krupa, Gene** (1909–73), jazz drummer and bandleader, born Chicago, Ill.; associated with Chicago style before becoming first drummer to win large public acclaim: *picture* J-425

**Krupp** [*krụp*], **Alfred** (1812–87), German "cannon King," born Essen; son of Friedrich and father of Friedrich Alfred Krupp; discoverer of method of casting steel in large pieces; made great guns used (1870–71) in the siege of Paris: A-660

**Krupp, Friedrich** (1787–1826), German ironmaster, born Essen; founder of house of Krupp and of great Krupp works at Essen; introduced manufacture of cast steel into Germany; died poor: E-290

**Krupp, Friedrich Alfred** (1854–1902), German industrialist, born Essen; son of Alfred and grandson of Friedrich Krupp; handed on the Krupp business to his daughter, Bertha.

**Krupp steelworks** E-290

**Krupp von Bohlen und Halbach, Bertha** (1886–1957), eldest daughter of Friedrich Alfred Krupp; brought up to manage Krupp works at Essen, which she inherited at 16; married **Baron Gustav von Bohlen und Halbach** (1870–1950), who added Krupp to his name and became chief director of works; their son **Alfried** (1907–67) became sole owner 1943; sentenced by U.S. tribunal at end of World War II, released from prison 1951; under his direction, firm recovered spectacularly without making armaments; Alfried's son, **Arndt** (born 1938), last heir; firm made foundation 1968.

**Krutch, Joseph Wood** (1893–1970), critic and essayist, born Knoxville, Tenn.; drama critic and associate editor *The Nation* 1924–32, literary editor 1933–37; professor of English 1937–43, of dramatic literature 1943–52, Columbia University ('Samuel Johnson'; 'The Twelve Seasons'; 'The Desert Year'; 'The Best of Two Worlds'; 'The Measure of Man'; 'The Great Chain of Life'; 'Human Nature and the Human Condition'; 'The Forgotten Peninsula'; 'If You Don't Mind My Saying So'; 'More Lives Than One', autobiography).

**Krylov** [*krĭ-lôf'*], **Ivan Andreevich** (1768–1844), noted Russian fabulist, born Moscow; wrote fables largely in language of peasants, satirizing life of his time: L-310, R-359

**Krypton** (Kr), a colorless, odorless gas, *tables* P-207, C-236
■ air contains, *picture* A-145
■ meter defined in terms of krypton 86 W-95
■ nuclear fission, *picture* N-377g

**Kryukovo,** Russia, "satellite city" of Moscow M-493b

**Kshatriya** [*kshăt'rĭ-yạ*], a Hindu of the soldier caste I-70, H-158

**Kuala Lumpur** [*kwäl'ạ lụm'pụr*], Malaysia, capital, on Malay Peninsula near w. coast; pop. 1,081,000: K-78d, *maps* I-162, E-36, *picture* M-67a
■ libraries L-241, 244
■ location K-78d, *locator map* K-78d

**Kuan Yin,** Buddhist divinity, goddess of mercy
■ enamel figure, *picture* E-202

**Kuban'** [*kụ-băn'*] **River,** in n. Caucasus, rises on slopes of Mt. El'brus; flows about 940 km (585 mi) to Sea of Azov; rushing mountain river becomes sluggish stream lower: *maps* C-178, R-349

**Kubasov, Valery N.** (born 1935), Russian cosmonaut, born Vyazniki, n.e. of Moscow; flight engineer in Soyuz 6: *table* S-348

**Kubelik** [*kụ'bě-lĭk*], **Jan** (1880–1940), Bohemian violinist; father of Jeronym Rafael Kubelik; popular and brilliant concert virtuoso.

**Kubelik, (Jeronym) Rafael** (born 1914), Czechoslovak conductor and composer, born near Prague; made tour as conductor and piano accompanist for father, Jan Kubelik, 1934–35; chief conductor Czech Philharmonic Orchestra, Prague, 1942–48; musical director Chicago Symphony Orchestra 1950–53, Covent Garden Opera Company, London, 1955–58; chief conductor Bavarian Radio, Munich, 1961–; music director Metropolitan Opera, New York, 1972–74.

**Kubelsky, Benjamin.** *see in index* Benny, Jack

**Kubik, Gail** (born 1914), composer, born South Coffeyville, Okla.; studied under Piston and Sowerby; chamber music, choral and orchestral works, film scores; won 1952 Pulitzer prize.

**Kubitschek** [*kụ'bĭ-chěk*], **Juscelino** (1902–76), Brazilian statesman, born Diamantina in state of Minas Gerais; president of Brazil 1956–60: B-408

**Kublai Khan** [*kū'blī kän*] (1216–94), one of greatest, most intelligent, and most cultured of Mongol rulers, grandson of Genghis Khan: M-435
■ completes Grand Canal, China C-119
■ Marco Polo visits P-441g, *picture* P-441g

**Kuching,** seaport, capital of Sarawak, Malaysia, on Borneo; pop. 37,949; Sarawak Museum, set in gardens: *map* E-36

**Kudu,** also **koodoo,** one of the largest of African antelopes; white stripe down the back and 8 or 10 vertical stripes descending from it down the sides: A-478

**Kudzu** [*kụd'zụ*], or **kudzu vine,** a perennial climber (*Pueraria thunbergiana*) of the pea family, native to China and Japan; leaves in 3 parts, flowers in purple clusters; in Japan, roots used as starch source and inner bark in cloth; in s. United States, plant used as forage crop, to enrich worn-out land, and to protect against erosion.

**Kufra** [*kụ'frä*] **Oasis,** group of oases in Sahara in s.e. Libya; pop. 9530; camels; dates, barley, grapes, olives; caravan trade.

**Kuhio, Prince,** in full **Jonah Kuhio Kalanianaole** (1871–1922), Hawaiian statesman, born Koloa on Kauai; descendant of last independent king of that island; Congressional delegate to U.S. 1903–22; obtained legislation for Hawaiian back-to-the-land movement
■ holiday (March 26) F-92

**Kuhlmann** [*kụl'män*], **Richard von** (1873–1948), German diplomat, born Constantinople; secretary of state for foreign affairs 1917–18, negotiating treaties with Russia and Rumania; opposition of army high command and Chancellor Hertling caused him to resign.

**Kuhn** [*kū'ěn*], **Bowie** (born 1926), lawyer, born Takoma Park, Md.; admitted to bar 1951; commissioner of baseball 1969–.

**Kuhn** [*kụn*], **Richard** (1900–1967), Austrian chemist, born Vienna; awarded 1938 Nobel prize in chemistry for work on carotenoids and vitamins, but declined because of a Nazi decree
■ Nobel prize, *table* N-294c

**Kuhn** [*kūn*], **Walt** (1877–1949), modernist painter, born New York City; simple, positive design; brilliant often raw color; paintings of women of stage and circus, also of flowers.

**Kuiper** [*koi'pẽr*], **Gerard Peter** (1905–73), American astronomer, born Netherlands; to U.S. 1933, became citizen 1937; with University of Chicago at Yerkes Observatory 1936–60, professor 1943–60, director of Yerkes and McDonald observatories 1947–49 and 1957–60; head Lunar and Planetary Laboratory, University of Arizona, 1960–73; author of books on astronomy: P-355, S-254e, b, 254

**Ku K'ai-chih** [*ḡụ'kī'ḡĭr'*] (350?–412), Chinese painter; remarkable expression with minimum detail; sure, rhythmic line; best known for a series of paintings on silk in British Museum, illustrating an essay 'The Admonition of the Instructress in the Palace'.

**Kukenaam** [*kụ-kạ-näm'*], **Falls,** in Kukenaam River, e. Venezuela, near Mount Roraima, *table* W-73c

**'Kukla, Fran, and Ollie',** puppet show on television, *picture* P-536

**Ku Klux** [*kū klŭks*] **Klan,** secret society in Reconstruction period K-78d–9, R-116, L-399
■ terror against Blacks B-294

**Ku Klux Klan, Knights of,** society founded in 1915 K-78d–9, U-187, *picture* H-31

**Kukri** [*kụk'rē*], a sword S-547, *picture* S-546

**Kukui** [*kụ'kụ-ē*], tropical tree (*Aleurites molluccana*), native to Malay region, found throughout tropics; state tree of Hawaii; also called candlenut, candleberry, lumbang, and varnish tree; fruit contains large seeds (candlenuts) useful in making candles, oil, dyes, paint, gum, food, and medicine: *picture* H-62
■ candlenut N-385

**Kukulcan,** Mayan name for the hero-god Quetzalcoatl M-180, M-253
■ temple, *picture* M-180

**Kulaks,** well-to-do Russian peasants S-404

**Külek Bogazi,** pass in Asia Minor. *see in index* Cilician Gates

**Kumamoto** [*kụ-mä-mō-tō*], Japan, city on w. coast of Kyushu Island; pop. 488,166; textiles, tile; Kumamoto Medical University, school of pharmacy: *map* J-418

**Kuma** [*kụ-mä'*], **River,** in n. Caucasus, Russia; flows e. until lost in swamps; reaches Caspian Sea in flood time only; about 580 km (360 mi) long: C-178, *maps* C-178, R-344, 349

**Kumasi** [*kụ-mä'sĭ*], formerly **Coomassie** [*kọ-măs'ĭ*], Ghana, city in w. Africa; pop. 260,286: G-121

**Kumkum,** forehead decoration worn by Indian girls and women, except orthodox Hindu widows: I-73

**Kumquat,** a small citrus fruit of the genus *Fortunella* L-278

**Kun, Béla** [*bā'lä kụn*] (1886–1938?), Hungarian leader; captured by Russia in World War I, he became follower of Lenin; organized revolution in Hungary and set up a Soviet rule; overthrown; became member of executive committee, Communist International: H-276

**Kunersdorf** [*kụ'nẽrs-dôrf*], Poland, former Prussian village 6 km (4 mi) e. of Frankfurt-an-der-Oder; Prussians defeated by Russians and Austrians 1759 (Seven Years' War); included in Poland since 1945.

**Kung, Hsiang-hsi** (H. H. Kung) (1881–1967), Chinese leader, born Shansi; governor, Central Bank of China, 1933–45; vice-president of executive department of national government 1933 and 1939; minister of finance 1933–44. *see also in index* Soong

**!Kung,** African language A-119

**Kunitz, Stanley (Jasspon)** (born 1905), poet, educator, and editor; born Worcester, Mass.; editor of a biographical series on authors; lecturer Columbia University 1963–66, adjunct professor Graduate School of the Arts 1967–; won 1959 Pulitzer prize for 'Selected Poems, 1928–1958'.

**Kuniyoshi** [*kọ-nĭ-yō'shĭ*], **Yasuo** (1893–1953), American painter and lithographer, born Okayama, Japan; identified with modernists; to U.S. 1906
■ 'Dream' D-184, *picture* D-184

**Kunlun** [*kụn'lụn'*] **Mountains,** in central Asia, in People's Republic of China, along n. border of Tibet: highest peak Ulugh Muztagh (25,340 ft; 7724 m): *maps* C-291 *picture* C-290

**Kunming** [*kụn'mĭng'*], People's Republic of China, capital of Yünnan Province; n.e. terminus Burma Road of World War II; pop. 1,100,000: C-293f, *maps* C-291, C-312

**Kunsthistorisches Museum.** *see in index* Art History Museum

**Kunz, George Frederick** (1856–1932), gem expert, born New York City; research curator of gems, American Museum of Natural History; kunzite named for him.

**Kunzite** [*kụnts'īt*], a semiprecious stone found in California and Madagascar; phosphorescent after exposure to radium: M-336

**Kuomintang** [*g̅wô'mĭn'däng'*], name for the Chinese Nationalist party, meaning "The People's Party," upholding principles of Dr. Sun Yat-sen: C-315, C-296, C-252, 253
■ Communist infiltration C-301–2

**Kuo-yü,** chief dialect of China C-295c

**Kuprin** [*kụp-ryēn'*], **Aleksandr Ivanovich** (1870–1938), Russian writer of novels, short stories, and sketches; born Narovchat, near Nizhni Lomov; power undisciplined by formal literary education: R-360a, 361

**Kura,** principal river of Transcaucasus, flowing n.e. and then s.e. into Caspian Sea; 1515 km (940 mi) long: C-178, *maps* C-178, T-299, R-344, 349
■ valley, *picture* C-178

**Kurbash,** or **courbash,** a whip of heavy hide; term also applied to forced labor under the lash which was outlawed in Egypt under British rule.

**Kurdistan,** mountainous region in s.e. Turkey, n. Iraq, n.w. Iran, and n.e. Syria: K-79

**Kurds,** Mohammedan tribes of Asia Minor K-79
■ Iran I-278
■ Iraq I-281
■ Turkey T-301

**Kure** [*kụr'ē*], Japan, naval port on Honshu Island and Inland Sea; pop. 242,655; shipbuilding; exporting; clothing and sake: *map* J-418

**Kurelek, William** (1927–77), Canadian author and illustrator, born Whitford, Alta.; wrote and illustrated 'O Toronto', 'Some-one With Me' (autobiography), 'Lumberjack'; Canadian Book of the Year for Children awards for 'A Prairie Boy's Winter' (1974) and 'A Prairie Boy's Summer' (1976).

**Kuria Muria** [*kụr'ĭ-ạ mụr'ĭ-ạ*] **Islands,** group of five high, rocky islands off s. coast of Arabia; area 28 sq mi (72 sq km); pop. about 70; British ceded to Oman 1967

**Kuril** [*kụ'rĭl*], **Islands,** or **Kurile Islands,** also **Chishima,** stretching n.e. from Hokkaido; 15,500 sq km (6000 sq mi); pop. 15,000; name from Russian *kurit* ("to smoke") in allusion to volcanoes; owned by Japan 1875–1945; occupied and annexed by Russia: *maps* R-345, J-419
■ seal herds S-99

**Kuroki** [*kụ-rō-kē*], **Tamesada** or **Tamemoto, Count** (1844–1923), Japanese general and samurai, born Kagoshima; distinguished in Sino-Japanese War of 1894–95; in Russo-Japanese War of 1904–5 commanded First Army, defeated Russians at Yalu River, and assisted Oyama at Mukden.

**Kuropatkin** [*kụ-rō-pät'kyĭn*], **Alexei Nikolaievich** (1848–1925), Russian general; in supreme command in East during Russo-Japanese War, until after battle of Mukden, in which he was defeated; again commanded an army 1916 in World War I; retired 1917.

**Kuroshio.** *see in index* Japan Current

**Kurta,** Pakistani shirt P-78

**Kurtz, Efrem** (born 1900), conductor, born St. Petersburg (now Leningrad), Russia; musical director Ballet Russe de Monte Carlo; conductor Kansas City (Mo.) Philharmonic Orchestra 1943–48; became U.S. citizen 1944; conductor Houston (Tex.) Symphony Society 1948–54.

**Kurumba,** a wild tribe of the Nilgiri Hills in s. India; live in mud and wattle huts; depend largely on jungle for food.

**Kurusu** [*kụ-rụ-sụ*], **Saburo** (1888?–1954), Japanese diplomat, born Yokohama; began diplomatic career 1910; ambassador to Germany 1939–40, signed pact with Nazis: W-271

**Kurzweil Reading Machine (KRM)** A-836

**Kusch** [*kụsh*], **P(olykarp)** (born 1911), American physicist, born Blankenburg, Brunswick, Germany; to U.S. 1912, became citizen 1922; professor of physics Columbia University 1949–72, academic vice-president and provost 1969–72; professor University of Texas at Dallas 1972–
■ Nobel prize, *table* N-294a

**Kushiro** [*kụ-shē-rō*], Japan, seaport city on Pacific Ocean on s.e. Hokkaido 20 mi (30 km) s.w. of Akkeshi; pop. 206,840; exports sulfur and lumber: *map* J-419

**Kuskokwim River,** one of chief rivers of Alaska; 550 mi (885 km) to Bering Sea: *maps* U-94, 39, N-308

**Kustenja,** Rumania. *see in index* Constanta

**Kut** [*kụt*], or **Kut al Imara** [*kụt äl ĭ-mär'ạ*], Iraq, a city on Tigris River, 105 mi (170 km) s.e. of Baghdad; railroad terminus; pop. 71,360.

**Kutaisi** [*kụ-tä'ĭ-sĭ*], or **Kutais** [*kụ-tü-ēs'*], Russia, city of Georgian S.S.R. 195 km (120 mi) n.w. of Tbilisi; pop. 161,000; coal-mining equipment, chemicals, textiles, leather products: G-95, *maps* R-344, 349, E-335

**Kutani ware,** Japanese porcelain made originally from materials found near Kutani-mura, village near Kanazawa, Japan; oldest and best period (1664–1750) widely collected; ware ranges from stoneware to fine porcelain, glazes from green through Indian red and brown.

**Kutaradja,** or **Koetaradja** [*kọ'tä-rä'g̅ä*], Sumatra, city with seaport (Ule-Lue, or Ulee Lheue) on n.w. tip of island; pop. 53,668: *map* E-36

**Kutb Minar,** tower at Delhi, India D-80, *picture* D-80

**Kutb-ud-Din** (died 1210), a Turki slave who became sultan of Delhi; appointed viceroy of India by Mohammed of Ghor 1192; founded Slave Dynasty in India (1206–88).

**Kutch,** or **Cutch** [*kŭch*], former state in w. India; since 1948 part of Gujarat state; bleak, treeless region with rocky hills; ruled for centuries by independent dynasties that kept it in virtual isolation. *see also in index* Rann of Kutch

**Kutchin** [*kŭ-chĭn'*], Indian tribe that lives in Yukon Territory, Canada, and Alaska: *map* I-134, *table* I-136

**Kutchuk-Kainardji** [*kụch'ụk-kī-när'g̅ē*], **Treaty of** (1774), between Turkey and Russia, giving Russia strong position on Black Sea.

**Kutenai** [*kụ'tē-nā*] **Indians,** or **Kootenay Indians,** two tribes of the Kitunahan stock, one living in Montana, the other in British Columbia, Canada: I-149

**Kutztown State College,** at Kutztown, Pa.; founded 1866; formerly a teachers college; arts and sciences, education, fine arts; graduate study.

**Kuvasz,** a working dog, originally from Tibet, *picture* D-146

**Kuwait,** or **Kuweit,** also **Kowait** [*kŭ-wāt'*], republic in n.e. Arabia; area about 7400 sq mi (19,000 sq km); pop. 1,031,000 (1976 est.); cap. and seaport, Kuwait (pop. 217,364 with suburbs): K-79–80, *maps* A-522 I-280, *picture* K-79
■ Arabian states A-521; *map* A-522
■ flag F-210, *picture* F-209
■ Israeli-Arab war I-320a
■ location K-79, *locator map* K-79
■ money, *table* M-428
■ National Day F-95
■ petroleum K-79, 80, P-229, *picture* K-79

**Kuybyshev,** or **Kuibyshev** [*kwē'bĭ-shĕf*], Russia, port city on Volga and Samara rivers 845 km (525 mi) s.e. of Moscow; pop. 1,047,000; flour milling; large trade; capital of the Soviet Union in World War II: *maps* R-344, 349, E-335
■ dam, *picture* V-383

**Kuybyshev Dam,** in Russia, on Volga River, *picture* V-383

**Kuznets** [*kŭz'nĕts*], **Simon** (born 1901), American economist, born Kharkov, Russia; to U.S. 1921; professor University of Pennsylvania 1930–54, Johns Hopkins University 1954–60, Harvard University 1960–71
■ Nobel prize, *table* N-294h

**Kuznetsk** [*kụz-nĕtsk'*] **Basin,** Russia, basin of Tom' River, Siberia; valuable mineral resources: S-189

**Kvutzoth** [*kvŭt-zōth'*], communal colonies in Palestine P-81

**Kwacha,** monetary unit of Malawi and Zambia, *table* M-428

**Kwajalein** [*kwä-g̅ŭ-lān'*], largest atoll in Marshall Islands, in Ralik group; pop. 5469; contains Kwajalein Island; occupied by U.S. 1944: W-276, 294, *map* P-4. *see also in index* Marshall Islands

**Kwakiutl** [*kwä-kē-ụ't'l*], a group of Indian tribes that live near Fort Rupert, B.C., Canada: *map* I-134, *table* I-137

**Kwammu,** also **Kwammu Tenno** (738?–805), emperor of Japan 782–805; conquered Ainus; moved capital twice in effort to free government from Buddhist influence: K-80

**Kwangchow,** People's Republic of China. *see in index* Canton

**Kwangju** [*g̅wäng'g̅ụ*], South Korea, city 40 mi (65 km) n.e. of Mokpo; pop. 607,058; railroad junction; textile center; Chonnam National University; radio station; historical site: *maps* K-77d, 75c

**Kwango** [*kwäng'g̅ō*], **River,** Portuguese **Cuango** [*kwäṅ'g̅ọ*], 700 mi (1150 km) long, rises in Angola and flows n. into Zaire, forming part of border.

**Kwangsi Chuang Autonomous Region,** in s.e. People's Republic of China; 84,000 sq mi (218,000 sq km); pop. 29,326,000; cap. Nanning: C-293f, *maps* C-293, C-312–13
■ people C-292

**Kwangtung** [*g̅wäng'dụng'*], province of s.e. People's Republic of China; 84,000 sq mi (218,000 sq km); pop. 50,149,000; cap. Canton: C-293f, *maps* C-293, C-313

**Kwanto Plain,** lowland in Japan. *see in index* Kanto Plain

**Kwantung** [*g̅wän'dụng'*], former Japanese leased territory on s. tip of Liaotung Peninsula, People's Republic of China; area 1337 sq mi (3463 sq km); Kwantung was leased to Japan by China in 1905, but, after World War II, most was included in Port Arthur-Dairen administrative district.

**Kwan-Yin.** *see in index* Kuan Yin

**Kwanza,** monetary unit of Angola, *table* M-428

**Kwashiorkor,** deficiency disease D-129g

**Kweichow** [*g̅wā'g̅ō'*], province of s. People's Republic of China; 66,000 sq mi (171,000 sq km); pop. 24,197,000; cap. Kweiyang: C-293f, *maps* C-293, C-312

**Kweiyang** [*g̅wā'yäng'*], People's Republic of China, capital of Kweichow Province; pop. 660,000; coal mining; textiles and chemicals; seat of higher education: C-293f, *map* C-312

**Ky, Nguyen Cao.** *see in index* Nguyen Cao Ky

**Kyakhta** [*kyäκ'tä*], Russia, city on n. border of Mongolian People's Republic, about 170 mi (275 km) n. of Ulan Bator; pop. 15,316; transit point for trade between Russia and Mongolia: *maps* R-345, M-433

**Kyanite** [*kī'ạ-nīt*], or **cyanite** [*sī'ạ-nīt*], an aluminum silicate; colorless, or blue, white, gray, green, or brown; cut as gem.

**Kyat** [*kyät*], monetary unit of Burma, *table* M-428

**Kyd** [*kĭd*], **Thomas** (1558–94), English dramatist, born London; important predecessor of Shakespeare: E-257

**Kyne, Peter B(ernard)** (1880–1957), novelist, born San Francisco, Calif.; clerk general store, lumber broker, reporter; served in Spanish-American War and World War I('Cappy Ricks', 'The Valley of the Giants', 'The Enchanted Hill').

**Kyodo** [*kē-ō'dō*], **News Service,** organization supplying news to Japanese press, radio, and television; founded 1945; headquarters, Tokyo.

**Kyogen** [*kē-ō'g̅ĕn*], in Japanese no drama J-397

**Kyokutei Bakin.** *see in index* Bakin

**Kyongju** [*kē'ông-g̅ŭ*], South Korea, town 38 mi (61 m) e. of Taegu; pop. 108,447; rail junction; coal mining; tourism; National Museum; 8th-century cave carvings; capital of Kingdom of Silla 57 B.C.–A.D. 935: *map* K-77d, *pictures* K-76a
■ ancient Korean capital K-76f

**Kyoto,** or **Kioto** [*kē-ōt'ō*], formerly **Heian-kyo** [*hā-än-kē-ō*], Japan, former capital; pop. 1,464,964 (1977 est.): K-80, J-405, 367, *maps* J-367, *inset* J-419
■ irimoya, roof style, *diagram* J-373
■ Kabuki, origin of J-398
■ libraries L-239
■ location K-80, *locator map* K-80
■ temples K-80, J-396, *pictures* J-389, 391

**Kyrie eleison** [*kĭr'ĭ-ē, kē'rĭ-ē, ē-lā'ĭ-sŏn*], Greek words, meaning "Lord have mercy upon us," used as prayer in Greek and Roman Catholic churches, and also (translated) in Anglican church.

**Kythēra,** island in Ionian Sea. *see in index* Cerigo

**Kyudo** [*kyụ-dō*], Japanese archery J-399

**Kyushu,** also **Kiushu** [*kyụ'shụ*], southernmost of four main islands of Japan; area 14,114 sq mi (36,555 sq km); pop. 12,666,000 (1977 est.); mountainous and volcanic; extensive coal mines; copper, rice, tea, tobacco: J-401, 402, 379, 381, 384, 367, *maps* J-418, 401
■ bridges, *picture* J-384
■ climate J-404, 403
■ folktale, *picture* S-418d
■ industry J-382, 383
■ offshore islands, *picture* J-402

**Kyzyl-Kum,** a desert in Russia R-324, *maps* R-344, D-93


## PRONUNCIATION KEY

cāpe, ăt, fär, fȧst, whạt, fạll; mē, yĕt, fẽrn, thêre;
īce, bĭt; rōw, wȯn, fôr, nŏt, dọ; cūre, bŭt, rụde, fụll, bûrn; *out*;
ü = French *u*, German *ü*; g̅em, g̅o; *th*in, *th*en;
ṅ = French nasal (Jeaṅ); *zh* = French *j* (*z* in *azure*); κ = German guttural *ch*.

# The letter L

probably started as a picture sign of an oxgoad, as in a very early Semitic writing used about 1500 B.C. on the Sinai Peninsula (1). A similar sign (2), denoting a peasant's crook, is found in earlier Egyptian hieroglyphic writing. About 1000 B.C., in Byblos and other Phoenician and Canaanite centers, the sign was given a linear form (3), the source of all later forms. In the Semitic languages the sign was called *lamedh,* meaning "oxgoad."

The Greeks first gave the sign some unbalanced forms (4) and renamed it *lambda.* Later they formed their sign symmetrically (5). The Romans adopted the earlier Greek forms (6). From Latin the capital letter came unchanged into English.

In late Roman times the small handwritten "l" was developed from the capital by rounding the lines. Later a form with an open loop in the vertical stroke was developed (7).

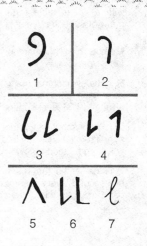

**Laaland,** Danish island. *see in index* Lolland

**Laban, Rudolf von** (1879–1958), dancer and teacher of dancing, born Hungary; taught many years in Germany; originated a new system of dance and devised a method of dance notation: D-25–6

**La Befana.** Italian Christmas character C-329–30

**Label,** heraldic charge, *picture* H-142

**Label,** on clothing C-406–7

**Labiatae** [*lā-bĭ-ā′tē*], plant family including mint, catnip, and ground ivy M-366

**Labium,** lower lip of insect I-198, *diagram* I-197

**La Boca,** artists' district in Buenos Aires, Argentina A-580

**Labor** L-81–91, *pictures* L-81–6, 89–90, *Reference-Outline* E-63. *see also in index* Industrial Revolution; countries by name, *subhead* labor; *also* topics beginning with Labor
- apprentice system G-257
- automation affects I-179
- banks B-64
- business cycle affects B-518
- capital and: Industrial Revolution I-173; Marxian views C-494a, S-234; Socialism and S-233
- child labor C-281: coal mines C-418; Oriental rugmaking R-313–14
- civil service C-371
- Communism C-494a, S-234
- convict labor P-505, 505c, d, *pictures* P-505, d
- cost of living L-315, T-280, U-191, *graph* L-315
- definition L-81, 82
- democracy in industry
  □ growth of labor movement L-85–6
  □ Industrial Revolution I-173
  □ rise in Middle Ages D-83
- economic factor in production E-56, 59: people engaged, *table* E-57
- employment. *see in index* Employment
- factories and factory laws F-12–13
- farm labor. *see in index* Agriculture, *subhead* labor
- fatigue and work W-235–6
- forced labor: displaced persons D-131; Hungary H-275; Poland P-415; Russia R-328; Tibet T-137
- government regulation. *see in index* Government regulation of industry; Labor legislation
- guilds G-256–7
- health of workers F-13
- homework, industrial. *see in index* Homework, industrial
- hours of L-91. *see also in index* Hours of labor
- immigration and I-57–8, C-83, T-135
- insurance: industrial I-213, E-201, I-184; old-age S-236–7; unemployment S-237
- international organizations L-91: International Labor Organization C-281, L-91, U-26
- journeymen G-257
- leisure created by machines L-185, *chart* I-182a
- machine age. *see in index* Machine age
- machinery, effects of L-185, M-13, *chart* I-182a
- Marxian doctrine C-494a, S-234
- Middle Ages G-256–7, *picture* L-83
- mining M-344–5, *pictures* M-342–3: coal C-419–20, 418, *pictures* C-415, 418
- Negro F-15
- on-the-job training, *picture* V-364
- Owen, Robert, theories of S-233–4
- pensions P-188–9, S-236–7
- peonage S-214. *see also in index* Peonage
- piecework. *see in index* Piecework
- problems studied, *picture* U-111
- productivity M-13, I-171, I-179, L-185
- railway workers R-75, 83–4, L-90, *pictures* R-85, W-173
- sabotage. *see in index* Sabotage
- safety S-4, 6–7. *see also in index* Safety; Safety devices and measures
- serfdom. *see in index* Serfdom
- slavery. *see in index* Slavery
- Socialism and S-234–6
- social security S-236–7, E-201
- specialization of labor. *see in index* Specialization of labor
- standard of living I-176, 179–80, L-185, U-186, *picture* I-176
- sweatshop system G-33
- tariff protects T-23
- unemployment: depression of 1930's H-222–3, R-268, U-187, 188, *graph* H-221; England E-247; technological I-185, M-13
- United States I-184–5, *picture* I-180
  □ age trends P-448–9, U-103, *chart* U-103
  □ Bureau of Census report C-192
  □ distribution, *chart* W-215c
  □ horsepower per employed worker, *chart* U-107
  □ Roosevelt, F. D., administrations R-269, 271, 272, 273
  □ Roosevelt, T., administrations R-284–5
  □ Southern labor U-67, 64, U-179: cotton C-588–9
  □ Truman administrations T-276, 278, 280
  □ workers, *chart* U-124
- veterans' aid U-208, P-188, *table* V-307: Canada V-308
- vocational education. *see in index* Agricultural education; Vocational education
- wages. *see in index* Minimum wage; Wages
- women W-214–15b, L-90, T-135, *chart* U-103, *pictures* W-215: distribution, *chart* W-215c
- working conditions and efficiency W-235–6: bonus L-171

**Labor, American Federation of** (A.F.L.). *see in index* American Federation of Labor

**Labor, Department of,** United States U-163–4, *list* U-157, *table* E-90
- building, *map* W-32, *picture* L-90
- Bureau of Labor Statistics U-164, L-315, S-6
- child labor laws C-281
- flag F-192, *picture* F-193
- secretary U-163: made Cabinet member C-4

**Labor, Knights of,** United States L-86
- Labor Day L-91

**Laboratory**
- Bell Telephone Laboratories. *see in index* Bell Telephone System, *subhead* laboratories
- crime, *picture* P-429: FBI F-81, *picture* F-81
- glass used, *pictures* G-139–40
- medical, bioengineering aids B-210: hormone manufacture H-229
- Menlo Park Laboratory E-70, 73, *pictures* E-71, N-195
- Naval Research Laboratory G-252, 255
- nuclear energy research N-250, F-269
- oceanography. *see in index* Oceanography, *subhead* research vehicles

**Labor boards**
- National Labor Relations Board L-88, 89, 90, U-166
- National Mediation Board, railway L-90
- National War Labor Board R-276–7, T-9
- War Manpower Commission R-276

**Labor Day** (September) L-91, F-94

**Labor Day, International** M-177b

**Labor legislation.** *see also in index* Factories and factory laws
- arbitration. *see in index* Arbitration, *subhead* labor
- child labor laws C-281
- Clayton Act M-450
- employers' liability E-201, I-217
- England E-247, L-85
- factory laws F-13
- Fair Employment Practices F-15
- Fair Labor Standards (Wage and Hour) Act R-273, L-91, C-281, U-164
- hours of labor L-91, C-281, R-273
- injunction L-88–9

- Labor-Management Relations (Taft-Hartley) Act L-88–9, 84–5, 90, U-191, T-278
- Mexico M-251–2
- National Industrial Recovery Act R-269–70
- National Labor Relations (Wagner) Act L-88, R-271
- old-age insurance S-236–7, P-188–9
- pensions S-236–7, P-188–9
- Social Security Act R-272, S-236–7
- Spain S-356
- state legislation L-90, C-281
- unemployment S-237: depression of 1930's U-188
- United States L-88–9, C-419–20, R-269, 271, 272, 273, U-166, W-175
- wages L-91, R-273
- workmen's compensation E-201, I-217, S-236, U-164

**Labor-Management Relations Act of 1947** (Taft-Hartley act), United States A-528, L-88–9, 84–5, 90, U-191, T-278

**Labor-Management Services Administration,** United States U-164

**"Labor pains,"** in childbirth R-151d

**Labor parties** L-91

**Labor party,** Australia A-816, L-91
- prime ministers. *see in index* Australian history, *table*

**Labor party,** Great Britain, formed 1906 to represent organized labor and Socialists; cooperated with Liberals, later adopted socialistic program: E-247, 248, 249, S-235–6, L-91
- Clement Attlee A-758
- prime ministers, *table* G-199a

**Labor party,** New Zealand L-91

**Labor Relations Act, National,** U.S. *see in index* National Labor Relations Act of 1935

**Labor Relations Board, National,** United States L-88, 89, 90, U-166

**Labors of Hercules** H-143–4

**Labor Statistics, Bureau of,** United States U-164
- *Consumer Price Index* published by L-315
- promotes safety S-6

**Labor unions** L-81–91, I-184–5, *pictures* L-81–2, 84–6, 89. *see also in index* Labor; Labor boards; Labor legislation; *also* names of labor unions and labor leaders
- American Federation of Labor (A.F.L.) L-86–7, G-157
- apprenticeships A-511
- arbitration A-528, L-89–90: Roosevelt, T. R-284–5
- boycott L-88
- China, People's Republic of C-298
- collective bargaining L-82, 83, 84, 85, L-184: escalator clauses L-91, I-185; individual vs. collective bargaining L-84; Labor-Management Relations (Taft-Hartley) Act L-88–9, 84–5,

---

A main entry may be divided into subentries. For example, look at the main entries on this page or following pages that are divided into alphabetically arranged subentries. Each subentry is marked with a ■. Some of these *first-level* subentries are important enough to be divided into alphabetically arranged *second-level* subentries, each marked with a □. A second-level subentry that has many references may be divided into alphabetically arranged *third-level* subentries, each marked with a △. In table form, the arrangement of subentry symbols is as follows:

**Main Entry Titles** are printed in boldface type.

■ is the symbol that marks each division of a main entry into the alphabetically arranged first-level subentries.

□ is the symbol that marks each division of a first-level subentry into alphabetically arranged second-level subentries.

△ is the symbol that marks each division of a second-level subentry into alphabetically arranged third-level subentries.

90, U-191, T-278; National Labor Relations (Wagner) Act L-88, R-271; under New Deal R-270, 271
■ Committee on Political Education L-91
■ Congress of Industrial Organizations (C.I.O.) L-87–8
■ contract I-185, L-88, 89–90
■ discrimination banned F-15
■ England L-85, 91, E-247, I-173, S-235, *picture* L-85
■ Europe L-91: trends in L-85–6
■ France L-91
■ Germany, West L-91
■ independent unions L-88
■ injunction L-88–9. *see also in index* Injunction
■ international organizations L-91: International Labor Organization U-26, L-91, C-281
■ Italy L-91
■ IWW. *see in index* Industrial Workers of the World
■ Japan J-387, 377, 410
■ Knights of Labor L-86
■ mediation L-90: Federal Mediation and Conciliation Service U-164
■ membership, number L-88, R-271
■ Mexico M-251
■ political activities L-91, P-434, S-234–5
■ postal service P-460c
■ railway brotherhoods L-88, R-83–4
■ Russia R-330a, 332c: libraries L-244
■ Second International promotes unity among workers S-234
■ Spain S-356
■ strike L-82, 85, 87, 88. *see also in index* Strike
■ Truman administrations T-280, 276, U-191, L-88
■ union security L-84–5
■ women in L-90

**Labouchère** [*lä-bọ-shêr'*], **Henry du Pré** (1831–1912), English journalist and radical political leader, editor of the weekly *Truth*, noted for exposure of public frauds.

**Labouchère, Pierre Antoine** (1807–73), French painter, born Nantes, France; known for paintings of the Reformation
■ painting of Calvin leading Geneva discussion, *picture* R-134

**Labrador,** a peninsula, most easterly part of the North American mainland; area 1,620,000 sq km (625,000 sq mi); e. triangle of Labrador Peninsula (area 292,218 sq km (112,826 sq mi); pop. 28,166), together with Newfoundland Island, forms Province of Newfoundland, Canada: L-92, N-165d, e, f, g, a, b, Q-9d–e, g, *maps* N-165c, k–l, C-73, 99, *picture* L-92
■ Cabot discovers C-9
■ Churchill Falls W-73c, L-92, *map* N-165c, *table* W-73c
■ Eskimos E-285
■ iceberg patrol, *picture* I-8
■ natural features L-92, L-163, N-165b, d, *map* N-165c
■ Viking landings E-283
■ work of Dr. Grenfell G-239

**Labrador Current,** or **Arctic Current,** cold ocean current along coast of Labrador; carries ice into important shipping lanes, *charts* O-397h, G-259b
■ causes fog F-286
■ effect on Labrador L-92

**Labrador duck,** an extinct black-and-white sea duck closely allied to eider duck; ranged north Atlantic coast of North America as far south as Long Island, N.Y.; believed to have bred in Labrador, Canada B-271

**Labrador ice sheet** I-5, *map* I-6

**Labradorite,** a gem J-454

**Labrador retriever,** a dog, *pictures* D-151, 141

**Labrador tea,** evergreen shrub (*Ledum groenlandicum*) of heath family; found in swamps of Greenland and Labrador, Canada; used for tea.

**La Brea tar pits,** Los Angeles, Calif., *list* L-354, *map* L-352
■ fossil remains F-353, 356

**Labrouste, Henri** (1801–1875), French architect A-562

**Labrum,** upper lip of insect I-198, *diagram* I-197

**La Bruyère** [*lá brü-yêr'*], **Jean de** (1645–96), French essayist and wit, a moralist, born Paris; one of best writers of classical French ('Caractères', 'Mémoires'): F-437–8

**Labuan** [*lä-bụ-än'*], island off n. Borneo; formerly one of Straits Settlements; in 1946 became part of North Borneo (now Sabah), a part of Malaysia since 1963; 35 sq mi (90 sq km); pop. 14,904: *map* E-36

**Laburnum,** small tree of pea family native to s. Europe; cultivated for showy yellow flowers, glossy foliage; all parts poisonous; called bean tree or golden chain in U.S.

**Labyrinth,** a name given by Greeks and Romans to buildings, entirely or partly underground, with intricate winding passages
■ myth A-62, T-159

**Labyrinth, membranous,** of ear, *diagram* E-4

**Labyrinthodont,** prehistoric amphibian A-461, *picture* A-460, *chart* G-64

**'Labyrinths',** work by Borges B-367

**Lac** [*lăk*], resinous substance emitted by lac insects L-98

**Lacatan,** banana variety B-53

**Laccadive** [*lăk'ạ-dīv*] **Islands,** coral islands in Arabian Sea w. of s. India; part of union territory of India, known as Lakshadweep, formerly Laccadive, Minicoy, and Amindivi Islands; pop. 13,109. *see also in index* Lakshadweep: *map* I-81

**Laccolith** [*lăk'ō-lĭth*], in geology, *diagram* G-59
■ Devils Tower, Wyoming N-35, *maps* N-30, W-327, *picture* W-325

**Lace** L-93–7, *pictures* L-93–7
■ baroque dress D-191, *picture* D-192
■ handmade L-93–7, *pictures* L-93, 95–7
■ history of lacemaking L-94–6
■ linen thread for L-290
■ machine-made L-93, *picture* L-94: history of development L-93; types L-96, 97
■ producing regions L-93, 95–6, 97: Belgium L-95, 97, Y-347, *picture* L-93; France L-95, C-18; Italy L-96, *picture* L-97

**Lace-bark tree,** tree of the West Indies (*Lagetta lintearia*); inner bark resembles coarse lace; used for collars, frills; also for making whips and rope.

**Lacedaemon** [*lăs-ē-dē'mŏn*], the ancient name of Laconia, in Greece, country of which Sparta was capital: S-369. *see also in index* Laconia

**La Ceiba,** Honduras, Caribbean port city; pop. 49,900; ships bananas, hides, fruits; brewery; soap and vegetable oil factories; U.S. fruit company headquarters: *map* N-309

**Lacertilia** [*lăs-ēr-tĭl'ĭ-ạ*], suborder of reptiles comprising lizards L-320

**Lacewing fly.** *see in index* Green lacewings

**Lacey Act of 1900,** United States, on mongoose importation M-436

**Lachaise** [*lá-shĕz'*], **Gaston** (1882–1935), sculptor, born Paris, France; in U.S. after 1906; best known for monumental female figures modeled in large, simple planes: S-91

**La Chaux de Fonds,** Switzerland. *see in index* Chaux de Fonds, La.

**Lachesis** [*lăk'ē-sĭs*], in Greek mythology F-74b, *picture* F-74b

**Lachine** [*lá-shēn'*], Que., Canada, manufacturing city and summer resort on Lake St. Louis connected with Montreal 10 km (6 mi) n.e. by Lachine Canal; pop. 44,423; structural steel and other metal products. Burned and inhabitants killed by Indians 1689: *maps* M-477, *insets* Q-11, C-99

**Lachine Canal,** near Montreal M-476a, 477

**Lachine Rapids,** in St. Lawrence River S-20, *diagram* S-20

**Lachish** [*lā'kĭsh*], ancient city in s. Palestine, often mentioned in Tell el-Amarna tablets and in Bible; destroyed by Joshua (Josh. x, 31–3) and assigned to tribe of Judah (Josh. xv, 39).

**Lachlan River,** in New South Wales, Australia; joins Murrumbidgee River near junction with Murray River; 1150 km (700 mi) long

**Lachrymal glands,** or **lacrimal** [*lăk'rĭ-mál*] **glands,** the tear-secreting organs E-369

**Lachrymator,** or **lacrimator,** a tear gas C-230

**Lac insect** L-98

**Lackawanna,** N.Y., industrial and railroad city on Lake Erie just s. of Buffalo; pop. 22,701; large steel plants, cement and concrete products: *map* N-260

**Lackland,** nickname for King John of England J-463

**Laclede** [*lá-klĕd'*], **Pierre** (1724–78), also called Pierre Laclede Liguest, American fur trader and founder of St. Louis, Mo.; born in Lower Pyrenees, France; emigrated to New Orleans 1755 and established a fur trade with the Indians of the Missouri River area
■ founds St. Louis S-21, *picture* M-401

**Laclede's Village,** old French town on site of St. Louis, Mo. S-22

**Lacombe, Albert** (1827–1916), Canadian Roman Catholic missionary, born St. Sulpice, Lower Canada; one of first missionaries sent to Northwest Territories; author of grammar and dictionary of Cree Indian language.

**La Condamine** [*lá kôn-dá-mēn'*], **Charles Marie de** (1701–74), French scientist, born Paris; explored the Amazon: R-305

**La Condamine,** district of Monaco M-425, *picture* M-425

**Laconia** [*lạ-kō'nĭ-ạ*], in ancient Greece, s.e. district of Peloponnesus of which Sparta was the capital: S-369, *map* G-221
■ origin of "laconic" S-369
■ Sparta conquers G-222

**Laconia,** N.H., resort and industrial city on Winnipesaukee River 28 mi (45 km) n. of Concord in beautiful lake region; pop. 15,575; knitting machines, shoes, hosiery, needles, ball bearings, skis: *map* N-183

**La Coruña** [*lä kō-rụ'nyä*], Spain, seaport on n.w. coast; pop. 200,955; sailing port of the Spanish Armada (1588); repulse of French by British under Sir John Moore in Peninsular War 1809: *maps* S-350, E-334

**Lacquer** [*lăk'ēr*] L-97–8, P-73, V-267
■ cellulose lacquers L-97, *table* C-184
■ furniture decoration I-227, *picture* F-484

**Lacquer ware** L-98, J-394, C-295g, *picture* M-248

**Lacrimal bone,** a small bone within orbit of eye S-210

**Lacrimal glands.** *see in index* Lachrymal glands

**La Crosse** [*lạ krạs'*], Wis., city on Mississippi River 120 mi (195 km) s.e. of St. Paul, Minn.; pop. 48,347; center of stock-raising and dairying region and tobacco market; heating and air-conditioning equipment, farm machinery, rubber footwear, beverage coolers, beer; University of Wisconsin–La Crosse; Viterbo College: W-194, *maps* W-207, 194, U-41
■ climate, *list* W-192

**Lacrosse,** a game L-98–100, *diagram* L-99, *pictures* L-98–9
■ field, *diagram* L-99
■ origin I-113

**Lacrosse,** guided missile, *picture* G-251d

**Lactarius pergamenus,** or **parchment lactarius,** a mushroom, *picture* M-553

**Lacteal,** any one of lymphatic vessels of intestinal canal.

**Lactic acid,** the acid formed in sour milk; chemical composition $C_3H_6O_3$
■ cheese making C-229, *picture* C-228
■ fermentation causes F-85
■ meat M-190
■ muscle action develops R-160
■ yeast culture Y-338

**Lactobacillus** [*lăk-tō-bạ-sĭl'ŭs*], a bacterium which makes lactic acid B-15

**Lactose,** or **milk sugar,** a double (disaccharide) sugar ($C_{12}H_{22}O_{11}$), reducible to galactose and glucose; differs from maltose and sucrose in structure of molecule; about one sixth as sweet as cane sugar: S-508, M-322, D-3

**Ladanum,** or **labdanum,** a resin obtained from the plants *Cistus ladaniferus* and *Cistus villosus*; used in the manufacture of heavy perfumes.

**Ladd, Edwin Fremont** (1859–1925), chemist, born Starks, Me.; on faculty of North Dakota Agricultural College 1890–1920; U.S. senator 1921–25; pioneer in pure food legislation.

**Ladd, George Trumbull** (1842–1921), philosopher, born Painesville, Ohio; one of first to introduce study of experimental psychology into America; founded Yale University psychological laboratory (translation, Lotze's 'Outlines of Philosophy', 6 vols.).

**Ladder**
■ fire department F-135, *pictures* F-134–5, 137, 132
■ in caisson, *diagram* C-17
■ lunar module, Apollo spacecraft S-346d, *picture* S-347
■ picking apples, *picture* F-53
■ safety measures S-7

**Ladder-back chair** I-229, *picture* I-233
■ in early American kitchen, *picture* F-488

**Ladder dredge** D-185

**Ladd-Franklin, Christine** (1847–1930), scientist, born Windsor, Conn.; first woman student at Johns Hopkins University and at universities of Göttingen and Berlin in Germany; distinguished career in mathematics, physics, and psychology; famous for her theory of color perception.

**Ladies' sorrel.** *see in index* Sorrel, wood

**Ladies tresses,** a wild flower of the genus *Spiranthes* of the orchid family; the flowers are small, white, yellowish- or greenish-white, in twisted spikes.

**Lading, bill of.** *see in index* Bill of lading

**Ladino** [*lä-dē'nō*], a person of mixed Spanish and Indian blood C-195, *charts* C-198, *picture* C-196. *see also in index* Mestizo

**Ladislaus** [*lăd'ĭs-lôs*], common form of **Laszlo'** [*läs'lō*] **I, Saint** (1040–95), king of Hungary; obtained Croatia for Hungary and Christianized it; most beloved of Hungarian kings; canonized 1198; festival June 27.

**Ladle,** a cuplike, long-handled spoon
■ carved wooden ladle, *picture* I-119

**Ladoga** [*läd'ō-gạ*], **Lake,** largest lake of Europe, in n.w. Russia; area about 18,000 sq km (7000 sq mi): L-100, *maps* R-322, 344, 348, E-335

**Ladrone Islands.** *see in index* Mariana Islands

**Lady,** title T-185

**"Ladybird, ladybird,"** nursery rhyme N-381c, *picture* N-381c

**Ladybug, ladybird,** or **lady beetle,** a small spotted beetle B-138, L-100, *pictures* L-100, I-202
■ hibernation H-151
■ preys upon: scale insects S-52f

**Ladycliff College,** at Highland Falls, near West Point, N.Y.; private control; primarily for women; founded 1933; liberal arts and sciences, teacher education.

**'Lady Elizabeth Delmé and Her Children',** painting by Reynolds P-47, *picture* P-47

**Ladyfinger,** banana variety B-53

**'Lady Jean',** painting by Bellows P-61, *picture* P-60

**Lady Margaret Hall,** one of the colleges at Oxford University, England O-515

**Lady of Christ's,** nickname of John Milton M-327

**Lady of the Lake,** water fairy and enchantress of Arthurian legend; treacherously imprisoned Merlin in an enchanted tower in the forest of Brécéliande; reared Lancelot in her palace, situated in the middle of an imaginary lake
■ King Arthur's sword A-655

**'Lady of the Lake, The',** poem by Sir Walter Scott S-73

**Ladysmith,** South Africa, trade center, and railroad junction in n. Natal; pop. 22,955; besieged

by Boers for 118 days (1899–1900) during Boer War, *map* S-264
■ siege, *table* W-8d

**Lady's-slipper,** a plant of the orchid type L-100, *picture* F-277e
■ floral emblem of Prince Edward Island, *picture* P-497
■ skin irritant P-409
■ state flower of Minnesota, *pictures* M-356, S-427

**'Lady with the Unicorn, The',** medieval story A-458

**Lae,** New Guinea, port on e. coast; pop. 4146; capital of Territory of New Guinea 1941–42; occupied by Japanese 1942–43; reoccupied by Allies Sept. 1943: *maps* E-37, P-4

**Laënnec** [*lā-nĕk'*], **René Théophile Hyacinthe** (1781–1826), French physician, born Brittany; invented the stethoscope and began practice of auscultation in medicine: M-215c, *picture* M-215c

**Laertes** [*lā-ẽr'tēz*], father of Odysseus O-409

**Laertes,** in Shakespeare's 'Hamlet', son of Polonius H-15

**La Farge** [*la färzh'*], **John** (1835–1910), painter, mural decorator, and designer of first stained glass made in U.S.; born New York City; grandfather of Oliver La Farge; exercised great influence on American art (lunettes, Supreme Court room, Minnesota State Capitol; 'Battle Window', Memorial Hall, Harvard University)

**La Farge, Oliver (Hazard Perry)** (1901–63), writer, anthropologist; born New York City, grandson of John La Farge; made archaeological and ethnological expeditions to Arizona for Harvard University and to Guatemala and Mexico for Tulane University; wrote with intimate knowledge and understanding of the Indians ('Laughing Boy', novel, won Pulitzer prize 1930; 'All the Young Men', 'A Pause in the Desert', short stories; 'Cochise of Arizona', biography; 'A Pictorial History of the American Indian'; 'Santa Fe', local history).

**Lafayette** [*lä-fĭ-ĕt'*, French *lȧ-fȧ-yĕt'*], **George Washington Motier de** (1779–1849), son of Marquis de Lafayette; aide-de-camp to General Grouchy.

**Lafayette, Gilbert Motier, marquis de** (1757–1834), French general and patriot L-101, *picture* L-101
■ American Revolution L-101, R-173
■ De Kalb and D-63
■ revisits United States, *picture* M-455

**LaFayette, Marie Madeleine, comtesse de** (1634–93), French novelist, born Paris; her masterpiece, 'La Princesse de Clèves', is first modern novel of sentiment in which story's interest depends not on the incident but on the character of persons involved: F-437

**Lafayette,** Calif., city 28 mi (45 km) n.e. of Berkeley; pop. 20,879; chiefly residential; settled 1834, incorporated 1968: *map, inset* C-52

**Lafayette,** Ind., city on Wabash River about 60 mi (95 km) n.w. of Indianapolis; pop. 43,011; aluminum products, prefabricated houses, gears, sponge rubber, meters; r.r. shops; Purdue University at West Lafayette: *maps* I-100, U-41

**Lafayette,** La., city about 52 mi (84 km) s.w. of Baton Rouge; pop. 81,961; railroad division point; agricultural and oil center; food products, aluminum products; The University of Southwestern Louisiana: *maps* L-380, 364

**'Lafayette',** submarine, *pictures* S-496

**"Lafayette, we are here,"** words reportedly uttered by General Pershing when laying wreath on tomb of Lafayette July 4, 1917; actually spoken by Col. Charles E. Stanton.

**Lafayette College,** at Easton, Pa.; Presbyterian; formerly for men, women admitted 1970; opened 1832 (chartered 1826); arts and sciences, education, engineering, international affairs.

**Lafayette Escadrille,** World War I W-257

**Lafayette Square,** Washington, D.C. public park north of the White House; contains statues of Generals Andrew Jackson, Lafayette, Kosciusko, and Steuben: *map* W-32

**La Fère** [*lȧ fĕr*], France, town on Oise River, 25 km (15 mi) n.w. of Laon; pop. 3095; scene of fighting in World Wars I and II.

**Lafitte** [*la-fēt'*], **Jean** (1780?–1826?), American pirate, slave trader, and smuggler; born France: L-101–2, *pictures* L-101, L-374
■ battle of New Orleans J-354
■ blacksmith shop L-101, *map* N-223a

**La Follette** [*la fŏl'ĕt*], **Philip F(ox)** (1897–1965), lawyer and political leader, born Madison, Wis.; son of Robert Marion La Follette; Progressive Republican; governor of Wisconsin 1931–33, 1935–39.

**La Follette, Robert Marion** (1855–1925), political leader, born Primrose, Wis.; called Fighting Bob; father of Philip F. and Robert M. La Follette, Jr.; governor of Wisconsin 1901–5; U.S. senator 1906–25; a Progressive Republican who subordinated party ties to his own principles; opposed U.S. entrance into World War I; many of the reforms he sought incorporated in the "Wisconsin idea"; Progressive party presidential candidate 1924: W-198, *picture* W-204
■ heads Progressives P-434: electoral vote, *chart* P-494
■ Insurgent leader T-8
■ Seamen's Act (author) S-173
■ Statuary Hall, *table* S-437b

**La Follette, Robert Marion, Jr.** (1895–1953), political leader, born Madison, Wis.; son of Robert Marion La Follette; Progressive Republican; U.S. senator from Wisconsin 1925–47; committed suicide.

**La Fontaine** [*lȧ fôn-tĕn'*], **Henri** (1854–1943), Belgian politician, born Brussels; prolific writer on international arbitration
■ Nobel prize, *table* N-294g

**La Fontaine, Jean de** (1621–95), French poet and fabulist L-102, *picture* L-102
■ fables F-2, F-437

**Lafontaine, Sir Louis Hippolyte** (1807–64), Canadian jurist and statesman, premier 1842–44 and 1848–51; chief justice of Lower Canada 1853–64: C-112, B-24

**Laforet, Carmen** (born 1921), Spanish novelist, born Barcelona S-366, 367, *picture* S-367

**Laforgue** [*lȧ-fôrḡ'*], **Jules** (1860–87), French symbolist poet, born Montevideo, Uruguay; one of first to write modern free verse.

**LAFTA** (Latin American Free Trade Association) L-147

**Lagado,** in 'Gulliver's Travels', the capital of Balnibarbi; here a celebrated Academy of Projectors engages in extracting sunbeams from cucumbers, in converting ice into gunpowder, and in similar ridiculous ventures.

**Lagan** [*lăḡ'ăn*], in law F-249
■ buoy marks, *picture* F-249

**Lagash,** ancient city-state in Babylonia, one of oldest centers of Sumerian civilization; on site of present Telloh, Iraq; reached peak about 3000 B.C. B-7, *map* B-4

**Lager beer,** alcoholic beverage B-132

**Lagerkvist, Pär Fabian** (1891–1974), Swedish poet, playwright, and novelist, born Växjö (plays: 'The Man Without a Soul', 'Let Man Live'; novels: 'The Eternal Smile', 'The Dwarf', 'Barabbas')
■ Nobel prize, *table* N-294f

**Lagerlöf** [*lä'ḡẽr-lûv*], **Selma (Ottiliana Lovisa)** (1858–1940), Swedish writer L-102–3, S-472
■ Nobel prize, *table* N-294f
■ 'Wonderful Adventures of Nils, The' L-102, R-111a

**Lago Argentino,** glacial valley, Argentina A-576

**Lagomorpha,** order of gnawing animals that differ from rodents in having 4 upper cutting teeth (incisors) instead of 2; includes hares, rabbits, and pikas.

**Lagoon,** a pool or lake, especially one connected with the sea
■ coral islands P-13, *pictures* P-13

**Lagos** [*lä'ḡōs*], a region (formerly province) of s. Nigeria; in w. Africa; 27,000 sq mi (70,000 sq km); low marshy coast, with countless lagoons; forested interior yields palm oil and kernels, mahogany, rubber; chief cities Ibadan (with surrounding suburban farm district, pop. 459,196) and Lagos: N-287

**Lagos,** Nigeria, capital and chief port, in s.w.; pop. 875,417: N-287, L-241, A-119
■ children's books L-310g

**Lagrange** [*lȧ-ḡränzh'*], **Joseph Louis** (1736–1813), French mathematician, one of greatest of 18th century, born Turin, Italy; contributed to verification of Newtonian theory of gravitation
■ Laplace and L-125c

**La Grange** [*la ḡrānġ'*], Ga., industrial city and trade center, 62 mi (100 km) s.w. of Atlanta; pop. 24,204; textiles, lumber products; La Grange College: *maps* G-92, U-41

**La Grange,** Ill., village 14 mi (22 km) s.w. of Chicago; pop. 15,681; named for Lafayette's home in France; nearby are diesel locomotive plant, aluminum rolling mill, and factory making parts of automobile bodies: *map, inset* I-50
■ manufacturing plant, *picture* I-36

**La Grange College,** at La Grange, Ga.; Methodist; chartered 1831; opened 1832; arts and sciences, teacher education; graduate studies; quarter system.

**La Grange Park,** Ill., village 14 mi (22 km) s.w. of Chicago; pop. 13,359; electronic components, plastic products: *map, inset* I-50

**La Granja,** Spain. *see in index* San Ildefonso

**Lagting** [*läg'tĭng*], in Norway N-368

**La Guaira** [*lä ḡwī'rä*], Venezuela, seaport for Caracas, on Caribbean Sea; artificial inner harbor; pop. 20,681: V-275, *map* S-298
■ tunnel, *table* T-292

**La Guardia** [*lȧ gwär'dĭ-ȧ*], **Fiorello Henry** (1882–1947), lawyer and public official, born New York City; member of U.S. Congress 1917–21, 1923–33; mayor of New York City 1934–45; director UNRRA 1946
■ organizes Civil Air Patrol C-366a

**La Guardia Airport,** New York, N.Y. N-273, *map* N-271

**La Guma, Alex,** novelist A-123

**Laguna** [*lä-ḡų'nä*] (Spanish "lagoon"), pueblo 42 mi (68 km) w. of Albuquerque, N.M.; pop. 4233; founded 1699; Laguna people belong to the Keresan language group of Pueblo Indians: *map* N-220

**Laguna Beach,** Calif., scenic city on Pacific Ocean about 45 mi (70 km) s.e. of Los Angeles; pop. 17,860; art center and resort; incorporated 1927: *map* C-53, *picture* U-88

**Laguna de Bay** [*lä-ḡų'nä thā vä'ē*], largest lake in Philippines, s.e. of Manila; 344 sq mi (891 sq km): P-256, 259

**La Habra,** Calif., city 17 mi (27 km) s.e. of Los Angeles; pop. 45,232; electronic components, metal products, processed foods, chemicals: *map, inset* C-53

**Lahaina** [*lą-hī'ną*], Hawaii, city on w. coast of Maui; pop. 3718; exports sugar; first white settlement of Hawaii was here: capital 1810–45: *map* H-71

**La Halle, Adam de.** *see in index* Adam de la Halle

**Lahn River,** West Germany, after s.w. course of 215 km (135 mi) joins Rhine opposite Coblenz: *map* G-115

**La Hogue** [*lą hōḡ'*, French *lą ōḡ'*], or **La Hogue, battle of,** fought 1692 near n.e. extremity of peninsula of Cotentin, Normandy, France; English and Dutch fleets under Admiral Russell defeated French fleet under Tourville: J-360

**Lahontan** [*lą-hŏn'tąn*], **Lake,** Nevada N-143

**Lahore** [*lą-hōr'*], Pakistan, capital of Punjab Province, near Ravi River, about 270 mi (435 km) n.w. of New Delhi, India; pop. 1,296,477; transportation center; silk and cotton cloths, carpets, vegetable oils; Punjab University: L-239, *map* I-66
■ Paisa Library L-310f

**Laibach,** Yugoslavia. *see in index* Ljubljana

**Laid paper,** paper marked with parallel lines
■ postage stamps S-405

**L'Aiglon** [*lĕ-ḡlôn'*], poetic name meaning "eaglet" given by Victor Hugo to duke of Reichstadt, son of Napoleon and Marie Louise; subject of play by Rostand.

**Laika,** Russian dog, first animal to orbit earth S-345, *table* S-344

**Laird, Melvin R(obert)** (born 1922), public official, born Omaha, Neb.; to Marshfield, Wis., at early age; member Wisconsin state Senate 1946–52; Republican congressman from Wisconsin 1953–69; U.S. secretary of defense 1969–73; chief adviser on domestic affairs 1973–74.

**Laissez faire** [*lĕ-sā fĕr'*] ("let it be"), the 18th-century (French) way of saying "less government in business"; in contemporary use means unrestricted industrial and commercial competition: I-170, 173, S-233, I-241

**Laity,** defined C-336

**Laius,** in Greek mythology, father of Oedipus O-409

**Lajoie, Napoleon** (Larry) (1875–1959), baseball second baseman, born Woonsocket, R.I.; second baseman chiefly Philadelphia, N.L., 1896–1900, and Cleveland, A.L., 1901–14; in 1901, batted .422, highest in A.L. history; lifetime average .339 B-93

**La Jolla** [*lą hoi'ą*], Calif., community in city of San Diego; Scripps Institution of Oceanography; cliffs, caves, and scenic stretches of ocean beach attract many tourists.

**La Jonquière, Jacques Pierre Taffanel, marquis de** (1680–1753), French naval officer, born near Albi in s. France; fought numerous engagements against British; governor of New France (Canada) 1749–53.

**La Junta** [*lą hŭn'tą*], Colo., city on Arkansas River 60 mi (100 km) s.e. of Pueblo; pop. 8338; railroad shops, food processing, livestock sales center; mobile homes: *maps* C-467, U-40
■ Bent's Fort. *see in index* Bent's Fort
■ Scouts portray Indians, *picture* C-463

**Lake, Simon** (1866–1945), naval architect and mechanical engineer, born Pleasantville, N.J.; inventor of even-keel type of submarine: S-493
■ O-class submarine, *picture* S-495

**Lake,** asphalt A-702

**Lake** L-103. For list of greatest lakes, *see table* on next page. *see also in index* names of individual lakes, as Erie, Lake
■ acid rain pollution A-19
■ climate affected by G-204
■ drained, effect on drought and floods F-226
■ extinct: Agassiz M-89a, R-120; Bonneville G-208, U-216; potassium salt deposits P-465–6
■ freshwater: largest S-518, L-103; longest T-15
■ glacial origin I-4, L-103
■ largest inland body of water L-103
■ oxbow E-16, L-103, R-210, *diagrams* E-17, R-210
■ part of river R-210, *diagram* R-210
■ pollution P-441c, d, *diagram* P-441d
■ salt L-103: Caspian Sea largest C-148; Dead Sea D-41, *picture* D-41; Great Salt Lake G-208; potassium salts P-465
■ seiche O-400a
■ water table and G-203–4

**Lake Charles,** La., port city in s.w. part of state, on Lake Charles, on direct channel to Gulf of Mexico; pop. 75,226; oil-refinery products, chemicals, synthetic rubber, wood products; meat-packing, rice milling; McNeese State

University: L-364, 365, *maps* L-380, 364, U-41
**Lake Chelan National Recreation Area,** in Washington N-40a, *map* N-30
**Lake Compounce,** amusement park, Bristol, Conn. A-385
**Lake District,** in n.w. England; has all principal English lakes: E-219, 218, *maps* G-199e
■ home of Wordsworth, *picture* W-234
**Lake dwellers,** Stone Age people who built huts on pile foundations along the shores of lakes: L-103, S-157, S-544, *picture* M-78
■ weaving T-138
**Lake Erie, battle of** (1813) P-209, W-13
**Lake Erie College,** at Painesville, Ohio; private control; for women; chartered 1856; opened 1859; arts and sciences, fine arts; coeducational division Garfield Senior College offers liberal arts, business, education.
**Lake Forest,** Ill., residential city on Lake Michigan, 30 mi (50 km) n. of Chicago; pop. 15,245; Barat College; Lake Forest College: *map* I-50
**Lake Forest College,** at Lake Forest, Ill.; private control, Presbyterian related; founded 1857; arts and sciences, teacher education; trimesters.
**Lake Geneva,** Wis., city in s.e. part of state, on Lake Geneva, 40 mi (65 km) s.w. of Milwaukee; resort; pop. 5607; Yerkes Observatory of University of Chicago, 6 mi (10 km) w. of city: *map* W-207
**Lakehurst,** N.J., borough about 55 mi (90 km) s. of New York City; pop. 2908: *map* N-203
**Lake Jackson,** Tex., city 50 mi (80 km) s. of Houston; pop. 19,102; metal products, store fixtures; dairy and fruit farms: *map* T-129
**Lakeland,** Fla., city about 30 mi (50 km) e. of Tampa; pop. 47,406; 12 lakes, resort center; citrus fruit, food-processing, machinery, tile products; phosphate mines: *maps* F-246, U-41
■ Florida Southern College, *picture* U-207
**Lakeland College,** near Sheboygan, Wis.; United Church of Christ; founded 1862; liberal arts, business administration, education, medical technology, music, science.
**Lakeland terrier,** dog, native of Lake District of England, *picture* D-148
**Lake Mead National Recreation Area,** in Arizona and Nevada N-40a, C-470, *maps* N-157, N-30, C-470, *picture* N-152
**Lake Nasser,** reservoir, Egypt A-732
**Lake of the Woods,** an island-dotted body of water of n. Minnesota and adjacent parts of Ontario, Canada; 1485 sq mi (3845 sq km); 105 mi (170 km) long: *maps* M-349, 362, U-70, M-89j, C-73, 98, O-456b. *see also in index* Northwest Angle
■ muskellunge fishing P-326
**Lake Oswego,** Ore., city 8 mi (13 km) s. of Portland; pop. 14,573; cement, infant's wear, wood products; incorporated 1918: *map, inset* O-492
**Lake Placid,** N.Y., village at s. end of Lake Placid (about 4 mi [6 km] long and ½ mi [1 km] wide); pop. 2490; a famous winter and summer resort in Adirondack Mts.; nearby is the grave of John Brown, the abolitionist, *map* N-261
■ Adirondack Mountains A-44
■ American Home Economics Association H-205
■ bobsled run S-216, *picture* N-254
■ Olympic Games O-453
**Lake Poets,** in England C-432
**Lake Regillus, battle of** (496 B.C.) R-242
**Lakeshores, national,** United States. *map* N-30, *picture* N-42
**Lakes-to-Gulf waterway** G-205, C-121, *picture* I-38
■ Illinois Waterway links I-38, C-255, *map* G-203
**Lake Success,** on Long Island, N.Y.; pop. 3254: *map, inset* N-260
■ UN temporary headquarters U-22
**Lake Superior State College,** at Sault Sainte Marie, Mich; founded 1946; arts and social sciences, science and technology; quarter system.
**Lake trout** T-269, *picture* F-172
■ lamprey an enemy L-104, P-114, *picture* L-104
■ propagation, *pictures* F-163
**Lakeview,** Mich., community 38 mi (61 km) n.e. of Grand Rapids; pop. 1139; farm produces: *map* M-285
**Lake Washington Floating Bridge,** in Washington W-42, S-103, 104, *map* S-103b

## LAKES—LARGEST IN THE WORLD

| | Area | |
|---|---|---|
| **Name** | **sq mi** | **sq km** |
| Caspian Sea | 143,550 | 371,795 |
| Superior | 31,820 | 82,415 |
| Victoria | 26,830 | 69,490 |
| Aral Sea | 25,000 | 64,750 |
| Huron | 23,010 | 59,595 |
| Michigan | 22,400 | 58,015 |
| Tanganyika | 12,700 | 32,895 |
| Great Bear | 12,275 | 31,790 |
| Baikal (Baykal) | 12,160 | 31,495 |
| Nyasa | 11,600 | 30,045 |
| Great Slave | 10,980 | 28,440 |
| Chad | 9,945 | 25,760* |
| Erie | 9,940 | 25,745 |

*At high water

**Lake Washington Ship Canal,** Washington S-103, 104, *map* S-103b
**Lakewood,** Calif., residential and commercial city 13 mi (21 km) s.e. of Los Angeles; pop. 74,654; incorporated 1954; annual Pan-American festival: *map, inset* C-53
**Lakewood,** Colo., residential city w. of Denver; pop. 112,860; artificial kidneys, aerospace equipment; Camp George West Military Reservation: *map* C-467
**Lakewood,** N.J., community 19 mi (30 km) s.w. of Long Branch; pop. 17,874; plastics, cosmetics, woodwork; winter resort: *map* N-203
**Lakewood,** Ohio, city on Lake Erie, just w. of Cleveland; pop. 61,963; originally East Rockport, took present name 1889: *map, inset* O-429
**Lake Worth,** Fla., city 9 mi (14 km) s. of Palm Beach, on Lake Worth, which opens into the Atlantic; resort; pop. 27,048; incorporated 1913: *map* F-247
**Laki, Mount,** volcano in Iceland I-10
**Lakshadweep,** formerly **Laccadive, Minicoy, and Amindivi Islands,** union territory, India; islands and coral reefs; 11 sq mi (28 sq km); pop. 31,810 (1971 census); grain, bananas, copra, fisheries: *maps* I-84c, 81
**Lalande** [*lȧ-länd'*], **Saint Jean de** (died 1646), Roman Catholic martyr; missionary in Canada and New York; companion of Father Jogues; murdered by Mohawks at Ossernenon, N.Y.; canonized 1930; feasts celebrated Sept. 26 and March 16 (by Jesuits).
**Lalande, Joseph Jérôme Le François de** (1732–1807), French astronomer, born Bourg-en-Bresse, France; professor Collège de France, director Paris observatory; popularized astronomy; established annual Prix Lalande for most useful work on astronomy.
**Lalemant** [*lȧl-män'*], **Saint Gabriel** (1610–49), Canadian Jesuit missionary, born Paris, France; came to Canada 1646; worked with Father Brébeuf among the Huron Indians and was killed by the Iroquois; canonized 1930.
**Lalique** [*lȧ-lēk'*], **René** (1860–1945), French jeweler, born Ay, near Reims; famous for carving in jewels and glass.
**'Lalla Rookh'** [*lä'lä ro̦k*], Oriental poem by Thomas Moore; an Indian princess, on her way to Sultan Aliris, her betrothed, is entertained by a Persian poet, with whom she falls in love; is later overjoyed to find that the poet was her betrothed in disguise.
**'L'Allegro'** [*läl-lā'grō*] ("the happy man"), poem by John Milton; companion poem of 'Il Penseroso'; describes quiet pleasures of a contented man: E-259
**Lalo** [*lȧ-lō'*], **Édouard** (1823–92), French composer, born Lille, France ('Le Roi d'Ys', opera; 'Symphonie Espagnole', 'Norwegian Rhapsody', orchestral works).
**Lamaism,** a religion of Tibet and Mongolia T-173, M-432, *pictures* T-172
■ Dalai Lama, or Grand Lama T-173: palace, *picture* T-173
**La Malbaie,** also **Murray Bay,** Que., Canada, town on St. Lawrence River at mouth of Malbaie River 124 km (77 mi) n.e. of Quebec (city); pop. 4307; summer resort: *map* Q-11
**La Mama Experimental Theatre Club,** forum for creating and performing new plays A-363
**Lamar, Lucius Quintus Cincinnatus** (1825–93), jurist and statesman, born Putnam County, Ga.; drafted Mississippi ordinance of secession; U.S. senator 1877–85; secretary of interior 1885–88; justice U.S. Supreme Court 1888–93; helped reconciliation between North and South after Civil War: *picture* M-384
**Lamar, Mirabeau Buonaparte** (1798–1859), soldier, born Louisville, Ga.; participated in Texas revolution and distinguished self at San Jacinto; president Texas Republic 1838–41; major general Mexican War; U.S. minister to Argentina, Nicaragua, Costa Rica.
**Lamarck** [*lȧ-märk'*], **Jean Baptiste Pierre Antoine de Monet, chevalier de** (1744–1829), French naturalist, born Bazentin, Picardy; in 1802 adopted the word "biologie" as name of new science to be devoted to study of all life considered as the same process whether in plants or animals
■ forerunner of Darwin D-35
■ heredity theory E-345, G-43a
**La Marque,** Tex., city s.w. of Texas City; pop. 15,372; chiefly residential; oil production and truck farming; established in 1860's, named 1890: *map* T-129
**Lamartine** [*lȧ-mȧr-tēn'*], **Alphonse de** (1790–1869), French poet, historian, and statesman; born Macon, France: F-438, 440
**Lamar University,** at Beaumont, Tex.; established 1923 as junior college; became state-supported senior college 1951; liberal arts, business, education, engineering, fine and applied arts, sciences, vocational training; graduate school.
**La Matanza,** Argentina, suburb of Buenos Aires; pop. 402,642: *map* S-299
**La Mauricie National Park,** in Quebec, Canada N-24d, Q-9h, *map* N-24b
**Lamb, Charles** (1775–1834), English essayist L-103–4, E-264, *picture* L-103
■ book annotations B-362
■ essays L-104, 103, E-290
■ letters L-197
■ on fairy tales and children S-466
■ opinion of Samuel T. Coleridge C-432
■ quoted on Shakespeare S-142
■ 'Tales from Shakespear' S-140, L-104
**Lamb, Mary** (1764–1847), English writer, sister of Charles Lamb L-104
■ 'Tales from Shakespear' S-140, L-104
**Lamb, William.** *see in index* Melbourne, Viscount
**Lamb, Willis E(ugene), Jr.** (born 1913), physicist, born Los Angeles, Calif.; professor of physics Stanford University 1951–56, Oxford University 1956–62, and Yale University after 1962
■ Nobel prize, *table* N-294a
**Lamb,** a young sheep S-146, *pictures* S-146, F-19, F-38
■ meat M-189, 190, M-192, 192a, 193, 194, S-146, 148, *diagrams* M-192b, *tables* M-189–90
■ skin L-174–5, G-144d
■ wool W-229, 230
**Lamballe** [*läṅ-bȧl'*], **Marie Thérèse de** (1749–92), French princess, born Turin, Italy; friend of Marie Antoinette; killed by revolutionists; her head carried past queen's prison windows.
**Lambaréné** [*läm-bạ-rā'nē*], Gabon, town on Ogooué River 95 mi (155 km) s.e. of Libreville; pop. 3750; Albert Schweitzer's medical center: S-56
**Lambeau, Earl Louis** (Curly) (1898–1965), football halfback and coach, born Green Bay, Wis.; founded Green Bay Packers 1919, halfback and head coach 1919–49: *list* F-337
**Lambert, Johann Heinrich** (1728–77), German physicist, mathematician, astronomer, and philosopher; born Mulhouse, Alsace; made important contributions to mathematical theory; measured intensity and absorption of light (Lambert, unit of intensity, named for him)
■ map projections improved M-101
**Lambert, Louis.** *see in index* Gilmore, Patrick S.
**Lambert, Richard Stanton** (born 1894), Canadian educator and writer, born London, England; promoted educational and cultural films and radio broadcasts; books for children include 'Franklin of the Arctic' (Canadian Book of the Year for Children award 1950) and 'The Adventure of Canadian Painting'; also author of books for adults.
**Lambeth, baron of.** *see in index* Davidson, Randall Thomas; Fisher, Geoffrey Francis
**Lambeth,** borough of Greater London, England; pop. 325,070: L-344, *map* L-337, *inset* G-199h
**Lambeth Council (1888),** defined essential positions of Anglican Church in the hope of reconciliation with other Christian denominations A-417
**Lambeth Palace,** in London, England; begun 1207; heavily damaged by bombing 1940–41: L-344
**Lambing Flat,** New South Wales, Australia
■ anti-Chinese riots A-785
**Lambkill,** or **sheep laurel,** evergreen shrub of heath family; grows to 1 m (3 ft); the flowers, which are purple or crimson, are arranged in flat-topped clusters: P-409, L-163
**Lambrequin,** or **mantling,** heraldic device H-142
**Lamb's-ears,** a perennial plant (*Stachys lanata*) of the mint family, native to w. Asia. Grows to 46 cm (18 in.), entire plant white, woolly, with oblong leaves and spikes of tiny, tubular, purple flowers; sometimes called woolly woundwort.
**Lambskin** L-174–5, G-144d
**Lamb's lettuce.** *see in index* Corn salad
**Lamb's quarters,** or **goosefoot,** an annual herb (*Chenopodium album*) of the goosefoot family with clusters of small greenish flowers and leaves shaped like the foot of a goose; although considered a

pest, delicious greens may be made from it.

**Lambuth College,** at Jackson, Tenn.; affiliated with United Methodist church; established 1843; arts and sciences and education.

**Lamb vulture** V-388

**Lamé** [*lá-mā'*], a fabric made of any of various fibers combined with tinsel threads, often of silver or gold; most frequently used for evening wear; also trade name for metallic yarns.

**Lame Duck amendment,** or **20th Amendment** H-223, U-146
■ text U-153

**'Lamentation, The',** drawing by Dürer D-181, *picture* D-182

**Lamentations,** book of Old Testament traditionally ascribed to Jeremiah; comprises five dirges bewailing the destruction of Jerusalem B-182

**Lamenting bird.** *see in index* Limpkin

**Lamer, Antonio** (born 1933), Canadian jurist, born Montreal, Que.; justice Superior Court of Quebec 1969–78, Quebec Court of Appeal 1978–80; justice Supreme Court of Canada 1980–.

**La Mesa,** Calif., residential city 8 mi (13 km) n.e. of San Diego; pop. 50,342; citrus fruit, avocados, poultry; incorporated 1912: *map* C-53

**Lamesa,** Tex., city 57 mi (92 km) s. of Lubbock; pop. 11,790; cotton and other farming, ranching; poultry; oil fields; cotton gins; garments; *map* T-128

**Lamia** [*lā'mĭ-ą*], in Greek mythology, a beautiful vampire; in John Keats's poem 'Lamia', a serpent that assumes human form to win a man's love.

**Laminar Flow Control,** or **LFC,** aerodynamics A-80, A-180

**Laminated fabric,** material consisting of two or more layers of goods put together with adhesive plastic, rubber, or other joining substance; term also applies to fabric joined to plastic sheet, as goods bonded to synthetic foam; used for women's dresses and coats.

**Laminating,** arranging in thin layers (laminae)
■ plastics P-383
■ plywood P-397, L-391, *picture* L-393
■ safety glass G-135

**La Mirada,** Calif., city located on freeway 17 mi (27 km) s.e. of Los Angeles; chiefly residential; pop. 40,986; Biola College; governed by city administrator system.

**Lammergeier** [*lăm'ĕr-gī-ĕr*], or **bearded vulture** V-388

**Lamoille** [*lą-moil'*] **River,** rises in n. Vermont near Hardwick; cuts w. through Green Mts.; flows into Lake Champlain; dam forms Lake Lamoille at Morrisville: *maps* V-286, 301

**Lamon** [*lăm'ŏn*], **Ward Hill** (1828–93), law partner, secretary, and biographer of Abraham Lincoln; born Frederick County, Va.; served as marshal of District of Columbia 1861–65; *picture* C-374

**Lamona,** a breed of poultry P-482

**Lamont, Robert Patterson** (1867–1948), U.S. secretary of commerce under President Hoover; born Detroit, Mich.; engineer and manufacturer; president American Steel Foundries 1912–29.

**La Motte-Fouqué** [*fo̦-kā'*], **Friedrich, baron de** (1777–1843), German romantic poet and novelist, born Brandenburg; extremely popular in early 19th century: G-98

**Lamp** L-105–6, *pictures* L-105–6. *see also in index* Light; Lighting
■ arc lamp, or light E-157: projectors S-444, *diagrams* S-444, M-507; signaling, *picture* S-193
■ Argand lamp L-106
■ colonial L-106. *see also in index* American Colonies, life in the, *subhead* lighting
■ electric lamp E-157–8, E-72–3, G-139, T-288, V-254, *pictures* E-157–8, E-69, 71, I-247, N-195: memorial tower, *picture* N-191
■ fluorescent. *see in index* Fluorescent lamp
■ glow lamp (neon type) E-170
■ Greece, ancient L-105–6, *pictures* L-105, G-225
■ interior decoration I-232–3
■ lanterns L-106, *pictures* L-106
■ lighthouse L-270
■ miner's safety lamps C-420, D-39, *pictures* D-39, C-420
■ oil L-105–6, P-232, *pictures* L-105–6, G-225
■ pottery as base, *picture* P-479
■ primitive L-105, *picture* L-105: Eskimo E-286
■ Rome, ancient L-106
■ signaling S-194
■ sodium vapor lamps S-247

**Lampblack,** or **carbon black,** a form of carbon G-41, C-132
■ ink I-190
■ paint pigment P-73
■ pencils P-158
■ tire manufacture G-41, R-303

**Lamp-eyed fish,** a deep-sea fish having an organ below each eye in which bacteria live; the bacteria secrete a luminous chemical; the fish may draw a lid over the organ when it wishes: F-160

**Lampman, Archibald** (1861–99), Canadian poet, born Morpeth, Ont.: C-113b, 116, *picture* C-114

**Lamprey,** an eel-shaped fish L-104, A-435, *pictures* L-104, P-114
■ animal groups, *chart* Z-366
■ evolutionary position F-162
■ invades Great Lakes P-114, L-104

**Lampsacus,** ancient Greek city of Mysia, Asia Minor, on Hellespont, opposite Gallipoli; settled by Ionian Greeks (654); known for its wines; center of worship of fertility god Priapus.

**Lamp shell,** bivalve S-151

**Län** [*lān*], administrative district in Sweden S-526

**Lana, Francesco de,** Italian monk A-200

**Lanai** [*lą-nī'*], island of Hawaii; 139.5 sq mi (361.3 sq km); 18 mi (29 km) long, 10 mi (16 km) wide; pop. 2204; highest point 3400 ft (1035 m); pineapple plantations since 1922; previously pastureland: H-53, *maps* H-52, 71, U-98, 117, P-5

**Lanao** [*lä-nä'ō*], **Lake,** second largest lake in Philippines, on island of Mindanao; 134 sq mi (347 sq mi): P-259, 255d, 256

**La Navidad,** in Haiti; Columbus' first settlement in New World: C-478, 479, H-7

**Lancashire** [*lăn'ką-shĕr*], or **Lancaster,** county of n.w. England; 3043 sq km (1175 sq mi); pop. 5,129,416; cap. Lancaster; iron and coal mines; textiles, machinery: L-106a, *map* E-218
■ textile industry M-82, L-314

**Lancaster, John of Gaunt, duke of.** *see in index* John of Gaunt

**Lancaster,** Calif., community 45 mi (72 km) n.e. of Los Angeles; in Antelope Valley region of Mojave Desert; pop. 48,027; cotton, citrus fruits, nuts; aircraft: *map* C-53

**Lancaster,** England, capital of Lancashire, on Lune River, 11 km (7 mi) from sea; pop. 48,170; L-106a, *map* G-199h
■ location L-106a, *locator map* L-106a

**Lancaster,** N.Y., village 11 mi (18 km) e. of Buffalo; pop. 13,056; in dairying area; stone quarries, glass products; settled 1810, incorporated 1849: *map* N-260

**Lancaster,** Ohio, city on Hocking River, 27 mi (43 km) s.e. of Columbus; pop. 34,953; glassware, machinery, boiler equipment, shoes, foundry products; birthplace of Gen. William Tecumseh Sherman; state industrial school for boys nearby: *map* O-429

**Lancaster,** Pa., city 34 mi (55 km) s.e. of Harrisburg; pop. 54,725: L-106a, *maps* P-185, 174, U-41
■ first chain store C-204
■ former state capital P-172
■ grave of Thaddeus Stevens S-445
■ location L-106a, *locator map* L-106a
■ Wheatland L-106a

**Lancaster, House of,** famous English royal family L-106a, *table* R-297. *see also in index* Roses, Wars of the
■ Henry IV founded H-136
■ rulers. *see in index* England, *table* of kings and queens

**Lancaster Turnpike,** historical road in United States R-215, T-196, *map* R-219, *pictures* P-175, W-25

**Lance,** long-shafted cavalry weapon with spearhead
■ medieval, *picture* M-302

**Lance corporal,** U.S. military rank
■ insignia, *picture* U-9

**Lancelet.** *see in index* Amphioxus

**Lancelot** [*lăn'sĕ-lŏt*], also **Lancelot of the Lake,** in Arthurian legend, bravest and most famous of the Knights of the Round Table; outstanding figure in Tennyson's 'Idylls of the King': R-299a, A-655
■ quest for Grail G-3

**Lancers,** a type of quadrille; introduced in 19th century; danced by 8 or 16 couples; also its music. *see also in index* Quadrille

**Lancewood,** name given to several trees of family *Annonaceae* native to West Indies and Guiana, and to their highly pliable and tough even-grained wood, which is used for fishing rods and for other articles requiring flexibility and strength.

**Lanchow** [*län'gō'*], People's Republic of China, capital of Kansu Province; pop. 732,000; petroleum refining; oil-field equipment, chemicals: C-293b, *maps* C-291, C-312

**Lanciani** [*län-chä'nē*], **Rodolfo** (1846–1929), Italian archaeologist, born Rome; professor ancient topography University of Rome; made important discoveries at Ostia, Tivoli, Rome ('Ancient and Modern Rome').

**Lancret** [*län-krĕ'*], **Nicolas** (1690–1743), French painter, born Paris; greatly influenced by Jean Antoine Watteau; gay portrayals of French society.

**Land, Edwin Herbert** (born 1909), American inventor and corporation executive L-106a–b, *pictures* L-106a, C-530
■ invents Polaroid Land camera P-300
■ theory of color vision L-106a–b, C-448

**Land, Emory S(cott)** (1879–1971), U.S. Navy officer, born Canon City, Colo.; chairman U.S. Maritime Commission 1938–46; chief of War Shipping Administration 1942–46; president Air Transport Association of America 1946–53.

**Land.** *see also in index* Agriculture; Irrigation and reclamation; Land grant; Lands, public; Land tenure; Land use; Soil, *subhead* conservation
■ ancient civilizations developed A-403
■ Aztec tribal organization A-892
■ description of townships, sections, and quarters, *diagram* L-108
■ earth's surface E-16, 17, *chart* E-13
■ economic factor in production E-56, 59: value, *table* E-57
■ eminent domain C-355
■ farmlands, United States U-104–5
■ homestead L-108, J-465, I-57, P-340
■ speculation P-335a
■ surveying S-520
■ taxation T-32
■ world cultivated land F-327, *chart* F-327

**Land Acts of 1870, 1881,** Ireland I-287

**Landau, Lev Davidovich** (1908–68), Russian physicist, born Baku; head of theoretical physics Vavilov Institute of Physical Problems
■ Nobel prize, *table* N-294b

**Land banks, federal,** United States F-36
■ farms financed by, *map* F-36

**Land bridges between continents.** *see in index* Geology, *subhead* land bridges between continents

**"Land down under"** (Australia) A-767

**Lander, Richard Lemon** (1804–34) and **Lander, John** (1807–39), English explorers, born Cornwall; determined course of Niger River 1830 and published journals; were brothers.

**Lander,** Wyo., town 120 mi (195 km) w. of Casper on Popo Agie River; pop. 9126; dairy farming, timber, stock raising, oil and coal mining; popular resort; nearby Wind River Indian Reservation; incorporated 1890: *map* W-326

**Lander College,** at Greenwood, S.C.; local control; coeducational, formerly for women; founded 1872; arts and sciences, education.

**Landes** [*länd*], region of s.w. France, vast tract of sandy marshland bordered by dunes: F-386
■ reclamation S-38

**"Land flowing with milk and honey,"** from Bible, Exod. iii, 8 and Jer., xxxii, 22; place of bounty or unusual fertility; phrase used to describe the abundance of heaven.

**Landform** C-395d
■ book about S-64d
■ evolution G-61

**Land grant** L-106b
■ educational L-106b, L-108, E-88, H-205, *table* E-92: South Dakota S-325; Texas T-115; Vermont V-288
■ railroad R-74, L-107, N-344, *map* L-107

**Landing,** airplane A-191

**Landing craft,** in warfare N-99, 94, *pictures* N-97, 100, 106, M-110, W-10

**Landing gear**
■ airplane A-184
■ glider G-144a, *diagram* G-144

**Landing net,** in fishing, *list* F-180

**Landis, James McCauley** (1899–1964), public official, born Tokyo, Japan, of American parents, missionaries; taught law, Harvard University, 1926–34; chairman SEC 1935–37; dean Harvard Law School 1937–46; director Office of Civilian Defense 1942–43; director U.S. economic operations in Middle East 1943–45; chairman CAB 1946–47; special assistant to President John F. Kennedy 1961.

**Landis, Kenesaw Mountain** (1866–1944), jurist and baseball commissioner, born Millville, Ohio; judge U.S. district court of n. Illinois 1905–22; tried Standard Oil rebate case in 1907: *profile* B-95
■ commissioner of baseball B-96

**Land League, Irish** I-287

**Landlord,** owner or master of land or of building rented to tenants: H-257a
■ cotton farms C-589
■ vassals in feudal system F-99, 100, *picture* F-98

**Land Management, Bureau of,** United States L-108, U-161

**Land measure,** units of, *tables* W-96, 97

**Land of Enchantment,** popular name for New Mexico N-206

**"Land office business, doing a"** U-177

**Land of Nod,** term used to designate the state of sleep; so called from the unknown land of "wandering," or Nod, to which Cain fled after the murder of Abel (Gen. iv).

**Land of the Five Rivers.** *see in index* Punjab

**Land of the Long White Cloud,** Maori name for New Zealand. *see in index* New Zealand

**Land of the Midnight Sun**
■ Norway N-363
■ Sweden S-522

**Landon, Alf(red) Mossman** (born 1887), political leader, born West Middlesex, Pa.; governor of Kansas 1933–37; Republican candidate for presidency 1936: R-272, *picture* K-14

**Landor, Walter Savage** (1775–1864), English author, born Warwick, England; a poet of distinction, also master of English prose style (poetry: 'Gebir', 'Rose Aylmer'; prose: 'Pericles and Aspasia': E-274

**Landowska** [*län-dôf'skä*], **Wanda** (1879–1959), Polish harpsichordist L-106b, *picture* L-106b

**Landrieu, Moon** (born 1930), lawyer and public official, born New Orleans, La.; member Louisiana house of representatives 1960–65;

councilman-at-large New Orleans 1966–70, mayor 1970–78; U.S. secretary of housing and urban development 1979–81.

**Landrum-Griffin labor law** L-91

**Lands, public** L-107–8, *map* L-107
■ Canada L-108: national parks N-24a–d, *map* N-24b, *pictures* N-24a, c–d
■ land grants, *see in index* Land grant
■ Mexico M-250
■ national parks N-22–4, *pictures* N-22–4
■ Rome (ancient) R-244, 246
■ surveying methods L-108, S-520
■ United States, *map* L-107
□ conservation C-546, R-285–6
□ exploited in Taft's administration T-8
□ Harrison's small tract policy H-43–4
□ Homestead Act of 1862 L-108, P-340
□ immigrants offered I-57
□ Indian interests I-148
□ irrigation and reclamation I-312–13, 315
□ Johnson's Homestead Bill J-465
□ national parks N-25–49, *maps* N-30, 48, *pictures* N-25–9, 31–49.
□ Northwest Territory N-362
□ public domain L-107–8, *map* L-107
□ railroad land grants R-74, L-107, N-344, *map* L-107
□ slave states oppose policy C-372

**Landsats,** earth resource satellites, *table* S-344

**Landscape** B-377

**Landseer, Sir Edwin Henry** (1802–73), English animal painter L-109, *picture* L-109

**Land's End,** or **Lands End,** promontory of Cornwall, forming westernmost point of England, *map* G-199h

**Landsgemeinde,** in Switzerland S-543, *picture* S-544a

**Landshut** [*länts'hu̇t*], West Germany, city on Isar River in Bavaria, 55 km (35 mi) n.e. of Munich; pop. 52,417; 14th- and 15th-century gabled houses; Napoleon defeated Austrians (1809): *map* G-115

**Landslide,** in U.S. politics
■ Democratic: Johnson, L. B. J-474, 469; Roosevelt, F. D. R-272
■ Republican: Eisenhower E-130; Nixon N-293, U-196a; prevented by 1948 upset T-278

**Landsmål** [*län'smạl*], a dialect of Norway N-366

**Land snail** S-221, 222

**Landsteiner, Karl** (1868–1943), American bacteriologist and pathologist, born Vienna, Austria; member Rockefeller Institute for Medical Research A-483, B-317, M-215d
■ Nobel prize, *table* N-294d

**Landsting** (from Norse *land,* "land," and *ting,* or *thing,* "parliament"), certain legislative bodies in Scandinavian countries; in Sweden, county councils.

**Land tenure.** *see also in index* Land grant; Lands, public
■ American pioneers P-340
■ Canada C-96b
■ Channel Islands C-207
■ eminent domain C-355
■ feudal system F-99, C-105, *diagram* M-296
■ Greece, ancient S-369: Solon's reforms S-255
■ Homestead Act L-108, P-340: first introduced J-465
■ Hungary H-276
■ Ireland I-287: tenants' rights I-287
■ Italy I-328: Sicily S-192
■ Japan J-380, 405
■ Latin America L-142–3; Central America C-195; Chile C-287; Ecuador E-65; Mexico M-250, L-142–3; Peru P-222
■ Mongolia M-432
■ Philippines P-261, 260
■ Rome, ancient R-244, 246
■ sovereignty of nations I-238

**Land use** L-109–13, *charts* L-111–12, *diagram* L-113, *map* L-110, *picture* L-109. *see also in index* Soil
■ Afghanistan, *chart* A-69
■ Algeria, *chart* A-275
■ Canada, *chart* C-88
■ Central America, *charts* C-199
■ China, People's Republic of, *chart* C-303
■ China, Republic of, *chart* C-317
■ deserts D-93
■ drought E-52
■ Egypt, *chart* E-116
■ erosion control C-542–3, E-50, 51–2, F-347, F-226, *pictures* C-544, 539, E-49
■ flood prevention methods F-226, E-51
■ food resources F-326–8, *chart* F-327
■ forestry F-343–4
■ France, *chart* F-396
■ future, changes that may affect L-113
■ Germany, East, *chart* G-108a
■ Germany, West, *chart* G-112a
■ good and bad uses L-109–11
■ grasslands G-193, 194
■ Great Britain G-198a, E-220, *chart* G-199
■ Greece, *chart* G-220
■ Italy I-332–3, *chart* I-335
■ Japan, *chart* J-379
■ Korea, *chart* K-75g
■ location factor H-253, L-112: flood zones F-224, F-221
■ Mexico, *chart* M-257
■ Netherlands, *chart* N-141
■ Norway, *chart* N-370
■ Philippines, *chart* P-255d
■ planning L-111–12
■ Portugal, *chart* P-457b
■ ruined land restored, *pictures* E-49
■ Russia, *chart* R-334: compared with U.S., *chart* R-336
■ South America, *chart* S-296
■ Spain, *chart* S-362
■ Sweden, *chart* S-528
■ Switzerland, *chart* S-545
■ United States L-109–13, U-101, *charts* L-111–12, U-118, *diagram* L-113, *map* L-110, *picture* L-109. *see also in index* states by name, *subhead* land use
■ world cultivated land F-327, *chart* F-327

**Lane, Edward William** (1801–76), English Arabic scholar, born Hereford; spent many years between 1825 and 1849 in Egypt; published 'Account of the Manners and Customs of the Modern Egyptians'
■ 'Arabian Nights' A-525

**Lane, Joseph** (1801–81), statesman, born Buncombe County, N.C.; to Vanderburgh County, Ind., 1820; served as Indiana senator 1844–46; made major general for heroic action in Mexican War; governor of Territory of Oregon 1848–50; Oregon delegate to Congress 1850–58, U.S. senator 1859–61; candidate for vice-president on secession ticket 1860.

**Lane, Ralph Norman Angell.** *see in index* Angell, Sir Norman

**Lane, Richard** (Night Train) (born 1928), football player, born Austin, Tex.; defensive back; Los Angeles Rams 1952–53; Chicago Cardinals 1954–59, Detroit Lions 1960–65: *list* F-337

**Lane, Sir William Arbuthnot** (1856–1943), English physician, born Ft. George, near Inverness, Scotland; consulting surgeon Guy's Hospital, Hospital for Sick Children, French Hospital, London; author books on operative treatment of fractures and of cleft palate.

**Lane College,** at Jackson, Tenn.; Christian Methodist Episcopal church; founded 1882; liberal arts, teacher education.

**Lane Theological Seminary,** Cincinnati, Ohio
■ Beecher family's association B-131

**Lanfranc** (1005?–1089), English prelate and scholar, born in Italy; archbishop of Canterbury 1070–89; as chief counselor of William the Conqueror played important part in fixing Norman rule upon English church and people.

**Lang, Andrew** (1844–1912), Scottish scholar, poet, and writer on many subjects; born Selkirk, Scotland ('Ballads in Blue China'; 'Custom and Myth'; 'History of Scotland'; 'Blue', 'Red', 'Yellow', and other fairy books): S-466, 465, R-111a
■ 'Arabian Nights, The' S-480

**Lang, Cosmo Gordon** (1864–1945), English divine, archbishop of Canterbury 1928–42; born Aberdeenshire, Scotland; canon of St. Paul's 1901–8; archbishop of York 1908–28.

**Langdell, Christopher Columbus** (1826–1906), lawyer and educator; born New Boston, N.H.; after 1870 dean of Harvard University Law School; introduced "case system" of teaching, which revolutionized methods of law schools.

**Langdon, John** (1741–1819), merchant and political leader, born Portsmouth, N.H.; an ardent supporter of the Revolution, he financed Stark's expedition against Burgoyne and built ships for Navy; signed United States Constitution; one of first senators from New Hampshire; governor of New Hampshire 1805–8, 1810–11.

**Lange** [*läng'ĕ*], **Christian Louis** (1869–1938), Norwegian pacifist and historian, born Stavanger; represented Norway at Hague Peace Conference (1907) and League of Nations
■ Nobel prize, *table* N-294g

**Langensalza,** also **Bad Langensalza** [*bät läng-ĕn-zäl'tsä*], East Germany, town on Salza River 19 mi (30 km) n.w. of Erfurt; pop. 16,304; Hanoverians defeated Prussians in 1866, but surrendered on arrival of Prussian reinforcements: *map* G-115

**Langer, William** (1886–1959), attorney and senator, born Everest, N.D.; governor of North Dakota 1933–34 and 1937–39; U.S. senator 1940–59; known for legislation for farmers; Republican: *picture* N-350

**Langerhans, islands of,** in pancreas, discovered by Paul L. Langerhans, German pathologist (1849–88)

**Langevin, Sir Hector-Louis** (1826–1906), Canadian political leader, born Quebec City: F-75e, *pictures* F-75c–d, *table* F-75a

**Langland, William** (1330?–1400?), English poet E-255

**Langley, Samuel Pierpont** (1834–1906), American physicist, astronomer, and inventor L-113, I-189, *picture* L-113
■ aerospace research A-77
■ flying machines A-201, *picture* L-113

**'Langley',** U.S. aircraft carrier N-105

**Langley Air Force Base,** Hampton, Va. A-164, N-297, *maps* N-297, V-349

**Langley Park,** Md., community situated 6 mi (10 km) n.e. of Washington, D.C.; pop. 11,564: *map, inset* M-138

**Langmuir, Irving** (1881–1957), chemist, born Brooklyn, N.Y.; engaged in research for General Electric Company 1909–50; invented gas-filled tungsten lamp and condensation vacuum pump; helped develop high-vacuum tube used in atomic hydrogen welding ('Atoms and Molecules')
■ Nobel prize, *table* N-294c
■ Pupin teaches P-535

**Langobards.** *see in index* Lombards

**Langres** [*län'grü*], France, ancient town in e. on Plateau of Langres; pop. 8945; makes cutlery; famous strategic point since time of Roman empire: *map* F-404

**Langshan,** a breed of poultry P-482, *picture* P-481

**Langston, John Mercer** (1829–97), public official, born Louisa County, Va.; first Negro elected to public office in United States 1855 (clerk Brownhelm Township, Ohio); elected 1888 for one term in U.S. Congress.

**Langston University,** at Langston, Okla.; state control; founded 1897; arts and sciences, applied sciences, education, technical and vocational education.

**Langton, Stephen** (1150?–1228), English cardinal and archbishop of Canterbury, credited with being first to divide Bible into chapters; agitator for Magna Carta
■ triumphs over King John J-463

**Langtry, Lily (Emily)** (1852–1929), English actress, noted for her beauty, born Island of Jersey and known as the "Jersey lily"; first great success in 'She Stoops to Conquer'.

**Language** L-114–20, *Reference-Outline* L-119–20. *see also in index* Alphabet; Grammar; Philology; Rhetoric; Writing; languages by name, as English language; and language groups, as Indo-European languages
■ art forms A-662
■ Asian A-682
■ bibliography L-120
■ bilingualism. *see in index* Bilingualism
■ brain perceives B-402
■ communication and C-489: information theory I-188a–d, *diagrams* I-188b–d, *table* I-188d
■ computers translate C-503, L-115c
■ dialect L-115f, g
■ Europe E-313–14, L-115c, e
■ language families L-115i–16, *diagrams* L-115i–j, 117–18
■ Latin once world language L-153
■ meanings, *diagrams* L-115–115a
■ public speaking P-526b
■ secret C-269
■ semantics C-488
■ sign, for deaf D-41b
■ teaching L-117–18
■ written W-310–310d, L-114

**Language arts** L-120–4, *pictures* L-121–4. *see also in index* Reading for recreation; Spelling
■ communication skills C-495–7, *pictures* C-495–7
■ report writing R-151a–b, *list,* R-151b, *picture* R-151a
■ writing, communication by W-308–9, *pictures* W-308–9
■ writing, creative W-310–12, *pictures* W-310–310d

**Language experience approach,** to reading R-103

**Languedoc** [*läng-dôk'*], former province in s. France; capital was Toulouse; wine: F-387

**Languedoc Canal.** *see in index* Canal du Midi

**Langue d'oil** [*läng dô-ēl'*], French dialect F-436

**Langur** [*lŭng-gu̇r'*], a monkey A-503, M-442–3, *pictures* A-502, M-442–3

**Lanham Act,** United States, *table* E-92

**Lanier** [*la-nēr'*], **Sidney** (1842–81), American lyric poet L-124, A-350, *pictures* G-90, L-124
■ Hall of Fame, *table* H-11

**Laniidae** [*la-nī'ĭ-dē*], the shrike family of birds. *see in index* Shrike

**Lankester, Sir Edwin Ray** (1847–1929), English biologist, born London; widely known as a teacher and as a writer of popular works on science; director of Natural History Museum in London 1898–1907 ('Science from an Easy Chair'; 'Secrets of Earth and Sea').

**Lanolin,** wool fat W-230

**Lansdale,** Pa., borough 9 mi (14 km) n.e. of Norristown; pop. 16,526; glue, building products, electronic components, tile, hosiery: *map* P-185

**Lansdowne, Henry Charles Keith Petty-Fitzmaurice,** 5th **marquis of** (1845–1927), British statesman, born London; governor-general of Canada 1883–88; viceroy of India 1888–93; secretary of foreign affairs 1900–1906, during which time an alliance was made with Japan and friendship cemented with France; leader of Unionist party in House of Lords; favored a moderate peace after World War I.

**Lansdowne, Henry Petty-Fitzmaurice, 3d marquis of** (1780–1863), English statesman, born London; chancellor of the exchequer at 25, a Liberal leader and advocate of parliamentary reform and abolition of slavery.

**Lansdowne,** Md., community 5 mi (8 km) s.w. of Baltimore; pop. 17,770; metal products, transportation equipment, electronic components: *map* M-139

**Lansdowne,** Pa., borough, residential suburb about 5 mi (8 km) w. of Philadelphia; pop. 11,891; some small industries; council-manager government; incorporated 1893: *map, inset* P-185

**Lansing, Robert** (1864–1928), lawyer and authority on international law, born Watertown, N.Y.; counsel for U.S. in Bering Sea and Alaska boundary arbitrations; secretary of state in President Wilson's Cabinet during World War I: W-177

**Lansing,** Ill., village 24 mi (39 km) s. of Chicago; pop. 29,039; truck farms; aluminum windows and doors; founded in 1860's, incorporated in 1893: *map, inset* I-50

**Lansing,** Mich., state capital, on Grand River 80 mi (130 km) n.w. of Detroit; pop. 130,414: L-125, *maps* M-285, 270, 276, U-41, *pictures* L-125
■ Capitol, State L-125, *pictures* L-125, M-279
■ location, *locator map* L-125

**Lanskneckt,** German mercenary band A-640

**Lanston, Tolbert** (1844–1913), inventor, born Troy, Ohio; patented Monotype in 1887, began production and marketing of machine 1897: M-451

**Lantana,** a perennial plant L-125

**Lantern** L-106, *pictures* L-106
■ colonial, *picture* L-106
■ lighthouse L-270
■ story of Diogenes D-119, *picture* D-119

**Lantern fish,** found in almost all seas; some deep-sea and some not; has luminescent organs in groups; family Myctophidae: F-161

**Lanthanide** [lăn´thā-nīd] **series,** of chemicals, *table* P-207

**Lanthanum** (La), a rare earth metal, *tables* P-207, C-236

**Lanuvium** [lə-nū´vĭ-ŭm] (modern **Lanuvio,** formerly **Civita Lavinia**), Italy, city of Latium, 30 km (19 mi) s.e. of Rome; member Latin League; conquered by Rome 338 B.C.; temple of Juno.

**Lao** [lä´ō], a native of Laos L-125a, I-161

**Laoag** [lä-wäg´], Philippines, city, seaport on Laoag River near n.w. coast of Luzon; pop. 61,727; rice, indigo, sugar: *maps* P-261d, P-4

**Lao Bridge,** bridge in southern Italy A-447

**Laocoön** [lā-ŏk´ō-ŏn], in Greek mythology, Trojan priest of Apollo, warns countrymen against wooden horse: T-267
■ statue of G-230

**'Laocoon',** book by Gotthold Ephraim Lessing (1766), in which the functions of poetry and painting are defined and distinguished; an important book in the history of art.

**Laodamia** [lā-ō-da-mī´ə], legendary Greek heroine, wife of Protesilaus; celebrated in William Wordsworth's 'Laodamia'. *see also in index* Protesilaus

**Laodicea** [lā-ŏd-ĭ-sē´ə], name of several ancient Asiatic cities in realms extending from Aegean Sea to India; **Laodicea ad Lycum** (modern **Denizli,** Turkey, 120 mi (195 km) s.e. of Smyrna), once wealthy trade center; founded probably 3d century, B.C.; site of one of 7 primitive churches of Asia (Rev. i, 11); **Laodicea ad mare** (modern **Latakia,** Syria), pride of the Caesars, noted for ruins of triumphal arch built possibly by Septimius Severus.

**Laoighis,** Ireland. *see in index* Leix

**Laomedon** [lā-ŏm´ē-dŏn], in Greek mythology, founder and king of Troy; father of Priam; lost Troy to Hercules but was killed by him for failure to deliver to Hercules the magic horses promised him.

**Laon** [län], France, city 130 km (80 mi) n.e. of Paris; pop. 25,623; fortified by Romans; Blücher defeated Napoleon 1814; captured by Germans 1870, 1914, and 1940: *maps* F-404, W-252
■ cathedral, *picture* C-158

**Laos** [lous], republic in s.e. Asia; area 91,429 sq mi (236,800 sq km); pop. 3,383,000 (1976 est.); cap. Vientiane: L-125a–b, *map* I-162, *pictures* L-125a–b
■ flag F-211, *picture* F-209
■ history L-125b, I-162, 163
■ location L-125a, *locator map* L-125a
■ Mekong River L-125a, b, M-217, *map* I-162, *picture* L-125a
■ national anthem, *table* N-52
■ natural features L-125a
■ neutrality L-125b, V-321
■ opium O-471
■ people L-125a: how the people live L-125a–b, *pictures* L-125b
■ Vietnam conflict V-321, 322, L-125b, *map* V-321

**Lao-tse** [loud´zŭ´] (604?–531? B.C.), Chinese philosopher and metaphysician; contemporary with Confucius; founder of Taoism: C-295c, L-229
■ teachings R-143

**Lap-and-lead lever,** in steam engine, *diagram* S-442

**La Parida,** in Venezuela. *see in index* Cerro Bolívar

**La Paz** [lä päs], Bolivia, largest city and seat of government; pop. 660,700: L-125c, B-335, *map* S-298, *pictures* L-125c, S-281a
■ Indian dance, *picture* D-18
■ location L-125c, *locator map* L-125c

**La Paz,** Mexico, port in Lower California, on Bay of La Paz; capital of Baja California Sur; pop. 70,219 (1976 est.); in agricultural area; pearl fishing center; silver mines: C-55, *map* M-260d

**La Peltrie, Marie Madeleine de** (1603–71), French Roman Catholic nun, born Alençon; founder of Ursuline convent at Quebec, Canada, 1639; conducted school for Indian and French girls until 1642, when she joined colonists under Maisonneuve and helped to found Montreal, Canada.

**Lapham, Silas.** *see in index* 'Rise of Silas Lapham, The'

**Lapidary** [lăp´ĭ-dĕr-ĭ], a cutter and polisher of gems J-451–2

**Lapido, Duro,** African writer A-121

**Lapis lazuli** [lăp´ĭs lăz´ū-lī], a semiprecious stone J-454
■ Sumerian culture, *picture* B-6

**Lapithae** [lăp´ĭ-thē], in Greek mythology, race related to the centaurs, dwelling in Thessaly
■ battle with centaurs C-192a: Theseus' aid C-192a

**Laplace** [lä-pläs´], **Pierre Simon, marquis de** (1749–1827), French mathematician and astronomer L-125c, *picture* L-125c

■ nebular hypothesis P-355, L-125c

**Lapland,** region in extreme n. of Norway, Sweden, Finland, and Russia A-571, L-125d–6, *map* L-125d, *pictures* L-125d, N-366
■ clothing L-125d, *pictures* L-125d, R-139
■ iron mining S-523, *pictures* S-526, E-316
■ people L-125d: children, *picture* N-366; how the people live L-125d–6, R-139, *pictures* L-125d, R-139

**La Plata** [lä plä´tä], Argentina, city 55 km (35 mi) s.e. of Buenos Aires and 8 km (5 mi) inland from Ensenada, its port on Plata estuary; pop. 391,247; National University; meat-packing and petroleum refining: *map* S-299

**La Plata, Río de,** South America. *see in index* Plata, Río de la

**La Plata, Viceroyalty of** S-290, 291

**La Porte,** Ind., city in lake area, 25 mi (40 km) w. of South Bend; pop. 21,796; farm machinery, airplane parts, heaters and radiators, furniture, wood products: *map* I-100

**Lappet-faced vulture,** bird B-280

**Lapping,** a polishing operation T-206

**Lapps,** people of Lapland L-125d–6, *pictures* L-125d, N-366, R-139
■ racial classification, *chart* R-26

**La Prensa,** newspaper, Argentina B-489

**'L'Après-midi d'un faune'** (The Afternoon of a Faun), tone poem by Debussy D-44
■ ballet B-31

**Lares** [lā´rēz], in Roman mythology, protecting deities of the household, associated with the Penates: M-577

**Laretta, Enrique** (1875–1961), Argentine writer and diplomat, born Buenos Aires; minister to France 1910–16: L-149a, *picture* L-151

**Large-scale integrated circuit,** or LSI, computers C-497d

**Largetooth aspen,** tree (Populus grandidentata) of willow family, native from Nova Scotia, Canada, to North Carolina, westward to Manitoba, Canada; grows to 18 m (60 ft); also called large poplar, popple, and large American aspen; wood is soft, weak, light, grayish-white; used for paper pulp, excelsior, matches.

**Larghetto** [lär-gĕt´ō], direction in music meaning slow and broad but not quite so slow as largo; term also refers to a passage or movement within a musical composition.

**Largo,** Fla., town 5 mi (8 km) s. of Clearwater; pop. 58,977; tourist center; citrus groves; incorporated 1905: *map* F-246

**Largo,** in music, *table* M-566a

**Largs** [lärgz], Scotland, yachting center and resort, on Firth of Clyde, 50 km (30 mi) s.w. of Glasgow; pop. 8908: *map* G-199g
■ battle of (1263) T-161

**Lariat,** noosed rope used by cowboys to catch cattle or horses C-176

**Laridae** [lăr´ĭ-dē], bird family, including gulls and terns. *see in index* Gull; Tern

**Lárisa,** or **Larissa** [la´rĭ-sa], Greece, city in Thessaly on

"starboard," the right side of a boat.

**Larceny,** in law, *table* L-165b

**Larch,** a tree L-126, *table* W-218
■ eastern L-126
■ western L-126, *pictures* L-126, *table* W-218

**Larcom, Lucy** (1824–93), poet, born Beverly, Mass. In her youth she was a factory worker, and some of her contributions to the factory magazine won praise of John Greenleaf Whittier, with whom she later compiled two books; editor Our Young Folks; outstanding for poems of life in New England ('Childhood Songs'; 'Wild Roses of Cape Ann and Other Poems').

**Lard,** rendered pork fat, *chart* F-77, *table* F-76
■ best hog type for H-197

**Larder beetle** B-140, *picture* I-210

**Lardner, Ring(gold Wilmer)** (1885–1933), writer of humorous stories showing keen insight and reproducing everyday conversation of ordinary persons; born Niles, Mich.; sportswriter on newspapers ('You Know Me, Al'; 'Gullible's Travels'; 'How to Write Short Stories'), which contains character sketch, 'The Champion'; 'Round Up'; 'First and Last'; 'The Portable Ring Lardner') A-360, *picture* M-282

**Laredo,** Tex., city in s. part of state on Rio Grande opposite Nuevo Laredo, Mexico; pop. 91,449; agriculture, stock raising, oil and gas; vegetable and fruit shipping; hats, garments, antimony smelting, brick; Laredo Air Force Base nearby: *maps* T-129, U-40

**Lares** [lā´rēz], in Roman mythology, protecting deities of the household, associated with the Penates: M-577

**Larsa,** ancient Sumerian city in s. Mesopotamia, on w. bank of old Euphrates River, 15 mi (25 km) s.e. of ancient Erech; temple libraries and important documents found in the ruins.

**Larsen Ice Shelf,** Antarctica, in n.w. Weddell Sea along e. coast of Antarctic Peninsula; named for Capt. C.A. Larsen, who sailed along edge of shelf in 1893

**Larson, (Lewis) Arthur** (born 1910), government official and lawyer, born Sioux Falls, S.D.; professor of law Cornell University 1948–53; dean University of Pittsburgh School of Law 1953–54; undersecretary of labor 1954–56; director U.S. Information Agency 1956–57; director Rule of Law Center, Duke University after 1958; author of 'A Republican Looks at His Party', 'Eisenhower: the President Nobody Knew'.

**Larva,** in zoology L-127, I-204–5
■ amphibians A-378
■ animal behavior experiment, *picture* A-440
■ ant A-469
■ bee B-125
■ beetle B-137, *picture* B-139; June J-482, *picture* J-482
■ caddis fly N-60d, *pictures* I-205, 201; protective coloration, *picture* P-512
■ caterpillar B-525, C-156–7, *pictures* C-157, B-521–523, 525, P-511–12: cage, *picture* N-73
■ clam and mussel C-380
■ crab C-598
■ eel E-103
■ flea F-219
■ housefly F-280, *picture* F-280
■ liver fluke W-298, *picture* W-298
■ lobster L-323
■ marine snail and slug S-222
■ mayfly M-183
■ mosquito, *pictures* M-497
■ oyster O-517–18, *picture* O-517
■ sphinx moth, *picture* I-201

Salambria River; pop. 72,336; transit trade, textiles; important city in ancient times: *maps* G-213, E-335

**Lark,** a group of small birds L-126–7, *picture* L-127
■ horned. *see in index* Horned lark

**Lark bunting,** *picture* C-460

**Lark sparrow,** bird of middle and w. U.S.; abundant in Mississippi valley; head streaked chestnut and white; tail white-edged; good singer; also called lark finch.

**Larkspur,** or **delphinium** L-127, *pictures* L-127, F-262
■ annual for fall planting G-22
■ annual for shade G-21
■ poison in P-408

**La Rocca, Dominick James** (Nick) (1889–1961), jazz cornetist, born New Orleans, La.; formed Original Dixieland Jazz Band during World War I; credited with composing 'Tiger Rag': J-425

**La Rochefoucauld** [lä rôsh-fo-kō´], **François, duc de** (1613–80), French courtier and writer, born Paris; engaged in court intrigues against Cardinals Richelieu and Mazarin: F-440

**La Rochelle** [lä rô-shĕl´], France, historic seaport of w.; pop. 72,075; once great maritime city and center of French Protestantism: *maps* F-381, 405, E-334
■ Edict of Nantes H-139
■ Richelieu besieges R-204

■ tadpole: frog F-449–50, *pictures* F-450; toad T-187
■ tussock moth, *picture* I-201
■ wasp, *pictures* W-56

**Lary, (Robert) Yale** (born 1930), football player, born Fort Worth, Tex.; defensive back for Detroit Lions 1952–53, 1956–64: *list* F-337

**Laryngitis** V-377

**Larynx** [*lăr'ĭngks*], the organ of voice A-391, V-377, *diagrams* V-377, L-395

**La Salle** [*lȧ săl'*], **René Robert Cavelier, sieur de** (1643–87), French explorer L-128–9, *map* L-129, *pictures* L-128
■ explorations L-128, 129, A-338, *maps* L-129, U-176: Illinois I-41, C-254, 262; Indiana I-91; Louisiana L-129, L-363, *pictures* L-128, L-369; Ohio O-419; Tennessee T-83; Texas T-117
■ Hennepin, his assistant H-133–4
■ Marquette's reports assist J-477

**La Salle,** Ill., city on Illinois River, adjacent to Peru and about 13 mi (21 km) w. of Ottawa; pop. 10,347; center of corn area; chemicals, electrical equipment, hydrotransmissions, zinc processing; Starved Rock State Park nearby: *map* I-50

**La Salle,** Que., Canada, residential city just s. of Montreal, at s. end of island of Montreal, overlooking Lachine Rapids in St. Lawrence River; pop. 76,713; named for La Salle, French explorer: Q-9h, *map* M-477, *inset* Q-11

**La Salle College,** at Philadelphia, Pa.; Roman Catholic; chartered 1863; arts and sciences, business, education; graduate work in theology; Pennyln Biostation.

**La Scala,** opera house in Milan, Italy M-316, *picture* I-327

**Las Casas** [*läs kä'säs*], **Bartolomé de** (1474–1566), Spanish historian and missionary L-129, L-149

**Lascaux** [*lă-skō'*] **Cave,** in s. France; Stone Age cave drawings found here A-531, *pictures* A-530, M-72
■ 'Stag Frieze, The', D-180, *picture* D-180

**Las Cruces** [*krụ'sās*], N.M., city 40 mi (65 km) n.w. of El Paso, Tex., in livestock and agricultural region; pop. 45,086; pecans, alfalfa, vegetables; cotton ginning, cottonseed oil; New Mexico State University; White Sands Missile Range nearby: *maps* N-221, 208, U-40

**Laser** [*lā'zẽr*] (light amplification by stimulated emission of radiation), also called "optical maser" L-129a–b, P-384, *diagrams* L-129a–b, *picture* L-129a
■ application tested, *picture* N-199
■ bibliography L-129b, S-64d
■ communication S-195b
■ holograms C-452, *pictures* C-452
■ medical use S-519a
□ eye repair B-312
■ modern book production B-358
■ reflector, on moon M-479
■ supermarket use A-834

**La Serena,** Chile, iron-shipping center about 360 km (225 mi) n. of Valparaiso; pop. 71,898; historic cathedral, convents; founded in 1544, in 1552 declared a city: C-284, *maps* C-282, S-299

**Lashio,** Burma, town 125 mi (200 km) n.e. of Mandalay; s.w. terminus of Burma Road: *map* I-162

**Lashkar,** India. *see in index* Gwalior

**Lashley, Karl Spencer** (1890–1958), psychologist, born Davis, W. Va.; professor of psychology University of Chicago 1929–35; professor of psychology Harvard University 1935–37, research professor of neuropsychology 1937–55.

**Lasker, Albert,** "the father of modern advertising" A-59

**Lasker, Eduard** (1829–84), Prussian statesman, born present Poznan, Poland; important service in civil consolidation of German empire.

**Lasker, Emanuel** (1868–1941), German chess master, born Berlinchen, Germany (now Barlinek, Poland); world chess champion 1894–1921; wrote books on chess, philosophy, and mathematics.

**Laski, Harold Joseph** (1893–1950), British liberal writer, born Manchester; professor political science (University of London after 1926); visiting lecturer in United States; author of many books, chiefly on contemporary political and social-political trends, also 'Letters, Correspondence, 1916–1935' with Oliver W. Holmes, jurist.

**Laskin, Bora** (born 1912), Canadian jurist, born Fort Williamson, Ont.; professor University of Toronto 1949–65; judge Supreme Court of Ontario 1965–69; judge Supreme Court of Canada 1970–, chief justice 1973–.

**Lasky, Jesse L(ouis)** (1880–1958), pioneer motion-picture producer, born San Jose, Calif.; coproducer of Hollywood's first full-length motion picture, 'The Squaw Man'; produced over 1000 motion pictures; specialized in biographical films ('I Blow My Own Horn', autobiography).

**Lasnier, (Marie) Rina** (born 1915), Canadian poet, born near Montreal, Que.: C-114

**Las Palmas** [*päl'mäs*], Grand Canary Island, port on n.e. coast; pop. 260,368; largest city of Canary Islands, *inset* S-350

**La Spezia** [*lä spĕt'syä*], Italy, city 80 km (50 mi) s.e. of Genoa, on Bay of Spezia; pop. 121,923; important naval harbor; shipbuilding; winter resort: *maps* I-338, 325

**Lassalle** [*lă-säl'*], **Ferdinand** (1825–64), German socialist, founder of German social democratic movement; born Breslau; his life was basis of George Meredith's 'Tragic Comedians': S-234

**Lassen Peak,** volcanic peak in n. California; erupted 1914–21; vast lava beds; height 10,453 ft (3186 m): N-40a, *maps* C-52, U-87

**Lassen Volcanic National Park,** in California N-40a, *maps* C-52, N-30

**Lassie,** famous dog, *list* D-137
■ book about D-154c, *picture* D-154c

**Lasso** [*läs'sō*], **Orlando di** (1532?–94), celebrated composer, forerunner of Palestrina; born Mons, Belgium, where he became choirboy; taken to Italy by patron, viceroy of Sicily; court musician to duke of Bavaria at Munich; composed more than 2000 works: M-556

**Lasso,** rope or a line of leather with a running noose; used for catching horses and cattle: *picture* C-173

**Last,** in shoemaking S-180, W-227, *picture* S-181

**'Last Communion of St. Jerome, The',** painting by Botticelli, *picture* D-93e

**'Last Days of Pompeii, The',** novel by Bulwer-Lytton giving detailed and vivid picture of life in Pompeii before city was destroyed by eruption of Mount Vesuvius (A.D. 79); realistic description of eruption.

**Lastex,** trade name for a rubber filament wrapped with cotton, silk, nylon, or rayon fibers; gives great stretch to fabrics woven from it; invented 1931.

**'Last Laugh, The'** (1925), motion picture, *picture* M-523

**'Last Leaf',** work by Oliver Wendell Holmes A-347

**'Last of the Mohicans, The',** novel by James Fenimore Cooper, one of the 'Leatherstocking Tales'; thrilling story of frontier life; romantic idealization of the Indian Uncas A-346, C-562

**'Last Picture Show, The',** work by McMurty A-362

**Last Supper.** *see in index* Lord's Supper

**'Last Supper, The',** painting by Leonardo da Vinci M-316, V-325, *picture* V-325

**Las Vegas** [*läs vā'gas*], Nev., largest city of state, 23 mi (37 km) n.w. of Hoover Dam; in irrigated agricultural area; pop. 164,674; tourist center; legalized gambling; campus of University of Nevada; Nevada Test Site, Nellis Air Force Base, Lake Mead Base, Las Vegas Air Force Station nearby: N-146, *maps* N-157, 144, U-40, *pictures* N-151
■ climate, *list* N-142
■ skiing on Charleston Peak, *picture* N-143

**Las Vegas,** N.M., livestock center 42 mi (68 km) e. of Santa Fe; composed of modern city (pop. 14,322) and old town (pop. 6307); livestock center; stone and wood products, garments; tourist trade; New Mexico Highlands University; established by Spanish about 1833: *maps* N-220, U-40
■ Fort Union National Monument N-37, *maps* N-30, N-220

**Laszlo.** *see in index* Ladislaus, Saint

**Latakia** [*lăt-a-kē'a*], French **Lattaquié** [*lȧ-tȧ-kyā'*], Syria, Mediterranean port 115 mi (185 km) n. of Beirut; pop. 67,799; produces famous Latakia tobacco; ancient Laodicea: *map* I-280

**Latchstring** P-331

**Lateen rig,** *picture* C-475

**'Late George Apley, The',** novel (1937) by John P. Marquand; won 1938 Pulitzer prize A-359

**Latent heat of fusion** W-68, F-433, H-112

**Latent heat of vaporization** W-68, H-112

**Lateral pass,** in football F-332

**Lateran,** basilica in Rome, Italy. *see in index* St. John Lateran

**Lateran, The,** palace in Rome, Italy; original building belonged to Lateranus family; taken from them by Nero; later given to pope by Constantine; used as residence by popes until 14th century; present palace, built in 16th century, now contains two museums.

**Lateran Councils,** a series of ecumenical church councils held in the Lateran Palace and St. John Lateran at Rome from the 12th to the 16th centuries.

**Lateran Treaty,** or **Concordat of 1929,** between Italy and Vatican V-267–8, 270–1, I-343c, P-347

**Laterite** [*lăt'ẽr-īt*], soil S-253

**Latex** [*lā'tĕks*], milky juice secreted by various plants G-266
■ concentrated R-302
■ frothed sponge R-305: from synthetic latex R-310
■ guayule G-249
■ synthetic R-310: paints P-72, 76
■ yields rubber R-301, 302, *pictures* R-302–3

**Latham, Hubert,** pioneer in aviation A-203

**Latham, Jean Lee** (born 1902), writer, born Buckhannon, W.Va.; editor in chief Dramatic Publishing Company, Chicago, 1930–36; author of plays presented on radio and television and of children's books ('Carry On, Mr. Bowditch', fictionalized biography awarded Newbery Medal 1956; 'This Dear-Bought Land'; 'On Stage, Mr. Jefferson'; 'Young Man in a Hurry'; 'Man of the Monitor'; 'Retreat to Glory: the Story of Sam Houston').

**Lathe** [*lāth*], machine tool T-201–2, *diagram* T-201, *pictures* T-201
■ early lathe, *picture* I-168
■ engine lathe T-201–2, *picture* N-287
■ turet lathe T-202, *diagram* T-201, *picture* T-201

**Lathing,** building material B-377

**Lathrop** [*lā'thrŭp*], **Dorothy Pulis** (1891–1981), writer and illustrator of children's books, born Albany, N.Y.; she illustrated 'Hitty', by Rachel Field, awarded Newbery Medal 1930; in 1938, Dorothy Lathrop's own book 'Animals of the Bible' was awarded the first Caldecott Medal ever given; among the 'books written and illustrated by her are: 'Who Goes There?'; 'Let Them Live'; 'The Littlest Mouse': R-111a

**Lathrop, George Parsons** (1851–98), journalist and poet, born Oahu, Hawaiian Islands; married Rose, daughter of Nathaniel Hawthorne; associate editor *Atlantic Monthly;* editor *Boston Courier;* founder American Copyright League.

**Lathrop, Julia Clifford** (1858–1932), social worker, born Rockford, Ill.; important work at Hull House, Chicago; chief 1912–21 U.S. Children's Bureau, first woman bureau chief; author of articles on child welfare, care of insane, and civil service.

**Latifundios,** also **latifundia,** large landed estates
■ Central America C-195
■ Italy I-328: Sicily S-192

**Latimer, Hugh** (1485?–1555), English Protestant reformer and martyr, bishop of Worcester; born Thurcaston, Leicestershire; his homely practical preaching largely drove the English Reformation home to the people; burned at stake (with Nicholas Ridley) exhorting his fellow-martyr, "Be of good cheer, Master Ridley, and play the man; we shall this day light such a candle by God's grace in England as I trust shall never be put out."

**Latina,** formerly **Littoria,** Italy, province on land reclaimed from Pontine Marshes s.e. of Rome; fertile farm lands; cap. Latina: *map, inset* I-339

**Latin America,** collective name for the 20 independent nations of southern North America, Central America, South America, and the West Indies: L-130–48, *pictures* L-130–48. *see also in index* Central America; South America; and names of separate countries
■ agriculture L-133, *pictures* L-131: land redistribution L-142–3, *picture* L-148
■ architecture L-136, *pictures* L-130, 134–5, 138, 141, 147
■ art L-136–7, *pictures* L-137–9: music M-561–2, L-136–7; painting P-67a–d, *pictures* P-67b–d, L-139, *Reference-Outline* P-71; sculpture, *picture* L-138
■ bibliography L-147–8, S-302–3
■ citizenship C-360: political posters, *picture* C-360
■ climate L-132–3
■ economic conditions and problems L-140–3, 131
■ education L-137–9, 142, *pictures* L-140–1, 146
□ illiteracy P-450
■ fundamental education program M-248, *picture* M-250
■ flags F-200, *pictures* F-201–2: historic F-200, *pictures* F-201–2
■ foreign investments L-140–1
■ good-neighbor policy L-146, R-273
■ government: dictatorship D-112: republican D-84
■ history L-139–40, 144–7, *picture* L-139: Alliance for Progress S-292, L-147; Bolivar's fight for freedom B-332; Indian civilizations L-136, *pictures* L-136–7; Organization of American States O-504, L-143; Pan American conferences L-145–6, M-457; Peace Corps L-147, P-143a, *picture* L-146; subversion, Cuban C-628a, 628b, L-146, O-504; World War II L-146, W-272
■ immigration L-134
■ labor L-131. *see also in index* Peonage
■ land tenure L-142–3
■ languages L-130
■ libraries L-233, 238, 244: Argentina L-233, 238, 240, L-310e; Brazil L-244, 245, 238, *picture* L-241; Mexico L-233, 240, *picture* M-250
■ literature. *see in index* Latin American literature
■ location, *locator map* L-130
■ meaning of name L-130
■ nations comprising L-130
■ natural features L-131–2
■ natural resources L-133, *pictures* L-132–3
■ nature protection, Pan American Convention on N-22
■ people L-133–5: children, *pictures* L-130, 134, 146; family life F-31; how the people live L-135, *pictures* L-130–1, 133–5, 139–46, 148
■ population L-135
■ recreation L-136–7, *pictures* L-139, 142–3
■ trade L-140, 147: prospects L-131
■ transportation L-142, *picture* L-132

**Latin American Economic System** (SELA) L-146

**Latin American Free Trade Association** (LAFTA) L-147

**Latin American literature** L-148–53, *pictures* L-149–52
■ bibliography L-153
■ children's literature L-310e–f, *list* L-310h–i, *picture* L-310e
■ folklore S-476–7, *list* S-481c
■ new voices, *list* L-306b

**Latin Empire,** established by Crusaders in 1204: C-618

**Latin language** L-153–5, E-80, *pictures* L-154–5
■ alphabet A-315
■ English language influenced by E-251–2, L-153
■ Romance languages derived from R-239, *map* L-153: French F-436; Italian I-321; Spanish S-353, 354, S-365
■ school curriculum E-82, 84, *picture* E-82

**Latin League,** confederation of cities of Latium in central Italy, existing from earliest historic times till 338 B.C.: R-244

**Latin literature** L-154–5
■ Augustan Age L-155, 154, *picture* R-241
□ Ovid L-155, M-579
□ Virgil. *see in index* Virgil
■ Caesar C-14, L-154–5, *picture* R-243
■ Cicero C-341, L-154, L-197, *picture* L-154
■ drama D-170–1, L-154, S-108a
■ Pliny the Elder R-124, L-155
■ Renaissance R-146
■ Seneca L-155, S-108a, D-170
■ Tacitus T-3, L-155

**Latin Quarter,** in Paris, France P-122, *map* P-120

**Latins,** in ancient times, inhabitants of Latium; also modern Italians, French, and Spanish
■ contribution to civilization C-370
■ early history R-240–2, 244

**Latinus,** in Roman mythology, king of Latium and father of Lavinia, wife of Aeneas; name also given to one of the heroes in Torquato Tasso's 'Jerusalem Delivered'.

**Latitude,** distance in degrees north and south from equator L-156–9, M-103a, c, *diagrams* L-157, 159, *maps* L-156, 158, *table* L-158. *see also in index* Longitude
■ climate control C-392–3, 395
■ high, low, and middle latitudes L-159, *diagram* L-159
■ "horse latitudes" W-181, *diagram* W-180–1
■ I.G.Y. studies I-236a
■ insolation and C-392–3, G-52, L-159
■ map location M-97
■ navigation N-88, L-158

**Latium** [*lā'shĭ-ŭm*], ancient district in middle Italy, inhabited by Latins R-240, 241, *map* I-338–9
■ Aeneas, legendary ruler A-63

**Latona.** *see in index* Leto

**La Tour, Charles Amador de** (1596–1666), French governor of Acadia 1628–35; quarreled with Charnisay over governorship; regained post after death of Charnisay in 1650.

**La Tour, Georges de** (1593–1652), French painter; contemporary of Nicolas Poussin; painter to duke of Lorraine.

**Latreille** [*lȧ-trĕ'y'*], **Pierre André** (1762–1833), French zoologist, born Brives-la-Gaillarde, Corrèze; noted for his classifications of insects.

**Latrobe, Benjamin Henry** (1764–1820), American architect and engineer, born Fulneck, Yorkshire, England; to U.S. 1796; surveyor of public buildings, Washington, D.C., 1803; in charge of rebuilding burned Capitol (1815–17), *profile* A-568

**Latrobe,** Pa., borough 33 mi (53 km) s.e. of Pittsburgh in industrial district: pop. 10,799; iron and steel, metal products, building materials, ceramics, die castings, plastics, ingot molds; St. Vincent College: *map* P-184

**Latsol,** a type of soil, *map* G-61

**Lattaquié,** Syria. *see in index* Latakia

**Latter-day Saints.** *see in index* Mormons

**Lattice,** of crystal C-621, 623, 624, 625, *diagrams* C-134, 623, 625

**Lattice,** in basketry B-103

**Lattice method,** in multiplication M-54b–3, D-135–135a

**Latticework,** in furniture design. *see in index* Fret

**Lattimore, Eleanor Frances** (Mrs. Robert Armstrong Andrews) (born 1904), American author and illustrator of children's books, born Shanghai, China; works based on own experiences ('Little Pear' series; 'Peachblossom'; 'Bells for a Chinese Donkey'; 'The Monkey of Crofton'; 'The Journey of Ching Lai'; 'Fisherman's Son').

**Lattimore, Owen** (born 1900), author and educator, born Washington, D.C.; director Walter Hines Page School of International Relations, Johns Hopkins University 1938–53; political adviser to Chiang Kai-shek 1941–42; deputy director Pacific operations Office of War Information 1942–44 ('High Tartary'; 'Solution in Asia'; 'Situation in Asia'; 'Ordeal by Slander'; 'Nomads and Commissars: Mongolia Revisited'; 'Studies in Frontier History').

**La Tuque** [*lȧ tük'*], Que., Canada, town and lumbering center on St. Maurice River 120 km (75 mi) n. of Trois-Rivières; pop. 13,099; pulp and paper, sashes and doors: *maps* Q-10, C-99

**'La Turista',** work by Shepard A-363

**Latvian Soviet Socialist Republic,** Russia, on Baltic Sea; 64,000 sq km (24,710 sq mi); pop. 2,365,000; cap. Riga; Russian rule not recognized by U.S.: L-159a, U-14, *maps* R-325, 344, 348, U-14
■ ballet, *picture* R-332f
■ cities L-159a, Riga R-207
■ folktales, *list* S-480, *picture* S-471
■ location L-159a, *locator map* L-159a

**Lauan** [*lä-wän'*], wood of several species of trees of lauan family (*Dipterocarpaceae*), native to Philippines, nearby islands, and s. Asia; often called Philippine mahogany.

**Laubach** [*lȯ'bäk*], **Frank Charles** (1884–1970), missionary and educator, born Benton, Pa.; ordained Congregational minister 1914; began career as missionary in Philippine Islands 1915; known as founder of worldwide campaign for teaching primitive and illiterate peoples to read, using principle of "each one teach one;" author, 'Toward World Literacy'; autobiography, 'Thirty Years with the Silent Billion'.

**Laud, William** (1573–1645), English prelate, archbishop of Canterbury; born Reading, England; tried to suppress dissent; beheaded on charge of treason
■ adviser of Charles I C-212, 213

**Laudanum,** tincture of opium
■ antidote P-411

**Lauder, Sir Harry Maclennan** (1870–1950), Scottish comedian, born Portobello, Scotland; a great favorite for his Scottish songs composed by him and sung in character; knighted 1919.

**Laudonnière** [*lō-dô-nyêr'*], **René Goulaine de** (died 1566), French Huguenot noble; accompanied Jean Ribaut's expedition (1562) to what is now South Carolina; established Fort Caroline colony on St. John's River (1564), but governed badly; wounded in Menéndez' attack, escaped to Europe; wrote memoirs.

**Laue** [*lou'ĕ*], **Max (Theodor Felix) von** (1879–1960), German physicist, born Pfaffendorf, near Coblenz; professor University of Berlin 1919–43; author of scientific books
■ Nobel prize, *table* N-294a
■ X-ray spectra X-334, C-624, S-254h

**Laugher pigeon** P-324

**Laughing gas,** or **nitrous oxide** ($N_2O$), an anesthetic A-413, M-215c, M-49a
■ aerosol propellant A-66
■ discovery of properties D-39, L-345

**Laughing gull** G-262

**"Laughing jackass,"** or **kookaburra,** an Australian bird A-782

**Laughing philosopher.** *see in index* Democritus

**Laughing Water,** or **Minnehaha Falls,** Minneapolis, Minn. M-346

**Laughlin** [*lăf'lĭn*], **James** (1806–82), American manufacturer and philanthropist, born Ireland; one of group which developed Pittsburgh, Pa., as an iron center.

**Laughlin, James Laurence** (1850–1933), political economist, born Deerfield, Ohio; head of department of political economy, University of Chicago, 1892–1916; prepared monetary reform scheme for Santo Domingo government, 1894–95; author of works on economics.

**Laughton, Charles** (1899–1962), American actor, born Scarborough, England; first appearance on N.Y. stage 1931 ('Payment Deferred'); in motion pictures from 1932; won Academy award 1933 for his role in 'The Private Life of Henry VIII' ('The Barretts of Wimpole Street'; 'Mutiny on the Bounty'; 'Hunchback of Notre Dame'; 'Rembrandt'; 'The Beachcomber'); popular theatrical dramatic reader; compiler of 'Tell Me a Story' A-27
■ Stephen Vincent Benét's association B-161

**Launceston** [*lăn'sĕs-tȯn*], England, quaint old town in Cornwall 34 km (21 mi) n.w. of Plymouth; pop. 4700; George Fox, the Quaker, imprisoned here (1655): *map* G-199h

**Launceston,** Tasmania, city in n.e. on Tamar River; pop. 62,181, including suburbs; wheat and potatoes grown in area; mining; trade with Victoria and South Australia

**Launching,** of ship S-172, *pictures* S-171, C-300
■ submarine, *picture* S-495b

**Launch vehicles,** in space travel S-342b, c, *pictures* S-348b, 341c–d
■ Saturns S-346d–e, 347, *diagrams* S-346c–e, *pictures* S-342c, 341d

**Laundry** L-159a–62, *pictures* L-159a–62
■ coin-operated L-162, *picture* L-162: dry-cleaning machines, *picture* D-200e
■ extractor L-159b, *picture* L-159b: principle C-200
■ history of laundering L-161–2, *picture* L-161
■ marking ink I-190
■ soap S-229–32
■ spot and stain removal D-200f–h, *picture* D-200g

**Launfal** [*lôn'fȧl*], **Sir,** knight of the Round Table and steward to King Arthur, in the Arthurian legends; hero of James Russell Lowell's 'Vision of Sir Launfal'.

**La Unión** [*lä ụn-yōn'*], El Salvador, chief port, on gulf of Fonseca at e. end of El Salvador; pop. 11,432; port handles about half of country's foreign trade; railroad terminus.

**Laura** (1308–48), lady loved by Petrarch and celebrated in his poems R-145

**Lauraceae** [*lô-rā'sē-ē*], the laurel family of plants, including laurel, bay, and sassafras: L-263

**Laura Ingalls Wilder Award,** established 1954 by Children's Library Association; awarded to authors or illustrators whose books have made "a substantial and lasting contribution to children's literature": L-303, *table* L-304b

**Laurana** [*lou-rä'nä*], **Francesco da** (1420?–1502), sculptor and medalist of Dalmatian origin; worked chiefly in Italy and France; stressed design rather than realism.

**Laurasia,** prehistoric continent G-65a

**Laureate, poet** P-402

**Laurel,** Miss., city 76 mi (122 km) s.e. of Jackson, in yellow pine region; pop. 21,897; petroleum center; Masonite, lumber, garments, poultry: M-375, *maps* M-387, U-41
■ lignocellulose plant P-379

**Laurel,** name given various flowering trees and shrubs L-163
■ camphor tree C-61
■ crown of poets, heroes P-402, L-163
■ lambkill. *see in index* Lambkill
■ mountain laurel. *see in index* Mountain laurel
■ myth of Daphne and Apollo L-163
■ source of word "laureate" P-402

**Laurelwood.** *see in index* Madrona

**Laurencin** [*lô-răn-săn'*], **Marie** (1885–1956), French painter, born Paris; a modernist with highly individual style; known for female portraits done in soft, pale colors.

**Laurens** [*lȧ-răṅs'*], **Henri** (1885–1954), French sculptor, born near Paris, France; identified with modernists who emphasized purely plastic forms: S-92

**Laurens, Henry** (1724–92), statesman, born Charleston, S.C.; father of John Laurens; president of Continental Congress 1777–78; one of commissioners to negotiate peace after Revolution: R-173, F-260

**Laurens, John** (1754–82), American soldier in Revolutionary War, born Charleston, S.C.; son of Henry Laurens; confidential secretary to George Washington; called the "Bayard of the Revolution"; killed in a skirmish shortly before peace with England was concluded.

**Laurens,** S.C., city 22 mi (35 km) n. of Greenwood; pop. 10,587; glass, textiles, carpets; cotton and peaches; vermiculite mines; incorporated 1785: *map* S-318

**Laurent, Robert** (1890–1970), American sculptor, born Concarneau, near Quimper, France; achieved vital beauty in direct carvings in stone, marble, and wood; noted for figures in alabaster and plant forms in wood; elected to National Institute of Arts and Letters 1970.

**Laurentian Library,** Florence, Italy L-231, *picture* L-232

**Laurentian Mountains,** or **Laurentides,** in Canada Q-9b, C-71, *picture* C-80
■ La Mauricie N.P. N-24d, *map* N-24b

**Laurentian Plateau,** also **Canadian Shield,** highland area in Canada, extending into n.e. United States: L-163, C-71, *maps* C-72–3, U-36, *pictures* N-301
■ Adirondacks A-44
■ Alberta A-263
■ geologic history L-163, N-300, G-63
■ lakes C-75
■ Manitoba M-89a, b, *map* M-89a
■ Michigan M-269, *map* M-270
■ Newfoundland N-165b, d, *map* N-165c
■ Ontario O-456c, b, 456, *map* O-456b
■ Quebec Q-9b, d, e, *map* Q-9a, *picture* C-80
■ Saskatchewan S-49c–d, *map* S-49c
■ Wisconsin W-193, *map* W-194

**Laurentides Provincial Park,** in Quebec, Canada, about 50 km (30 mi) n. of Quebec City; 9358 sq km (3613 sq mi), 1500 lakes; trout fishing: *map* Q-11

**Laurentius, Saint.** *see in index* Lawrence, Saint

**Laurier** [*lạr'ē-ā*], **Sir Wilfrid** (1841–1919), Canadian statesman L-163–4, C-112d, e, *picture* L-163
■ King, Mackenzie K-56
■ Sir Wilfrid Laurier's House N.H.S. N-24d, *map* N-24b

**Lauritsen, Charles Christian** (1892–1968), American physicist, born Holstebro, Denmark; professor at California Institute of Technology 1935–62; research on nuclear physics.

**Laurium,** or **Laurion,** Greece, hill range 30 km (20 mi) below Athens; in ancient times known for silver mines worked until 400 B.C., reopened by French 1864; remains of a Poseidon temple nearby: *map* G-221

**Lausanne** [*lō-zän'*], Switzerland, historic city on n. shore of Lake Geneva; pop. 137,383; 13th-century cathedral; university: S-542, 543, 544a, *maps* S-537, E-334

**Lausanne, Treaty of** (1912), closed Turko-Italian War; gave Tripoli to Italy; granted Italians right to occupy Dodecanese Islands and Rhodes; settlement made after Balkan states attacked Turkey.

**Lausanne, Treaty of** (1923), revised Treaty of Sèvres, extending Turkey's territory: W-263, G-218
■ Bosporus B-371
■ Dardanelles D-34

**Laut, Agnes Christina** (1871–1936), Canadian author, born Stanley, Ont.; authoritative historical books on early explorers and pioneer life in the Northwest ('The Conquest of the Western Empire'; 'Pathfinders of the West'; 'Vikings of the Pacific'; 'Life of Cadillac').

**Lauterbrunnen** [*lou'tēr-brun-ĕn*], Switzerland, village 55 km (34 mi) s.e. of Bern; pop. 3216; lace manufactures: *picture* E-307

**Lautrec, Henri de Toulouse.** *see in index* Toulouse-Lautrec

**Lauzon** [*lō-zôn'*], Que., Canada, city on St. Lawrence River opposite Quebec (city) and adjoining Lévis; pop. 12,809; shipbuilding center: *map* Q-11

**Lava** [*lä'va*], molten rock discharged from volcanoes or intruded between rock strata under the ground: L-164, *pictures* E-25, H-64. *see also in index* Lava soil
■ basalt B-86
■ cave C-178c
■ Etna lava fields E-303
■ Idaho I-17
■ igneous rocks formed R-229, M-337, G-59, E-25, *chart* R-229, *diagram* G-59
■ kimberlite D-100, *diagram* D-102
■ Vesuvius, eruptions of V-305: destruction of Pompeii and Herculaneum P-442–3
■ volcanoes V-378, 380, 383, *diagram* V-379, *picture* V-381

**Lava Beds National Monument,** in California N-40a, *map* N-30

**Laval** [*la-väl'*], **Pierre** (1883–1945), French political leader, born near Clermont-Ferrand, France; rose in few years from obscurity to dominant position in French politics; minister of public works 1925; later was undersecretary of state, senator, minister of labor, foreign minister, and in 1931–32 and 1935–36 premier; vice-premier 1940; collaborated with Hitler, serving as chief of Vichy government April 1942–Aug. 1944; convicted of treason and shot.

**Laval,** Que., Canada, city comprising island n.w. of Montreal; pop. 228,010: Q-9e, h, *map* M-477, *inset* Q-11

**Lavalava** [*läv-a-läv'a*], Samoan clothing, *picture* C-398

**Lavalleja** [*lä-vä-yä'hä*], **Juan Antonio** (died 1853), liberator of Uruguay from Brazilian rule 1825–28; dictator 1827–28; insurgent against later governments.

**Laval-Montmorency, François Xavier de** (1623–1708), first Roman Catholic bishop of Quebec, Canada, born Montigny-sur-Avre, France; arrived in Quebec 1659 as vicar apostolic of New France; founded Seminary of Quebec 1663; Laval University named for him: C-106

**Laval University** (Université Laval), at Ste-Foy, near Quebec, Que., Canada; Roman Catholic; founded 1852 by the Seminary of Quebec (1663); arts, agriculture, canon law, commerce, law, letters, medicine, nursing, pedagogy, philosophy, sciences, social sciences, surveying and forest engineering, theology; graduate school; affiliated schools; teaching in French: Q-15, *pictures* U-210, Q-13, 9e

**'L'Avare'.** *see in index* 'Avare, L''.

**Lava soil,** from volcanoes S-249, V-378
■ Central America C-194
■ Java J-422
■ United States U-84: Hawaii H-54; Idaho I-17

**Lavater** [*lä-vä-tēr'*], **Johann Kaspar** (1741–1801), Swiss poet and mystic, born Zurich; founder of physiognomy, the art of reading character, especially from facial features.

**Lavatera** [*lăv-a-tē'ra*], a genus of plants and shrubs of the mallow family, native to warm regions of the world. Leaves lobed, often maplelike; flowers, 5 petals, in axils of leaves or in loose clusters, white through red; entire plant somewhat hairy or grayish; tall species used as windbreaks; also called tree mallow.

**Lavelli, Dante** (Glue Fingers) (born 1923), football player, born Hudson, Ohio; Cleveland Browns 1946–56: *list* F-337

**Lavender,** an aromatic shrub of the mint family native to s. Europe
■ perfume made from, *pictures* P-204, F-386

**Lavender laceflower.** *see in index* Trachymene

**'Lavengro',** a semiautobiographical story by George Henry Borrow dealing with his early adventures and his wanderings with the gypsies.

**Laver,** algae A-284

**Laver, Rod(ney George)** (born 1938), Australian tennis player, born Gladstone, Queensland; on Australia's Davis Cup team 1959–61; won many top titles; in 1962 and 1969 he won the world's four major singles championships (Australian, French, British, and United States), the first player to achieve this grand slam more than once; professional since 1963 ('The Education of a Tennis Player' with Bud Collins).

**Laveran** [*là-vrän'*], **Charles Louis Alphonse** (1845–1922), French physician, born Paris: M-498, M-215c
■ Nobel prize, *table* N-294d

**La Vérendrye** [*là vā-rän-drē'*], **Pierre Gaultier de Varennes, sieur de** (1685–1749), French Canadian explorer and fur trader, born at Trois-Rivières, Canada; pushed westward in search of the Western Sea; visited Mandan Indian villages on the Missouri; two of his sons, Francois, chevalier de la Vérendrye, and Louis Joseph de la Vérendrye, visted North Dakota and possibly reached the foothills of the Rocky Mts.: M-353, *picture* F-495
■ Manitoba M-89d: monument M-89f
■ North Dakota N-344, *picture* N-345
■ route, *map* C-109

**La Verne College,** at La Verne, Calif.; Church of the Brethren; founded 1891; liberal arts and teacher education; graduate study.

**Lavery** [*lă'vēr-ĭ*], **Sir John** (1856–1941), British painter, born Belfast, Ireland; renowned chiefly for portraits and figure work done in a broad style; also landscape and historical works; knighted 1918.

**Lavinia,** in Roman mythology, daughter of Latinus and Amata; betrothed to Turnus but married Aeneas who killed Turnus in single combat (Vergil's 'Aeneid' books 7, 10, and 12).

**Lavinium,** ancient town of Latium, 27 km (17 mi) s. of Rome, Italy; said to have been founded by Aeneas and named after his wife, Lavinia.

**Lavisse** [*là-vēs'*], **Ernest** (1842–1922), French historian, born France; professor at Sorbonne; member of French Academy; wrote and edited histories of Prussia, France, and Europe.

**Lavoisier** [*lav-wäz'ē-ā*], **Antoine Laurent** (1743–94), French chemist L-164–5
■ combustion explained by S-57j, F-122, C-243, O-516, *picture* S-57j
■ head of powder works W-169
■ theories about heat H-114

**Lavra,** famous monastery of Greek church, at Kiev, Russia K-49

**Law, Andrew Bonar** (1858–1923), British statesman, born New Brunswick, Canada, of Scottish parentage; taken to Scotland as child; made a fortune as iron merchant; began career in Parliament in 1900, becoming leader of Conservative party; helped to form coalition government in World War I; prime minister 1922.

**Law, John** (1671–1729), Scottish financier, born in Edinburgh; lived in London until convicted of killing a man in a duel; fled to the Continent, where he proposed new government credit systems based on paper money and colonial exploitation; appointed controller-general of French finance (1720); inflation beyond his control followed; escaped to Italy and died in Venice: M-379

**Law** L-165, *table* L-165a–b. *see also in index* Commercial law; Factories and factory laws; Government; Government regulation of industry; International law; Jury; Labor legislation; Social legislation
■ administrative A-46
■ advertising codes A-60
■ air pollution A-147
■ apprenticeship programs A-511
■ Arabs A-526
■ arbitration. *see also in index* Arbitration
■ bankruptcy B-74
■ Beccaria's contribution B-122
■ bill of rights B-193
■ canon L-165
■ citizenship C-353
■ civil L-165, C-593, 595–6, J-485
■ codes, historic L-165
□ Greek G-223, L-398, S-255
□ Hammurabi (Babylon) P-506
□ Justinian J-485, B-534
□ Napoleonic N-11
□ Ten Commandments M-495
■ common, defined E-233, L-165
■ Constitution, United States U-139–54, *pictures* U-139, 141, 143, 145. *see also in index* United States Constitution
■ counterfeiting C-592
■ courts of justice C-593–6, *pictures* C-593–5. *see also in index* Courts of Justice
■ criminal L-165, C-593, 595–6
■ etiquette adapted E-298
■ flotsam, jetsam, and lagan F-249
■ habeas corpus H-1–2
■ initiative and referendum I-189–90
■ libraries L-208, 209, 234, 243, 244, *picture* L-239: librarian L-226
■ local option P-506
■ marriage M-114–15
■ martial C-594, L-165
■ Mesopotamian B-4
■ Mohammedan Koran K-74
■ Mongolian law G-45
■ Mosaic law B-181, M-495
■ parliamentary law P-132a–3, *table* P-132b
■ practice: women W-215a
■ purpose of G-163
■ Roman. *see in index* Roman law
■ state constitutions S-428–9
■ United Kingdom U-19: Edward I reorganizes E-100d; Henry II reforms H-136, E-233; Magna Carta foundation of M-45
■ United States: how made C-516, 518, *pictures* C-517; statehood S-429a–b
■ veto V-308–9. *see also in index* Veto
■ wills W-160

**Law Enforcement Assistance Administration,** United States U-160

**Law, merchant,** for regulating medieval trade R-149

**Law, scientific.** *see in index* name of law, as Ohm's law

**Law, The,** division of the Old Testament P-509

**Law Day USA** (May 1), in United States F-93

**Lawes, Sir John Bennet** (1814–1900), English agriculturist, born Rothamsted, England; there founded experimental farm on family estate; developed a fertilizer by treatment of phosphates with sulfuric acid.

**Lawler, Ray,** Australian playwright A-799

**Lawless, Theodore Kenneth** (1892–1971), dermatologist, born in Thibodaux, La.; began practice in Chicago 1924; taught at Northwestern University 1924–41; 1954 Spingarn medal (dermatology).

**Law lords,** in British Parliament P-131a

**Lawn,** formerly a fine linen fabric made in Laon, France; now a light thin cotton material, white, dyed, or printed.

**Lawn,** grass-covered grounds G-189, *picture* H-247
■ mowing, *picture* F-28: power mower, noise level P-441e
■ planting G-24–5
■ sprinkler, *picture* J-444
■ weeds W-92, *pictures* W-92a–b

**Lawn bowling,** or **bowls,** outdoor game of ancient origin, played on grass plot, the green; players roll balls (bowls), about 13 centimeters (5 inches) in diameter, at a smaller ball called the jack B-386

**Lawndale,** Calif., city near Pacific Ocean 12 mi (19 km) s.w. of Los Angeles; pop. 23,460; electronic devices, aircraft parts, candy manufacturing: *map, inset* C-53

**Lawn tennis.** *see in index* Tennis

**Lawrance, Charles Lanier** (1882–1950), aircraft engineer, born Lenox, Mass.; designed and perfected radial, air-cooled engine called "Wright Whirlwind"; organized Lawrance Engineering and Research Corp.

**Lawrence, Saint,** also **Laurentius,** or **Lorenzo** (died 258?), Christian martyr, called "the Deacon," friend of the poor; commemorated August 10; meteorites appearing about that time known as "tears of St. Lawrence"
■ martyrdom M-120

**Lawrence, Abbott** (1792–1855), manufacturer and diplomat, born Groton, Mass.; brother of Amos A. Lawrence; minister to Great Britain 1849–52; founded Lawrence Scientific School of Harvard University
■ Lawrence, Mass., named for L-166

**Lawrence, Amos Adams** (1786–1852), merchant and philanthropist, born Groton, Mass.; brother of Abbott Lawrence; did much to establish cotton textile industry in New England; gave freely to schools and charities. His son **Amos Adams** (1814–86) was chief founder of Lawrence College, now Lawrence University, at Appleton, Wis.

**Lawrence, Charles** (1709–60), English soldier and statesman, born Portsmouth, England; lieutenant governor of Nova Scotia, Canada, 1754–56, governor 1756–60.

**Lawrence, D(avid) H(erbert)** (1885–1930), English novelist, poet, and painter; born Eastwood, near Nottingham; novels characterized by a sensitive delineation of nature and individual emotion ('Sons and Lovers'; 'Women in Love'; 'Kangaroo'); also wrote essays ('Twilight in Italy') which have an enduring quality of richness of description, and poems, some of which were illustrated by his own drawings ('Birds, Beasts and Flowers'): E-271, 276, W-310b

**Lawrence, Ernest O(rlando)** (1901–58), physicist, born Canton, S.D.; on faculty University of California 1928–58, director radiation laboratory 1936–58; Fermi award 1957 for invention of cyclotron and other contributions to atomic energy, *picture* S-332
■ Nobel prize, *table* N-294a

**Lawrence, Gertrude** (1898–1952), English actress, born London; won first success singing 'Limehouse Blues' 1924; starred in stage shows in England and U.S. ('Private Lives'; 'Tonight at 8:30'; 'Susan and God'; 'Skylark'; 'Pygmalion'; 'The King and I'); author of 'A Star Danced', autobiography.

**Lawrence, Sir Henry Montgomery** (1806–57), English brigadier general and colonial administrator, brother of John L. M. Lawrence
■ at siege of Lucknow L-387

**Lawrence, Jacob** (born 1917), artist, teacher, and humanitarian; born Atlantic City, N.J.; paintings on Negro life and history in U.S.; widely represented in permanent collections of American museums; teacher of art at Pratt Institute, Brandeis University, and many other schools; won 1970 Spingarn medal.

**Lawrence, James** (1781–1813), American naval hero L-166, *pictures* L-166, N-200

**Lawrence, John Laird Mair Lawrence, Baron** (1811–79), British viceroy and governor-general of India, called "savior of India" because his relief of Delhi during the Mutiny (1857) maintained British dominion; brother of Sir Henry M. Lawrence.

**Lawrence, Josephine** (1890–1978), author and journalist, born Newark, N.J.; wrote first children's story ever broadcast, 1921; adult books: 'If I Have Four Apples' and 'All Our Tomorrows'.

**Lawrence, Sir Thomas** (1769–1830), English court painter, born Bristol; supported family with portrait sketches at age of 10; flattering but often superficial likenesses of English beauties and European sovereigns; the successor of Sir Joshua Reynolds as most celebrated portrait painter of his day ('Mrs. Siddons', 'Princess Lieven', 'Calmady Children', 'Pinkie').

**Lawrence, T(homas) E(dward)** (1888–1935), British soldier, explorer, and scholar; called Lawrence of Arabia: L-166, *picture* L-166

**Lawrence, William** (1850–1941), Episcopal bishop, born Boston, Mass.; grandson of Amos and son of Amos Adams Lawrence; bishop of Massachusetts 1893–1926 ('Life of Amos A. Lawrence'; 'Memories of a Happy Life'; 'Life of Phillips Brooks').

**Lawrence,** Ind., town just n.e. of Indianapolis; pop. 25,591; settled 1849 on site bought from Miami Indians 1783; incorporated 1929: *map* I-100

**Lawrence,** Kan., city on Kansas River about 35 mi (55 km) s.w. of Kansas City, Kan.; pop. 52,738; chemicals, paper products, pipe organs; Haskell Institute, for Indians: K-7–8, 9, *maps* K-17, U-41
■ attack in 1856, *picture* P-321
■ Kansas, University of, *picture* K-11
■ railroad station, *picture* R-73

**Lawrence,** Mass., manufacturing city on Merrimack River, 30 mi (50 km) from sea; pop. 63,175; L-166, *maps* M-161, U-41, M-152
■ temperature, *list* M-143

**'Lawrence',** Perry's flagship, in battle of Lake Erie S-177g–h, P-209

**Lawrence of Arabia.** *see in index* Lawrence, T(homas) E(dward)

**Lawrence University,** at Appleton, Wis.; founded 1847; named for Amos A. Lawrence, a Boston merchant who was its chief founder; arts and sciences, music; quarter system.

**Lawrencium** (Lw), chemical element, *tables* P-207, C-236

**Lawrie, Lee** (1877–1963), American sculptor, born Berlin, Germany; instructor Yale University 1908–18; sculptures for Bok Singing Tower, U.S. Military Academy, Nebraska and Louisiana Capitols; Atlas statue, Rockefeller Center
■ carving, *picture* P-143d

**Lawson, Don** (born 1917), writer and editor, born Chicago, Ill.; author of books for young people; editor in chief 'Compton's Encyclopedia' 1965–73; editor American Educator Encyclopedia 1973–74, editor in chief 1974– (adult novel: 'A Brand for the Burning'; history books for young people: 'Young People in the White House', 'The United States in World War I', 'The United States in World War II', 'The United States in the Korean War', 'The War of 1812', 'The Colonial Wars', 'The American Revolution', 'The United States in the Indian Wars', 'The United States in the Spanish-American War', 'The United States in the Mexican War', 'Famous Political Families', 'Frances Perkins: First Lady of the Cabinet', 'The Lion and the Rock: the Story of the Rock of Gibraltar'; anthologies: 'Great Air Battles', 'Youth and War', 'Ten Fighters for Peace').

**Lawson, Henry** (1867–1922), Australian short-story writer and poet, born near Grenfell, New South Wales A-797

**Lawson, John Howard** (1895–1977), playwright and motion-picture scriptwriter, born New York City ('Roger Bloomer' and 'Processional', plays exemplifying expressionism).

**Lawson, Robert** (1892–1957), author and illustrator of children's books, born New York City; drawings are a fine combination of imagination and humor; illustrated 'The Story of Ferdinand' by Munro Leaf; wrote and illustrated 'They Were Strong and Good' (1941 Caldecott Medal), 'Mr. Revere and I', 'The Tough Winter', 'Captain Kidd's Cat', 'The Great Wheel': R-111a
■ 'Ben and Me' R-108, *picture* R-111
■ 'Rabbit Hill' (1945 Newbery Medal) R-110a

**Lawson, Victor Fremont** (1850–1925), editor and newspaper publisher, born Chicago, Ill.; owner of *Chicago Daily News,* which he endeavored to maintain without political bias; president Associated Press 1884–1900; advocacy of government savings bank caused him to be called "the father of the postal savings bank in America."

**Lawson quintuplets** M-542a

**Lawson's cypress.** *see in index* Port Orford cedar

**Lawton, Henry Ware** (1843–99), U.S. Army officer, born Manhattan, Ohio; in Civil War rose from sergeant to brevet colonel; commanded troops which took El Caney in Cuba in 1898; promoted to major general; killed in attack upon Filipinos at San Mateo, Luzon, Philippines.

**Lawton,** Okla., city about 80 mi (130 km) s.w. of Oklahoma City, in farm district and oil region; pop. 80,054; stock feed, dairy products, meat-packing, cement products, trailer homes, boxes, hats, men's slacks; Museum of the Great Plains; Fort Sill and a wildlife refuge nearby: O-436, *maps* O-446, 435, U-40
■ wildlife refuge, *picture* O-442

**Lawyer,** or **attorney,** vocation L-165, V-367, *picture* P-526b
■ India, *picture* L-239

**Lawyer,** fish. *see in index* Burbot

**Laxative,** or **physic** H-87–8, *table* D-200a

**Laxness** [*läks′nĕs*], **Halldor (Kiljan)** (real name Halldor Gudjonsson) (born 1902), Icelandic novelist, born Reykjavik, Iceland; traveled widely; in U.S. 1927–30 ('Salka Valka'; 'Independent People')
■ Nobel prize, *table* N-294f

**Layamon** [*lā′a-mŏn*], English poet and priest, lived about 1200; author of the 'Brut', metrical chronicle of Britain, one of monuments of early English language.

**Layard, Sir (Austen) Henry** (1817–94), English diplomat, archaeologist, and writer; born Paris; excavated ruins of Nineveh ('Monuments of Nineveh') A-532

**Laye, Camara,** Francophone author A-122

**Layering,** in horticulture G-178, P-361–2

**Laying,** ropemaking process, *picture* R-293

**Layne, Robert** (Bobby) (born 1926), football quarterback, born Santa Anna, Tex.; quarterback Chicago Bears 1948; New York Bulldogs 1949; Detroit Lions 1950–58 and Pittsburgh Steelers 1958–62: *list* F-337

**'Lay of the Last Minstrel, The',** poem by Scott S-73

**Layout** P-499
■ advertising V-365, 370

**Laysan** [*lä′ē-sän*] **Island,** small coral island belonging to U.S., in Pacific in group lying n.w. of Hawaiian Islands; breeding place for many birds: *maps* P-5, H-71

**'Lays of Ancient Rome',** a collection of ballads by Macaulay M-3
■ 'Horatius at the Bridge' M-3

**Layton, Irving** (born 1912), Canadian author and editor C-114, 116

**Layton,** Utah, city 10 mi (16 km) s. of Ogden; lies between Wasatch Range and Great Salt Lake at altitude of 4356 ft (1328 m); pop. 22,862; irrigated farm area; sugar refining: *map* U-232

**Lazarus,** beggar in parable of the rich man and the poor man (Luke xvi, 19–30); short form of Hebrew name Eleazar meaning "God has helped."

**Lazarus,** man of Bethany, brother of Martha and Mary; raised from the dead by Christ after four days (John xi); his tomb and house were visited by 4th-century pilgrims.

**Lazarus, Emma** (1849–87), poet, born New York City; published first poems and translations at 18; did philanthropic work among Jewish refugees from Russia; worked for Jewish nationalism ('Alide'; 'Songs of a Semite')
■ poem inscribed on Statue of Liberty L-205

**Lazear, Jesse William** (1866–1900), physician, born Baltimore, Md.; with U.S. Army Yellow Fever Commission in Cuba; for experimental purposes allowed himself to be bitten by mosquito carrying yellow fever germ and died: M-499, *picture* R-121

**Lazuli** [*lăz′ū-lī*], **bunting,** a bird of the finch family B-503

**"Lazy heart,"** in space travel S-346a

**L.C.L.** (less than carload), freight shipments R-82

**$LD_{50}$,** measurement A-449

**Lea, Henry Charles** (1825–1909), publisher and church historian, born New Orleans, La.; remembered for 'A History of the Inquisition of the Middle Ages' and 'A History of the Inquisition of Spain', the standard books in English in their fields.

**Lea, Homer** (1876–1912), soldier and author, born Denver, Colo.; although a hunchback, he became a general in the service of Sun Yat-sen in China; author of two prophetic works on Japan's plans for expansion—'The Valor of Ignorance' and 'The Day of the Saxon': *picture* C-464

**Lea, Tom** (born 1907), painter and writer, born El Paso, Tex.; painted many murals; illustrated J. Frank Dobie's 'Apache Gold & Yaqui Silver' and 'The Longhorns'; wrote and illustrated 'The Brave Bulls', 'The King Ranch'.

**Leaching,** in metallurgy M-228

**Leach's petrel** P-227, *picture* P-227

**Leacock** [*lē′kŏk*], **Stephen Butler** (1869–1944), Canadian educator and humorist, born Swanmoor, Hampshire, England; professor of political economy at University of Chicago 1899–1903, at McGill University, Montreal, Canada, 1908–36; author of biographies of Charles Dickens and Mark Twain, and of books on history, economics, and political science; won a wider public with nonsensical sketches: C-114, *picture* C-115

**Lead** [*lēd*], S.D., city in Black Hills; pop. 5420; timber, stock raising; gold mining; tourist center; Homestake Mine, largest gold mine in U.S.; incorporated 1890: *maps* S-334, U-40
■ Homestake Mine B-306, S-323, G-150b–c, d, *picture* S-331

**Lead** [*lĕd*] (Pb), a metalic chemical element L-167, *picture* L-167, *tables* P-207, M-229, C-233, 236
■ acetate, in secret ink I-190
■ alchemy A-273
■ alloys L-167; brass B-410; bronze B-463
■ automobile exhaust A-848
■ carbonate, basic (white lead) P-73
■ chemical test for, *table* Q-4
■ chromate (chrome yellow) C-335
■ electrochemical activity E-167
■ end-product of radioactivity R-64, 68, G-62
■ gasoline, antiknock G-42 L-167
■ glassmaking G-137, 142, L-167, *picture* G-143
■ isotopes L-167
■ melting point, *table* F-433
■ metalworking M-230
■ monoxide (litharge) L-167
■ native form M-332
■ ore deposits, *map* O-497
■ paints and driers P-73
■ poisoning L-167
■ producing regions L-167
□ United States L-167, U-106: Idaho I-18, *map* I-20; Missouri M-397, *map* M-400; Oklahoma O-436, *map* O-438
■ protection against radioactivity L-167, *picture* R-64
■ radioactive minerals contain L-167, M-335
■ red lead (minium) L-167, P-73
■ refining L-167: cadmium a by-product C-10
■ silver associated in ores S-204
■ sulfide (galena) L-167
■ supercold affects C-620b
■ tetraethyl C-239, G-42, L-167
■ white lead P-73, 76

**'Lead, Kindly Light',** hymn by Cardinal Newman N-205

**Lead arsenate,** an insecticide I-194

**Leadbelly.** *see in index* Ledbetter, Huddie

**Leader,** in fishing F-177, *list* F-180

**Leading,** in boxing B-390

**Lead** [*lĕd*] **line,** in navigation N-86

**Lead mold,** in electrotyping E-173

**Lead pencil** P-158–9, *pictures* P-158–9

**Leadville,** Colo., mining and tourist city in w.-central part of state, about 80 mi (130 km) s.w. of Denver; almost 2 mi (3 km) above sea level; pop. 3879; gold, silver, molybdenum mines; important center of American mining history: C-457, *maps* C-466, U-40
■ Tabor, first mayor T-2

**Leadwort,** a plant. *see in index* Plumbago

**Leadwort family,** or **Plumbaginaceae** [*plŭm-băġ-ĭ-nā′sē-ē*], a family of plants and shrubs including the prickly thrifts, sea lavender, leadwort, and statice, or thrift.

**Leaf, Munro** (1905–76), author of children's books, born present Baltimore, Md. ('The Story of Ferdinand', 'Wee Gillis', illustrated by R. Lawson; 'Reading Can Be Fun', 'Three Promises to You', 'Science Can Be Fun', 'Who Cares? I Do', illustrated by author).

**Leaf,** of metal. *see in index* Foil

**Leaf,** of plant. *see in index* Leaves

**Leaf beetle,** *picture* B-141

**Leaf butterfly.** *see in index* Oriental leaf butterfly

**Leaf-cutting ant,** ant which cuts and carries away leaves and petals of trees and other plants; found chiefly in tropical America A-468, *picture* N-63

**Leaf-cutting bee** B-124
■ egg, *picture* E-106

**Leaf fish,** a freshwater fish (*Monocirrhus polyacanthus*) of northern South America; belongs to family *Nandidae: picture* F-157

**Leafhoppers,** a group of insects of the order *Hemiptera;* especially the red-banded leafhopper (*Graphocephala coccinea*) which infests various flowers, vegetables, shrubs, and weeds: *picture* I-200

**Leaf insect,** an insect of tropical regions, with wings amazingly leaflike in form and color; family *Phasmidae.*

**Leaflet** L-177

**Leaflet bomb,** a weapon B-337

**Leaf lettuce** L-201, *picture* L-201

**Leaf monkey.** *see in index* Langur; Guereza

**Leaf rollers,** popular name of the *Tortricidae,* a family of small moths, many of whose larvae roll leaves to form a shelter: I-209

**Leaf rust,** a fungus growth R-363

**League,** an ancient unit of long measure which in modern usage varies in different countries from about 2 to about 4 miles (about 3¼ to about 6½ kilometers): *table* W-96
■ marine league, *table* W-96

**League Island Navy Yard.** *see in index* Philadelphia Navy Yard

**'League of American Wheelmen, The',** organization B-189

**League of Arab States.** *see in index* Arab League

**League of Nations** L-168. *see also in index* Mandates; Plebiscite
■ council meeting, *picture* W-264
■ Danzig under protection of D-33
■ Harding's policy H-30
■ headquarters at Geneva G-44
■ International Labor Organization L-91, U-26, C-281
■ limitation of armaments P-143c
■ Permanent Court of International Justice L-168, H-4, E-322
■ supporters: Roosevelt, F.D. R-263; Taft T-9; Wilson L-168, W-177

■ United States rejects U-185, W-263
■ Versailles, Treaty of W-263

**League of Swiss Cantons** (1291), *table* T-251a

**League of the Three Petticoats,** in Seven Years' War S-117

**League of Women Voters,** nonpartisan association of women interested in the promotion of good citizenship and government: C-160, W-215d

**Leah,** elder daughter of Laban and unloved first wife of Jacob (Gen. xxix); from her the tribes of Levi, Simeon, Reuben, Judah, Issachar, and Zebulon descend.

**Leahy** [*lā'hē*], **William Daniel** (1875–1959), U.S. Navy officer, born Hampton, Iowa; chief of naval operations 1937–39; governor of Puerto Rico 1939–40; ambassador to Vichy, France, 1940–42; chief of staff to president of the United States 1942–49; appointed fleet (5-star) admiral 1944.

**Leakey, Caroline,** Australian writer A-797

**Leakey, Louis Seymour Bazett** (1903–72), British archaeologist, born Kabete, near Nairobi, Kenya; curator Coryndon Memorial Museum, Nairobi, 1945–61; leader of many East African expeditions: F-356, M-76

**Leamington** [*lĕm'ĭng-tŏn*], England, health resort in Warwickshire, 145 km (90 mi) n.w. of London; pop. 45,090; mineral springs: *map* G-199h

**Leander,** lover of Hero H-146

**Leaning tower of Pisa,** in Pisa, Italy P-343, *picture* P-343
■ Galileo's experiment G-195, F-23, *picture* G-195

**Lean-to,** shelter C-63–4, *picture* V-241
■ Whelan, *diagram* T-105

**"Lean-to" fire,** *pictures* C-65

**Leap year** C-28, Y-337, *diagram* Y-337

**Lear, Edward** (1812–88), English writer and artist L-168, R-106, *picture* L-168

**Learning** L-169–72, E-75, *pictures* L-169–72
■ animals P-521, L-170–1, *pictures* P-520, 522–3, L-170–1
■ child development C-265–80, *pictures* C-265–73, 275–80
■ education E-74–100c, *chart* E-94, *pictures* E-74, 78–80, 82–6, 88–9, 91, 93, 95–6, 98–9, 100a, *tables* E-76–7, 90, 92, 97
■ educational television. *see in index* Education, *subhead* television as medium
■ exceptional children. *see in index* Exceptional children
■ expository method S-238–9
■ factors in efficient learning L-171–2
■ growth and decline of learning ability L-172
■ habit H-2, L-169
■ inquiry method S-239–40
■ intelligence tests measure I-218–23, *graph* I-219, *pictures* I-218, 220–1, 223
■ kindergartens and nursery schools K-51–3, *pictures* K-51–3
■ memory M-220, *picture* M-220
■ new math concepts M-164f
■ play P-385–90b, *pictures* P-385, 387–90
■ psychological theories P-521, 524
■ readiness C-265, 276, *picture* C-276: reading R-101, 102–3, *pictures* R-100–101, 101d
■ study S-491–2
■ teaching machines T-45–7, *pictures* T-45–6

**Learning Center**
■ alternative schools A-321

**Leary, Herbert Fairfax** (1885–1957), U.S. Navy officer, born Washington, D.C.; commander of Allied naval forces in s.w. Pacific 1942–43; commander of eastern sea frontier, U.S., 1943–45.

**Lease,** in law, *table* L-165b

**Lease-lend.** *see in index* Lend-lease

**Leasing system**
■ shoe manufacturing S-180

**Least flycatcher,** or **chebec** F-282

**Least grebe** G-210

**Least sandpiper** S-40
■ silhouette, *picture* B-189

**Least tern** G-262

**Leather** L-173–6, *pictures* L-174–6
■ armor A-630
■ artificial L-175
■ by-products L-173
■ embossing L-174, E-191, *picture* L-176
■ gloves G-144d
■ history L-175–6
■ kinds L-174–5, *map* L-173
□ chamois C-205
□ crocodile C-611
□ goatskin G-147
□ parchment and vellum L-229, D-200e
□ shagreen: sawfish S-52d; shark S-144
■ leathercraft, *picture* H-186: books on H-186
■ manufacture L-173–4, *pictures* L-174–6
■ shoes L-174, 175, 176, 173, S-179, 180–1, *diagrams* S-179, *pictures* S-180–1
□ labels C-407
■ sources L-173, *map* L-173

**Leatherback turtle** T-308, 310, *picture* T-309

**Leather beetle,** *Dermestes vulpinus;* one of family of small, destructive insects sometimes classed as museum beetles; larvae feed on animal substances, especially skins.

**Leather carp,** fish C-141

**Leathernecks,** nickname of United States Marines M-109

**Leather splits.** *see in index* Splits

**'Leatherstocking Tales',** series of five fast-paced adventure novels by James Fenimore Cooper starring Leatherstocking, the ideal American frontiersman: C-562, A-346

**Leavening** B-428
■ yeast Y-338

**Leavenworth, Henry** (1783–1834), U.S. Army officer and Indian fighter, born New Haven, Conn.; built Army posts, later known as Ft. Snelling (1819) and Ft. Leavenworth (1827); stationed at Ft. Atkinson, Neb. (1821–24).

**Leavenworth,** Kan., city in n.e. on Missouri River; pop. 33,656; steel fabricating and products, paper products, plastics; nearby are state and U.S. penitentiaries and Veterans Administration Hospital; in early days outfitting point for cross-prairie wagon trains; K-7, *maps* K-17, U-41

**Leavenworth Prison** P-505b, K-14d

**Leaves** L-177–80, *pictures* L-177–9
■ arrangement L-177
■ autumn coloration L-178, *picture* L-179
■ chlorophyll L-178. *see also in index* Chlorophyll
■ clocklike rhythms B-224
■ collecting L-180, *picture* L-178
■ evaporation from T-253, L-178
■ experiments with P-363c
■ growth of, *pictures* H-154
■ light, response to L-177–8, P-363: compass plants C-501; eucalyptus E-304
■ modifications L-177
□ carnivorous, or insect eating P-344, S-517, V-280, *pictures* N-60a, S-517, V-280
□ drought resisting G-189
□ fronds F-86, 87, *diagram* F-87, *pictures* F-86–8
□ needlelike (conifers) P-329
■ parts L-177
■ photosynthesis L-178. *see also in index* Photosynthesis
■ plant adaptation A-39
■ reduction by desert plants C-9
■ respiration P-373, W-75, R-159, *diagram* P-373
■ stomata L-178, P-358, P-372, *picture* L-177
■ transpiration L-178, P-372, P-359, W-69
■ tree L-177–80, T-253, *pictures* L-177–9, T-254–7. *see also in index* trees by name, *subhead* leaf
■ venation (veins) L-177, P-360: parallel, palmate, and pinnate L-177
■ water plants W-75

**'Leaves of Grass',** poems by Walt Whitman W-157, A-349

**Leawood,** Kan., residential city 15 mi (25 km) s. of Kansas City; pop. 13,360; incorporated in 1948: *map* K-18

**Lebanon** (from Arabic *laban,* "to be white"), republic on Mediterranean n. of Israel; cap. Beirut; area 4015 sq mi (10,400 sq km); pop. 3,254,000 (1979 est.); cedars of Lebanon supplied by Hiram of Tyre for Solomon's temple (I Kings v): L-180–180b, *map* I-280, *pictures* L-180–180a
■ cities L-180a. *see also in index* Beirut and other cities by name
■ climate L-180a
■ education L-180a, *picture* L-180a
■ flag F-211, *picture* F-209
■ government L-180a, b: elections L-180b
■ history L-180a–b: Arafat's occupation A-527; opposes Israel I-320, L-180b
■ location L-180, *locator map* L-180
■ money, *table* M-428
■ national anthem, *table* N-52
■ people and language L-180a
■ railroad mileage, *table* R-85
■ trade L-180a

**Lebanon,** N.H., city 47 mi (76 km) n.w. of Concord; pop. 11,134; dairy products and poultry, textiles, wood products, machinery, leather goods; founded 1761: *map* N-183

**Lebanon,** Pa., industrial city 25 mi (50 km) n.e. of Harrisburg; pop. 25,711; in limestone and iron-mining district; chemicals, iron and steel products, textiles, food products, paper boxes, pharmaceuticals: *map* P-185

**Lebanon,** Tenn., city 30 mi (50 km) n.e. of Nashville; pop. 11,872; livestock, timber, Burley tobacco, and limestone; Sam Houston practiced law here: *map* T-96

**Lebanon, cedar of** C-179, *picture* C-179
■ Beirut landmark B-144
■ Lebanese flag depicts F-211, *picture* F-209
■ ships S-164

**Lebanon Mountains,** range in Lebanon close to the coastal plain; highest point 10,131 ft (3088 m) B-143, L-180, 180a

**Lebanon Valley College,** at Annville, Pa.; United Methodist church; founded 1866; arts and sciences, education; member cooperative University Center at Harrisburg.

**Le Bel** [*lē bĕl'*], **Joseph Achille** (1847–1930), French chemist, born Pechelbronn, Alsace; in 1874 set forth concept of asymmetric carbon atom independently of his contemporary, Van't Hoff; carried on many experiments in organic chemistry.

**Lebensraum** [*lā'bĕns-roum*], German word, meaning "living space," slogan of German imperialism; used by Adolf Hitler to express Germany's demand for new territories and economic self-sufficiency.

**Leblanc** [*lē-bläṅ'*], **Maurice** (1864–1941), French writer, born Rouen; wrote stories about Arsène Lupin, gentleman-burglar who turned detective.

**Leblanc, Nicolas** (1742–1806), French chemist, born Issoudun; in 1789 discovered method of making soda from common salt; lost both property and his patent rights in French Revolution.

**Leblanc process,** for making soda and by-products S-247

**Le Blon** [*lē blôṅ'*], **Jacques Christophe** (1667–1741), French painter and engraver, born Frankfurt, Germany; the father of modern color printing.

**Le Bourget** [*lē bor-zhā'*] **Flying Field,** Paris, France L-289

**Le Bris** [*lē brē'*], **Jean Marie** (died 1872), French sea captain and inventor; patterned first glider after albatross: G-144b, A-201

**Lebrun** [*lē-brûṅ'*], **Albert François** (1871–1950), 14th president of France under the Third Republic, born Mercy-le-Haut, n.e. France; president of the Senate 1931–32; president of France 1932–40.

**Lebrun, Charles** (1619–90), French artist, born Paris; as one of founders of the Royal Academy of Painting and Sculpture and director of Gobelin tapestry manufactory, he practically directed French art tendencies during his lifetime; court artist under Louis XIV.

**Lebrun, Elisabeth Vigée-.** *see in index* Vigée-Lebrun

**Le Caron** [*lē kà-rôṅ'*], **Joseph** (1586–1632), French Roman Catholic missionary, born near Paris; pioneered among Huron Indians in Canada; compiler of first Huron dictionary; sent back to France (1629) by British after capture of Quebec, Canada.

**Le Chatelier** [*lē shä-tē-lyā'*], **Henry Louis** (1850–1936), French chemist, born Paris; known for law of chemical equilibrium: C-241

**Lechfeld** [*lĕk'fĕlt*], **battle of** (955), on plain of Lechfeld in Bavaria; Magyars defeated by Otto I: A-828, H-275

**Lechon,** Philippine food P-253d

**Lech** [*lĕk*] **River,** rapid and tortuous stream rising in Vorarlberg Alps at height of 1865 m (6120 ft); flows n. through Bavaria 290 km (180 mi), joining Danube below Donauwörth: *maps* G-99a, 115, D-32

**Lecithin** [*lĕs'ĭ-thĭn*], a fatty substance found in plant and animal cells S-340

**Lecky, William Edward Hartpole** (1838–1903), Irish historian and publicist, born Newton Park, near Dublin ('A History of European Morals'; 'History of England in the Eighteenth Century')
■ quoted G-75

**Leclaire** [*lē-klĕr'*], **Edmé Jean** (1801–72), French social scientist; founded system of profit sharing at his interior decorating firm in Paris 1842.

**Leclanché** [*lē-kläṅ-shā'*], **Georges,** French inventor B-108

**Leclerc, Jacques Philippe,** real name Jacques Leclerc de Hauteclocque (1902–47), French army officer, born Belloy-Saint-Léonard, n. France; prisoner of Germans 1940; escaped, joined Free French; led force across Sahara to meet General Montgomery 1943; led French into Paris Aug. 1944; signed for France at Japanese surrender on U.S.S. *Missouri* Sept. 2, 1945.

**Lecocq** [*lē-kôk'*], **Alexandre Charles** (1832–1918), French composer, born Paris; produced many light operas, melodious, gay, and lively ('La Fille de Madame Angot'; 'Giroflé-Girofla').

**Lecompton,** Kan., town on Kansas River, 15 mi (25 km) e. of Topeka; pop. 576; settled 1854 by proslavery men and was their headquarters during contest with free-state settlers for control of the state: *map* K-17

**Lecompton Constitution,** adopted by proslavery faction of Kansas in 1857
■ Buchanan urges acceptance B-476

**Le Conte** [*lē kŏnt'*], **Joseph** (1823–1901), scientist, born Liberty County, Ga.; helped popularize geology ('Elements of Geology'; 'Religion and Science').

**Leconte de Lisle** [*lē-kônt' dē lēl*], **Charles Marie** (1818–94), French poet, born island of Bourbon (now Réunion); chief of modern Parnassian school ('Poèmes antiques').

**Lecoq de Boisbaudran** [*lē-kôk' dē bwä-bō-dräṅ'*], **Paul Émile,** called François (1838–1912), French chemist, discoverer of gallium, samarium, dysprosium, holmium.

**Le Corbusier** [*lē kôr-bü-zyā'*], pseudonym of Charles Édouard Jeanneret-Gris (1887–1965), Swiss architect, born La Chaux-de-Fonds, Switzerland; Visual Arts Center at Harvard University, his first building in U.S., completed 1963 ('Towards a New Architecture'): D-94–94a, A-565, *picture* A-564, *profile* A-568

**Lecouvreur, Adrienne,** French actress A-27

**Le Creusot** [*krû-zō'*], France, town in e.-center, 120 km (75 mi) n.w. of Lyons; pop. 33,581; famous iron and armaments works: *map* F-405

**Lectern** [*lĕk'tẽrn*], a reading desk
■ medieval, *picture* M-303

**Lectum, Cape.** *see in index* Baba, Cape

**Lecturer,** in college U-206

**Lecuona** [*lā-kụ-ō'nạ*], **Ernesto** (1895–1963), Cuban composer, conductor, and pianist; born Guanabacoa, Cuba; piano debut at 5; composed first work at 11 ('Malagueña'; 'Andalucía'): M-561

**Leda** [*lē′da*], in Greek and Roman mythology, a fair mortal wooed by Zeus (Jupiter) in guise of swan; mother of twins Castor and Pollux, of Helen, and of Clytemnestra.

**Ledbetter, Huddie,** known as **Leadbelly** (1888–1949), folksinger, born Mooringsport, La. B-302

**Lederberg, Joshua** (born 1925), geneticist, born Montclair, N.J.; professor University of Wisconsin 1954–59, Stanford University 1959–
■ Nobel prize, *table* N-294e

**Ledger lines,** in musical notation M-564, *picture* M-564

**Ledo Road.** *see in index* Stilwell Road

**Ledyard, John** (1751–89), adventurer, born Groton, Conn.; dreamed of opening up fur trade in Pacific Northwest, glimpsed on voyage (1776–80) with Captain Cook; enlisted interest of John Paul Jones, Thomas Jefferson, Sir Joseph Banks; failed in two attempts to cross Siberia on foot; died during expedition into Africa.

**Ledyard,** Conn., 7 mi (11 km) n.e. of New London in agricultural area; pop. of township 13,735; plastics; incorporated 1836: *map* C-533

**Lee, Ann** (1736–84), "Mother Ann," founder of the American Society of Shakers, born Manchester, England; to America 1774; set up first Shaker colony near Albany, N.Y., 1776.

**Lee, Arthur** (1740–92), diplomat, born Stratford, Va.; brother of Richard Henry Lee; served as American representative in various European countries during Revolutionary War.

**Lee, Charles** (1731–82), American Revolutionary War general, born Dernhall, Cheshire, England; dismissed for insubordination; involved in treasonable intrigues not discovered until after his death: R-168, 172

**Lee, Dennis** (born 1939), Canadian poet and author, born Toronto (children's poetry: 'Wiggle to the Laundromat'; 'Alligator Pie', won Canadian Book of the Year for Children award 1975; 'Nicholas Knock and Other People'; 'Garbage Delight', won Canadian Book of the Year for Children award 1978).

**Lee, Doris (Emrick)** (Mrs. Arnold Blanch) (born 1905), modernist painter, muralist, and book illustrator, born Aledo, Mercer County, Ill.; known for rural scenes done with humor and charm; work represented in Metropolitan Museum of Art and major galleries ('Thanksgiving Dinner', 'Country Wedding').

**Lee, Fitzhugh** (1835–1905), Confederate Civil War general, born Fairfax County, Va.; nephew of Robert E. Lee; military governor of Havana, Cuba, after Spanish-American War.

**Lee, Francis Lightfoot** (1734–97), signer of Declaration of Independence, born Stratford, Va.; brother of Richard Henry Lee
■ signature reproduced D-55

**Lee, Harper** (Nelle Harper Lee) (born 1926), novelist, born Monroeville, Ala.; won 1960 Pulitzer prize for her first novel, 'To Kill a Mockingbird': R-111i

**Lee, Henry,** called "Light Horse Harry" (1756–1818), statesman and American Revolutionary War general, born Dumfries, Va.; member of Continental Congress 1785–88; governor of Virginia 1792–95; father of Robert E. Lee
■ quoted on Washington W-29

**Lee, Jason** (1803–45), American Methodist missionary and Oregon pioneer, born Stanstead, Que., Canada, then part of Vermont; went west with Wyeth's expedition (1834) to open mission among Flathead Indians; aided by Dr. McLoughlin in settling in Willamette Valley; established other missions in Clatsop region and at The Dalles: O-484, *picture* O-490
■ Statuary Hall, *table* S-437b

**Lee, Joseph** (1862–1937), social worker, born Brookline, Mass.; known as "father of American playground movement"; organized and was president of National Recreation Association from 1910; president War Camp Community Service during World War I ('Play in Education'). National Joseph Lee Day celebrated July 28.

**Lee, Manfred B.** *see in index* Queen, Ellery

**Lee, Mary Randolph Custis** (Mrs. Robert E. Lee) L-180b

**Lee, Richard Henry** (1732–94), American Revolutionary War leader L-180b, D-51
■ signature reproduced D-55

**Lee, Robert E(dward)** (1807–70), Confederate general L-180b-3, *pictures* L-181, V-342
■ birthday celebrated F-92
■ birthplace, *picture* V-335
■ captures John Brown L-182
■ Christ Church, *picture* V-334
■ Civil War L-182–3, C-376–7, 378
□ Antietam M-5
□ Chancellorsville C-206, 207, *map* C-206
□ Fredericksburg F-430–1, *map* F-431
□ Gettysburg G-119–20, *map* G-119: statue, *picture* P-178
□ Grant and G-171, 172, L-183, *pictures* C-511, L-284g, V-337: surrender site, *picture* V-334
■ Custis-Lee Mansion N-35, L-180b, *map* W-32, *picture* L-183
■ Hall of Fame, *table* H-11
■ horse, Traveller, *list* H-232e
■ quoted S-490b
■ Statuary Hall, *table* S-437b
■ Stone Mountain, *picture* G-82

**Lee, Sir Sidney** (1859–1926), English author and educator, born London; editor 'Dictionary of National Biography'; works include 'Life of Shakespeare', 'Life of Queen Victoria': S-142

**Lee, Isung Dao.** *see in index* Tsung Dao-lee

**Lee, William** (died 1610), English clergyman and inventor K-67, 69

**Lee,** river in Ireland C-573, *map* G-199h

**Leeboard,** a slab of wood or metal hung over the leeward side of sailing canoes and other small craft to prevent drifting sideways: C-125

**Leech, John** (1817–64), English caricaturist, whose *Punch* cartoons John Ruskin called "the finest definition and natural history of the classes of our society, the kindest and subtlest analysis of its foibles."

**Leech,** a bloodsucking worm L-183–4, *picture* W-298

**Leech,** nautical, *diagram* B-326

**Leechee.** *see in index* Litchi

**Leech Lake,** in n. Minnesota, 20 mi (30 km) long, *maps* M-349, 362

**Lee College,** at Cleveland, Tenn.; Church of God; founded 1918; arts and sciences, education, religion.

**Leeds,** England, city on Aire River; pop. 503,720: L-184, *map* G-199h
■ location, *locator map* L-184

**Leeds and Liverpool Canal,** England L-184

**Leek,** herb similar to onion O-455, F-95

**Leemans, Alphonse** (Tuffy) (1912–79), football player, born Superior, Wis.; halfback, fullback; New York Giants 1936–43: *list* F-337

**Leeming, Joseph** (1897–1969), author, editor, and publicist, born Brooklyn, N.Y.; writer of books for children, chiefly on making and doing things: 'The Costume Book', 'Fun with Magic', 'Fun with Clay', 'Fun with Puzzles', 'Fun with Beads'.

**Leesburg,** Fla., city 36 mi (58 km) n.w. of Orlando; pop. 13,191; citrus fruit and vegetable raising and packing; wood products, mobile homes, plastics: *map* F-246

**Lee's Summit,** Mo., city 17 mi (27 km) s.e. of Kansas City; pop. 28,741; electric components, chemicals, plastics; incorporated 1865: *map, inset* M-409

**Leeuwarden** [*la′vär-dĕn*], Netherlands, capital of province of Friesland; pop. 78,247; flourishing trade in cattle, grain, fish: *map* N-133

**Leeuwenhoek** [*lā′vĕn-ho̦k*], **Anthony van** (1632–1723), Dutch naturalist and microscopist, born Delft; first to describe red corpuscles of the blood; described and illustrated bacteria, yeast plants, hydra, and other microscopic life: M-215b, M-290, B-228, C-182

**Leeuwin** [*lo̦′wĭn*], **Cape,** extreme s.w. point of the continent of Australia

**Leeward** [*lē′wẽrd* or *lū′ẽrd*] **Islands,** n. group of Lesser Antilles, West Indies; includes Virgin Islands of the United States; the island St. Martin (French and Dutch); the islands Saba and St. Eustatius (both Dutch); Guadeloupe and dependencies (French); and the British possessions St. Kitts-Nevis, Anguilla, Antigua, Montserrat, and British Virgin Islands; pop. 566,000: *map* W-105
■ name, origin W-102

**Lefebvre** [*lĕ-fĕ′vr*], **Jules Joseph** (1836–1912), French painter; eminent as a painter of ideal heads; celebrated also for historical and allegorical paintings ('Lady Godiva'; 'Mignon').

**Lefèvre d'Étaples** [*dā-tȧ′pl*], **Jacques** (1455?–1537), French theologian and scholar, born Étaples; also known as Jacobus Faber Stapulensis; pioneer of French Protestantism; condemned by Sorbonne for certain critical works on Bible, but protected by Francis I and Margaret of Navarre; translated Bible into French.

**Left,** in politics, origin P-434

**Left and right** D-120, *picture* D-122

**Left-handedness** C-268, H-20, D-120

**Leg** F-328, 330, *pictures* F-329
■ bones S-210, *diagrams* S-208–10
■ evolution A-461
■ fractures, *pictures* F-378: in traction, *picture* F-378

**Legacy,** in law, *table* L-165b

**Legal Counsel, Office of,** United States U-160

**Legal holidays** F-90

**Le Gallienne** [*lĕ gȧl-yĕn′*], **Eva** (born 1899), American actress, born London, England; daughter of Richard Le Gallienne; educated in France; made American debut at 16; founder and director of Civic Repertory Theatre, New York City, in which she produced plays of high quality and presented them at popular prices ('The Swan'; 'The Master Builder'); author of 'At 33' and 'With a Quiet Heart', autobiographies.

**Le Gallienne, Richard** (1866–1947), American critic, essayist, and poet; born Liverpool, England; father of Eva Le Gallienne; 'Prose Fancies', 'The Quest of the Golden Girl', 'Pieces of Eight' are imaginative prose sketches; 'Odes from the Divan of Hafiz', 'English Poems', and other volumes of poems include many graceful lyrics.

**Legal tender,** coins and paper money that may legally be offered in payment of any money debt M-426

**Legal terms,** *table* L-165a–b

**Le Gascon** (the Gascon), French bookbinder of the 17th century; real name unknown

**Legaspi** [*lā-gȧs′pē*], formerly **Albay** [*ȧl-bī′*], Philippines, seaport of Luzon on Bay of Albay; pop. of municipality, 84,090; cap. of Albay Province: *maps* P-261d

**Legate** (from Latin *legare,* "to appoint"), specifically an ecclesiastical or diplomatic representative of the pope; term occasionally used to signify any ambassador or diplomat.

**Legato,** *table* M-566a

**Legend** (from Latin *legere,* "to read," originally "to gather"), a fictitious or improbable story based on tradition and some fact, as the legends of King Arthur; originally stories of saints and martyrs. *see also in index* Folklore

**Legend,** the title or description under a picture, diagram, or graph.

**'Legend of Sleepy Hollow, The',** story by Washington Irving A-345, I-316, *picture* S-184

**Legendre** [*lĕ-zhäṅ′dr*], **Adrien Marie** (1752–1833), French mathematician, born Toulouse, France; a leader in introducing the metric system; helped prepare great centesimal trigonometric tables; made important contributions to geodesy.

**Léger** [*lā-zhā′*], **Alexis Saint-Léger** (1887–1975), pseudonym St.-John Perse, French poet, born on island near Guadeloupe; went to France when 11; general secretary of ministry of foreign affairs 1933–40; in U.S. after 1940 ('Éloges', 'Anabase', 'Exil')
■ Nobel prize, *table* N-294f

**Léger, Fernand** (1881–1955), French painter, born Argentan; early work simple abstractions, later turned to cubism and flat-patterned landscapes: M-527, T-20
■ 'Interior' D-178, *picture* D-179
■ United Nations murals U-22

**Léger, Jules** (1913–80), Canadian political leader, born St. Anicet, Que.; held Canadian government posts from 1940, governor-general 1974–79.

**Léger, Paul Émile, Cardinal** (born 1904), Canadian prelate, born Valleyfield, Que.; ordained Roman Catholic priest 1929; became archbishop of Montreal 1950, resigned 1967 to do missionary work in African leper colonies; created cardinal 1953.

**Legerdemain** [*lĕg-ẽr-dĕ-mān′*], sleight of hand M-42–3, *pictures* M-41, 44

**Leggings,** garment D-190, *picture* D-191

**Leghorn,** Italian **Livorno** [*lē-vōr′nō*], Italy, Tuscan port on w. coast; pop. 161,077; Leghorn straw hats; glass, metal products, chemicals; shipbuilding: I-327, *maps* I-338, 325, E-334
■ Mascagni's birthplace M-141

**Leghorn,** a breed of fowls P-482, *pictures* P-480–1

**Legion,** originally name given to Roman citizen-army, from Latin *legere,* "to gather"; in modern times applied to organizations whose members have performed unusual services either civil or military
■ Foreign Legion, of France. *see in index* Foreign Legion
■ Roman A-636, W-9, C-535, *diagram* W-8

**Legionary ant,** or **Army ant** A-468

**Legion of Honor,** French order of merit, reward for civil and military services: D-59, *picture* N-8

**Legion of Merit Medal,** United States D-56

**Legion of Valor of the United States of America** P-140

**Legislative Assembly,** body in France during Revolution (1791–92) which succeeded National Assembly of 1789–91: F-444
■ Louis XVI deposed L-361

**Legislative assembly,** in state government A-804, S-429

**Legislative Council,** in Australian government A-804

**Legislative courts,** United States C-594

**Legislature,** the lawmaking body of a government. *see also in index* Diet; entries beginning Congress and Parliament; *see also* Fact Summary with each state article
■ bicameral P-129–30, S-429
■ states of United States S-429
■ unicameral. *see in index* Unicameral legislature
■ United Kingdom, defined U-17

**Legitimate theater** T-148. *see also in index* Theater

**Legitimists,** party in France which after Revolution of 1830 supported elder line of Bourbons; now any supporter of monarchy by hereditary right.

**Legler, Henry Eduard** (1861–1917), American librarian and writer, born Palermo, Italy; came to U.S. in early youth; secretary Wisconsin Library Commission 1904–9; librarian, Chicago Public Library after 1909.

**Legnano** [*lān-yä′nō*], Italy, city 26 km (16 mi) n.w. of Milan;

pop. 42,460; cotton and silk manufactures; Lombard League defeated Frederick Barbarossa nearby in 1176.

**Legnica** [*lĕḡ-nē'tsä*], German **Liegnitz** [*lēḡ'nĭts*], Poland, former Prussian manufacturing and trade town in Silesia, 60 km (40 mi) n.w. of Wroclaw; pop. 75,900; decisive victory of Frederick the Great over Austrians (1760); included in Poland since 1945.

**Legree, Simon,** a brutal slave driver in Harriet Beecher Stowe's 'Uncle Tom's Cabin'; name later used symbolically for any overbearing and unreasonable taskmaster.

**Legros** [*le-ḡrō'*], **Alphonse** (1837–1911), French painter and etcher, born Dijon, France; for nearly 30 years a teacher in London, where his severe yet dignified realism, simple technique, and respect for European painting traditions exerted a powerful influence on English art.

**Legumes** [*lĕḡ'ūmz*], pod-bearing plants of pea and bean type; form family *Leguminosae:* P-376
- ■ Australian flora classified A-783
- ■ clover C-409
- ■ cowpea C-596, *picture* C-596
- ■ lentil L-196
- ■ locust L-330, *picture* L-330
- ■ mesquite M-227, *picture* M-227
- ■ nitrogen-fixing bacteria on roots N-291, C-409–10, P-363a, *picture* C-410
- ■ pea P-142b, *pictures* P-142b
- ■ peanut P-146–7, *picture* P-147
- ■ soybean S-340, *picture* S-340
- ■ sweet pea S-529
- ■ tamarind T-13
- ■ uses: hay H-77
- ■ vetch V-305

**Leguminosae.** *see in index* Legumes

**Lehar** [*lā'här*], **Franz** (1870–1948), Hungarian composer, born Komarno; fame rests on operetta, 'The Merry Widow'.

**Le Havre** [*lē ä'vr'*], France, 2d seaport, at mouth of Seine River; pop. 198,021: H-50, *maps* F-381, 404, E-334, *picture* F-394
- ■ location H-50, *locator map* H-50

**Lehigh River,** tributary of Delaware River, about 120 mi (190 km) long; rises in Wayne County, e. Pa.; empties into the Delaware at Easton; navigable by locks for 84 mi (135 km): *map* P-165

**Lehigh University,** at Bethlehem, Pa.; private control; formerly for men, women admitted 1971; founded 1865; arts and science, business administration, education, engineering; graduate school.

**Lehman** [*lē'măn*], **Herbert H(enry)** (1878–1963), banker and statesman, born New York City; banker 1908–28; lieutenant governor of New York State 1928–32; governor 1932–42; director general UNRRA 1943–46; U.S. senator, (Democrat) 1949–56; awarded Presidential Medal of Freedom 1963.

**Lehman Caves National Monument,** in Nevada N-40a, *maps* N-30, N-156, *pictures* C-178a, N-153

**Lehmann** [*lā'män*], **Lilli** (1848–1929), German dramatic soprano, born Würzburg, Germany; because of superb quality and volume of her voice became famous as Brünnhilde, Isolde, and in other Wagnerian roles; also as interpreter of Mozart.

**Lehmann, Liza** (1862–1918), English soprano and composer, born London; remarkable success as concert singer; married Herbert Bedford, composer, 1894, and retired, devoting herself to composition of songs and song cycles ('In a Persian Garden').

**Lehmann, Lotte** (Mrs. Otto Krause) (1888–1976), American soprano, born Perleberg, Brandenburg, Germany; became U.S. citizen 1943; member Vienna State Opera, also of Chicago, New York, and other leading opera companies of U.S.; noted lieder singer; retired from stage 1951; author of 'Five Operas and Richard Strauss'.

**Lehmbruck** [*lām'bruk*], **Wilhelm** (1881–1919), German sculptor, born Meiderich (now Duisburg), Germany; by the use of exaggerated lines attained great esthetic and rhythmic force ('Kneeling Woman'): S-91

**Lehr** [*lēr*], oven, in glassmaking G-138, *picture* G-138

**Lei** [*lā'ē* or *lā*], a rope of flowers worn by Hawaiians; often used as a token of greeting or farewell; also chain or crown of shells, leaves, or flowers given as a sign of friendship by Polynesians: *pictures* H-54, E-136

**Lei,** monetary unit. *see in index* Leu

**Leibnitz,** lunar mountain range M-485, *map* M-481

**Leibniz,** or **Leibnitz** [*līp'nĭts*], **Gottfried Wilhelm, baron von** (1646–1716), German philosopher, mathematician, and scientist; born Leipzig; a many-sided genius, versed in law, theology, and politics; spent much of his time at courts of German nobles and took part in affairs of state. Most famous for his contributions to philosophy and mathematics; his differential method in calculus prevailed over Newton's earlier system; founder of Academy of Sciences: S-57h, *picture* C-21
- ■ computer history C-497c
- ■ controversy with Newton N-234

**Leicester** [*lĕs'tēr*], **Robert Dudley, earl of** (1532?–88), English statesman and soldier; his supposed secret marriage to Amy Robsart is the theme of Sir Walter Scott's 'Kenilworth': E-185

**Leicester, Simon de Montfort, earl of.** *see in index* Montfort

**Leicester,** or **Leicestershire,** England, n. midland county; 2155 sq km (832 sq mi); pop. 682,568; cap. Leicester; on Soar and Wreak rivers; sheep raising; farming; limestone and slate quarries: *map* E-218

**Leicester,** England, capital of Leicester county, on Soar River, 140 km (90 mi) n.w. of London; pop. 578,470; hosiery, boots and shoes, typewriters; Roman remains: *map* G-199h

**Leicester,** breed of sheep S-147

**Leicester Square,** in London L-343, *map* L-339

**Lei Day,** Hawaii F-93

**Leiden,** or **Leyden** [*līd'n*], Netherlands, city on Old Rhine River 35 km (22 mi) s.w. of Amsterdam; pop. 95,964; metal products, textiles; printing, food processing; birthplace of Rembrandt: *map* N-133
- ■ bulb industry B-379
- ■ Dutch home of Pilgrims M-181
- ■ libraries L-233, 243
- ■ siege (1574) *table* W-8d

**Leidesdorff, William** (1810–48), businessman, born in Danish Virgin Islands; to California 1841; served as American consul in California and city treasurer of San Francisco: *picture* C-48

**Leidy** [*lī'dĭ*], **Joseph** (1823–91), naturalist, born Philadelphia, Pa.; professor anatomy 1853–91 and director biology dept. 1884–91, University of Pennsylvania; research in vertebrate paleontology of America ('On the Fossil Horse of America').

**Leif Ericson.** *see in index* Ericson

**Leigh** [*lē*], **Vivien** (1918–67), English actress of stage and screen, born in Darjeeling, India, as Vivian Mary Hartley; twice won Academy award (motion pictures) for acting in 'Gone with the Wind' (1939) and 'A Streetcar Named Desire' (1951); married to Sir Laurence Olivier 1940–60
- ■ 'Gone with the Wind', *picture* M-527

**Leigh,** England, town in Lancashire, 30 km (20 mi) n.e. of Liverpool; pop. 46,200; coal mining; textiles, electric cable: *map* G-199g

**Leigh-Mallory, Sir Trafford Leigh** (1892–1944), British air officer, born Mobberley, near Manchester, England; headed Allied air forces for invasion of Europe 1944; lost in flight to command in s.e. Asia.

**Leighton** [*lā'tn*], **Frederick, Baron Leighton of Stretton** (1830–96), English painter and sculptor, born Scarborough, England; best known for classical subjects: S-90

**Leighton, Margaret** (born 1896), author, born Oberlin, Ohio; daughter of Thomas Nixon Carver, professor of political economy at Harvard University for many years; books for children: 'The Singing Cave'; 'Judith of France'; 'The Sword and the Compass'; 'Journey for a Princess'.

**Leinsdorf** [*līns'dôrf*], **Erich** (born 1912), American conductor, born Vienna, Austria; to U.S. 1937, became citizen 1942; chief conductor of German opera Metropolitan Opera House, New York City, 1939–43; conductor Cleveland (Ohio) Orchestra 1943–44, 1945–47, Rochester (N.Y.) Philharmonic Orchestra 1947–56; musical director and conductor Boston Symphony Orchestra 1962–69.

**Leinster** [*lĕn'stēr*], one of 4 provinces of Ireland, in middle and s.e. part s. of Ulster and s.e. of Munster provinces; bordered on e. by Irish Sea, on s.e. by St. George's Channel; 19,630 sq km (7580 sq mi); pop. 1,414,415: *map* I-283

**Leipzig** [*līp'sĭḡ*], East Germany, city in Saxony, 110 km (70 mi) n.w. of Dresden; pop. 584,365: L-184, L-233, *maps* G-115, 99a, E-334
- ■ Bach: bust, *picture* M-557
- ■ location L-184, *locator map* L-184

**Leipzig, battle of** (1813) N-13

**Leipzig, battle of,** or **battle of Breitenfeld** (1631) G-265

**Leipzig, University of** (renamed Karl Marx University 1953 by East Germany's Communist government), 3d in size and 3d in age of the universities of Germany; established 1409 by 400 teachers and students who seceded from University of Prague as result of Hussite agitations; medicine, law, theology, and liberal arts and sciences: L-184, L-233

**Leisler** [*līs'lēr*], **Jacob** (1640–91), popular leader in colonial New York, born Frankfurt, Germany; executed for insurrection: N-248

**Leisure** L-185–7, *pictures* L-185–6. *see also in index* Hobby; Reading for recreation; Recreation; Sewing
- ■ bibliography L-187
- ■ cultural institutions U-113. *see also in index* Libraries; Museums and art galleries
- ■ dance, stage D-26, 28, 29
- ■ dancing D-16–17, F-289–90, H-182, *pictures* D-16–17, F-290
- ■ family life F-28, 26, 27, *pictures* F-26–31
- ■ farm life F-47–8, *pictures* F-46–9
  - □ folk dance F-290, *picture* F-290
- ■ home improvement I-224, 230–3, F-485, W-5, *picture* T-200: painting P-76, *pictures* P-76
- ■ increase L-185, U-103, *chart* I-182a
- ■ motion pictures M-504, 524–5, 529
  - □ development M-517, 518–19, *pictures* M-517, 519
  - □ silent era M-519, 520, 521–2
  - □ sound first used M-523
- ■ music M-554, H-183, O-464b, O-474, *pictures* L-244, 240, F-359, H-182, T-278
- ■ outdoor cooking F-315, *pictures* F-315, H-185
- ■ plays D-169, T-148–9, *picture* T-155
- ■ radio R-43, 48, 57
- ■ television T-66, 68, 69, 75, P-535, *pictures* T-66

**Leith** [*lēth*], Scotland, seaport and shipbuilding center on s. shore of Firth of Forth; port for Edinburgh, with which it was incorporated 1920; pop. 51,378: *map* G-199g

**Leitmotiv** [*līt'mō-tēf*], in music O-463–4, M-559

**Leitrim** [*lē'trĭm*], county in Connaught province, Ireland; 1526 sq km (589 sq mi); pop. 30,572; lost more by emigration than any other county; beautiful scenery, especially along River Shannon; organized as county 1583: *map* I-283

**Leix** [*lāks*], also **Laoighis** [*lā'ĭsh*], formerly **Queen's,** county in s.e. Ireland, in Leinster Province; 1720 sq km (664 sq mi); pop. 44,595; farming, dairying, textile manufacturing; county town Port Laoighise (Maryborough): *map* I-283

**Le Jeune, Paul** (1591–1664), French Jesuit missionary, born Châlons-sur-Marne; 1632–39 was in Quebec, Canada, as superior of Canadian missions.

**Lek,** monetary unit of Albania, *table* M-428

**Leland, Charles Godfrey** (1824–1903), poet, ethnologist, traveler, and pioneer educator in art handicraft, born Philadelphia, Pa. ('Hans Breitmann's Ballads', poems in Pennsylvania Dutch dialect).

**Leland, Henry Martyn** (1843–1932), pioneer automobile manufacturer; founder Cadillac Motor Car Company, Lincoln Motor Company A-858, *profile* A-856

**Leland Stanford Junior University.** *see in index* Stanford University

**Leloir** [*lĭ-l'wôr'*], **Luis F(ederico)** (born 1906), Argentine biochemist, born Paris, France; director Institute of Biochemical Research, Buenos Aires, 1947–
- ■ Nobel prize, *table* N-294d

**Lely** [*lā'lĭ*], **Sir Peter,** real name Pieter van der Faes (1618–80), English court painter, born Westphalia, Germany, of Dutch family; portraits of beautiful women of court of Charles II.

**Lemaître** [*lē-mê'tr'*], **Jules** (1853–1914), French critic and dramatist, born Vennecy, near Orléans, France ('Impressions of the Theatre' and 'Contemporaries', widely read critical essays; 'The Pardon', 'The Poor Little Thing', plays).

**Léman, Lac.** *see in index* Geneva, Lake

**Le Mans** [*lē mäṅ'*], France, commercial and manufacturing city on Sarthe River, 185 km (115 mi) s.w. of Paris; pop. 140,520; French under General Chanzy defeated 1871 by Germans; again fell to Germans 1940: *maps* F-381, 404
- ■ Grand Prix auto race A-874

**Lemare, Edwin Henry** (1866–1934), English organist and composer, born Ventnor, Isle of Wight; organist in London, England, at Carnegie Institute, Pittsburgh, Pa., San Francisco, Calif., Portland, Me., and Chattanooga, Tenn.; composed organ and choral works, and made transcriptions of orchestral works for organ.

**LeMay** [*lē-mā'*], **Curtis E(merson)** (born 1906), U.S. Air Force officer, born Columbus, Ohio; Air Force deputy chief of staff for research and development 1945–47; commanding general U.S. Air Forces in Europe 1947–48, Strategic Air Command 1948–57; became 4-star general 1951; Air Force vice-chief of staff 1957–61, chief of staff 1961–65; American Independent vice-presidential candidate 1968; author of 'America Is in Danger' A-159

**Lemay** [*lē-mā'*], **Léon-Pamphile** (1837–1918), Canadian poet and novelist, born Lotbinière, near Quebec; educated in theology and law; librarian to Quebec legislature 1867–92 ('Les Vengeances', 'Petits poèmes', 'Les Gouttelettes', 'Reflets d'antan', poetry; 'Le Pèlerin de Sainte Anne', 'L'Affaire Sougraine', fiction): C-113a, b, 116

**Lemay,** Mo., residential city bordering St. Louis on south; pop. 40,516; stone quarries: *map, inset* M-409

**Lemberg,** Russia. *see in index* L'vov

**Lemelin, Roger** (born 1919), French-Canadian writer, born Quebec: C-115

**Lemke, William** (1878–1950), political leader, born Albany, Minn.; attorney general of North Dakota 1921–23; Republican representative from North Dakota 1933–50: *picture* N-350

**Lemming,** a small rodent of the mouse family, *Miridae*

**Lemmon slave case** (1854) A-652

**Lemnitzer, Lyman L(ouis)** (born 1899), U.S. Army officer, born Honesdale, Pa.; commissioned 2d lieutenant 1920, became 4-star general 1955; Army deputy chief of staff (plans and research) 1952–55; commander in chief of Far East command and of UN command 1955–57; Army vice-chief of staff 1957–59, chief of staff 1959–60; chairman Joint Chiefs of Staff 1960–62; supreme allied commander in Europe 1963–69; first person to receive distinguished service medals of Army, Navy, and Air Force at same time (July 1969).

**Lemnos,** island in n. Aegean; 390 sq km (150 sq mi); held in turn by ancient Greeks, Byzantine Empire, Italians, and Turks; Greek after World War I: *map* G-213
■ fabled home of Hephaestus H-141

**Lemon, Robert Granville** (Bob) (born 1920), baseball player, born San Bernardino, Calif.; A.L. infielder-outfielder 1941–42, pitcher 1946–58.

**Lemon,** a citrus fruit L-187–8, *chart* L-188, *picture* L-187
■ blossom and fruit L-188, *pictures* L-187, F-469
■ cultivation of B-178
■ introduced into Europe C-618
■ invisible ink I-190
■ perfume making L-188, *picture* P-204: synthetic odor P-204
■ pests and diseases S-52e–f
■ producing regions L-187–8, *chart* L-188, *picture* F-476
■ vitamins V-356

**Lemon chrome,** a pigment C-335

**Lemon Grove,** Calif., community just s.e. of San Diego; chiefly residential; pop. 19,690: *map* C-53

**Lemonnier** [*lĕ-mô-nyā'*], **Pierre Charles** (1715–99), French astronomer, born Paris; made many observations of Uranus before its discovery as a planet; these led to the discovery of the planet Pluto.

**Lemon verbena,** a perennial plant (*Lippia citriodora*) related to lantana; flowers white or lilac in a 3-spike cluster; leaves lemon-scented, with glandular dots; native to South America.

**Le Moyne** [*lĕ mwȧn'*], **Charles** (1626–85), French colonist in Canada; father of famous explorers and soldiers better known by territorial titles. *see also in index* Bienville; Iberville

**Le Moyne** [*lĕ-moin'*] **College,** at Syracuse, N.Y.; Roman Catholic; founded 1946; arts and sciences, business administration, and teacher education.

**LeMoyne-Owen College,** at Memphis, Tenn.; affiliated with United Church of Christ and Tenn. Baptist Convention; founded 1870; liberal arts, education.

**Lempira** [*lĕm-pē'rä*], monetary unit of Honduras, historic value about 50 cents, *table* M-428

**Lemur** [*lē'mŭr*], a fox-faced monkey-like animal L-188, *pictures* L-188, A-98
■ ring-tailed L-188

**Lemur, flying.** *see in index* Flying lemur

**Le Nain** [*lĕ năn'*], **Antoine** (1588–1648), **Louis** (1593–1648), and **Mathieu** (1607–77), French painters, brothers, born Laon, France; depicted interiors; also portrayed scenes of everyday life of peasants; pictures grayish and dull in color.

**Lenape,** Indians. *see in index* Delaware

**Lenard** [*lā'närt*], **Philipp** (1862–1947), Hungarian physicist, born present Bratislava, Czechoslovakia; head of radiological institute at Heidelberg, Germany, 1909: X-334
■ Nobel prize, *table* N-294a

**Lena River,** in n.e. Siberia; empties into Arctic, forming vast delta; length 4600 km (2860 mi): *maps* R-322, *picture* S-190
■ length, comparative. *see in index* River, *table*

**Lenau** [*lā'nou*], **Nikolaus,** pseudonym of Nikolaus Franz Edler von Niembsch von Strehlenau (1802–50), Austrian poet, born Hungary; intense melancholia gave his lyrics somber, pessimistic tone; died insane ('Faust'; 'Savonarola'; 'Die Albigenser').

**Lenbach** [*lĕn'bäκ*], **Franz von** (1836–1904), German portrait painter, born Schrobenhausen, near Ingolstadt, Germany; called "greatest of his generation"; painted Emperor William I and Bismarck.

**Lend-lease** R-275, W-270
■ Lend-lease Act (1941) R-275, 277, W-270

**Lenepveu** [*lĕn-vû'*], **Jules Eugène** (1819–98), French painter; best known for classical and historical paintings and for decorative frescoes in theaters, churches, and public buildings ('The Martyrs in the Catacombs')
■ 'Joan of Arc', *picture* H-273

**L'Enfant** [*läṅ-fäṅ'*], **Pierre Charles** (1754–1825), French architect and engineer, who planned Washington, D.C., born Paris; came to fight in American Revolution before Lafayette; served as captain of engineers under Steuben and later was wounded in action at Savannah, Ga., and captured by British at Charleston, S.C. After war, worked as architect in New York City until called (1791) by President Washington to prepare plans for federal capital: W-30
■ Banneker's collaboration B-74
■ grave N-20

**L'Engle, Madeleine** (born 1918), actress, teacher, and author; born New York, N.Y.; awarded Newbery Medal 1963 for 'A Wrinkle in Time' ('The Young Unicorns'; 'The Journey with Jonah').

**Lenglen, Suzanne** (1899–1938), French tennis player, born Compiègne; six-time Wimbledon champion in women's singles, 1919–23 and 1925; also starred in doubles; professional 1926–27.

**Length,** in physics. *see in index* Measurement; Metric system; Relativity; Weights and measures

**Length of life.** *see in index* Life, *subhead* length of; Vital statistics

**Lenin** [*lĕn'ĭn*], **Nikolai,** real name Vladimir Ilich Ulyanov (1870–1924), Russian Bolshevist leader L-188–188a, C-494a, R-354–5, S-235, *pictures* L-188a, U-15, R-357
■ Chinese Communists C-300, 301
■ educational system E-99: university libraries L-243
■ government from Kremlin M-493b
■ Leningrad named for him L-188b
■ motion pictures M-522
■ portrait, *picture* R-326: in flowers, *picture* R-328
■ Stalin and S-403, *picture* R-355
■ tomb L-188a, M-493b, *diagrams* M-493b, *map* M-493a, *pictures* M-493, 494, R-356
■ Trotsky and T-268
■ wife L-188a, *picture* L-188a

**'Lenin',** Russian icebreaker S-170

**Leninakan** [*lĕ-nē-nä-kän'*], Russia, city in Armenian S.S.R. 140 km (85 mi) s.w. of Tbilisi; pop. 164,000; textile center; much destruction by earthquake 1926: *maps* R-344, 349, E-335

**Leningrad** [*lĕn'ĭn-grăd*], formerly **St. Petersburg** and **Petrograd,** Russia, industrial and commercial city, former capital of Russia; pop. 3,513,000: L-188b–90, *maps* L-189, R-322, 344, 348, E-335, W-253, F-119, *pictures* L-188b, 190
■ cities, world's largest. *see in index* City, *table*
■ climatic region, *map* R-344: temperature and precipitation, *graph* R-334
■ Hermitage L-189, *map* L-189: Michelangelo's 'Crouching Boy', picture L-190
■ libraries L-239, 240, 237, L-189, *map* L-189
■ location L-188b, *locator map* L-188b
■ New Year's custom N-235
■ places of interest L-189–90, *map* L-189, *pictures* L-188b, 190
■ St. Isaac's Cathedral L-189, *map* L-189, *pictures* L-188b, R-353
■ school, *picture* R-332d
■ siege (1941–44) L-190, *table* W-8d
■ statue of Peter the Great, *picture* R-354
■ Summer Palace of czars, *picture* R-354

**Lenin Peak,** on border between Kirghiz, S.S.R. and Tadzhik S.S.R.; height 7132 m (23,399 ft); highest point in Trans-Alai Range; former name Mount Kaufman.

**Lenin State Library,** Moscow, Russia L-240, *map* M-493a

**Lennep, Jacob van** (1802–68), Dutch poet and novelist, born Amsterdam; wrote patriotic songs and historical romances of which 'De Pleegzoon' (The Adopted Son) is most famous.

**Lenni-Lenape,** Indians. *see in index* Delaware

**Lennon, John** (1940–80), British singer B-119
■ assassination A-703

**Lennox,** Calif., community 10 mi (16 km) s.w. of Los Angeles; pop. 16,121; industrial and farming area: *map, inset* C-53

**Lenoir** [*lĕ-nwȧr'*] **(Jean Joseph) Étienne** (1822–1900), French inventor of practical gas engine, born Mussy-la-Ville, Luxemburg: I-234, A-858, *profile* A-856

**Lenoir, William Benjamin** (born 1939), astronaut candidate, born Miami, Fla.; electrical engineer chosen for NASA scientist-astronaut program 1967.

**Lenoir,** N.C., town 62 mi (100 km) n.w. of Charlotte; resort, set in foothills of Blue Ridge Mountains; pop. 13,748; furniture, textiles, hosiery; incorporated 1851: *map* N-336

**Lenoir-Rhyne College,** at Hickory, N.C.; affiliated with Lutheran Church in America; established in 1891; arts and sciences, nursing, and teacher education.

**Lenormand** [*lē-nôr-mäṅ'*], **Henri René** (1882–1951), French dramatist, born Paris; plays deal with psychoanalytical and often abnormal themes ('The Failures'; 'Time Is a Dream').

**Lenôtre** [*lĕ-nō'tr'*], or **Le Nôtre, André** (1613–1700), French landscape architect, born Paris; style formal, classical, symmetrical; designed Versailles, Fontainebleau, and other royal gardens for Louis XIV; also English gardens for Charles II.

**Lenox, Walter Scott** (1859–1920), potter, born Trenton, N.J.: P-477

**Lenox porcelain** P-477

**Lenroot, Katharine Fredrica** (born 1891), social worker, born Superior, Wis.; served in Children's Bureau, U.S. Department of Labor, 1915–34, and was chief 1934–51.

**Lens** [*läṅs*], France, coal-mining and iron-manufacturing city 27 km (17 mi) s.w. of Lille; pop. 41,800; victory of French under prince of Condé over Spaniards (1648): *map* F-404

**Lens** [*lĕnz*], in optics L-190–6, *diagrams* L-191–5, *picture* L-190
■ aberration. *see in index* Aberration, *subhead* in lenses
■ burning glass L-192, *diagram* L-192
■ camera P-284–5, L-193–4, *diagrams* P-284, L-194, *pictures* P-284: motion pictures M-504–5, *diagram* M-505
■ contact, for eye S-370
■ derivation of word L-191
■ eye, human (crystalline lens) E-366, 369–70, *diagram* E-366
■ fluorite M-335
■ fused quartz, properties Q-7
■ glass employed G-139
■ limits of enlargement M-292
■ microscope M-290, 292, *diagram* M-290
■ quartz Q-7
■ refractive index L-196
■ shapes, *picture* L-190
■ spectacles S-370
■ stereopticon S-443, 444, *diagrams* S-444
■ stereoscopic camera S-444
■ telephoto P-285, M-505
■ telescopic A-730, T-62–3, 65
■ zoom P-285, M-505

**Lenski, Lois** (1893–1974), writer and illustrator of books for children, born Springfield, Ohio; historical backgrounds are based on old records and diaries ('Bound Girl of Cobble Hill'; 'Ocean-Born Mary'; 'Indian Captive'); regional stories based on her experiences ('Strawberry Girl', winner of Newbery Medal in 1946; 'Prairie School'; 'San Francisco Boy'); picture books for small children ('Little Airplane'; 'Mr. and Mrs. Noah'; 'Cowboy Small'; 'Papa Small'); awarded Regina Medal 1969; autobiography, 'Journey into Childhood': L-310c

**Lent, Blair** (born 1930), illustrator, born Boston, Mass.; 1973 Caldecott winner for 'The Funny Little Woman' (author and illustrator 'Pistachio', 'John Tabor's Ride', 'Baba Yaga'; compiler and illustrator 'From King Boggen's Hall to Nothing-at-all'; illustrator 'The Wave'): R-106.

**Lent,** in Christian church E-33–4
■ Mardi Gras. *see in index* Mardi Gras
■ Mexican festival, *picture* M-246

**Lentil,** a leguminous plant L-196

**Lento,** *table* M-566a

**Lenz's law,** of electromagnetic induction E-150, *diagrams* R-59

**Leo,** saints and popes, *table* P-99

**Leo I, the Great, Saint** (died 461), pope, commemorated as saint April 11: L-196
■ Attila and H-277

**Leo III, Saint** (died 816), pope, commemorated as saint June 12: L-196, *picture* M-295
■ crowns Charlemagne C-209–10, *picture* G-112d

**Leo IV, Saint** (800?–855), pope, commemorated as saint July 17: L-196

**Leo IX, Saint** (1002–54), pope, commemorated as saint April 19: L-196
■ Great Schism B-536

**Leo X** (1475–1521), pope L-196, M-211

**Leo XIII** (1810–1903), pope L-196

**Leo III, the Isaurian** (680?–741), Byzantine emperor 717–41; in 718 saved empire from Saracens; freed serfs and reduced taxation
■ campaign against Arabs B-535

**Leo VI, the Wise** (866–912), Byzantine emperor 886–912; noted for legislative works ('Basilica', revision of Justinian laws; 'Book of Prefect', applied to guilds of Constantinople; 'Tactics', for the army and navy).

**Leo,** or **Lion,** a constellation, *charts* S-418, 422
■ Regulus in, *charts* S-418, 422
■ zodiac Z-356, *chart* A-708, *picture* Z-356. *see also in index* Zodiac, *table*

**Leofric** [*lā'ōf-rēk*], earl of Mercia (died 1057), husband of Lady Godiva; in 1051 acted as mediator between Edward the Confessor and Earl Godwin: C-596

**Leominster** [*lĕm'ĭn-stẽr*], Mass., industrial city about 19 mi (31 km) n. of Worcester; pop. 34,508; plastic and paper products, clothing, furniture: *map* M-160

**León,** Mexico, city 320 km (200 mi) n.w. of Mexico City; pop. 209,870; center of agricultural and mining district; cereals, potatoes, fruit, livestock; shoes, textiles: *maps* M-241, 260d

**León,** Nicaragua, city 70 km (45 mi) n.w. of Managua; pop. 55,347; in fertile farming district; corn, coffee, sugarcane, cattle and dairy products; National University; cathedral (completed 1780); city founded 1524 on shore of Lake Managua; after destruction by earthquake, city was moved in 1610 to present site; former capital of Nicaragua: *maps* C-194, N-309

**León,** Spain, ancient kingdom and modern province in n.w.; cap. León (pop. 73,483)
■ early history S-358
■ Isabella, queen of I-317

**Leonard, Benny,** boxer B-392

**Leonard, Walter Fenner** (Buck) (born 1907); baseball first baseman, born North Carolina; famed as home run hitter for Homestead Grays; in Negro and Mexican leagues 1933–55.

**Leonard, William Ellery** (1876–1944), poet and educator, born Plainfield, N.J.;

professor of English, University of Wisconsin ('Two Lives', 'A Son of Earth', poems; 'The Locomotive God', autobiography).

**Leonardo da Vinci.** *see in index* Vinci, Leonardo da

**Leoncavallo** [*lā-ōn-kä-väl'lō*], **Ruggiero** (1858–1919), Italian composer L-196–196a, *picture* L-196
■ 'Pagliacci, I' L-196, 196a, *picture* O-462: story O-467

**Leone,** monetary unit of Sierra Leone, *table* M-428

**Leonidas** [*lē-ŏn'ĭ-dǎs*], king of Sparta, killed 480 B.C. at Thermopylae P-215

**'Leonore',** work by Beethoven B-136

**Leonov** [*lyĭ-ô'nôf*], **Aleksei Arkhipovich** (born 1934), Russian cosmonaut, born near Irkutsk; parachute instructor; copilot of Voskhod II spaceship; Soyuz commander of 1975 Apollo-Soyuz flight: S-346f, *picture* U-196b, *table* S-348

**Leonov, Leonid Maksimovich** (born 1899), Russian novelist, born Moscow: R-360b, 361

**Leontes** [*lē-ŏn'tēz*], in Shakespeare's 'The Winter's Tale', king of Sicily W-188, 189

**Leontief, Wassily** (born 1906), American economist, born Leningrad, Russia; came to U.S. 1931, naturalized citizen; did pioneer work in input-output analysis; professor Harvard University 1946–
■ Nobel prize, *table* N-294h

**Leopard** [*lĕp'ērd*], animal of the cat family L-196a, *picture* L-196a
■ protective coloration, *picture* P-513

**'Leopard',** British warship W-11

**Leopard cat,** *picture* C-154c

**Leopard frog** F-448, 449, 451

**Leopardi** [*lā-ō-pär'dē*], **Giacomo, Count** (1798–1837), Italian lyric poet, prose writer, and scholar; born Recanati, near Macerata, Italy; master of finished style and slave of pessimism ('La Ginestra'): I-322

**Leopard's-bane.** *see in index* Doronicum

**Leopard seal,** or **harbor seal** S-98, 100

**Leopold I** (1640–1705), Holy Roman emperor L-196a

**Leopold II** (1747–92), Holy Roman emperor L-196a, A-830

**Leopold I** (1790–1865), king of Belgium L-196a–b, B-149

**Leopold II** (1835–1909), king of Belgium B-149, L-196b
■ patron of Stanley S-410

**Leopold III** (born 1901), king of Belgium; abdicated 1951: L-196b, B-149
■ Baudouin as follower of B-110

**Leopold I** (died 994), margrave of Austria A-828

**Leopold V** (1157–94), duke of Austria, succeeded 1177; went on Crusades 1182 and 1190; quarreled with Richard I in Palestine, R-202, A-828

**Leopold, Order of,** Belgian military decoration D-59

**Léopoldville,** Republic of Zaire. *see in index* Kinshasa

**Lepachys** [*lĕp'ą-kĭs*], annual or perennial plants of the composite family, native to North America. Grow 0.6 to 1.5 m (2 to 5 ft); leaves finely cut; flowers solitary, on wiry stems, ray florets, 6 or 7, yellow or purple, droop from the cylindrical thimblelike center of disk florets that are first silver gray, later brown; called yellow, gray-headed, or longheaded coneflower.

**Le Pan, Douglas Valentine** (born 1914), Canadian poet C-114, 116

**Lepanto** [*lē-păn'tō*], **battle of** (1571), fought in Gulf of Corinth near Lepanto, Greece T-305
■ Cervantes at C-201
■ galleys N-104

**Lepaya,** Latvian S.S.R. *see in index* Liepaja

**Lepidolite,** a mineral M-336

**Lepidoptera,** the order of scaly-winged insects including butterflies, moths, and skippers B-521, *list* I-207

**Lepidus, Marcus Aemilius** (died 13 B.C.), Roman consul and army commander; triumvir with Antony and Octavian (Augustus); his army betrayed him when he attempted a revolt against Octavian A-462, 496

**Leporidae** [*lē-pŏr'ĭ-dē*], a family of rodents including hares and rabbits. *see in index* Rabbit and hare

**Leprechaun** [*lĕp'rĕ-kôn*], in Irish superstition a pygmy sprite sometimes inhabiting wine cellars, sometimes farmhouses, and aiding in work; possesses treasure which human may get by keeping his eye fixed on sprite: F-16

**Le Prince de Beaumont, Jeanne Marie** (1711–80), French writer, born Rouen, France: S-475

**Leprosy,** or **Hansen's disease,** chronic communicable disease of skin, mucous membranes, and peripheral nerves; known since ancient times; bacillus, discovered 1879 by G. H. A. Hansen (1841–1912) of Norway; treatment with sulfones, begun 1943, made possible cure or arrest of disease and eliminated need for traditional isolation of victims from society, *table* D-128e

**Leptis Magna,** Libya, ancient seaport 100 mi (160 km) e. of Tripoli; founded by Phoenicians; became splendid Roman city; birthplace of Emperor Septimius Severus; ruins of harbor, beautiful sculptures, and buildings have been uncovered; L-249, *picture* L-248

**Lepton** [*lĕp'tŏn*], plural **lepta,** a minor coin of ancient times, worth about 1⁄10 cent; Jerusalem lepton famed in Bible as "widow's mite"; also a modern bronze Greek coin worth 1⁄100 drachma.

**Leptons,** elementary particles A-750, M-172

**Leptospirosis** [*lĕp-tō-spī-rō'sĭs*], dog disease D-153

**Lepus,** or **Hare,** a constellation, *chart* S-421

**Le Puy** [*lē pü-ē'*], France, city 225 km (140 mi) n.w. of Marseilles; pop. 22,396; 12th-century cathedral; lace, textiles, spirits: F-385, *map* F-405

**Lerici, Carlo,** Italian archaeologist A-533

**Lérida** [*lā'rē-dä*], Spain, walled cathedral city 130 km (80 mi) w. of Barcelona; pop. 50,047; leather, glass, textiles; as a Celtiberian city, **Ilerda,** heroically resisted Romans.

**Lérins** [*lā-răns'*], **Monastery of,** on islet of Lérins group in Mediterranean off Cannes, France M-445

**Lerma** [*lĕr'mä*] **River,** rises 29 km (18 mi) w. of Mexico City and flows 452 km (281 mi) w. to Lake Chapala, from which it emerges as Río Grande de Santiago and flows 452 km (340 mi) n.w. to Pacific Ocean; Santiago noted for scenic beauty of its canyon and, near Guadalajara, for the Juanacatlán Falls, which are 15 meters (50 feet) high and 130 meters (430 feet) wide, *map* M-241

**Lermontov** [*lyĕr'mŏn-tŏf*], **Mikhail Yurievich** (1814–41), Russian poet and novelist, born Moscow; ranked next to Pushkin as greatest Russian poet; despised society; felt at home only in Caucasus ('On the Death of a Poet', 'Song of the Merchant Kalashnikov', poems): R-360, 361

**Lerner, Alan Jay** (born 1918), author and lyricist, born New York City; collaborated with **Frederick Loewe** (born 1904), Austrian composer, born Vienna ('Brigadoon', 'Camelot', musicals; 'An American in Paris', 'Gigi', films)
■ 'My Fair Lady' O-464a, M-567b

**Le Roy, Pierre** (1717–85), French horologer
■ chronometer L-158

**Lerwick,** Scotland, capital and chief town of Shetland Islands, on s.e. coast of Mainland Island; pop. 5919: *maps* E-334, *inset* G-199g

**Le Sage** [*lē sȧzh'*], **Alain René** (1668–1747), French novelist and dramatist, born Sarzeau, near Vannes, France; a satiric realist ('Gil Blas', comic masterpiece of adventurous roguery).

**Lesage, Jean** (1912–80), Canadian political leader, born Montreal, Que.; crown attorney 1939–44; member House of Commons 1945–58; delegate to UN 1950, 1952; leader Quebec Liberal party 1958–70; prime minister province of Quebec 1960–66.

**Les Baux** [*lā bō*], formerly **Les Beaux,** France, village in s., near Arles; pop. 87

**Lesbos** [*lĕz'bŏs*], modern Greek **Mytilini** [*mē-tē-lyē'nyĭ*], Greek island in Aegean Sea off coast of Asia Minor; about 1680 sq km (650 sq mi); pop. 114,797; important naval and colonizing power in early history of Greece; famed for school of poets (7th century B.C.) and as birthplace of Sappho; passed to Turkey 1462, to Greece 1912; cap. Mytilene; olives, grapes, grain: *maps* G-213, 221, T-299, E-335, *picture* G-212

**Lescarbot, Marc** (1570?–1630?), Canadian historian C-113

**Lescaze** [*lĕs-käz'*], **William** (1896–1969), American architect, born Geneva, Switzerland; came to U.S. 1920; leader in modernism

**Leschetizky** [*lā-shā-tĭts'kē*], **Theodor** (1830–1915), Polish teacher of piano, born Lancut, near Rzeszów, Poland; pupil of Czerny, he became eminent pianist; taught in St. Petersburg and Vienna; won chief fame as teacher of Paderewski; composed opera 'Die Erste Falte' and piano numbers.

**Leskov** [*lyĕ-skôf'*], **Nikolai Semenovich** (1831–95), Russian author, born St. Petersburg: R-360a, 361

**Leslie, Sir John** (1766–1832), Scottish mathematician and physicist, born Fife County, Scotland; inventor of a differential thermometer, photometer, and hygrometer; used air pump and sulfuric acid to freeze water and thus invented a process of artificial refrigeration.

**'Les Misérables'** [*lā mē-zā-rȧ'bl'*], novel by Victor Hugo H-268

**Lesotho,** formerly **Basutoland,** nation in s. Africa; 11,716 sq mi (30,344 sq km); pop. 745,000 (1965 est.); cap. Maseru: L-196b–7, *map* S-264, *picture* L-196b
■ flag F-207, *picture* F-205
■ location, *locator map* L-196b
■ money, *table* M-428

**Lespedeza** [*lĕs-pĕ-dē'zą*], a plant C-410

**Lespinasse** [*lĕs-pē-nȧs'*], **Julie Jeanne Eléonore de** (1732–76), French letter writer and social leader, noted for her love letters: C-551

**Lesseps** [*lĕ-sĕps'*], **Ferdinand, vicomte de** (1805–94), French engineer, born Versailles; served as consul at Cairo, Rotterdam, and Barcelona: P-92, S-503, 504

**Lesser Antilles,** eastern islands of West Indies; 5500 sq mi (14,200 sq km); pop. 2,088,226: W-101, *map* W-105

**Lesser Himalayas,** region of Bhutan B-180

**Lesser panda** P-97, *picture* P-97

**Lesser Slave Lake,** in central Alberta, Canada; about 1230 sq km (475 sq mi): *map* C-98

**Lesser Sunda Islands.** *see in index* Sunda Islands

**Lessing, Doris (May)** (born 1919), Rhodesian writer, born Kermanshah, Persia (now Iran); (novels: 'The Grass is Singing', 'Children of Violence', 'The Golden Notebook'; plays: 'Maria', 'Play With a Tiger'; short stories: 'The Habit of Loving', 'African Stories.').

**Lessing, Gotthold Ephraim** (1729–81), German critic and dramatist, born Kamenz; famous for 'Laocoon', critical work on poetry and plastic arts ('Minna von Barnhelm', comedy; 'Emilia Galotti', tragedy; 'Nathan the Wise', noble poetic drama of religious tolerance; 'The Education of the Human Race', religious study): G-96b, 98, D-173, *picture* G-96a

**Lester, Julius** (born 1939), author, musician, singer; born St. Louis, Mo.; ('Black Folktales'; 'Search for the New Land', 'Long Journey Home: Stories from Black History', 'Two Love Stories')
■ 'To Be a Slave' R-111d

**Lesueur** [*lĕ-sü-ûr'*], **Charles Alexandre** (1778–1846), French zoologist and artist; did earliest American work on marine invertebrates and fishes of Great Lakes; called "Raphael of zoological painters"; with Owen's colony at New Harmony, Ind.

**Le Sueur, Pierre Charles** (1657?–1705?), French explorer and fur trader; in 1700 traveled up Mississippi River, explored Minnesota River, and built fort near site of Mankato, Minn.; town and county in Minnesota named for him.

**Lesueur rat kangaroo** A-779

**Lethal genes** H-144

**Lethbridge,** Alta., Canada, city on Oldman River 174 km (108 mi) s.e. of Calgary; pop. 41,217; cattle ranching; wheat and vegetable farming, the latter under irrigation; coal deposits; flour, beet sugar; food processing: C-98
■ University of Lethbridge A-266

**Lethe** [*lē'thē*], in Greek mythology, river of oblivion H-2

**Leto,** in Greek mythology, mother of Apollo and Artemis, children of Zeus; goddess of fertility; protected graves; Roman Latona.

**LeTourneau College,** at Longview, Tex.; private control; founded 1946; liberal arts, engineering, technology.

**Lettering,** in mechanical drawing M-200, *picture* M-201

**Lettering,** writing B-346, *picture* B-349
■ pencil M-197

**Letterpress printing**
■ color engravings P-278
■ halftone engravings P-276–7, *pictures* P-276–7
■ line engravings P-275–6

**'Letters from an American Farmer',** work by Crèvecoeur A-344

**Letters of marque** [*märk*], commissions given by a government authorizing private persons to fit out armed vessels and to sail as privateers against the enemy.

**Letters of the alphabet.** *see in index* Alphabet

**'Letters on the Regicide Peace',** work by Burke B-507

**Letters patent,** official, public documents granting specific privileges or authority to an individual or corporation; issued by government or sovereign; typically contains signature and seal; used to confer exclusive rights to inventions and in England to bestow titles of nobility.

**Letter writing** L-197–200
■ address, forms of, *table* E-297
■ bibliography L-200
■ business letters L-199–200: dictating machine D-111–12, *picture* D-111
■ letters as literature L-306a: Gray G-197; Sévigné, Madame de S-118
■ Santa Claus S-46, *picture* S-46

**Letts,** people of Latvian S.S.R. L-159a

**Lettuce,** a plant L-201, *pictures* L-201
■ cultivating, *picture* F-60
■ harvesting, *picture* P-191

**Leu** [*lĕ'ų*], plural **lei** [*lā*], monetary unit of Rumania; historic value less than 1 cent, *table* M-428

**Leucippus** [*lū-sĭp'ŭs*], Greek philosopher about 5th century B.C.; regarded as founder of the atomic theory, adopted and improved by Democritus.

**Leucite** [*lū'sīt*], a rock-forming mineral of potassium and aluminum metasilicate, found in basaltic lavas, and sometimes used as fertilizer.

**Leuconostoc,** bacteria B-15

**Leuctra** [*lūk'trą*], **battle of** (371 B.C.) named for village of Leuctra in Boeotia T-158

**Leukemia** [*lū-kē'mĭ-ą*], D-129b
■ virus, *picture* V-353

**Leukocytes.** *see in index* White cells

**Leutze** [*loi'tsē*], **Emanuel** (1816–68), American portrait painter, also painter of historical subjects, born Gmünd, near Stuttgart, Germany; painted the well-known 'Washington Crossing the Delaware'.

**Leuven,** Belgium. *see in index* Louvain

**Lev** [*lěv*], plural **leva,** monetary unit of Bulgaria since 1928, historic value less than 1 cent; at one time was equal to gold franc, worth 19.3 cents, *table* M-428

**Levalloisian** [*lěv-ạ-loi'zē-ạn*] **culture,** from Levallois-Perret, near Paris, France, where remains were found: M-75

**Levant** [*lě-vănt'*], **Oscar** (1906–72), composer, pianist, motion-picture actor; born Pittsburgh, Pa.; author of 'A Smattering of Ignorance', 'The Memoirs of an Amnesiac', 'The Unimportance of Being Oscar'.

**Levant,** term meaning "rising (of the sun)" applied to the countries along e. Mediterranean; name originated with Italians; includes Greece, Turkey, Syria, Lebanon, Egypt, and Palestine.

**Levantine** [*lěv'ạn-tīn*] **Sea** M-216

**Levee,** an embankment F-224, 225, *picture* F-224. *see also in index* Dike
- flood control, Mississippi River M-390, *pictures* U-60, M-391, M-383
- natural formation R-211, *diagram* R-210

**Level.** *see in index* Spirit level

**Levelland,** Tex., city 35 mi (55 km) w. of Lubbock; pop. 13,809, in agricultural region; cotton; grain, cattle; oil and gas; incorporated 1926: *map* T-128

**Levene, Phoebus Aaron** (1869–1940), American biochemist, born Sagor, Russia; member Rockefeller Institute 1907–39; worked out formula for structure of nucleic acids; in 1930 purified and concentrated vitamin $B_2$.

**Lever,** a mechanical device M-206–7, 208, *diagrams* M-207–8
- Archimedes A-541
- brake operation B-405
- in voting machines, *picture* V-387
- in weighing machines W-93

**Leverhulme** [*lē'vẽr-hūm*], **William Hesketh Lever,** first **Viscount** (1851–1925), English businessman, born Bolton, England; founded soap works (Lever Brothers) with associated companies all over world; model industrial village at Port Sunlight near Liverpool; instituted profit-sharing plans.

**Leverrier** [*lē-vě-ryā'*], **Urbain Jean Joseph** (1811–77), French astronomer, born Saint-Lô, France; studied motion disturbance of Uranus; calculations indicated presence of then unknown planet Neptune A-714, P-354

**Levertov, Denise** (b. 1923), American poet A-364

**Lévesque, René** (born 1922), Canadian political leader and journalist, born New Carlisle, Que.; member Quebec legislature 1960–70, reelected 1976; premier Quebec 1976–; one of founders and first president of Parti Québécois.

**Levey, Barnett,** theater developer A-798

**Levi,** Hebrew patriarch, 3d son of Jacob and Leah, ancestor of tribe of Levi, or Levites, from which came the Jewish priests and keepers of the sanctuary.

**Levi, Edward Hirsch** (born 1911), government official, born Chicago, Ill.; dean law school University of Chicago 1950–62, university provost 1962–68, university president 1968–75; U.S. attorney general 1975–77.

**Leviathan** [*lē-vī'ạ-thán*], Hebrew name for sea monster; also dragon of turmoil which contested against God; mentioned in Job ix, 13 and Isa. xxvii, 1.

**'Leviathan',** ocean liner; before World War I was German liner *Vaterland;* acquired by United States; scrapped 1937: *picture* W-256

**Levin, Harry (Tuchman)** (born 1912), writer and educator, born Minneapolis, Minn.; on faculty of Harvard University 1939–('James Joyce: A Critical Introduction', 'Contexts of Criticism'): W-310d

**Levin, Meyer** (born 1905), writer, born Chicago (novels: 'The Old Bunch', 'Citizens', 'Yehuda', 'My Father's House', 'Compulsion', 'The Fanatic', 'The Settlers').

**Levine, Charles,** aviator A-205, *picture* A-204

**Levine** [*lě-vēn*], **Jack** (born 1915), artist, born Boston; gained early fame for expressionistic and satirical works on modern social subjects; rich, glowing colors.

**Levine, Philip** (born 1900), American bacteriologist and serologist, born Kletsk, Russia; director of biological division, Ortho Research Foundation, Raritan, N.J., from 1944; his research on Rh factors contributed greatly to success of blood transfusions used to save babies at birth.

**Levinson, Salmon Oliver** (1865–1941), lawyer and advocate of peace, born Noblesville, Ind.; leader of movement to outlaw war; author of plan for readjustment of German reparations, Allied debts, and world peace (1927).

**Lévis** [*lā-vē'*], Que., Canada, city on St. Lawrence River opposite Quebec (city) and adjoining Lauzon; pop. 15,627; furniture, boilers, tobacco products; base for Wolfe's siege of Quebec, 1759: *map, inset* Q-11

**Lévi-Strauss, Claude,** French anthropologist A-486

**Levites,** tribe of Israelites J-456

**Leviticus,** the 3d book of the Old Testament, containing the ceremonial laws of the priests; parts of book (chapters xix–xxii) among oldest surviving fragments of Bible, found with Dead Sea Scrolls 1956
- Golden Rule E-299
- quarantine and sanitation M-215

**Levittown,** N.J. *see in index* Willingboro

**Levittown,** N.Y., residential village on Long Island, 6 mi (10 km) e. of Mineola; pop. 65,440; unincorporated housing development of Levitt and Sons, Inc., Manhasset, N.Y., motivated by veterans' housing demands; built by mass production methods 1947–51: *map, inset* N-260

**Levittown,** Pa., private housing project 8 mi (13 km) from Trenton, N.J.; pop. 68,793; built 1952–58 by Levitt and Sons, Inc., builders of Levittown, N.Y.; more than 17,000 homes in identifiable neighborhoods; conspicuous example of city planning to meet all needs: *map* P-185

**Levulose,** or **fructose** S-508, 509, H-214. *see in also index* Fructose

**Lewes** [*lū'ĭs*], **George Henry** (1817–78), English philosopher and critic, born London; founded and edited *Fortnightly Review*
- George Eliot and E-182–3

**Lewes,** Del., resort town on Delaware Bay; pop. 2197; founded 1631 by Dutch as Fort Opdike, first settlement in Delaware; scene of first and last naval battles of Revolution: D-69, F-165, *maps* D-77, 66
- Zwaanendael Museum D-68, *picture* D-69

**Lewes,** England, county seat of Sussex, 70 km (45 mi) s. of London; pop. 14,030: *map* G-199h
- battle of (1264) M-475
- Glyndebourne Opera Festival, *picture* O-464a

**Lewin** [*lě-vēn'*], **Kurt** (1890–1947), German psychologist, born Mogilno, near Inowroclaw, present Poland; to U.S. 1932; professor of child psychology University of Iowa 1935–44; director Research Center for Group Dynamics, Massachusetts Institute of Technology, 1944–47: *table* E-90

**Lewis, Andrew** (1720?–81), American soldier, born Ireland; brother of Charles Lewis; major in Washington's Virginia regiment; brigadier general Continental army
- victory of Point Pleasant W-112

**Lewis, Andrew L., Jr.** (Drew) (born 1931), public official, financial and management consultant, born Philadelphia, Pa.; U.S. secretary of transportation 1981–.

**Lewis, Sir Arthur** (born 1915), British economist, born Castries, Saint Lucia; moved to England as teenager; professor of political economy University of Manchester 1948–58; at University of West Indies 1959–63; professor at Princeton University 1963–; president Caribbean Development Bank 1970–73; Lewis Model describes transition from agrarian to industrialized economy: *picture* N-294h
- Nobel prize, *table* N-294h

**Lewis, Cecil Day-.** *see in index* Day-Lewis

**Lewis, C(live) S(taples)** (1898–1963), writer, born Belfast, Northern Ireland; professor Medieval and Renaissance English, Cambridge University, 1954–63; wrote scholarly, philosophical, and religious books ('Miracles'; 'Mere Christianity'); also children's books ('The Magician's Nephew'; 'The Last Battle'); pseudonym, Clive Hamilton: E-276, R-111b

**Lewis, D(ominic) B(evan) Wyndham** (1894–1969), English author; of an old Welsh family; columnist on *London Daily Express;* contributor *Daily Mail;* his studies and writings chiefly concerned with Middle Ages ('François Villon'; 'King Spider', on Louis XI of France; 'The World of Goya').

**Lewis, Elizabeth Foreman** (1892–1958), writer, born Baltimore, Md.; missionary teacher in China; Newbery Medal (1933) for first book 'Young Fu of the Upper Yangtze' ('Ho-ming, Girl of New China'; 'To Beat a Tiger One Needs a Brother's Help').

**Lewis, Francis** (1713–1802), signer of Declaration of Independence as N.Y. delegate; born Wales; a founder of Sons of Liberty
- signature reproduced D-55

**Lewis, Gilbert Newton** (1875–1946), chemist, born Weymouth, Mass.; taught chemistry at Harvard University, Massachusetts Institute of Technology, and (after 1912) University of California; proposed (1916) his theory of atomic structure.

**Lewis, Isaac Newton** (1858–1931), U.S. Army officer and inventor, born New Salem, Pa.; invented Lewis machine gun, which he manufactured in Belgium and supplied to the Allies in World War I.

**Lewis, John** (born 1920), jazz innovator and pianist, born in La Grange, Ill.; was reared in Albuquerque, N.M.; leader of Modern Jazz Quartet: J-426, *picture* N-218

**Lewis, John Llewellyn** (1880–1969), American labor leader L-201, L-87, R-271, T-276, *pictures* L-201, I-272

**Lewis, Matthew Gregory** (1775–1818), English romance writer and dramatist, born London; nicknamed "Monk" after his most popular romance 'Ambrosio, or the Monk', which was suppressed; later reprinted in expurgated form: E-264, 274

**Lewis, Meade Lux** (1905–64), jazz pianist, born in Louisville, Ky.; popularized boogie-woogie upon emerging from obscurity several years after making a memorable record, 'Honky Tonk Train Blues' (1929).

**Lewis, Meriwether** (1774–1809), American explorer L-202, *pictures* L-202, M-463
- Lewis and Clark Expedition L-202–3, *map* L-203, *picture* L-203

**Lewis, Sinclair** (1885–1951), American novelist L-202, A-359, N-376–7, *pictures* L-202, N-375, M-360
- Nobel prize, *table* N-294f

**Lewis, William Berkeley** (1784–1866), friend, adviser, and campaign manager of Andrew Jackson and member of famous "Kitchen Cabinet."

**Lewis, Wyndham** (1884–1957), English author and artist, born in Maine; brought up in England; leader of vorticist painters ('Tarr', novel; 'Time and Western Man', philosophy; 'The Revenge for Love', a political satire; 'Rotting Hill', short stories).

**Lewis and Clark Centennial Exposition,** also called **American Pacific Exposition,** held June I to Oct. 15, 1905, in Portland, Ore., to celebrate 100th anniversary of exploration of the Oregon country; cost about $7,000,000; attendance 2,545,509.

**Lewis and Clark College,** at Portland, Ore.; private control; chartered 1867; opened as Albany College 1867; name changed 1942; arts and sciences, education, law; graduate studies; quarter system.

**Lewis and Clark Expedition** (1804–6) L-202–3, F-65, *maps* L-203, U-176, *pictures* L-203, J-433, E-358
- book about R-111c
- Clark, William C-381, *picture* C-381
- council with Indians, *picture* N-113
- Idaho I-20, *picture* I-21
- Lewis, Meriwether L-202, *picture* L-202

**Lewis Carroll.** *see in index* Carroll, Lewis

**Lewis College,** since 1973 **Lewis University,** at Romeoville, Ill.; private control; founded as technical school 1930, senior college 1950; liberal arts, aviation technology, education, and natural sciences; graduate studies.

**Lewis Institute.** *see in index* Illinois Institute of Technology

**Lewisite,** a poison gas C-230

**Lewisohn** [*lų'ĭ-sŏn*], **Ludwig** (1883–1955), American writer, born Berlin, Germany; to U.S. 1890; books show his attempted complete assimilation in Nordic civilization, his disappointment, and return to identification with Judaism (autobiography, 'Up Stream'; novel, 'The Island Within'; criticism, 'The Story of American Literature').

**Lewisohn Stadium,** in New York City; belongs to and is on the campus of the City College of the City University of New York; site of summer concerts.

**Lewisporte,** Newf., Canada, port town on Notre Dame Bay 260 km (160 mi) n.w. of St. John's; pop. 2892; former names include Big Burnt Bay and Marshallville; present name for English lumberman Lewis Miller who founded business here 1900: *map* N-165l

**Lewiston,** Idaho, port city on Snake and Clearwater rivers, 90 mi (140 km) s.e. of Spokane, Wash.; pop. 27,986; wheat, livestock, fruit, vegetables; lumber, plywood, cartridges, paper; food processing; first capital of Idaho Territory 1863–64; annual Lewiston Roundup: I-18, 19, *maps* I-28, 17, U-40
- climate, *list* I-15

**Lewiston,** Me., 2d city of state, on Androscoggin River opposite Auburn, 30 mi (50 km) n. of Portland; pop. 40,481; textiles, shoes, printing, wire goods, electronic tube and lighting equipment; Bates College: M-54, *maps* M-65, 53, U-41
- textile plant, *picture* M-54

**Lewiston-Queenston International Bridge,** over Niagara River between New York and Ontario, *map* N-281

**Lewistown,** Mont., city at geographic center of state in farming, stock-raising, oil, and mining district; pop. 7104; brick and tile, lumber, campers; honey, feed: *map* M-471

**Lewistown,** Pa., borough on Juniata River 43 mi (69 km) n.w. of Harrisburg; pop. 9830; in farm and dairy area; iron and steel products, clothing: *map* P-184–5

**Lewis-with-Harris,** island, largest of Outer Hebrides; area 2135 sq km (825 sq mi): H-121, *map* G-199g

**Lex Canuleia,** Roman law R-243

**Lex Hortensia,** Roman law R-244

**Lexical meaning,** of words G-168

**Lexington,** Ky., 2d city of state; in Bluegrass region, about 70 mi (110 km) e. of Louisville; pop. 204,165; horses, livestock, tobacco; machine products, tobacco processing, distilling, food products; Transylvania College; state and federal institutions: K-29, 31, *maps* K-41, 28, U-41
- climate, *list* K-26
- home of Henry Clay, *picture* K-37
- Kentucky, University of, *picture* K-35

**Lexington,** Mass., 12 mi (19 km) n.w. of Boston; pop. of township 29,479; scene of first battle of Revolution (Lexington and Concord): L-203–4, *maps* L-204, *inset* M-160
■ 'Minute Man at Lexington', statue, *picture* M-150
■ Minute Man N.H.P. L-204, N-40b, *map* N-30
■ Revere reaches, *picture* R-161

**Lexington,** N.C., city 20 mi (30 km) s. of Winston-Salem; pop. 15,711; furniture, textiles, clothing, electronic and food products: *map* N-336

**Lexington,** Va., city in farming district 30 mi (50 km) n.w. of Lynchburg; pop. 7292; Washington and Lee University, Virginia Military Institute; tombs of Stonewall Jackson and Robert E. Lee: *map* V-348

**'Lexington',** U.S. Navy aircraft carrier W-292, *picture* W-293

**Lexington and Concord, battle of** L-203–4, S-193, *map* L-204, *picture* R-168
■ Patriots' Day F-93
■ Revere's ride R-161, *picture* R-161

**Lex Valeria,** Roman law R-242–3

**Ley** [*lī*], **Robert** (1890–1945), German Nazi official, born Niederbreidenbach, Rhine Province; committed suicide when captured at end of war: G-105

**Ley** [*lā*], **Willy** (1906–69), American rocket authority and author, born Berlin; to U.S. 1935, became citizen 1944; consultant office of technical services, U.S. Department of Commerce; wrote on space travel ('Conquest of Space'; 'Rockets, Missiles, and Men in Space'; 'The Exploration of Mars', with Wernher von Braun) and natural science ('Dragons in Amber'; 'Salamanders and Other Wonders'; 'Exotic Zoology'; 'Watchers of the Skies'; 'The Dawn of Zoology').

**Leyden, Lucas van.** *see in index* Lucas van Leyden

**Leyden,** Netherlands. *see in index* Leiden

**Leyden jar,** an electrical condenser E-153, *diagrams* E-151

**Leyte** [*lāt'ē*], island of the Philippines; 2786 sq mi (7216 sq km); pop. 1,223,667; hemp, sugar, sulfur; cap. Tacloban (pop. of municipality, 53,551): P-259, 255d, 256, *maps* P-259a, 261d
■ population P-253b, *chart* 253b
■ World War II W-276, 296: General MacArthur lands M-2

**LFC,** or **Laminar Flow Control,** aerodynamics A-80

**Lhasa** [*lä'sa*], People's Republic of China, capital of Tibet; in s.e.; pop. 175,000: T-172, 173, *maps* C-291, C-312, *picture* T-173
■ climatic region, *map* C-304: temperature and precipitation, *graph* C-304

**Lhasa apso,** terrier, native of Tibet, *table* D-150

**Lhévinne, Josef** (1874–1944), American pianist, born Russia; U.S. debut 1906; taught in Berlin, Germany, later in New York City.

**Liabilities,** in accounting A-15

**Liakoura** [*lyä'kọ-ra*], modern name for Mt. Parnassus. *see in index* Parnassus, Mount

**Liana** [*lĭ-ä'nạ*], a climbing plant P-359

**Liao** [*lĭ-ou'*], river in n.e. part of People's Republic of China; flows e. and s. to Gulf of Liaotung; 900 mi (1450 km) long: M-83, *map* M-84

**Liaoning** [*lĭ-ou'nĭng'*], province in n.e. part of People's Republic of China; area 56,000 sq mi (145,000 sq km); pop. 41,718,000; cap. Mukden: M-83, C-293a, *maps* M-84, C-293, C-313, *picture* C-295
■ health center, *picture* C-301
■ minerals M-84

**Liaotung Peninsula,** People's Republic of China, projects s.w. into Yellow Sea between gulfs of Liaotung and Korea; Port Arthur at tip: M-84, *map* C-313
■ Dairen. *see in index* Dairen
■ history M-85
■ Russo-Japanese War R-362

**Liaoyang** [*lĭ-ou'yäng'*], People's Republic of China, city in Liaoning Province s.w. of Mukden; pop. 250,000; cotton milling, scene of Russian defeat in Russo-Japanese War: R-362, *maps* C-313, R-362

**Liard River,** Canada, 2d largest tributary of Mackenzie River; rises in s. Yukon Territory and flows through n. British Columbia; enters Mackenzie at Fort Simpson, about 240 km (150 mi) west of Great Slave Lake: *maps* C-72, 98

**Liatris** [*lī-ā'trĭs*], or **blazing star,** a genus of perennial plants of the composite family, native to North America. Tall wandlike flower spikes, purple or white, rise from clusters of narrow, ribbed leaves. Also called gayfeather and button snakeroot.

**Libby, W(illard) F(rank)** (1908–80), chemist, born Grand Valley, Colo.; professor of chemistry Institute for Nuclear Studies, University of Chicago, 1945–54; member of Atomic Energy Commission 1954–59; professor of chemistry University of California at Los Angeles 1959–80: A-535, M-73, *picture* C-464
■ Nobel prize, *table* N-294c

**Libby Prison,** prison for captured Union officers at Richmond, Va., hastily established in Libby and Son's tobacco warehouse during Civil War; moved to Chicago 1889 and became the Libby Prison Museum; razed 1899; Libby Prison bricks used in North Wall of Civil War Room in Chicago Historical Society building.

**Libel,** in law, *table* L-165b

**Liberal,** Kan., city in s.w. near Oklahoma boundary; pop. 13,789; trade center in agricultural region; oil, natural gas; food products, aircraft; incorporated 1888; International Pancake Race: *map* K-16

**Liberal arts** U-204–5
■ history U-209, E-80, 81
■ Morrill Act, *table* E-92
■ Russia lacks R-332d

**Liberal-Country Coalition,** political party, Australia A-816

**Liberal-Democratic party** (Japan) J-377, 411, *table* J-378

**Liberal party** (Canada) C-112c, d, e, g
■ Brown, George F-75, 75a, C-112b
■ King, Mackenzie K-56, *picture* K-56
■ Laurier leads L-164
■ Pearson P-150
■ St. Laurent S-18
■ Trudeau T-272

**Liberal party** (Great Britain), also called **Whig party** P-434, E-245, V-313. *see also in index* Whig party (England)
■ Churchill C-339
■ conference, *picture* U-17
■ Gladstone G-133–4
■ Irish question G-134, I-287
■ Lloyd George L-321–2
■ Melbourne V-312
■ prime ministers, *table* G-199a
■ reforms E-246, 247–8
■ Russell R-319

**Liberal Republican party** (U.S.), formed 1872 by Republicans opposed to political abuses under President Grant; nominated candidates 1872 and 1876
■ Greeley G-236
■ Schurz a leader G-173

**Liberals,** or **progressives,** in education E-74, 85, 89, 91, 93–4, 95–6, 97–9, D-98, M-474, *tables* E-76–7, 90

**Liberal Unionist party** (Great Britain) C-204a

**'Liberator',** abolitionist paper A-10, A-291, G-34, 35, *pictures* J-352, M-153

**Liberec** [*lĭ'bĕ-rĕts*], German **Reichenberg** [*rī'kĕn-bĕrk*], Czechoslovakia, city in n. Bohemia; pop. 66,365; founded in 13th century; development began when first textile factory was established in 1823.

**Liberia,** Negro republic on w. coast of Africa; 43,000 sq mi (111,400 sq km); pop. 1,716,900 (1978 est.); cap. Monrovia: L-204
■ Africa's independence A-111
■ anti-slavery movement A-10
■ flag F-207, *picture* F-205
■ government L-204: elections L-204
■ holidays F-96
■ location, *locator map* L-204
■ money, *table* M-428
■ national anthem, *table* N-52
■ Peace Corps aid, *picture* P-143a
■ people L-204
■ political assassination A-704
■ railroad mileage, *table* R-85
■ ship tonnage, *table* S-176a
■ university library L-239

**Liberty,** Mo., city 13 mi (21 km) n.e. of Kansas City; pop. 16,251; corn, wheat, tobacco; William Jewell College: *map* M-408

**Liberty.** *see also in index* Freedom; Freedom of speech; Freedom of the press; Religious liberty
■ birth of democracy W-245–6, D-82
■ Christian doctrine W-247
■ Henry, Patrick H-140
■ Magna Carta provisions M-45, D-84
■ Mill, John Stuart, on E-269
■ Napoleon I F-445
■ Western liberal traditions W-245–7, 248

**'Liberty',** sloop belonging to John Hancock H-16

**'Liberty',** U.S. communications ship I-320a

**Liberty, Statue of,** in New York Harbor L-205, *map* N-271, *pictures* L-205, N-263, U-115, U-28
■ Statue of Liberty N. Mon. N-45, *map* N-30

**Liberty Bell** D-53, U-115, *pictures* D-52, U-115, P-178

**Liberty bonds,** United States, in World War W-262

**Liberty Bowl,** at Memphis, Tenn. F-333

**Liberty cap,** symbol of freedom which appears on Goddess of Liberty and on many coins and coats of arms: H-47, F-395, *picture* F-395

**Liberty Day,** Virgin Islands of the United States F-95

**Liberty Island,** formerly **Bedloe's Island,** in New York Harbor, site of Statue of Liberty: *map* N-271. *see also in index* Liberty, Statue of

**Liberty party,** United States, founded 1839 to oppose slavery; ran James Gillespie Birney for U.S. president 1840 and 1844; joined Free-Soil party 1848: C-373, P-433
■ presidential vote (1844), *table* P-495a

**Liberty Tree Day** (Aug. 14) F-94

**Liberty Tunnel,** at Pittsburgh, Pa., *table* T-292

**Libra** [*lī'brạ*], unit of weight W-94

**Libra,** also **Balance,** or **Scales,** a constellation, *charts* S-419
■ zodiac Z-356, *chart* A-708, *picture* Z-356. *see also in index* Zodiac, *table*

**Librarian** L-224–7, 212, 246, 247, 233, 239, V-366, *pictures* L-226, V-367
■ academic L-226
■ ancient times L-229
■ associations L-227
■ bibliography L-247
■ children's L-225, 211, L-310a, c, g, *pictures* L-238, 209
■ library schools L-227, *table* L-228: Ugandan students, *picture* L-227
■ Middle Ages B-350, L-231
■ public L-225–6, 240, *pictures* L-209, 211–12
■ reference L-225, R-122, *pictures* R-122, L-211
■ research L-226
■ school L-226, 224, 225, *picture* K-51
■ special L-226, 227
■ young adult L-225, 211–12

**Libraries** L-206–47, *diagrams* L-215, *pictures* L-206, 208–14, 216–27, 229–46, *tables* L-214–15, 228. *see also in index* Books and bookmaking; Libraries, history of; Libraries of the world; Reading for recreation; Storytelling
■ arrangement L-213–16, *pictures* L-216–17, *tables* L-214–15
■ associations L-227
■ bibliography L-247
■ book preservation A-149
■ catalog L-216–18, 210, 225, *picture* L-214; cards L-216–17, *diagrams* L-215, *picture* L-227 L-214; Uganda, *picture* L-227
■ children's L-210–11, 225, 244, *pictures* L-213, 236–8, 240–1
□ bibliography L-247
□ history L-310a, c, d, e, f, g, *pictures* L-236, L-310b
□ home R-101d: books R-105–11e, H-182–95, S-478–82
□ storytelling S-461–2, *pictures* L-209, 237, 243
■ choosing a book L-218–19
■ college and university L-207–8, 212, 214, 233, 237–8, 239, 242–3
□ ancient L-229
□ Canada L-246, 233, 238, 243
□ England L-231: Oxford's Bodleian L-233, S-140, *pictures* O-515, L-235
□ Israel L-239: Hebrew University, *picture* L-223
□ Latin America L-233, 238, *picture* M-250
□ librarians L-226
□ Middle Ages L-230, 231
□ Poland L-231, 233, 243, *picture* L-241
□ Russia L-237, 243, *picture* L-239
□ Uganda L-243, *picture* L-227
□ United States L-233, 237, 243, 246
△ Brown University P-516
△ Chicago, University of L-239, *picture* I-40
△ City College, *picture* C-433
△ Cornell University *picture* N-247
△ Delaware, University of, *picture* D-73
△ Harvard University, *see in index* Harvard University Library
△ Howard University, *pictures* U-208
△ Nebraska at Lincoln, University of, *picture* N-115
△ Northwestern University, *picture* I-40
△ Notre Dame, University of, *picture* I-90
△ Oklahoma, University of, *picture* O-441
△ Princeton University L-237
△ South Dakota, University of, *picture* S-329
△ Tennessee, University of, *picture* T-87
△ Texas, University of, *picture* T-122
△ Vermont, University of, *picture* V-293
△ Washington, University of, *picture* W-47
△ Wayne State University, *picture* D-96d
△ Yale University L-237
■ computers L-225, 226, 247, *pictures* L-245–6, 225
■ cooperation L-210, 226, 246, *picture* L-226: Middle Ages L-230
■ Dewey decimal classification system L-214, 215, *picture* L-217, *table* L-214
■ finding a book L-217–18
■ law L-208, 209, 234, 243, 244, *picture* L-239: librarians L-226
■ Library of Congress classification system L-214–15, *table* L-215
■ library schools L-227, *table* L-228: Ugandan students, *picture* L-227
■ machines L-246–7, 210, 212, 223, 226, M-288, *pictures* L-244–6, 221–3, 237, 213, M-288: bookwheel L-230, *pictures* L-233; record player, *pictures* L-244, 240–1, 211; Telex, *picture* L-226
■ medical L-208, 238, 244
■ microforms L-247, 212, 223, M-288, *pictures* L-221–3, M-288
■ national L-209, 241–2, 244, 245, 246, 231, 233–4, 237, 238, 239, *pictures* L-238, P-154. *see also in index* Library of Congress
□ ancient L-229
■ newspaper N-230
■ nonbooks L-221–3, 246–7, 207, 208, 210, 211–12, 217, *pictures* L-220–5, 243–6, 240–1, 237, 208, 211, 213: bibliography L-247; indexes L-221–2, *pictures* L-218–19
■ public L-207, 209, 210–11, 212, 214, 216, *pictures* L-209–13, 224, 236–7, 240, 243–4, 246
□ bibliography L-247
□ Canada L-237, 239, 241, 246, L-310d, C-91, *picture* L-243: shut-in service, *picture* L-211
□ England L-234, 237, 240
□ history L-234, 237, 239–41, *pictures* L-236: ancient L-229, 234, 207; Middle Ages L-230, 231, 234
□ India L-239, *picture* L-237
□ librarians L-225–6, 240, *pictures* L-209, 211–12
□ Russia L-239, 240, *picture* L-240
□ United States L-234, 237, 239, 241, 246, *pictures* L-209–13, 224, 236, 243–4, 246
△ Boston L-234, 237. *see also in index* Boston Public Library
△ Carnegie C-138: first L-241, *picture* H-40; storytelling S-461, L-310c
△ Chicago, *list* C-260, *map* C-261, *picture* L-243
△ Cincinnati, *pictures* L-244, 224
△ Cleveland C-390b, L-310c, S-461, *picture* L-310b
△ Evanston, *picture* L-236
△ Newark, N.J. N-160: reading room, *picture* R-122

△ New Bedford, Mass. N-160, *picture* N-160
△ New Orleans, *picture* N-225
△ New York, N.Y. L-234: Brooklyn Public Library, *pictures* L-210, 212; New York Public Library N-270, R-122, L-310c, *map* N-264, *pictures* L-246, R-123; Queens Public Library, *picture* L-236
△ Peterborough, N.H. N-173, L-239
△ Philadelphia P-251, *map* P-251b, *picture* R-131: Library Company of Philadelphia L-234, 237, F-424, *list* P-251d
△ Pittsburgh L-241, L-310c, S-461, *picture* H-40
△ San Antonio C-350
■ reference books, R-122–31, L-219–21, *pictures* R-122–31: indexes L-220, 221–2, R-128–9, *pictures* L-218–19
■ research L-208–9, 212, 231, 239, 244, 245, *picture* S-59c: librarians L-226
■ rural service L-212, *picture* L-211: Singapore, *picture* L-238
■ school L-207, 210, 211, 212, 214, 216, *pictures* L-245, M-288: bibliography L-247; early L-237; librarians L-226, 224, 225, *picture* K-51; Thailand, *picture* L-208
■ services provided L-210–12, 223, 225, 226, 244, 245–6, 247, *pictures* L-209–13, 224, 226, 236–8, 240–1, 243–4, 246
■ special L-208, 209, 243–5, 246, *pictures* L-213, 225, 239: librarians L-226, 227
■ state and provincial L-246, 209, N-246: film about L-247
■ subscription L-234, 237, 243
■ traveling L-212, *pictures* L-210–11, 236: miniature books, *picture* L-234; railroad trains L-237; Singapore, *picture* L-238
■ types L-207–10, 234, 237
■ vertical file L-222–3, *picture* L-220
■ workers L-224–7, *pictures* L-224–7, 236, 243. *see also in index* Librarian
□ bibliography L-247
■ young adult, *pictures* L-213, 246: librarians L-225, 211–12

**Libraries, history of** L-227, 229–45, *pictures* L-229–36
■ ancient times L-227, 229–30, 243, *picture* L-229: Alexandria L-229; Babylonia and Assyria L-229; China L-229; Greece L-229, 234, 207; Hittites H-179–80; India L-229; Kish K-61; Rome L-229, 234, 207, S-212–13
■ Carnegie C-138: first library L-241, *picture* H-40; storytelling S-461, L-310c
■ Middle Ages L-230–1, 234, M-446, *pictures* L-230–3
■ Renaissance R-146, *picture* L-232

**Libraries of the world** L-229–47, *pictures* L-229–46. *see also in index* Libraries; Libraries, history of
■ Africa L-241, 242–3, 239, 227, 230–1, L-310g
□ Egypt L-239, 241, 242, 245, 230: ancient L-229, 243
□ Ghana L-242, *picture* G-121
□ Kenya L-243, L-310g, *picture* L-238
□ Uganda L-243, *picture* L-227
■ Asia L-239, 238, 241, 242, 244, 245, *pictures* L-237–40, 211, 213: ancient L-227, 229, 243; China L-241, 242, 239, 229, 231, C-317, T-283, *pictures* L-230, P-154; Middle Ages L-230–1, *picture* L-230; India L-239, 245, 229, *pictures* L-239, 237; Israel L-239, *picture* L-223; Singapore L-237, 242, *picture* L-238; Thailand L-241, 242, 244, *picture* L-208
■ associations L-227
■ Australia and New Zealand L-237, 239, 242, 244: Canberra L-241–2; Melbourne M-217b, *map* M-217b; Sydney S-549a, L-244, *map* S-549a
■ Canada L-245–6, 244, 238, 242, 243, C-91, *pictures* L-242–3. *see also in index* provinces by name, *subhead* libraries
□ associations L-227
□ library schools, *table* L-228
□ public L-237, 239, 241, 246, L-310d, C-91, *picture* L-243: shut-in service, *picture* L-211
■ Europe L-231–4, 237, 238, 239, 240–1, 242, 243–4, *pictures* L-232–5, 240–1
□ ancient L-229, 234, 209, S-212–13
□ Belgium L-238, 243, 244, 234, L-385
□ England L-240, 239, 243, 244, 234, 237, *pictures* L-234–5. *see also in index* British Museum
△ Middle Ages L-230, 231, 234
△ Oxford's Bodleian L-233, S-140, *pictures* O-515, L-235
□ France L-230, 231, 233, 234, 237, 243, F-397
□ Germany L-244, 239, 233, 234, 237, G-112b, *picture* L-241
△ Middle Ages L-230, 231
□ Italy L-230, 231, 233, 238, 239, I-336, *picture* L-232
△ Vatican L-231, R-254
□ Middle Ages L-230, 231, 234, *pictures* L-232–3
□ Netherlands L-233, 238, 241, 243, *picture* L-226
□ Poland L-239, 243, 231, 233, C-599, *picture* L-241
□ Scotland L-234, *picture* L-235
□ Spain L-233, 237, 243, 230, 231
■ Latin America L-233, 238, 244: Argentina L-233, 238, 240, L-310e; Brazil L-244, 245, 238, *picture* L-241; Mexico L-233, 240, *picture* M-250
■ Russia L-237, 239, 240, 243, 244, R-334b, *pictures* L-239–40
■ United States L-245–6, 244, 243, 241, 237, 238, 239, U-121–2, *pictures* L-243–6, 236, 209–13, 224–5. *see also in index* Libraries, *subhead* college and university, United States; Libraries, *subhead* public, United States; states by name, *subhead* libraries
□ associations L-227
□ Boston Athenaeum L-243
□ colonial L-233, 234, 237
□ Eisenhower, Abilene, Kan. E-137, *picture* K-12
□ F.D. Roosevelt, Hyde Park, N.Y., *picture* R-279
□ Folger Shakespeare, Washington, D.C. S-140, L-209, 244, *map* W-32
□ Hammarskjold, New York, N.Y. U-22
□ Hoover, California and Iowa H-224
□ Huntington, San Marino, Calif. *see in index* Henry E. Huntington Library and Art Gallery
□ Library of Congress. *see in index* Library of Congress
□ Library of Hawaii, *picture* H-58
□ library schools, *table* L-228
□ Mount Angel Abbey, Ore., *picture* D-93b
□ Newberry Library. *see in index* Newberry Library
□ Truman, Independence, Mo. T-280, *pictures* T-280, M-404

**Library Company of Philadelphia** L-234, 237
■ Library Hall, *list* P-251d

**Library of Congress,** Washington, D.C. L-238, 246, W-31, 33, *picture* W-31
■ building, *map* W-32
□ concert hall, *see in index* Coolidge, Elizabeth Sprague
■ film about L-247
■ historic buildings N-27
■ Jefferson collection J-434
■ phonograph records F-304, F-307: recorded, *picture* F-307; talking books, *picture* L-211

**Library of Congress classification,** of library books L-214–15, *table* L-215

**Library of Parliament,** Ottawa, Ont., Canada L-238, O-507, *picture* L-242

**Library organizations** L-227. *see also in index* American Library Association; Canadian Library Association

**Library science** L-226
■ library schools L-227, *table* L-228; Uganda, *picture* L-227

**Libration,** in astronomy, an apparent slow balancing movement of a heavenly body on each side of its mean position
■ moon M-482

**Libretto,** *table* M-566a

**Libreville** [*lē-brē-vēl'*], Gabon, capital and seaport, on Gulf of Guinea; pop. 57,000; Roman Catholic mission established here 1843; city settled 1849 by Negroes from slave ship; site of British and Free French occupation 1940.

**Libya** [*lĭb'ē-ə*], Italian **Libia** [*lē'byä*], republic in n. Africa; 679,360 sq mi (1,759,530 sq km); pop. 1,564,369 (1964 census), 1,682,000 (1966 est.); cap. Tripoli: L-248–9, *map* P-212, *pictures* L-248–9
■ earthquakes (1963) E-32
■ flag F-207, *picture* F-205
■ high temperature record, *list* W-88
■ Israeli-Arab war I-320a
■ location L-248, *locator map* L-248
■ money, *table* M-428
■ railroad mileage, *table* R-85
■ Sahara S-14–16a, *map* S-15, *pictures* S-15–16
■ World War II W-271

**Libyan Desert,** part of the Sahara in Egypt and Libya extending from the Mediterranean to the Sudan L-248, *maps* E-109, D-93
■ Libyan Erg S-15

**Lice.** *see in index* Louse

**License**
■ dog, *list* D-137
■ driver S-5
■ fishing F-170, F-164
■ franchise differentiated from F-417
■ hunting H-279
■ logging operations Q-9d, O-456e
■ marriage M-114
■ merchant ships S-176a: officers S-174
■ osteopath O-505d
■ pharmacist P-248a
■ physician M-212c, a
■ practical nurse N-383
■ radio amateurs R-55
■ radio set owners R-54
■ radio stations R-53–4, 55
■ taxation, form of T-32
■ teacher E-100a, 100

**Lichens** [*lī'kĕnz*] L-250, P-370, *pictures* A-474, L-250
■ agents in soil formation S-251, L-250, N-55
■ Mars supports A-717

**Lichfield,** England, city in Staffordshire, 25 km (15 mi) n. of Birmingham; pop. 22,930: *map, inset* G-199g
■ birthplace of Dr. Johnson J-477

**Lichtenstein, Roy** (born 1923), artist, born New York, N.Y.; used old-West theme in early paintings; pioneered pop-art movement of 1960's
■ 'Girl with a Ball' P-67, *picture* P-69

**Licinian laws,** six laws of ancient Rome passed 367 B.C. in tribuneship of Gaius Licinius; practically ended the struggle between patricians and plebeians: R-244

**Licinius** (250?–324), Roman emperor 307–323; defeated Maximinus and became sole ruler in East; married Constantine's half-sister; executed for treason.

**Lick, James** (1796–1876), philanthropist, born Fredericksburg, Pa.; established Lick Observatory in California; buried in vault under its large telescope.

**Licking River,** rises in Cumberland Mountains in e. Kentucky and flows n.w. 220 mi (350 km) to Ohio River: K-29, *maps* K-28, 41

**Lick Observatory,** California O-392

**Licorice,** or **liquorice** [*lĭk'ō-rĭs*], a plant L-251

**Lictor** [*lĭk'tẽr*], official attendant of magistrates in ancient Rome; a dictator had 24 lictors; a consul 12, a propraetor 6, a praetor 2: F-71

**Licuri.** *see in index* Ouricury

**Liddell, Henry George** (1811–98), English clergyman, born Binchester, near Bishop Auckland, England; with R. A. Scott prepared 'Greek Lexicon' (1843), still used; dean of Christ Church College, Oxford University, England, 1855–91; his daughter Alice was original of 'Alice in Wonderland'.

**Lido** [*lē'dō*], Venice, Italy V-278

**Lie** [*lē*], **Jonas** (1833–1908), Norwegian novelist, born Modum, near Drammen, Norway; friend of Ibsen; insight into character is softened by humor and sympathy ('The Visionary'; 'The Commodore's Daughter'; 'Niobe'; 'The Pilot and His Wife').

**Lie, Trygve** [*trüg'vĕ*] (1896–1968), Norwegian statesman, born Oslo; legal adviser to Labor party 18 years; minister of foreign affairs 1941–46; secretary-general of the United Nations 1946–53; governor of Oslo and Akershus 1955–63; author of 'In the Cause of Peace': U-22, 24, *picture* U-25

**Liebermann** [*lē'bẽr-män*], **Max** (1847–1935), German painter, born Berlin; an exponent of impressionist school in Germany; ('Jesus Among the Scribes'; 'Spinners'; also landscapes and portraits).

**Liebig** [*lē'bĭĸ*], **Justus, baron von** (1803–73), German chemist and teacher L-251, *picture* L-251
■ mirrors T-63

**Liebknecht** [*lēp'k'neĸt*], **Karl** (1871–1919), German Socialist leader; son of Wilhelm Liebknecht, friend of Marx and Engels; only member of Reichstag to oppose World War I; shot by soldiers while on his way to prison after Spartacan uprising
■ Spartacans S-370

**Liebknecht, Wilhelm** (1826–1900), German socialist and journalist, born Giessen, Germany; father of Karl Liebknecht; with August Bebel helped form German Social Democratic party; writing had great influence: S-234

**Liebman, Joshua Loth** (1907–48), rabbi and writer, born Hamilton, Ohio; rabbi of K.A.M. Temple, Chicago, Ill., 1934–39; rabbi of Temple Israel, Boston, Mass., 1939–48 ('Peace of Mind').

**Liechtenstein** [*lĭĸ'tĕn-shtīn*], principality of Europe on upper Rhine; borders Switzerland s. of Lake Constance; cap. Vaduz; area 158 sq km (61 sq mi); pop. 21,078 (1970 census): L-251–2, *Fact Summary* E-328, *maps* S-537, E-334
■ flag F-202, *picture* F-203
■ location L-251, *locator map* L-251
■ money, *table* M-428
■ national anthem, *table* N-52

**Lied** [*lēt'*], plural **lieder** [*lēd'ẽr*] (from German for "song"), German art song M-558
■ Franz. *see in index* Franz, Robert
■ Mahler M-50
■ Schubert M-558, S-54, 55
■ Schumann M-558, S-55
■ Wolf M-561. *see also in index* Wolf, Hugo

**Lie detector** L-252, *picture* L-252

**Liège** [*lē-āzh'*], Belgium, city on Meuse River; pop. 153,240: L-252, *maps* E-334, W-252
■ Charles the Bold takes C-218
■ location, *locator map* L-252

**Liegnitz.** *see in index* Legnica

**Lien,** in law, *table* L-165b

**Liepaja,** or **Lepaya** [*lyĕ'pä-yä*], Latvian S.S.R., Baltic port, railroad terminus, and manufacturing city; pop. 71,464; ice-free artificial harbor; large export trade; metal-working: *maps* R-344, 348

**Lieutenant** [*lū-tĕn'ănt*]
■ Canadian Armed Forces, *table* C-100f
■ U.S. Air Force: insignia, *picture* U-8
■ U.S. Army A-634, insignia, *picture* U-8
■ U.S. Marine Corps: insignia, *picture* U-8
■ U.S. Navy, *table* N-96: insignia, *picture* U-8

**Lieutenant, junior grade,** U.S. Navy
■ insignia, *picture* U-8

**Lieutenant colonel**
■ Canadian Armed Forces, *table* C-100f
■ U.S. Air Force: insignia, *picture* U-8
■ U.S. Army A-634, insignia, *picture* U-8
■ U.S. Marine Corps: insignia, *picture* U-8

**Lieutenant commander,** in U.S. Navy, *table* N-96
■ insignia, *picture* U-8

**Lieutenant general**
■ Canadian Armed Forces C-100a, c, *table* C-100f
■ U.S. Air Force: insignia, *picture* U-8
■ U.S. Army A-634, insignia, *picture* U-8
■ U.S. Marine Corps: insignia, *picture* U-8

**Lieutenant governor,** an officer authorized to perform the duties of a governor during his absence or to take his place if he dies or resigns.

**Life** L-253–9, *pictures* L-253–9. *see also in index* Animals; Biology; Embryology; Man; Physiology; Plants; Prehistoric life; Reproduction
■ bioethical issues B-214
■ earliest appearance on earth E-344, G-63, P-487
■ earth suitable for E-6, 7
■ evolution E-343–5b, *diagrams* E-344, 345a, *pictures* E-345b. *see also in index* Evolution
■ functions of living L-254
■ group, study of S-242–4
■ length of
□ animals A-126
△ birds: parrot P-135; peacock, *picture* P-146
△ dog D-140
△ frog F-450
△ horse H-232d

△ insects: cicada C-340; mayfly M-183
△ turtle T-309
□ man P-446, H-93, I-213, I-68, J-366, K-75b
□ trees T-252–3, 258: bristlecone pine, *pictures* C-32, T-253; sequoia S-112; yew Y-341, 342
■ light important to L-260, *picture* L-260
■ origin E-343–4, *diagram* E-344
■ outside earth E-6–7, 9; absent in moon samples, *picture* M-479; may exist on Mars P-352, 353
■ temperature range for, *chart* H-111

**Lifeboat** S-177e

**Life buoy,** or **life preserver**
■ kapok K-21

**Life community,** in ecology E-46. *see also in index* Ecology, *subhead* communities of animals and plants

**Life expectancy** H-93
■ India I-68
■ Japan J-366
■ Korea K-75b
■ life insurance based on I-213

**Life in many lands** P-190–6, *pictures* P-190–6, *Reference-Outline* P-195–6

**Life insurance** I-213–15
■ endowment policy I-214
■ first policy issued I-218
■ guides in buying I-213
■ how sold I-212–13, 218
■ income provisions I-214
■ loan I-214
■ mutual companies I-213
■ stock companies I-213
■ term I-214
■ trusts T-282
■ variable life insurance I-214
■ veterans' I-216–17, *table* V-307: Canada V-308

**'Life of Samuel Johnson LL.D., The',** biography by Boswell B-222, 376

**'Life on the Mississippi',** work by Twain A-352

**Life preserver.** *see in index* Life buoy

**Lifesaving,** training in emergency medical service for nonprofessional personnel. *see also in index* First aid; Safety devices and measures
■ artificial respiration F-148, *pictures* F-147
■ Australian service A-789
■ Canadian service C-100c, *picture* C-100d
■ Coast Guard C-420a, b, *picture* C-420b
■ drowning person S-535
■ fire department F-134, 137, *pictures* F-134–5, 137–8
■ helicopters, *pictures* H-241a, P-429, F-222
■ MERVAN unit, *picture* H-241c
■ police P-425, 428
■ quicksand Q-17
■ Red Cross R-118
■ St. Bernard dogs D-140, *picture* D-146
■ wireless (radio) saves life at sea M-106, R-56

**'Life Studies',** work by Lowell A-364

**Life Support Systems** B-210

**Life zones,** or **zoogeographical regions** Z-365, *Reference-Outline* Z-367
■ North America N-311–16, *map* N-311
■ plants, distribution of P-363e–4, *pictures* P-363e–f

**Liffey** [*lĭf' ĭ*] **River,** Ireland, 110-kilometer (70-mile)-long stream rising s. of Dublin and flowing w., n., and e. into Dublin Bay: *map* G-199h
■ Dublin on D-201, *picture* D-201

**Lift,** in aviation
■ airplanes A-175
■ gliders G-144a
■ icing decreases

**Lift bridge, vertical,** *picture* M-348

**Lifting by one's bootstraps** M-209

**Ligament** (from Latin *ligare,* "to bind"), a tough, fibrous band which connects bones or supports viscera: B-342, S-210

**Ligases,** enzymes E-281, *table* E-281

**Ligature,** surgical thread used for tying blood vessels; may be absorbable (as catgut) or nonabsorbable (as silk, cotton, nylon, and fine steel wire).

**Liggett, Hunter** (1857–1935), U.S. Army officer, born Reading, Pa.; in World War I commanded 1st Army, A.E.F. ('Commanding an American Army'; 'Recollections of the World War').

**Light, Col. William,** South Australian surveyor general A-41

**Light** L-260–9, *chart* L-268, *diagrams* L-261–2, 264–8, *pictures* L-260, 263, 266, 269, *Reference-Outline* P-309. *see also in index* Electric lighting; Gas, for heating and lighting; Lamp; Lighting; and chief topics below
■ absorption C-445, 447–8, 450, 451–2: analyzing the sun S-371–2
■ atoms as source L-268–9, C-447, R-38, *diagrams* L-268, R-38
■ bibliography L-269, S-64d, P-310
■ black hole B-306
■ circadian rhythm B-226
■ color L-263, 266, C-443–5, 446, 447–8, 449, 451–2, S-254h, *charts* C-444–5, *diagrams* C-450–1, *pictures* L-266, C-443: lasers L-129a, b, C-452, *diagrams* L-129a–b, *pictures* L-129a, C-452
■ corpuscular, or particle, theory L-265–6, 267, 268, 269, N-243, R-37, P-306
■ diffraction L-266–7
■ diffuse reflection L-262, *diagram* L-262
■ dispersion S-371, L-263: diamonds D-100; spectroscope S-372
■ electromagnetic nature L-260, 267–8, 269, R-33–4, *diagrams* L-267–8
■ ether theory L-265, E-292: drift experiment R-140, 141, L-264, M-267
■ eye, action on E-366–7
■ fluorescent F-278, *pictures* F-278, L-269
■ glow in electron tubes E-170
■ heavenly bodies A-710
■ history of theories L-265–9, 263–4, P-306, *diagrams* L-264–8
□ Einstein R-141, 142, 143, L-264–5, 268
□ Kepler K-46
□ Newton L-263, 265–6, 267, N-234, P-306: experiment, *picture* S-57g
■ intensity L-261, *diagram* L-261
■ interference L-266–7, S-372, *diagrams* L-266, M-170: holograms C-452, *pictures* C-452; in soap bubbles S-232–3; stars measured by S-414
■ laser and maser L-129a–b, *diagrams* L-129a–b, *picture* L-129a. *see also in index* Laser
■ lens action L-190–6, *diagrams* L-191–5, *picture* L-190
■ line spectrum N-377c
■ luminescence. *see in index* Luminescence
■ mass of photon M-169
■ measurement L-261–2, *diagram* L-261
■ mirage M-370–1, *pictures* M-370
■ phosphorescence of animals. *see in index* Phosphorescence
■ photoelectric devices P-273–5, *pictures* P-273–4
■ photography. *see in index* Photography
■ photosensitization P-408
■ photosynthesis. *see in index* Photosynthesis
■ polarization L-265, 267, *diagram* L-265, *picture* M-293: polarimeter Q-6, *picture* Q-3; tartaric acid T-27
■ rainbow R-88: weather saying, *list* W-88
■ reflection L-262, *diagrams* L-262: diamonds D-100; mirages M-370–1, *pictures* M-370; mirrors M-371, L-262
■ refraction L-262–3, 265, S-371, R-39, *diagram* S-371, *pictures* L-263, 266: diamonds D-100; lens L-190–6, *diagrams* L-191–5, *picture* L-190; mirages M-370–1, *pictures* M-370; rainbows R-88; twilight and dawn T-311
■ selenium affected by S-108
■ sources L-260–1, *picture* L-260
■ spectrum and spectroscope S-371–4, L-268–9, C-444, *chart* C-444, *diagrams* S-371–2, *pictures* S-373, C-443
■ speed L-263–5, 267, 262, L-196, S-512, *diagram* L-264, *picture* L-266: constant speed in Einstein theory R-141; measured by Michelson M-267
■ waves L-265–9, S-372, R-37, E-211, *chart* L-268, *diagrams* L-265–7, M-170, *table* R-34: lasers L-129a–b, *diagrams* L-129a–b

**Lighters, automatic,** *picture* F-123

**Lighter-than-air craft.** *see in index* Airship; Balloon

**Light heavyweight,** in boxing B-388

**Light Horse Harry.** *see in index* Lee, Henry

**Lighthouse** L-270–1, 273, *pictures* L-270–1
■ ancient, *picture* C-491
■ Baltimore, *picture* C-420b
■ Boulogne L-270, *picture* L-270
■ Cape Hatteras, N.C., *picture* N-327
■ Fenwick Island, Del.: *picture* D-74
■ Genoa, Italy, *picture* G-45
■ Grand Manan Island, *picture* N-162e
■ lantern L-270, *picture* L-270
■ light cycle N-86–7, *diagram* N-86
■ lightships and light towers L-270, 273: Buzzards Bay tower, *picture* L-273
■ Marblehead Lighthouse in Ohio, *picture* O-425
■ Minot's Ledge L-270
■ Montauk Point, *picture* N-254
■ nuclear, *picture* C-420b
■ Pharos of Alexandria S-116, L-270, *picture* S-116
■ plastic sculpture depicts, *picture* P-381
■ Portland Head Light, in Maine, *picture* M-51
■ Prince Edward Island, *picture* P-497b
■ Roman ruins at Dover D-164f
■ Split Rock, Minn., *picture* M-348

**'Light in August',** work by Faulkner A-360

**Lighting** L-272–3, *pictures* L-272. *see also in index* Lamp; Light
■ airport A-212, *pictures* A-213
■ aquarium A-515
■ arc lamp, or light E-157; projectors S-444, *diagrams* S-444, M-507; signaling, *picture* S-193
■ automobile A-845
■ calcium light L-278
■ colonial. *see in index* American Colonies, life in the, *subhead* lighting
■ electric. *see in index* Electric lighting
■ electric lamp or bulb E-157–8, T-288, *pictures* E-157–8, I-247
■ fire prevention F-143
■ fluorescent light. *see in index* Fluorescent lamp
■ gas G-38, *pictures* I-251, M-455
■ healthful practices H-89
■ houses I-232–3, L-272–3, *pictures* L-272: style, *pictures* I-225, 227–8, 230–2
■ indirect E-158, L-273, *pictures* L-272
■ limelight L-278
■ measuring intensity of illumination L-261
■ oil L-105–6
■ photography P-288–9, *diagram* P-289, *pictures* P-282, 287, 289: mercury lamp used E-157; motion pictures M-511, *picture* M-512
■ pioneer American P-333
■ primitive L-105, *picture* L-105: Eskimo E-286
■ sculpture, how lighting affects S-80, *picture* S-80
■ sodium vapor S-247
■ solar power S-516
■ stage T-153, 154
■ stroboscopic light C-200

**Light meter,** for photography P-288–9, *diagram* P-289
■ motion pictures M-511

**Lightner Museum of Hobbies,** deeded in trust to the city of St. Augustine, Fla., 1947 by **Otto C. Lightner** (1887–1950), founder-publisher of *Hobbies* magazine, born Norwich, Kan.; museum houses thousands of varied collections from all over the world, including cut glass, metal matchboxes, chandeliers, old musical instruments, and costumes; opened to public 1948.

**Lightning** L-274–5, *pictures* L-274–5
■ accident prevention S-12
■ burn cause B-511
■ distance, test S-259
■ evolution role E-343, *diagram* E-344
■ Franklin's experiments E-153, L-274
■ nitrogen, atmospheric, fixed by N-291
■ scientific studies, *picture* P-301
■ Thor's hammer T-165
■ thunder caused by L-275
■ "whistlers" begin in I-236b

**Lightning bug,** another name for a firefly. *see in index* Fireflies

**Lightning conch,** or **left-handed whelk** (*Busycon perversum*), snail
■ shell, *picture* S-150

**Lightning rod,** or **lightning shield,** for protecting buildings from lightning L-275
■ Franklin invents F-426

**'Light of Asia',** poem by Sir Edwin Arnold about Buddha.

**Light opera** O-460. *see also in index* Opera, *subhead* light opera

**Light Pen,** medical device B-213

**Lightship** L-270, 273

**'Lights of New York, The'** (1928), motion picture M-523

**Light soil** S-250

**'Light That Failed, The',** a story by Kipling of an artist-journalist who becomes blind K-60

**Light tower** L-273, *picture* L-273

**Lightweight,** in boxing B-388

**Light-year,** in astronomy E-9, S-413, S-254, A-719, U-199

**Lignin,** or **lignone,** complex chemical substance which, with cellulose, forms the woody structure of plants and trees; used as basis of certain new plastics: W-217, C-182, S-254g
■ products W-222, P-107

**Lignite,** a low-grade coal C-411
■ Germany, East G-100, G-108: works, *picture* G-107
■ Germany, West G-100
■ United States deposits: North Dakota N-341, 342, 340, *maps* N-344, C-419, *picture* N-342

**Lignocellulose,** from wood P-379

**Lignum vitae** [*lĭg' nŭm vī' tē*], a tropical tree of the genus *Guaiacum* of the caltrop family, native to s. Florida, Central and South America. Grows to 9 m (30 ft); leaves oblong, leathery; flowers blue, rarely white. Wood extremely hard; fibers much interwoven, heavy, contain a gum-resin that acts as a natural lubricant. Used for propeller-shaft bearings of ships and other bearing parts permanently underwater, pulleys, and mallet heads. Guaiac gum or resin collected from living tree is used in medicine.

**Ligny** [*lēn-yē'*], Belgium, village 40 km (25 mi) s.e. of Brussels; pop. 1930; victory of Napoleon I over Prussians under Blücher (1815) prelude to battle of Waterloo: W-74

**Liguest, Pierre Laclede.** *see in index* Laclede, Pierre

**Ligugé,** monastery of M-445

**Liguria** [*lĭ-gū' rĭ-ą*], in ancient Roman days, the part of n. Italy between the Po and the Mediterranean, and from the Gulf of Genoa to the Gaul border, or even at one time to the Rhone; also region of modern Italy; 5416 sq km (2091 sq mi); pop. 1,735,349; cap. Genoa: I-326, *map* I-338

**Ligurian Republic,** the government instituted in Genoa 1797 by Napoleon I; incorporated in France 1805.

**Ligurians,** a pre-Roman and pre-Tuscan people, organized in tribes; they were considered by some authorities the aboriginal inhabitants of n. Italy
■ in France F-389

**Ligurian Sea,** *maps* I-338, 325. *see also in index* Genoa, Gulf of

**Li Hung-chang** [*lē hụng' -ġăng'*] (1823?–1901), Chinese statesman; aided General Gordon in suppressing the Taiping rebellion; bore chief burden of Sino-Japanese War of 1894; for many years "buffer" between China and outside world.

**Like charges repel and unlike charges attract** E-139

**Lilac,** shrub of olive family L-276, *pictures* L-276, F-264
■ hedges H-123
■ state flower of New Hampshire, *pictures* N-176, S-427

**Liliaceae** [*lĭl-ĭ-ā' sē-ē*], the lily family. *see in index* Lily

**Liliencron** [*lē' lē-ĕn-krōn*], **Detlev, baron von** (1844–1909), German soldier, lyric poet, realistic novelist, and author of short stories; born Kiel ('Adjutantenritte', poems; 'Poggfred', humorous epic).

**Lilienthal** [*lĭl' yĕn-thąl*], **David E(li)** (1899–1981), lawyer, born Morton, Ill.; practiced law in Chicago 1923–31; director of Tennessee Valley Authority

1933–41, chairman 1941–47; chairman United States Atomic Energy Commission 1947–50; author, 'Change, Hope and the Bomb', 'The Journals of David E. Lilienthal'.

**Lilienthal, Gustav,** German inventor A-201, B-233

**Lilienthal** [*lē'lē-ĕn-täl*], **Otto** (1848–96), German inventor, born Anklam, Prussia; one of the early experimenters in aviation
■ glider A-64, 201, G-144b
■ bionic techniques B-233

**'Liliom',** play by Ferenc Molnár D-174
■ 'Carousel' adapted from D-174, *picture* D-172

**Lilith** [*lĭl'ĭth* or *lĭ'lĭth*], in Hebrew folklore, a demon in the form of a beautiful woman who works mischief at night, especially among children; said to have been the first wife of Adam.

**Liliuokalani** [*lē-lē-ų-ō-kä-lä'nē*], (1838–1917), queen of Hawaiian Islands 1891–93; wrote words of famous song 'Aloha Oe': H-60, D-154d, *picture* H-66

**Lille** [*lēl*], France, manufacturing city of n., on Deule River; pop. 189,697: L-276, *maps* F-381, 404, E-334, W-252

**Lille lace** L-97

**Lille University** (founded 1530) L-276

**Lillie, Beatrice** (Lady Peel) (born 1898), actress, born Toronto, Ont., Canada; made stage debut, London, England, 1914; first N.Y. appearance, André Charlot's Revue, 1924; best known as a comedienne; appeared also in movies, on radio, and T.V.; autobiography, 'Every Other Inch a Lady'.

**Lillie, Gordon William** (Pawnee Bill) (1860–1942), pioneer, born Bloomington, Ill.; official interpreter to Pawnee Indians; managed Pawnees in first Buffalo Bill Wild West Show 1883–86; later professional showman; led Oklahoma land rush 1889.

**Lilliputians** [*lĭl-ĭ-pū'shanz*], in Jonathan Swift's 'Gulliver's Travels', tiny inhabitants of Lilliput: G-260, S-532, *picture* S-532

**Lillo, George** (1693–1739), English dramatist, born London D-173

**Lilly, Robert** (Bob) (born 1939), football player, born Olney, Tex.; defensive tackle for Dallas Cowboys 1961–74: *list* F-337

**Lilly Endowment, Inc.,** established 1937 F-363, *table* F-362

**Lilly the Euphuist.** *see in index* Lyly

**Lilongwe,** Malawi, capital since 1975; pop. 75,000; founded 1947 as agricultural marketing center: M-67

**Lily,** a plant L-276–7, *pictures* L-276, F-257
■ day lily, *picture* F-262
■ Easter lily L-277
■ golden clarion lily, *picture* F-263
■ Madonna lily L-277: floral emblem of Quebec, *picture* Q-8
■ microscopic study of stem, *picture* M-293
■ poison in P-408
■ prairie lily, floral emblem of Saskatchewan, *picture* S-49a
■ structure of flower, *pictures* F-257
■ water lily W-73d, *picture* W-73d
■ wild yellow lily, *picture* F-277e
■ wood, or wild orange-red, lily, *picture* F-277b
■ yellow snow lily, *picture* P-359

**Lilybaeum** [*lĭl-ĭ-bē'ŭm*], ancient city on Lilybaeum Promontorium (Cape Boeo), w. extremity of Sicily, founded by Carthaginians; starting point of Romans on African military expeditions; modern Marsala; pop. 81,327; famed wine: *maps* I-339, G-221

**Lily family,** or **Liliaceae** [*lĭl-ĭ-ā'sē-ē*] L-277

**Lily of the Mohawks.** *see in index* Tekakwitha, Kateri

**Lily of the valley** L-277, *pictures* L-277, F-255

**Lima** [*lī'ma*], Ohio, industrial city 70 mi (110 km) s.w. of Toledo; pop. 47,381; petroleum refining and pipeline center; electric motors, school buses, aircraft parts, machine tools, neon signs, power shovels and cranes, steel products; food products; state hospital for criminal insane: *maps* O-428, O-420, U-41

**Lima** [*lē'mä*], Peru, capital; pop. 1,436,231, with suburbs: L-277, *maps* S-298, P-224, *picture* P-222
■ Christmas carnival C-330
■ factory technician, *picture* S-288
■ libraries L-233, 238
■ location, *locator map* L-277
■ San Marcos, University of L-277, L-233, *picture* L-141
■ Torre-Tagle Palace L-277, *picture* L-138

**Lima, Declaration of** (1938) L-146

**Liman von Sanders, Otto** (1855–1929), Prussian general, born present Slupsk, Poland; in command of Turkish army which defeated allied attack on Gallipoli Peninsula 1915; in 1918 his army in Palestine was crushed by General Allenby.

**Limber pine,** evergreen tree (*Pinus flexilis*) of pine family, found at high altitudes in scattered localities from Alberta to Mexico and California; grows to 15 m (50 ft); trunk short, thick; leaves in fives, to 8 cm (3 in.) long, dark yellowish green, bunched at ends of branches; cones oval, to 15 cm (6 in.) long, light brown.

**Limbic system,** of brain A-373, B-402, *diagram* B-399

**Limbo,** in Roman Catholic doctrine, abode of souls between heaven and hell; also place of oblivion.

**Limbourg, Pol, Hermann,** and **Hannequin, de,** French painters, three brothers, of 15th century; Pol was most talented; chief work 'Très riches Heures du Duc de Berry' an illuminated Book of Hours in which landscapes dotted with figures were painted with a remarkable sense of design and of realism; said to have established a typical French tradition of landscape painting
■ 'Très riches Heures du Duc de Berry', *picture* L-83

**Limburger cheese,** named for Limburg, Belgium; made in northern Europe and U.S.: C-229, *picture* C-229

**Lime,** chemical compound of calcium L-278. *see also in index* Limestone
■ agricultural chemistry A-137
■ cement contains C-187, 188
■ coal gas purified G-38
■ glass manufacture G-136–7
■ mortar L-278
■ plaster uses C-18
■ quicklime L-278, C-18
■ shells yield S-148
■ slaked L-278
■ soil acidity corrected by S-253, *picture* S-253
■ whitewash P-72

**Lime,** fruit of lime tree B-178, L-278

**Lime-juicers,** British sailors L-278

**Limelight,** use in stage lighting caused it to be metaphoric expression for prominence L-278

**Limequat,** a citrus fruit L-278

**Limerick,** county of s.w. Ireland, in province of Munster; area 2686 sq km (1037 sq mi); pop. 137,357; comprises most of Golden Vale, most fertile district in all Ireland: *map* I-283

**Limerick,** Gaelic **Luimneach** [*lĭm'năk*], Ireland, county borough in Limerick County; pop. 55,912; chief port on Ireland's w. coast; at head of Shannon River estuary; lace, flour, salmon, bacon; gave name to limerick verse: *maps* G-199h, E-334

**Limerick,** humorous and often ungrammatical verse; became popular in mid-19th century; believed to have originated at Irish parties; rhyme scheme *aabba*
■ Lear, Edward L-168

**Limerick, Treaties of** (1691), *table* T-251a

**Limerick lace** L-97

**Limes Germanicus,** frontier of Roman Empire in Germany, heavily fortified: G-102

**Lime-soda process,** for softening water W-70a

**Limestone,** calcium carbonate ($CaCO_3$) L-278, *picture* R-229a
■ algae secretes A-283
■ cave formation C-18, G-60, *picture* N-28
■ cement, use in C-187, 188, 189
■ chalky forms C-204a
■ corals secrete C-572, *picture* C-572
■ dolomite M-335
■ ironmaking uses I-299, 299a, *chart* I-299a, *diagram* I-299b
■ marble M-104, G-59, R-229a, *chart* R-229, *diagram* G-60
■ mine, *picture* O-417
■ oceans G-60, L-278, *diagram* G-59
■ quarrying Q-6–7, *pictures* I-86, N-243, M-337, M-273
■ rock cycle, *chart* R-229
■ rock-dusting C-420, *picture* C-415
■ soil acidity corrected by L-278, S-253, *picture* S-253
■ steelmaking uses I-299, *diagrams* I-299c–d

**Limestone College,** at Gaffney, S.C.; private control; coeducational, formerly for women; established 1845; arts and sciences, education.

**Lime tree,** citrus tree yielding a small green fruit L-278
■ introduced into Europe C-618

**Lime tree,** the linden tree L-290

**Limewater,** solution of slaked lime in water L-278

**Limeys,** British sailors L-278

**Limitation of armaments.** *see in index* Armaments, limitation of

**Limitations, Statutes of,** laws setting a time limit on prosecution for certain crimes and on other legal enforcement of rights.

**Limited-access highway** R-214
■ cloverleaf, *picture* R-215
■ Los Angeles, Calif. L-355

**Limited liability,** in business C-581

**Limited monarchy,** or **constitutional monarchy** G-164, D-84, 85, U-17

**Limko** [*lŭm'gō*], People's Republic of China, town on n. Hainan
■ climatic region, *map* C-304: temperature and precipitation, *graph* C-304

**Limmat** [*lĭm'ät*], river of Switzerland; rises at n. end of Lake Zurich, flows n.w. 29 km (18 mi) to Aare River; upper course called Linth
■ Zurich on Z-370

**Limnology** S-61e

**Limoges** [*lē-mōzh*], France, city in w. center, on Vienne River; pop. 127,605; taken by Black Prince 1370; porcelain manufacturing center: F-385, *maps* F-381, 405, E-334
■ enamelware E-202

**Limón, José (Arcadio)** (1908–72), dancer, choreographer, and teacher; born Culiacán, Mexico; to U.S. 1915; member Humphrey-Weidman Co. 1930–40; dancer, choreographer Broadway musicals ('Roberta'); formed own company ('The Moor's Pavane'; 'Missa Brevis'): D-26

**Limón** [*lē-mōn'*], Costa Rica, major seaport, on Caribbean; pop. 35,000; ships coffee and bananas; Columbus may have been here 1502; founded 1874: C-584, *maps* C-194, N-309

**Limonite** [*lī'mō-nīt*], also called **brown ore,** an important iron ore I-295, M-332, *table* M-229

**Limousine,** automobile A-844

**Limpet,** a gastropod mollusk which clings to rocks M-424
■ plate limpet (*Acmaea patina*): shell, *picture* S-151

**Limpkin,** a large raillike bird (*Aramus pictus pictus*) closely related to cranes; plumage dark brown with white markings; frequents swamps of Florida, West Indies, and Central America; feeds on aquatic insects and frogs; its mournful wail suggested its nicknames "the lamenting bird" and "mad widow."

**Limpopo** [*lĭm-pō'pō*] **River,** in e. part of south Africa; forms n. boundary of Transvaal, then flows s.e. through Mozambique 1000 mi (1600 km) into Indian Ocean; scene of Kipling's 'Elephant's Child': *maps* S-264

**Linaceae.** *see in index* Flax family

**Linacre** [*lĭn'a-kẽr*], **Thomas** (1460?–1524), English humanist, physician and divine; physician to Henry VII and Henry VIII; helped found College of Physicians, of which he was first president; but famed chiefly as classical scholar.

**Linanthus,** low-growing annual plants of the phlox family, native to western North America. Leaves threadlike; flowers tiny starlike funnels or saucers, white through purple, completely cover plant in mass of bloom; used in rock gardens; often called ground pink.

**Linaria,** a genus of plants of the figwort family, including the toadflax, or butter-and-eggs, and Kenilworth ivy. *see also in index* Butter-and-eggs; Kenilworth ivy

**Lincoln, Abraham** (1809–65), 16th president of United States L-279–86, *pictures* L-279, 282, 284–284a, d–g, 285–6, I-48. *see also in index* Civil War, American
■ abolitionist movement A-10
■ administrations (1861–65), major events L-284f–6, *list* L-280, *pictures* L-284g
□ Cabinet L-284f: Seward S-119; Stanton S-411
□ Civil War C-374–9, *maps* C-375–7, *pictures* C-372, 379
□ Confederate States of America C-509–11
□ Emancipation Proclamation E-190: Lincoln reading, *picture* L-284g
□ Gettysburg Address L-284h–5: text L-284h
□ immigration encouraged I-57
□ new states: Nevada N-148; West Virginia W-116
□ reconstruction views R-114
□ reelection L-285, M-4
□ second inauguration L-285, *picture* T-146
□ *Trent* affair T-259
□ world events, *map* L-284f
■ arrival in capital, *picture* C-374
■ assassination A-703, L-286
□ Ford's Theater N-36, W-35, L-286
□ 'Our American Cousin'. *see in index* 'Our American Cousin'
■ bibliography L-286
■ birthday celebrated F-92, 91
■ birthplace L-280, *picture* L-280
■ Black Hawk War (1832) L-283–4
■ business career L-283, 284: Lincoln-Berry general store, *picture* L-283
■ cartoon subject C-145e
■ Douglas debates L-287–8, L-284c–d, D-164c, *pictures* L-288, I-43
■ early life: Kentucky and Indiana L-280–2; New Salem and Springfield, Ill. L-283–4c, I-39, *pictures* L-282–3, I-46
■ early political career L-284–5
■ education L-279, 280, 281, 284
■ election: of 1860 L-284d; of 1864 L-285, M-4
■ Hall of Fame, *table* H-11
■ handwriting reproduced L-284e, 279
■ home, *pictures* L-284b–c
■ lawyer L-284a, c
■ Lincoln, Neb., named for L-287
■ memorials: Abraham Lincoln Birthplace N.H.S. N-29, L-280, *pictures* K-31, L-280; Lincoln Boyhood N. Mem. N-40a, *picture* I-97; Mount Rushmore, S.D. S-324, N-41, *map* S-334, *pictures* S-79, S-321; New Salem, Ill. I-39, *pictures* L-283, I-46; Springfield, Ill. S-397, *pictures* L-284c, I-46; Washington, D.C. W-35, N-36, 40a, *map* W-32, *picture* L-286
■ Mexican War opposed L-284c
■ political literature A-350
■ portrait: on cent M-367, *picture* M-425b; on $5 bill, *table* M-429
■ quoted L-280, 281, 282, 283, 284, 284a, b, c, d, f, h, 285, 287, 288, N-16
■ "rail splitter" L-283, *picture* L-284
■ Sherwood's play on, *picture* D-175
■ signature reproduced L-279
■ slavery views and policy L-284c, f, h, L-288, B-291; Douglass, Frederick D-164f
■ statues: Borglum, *picture* N-159; French F-435, *picture* L-286; Saint-Gaudens, *picture* S-90
■ storyteller L-281–2, 284c, h, *picture* F-305
■ time line, *chart* L-279
■ tomb at Springfield, Ill. S-397, *picture* I-46
■ wife and family W-146–7, 152a–b, L-284a–c, f, h, *pictures* W-147, 152a, L-284d
■ wrestler L-283, *picture* L-282

**Lincoln, Benjamin** (1733–1810), American general, prominent in Revolutionary War, born Hingham, Mass.; secretary of war 1781–84; commanded Massachusetts militia and suppressed Shays' Rebellion (1787): R-172

**Lincoln, Mary Todd** (1818–82), wife of President Lincoln W-146–7, 152b, L-284a–b, f, *pictures* W-147, 152a, L-284d

**Lincoln, Nancy Hanks** (1784?–1818), mother of Abraham Lincoln, born Virginia: L-279–80, 281

**Lincoln, Robert Todd** (1843–1926), American lawyer, son of Abraham Lincoln; secretary of war 1881–89; minister to Great Britain 1889–93: W-147, 152a, L-284b–c, *pictures* W-152a, L-284d

**Lincoln, Sarah Bush Johnston,** 2d wife of Thomas Lincoln L-281

**Lincoln, Thomas** (1778?–1851), father of Abraham Lincoln L-279–81
■ home, near Hodgenville, Ky. L-280, *picture* L-280

**Lincoln,** or **Lincolnshire,** agricultural county in e. England; 6897 sq km (2663 sq mi); pop. 743,596; divided into Parts of Holland, Parts of Kesteven, and parts of Lindsey; cap. Lincoln: *map* E-218

**Lincoln,** England, capital of Lincoln County, on Witham River 200 km (125 mi) n. of London; pop. 75,770; metal products; Roman remains: *maps* G-199h, B-341
■ cathedral, *map* G-199e, *picture* E-244: contains copy of Magna Carta M-45

**Lincoln,** Ill., city 28 mi (45 km) n.e. of Springfield in agricultural region; pop. 16,327; corrugated boxes glass products; named for Abraham Lincoln when founded in 1853: *map* I-50

**Lincoln,** Neb., state capital, in s.e.; 2d city of state; pop. 171,932: L-287, N-110, *maps* N-121, 108, U-40–1, *picture* L-287. *see also in index* Nebraska at Lincoln, University of
■ Capitol, State L-287, *pictures* L-287, N-115
■ location L-287, *locator map* L-287

**Lincoln,** R.I., township 2 mi (3 km) n.e. of Pawtucket; pop. 16,949; composed of several villages including Lonsdale and Saylesville; limestone quarries: *map* R-191

**Lincoln Boyhood National Memorial,** in Indiana N-40a, *picture* I-97

**Lincoln Center for the Performing Arts,** New York, N.Y. N-272, O-464b, R-230, *map* N-264

**Lincoln College,** Oxford University, England O-515

**Lincoln-Douglas debates** L-287–8, L-284c–d, D-164c, *pictures* L-288, I-43

**Lincoln Highway,** United States, a coast-to-coast national highway R-217

**Lincoln Memorial,** Washington, D.C. W-35, N-40a, *map* W-32, *picture* L-286
■ design on $5 bill, *table* M-249
■ 'Seated Lincoln', *picture* L-286

**Lincoln Memorial Garden,** Springfield, Ill. S-397

**Lincoln Memorial University,** at Harrogate, Tenn.; private control; chartered 1897; arts and sciences, education.

**Lincoln Museum,** in Ford's Theater, Washington, D.C. N-36

**Lincoln Park,** Mich., suburb of Detroit about 10 mi (16 mi) s.; pop. 45,105; manufactures tools; incorporated as village 1921, as city 1925: *map, inset* M-285

**Lincoln sheep** S-147, *picture* S-147

**Lincolnshire,** county, England. *see in index* Lincoln

**Lincoln's Inn Fields,** a square in London, England, laid out by Inigo Jones; named for Lincoln's Inn, on e. side, occupied by a guild of lawyers
■ law library L-243
■ Old Curiosity Shop, *picture* D-107

**Lincoln Tunnel,** in New York, N.Y. T-291, *map* N-264, *table* T-292

**Lincoln University,** at Jefferson City, Mo.; state control; founded 1866; arts and sciences, journalism, music, and teacher education; graduate division.

**Lincoln University,** at Lincoln University, Pa.; private control; established 1854; liberal arts.

**Lincolnwood,** Ill., village just n. of Chicago; pop. 12,929; photographic equipment and tape recorders: *map, inset* I-50

**Lind, Don L.** (born 1930), astronaut candidate, born Murray, Utah; physicist NASA Goddard Space Flight Center 1964–66; chosen for NASA program 1966.

**Lind, Jenny** (1820–87), called "Swedish nightingale," beloved soprano singer, born Stockholm; pupil of Adolf Lindblad; toured U.S. 1850–52 under management of P.T. Barnum; married her accompanist, Otto Goldschmidt: *picture* F-113

**Lindbergh, Anne Spencer Morrow** (born 1906), aviatrix and writer, born Englewood, N.J.; wife of Charles A. Lindbergh; first woman to receive Hubbard gold medal of National Geographic Society 1934 for work as copilot and radio operator ('Bring Me a Unicorn', 'Hours of Gold, Hours of Lead', letters and diaries): L-289–90
■ 'North to the Orient' L-290

**Lindbergh, Charles Augustus** (1859–1924), American congressman, born Stockholm, Sweden: L-288
■ wife and son, *pictures* L-288–9

**Lindbergh, Charles Augustus** (1902–74), American aviator A-170, L-288–90, *pictures* L-288–9, M-360
■ aerial survey for archaeologists A-532
■ book about R-110
■ books by: 'Spirit of St. Louis, The' L-290; 'Wartime Journals of Charles A. Lindbergh, The' L-290
■ Maya ruins photographed, *picture* E-356
■ Medal of Honor D-56
■ mother, *picture* L-288
■ New York to Paris flight L-289, A-205, *picture* A-204

**Lindblad, Adolf** (1801–78), Swedish composer, born near Stockholm; wrote many songs introduced by Jenny Lind, who was his pupil.

**Lindblad, Otto** (1809–64), Swedish composer, born Karlstorp, s. Sweden; best known for quartets; wrote music for national song 'Ur svenska hjertans djup' (From the Depth of Swedish Hearts).

**Linde** [*lĭn'dĕ*], **Carl von** (1842–1934), German engineer, born Berndorf, near Baden, Austria; devised process of liquefying air 1895.

**Linden,** N.J., city about 3 mi (5 km) s.w. of Elizabeth; pop. 41,409; oil, gasoline; site purchased from Indians 1664: *map* N-202

**Linden,** a shade tree L-290
■ American. *see in index* Basswood

**Linden family,** or **Tiliaceae** [*tĭl-ĭ-ā'sē-ē*], a family of plants, shrubs, and trees; includes basswood, lindens, grewias, jute, Jewsmallow; often called basswood family.

**Lindenhurst,** N.Y., village 32 mi (52 km) s.e. of New York City; pop. 26,919; resort area; some manufacturing; settled 1869: *map, inset* N-260

**Lindenwold,** N.J., borough 6 mi (10 km) s.e. of Haddonfield; pop. 18,196; mill work, plumbing fixtures; meat-packing; settled 1742, incorporated 1929: *map, inset* N-203

**Lindenwood Colleges, The,** at St. Charles, Mo.; affiliated with United Presbyterian Church in the U.S.A.; coordinate colleges for men and women; founded 1827; arts and sciences, teacher education.

**Lindgren, Astrid** (born 1907), Swedish author of children's books, born Vimmerby, 110 km (70 mi) s. of Norrköping; children's book editor, Raben and Sjögren Publishers, Stockholm 1946–70; many awards
■ 'Pippi Longstocking' R-110a

**Lindsay, Howard** (1889–1968), actor, director, author, and producer; born Waterford, N.Y.; with Russel Crouse wrote and produced many plays ('Life with Father', in which he also acted; 'Arsenic and Old Lace'; 'State of the Union', awarded 1946 Pulitzer prize).

**Lindsay, John V(liet)** (born 1921), public official, born New York, N.Y.; U.S. congressman (Republican) from New York 1959–65; mayor of New York City 1965–73; joined Democratic Party 1971.

**Lindsay, (Nicholas) Vachel** (1879–1931), poet and lecturer, born Springfield, Ill.; several times wandered through country on foot reciting and selling his verses for bread; wrote virile, rhythmic verse, which he held should be read aloud or chanted A-354

**Lindsay,** Ont., Canada, town on Scugog River 90 km (56 mi) n.e. of Toronto in fertile farming area and scenic lake region; pop. 12,746; flour, machinery, brakeshoes, woolens, chemicals, lumber, meat and dairy products: *maps* O-457

**Lindsey, Benjamin Barr** (1869–1943), judge and social reformer, born Jackson, Tenn.; admitted to Colorado bar 1894; revolutionized methods of handling delinquent children ('Problems of the Children'; 'Revolt of Modern Youth'; 'House of Human Welfare'; 'Companionate Marriage'): J-486

**Lindstrom, Frederick Charles** (Fred) (born 1905), baseball player, born Chicago, Ill.; N. L. third baseman 1924–36.

**Line**
■ algebra A-295
■ calculus C-21, 23, *graphs* C-22–5
■ geometry G-66, 67, 72, 73, *diagrams* G-66: directrix G-69–70, 71, *diagram* G-70
■ latitude and longitude L-156–9, *diagrams* L-157, 159, *maps* L-156, 158, *picture* L-159, *table* L-158
■ mechanical drawing M-201, 202, *pictures* M-197–8, 201

**Line,** in dress design D-198

**Line,** in interior decoration I-231

**Linear accelerator** A-323, N-377e, *picture* N-377f

**Linear equation** A-297

**Linear function** A-297
■ Linear induction motor, B-405

**Linear measure** M-185, *tables* W-96, 97
■ origin of the foot F-330

**Linear perspective** P-220, D-93d

**Linear Scripts A and B** A-61, 62, 537, *picture* A-531

**Line dancing** D-28, *picture* D-27

**Line drawing** D-178–9
■ Persian sketch, 'Camel with Driver' D-178–9, *picture* D-179

**Line engraving**
■ on metal E-278–9
■ on wood E-278

**Line graph** G-182–3, 184–5, *graphs* G-182, 184–5

**Linen** L-290
■ Belfast trade B-144
■ burning test to identify, *table* F-9
■ flax source of F-217, 218
■ laundering L-159a, b, *picture* L-160
■ manufacturing centers I-289
■ uses L-290: ancient T-138, 139

**Linen-fold carving,** on furniture, *picture* W-226

**Line of Demarcation,** imaginary line from North Pole to South Pole.

**Line officer,** army rank A-634

**Line of position,** in navigation N-86, 88, *diagram* N-89a

**Line printer,** computer output C-501, *picture* C-499

**Liner.** *see in index* Ocean liner

**Linesman,** in football F-333
■ signals, *diagrams* F-332b

**Lines of force, magnetic,** imaginary lines along which magnetic force is exerted E-142, 147, M-47–8, 49
■ electric generator and motor, action in E-148–50, *diagrams* E-148–9
■ induction coil, action in E-151
■ iron filings show M-47, *pictures* M-48

**Line squall** W-183

**Linfield College,** at McMinnville, Ore.; affiliated with American Baptist convention; founded 1849; arts and sciences, education; graduate study.

**Ling** [*lĭng*], **Per Henrik** (1776–1839), Swedish playwright and poet, born Ljunga, s. Sweden; created system of gymnastics used in therapeutics; founded Royal Gymnastic Central Institute at Stockholm 1813.

**Ling.** *see in index* Heather

**Ling,** fish. *see in index* Burbot

**Lingala,** language A-119

**Lingonberry** [*lĭng'gĕn-bĕr-ĭ*], or **cowberry,** a low-growing shrub (*Vaccinium vitis-idaea*) of heath family, native to n. Europe and Asia. Creeping evergreen; leaves oblong; flowers white or pink in small clusters; fruit small, dark red, oblong, in clusters. Named "lingon" or "kroesa" in Denmark and Sweden. North American variety is smaller; native from Massachusetts to Alaska; also called mountain cranberry and foxberry.

**Lingua franca,** a hybrid language L-115g, h, A-119

**Linguistic approach,** to reading R-103

**Linguistics** S-61h
■ anthropology A-481
■ Bloomfield's theories B-318

**Link, Edwin,** aviator A-208

**Link,** unit of length in surveying S-520

**Link Foundation,** a fund established in 1953 by Edwin A. Link, who developed the Link trainer, to advance aviation education and training by grants in aid to other agencies engaged in such projects; a Link Foundation fellowship program has been started; headquarters, Smithsonian Institution, Washington, D.C.

**Linking verb,** in grammar V-281, S-110

**Linlithgow** [*lĭn-lĭth'gō*], **Victor Alexander John Hope,** 2d **marquess of** (1887–1952), English political leader, formerly a banker; viceroy and governor-general of India 1936–43.

**Linnaea** [*lĭ-nē'a*], or **twinflower,** a delicate, creeping evergreen wild flower (*Linnaea borealis*) of honeysuckle family, with threadlike, upright flower stalks, each topped with two fragrant drooping, bell-shaped rose or white flowers; named after Linnaeus (Carl von Linné).

**Linné** [*lĭn-nā'*], or **Linnaeus, Carl von** (1707–78), Swedish botanist and naturalist L-290–1
■ classification system B-229, S-57i
■ clock garden B-224

**Linnet,** a small European songbird (*Carduelis cannabina*) of the finch family, so called because it feeds on the seeds of flax; also the common house finch of w. United States and Mexico. *see also in index* House finch

**Linoleum** L-291, *picture* C-574

**Linotype** L-292–5, *pictures* L-292–5
■ assembling, or composing, matrices L-293–4, *picture* L-294
■ casting a line L-294, *picture* L-294
■ distributing matrices L-294–5, *picture* L-294
■ invention L-293, I-249
■ newspapers use L-293–5, N-227, *picture* N-228
■ spacing, or justifying, a line L-294, *picture* L-294

**Lin Piao** (1907–71), Chinese Communist leader, born Hupei Province; member politburo of Red China 1955–71; defense minister 1959–71; commander in chief of Red Guards 1966–71; Communist party vice-chairman 1969–71; named eventual successor to Mao Tse-tung 1969: C-302

**Linseed oil** F-217
■ drying oil F-76, 77
■ paints P-73

**Linsey-woolsey,** a cloth P-333

**Lint, cotton** C-589, 591

**Linters,** fibers from cottonseed
■ cellulose, source of R-99, C-184
■ uses C-589, C-184, 185

**Linton, Ralph** (1893–1953), anthropologist, born Philadelphia, Pa.; professor at Wisconsin, Columbia, and Yale universities; extensive field work ('The Study of Man'; 'The Tree of Culture').

**Linton, William James** (1812–97), English wood engraver and republican reformer, born London; in later years lived in New Haven, Conn.; considered greatest wood engraver of his day; also wrote lives of John Greenleaf Whittier and Thomas Paine.

**Linum** [*lī'nŭm*], the flax genus of herbs; includes the blue-flowered commercial flax (*Linum usitatissimum*); yellow linum or flax (*L. flavum*) and scarlet flax (*L. grandiflorum coccineum*), in gardens.

**Lin Yutang** (1895–1976), Chinese philosopher and writer, born Changchow, Fukien Province; son of pastor of American Reformed church mission; professor at Peking National University 1923–26; in U.S. 1935–66; returned to Asia 1966; interpreted China with urbane humor (nonfiction: 'My Country and My People', 'The Importance of Living', 'On the Wisdom of America', 'The Importance of Understanding'; novels: 'Moment in Peking', 'A Leaf in the Storm', 'Chinatown Family', 'Vermilion Gate', 'The Secret Name').

**Linz** [*lĭnts*], Austria, Danube River port city 150 km (95 mi) w. of Vienna; pop. 195,978; shipbuilding; iron and steel, chemicals, footwear, textiles, tobacco products A-826, *maps* D-32, E-334

**Lion** L-296–7, C-154a, *picture* L-296–7
■ circus animal, *picture* C-346: training, *picture* C-351
■ critical zone, *picture* A-444
■ cub L-297, *picture* L-297
■ distinguished from tiger T-176
■ food in captivity Z-361d
■ heraldic device H-142
■ Livingstone attacked by L-316
■ portrayed in art: sculpture, *pictures* R-193, T-166
■ range L-296
■ stories: 'Androcles and the Lion' L-296; 'Animals Sick of the Plague' F-2; 'Fox and the Lion, The' F-3; 'Lion and the Mouse, The' F-1, *picture* F-2
■ taxidermist's art, *pictures* T-36
■ teeth and jaws, *pictures* L-296
■ zoo animal, *picture* Z-358

**Lion,** or **Leo,** in astronomy. *see in index* Leo

**'Lion and the Mouse, The',** fable F-1, *picture* F-2

**Lion dance**
■ Kabuki drama, *picture* J-398
■ Watusi, *picture* D-18

**'Lion in Winter, The',** play by James Goldman, *picture* T-148

**'Lion of Lucerne',** sculpture by Thorvaldsen T-166, *picture* T-166

**Lion of the North,** name sometimes given to Gustavus II, Adolphus, of Sweden; military genius whose forces swept south to save Protestantism in Germany in 1631 and 1632.

**Lion Rock Tunnel,** in Hong Kong, *table* T-292

**Lions, Court of,** in Alhambra, *picture* S-358

**Lions, Gulf of,** wide bay of Mediterranean washing most of s. coast of France: F-387, *maps* F-381, E-334

**Lions Gate Bridge,** over Burrard Inlet, Vancouver, B.C., Canada, *map* V-264, *picture* V-263

**Lions International,** association founded 1917; more than 995,000 businessmen in over 26,000 clubs in 148 countries; a Lions Club has 11 standing activities: agriculture, boys and girls, citizenship, civic improvement and community betterment, education, health, safety, sight saving and work for blind, work for deaf, international relations, youth exchange; headquarters, Chicago, Ill.

**Lion's paw** (*Pecten nodosus*), clam shell, *picture* S-150

**Lion-tailed macaque,** a monkey, *picture* M-441

**Lipari** [*lē'pä-rē*] **Islands,** or **Aeolian Islands,** Italy, group of volcanic islands in Mediterranean n. of Sicily; 116 sq km (45 sq mi); pop. 11,037; largest Lipari; fruit, olives, pumice stone: *maps* I-339, 325
■ volcanoes L-164

**Lipase,** an enzyme D-117, E-281, *table* E-281

**Lipchitz** [*lĕp-shēts'*], **Jacques** (1891–1973), American sculptor, born near Grodno, present Lithuania; to U.S. 1941, became citizen 1958; early work influenced by cubists: S-92, 93
■ 'Prometheus Strangling the Vulture', *picture* S-93

**Lipides** [*lĭp'īdz*], a class of compounds P-312

**Lipit-Ishtar,** Babylonian king
■ code of law L-165

**Lipizzan,** or **Lippizan** [*lĭp'ĭt-sän'*], horse H-234a, *pictures* H-234a, 232i, H-275, *table* H-232f

**Lipkind, William** (1904–74), pen name Will, anthropologist and author, born New York City; spent 1938–40 in wilds of central Brazil studying Caraja Indians; wrote children's books illustrated by Nicolas Mordvinoff: 'The Two Reds', 'Finders Keepers' (1952 Newbery Medal), 'Circus Ruckus', 'Perry the Imp', 'Four-Leaf Clover': R-108
■ 'Finders Keepers' D-154c

**Lipmann, Fritz Albert** (born 1899), American biochemist, born Königsberg, Germany (now Kaliningrad, Russia); became U.S. citizen 1944; professor of biological chemistry Harvard University medical school 1949–57; professor Rockefeller University 1957–
■ Nobel prize, *table* N-294e

**Li Po** [*lē'bô'*], or **Li T'ai-po** [*lē' tī'bô'*], (701?–762?), Chinese poet; wrote of love, wine, and beauties of nature; supposedly drowned kissing the moon's reflection: C-295e

**Lipotropic hormone** (LPH) H-225, *table* H-226

**Lippe** [*lĭp'ŭ*], former state in w. Germany; 1215 sq km (469 sq mi); after World War II became part of state of North Rhine-Westphalia.

**Lippershey, Hans** (died 1619), Dutch spectaclemaker, traditionally credited with inventing the telescope 1608: T-62, P-306

**Lippi** [*lēp'pē*], **Filippino** (1457?–1504), Italian painter, born Prato, near Florence; son of Fra Filippo Lippi; pupil of Botticelli; masterpieces include 'Vision of Saint Bernard' and 'The Adoration of the Magi', both at Florence.

**Lippi, Fra Filippo** (1406–69), Italian painter, born Florence; father of Filippino Lippi; probably the greatest colorist of his day; his pictures reveal a strong, naive nature, with a lively and somewhat whimsical observation B-383

**Lippmann** [*lēp-män'*], **Gabriel** (1845–1921), French physicist, born Hollerich, Luxemburg
■ Nobel prize, *table* N-294a

**Lippmann** [*lĭp'măn*], **Walter** (1889–1974), writer, editor, and social philosopher; born New York City; studied at Harvard University under George Santayana and William James; one of founders of *New Republic;* editor *New York World* 1929–31; editorial writer *New York Herald Tribune* 1931–62; syndicated by *Los Angeles Times* and *Washington Post* 1963–69; Pulitzer awards 1958 and 1962; Presidential Medal of Freedom 1964 ('Public Opinion'; 'U.S. Foreign Policy'; 'Essays in the Public Philosophy').

**Lippold, Richard** (born 1915), sculptor, born Milwaukee, Wis.; professor of art Hunter College 1952–67; commissioned sculpture for architects, Metropolitan Museum of Art, Lincoln Center for the Performing Arts.

**Lip reading,** aid to deaf D-41b

**Lips,** *diagrams* T-197
■ cancer T-190a
■ speech C-552, V-279

**Lipscomb, William N., Jr.** (born 1919), chemist, born Cleveland, Ohio; faculty University of Minnesota 1946–59, professor 1954–59; professor Harvard University 1959–; research in chemical bonding of boranes
■ Nobel prize, *table* N-294d

**Lipstick,** cosmetic
■ color classification C-446
■ stain removal D-200f

**Lipton, Sir Thomas** (1850–1931), British merchant and yachtsman, born Glasgow, Scotland; son of poor Irish parents; made start by advertising small provision store; developed business until he amassed great wealth and owned large tea, coffee, and cocoa plantations; also known for yachts (*Shamrock*) entered in America's Cup races.

**Liquefaction,** of gases C-620a, b, G-37–8, *diagrams* C-620a–b
■ air L-301: to produce nitrogen, *diagram* N-292
■ chlorine C-320
■ Faraday discovers methods F-34
■ helium C-260a, b, *diagram* C-260a
■ LP-Gas G-41

**Liquefied petroleum gas.** *see in index* LP-Gas

**Liqueur** A-276

**Liquid,** in physics L-298–301, *diagrams* L-298–301. *see also in index* liquids by name, as Gasoline
■ apparent solids C-621, S-254g
■ Archimedes' principle L-298, *diagram* L-299
■ boiling point W-68, L-299–300
■ capillarity C-130b, L-301, *diagrams* L-300
■ colloids C-434–7, *pictures* C-435–7, *table* C-435
■ density determined H-288
■ dew formation D-97
■ distillation D-132–132a, *diagram* D-132a
■ drop formation L-298, *diagram* L-300
■ emulsions C-435
■ evaporation E-342–3
■ freezing F-433–4, S-254f, M-167
■ incompressibility L-298
■ ionization I-257–8, *diagram* I-257
■ liquid-vapor equilibrium C-241
■ melting S-254f, M-167
■ mixtures explained S-256
■ molecules in, *diagram* M-167
■ osmosis L-301, P-359, *diagram* L-301
■ siphon S-205–6, *picture* S-206
■ superfluidity C-620b
■ surface tension L-298, M-167, *diagrams* L-299–300
■ waves W-81–2: sound S-259, *graph* S-260
■ wetness explained L-300
■ wetting agents S-231–2, L-300–1, *diagram* L-299

**Liquid air** L-301, *diagram* N-292

**Liquidambar** (*Hamamelidaceae*), deciduous trees of witch-hazel family; native to Asia and America; small flowers; spiny, round fruit filled with encapsulated seeds, many of them unsound. *see also in index* Red gum

**Liquid Fuels Act, Synthetic** (1944), United States P-230

**Liquid helium** C-620a, b, *diagram* C-620a

**Liquid-hydrogen** N-377e

**Liquid measure,** *tables* W-96, 97

**Liquid nitrogen** C-620a, L-301, *diagram* C-620a: uses in carbon dating, *picture* C-132

**Liquid oxygen,** or **lox,** oxygen condensed to a bluish liquid: *diagram* C-620a
■ explosives E-361
■ liquid air L-301
■ rocket propellant S-342a, 346d, *diagram* R-232

**Liquorice,** or **licorice** [*lĭk'ō-rĭs*], a plant L-251

**Liquor laws.** *see also in index* Prohibition
■ ancient P-506
■ foreign P-507
■ United States P-506–7, R-269: temperance movement T-76

**Lira** [*lē'rä*], plural **lire,** (from Latin *libra,* "pound"), monetary unit of Italy and Turkey; historic value of Italian coin 5¼ cents; at one time worth 19.3 cents; name also applied to Turkish gold 100-piaster piece, historic value about $7.45; Turkish lira often called pound: *table* M-428

**Liripipe,** a headdress D-190

**Lisa** [*lē'sa*], **Manuel** (1772–1820), fur trader, born New Orleans; led first important expedition up the Missouri 1807 and built Fort Manuel at mouth of Bighorn River; with Andrew Henry, Jean Pierre Chouteau, and others founded Missouri Fur Company (1808–9) and built Fort Lisa near mouth of Big Knife River in North Dakota; erected Fort Manuel in n. South Dakota 1812; traveled up and down Missouri at least 12 times: F-497–8, S-326

**Lisboa, António Francisco** (1730–1814), Brazilian sculptor; crippled, he worked with tools fastened to his arms B-418
■ sculpture, *picture* L-138

**Lisbon,** also **Lisboa,** Portugal, capital; pop. 822,000: L-302, P-454, 457, *maps* P-455, S-350, E-334, *picture* P-457
■ cable connections C-8, *map* C-5
■ climate P-455, *graph* P-457b
■ Columbus in C-475
■ earthquake (1755) E-32, L-302
■ location L-302, *locator map* L-302
■ national library L-238

**Lisgar, John Young, Baron** (1807–76), English statesman, born Bombay, India; chief secretary for Ireland, lord high commissioner of Ionian Islands, and governor of New South Wales, Australia; governor-general of Canada 1869–72.

**Lisle, Leconte de.** *see in index* Leconte de Lisle

**Lisle, Rouget de.** *see in index* Rouget de Lisle

**Lisle,** a hard, twisted thread originally of linen, now often of specially prepared cotton
■ origin of name L-276

**Lisping,** in speech C-269

**Listening,** a learning tool C-496, 495, *picture* C-496
■ language art L-121, *pictures* L-121, 123
■ spelling S-376, *picture* S-375

**'Listen to Living',** painting by Matta P-67d, *picture* P-67d

**Lister, Joseph, Baron** (1827–1912), English surgeon, born Upton, Essex; developed antiseptic surgery; first to use various instruments and to try a number of new operations: M-215c

**Lister,** or **middlebuster,** farm implement, *picture* F-58

**Listing,** in agriculture C-542

**Liston, Charles** (Sonny) (1932–70), boxer, born Pine Bluff, Ark.
■ Ali's championship dispute A-306
■ heavyweight champion B-392, *table* B-391

**Lists,** in medieval tournament K-66

**List system,** of voting. *see in index* Proportional representation

**Liszt** [*lĭst*], **Franz** (1811–86), Hungarian composer L-302, M-559, P-318, *picture* L-302

**Li T'ai-po.** *see in index* Li Po

**Litani River,** in s. Lebanon; about 90 mi (140 km) long: L-180–180a

**Litany,** liturgical prayers in which the clergy leads and the choir or congregation responds (from Latin *litania,* "a prayer"); used in Catholic and in Episcopal and some other Protestant churches.

**Litchfield,** Conn., borough 23 mi (37 km) w. of Hartford; pop. 1489; birthplace of Harriet Beecher Stowe, Henry Ward Beecher, and Ethan Allen; first school of law (1784): *map* C-532, *picture* C-519
■ first law school in United States, *picture* C-525
■ first temperance society T-76

**Litchi, lichee,** or **leechee,** a Chinese tree (*Litchi chinensis*) having leathery pinnate leaves and delicious strawberrylike fruit; also grown in southern Vietnam and Malay Archipelago: N-385

**Liter** [*lē'tēr*], unit in metric system (1.0567 liquid qts.) W-95, *diagram* W-95
■ conversion equivalents, *table* W-97

**Literacy** P-450
■ American Colonies A-342
■ immigrants tested I-58
■ Russia E-99, P-450

**Literacy tests** P-450, S-505, I-58

**Literary agent** B-363

**Literary awards** L-303–4, *pictures* L-303, *tables* L-304–304b. *see also in index* Awards

**Literature** L-305–8, *pictures* L-305–6a, *Reference-Outline* L-306f–8. *see also in index* Books and bookmaking; Reading for recreation; Satire;

also chief topics below and individual writers by name
■ African A-120
■ American A-340
■ Arabian M-421
■ art forms A-662
■ Arthurian legends A-655
■ Australian A-797
■ autobiography A-831
■ awards, literary. *see in index* Awards
■ bibliography L-308
■ Buddhist B-484
■ Canadian C-113–17, *pictures* C-113–15
■ Celtic C-185
■ children's. *see in index* Literature for children
■ Chinese C-295d–e: tea legend T-41
■ conversation of famous masters C-550
■ diary D-104
■ drama D-169–77, *pictures* D-169–76
■ Egypt, ancient E-125
■ English E-253–76, *pictures* E-253–72
■ essay E-289–90
■ fables F-1–3, *pictures* F-1–2
■ Fathers of the Church F-75f: Bede, Saint E-253
■ folklore and folktales F-291–306, S-460–1, 465–82, *pictures* F-291–306, S-465–82. *see also in index* Folklore; Folktales
■ French F-436–41, *pictures* F-436–9
■ German G-96a–8, *pictures* G-96a–7
■ giant steps L-310g–12
■ Greek G-232–6, *pictures* G-232–5
■ Hebrew H-120–1
■ Hindu I-78
■ humor H-270
■ Icelandic I-13
■ Irish I-291–2, *pictures* I-291–2
■ Italian I-321–2, *pictures* I-321–2
■ Japanese J-391, *picture* J-391
■ Korean K-76b
■ Latin L-154–5
■ Latin American L-148–53, *pictures* L-149–52
■ letters, and their writers L-197
■ magazines M-33–5, *picture* M-33
■ Middle Ages N-375–6, R-239. *see also in index* Middle Ages, *subhead* literature
■ mythology M-579–80
■ naturalism N-376
■ Netherlands N-138
■ new voices, *list* L-306b–e
■ Northmen N-361
■ novel N-375–7, *pictures* N-375
■ origin of P-403
■ Persian P-213–14
■ Philippine P-257c–d
■ poetry P-403–7
■ realism N-376
■ Renaissance R-145–6, *Reference-Outline* R-150
■ romance R-239, N-375–6, F-436
■ romanticism N-376
■ Russian R-359–62, *pictures* R-359–60b
■ Scandinavian S-52g
■ science fiction. *see in index* Science fiction
■ short story S-183–4, *pictures* S-183–4
■ Spanish S-365–8, *pictures* S-365–7

**Literature for children** L-309–12, *pictures* L-309–11
■ Africa L-310g, *list* L-311, *picture* L-310g
■ Asia L-310f, *list* L-310j–11, *pictures* L-309, 310f
■ Australia and New Zealand L-310f–g, *list* L-311
■ awards, literary L-303, N-161, *pictures* L-303, *tables* L-304–304b
■ battledore L-309, *picture* L-310
■ bibliography L-312
■ books for home library R-105–11e, H-182–95, S-478–81d, 464
■ 'Bounty of Books, A' R-104–11e, *pictures* R-104–11e
■ Caldecott, Randolph C-26–7, *picture* C-26: illustrations, *picture* C-27
■ Canada L-310d–e, *list* L-310h, *picture* L-310d
■ Carroll, Lewis C-141–2, E-268. *see also in index* 'Alice's Adventures in Wonderland'
□ letter, facsimile L-197
■ classics retold S-140, L-104
■ fables F-1–3, *pictures* F-1–2. *see also in index* Fables
■ fairy tales. *see in index* Fairy tales
■ first children's books L-309–10
■ folklore and folktales F-291–306, S-465–82, 460–1, *pictures* F-291–306, S-465–82. *see also in index* Folklore; Folktales
■ giant steps, *list* L-310h–11
■ hobbies, list of books H-182–95
■ hornbook L-309, E-84, *picture* E-84
■ illustration, value R-105
■ Latin America L-310e–f, *list* L-310h–i, *picture* L-310e
■ libraries L-210–11, 244, S-461–2, *pictures* L-209, 213, 236–8, 240–1, 243: bibliography L-247; history L-310a, c, d, e, f, g, *pictures* L-236, L-310b; librarian L-225, *picture* L-238
■ McGuffey's readers M-8, E-88, *pictures* M-8, E-89
■ magazines L-310, 310c, d, e, f, *picture* L-310e
■ Mother Goose. *see in index* Mother Goose
■ myths M-579–80. *see also in index* Mythology
■ nature study, list of books N-80–1
■ Newbery, John N-161, *picture* N-161. *see also in index* Newbery, John
■ nursery rhymes N-381a–d, *pictures* N-381a–d. *see also in index* Nursery rhymes
■ picture books. *see in index* Picture books for children
■ stories. *see in index* Stories
■ storytelling S-460–82, *pictures* S-460, 462–3, 465–82, L-209, 237, 243
■ textbooks. *see in index* Textbooks, *subhead* elementary

**Litharge,** lead monoxide L-167

**Lithium** (Li), an alkali chemical element A-307, *tables* M-229, P-207, C-236
■ chloride V-255
■ electrochemical activity E-167, *diagram* I-257
■ electronic structure, *diagram* C-235
■ ore M-336
■ photosensitivity P-274
■ spectrum, *diagram* S-372
■ stability R-67

**Lithography** L-312, P-500–1
■ cartooning increased C-145c
■ Currier and Ives prints C-631, *picture* C-631
■ photolithography P-277–8, P-501, *pictures* P-278. *see also in index* Offset process

**Lithopone** P-73

**Lithosphere,** the solid body of the earth E-17, *picture* A-749

**Lithuanian Soviet Socialist Republic,** Russia, area 65,000 sq km (25,100 sq mi); pop. 3,129,000; cap. Vilna; L-312–13, U-14–15, P-413, 414, *maps* R-325, 344, 348–9, U-14
■ literature, *list* L-306c
■ location, *locator map* L-312
■ stamp, *picture* S-409
■ university library L-233

**Litmus,** purplish coloring matter; used as an acid-base indicator; turns red in acid, blue in alkali solution: Q-6

**Litotes** [*lī'tō-tēz*], a figure of speech F-109

**Litterae humaniores** [*lĭt'ĕr-ē hŭ-măn-ĭ-ō'rēz*] R-146

**Little, Arthur Dehon** (1863–1935), chemical engineer, born Boston, Mass.; expert on papermaking, processes for chrome tanning.

**Little America,** Admiral Byrd's base in Antarctica B-532, P-423, *map* W-242, *picture* P-418
■ ozone percentage I-236c

**Little Bear,** or **Ursa Minor,** a constellation, *charts* S-416, 419, 422, D-123

**Little Belt,** strait between Fyn Island and mainland of Denmark: D-89, B-46, *map* D-91

**'Little Belt',** British sloop W-11

**Little Belt Mountains,** range of Rocky Mountains, in Lewis and Clark National Forest, Montana: *map* M-460

**Little Bighorn River,** in s. Montana, flows n. across Crow Indian Reservation for 60 mi (100 km) to Bighorn River: *map* M-471
■ scene of Custer massacre C-631, *pictures* M-463, 467

**Little blue heron** H-147

**'Little Brown Church in the Vale, The',** hymn written 1857 by William S. Pitts, inspired by valley at Bradford, Iowa
■ church, *picture* I-265

**Little brown crane** C-601

**"Little Church Around the Corner,"** Church of the Transfiguration (Episcopal), in New York City on 29th St.; founded 1848 by George Hendric Houghton (1820–97), rector 1849–97; received nickname, 1870, when Joseph Jefferson, arranging funeral for an actor friend, was turned away from one church and advised, "There's a little church around the corner that might accommodate you"; nickname persisted and church remained a favorite with theatrical people: *map* N-264

**Little Colorado,** or **Colorado Chiquito,** river in Arizona, a tributary of Colorado River C-470, *maps* C-470, U-81

**Little Corporal,** Napoleon N-10

**Little Diomede Island.** *see in index* Diomede Islands

**Little Dipper,** seven stars corresponding to constellation Little Bear; tip of handle is North Star. *see also in index* Little Bear

**Little Dog,** or **Canis Minor,** a constellation, *charts* S-415, 421, 423

**'Little Dorrit',** novel by Charles Dickens; Little Dorrit is born, brought up, and wed in the prison where her father was confined for debt: D-107

**Little Egypt,** in Illinois I-33

**Little Entente** [*ăn-tänt'*], alliance between Czechoslovakia, Yugoslavia and Rumania: E-322, 323, Y-351

**Little Falls,** Minn., city on Mississippi River 30 mi (50 km) n.w. of St. Cloud; pop. 7250; paper, garments, boats; granite quarry nearby: *map* M-363
■ boyhood home of Charles A. Lindbergh L-288

**Little Falls,** N.J., 5 mi (8 km) s.w. of Paterson on Passaic River; pop. of township 11,496; ornamental iron, carpets, scissors: *map* N-202

**Little Falls,** N.Y., manufacturing city on Mohawk River and Barge Canal 18 mi (29 km) e. of Utica; pop. 6156; waterpower from cascades in river; food-processing equipment, food products, bicycles, footwear, textile products, paper; Gen. Nicholas Herkimer's grave nearby: *map* N-261

**Littlefield, Catherine** (1908–1951), ballet dancer and choreographer, born Philadelphia, Pa.; première danseuse Philadelphia Grand Opera Co. 1926–33; founded Littlefield Ballet 1935; created several ballets on American themes: 'Barn Dance' and 'Terminal'; restaged 'The Fairy Doll', 'Daphnis and Chloe'.

**Little fox mitre** (*Mitra vulpecula*), mollusk shell, *picture* S-152

**"Little Jack Horner,"** nursery rhyme N-381a

**Little John,** a member of Robin Hood's band of outlaws R-225

**Little Kanawha River,** in West Virginia. *see in index* Kanawha

**Little Khingan** [*shĭng'ăn'*] **Mountains,** in n.e. part of People's Republic of China; continuation of Great Khingan Mountains; in Heilungkiang Province w. of Amur R.; highest point about 4665 ft (1422 m): *map* M-84

**Little League,** in baseball B-94, *picture* B-96
■ game, *pictures* H-195, V-239, P-179

**'Little Lord Fauntleroy',** story by Mrs. Frances Hodgson Burnett of the seven-year-old Little Lord Fauntleroy whose curls and velvet suits set a fashion for small boys.

**Little Magician,** one of the nicknames of Martin Van Buren V-261

**'Little Mermaid',** statue, C-566, *picture* D-90

**Little Miami River,** in Ohio, tributary of Ohio River; 140 mi (225 km) long: *map* O-429

**'Little Minister, The',** novel by Sir James Barrie; Babbie, daughter of a village squire, in the guise of a gypsy, wins the love of Gavin Dishart, the little minister; background of Scottish village life.

**Little Missouri River,** tributary of the Missouri, rising in Wyoming and flowing 450 mi (720 km) through Montana and North and South Dakota: *maps* N-340, U-40
■ Bad Lands along, *picture* N-341: Theodore Roosevelt N. Mem. P. N-45, *map* N-352, *pictures* N-348

**'Little Murders',** work by Feiffer A-363

**Littleneck.** *see in index* Hard-shelled clam

**'Little Organum For the Theater, A',** work by Brecht B-433

**'Little Orphan Annie',** comic strip C-145d, *picture* C-145b

**Little Pee Dee River,** tributary of Pee Dee in e. South Carolina, *map* S-319

**'Little Pretty Pocket Book, A',** child's book published by John Newbery N-161, L-306

**Little Rhody,** popular name for Rhode Island R-180

**Little River Turnpike,** historical road in United States R-221

**Little Rock,** Ark., state capital; largest city of state; on Arkansas River; pop. 158,461: L-313, *map* U-41
■ Capitol, State L-313
■ location L-313, *locator map* L-313
■ veterans' hospital, *picture* H-239

**Little St. Bernard Pass,** Alpine pass (2190 m; 7180 ft) in Italy s. of Mont Blanc; connects valleys of Dora Baltea and Isère: *map* S-537

**Little Sisters of the Poor,** founded in France 1840, extended to U.S. 1868; for relief and nursing
■ vows M-448

**Little spotted cat,** *picture* C-154d

**Little Steel formula,** system of U.S. wage increases in smaller steel plants to cover 15 percent rise in living costs between Jan. 1, 1941, and May 1, 1942; adopted by War Labor Board July 1942 to stabilize wages in World War II.

**Little theater,** a theater in which an amateur group produces dramas T-148, 157

**Littleton, Sir Thomas** (1422–81), English judge and writer on law; 'Treatise on Tenures', dealing with English land laws of his day, is still used as an authority.

**Littleton,** Colo., town 8 mi (13 km) s. of Denver on South Platte River; pop. 26,466; missiles, light industry; oil research center: *map* C-467

**Little Trianon,** or **Petit Trianon,** palace at Versailles, France V-303

**Little Turtle** (1752?–1812), chief of Miami Indians, born near Fort Wayne, Ind.; kept his people from joining Tecumseh's confederacy against white men: I-87

**'Little Women',** novel by Louisa M. Alcott A-277, R-111c

**Littoral nation,** one with shorelines I-238

**Littoral (tidal) zone,** area along the shore between the high-tide and low-tide levels
■ Atlantic Ocean's marine life A-745

**Littoria,** Italy. *see in index* Latina

**Liturgical music,** or **church music** M-556, 557, 562
■ Gregorian chants M-555, G-238

**Liturgy** (from Latin *liturgia,* meaning "a public service"), term applied to any or all of the services used in public worship; especially in Roman Catholic, Eastern Orthodox, and Episcopal churches.

**Litvinov** [*lĭt-vē'nôf*], **Maxim Maximovich** (1876–1951), Russian statesman, born Bialystok, Russia (now Poland); diplomatic agent in England after Bolshevik revolution; commissar for foreign affairs 1930–39; ambassador to the U.S. 1941–43; deputy commissar for foreign affairs March-Aug. 1946.

**Liukiu Islands,** between Formosa and Kyushu. *see in index* Ryukyu

**Liu Shao-ch'i** [*lyu̦' shou'chē'*] (1898?–1974), Chinese Communist party theorist, born Hunan Province, China: became chairman People's Republic of China 1959; expelled from Chinese Communist party 1969.

**Live-forever, houseleek,** or **hen-and-chickens,** perennial plants of the family *Crassulaceae;* thick, succulent leaves, often in rosettes close to the ground; white, green, rose, or yellow star-shaped flowers.

**Live oak,** an evergreen oak O-387, 388
■ state tree of Georgia, *picture* G-86

**Liver,** in human body A-391, L-313–14, D-117, *diagrams* D-114–15
■ alcohol effects A-276
■ blood and B-314, L-313–14
■ hormones regulate, *table* H-226
■ poisoning A-254, M-226

**Liver fluke** W-298, *pictures* W-298

**Liverleaf.** *see in index* Hepatica

**Livermore, Mary Ashton Rice** (1820–1905), reformer, early advocate of abolition of slavery, prohibition, and woman's suffrage; born Boston, Mass.; won reputation in Civil War as worker for Sanitary Commission.

**Livermore,** Calif., city 35 mi (55 km) s.e. of San Francisco; pop. 37,703; wine; nuclear research center; annual rodeo; incorporated as town 1876; as city 1930: *map, inset* C-52

**Liverpool,** England, seaport of Great Britain; on estuary of Mersey River; pop. 677,450: L-314, *maps* E-334, *inset* G-199g
■ bridges L-314
■ cathedral C-158
■ location L-314, *locator map* L-314
■ Queensway Road Tunnel (Mersey Tunnel) T-291, *table* T-292
■ wheat market W-134

**Liverpool,** N.S., Canada, port town 116 km (72 mi) s.w. of Halifax; pop. 3607; fishing; papermaking, yeast manufacture; metal products: *map* N-373k

**Liverpool, University of,** at Liverpool, England L-314

**Liverpool and Manchester Railway,** England, early railroad L-327, R-73
■ Stephenson, George S-443

**Liverwort** L-314–15, P-370–1, *pictures* L-314, P-371, N-54b, i
■ confused with mosses M-501

**Livesay, Dorothy** (born 1909), Canadian poet and journalist, born Winnipeg, Man.: C-114

**'Lives of the English Poets',** biographies by Samuel Johnson B-222

**Livestock.** *see also in index* Animals, domestic; Breeding, animal; Dairying; Forage crops; Meat; Meat industry; and chief topics below
■ animals injurious to, *Reference-Outline* Z-367
■ alligators and crocodiles A-311
■ cattle C-161–9, *pictures* C-161–3, 165–8
■ farming improvements A-136
■ goats G-146–7, *pictures* G-146
■ hogs H-196–9, *pictures* H-196–9
■ horses H-231–8, *diagrams* H-232c, 234b–c, e–f, h–i, *lists* H-232a, *map* H-234i, *pictures* H-231, 232d–4a, 234g, 234j–8, *tables* H-232, 232f
■ plants injurious to P-408–9, C-169: locoweed and halogeton W-92; yew Y-342
■ poultry P-480–3, *pictures* P-480–2
■ reindeer R-139, *pictures* R-139
■ sheep S-146–8, *pictures* S-146–7
■ stock car for transporting, *pictures* R-82, W-257

**Living, ways of**
■ family F-26–32, *pictures* F-26–31
■ in many lands P-190–6, *pictures* P-190–6, W-238–40, *Reference-Outline* P-195–6

**Living costs** L-315, *graph* L-315
■ hospital care H-241d, b
■ index numbers show relationships L-315, S-437, P-202, *graphs* L-315, S-437
■ UAW contract adjusts wages to L-91
■ United States: Truman's administrations T-280, U-191

**Livingston, Edward** (1764–1836), lawyer and statesman, born Clermont, N.Y.; brother of Robert R. Livingston; served as congressman, U.S. senator, secretary of state under President Jackson, and minister to France 1833–35.

**Livingston, Philip** (1716–78), signer of Declaration of Independence, born Albany, N.Y.
■ signature reproduced D-55

**Livingston, Robert R.** (1746–1813), statesman, jurist, and experimental farmer; born New York City; brother of Edward Livingston; first chancellor New York State 1777–1801, secretary of foreign affairs 1781–83; minister to France 1801–5
■ aids Fulton F-479
■ Declaration of Independence D-51, *picture* R-162
■ defends Constitution U-142
■ Louisiana Purchase L-383
■ Statuary Hall, *picture* S-437b, *table* S-437b

**Livingston, William** (1723–90), lawyer, born Albany, N.Y.; attacked English Parliament's interference in provincial matters and Anglican domination of King's College; representative from New Jersey to 1st and 2d Continental Congress; signed United States Constitution; governor of New Jersey 1776–90: N-194

**Livingston,** Mont., city on Yellowstone River, 45 mi (70 km) n. of Yellowstone Park; pop. 6994; hunting, fishing, resort area; livestock; timber; mobile homes; railroad shops: *maps* M-470, U-40

**Livingston,** N.J., urban township 9 mi (15 km) n.w. of Newark; near Passaic River; pop. 28,040; beverages, poultry, dairy products: *map* N-202

**Livingstone, David** (1813–73), Scottish missionary explorer of Africa L-316–17, *picture* L-316
■ books by and about L-317
■ Stanley's search for S-410–11
■ Victoria Falls V-315
■ watermelons W-74

**Livingstone College,** at Salisbury, N.C.; affiliated with African Methodist Episcopal Zion church; chartered 1885; liberal arts, education and theology; graduate studies.

**Livingstone Mountains,** range in mainland Tanzania bordering n.e. shores of Lake Nyasa.

**Livingston University,** at Livingston, Ala.; state control; incorporated as private academy 1840; arts and sciences, business education and administration, teacher education; graduate study; quarter system.

**Living theater** A-363, T-148. *see also in index* Theater

**Living things.** *see in index* Nature study

**Livius Andronicus** [*ăn-drō-nī'kŭs*], **Lucius** (284?–204? B.C.), first known Roman poet, a Greek; enslaved but later freed; became actor and teacher, introducing Greek literature to Rome: L-154

**Livonia,** district in s. Estonian S.S.R. and n. Latvian S.S.R.; a former Baltic province of imperial Russia with capital at Riga; 45,516 sq km (17,574 sq mi): L-159a

**Livonia,** Mich., city 18 mi (29 km) n.w. of Detroit; pop. 104,814; automobile parts; automotive research laboratory; food processing; horse racing; Madonna College: *map* M-285

**Livorno,** Italy. *see in index* Leghorn

**Livre** [*lē'vẽr*], an old French silver coin worth about 19.3 cents, replaced by franc in 1795; originally equaled English pound in value (from *libra,* Latin for "pound").

**Livy** [*lĭv'ĭ*], anglicized name of Titus Livius (59 B.C.–A.D. 17), Roman historian, great prose writer; 35 of the 142 books of his history of Rome still exist: L-155

**Livyeres,** in Labrador, Canada L-92

**Lizard,** scaly-bodied, four-legged reptile L-317–20, R-152, *pictures* L-317–20
■ embryo, *pictures* E-194
■ foot, *pictures* F-329
■ heart R-152
■ kinds L-317–20, *pictures* L-317–20
□ chameleon C-204b–5, *pictures* C-204b
□ dragon, or giant L-320, *picture* L-318
□ flying dragon F-283, D-166, *picture* L-319
□ horned toad. *see in index* Horned toad
□ iguana I-31
□ monitor L-320, *picture* P-10
■ legendary, *picture* S-481b
■ place in evolution, *chart* G-64
■ prehistoric A-462, *picture* A-460, R-155, 157, *pictures* R-153, 155
■ reproduction A-426
■ salamander mistaken for S-25

**Lizard, The,** or **Lizard Head,** a bold promontory of Cornwall; the most southerly point of Great Britain; small bays and hazardous reefs line the coast.

**Ljubljana** [*lyụ'blyă-nä*], German **Laibach** [*lī'băk*], Yugoslavia, Slovenian city 80 km (50 mi) n. of Fiume; pop. 183,000; old castle and cathedral; Congress of Laibach 1821, which emperors of Austria and Russia attended, restated basic principles of Holy Alliance: *map* E-334
■ university library L-233

**Ljusne** [*yụs-nĭ'*] **River,** also **Ljusnan** [*yọs-năn'*] **River,** Sweden, rises in mountains on border of Norway; winds 510 km (320 mi) s.e. into Gulf of Bothnia; source of hydroelectric power; logging route; salmon: *map* S-524

**Llama** [*lä'mạ*], South American animal of camel family B-334, L-321, *picture* L-321
■ ancestry C-57
■ Indian herders, *picture* P-191
■ pack animal L-321, *pictures* L-321, S-289
■ ruminant R-318
■ zoo animal, *picture* Z-361a

**Llaneros** [*lyä-nä'rōs*], cattlemen of Venezuela V-275

**Llano culture.** *see in index* Elephant Hunter culture

**Llano Estacado** [*lăn'ō ĕs-tạ-kä'dō*], or **Staked Plain,** arid plateau in n.w. Texas and s.e. New Mexico; over 40,000 sq mi (103,600 sq km): T-110, N-207, *maps* T-111, N-208, U-62

**Llanos** [*lä'nōz,* Spanish *lyä'nōs*], plains
■ South America S-275, *map* G-193: Colombia C-439; Venezuela V-275, G-192
■ Texas plains C-171

**Llanquihue** [*yăng-kē'wä*], **Lake,** in s. Chile; 620 sq km (240 sq mi); extends north of Puerto Montt, which is its outlet to the Pacific.

**Llareta,** a plant. *see in index* Yareta

**Llewellyn, Richard,** pen name of Richard David Vivian Llewellyn Lloyd (born 1907?), Welsh writer (trilogy: 'How Green Was My Valley', 'Up, into the Singing Mountains', 'And I Shall Sleep . . . Down Where the Moon Is Small'): E-276

**Lloyd, Harold (Clayton)** (1894–1971), motion-picture actor, born Burchard, Neb.; began as "extra" at 19; famous for comedy roles in which he wore horn-rimmed glasses; formed own company 1923 ('Safety Last'; 'The Freshman'; 'Harold Lloyd's World of Comedy').

**Lloyd, John Henry** (Pop) (1884–1965), baseball player, born Gainesville, Fla.; shortstop Negro leagues 1905–31.

**Lloyd, (John) Selwyn (Brooke)** (born 1904), English statesman, born West Kirby, near Liverpool; Conservative member of Parliament 1945–; minister of state 1951–54, of supply 1954–55, of defence 1955; foreign secretary 1955–60; chancellor of the exchequer 1960–62; leader of House of Commons 1963–64, speaker 1971–.

**Lloyd Barrage,** also called **Sukkur Barrage,** in the Indus River at Sukkur in Sind region, Pakistan; a dam 4620 ft (1410 m) long, completed in 1932; irrigates 5,300,000 acres (2,145,000 hectares).

**Lloyd George, David, earl of Dwyfor** (1863–1945), British statesman L-321–2, *picture* L-321
■ Irish home-rule policy I-288
■ social legislation E-247, L-321–2

**Lloydminster,** Alta. and Sask., Canada, city on boundary of the two provinces, 225 km (140 mi) s.e. of Edmonton; pop. (Alberta) 4738, (Saskatchewan) 3953; petroleum and farm products: S-49e, h, *map* S-49k

**Lloyd's of London,** insurance organization I-218, L-339, *picture* I-217
■ marine insurance, *Titanic* S-177d

**Lluchu,** South American wool hat B-335

**Loading,** in papermaking P-102

**Loading coils,** in telephone
■ Pupin invents P-535

**Load line,** of ship, *diagram* S-176

**Loalach,** a mudfish M-540

**Loam,** soil S-250, 253, G-19

**Loan,** financial B-64, C-603. *see also in index* Bank and Banking; Bond; Credit; Mortgage
■ credit in business C-602–4, *picture* C-602
■ farm credit F-35–6, *map* F-36
■ housebuilding H-253
■ interest, how to compute P-199–202
■ life insurance I-214
■ savings and loan associations S-52c–d, H-254
■ United States, Bank of B-73
■ veterans, loan provisions for V-306, *table* V-307: Canada V-308

**Loan, interlibrary** L-210, 246, *picture* L-226
■ Middle Ages L-230

**Loanda,** Angola. *see in index* Luanda

**Lobachevski, Nikolai Ivanovich** (1793–1856), Russian mathematician, born Makariev, Nizhniy Novgorod; helped to found non-Euclidean geometry ('New Principles of Geometry').

**Lobbying,** practice of influencing legislators and other public officials; word taken from *lobby,* part of assembly hall where private persons are permitted to interview legislators; may be influence for public good or for promoting private or corporate interests to public detriment; under Regulation of Lobbying Act (1946) lobbyists must register and give source and disbursement of their finances
■ Japan J-377

**Lobe,** of lungs L-395, *diagram* L-395

**Lobe-fin,** or **Crossopterygian,** primitive crawling fish A-461

**Lobelia,** a genus of herbs of the family *Campanulaceae* with alternate leaves and white, blue, or red flowers; corolla very irregular; includes *Lobelia inflata* (Indian tobacco) used in medicine; *L. cardinalis,* cardinal flower. *see also in index* Cardinal flower

**Lobengula** [*lō-bĕng-gū'lạ*] (1833–94), king of the Matabele tribe in Southern Rhodesia (now Rhodesia); ruled 1870–94; died in exile after 1893 attack on British settlers failed: R-195, R-193

**Lobito** [*lọ-vē'tọ*], Angola, one of best seaports on w. coast of Africa; terminus of Benguela railway; pop. 23,897.

**Loblolly pine** P-328, 329

**Lob Nor,** in People's Republic of China. *see in index* Lop Nor

**Lobster** L-322–4, *pictures* L-322–3
■ catching L-323, *pictures* L-323, M-60, N-373d
■ eggs A-426
■ spiny lobster, or sea crawfish, related to L-324

**Lobster pot,** or **lobster trap** L-323, *pictures* L-323, F-384, M-60

**'Lobster Trap and Fish Tail',** mobile by Calder, *picture* S-93

**Lobworm,** a marine annelid (*Arenicola marina*) about 20 centimeters (8 inches) long, with bright red gills on its central segments; burrows in sandy shores between tide marks; used for bait; also called lugworm and lugbait.

**Local apparent time** T-179. *see also in index* Solar time

**Local government.** *see also in index* City; Municipal government; State government
■ ancient C-366
■ Board of Estimate, New York N-274
■ censorship C-487
■ census C-192
■ city C-363–4
■ county, United States C-592
■ education, United States E-84, 87–8
■ health agencies H-97–8, *picture* H-97
■ town T-219

■ United Kingdom U-18–19, *pictures* U-18–19: hundred D-83

**Local Group,** of galaxies E-9

**Local option** P-506

**Locarno,** Switzerland, town at n. end of Lake Maggiore; pop. 10,200; Madonna del Sasso sanctuary; Treaties of Locarno signed here: S-542, *map* S-537

**Locarno, Treaties of** (1925) W-265, *table* T-251a
■ signatures, *picture* W-265

**Location, relative, exact, and natural** G-48, *maps* G-47

**Loch** [*lŏĸ*], Scottish word for lake. *see in index* names of lakes, as Lomond, Loch

**Lochinvar** [*lŏĸ-ĭn-vär'*], in Sir Walter Scott's 'Marmion', hero of ballad 'Lochinvar', "so faithful in love, and so dauntless in war."

**Lochner** [*lōĸ'nẽr*], **Stephan** (born 1405–15, died 1451), German painter; birthplace probably Meersburg; his altarpiece is chief treasure of Cologne cathedral.

**Loch Ness monster** A-462

**Loch Raven,** Md., community at s.e. end of Loch Raven Reservoir; n.e. suburb of Baltimore; pop. 25,000: *map* M-139

**Lochy, Loch,** w. Scotland, *map* G-199g

**Locke, Alain Le Roy** (1886–1954), American author and historian B-294, L-324

**Locke, David Ross.** *see in index* Nasby, Petroleum V.

**Locke, John** (1632–1704), English philosopher L-324–5, *picture* L-324
■ bioethical bill of rights B-214
■ draws Carolina constitution S-310, 311
■ ideas embodied in Declaration of Independence D-51, L-324
■ political science P-434
■ theory of mind E-82–3, L-324

**Locke, William John** (1863–1930), English novelist and playwright, born Georgetown, British Guiana; first interest in architecture, secretary of Royal Institute of British Architects 1897–1907; a whimsical romanticist ('The Morals of Marcus Ordeyne'; 'The Beloved Vagabond'; 'Stella Maris'; 'Septimus').

**Lockhart, John Gibson** (1794–1854), Scottish writer and lawyer, born Cambusnethan, near Glasgow; famous as biographer of his father-in-law, Sir Walter Scott; also wrote life of Burns and novels.

**Lock Haven,** Pa., city on West Branch of Susquehanna River about 25 mi (40 km) s.w. of Williamsport; pop. 9617; paper, electronic equipment, aircraft, metal products, dyes, textiles; Lock Haven State College: *map* P-185

**Lock Haven State College,** at Lock Haven, Pa.; established 1870; formerly a teachers college; liberal arts, education.

**Lockheed S-3A,** Viking airplane, *picture* A-178

**Lockjaw.** *see in index* Tetanus

**Lockport,** N.Y., city on New York State Barge Canal, n.e. of Buffalo; named for two large locks situated there; pop. 25,399; grain and fruit; flour, textiles, wallboard, auto radiators and heaters, air conditioners, plastics, paper, steel products: *map* N-260

**Locks, canal** C-118
■ how they work C-118, *picture* C-119: Panama Canal P-89–91, *diagram* P-88, *pictures* P-88–9, 94–5
■ Panama Canal. *see in index* Panama Canal, *subhead* locks
■ St. Lawrence in 1781, *picture* C-101
■ St. Lawrence Seaway S-20, 21, *map* S-20, *pictures* S-19, U-51
■ Sault Sainte Marie Canal S-52b, *pictures* S-52b, C-119, M-277, M-281
■ Welland Ship Canal W-98, *pictures* C-117, O-456d

**Locks and keys** L-325, *diagrams* L-325

**Lock stitch,** sewing machine S-127

**Lockwood, Belva Ann Bennett** (1830–1917), lawyer, born Royalton, N.Y.; first woman permitted to practice before U.S. Supreme Court; active in woman suffrage movements; nominated for president of U.S. 1884 and 1888 by Equal Rights party.

**Lockyer, Sir (Joseph) Norman** (1836–1920), English astronomer and physicist, born Rugby, England; pioneer in application of spectroscope to sun and stars; explained sunspots; between 1870 and 1905 conducted eight British expeditions for observing total solar eclipses ('The Sun's Place in Nature'; 'Recent and Coming Eclipses'; 'The Chemistry of the Sun'; 'Inorganic Evolution')
■ discovers helium in sun S-372, H-131

**Loco-foco,** obsolete popular name for friction matches; also applied to a New York City faction of Democratic party, because a meeting at Tammany Hall (1835) was held by the light of candles and matches after a rival faction had turned off the lights.

**Locomotive** L-326–9, *pictures* L-326–9
■ diesel-electric D-113–14, R-78, L-326–7, *pictures* L-326–7, I-36
■ electric R-77–8, L-327, *pictures* L-327–8, R-75
□ mine locomotive L-327, M-343, *diagram* C-416, *pictures* C-417, V-333
□ towing locomotive, Panama Canal P-90, *pictures* P-94–5
■ pneumatic P-399
■ steam L-326, *pictures* L-328–9, S-438, N-179
□ Civil War, *picture* C-379
□ development R-72–3, 76–7, L-327, *pictures* R-74–5, L-328–9: Stephenson's inventions S-442, 443
□ early locomotive in Scotland, *picture* I-172
□ how it works, *diagrams* S-439–41
□ reversing mechanism, *diagrams* S-441
□ speed L-326
□ types R-76–7
■ toy, *picture* F-74a

**Locoweed** W-92, C-169, *picture* W-92b
■ can become poisonous P-408

**Locris,** name for two separate districts of ancient Greece: **East Locris,** on e. coast opposite Euboea; **West Locris,** on Gulf of Corinth, s. of Doris: *map* G-221

**Locust,** an insect L-330
■ animal migration A-452
■ beetle parasite B-141
■ cicada L-330, *picture* L-330
■ foot, *picture* F-329
■ grasshopper G-189–92, *pictures* G-189–92
■ "seventeen-year," a cicada C-340, *picture* C-340

**Locust,** a rough-barked tree of the pea family L-330, *pictures* L-330
■ black locust L-330, *picture* L-330: leaf, *picture* L-330; weight of wood H-155
■ flower, *picture* T-258

**Locust, honey.** *see in index* Honey locust

**Lod,** Israel. *see in index* Lydda

**Lode,** or **vein,** of minerals G-150b

**Lodestone,** a magnetized magnetite M-332, M-46
■ compass, early C-498, *picture* C-498

**Lodge, Henry Cabot** (1850–1924), political leader and historian, born Boston, Mass.; grandfather of Henry C. Lodge, Jr.; U.S. senator from Massachusetts 1893–1924; led Republican party in blocking U.S. entrance into League of Nations ('The Story of the Revolution'; 'Life of Alexander Hamilton'; 'Life of George Washington'; 'The Senate and the League of Nations'): W-177

**Lodge, Henry Cabot, Jr.** (born 1902), political leader, born Nahant, Mass.; grandson of Henry Cabot Lodge; U.S. senator (Republican) from Massachusetts 1937–53 (resigned 1944 to serve in World War II, reelected 1946); directed campaign which won Republican presidential nomination for Dwight D. Eisenhower 1952; chief U.S. delegate to the United Nations 1953–60; Republican vice-presidential nominee 1960; ambassador to South Vietnam 1963–64, 1965–67, to West Germany 1968–69; chief U.S. negotiator at Vietnam peace talks in Paris 1969; presidential emissary to Vatican 1970–75: N-293d, K-24d

**Lodge, Sir Oliver Joseph** (1851–1940), English physicist, exponent of psychic research, and author; born Penkhull, Staffordshire; did valuable foundation work in electricity and radio; principal of University of Birmingham 1900–1919; in addition to autobiography and many scientific works, wrote 'Raymond, or Life and Death', and other books setting forth his belief in possibility of communication with the dead.

**Lodge, Thomas** (1558?–1625), English poet, dramatist, and writer of romances; his pastoral romance 'Rosalynde' gave plot to Shakespeare for 'As You Like It'.

**Lodgepole pine,** slender evergreen tree (*Pinus contorta*) of pine family. Grows 9 to 24 m (30 to 80 ft); thin bark peels off in scales. Leaves in twos, 6⅖ (2½ in.) long; cones oval. Sometimes called jack pine, spruce pine, blackjack, knotty pine, tamarack, scrub pine, and yellow pine: *table* W-218

**Lodi** [*lō'dī*], Calif., city 32 mi (52 km) s. of Sacramento; pop. 35,221; wines and brandies, food processing and canning, tire molds; grape festival and national wine show in September: *maps* U-40, *inset* C-53

**Lodi** [*lô'dē*], Italy, town 29 km (18 mi) s.e. of Milan on right bank of Adda River; pop. 38,158; French victory over Austrians (1796); founded 5th century B.C.; destroyed in 12th-century wars; reestablished by Frederick Barbarossa: *map* I-338
■ Napoleon I at N-10

**Lodi** [*lō'dī*], N.J., borough on Saddle River just n.e. of Passaic; pop. 25,213; textile dyeing and finishing, chemicals, plastics: *map, inset* N-202

**Lodz** [*lọġ*], Poland, city 120 km (75 mi) s.w. of Warsaw; pop. 761,760; enormous recent growth due to large textile industry; battle of Lodz (1914): P-413, *maps* E-334–5, W-253
■ university library L-243

**Loeb** [*lōb*], **Jacques** (1859–1924), American biologist, born Mayen, near Coblenz, Germany; in U.S. after 1891; fertilized sea-urchin eggs chemically ("artificial parthenogenesis"); developed theory that many so-called "intelligent" actions of animals are physical or chemical in nature ("tropism").
■ aging experiments A-127

**Loeffler** [*lĕf'lẽr*], **Charles Martin** (1861–1935), American composer and violinist, born Mulhouse, Alsace; with Boston Symphony Orchestra 1883–1903; wrote songs, orchestral and chamber music; impressionistic style ('The Death of Tintagiles'; 'La Bonne Chanson'; 'A Pagan Poem'; 'Canticle of the Sun'): M-562

**Loening** [*lō'nĭng*], **Grover** (1888–1976), American aeronautical engineer, born Bremen, Germany; invented first flying boat; designed Loening monoplane and seaplane.

**Loess** [*lō'ĕs* or *lûs*], a type of soil S-249, *picture* S-250
■ Argentina A-575
■ China C-293b
■ origin M-337

**Loesser** [*lĕs'sẽr*], **Frank** (1910–69), songwriter and playwright, born in New York, N.Y.; won Academy award 1948 for song 'Baby, It's Cold Outside'; New York Drama Critics Circle Award 1950 for 'Guys and Dolls', 1956 for 'The Most Happy Fella', and 1961 for 'How to Succeed in Business Without Really Trying', which also won Pulitzer Prize for drama: O-464a

**Loewe, Frederick.** *see in index* Lerner, Alan Jay

**Loewe** [*lû'vẽ*], **Johann Karl Gottfried** (1796–1869), German composer, born near Halle, Germany; cantor and teacher in Stettin; one of first to give artistic form to ballad.

**Loewi** [*lû'vē*], **Otto** (1873–1961), American pharmacologist, born Frankfurt, Germany; worked with H. H. Dale on nerve impulses and their chemical transmission; to U.S. 1940, became citizen 1946
■ Nobel prize, *table* N-294d

**Loewy, Raymond Fernand** (born 1893), American industrial designer, born Paris, France; in United States after 1919, became citizen in 1938; designed streamlined trains, ships, and automobiles, also buildings for New York World's Fair 1939–40; author 'The Locomotive—Its Esthetics': D-94d

**Löffler** [*lûf'lẽr*], **Friedrich August Johannes** (1852–1915), German bacteriologist, born Frankfurt-an-der-Oder; discovered causative organism of glanders, of diphtheria (with E. Klebs), and of foot-and-mouth disease (with Paul Frosch).

**Lofoten Islands,** also **Lofoden Islands,** group of rocky islands off n.w. coast of Norway; 4040 sq km (1560 sq mi); pop. 28,980: N-364, *map* N-365

**Loft,** in golf G-155, *diagram* G-155a

**Lofting, Hugh** (1886–1947), writer and illustrator, born Maidenhead, Berkshire, England; resident of U.S.; creator of character "Doctor Dolittle" and author of whimsical poetry and stories for young children; awarded Newbery Medal 1923 for 'Voyages of Doctor Dolittle' ('Story of Doctor Dolittle'; 'Porridge Poetry'): R-110a

**Log,** oil-well record P-236

**Log, ship's,** device for measuring speed; term also used for ship's record book: B-324, L-331, *pictures* L-331

**Logan, George** (1753–1821), statesman, born Stenton, Pa. (now a part of Philadelphia); U.S. senator from Pennsylvania 1801–7; his attempt to settle difficulties between France and United States (1798) without authority from the government led Congress to pass Logan Act, forbidding such activities by nonaccredited persons.

**Logan, James** (1674–1751), American colonial political leader, born Ireland; a Quaker and secretary to William Penn; chief justice Pennsylvania Supreme Court 1731–39: P-171

**Logan, John** or **James** (1725?–80), English name of Cayuga Indian chief Tahgahjute; birthplace probably Shamokin, Pa.; friend of the whites until the massacre of his family by the whites 1774; joined English and became a leader in Lord Dunmore's War.

**Logan, John Alexander** (1826–86), Civil War general and U.S. senator, born Jackson County, Ill.; admitted to bar 1851; distinguished service in Civil War; except for 2-year interval was member of U.S. Senate 1871–86; candidate for presidential nomination on Republican ticket 1884; author 'The Great Conspiracy' dealing with Civil War
■ Illinois statesman I-41
■ originates Memorial Day F-93

**Logan, Joshua** (born 1908), producer and director, born Texarkana, Tex.; plays: 'Mister Roberts', 'The Wisteria Trees', 'Picnic'; musical plays: 'South Pacific' (awarded 1950 Pulitzer prize), 'Fanny'; also motion-picture adaptations.

**Logan, Rayford W(hittingham)** (born 1897), educator, born in Washington, D.C.; professor of history Howard University, Washington, D.C., 1938–65, head of department 1942–64; edited 'What the Negro Wants'; author of 'The Negro and the Post-War World: a Primer' and 'The Negro in American Life and Thought'.

**Logan, Stephen Trigg** (1800–1880), jurist, born in Franklin County, Ky.; judge of circuit court; delegate to Republican convention of 1860, which nominated Lincoln, his former law partner.

**Logan, Sir William Edmond** (1798–1875), Canadian geologist, born Montreal; mapped coal basin in Wales; first director Geological Survey of Canada 1842–70.

**Logan,** Utah, city 67 mi (108 km) n. of Salt Lake City; pop. 26,844; dairy products; textiles, pianos, farm machinery; vegetable canning; Utah State University: U-218, *maps* U-232, 217, U-40.

**Logan, Mount,** 2d highest peak (6050 m; 19,850 ft.) of North America, situated in s.w. Yukon Territory: C-74, *maps* C-88, 98
■ height, comparative. *see in index* Mountain, *table*
**Loganberry** L-332, *picture* L-332
**Logania** [*lō-gā'nĭ-ạ*] **family,** or **Loganiaceae** [*lō-gā-nĭ-ā'sē-ē*], a family of plants, native chiefly to warm regions, including Carolina yellow jessamine, buddleia, pinkroot, ignatius bean, strychnine, natal orange, and summer lilac.
**Logansport,** Ind., city on Wabash and Eel rivers about 70 mi (110 km) n. of Indianapolis; pop. 17,899; railroad division point; electrical products, hydraulic machinery, springs; state mental hospital and Bunker Hill Air Force Base nearby: *map* I-100
**Logarithmic chart** G-186–8, *graph* G-187
**Logarithms** A-595, L-332–3, *table* L-333
■ information computation I-188b
■ slide rule S-217, C-21
**Logbook** L-331
**Log cabin.** *see in index* Shelter, *subhead* log cabin
**Log-cabin campaign,** of William Henry Harrison H-44, *picture* H-44
**Log-cabin fire** C-65, 66
**Loggerhead shrike,** or **migrant shrike** S-186, *pictures* S-186
**Loggerhead turtle** (genus *Caretta*) T-310
**Loggia dei Lanzi** [*lôd'gä dā'ē länt'sē*], gallery in Florence F-229, *map* F-229, *picture* F-229a
**Logging.** *see in index* Lumbering
**Logic** L-334, P-264, 266
■ algebra A-294
■ Aristotle's writings A-589
■ Boolean principles B-364
■ computer hardware systems C-501
■ dialectical, of Hegel P-266, H-124
■ new math concepts M-164e, *diagrams* M-164e
**Logistics** [*lō-gĭs'tĭks*], in military science, details of moving, quartering, and supplying troops.
**Logogram,** in writing W-306a
**Logography,** system of writing W-306a
**Logo-syllabic writing.** *see in index* Word-syllabic writing
**Logrolling.** *see in index* Birling
**Logroño** [*lō-grō'nyō*], Spain, ancient walled city in n., capital of province of same name; on Ebro River; pop. 58,545; wine trade.
**Logwood** L-334
**Lohengrin** [*lō'ĕn-grĭn*], in German legend L-334
■ opera by Wagner, *picture* O-464d: story O-465
**Loin,** cut of meat M-194, 192a, *diagrams* M-192b, *table* M-189
**Loincloth,** garment D-188
**Loire** [*lō-wär'*] **River,** longest river in France (1000 km; 620 mi) L-334, *maps* F-381, E-334, W-277
■ location, *locator map* L-334
■ Plessis-les-Tours, *picture* F-380
**Loki** [*lō'kē*], in Norse mythology, mischievous god
■ Balder and M-416
■ in 'Nibelungenlied' N-282
**'Lolita',** work by Nabokov A-361
**Lolland** [*lŏl'änd*], or **Laaland** [*lŏl'län*], Danish island in Baltic Sea; 1241 sq km (479 sq mi); pop. 83,170; sugar beets: *map* D-91
**Lollards,** name applied to followers of John Wycliffe in 14th century; originally a Dutch word meaning "mumbler"
■ Wycliffe W-312
**Lollipop** C-123
**Loma, Point,** Calif., promontory at entrance to San Diego Bay S-39, *picture* S-40
■ Cabrillo N. Mon. N-32, *map* N-30
**Loma Linda University,** at Loma Linda and Riverside, Calif.; Seventh-day Adventist; founded 1905; arts and science, allied health professions, dentistry, education, medicine, nursing, and public health; graduate studies at Loma Linda.
**Lomax** [*lō'măks*], **John Avery** (1867–1948, born Goodman, Miss.) and his son, **Alan** (born 1915, Austin, Tex.), ballad collectors ('American Ballads and Folk Songs'; 'Cowboy Songs and Other Frontier Ballads'; 'Negro Folk Songs'; 'The Folk Songs of North America'): F-307, S-477
**Lombard, Peter.** *see in index* Peter Lombard
**Lombard,** Ill., residential village 21 mi (34 km) w. of Chicago; pop. 37,295; lilac nurseries; Morton Arboretum nearby: *map, inset* I-50
**Lombard College,** at Galesburg, Ill.; founded 1851; merged with Knox College 1930.
**Lombardi, Vince(nt Thomas)** (1913–70), football coach and administrator, born Brooklyn, N.Y.: *list* F-337
**Lombard League,** of cities of n. Italy against Frederick I F-429
**Lombardo, Guy (Albert)** (1902–77), American orchestra leader, born London, Ont., Canada; became U.S. citizen 1937; orchestra (Royal Canadians) noted for "sweet" music; a national champion speedboat racer.
**Lombards,** also **Langobards** ("long beards"), Germanic tribe which settled in n. Italy L-335
■ Charlemagne conquers L-335, C-209
■ Gregory I and G-238
**Lombardy,** a region of n. Italy; area 23,804 sq km (9191 sq mi); pop. 7,406,152; cap. Milan: L-335, I-326, *map* I-338, *picture* I-323
■ history I-343b
■ Po River P-400
**Lombardy, iron crown of.** *see in index* Iron crown of Lombardy
**Lombardy poplar** P-446
**Lombok,** island of Indonesia, e. of Bali; about 1810 sq mi (4690 sq km); pop. 1,581,193; rice, coffee, indigo, sugar: I-164, 165, *maps* E-36
**Lombroso** [*lōm-brō'sō*], **Cesare** (1836–1909), Italian criminologist, born Verona; founded criminal anthropology; originated theory that there is a "criminal type" marked by physical signs ('The Criminal').
**Lomé** [*lō-mā'*], Republic of Togo, capital and seaport, on Gulf of Guinea; pop. 148,443: T-191
■ national library L-241
■ people, *picture* T-191
**Lomita,** Calif., residential community 13 mi (21 km) n.w. of Long Beach; pop. 17,191; Lomita Railroad Museum: *map, inset* C-53
**Lomond, Ben,** Scotland. *see in index* Ben Lomond
**Lomond, Loch,** largest lake in Scotland, in counties of Stirling and Dumbarton; 70 sq km (27 sq mi); length 37 km (23 mi): *map* G-199g
**Lomonosov** [*lŏ-mŏ-nô'sôf*], **Mikhail Vasilievich** (1711–65), Russian poet and philologist; set up principle of latter-day Russian language; called "Father of Russian Literature" ('Ode on the Capture of Khotin'): R-359, 361, *picture* R-359
**Lompoc,** Calif., city near Pacific Ocean 48 mi (77 km) n.w. of Santa Barbara; pop. 26,267; oil, diatomite, missiles; Vandenberg Air Force Base nearby; established 1874: S-342c, *map* C-53
**London, George,** real surname Burnstein (born 1920), American bass baritone, born Montreal, Que.; to U.S. 1935; with Metropolitan Opera Company 1951–68; artistic administrator John F. Kennedy Center for the Performing Arts 1968–71; director National Opera Institute 1971–77; director Opera Society of Washington from 1975; radio, television, and concert singer.
**London, Jack** (John Griffith London) (1876–1916), American novelist and short-story writer L-335, *pictures* L-335, C-48
■ 'Call of the Wild, The' L-335, D-154c
■ ranch home, *picture* C-46
■ Russia publishes R-332f
**London,** England, one of the largest cities in the world; capital of Great Britain; pop. Greater London 7,703,410; L-336–44, *maps* L-337–9, E-334, *inset* G-199h, *pictures* L-336–7, 340–4
■ art galleries and museums L-343–4. *see also in index* British Museum; National Gallery, Victoria and Albert Museum
■ Bank of England L-339, *map* L-339
■ Big Ben L-342, W-65, *pictures* G-198, W-64, P-131, E-325
■ boroughs L-337, *map* L-337
■ button wear B-528
■ Charing Cross L-338, *map* L-339
■ circus C-344, *picture* C-348c
■ City of London L-336–7: lord mayor L-339–40
■ clothing shops C-401
■ coffeehouses C-550: businessmen frequent I-218; Cheshire Cheese, *picture* C-551
■ crown jewels of Great Britain L-340–1, *picture* J-451
■ Dickens' Old Curiosity Shop, *picture* D-107
■ East End L-344
■ Elizabethan houses, *picture* E-239
■ fires L-336, 337
■ Girl Scout Ark G-131
■ government U-19, L-336, *pictures* U-19: Middle Ages D-84
■ Greater London L-337, *maps* E-218, L-337, *picture* H-250
■ Great Exhibition (1851) F-20
■ Greenwich L-156, 159, L-344, *map* L-337, *inset* G-199h, *picture* L-159
■ harbor and docks L-334, H-27
■ history L-336–7
□ Alfred the Great A-282
□ Cade's rebellion H-137
□ charter granted, *picture* W-163
□ Fawkes's plot F-78
□ Pepys, Samuel P-197b–8, E-258–9
□ Wat Tyler's Rebellion T-315
□ World War II, *map* W-277: air raids W-287, L-337, 339, *picture* E-248; evacuation of children, *picture* E-248; V-1's G-253; V-2's G-254–5
■ industry L-337
■ libraries L-231, 234, 239, 243
■ location, *locator map* L-336
■ palaces L-342, 341, 344, *map* L-338, *picture* L-343. *see also in index* Buckingham Palace
■ parks L-342–3, *map* L-338, *picture* G-198d
■ Parliament buildings L-342, *map* L-339, *pictures* L-341, G-199, P-131–131a, E-325
■ police P-430, 430b, *picture* P-430a: Scotland Yard L-341–2
■ postal service P-463, 465
■ procession to Parliament, *picture* E-217
■ St. Paul's Cathedral. *see in index* St. Paul's Cathedral
■ skyscraper, *picture* E-223
■ smog problem P-441b, c
■ streets L-338–9, 341–2, 343, *map* L-338–9
■ subway L-338, S-488
■ temperature and precipitation, *graph* G-199
■ Thames River. *see in index* Thames River, *subhead* London
■ theaters L-344, 338, T-155–6
■ Tower Bridge, *map* L-339, *pictures* L-336, E-317
■ Tower of London. *see in index* Tower of London
■ trade L-336, G-198c: medieval period R-149; tea auction T-43
■ Trafalgar Square L-338, *map* L-339, *picture* L-337
■ water system in early times W-70b
■ West End L-343
■ Westminster Abbey W-109, *picture* W-109
■ Whitehall, district L-341–2, *map* L-339, *pictures* L-341, U-12
■ zoo Z-364, 357; panda, *picture* P-97
**London,** Ont., Canada, city on Thames River; pop. 223,222: L-345, *maps* O-456l, b, e, C-99
■ location L-345, *locator map* L-345
■ shut-in library service, *picture* L-211
**London, Declaration of.** *see in index* Declaration of London
**London, Tower of.** *see in index* Tower of London
**London, treaties of**
■ 1913 (Balkan States-Turkey), *table* T-251a
■ 1915 (secret treaty) W-254, *table* T-251a
■ 1930 (naval armaments) P-18, N-105
■ 1936 (naval armaments) P-143c, *table* T-251a
**London, University of,** educational institution at London, England; grew out of University College, founded 1827; by royal charter of 1836 had been examining body only, for conferring degrees; reorganized 1900 to include also teaching, research, and extension work: L-344
**London Bridge,** historic bridge over the Thames River, London, England; original, completed in early 13th century, bore rows of houses with chapel in center; second bridge, completed 1831, of granite, was 65 ft (20 m) wide with 5 arches of varying sizes; purchased 1968 by American land developers and moved to Arizona desert, near Lake Havasu, as a tourist attraction; third bridge, 860 ft (262 m) long, opened 1973: B-445, *map* L-339
■ Shakespeare's time, *picture* S-134
**"London Bridge,"** nursery rhyme N-381b
**London Company,** also known as Virginia Company of London, organized 1606 by King James I of England to establish colonies in North America between 34th and 41st degree of n. latitude; dissolved 1624; was the s. branch of a joint land stock company of which Virginia Company of Plymouth was n. branch. *see also in index* Plymouth Company
■ grant to Pilgrims M-181
■ Hakluyt promotes H-8
■ Jamestown J-361–2, V-335
**London Conference** (1866) F-75, C-112b, *picture* C-112b, *table* S-495a
**London Conference on Naval Armament**
■ 1930 N-105, H-223
■ 1936 P-143c, P-18
**London Convention for the Protection of African Fauna and Flora** N-22
**Londonderry, 2d marquis of.** *see in index* Castlereagh
**Londonderry,** also **Derry,** Northern Ireland, port on Foyle River about 105 km (65 mi) n.w. of Belfast; pop. 55,000; linen; besieged by James II in 1689; county borough and chief town of Londonderry County (land area 2074 sq km [801 sq mi]), pop. 174,658, including county borough): I-290, *maps* G-199g, I-283
**London Missionary Society** C-338
■ Livingstone L-316
**London Prize Ring Rules,** boxing B-390
**London Round Table Conferences on India** I-81
**'Lonely House, The',** etching by Hopper, *picture* A-663
**Lone Mountain College,** at San Francisco, Calif.; Roman Catholic; founded 1930 as San Francisco College for Women; arts and sciences; graduate school.
**Lone Star State,** nickname for Texas T-110
**Long, Crawford Williamson** (1815–78), American surgeon L-345, *picture* G-90
■ ether's discovery A-413
■ first operation on anesthetized patient L-345, *pictures* G-85, T-314
■ Statuary Hall, *table* S-437a
**Long, Huey Pierce** (1893–1935), Democratic leader, born Winnfield, La.; governor of Louisiana 1928–31; U.S. senator 1931–35; nicknamed "the Kingfish"; shot to death by Dr. Carl A. Weiss, Jr.; (autobiography 'Every Man a King'): *picture* L-374
■ assassination, *list* A-704
■ birthday celebrated F-94
■ bridge at New Orleans named for N-223b, *map* N-223b
■ Statuary Hall, *table* S-437a
**Long, John Davis** (1838–1915), public official, born Buckfield, Me.; governor of Massachusetts 1880–83; member of Congress 1883–89; secretary of navy 1897–1902, during Spanish-American War.
**Long, John Luther** (1861–1927), novelist and dramatist, born Hanover, Pa. ('Madame Butterfly'; 'The Darling of the Gods').
**Long, Russell B(illiu)** (born 1918), political leader, born

Shreveport, La.; son of Huey Pierce Long; U.S. senator (Democratic) from Louisiana 1948–, assistant majority leader (majority whip) 1965–69.

**Long, Stephen Harriman** (1784–1864), U.S. Army surveyor and engineer, born Hopkinton, N.H.; led exploring expedition to Rocky Mts. 1819–20; discovered Longs Peak; authority on railroads: F-66, N-112, C-458, *picture* M-455
■ located 49th parallel M-353

**Long Beach,** Calif., city on s. coast about 20 mi (30 km) s. of Los Angeles; pop. 361,334; L-345, *maps* U-40, *inset* C-53
■ harbor L-354–5
■ location L-345, *locator map* L-345
■ Signal Hill L-345, *picture* C-39

**Long Beach,** N.Y., residential and resort city on island off s.w. shore of Long Island, 21 mi (34 km) s.e. of New York City; pop. 361,334; commercial fisheries, lobster beds: *map, inset* N-260

**'Long Beach',** U.S. Navy nuclear-fueled cruiser N-98, *picture* N-94

**Long-billed curlew.** *see in index* Curlew

**Longbow** A-639
■ Hundred Years' War H-271, 272, *pictures* H-271, 273, H-137
■ influence on knighthood K-67
■ influence on warfare W-9

**Long Branch,** N.J., resort city on Atlantic coast about 6 mi (10 km) n. of Asbury Park; pop. 29,819; electronics, clothing, mill products; fishing pier and boardwalk; Monmouth College at West Long Branch: *maps* N-202, 188

**Longchamps,** or **Longchamp** [*lôṅ-shäṅ'*], part of the Bois de Boulogne, w. of Paris, France; site of an abbey founded 1260 by Isabel, sister of St. Louis, and suppressed 1792; now a racecourse.

**Longcloth,** plain, lightweight, cotton fabric; soft, closely woven; used for children's clothes and underwear.

**'Long Day's Journey into Night',** drama by Eugene O'Neill O-455, *picture* D-174

**Long-distance telephone** T-60

**Long division** D-135–135a, b

**Long-eared sunfish** S-518

**Longevity,** length of life. *see in index* Life, *subhead* length of; Vital statistics

**Longfellow, Henry Wadsworth** (1807–82), American poet L-346–8, A-348, *pictures* L-346, M-62
■ books by L-348
■ bust in Westminster Abbey, *picture* L-342
■ Cambridge home C-56b, L-347, 348, *picture* L-347
■ 'Courtship of Miles Standish, The' L-348, S-410, *picture* L-348
■ 'Evangeline' A-14
■ Hall of Fame, *table* H-11
■ 'Santa Filomena', poem N-289
■ 'Song of Hiawatha, The' H-150, L-348, M-274
■ statue, *picture* M-60
■ translated 'Frithjof's Saga' S-526
■ 'Village Blacksmith, The' B-308

**Longfellow-Evangeline State Park,** near St. Martinville, La.
■ Acadian House Museum, *picture* L-367

**Longford,** agricultural county in Leinster Province, e.-central Ireland; 1044 sq km (403 sq mi); pop. 28,989; also name of town in county (pop. 3454): *maps* I-283, G-199h

**Long-haired cats,** C-153b, *pictures* C-153d
■ standards C-153d

**Longhorn cattle** C-162–3, 164, *pictures* C-171, N-117
■ ranching C-170, 171, 173–5, *picture* C-171

**Longhorn Cavern,** at Burnet, Tex., *picture* C-178b

**Long-horned beetle,** a beetle of the family *Cerambycidae, pictures* B-139, B-141

**Longhouse,** dwelling used by certain primitive peoples
■ Iroquois Indians, *picture* I-106

**Longinus** [*lŏn-ġī'nŭs*], **Cassius** (213?–273), Greek critic G-235

**Long Island,** N.Y., island s. of Connecticut forming s.e. portion of New York State; 1401 sq mi (3628 sq km); pop. 6,728,074; L-349, N-238, *maps, inset* N-239, 260, *picture* L-349
■ Brooklyn. *see in index* Brooklyn, Borough of
■ Jones Beach, *pictures* L-349, N-247
■ location, *locator map* L-349
■ national rifle matches R-206

**Long Island, battle of** (1776) L-349

**Long Island Sound,** arm of Atlantic Ocean between Long Island and mainland; 76 mi (122 km) long: N-237, *maps, inset* N-239, 260

**Long Island University,** at Greenvale, N.Y., and Brooklyn, N.Y.; private control; founded 1926; liberal arts, business administration, education, library science, and pharmacy; graduate study; centers at Greenvale and Southampton.

**Longitude,** distance in degrees east or west on earth's surface L-156–9, M-103c–d, *diagram* L-157, 159, *maps* L-156, 158, *picture* L-159, *table* L-158. *see also in index* Latitude
■ map location M-97
■ navigation N-88, L-158
■ time and T-178–80, 181, L-158, 159

**Longitudinal arch,** of the foot F-330

**Long Lake,** N.Y., in Adirondacks; 14 mi (22 km) long, 1 mi (1.6 km) wide: *map* N-261

**Longleaf pine, Southern yellow pine,** or **Georgia pine** P-328, 329, G-78, 80, *table* W-218

**Longman, (Mary) Evelyn Beatrice** (Mrs. Nathaniel Horton Batchelder) (1874–1954), sculptor, born Winchester, Ohio; designed bronze doors for chapel of U.S. Naval Academy, Annapolis.

**Longmeadow,** Mass., 3 mi (5 km) s. of Springfield on Connecticut River; pop. of township 16,301; settled 1644, incorporated 1783: *map* M-160

**Longmont,** Colo., city 12 mi (19 km) n.e. of Boulder; in agricultural area; pop. 42,942; electronic equipment, trailers and campers; food processing; established about 1870, incorporated as town 1873, as city 1885: *map* C-467

**Long Parliament** C-212–13, E-238
■ Cromwell dismisses, *picture* C-613
■ Hampden H-16
■ Rump Parliament C-213, C-612–13, E-238, *picture* C-613

**Long primer,** a size of type T-316

**Longshanks,** nickname of Edward I of England E-100d

**Longshoreman** H-25–6

**Longs Peak,** Colo., one of highest peaks of Rocky Mts. (14,256 ft; 4345 m), Rocky Mountain National Park, 50 mi (80 km) n.w. of Denver: *maps* C-466, U-80–1, *picture* C-453
■ climatic region, *map* U-119: temperature and precipitation, *graph* U-119

**Longstreet, Augustus Baldwin** (1790–1870), newspaper editor, educator, and Methodist minister; born Augusta, Ga.; president Emory College, University of Mississippi, and University of South Carolina ('Georgia Scenes').

**Longstreet, James** (1821–1904), Confederate Civil War general, born Edgefield District, S.C.; distinguished himself at Bull Run, Fredericksburg, Chickamauga, and in battle of the Wilderness; U.S. minister to Turkey 1880–81; U.S. Railway Commissioner 1898–1904: R-115
■ Bull Run, second battle C-376
■ Chickamauga battle C-378
■ Gettysburg G-119–20

**Long-tailed shrew** S-186

**Longview,** Tex., city about 125 mi (200 km) e. of Dallas; pop. 62,762; oil production; earth-moving equipment, industrial machinery, oil field supplies, chemicals, LeTourneau College: *maps* T-128, U-41

**Longview,** Wash., port city in s.w. part of state at confluence of Cowlitz and Columbia rivers; pop. 31,052; lumber, paper products, aluminum; incorporated 1924: W-41, *maps* W-52, U-40

**Longwall method,** in coal mining C-416, 414

**Longwood College,** at Farmville, Va.; state control; founded 1839; arts and sciences, education; graduate studies.

**Longworth, Nicholas** (1869–1931), political leader, born Cincinnati, Ohio; Ohio Republican congressman 1903–13, 1915–31; speaker of House 1925–31: *picture* W-153
■ wife, Alice Roosevelt W-154, *picture* W-153

**Lonicera** [*lŏ-nĭs'ēr-ạ*], the honeysuckle genus of plants H-214, *picture* H-214

**Lönnrot** [*lûn'rŏt*], **Elias** (1802–84), Finnish folklorist, philologist, and physician; born Sammatti, s. Finland; best known as compiler of 'Kalevala': S-470, F-119–20

**'Look Back in Anger'** (1958), motion picture M-525

**'Look Homeward, Angel',** autobiographical novel by Thomas Wolfe A-359, W-211

**'Looking Backward',** novel by Edward Bellamy N-376

**'Looking for Mr. Goodbar',** work by Rossner A-363

**Lookout, Cape,** North Carolina, 70 mi (110 km) s.w. of Cape Hatteras N-322, *maps* N-323, 337, U-41
■ Cape Lookout N.S. N-32, *map* N-30

**Lookout Mountain,** ridge in n.w. Georgia extending into Tennessee and Alabama C-221, *maps* T-97, A-223, *pictures* C-220, T-88
■ battle in Civil War C-221, *maps* C-221, C-376
■ cable railway, *picture* T-81

**Loom**
■ development S-390–2: Industrial Revolution I-170, 171
■ handloom, *picture* C-400
□ American Colonies S-392
□ ancient loom of South America, *picture* T-138
□ Egyptian, ancient, *picture* T-137
□ England, *picture* E-242
□ Guatemala, *picture* G-247–8, T-138
□ Hopi, *picture* I-109
□ Mexico, *pictures* M-249
□ Navajo S-391, *pictures* S-390, I-126
□ practice, *pictures* S-391
□ rugs, *picture* T-301
□ tapestry T-18
■ power loom C-590, *pictures* T-133–4, C-403
□ first in America T-134–5
□ Jacquard S-392, F-5, *picture* T-134: rugs R-316, 312, *pictures* R-315
□ 19th century, *picture* N-175
■ principle F-5

**Loon,** a diving waterbird L-350, *picture* A-426
■ state bird, *picture* M-356

**Loop,** in Chicago, Ill. C-255, 258, *map* C-261

**Loop antenna,** in radio, *picture* R-55

**Looper.** *see in index* Cankerworm

**Loos, Adolf** (1870–1933), Austrian architect, *profile* A-569

**Loos, Anita** (born 1893), novelist, playwright, and motion-picture scenarist, born Sisson, Calif. (novel, 'Gentlemen Prefer Blondes', later dramatized).

**Loos-en-Gohelle** [*lō-ō-zäṅ-gō-ĕl'*], called **Loos** [*lō-ōs'*] until 1937, town in n. France, about 5 km (3 mi) n.w. of Lens; pop. 3918; scene of British offensive 1915; town captured but British lost about 70,000 men.

**Loosestrife,** leafy-stemmed perennial herbs embracing the genus *Lysimachia* of the primrose family; common loosestrife is *L. vulgaris,* a tall coarse plant with large yellow flowers in terminal leafy panicles; *L. nummularia* (creeping Charlie, moneywort, or creeping jenny) is a trailing plant with large yellow flowers which are often used in rock gardens.

**Loosestrife family,** or **Lythraceae** [*lĭth-rā'sē-ē*], a family of plants, shrubs, and trees, native chiefly to tropical America, including swamp loosestrife, loosestrife, henna, crape myrtle, cigar flower, purple loosestrife, and blue waxweed.

**Lop-eared rabbit** R-22–3

**Lope de Vega.** *see in index* Vega Carpio

**López, Alfonso Ramon** (Al) (born 1908), baseball catcher and manager, born Tampa, Fla.; managed A.L. pennant winners, Cleveland Indians 1954, Chicago White Sox 1959.

**López** [*lō'pās*], **Carlos Antonio** (1790–1862), dictator of Paraguay, born near Asunción; teacher and lawyer; established country's first newspaper; rule marked by uneasy relations with U.S. and neighboring countries: P-112

**López, Francisco Solano** (1826–70), dictator of Paraguay P-112–13

**López de Legaspi, Miguel** (1524–72), Spanish soldier, born Zumarraga, near Tolosa, Spain; conquered Philippines and founded Manila: P-259c

**López de Villalobos** [*vēl-yä-lō'bōs*], **Ruy** (1500?–1546), Spanish navigator; in 1542 attempted conquest of Philippines for Spain and named the islands "Las Filipinas."

**López Mateos, Adolfo** (1910–69), Mexican lawyer and statesman, born near Mexico City; minister of labor and social welfare 1952–57; president 1958–64: M-256

**López Portillo, Josó** (born 1920), Mexican political leader, born Mexico City; former professor of law National University of Mexico; finance minister 1973–75; president 1976–: M-256

**Lop Nor,** or Lob Nor [*lôp nôr*], marshy, salty depression in Sinkiang-Uigur Autonomous Region, People's Republic of China; receives Tarim River: *maps* C-291, C-312

**Loquat** [*lō'kwŏt*], a small evergreen tree or shrub (*Eriobotrya japonica*) of the rose family and its fruit; originated in Asia; now widely cultivated in tropical and subtropical areas; fruit used for jellies, jams, and preserves.

**Lorain,** Ohio, port and industrial city on Lake Erie, 26 mi (42 km) w. of Cleveland; pop. 75,416; ships steel products, coal, iron ore; steel tubes and pipe, pumps, clothing, chemicals, communications and navigation equipment, toys, gypsum: *maps* O-428, 420

**Loran,** in radar R-32, *picture* N-89
■ iceberg location I-8
■ navigational equipment A-886, S-495a, N-87, S-194, *picture* N-89

**Loras College,** at Dubuque, Iowa; Roman Catholic; established in 1839; arts and sciences, and teacher education; graduate studies.

**Lorca, Federico García.** *see in index* García Lorca, Federico

**Lorca** [*lôr'kä*], Spain, ancient city in s.e., on river Sangonera; pop. 19,854; trade center; many battles between Christians and Moors: *map* E-334

**Lord,** a British title borne by bishops, marquises, earls, viscounts, and barons; also borne as courtesy title by eldest sons of dukes, marquises, and earls, and younger sons of dukes and marquises; title of office borne by lord chancellor: T-185

**Lord & Thomas,** advertising agency A-58

**Lord Dunmore's War,** named for John Murray, earl of Dunmore, governor of Virginia; expedition by American colonists against Indian coalition formed to check westward expansion of Virginia; ended at battle of Point Pleasant (now Tu-Endie-Wei Park, W. Va.) 1774
■ battle W-112: monument, *picture* W-115

**Lord Howe Island,** dependency of New South Wales, Australia, in Pacific 700 km (435 mi) n.e. of Sydney; resort; 13 sq km (5 sq mi); pop. 223: *map* P-4

**'Lord Jim',** novel by Joseph Conrad E-270

**Lord mayor,** title given to mayors of cities of York, Dublin, and London
■ London L-339–40

**Lord Mayor's Day** (Nov. 9), London, England L-340

**Lord of Misrule** C-330, 331, *picture* C-331

**Lords, House of,** upper house of British Parliament P-131–131a, b, U-18
■ appeal court, serves as C-595
■ Cabinet members chosen from C-4
■ Reform Bill crisis R-319
■ veto power limited L-322

**Lord's Day** S-1

**Lord's Prayer, The** (Matt. vi, 9–13), commonly used in religious worship; variations exist among denominations; King James version follows:
"Our Father which art in heaven, Hallowed be thy name.
Thy kingdom come. Thy will be done in earth as it is in heaven.
Give us this day our daily bread.
And forgive us our debts, as we forgive our debtors.
And lead us not into temptation, but deliver us from evil: For thine is the kingdom, and the power, and the glory, for ever. Amen."
■ hornbook contains, *picture* E-84

**Lord's Supper,** or **Holy Eucharist,** also **Communion,** Christian rite in which bread and wine are taken in commemoration of Christ's death. This sacrament was instituted by Christ at his supper (Lord's Supper, or Last Supper) with his disciples the night before his death (Matt. xxvi, 26–29; Mark xiv, 22–25; Luke xxii, 14–20)
■ Anglicans A-417
■ tabernacle T-1

**Lorelei** [*lôr'ĕ-lī*], fabled Rhine siren; legend probably from an echoing rock of that name on the Rhine; in poem by Heine and other literature, also Mendelssohn and Lachner operas
■ rock, *picture* G-99

**Lorentz, Hendrik Antoon** (1853–1928), Dutch physicist, born Arnhem, Netherlands; sought consistent theory for magnetism, electricity, and light; explained the Zeeman effect
■ contraction of matter R-140, 141
■ Nobel prize, *table* N-294a

**Lorentz, Pare** (born 1905), motion picture producer and director, born Clarksburg, W. Va.; chief of films section U.S. War Department, Civil Affairs Division, 1946: M-529, *picture* W-122

**Lorenz** [*lō'rĕnts*], **Adolf** (1854–1946), Austrian orthopedic surgeon; devised bloodless operation (forcible manipulation) for congenital dislocation of hip joint; also operation for clubfoot.

**Lorenz, Konrad Zacharias** (born 1903), Austrian naturalist, born Vienna; noted for study of wild animal behavior; head of Max Planck Institute 1961–
■ Nobel prize, *table* N-294e

**Lorenzetti** [*lō-rān-tsāt'tē*], **Ambrogio** (active 1319–48), and **Pietro** (active 1305–48), two Sienese painters, brothers; noted chiefly for religious frescoes; Ambrogio was most gifted, and in vigorous, colorful, and naturalistic works showed influence of Giotto; he painted a series of allegories representing good and bad government.

**Lorenzo, Saint.** *see in index* Lawrence, Saint

**Lorenzo de' Medici** [*lō-rent'sō dā mā'dē-chē*], or **Lorenzo the Magnificent,** (1449–92), Florentine statesman and patron of arts M-211, F-230 L-231, *picture* M-211
■ Michelangelo M-264, S-87

**Lorenzo de' Medici** (1492–1519), duke of Urbino, grandson of Lorenzo the Magnificent, father of Catherine; succeeded as ruler of Florence when uncle, Giovanni, became Pope Leo X.

**Lorenzo Monaco** (1370?–1425), Italian painter A-415

**Loretto Heights College,** at Denver, Colo.; private control, Catholic related; opened 1918; arts and sciences, nursing, teacher education.

**Lorgnette** [*lôr-nyĕt'*], eyeglass S-370

**Loricata.** *see in index* Crocodilia

**Lorient** [*lô-ryäṅ'*], France, fortified naval port in n.w. on Bay of Biscay at junction of Scorff and Blavet rivers; pop. 66,023; fisheries: *maps* F-404, W-277

**Lorimer, George Horace** (1868–1937), editor, born Louisville, Ky.; editor in chief of *Saturday Evening Post,* 1899–1936; popular books on success ('Letters from a Self-Made Merchant to His Son').

**Loring, Eugene,** real name LeRoy Kerpestein (born 1914), dancer and choreographer, born Milwaukee, Wis.; danced with Fokine's ballet, Ballet Caravan, Ballet Theatre; formed own company, Dance Players, in New York City, 1941; created ballet 'Billy the Kid'.

**Loris,** a species of short-tailed lemur; round-eyed with soft fur, poorly formed index fingers; slender type, smaller than squirrel, inhabits forest regions of Sri Lanka and s. India; slow, heavy kind found in other Indo-Malay areas.

**'Lorna Doone'** [*dọn*], novel by Richard Doddridge Blackmore which made the Exmoor country famous; the heroine is an heiress kidnaped by outlaws and brought up in their fortress B-306

**Lorne, marquis of.** *see in index* Argyll, duke of

**Lorne, Firth of,** inlet of Atlantic, w. coast of Scotland; terminus of Caledonian Canal: *maps* G-199g

**Lorrain** [*lô-răṅ'*], **Claude,** real name Claude Gelée or Gellée [*zhĕ-lā'*] (1600–1682), French landscape painter, born Lorraine; influenced by Italian Renaissance and classical art.

**Lorraine** [*lō-rān'*], district of n.e. France (also called Lotharingia and Lothringen) F-389. *see also in index* Alsace-Lorraine
■ Charles the Bold invades C-218
■ iron and steel mill, *picture* F-388

**Lorraine, House of** A-830

**Lory,** also **lorikeet,** any of a large group of parrots, chief genera *Domicella, Lorius, Trichoglossus, Chalcopsitta,* and *Eos;* distinguished from other parrots by its brushlike tongue with which it extracts nectar from flowers; chiefly in Australia and New Guinea.

**Los Alamos,** N.M., in Los Alamos County, 24 mi (39 km) n.w. of Santa Fe; pop. 11,310; nuclear research and development center; atomic bomb designed and tested in laboratories in this area: N-212, 210, *maps* N-220, U-40

**Los Altos,** Calif., city in Santa Clara County 27 mi (43 km) s.e. of San Francisco; pop. 25,769; chiefly residential, incorporated 1952: *map, inset* C-52

**Los Angeles, Victoria de,** real name Victoria Gamez Cima (born 1923), Spanish lyric soprano, born Barcelona; appeared in leading opera theaters of world; French, Italian, and German roles.

**Los Angeles,** Calif., largest city on Pacific coast; pop. 2,966,850: L-350–7, *maps* L-352–3, C-33, 42, U-40, *inset* C-53, *pictures* L-350–1, 354–7
■ airports L-357, *list* L-354, *map* L-352–3
■ black youth revolts B-297
■ Civic Center L-355, *map, inset* L-352, *picture* L-350
■ climate, *list* L-351: climatic region, *map* U-119; smog P-441b; temperature and precipitation, *graph* U-119
■ district laboratory, *picture* H-96
■ earthquake E-32
■ education L-356, *list* L-354, *map* L-352–3
■ fire department, cost of F-139
■ fisheries L-355, C-39
■ furniture market F-484
■ government L-356, 355; buildings, *map, inset* L-352
■ harbor L-354–5, L-345, *picture* L-355
■ highways and streets L-355, *map* L-352–3: freeways L-355, *pictures* L-351, C-36
■ history L-356–7, *picture* L-356
■ industries L-351, 354–5, *lists* L-351, 354: ceramics P-477
■ libraries, *list* L-354, *map* L-353
■ location L-350–1, *locator map* L-350
■ motion pictures M-520, L-351: Grauman's Chinese Theater, *picture* L-355; studios, *list* L-354
■ museum, *list* L-354, *map* L-353
■ parks L-356, *list* L-354, *map* L-352–3
■ people L-355
■ places of business, of culture, and of interest, *list* L-354, *map* L-352–3
■ population L-355, *list* L-351
■ rapid growth L-351, 357, *graphs* G-187
■ Spanish Americans H-251
■ trade, *list* L-351
■ water supply, aqueducts L-357, C-35
■ Watts riot U-196, K-55
■ zoo, *map* L-353: tarpan, *picture* H-232e

**Los Angeles Music Center for the Performing Arts** L-356, *picture* C-46

**Los Gatos,** Calif., town 8 mi (13 km) s.w. of San Jose; pop. 29,593; chiefly residential; service industries; incorporated 1887: *map* C-53

**Losing checkers,** game B-322

**Lossing, Benson John** (1813–91), historical writer, editor, illustrator, born Beekman, N.Y.; his 'Pictorial Field-Book of the Revolution' a pioneer historical work.

**"Lost Battalion, The,"** 554 men in World War I from the 77th (New York) Division, who were not lost, but cut off during advance and surrounded by enemy Oct. 2–7, 1918, during Meuse-Argonne battle; under command of Maj. Charles W. Whittlesey, troops refused to surrender in spite of repeated attacks, lack of food, extreme cold, and mistakenly placed artillery barrage from own army; only 194 were rescued
■ Meuse-Argonne battle M-237
■ pigeon takes message P-324

**Lost Colony of Virginia,** English colony in what is now North Carolina which disappeared in 1591; the Croatan Indians in North Carolina claim to be descendants of an Indian tribe which these colonists joined; they intermarried with its members; thus an explanation is given for the mixed blood and occasional English names of the Croatans: N-327
■ carving "Croatoan," *picture* N-329
■ pageant by Paul Eliot Green P-20
■ symphonic drama, *picture* N-332

**Lost Dauphin** L-361, *pictures* L-361, F-443

**"Lost generation"** F-181

**Lost Ten Tribes,** ten of twelve tribes of United Kingdom of Israel which seceded to form separate kingdom of Israel: J-456–7

**Lost-wax process,** in casting metals S-81

**Lota** [*lō'tä*], Chile, mining town and seaport about 30 km (20 mi) s. of Concepción; pop. 51,548; coal shipping, copper smelting; Cousiño Park nearby, noted for worldwide collection of plants.

**Lothair I** (795–855), Holy Roman emperor, grandson of Charlemagne; became joint ruler 817 when Louis I, his father, divided the empire among his sons; after years of strife with his brothers received Italy and imperial title together with lands along Rhine and Rhone rivers (Partition of Verdun, 843) A-320
■ land, *map* F-400

**Lothair II,** sometimes called Lothair III (1070?–1137), Holy Roman emperor 1133–37; created duke of Saxony 1106, and elected German king 1125; his reign was regarded as a golden age for Germany.

**Lothair II** (825–869), king of Lorraine, son of Lothair I; received as his kingdom district w. of Rhine between North Sea and Jura Mts., called after him Lotharingia or Lorraine (German *Lothringen*)
■ medallion, *picture* J-450

**Lotharingia,** France. *see in index* Lorraine

**Lothian, Philip Henry Kerr,** 11th **marquis of** (1882–1940), British statesman; member of Liberal party; secretary of prime minister Lloyd George 1916–22; undersecretary of state for India 1931–32; ambassador to U.S. 1939–40.

**Lothringen,** France. *see in index* Lorraine

**Loti** [*lō-tē'*], **Pierre,** pen name of Louis Marie Julien Viaud [*vē-yō'*] (1850–1923), French naval officer and novelist, born Rochefort, France
■ chief works F-440

**Lötschberg Tunnel,** in Switzerland, *table* T-292

**Lottery,** draft C-536, *picture* C-535
■ World War I, *pictures* W-260, W-174

**Lottery,** gambling scheme in which a sum of money is paid for the chance of drawing a prize of greater value than the amount invested; state-sponsored lottery in New Hampshire, first in any state since 1894, adopted 1963.

**Lotus,** plant L-357, W-73d, *picture* L-357
■ Egyptian hieroglyphics N-379
■ sacred flower L-357, F-271
■ used for food F-259, L-357

**Lotus eaters** L-357
■ Odysseus' men O-406

**Lotze** [*lōt'sĕ*], **Rudolf Hermann** (1817–81), German philosopher, born Bautzen, Saxony; assumed that the orderly functioning of nature implied a motivating, ideal principle; helped to develop physiological psychology.

**Loubet** [*lọ-bĕ'*], **Émile** (1838–1929), French statesman, born Marsanne, near Montélimar, France; 7th president of Third Republic 1899–1906; remitted Alfred Dreyfus' sentence.

**Loucks, Henry Langford** (1846–1928), American farmer and political leader, born Hull, Que., Canada; settled 1884 on homestead in Deuel County, Dakota Territory; founder of *Dakota Ruralist;* president National Farmers' Alliance 1892, leader of successful fight for initiative and referendum in South Dakota.

**Loudness,** of sound S-260, P-441e
■ noise meter, *picture* P-441e

**Loudspeaker**
■ phonograph P-269–70, *diagram* P-268d
■ radio, *diagram* R-47: symbol for, *diagram* R-56

**Lough** [*lŏκ*], Irish name for lake. *see in index* lakes by name, as Neagh, Lough

**Lougheed, Peter** (born 1928), Canadian public official and lawyer, born Calgary, Alta.; member Legislative Assembly, Calgary West, 1967–72; premier of Alberta 1972–.

**Louis, Saint.** *see in index* Louis IX

**Louis I** [*lü' ē*], Holy Roman emperor. *see in index* Louis I, the Pious, king of France

**Louis II** (827–75), Holy Roman emperor (crowned 850) and king of Italy (came to throne 839), son of Lothair I; fought Saracens and restored order in Italy.

**Louis III, the Blind** (880?–928), Holy Roman emperor (crowned 901) and king of the Lombards (chosen 900), grandson of Louis II; his eyes were put out 905 by Berengar, rival king of the Lombards; exiled to Provence.

**Louis IV, the Bavarian** (about 1287–1347), Holy Roman emperor (crowned 1328) and king of Germany (elected 1314); despite his being almost constantly at war, first with his brother over Bavaria, then with the pope over Germany, Louis enlarged his domains, and fostered trade and learning.

**Louis,** kings of Bavaria. *see in index* Ludwig

**Louis II, the German** (804–76), king of East Franks; 3d son of Louis the Pious and grandson of Charlemagne; his share of Charlemagne's empire after Partition of Verdun (843) formed nucleus of modern Germany: *map* F-400

**Louis I, the Pious** (778–840), king of France and Holy Roman emperor, youngest son of Charlemagne whom he succeeded: L-358, A-411, C-210

**Louis VI, the Fat** (1081–1137), king of France L-358
■ flag, *picture* F-401

**Louis VII** (1120–80), king of France L-358
■ fleur-de-lis emblem F-395, I-290, *picture* F-395
■ Second Crusade C-616

**Louis VIII** (1187–1226), king of France L-358

**Louis IX,** or **Saint Louis** (1214–70), king of France; canonized in 1297; festival August 25: L-358–9, *picture* L-358
■ builds Sainte Chapelle P-122
■ in Crusades C-618

**Louis X** (1289–1316), king of France, son of Philip IV; ruled 1314–16; nicknamed "the Quarreler"; inherited kingdom of Navarre from mother Joan 1305; resigned to succeed his father to French throne.

**Louis XI** (1423–83), king of France L-359, *picture* L-359
■ Charles the Bold opposes C-218
■ library L-231
■ Plessis-les-Tours built by, *picture* F-380
■ silk industry started T-140

**Louis XII** (1462–1515), king of France L-359

**Louis XIII** (1601–43), king of France L-359
■ dueling in reign S-546–7
■ Richelieu R-203–4, *picture* R-203

**Louis XIV** (1638–1715), king of France L-359–60, *picture* L-360
■ architecture A-557
■ button adornment B-528
■ Cadillac in New France C-10
■ Canal du Midi C-119
■ Colbert aids C-431
■ court etiquette E-300
■ dance promoted by B-33, D-24
■ engraving of period E-279
■ French Bourbons B-384
■ furniture of period I-227
■ Gobelin tapestries T-20
■ James II aided by J-360
■ La Salle explores the Mississippi L-129, *map* L-129
■ Man in the Iron Mask. *see in index* Iron Mask, Man in the
■ Marquise de Maintenon M-67
■ marriage V-272
■ rivalry with English in fur trade F-496
■ Versailles palace V-303
■ wars L-359–60: Leopold I, emperor L-196a; Marlborough M-112; Spanish Succession A-829; William III W-164–5, N-139, C-1, K-58
■ wigs originated in his reign H-47

**Louis XV** (1710–74), king of France L-360
■ builds Petit Trianon V-303
■ furniture of period I-227, *picture* I-232
■ Voltaire and V-385

**Louis XVI** (1754–93), king of France L-360–1, F-442, 443–4, *picture* F-443
■ American Colonies, aid for F-427
■ calls Estates-General E-291, F-442
■ French fashions D-192
■ furniture of period I-227
■ Marie Antoinette. *see in index* Marie Antoinette
■ Mirabeau M-369
■ popularizes potato P-467
■ Robespierre demands death R-223

**Louis XVII** (1785–95?), the lost dauphin L-361, *pictures* L-361, F-443

**Louis XVIII** (1755–1824), king of France L-361
■ Talleyrand T-13

**Louis I** (1838–89), king of Portugal, born Lisbon; came to throne 1861; abolished slavery in Portuguese colonies; promoted literature, translated Shakespeare and works from French.

**Louis II** (1870–1949), prince of Monaco, born Baden-Baden, Germany; succeeded to throne of principality of Monaco 1922; son of Albert I; served in French army with rank of major general.

**Louis** [*lü'ĭs*], **Joe** (Joseph Louis Barrow) (1914–81), boxer, born near Lafayette, Ala.
■ burial at Arlington National Cemetery N-21
■ heavyweight champion B-392, *table* B-391

**Louisbourg, Fortress of,** on Cape Breton Island, N.S., Canada C-106
■ captured 1745 by American colonists K-57, C-106
■ captured 1758 by British N-373g: Wolfe at W-211
■ national historic park N-24c, N-373e, C-130, *map, inset* N-24b, *pictures* N-373f, N-24c

**Louise** (1776–1810), queen of Frederick William III of Prussia, born at Hanover; her beauty and goodness and the fortitude with which she bore the hardships of the Napoleonic Wars made her a popular heroine.

**Louise, Lake,** Alberta, Canada, in Canadian Rocky Mountains, *picture* C-82

**Louis-Hippolyte Lafontaine bridge-tunnel complex** T-291, 293, M-476a

**Louisiade** [*lụ-ē-zē-äd'*] **Archipelago,** group of islands off s.e. coast of New Guinea, belonging to Papua New Guinea; pop. 11,451: *maps* E-37, P-4

**Louisiana** [*lụ-ē-zē-ăn'ạ*], a gulf state of the U.S.; 48,523 sq mi (125,674 sq km); pop. 4,203,972; cap. Baton Rouge: L-362–82, *Fact Summary* L-375–8, *maps* L-380–1, 364, 368, 375, U-41, 58, *pictures* L-362–3, 365–7, 369–74
■ agriculture L-364–5, 376, 363, 370, *charts* L-376, *map* L-368, *picture* L-365
■ bibliography L-378
■ bird, state, brown pelican P-156, P-441d, *pictures* P-155, L-370
■ Capitol, State, *picture* L-371: former, *picture* L-371
■ cities L-364, 378, *map index* L-379, 382, *see also in index* cities listed below and other cities by name
□ New Orleans N-223–6, *pictures* N-223–223a, 224–6
□ Shreveport S-185
■ climate L-363, *list* L-362
■ communication L-377
■ conservation L-363–4, *picture* L-372
■ education L-366–7, 375, 370, *picture* L-371
■ elevation L-363, *list* L-362, *map* L-375
■ employment, *chart* L-377
■ extent L-363, *list* L-362, *map* L-375
■ fisheries L-365, 376, *chart* L-376, *map* L-368
■ flags F-194, *picture* F-195: French (1803) F-188a
■ flower, state, magnolia M-49b, *pictures* L-370, F-265, S-427
■ forests L-363, 364, 376, *chart* L-376, *map* L-368
■ furs L-365, *picture* L-366
■ geographic center, *list* L-362, *map* L-375
■ geographic region: South, the U-56–67, *map* U-58–9, *pictures* U-56–7, 60, 64, *Reference-Outline* U-133–4
■ government L-367, 375
□ elections L-367, 375
■ harbors and ports N-223–223a, H-24, *pictures* N-223–223a
■ history L-367–8, 364, 365–6, 369, N-225–6, *pictures* L-367, 369
□ Cadillac governs C-10
□ Civil War C-509, F-64, L-368, *map* C-376
□ La Salle claims L-129, *pictures* L-128, L-369
□ New Orleans founded N-225
□ Reconstruction R-114, 116, N-226, L-368, *picture* R-115
□ United States purchases L-383
□ War of 1812. *see in index* New Orleans, battle of
■ industries L-364, 362, *charts* L-376, *map* L-368, *pictures* L-365–6: sugar L-364–5
■ land use, *list* L-362, *map* L-368
■ laws L-362
■ levees M-390, L-363
■ libraries L-375: New Orleans, *picture* N-225
■ location L-362, 363, *locator map* L-362
■ minerals L-365, *charts* L-376, *map* L-368
□ petroleum P-230–1, *picture* P-234
□ salt S-30
□ sulfur S-509
■ motto L-370
■ name L-363
■ natural regions L-363, map L-364
■ natural resources L-363, 365, 376, *charts* L-376, *map* L-368, *pictures* L-366
■ parishes L-375, *map index* L-379
■ parks and other areas L-378, *pictures* L-371–2: Chalmette N.H.P. N-33, L-366, *maps* N-30, N-223b, *picture* L-372; Longfellow-Evangeline State Park, *picture* L-367
■ people L-364: famous L-368, *pictures* L-374
■ places of interest L-378
■ population L-364, 368, *chart* L-375, *list* L-362
■ products L-364–5, *charts* L-376, *map* L-368, *pictures* L-365–6
■ profile L-370–4, *pictures* L-370–4
■ recreation L-366, *pictures* L-372–3
■ rivers L-363, *maps* L-364, 380–1: Mississippi M-389–92, *picture* L-372
■ seal, state, *picture* L-370
■ song, state L-370
■ special days F-92, 93, 94, 95
■ Statuary Hall, *table* S-437a
■ trade L-376
■ transportation L-365–6, 377: roads L-366, 377, *map* L-380–1. *see also in index* New Orleans, *subhead* bridges
■ tree, state, bald cypress C-634, *pictures* L-370, P-357
■ waterways L-363, 365, N-223a, 226

**Louisiana College,** at Pineville, La.; affiliated with Southern Baptist convention; established in 1906; arts and sciences, education, and professional studies.

**Louisiana Purchase** L-383, *map* U-177
■ completion, *picture* U-175
■ effect on New Spain S-339, N-225
■ Lewis and Clark Expedition L-202–3, *map* L-203, *picture* L-203
■ Monroe negotiates M-456, *picture* J-433

**Louisiana Purchase Exposition,** at St. Louis, Mo., from April 30 to Dec. 1, 1904; recorded admissions were 19,694,855; amusements on the "Pike"; 500 buildings; floral clock with 50-ft (15-m) hands: S-22, T-43

**Louisiana State University,** since 1976 **Louisiana State University and Agricultural and Mechanical College,** at Baton Rouge, La.; opened 1860; arts and sciences, agriculture, business administration, chemistry and physics, education, engineering, environmental design, law, library, music, social welfare, veterinary medicine, and graduate studies; four-year branches at Shreveport and New Orleans (University of New Orleans); Louisiana State Medical Center also at New Orleans; two-year branches at Alexandria and Eunice: L-366, B-106
■ War Memorial Tower, *picture* L-371

**Louisiana Tech University,** at Ruston, La.; state control; founded 1894; formerly called Louisiana Polytechnic Institute; arts and sciences, agriculture and forestry, business administration, education, engineering, home economics; graduate studies; quarter system.

**Louis Napoleon.** *see in index* Napoleon III

**Louis Philippe** [*lụ-ē' fē-lēp'*] (1773–1850), "citizen-king" of France L-361, B-384
■ daughter marries Leopold I L-196b
■ Paris, improvements P-123

**Louis style,** name of various periods of furniture I-227–8, *picture* I-232, *table* I-226

**Louisville,** Ga., city on Ogeechee R. 40 mi (60 km) s.w. of Augusta; pop. 2823; capital of Georgia 1796–1805
■ Old Market, *picture* G-83
■ temperature, *list* G-77

**Louisville,** Ky., largest city of state on Ohio River; pop. 298,840: L-383–4, *picture* K-35, *maps* K-40, 28, 32, U-41
■ Bluegrass Music Festival F-91
■ Churchill Downs, *pictures* K-27, 33
■ City Hall, *picture* K-28
■ climate, *list* K-26
■ dam D-7
■ Sherman Minton Bridge, *picture* L-383

**Louisville, University of,** at Louisville, Ky.; state control; founded 1798; arts and sciences, business, dentistry, education, law, medicine, music, police administration, science, and social work; graduate school: L-384

**Louisville and Portland Canal** L-383, *map* C-118

**Lounsbury, Thomas Raynesford** (1838–1915), scholar, born Ovid, N.Y.; professor English language and literature, Sheffield Scientific School of Yale University, for more than 30 years; distinguished for his studies in development of English language ('History of the English Language'; 'Studies in Chaucer'; 'The Text of Shakespeare').

**Lourdes** [*lụrd*], France, town 132 km (82 mi) s.w. of Toulouse; pop. 17,627: L-384, F-386, *map* F-405
■ location L-384, *locator map* L-384

**Lourenço Marques,** Mozambique. *see in index* Maputo

**Louse,** a wingless blood-sucking insect of the order *Siphunculata* (also called *Anoplura*); eggs are called nits: I-208
■ bird, or biting P-114, *picture* I-200
■ body, or sucking P-114, *pictures* P-115, I-200
■ crab, V-274, *picture* P-115
■ egg (head louse), *picture* E-106
■ leg, *picture* I-197
■ plant. *see in index* Aphids
■ vaccine source V-251

**Louse fly,** name for flies of family *Hippoboscidae* that spend adult lives like lice as parasites; some adults wingless, notably the sheep tick (*Melophagus ovinus*); others winged (*Lynchia americana,* which infests owls); still others lose wings during parasitic life (*Lipoptena depressa,* which preys on deer): F-281

**Lousma, Jack R.** (born 1936), astronaut, born Grand Rapids, Mich.; U.S. Marine Corps officer selected for NASA program 1966; member Skylab 1973: *table* S-348

**Louth** [*louth*], agricultural and fishing county in Leinster Province, n.e. Ireland; 821 sq km (317 sq mi) (smallest county in Ireland); pop. 69,519; county seat Dundalk: *map* I-283

**Louvain** [*lụ-văn'*], Flemish **Leuven,** Belgium, city in center; pop. 32,524: L-385
■ bells production B-156
■ location L-385, *locator map* L-385

**L'Ouverture, Pierre Dominique Toussaint.** *see in index* Toussaint L'Ouverture

**Louvois** [*lụ-vwä'*], **François Michel Le Tellier, marquis de** (1641–91), French statesman, born Paris; Louis XIV's war minister who wasted prosperity of France and destroyed peace of Europe for military "glory."

**Louvre** [*lụ'vr'*], art museum in Paris, France P-121, *map* P-120, *picture* E-324
■ art treasures
□ Cimabue: 'Madonna of the Angels, The' P-28–9, *picture* P-29
□ Goujon: 'Fountain of the Nymphs', *picture* S-89
□ Hals: 'Gypsy Girl, The', P-43, *picture* P-43
□ Holbein portraits: 'Anne of Cleves' P-39, *picture* P-39; Erasmus H-201, *picture* R-148; Kratzer, Nicholas, *picture* H-201
□ Michelangelo: 'Bound Slave', *picture* S-86
□ Sumerian sculpture, *picture* S-81
□ 'Venus de Milo' G-229
□ Vinci, da: 'Madonna of the Rocks', *picture* V-326; 'Mona Lisa' P-37, V-326, *picture* P-36
□ 'Winged Victory', or 'Nike', of Samothrace S-83, G-230, *picture* S-83

**Louÿs** [*lwē*], **Pierre,** real name Pierre Louis (1870–1925), French poet and novelist, born Ghent, Belgium; competent translator, fooled experts with original poems represented as Greek works ('Chanson de Bilitis'): F-440

**Love, John Arthur** (born 1916), public official, born Gibson City, Ill.; governor of Colorado 1962–73; director U.S. Energy Policy Office 1973.

**Love**
■ child development C-280, 277, 270
■ love stories, *pictures* L-305–6
■ motivating force E-198

**Lovebird** P-135

**Love-in-a-mist,** a flower. *see in index* Nigella

**'Love in a Police Station',** motion picture, *picture* M-522

**Lovejoy, Elijah Parish** (1802–37), abolitionist, born Albion, Me.; editor of an antislavery paper which was published in Alton, Ill.; killed by mob while trying to save his

press. His brother **Owen Lovejoy** (1811–64) carried on antislavery movement in Illinois and as member of Congress 1857–64; an early supporter of Abraham Lincoln
■ Beecher family influenced by B-131
■ Phillips condemns murder P-263

**Lovelace, Maud Hart** (born 1892), author, born Mankato, Minn.; known for Betsy-Tacy series of books for girls, also for 'The Tune Is in the Tree', 'The Trees Kneel at Christmas', and 'Early Candlelight'.

**Lovelace, Richard** (1618–58), English Cavalier poet, born London; immortalized by two lyrics ('To Lucasta, on Going to the Wars'; 'To Althea, from Prison').

**Loveland,** Colo., city 12 mi (19 km) s. of Fort Collins; pop. 30,244; in farm area; electronic instruments; entrance to Rocky Mountain National Park; incorporated 1881: *map* C-467

**Love-lies-bleeding,** a hardy annual garden herb (*Amaranthus caudatus*) with clusters of dark purplish flowers; native to the tropics.

**Lovell, James Arthur, Jr.** (born 1928), business executive, former astronaut, born Cleveland, Ohio; U.S. Navy officer selected for NASA program 1962; resigned from Navy and space program 1973: S-346f, 347, *table* S-348

**Lovely fir.** *see in index* Silver fir

**Loveman, Robert** (1864–1923), poet, born Cleveland, Ohio; lived much of life in South; wrote poems of nature ('Songs from a Georgia Garden'; 'On the Way to Willowdale').

**'Love of the Three Kings, The'.** *see in index* 'Amore dei Tre Re, L' '.

**Lover, Samuel** (1797–1868), Irish novelist and poet, born Dublin; tendency to caricature Irish life; author of 'Handy Andy', a roaring farce; 'Rory O'More', equally popular as novel and play.

**'Love's Labour's Lost',** comedy by Shakespeare, written about 1591, in which princess of France and her three ladies cause King Ferdinand of Navarre and his three friends to break vows
■ chronology of play S-133
■ rank of play S-139

**'Love Song of J. Alfred Prufrock, The',** poem by T. S. Eliot A-355, W-310b

**Loves Park,** Ill., city 4 mi (6 km) n.w. of Rockford; pop. 13,192; machine tools; incorporated 1947: *map* I-50

**Lovett, Robert Abercrombie** (born 1895), banker and public official, born Huntsville, Tex.; special assistant to secretary of war 1940–41; assistant secretary of war for air 1941–45; undersecretary of state 1947–49; assistant secretary of defense 1950–51; secretary of defense 1951–53.

**Lovett, Robert Morss** (1870–1956), educator and writer, born Boston, Mass.; professor of English, University of Chicago 1909–36; government secretary of Virgin Islands 1939–43 ('A History of English Literature', with W. V. Moody; 'Richard Gresham' and 'A Winged Victory', novels; 'Cowards', play).

**Lovington,** N.M., town near Texas border 20 mi (30 km) n.w. of Hobbs; pop. 9727; grain, cotton, cattle; in oil-producing region; founded 1908: *map* N-221

**Low, Archibald Montgomery** (1888–1956), British engineer and writer, born Purley, near London; invented system of radio signaling, television system, and radio controls for torpedoes and rockets.

**Low, Sir David** (1891–1963), British cartoonist, born Dunedin, New Zealand; created Colonel Blimp as a symbol of stupidity: political cartoonist *Manchester Guardian* 1953–63; autobiography and cartoons.

**Low, Juliette Gordon** (1860–1927), founder of Girl Scout movement in the U.S.: L-385, *picture* G-90
■ birthplace, *pictures* G-130, G-89
■ Girl Scouts G-129

**Low, Seth** (1850–1916), merchant, educator, and administrator, born Brooklyn, N.Y.; mayor of Brooklyn 1882–86 (enforced first municipal civil-service rules adopted in America); president Columbia University 1890–1901; mayor of Greater New York 1901–3.

**Low, Will Hicok** (1853–1932), decorative painter, designer of stained glass, and illustrator, born Albany, N.Y. (illustrations for Keats's 'Lamia'; frieze in legislative library, New York State Capitol).

**Low,** or **low atmospheric pressure center** W-84, *map* W-86–7

**Low Archipelago,** in s. Pacific. *see in index* Tuamotu

**Lowboy,** a piece of furniture
■ Queen Anne, *picture* I-227

**Low Countries,** name applied to a region in Europe comprising Belgium, Luxemburg, and the Netherlands. *see in index* Belgium; Luxemburg; Netherlands

**Lowden** [*lou'd'n*], **Frank O(rren)** (1861–1943), lawyer and political leader, born Sunrise City, Minn.; from poor farm boy became successful lawyer, notable congressman; governor of Illinois 1917–21; also farmer who promoted cooperative marketing.

**Lowe, Sir Hudson** (1769–1844), English general, born Galway, Ireland; fought in Napoleonic Wars; custodian of Napoleon I on St. Helena.

**Lowe, Thaddeus Sobieski Coulincourt** (1832–1913), aeronaut and inventor, born Jefferson Mills, now Riverton, N.H.; as chief of aeronautic section of U.S. Army used balloons for observation in Civil War.

**Lowell, Abbott Lawrence** (1856–1943), educator and political scientist, born Boston, Mass.; brother of Amy and Percival Lowell; president of Harvard University 1909–33; developed social life among students through freshman dormitories ('The Government of England'; 'Governments and Parties in Continental Europe'; 'Conflicts of Principle').

**Lowell, Amy** (1874–1925), American poet and critic L-385

**Lowell, Francis Cabot** (1775–1817), Boston merchant, founder of U.S. cotton manufacturing industry, born Newburyport, Mass.; son of John Lowell: T-135
■ Lowell, Mass. L-386

**Lowell, James Russell** (1819–91), American poet, essayist, and critic L-385–6, A-348, *picture* L-385
■ abolitionist writings C-373
■ Cambridge home C-56b
■ Hall of Fame, *table* H-11

**Lowell, John** (1743–1802), American jurist, born Newburyport, Mass.; said to have been author of clause in Massachusetts state constitution declaring "all men are born free and equal"; this clause was interpreted in 1783 by the Supreme Court of state to mean that slavery was abolished; father of Francis Cabot Lowell and grandfather of James Russell Lowell.

**Lowell, Percival** (1855–1916), astronomer, born Boston, Mass.; brother of Amy and Abbott L. Lowell; established Lowell Observatory 1894 near Flagstaff, Ariz.; discovery here of planet Pluto in 1930 direct result of his mathematical prediction ('The Genesis of Planets'): A-714

**Lowell, Robert (Traill Spence, Jr.)** (1917–77), poet, born Boston, Mass.; great-grandnephew of James Russell Lowell; awarded Pulitzer prize 1947 for 'Lord Weary's Castle' ('For the Union Dead'; 'Near the Ocean'; 'Notebook 1967–68'): A-364

**Lowell,** Mass., one of the oldest industrial cities of the United States; pop. 92,418: L-386, *maps* M-145, 161, 152, U-41
■ carpet industry R-316
■ location, *locator map* L-386

**Lowell, University of,** at Lowell, Mass.; state control; established 1975 by merger of Lowell State College and Lowell Technological Institute; arts and sciences, education, engineering and technology, music, nursing.

**Lowell Observatory,** Flagstaff, Ariz. A-601, 604, *picture* A-605
■ Saturn photograph, *picture* S-52

**Lowell State College,** at Lowell, Mass.; chartered 1894. *see also in index* Lowell, University of

**Lowell Technological Institute,** at Lowell, Mass.; state control; established 1895. *see also in index* Lowell, University of

**Lower Austria,** a province in n.e. Austria; area 19,171 sq km (7402 sq mi); pop. 1,374,012; wooded hill country; capital Vienna; ruled by Hapsburgs until 1918.

**Lower Burrell,** Pa., city of Westmoreland county 16 mi (26 km) n.e. of Pittsburgh; in coal-mining area; pop. 13,200; incorporated 1958: *map* P-184

**Lower California,** Mexico. *see in index* California, Lower

**Lower Canada,** name formerly given to province of Quebec C-108, 112, Q-9g, O-456g, *map* C-112a

**Lowercase letters,** or **small letters** B-356, T-316, 317, *pictures* T-317

**Lower Egypt,** that part of Egypt north of 30° N. latitude E-108

**Lower Fort Garry National Historic Park,** in Manitoba, Canada M-89f, N-24d, *map* N-24b

**Lower house,** in national legislatures P-130
■ Commons, House of
□ Canada P-132, C-86, F-75b
□ Great Britain. *see in index* Commons, House of, British
■ Representatives, House of
□ Australia P-131
□ Japan J-376, 377, 407, *table* J-378
□ New Zealand N-277a
□ United States. *see in index* Representatives, House of, United States

**Lower Merion,** Pa., urban township on Schuylkill River just w. of Philadelphia; pop. 63,392; consists of 13 unincorporated communities.

**Lower Saxony,** German **Niedersachsen** [*nē'dĕr-zäk-sĕn*], state in West Germany, former state in British zone, Germany: *maps* G-114, 109, *table* G-109

**Lower Silesia,** former province of Germany. *see in index* Silesia

**Lower Southampton,** Pa., urban township situated in Bucks County just n.e. of Philadelphia; pop. 17,578; largely residential.

**Lowes, John Livingston** (1867–1945), educator and author, born Decatur, Ind.; professor of English literature Harvard University 1918–39; noted for critical works on Chaucer, Shakespeare, Coleridge ('The Road to Xanadu'; 'Art of Geoffrey Chaucer'; 'Essays in Appreciation').

**Lowestoft** [*lōz'tŏft*], England, seaport and resort of Suffolk, 180 km (110 mi) n.e. of London; pop. 50,730; fisheries; captured by Cromwell 1643; Dutch fleet defeated by duke of York 1665: *map* G-199h
■ porcelain P-476

**Low-fat milk** M-323, *table* M-322

**Low German,** dialect G-96, G-96a

**Lowlands,** Alberta, Canada A-262

**Lowlands,** in England E-219, *map* E-219

**Lowlands,** of central Scotland S-67, *map* S-67, *picture* S-68

**Low latitudes** C-392–3, L-159, *diagram* L-159

**Lownsbery, Eloise** (1888–1967), writer, born Pawpaw, Ill.; brings medieval history to life in her books for boys and girls ('Boy Knight of Reims'; 'Out of the Flame'; 'Marta the Doll').

**Low-pressure belt,** in meteorology W-83, 84, E-21

**Low relief,** or **bas-relief** [*bär-ĭ-lēf'*], in sculpture S-80, *picture* P-264

**Lowry, Malcolm** (1909–57), Canadian novelist, poet, and traveler, born Cheshire County, England: C-116

**Low wave,** *tables* R-34, R-50

**Lox.** *see in index* Liquid oxygen

**Loyalist,** or **Tory,** in American Colonies R-167, P-432, *picture* R-166
■ after Revolution R-174, C-107–8, *picture* C-108. *see also in index* United Empire Loyalists

**Loyalists, United Empire.** *see in index* United Empire Loyalists

**Loyal Legion, Military Order of the,** patriotic society founded 1865 at Philadelphia, Pa., on the day following Lincoln's assassination; organized by U.S. Army and Navy officers; membership limited to such officers and their direct male descendants; purposes: fellowship among and welfare of U.S. soldiers and sailors, care of widows and orphans of deceased members.

**Loyal Order of Moose.** *see in index* Moose, Loyal Order of

**Loyalty,** to one's country. *see in index* Patriotism

**Loyalty Day** (May 1), designated by Congress in 1958 to reaffirm loyalty to the United States and to acknowledge the heritage of American freedom.

**Loyalty Islands,** French **Îles Loyauté,** Pacific group 100 km (60 mi) e. of New Caledonia, of which it is a dependency; 2072 sq km (800 sq mi); pop. 13,378; copra, rubber: *map* P-4

**Loyang,** People's Republic of China, city in Honan Province 100 mi (160 km) w. of Kaifeng; pop. 580,000; farming, stock raising; trucks, cement, textiles: C-293b, *map* C-313, *picture* C-293b

**Loyola** [*loi-ō'lă*], **Saint Ignatius of** (1491–1556), founder of Jesuit Order; festival July 31: L-386–7, *pictures* L-386, R-134
■ Counter Reformation R-135, L-387
■ influence on Francis Xavier X-329

**Loyola College,** at Baltimore, Md.; Roman Catholic; established in 1852; arts and sciences, business administration, and teacher education; graduate division.

**Loyola Marymount University,** at Los Angeles, Calif.; Roman Catholic; formed 1973 by merger of Marymount College (chartered 1948) and Loyola University of Los Angeles (established 1929); arts and sciences, business administration, education, and engineering; graduate division.

**Loyola University in New Orleans,** at New Orleans, La.; Roman Catholic; established 1912; arts and sciences, business administration, dentistry, law, music, and teacher education; graduate studies: *map* N-223b

**Loyola University of Chicago,** at Chicago, Ill.; Roman Catholic; founded 1870; arts and sciences, business administration, education, law, nursing, social work; graduate school; Medical Center (medicine and dentistry) at Maywood; center for humanities at Rome, Italy: *map* C-261

**Loyson** [*lwä-zôṅ'*], **Charles** (1827–1912), French preacher, born Orléans, France; called "Père Hyacinthe"; eloquent speaker but his unorthodox beliefs caused his excommunication from Roman Catholic church.

**Lozeau** [*lô-zō'*], **Albert** (1878–1924), Canadian poet and journalist, born Montreal; an invalid from youth; ranks high for sensitiveness and imagination: C-113a

**Lozenge,** candy C-123

**Lozier, Jean Baptiste Charles Bouvet de.** *see in index* Bouvet de Lozier

**LP-Gas,** or **LPG** (liquefied petroleum gas) G-41, *chart* P-241a

**LSD** (lysergic acid diethylamide), a hallucinatory drug synthesized by Dr. Albert Hofmann, Basle, Switzerland, 1938; used to treat terminal cancer patients; may become valuable in psychotherapy; nonmedical use considered dangerous: D-200d

**LSI,** or **Large-scale integrated circuit,** computers C-497d

**Luanda** [*lụ-än'dạ*], or **Loanda** [*lō-än'dạ*], also **So Paulo de Loanda** [*souṅ pou'lọ thĕ lwäṅn'dạ*], Angola, capital and seaport; pop. 480,613; founded 1575; for about three centuries, a center of slave trade A-419

**Luang Prabang** [*lwäng' prä-bäng'*], Laos, city in n., on Mekong River; pop. 43,924; historic royal residence; also name of former kingdom: L-125b
- palace, *picture* L-125a

**Luau** [*lụ-ä'ụ*], Hawaiian feast H-57, *picture* H-53

**Lubang** [*lụ-bäng'*] **Islands,** small group off s.w. coast of Luzon, in the Philippines; pop. 19,904; largest island Lubang (74 sq mi; 192 sq km) commands entrance to Manila Bay: *map* P-261d

**Lubber's knot,** or **granny knot** K-70

**Lubber's line,** on compass C-494d, *diagram* C-500

**Lubbock, Sir John.** *see in index* Avebury, John Lubbock, Baron

**Lubbock,** Tex., city about 110 mi (180 km) s. of Amarillo; pop. 173,979; oil wells in area; cotton and cotton products, packed meats, grain sorghums; Texas Tech University; Mackenzie State Park; Reese Air Force Base nearby: *maps* T-128, U-40

**Lübeck** [*lü'bĕk*], West Germany, seaport on Trave River, 19 km (12 mi) from Baltic Sea; pop. 239,339; shipbuilding; machinery: *map* G-114
- free city F-431
- head of Hanseatic League H-22

**Lubin, David** (1849–1919), agricultural organizer, born Klodowa, Russian Poland; brought to U.S. in 1855; founded dry-goods and mail-order business in California, 1874; devoted last part of his life to agricultural problems. *see also in index* International Institute of Agriculture

**Lubitsch** [*lụ'bĭch*], **Ernst** (1892–1947), motion-picture director and producer, born Berlin, Germany; to U.S. 1922; brilliant style and sophisticated humor ('Lady Windermere's Fan'; 'Merry Widow'; 'Ninotchka').

**Lübke** [*lüp'kĕ*], **Heinrich** (1894–1972), West German political leader, born Enkhausen, near Dortmund, Germany; minister of Food, Agriculture, and Forestry, Federal Republic of Germany, 1953–59, president 1959–69.

**Lublin** [*lụ'blēn*], Poland, city 150 km (95 mi) s.e. of Warsaw; pop. 197,100; flourished in 12th century; scene of Russian victory over Austrians in World War I: *maps* P-414, E-335

**Lublin, Treaty of** (1569), *table* T-251a

**Lubricant,** oily or greasy substance used to diminish friction L-387
- automobile, *picture* A-848
- graphite G-178
- petroleum L-387, *charts* P-241–241b

**Lubumbashi,** formerly **Elisabethville,** Zaire, city in s.e.; pop. 525,154; copper- and tin-mining center: Z-353a

**Luca della Robbia.** *see in index* Robbia, Luca della

**Lucan** (Marcus Annaeus Lucanus) (A.D. 39–65), Roman poet, author of 'Pharsalia', epic on civil war between Caesar and Pompey.

**Lucania,** region in Italy. *see in index* Basilicata

**Lucas** (originally **Luchich), Anthony Francis** (1855–1921), American mining engineer and geologist, born Dalmatia; to U.S. 1879, became citizen 1885: T-119

**Lucas, Edward Verrall** (1868–1938), English essayist, novelist, and biographer; born Eltham, Kent; "the modern Charles Lamb"; widely popular for his genial humor and broad sympathies ('The Open Road', anthology; 'The Life of Charles Lamb'; 'Over Bremerton's' and 'London Lavender', novels; 'Pleasure Trove', essays; 'A Wanderer in London' and 'A Wanderer in Paris', travel).

**Lucas, Eliza.** *see in index* Pinckney, Elizabeth (or Eliza) Lucas

**Lucas, Jerry** (born 1940), basketball player, born Middletown, Ohio; center, Ohio State University, selected as all-America player 1960, 1961, and 1962; with Cincinnati Royals 1963–69, Golden State Warriors 1969–71; New York Knickerbockers 1971–74.

**Lucas, John Seymour** (1849–1923), English historical and portrait painter, born London
- painting, *picture* W-163

**Lucas Van Leyden** [*lī'dĕn*] (1494?–1533), Dutch painter and engraver, born Leiden, Netherlands; superb technician; influenced by Albrecht Dürer, later by Marcantonio.

**Lucca** [*lụk'kä*], Italy, old and picturesque city 19 km (12 mi) n.e. of Pisa; pop. 88,428; many antiquities; large trade: *map* I-338

**Luce, Clare Boothe** (Mrs. H. R. Luce) (born 1903), writer and diplomat, born New York City; edited *Vogue* 1930, *Vanity Fair* 1931–34, then turned to writing plays ('The Women'; 'Kiss the Boys Goodbye'); later became a war correspondent ('Europe in the Spring'); member U.S. Congress 1942–46; U.S. ambassador to Italy 1953–56.

**Luce, Henry Robinson** (1898–1967), editor and publisher, born Shantung Province, China; son of American missionary; husband of Clare Boothe Luce; in 1923 became co-founder and editor in chief of Time, Inc., editorial chairman 1964–67.

**Lucerne** [*lụ-sẽrn'*], German **Luzern** [*lụt-sẽrn'*], Switzerland, capital of canton of Lucerne at n.w. end of Lake Lucerne; pop. 69,879; tourist resort: *map* S-537
- 'Lion of Lucerne' T-166, *picture* T-166
- medieval bridge, *picture* S-544

**Lucerne.** *see in index* Alfalfa

**Lucerne, Lake,** also **Luzern (Vierwaldstättersee),** beautiful mountain-rimmed lake in central Switzerland; 39 km (24 mi) long: *map* S-537

**Lucia, Santa.** *see in index* Lucy, Saint

**Lucia Day,** in Sweden S-525

**'Lucia di Lammermoor'** [*lụ-chē'ä dē läm-mĕr-mọr'*], opera by Gaetano Donizetti
- story O-465

**Lucian** [*lū'shạn*] (120?–180?), Greek satirist and humorist G-235, S-341c, 348d

**Lucifer** [*lū'sĭ-fẽr*], a cat that belonged to Cardinal Richelieu, *list* C-152

**Lucifer** [*lū'sĭ-fẽr*], name of Venus as morning star; applied by Isaiah to king of Babylon ("How art thou fallen from heaven, O Lucifer, son of the morning!"), and, through misunderstanding of this passage by later writers, to Satan.

**Luciferase,** an enzyme manufactured in the cells of certain animals, the function of which is to control that slow process of oxidation known as bioluminescence or luminescence.

**Luciferin,** a chemical substance occurring in luminescent animals, which, when acted upon by the enzyme luciferase, produces light: P-270
- firefly F-142

**Lucilius, Gaius** (180?–103 B.C.), Roman satirist L-154

**Lucin Cutoff** G-208, U-218

**Lucite** P-383, *picture* P-381

**Luckhardt, Arno Benedict** (1885–1957), physiologist, born Chicago, Ill.; professor of physiology, University of Chicago 1923–46 (chairman of department 1941–46); with J. Bailey Carter discovered value of ethylene gas as an anesthetic.

**Luckman, Sid(ney)** (born 1916), football quarterback, born Brooklyn, N.Y.; played for Chicago Bears 1939–50: *list* F-337

**Luckner, Felix von, Count** (1881–1966), German naval officer and adventurer, born Dresden; sailor at age of 13; gained title "Sea Devil" by daring exploits in World War I; lived in U.S. 1926–34 then returned to Germany; hero of 'The Sea Devil', by Lowell Thomas.

**Lucknow,** India, manufacturing and rail center, capital of Uttar Pradesh state; pop. 750,512: L-387, *maps* I-66
- location L-387, *locator map* L-387
- siege (1857) L-387, *table* W-8d

**'Luck of Roaring Camp, The',** work by Harte A-351

**Lucretia** [*lū-krē'shĭ-ạ*], Roman matron whose suicide because of outrage inflicted by Sextus, son of King Tarquin the Proud, provoked expulsion of the Tarquins.

**Lucretius** [*lụ-krē'shŭs*] (Titus Lucretius Carus) (96?–55 B.C.), Roman poet-philosopher; preached against the idea of the immortality of the soul: L-155, P-265

**Lucullus** [*lū-kŭl'ŭs*], **Lucius Licinius** (110?–56? B.C.), immensely wealthy Roman noble, helped conquer Mithradates; "Lucullan luxury" has become proverbial.

**Lucy, Saint,** Italian **Santa Lucia** [*sän'tä lụ-chē'ä*] (283?–304?), noblewoman of Syracuse, Sicily; two attempts at torturing her having failed, she was finally killed by sword; festival December 13
- Lucia Day in Sweden S-525

**Lucy, Sir Thomas** (1532–1600), English squire, justice of peace, said to have prosecuted Shakespeare; supposedly portrayed in 'Henry IV' as Justice Shallow: S-130

**Luddites,** bands of workmen organized in England to smash machinery 1812–18 in protest against displacement of hand labor.

**Ludendorff, Erich von** (1865–1937), German general, born Prussia; expert strategist; worked with Hindenburg in World War I and with him responsible for many successful campaigns; fled to Sweden after Germany's defeat; returned to Munich 1919; supported Hitler for a time; later became a mystic; author of several books about World War I: H-179, *picture* G-104
- offensive of 1918 W-258

**Lüderitz** [*lụd'ĕ-rĭts*], South-West Africa, port and health resort in s.w.; pop. 3604; fish, rock lobsters; center for diamond-producing region: *maps* S-264

**Ludington, Sybil** (1761–1839), Revolutionary War heroine; at age 16 made night ride by horseback to arouse members of her father's volunteer regiment to muster for fight against British; ride was three times longer than Paul Revere's.

**Ludington,** Mich., commercial city and resort on Lake Michigan and Marquette River 70 mi (110 km) n.w. of Grand Rapids; pop. 8937; watchcases and jewelry, game boards, furniture, chemicals, vibrator machinery: *map* M-285
- car ferry M-287

**Ludlow,** England, old town in s. Shropshire; pop. 6796: *map* G-199h

**Ludlow,** Mass., community 7 mi (11 km) n.e. of Springfield; pop. of township 18,150; near Westover Air Force Base; plastics; incorporated 1774: *map* M-160

**Ludlow,** machine for casting lines of type L-295, *picture* L-295

**Ludwig** [*lụt'vĭk*] **I** (1786–1868), king of Bavaria, grandfather of Ludwig II; born Strasbourg; munificent patron of art; forced to abdicate by revolution in 1848
- beautifies Munich M-546–7

**Ludwig II** (1845–86), king of Bavaria, grandson of Ludwig I and cousin of Ludwig III; born Nymphenburg, near Munich; succeeded 1864; patron of Richard Wagner; died insane
- Neuschwanstein Castle, *picture* G-112
- Wagner W-2

**Ludwig III** (1845–1921), king of Bavaria; cousin of Ludwing II; born Munich; succeeded 1913, abdicated 1918.

**Ludwig, Emil** (1881–1948), American author, born Breslau, Germany; lived early life in Switzerland; became U.S. citizen 1941; in his youth wrote plays, sketches, and novels but found greatest success in his "humanized" historical biographies, including those of Napoleon I, Bismarck, Goethe, Lincoln; 'Gifts of Life', autobiography.

**Ludwig, Otto** (1813–65), German dramatist and novelist, born Eisfeld, near Coburg, Germany; one of leading German writers of fiction in middle 19th century: G-98

**Ludwigia,** plants of swamps, ditches, pond margins, and wet pine barrens; a genus of the evening primrose family, *Onagraceae;* used in aquariums: N-74, *picture* N-74

**Ludwigshafen** [*lụt'vĭĸs-hä-fĕn*], West Germany, city on Rhine opposite Mannheim; pop. 171,510; large chemical works and other manufactures; known for large trade in coal, timber, iron: *map* G-115

**Lufbery, Raoul** (1884–1918), American aviator, born Clermont, near Beauvais, France; World War I ace; credited with 17 victories; killed in combat.

**Luff,** *diagram* B-326

**Lufkin,** Tex., city about 115 mi (185 km) n.e. of Houston; pop. 28,562; livestock, lumbering; oil-field equipment, paper products, machinery; Angelina and Davy Crockett National Forests nearby: *map* T-128

**Lufthansa German Airlines** G-112

**Luftwaffe** [*lụft'väf-ĕ*], German air force, including antiaircraft units, under Hitler. Word means "air weapon"
- World War II A-158, 205, W-266, 268–9, 286, 287, 290

**Lugano** [*lụ-gä'nō*], **Lake,** deep and narrow lake enclosed by mountains, partly in Switzerland, partly in n. Italy, between Lakes Maggiore and Como; 30 km (20 mi) long: I-324, *maps* S-537, I-325

**Lugbait,** or **lugworm.** *see in index* Lobworm

**Lugh** [*lụ*] **the Long-Handed,** in Irish mythology I-291

**Lug pole,** camp cooking device C-64, *picture* C-69

**Luimneach,** Ireland. *see in index* Limerick

**Luini** [*lụ-ē'nē*], **Bernardino** (1475?–1532?), Italian artist, born Luino, near Varese, Italy; most noted as a fresco painter; excelled at depicting sacred and mythological subjects.

**Luke, Saint,** one of apostolic assistants, traditional author of the Third Gospel and of the Acts; patron of physicians; festival October 18 A-507

**Luke, Frank** (1897–1918), aviator, born Phoenix, Ariz.; as World War I ace downed 18 or 19 enemy balloons and airplanes; was killed in combat; posthumously awarded the Medal of Honor.

**Luke, Gospel of Saint,** Third Gospel and 3d book of New Testament.

**Lukeman, (Henry) Augustus** (1871–1935), sculptor, born Richmond, Va.; successor to Gutzon Borglum in charge of Confederate memorial, Stone Mountain, Ga.; portrait busts, statues, monuments (portrait statues of William McKinley and Jefferson Davis; equestrian statue of Kit Carson; 'Manu the Law Giver of India').

**Luks, George Benjamin** (1867–1933), painter, born Williamsport, Pa.; war correspondent and illustrator in Spanish-American War. His paintings of poorer classes, street scenes, portraits, and his interpretations of childhood show free, virile, and spontaneous technique ('The Spielers'; 'Old Clothes Man')

**Luleå** [*lụ-lē-ō*], Sweden, seaport on Gulf of Bothnia; pop. 30,488; shipbuilding; lumber and iron; chartered 1621, moved 6 km (4 mi) to present site 1648–9: S-523, *maps* S-524, E-335, F-119

**Lule** [*lụl'ĕ*] **River,** in n. Sweden, flows 320 km (200 mi) to Gulf of Bothnia: *maps* S-524, F-119

**Lulli** [*lụl'lē*], **Giovanni Battista,** French, **Jean Baptiste Lully** (1632–87), celebrated composer, born Italy, called "father of French opera"; taken to Paris, France, as boy, worked as servant; rose to position of court musician to Louis XIV; introduced lively ballets; dominated French opera for almost a century: B-33, O-461-2

**Lully, Raymond** (Ramón Lull or Raymundus Lullius) (1235?–1315), Spanish scientist and missionary, born Palma, Majorca; authority on Arabic; founder of western orientalism
■ forerunner of modern chemists C-242-3

**Luluabourg,** Zaire. *see in index* Kananga

**Lumbar vertebra,** vertebra in the lower back S-209

**Lumber and timber** L-388–94, *pictures* L-388–94. *see also in index* Forests and forestry; Lumbering; Wood; *also* names of trees
■ beech uses B-130
■ building construction B-491
■ commercial varieties L-393
■ hardwood F-345, W-217, *pictures* T-254–7, *table* W-219
■ heaviest in United States H-155
■ manufactured lumber W-221, P-397
■ pine most useful to man P-327–9
■ plywood P-397, *pictures* W-222, L-392
■ producing regions L-393, 392, 388
□ Asia A-688
□ Australia A-809
□ Beaumont B-119
□ Canada C-76–7, 79, *chart* C-94: New Brunswick N-162d, h, 162–162a, *chart* N-162h, *map* N-162d; Ontario O-456e, j, O-507, *chart* O-456j, *map* O-456l, *picture* O-507; Quebec Q-9d, i, *map* Q-9c
□ Finland F-118
□ Japan J-381, 401, *graph* J-381
□ Norway N-364
□ Philippines P-257, 259b
□ South America S-286, *picture* S-281b
□ Sweden S-523, 524, *chart* S-528, *pictures* S-525, E-308
□ United States U-64, 65, 82, 90–1, 105, *charts* U-127, *map* U-105: Alaska A-243 California C-35, 37, *map* C-42; Florida F-233, *map* F-238; Georgia G-79, 80, *map* G-84, *pictures* G-80; Idaho I-16–17, *map* I-20; Michigan M-270, *map* M-276; Mississippi M-373, 374, 375, *map* M-378, *picture* M-376; national, state, and community forests N-48, 49, F-347, *map* N-48, *pictures* N-48–9; North Carolina N-323, *map* N-328; Oregon O-481, 482, *map* O-484, *pictures* O-482, 487–8; Virginia V-331, 332, *map* V-336; Washington W-40, 39, *map* W-44, *pictures* W-41, 45
■ pulpwood timber, *pictures* P-104
■ reforestation and reserves
□ United States: Michigan M-271; Pennsylvania P-165–6; Wisconsin W-194
■ seasoning or drying L-391, W-221, *picture* L-393
■ softwood W-217, F-345, *table* W-218
■ substitutes P-379
■ United States, annual board feet cut, *chart* U-127
■ uses W-220, 221, L-392, *tables* W-218–19
■ veneer V-272

**Lumbering** L-388–94, *pictures* L-388–94. *see also in index* Lumber and timber
■ block logging F-343
■ conservation practices F-343, L-388, *pictures* F-344, E-50
■ felling trees L-389, *pictures* L-388, O-482, M-52
■ hauling logs L-390, *pictures* L-389
■ logging camp to sawmill L-390–1, *pictures* L-389, 394: Canada, *picture* C-76; Europe, *pictures* E-308, F-120; South America, *picture* S-277
■ Paul Bunyan stories F-295, L-394, S-481d, *pictures* F-296, M-352
■ sawmill L-390–1, *pictures* L-390–2
■ selective logging F-343, L-388
■ Tony Beaver stories F-295

**Lumberjack,** a lumberman
■ folklore F-295–6
■ how he lives L-394, *pictures* L-394
■ memorial, *picture* M-275
■ Paul Bunyan stories F-295, L-394, S-481d, *pictures* F-296, M-352
■ timber festival, *picture* O-488
■ work of L-388–90, *pictures* L-394, 388–9. *see also in index* Lumbering

**Lumberton,** N.C., city on Lumber River 30 mi (50 km) s. of Fayetteville; pop. 18,340; tobacco marketing and processing; textiles, electric equipment; All America City 1970: *map* N-336

**Lumen,** unit of light intensity L-261–2

**Lumière** [*lü-myėr'*], **Auguste Marie Louis Nicolas** (1862–1954), French chemist and industrialist, born Besançon, France; brother of Louis J. Lumière, whom he helped in development of the cinématographe and with whom he manufactured photographic plates and paper; research on vitamins: M-519, P-300

**Lumière, Louis Jean** (1864–1948), French chemist and industrialist, born Besançon, France; brother of Auguste M. L. N. Lumière; in 1895 invented cinématographe, the first motion-picture projector using intermittent movement of film; pioneer (1907) in natural-color photography and in three-dimensional movies (1935): M-519, P-300

**Luminal,** a sedative drug N-15

**Luminance signal,** in television T-72–3, *diagram* T-74

**Luminescence,** emission of light resulting from causes other than high temperature P-270. *see also in index* Fluorescence; Phosphorescence
■ beetle B-137
■ dinoflagellates O-398b
■ fish F-160–1, 154, O-395c, E-166b, *picture* F-161
■ Jack-o'-lantern mushrooms M-552

**Luminiferous ether** R-140

**Luminous flux** L-261–2

**Luminous paint** P-73, R-70

**Lummis, Charles Fletcher** (1859–1928), explorer and writer, born Lynn, Mass.; became an authority on history and archaeology of Southwest; learned language and customs of Indians and did much to improve their conditions ('The Land of Poco Tiempo'; 'The Man Who Married the Moon, and Other Pueblo Indian Folk-Stories'; 'Mesa, Cañon and Pueblo').

**Lumpsucker,** a mail-cheeked fish of the spiny-finned group; imperfect first dorsal fin forms lump on back; ventral fins shape circular sucker which may attach to rocks; short thick body with rough, scaleless skin; weighs to 9 kg (20 lbs).

**Lumumba** [*lụ-mụm'bą*], **Patrice (Emergy)** (1925–61), Congolese political leader, born Katako Kombe, Kawai Province; first premier Democratic Republic of the Congo (now Zaire) June–September 1960; Z-353a
■ assassination, *list* A-704

**Luna,** in Roman mythology, the goddess of the moon and of months; although not a major object of worship, she had shrines on the Aventine and Palatine hills in Rome.

**Luna,** Russian spacecraft. *see in index* Lunas

**Lunacharski** [*lụ-nŭ-chär'skĭ*], **Anatoly Vasilievich** (1875–1933), Russian political leader and author, born Poltava, Russia, of wealthy parents; became revolutionary in 1892; as people's commissar for education in Soviet government prevented destruction of books and works of art after revolution.

**Luna moth** B-521, 528, *picture* B-523

**Luna Park,** amusement park, Coney Island, N.Y. A-384

**Lunar caustic.** *see in index* Silver nitrate

**Lunar eclipse** E-44, M-482, *diagram* M-482

**Lunar flights.** *see in index* Space travel, *subhead* moon

**Lunaria** [*lū-nā'rĭ-ạ*], a genus of plants of mustard family, native of Eurasia, and one of common flowers of old-time gardens. Heart-shaped leaves; tiny, scented purple or white flowers; seedpod 5 cm (2 in.) long, transparent; used as everlasting. Also called moonwort, honesty, satin flower, and silver dollar.

**Lunar module** (LM), of Apollo spacecraft S-346c–d, b, 347, 341, *diagrams* S-346c–e, *pictures* S-341, 347, *table* S-348
■ crash impact on moon M-479
■ stamp honors, *picture* S-405

**Lunar month,** or **synodic month** M-476, M-483, *diagram* M-483

**Lunar Orbiters,** space-moon probes M-485, *table* S-344

**Lunar Roving Vehicle** S-347

**Lunar year** Y-336, C-28

**Lunas,** Russian man-made satellites M-486, *table* S-344
■ moon's far side photographed, *picture* M-482

**Lundy, Benjamin** (1789–1839), a philanthropist, prominent in antislavery movement, born Hardwick, N.J.; published antislavery magazine and lectured against slavery.

**Lundy's Lane, battle of,** in War of 1812, between British and American forces near Niagara Falls on Canadian side: W-14

**Lüneburg** [*lü'nĕ-burg̃*], West Germany, city of Lower Saxony s.e. of Hamburg; pop. 60,900; was prominent in Hanseatic League; cement works, salt spring: *map* G-114

**Lüneburger Heide,** heath s.w. of Lüneburg, in Lower Saxony, West Germany: *map* G-114

**Lunenburg,** N.S., Canada, industrial and fishing town 60 km (40 mi) s.w. of Halifax; pop. 3154: N-373d, g, b, *maps* N-373k, b, C-99

**Luneta Park,** in Manila, Philippines P-255, *pictures* P-257b, M-87

**Lunéville** [*lụ-nā-vēl'*], France, town 29 km (18 mi) s.e. of Nancy; pop. 22,961; treaty between France and Austria (1801): *map* F-404

**Lunéville, Treaty of** (1801), *table* T-251a

**Lung, Momsen,** for submarine escape, *picture* S-495b

**Lungfish,** or **mudfish** M-539–41, *pictures* M-540, F-162
■ place in evolution A-461, *chart* G-64, *picture* A-460

**Lungs,** organs of respiration in airbreathing animals
■ Carrel-Lindbergh machine L-289
■ evolution A-461
■ human L-395, A-391, R-159–60, *diagram* L-395
□ artificial B-211
□ diseases D-129d, P-441b, c, T-190a, b. *see also in index* Tuberculosis
△ diagnosis, *picture* D-129d
■ mudfish M-539, 540

**Lungworm** W-299

**Lungwort, Virginia cowslip,** or **bluebell,** a perennial plant (*Mertensia virginica*) of the borage family with pale-green leaves and clusters of purplish-blue trumpet-shaped flowers; often cultivated in gardens; herbalists once used extract made from leaves to treat lung diseases: *pictures* F-277a, P-358

**Luniks,** Russian moon probes. *see in index* Luna, Russian spacecraft

**Lunokhod,** Soviet lunar landing vehicle, *table* S-344

**Lunt, Alfred** (1893–1977), actor and director, born Milwaukee, Wis.; starred with wife, Lynn Fontanne, in numerous theater productions and motion-picture version of 'The Guardsman': A-27, *picture* W-204. *see also in index* Fontanne, Lynn

**Lupercalia,** Roman festival in honor of ancient god Lupercus, protector of flocks against wolves, sometimes identified with Faunus: F-91
■ dance D-21

**Lupines,** various plants of the bean family, with white, yellow, or blue flowers on a central spike; contain poison: *picture* F-277
■ annual for fall planting G-22
■ annual for shade G-21
■ bluebonnet. *see in index* Bluebonnet
■ New Zealand, *picture* N-276a
■ tree variety, *picture* F-273

**Lupulin,** an alkaloid, the active principle of hops H-224

**Lupus,** constellation, *chart* S-419

**Lupus,** disease D-129h

**Luque** [*lọ'kā*], **Hernando de,** partner of Pizarro P-349

**Luray Cavern,** large limestone cave in Page County, Va. C-178a

**Lurçat, Jean** (1892–1966), French modernist painter and tapestry designer, born Bruyères, near Épinal, France; influenced revival of French tapestry-weaving industry: T-20

**Lure,** in falconry F-23

**Lure, artificial,** in fishing F-176
■ bait casting, *pictures* F-175
■ fly fishing F-178, *pictures* F-176
■ spinning F-179

**Luria, Salvador E(dward)** (born 1912), American biologist, born Turin, Italy; to U.S. 1940, citizen 1947; professor Massachusetts Institute of Technology 1959–
■ Nobel prize, *table* N-294e

**Lurs** [*lụrz*], nomadic people of Iran, probably of Aryan origin I-278

**Lusaka** [*lụ-sä'kạ*], Zambia, capital; pop. 559,000; Z-353b

**Lüshun,** People's Republic of China. *see in index* Port Arthur

**'Lusiads** [*lū'sĭ-ădz*], **The',** Portuguese **Os Lusiadas** ("the sons of Lusus," or "the Portuguese"), one of greatest epic poems of world literature, by Camoens: P-456

**Lusitania** [*lū-sĭ-tān'yạ*], ancient Roman province comprising most of modern Portugal and s.w. Spain; name comes from Lusitani, group of tribes who held off Roman domination until the death of their leader.

**'Lusitania',** ocean liner, S-177e–f, 177a, W-254–5, W-176, *pictures* W-173, W-254
■ submarine that sank ship, *picture* W-256
■ warning ad, *picture* S-177e

**Lüta,** People's Republic of China, municipality in Liaoning Province; made up of cities Port Arthur and Dairen and two counties; pop. 3,086,000 (1975 est.): *maps* M-84, C-291, C-313. *see also in index* Dairen; Port Arthur
■ location, *locator map* D-1a

**Lute,** ancient pear-shaped stringed instrument of Arabian origin
■ ancient Egyptian, *picture* E-122

**Lutetia** [*lū-tē'shĭ-ạ*], ancient name of Paris, France P-122

**Lutetium** (Lu), a transitional chemical element, *tables* P-207, C-236

**Lutfisk** [*lụt'fĭsk*], Scandinavian dish C-327

**Luther** [*lụt'ĕr*, English *lū'thĕr*], **Hans** (1879–1962), German statesman, born Berlin; in 1924 concluded Dawes loan for Germany; chancellor 1925–26; instituted taxation and tariff reform; president of Reichsbank 1930–33; ambassador to U.S. 1933–37.

**Luther, Martin** (1483–1546), leader of the Reformation L-396–7, R-133–4, G-98, *pictures* L-396–7, G-96a, G-112d, R-133
■ burns papal bull L-396, *picture* L-397
■ Charles V opposes C-212
■ Christmas tree legend C-326
■ Dürer D-210
■ Henry VIII opposes H-138
■ influence on German language G-96a
■ Ninety-five Theses L-396, *picture* R-133
■ Zwingli and Z-370

**Lutheranism,** religious movement that grew out of teachings of Martin Luther
■ American Colonies C-337
■ Denmark D-90
■ early spread of R-134, 135
■ Norway N-366, 368
■ Sweden S-524, 527
■ United States C-338

**Luther College,** at Decorah, Iowa; affiliated with American Lutheran church; established 1861; liberal arts and teacher education.

**Luther League of America,** an organization of several Lutheran Young People's Societies established 1895 at Pittsburgh, Pa.; originally nonsynodical; adopted by United Lutheran church in America, 1920.

**Luthuli, Albert John** (1898–1967), South African liberation leader, born Rhodesia; Zulu chieftain 1936–52; president general of

the proscribed African National Congress; charged with treason 1952, acquitted; movements restricted by banishment orders 1959–67; author 'Let My People Go'.
■ Nobel prize, *table* N-294h

**Lutine Bell,** in Lloyd's of London; came from the frigate *La Lutine* which sank in 1799 with a cargo of gold; Lloyd's underwriters had insured the cargo and had suffered heavy loss.

**Luton** [*lū'tŏn*], England, town 50 km (30 mi) n.w. of London; pop. 156,690; automobiles, ball bearings, hats, chemicals: *map* G-199h

**Luttrell Psalter,** illuminated manuscript of 14th century, *pictures* E-234

**Lutyens** [*lŭch'ĕnz*], **Sir Edwin Landseer** (1869–1944), British architect, born London; designer of public buildings and homes; planned New Delhi, India; works include Government House, New Delhi, Whitehall Cenotaph, London, and British Embassy, Washington, D.C.; Royal Academy 1920, Order of Merit 1943.

**Lutz, Frank Eugene** (1879–1943), biologist, born Bloomsburg, Pa.; with American Museum of Natural History, New York City, from 1909; curator of its Department of Insects and Spiders 1921–43 ('Field Book of Insects').

**Lützen** [*lüt'sĕn*], East Germany, town 21 km (13 mi) s.w. of Leipzig; pop. 4819
■ battle (1632) G-265, *picture* G-264

**Luxemburg, Rosa** (1870–1919), German socialist agitator and fiery orator, born Russian Poland; killed in Berlin riots.

**Luxemburg,** also **Luxembourg,** country of n.w. Europe, surrounded by France, Germany, and Belgium; 2585 sq km (998 sq mi); pop. 334,790 (1966 census); cap. Luxemburg: L-397–8, *Fact Summary* E-329, *maps* E-334, W-252, 277, *picture* L-398
■ Benelux N-136, E-326
■ cemetery, United States permanent military N-20
■ European Economic Community E-341–2, I-243
■ flag F-202, *picture* F-203
■ government L-398: elections L-398
■ invasion by Germany W-267
■ location, *locator map* L-397
■ money, *table* M-428
■ national anthem, *table* N-52
■ railroad mileage, *table* R-85

**Luxemburg,** also **Luxembourg,** capital of grand duchy of Luxemburg; pop. 76,143: L-397–8, *picture* L-398
■ Court of Justice E-341

**Luxor,** village in Upper Egypt on part of site of ancient Thebes, near El Karnak: T-157, *map* E-109
■ "Avenue of Sphinxes" S-379
■ Medinet Habu temple, *picture* E-125

**Luzern,** Switzerland. *see in index* Lucerne

**Luzon** [*lụ-sŏn'*], largest and most important island of Philippines; area 40,420 sq mi (104,690 sq km); pop. 20,851,000; contains Manila, largest city, and Quezon City, official capital of country: P-259, 259b, 253a, b, 257, 257c, *maps* P-259a, 261d, P-4
■ agriculture P-255d, 256
■ population P-253b, *chart* P-253b
■ transportation P-257a
■ volcanoes P-259
□ Mayon P-259, *maps* P-259a, 261d, *picture* P-253
□ Taal, *picture* P-259
■ World War II W-278, 296–7, *picture* W-296

**Luzzone Dam,** in Switzerland, on Brenno di Luzzone River, *table* D-12

**L'vov** [*lə-vôf'*], Polish **Lwow** [*lə-vọf'*], German **Lemberg,** Russia, former Polish fortified city 460 km (285 mi) s.w. of Kiev; pop. 553,000; capital of Austrian Galicia in 18th century; returned to Poland after World War I; included in Russia since 1945: P-412, U-2, *maps* R-344, 349, E-335, W-253

**Lwoff, André** (born 1902), French biologist, born Allier Department; with Pasteur Institute in Paris; professor Sorbonne 1959–68
■ Nobel prize, *table* N-294e

**Lyallpur** [*lī'ăl-pụr*], Pakistan, city 75 mi (120 km) s.w. of Lahore; pop. 425,248; railroad junction; wheat and cotton center; food products, farm implements, chemicals.

**Lyases,** enzymes E-281, *table* E-281

**Lyautey** [*lyō-tā'*], **Louis Hubert** (1854–1934), French marshal, born Nancy; as resident general and high commissioner of Morocco (1912–25) put the government on a sound basis.

**Lycabettus** [*lĭk-ạ-bĕt'ŭs*], **Mount** (modern Mount St. George), hill n.e. of Athens 339 meters (1112 feet) high; modern section of city spreads to its base; reservoir on its side built by Hadrian and Antoninus Pius still in use A-734, *picture* A-734

**Lycaenidae,** butterflies B-528

**Lycée** [*lē-sā'*], French school F-391, E-98
■ American college compared C-433

**Lyceum** [*lī-sē'ŭm*], Aristotle's school in ancient Athens A-14
■ Aristotle's teaching A-589
■ Theophrastus continued G-235

**Lyceum,** in United States A-51

**Lychnis, scarlet.** *see in index* Jerusalem cross

**Lycia** [*lĭsh'ĭ-ạ*], ancient division of s.w. Asia Minor on Mediterranean, conquered by Persia 6th century B.C., then subject in turn to Macedon, Egypt, Syria, and Rome: *maps* P-212, M-7

**'Lycidas'** [*lĭs'ĭ-dás*], poem by John Milton commemorating death of his friend Edward King, drowned at sea: E-259

**Lycoming College,** at Williamsport, Pa.; United Methodist; founded as Williamsport Academy 1812, as college 1947; arts and sciences, education.

**Lycoperdon bovista,** a mushroom, one of the puffballs, *picture* M-553

**Lycopodium,** a genus of nonflowering mosslike plants of the club moss family (*Lycopodiaceae*) with trailing stems and numerous small evergreen leaves; the sulfur-yellow, highly inflammable powderlike spores produced by erect fruiting spikes are sometimes used in making fireworks.

**Lycoris** [*lī-kō'rĭs*], a genus of perennial plants of the amaryllis family, native to eastern Asia; root a bulb; leaves long, narrow, disappearing before flowers develop; flowers yellow, red, or rose-lilac, fragrant, grow in cluster at top of tall stem, stamens project beyond flower tube; one species called golden spider lily.

**Lycurgus** [*lī-kûr'gŭs*] (late 9th or early 8th century B.C.), lawgiver of ancient Sparta L-398

**Lydda** [*lĭd'ạ*], Hebrew **Lod** [*lōd*], Israel, ancient town 10 mi (16 km) s.e. of Tel Aviv-Jaffa; pop. 21,000; international airport: *map* I-320
■ Israeli-Arab war I-320a
■ legend of St. George G-74

**Lyddite,** an explosive derived from picric acid E-361

**Lydgate, John** (1370?–1451?), English poet, scholar, and monk, born at Lydgate near Newmarket; contemporary of Geoffrey Chaucer and acknowledged him as his "master"; voluminous writer; style rough and verbose; founder of English literary school between Chaucer and Edmund Spenser: E-273
■ Canterbury tale, *picture* C-224

**Lydia,** ancient kingdom in Asia Minor; early seat of Asiatic civilization with important influence on Greeks; later part of Roman province of Asia: C-611, *maps* G-221, M-7
■ coins C-430d, *picture* C-430c

**Lydian stone.** *see in index* Touchstone

**Lye** [*lī*], a caustic, *see also in index* Caustic potash
■ antidotes F-148
■ soaps S-229, 231

**Lyell, Sir Charles** (1797–1875), British geologist, born Kinnordy, near Kirriemuir, Scotland; established James Hutton's "uniformitarian" theory of earth's evolution: E-345

**Lyle, David Alexander** (1845–1937), U.S. Army officer, born Lancaster, Ohio; attained rank of colonel 1907; inventor of Lyle lifesaving gun.

**Lyly** [*lĭl'ĭ*], or **Lilly, John** (1554?–1606), English romancer and dramatist, born The Weald; created euphuism, a writing style: D-171, E-273

**Lyman, Roy** (Link) (1898–1972), football tackle; with Canton Bulldogs 1922 and 1924, Cleveland Browns 1923, and Chicago Bears 1925–34: *list* F-337

**Lyme** [*līm*] **grass,** or **wild rye,** a coarse perennial grass of erect growth found in temperate climates.

**Lyme Regis** [*līm rē'gĭs*], England, seaside resort of Dorsetshire, 217 km (135 mi) s.w. of London; pop. 3310; fine beach: *map* G-199h

**Lymph,** a colorless liquid exuded through the capillaries to nourish tissues of the body A-391

**Lymphatic glands,** small glands scattered throughout lymphatic system, but especially in the neck, armpits, groin, thighs, and body organs; produce corpuscular elements of lymph: D-128a

**Lymphatic system,** a system of vessels for collecting lymph and carrying it back into the blood: B-314, D-128a

**Lymphocyte,** one kind of white blood cell B-314, D-128a, b, S-519c, *table* B-317

**Lymphogranuloma venereum** [*lĭm-fō'grăn-yŭ-lō'mạ vē-nĭ'rē-ŭm*], a venereal disease: V-274

**Lynbrook,** N.Y., resort city on shore of Long Island, near New York City; pop. 23,776; chiefly residential: *map, inset* A-260

**Lynch, Charles** (1736–96), American political leader and soldier: L-399

**Lynch, John Roy** (1847–1939), black leader of Reconstruction period, born Concordia Parish, La.; in U.S. Congress 1873–77, 1882–83; in army 1898–1911 B-292

**Lynch, Thomas, Jr.** (1749–79), signer of Declaration of Independence, born South Carolina: S-310
■ signature reproduced D-55

**Lynchburg,** Va., industrial city on James River, about 95 mi (150 km) s.w. of Richmond; pop. 66,743; foundries, communications products, nuclear reactors; Randolph-Macon Woman's College, Lynchburg College; supply depot for Confederates during Civil War: *maps* V-348, 331, 336, U-41

**Lynchburg College,** at Lynchburg, Va.; private control; opened 1903; arts and sciences, teacher education; graduate studies.

**Lynching** L-399, *picture* N-293

**Lynd, Robert Staughton** (1892–1970), sociologist, born New Albany, Ind.; professor of sociology Columbia University 1931–60; with wife, **Helen Merrell Lynd** (born 1897), wrote 'Middletown' and 'Middletown in Transition', studies of a Middle Western city (Muncie, Ind.).

**Lyndhurst,** N.J., urban township 6 mi (10 km) n.e. of Newark on the Passaic River; pop. 22,729; incorporated 1852: *map, inset* N-202

**Lyndhurst,** Ohio, residential city 4 mi (6 km) n.e. of Cleveland Heights; pop. 18,092; incorporated 1917: *map, inset* O-429

**Lyndon B. Johnson Space Center,** near Houston, Tex. S-346b, H-262, *map* H-261, *pictures* S-342b, T-123

**Lyndon State College,** at Lyndonville, Vt.; founded 1911; formerly a teachers college; liberal arts, education; graduate studies.

**Lynen, Feodor** (1911–79), German biochemist, born Munich; director Max Planck Institute for Cell Chemistry, University of Munich
■ Nobel prize, *table* N-294e

**Lynn, James Thomas** (born 1927), lawyer and government official, born Cleveland, Ohio; general counsel Department of Commerce 1969–71, undersecretary 1971–73; secretary of housing and urban development 1973–75; director Office of Management and Budget 1975–77

**Lynn** [*lĭn*], Mass., a city near Boston; pop. 78,471: L-399, *map, inset* M-160
■ early shoe factory S-179
■ location L-399, *locator map* L-399

**Lynnhaven Bay,** on coast of Virginia e. of Norfolk
■ oysters O-517

**Lynnwood,** Wash., city 16 mi (26 km) n. of Seattle on Puget Sound; pop. 21,937; prefab homes and panels, fireplaces, doors: *map* W-52

**Lynwood,** Calif., city 9 mi (15 km) s. of Los Angeles; pop 48,548; metal products, chemicals; incorporated 1921: *map, inset* C-53

**Lynx** [*lĭnks*], a member of the cat family L-399–400, *pictures* A-436, L-399
■ Canada lynx L-399–400, *picture* C-154d
■ European lynx, *picture* C-154b

**Lyon, Mary** (1797–1849), pioneer in higher education for women, born near Buckland, Mass.; opened Mt. Holyoke Female Seminary (later Mt. Holyoke College) 1837
■ Hall of Fame, *table* H-11

**Lyon, Nathaniel** (1818–61), soldier, prominent opponent of states' rights and slavery, born Ashford, Conn.; organized Unionist troops in Missouri; killed at Wilson's Creek: M-400

**Lyonesse** [*lī-ō-nĕs'*], fabled land in Arthurian legends, off s. coast of Cornwall, England; reputedly engulfed by sea.

**Lyons, Joseph Aloysius** (1879–1939), Australian political leader, born Circular Head, Tasmania; premier, treasurer, and minister for railways 1923–28; prime minister 1932–39; founded United party 1931.

**Lyons, Theodore Amar** (Ted) (born 1900), baseball pitcher and manager, born Lake Charles, La.; pitcher Chicago, A.L., 1923–42, manager-pitcher 1946, manager 1947–48; won 260 games, lost 230; won over 20 games in each of 3 seasons; pitched no-hit game against Boston, Aug. 21, 1926.

**Lyons** [*lī'ŭnz*], French **Lyon** [*lē-ôṅ'*], France, city at junction of Rhone and Saône rivers; pop. 524,500: L-400, F-388, *maps* F-381, 405, E-334
■ Botanic Garden, *table* B-379
■ Croiz Rousse Tunnel, *table* T-292
■ libraries L-234
■ location, *locator map* L-400

**Lyra,** or **Lyre,** constellation across North Pole from Little Bear; represents lyre of Orpheus or of Mercury: *charts* S-419–20, 423

**Lyre** [*līr*], form of harp M-568, *picture* E-78
■ ancient Egyptian, *picture* E-122
■ bell-lyra, *picture* M-569
■ legendary invention H-145
■ Nero's "fiddle" N-128
■ Orpheus, *picture* O-464

**Lyre-back chair,** *picture* I-232

**Lyrebird** L-400, A-782, *pictures* L-400, P-110

**'Lyrical Ballads'** (1798), book of poems by Wordsworth and Coleridge W-234

**Lyric poetry** P-407
■ Greek G-234
■ Muse of M-550

**Lyrics,** in musical comedy M-567a

**Lysander** [*lī-săn'dĕr*] (died 395 B.C.), able unscrupulous Spartan admiral; defeated Athens at Aegospotami and terminated Peloponnesian War.

**Lysergic acid diethylamide.** *see in index* LSD

**Lysias** [*lĭs'ĭ-ás*] (459–380 B.C.), one of great Attic orators; originator of eloquent but plain style in Greek rhetoric.

**Lysippus** [*lī-sĭp'ŭs*] (4th century B.C.), Greek sculptor G-230
■ Hercules H-144

**'Lysistrata',** play by Aristophanes A-588

**Lysozyme** [*lī'sō-zīm*], germ-killing enzyme in most body fluids B-234, *table* E-281

**Lys** [lēs] **River,** a tributary of the Scheldt; rises in extreme n. of France and flows n.e. 190 km (120 mi) joining Scheldt at Ghent; scene of terrific fighting in World War I: *map* W-252

**Lyster, William,** Australian opera director A-800

**Lyte, Henry Francis** (1793–1847), British divine and hymn writer, born near Kelso, Scotland; author of popular hymns 'Abide with Me', 'Jesus, I My Cross Have Taken'.

**Lythraceae.** *see in index* Loosestrife family

**Lythrum** [lĭth'rŭm], or **purple loosestrife,** a perennial plant (*L. salicaria*) of the loosestrife family, found from New England to Utah; grows to 1 m (3 ft); leaves narrow, 10 cm (4 in) long; flowers purple, in dense spikes; also called spiked loosestrife.

**Lytton, Edward George Earle Bulwer-Lytton,** first **Baron** (1803–73), English novelist, playwright, and political leader; born London; member of Parliament 1831–41, 1852–66; made secretary for the colonies 1858; historical novels; known for 'Last Days of Pompeii'.

**Lytton, Edward Robert Bulwer-Lytton,** first **earl of** (1831–91), pen name Owen Meredith, English statesman and poet, born London; son of Baron Lytton; viceroy of India 1876–80 ('Lucile', novel).

---

**PRONUNCIATION KEY**

cāpe, ăt, fär, fást, whąt, fạll; mē, yĕt, fērn, thêre;
īce, bĭt; rōw, wŏn, fôr, nŏt, dọ; cūre, bŭt, rўde, fўll, bûrn; out;
ü = French u, German ü; ǥem, ḡo; thin, then;
ṅ = French nasal (Jeaṅ); zh = French j (z in azure); к = German guttural ch.